International Encyclopedia of
Housing and Home

INTERNATIONAL ENCYCLOPEDIA OF HOUSING AND HOME

Editor-in-Chief
SUSAN J. SMITH
*Girton College and Cambridge University,
Cambridge, UK*

Associate Editors-in-Chief
MARJA ELSINGA
*Delft University of Technology,
Delft, The Netherlands*

ONG SEOW ENG
*National University of Singapore,
Singapore*

LORNA FOX O'MAHONY
*University of Durham,
Durham, UK*

SUSAN WACHTER
*University of Pennsylvania,
Philadelphia, PA, USA*

ELSEVIER

AMSTERDAM BOSTON HEIDELBERG LONDON NEW YORK OXFORD
PARIS SAN DIEGO SAN FRANCISCO SINGAPORE SYDNEY TOKYO

Elsevier
Radarweg 29, PO Box 211, 1000 AE Amsterdam, Netherlands
The Boulevard, Langford Lane, Kidlington, Oxford OX5 1GB, UK
225 Wyman Street, Waltham, MA 02451, USA

Copyright © 2012 Elsevier Ltd. All rights reserved

The following articles are US Government works in the public domain and not subject to copyright.
Housing Subsidies and Work Incentives
Mortgage Choice: Behavioural Finance
Mortgage Default: Determinants

No part of this publication may be reproduced, stored in a retrieval system or transmitted in any form or by any means electronic, mechanical, photocopying, recording or otherwise without the prior written permission of the publisher

Permissions may be sought directly from Elsevier's Science & Technology Rights Department in Oxford, UK: phone (+44) (0) 1865 843830; fax (+44) (0) 1865 853333; email: permissions@elsevier.com. Alternatively you can submit your request online by visiting the Elsevier web site at http://elsevier.com/locate/permissions, and selecting *Obtaining permission to use Elsevier material*

Notice
No responsibility is assumed by the publisher for any injury and/or damage to persons or property as a matter of products liability, negligence or otherwise, or from any use or operation of any methods, products, instructions or ideas contained in the material herein, Because of rapid advances in the medical sciences, in particular, independent verification of diagnoses and drug dosages should be made

British Library Cataloguing in Publication Data
A catalogue record for this book is available from the British Library

Library of Congress Catalog Number: 2012935706

ISBN (print): 978-0-08-047163-1

For information on all Elsevier publications
visit our website at books.elsevier.com

Printed and bound in Spain

12 11 10 9 8 7 6 5 4 3 2 1

Working together to grow
libraries in developing countries

www.elsevier.com | www.bookaid.org | www.sabre.org

ELSEVIER   BOOK AID International   Sabre Foundation

Editorial: Richard Berryman, Scott Bentley
Production: Mike Nicholls

EDITORS

EDITOR-IN-CHIEF
Susan J. Smith
Cambridge University
Cambridge
UK

ASSOCIATE EDITORS-IN-CHIEF
Marja Elsinga
Delft University of Technology
Delft
The Netherlands

Ong Seow Eng
National University of Singapore
Singapore

Lorna Fox O'Mahony
Durham Law School
Durham
UK

Susan Wachter
University of Pennsylvania
Philadelphia, PA
USA

SECTION EDITORS
David Clapham (Approaches)
Cardiff University
Cardiff
UK

Kavita Datta (Policy)
Queen Mary University of London
London
UK

Robyn Dowling (Home/Homelessness)
Macquarie University
Sydney, NSW
Australia

Suzanne Fitzpatrick (Home/Homelessness)
Heriot-Watt University
Edinburgh
UK

Kenneth Gibb (Approaches)
University of Glasgow
Glasgow
UK

Richard K. Green (Economics/Finance)
University of Southern California
Los Angeles, CA
USA

Chris Hamnett (Welfare/Well-Being)
Kings College London
London
UK

Kyung-Hwan Kim (Economics/Finance)
Sogang University
Republic of Korea
and
Singapore Management University
Singapore

Heather Lovell (Environment)
University of Edinburgh
Edinburgh
UK

Montserrat Pareja Eastaway (Environment)
University of Barcelona
Barcelona
Spain

Richard Ronald (Institutions)
Delft University of Technology
Delft
The Netherlands

Anthony B. Sanders (Economics/Finance)
George Mason University
Fairfax, AZ
USA

Sasha Tsenkova (Institutions)
University of Calgary
Calgary, AB
Canada

Peter M. Ward (Welfare/Well-Being)
University of Texas at Austin
Austin, TX
USA

Gavin Wood (Policy)
RMIT University
Melbourne, VIC
Australia

EDITORIAL ADVISORY BOARD

Antonio Azuela
National Autonomous University of Mexico
Mexico

Robert Buckley
The New School
New York, NY
USA

Karl E Case
Wellesley College
Wellesley, MA
USA

Rebecca L H Chiu
University of Hong Kong
Hong Kong

Alan Gilbert
University College London
London
UK

Deniz O Igan
International Monetary Fund
Washington
USA

Hugo Priemus
Delft University of Technology
Delft
The Netherlands

Freek Spinnewijn
FEANTSA
Brussels
Belgium

Judith Yates
University of Sydney
Sydney, NSW
Australia

GUIDE TO USING THE ENCYCLOPEDIA

STRUCTURE OF THE ENCYCLOPEDIA

The encyclopedia contains 521 entries, arranged in alphabetical order, and split across 7 volumes. There are five features to help you either browse the contents or to access specific topics which interest you.

1. ALPHABETICAL CONTENTS LIST

The full alphabetical contents list follows the editorial introductions. Titles, authors, volume and page numbers are provided.

2. SECTION IDENTIFIERS

The encyclopedia was developed around 7 thematic Sections, each with its own commissioning and editorial team. A list of entries organised by Section appears next. This is useful in providing a conceptual map of the contents, as well as for making quick connections between entries.

Most entries are around 4000 words. However, in every Section there are up to seven rather longer scene setting or 'overview' articles. These are identified in the main contents list.

On an entry by entry basis, a Section identifier is listed at the foot of the opening page, where there is also an indicator to identify Overview articles.

3. CROSS REFERENCES

Most entries in the encyclopedia are cross-referenced. The cross references, which appear at the end of an entry as a 'See also' list, serve four different functions:

  i. To draw the reader's attention to related material in other entries
  ii. To indicate material that broadens and extends the scope of the article
  iii. To indicate material that covers a topic in more depth
  iv. To direct readers to other articles by the same author(s)

4. CONTRIBUTORS

In addition to the comprehensive contents and author list, each of the seven alphabetical volumes includes a list of the specific authors whose entries appear in its pages.

5. INDEX

There is a comprehensive index for the whole work provided at the back of Volume 7. This index includes page numbers for quick reference to the information you are looking for. The index differentiates between references to a whole entry, a part of an entry, and a table or figure.

LIST OF ARTICLES BY SECTION

APPROACHES

Actor–Network Theory
Appraisal and Cost-Benefit Analysis
Austrian Economics
Behavioural Economics
Case Studies
Comparative Housing Research
Complexity
Construction of Housing Knowledge
Critical Realism
Cultural Analysis of Housing and Space
Democracy and Accountability
Demographic Perspectives in Economic Housing Research
Difference
Discourse Analysis
Econometric Modeling
Economic Approaches to Housing Research
Ethnography
Evolutionary Economics
Filtering
Forecasting in Housing Research
Foucauldian Analysis
Game Theory
Gentrification
Globalisation
House Biographies
House Price Indexes: Methodologies
House Prices and Quality of Life: An Economic Analysis
Housing Careers
Housing Classes and Consumption Cleavages
Housing Indicators
Housing Market Search
Housing Preferences
Housing Statistics
Inequalities in European Cities
Institutional Economics: New
Institutional Economics: Traditional
Life Course
Neighbourhood Effects: Approaches
Neoclassical Models of the Housing Market
Neural Networks and Analytic Hierarchy Processes
New Urban Economics and Residential Location
Path Dependency
People and the Built Form
Political Ideologies
Post-Bubble Housing in Japan
Power
Property Rights Approaches
Qualitative Interviewing
Qualitative Methods in Housing Research
Regulation Theory
Residential Segregation: Measurement
Rurality and Housing
Simulation Models for Housing Analysis
Small-Area Spatial Statistics
Social Class and Housing
Social Construction
Social History
Social Policy Approaches
Social Theory and Housing
Socio-Legal Perspectives
Spatial Economics
Stakeholder Analysis for Housing
Structure and Agency
Sustainability
Systems Theory
Textual and Linguistic Analysis
Visual Research Methods
Welfare States and Housing

ECONOMICS/FINANCE

Covered Bonds
Credit Derivatives
Credit Derivatives and the Housing Market
Discrimination in Mortgage Markets
Economics of Housing Choice
Economics of Housing Externalities
Economics of Housing Market Segmentation
Economics of Social Housing
Financial Deregulation
Financial Regulation
Hedging Housing Risk
Home Ownership: Economic Benefits
Home Ownership: Non-Shelter Benefits
House Price Expectations
House Price Indexes
Housing and Wealth Portfolios
Housing Demand
Housing Equity Withdrawal in the United Kingdom
Housing Finance: Mexico
Housing Finance: Global South
Housing Markets and Macroeconomic Policy

Housing Subsidies in the Developing World
Housing Wealth and Consumption
Housing Wealth and Inheritance in the United Kingdom
Housing Wealth as Precautionary Savings
Housing Wealth Over the Life Course
Housing Wealth Distribution in the United Kingdom
Industrial Organisation of the US Residential Mortgage Market
Islamic Housing Finance
Microfinance for Housing
Mortgage Choice: Behavioural Finance
Mortgage Choice: Classical Economics
Mortgage Contracts: Flexible
Mortgage Contracts: Traditional
Mortgage Default: Consequences
Mortgage Default: Determinants
Mortgage Equity Withdrawal
Mortgage Innovation
Mortgage Insurance
Mortgage Market Functioning
Mortgage Market Regulation: Europe
Mortgage Market Regulation: North America
Mortgage Market, Character and Trends: Africa
Mortgage Market, Character and Trends: Brazil
Mortgage Market, Character and Trends: China
Mortgage Market, Character and Trends: France
Mortgage Market, Character and Trends: Germany
Mortgage Market, Character and Trends: India
Mortgage Market, Character and Trends: Italy
Mortgage Market, Character and Trends: Japan
Mortgage Market, Character and Trends: Korea
Mortgage Market, Character and Trends: Mexico
Mortgage Market, Character and Trends: United Kingdom
Mortgage Market, Character and Trends: United States
Mortgage Markets and Macro-Instability
Mortgage Payment Protection Insurance
Neighbourhood Effects
Price Determination in Housing Markets
Price Dynamics in Housing Markets
Residential Property Derivatives
Residential Real Estate Investment Trusts
Risk in Housing Markets
Simulation Models for Urban Economies
Social Housing: Finance
Spatial Mismatch
Submarkets
Subprime Mortgages
Supply Elasticity of Housing
Taxation and Subsidies: The US Case
Time and the Economic Analysis of Housing Systems
Transaction Costs in Housing Markets
User Cost, Home Ownership and Housing Prices: United States

ENVIRONMENT

Abandonment
Adaptable Housing
Building Regulations for Energy Conservation
Climate Change
Climate Change: Adaptations
Community Energy Systems
Construction and Demolition Waste
Construction Methods
Crime Prevention Through Environmental Design
Defensible Space
Demolition
Eco-Communities
Ecological Footprint
Eco-Renovation
Energy Saving
Environmental Consciousness
Environmental Risks: Earthquakes
Environmental Risks: Flooding
Ethnic Minorities and Housing
Eviction
Fuel Poverty
Gated Communities
Gender and Space
Gentrification and Neighbourhood Change
Ghetto
Gypsy/Roma Settlements
Health and Housing
Health Risks: Damp and Cold
Health Risks: Overcrowding
High Rise
Household Waste Recycling
Housing and Sustainable Transport
Housing Developers and Sustainability
Housing Dynamics: Environmental Aspects
Housing Estates
Housing Pathology
Maintenance and Repair
Modern Methods of Construction
Multiple Homes
Neighbourhood Design: Green Space and Parks
Neighbourhood Design: Public Spaces
Neighbourhood Design: Urban Outdoor Experience
Neighbourhood Disadvantage
Neighbourhood Governance
Neighbourhood Incivilities
Neighbourhood Planning
Neighbourhood Reputation

Neighbourhood Watch
NIMBYism
Peripheral Neighbourhoods
Place Attachment
Residential Segregation
Residential Urban Form and Transport
Restorative Housing Environments
Rural Communities
Rural Housing
Second Homes
Self-Build: Global North
Self-Build: Global South
Shanty Towns
Slums
Social Spaces and Urban Policies
Social Sustainability
Sustainable Communities
Sustainable Housing Cultures
Sustainable Lifestyles
Sustainable Regeneration
Sustainable Urban Development
Temporary Housing
Vacancy Chains
Vernacular Housing
Water Supply and Sanitation

HOME/HOMELESSNESS

Anthropological Perspectives on Home
Children and Parenting
Cost Analyses of Homelessness: Limits and Opportunities
Criminological Perspectives on Homelessness
Do-it-Yourself
Domestic Technologies and the Modern Home
Domestic Violence
Domesticity
Domestic Pets
Domicide
Economic Perspectives on Homelessness
Emotions at Home
Ethnographies of Home and Homelessness
Experiencing Home
Experiencing Home: Sexuality
Feminist Perspectives on Home
Feminist Perspectives on Homelessness
Gender Divisions in the Home
Hidden Homelessness
High-Rise Homes
Home and Homelessness
Home as a Space of Care
Home as Inheritance
Home as Investment
Home as Leisure Space
Home as Workplace
Home Environments: Aesthetics, Fashion, Status
Home in Temporary Dwellings
Home Objects
Home: Paid Domestic Labour
Home: Unpaid Domestic Labour
Homeless Families: United Kingdom
Homeless Families: United States
Homelessness: Causation
Homelessness: Definitions
Homelessness: Measurement Questions
Homelessness: Prevention in the United States
Homeless People in China/East Asia
Homeless People: African Americans in the United States
Homeless People: Care Leavers
Homeless People: Care Leavers in the United Kingdom
Homeless People: Disasters and Displacement
Homeless People: Economic Migrants in Southern Europe
Homeless People: Ex-Prisoners in England and Wales
Homeless People: Ex-Service Personnel/Veterans in the United Kingdom
Homeless People: Indigenous/Aboriginal
Homeless People: Older People
Homeless People: Polish Migrants in the United Kingdom
Homeless People: Refugees and Asylum Seekers
Homeless People: Single Men in Japan
Homeless People: Street Children in Africa
Homeless People: Street Children in Asia
Homeless People: Street Children in Mexico
Homeless People: Street Children in the United Kingdom
Homeless People: Youth in Australia
Homeless People: Youth in the United Kingdom
Homes as a Space of Worship
Homestead and Other Legal Protections
Ideal Homes
Illicit Drug Use and Homelessness
Impairment and Experience of Home
Kitchens
Living Rooms
Material Cultures of Domestic Interiors: Africa
Material Cultures of Domestic Interiors: India
Material Cultures of Domestic Interiors: Japan
Material Cultures of Domestic Interiors: Transnationalism
Material Cultures of Home
Meanings of Home
Meanings of Home for Moveable Habitats
Meanings of Home for Older People
Meanings of Home: Gender Dimensions

Meanings of Home in Popular Culture
Memory and Nostalgia at Home
Mental Health and Homelessness
Migration: Ethnicity, Race and Mobility
Nature in the Home
Ontological Security
Philosophical Perspectives on Home
Policies to Address Homelessness
Policies to Address Homelessness: Criminalisation and Control of Public Space
Policies to Address Homelessness: Housing First Approaches
Policies to Address Homelessness: Partnership-Based Approaches in Ireland
Policies to Address Homelessness: Prevention in the United Kingdom
Policies to Address Homelessness: Rights-Based Approaches
Policies to Address Homelessness: 'Staircase' Models
Privacy, Sanctuary and Privatism
Representations of Home: Literature and Language
Representations of Home: Painting
Representations of Home: Photos and Film
Representations of Homelessness
Rural Homelessness in India
Rural Homelessness: An International Perspective
Shelter and Development
Social Psychological Perspectives on Homelessness
Squatting: Developing World
Squatting: United Kingdom
Suburban Homes
Technology and Surveillance in the Home

INSTITUTIONS

Affordable Housing Strategies
Architects
Central Government Institutions
Civil Sector Institutions and Informal Settlements
Community- and Neighbourhood-Based Organisations in the United States
Cooperative Housing/Ownership
Demand Subsidies for Low-Income Households
Ethnicity and Housing Organisations
Government Mortgage Guarantee Institutions
Government/Public Lending Institutions: Asia-Pacific
Government Sponsored Enterprises in the United States
Homeowners' Associations in Post-Socialist Countries
House Building Industries: Africa
House Building Industries: Asia Pacific
House Building Industries: Latin America
House Building Industries: Post-Socialist
House Building Industries: Western Europe and North America
Households and Families
Housing Agents and Housing Submarkets
Housing Auctions
Housing Developers: Developed World
Housing Developers: Developing World
Housing Finance Institutions: Africa
Housing Finance Institutions: Asia
Housing Finance Institutions: Latin America
Housing Finance Institutions: Transition Societies
Housing Institutions in Developing Countries
Housing Market Institutions
Housing Paradigms
Housing Policy: Agents and Regulators
Human Rights and Housing
Informal Housing: Asia
Informal Housing: Latin America
Institutions and Governance Networks in Housing and Urban Regeneration
Institutions for Housing Supply
Institutions for Neighbourhood Renewal
Institutions that Represent Housing Professionals
Land Owners
Land Registration Institutions: Developed World
Master Plan Developers
Mortgage Lenders and Loans
Neighbourhood Improvement: The Role of Housing and Housing Institutions
New Urbanism and Smart Growth Movements
Notaries and Legal Professionals
Older People: Housing Institutions
Planning Institutions: Canada/United States
Planning Institutions: China
Planning Institutions: Post-Socialist
Post-Conflict Housing Restitutions
Private Protection and Housing Property Insurers in the United States
Private Rental Landlords: Developing Countries
Private Rental Landlords: Europe
Private Rental Landlords: North America
Private Sector Housing Management: Asia Pacific
Private Sector Housing Management: Europe
Private Sector Housing Management: North America
Private Sector Housing Management: Post-Socialist
Public-Private Partnerships
Real Estate Agents
Research Networks and Professional Institutions in Housing
Resident and Neighbourhood Movements

Rights to Housing Tenure
Rights to Housing: Developing Societies
Rights to Housing: International Instruments
Rights to Housing: Marginalised Housing Groups
Rights to Land Tenure
Security of Tenure in Muslim Communities
Self-Help Housing Organisations
Self-Provided Housing in Developed Societies
Social Housing Institutions in Europe
Social Housing Landlords: Asia Pacific
Social Housing Landlords: China
Social Housing Landlords: Europe
Social Housing Landlords: Latin America
Social Housing Landlords: North America
Social Housing Landlords: Post-Socialist
Subprime and Predatory Lending: Legal Regulation
Supply-Side Subsidies for Affordable Rental Housing
Taxation
Tenant Cooperatives, Shareholders' Housing Companies
Tenure as an Institution
Welfare Agencies and Assistance: United States
Women and Housing Organisations

POLICY

Access and Affordability: Homeowner Taxation
Access and Affordability: House Purchase Certificates
Access and Affordability: Housing Allowances
Access and Affordability: Housing Vouchers
Access and Affordability: Mortgage Guarantees
Access and Affordability: Rent Regulation
Brownfield Development and Housing Supply
Choice and Government Intervention in Housing Markets
Contract Saving Schemes
Deposit Assistance Schemes for Private Rental in the United Kingdom
Development Land Tax
Discrimination in Housing Markets
Education Programmes for Home Buyers and Tenants
Energy Consumption, Housing, and Urban Development Policy
Exclusionary Zoning
First Home Owner Grants
Foreclosure Prevention Measures
HOPE VI
Housing and Labour Markets
Housing and Neighbourhood Quality: Home Improvement Grants
Housing and Neighbourhood Quality: Urban Regeneration
Housing Construction Industry, Competition and Regulation
Housing Finance Deposit Guarantees
Housing Governance
Housing Markets and Macroeconomic Policy
Housing Policies in Developing Countries
Housing Policies in Developing Countries: Microfinance
Housing Policies in Developing Countries: Sites-and-Services and Aided Self-Help
Housing Policy and Regeneration
Housing Policy Trends
Housing Standards: Regulation
Housing Subsidies and Work Incentives
Housing Supply
Housing Supply: Green Belts
Housing Supply: Urban Growth Boundaries
Housing Trust Funds
Immigration and Housing Policy
Impact Fees
Inclusionary Zoning to Support Affordable Housing
Intermediate Housing Tenures
Key Worker Housing Policies
Local Government Property Taxes
Low-Income Housing Tax Credits
Mobility Programmes for Disadvantaged Populations: The Moving to Opportunity Programme
Monetary Policy, Wealth Effects and Housing
Mortgage Interest Rate Regulation
Mortgage Markets: Regulation and intervention
Policies to Address Redlining
Policies to Address Social Mix in Communities
Policies to Address Spatial Mismatch
Policies to Promote Housing Choice in Transition Countries
Policies to Promote the Environmental Efficiency of Housing
Policies to Support Access and Affordability of Housing
Policy Instruments that Support Housing Supply: Social Housing
Policy Instruments that Support Housing Supply: Supply-Side Subsidies
Privatisation of Social Housing
Rent Policies For Social Housing
Securing Land Rights and Housing Delivery
Security of Tenure Legislation in Private Rental Housing
Self-Help: Policy Assistance
Shared Equity
Social Housing and Employment
Social Housing: Measures to Attract Private Finance
Taxation Policy and Housing
Upgrading Informal Settlements

WELFARE/WELLBEING

Access and Affordability: Developed Countries
Asset-Based Welfare
Asset-Based Well-Being: Use Versus Exchange Value
Collective Ownership
Disability and Enablement
Foreclosure Vulnerability
Gated Communities: Developed Countries
Gated Communities: Global South
Gender and Urban Housing in the Global South
Gentrification and Well-Being
Health and Well-Being
Health and Well-Being: Vulnerable Populations
Household Organisation and Survival in Developing Countries
Housing and the State in Australasia
Housing and the State in China
Housing and the State in Latin America
Housing and the State in South Africa
Housing and the State in South Asia
Housing and the State in the Middle East
Housing and the State in the Soviet Union and Eastern Europe
Housing and the State in Western Europe
Housing Need in the United Kingdom
Housing Subsidies and Welfare
Immigration and Housing: North-Western Europe
Immigration and Housing: United States
Informal Housing: Colonias in the United States
Migration and Housing: Global South
Migration and Population Mobility
Migration and Urban Living in Less Developed Countries
Mobility and Community
Mortage Default and Well-Being in the United States
Older People: Well-Being
Older People: Well-Being, Housing and Neighbourhoods
Politics of Housing
Post-Disaster Housing and Reconstruction
Privatisation of Housing: Implications for Well-Being
Remittances and Well-Being
Rental Market and Rental Policies in Less Developed Countries
Residential Segregation and Education
Residential Segregation and Ethnic Diversity in US Housing
Residential Segregation: Apartheid
Residential Segregation: Experiences of African Americans
Residential Segregation: Race and Ethnicity
Rights, Citzenship, and Shelter
Rights to the City
Self-Build: Latin America
Self-Help: Land Development
Self-Help and Informal Sector Housing in the United States and Canada
Shelter and Settlement for Forcibly Displaced People
Slum Clearance
Social Exclusion and Housing
Social Housing and Social Problems
Social Housing in the United States: Overview
Social Housing: Allocation
Social Justice
Social Mix in Western Countries
Social Movements and Housing
Squatter Settlement Clearance
Supported Housing
Urbanisation and Housing the Poor: Overview
Urban Regeneration in Latin America
Well-Being and Housing in the Caribbean

CONTRIBUTORS TO VOLUME 1: A–D

Kwame Addae-Dapaah
National University of Singapore, Singapore

Chris Allen
Manchester Metropolitan University, Manchester, UK

Rowland Atkinson
University of York, York, UK

Blair Badcock
Housing New Zealand Corporation, Wellington, New Zealand

Steven Bourassa
University of Louisville, Louisville, KY, USA

David Byrne
Durham University, Durham, UK

Thomas Byrne
University of Pennsylvania, Philadelphia, PA, USA

Pamela Carlisle-Frank
The Foundation for Interdisciplinary Research and Education Promoting Animal Welfare (FIREPAW, Inc.), Houston, TX, USA

Irene Cieraad
Delft University of Technology, Delft, The Netherlands

Melek Cigdem
RMIT University, Melbourne, VIC, Australia

David Clapham
Cardiff University, Cardiff, UK

Paul Cozens
Curtin University of Technology, Bentley, WA, Australia

Jeff Crump
University of Minnesota, St. Paul, MN, USA

Dennis Culhane
University of Pennsylvania, Philadelphia, PA, USA

Ritske Dankert
Delft University of Technology, Delft, The Netherlands

Timothy Dixon
Oxford Brookes University, Oxford, UK

Gary Dymski
University of California Riverside, Riverside, CA, USA

Marja Elsinga
Delft University of Technology, Delft, The Netherlands

Tina Fawcett
University of Oxford, Oxford, UK

Kenneth Gibb
University of Glasgow, Glasgow, UK

Tony Gilmour
University of New South Wales, Sydney, NSW, Australia

Matthew Gregg
Oxford Brookes University, Oxford, UK

Rajat Gupta
Oxford Brookes University, Oxford, UK

Marietta Haffner
Delft University of Technology, Delft, The Netherlands

Malcolm Harrison
University of Leeds, Leeds, UK

Laura Hemingway
University of Leeds, Leeds, UK

David Hillier
University of Glamorgan, Wales, UK

Joris Hoekstra
Delft University of Technology, Delft, The Netherlands

Clare Holdsworth
University of Liverpool, Liverpool, UK

Joanne Hollows
Nottingham Trent University, Nottingham, UK

Kath Hulse
Swinburne University of Technology, Melbourne, VIC, Australia

Rita Jacinto
King's College London, London, UK

Peter Kemp
University of Oxford, Oxford, UK

Charles King
Simon Fraser University, Vancouver, BC, Canada

Michael Lea
Cardiff Economic Consulting, Cardiff, CA, USA

Tang Lee
University of Calgary, Calgary, AB, Canada

Thomas Lindh
Institute for Futures Studies, Stockholm, Sweden

Stuart Lowe
University of York, York, UK

Duanfang Lu
University of Sydney, Sydney, NSW, Australia

Vincent Lyon-Callo
Western Michigan University, Kalamazoo, MI, USA

Duncan Maclennan
University of St Andrews, St Andrews, UK

Bo Malmberg
Institute for Futures Studies, Stockholm, Sweden

Tony Manzi
University of Westminster, London, UK

Paula Meth
University of Sheffield, Sheffield, UK

Vivienne Milligan
University of New South Wales, Sydney, NSW, Australia

Diana Mitlin
International Institute for Environment and Development (IIED), London, UK

Lorraine Murphy
Delft University of Technology, Delft, The Netherlands

Laurence Murphy
University of Auckland, Auckland, New Zealand

Mike Oxley
De Montfort University, Leicester, UK; Delft University of Technology, Delft, The Netherlands

Kelly Patterson
University at Buffalo, Buffalo, NY, USA

Andrey Pavlov
Simon Fraser University, Vancouver, BC, Canada

Douglas Robertson
University of Stirling, Stirling, UK

Richard Ronald
University of Amsterdam, Amsterdam, The Netherlands

Julie Rugg
University of York, York, UK

Ann Rutledge
R&R Consulting, New York, NY, USA

David Satterthwaite
International Institute for Environment and Development (IIED), London, UK

Beverley Searle
St Andrews University, St Andrews, UK

Robert Silverman
University at Buffalo, Buffalo, NY, USA

Neil Simcock
Lancaster University, Lancaster, UK

Janet Smith
University of Illinois at Chicago, Chicago, IL, USA

Peter Somerville
University of Lincoln, Lincoln, UK

Dag Einar Sommervoll
Research Department of Statistics Norway, Oslo, Norway

Lynn Spigel
Northwestern University, Evanston, IL, USA

Eli Støa
Norwegian University of Science and Technology, Trondheim, Norway

Marion Steele
University of Guelph, Guelph, ON, Canada; University of Toronto, Toronto, ON, Canada

Graham Steventon
Coventry University, Coventry, UK

Ray Struyk
NORC, Bethesda, MD, USA

Chi Ming Tam
City University of Hong Kong, Hong Kong, China

Vivian Tam
University of Western Sydney, Sydney, NSW, Australia

Marilyn Taylor
University of the West of England, Bristol, UK

Robert Van Order
George Washington University, Washington, DC, USA

Gordon Walker
Lancaster University, Lancaster, UK

Nicholas Walliman
Oxford Brookes University, Oxford, UK

Matt Watson
University of Sheffield, Sheffield, UK

Gavin Wood
RMIT University, Melbourne, VIC, Australia

PREFACE AND ACKNOWLEDGEMENTS

The urge to collect and catalogue is as old as humanity itself. Perhaps there is something about being human that insists on scholars pausing from time to time to gather up everything they know and set it down en masse. Certainly, encyclopedias have existed, pretty much in the form we know them now, for at least two millennia. Furthermore, most dictionary definitions of the term 'encyclopedia' contain phrases like 'complete education', 'comprehensive', and 'covering all knowledge'. Roget's Thesaurus likewise directs those looking for synonyms and antonyms of 'encylopedical' to the headings 'generality' and 'knowledge'. In short, anyone with an encyclopedic knowledge of a subject simply knows it all.

It cannot be denied that there is something satisfying about the thought of coordinating a project designed to pull the housing world together in this way. Housing studies, after all, is a quintessentially interdisciplinary and international enterprise whose research and teaching spans a wide range of social science, health, and environmental disciplines. Its relevance ranges from sociology and geography to law, from politics to public health, from economics to accountancy, and from architecture to planning, engineering, and environmental science. The meaning and materiality of home has likewise moved to centre stage in a broad sweep of cultural studies, English, and humanities research. Housing and home together are hot media topics, the staple diet of dinner parties, the heart of practical politics, and very big business in the sale of financial services, do-it-yourself (DIY), home interiors, and garden design. The thought of gathering 'everything you ever wanted to know' about housing and home together into a single massive reference work is enticing.

The *International Encyclopedia of Housing and Home* is not, however, an oracle of this kind. To pretend that it is would be tantamount to claiming that a map of Spain were as complete as Spain itself. But if the map were that comprehensive, it would *be* Spain! Subjects as diverse, dynamic, lively, changeable, topical, and important as housing and home could never be crammed into, or pinned onto, the pages of a book, no matter how many volumes or innovative media platforms were brought to bear. So, in a sense, we have broken the encyclopedic mould. The aim was always to produce a work that is wide-ranging enough to embrace the cutting edges of research, to probe the inner core and outer limits of the worlds of housing and home, to capture the sheer colour and vibrancy wrapped into these subjects, and to recognise the critical importance they hold for economic management, social policy, and public well-being. At the same time, however, the enterprise is designed to set hares running: to identify, as much as to fill, key gaps in the literature; to point to new themes and research agendas which might, in time, make the current work redundant.

Cataloguing the spheres of housing and home is, then, a dynamic and open-ended project. It is a venture that began in earlier works, for example, in Willem van Vliet's (1998) single-volumed *Encyclopedia of Housing*, and its companion work, David Levinson's (1998) *Encyclopedia of Homelessness* (both published by Sage). It is a process extended into more specialised compilations, such Jack Guttentag's (2004) *Mortgage Encyclopedia* (McGraw-Hill) and Andrew Arden's (1997) *Encyclopedia of Housing Law and Practice* (Sweet and Maxwell). Then there are Jack Rostron and Michael Nutt's *Dictionary of Housing* and Jack Rostron, Robert Hardy-Pickering, Laura Tatham and Linda Wright's *Dictionary of Property and Construction Law* (published by Arena in 1997, and Routledge in 2001, respectively). And there are numerous single-volume collections, most notably and recently, the *Handbook of Housing Studies* (Sage, 2011), edited by David Clapham, William Clark and Kenneth Gibb. Who knows where it might end? Not here, and not yet; I am sure. But one other thing is certain: there is nothing published, in press, or yet planned, which offers the sheer scale, complexity, and range of content now packed into the *International Encyclopedia of Housing and Home*. This is a massive work, equivalent in size to around 25 standard edited collections. We offer it, therefore, notwithstanding its partial, uneven, and evolving character, as the major single reference work for housing professionals – for academics and practitioners – for all teaching, learning, and research needs.

It is probably clear, but the words should be said, that the encyclopedia is very much a collective enterprise and a labour of love. Academic authors get little credit for an undertaking like this in the counting and ranking exercises that so many governments now engage in. To be sure, small payments have been made, and the publisher no doubt seeks a profit. But you can be certain that those who brought this project to life did so, above all, as a service to colleagues, reflecting absolute passion for the subject. That sense of imagination and excitement is, I think, reflected in the quality of the articles and the coherence of the work.

The project has been ongoing since 2007; fully 20 senior scholars have spent, on and off, at least 5 years planning, commissioning, debating, and editing the 2 million words that are published herein. They have worked with over

350 authors, and been supported by an enthusiastic international advisory board drawn from all walks of life around housing and home. There is input from most world regions and from every key centre for housing research as well as from the non-university sector. The result is in every sense a collaborative work: it reflects the expertise of the authors, the insight and efficiency of the section editors, the vigilance of the associate editors-in-chief, and the good humoured energy of the entire scholarly team. That, I feel is the main strength of the work, and key to its endurance.

I am sure there are many acknowledgements to funding agencies, institutions, projects, colleagues, and friends that everyone involved with this work would wish to make. My personal debt is to the UK's Economic and Social Research Council, whose Professorial Fellowships scheme made time for the plot to be hatched (RES 051-27-0126); to the members of the first Think Tank on Housing Wealth who debated its feasibility; and to Elsevier's Mary Malin who turned a modest proposal into a Major Reference Work.

If I had enough space, and readers had the patience, I would wish at this point to mention every editor, and many authors, by name, and list the distinctive qualities that each has brought to this amazing collective work. It has been a privilege to be part of that team. The work of the authors is, I feel sure, clear from the content of the articles. The achievements of the section editors can been seen from the coherence of the thematic volumes and the energy in their introductory statements. The role of the associate editors-in-chief is perhaps less obvious, because they have worked between sections to explore synergies, look for overlap, encourage themes that cross section boundaries, and of course they have worked as a resource for the sections themselves. Marja Elsinga steered 'Environment' and 'Policy'; Lorna Fox O'Mahony anchored 'Home and Homelessness' and 'Institutions'; Susan Wachter and Ong Seow Eng kept an eye on 'Economics and Finance' across the board. The editors in turn owe special thanks to Jim Follain and Jim Shilling for their work as reviewers in 'Economics and Finance'. We are all grateful to Mike Nicholls for his meticulous coordination of the proofs. If, however, there is one person without whom the project would have foundered, it is Richard Berryman, development editor for Elsevier's Major Reference Works. He has far exceeded his brief, keeping track of all the articles, managing the process of electronic manuscript submission (circumventing it where necessary), and bringing unfailing energy, good humour, and consummate professionalism to an otherwise impossible task.

Susan J Smith
Cambridge, October 2011

INTRODUCTION

Housing has never been more squarely in the spotlight; homes have rarely been closer to people's hearts. For the first time ever, we appreciate the full extent to which housing market dynamics can challenge macroeconomic stability, and expose the fragility of households' primary asset base. Residential mortgage markets have proved sufficiently volatile to trigger a global credit crisis, and to bankrupt entire residential neighbourhoods; yet, they have also added unprecedented financial flexibility to home-occupiers' domestic accounts. Meanwhile, the social aspects of housing (including issues around exclusion, inequality, and identity) are under intense scrutiny by politicians and social researchers alike. Many governments have rekindled their in-house, and commissioned, housing research programmes and revitalised housing policy. The search is on for housing solutions to a wide range of enduring social problems and for ways to manage a new suite of financial and environmental risks. As a result, the inherently multidisciplinary field of housing studies is undergoing a major renaissance. The time seems right to publish a comprehensive *International Encyclopedia of Housing and Home* designed to meet a suite of teaching, research, practical, professional, and policy needs among a wide-ranging readership.

Encyclopedias come in many shapes and sizes: some are little more than elaborate dictionaries, full of long words and short definitions; others seem more like edited books, with extended manuscripts covering a few core themes. This encyclopedia occupies neither extreme. It is, well, 'encyclopedic' in every sense. It is based on over 500 substantial contributions, enough to touch practically every core theme relating to housing and home. Most articles run to at least 4000 words, sufficient for subject experts to address their topics in depth, without sacrificing accessibility. This melée is structured around a series of longer keynote or overview articles, which set the scene for the seven thematic volumes or sections comprising the larger work. The result is a comprehensive, authoritative source of facts, ideas, and concepts anchored on housing and home. The contents are international in scope, engaging with trends in every world region; the authors are drawn from a wide range of countries, and the work as a whole collates a mix of expertise from academics, policy-makers, professionals and practitioners.

There is an infinite number of ways to collect and organise the contents of a publication like this. In the end, the encyclopedic tradition is to list articles alphabetically, and we feel this works for housing and home. 'Housing studies' is, after all, a tradition founded on 'mix and match' across sectors and disciplines; the uneasy jostling of incongruous ideas has already proved to be an exciting route to new knowledge. With that in mind, why not experiment with the alphabet?

For those who seek more structure, there are other ways of navigating the text. For example, readers may wish to search by 'discipline' (there are contributions from housing economics, housing law, the sociology of housing, psychology and housing, housing and health, cultures of housing, and politics of housing), by 'world region' (coverage extends to Europe, Australasia, North and South America, Africa, and Asia), 'thematically' (through topics such as housing finance, housing policy, and housing management), 'sectorally' (owner-occupation, social renting, private renting, buy-to-let, co-operative housing, self-build, etc.), 'conceptually' (housing markets, price mechanisms, housing need, housing allocation, housing consumption, and meanings of home), 'theoretically' (housing and the macroeconomy, the microstructures of housing markets, social theory and housing), 'methodologically' (life-course approach, behavioural economics, hedonic analysis, microsociology, ethnography, and synoptic reading), and 'practically' (housing interventions, planning, buying and selling, professional training, needs assessment, price index construction, taxation, etc.).

Notwithstanding these multiple organisational possibilities, the main conceptual map of the encyclopedia is constructed from seven broad themes, each of which was commissioned, written, and edited as a separate volume or section. Other than an alphabetical list, section headings are the main way in which the work is structured. Introductions to each section, written by the editors who devised them, appear next. In brief, the sections are as follows. 'Approaches' contains articles on the main concepts and theories used in housing research, and on the methodologies commonly used to explore key themes around housing, home, and homelessness. 'Economics and Finance' engages with all aspects of housing and economy, including housing economics, housing market dynamics, housing wealth, and housing finance. 'Environment' includes articles on the physical and social environments, including environmental sustainability, energy efficiency, neighbourhood trajectories, and residential segregation. 'Home and Homelessness' addresses the full range of ideas about homemaking, home cultures, home values, domestic interiors, design, and meanings of home; it also considers the absence of home – the predicament of homelessness – in its many and varied forms. 'Institutions' documents all the main institutions of the housing system: legal frameworks, housing tenures, lenders, insurers, valuation, marketing, intermediation, and so on. 'Policy' is concerned with all aspects of housing governance and regulation: access and affordability of housing, housing production, tax policies, and links between housing, labour markets, and mortgage markets. 'Welfare and Well-Being' is concerned with the social aspects of housing. It examines the links between housing, welfare, and well-being; it considers housing needs, risks, and affordability; and it touches on health, safety, and security.

There are, of course, aspects of housing and home that this work does not cover. Some areas are simply not in the brief: they would have made the project too large, and in some important respects unbalanced. These include: commercial real estate; aspects of welfare, urban studies and planning that do not pertain to housing; technical building regulations; and aspects of home not relating to dwelling or residential property. Some topics cried out for attention, but simply refused to be attached to an author: maybe that will change next time round, as key themes blossom; perhaps it is already a pointer to topics that will in future fail to thrive. Some authors, bluntly put, did not submit their articles, despite extended deadlines. But that is the messy reality of creating a major reference work. Encyclopedias can no longer be produced by a single person; the shape they take is in every sense a reflection of the busy worlds they inhabit. One thing is clear, however: the encyclopedia is not only the print in your hands or the text on an electronic platform. It has created the community that made it and that network will hopefully widen as time goes on: connecting scholars across spaces, disciplines, and languages; sparking new alliances, friendships, and debates; indeed, giving shape to areas of scholarship that were overlooked or taken for granted before. In that sense, the encyclopedia can never be finished. It has a life of its own which has already burst free of its covers.

M Elsinga, L Fox O'Mahony, SE Ong, SJ Smith, and S Wachter

APPROACHES

Housing is a complex entity that has many different dimensions and impacts on many areas of private and public life. Housing is at the same time shelter, the scene of people's most emotional moments, the place we call home, an indicator of status, and a point of access to employment as well as to a range of public and private facilities. Housing is also the most expensive purchase the majority of households will make and a repository for the majority of personal wealth. The complexity of housing is fascinating, but this presents problems as well as opportunities for housing analysts.

The peculiarities of housing (as a locationally fixed commodity, a strangely indivisible investment, an object of consumption, and a crucible of housing services) demand special methodological and conceptual attention. That is one reason why we have devoted an entire section of the encyclopedia to it. Some aspects of housing can readily be explored using tried and tested tools borrowed from cognate areas of social and economic research. Others demand a more bespoke range of approaches. More than anything else, while acknowledging that certain elements of housing – one or two attributes at once, perhaps – can readily and productively be subject to discipline-specific analyses, the articles in this section of the encyclopedia point to the opportunity, and incentive, which housing studies provides to undertake comprehensive and transdisciplinary research.

There are 67 articles in this section. They provide both theoretical depth and methodological detail; they span qualitative and quantitative, as well as social and economic, approaches to housing research. They can therefore be used in conjunction with substantive articles in many other sections. For example, the article on the methodology of house price indexes in this section has a counterpart in the section 'Economics and Finance' on the uses and application of such indexes. Similarly, an article on neighbourhood effects in this section has a bearing on several substantive articles in the section 'Environment'. By way of a more systematic introduction to the diverse approaches collected here, we briefly consider theories, methods, and social and economic approaches as applied to housing studies.

Theory has become increasingly important in housing studies in recent years. Only two decades ago, Jim Kemeny (1992) made a haunting plea for more theoretically-aware housing research. He was critical of the then-dominant empirical paradigm for its excessively policy-driven approach, around an agenda shaped by government agencies. He argued that this style of housing studies lacked an explicit research epistemology or ontology and was isolated from the societal context within which specific problems were situated. Instead, most research addressed questions set and problems defined by powerful agents – most notably by governments. This made housing studies useful in an instrumental sense (and this is still the case), but limited its explanatory power and capacity to imagine change.

To an extent, Kemeny solved the problem himself, taking a lead role in establishing the journal *Housing and Social Theory*. However, the success of that journal is just one indicator of a steady increase in the amount of theoretically aware housing research now under way. Many articles in this section testify to this continuing trend, profiling the wide array of theoretical perspectives that are now used to illuminate housing and home. Some of those ideas are 'borrowed' – drawn from the wider social sciences, as epitomised in the application of the concept of ontological security, drawn from the work of the sociologist Anthony Giddens (1984), to research on owner-occupation. But others are, or have been made, very specific to housing research. The scene is set in Jago Dodson's overview article: Social Theory and Housing.

The 'theoretical' picture is fairly comprehensive. Articles range from actor–network theory through constructionism, critical realism, Foucauldian approaches, housing classes, and welfare regimes. There are, inevitably, gaps in this coverage, and it is important to be aware that new theoretical ideas are coming to light all the time. The articles in this section pick up on that dynamism. For example, there is no consensus on the nature of the micro-foundations of housing market dynamics. Traditional neoclassical economic approaches have their place in this section, but they have been increasingly criticised by adherents of institutional economics, behavioural economics, and other approaches such as material sociology. Some of this jostling is apparent in the selection of articles herein.

Hence, one question that arises is whether there can, or should, be any comprehensive or all-embracing 'grand theory' to guide housing research. On the one hand, the lack of a 'general' theory of housing may be something to worry about. Some regard the absence of a coherent and comprehensive theoretical framework as a substantial weakness, making it impossible to transcend individual partial analyses. How do you put different insights together and understand how they relate or make up a larger whole? How do you devise a policy when all you have to go on are partial findings from varying approaches? On the other hand, the theoretical eclecticism that now exists is a fair reflection of the complexity of housing and of the many different analytical or policy questions that it poses. Even single issues, such as consumer market behaviour (e.g., the notion of housing choice), can be viewed in many different ways, and each can offer its own particular inspiration. The theoretical angle adopted in a specific piece of housing research may therefore rightly be adjusted to or dictated by the precise research question being addressed.

If the lack of a comprehensive theoretical framework in housing studies is problematic, it reflects a wider challenge for the social sciences more broadly. What is exciting, and to an extent reflected in the ideas in this section, is that housing is already the focus of transdisciplinary work in a variety of areas – for example, in behavioural and institutional economics – because of its unique features. Perhaps this is why King (2009) has argued that housing provides a good base from which to devise theory from a vantage point at the forefront of transdisciplinary research. Clearly, there is much work to be done before progress can be made in this direction, but the scope of this encyclopedia, if nothing else, provides a good testing ground for such endeavours.

Methods are as important to 'Approaches' as theories, and the articles in this section also illustrate the application of many different elements of the methodological toolkit to a range of housing topics. Reflecting a broad array of disciplines and approaches, these 'how-to' articles range widely, and they are not just about practicalities; they include some fundamental methodological concerns. For example, Flood's analysis of housing indicators reflects on their intrinsic meaningfulness as well as commenting on good and bad practice at a more prosaic level. Other articles relevant at this juncture include those on housing statistics, small area spatial statistics, forecasting, and econometric modelling. There are also reflections on comparative methods, qualitative methods, cultural analysis, visual methods, and so on. There is probably something here for everyone who is in search of a methodological starting point for research on housing and home.

There is insufficient space to profile all the 'how-to' articles, but it is perhaps worth taking one example from an overview article by Mike Oxley that provides a critique of comparative housing research. This article shows that an important development in housing research in the past 20 years has been an increase in international research, comparing housing systems for deeper insights about policy, process, and practice. While it is relatively easy to provide a superficial analysis of different national housing systems, going 'deep' into contexts, institutions, and markets requires ongoing commitment, as well as exceptional conceptual and methodological clarity. Such articles encourage commentators on housing research to recognise the scope for policy transfer and to be more willing to address the complexities of housing systems in other countries.

A sea change in the social sciences across the last decade has been the reconciliation between economics and other styles of social research. Some of this rapprochement is evident in articles of this section. However, 'housing economics' (like economics generally) addresses some very specific problems using some very distinctive tools, and this particularity is well-reflected among contributors to the encyclopedia. Approximately 17 articles are apposite here, spanning the neoclassical mainstream as well as the emerging heterodox panoply. Interestingly, while the section 'Economics and Finance' properly contains articles with a mainstream flavour, a large part of the discussion in 'Approaches' represents the heterodox challenge. At the very least, it grapples with the heterogeneity of housing research and aptly illustrates the wealth of alternative economics approaches now in play. There is, for example, discussion of institutions, property rights, Austrian economics, evolutionary perspectives, new institutional economics, behavioural economics, and neural networks. The sheer range of these ideas is pulled together in a compelling overview article by Alex Marsh on economic approaches.

More than any other applied area of economics, the housing and land market seems disposed to nonmainstream approaches, even if only a few such approaches are commonly published in key disciplinary journals (with the exception of behavioural economics which has taken the discipline by storm). Perhaps there are specific features of housing and human interactions with real estate that lend themselves to broader analyses of economics – analyses which take appropriate account of local context, bounded rationality, power over resources, the importance of the elapsing of real time, durability and spatial fixity, the joint nature of housing (with neighbourhoods, local government, and finance markets, to name three important links), and the way households, firms, and the state cope with decision-making in the face of this complexity. Other commodities have some of these attributes but, as has often been said, housing is unique in possessing them all. This, however, is not to deny the continuing importance of the insights of neoclassical economics and the evidence base built up around it, including in the sphere of housing economics. Regardless of philosophical and methodological disputes, the study of housing would be much poorer if we were to ignore the mainstream, just as housing research would be sorely limited if we only had 'orthodox' economics to rely on.

Social research in housing has a heterodox history and there is no parallel here to the challenge now facing orthodox housing economics. However, there is no shortage of articles illustrating the diversity of social approaches, and capturing the tensions, as well as opportunities, these engender. We have attempted to make it clear that the distinction between economic and social approaches is one of practicality rather than ontology. It is equally important to avoid characterising one as demanding quantitative methods and the other as more fitted to qualitative understandings. However, notwithstanding recent interests among economists in focus groups and related approaches, some of the major contributions to the development of qualitative methods have come from the sociological and anthropological disciplines. It is these cutting-edge approaches that are profiled herein. That is why there is an overview article on qualitative methods in housing research by Henry Coolen, providing context for other articles on ethnography, discourse, house biographies, life-course perspectives, and so on. There is also an emphasis in the social research articles on approaches relating to welfare, well-being, and the monitoring of inequality. While 'approaches' are not usually thought of in terms of normative theory, by sensitising readers to historical methods, matters of sustainability, and questions of power, political ideology, and policy futures, this section builds a platform for articles elsewhere in the encyclopedia to take on this broader mantle.

To return, in conclusion, to the start. Even given the extensive section that 'Approaches' has become, there is more to say, gaps to fill, and potential to realise. There is no objective sense of resolution to many key debates, and no conclusion to the various conversations the articles open up. And nor should there be. Housing studies has blossomed through diversity, and a diverse array of 'approaches' is key to this continuing. To be sure, such breadth may pose a challenge to readers and their disciplinary priors. However, the section editors, themselves coming from different disciplines, have shaped this volume with engagement and rapprochement firmly in mind.

D Clapham and K Gibb

References

Giddens A (1984) *The Constitution of Society*. Polity Press: Cambridge.
Kemeny J (1992) *Housing and Social Theory*. Routledge: London.
King P (2009) Using theory or making theory: Can there be theories of housing? *Housing, Theory and Society* 26.1: 41–52.

ECONOMICS AND FINANCE

Overview

Economics as a discipline has a long history of engagement with housing research. However, it is fair to say that, until the last decade, housing rarely took the centre stage. Now, however, it is clear how crucial housing, mortgage, and related capital markets are for the financial fortunes of whole economies and for individual households. This section consists of 72 articles, selected to illustrate this. The essays cover a wide range of topics concerning the real (physical) side of housing, as well as housing finance. They address microeconomic issues as well as macroeconomic concerns, and are complementary to articles in the sections 'Policy' (in areas such as housing supply, zoning and land-use regulation, and taxation), 'Institutions' (where there are common themes around taxes and subsidies), and 'Approaches' which, for example, contains methodological details on the calculation of housing price indexes, as well as an overview of institutional, behavioural, and neoclassical analyses of the housing economy). Although most of the articles in this section are based on the US and UK literature, reflecting the bulk of academic research, some articles cover both developed and developing countries, especially on the subject of mortgage markets and their regulations as well as housing subsidies.

This brief introduction is organised around the major themes addressed in the collection. These may be grouped into seven categories: housing demand, supply, and markets; house prices; government intervention in housing markets in the form of regulations and the direct provision of social housing; government intervention in the form of taxes and subsidies; housing wealth; housing and the macroeconomy; and housing finance (which has traditionally been jurisdiction-specific) together with an emerging international perspective on mortgage markets. Each is introduced below.

Thematic Review

Housing Demand, Supply, and Markets

Housing is not a simple commodity, like grains or metals. It is rather a complex, composite commodity, which is hard to price and whose supply is determined by policy and politics as much as markets. Moreover, housing is an investment asset as well as a consumption good. And when people discuss house 'prices', they often refer to an asset price, rather than a commodity price: the true 'price' of the commodity known as housing is rent.

Many of the articles in this section engage with this dilemma, recognising that when households demand housing, they are in fact demanding a bundle of services. Part of the bundle is physical: houses embody different quantities of interior space, exterior space, materials, plumbing, heating, and so on. Some part of the bundle is not physical. The location of a house, for example, determines the government services that it and its occupants receive. To give but one instance, it has been known that the demand for houses in 'good' school districts exceeds the demand for housing in less good school districts. Housing demand changes with price and income, just as with any other good, and in this, a remarkable similarity of housing demand is found across countries. But house price is also sensitive to household type, household tastes, and a host of other variables.

Housing demand also involves the choice of tenure, that is, whether to own or to rent, which is often made simultaneously with choices about the quantity of housing. The tenure decision is affected by the relative price of owning and renting, access to housing finance, and terms of mortgage loans. Homeownership is attractive to individual households because it generates private economic benefits. Social benefits emanating from homeownership form a basis for government support to it. Renting is more difficult in that landlords essentially serve as a financial intermediary between users of property and property itself. Rental housing therefore produces principal–agent issues that are solved via home-owning. Homeownership also allows the hedging of rent increases as the owner-occupant household is effectively renting to itself. All these themes are covered by the articles in this section.

Housing supply is more complicated. It includes new construction and alteration of the existing stock, and these two sources of supply are determined by two distinct sets of players, with different motivations: developers, on the one hand, and owner-occupiers, on the other hand. New homes are generally manufactured at the place where they are occupied, and the materials used for construction can vary from one part of the world to another. Even when manufactured homes and materials for home buildings are shipped around, the land component of supply is fixed locally. Natural barriers can also create impediments to housing supply. Bangladesh, for example, a country that is especially susceptible to flooding, faces supply challenges that are considerably greater than most other countries, and topography constrains housing supply in some coastal cities in the United States.

Political attitudes have, arguably, the greatest impact on housing supply. That is why there are synergies between the section economics and finance, on the one hand, and that on policy, on the other hand. The American city of Houston has virtually no limitations on housing construction, and as such, the supply curve for housing there is highly elastic. Mumbai, on the other hand, is among the densest large cities in the world, and yet has for many years imposed regulations and requirements that substantially limit its ability to supply housing. The elasticity of housing supply is affected by both natural constraints and regulatory barriers; the balance is weighed up by the relevant articles.

Finally, the articles in this section recognise that there is no single national housing market but a large number of local housing markets; such markets are also segmented. Identifying the submarkets is an important issue for both market analysis and policy formulation; a number of articles on housing supply, demand, and markets investigate the implications of such heterogeneity.

House Prices

The recent global financial crisis has shown that understanding house price fundamentals and dynamics has many important implications for wealth profiles, for lending and borrowing, and for policy. But understanding house price trends and volatilities is not a trivial matter. This is clear from the cluster of articles concerned with the measurement and determinants of house prices through time and spatially.

One can view house prices from several perspectives. Even terminology is not straightforward: from an economic perspective, the 'price' of a house is the rent one pays (or implicit rent in the case of owner-occupied housing) to receive the flow of housing services. To be precise, the term housing price or rent in its common use is in fact expenditure on housing and equals the unit price of housing multiplied by the quantity of housing consumed in a particular housing unit. Differentiating housing expenditure into price and quantity of housing is itself a challenge for housing researchers. The transaction price of a house is its asset value, which can be looked at as the present discounted value of its service flow.

Measuring discounted value is difficult, particularly for owner-occupied housing. In the first place, one would need to measure and forecast the rent that a particular owner-occupied house might fetch in the market; second, one would need to choose a correct discount rate. A further complication is the tendency for the market price of housing assets in any given point in time to deviate from what is explained by fundamental values. The discrepancy is called a bubble, which is often driven by expectations about future price appreciation. The difficulties in establishing fundamental values may explain why, at the time housing bubbles appeared to be developing around the world in the middle of the first decade of the twenty-first century, there was no consensus among economists as to whether this was, or was not, a departure from fundamentals.

Another method for determining fundamental house price is simply to sum the construction costs of improvements with land value. But getting construction costs right is difficult enough; getting land value right as well requires one to determine the fundamental value of land. This in turn depends on calculating land rent and a discount rate, which puts us in the same predicament mentioned in the previous paragraph. Residential property prices are, as a result, still one of the most researched, yet least understood, topics in housing economics.

Government Interventions: Regulations and Direct Provision of Social Housing

Government intervenes in the housing market in a variety of ways: land-use regulation and the provision of social housing are two of the most critical factors where economics and finance are concerned. Planning regulations, for example, directly affect how housing developers meet housing demand. It is almost certain that the demand for large blocks of flats in cities in India exceeds supply. Important reasons for the shortage are that regulations have made it difficult for developers to assemble parcels of vacant land and have produced binding limits on floor area ratios. Washington, DC, is a city whose housing supply is shaped in part by height limits, which in turn leaves demand unmet. Government regulation, in short, does much to shape both the price of housing and development densities in cities around the world.

The social housing sector is important because it effectively (to an extent) suspends the price mechanism in housing markets. The size and significance of this sector varies across countries, and is covered in most detail in other sections (see 'Institutions', 'Policy', and 'Home and Homelessness'). However, there are articles in this section on the economics and the financing of social housing which provide important points of contrast with a literature more generally focused on owner-occupation.

Government Interventions: Taxation and Subsidies

Taxation exerts a powerful effect on the shape of the world's housing systems. Most interest, in practice, centres on the implications of taxation for the role and relevance of owner-occupation. This in turn varies across countries. Many countries provide homeowners with a subsidy in the form of mortgage interest deduction; almost all countries give a tax break to owner-occupied housing by not taxing imputed rents, or capital gains, on primary residences. The mortgage interest deduction can affect the user cost of housing (i.e., the economic cost of owning a house) and make homeownership more attractive than it would otherwise be. However, it almost certainly will get capitalised into house prices to a varying extent depending on the supply elasticity. So it is not really clear how mortgage interest deductibility affects homeownership rates or home prices. Some argue that its impact is more on the size of properties than on whether they are purchased or not.

Many, if not most, countries provide some form of subsidy (other than tax breaks) to some households, and while the nature of the subsidy varies, generally the subsidy favours homeownership. This is done because homeownership is believed to generate social benefits. Some countries, such as Singapore, have a long history of directly subsidising owner-occupied housing, and this has helped drive ownership rates to high levels. Other countries also subsidise renters, through provision of social housing (supply-side subsidy), through vouchers (demand-side subsidy), or through tax incentives to landlords. Several such themes are aired in this section.

Housing Wealth

A number of articles address the various dimensions of housing wealth, the ways households can tap into it, and the impact of housing wealth on consumption. We now know with a great deal of confidence that housing wealth is important – it is the world's largest single asset class, it makes up an enormous share of global wealth, accounts for the bulk of personal wealth in most national economies, and for the majority of owner-occupiers, is by far their largest, sometimes their only, asset. We do not, on the other hand, have as much confidence in knowing the total value of individual, national, or global housing assets, not least because of uncertainty about the fundamental value of houses.

This section also reflects the fact that there is not yet any consensus concerning the implications of housing wealth for the broader economy. There is, to be sure, extensive debate on the link between home prices and consumption, and on what the causal mechanisms might be. There have also been a number of estimates of the marginal propensity to consume out of housing wealth (rather than other parts of the wealth portfolio), but these estimates have a wide range. Part of the difficulty is that the fungibility of housing wealth – the ability to mobilise or 'cash in' home equity – varies between jurisdictions, according to the 'completeness' of mortgage markets, and the transactions costs in housing markets. The means of extracting equity also varies across the life course. For example, for households attached to a job, it is difficult to cash in on house value by moving from an expensive city to an inexpensive city; retirees, conversely, do have that option. On the other hand, home-buyers in work have more opportunities to borrow-up against owned homes (to engage in mortgage equity withdrawal) than do older outright owners without an income stream. There is some agreement that the collateral channel has increased in importance; that increased leverage together with equity borrowing accounts for a significant proportion of housing's wealth effects. However, on the subject of tapping into home equity via loans, there is a mix of evidence, some of which suggests that the ability to use that mechanism can be fleeting.

That is, mortgage equity withdrawal may not improve the household balance sheet in the long run, because the asset extracted (cash) is offset by a new liability (a future stream of mortgage payments). Nevertheless, as the articles in this section show, mortgage equity withdrawal is one means by which some homeowners smooth both incomes and consumption across the life course.

Housing and the Macroeconomy

The interplay between the housing sector and the macroeconomy has attracted growing attention in recent years. Research indicates that the housing sector interacts with the macroeconomy through three major channels: the investment, consumption, and banking channels. Regarding the first channel, it is sometimes argued that housing 'is the business cycle'. Indeed, variations in housing construction explain a disproportionate amount of variation in the broader economy. The question is why. The second channel, the housing wealth effect, has been discussed above. As for the third channel, the performance of mortgage loans, conditioned by the fluctuation in housing price, influences the balance sheet of lending institutions. This affects their ability to expand new credit to households and businesses, and hence the level of consumption and investment activities. The housing–macroeconomy linkages operate in the other direction as well. For example, changes in the interest rate and the supply of credit have an impact on housing demand and the supply of new housing.

Mortgage Markets: Character and Trends

Because housing is a long-lived and 'lumpy' (indivisible) consumer durable, and because households generally wish to smooth consumption over the lifetime, it is only natural that mortgage markets have expanded hand in hand with housing markets. When housing finance is not available, households must save for many years before they have the opportunity to purchase a house. The behaviour of borrowers regarding the choice of mortgage products and repayment of mortgage debt (or default there on) and the factors that affect their behaviour are covered by several articles in this section.

The size of the housing finance sector varies considerably across countries. Some developed countries, particularly the United States, the United Kingdom, Denmark, and the Netherlands, have very large mortgage markets relative to their economies. Most emerging countries have relatively small mortgage markets, but some high-income countries, including Italy and France, have relatively small markets too. Mortgage products are highly heterogeneous across countries and jurisdictions vary in the 'completeness' of the mortgage markets they support. The United States features a large variety of mortgage products, even now, and is, like Denmark, unusual in that fixed-rate, long-term, freely-prepayable mortgages are common. In Canada mortgages generally have terms of medium length (5 years is usual). The UK and Australian mortgage markets, in contrast, where long-term fixes are less common, support a wide range of loan products in the amortising adjustable rate and equity borrowing ranges.

In short, and until recently, mortgage markets have been stubbornly national in character, notwithstanding an otherwise-globalising economy. To illustrate that diversity, there are several articles on mortgage markets, character, and trends in specific illustrative jurisdictions, from Germany (with notably low rates of homeownership) to the United Kingdom and the United States (with reasonably high rates of highly mortgaged owner-occupation) in the developed world, and spanning all other world regions, from Africa to China.

Mortgages, because they are secured debt, allow households with a relatively small asset base to borrow at narrow spreads over risk-free assets. This is because properly underwritten loans consider both the ability of the borrower to repay the loan and the quality of the collateral underpinning it. In recent years, many lenders departed from good underwriting practices, for reasons that are currently subject to debate. Nevertheless, during those years when mortgages were carefully underwritten, they were very safe investments for lenders.

This might explain why, to meet a growing demand for credit in some parts of the more developed world, mortgage-linked instruments emerged during the 2000s as an important financial market. Mortgage-linked securities helped lending institutions tap the capital market as well as contributing to the development of capital markets. Countries vary in how mortgage finance is sourced, the major division being between those that rely on capital markets for housing finance and those that rely on depositories. Germany, Denmark, and the United States tend to rely on capital markets, while Australia, the United Kingdom, and Canada rely more on depositories. These themes are taken up in the remaining articles for this section.

Research Agenda Going Forward

The articles collected here cover a wide range of subjects in the economics and finance of housing. Already, however, they point out new directions and identify areas in which further research is needed. For example, a clear and encouraging trend in housing research in recent years is increased interest in housing supply. Additional research on supply elasticity, the role of regulations on supply, and the impact of the supply elasticity on the volatility in housing price and quantity would be helpful. Second, the effects of ageing, and cohorts, on the place of housing and mortgage debt in the household portfolio, have important policy implications and merit greater attention. Third, the relationship between the structure of mortgage markets (funding mechanisms and mortgage products) and the stability of housing markets requires far more careful study. A related topic worth exploring is the role of macroprudential measures in promoting housing market stability. Finally, explaining the driving forces of the co-movement of housing prices in many developed countries during the latest housing boom, and the different pathways to unwinding the boom, is a pressing topic for research, which may be feasible once internationally comparable housing price data become more widely available.

RK Green, K-H Kim, AB Sanders, and S Wachter

ENVIRONMENT

Aims and Objectives

The broad aims of this section echo that of the overall encyclopedia, namely to provide an international perspective on housing and to engage with academic and practitioner audiences. The objective is to provide an insight into the main issues associated with housing and the environment. This section brings together the key environmental issues for housing globally, including those relating to the physical and the social spheres, and the interaction between them. The dynamic relationship established between space and society over time is explored, with many of the articles covering issues at the intersection of the social and the physical, and recognising that this relationship is multidirectional. How do individuals and communities affect the housing and wider environment? How do physical circumstances, including housing environments, influence behaviours and social relationships?

The section comprises 68 core articles written by recognised experts in the field and providing comprehensive overviews of a wide range of environmental topics from climate change to ghettos, and from health risks to household waste recycling. To provide orientation, we commissioned a small number of longer overview articles on Sustainable Communities by Alina Congreve, Climate Change by Tina Fawcett, Housing Dynamics: Environmental Aspects by Gareth Powells, and Social Spaces and Urban Policies by Wim Ostendorf. The breadth and depth of the articles in this section provide evidence of a growing interest in environmental issues for housing research and practice.

Structure and Organisation

The articles in this section are broadly divided into two categories: social and physical. The reciprocal influences created around the physical and social domains in housing are barely extricable; however, a distinction was made to facilitate the design of the section, the identification of authors, and the categorising of key concepts and issues covered by the term 'environment'. The articles were commissioned as being primarily about either the social environment or the physical environment, though in practice, of course, the two themes often overlap.

The more physical-oriented articles (encompassing both the dwelling and the built environment) cover topics about housing and environmental change, the impact of housing on the biosphere, and housing environmental sustainability issues as well as articles about the material infrastructure of housing: the bricks and mortar and its physical layout. The articles concentrate on either the dwelling or the neighbourhood/city scale, or undertake a more generic 'theory and approaches' review. Thus, for instance, we have an article by Erling Holden that is primarily about the dwelling (Ecological Footprint), Gordon Walker deals with the scale of the neighbourhood (Community Energy Systems), and Rajat Gupta deals with more general matters of theory and approaches (Climate Change: Adaptations). For essays concentrating on built environment issues, topics relating to the dwelling are explained and developed in articles on rural housing by Mark Shucksmith and on second homes by Fernando Diaz Orueta. Built environment concepts associated with the neighbourhood and the city are also discussed, for example in articles on Green Space and Parks by Nicola Dempsey and on Housing and Sustainable Transport by Erling Holden.

Essays addressing the social perspective are concerned with the interactions between housing and householders, and more broadly with environment and society. The social dimension comprises both the individual and the community, and includes topics and ideas that go from individual perceptions to collective actions related to the physical environment, embodying several scales like the dwelling, the neighbourhood, or the city. For instance, the scale of the dwelling and the role of householders are evidenced in a few articles (Place Attachment by Barbara Brown, Irwin Altman, and Carol Werner and Household Waste Recycling by Matt Watson), while others concentrate on a larger environmental scale (Neighbourhood Design: Urban Outdoor Experience by Nicola Dempsey, Neighbourhood Watch by Richard Yarwood, and Eco-Communities by Heather Lovell). This perspective also includes articles that are more conceptually focused on 'theories and approaches' (Sustainable Housing Cultures by Eli Støa).

Certain entries reflect more than others the difficulties associated with disentangling the predominance of one approach or another. Examples of this include essays on the undesired effects on the environment of negative behaviours like crime (see Neighbourhood Incivilities by Ralph Taylor), the individual health risks associated with poor environmental conditions (see Health Risks: Damp and Cold by Jeroen Douwes), and the particularities and specificities of the relationship established between groups or collectives and the environment (see Vernacular Housing by Laida Memba Ikuga or Gypsy/Roma Settlements by Teresa San Román).

Over time, housing research has changed its focus to embrace problems and issues in the real world. Until the mid- to late 1990s, the majority of the wider housing studies literature tended to concentrate on either social issues (such as low-income housing and welfare) or economic issues (notably housing finance and the operation of housing markets), and the physical environment was rather overlooked. But in the last few decades, this has begun to change with a growing body of work researching environmental issues, including householder studies (on energy and water consumption and waste management), the design and production of sustainable housing, and attitudes in the house building industry towards the environment. Exemplifying this, the articles broadly grouped as pertaining to the physical environment section consider both traditional research issues related to housing and urban studies (Maintenance and Repair by Ad Straub, Housing Estates by Frank Wassenberg, and Ethnic Minorities and Housing by Gideon Bolt) as well as newer more contemporary housing research topics (Defensible Space by Paul Cozen and David Hillier, Eco-Renovation by Gavin Killip, and Eco-Communities by Heather Lovell).

The physical environment articles address a wide range of international perspectives covering the environmental issues at stake not only in the rich and developed part of the world but also in poorer, developing countries. To this end, leading researchers from around the world discuss international debates and case studies which include examples of community planning in Vancouver, Canada, in Seattle, USA and in Brisbane, Australia (see Neighbourhood Planning by Simon Pinnegar). There is also a comparison of self-build techniques between the Gaza Strip (Autonomous Palestinian Territories), Khartoum (Sudan), Kigali (Rwanda), Rio de Janeiro (Brazil), and Buenos Aires (Argentina) (see the article on Self-Build: Global South by Fernando Murillo).

Several transversal concepts of paramount importance for the whole section feature as a *leitmotiv* across many of the articles. They are mainly related to the impact of recent changes and shifts in societal cultures and lifestyles and its relation to the environment. The three pillars of sustainability, for instance, have been acknowledged in many of the articles as has the growing attention researchers pay to safety-related issues and environmental impacts on health. Another topic that demands attention is the way deprivation and persistent inequalities at the social level are reflected in territorial outcomes.

This section deals explicitly with processes and dynamics over the territory inspired (or not) by certain attitudes and behaviours of the population and its evolution over time. In that sense, the section puts a particular emphasis on the preconditions, requirements, and determinants over time for processes to develop. A few articles (Temporary Housing by Claire Lévy-Vroelant, Gated Communities by Rowland Atkinson and Sarah Blandy, and Gentrification and Neighbourhood Change by Marco van der Land, Alexander Curley and G van Eijk) are key examples here relating to social issues, whilst others (Adaptable Housing by Eli Støa or Construction and Demolition Waste by Vivian Tam) show a certain degree of progression and development on the physical side.

More than just theoretical analysis, many of the articles in this section discuss and debate the impact of policies, programmes, and actions: that is, both analytic and normative approaches are incorporated within the section. This is perhaps most evident in a series of case studies: for instance, Amsterdam's pattern of social segregation (Social Spaces and Urban Policies by Wim Ostendorf and Sako Musterd), Danish practices related to energy consumption (Sustainable Lifestyles by Kirsten Gram-Hanssen), the design of teahouses in Shanghai or the *favelas* in Brazil (Vernacular Housing by Laida Memba Ikuga), and the evolution of second homes at the Spanish Mediterranean coast (Second Homes by Fernando Diaz Orueta).

Finally, a few umbrella concepts considered in this section are also reflected in other sections of the encyclopedia. This is the case, for instance, with neighbourhood governance (Ali Madanipour), social sustainability (Monterrat Pareja-Eastaway), and sustainabe housing cultures (Eli Støa). There are also essays on sustainable lifestyles (Kirsten Gram-Hanssen) and on gender and space (Irene Molina).

In summary, housing and the home cannot be seen, experienced, or studied apart from in their environmental contexts and effects. The physical and the social environment contribute to what housing and home represents for individuals; that wider environment is itself shaped by the practices associated with housing and home. This section aims to provide the reader with an overview of the many different international dimensions of this interplay. The hope is that it provides a way into these issues for the nonexpert, that it opens new dimensions for those already well-read in the field, and that it inspires the research community towards fresh ways of thinking.

H Lovell, M Pareja Eastaway, and M Elsinga

HOME AND HOMELESSNESS

'Home' is a concept found across the natural and social sciences, referring in its broadest sense to the habitats of animals and plants. In the context of housing, home denotes the feelings, values, cultures, and practices associated with the physical structures of human dwelling. This concept of home refers to the ways in which dwelling structures become sites of emotional, cultural, and personal significance; the ways in which a sense of belonging in the world is constructed in and through the residential environment. The articles in this section reflect and expand upon this conceptualisation of home, and on the impacts (largely in the material sense) of absence of home ('homelessness'). There are 98 articles in this section, spread more or less evenly across topics relating to home and to homelessness.

Home: A Multidisciplinary Affair

Reflecting on the multiple meanings and experiences of the term 'home', a hallmark of the scholarship in this section – perhaps more so than in any other part of the encyclopedia – is its multidisciplinary character. To illustrate this, particular editorial effort has been made to ensure that all principal disciplinary perspectives on home are elaborated to some extent, each taking different theoretical points and hence conceptualising home in subtly different ways. Philosophical perspectives, for example, are primarily concerned with the ways in which homes – material or imaginative – are connected with our sense of 'being-in-the-world', with personhood most generally. Anthropology is more focused on the collective, rather than the self, in its emphasis on the built forms of housing and different meanings of home associated with different cultures and, more recently, with its recognition of the importance of objects and material culture more generally in making home. In literature, film studies, and popular culture, the creation and maintenance of normative definitions of home is paramount, highlighting, for example, the omnipresence of representations of home across diverse forms like Flemish painting, American postwar television, and women's magazines. Feminist perspectives are critical in understanding the 'house-as-home', initially in refuting the overly romanticised and gender-blind perspectives that dominated early housing studies, and more recently in elaborating the complex links between home and both masculinity and femininity. Feminist frameworks in fact underpin a number of articles in this section, including those on sexuality, emotions, home and work, and meanings of home.

Although the individual lenses through which home is comprehended varies across these disciplines, collectively three key themes emerge.

The first, reflecting the importance of feminism in scholarship on home, is the centrality of gender when both experiencing and conceptualising home. Men and women experience home in different ways. Whether home is a place of relaxation or a place of unpaid (or paid) work, whether a safe haven or site of violence and antagonism, for example, are experiences strongly correlated with gender. While gender differences remain critical to understanding home, recent feminist scholarship has also turned attention to new types of relations between gender and home, such as through migration, temporary dwelling, and technology. Furthermore, gender is central to key concepts used to understand home. The chain of association linking home with the domestic sphere, and infusing the domestic sphere with connotations of privacy, for instance, can be traced back to the eighteenth-century notion of separate spheres in which it was presumed that the realms of daily life for men and women were, and should be, completely different. Feminist critiques of this public–private dichotomy, and the reformulation of this dualism to stress the necessary interconnections of public and private, drive contemporary feminist theorisations of house-as-home.

A second key theme concerns the ways in which experiences of home reflect and reproduce patterns of historical, geographical, and social differentiation. How home is understood, practiced, and represented varies considerably depending on age (compare the way home is imagined by a child and by an elderly person), race, religion, and sexuality, as many of the articles demonstrate. These socially differentiated experiences of home are critical in shaping both people's life chances and their senses of themselves. Historical variations are also implicit in this section, exemplified in the changing representations of home in literature and film, and the altering technological foundations of the modern house-as-home. Perhaps not surprisingly, given the volume's emphasis on houses, the importance of geographical context in shaping home underpins many of the articles. Geographical context is approached at a number of scales: national–regional differences as exemplified in the different material cultures of home and home objects; the common and varying elements of home found in high-rise and suburban housing; and the experiences of domestic workers across the global North and South. This section also advances scholarship on home through its emphasis on the importance of transnational movements of people and ideas in transforming home.

A final key theme concerns the strong linkages between home and the myriad economic, political, and legal institutions of housing. While home is a more cultural concept than house, and scholarship on home draws less on political science, law, and economics than other dimensions of housing studies, what home means remains strongly connected to socioeconomic, political, and legal differentiation. Homeownership is a critical investment and wealth-building activity across the Western world that underpins many national economies and has been linked to a sense of 'ontological security'. The legal protection of homeownership underpins the experience of homeownership, and may even be the basis for claiming new legal rights, for example, through 'defensive homeownership'. Finally, institutions such as planning and welfare systems silently support homeownership and middle-class definitions of home through their continuing preference for homeownership and nuclear family/individualised patterns of social life.

Future scholarship on home will probably be influenced by broader intellectual trends across the social sciences, in concert with the changing social, political, cultural, and economic context. Within this frame, a number of likely directions can be identified. Empirically, many of the recent trends identified in this section will endure impacts of transnational movements on housing and home, imprint of social constructions of home across diverse policy and institutional fields, and increasingly complex identity formation in and through home. The implications of climate change for experiences of home are likely to become a key issue, as scholars explore the links between carbon-intensive practices and meanings of home, on the one hand, and the meanings of home (shared living spaces, more high rises?) that could underpin a carbon-reduced future, on the other hand.

Theoretically, the trend towards more integrative approaches is also likely to continue. While much scholarship on home already draws upon diverse social science and humanities disciplines, the current moment sees increasing dialogue across natural and social sciences through perspectives such as 'science and technology' studies in which the processes of the natural and social worlds are considered simultaneously. In relation to home, it may be that existing scholarship on material cultures and pets, which draw from an understanding of the 'more-than-human' world and dispute the separation of nature and culture, will take housing studies in new directions, such as recent work on the ways in which social networks and technologies are assembled to constitute home in an increasingly technologically embedded world. These new frameworks will enable housing studies to address changing contours of home into the future.

Homelessness: A Multifaceted Condition

'Homelessness' can, conceptually, be understood as the absence of 'home', but practical definitions tend to prioritise the material aspects of inadequate housing conditions. Such definitions vary in breadth across the developed world, from the categorisation of 'literal homelessness' traditionally found in the United States and elsewhere, which is confined to those sleeping rough or in homeless shelters, to the much wider definition employed in the United Kingdom, for example, which covers all those without a legal right to occupy 'reasonable' accommodation, and the 'cultural' definition used in Australia. The European Federation of National Organisations Working with the Homeless (FEANTSA) 'ETHOS' typology, which offers a homelessness definition encompassing aspects of 'rooflessness', 'houselessness', 'insecure housing', and 'inadequate housing', has been increasingly influential in Europe and beyond. But such broad-ranging definitions are inappropriate in the developing world, where the imposition of such 'Western' notions of housing security and adequacy would label most of the population as homeless. In India, for example, reference is more often made to those who are 'houseless' or 'shelterless', emphasising the absence of any form of shelter.

Homelessness is recognised as a major social policy concern in many developed countries, and as a feature of extreme poverty throughout the developing world. Homelessness can also happen dramatically as the result of human conflicts or natural disasters, with the needs of refugees and internally displaced people representing a major humanitarian challenge in many parts of the world. The material circumstances giving rise to homelessness differ across the globe, and its manifestations differ too: street children, informal settlements, and large refugee camps are key concerns in Asia, Africa, and Central and South Americas, whereas single adults sleeping rough or in shelters, families living in temporary accommodation, and 'hidden' homeless groups 'doubling up' with friends and relatives are core issues in much of the developed world. While most identifiable homelessness is located within urban settings, there is a growing understanding of the particular dimensions of rural homelessness in countries as diverse as India, the United States, New Zealand, Spain, Ireland, and Finland.

There are clear patterns, at least within the developed world, of the characteristics of the people most vulnerable to 'literal homelessness'. This group tends to be male, single, middle-aged, unemployed, or disabled, with a strong overrepresentation of ethnic minorities and recent migrants. Men leaving institutional settings – such as prison and the armed forces – are often at particular risk of street homelessness. However, the broader one's definition of homelessness, the more 'feminised' it becomes, with women and children predominating among refugees and internally displaced people in the developing world.

Understandings of homelessness, like meanings of 'home', have benefited from multidisciplinary scholarship, though major challenges remain in integrating the varying perspectives that these different disciplines offer. Economists tend to focus on aggregates and macroexplanatory levels, often giving overwhelming importance to housing market conditions in explaining homelessness, whereas applied social psychologists, for example, focus on the ways in which homeless people's self-identity influences their propensity to engage with housing and support services. Added to this rich intellectual mix are distinctive theoretical and methodological approaches, which cut across disciplinary boundaries. Social constructionist perspectives have explored the meanings attached to homelessness by various actors, and the impacts that these representations can have on policy responses. Ethnographers provide rich and culturally sensitive details on the lives of marginalised people, such as homeless people, that enable their perspectives to be 'included' in debate and policy formulation. Explanatory frameworks have been offered from a 'critical realist' perspective, which contends that complex causal mechanisms operate across a wide range of social strata, and no single factor is likely to be 'necessary' or 'sufficient' for the generation of homelessness. As with scholarship on 'home', feminist perspectives have been influential, and have gained in sophistication and subtlety over time.

At its core, the study of homelessness reflects a concern with human suffering and exclusion and a desire to prevent and resolve it, with an increasing emphasis on commitments to 'end homelessness' by governments and NGOs across the developed world. Demands for 'rights-based' approaches have come to dominate political discourse in recent years, although there are also counter voices arguing for less adversarial 'social partnership' models. Another key schism is between those who advocate 'continuum of care' models, whereby homeless people move through a series of accommodation and support 'steps' to render them 'housing ready' before accessing mainstream accommodation, and the 'Housing First' model, rapidly gaining ground across the developed world, whereby ordinary housing is provided immediately with support services configured around this permanent accommodation. There is encouraging evidence from a range of countries on improved specialist responses to diverse homeless groups – including young people, older people, people with mental health, drug or alcohol problems, and women fleeing domestic violence – but these targeted programmes sometimes attempt to compensate for the absence, or retrenchment, of mainstream welfare protection. Another cause for concern in many quarters is the 'criminalisation' of homelessness in nations as diverse as India, Australia, Brazil, Japan, England, Hungary, and Rwanda.

Future scholarship on homelessness will doubtless be informed by intellectual trends across the academic world, as with other areas of study, but two important practical points stand out.

First, improved quantitative data on homelessness are required. The availability of robust statistical evidence on homelessness is extremely patchy, even if one confines oneself to the developed world. The United States has by far the best quantitative research, based on large sample sizes and robust methodologies, including the use of longitudinal and control/comparison group techniques to assess rigorously the effectiveness of specific homelessness programmes. Elsewhere, there is a dearth of quantitative research on homelessness, aside from basic, descriptive work on the characteristics of homeless people. Cost–benefit analysis and associated economic techniques designed to demonstrate the efficient use of public resources are a key concern in this regard. These types of economic analyses are relatively well developed within the homelessness sector in only Australia and the United States at the moment, but it seems inevitable that their importance will grow in the coming years, especially given ongoing downward pressures on public expenditure following the global economic crisis.

Second, there is a clear need for international comparative research on homelessness (both qualitative and quantitative). Key research questions on, for example, the impact of structural contexts on the scale and nature of homelessness cannot be answered without such evidence. Conducting cross-country empirical research on homelessness requires significant resources which are rarely made available, and there are also considerable methodological challenges to overcome with respect to conceptual equivalence, data harmonisation, and, perhaps most profoundly, institutional divergence in responses. However, there are many other areas of housing studies where such barriers are, if not overcome, at least worked around in order to deliver useful comparative findings. There is, in principle, no reason why similar progress cannot be made in the homelessness field.

R Dowling and S Fitzpatrick

INSTITUTIONS

The Purpose and Place of Housing Institutions

While housing is a basic human need that can be provided at a rudimentary level of shelter, and the home is a quintessentially personal realm where intimacy and privacy is realised, the provision and consumption of homes has become a highly regulated practice, mediated by various institutions and agencies. Housing agents and organisations are, especially in developed societies, regulated by the state or even civil sector organisations run on a nonprofit basis. At the same time, private enterprises concerned with housing have increasingly organised themselves into larger units in order to represent their own interests, often in tandem with the institutional and legislative mobilisation of governments. This section of the encyclopedia addresses the diversity and complexity of institutions and institutional relationships in the realisation of housing.

One conventional understanding of housing institutions is focused on the social organisations that support the specific housing and housing-related needs of society. Other approaches emphasise the need to see institutions more broadly as the norms, rules, and regulations – the entire body of mechanisms and structures of social order and cooperation – that govern the behaviour of a set of individuals. From this perspective, housing institutions encompass the norms and rules that enable a society to fulfil its need for adequate housing, including the complex interactions of housing supply and demand, and housing needs. 'Institutions' may thus refer to organisations that perform specific tasks within society, the laws and regulations formulated at different levels of government, and informal values and norms concerning how housing is used and circulated.

In order to be as inclusive and comprehensive as possible, we have assumed a broad definition of institutions in this volume. The literature on institutions within housing studies has usually taken the existence of 'typical' institutional entities and practices as givens, and thus become a normative force that has inadequately questioned the nature and role of housing institutions. Indeed, examples of housing practices in places like Africa, Latin America, and East Asia as set out in this section illustrate considerable complexity and diversity in institutional arrangements concerning the home and processes of housing.

Approaches

Understanding institutions in housing is a formidable task that requires, on the one hand, considerable sensitivity to social and cultural variations, and on the other hand, appreciation of the growing influence of global economic and regulatory forces. Recently, the changing institutional relationships around housing markets have heightened the 'interconnectedness' of households to an international institutional network, subjugating the 'micro' phenomenon of 'home', and the security and orientation of the family within the home, to the influence of multiscalar flows of capital and finance. This became particularly evident in the international property price bubble that emerged at the beginning of the twenty-first century, which helped to stimulate irresponsible lending and borrowing, especially in subprime mortgage sectors, and which was followed by the credit crunch and a global recession that has spread far beyond housing markets and mortgage finance. Housing institutions, regulators, and agencies not only triggered the unfolding of the latest financial crisis; their alignment around a particular mode of market housing provision, and commodity consumption, albeit manifest differently in each local context, helped reconfigure housing processes on a global scale while at the same time reconstituting the very meaning and experience of home at the individual level.

This is not to say that institutional relationships in each society have converged in line with neoliberal forms of capitalism. Indeed, the meaning and nature of housing and home in each culture or community reflects the complexity and idiosyncrasy of housing systems, which are locally and historically contingent and demonstrate considerable path dependency.

The articles collected in this volume attempt to capture the diversity of institutions that intersect with housing as well as differences in the formation and development of institutional constellations in different countries. As researches on, for example, welfare regimes and varieties of capitalism have demonstrated, institutions and institutional frameworks both shape the interaction of political, economic, and social dimensions and are shaped by the context with which they arise and evolve. Consequently, there is a particularly comparative focus to this volume with a number of articles and clusterings of articles that address comparable institutional phenomena in different societies and regions of the world. On the one hand, this helps demonstrate local institutional relations and their impact on housing markets, policies, and practices, as well as change and development over time. On the other hand, it illustrates how much the impact of individual agency, political intervention, and global forces is contingent on historic frameworks of organisational formations and relations. What is apparent across the articles here is how often relatively similar housing policy developments are mediated by different institutional structures and networks, leading to highly variegated social and market outcomes.

While the geographic separation of countries and regions provides one way to approach this text, it is also possible to consider different institutional dimensions. In terms of scale, the range runs from international and state agencies to neighbourhood associations to individual professionals. In terms of institutions as regulations, or rules of the game, there is also considerable variety, from the laws that define rights of ownership and access to housing, to the means by which management decisions are made, and to the cultural norms that regulate the exchange of shelter and housing wealth within the family or household unit. This volume also touches on important social issues such as ageing, gender, and race and how different institutional relations and practices affect these. There are also the more familiar topics concerning housing supply and demand, housing markets, and public policy.

Themes and Issues

More theoretically or conceptually driven approaches to scientific collections like this one can often impose frameworks for understanding the phenomena and the nature of relationships between them. However, in compiling this section we have considered eclecticism a merit, and the diversity of topics and approaches as an opportunity to re-engage with the dynamism and complexity of housing relations. One of the distinctive contributions offered by a focus on 'institutions' of housing and home within the framework of an encyclopedia is considerable freedom to move between topics and thereby make unanticipated connections and associations between ideas, practices, and places. It is useful, nonetheless, to highlight a number of key themes and issues, as well as make some illustrative links between topics.

The contributions in this section essentially explore differences in housing regimes and housing institutions. Housing institutions are viewed as culturally embedded in the overall process of economic, social, and political transformation, while recognising the power of specific local imperatives and market pressures to shape their response. The main argument is that housing institutions have differential capacities to direct these processes of change, leading to divergent responses in the housing provision system. The section explores these differences as well as the institutional relationships in four principal domains: (1) housing tenure and housing rights; (2) housing institutions providing affordable housing; (3) institutions for the supply of housing; and (4) housing markets and the myriad of formal and informal institutions involved in the provision of housing. While the articles themselves reveal the complexities of housing institutions, it is possible to identify some of the most significant issues addressed in relation to each of these domains. These issues are likely to dominate the discourse in the housing literature for years to come.

Institutional Perspectives on Housing Rights and Housing Tenure

Housing tenure is one of the central social institutions in the field of housing. Tenures provide users with rights and burden them with responsibilities related to the consumption of housing. Several articles provide comparative perspectives on a variety of housing tenures, their evolution, and specific forms. Types of tenure are constructed by abstracting from the variety of empirically and historically existing forms – owner-occupation and renting – with major differences in terms of user rights, control, and disposition provided to the resident. Tenure differences are qualified by specific institutional arrangements in different societies with a particular emphasis on provisions ensuring the right to housing for marginalised groups in society as well as housing challenges in postconflict situations.

Housing Institutions Providing Affordable Housing

Meeting the growing need for affordable housing is one of the biggest challenges in both developed and developing countries. A number of articles explore the institutional context and the myriad of arrangements to finance, provide, allocate, and manage affordable housing through public and nongovernment models. They review a variety of approaches that have been adopted as well as the roles and contributions of different institutions across the housing system – governments, private agencies, not-for-profit organisations, and market intermediaries. Characteristics of the historic and contemporary contributions of these institutions to the provision of affordable housing highlight divergent pathways in different countries and regions. The policy debate centres on policy instruments – fiscal, financial, and regulatory – supporting the production (supply side) or the consumption (demand side) of housing. Strategies to promote, produce, and manage affordable housing are also differentiated by tenure – renting versus homeownership – and classified by the degree of targeting and efficiency.

Institutions for Housing Supply

National systems of housing supply involve dynamic public, private, and not-for-profit institutions. Although their relationships are influenced by the country (or regional) context, historic tenure mix, the place of housing in the welfare system, and local structures of housing provision, converging trends are evident. Several articles highlight a broad shift away from direct provision of affordable housing by public agencies in favour of approaches involving the private and not-for-profit sectors, either separately or in partnership. This has resulted in a complex landscape of housing finance, ownership, and management. The growth of new institutions, coupled with the more general emphasis on competitive supply by market agents (landowners, developers, house-builders, managers), has led to new forms of housing provision and 'hybrid' organisations. The contributions explore several major forms of new housing supply, including public/private partnerships, speculative house building, self-help, and informal housing. They review regional patterns and country-specific trends and relationships among key institutions related to the promotion, production, allocation, and consumption of housing.

Housing Markets: Informal and Formal Institutions

Housing markets are culturally embedded in society and the efficiency of their institutions is critical for the provision of adequate and affordable housing. Several articles explore housing market institutions in developing countries, highlighting the importance of informality and difference. Major activities – access to housing, maintenance, services (water, sanitation, access roads), tenure security (to prevent eviction), finance for construction, purchase, or renting – occur through a combination of more or less formal processes. Depending on the social, economic, political, and legal context, some of these activities have been institutionalised over time into more permanent norms and rules implemented with varying degrees of formality by agencies or organisations of the state, market, or civil society. Such informality is very much part of the institutional transformation of post-socialist housing markets and is likely to distinguish them from some of their more mature, well-established European counterparts.

Concluding Remarks

Despite the common challenges facing housing systems in different countries, there are historical and deeply embedded differences in the nature of their housing institutions. There are also significant differences in the political, economic, and social drivers affecting housing policy reforms and the transformation of these institutions, which challenge the idea of convergence. The volume examines the range of strategies used in contemporary societies to protect housing rights, to improve housing quality and affordability, and to enhance the efficiency of housing markets through the lens of housing institutions. This approach brings into focus the role and respective contributions of government, private sectors, and not-for-profit agencies in the provision of housing. In 83 articles, this section addresses the diversity of institutions that have developed around the financing, production, and consumption of housing, accounting for differences between countries and institutional transformation. While capturing diversity is an exhaustive task beyond the scope of this work, this section, nonetheless, illustrates core differences in institutional configurations and relationships regarding housing markets, housing management, construction, planning, tenure, and housing rights.

R Ronald and S Tsenkova

POLICY

Aims and Structure

The aim of this section is to provide a global overview of housing policies and to engage with academic and practitioner audiences. A well-functioning housing market that provides shelter for all regardless of income is of key importance in societies all over the world, and therefore a primary objective of housing policy. During the global financial crisis, we learned that low incomes, subprime loans, and a global financial market proved to be an explosive combination. As a consequence, housing policies and financial policies are being reconsidered as is evident from several articles in this and in other sections. This section of the encyclopedia focuses upon various aspects of housing policy in developed, developing, and transitional economies, collectively reflecting the evolution of housing policy formulation and implementation in a variety of economic, political, and social contexts.

This section comprises 58 core articles and 7 longer overview essays written by recognised experts in the field, providing a comprehensive guide to a wide range of policy topics. Together, the articles are organised around the following seven key themes.

Housing Policy Development

Two essays by John Doling and Peter Ward provide a comprehensive overview of the evolution of housing policy in advanced, transitional and developing economies. Doling suggests a framework that emphasises processes of convergence and divergence with respect to broad historical trends in housing policy (Housing Policy Trends). He shows that over time, with economic development and urbanisation, countries' housing policies are characterised by increased state intervention in housing, but over the course of the last half century, they have relied more on market processes, with an increasing emphasis on homeownership. While Doling's primary focus is on the advanced economies, he also considers transition and developing countries.

Ward, in contrast, provides an overview of housing policies in developing countries. Detailing the evolution of housing policies from the 1950s onwards, Ward argues that housing policies and their implementation are shaped by broader economic and political ideologies, levels of development and urbanisation, and rates of urban growth. Exploring this in relation to changing development paradigms ranging from modernisation to neoliberalism, he charts the changing nature of state intervention in the housing arena from the very direct role played by governments in various sites and service schemes in the 1980s to the subsequent rolling back of the state associated with neoliberal economics and politics. The latter era has been marked by an emphasis on decentralisation, good governance, urban sustainability, and greater efficiency of urban management and city planning.

Self-Help

Articles by Richard Harris (Self-Help: Policy Assistance) and Diana Mitlin (Housing Policies in Developing Countries: Sites-and-Services and Aided Self-Help) both focus on one of the most prominent housing initiatives across the developing world, namely aided self-help or site and service schemes. Harris's article provides a rare insight into the evolution of self-help policies which he traces back to the early years of the twentieth century when a number of European nations (including Germany, Scandinavia, Austria, and Canada) began to help those on low incomes to construct their own housing. Articulated in the writings of Crane in the 1940s and Turner in the 1960s, the key principles of self-help were to afford poorer individuals and households the 'freedom to build' and for the state to facilitate this through the (varied) provision of serviced land, advice, finance, building materials, and training in management and construction.

These arguments are further developed in Mitlin's article which concentrates on the experience of developing countries from the 1970s onwards. She attributes the growing popularity of site and service programmes among both international agencies (such as the United Nations and the World Bank) and national governments to rapidly expanding urban populations as well as an urbanisation of poverty. Within this context, self-help housing initiatives provided a viable alternative in relation to previous (failed) interventions including squatter eviction and relocation as well as publically provided housing. This said, drawing upon a range of examples, both Harris and Mitlin identify the limitations of site and service programmes including the limited scale of many programmes, speculative investment, downward raiding by the rich and powerful, and demanding building standards. On a more ideological note, site and service programmes have also been criticised for shifting the responsibility of housing provision from the state to vulnerable individuals and households and for depressing wage levels. The article by David Satterthwaite on upgrading presents a type of self-help initiative undertaken by poor urban populations living in 'slum' or informal settlements to improve their housing.

Access and Affordability

Judith Yates and Vivienne Milligan provide an overview of policies that promote access to housing opportunities and the affordability of housing. They explain a rationale for policies that improve access and affordability, which highlights their impact on individual households and on the economy as a whole. A taxonomy of policies is proposed that gives insight into the diverse range of direct and indirect forms of assistance that can be provided. The authors highlight the importance of evaluating these policies against a broad rather than narrow range of objectives. The group of articles addressing access and affordability issues includes programmes that aim to directly alleviate housing costs burdens (Peter Kemp writes on housing allowances, and Marion Steele on housing vouchers). Marietta Haffner, Marja Elsinga and Jap Hockstra examine private renting, Hugo Priemus writes on administered rents in public housing, Jenny Schuetz and Rebecca Meltzer address inclusionary zones, and Hans Lint reviews the legislation on security of tenure. In more recent times, state intervention in the form of regulatory controls has been relaxed and direct provision via social housing has contracted. Innovative attempts to improve low-income households' access to housing opportunities are tackled in two articles (Intermediate Housing Tenures by Marja Elsinga and Social Housing: Measures to Attract Private Finance by Peter Phibbs). As John Doling, (mentioned above), points out, advanced countries have increasingly concentrated on expanding homeownership. Government policies to improve access for first-time home-buyers are reviewed in two articles (Contract Saving Schemes by Richard Ronald and First Home-Owner Grants by Tony Dalton), while measures to improve access to private rental housing are discussed in one article (Deposit Assistance Schemes for Private Rental in the United Kingdom by Julie Rugg). Finally, there is an article on schemes in developing countries that aim to improve access to housing loans. The programmes reviewed by Peer Smets (Housing Policies in Developing Countries: Microfinance) usually consist of small loans obtained for a short period of time and are suited to the ways in which poorer households manage their finances, as well as the ways in which they build their housing – incrementally and progressively.

Taxation and Housing

Housing and the land that housing is built on are an important source of tax revenue to most governments. A broad range of taxes are applied to housing and land. They can significantly shape how land is used, the structures that are built, and the cost of housing to the tenant or home-buyer. In most countries, the taxation of housing poses difficult challenges for policy-makers. The key policy issues are outlined by Miranda Stewart (Taxation Policy and Housing), an overview article that also describes the wide range of transaction, income, and wealth tax measures applied to housing. From this article, we learn that taxes can impact on market efficiency by influencing the allocation of resources between different housing tenures, as well as being an important determinant of housing affordability. A key feature of the taxation of housing is homeowner tax expenditures that are departures from the benchmark tax treatment of income, assets, or transactions benefiting homeowners. These have tended to attract critical attention from policy analysts (see Steven Bourassa's article on this theme). Local governments frequently derive much of their tax revenue from local government property taxes (see the article Local Government Property Taxes by Gavin Wood and Rachel Ong) that are commonly levied on the unimproved capital value of buildings, including housing. These taxes are the subject of a large literature that addresses a wide range of housing-related issues, but which also tackles impacts on neighbourhoods and residential segregation. Policy-makers have periodically considered the lift in land values accompanying changes in zoning or the grant of planning permission as an 'unearned' income that should be subject to tax. In some countries, they will be captured by a capital gains tax; but where this is not the case, a development land tax (as discussed by Michael Oxley) is commonly advocated.

Housing Supply and Neighbourhoods

Access to housing opportunities and the affordability of dwellings in market-driven housing systems will in part depend upon an ample supply of housing that is also responsive to changing market conditions. Policies that address these housing supply issues are overviewed in Kerry Vandell's article on housing supply. Extreme supply shortages that follow severely disruptive events such as wars commonly motivate programmes of investment in social housing to support housing supply (see Michael Berry's entry). But in more normal circumstances, supply responses from private developers and builders can be stimulated by supply-side subsidies (as discussed by Melek Cigdem); the competitiveness of the developer and construction industries will help shape the efficiency of housing supply, and this is addressed by governments through competition policy and regulation (as explained by David Hayward). Urban planning is a key influence on the size, location, and design of housing supply. Three articles by, respectively, Kyung-Hwan Kim, Michael Buxton and Lucy Groenhart, and Timothy Dixon, describe how governments use green belts, urban growth boundaries, and brownfield development to influence where housing is built and supplied. The location of housing and its size help shape a city's 'carbon footprint'; this important subject is explored in the article by Anthony Yezer. Finally, government approaches to the design and enforcement of residential building standards are described by Henk Visscher.

Housing also has a critically important role in driving neighbourhood dynamics, and, as a consequence, housing programmes are a component of policies addressing neighbourhood decline. Urban regeneration policies are reviewed by Ronan Paddison, while Reinout Kleinhans explains how housing programs are integrated into urban regeneration policies. There are also individual articles in this section that address issues with a strong neighbourhood dimension

(Exclusionary Zoning by Alan Mallach), and others that are focused on specific housing programmes with a strong spatial focus (HOPE VI by Diane Levy).

Labour Markets and Mortgage Markets

Housing systems are vital to the efficient functioning of economies, and the interrelationships between housing, labour markets, and the finance sector are vital in this respect. Labour market issues that have attracted concern among housing policy-makers are overviewed by Paul Flatau (in a piece on Housing and Labour Markets). Individual articles explore the following: policy responses to the efficiency and equity consequences of spatial mismatch between the residential location of workers and job sites: (Donald Houston considers the general policy response); policies that aim to retain key workers (e.g., teachers and firefighters) in regions where housing costs are high are set out by Nicola Morrison; housing subsidy programmes and incentives to work are discussed by Mark Shroder; the use of housing programmes to encourage mobility among disadvantaged subgroups are illustrated in the 'Moving to Opportunity' Programme introduced by William Clark; and finally, the relationship between social housing and employment outcomes is discussed by Kath Hulse.

Housing systems are a major sector of the national economy and are closely linked to the finance sector through mortgage markets. Housing and macroeconomic policy is discussed by Stephen Whelan and regulation and intervention in mortgage markets is addressed by Martin Flanagan; more specific regulatory instruments are described in articles dealing with mortgage guarantees by Robert Van Order, deposit guarantees for housing finance institutions by James Barth and Harris Hollans, and mortgage interest rate regulation by Ian Harper and Lachlan Smirl. The importance of housing finance and housing equity in personal wealth portfolios has meant that housing asset values and mortgage debt are an important consideration in the application of monetary policy, as discussed by John Muellbauer (Monetary Policy, Wealth Effects, and Housing).

Choice and Discrimination

We have witnessed a transformation in the role of governments in housing policy over the last few decades with an increasing emphasis on market-based solutions to housing problems. These trends and the policies that use market mechanisms to increase choice and promote individual responsibility are examined in Melek Cigdem and Gavin Wood's overview article (Choice and Government Intervention in Housing Markets). One of the first and most important policy initiatives of this kind was the sale and transfer of public housing (Privatisation of Social Housing by Manuel Aalbers); other market-based policy initiatives reviewed in this section include articles by Andrew Caplin (Shared Equity), Ray Struyk (Access and Affordability: House Purchase Certificates), and Freidman Roy and Richard Ronald (Contract Saving Schemes). Policies in transition countries are reviewed in Martin Lux's article (Policies to Promote Housing Choice in Transition Countries). The enthusiasm for neoliberal market-oriented housing policies is tempered by market imperfections that can impede choice among disadvantaged groups. Policies to address discrimination in housing markets, to tackle redlining, and to provide education programmes for home buyers and tenants have been motivated by these concerns. They are discussed here by Dag Einar Sommervoll, Manuel Aalberts, and Anitra Nelson, respectively. Finally, Val Colic-Peisker's article on immigration and housing policy is especially pertinent given the importance of migration in a globalising world.

The *International Encyclopedia of Housing and Home* has a separate section on 'Policy' because housing is a basic need and a substantial sector of the economy. Housing policy is therefore of a key concern for governments all over the world. The 65 articles in this section aim to provide the reader with an overview of the diverse housing policies in different parts of the world.

G Wood and K Datta

WELFARE AND WELL-BEING

Why Well-Being?

The *International Encyclopedia of Housing and Home* would not be complete without a set of articles which very directly tackles issues of human welfare and well-being. Of course, this theme appears, tacitly or more explicitly, in a very wide range of essays across all the main sections. Nevertheless, a central aim of very many areas of housing studies has been to engage with the importance of housing systems not only in reflecting wider patterns of exclusion and inequality but also as way of documenting and intervening in processes of discrimination, exclusion, and impoverishment. Many of the contributions in this section of the encyclopedia aim to profile such matters.

The entire encyclopedia, in its aim to appeal internationally, is challenged by the variety of meanings and implications attached in politics, policy, and practice to certain key words. There are, however, few concepts that introduce more confusion than those used to describe welfare and well-being. In the United Kingdom, and in many other European countries, for example, the term 'welfare' has a very broad meaning, which includes individuals' material conditions as well as the range of services and policy instruments that aim to secure certain levels of welfare across the population. In this sense, improving human welfare and securing well-being have very similar connotations. In addition, many, if not most, developed countries have forms of social welfare policy which commonly include housing policy, and there are extensive debates about the nature, variety, and direction of what are often termed 'welfare state regimes'. While the scope and scale of social housing provision and subsidy has frequently been scaled back or privatised in recent decades, the legacy and extent of social housing is still important in many countries; for example, see articles on social housing and the welfare state in Western Europe by Peter Boelhouwer, on social housing in the United States by Rachel Bratt, on housing finance and welfare by Peter King, and on privatization by Peter Malpass. Thus, welfare in this context is equally an individual or collective state, an ideal, and a set of policy instruments. In the United States and elsewhere, by contrast, the term 'welfare' carries the baggage of formal social welfare programmes which have in some contexts a variety of derogatory connotations, as well as limited applicability in many developing countries. Hence, our choice of the terms 'welfare' and 'well-being' to try to embrace the variety of different understandings involved.

The 62 articles in this section gathered under the collective heading of 'Welfare and Well-Being' make an important statement. Housing and home lie at the centre of many issues concerning individual and social welfare and well-being in the broadest sense, which impact on the quality of life that people experience through housing across the life course. So while some researchers and policy-makers examine housing in the context of structure, tenure, location, asset values, affordability, and accessibility, and while others consider patterns of residential and social segmentation, and the opportunities they contain for social and political mobilization, the articles in this section also look to other possibilities for the meanings of housing and home, in particular, their role in securing a better quality of life for individuals, households, and communities.

It is important, finally, to note that the section 'Welfare and Well-Being' for the purpose of the encyclopedia refers neither to the subjective measures that have become popular in health studies, nor to the 'happiness benchmark' that has come into vogue as a policy goal. It is a treated as material condition as well as a meaningful experience, and the articles are concerned as much with what produces its absence – what strips households of well-being – as with what guarantees its presence. So there are articles on housing and the state in a variety of countries, on housing wealth and quality of life, and on the reciprocal link between housing and health that is shaped by environments, policies, and institutions.

At Home with Well-Being

Several decades ago, Lee Rainwater (1966) wrote a paper entitled *Fear and the House-as-Haven in the Lower Class* in which he analysed the value and significance of the home as a refuge from human and non-human threats. Whether a single family dwelling, a self-built squatter home, a terraced cottage, or a high-rise flat, the idea is that home can be a haven – a space that is both defensible and secure. Although feminist scholarship over the years has questioned such visions (showing that for many women, home is anything but refuge (see Gender and Urban Housing in the Global South by Sylvia Chant)), the articles in this section do encourage us to think about the complex role of housing in relation to well-being: in terms of physical and economic security (or insecurity); a place to relax and have fun, or to simply get by and survive; a place of quiet and privacy (or noise and intrusion); and an asset that can be used to meet needs, now, in older age, or for children (see Asset-Based Well-Being: Use Versus Exchange Value by Beverley Searle). Housing generally, and the home in particular, has multiple significances at the individual level and this applies in both developed and less developed worlds.

In Latin American squatter and informal settlements, young households embrace the risks and social costs of living in neighbourhoods without services or secure tenure, and face having to self-build their homes, because such settlements offer a space for family life, a place to live hassle free (*vivir tranquilo*), and the eventual prospect of leaving a legacy to children (*tener un patrimonio para los hijos*). Several articles in this section examine these processes of settlement and home creation, and elsewhere there are reflections on the meanings of the home for those that live out that experience.

Interestingly, too, a high proportion of original homeowners who settled peripheral unserviced land informally some 30 or more years ago continue to live on those same lots, in dwellings that are today fully consolidated, serviced, and located in the intermediate ring of the city (see Urban Regeneration in Latin America by Peter Ward). Physical immobility appears to be the order of the day – at least among low-income homeowners. It seems likely that the meaning of those homes and the significance of their sacrifices have changed over time as people consolidated and expanded the physical space of their dwellings. For many of their (now adult) children, the home is already a patrimony, since they continue to live on the lot with their own families and fully expect to continue to do so once their parents die. How second and even third generations perceive and construct meanings about the family home is only now beginning to be researched.

In developed countries, housing markets operate to allow households to adjust home and housing to needs through residential mobility: moving out or moving inwards; building assets or drawing down on equity; upsizing or downsizing; moving into school catchment areas; and searching for amenity of one sort or other. Here the constraints are largely market based – affordability – although ethnicity and race may also be important, as are national and subnational housing policies. Nevertheless, the wider point is that housing is more than an artefact, or an asset, or a space in which to live; it carries meanings and significance which change in the life course and which are likely to be shaped or constructed by class, ethnicity, social trends and fads, advertising and real estate promotions, national ideology, and so forth As the articles in this section show, this all has a bearing on both welfare and well-being.

Scales of Welfare and Well-Being

Whether in the developed or emerging world, the articles in this section identify a range of scales at which welfare and well-being can be considered, from the macro to the micro.

At the 'macroscale', as we have clearly seen with the recent financial crisis, housing is important in terms of the role it plays in the economy (especially in the developed world) through housing-related construction and spending, in the growth of mortgage debt, and in national economic policy. The inflation of a home price and mortgage lending bubble is implicated in the financial turmoil precipitated by subprime mortgage lending and by mortgage heavy-credit derivatives which proved unsustainable. The subsequent credit crisis, with sharp contractions in mortgage lending, sudden illiquidity in housing markets, dips in price, and a rise in repossessions, particularly in the United States, dealt a major blow to households who are vulnerable to the social and financial consequences of negative equity, bankruptcy, and homelessness. In a number of cities, particularly in the United States, the level of repossessions has led to stagnant or cratering housing markets, which are associated with high levels of vacancies and abandonment and a variety of consequent social and economic problems. While many of these issues are, appropriately, explored in the section 'Economics and Finance', their implications for the financial and wider welfare of home-buyers are drawn out in several of the articles of this section, including those of Lucy Delgadillo and Dan Immergluck.

As a result of recession, which has destabilised the economies and finances of a number of countries, including the United States, the United Kingdom, Spain, and Ireland, all of which had major housing booms, many governments have now embarked on austerity policies in order to try to rein in their national debt. This in turn has created problems in terms of rising unemployment and falling incomes and welfare cuts. There are also cuts in housing-related expenditures and subsidies which have increased housing costs and added to problems of affordability. And, as mentioned earlier, housing is also important as an asset whose erosion can undermine the well-being of homeowners, particularly older homeowners who may rely on live-in adult children to care for them in old age (as in Latin America) or who seek to trade down and release equity for retirement (increasingly the case in developed nations). These issues are explored in articles by Laurence Murphy (Asset-Based Welfare), Beverley Searle (Asset-Based Well-Being: Use Versus Exchange Value), and Hal Kendig (Older People: Well-Being, Housing and Neighbourhoods).

In short, at a macroeconomic level, housing is of importance for social well-being across the board. This is clear even when it is examined from a variety of perspectives, ranging from free-market economics to welfare state regime theory.

Moving to the 'urban scale', housing has a bearing on well-being, in particular, through its role in mediating the practice of segregation between different social and income groups. As is well known, this operates in a variety of different ways in both developed and developing countries. It includes the concentration of low-income groups into low-price, low-quality housing in inner cities or in peripheral social housing estates and irregular settlements; the flight of some higher-income households to suburban or periurban areas; and the creation of segregated housing in inner cities based upon race, class, and ethnicity. The concentration of different income and ethnic groups in different segments of the housing market can generate major differences in social conditions and quality of life: at one extreme, deprived groups are segregated within the poorest housing enclaves, and at the other extreme, highly privileged groups lock themselves away in gated communities. These themes are picked up in several articles, including those of James De Filippis (Social Movements and Housing), Anthony Lemon (Residential Segregation: Apartheid), William Wilson (Residential Segregation: Experiences of African Americans), Edward Geotz (Slum Clearance), Nora Libertun de Duren (Gated Communities: Global South), and Elena Vesselinov (Gated Communities: Developed Countries). These authors also indicate the extent to which such housing issues are tied to political struggles and campaigns. Examples include low-income self-builders mobilizing for legal recognition and for basic services, renters demonstrating to resist eviction, and sometimes – as in Mugabe's Zimbabwe – struggles over blatant ethnic cleansing. Commonplace, too, are protests to challenge rent hikes or threats of gentrification and displacement. In all of these cases, housing and neighbourhoods are the medium through which affected groups attempt to influence or change central or local government policy or to halt new developments which are seen as prejudicial to neighbourhood quality or residents rights (see the articles by Roger Zetter (Shelter and Settlement for Forcibly Displaced People), James DeFilippis (Social Movements and Housing) and others). All this engages with well-being in the broader sense.

At the 'neighbourhood level', processes such as housing abandonment, clearance and redevelopment, gentrification, condominium conversion, and the sale of social housing can contribute to changes in both the availability and the quality and affordability of the housing stock, in ways that adversely affect well-being (see articles by Alan Morris (Social Housing and Social Problems), Alan Smart (Squatter Settlement Clearance), Peter Malpass (Privatisation of Housing: Implications for Well-Being), and others). The form of housing and the environment in which it is located are also important for social interaction and quality of life. There are major differences between homes with gardens in green, communal areas, and life in high-rise blocks in a depressing environment where residents may live in fear or in a state of virtual imprisonment. Housing and home are also important for specific social groups in terms of availability, access, and exclusion. While some groups, particularly the more affluent and able bodied, have relatively few problems in finding appropriate housing, others, such as travellers, refugees, and asylum seekers in the United Kingdom, have difficulties in finding affordable homes that meet their needs. In developing countries, of course, the majority of city populations struggle to find affordable housing at all, and can only do so through informal mechanisms of self-help. It is sobering to note, nevertheless, that self-help and self-managed housing is increasingly observed as a means to homeownership among low-income groups in the United States (see articles by Richard Harris (Self-Help and Informal Sector Housing in the United States and Canada), and Vinit Mukhija (Informal Housing: Colonias in the United States)).

Everywhere there is evidence that older people, and those suffering from various health conditions and disabilities, experience difficulty in finding appropriate, accessible, enabling housing which enhances quality of life. The design and layout of housing, environmental quality, and other features of dwelling that are linked to physical and mental health are dealt with in the articles by Philippa Howden-Chapman (Health, Well-Being, and Housing), Mary Godfrey (Supported ousing), Rita Jacinto (Disability and Enablement), Diana Olsberg (Older People: Well-Being), Jason Prior (Health, Well-Being and Vulnerable Populations), and others. There are links here, too, to the articles in the section 'Environment'.

As mentioned at the outset, at the individual household level, housing is significant in terms of its role in social reproduction. Homes provide the locale for a great deal of day-to-day life, from cooking and eating to sleeping and a host of other activities, such as school homework, all of which require adequate and appropriate spaces. Some households are fortunate in having sufficient spaces for these activities, while others may be overcrowded and lack appropriate space or facilities. At the most basic level, homes are where occupants can express individuality in the way they personalise and use space. Some types of housing and environments permit this much more easily than others.

Similarly, the scope to remodel or revamp one's housing at the individual level varies. Renters, by and large, have little opportunity or incentive to undertake major remodels or retrofits (although some tenants in low-rent settings may find redecorating or housing improvement investment worthwhile). But most households do take the opportunity to redecorate, improve, or extend their homes, particularly where they have become invested in the neighbourhood, and where the home and actual dwelling itself is imbued with a special significance. Whether through contracting out, or through do-it-yourself (DIY), or through self-building and mutual aid, the housing stock generally, and the home specifically, may be refurbished over time.

Sustainable Well-Being?

'Greening' the home is a contemporary arena for physical improvements. Energy-efficient homes are on the increase and many householders are retrofitting their homes to add solar panels, improve insulation, install more energy-efficient appliances, and engage in rainwater harvesting, garbage, and other recycling, as well as undertaking garden/yard microenvironmental improvements and uses. While sustainable housing applications have traditionally been the preserve of middle-income and better-off groups, the challenge in developing countries especially will be to extend participation in sustainable housing practices to working and lower-income homeowners.

In the United States, 'weatherization' campaigns for homes using resources of the American Reinvestment and Recovery Act has targeted poorer and working-class households, and in countries such as Brazil and Mexico, one observes a quickening of interest in applying green technologies to new housing and to retrofitting older homes in working-class neighbourhoods. Indeed, the savings from making homes more energy efficient and sustainable form a much larger proportion of income among the poor than the rich. We expect interest in sustainable home buildings and retrofits to become more widespread in the future. As such, they are likely to add significant new (green) 'meanings' to housing and the home, especially among younger generations.

In the same vein, cutting across many of these scales are issues of housing rights and social justice. Such issues are rarely simple, as the current 'right to the city' debates illustrated in the article by Edesio Fernandes. While the 'right to the city' is a powerful political slogan, it tends to gloss over the crucial questions of rights for whom, and rights to what. Do landlords and developers have rights to the city or rights to housing, and if so, what form do they take and how are they to be evaluated against the rights of the overcrowded or the homeless? Equally, issues of rights for refugees or rights for travellers need to be evaluated against the rights of long-term residents in an area who may feel that their rights are being ignored or pushed to one side. In this respect, housing, whether viewed as an economic good, an individual possession, or a social right, is at the heart of wider economic, social, and political debates about the structure of society and the pursuit of social well-being.

C Hamnett and P Ward

References

Rainwater L (1966) Fear and the house-as-haven in the lower class. *Journal of the American Institute of Planners* 32: 23–31.

CONTENTS

VOLUME 1

Abandonment	SG Lowe	1
Access and Affordability: Developed Countries	JL Smith	7
Access and Affordability: Homeowner Taxation	SC Bourassa	13
Access and Affordability: House Purchase Certificates	RJ Struyk	18
Access and Affordability: Housing Allowances	PA Kemp	23
Access and Affordability: Housing Vouchers	M Steele	30
Access and Affordability: Mortgage Guarantees	R Van Order	36
Access and Affordability: Rent Regulation	M Haffner, M Elsinga and J Hoekstra	40
Actor–Network Theory	R Dankert	46
Adaptable Housing	E Støa	51
Affordable Housing Strategies	V Milligan and T Gilmour	58
Anthropological Perspectives on Home	I Cieraad	65
Appraisal and Cost–Benefit Analysis	K Addae-Dapaah	70
Architects	TG Lee	76
Asset-Based Welfare	L Murphy	81
Asset-Based Well-Being: Use Versus Exchange Value	BA Searle	87
Austrian Economics	D Maclennan	93
Behavioural Economics	K Gibb	97
Brownfield Development and Housing Supply	TJ Dixon	103
Building Regulations for Energy Conservation	L Murphy	110
Case Studies	D Robertson	117
Central Government Institutions	B Badcock	122
Children and Parenting	C Holdsworth	131
Overview Article Choice and Government Intervention in Housing Markets	M Cigdem and G Wood	137
Civil Sector Institutions and Informal Settlements	D Mitlin and D Satterthwaite	144
Overview Article Climate Change	T Fawcett	150
Climate Change: Adaptations	R Gupta and M Gregg	164
Collective Ownership	D Robertson	180
Community- and Neighbourhood-Based Organisations in the United States	RM Silverman and KL Patterson	186
Community Energy Systems	G Walker and N Simcock	194
Overview Article Comparative Housing Research	M Oxley and M Haffner	199
Complexity	DS Byrne	210
Construction and Demolition Waste	VWY Tam and CM Tam	215

Construction Methods	N Walliman	219
Construction of Housing Knowledge	C Allen	227
Contract Saving Schemes	R Ronald	233
Cooperative Housing/Ownership	D Clapham	243
Cost Analyses of Homelessness: Limits and Opportunities	T Byrne and D Culhane	248
Covered Bonds	M Lea	255
Credit Derivatives	A Rutledge	262
Credit Derivatives and the Housing Market	C King and A Pavlov	269
Crime Prevention through Environmental Design	G Steventon	280
Criminological Perspectives on Homelessness	V Lyon-Callo	285
Critical Realism	P Somerville	291
Cultural Analysis of Housing and Space	D Lu	296
Defensible Space	P Cozens and D Hillier	300
Demand Subsidies for Low-Income Households	K Hulse	307
Democracy and Accountability	M Taylor	314
Demographic Perspectives in Economic Housing Research	T Lindh and B Malmberg	319
Demolition	J Crump	325
Deposit Assistance Schemes for Private Rental in the United Kingdom	J Rugg	330
Development Land Tax	M Oxley	335
Difference	M Harrison and L Hemingway	341
Disability and Enablement	R Jacinto	347
Discourse Analysis	T Manzi	354
Discrimination in Housing Markets	DE Sommervoll	359
Discrimination in Mortgage Markets	GA Dymski	364
Do-it-Yourself	M Watson	371
Domestic Pets	P Carlisle-Frank	376
Domestic Technologies and the Modern Home	L Spigel	383
Domestic Violence	P Meth	399
Overview Article Domesticity	J Hollows	405
Domicide	R Atkinson	415

VOLUME 2

Eco-Communities	H Lovell	1
Ecological Footprint	E Holden	6
Econometric Modeling	E Deutsch	12
Overview Article Economic Approaches to Housing Research	A Marsh	26
Economic Perspectives on Homelessness	B O'Flaherty	37
Economics of Housing Choice	M van Ham	42

Economics of Housing Externalities	E Rossi-Hansberg and P-D Sarte	47
Economics of Housing Market Segmentation	I Ellen	51
Economics of Social Housing	K Gibb	55
Eco-Renovation	G Killip	61
Education Programmes for Home Buyers and Tenants	A Nelson	68
Emotions at Home	L Murphy and D Levy	75
Energy Consumption, Housing, and Urban Development Policy	AM Yezer, F Liu and W Larson	80
Energy Saving	E Löfström and J Palm	87
Environmental Consciousness	E Löfström, J Palm and E Gullberg	92
Environmental Risks: Earthquakes	F Akinci	99
Environmental Risks: Flooding	Y Chen and G Pryce	104
Ethnic Minorities and Housing	G Bolt	109
Ethnicity and Housing Organisations	H Beider	114
Ethnographies of Home and Homelessness	I Glasser	119
Ethnography	P Luken	124
Eviction	M Slatter	129
Evolutionary Economics	R McMaster and C Watkins	135
Exclusionary Zoning	A Mallach	139
Experiencing Home	KJ Mee and N Vaughan	146
Experiencing Home: Sexuality	A Gorman-Murray	152
Feminist Perspectives on Home	R Longhurst	158
Feminist Perspectives on Homelessness	J Wardhaugh	163
Filtering	L Magnusson Turner	172
Financial Deregulation	P King	176
Financial Regulation	A Gelpern	181
First Home Owner Grants	T Dalton	189
Forecasting in Housing Research	G Meen	196
Foreclosure Prevention Measures	A Nelson	202
Foreclosure Vulnerability	D Immergluck	210
Foucauldian Analysis	K McKee	216
Fuel Poverty	B Boardman	221
Game Theory	B Bengtsson	226
Gated Communities	R Atkinson and S Blandy	232
Gated Communities: Developed Countries	E Vesselinov	237
Gated Communities: Global South	N Libertun de Duren	244
Gender and Space	I Molina and K Grundström	250
Gender and Urban Housing in the Global South	S Chant	255
Gender Divisions in the Home	S Punch	264
Gentrification	R Atkinson	269
Gentrification and Neighbourhood Change	M van der Land, A Curley and G van Eijk	275
Gentrification and Well-Being	L Freeman	280

Contents

Ghetto	A Madanipour	287
Globalisation	F Wu	292
Government Mortgage Guarantee Institutions	MG Elsinga	298
Government/Public Lending Institutions: Asia-Pacific	E Oizumi and S Kim	304
Government Sponsored Enterprises in the United States	M Haffner and H van der Heijden	311
Gypsy/Roma Settlements	T San Román-Espinosa and Ó López-Catalán	316
Health and Housing	R Lawrence	323
Health Risks: Damp and Cold	J Douwes, P Howden-Chapman and J Crane	332
Health Risks: Overcrowding	R Lawrence	339
Overview Article Health, Well-Being and Housing	P Howden-Chapman, J Crane, M Baker, H Viggers, R Chapman and C Cunningham	344
Health, Well-Being and Vulnerable Populations	J Prior and S Harfield	355
Hedging Housing Risk	S Swidler	362
Hidden Homelessness	D Robinson	368
High Rise	JM Jacobs	371
High-Rise Homes	R Fincher and I Wiesel	379
Overview Article Home and Homelessness	F Klodawsky	384
Home as a Space of Care	S Bowlby	388
Home as a Space of Worship	L Kong and S Nair	394
Home as Inheritance	A Dupuis	399
Home as Investment	F Allon	404
Home as Leisure Space	E Casey	410
Home as Workplace	KV Gough	414
Home Environments: Aesthetics, Fashion, Status	D Leslie and M Hunt	419
Home in Temporary Dwellings	C Brun	424
Home Objects	G Noble	434
Home Ownership: Economic Benefits	A Díaz and MJ Luengo-Prado	439
Home Ownership: Non-Shelter Benefits	DR Haurin	446
Home: Paid Domestic Labour	BSA Yeoh and S Huang	451
Home: Unpaid Domestic Labour	L Craig	456

VOLUME 3

Homeless Families: United Kingdom	S Fitzpatrick	1
Homeless Families: United States	VA Fusaro, EL Bassuk, M Grandin, L Guilderson and M Hayes	8
Overview Article Homelessness: Causation	S Fitzpatrick	15
Overview Article Homelessness: Definitions	D MacKenzie	25

Homelessness: Measurement Questions	C Chamberlain	36
Homelessness: Prevention in the United States	J Apicello, W McAllister and B O'Flaherty	42
Homeless People: African Americans in the United States	RA Johnson	50
Homeless People: Care Leavers	P Mendes and G Johnson	57
Homeless People: Care Leavers in the United Kingdom	C Baker and S Baxter	62
Homeless People: Disasters and Displacement	S Breau	68
Homeless People: Economic Migrants in Southern Europe	A Tosi	74
Homeless People: Ex-Prisoners in England and Wales	A Jones	80
Homeless People: Ex-Service Personnel/Veterans in the United Kingdom	S Johnsen	86
Homeless People in China/East Asia	P Kennett, H-G Jeon and T Mizuuchi	90
Homeless People: Indigenous/Aboriginal	P Memmott and C Chambers	97
Homeless People: Older People	M Crane and AM Warnes	104
Homeless People: Polish Migrants in the United Kingdom	C McNaughton Nicholls	111
Homeless People: Refugees and Asylum Seekers	JA Sweeney	116
Homeless People: Single Men in Japan	Y Okamoto and J Bretherton	122
Homeless People: Street Children in Africa	L Van Blerk	127
Homeless People: Street Children in Asia	DOB Lam and FC Cheng	132
Homeless People: Street Children in Mexico	GA Jones and S Thomas de Benítez	138
Homeless People: Street Children in the United Kingdom	E Smeaton	145
Homeless People: Youth in Australia	G Johnson	151
Homeless People: Youth in the United Kingdom	D Quilgars	156
Homeowners' Associations in Post-Socialist Countries	J Hegedüs	161
Homestead and Other Legal Protections	DB Barros	167
HOPE VI	DK Levy	172
House Biographies	H Jarvis	176
House Building Industries: Africa	DCI Okpala	182
House Building Industries: Asia Pacific	Y Yau	187
House Building Industries: Latin America	A de Castro	195
House Building Industries: Post-Socialist	S Tsenkova	203
House Building Industries: Western Europe and North America	C Moore and D Adams	211
Household Organisation and Survival in Developing Countries	S Chant	217
Households and Families	R Simpson	227
Household Waste Recycling	M Watson	234
House Price Expectations	R Martin	239
Overview Article House Price Indexes	SC Bourassa	247
House Price Indexes: Methodologies	NE Coulson	252
House Prices and Quality of Life: An Economic Analysis	JF McDonald	258
Housing Agents and Housing Submarkets	C Donner	265
Overview Article Housing and Labour Markets	P Flatau	273
Housing and Neighbourhood Quality: Home Improvement Grants	P Leather	281

Housing and Neighbourhood Quality: Urban Regeneration	R Paddison	288
Housing and Sustainable Transport	E Holden and K Linnerud	294
Overview Article		
Housing and the Macroeconomy	J Muellbauer	301
Housing and the State in Australasia	B Badcock	315
Housing and the State in China	F Wu	323
Housing and the State in Latin America	C Zanetta	330
Housing and the State in South Africa	C Lemanski	337
Housing and the State in South Asia	S Kumar	340
Housing and the State in the Middle East	AM Soliman	346
Housing and the State in the Soviet Union and Eastern Europe	I Tosics	355
Overview Article		
Housing and the State in Western Europe	P Boelhouwer and J Hoekstra	363
Housing and Wealth Portfolios	M Flavin	374
Housing Auctions	D Brounen	380
Housing Careers	M Abramsson	385
Housing Classes and Consumption Cleavages	SG Lowe	390
Housing Construction Industry, Competition and Regulation	D Hayward	395
Housing Demand	S Malpezzi and SM Wachter	404
Housing Developers and Sustainability	A Congreve	408
Housing Developers: Developed World	W Amann and A Mundt	415
Housing Developers: Developing World	C Acioly Jr. and M French	422
Overview Article		
Housing Dynamics: Environmental Aspects	G Powells	429
Housing Equity Withdrawal in the United Kingdom	A Holmans	436
Housing Estates	F Wassenberg	444
Housing Finance: Deposit Guarantees	JR Barth and H Hollans	450
Overview Article		
Housing Finance: Global South	K Datta	456
Housing Finance: Mexico	M Lea	463
Housing Finance Institutions: Africa	F Roy	470
Housing Finance Institutions: Asia	H Zhu	480
Housing Finance Institutions: Latin America	WB Gwinner	486
Housing Finance Institutions: Transition Societies	W Amann and E Springler	491
Housing Governance	A Beer	497
Housing Indicators	J Flood	502
Overview Article		
Housing Institutions in Developing Countries	A Pal and W Van Vliet	509
Housing Market Search	WAV Clark	518
Housing Markets and Macroeconomic Policy	S Whelan	523
Overview Article		
Housing Market Institutions	K Hawtrey	528
Housing Need in the United Kingdom	A Clarke	538

Housing Paradigms	T Iglesias	544
Housing Pathology	A Thomsen	550
Overview Article		
Housing Policies in Developing Countries	PM Ward	559
Housing Policies in Developing Countries: Microfinance	P Smets	573
Housing Policies in Developing Countries: Sites-and-Services and Aided Self-Help	D Mitlin	579
Overview Article		
Housing Policy: Agents and Regulators	P Boelhouwer and J Hoekstra	585
Housing Policy and Regeneration	RJ Kleinhans	590
Overview Article		
Housing Policy Trends	J Doling	596
Housing Preferences	HCCH Coolen and SJT Jansen	606
Housing Standards: Regulation	HJ Visscher, FM Meijer and JP Branco	613
Housing Statistics	M Steele	620
Housing Subsidies and Welfare	P King	627
Housing Subsidies and Work Incentives	M Shroder	632
Housing Subsidies in the Developing World	A Gilbert	638
Overview Article		
Housing Supply	KD Vandell	644
Housing Supply: Green Belts	K-H Kim	659
Housing Supply: Urban Growth Boundaries	M Buxton and L Groenhart	664
Housing Trust Funds	KE Larsen	668
Housing Wealth and Consumption	M Iacoviello	673
Housing Wealth and Inheritance in the United Kingdom	C Hamnett	679
Housing Wealth as Precautionary Savings	R Martin	685
Housing Wealth Distribution in the United Kingdom	G Pryce	691
Housing Wealth over the Life Course	T Davidoff	697
Human Rights and Housing	P Kenna	703
Ideal Homes	T Chapman	709
Illicit Drug Use and Homelessness	J Neale	714

VOLUME 4

Immigration and Housing Policy	V Colic-Peisker	1
Immigration and Housing: North-Western Europe	J Doherty	8
Immigration and Housing: United States	C Flippen	16
Impact Fees	J Flood	22
Impairment and Experience of Home	R Wilton and E Hall	26
Inclusionary Zoning to Support Affordable Housing	J Schuetz and R Meltzer	32
Industrial Organisation of the US Residential Mortgage Market	WS Frame and LJ White	37
Inequalities in European Cities	S Musterd and W Ostendorf	49
Informal Housing: Asia	E Berner	56

Informal Housing: Colonias in the United States	V Mukhija	63
Informal Housing: Latin America	C Klaufus and P Van Lindert	70
Institutional Economics: New	SCY Chen and C Webster	78
Institutional Economics: Traditional	R McMaster	86
Institutions and Governance Networks in Housing and Urban Regeneration	G van Bortel	93

Overview Article

Institutions for Housing Supply	B Needham	99
Institutions for Neighbourhood Renewal	H Vestergaard	109
Institutions that Represent Housing Professionals	P Gray, M Chivunga, U McAnulty and P Shanks	114
Intermediate Housing Tenures	M Elsinga	124
Islamic Housing Finance	M Samers	130
Key Worker Housing Policies	N Morrison	139
Kitchens	L Johnson	145
Land Owners	R Grover and A Ng'ombe	152
Land Registration Institutions: Developed World	E Cooke	157
Life Course	C Holland and S Peace	163
Living Rooms	P Garvey	169
Local Government Property Taxes	G Wood and R Ong	174
Low-Income Housing Tax Credits	K McClure	180
Maintenance and Repair	A Straub	186
Master Plan Developers	L Cheshire	195
Material Cultures of Domestic Interiors: Africa	R Grant	200
Material Cultures of Domestic Interiors: India	I Bryden	206
Material Cultures of Domestic Interiors: Japan	I Daniels	211
Material Cultures of Domestic Interiors: Transnationalism	H van der Horst	217

Overview Article
Material Cultures of Home — S Chevalier — 222

Overview Article
Meanings of Home — L Fox O'Mahony — 231

Meanings of Home for Moveable Habitats	M Bevan	240
Meanings of Home for Older People	B Tanner, D De Jonge and T Aplin	246
Meanings of Home: Gender Dimensions	A Gorman-Murray	251
Meanings of Home in Popular Culture	J Lloyd	257
Memory and Nostalgia at Home	I Cieraad	262
Mental Health and Homelessness	K Amore and PL Howden-Chapman	268
Microfinance for Housing	SR Merrill	274
Migration and Housing: Global South	K Datta	282
Migration and Population Mobility	AG Champion	287
Migration and Urban Living in Less Developed Countries	A Datta	294
Migration: Ethnicity, Race and Mobility	EL-E Ho and P Kissoon	298
Mobility and Community	J Richardson	302

Mobility Programmes for Disadvantaged Populations: The Moving to Opportunity Programme	WAV Clark	307
Modern Methods of Construction	H Lovell	312
Monetary Policy, Wealth Effects and Housing	J Muellbauer	317
Mortgage Choice: Behavioural Finance	JK Dokko	326
Mortgage Choice: Classical Economics	D Leece	330
Mortgage Contracts: Flexible	M Munro	336
Mortgage Contracts: Traditional	D Leece	341
Mortgage Default: Consequences	J Ford and A Wallace	346
Mortgage Default: Determinants	PS Willen	354
Mortgage Default: Well-Being in the United States	LM Delgadillo	358
Mortgage Equity Withdrawal	M Munro	364
Mortgage Innovation	MS Chambers	370
Mortgage Insurance	J Guttentag	376
Mortgage Interest Rate Regulation	I Harper and L Smirl	382
Mortgage Lenders and Loans	MB Aalbers	389
Overview Article Mortgage Market Functioning	VC Warnock and FE Warnock	394
Mortgage Market Regulation: Europe	MB Aalbers	399
Mortgage Market Regulation: North America	A Levitin and S Wachter	403
Mortgage Market, Character and Trends: Africa	D Makina	410
Mortgage Market, Character and Trends: Brazil	E Haddad and J Meyer	415
Mortgage Market, Character and Trends: China	Y Deng and P Fei	422
Mortgage Market, Character and Trends: France	A Laferrère and D Le Blanc	434
Mortgage Market, Character and Trends: Germany	I Helbrecht and T Geilenkeuser	445
Mortgage Market, Character and Trends: India	P Tiwari	451
Mortgage Market, Character and Trends: Italy	A Calza	459
Mortgage Market, Character and Trends: Japan	M Seko and K Sumita	465
Mortgage Market, Character and Trends: Korea	M Cho and K-H Kim	474
Mortgage Market, Character and Trends: Mexico	TM Fullerton and JA Ibarra Salazar	482
Mortgage Market, Character and Trends: United Kingdom	SJ Smith	488
Mortgage Market, Character and Trends: United States	A Levitin and S Wachter	492
Mortgage Markets and Macro-Instability	H Schwartz	501
Mortgage Markets: Regulation and Intervention	M Flanagan	507
Mortgage Payment Protection Insurance	J Ford	518

VOLUME 5

Multiple Homes	C Paris	1
Nature in the Home	ER Power	6
Neighbourhood Design: Green Space and Parks	N Dempsey	12
Neighbourhood Design: Public Spaces	R Sendi and B Goličnik Marušić	21

Neighbourhood Design: Urban Outdoor Experience	N Dempsey	29
Neighbourhood Disadvantage	J Prior	43
Neighbourhood Effects	T Kauko and M d'Amato	50
Neighbourhood Effects: Approaches	M van Ham and D Manley	55
Neighbourhood Governance	A Madanipour	61
Neighbourhood Improvement: The Role of Housing and Housing Institutions	T Carter	67
Neighbourhood Incivilities	RB Taylor	73
Neighbourhood Planning	S Pinnegar	78
Neighbourhood Reputation	M Permentier	85
Neighbourhood Watch	R Yarwood	90
Neoclassical Models of the Housing Market	M Andrew	96
Neural Networks and Analytic Hierarchy Processes	T Kauko	103
New Urban Economics and Residential Location	R Arnott	111
New Urbanism and Smart Growth Movements	JL Grant and S Tsenkova	120
NIMBYism	K Burningham	127
Notaries and Legal Professionals	NM Davidson	131
Older People: Housing Institutions	R Gilroy	136
Older People: Well-Being	D Olsberg	143
Older People: Well-Being, Housing and Neighbourhoods	H Kendig, L Clemson and L Mackenzie	150
Ontological Security	A Dupuis	156
Path Dependency	B Bengtsson	161
People and the Built Form	R Lawrence	167
Peripheral Neighbourhoods	S Mugnano	174
Philosophical Perspectives on Home	K Jacobson	178
Place Attachment	BB Brown, I Altman and CM Werner	183
Planning Institutions: Canada/United States	I Skelton	189
Planning Institutions: China	Y Song	196
Planning Institutions: Post-Socialist	Z Nedović-Budić	202
Policies to Address Homelessness	P Flatau	209
Policies to Address Homelessness: Criminalisation and Control of Public Space	J Wardhaugh	215
Policies to Address Homelessness: Housing First Approaches	V Stanhope, DK Padgett and BF Henwood	230
Policies to Address Homelessness: Partnership-Based Approaches in Ireland	E O'Sullivan	237
Policies to Address Homelessness: Prevention in the United Kingdom	H Pawson	243
Policies to Address Homelessness: Rights-Based Approaches	I Anderson	249
Policies to Address Homelessness: 'Staircase' Models	I Sahlin	255
Policies to Address Redlining	MB Aalbers	261
Policies to Address Social Mix in Communities	G Meen	268
Policies to Address Spatial Mismatch	D Houston	274

Policies to Promote Housing Choice in Transition Countries	M Lux	280
Policies to Promote the Environmental Efficiency of Housing	RE Horne	286

Overview Article

Policies to Support Access and Affordability of Housing	J Yates and V Milligan	293
Policy Instruments that Support Housing Supply: Social Housing	M Berry	306
Policy Instruments that Support Housing Supply: Supply-Side Subsidies	M Cigdem	311
Political Ideologies	P King	317
Politics of Housing	B Bengtsson	322
Post-Bubble Housing in Japan	Y Hirayama	328
Post-Conflict Housing Restitutions	A Buyse	336
Post-Disaster Housing and Reconstruction	C Johnson and G Lizarralde	340
Power	P King	347

Overview Article

Price Determination in Housing Markets	G Meen	352
Price Dynamics in Housing Markets	M Cho and K-H Kim	361
Privacy, Sanctuary and Privatism	R Dowling	367
Private Protection and Housing Property Insurers in the United States	RW Klein	372
Private Rental Landlords: Developing Countries	A Gilbert	381
Private Rental Landlords: Europe	J Hoekstra, M Haffner, H van der Heijden and M Oxley	387
Private Rental Landlords: North America	A Mallach	393
Private Sector Housing Management: Asia Pacific	EC-M Hui and TH Khan	401
Private Sector Housing Management: Europe	N Nieboer	407
Private Sector Housing Management: North America	J Londerville	414
Private Sector Housing Management: Post-Socialist	S Tsenkova	420
Privatisation of Housing: Implications for Well-Being	P Malpass	427
Privatisation of Social Housing	MB Aalbers	433
Property Rights Approaches	CA Nygaard	439
Public-Private Housing Partnerships	T Brown and N Yates	446

VOLUME 6

Qualitative Interviewing	D Thorns	1

Overview Article

Qualitative Methods in Housing Research	HCCH Coolen	8
Real Estate Agents	P Cucchiarelli and S McGreal	16
Regulation Theory	M Goodwin	22
Remittances and Well-Being	M Orozco	28

Overview Article

Rental Market and Rental Policies in Less Developed Countries	A Gilbert	35
Rent Policies for Social Housing	H Priemus	46
Representations of Homelessness	M Filipovič Hrast	54
Representations of Home: Literature and Language	K Mezei	59

Representations of Home: Painting	A LeZotte	64
Representations of Home: Photos and Film	P King	67
Research Networks and Professional Institutions in Housing	C Watson	72
Resident and Neighbourhood Movements	P Somerville	77
Residential Property Derivatives	P Englund	83
Residential Real Estate Investment Trusts	B Case	88
Residential Segregation	J Leal	94
Residential Segregation and Education	W Clark	100
Residential Segregation and Ethnic Diversity in the United States	K Brown	105
Residential Segregation: Apartheid	A Lemon	111
Residential Segregation: Experiences of African Americans	JM Quane and WJ Wilson	121
Residential Segregation: Measurement	C Peach	126
Residential Segregation: Race and Ethnicity	C Peach	132
Residential Urban Form and Transport	I Hamiduddin	137
Restorative Housing Environments	T Hartig	144

Overview Article

Rights, Citzenship, and Shelter	B Bengtsson, S Fitzpatrick and B Watts	148
Rights to Housing: Developing Societies	X Ren	158
Rights to Housing: International Instruments	S Leckie	164
Rights to Housing: Marginalised Housing Groups	L Weinstein	170
Rights to Housing Tenure	C Hunter and S Blandy	176
Rights to Land Tenure	R Home	182
Rights to the City	E Fernandes	187

Overview Article

Risk in Housing Markets	N Berg, N Jha and JC Murdoch	193
Rural Communities	M Shucksmith and N Thompson	204
Rural Homelessness: An International Perspective	P Milbourne	210
Rural Homelessness in India	J Wardhaugh	216
Rural Housing	M Shucksmith and J Sturzaker	226
Rurality and Housing	P Milbourne	232
Second Homes	F Diaz Orueta	237

Overview Article

Securing Land Rights and Housing Delivery	R Sietchiping and C Augustinus	243
Security of Tenure in Muslim Communities	S Sait	251
Security of Tenure Legislation in Private Rental Housing	H Lind	254
Self-Build: Global North	N Walliman	259
Self-Build: Global South	F Murillo	265
Self-Build: Latin America	C Clarke	278
Self-Help and Informal Sector Housing in the United States and Canada	R Harris	286
Self-Help Housing Organisations	A Curley	292

Self-Help: Land Development	G Payne	297
Self-Help: Policy Assistance	R Harris	304
Self-Provided Housing in Developed Societies	K Dol, C Lennartz and P De Decker	310
Shanty Towns	V Neves	316
Shared Equity	A Caplin	321
Shelter and Development	H Dandekar	325
Shelter and Settlement for Forcibly Displaced People	R Zetter	330
Simulation Models for Housing Analysis	G Meen	336
Simulation Models for Urban Economies	R Arnott	342
Slum Clearance	EG Goetz	350
Slums	A Olotuah	355
Small-Area Spatial Statistics	E Ferrari	362
Social Class and Housing	C Allen	368
Social Construction	K Jacobs	374
Social Exclusion and Housing	S Münch	377
Social History	K Jacobs	381
Social Housing: Allocation	S Kromhout and M van Ham	384
Social Housing and Employment	K Hulse	389
Social Housing and Social Problems	A Morris	395
Social Housing: Finance	J Flood	401
Overview Article Social Housing Institutions in Europe	H Priemus	410
Overview Article Social Housing in the United States: Overview	RG Bratt	416
Social Housing Landlords: Asia Pacific	NM Yip	426
Social Housing Landlords: China	B Tang	432
Social Housing Landlords: Europe	M Norris	438
Social Housing Landlords: Latin America	P Jiron	444
Social Housing Landlords: North America	CT Koebel	449
Social Housing Landlords: Post-Socialist	M Lux	454
Social Housing: Measures to Attract Private Finance	P Phibbs	460
Social Justice	P King	464
Social Mix in Western Countries	S Musterd and W Ostendorf	469
Social Movements and Housing	J DeFilippis	473
Social Policy Approaches	P Spicker	478
Social Psychological Perspectives on Homelessness	J Christian and D Abrams	484
Overview Article Social Spaces and Urban Policies	W Ostendorf and S Musterd	489
Social Sustainability	M Pareja-Eastaway	502
Overview Article Social Theory and Housing	J Dodson	506
Socio-Legal Perspectives	S Blandy and C Hunter	514

VOLUME 7

Spatial Economics	J Lauridsen	1
Spatial Mismatch	L Gobillon and H Selod	5
Squatter Settlement Clearance	A Smart	11
Squatting: Developing World	S Jiusto	16
Squatting: United Kingdom	K Reeve	23
Stakeholder Analysis for Housing	J Sousa	28
Structure and Agency	D Clapham	34
Submarkets	C Watkins	39
Subprime and Predatory Lending: Legal Regulation	D Reiss	45
Subprime Mortgages	MJ Courchane and DJ Kogut	51
Suburban Homes	R Dowling	60
Supply Elasticity of Housing	KH Kim, SY Phang and S Wachter	66
Supply-Side Subsidies for Affordable Rental Housing	M Oxley	75
Overview Article Supported Housing	M Godfrey	81
Sustainability	RLH Chiu	91
Overview Article Sustainable Communities	A Congreve	97
Sustainable Housing Cultures	E Støa and M Aune	111
Sustainable Lifestyles	K Gram-Hanssen	117
Sustainable Regeneration	JP Evans	124
Sustainable Urban Development	J Callender	129
Systems Theory	ML Rhodes	134
Taxation	J Yates	138
Taxation and Subsidies: The US Case	MS Chambers	148
Overview Article Taxation Policy and Housing	M Stewart	152
Technology and Surveillance in the Home	M Nelson	167
Temporary Housing	C Lévy-Vroelant	172
Tenant Cooperatives, Shareholders' Housing Companies	H Ruonavaara	180
Tenure as an Institution	H Ruonavaara	185
Textual and Linguistic Analysis	A Hastings	190
Overview Article Time and the Economic Analysis of Housing Systems	D Maclennan	196
Transaction Costs in Housing Markets	J Van Ommeren	201
Upgrading Informal Settlements	D Satterthwaite	206
Urbanisation and Housing the Poor: Overview	V Desai	212
Urban Regeneration in Latin America	PM Ward	219
User Cost, Home Ownership and House Prices: United States	A Díaz and MJ Luengo-Prado	228

Vacancy Chains	L Magnusson Turner	235
Vernacular Housing	L Memba Ikuga and T Murray	241
Visual Research Methods	I Ortega-Alcázar	249
Water Supply and Sanitation	K Welle and A Walnycki	255
Welfare Agencies and Assistance: United States	SJ Newman	261
Welfare States and Housing	H Schwartz	267
Well-Being and Housing in the Caribbean	C Clarke	273
Women and Housing Organisations	KW Chan	282
Subject Index		289

A

Abandonment

SG Lowe, University of York, York, UK

© 2012 Elsevier Ltd. All rights reserved.

Glossary

Counterurbanisation The process by which households relocate from city and town centres to suburban and rural areas.

Deindustrialisation A macroeconomic process that generally refers to the loss of 'traditional' manufacturing and mining industries. An example of this is the rapid decline of textiles and finished garment production during the 1980s in the cities of northern England.

Low demand for housing A situation sometimes occurs in local housing markets in which there is a surplus in the stock of dwellings compared to demand from households, typically occurring when there is population decline.

Subprime mortgages Mortgages that are sold by unregulated companies to households with insufficient income to cover repayments. Households are tempted to remortgage their property (to release equity) by cheap introductory low-interest offers which then become unsustainably high at the end of the deal.

Introduction

Abandonment of housing is the process by which properties in either the public or private sectors become detached from the housing market and eventually fall into disuse. It is a juncture in the life of a property several stages removed from simply becoming vacant, and at the end of which the owner takes no active steps to rehabilitate the property into the housing market. Households that once lived there relinquish their right to the title or possession of the property. This article focuses on the problem of housing abandonment in Britain during the 1990s, looking at the underlying causes and consequences of abandonment, particularly the process of deindustrialisation that came to a peak during the 1980s and the early 1990s. This story has antecedents in the US economy, and reference is made to this case to help explain the processes at work. The collapse of the American subprime housing market in 2007–08 has given rise to a renewed bout of foreclosures, leading to large-scale abandonment. The article ends by outlining this new source of abandonment.

Abandonment in History

Abandonment of housing occurs in many circumstances and has been a feature of human settlement throughout history. The phenomenon generally occurs when something happens to disturb a local community to such an extent that the population has to leave the habitation permanently or when something catastrophic happens that causes populations to decline. A dramatic example of this concerns the thousands of villages abandoned as a result of plague in medieval Europe. The population of most European countries fell sharply in the 100 years between 1350 and 1450. The population of England in 1350 has been estimated at 4–5 million; 40% of this population was wiped out by the outbreak of 'Black Death' in 1384, which killed about one-and-a-half million people. Thousands of villages simply disappeared off the map.

In the advanced, industrialised economies of the twentieth and twenty-first centuries, housing abandonment is not as dramatic as in the past but is commonplace and sometimes occurs on a very large scale. There are various reasons for this. The most important are:

- Failures of the planning system when land-use planning decisions are made that create 'blight'.
- Underlying restructuring of economies that impacts on the type and location of employment.
- Policy failures when centralised decision making is out of touch with rapidly changing local economic conditions.
- Oversupply of certain types/sizes of property compared with household structures.

- The collapse of subprime mortgage markets.

'Planning blight' was common in UK cities in the 1960s when slum clearance programmes began to encroach on areas of good quality housing. Announcements of new clearance zones caused property prices to collapse, and spillover effects into neighbouring communities were difficult to contain. Until changes in planning law in the early 1960s and the introduction of the idea of public participation, local residents had few defences except through the courts. A spate of local community action groups often successfully put up resistance to the planning process and eventually housing policy priorities changed. But for a while, most large UK cities had urban landscapes that looked rather like bombsites, with some houses still standing but many abandoned. A few owner-occupiers refusing to quit often delayed the implementation of clearance schemes. Planning blight continues to be a problem because the process of public objections makes the planning system very slow.

Another perhaps rather modest source of abandonment of housing can be the mismatch in some areas between the structure of households and the type of property available or that certain dwelling types were unpopular (e.g., maisonettes, high-rise flats, and small houses). Imbalances in the supply and demand for housing of these types can occur widely but are relatively of less importance in the overall pattern of abandoned housing compared with major macroeconomic issues.

Globalisation and Economic Restructuring

The main cause of housing abandonment in the modern period is profound economic restructuring. This was the case in the United Kingdom during the 1980s and 1990s, when traditional manufacturing and mining industries contracted very rapidly and in some cases almost completely disappeared. Underneath this is the impact of globalisation on the British economy, which was particularly vulnerable to change because it had previously been the 'workshop of the world', famous for its manufacturing and export-based economy. In brief, what happened was that from about the mid-1970s onwards, the centres of manufacturing shifted from the Northern Hemisphere to the Asian Pacific Rim and less economically developed nations in South America. The new workshop of the world is China, which currently accounts for 25% of the world's manufactured goods.

With the liberalisation of world trade in the 1980s and the speeding up of globalisation, trade barriers were broken down, and industries that had previously been protected by import taxes found themselves exposed to the full force of global competition. In the United Kingdom, during the 1980s and 1990s once-secure jobs in manufacturing, textiles, mining, and horticulture disappeared rapidly. For example, in the Pennine towns of England (centred on Huddersfield and Halifax, the cradle of the Industrial Revolution) in the period between 1971 and 1997 manufacturing and textiles declined by 48%. In the space of 25 years, 40 000 jobs were lost. Meanwhile, in just one decade between 1981 and 1991, in Vietnam, 900 000 jobs in manufacturing – many of these in textiles and finished garment production – were created. Finished garments accounted for 50% of Vietnam's exports in 1991. China's ability to put tens of millions of workers into low-cost production has fuelled a huge export-led boom in the Chinese economy, especially since they joined the World Trade Organization in 2001.

The economies of Britain and the United States are now described as 'postindustrial' because they have replaced large sections of their manufacturing core with services. Product design, marketing, retailing, and research are still mainly done in these nations so that they retain a high proportion of the value of the goods. Added to this has been a massive expansion in global trading of financial assets, money, stocks, government bonds, and insurance, much of it arising from the 'virtual' economy since the invention of the Internet in the 1980s. Before the 'credit crunch' and the recession in the world economy that began in 2007, London had become the largest centre for the trading of financial assets in the world. In addition, the modern state itself had become a very large-scale service industry employer. Government statistics show that one in five employed people works directly for the government, and if outsourced work is included, such as Capita call centres, the figure is nearly 7 million, or one in four of the employed workforce (*The Telegraph*, 29 July 2003: 32).

This is not the place to develop this argument; suffice it to say that there is a new geography of world trade and crucially for the issue of abandonment there is an accompanying massive shift of populations in every country that has been involved in the new global economy. In Britain, this has taken the form of a process of counterurbanisation, of a major movement of households out of the old industrial cities towards smaller towns and suburban locations. Out-of-town shopping precincts, science parks connected to universities (which have themselves expanded dramatically), and new sporting and cultural facilities have become familiar features around the country, alongside which has appeared a new owner-occupied suburban-built environment.

The work of Turok and Edge (1999) shows clearly that during the 1980s and 1990s employment grew sharply in smaller towns and rural areas but fell in bigger cities. Old industries were replaced by new ones and *in different places*. During the 1990s, about 40 000 people migrated out of the Northern and Midland conurbations annually, with much of the movement being to other parts of the same or adjacent regions, rather than to the South of England. It is interesting to note that a large proportion of the 'new' work was part-time female employment taking the place of full-time male jobs in manufacturing. Together, this relocation and changing pattern of household incomes impacted on the growth of homeownership, which was also a feature of this period. Suburbanisation continued to attract people away from city centres. The point, however, for the issue of abandonment is that it was the pattern of deindustrialisation that accompanied this restructuring that caused a huge scale of low and collapsing demand for housing leading to disuse and eventually abandonment and demolition in UK inner cities.

Abandonment in American Cities

This situation is not unique to Britain. Housing abandonment was identified in the mid-1960s as a major problem facing American cities, and there is ample documentation of it (see Further Reading). These studies showed how housing markets failed under the impact of depopulation as old industries moved away. In some cases, banks and mortgage companies 'red-lined' specific neighbourhoods (where they would not lend) to screen out low-income households, leading to disinvestment and neglect of property. Processes associated with depopulation depleted the urban tax base and quickly stripped once-viable neighbourhoods of their economic and social energy. There was an underlying theme in all this work that whole areas of US inner cities were left to decay and became virtually uninhabitable. The process appeared to continue and make a resurgence following the subprime mortgage scandal that broke in 2007 and led to the collapse of the US housing market and widespread abandonment as property owners in hundreds of thousands walked away from impossible debts.

The American Rust Belt cities are the best documented example of industrial collapse, dating from the mid-1960s, which anticipates what happened in Britain by some considerable time. But in many ways there is a close parallel with the causes of housing abandonment in Britain during the 1980s and 1990s. This area of the Northeastern, Mid-Atlantic, and portions of the Upper Midwest United States was the centre of heavy industry and manufacturing based around steel production. The term 'Rust Belt' signifies the collapse of the steel industry and related manufacturing over a long period since the 1960s. New employment opportunities developed around railheads and in rural/small town locations because the work was less geographically dependent on raw materials. This process was described in the Kerner Commission Report (1968), which showed the dramatic decline of population leading to loss of demand for housing and consequent abandonment that accompanied this shift away from the heartlands of the old manufacturing industries in cities such as Syracuse, Duluth, Milwaukee, Detroit, Toledo, Cleveland, and Pennsylvania. It was also associated with the expanding suburbanisation of employment opportunities that exerted further pressure on declining inner cities, a situation that was to impact the Northern cities of the United Kingdom, but 10 to 20 years later.

Abandonment and Low Demand for Housing in the United Kingdom

The first signs that all was not well was the development of 'difficult to let' council housing in Northern cities with housing officers accused of being inefficient in re-letting vacant properties. There was, however, a clear difference between estates that were lettable but unpopular and the situation in the 1990s when even newly built and refurbished properties could not be let. Later evidence of a trend towards low and falling demand came through local councillors reporting on the social chaos that was resulting from households draining away from certain localities and that local authorities were quietly engaged in the demolition of surplus stock, properties that had sometimes been expensively refurbished under central government schemes such as City Challenge. There was a suggestion that policy in this field significantly lagged behind reality on the ground, with local authorities tied into these expensive but inappropriate regeneration programmes. At first, this problem was confined to social housing, but it quickly came to affect the private sector, with landlords unable to re-let properties and house prices collapsing. In the West End of Newcastle, along the banks of the River Tyne, some 20 000 jobs were lost from the Vickers shipyard and munitions factory in the space of only a few years in the late 1980s. Families able to move to new work did so, leaving behind traumatised neighbourhoods where normal life became impossible. At first, abandoned houses were boarded up, but such was the scale of the problem that local authorities eventually decided on wholesale demolition. Pockets of owner-occupied properties (**Figure 1**) were left abandoned because houses lost all their value with owners, who were unable to sell, simply walking away from their liabilities. In Newcastle, as elsewhere, following wholesale demolitions, a strange new landscape of grassed-over terraces emerged leaving behind a curious, postindustrial archeology made visible by nameless streets and kerbs marking the layout of once-vibrant communities.

The evidence of abandonment leading to demolition began to be documented rather belatedly in the 1980s and 1990s. Webster, for example, reported that about 10% of Glasgow's council housing had been demolished between 1981 and 1999, some 20 000 units. Research

Figure 1 Abandoned owner-occupied properties in the West End of Newcastle, '...a strange new landscape of grassed-over terraces'.

commissioned by the government discovered that between 1991 and 1997, council houses demolished per annum in England and Wales stood at 40 000, representing 1% of the total social housing stock. Abandonment of fit housing in all tenures in the north of England was reported in a number of studies (Bramley et al., 2000; Lowe et al., 1999; Power and Mumford, 1999). In all these cases, the principal reason for the existence of large surpluses of housing was population decline arising from deindustrialisation.

The Impact of Abandonment on Local Communities

It is readily apparent that population decline is the general context for the existence of surplus housing, leading quite quickly to the collapse of local housing markets and abandonment. This does not explain one of the most complex issues related to the abandonment phenomenon that arises from the social processes that accompany and eventually accelerate neighbourhood decline. In the UK case, evidence showed that abandonment was characteristic of the most deprived wards, but it was also clear that not every neighbourhood was equally affected. Why this should be the case when set against a general economic malaise is probably a result of microlevel features of the communities likely to be affected. Social studies showed that streets literally round the corner from those with empty properties seemed to be more stable and unaffected by the problems created by abandonment. It seems that the existence of only one or two abandoned houses created a kind of contagion, spreading out from one or two empty properties until clusters of dwellings or a whole street were affected. There are some clues here in earlier American studies that showed just such a 'contagion' effect from an original single problem, rather like the spread of a virus. Once this happens, perhaps randomly, neighbouring houses come under pressure and house prices already affected by low demand can plummet. When an entire street becomes infected by problems, communities enter a spiral of decline – corner shops close, people able to move do so, and bus services are curtailed and eventually stop; meanwhile drug abusers and squatters colonise the area and petty or serious crime takes hold. The economic and social life of once-stable communities ebbs away with remarkable speed.

The social processes that underlie this 'contagion' leading to housing abandonment has rarely been researched or understood. However, in a remarkable study in Newcastle, Keenan tracked over 700 moving households in the West End of the city, an area that was at the time badly affected by low-demand problems. Keenan found that these households moved frequently (many two or three times during the previous year) over short distances, and he concluded that this pattern of 'serial moving' was a perverse consequence of the number of empty properties in the area. Very few movers improved their housing situation as a result of the move. Subsequent interviews discovered that these residents were subject to multiple pressures, reporting high levels of stress due to crime and vandalism, often combined with mounting personal debt. For almost half these movers, there were disputes with neighbours, or a perception that their neighbours were a problem in some way. Rather than being resigned to the situation, the households – single parents, young childless couples, single-person households – moved elsewhere within the community, staying with relatives or friends, sometimes with different partners, but in the end most of them were forced to move out of the area (Keenan, 1998).

Once houses are abandoned, there is a slippery slope that often leads to the collapse of once-healthy communities. There was evidence in these chaotic, rough-and-tumble neighbourhoods not only of serial movers but also of housing benefit fraud by private landlords anxious because of declining income. As a result, this mélange of problems also incorporated illegal ghost tenancies against which housing benefit was claimed. The 'churning' that took place in these low-demand neighbourhoods was thus not a new-found housing market freedom but a catalogue of problems – women escaping abusive relationships, people running from debt, overbearing landlords, corrupt property agencies, and vulnerable single parents on 24-h burglar watch and dealing with disruptive neighbours. One of the more alarming aspects of low demand for housing and eventual abandonment was that under the weight of these problems, personal relationships were badly affected, rather perversely, by opportunities to move round the area, even to occupy more than one house, possibly with different partners or possibly none. If people become unable to conduct long-term relationships, the glue that sticks communities together starts to weaken and the stability of decades of shared life turns to insecurity.

The Subprime Crisis in the US Housing Market

Similar stories of rapidly deteriorating communities are evident in the recent subprime mortgage scandal in America. Foreclosure (repossession), family stress, and neighbourhoods in crisis are widely reported in the US literature. Abandonment arises in this case from the unregulated selling of subprime mortgages that entrap households into unsustainable debt. This problem had been apparent for some years, and as early as 2006, reports were released documenting a pattern of increasing foreclosures leading to abandonment. For example, the Minnesota Family Housing Fund described a 'foreclosure epidemic' and announced a $11 million scheme to buy up foreclosed homes. A 2006 report published by the city of St Paul found that there were more than 800 abandoned buildings in the city, the highest number since records began in the 1980s. This is now commonplace across the United States. The problem originated from misselling of mortgages by predatory banks and building societies. The problem emerged with increasing house prices during the early years of the new millennium

Figure 2 Thousands of abandoned properties litter US suburbs with no hope of being reintegrated because there is an oversupply of properties.

and growth in equity. Lenders gained access to most of this value by extending high-cost credit that has subsequently to be refinanced by new loans. This 'loan churning' created profitable fees for lenders, but each time a refinance occurred, the homeowner lost some of the equity, eventually leaving none at all, with foreclosure the only option. This form of asset stripping by predatory loan companies and banks was conducted on a massive scale and bound in millions of vulnerable low-income households who often had few choices and originally were offered attractive short-term low-interest loans. This corrupt behaviour was not only the trigger to the global financial meltdown due to the discovery of huge quantities of unregulated mortgage-backed securities – a type of the so-called toxic assets – but it is also the cause of housing abandonment – now endemic in the US housing market – with thousands of communities having entered a spiral of decline (**Figure 2**).

Conclusion

Housing abandonment has been a problem throughout history often due to cataclysmic events, leading to rapid population decline. In the modern period abandonment is the end product of a complex interaction between international, national, and local factors. The globalisation of the world economy and its banking system binds the world together in ways that were previously impossible. The restructuring of the global economy, particularly the redeployment of manufacturing to China and the Asian Pacific Rim, has impacted on the streets of the United States, Britain, and many other nations. New geographies have been created by the shift of populations away from the centres of 'old manufacturing' in the great industrial cities towards small towns and suburban communities. Here is where the new economy of Britain with its research centres, universities, science parks, retail outlets, and footloose service industries with no special locational needs tends to congregate. A new services economy has brought with it a demand for living in the homeowning suburbs, not council housing built for the purpose of housing male-breadwinner manufacturing families during the heyday of the old industries. Abandonment of housing inevitably follows as population decline sets in.

A new source of abandonment has recently become much more prevalent due to the crash in the American housing market with a massive scale of housing repossessions, leading eventually to abandonment as the corrupt practices of the mortgage industry take a heavy toll on communities across the country. Vulnerable neighbourhoods have been badly affected, and abandonment seems to be an inevitable consequence of a housing market oversupplied with properties. In this respect, the UK case is different because the scale of subprime lending has been much smaller and the balance of households to dwellings is a persistent problem due to planning constraints and, recently, because the building industry has contracted. In Britain, the 'Pathfinder' regeneration projects have had a significant impact in mitigating the worst of the 'low-demand' problems from the 1980s and 1990s. Outright housing abandonment is a persistent problem, but is at a lower level than in recent decades. But for the worst-affected inner cities, the consequences of neighbourhoods drained of their population, economic stability, and social life blood remain a legacy of economic restructuring. Wherever it occurs, the sure sign of an abandoned property is that it is neglected, boarded-up, vandalised and with no apparent owner, often in the end leading to demolition. Ultimately, this situation is the consequence of the shaping and reshaping of the global economy.

See also: Demolition; Globalisation; Housing and Labour Markets; Housing and Neighbourhood Quality: Urban Regeneration; Housing Pathology; Migration and Population; Mortgage Default: Consequences; Neighbourhood Disadvantage; Subprime Mortgages; Sustainable Communities; Time and the Economic Analysis of Housing Systems.

References

Bramley G, Pawson H, and Third H (2000) *Low Demand Housing and Unpopular Neighbourhoods*. London: DETR.
Keenan P (1998) Residential mobility and low demand: A case history from Newcastle. In: Lowe S, Keenan P, and Spencer S (eds.) *Housing Abandonment in Britain: Studies in the Causes and Effects of Low Demand Housing*. York: Centre for Housing Policy, University of York.
Kerner Commission Report (1968) *U.S. National Advisory Commission on Civil Disorders*. Washington, DC: US Government Printing Office.
Lowe S, Keenan P, and Spencer S (1999) Housing abandonment in inner cities: The politics of low demand for housing. *Housing Studies* 14(5): 703–716.
Power A and Mumford K (1999) *The Slow Death of Great Cities?* York: Joseph Rowntreee Foundation.
Turok I and Edge N (1999) *The Jobs Gap in Britain's Cities: Employment Loss and Labour Market Consequences*. Bristol: The Policy Press.

Further Reading

Hoover EM and Vernon R (1962) *Anatomy of a Metropolis*. New York: Doubleday.
Wilson D, Margulis H, and Ketchum J (1994) Spatial aspects of housing abandonment in the 1990s: The Cleveland experience. *Housing Studies* 9(4): 493–510.

Access and Affordability: Developed Countries

JL Smith, University of Illinois at Chicago, Chicago, IL, USA

© 2012 Elsevier Ltd. All rights reserved.

Glossary

Affordable housing Dwellings built specifically for those whose income denies them the ability to purchase or rent on the open market.

Housing assistance Subsidy to offset full cost of market rate housing that can take several forms: an allowance based on a formula relative to income, a direct payment to a property owner to reduce rent cost (see rental housing assistance), and assistance with initial payment to secure housing (down payment, security deposit). While most countries use income level to qualify, not all end assistance if income increases.

Market failure An economic term describing a situation in a market where supply and demand are not in equilibrium. In housing markets, this can occur when the cost of producing a housing unit exceeds the price consumers can pay for it without subsidy.

Rental housing assistance A form of subsidy to make monthly rent affordable to a tenant. Assistance can be tied to housing or to the tenant, who can then take the assistance when moving and use it at another location.

Shelter poverty A family is in shelter poverty if its income is insufficient to cover the subsistence-level costs for food, clothing, transportation, and health care plus the actual cost of housing.

Social exclusion Term used to describe contemporary forms of social disadvantage generally affecting entire communities of people that are denied or prevented access to the benefits those who are socially advantaged can access.

Social housing Housing that is funded by and/or owned by the public sector and is for an established social benefit (e.g., providing affordable housing) and may be developed and managed by a government, nonprofit, or for-profit entity; also known as public housing in some countries.

Introduction

In most cultures, housing is considered a foundation for well-being. Not only does it provide basic shelter and security, a home's location also affects access to economic opportunities, quality food, social services, and material goods.

The challenge for many families is being able to access housing that offers the best combination of features, quality, and locational amenities. A key barrier usually is the cost of housing. In market economies, housing access is primarily determined by a family's resources and what is available to rent or buy. The cost of a housing unit will depend on the size, features, amenities, and location. While it is assumed that supply is built to meet demand, most housing built by private developers and real estate investors in recent years have targeted higher-income households rather than a full spectrum of consumers. As a result, not all families can afford to rent or buy a portion of the private sector housing stock, or when they can, it may not be in a location that allows easy access to transportation and other services and amenities that promote well-being. While the public sector via government programmes and nonprofit agencies has aimed to provide affordable housing, it has not always been of highest quality, well located, or without social problems.

To a certain extent, what makes housing affordable or unaffordable is the cost of other goods and services essential to well-being. This concern is evident in how affordability is typically defined and measured across developed countries, though not all view access to affordable housing from the same vantage point. There are notable differences regarding when government can and should intervene in the private market to make housing affordable to lower-income populations. Along these lines, there are a growing number of countries employing a human rights framework that requires government to engage in some way to make housing affordable to those with limited resources, though the means for doing so varies and the extent to which it is actually being employed is unknown.

Defining Affordability

Affordability is generally a relative term. Researchers, policy-analysts, and public officials gauge whether or not a house is affordable by comparing its cost to something else. Typically, income is the common referent. For example, in the United States, an apartment is affordable when you pay no more than 30 or 35% of income towards rent and utilities every month, or when buying a home, the price paid is no more than three times your annual salary. The basis for these ratios is usually some combination of average rates and assumptions about what resources are required to fulfil other basic needs such as food and clothing.

In contrast, most economists examine affordability in terms of demand and supply, assuming that whatever price is paid for a good reflects a consumer's ability to afford it and a willingness to pay for it. This means some families may be willing and able to pay more or less than a fixed percentage of their income. However, if a good is not valued correctly in the market, then prices should adjust to meet demand. Using this logic, when prices exceed the proportion of income that people are willing and able to pay for housing, then an excess of supply should cause prices to drop in order to meet demand. When this optimisation cannot occur, it is assumed that there is some form of market failure. In housing production analysis, economists often attribute higher prices to regulation on land use and construction, which then can drive up materials' costs and land values. While empirical research suggests that regulating the housing market causes prices to be higher, there is no clear agreement as to how 'free' the market should be, given concerns for health, safety, and privacy. Furthermore, lower costs in housing might mean higher costs for other items. For example, families seeking lower-cost housing in suburbs and exurbs may have to pay more for transportation if the location requires an automobile to get to and from work, school, and shopping.

A measurement specifically used to gauge the general affordability of for-sale housing compares median house price to median income. This ratio, which is used primarily to determine and compare the housing market affordability of different urban areas, accounts for variation within and across markets while retaining a relative measurement of income to price. Some researchers assume that a ratio of 3 or below means housing is affordable. Using this threshold, the 2009 data for 272 urban housing markets (with 100 000 or more units) in Australia, Canada, Ireland, New Zealand, the United Kingdom, and the United States suggest that many housing markets in the sample are affordable or moderately unaffordable (see **Table 1**), though the majority of markets in Australia, New Zealand, and the United Kingdom are severely unaffordable. In comparison to 2008, the overall pattern for these markets had not changed though there were more affordable markets in the United States in 2009, which is likely due to the housing market crisis that began a few years before. In contrast, ratios are much higher in Asian markets – often at double digits. While such a ratio can allow for comparisons, it does not account for local context including current vacancy rate, days homes have been on the market and/or unoccupied, transaction costs, and the availability of credit. It also does not reveal the role that international capital plays in determining development decisions and housing prices – a concern in many urban areas with rapid expansion of high-density condominium developments in the late twentieth century.

Clearly, using a fixed percentage of income or a ratio of income to home price is an artificial and arbitrary measure of affordability. Still, most developed countries look at affordability in this way, and in many cases, the thresholds set appear to align well with the average percentage paid. In the United States, the affordability threshold is up to 30% of monthly income to cover rent or mortgage payment (or up to 35% when the cost of utilities is included), while the UK standard is lower at 20% or less for mortgage payment and 25% for rent. In these cases, both thresholds generally reflect average conditions; housing comprised 18.7% of total consumption in the United Kingdom in 2004 (21.2% in the European Union) and in 2008 the median rent paid including utilities was 29.8% of income in the United States.

While it would appear that fixed thresholds do indeed reflect some form of market equilibrium, it is important to keep in mind that there are an equal number of families paying more and less than the median. For those families

Table 1 Distribution of housing affordability ratio in selected countries, 2009

Country	Ratio of median housing price to median income					Total	National median
	3.0 and under	3.1–4.0	4.1–5.0	5.1–6.0	6.0 and over		
Australia	0	0	1	8	14	23	6.8
Canada	5	13	5	2	3	28	3.7
Ireland	0	3	2	0	0	5	3.7
New Zealand	0	0	3	2	3	8	5.7
United Kingdom	0	0	14	11	8	33	5.1
United States	98	58	8	4	7	175	2.9
Total	103	74	33	27	35	272	

Source: 6th Annual Demographia International Housing Affordability Survey, 2010.

paying more than the median, the concern is that fewer resources are then available for other goods and services that also improve well-being. In the United States, these families are considered 'burdened' by their housing cost. However, the burden is presumed to be less for those with higher incomes since they will have more income overall to spend after paying for housing (e.g., 30% of $10 000 on housing means $7000 available, but 30% of $100 000 means $70 000 available). A better measure of burden among lower-income families is 'shelter poverty', which is determined by first calculating the subsistence level costs for food, clothing, transportation, and health care and then adding actual housing costs to determine if income is sufficient to cover all costs. If not, the family is considered to be in shelter poverty. Interestingly, little attention is given to those paying less than median or the set threshold, possibly because it is assumed that there are no negative effects on well-being.

There are many limitations to using income thresholds and ratios to gauge affordability and then make comparisons across countries. The first is the assumption that whatever is left at a given threshold will be sufficient to cover other needs such as food, clothing, transportation, education, and health care in that country; this obviously depends on many factors, local and national. Complicating matters are tracking these costs with housing over time. Until the global economic crisis of 2008, the cost of housing in most developed countries had been increasing at rates much faster than the rate of inflation for nearly a decade. At the same time, the cost of living too was increasing, particularly fuel and food. However, income and real wages did not increase at the same rate in all countries.

Another challenge is to discern what basic goods and services are provided via the state – including housing – from what are solely purchased in the private market. However, to complicate this further, one would need to know how much of income goes towards taxes, which then translate into public benefits. A good example to illustrate this point is Sweden, which historically has had not only high personal taxes but also wide-scale government-subsidised housing development and rehabilitation. Finally, preferences are not accounted for in this measure; so it is unknown how many households are paying more (or less) than the threshold to satisfy other housing goals, such as reducing travel time. People may be willing to pay more for housing if the location is close to work or shopping, which can save time and money. However, for lower-income households, location may not be a choice when transportation is limited, which may mean trading off higher housing cost to assure easy access to employment, or conversely, paying less for housing but having to travel longer distances for work and basic goods and services.

Government Involvement

In market economies, the role of government in shaping housing prices is a controversial subject. The debates generally centre on what public benefit justifies expending the resources and intervening in the private market. The main arguments supporting government involvement of any sort are strongly tied to concerns about economic growth and the need for worker housing, as well as a broad range of social, political, and health concerns. All are interdependent, given the distribution of housing and the spatial patterns formed over the past century relative to income, and also what people are willing to spend on housing relative to other essential and nonessential items.

Worker Housing

In most developed countries, some amount of affordable housing is needed for lower-income workers and others essential to the expansion and sustainability of an economy. While most market economies are premised on the assumption that the private market will respond to increased demand, the supply generally has not been adequate either in number or in quality. From the industrial period onwards, the market response to growing employment bases generally has been to underproduce housing for lower-income families. An extreme response to this shortage in developing countries has been workers and other marginal labour, building and living in shanty towns, and unregulated housing developments. In developed countries, the market responded during industrialisation with newly built tenements, which often were of poor quality in terms of light and ventilation and not really affordable unless there were multiple workers contributing to pay the rent. Relatively speaking, this has not changed much, though instead of new housing, most workers move into old housing stock that either has filtered down from higher-income people who have left the community for better housing options elsewhere or has been sitting relatively vacant. In either case, these housing units are likely to be of poor quality and with many of the same problems of previous tenements.

Historically, many European countries and later the United States and Canada responded to these conditions with social housing, which was publically built and owned, to meet some of this need for good-quality, affordable, worker housing. In general terms, this type of housing was built to meet existing standards but at the same time be affordable to low-wage workers. With some exceptions, efforts were made to produce housing that could also demonstrate modern construction technology and new efficiencies for working within the home as well as promoting social values. A good example is the social housing built by architects from Germany's Bauhaus era in the 1930s, which was often large-scale developments with open space.

Social housing often replaced poor-quality private rental housing, which, in part, was the justification for its development, more so than making it affordable to workers. Over time, however, affordability became the driving factor as policy-makers responded to the housing needs of different segments of the population who did not or could not work, including an ageing population, people with disabilities, and single parents. Besides being unable to afford housing, these populations often need specific housing features that are not readily found in the market (e.g., accessible entries and kitchens). A 2009 survey of social housing in Austria, Denmark, England, France, Germany, Hungary, Ireland, the Netherlands, and Sweden finds that most of the social stock is directed at people who 'cannot serve their own housing needs'. This is also the case in the United States where all public-owned and assisted housing is means-tested and income-targeted.

Not all developed countries support direct government intervention in the market. As a result, not all public or social housing is necessarily developed and owned by a state or local housing agency. A common alternative strategy is to provide financial incentives to private developers to produce affordable housing and in some cases even mandate the inclusion of affordable units in new private sector market rate development. Another approach is to allow government to control rents and even for-sale housing prices. An alternative employed in many countries is some form of housing allowance or assistance to help families purchase a home and/or reduce the monthly payment for rent or mortgage. A large portion of affordable housing, however, has also been developed by nonprofit, nongovernmental, and charitable organizations. This includes both rental and for-sale housing. In some countries, this came about in response to the public sector, reducing its role in housing production and shifting towards direct housing assistance to families. Finally, a truly private sector approach used in some countries (e.g., the United States) is filtering, which assures housing at the higher-income spectrum is produced to then free up housing for people in lower-income categories. This assumes a certain level of mobility in a society but also requires creating demand among households so they will actually move out of lower-cost housing.

Social Exclusion

A contemporary concern in most developed countries is the issue of segregation or social exclusion caused by past housing development practices and policy. Until recently, modern housing production has generated a collection of homogeneous neighbourhoods rather than a mix of types affordable to a variety of income groups. The cost of housing is generally correlated with the quality of the neighbourhood; the higher the cost, the better the quality of the schools and other amenities that can advantage children. Families that cannot afford to buy or rent a home in a good neighbourhood are assumed disadvantaged and likely to continue to be so in generations to come.

Housing policy has been devised to change uneven development and other problematic spatial patterns. A growing concern in the United States, the United Kingdom, Europe, and Australia is the social exclusion of poor people often concentrated in substandard social housing in urban areas and isolated from much of the rest of society. To change this, housing policy was created to permit government to demolish these communities and replace them with new mixed-income developments on the premise that this will help poor people become included in society and improve their situations. Similar assumptions underpin efforts to promote racial and ethnic integration. Still, in most countries, the pattern of private sector housing development continues to be relatively segregated by income as well as by ethnicity and race.

Civic Engagement

Tied to the issue of segregation and social exclusion are democratic and political participation and civic engagement. In many countries, housing segmented by income has been linked to a bifurcated involvement of people in shaping the policies, institutions, and organisations that affect what rights, opportunities, and resources are available. With few exceptions, the pattern in developed countries is fairly consistent with higher rates of participation, whether by voting or voice, coming from the middle-class and higher-income neighbourhoods. While housing affordability itself does not determine how someone votes, the distribution of it can affect what issues the majority of voters care about. In the United States and some European countries, political participation has become more suburbanised and even exurban, while it has remained relatively urbanised in other countries where the majority of middle- and higher-income families remain in large city centres. In turn, this may, for example, mean more political support for expanding roads in some countries, while others will support public transport.

Health

Public health concerns long have been reason for government involvement in housing. However, beginning in the late 1990s, the link between health and affordability has been emphasised more so than housing quality. In part, this is likely so due to the dwindling problem of poor-quality housing overall as most developed countries have replaced or rehabilitated the vast majority of below-standard homes. Attention has shifted towards the presumed causal relationship between health and neighbourhood conditions in which housing affordability is the intervening variable. As the social exclusion research suggests, families that live in low-cost housing often are in poor communities with limited resources. In addition, these communities may be more likely to have environmental hazards, pollution, and other threats to health, often attributed to historical patterns of industrial development and lower land values. As with social exclusion, many countries are employing regeneration strategies to improve both the housing and the built environment of social housing communities. This includes not only adding basic health-care services but also assuring better access to healthy foods, exercise, and green space.

Right to Housing

In most developed countries, housing policy has long aimed to respond to housing need not met by the market. In some, there is a genuine shortage of units at any price point, while in some the 'need' is due to a shortage of housing at certain price points rather than a lack of units. The distinction is important since the latter does not necessarily require housing to be built to meet the needs of lower-income families. Furthermore, it shifts attention to the question of why some families have insufficient resources. In part, this is what strategies aimed at reducing social exclusion do as well. However, creating more access to resources by reducing isolation does not necessarily assure housing affordability; rather the outcome expected is that the income of some families will increase, which in turn can expand their housing options.

Using human rights instruments and mechanisms, such as the United Nations Universal Declaration of Human Rights adopted in 1948 and the International Covenant on Economic, Social and Cultural Rights adopted in 1966, links housing affordability to the problem of why we do not have adequate resources to afford housing. A human rights framework assumes housing is fundamental to individual well-being and also to assure a means of livelihood. Adequate housing, as defined by the United Nations, is not just a house but also a community and a "territory where people can have access to the means of livelihood – to land, to water, to resources, to sources of income – and not only being sheltered somewhere." While this framework does not explicitly address housing affordability, it often does when translated to policy. For example, all countries that have signed and ratified the Revised European Social Charter (RESC) agree to make housing affordable as outlined in Article 31:

The right to housing – with a view to ensuring the effective exercise of the right to housing, the Parties undertake to take measures designed:

- to promote access to housing of an adequate standard;
- to prevent and reduce homelessness with a view to its gradual elimination;
- to make the price of housing accessible to those without adequate resources.

These three measures are not mutually exclusive; however, they each likely have a different degree of acceptance and support in developed countries. Generally speaking, most will have some form of regulations and means to make housing adequate, that is, it meets certain standards to assure health and safety. Fewer countries, however, directly link affordable housing to the problem of homelessness. Those that do are likely to also support a right to housing on the premise that society should assure everyone has some form of permanent shelter available to them. From this perspective, the lack of affordable housing contributes to homelessness, and in order to prevent people from becoming homeless as well as help those who are homeless requires a sufficient supply of affordable housing or means to make it affordable. The right to housing can thus literally mean the right to home of some minimum standard. The question is who pays for that housing to be produced and maintained, especially now as many countries are relying on private market developers to produce social housing.

The most challenging of the three to operationalise, perhaps, is framing the right to housing as a pricing problem in which people do not have sufficient resources to afford what housing costs in the market. While the RESC solution is to make the price accessible to people who cannot afford it otherwise, the challenge is deciding what the correct price should be. For example, if we assume that it is a shelter poverty problem, then a solution would be to reduce the price so that there is sufficient income remaining to fulfil other basic needs like food and clothing. This approach assumes the cost of meeting basic needs is constant and not relative to income. As a result, a right to housing would primarily be guaranteed to lower-income families. However, absence of some reference to other costs and simply framed as not having 'adequate resources' to access housing broadens the right to housing to include families of all income levels. Adjusting the price to make it accessible could be in the form of a housing allowance, which some countries currently provide, often graduated relative to income. The alternative might be to set prices so that market cost is better matched to income. This approach would require extensive government involvement in the housing market, which most countries with market-based economies avoid. However, if instead of focusing on making the housing affordable, attention is shifted towards making sure families have adequate resources to afford what housing costs on the market, then housing affordability is no longer the problem we are trying to solve. The limit here is that this approach to a right to housing does not automatically guarantee access to a home – only the potential to have funds to afford one.

See also: Access and Affordability: Housing Allowances; Access and Affordability: Housing Vouchers; Affordable Housing Strategies; House Price Indexes; Housing Paradigms; Housing Supply; Human Rights and Housing; Policies to Support Access and Affordability of Housing; Urbanisation and Housing the Poor: Overview.

Further Reading

Stone M (1993) *Shelter Poverty: New Ideas on Housing Affordability*. Philadelphia, PA: Temple University Press.
Van Vliet W (1998) *The Encyclopedia of Housing*. Thousand Oaks, CA: Sage Publications.
Whitehead C and Scanlon K (2007) *Social Housing in Europe*. London: LSE London, London School of Economics and Political Science.

Relevant Websites

www.cecodhas.org – Comité Européen de Coordination de l'Habitat Social.
www.demographia.com – Demographia.
http://ec.europa.eu – European Commission, Public Health.
www.feantsa.org – European Federation of National Organisations working with the Homeless.
www.globalpropertyguide.com – Global Property Guide.
http://housingisahumanright.org – Housing is a Human Right.
www.federcasa.it – Housing Statistics in the European Union 2005/2006.
www.realtor.org – National Association of Realtors.
www.unece.org – United Nations Economic Commission for Europe.

Access and Affordability: Homeowner Taxation

SC Bourassa, University of Louisville, Louisville, KY, USA

© 2012 Elsevier Ltd. All rights reserved.

Glossary

Capital gain The increase in the value of a home between sales, adjusted for the cost of capital improvements. Capital gains may be expressed in real (adjusted for general inflation) or nominal terms.
Debt The portion of the cost of a home that is financed with a mortgage or other type of loan.
Equity The portion of the cost of a home that is financed using the home owner's own funds.
Home ownership expense Home ownership expenses include various costs such as mortgage interest payments, hazard insurance, property taxes, maintenance, and condominium fees. They do not include repayment of mortgage principal or the costs of capital improvements.
Imputed rent The hypothetical rent that a home-owning household would pay to itself if it were treated in the income tax code as both a landlord and a tenant.
Tax credit A reduction in the amount of income tax owed.
Tax deduction A reduction in the amount of taxable income.
Tax exemption An exclusion from taxation of a category of income that would otherwise be taxable.
Tax expenditure A subsidy built into the income tax regulations in the form of a tax credit, deduction, or exemption.

Types of Tax Expenditures

National and other levels of government offer a variety of incentives to encourage home ownership. One important class of incentives is tax expenditures, also referred to as tax preferences or tax concessions. Tax expenditures are subsidies that are built into the income tax regulations, which are largely intended to reduce the cost of purchasing and occupying a home and thereby encourage owner-occupation. Tax expenditures can be in the form of deductions or credits for various expenses or exemption of certain types of income from taxation. There is considerable variation in the range and type of tax expenditures built into countries' income tax regulations.

Deductions and Credits

Tax deductions reduce taxable income, while tax credits reduce the amount of tax due. Thus a given amount of tax credit is worth more than the same amount of tax deduction, because the latter must be multiplied by the taxpayer's marginal tax rate to yield the tax savings. Tax deductions are more common than tax credits, and they typically apply to expenses such as mortgage interest payments or property taxes. Federal and some state governments in the United States allow deduction of mortgage interest and property taxes, although there are various limits such as caps on the amount of interest that can be deducted. The United Kingdom used to allow deduction of mortgage interest, but this was gradually phased out starting in the mid-1970s; it was completely eliminated by 2000. Switzerland allows deduction of mortgage interest and other housing expenses, although these deductions are offset by taxation of imputed rent. Countries such as Australia and New Zealand do not allow for any housing deductions or credits, and they exempt imputed rent and capital gains from taxation.

Exemptions

Tax exemptions or exclusions for owner-occupied housing include those for imputed rent and capital gains. Taxation of imputed (or implicit) rent involves treating home owners as if they were landlords by taxing an estimate of the rent that would be paid to occupy the dwelling while typically allowing deduction of at least some expenses. The logic behind this idea is that it provides a means for making the tax treatment of owner-occupied housing more like that of other capital investments, such as rental housing, thus resulting in a more efficient allocation of resources across different types of assets. On the negative side, taxing imputed rent adds complexity to the income tax system and is likely to be politically unpopular, particularly in countries where a majority of households are home owners. Introduction of an imputed rent tax may also have an inequitable effect on some households, particularly elderly home owners with reduced incomes and relatively small deductible expenses (because they no longer have a mortgage). Moreover, many countries have a policy of encouraging investment in owner-occupied housing and are not particularly concerned with equalising investment incentives across assets.

Switzerland, which has the lowest home ownership rate in the developed world (about 34%), is one of the few countries to tax imputed rent. With a well-established majority of renters, there is little political support for policies that encourage ownership. Nevertheless, imputed rent is calculated using relatively conservative assumptions (the Swiss federal authorities aim to capture an imputed rent that is no less than 70% of market rent) and on average is less than the offsetting deductible expenses, which include mortgage interest, property taxes, maintenance, insurance, and condominium fees.

Capital gains are also commonly exempt, or at least partially exempt, from income taxation. Also, capital gains may be subject to tax rates that are less than those applicable to other income such as salaries and wages. One of the issues with capital gains is that in their optimal form they are difficult to administer. Ideally, only real (inflation-adjusted) gains would be added to income and taxed and real losses would be deducted. Gains or losses would be taxed or deducted as they accrue. The somewhat complex translation from nominal to real terms is further complicated by the need to adjust for the amount and timing of any capital improvements. As a consequence of these complications, countries may choose to tax only nominal gains, but at favourable rates (relative to other income). Moreover, home owners often sell one house in order to buy another and not infrequently this is due to a change in employment. Capital gains taxes thus could interfere with labour mobility. These and other considerations lead most countries to exempt all or most capital gains on owner-occupied homes from income taxation.

Examples of countries that exempt owner-occupiers' capital gains include Australia and New Zealand, where they are completely exempt, and the United States, where they are mostly exempt. In the United States, single persons or couples can exclude $250 000 or $500 000 in nominal gains per transaction, subject to some restrictions including a minimum occupancy period. In contrast, capital gains are taxed relatively heavily in Switzerland, where applicable tax rates have an inverse relationship with the holding period and, in at least some cantons, increase with the magnitude of the capital gains. The relationship between tax rates and the holding period is evidently intended to discourage speculative behaviour. In the canton of Geneva, for example, the capital gains tax rate is 50% if the property is resold within 2 years, and there is no tax if the property is sold after 25 years. However, in all cantons, the tax is postponed if the proceeds are used to purchase another home (subject to some restrictions).

Policy Considerations

Some of the policy questions regarding tax expenditures for owner-occupied housing have been touched on in the preceding paragraphs. Broadly speaking, there are two main sets of issues that need to be addressed. The first question concerns whether home ownership should be subsidised. If the answer to this first question is affirmative, then the second question arises concerning the choice between tax expenditures and other forms of subsidy, such as direct grants or income supplements.

Should Home Ownership be Subsidised?

Various public and private benefits have been attributed to home ownership. The public benefits include greater involvement in and commitment to the community on the part of home-owning households, better upkeep of homes, and improved children's outcomes, such as higher high school graduation rates and lower pregnancy rates among teenagers. Although empirical analyses have attempted to control for it, there remains a question about whether most or all of these benefits are due to the greater stability associated with home ownership. In a country such as Switzerland, with a tradition of long-term rental tenancy, the relationship between these benefits and home ownership may be less pronounced or nonexistent. Private benefits include the ability to accumulate wealth and to have more control over interior and exterior decoration.

Costs associated with government support of home ownership include the costs of the subsidies (i.e., the foregone revenues), which are not negligible. For example, the mortgage interest deduction in the United States is the second largest tax expenditure in that country (after the deductibility of health insurance premiums paid by employers). The revenue gain is actually somewhat less than the official figures, because eliminating the deductibility of mortgage interest would cause buyers to shift from debt to equity financing, and since income from alternative investments of that equity would presumably be taxed there is a partial offsetting revenue loss. Another cost is associated with reductions in labor mobility, particularly in declining markets where houses may be difficult to sell. This is clearly a problem in many markets today in the United States and other countries. It is also evident that home ownership is not sustainable for many households. In more than a few markets, home ownership has proven to be a bad investment. Finally, subsidies for home ownership may lead to overinvestment in that sector at the expense of more productive uses of resources.

On balance, it is difficult to make a strong case in support of subsidies for home ownership, given that there seem to be as many drawbacks as advantages. Moreover, even if home ownership does yield social benefits, getting the policy just right would seem to be an impossible task. Nevertheless, home ownership seems firmly rooted in many national cultures, as evidenced by terms such as The American Dream, The Great Australian Dream, or The Great New Zealand Dream. Consequently, policies to subsidise home ownership continue to be supported regardless of their merits. In the United States, for example, the President's Advisory Panel on Federal Tax Reform recommended in 2005 that the mortgage interest deduction be eliminated and replaced with a much more targeted tax credit. Even this relatively tepid policy proposal was strongly opposed by various housing industry groups. This and the other recommendations of the panel were quickly shelved.

Tax Expenditures Versus Alternatives

Tax expenditures are indirect subsidies in the sense that they reduce tax revenues and do not involve cash grants that must be budgeted and appropriated by governments. Alternatives to tax expenditures include direct subsidies in the form of grants to first-time buyers as have been used in Australia, for example. The US government provides funds to state and local governments that can be used as grants towards home purchase by households meeting certain income criteria. Sometimes these grants are in the form of soft second mortgages, which need not be repaid if the buyer remains in the home for a minimum period of time, such as 5 years. Another option is housing allowances, which are income supplements for low-income households, including owner-occupiers. Housing allowances in New Zealand, for example, benefit low-income households regardless of housing tenure.

There are at least two broad policy concerns that speak against the use of tax expenditures. One is the issue of transparency. While direct subsidies must periodically be reviewed and approved by governments, once tax expenditures are included in the income tax regulations, they no longer need to be addressed explicitly in any budgeting process. Consequently, they are relatively hidden compared to direct subsidies. Regressive subsidies, such as the mortgage interest deduction in the United States, survive in the form of a tax expenditure, but would be highly unlikely to be supported in the form of a direct subsidy. The other issue concerns tax simplification. This is particularly an issue in the United States, where the individual income tax code has become increasingly complex over time, and compliance requires the expenditure of considerable resources on the part of individuals and government. Tax credits and deductions in the code make compliance more costly. In contrast, New Zealand has greatly simplified its income tax code, to the point that many individuals no longer need to file any paperwork. Obviously, tax expenditures cannot play a role if the aim is to simplify the tax rules.

Evidence on Their Impacts

There is also a question about whether tax expenditures have desired policy impacts with respect to home ownership. In the United States, for example, the mortgage interest deduction was introduced at a time when few households actually paid income tax and so it was clearly not intended to encourage home ownership to any significant extent. Subsequently, however, a significant constituency has come to rely on the deduction and it has become politically impossible to change it substantially. In the United Kingdom, the mortgage interest deduction was also quite popular, but it was phased out very gradually, so that by the time it was completely eliminated in 2000, it was not having much of an impact.

Mortgage Interest Deduction

Most of the research on the impacts of the mortgage interest deduction has focussed on the United States. The impact of the deduction in the United States is somewhat blunted by the fact that some home buyers, particularly those with lower incomes, cannot take advantage of it because their total deductions do not meet certain threshholds. Consequently, they take a standard deduction rather than itemised deductions and the mortgage interest deduction is effectively wasted. Many of the individuals and households who receive the most benefit from the deduction do not really need it as they would be able to afford home ownership in any case. For these households, the deduction is probably just helping to subsidise the purchase of larger homes. Moreover, much of the value of the deduction appears to be capitalised into land prices, meaning that houses are more costly than they otherwise would be. This is particularly an issue for first-time buyers, for whom any savings provided by the deduction may be offset by higher prices.

Recent empirical research on housing tenure choice in US metropolitan areas suggests that for young adults the impacts of the deductions on house prices may well offset the savings in taxes. Moreover, a more targeted tax credit – such as that proposed by the President's Advisory Panel on Federal Tax Reform – also would not encourage home ownership on average, although it would change the geography of housing tenure somewhat by raising ownership rates in expensive locations and lowering them in less costly places. On balance, it seems that neither tax deductions nor tax credits for mortgage interest are effective in encouraging home ownership.

Some policy analysts have defended the mortgage interest deduction on the grounds that it equalises the after-tax cost of debt and equity financing and that the real tax expenditure is the failure to tax imputed rent. At least two Nobel laureates in economics (Herbert Simon and William Vickrey) have advocated taxation of imputed rent for this reason.

Imputed Rent

The main policy objective of taxing imputed rent is to attempt to equalise the cost of investing in owner-occupied housing with the costs of investing in other capital assets. Nevertheless, much of the policy discussion has focussed on the impacts on ownership rates of taxing imputed rent and on the distribution of the income tax burden across different income groups.

Recent research on Switzerland has considered the impacts of a range of factors on housing tenure in an attempt to explain the country's extraordinarily low ownership rate. While high prices appear to have the biggest impact on tenure choice, the second most important factor is the tax on imputed rent, which is estimated to reduce the ownership rate by 9 percentage points. However, if the related deductions (mortgage interest and so forth) were also removed, then the ownership rate would drop slightly, due to the fact that the deductions are typically worth more than the conservatively estimated imputed rent. It is probably inappropriate to extrapolate this finding to other countries where circumstances are quite different.

Empirical research in Australia has explored the distributional effects of a hypothetical tax on imputed rent on different income and age groups. The main findings are that the tax burden does not fall more heavily on low-income households when net imputed rent (i.e., net of deductible expenses) is included in owners' incomes and life cycle effects are controlled for. Nevertheless, this does not really overcome the practical problem that would be faced by those low-income, particularly elderly, households who are house-rich and income-poor.

Policy Implications

This overview has been based primarily on the experiences of a small number of countries, specifically Australia, New Zealand, Switzerland, the United Kingdom, and the United States. Nevertheless, these cases suggest some general policy conclusions that may be relevant elsewhere.

One conclusion is that it is impossible to satisfy all possible policy objectives. For example, one policy objective is efficiency in resource allocation. If it is assumed that home ownership does provide social benefits, then the goal of efficiency might justify subsidies to increase the ownership rate. If home ownership is not the source of social benefits, then efficiency is achieved by equalising costs across different assets to avoid overinvestment in owner-occupied housing. In this case it would be desirable to fully tax imputed rent and real capital gains, allowing deductions for expenses and real losses. But it is difficult to accurately measure imputed rent and real gains and losses, leading to significant administrative and compliance issues. Switzerland adopts a second-best approach to this by taxing a very conservative and rough estimate of imputed rent and nominal, rather than real, capital gains. The United States, in contrast, does not bother with trying to tax imputed rent (it does not even consider imputed rent to be a form of income) and exempts most capital gains from taxation. The capital gains that are taxed are nominal, rather than real.

But the US tax code retains two significant deductible expenses – mortgage interest and property taxes – which, from an efficiency point of view, probably does not make sense given that the relevant income (imputed rent) remains untaxed. Moreover, it is unclear that these deductions have the positive impact on home ownership attributed to them. Instead their effects seem to be higher land prices and consumption of larger homes by households who do not need subsidies to afford home ownership. Consequently, there appears to be a strong argument for eliminating deductions if imputed rent is not taxed. The goals of tax simplification and transparency also strongly suggest that these deductions should be eliminated.

This does not mean that governments desiring to encourage home ownership are left without any tools. Australia has successfully used grants for first-time home buyers to encourage home ownership. There is, however, some evidence to suggest that these grants merely speed up access to ownership for households who would eventually become home owners in any case. If encouraging home ownership is not a policy objective, there are subsidies that may be attractive for other reasons. New Zealand's housing allowances are available to both renters and owners (and therefore do not introduce any tenure bias) and may be particularly helpful in avoiding foreclosure in the case of households whose income has been reduced due to job loss, illness, or retirement. Such allowances could be particularly helpful in avoiding both household distress and housing market disruptions in times of recession.

See also: Access and Affordability: Housing Allowances; First Home Owner Grants; Home Ownership: Economic Benefits; Low-Income Housing Tax Credits; Taxation Policy and Housing.

Further Reading

Bourassa SC, Greig AW, and Troy PN (1995) The limits of housing policy: Home ownership in Australia. *Housing Studies* 10: 83–103.

Bourassa SC and Grigsby WG (2000) Income tax concessions for owner-occupied housing. *Housing Policy Debate* 11: 521–546.

Bourassa SC and Hendershott PH (1994) On the equity effects of taxing imputed rent: Evidence from Australia. *Housing Policy Debate* 5: 73–95.

Bourassa SC and Hoesli M (2010) Why do the Swiss rent? *Journal of Real Estate Finance and Economics*, 40: 296–309.

Bourassa SC and Yin M (2006) Housing tenure choice in Australia and the United States: Impacts of alternative subsidy policies. *Real Estate Economics* 34: 303–328.

Bourassa SC and Yin M (2008) Tax deductions, tax credits, and the home ownership rate of young urban adults in the United States. *Urban Studies* 45: 1141–1161.

Capozza D, Green R, and Hendershott PH (1996) Taxes, mortgage borrowing, and residential land prices. In: Aaron HJ and Gale WG (eds.) *Effects of Fundamental Tax Reform*, pp. 171–210. Washington, DC: Brookings Institution.

Follain JR, Ling DC and McGill GA (1993) The preferential tax treatment of owner-occupied housing: Who really benefits? *Housing Policy Debate* 4: 1–24.

Follain JR and Melamed LS (1998) The false messiah of tax policy: What elimination of the home mortgage interest deduction promises and a careful look at what it delivers. *Journal of Housing Research* 9: 179–199.

Goode R (1960) Imputed rent of owner-occupied dwellings under the income tax. *Journal of Finance* 15: 504–530.

Green RK and Vandell KD (1999) Giving households credit: How changes in the U.S. tax code could promote homeownership. *Regional Science and Urban Economics* 29: 419–444.

Hendershott PH and White M (2000) The rise and fall of housing's favored investment status. *Journal of Housing Research* 11: 257–275.

Laidler D (1969) Income tax incentives for owner-occupied housing. In: Harberger AC and Bailey MJ (eds.) *Taxation of Income from Capital*, pp. 50–76. Washington, DC: Brookings Institution.

Rohe WM and Watson HL (eds.) (2007). *Chasing the American Dream: New Perspectives on Affordable Homeownership*. Ithaca, NY: Cornell University Press.

Woodward SE and Weicher JC (1989) Goring the wrong ox: A defense of the mortgage interest deduction. *National Tax Journal* 42: 301–313.

Access and Affordability: House Purchase Certificates

RJ Struyk, NORC, Bethesda, MD, USA

© 2012 Elsevier Ltd. All rights reserved.

Glossary

Down payment The funds a homeowner provides at the time he purchases the unit, which are applied against the purchase price of the dwelling, the balance being financed by a loan.

Equity The portion of the cost of a home that is financed using the homeowner's own funds, which he may obtain through savings, sales of assets, or as a subsidy. Over time it consists of the down payment and increase in the value of the property.

Interest rate subsidy A reduction in the interest rate from the prevailing market interest rate with the difference in monthly payments between those under the market rate and effective rates paid to the lender by a government agency.

Voucher A subsidy that grants limited purchasing power to an individual to choose among a restricted set of goods and services.

Introduction

Housing purchase certificates (HPCs) are vouchers for the purchase of a dwelling unit. They are vouchers that can be either for the full price (up to a programme-determined maximum) or for a partial payment (i.e., a downpayment subsidy). HPCs for the full purchase price of a unit appear to have been pioneered within Europe in Norway in 1982 and in the Eastern Europe–CIS (Commonwealth of Independent States) region by the Russian Officer Resettlement Program, which facilitated the relocation of the former Soviet military officers from the Baltic Republics to Russia in 1993–94. Downpayment subsidies (whether or not in a voucher format) are best known for their long use in Chile; they have also been employed in Costa Rica, Colombia, South Africa, Egypt, Hungary, Russia, and a number of other countries. Because HPCs have a short history, the empirical literature on them is limited.

Like other vouchers, HPCs have several desirable features. They empower beneficiaries to choose among providers, and in this way, it can stimulate greater efficiency in housing construction as developers are forced to compete against each other on price and quality. The value of HPCs is clear to recipients and to those appropriating the funds – something less true of interest rate subsidies or deductions of housing-related expenses from the personal income tax. And they are easy to use in conjunction with the recipient's own resources. Finally, governments' budget spending on HPCs constitutes capital outlays made in a single year; that is, they do not have recurrent yearly obligations to fulfil such as those under interest rates subsidies, for example. Such ongoing commitments reduce governments' freedom to respond to future priorities and can expose borrowers and lenders to the risk that governments fail to meet their obligations in times of severe budget stress.

Following a short overview of home purchase vouchers, we first outline the basic administrative steps for an HPC programme. The article then focuses on HPCs that pay for the full cost of a dwelling before turning to partial purchase certificates that subsidise downpayments. The article finishes with some brief conclusions.

Vouchers

Today, vouchers are a widely used form of subsidy. They are employed to provide assistance in an extraordinarily broad range of areas. Among their more common uses are in the provision of food, higher education, primary and secondary education, housing, training, childcare, and medical insurance for the nonelderly.

Steuerle (2000) defines a voucher as a subsidy that grants limited purchasing power to an individual to choose among a restricted set of goods and services. More specifically:

- Vouchers can give purchasing power to an individual directly or indirectly. Food stamps can be spent directly at a grocery store, while under housing vouchers the beneficiary chooses the dwelling but payments are generally made to the owner through an agent (e.g., a bank); in other words, the buyer does not hand over the voucher to the seller but rather to the agent who then pays the seller.
- A voucher can be structured as an expenditure or a tax subsidy.
- Typically, a voucher provides a limited benefit to the client, for example, a fixed value per month for food

stamps. Usually, the client can supplement the value of the voucher with her own money.
- A voucher both prescribes and proscribes. On the one hand, the client must have a range of choice of providers of goods or services. On the other hand, it limits the type of goods or services that can be purchased.

Vouchers are viewed on efficiency grounds as superior to in-kind subsidies (e.g., public housing) because they give beneficiaries a choice among providers. They can also intensify competition among providers, increasing efficiency compared with, say, delivery of services by monopolistic government social service agencies.

In the housing arena, vouchers have become closely associated with housing allowances – means-tested payments to assist with the payment of rent or, for homeowners (as in New Zealand, for example), operating costs. Housing allowances are widely employed, including in some Eastern Europe countries and the former CIS. 'Voucher', in this context, is a general term encompassing housing allowance programmes, whether or not participants receive an actual voucher. But in the United States, vouchers are a term typically used in the context of their rental housing allowance programme, where a voucher is actually received by eligible participants (see article Access and Affordability: Housing Vouchers). This article is about 'homeowner' housing voucher programmes, or housing purchase certificates as they are commonly termed.

Basic Programme Operations

The workings of an HPC programme are very simple – an eligible household is given a certificate backed by funds at a credible institution and uses it to negotiate the purchase of a dwelling unit selected in the open housing market. The actual operation of a programme involves seven distinct elements working together, which are listed below.

(a) Identification of certificate recipients – establishing eligibility rules.
(b) Establishing the validity period of the certificate.
(c) Certificate registration – recording the award of the certificate to a family, which initiates housing search and the use-tracking process, that is, at a minimum whether the certificate is used within the prescribed time period.
(d) Pricing the certificates in such a way that they reflect the unit size and location of housing demanded by an eligible household.
(e) Supply-side promotion and dissemination of market information – efforts to increase the supply of units on offer and to increase the efficiency of the housing search process.
(f) Selection of an administering agent for sales closing and payments and determination of fees for these services – local commercial banks, for example.
(g) Case review – an external party to review all documents prior to closing the sale, ranging from the HPC to the property title – an accounting firm, for example.

Full Purchase Certificates

Certificates covering the full cost of a dwelling unit have not often been employed. They have been used to meet emergency housing needs and to fulfil explicit government obligations to provide full housing solutions to specified classes of individuals. Examples of their use to meet emergency housing requirements include the Russian Officers Resettlement Program that was designed to quickly repatriate Russian officers in the Baltic Republics to avoid confrontations after the Soviet Union's break-up; the issuance of home purchase vouchers to earthquake victims on Sakhalin Island, as well as other locations in Russia, that could be used to purchase housing anywhere in the country; and in the Armenian Earthquake Zone Recovery Program (EQZRP) beginning in 1998 to provide substitute housing to victims of the severe 1988 earthquake. (Earthquake victims were first assisted with programmes to construct new housing and HPCs were only introduced 10 years after the event.) Nonemergency cases include the distribution of home purchase vouchers to households wishing to relocate from Russia's Far North where there was no longer employment for them and to retired Russian military officers who by the terms of their contract are entitled to an apartment upon retirement as part of their compensation. Success rates, as measured by the share of voucher recipients who were able to purchase a unit with it, have been consistently high in these programmes.

Issues

The examples discussed demonstrate that housing purchase subsidy programmes are indeed workable. Still there are three programme elements that can be particularly challenging. Countries will need to be confident that they can execute these successfully if they are to adopt this type of programme.

Administrative complexity

The home purchase voucher programmes outlined above are moderately complex. There are several distinct actors – those selecting the beneficiaries, banks, the realty firm or others developing price information, and the final-stage reviewer – whose actions must be coordinated and actively monitored. The programme manager has a challenging job but it is certainly within the competence of organisations in most countries. An open question is whether a government should contract out for the overall management services or assign it to staff at the finance or housing ministry.

Limited supply of units for sale

A common and legitimate concern is that downpayment vouchers will drive up housing prices unless there is an adequate supply of housing on the market. Indeed, some certificate programmes have been initiated following a pilot programme designed to test if there would be a sufficient supply response to the effective housing demand created by the programme. In fact, experience with both the pilot and main programmes indicates that supply responses were larger than anticipated, as families doubled up to be able to sell a unit and use the cash received to meet daily expenses. One of the main findings from studies of certificate programmes is the high degree of supply responsiveness from the existing housing stock.

Price data

A particular challenge for programme implementation has been determining the price of housing in markets where home purchase vouchers will be used. The challenge typically arises when there is a low volume of sales, and when tax regimes create incentives for those purchasing and selling units to understate the sales prices in official documents. This problem can be compounded by the absence of local real estate professionals who track prices for their own purposes. The reality has been that implementers have often had to settle for an average value for each unit size and occasionally even for a simple average price per square metre over all unit sizes. And these frequently have been based on smaller sample sizes than preferred. While this is less precise than is desirable, these estimates can prove serviceable.

Partial Purchase (Downpayment) Certificates

Partial purchase (or downpayment) certificates cover only a fraction of the purchase price and therefore assist households to meet a downpayment requirement. They differ from first homeowner grants because partial purchase certificate programmes are voucher based, which gives governments greater scope to prescribe the types of (in this case) housing that can be acquired. In addition, the certificate programmes are not typically restricted to first-home buyers (see article First Home Owner Grants).

Chile is credited with pioneering certificates as a downpayment subsidy approach to improve access to owner-occupied housing, beginning in 1977. Its primary motivation was dissatisfaction with a traditional programme of government construction of units for the poor. Private companies competed for contracts to produce dwellings meeting minimum standards. Competition between companies encouraged the production of housing that better matched consumers' preferences, and was also responsible for efficiency gains in the form of lower production costs as compared to government construction of housing units. Participants received vouchers to help meet the downpayment and were targeted on those who were both poor and prepared to help themselves. The latter was signalled by applicants accumulating savings in special accounts (see Contract Saving Schemes). The longer their savings record and the greater the amount saved, the higher the chances of getting the subsidy. While there have been criticisms, the programme is widely viewed as successful, particularly in its transparency and administrative integrity. One criticism is that the poorest families who most need assistance are those least able to accumulate savings.

Partial payment certificates have also been utilised in Western Europe. Norway turned to needs-tested certificates in 1982 as a replacement for a universal homeownership grant. Recent analyses show that the programme works well and that these grants are well targeted vertically but have some horizontal equity issues.

The analysis that follows relies primarily on an excellent comparative article by Alan Gilbert (2004) that discusses certificate programmes in Chile, Colombia, and South Africa, which he believes represent the best examples of how the policy has been applied. The programmes have a similar structure, except that South Africa's does not use the savings record of potential beneficiaries to qualify and rank applicants. These programmes have all been adjusted over time. Hence, it is difficult to give a simple characterisation of any of them, since the relative strengths and weaknesses of each have been different at various times. We try to provide balanced characterisations.

Production Levels

Table 1 shows that the absolute number of downpayment certificate subsidies allocated in each country was large. When considered relative to a country's housing deficit (the excess of households over dwelling units) and population, Colombia's programme is seen to be an order of magnitude smaller than the others. Chile and South Africa's downpayment certificate subsidies represented more than 7% of their housing deficits over the time periods indicated in the top row of **Table 1**. Even at these production levels, however, there was no reduction in the number of applications for assistance. Deficits, on the other hand, were cut in Chile and South Africa – a highly unusual feat among developing countries. In all three countries programme funding has been limited, and this posed challenges for policy-makers because

Table 1 Subsidies approved relative to housing need in Chile, Colombia, and South Africa (years for which the data or estimates apply are in parentheses)

Indicator	Chile	Colombia	South Africa
Number of subsidies approved per annum	91 130 (1990–99)	37 977–58 755[a] (1990–2000)	196 030 (1994–2000)
Number of subsidies relative to the housing deficit (in %)	10.5–12.2 (1996)	1.7–2.6 (1993)	7.5 (1998)

[a]Official estimates do not agree on the number of subsidies delivered.
Source: Gilbert A (2004) Helping the poor through housing subsidies: Lessons from Chile, Colombia, and South Africa. *Habitat International* 28: 13–40, Table 5.

achieving some satisfactory quality of housing for beneficiaries limits the number that can be assisted and requires more stringent targeting of certificates.

An idea of per-unit subsidy cost is provided in **Table 2**. Focusing on purchasing power of parity (PPP) figures and subsidies as a percent of per capita GNP, it is clear that they are large. The lowest PPP subsidy value is for South Africa at nearly US$7000 per dwelling. As a percent of per capita GDP, costs range from 83 to 175%, for South Africa and Colombia, respectively. Columbia's high per-unit cost has, however, been accompanied by low production levels so that the subsidy is a low overall share of total central government budget expenditure – under 1%. Chile had the highest budget share at 5.8%.

Issues

These programmes have in common several implementation issues deserving comment: target proliferation, targeting on the poor and needy, and subsidy depth versus programme breadth.

Too many targets

All these programmes had multiple objectives, including increasing homeownership, discouraging land invasions and illegal subdivisions, and involving the private sector in low-income housing construction and finance. Getting private banks to make loans has been especially challenging, particularly in South Africa and Colombia. The initial version of the Colombian programme required participants to obtain a housing loan. Banks were reluctant to lend to many poor families and targeting suffered accordingly.

Beyond these basic goals, others have been added that at times work against the basic objectives. Colombia wanted to use the programme as an employment generator and sought at different times to achieve this aim by making downpayment certificates only available to the purchasers of newly constructed housing. The programme was also used as a frontline resource in response to natural disasters that destroyed dwelling units. In South Africa, the government did not want to employ the old 'apartheid' construction firms, and tried to use the programme to foster the development of black construction firms. While the additional goals are laudable, they have often undermined programme efficiency and may even work against achieving the primary goals.

Targeting the poor

All three countries have limited entitlement programmes and the same general criteria for targeting these subsidies – directing them in principle to the poor families rather than one-person households, those wanting to become homeowners, and nationals rather than foreigners. Here, we focus on the extent of targeting on the poor.

South Africa's downpayment certificates are available to all families earning less than R3500 per month (US$422 using an October 2008 exchange rate). While there is broad agreement that poor families have been a large share of beneficiaries, it is hard to be certain because there is no system for checking the incomes stated by applicants.

Table 2 Approximate per-dwelling unit subsidy value (US dollars): Chile, Colombia, and South Africa, *c.* 1998 (years for which the data apply are in parentheses)

Indicator	Chile[a]	Colombia	South Africa
Subsidy value at current exchange rate	4200 (1998)	3750 (1998)	2623 (1999)
Subsidy at purchasing power of parity (PPP)	10 111	11 776	6904
Subsidy as percent of GDP per capita	86%	175%	83%

[a]Subsidy for basic housing unit.
Source: Gilbert A (2004) Helping the poor through housing subsidies: Lessons from Chile, Colombia, and South Africa. *Habitat International* 28: 13–40, Table 6.

Chile and Colombia have had real problems reaching the poorest families. In Chile, after 1990 when targeting was significantly improved, only 27% of beneficiaries came from the lowest income quintile while 11% were from the highest. The result is a consequence of allocation rules that favour those able to make large contributions to savings. Nevertheless, it is believed that a majority of programme resources reached the poor. In Colombia during the early years, participation was conditional on obtaining a bank loan, which worked strongly against the poor. The major change that sharply improved targeting was due to a shift away from exclusive support of newly constructed units to a much higher proportion of certificates granted for upgrading projects with allocations to groups of households.

Overall, targeting appears to have been fairly good, although programme variations make it difficult to characterise. Programme design has at times worked against targeting the poor, and often programme features could be changed to overcome such problems. These, of course, would likely conflict with budget constraints. At the same time, it appears that limited effort has gone into implementing procedures to more precisely identify the poor with some precision.

Conclusions

The evidence reviewed points to several strengths and a basic issue to consider when employing HPCs, either as a full or partial purchase certificate subsidy programme. Success rates were unambiguously high since those who received a grant were able to use it. Similarly, national governments were able to control their budgets from unintended or undesired outlays by limiting spending to funds appropriated each year, that is, these were limited entitlement programmes.

In the two programme types reviewed, targeting has different meanings. The target groups for the full purchase subsidies were defined by a particular household status, independent of economic resources, for example, victim of a national disaster or a military officer whose contract entitles him to a dwelling unit upon retirement. Rigorous administrative screening appears to have correctly allocated the home purchase vouchers. In targeting downpayment certificates, two forms of screening were employed in the programmes reviewed: (a) income or economic status certification similar to that for other means-tested programmes, and (b) the lender screening for creditworthiness as a condition to issue a loan to supplement the subsidy and savings. Evidence on (a) suggests that targeting was generally acceptable, although variable. Evidence on (b) shows that lenders screened strongly for ability to pay, and this worked against targeting on poor households. Only Chile, among the countries reviewed above, stepped in with government-provided loans.

Finally, there is the trade-off between the housing quality standard and the number of assisted households, given a binding budget constraint. In the full purchase certificate programmes reviewed, voucher values were set high enough for the programmes to work effectively. Only existing units (or fully completed new units) were eligible for purchase, so that voucher holders could assess location and quality and select the combination best for them. Downpayment subsidy programmes tied to new dwelling estates with poor locations can be problematic because home purchase voucher holders have little or no ability to trade off location against other housing features. Downpayment certificate subsidies confronted the quality versus quantity trade-off more often and more strongly, one that was exacerbated by the lack of mortgage loans to poor borrowers. Allowing families to upgrade existing units appears to be a reasonable option for reducing the quality–quantity tension.

Overall, upfront HPC programmes show a good deal of promise. One would hope that governments and donors will in future give greater consideration to the use of HPCs in postdisaster situations, as well as a substitute for less efficient subsidies designed to encourage home purchase.

See also: Access and Affordability: Housing Vouchers; Contract Saving Schemes; First Home Owner Grants; Policies to Support Access and Affordability of Housing.

References

Gilbert A (2004) Helping the poor through housing subsidies: Lessons from Chile, Colombia, and South Africa. *Habitat International* 28: 13–40.
Steuerle CE (2000) Common issues for voucher programs. In: Steuerle CE, Doorn Ooms V, Peterson GE, and Reischauer RD (eds.) *Vouchers and the Provision of Public Services*, pp. 3–39. Washington, DC: Urban Institute Press.

Further Reading

Anlian S and Struyk R (2003) Home purchase certificates: The other housing vouchers. *European Journal of Housing Research* 3: 227–241.
Bradford DF and Shaviro DN (2000) The economics of vouchers. In: Steuerle CE, Doorn Ooms V, Peterson GE, and Reischauer RD (eds.) *Vouchers and the Provision of Public Services*, pp. 40–91. Washington, DC: Urban Institute Press.
Gobillon L and le Blanc D (2008) Economic effects of upfront subsidies to ownership: The case of the pret a taux zero in France. *Journal of Housing Economics* 17: 1–33.
Romanik C and Struyk R (1995) Assisting demobilized Russian officers obtain housing: The housing certificate option. *Review of Urban and Regional Development Studies* 7: 97–118.
Stamso MA (2008) Grants for first-time homeowners in Norway – distributional effects under different market conditions. *European Journal of Housing Policy* 8: 379–397.

Access and Affordability: Housing Allowances

PA Kemp, University of Oxford, Oxford, UK

© 2012 Elsevier Ltd. All rights reserved.

Glossary

Demand subsidies Financial assistance paid to eligible households to help them afford their rent or mortgage costs. Housing allowances are a particular type of demand subsidy.

Housing allowances Income-related subsides that are paid on a regular basis to eligible households to help them afford their rent or mortgage costs.

Housing benefit A synonym for housing allowances.

Housing vouchers Housing allowances that are paid in the form of a promissory note or certificate that the eligible tenant hands over to the landlord, who then redeems it for the monetary equivalent from the administering agency. The term is sometimes used as a synonym for housing allowances and also to refer specifically to *ex ante* housing allowances where the amount paid is not related to the recipient's actual rent or mortgage costs.

Introduction

Income-related housing allowances are one of the most widely used housing policy instruments in the advanced welfare states. They are one of a wide array of mechanisms through which public policy seeks to influence the cost of housing to the consumer. In addition to housing allowances, this menu of policy instruments includes rent controls, 'bricks and mortar' subsidies to housing suppliers, tax reliefs, and land-use regulation. The aim of this article is to present an overview of the nature, roles, and policy issues surrounding income-related housing allowances.

What Are Housing Allowances?

Housing allowances are subsidies tied to housing, which are paid to consumers or directly to landlords or mortgage lenders on the consumer's behalf. Hence, this policy instrument is focused on the demand-side of the housing market. They contrast with supply-side policy instruments such as bricks and mortar subsidies and rent controls (see article Policy Instruments that Support Housing Supply: Supply-Side Subsidies).

Housing allowance eligibility invariably extends to tenants but in some schemes may also include low-income owner-occupiers. However, in the remainder of this article, for ease of exposition, we refer simply to 'tenants'. Although 'housing allowances' is the generic term to describe this policy instrument, policy-makers may give them other names. These include housing benefit, rent assistance, shelter allowances, accommodation supplement, housing vouchers, rent certificates, and rent rebates (see article Policies to Support Access and Affordability of Housing).

Housing allowances most commonly involve a cash payment – or, increasingly, its electronic equivalent in the form of an automated credit transfer – to the consumer. However, other ways of paying the allowance also exist. A housing voucher, for example, is not cash but rather a promissory note – that is, a promise to pay – that is issued by the administering agency to the tenant. Once entitled tenants have obtained their accommodation, they give the voucher to the landlord, who in turn redeems it for its monetary value from the administering agency (see article Access and Affordability: Housing Vouchers).

In some jurisdictions – including Australia, Canada, and Ireland – social housing landlords charge income-related rents, that is, rents set at a defined percentage of the income of each tenant. This type of arrangement is sometimes called 'rents geared to income' or 'differential rent schemes'. Income-related rents can be regarded as an implicit housing allowance and are functionally equivalent to them. Such schemes involve an explicit judgement about the proportion of household income that tenants should be paying in rent.

In some countries, such as Australia, only social security recipients are eligible for housing allowances, but more commonly other low-income households – including people in work – may claim them. In the latter case, housing allowances are typically a supplementary form of income transfer, which is often administered separately from social security benefits (social insurance, social assistance, and other income support programmes such as universal child benefits) and tax credits. Income-related assistance with housing costs may also be incorporated implicitly or explicitly into social security benefits. This may involve a notional contribution to housing within the social security payment, with additional help being available from a separate housing allowance scheme; or a full payment of 'reasonable' housing costs that is added to the social security benefit paid to the claimant.

What Are the Goals of Housing Allowances?

Income-related housing allowances commonly have either housing policy or income support objectives. Less often, they may also be used to promote the take up of employment or to enable households to relocate out of poverty neighbourhoods.

As a housing policy instrument, the most common goal of housing allowances is to enable low- or moderate-income households to occupy better-quality accommodation than they would otherwise be able to obtain. In some countries, such as the United States, entitlement to a housing allowance is explicitly conditional upon the recipient living in accommodation that meets a minimum standard of fitness. If the household does not live in accommodation that meets the minimum standard, they must either upgrade it (or persuade the landlord to do so) or move to a dwelling that meets the standard, in order to qualify for the allowance.

Perhaps because, in general, the standard of housing has improved considerably since the Second World War, concerns about housing allowance recipients living in poor-quality housing have become less prominent than they previously were. As a result, it is less common than it once was to require housing allowance recipients to live in accommodation above a minimum standard. Indeed, as discussed below, in some countries (such as Britain), there is now as much, if not more, concern about recipients living in housing that is too expensive than about them living in sub-standard accommodation.

Because of improvements in housing conditions, the housing policy role of allowances has become less important in recent decades (see below). Instead, much more attention is focused on the income support (or social security) role of housing allowances. Here, the issue of concern is to ensure that low-income households do not devote an unduly large share of their income to housing payments. In other words, from an income support perspective, the role of housing allowances is to ensure that housing is 'affordable' to low- and moderate-income households.

In this context, affordability is often conceived in terms of rent-to-income ratios. Thus, from this perspective, housing allowances are seen as a way of reducing the rent-to-income ratio of low-income households to an acceptable level, sometimes expressed as a given percentage of their income. It follows that, by reducing the share of their income that is spent on rent, low-income tenants will be able to allocate more of it to nonhousing items, such as food or clothing.

There is often a tension between the housing policy and the income support goals of housing allowances especially in relation to the cost of the scheme, which is generally borne in whole or in part by either the housing or the social security ministry at a national level. Whereas the housing ministry is likely to see housing allowances as an instrument of housing policy, the social security ministry is more likely to be concerned about their income support function.

In the United States, a third goal of housing allowances has been especially important, namely as a policy instrument to promote 'spatial mobility' among recipients. For example, the Moving to Opportunity experimental programme tested the use of housing vouchers as a means of enabling recipients to move to low-poverty neighbourhoods. Likewise, the Housing Choice Voucher Program aims not only to enable low-income households to live in decent-quality housing, but also to give them an incentive to move to areas that have better job, education, and other opportunities.

The spatial mobility goal of housing allowances is based on the fact that this policy instrument is tied to the individual and not to the dwelling. The housing policy and income support goals can – and have – also been pursued through dwelling-based policy instruments such as rent control and social housing. These supply-side subsidies may be more or less good than housing allowances at enabling low-income households to live in decent-quality dwellings and at rents that do not absorb an excessively high share of their income; but, unlike housing allowances, they do not facilitate spatial mobility. Indeed, one of the criticisms sometimes made about rent controls and social housing is precisely the opposite: that they can often inhibit residential mobility (see article Access and Affordability: Rent Regulation). For example, it is claimed that households may be reluctant to leave their rent-controlled housing if it means moving to accommodation that is not subject to rent control, and which is therefore more expensive. By contrast, housing allowances are generally not tied to particular houses; instead, they are portable in the sense that, if the recipient moves home, their entitlement moves with them.

What Are the Key Features of Housing Allowances?

In general, housing allowances are income-related ('means tested') subsidies, that is, the amount of payment is related in some way to the income of the recipient. This enables payments to be targeted on low- or moderate-income households. The relationship between income and the size of the allowance is such that, other things being equal, poorer claimants are awarded a larger payment than less-poor households. The means test simultaneously identifies whose income is low enough to qualify for the allowance and the amount of payment they will be entitled to receive.

However, it is possible to have a housing allowance scheme in which eligibility is restricted to people below a given income level but the amount of payment is the same for all recipients, or for all recipients in a given category (e.g., pensioners, families, and single people). Elsewhere, I have referred to these as income-tested schemes as distinct from income-related ones (see Kemp, 1997). All households who qualify via the income test receive the allowance and the amount they receive is the same.

Housing allowances can also be payments that are neither income-related nor subject to an income test. In this case, the allowance is not necessarily restricted to low- or moderate-income households. These payments are usually called 'universal' housing allowances. They may be confined to certain categories of households (e.g., pensioners) rather than to all households, but all households of that type are entitled to the allowance.

Occupational housing allowances (i.e., ones paid by employers) are often universal in the sense that all people working for the employer receive one (or receive one if the employer is unable to give them with the subsidised accommodation that is more commonly provided to their other employees). In Britain, for example, occupational housing allowances have at times and in places been paid to coalminers, agricultural workers, and police officers. They are, in effect, a form of wage supplement. Where they are paid to people who are working in a low-paid occupation, then that amounts to an indirect form of earnings test.

In contrast, income-related housing allowances are typically calculated not only on the income of the applicant, but also on their partner's (if any) and, in some cases, the incomes of other household members. In addition, income is often adjusted to take into account household size or type. In general, housing allowances are assessed, funded, and administered by public agencies and paid only to low- or moderate-income households. The remainder of this article is focused solely on housing allowances of this type.

The defining characteristic of income-related housing allowances, though, is not that they are income-related, for the same is true of many other government programmes in social protection, such as means-tested pensions and unemployment assistance. What distinguishes housing allowances from these other means-tested schemes is that they are tied to housing. They are tied either (1) in the sense that the amount paid is related in some way to the cost of housing or (2) because they may only be used to pay for housing.

Housing vouchers are an example of the latter because they can only legally be used to pay for housing; the recipient hands them over to the landlord in lieu of rent. In Britain, rent rebates (part of the Housing Benefit scheme) are also explicitly tied to the payment of housing. The administering agency and the landlord are the same organisation (the local council) and the Housing Benefit office transfers the payment directly into the recipient's rent account. Hence the tenant hands over to their council only the net rent, that is, the rent that is left after the rebate is deducted, which in many cases is nil because the rebate can cover all of the rent.

Where, as is often the case, the amount of the housing allowance is related in some way to the cost of housing, it is useful to distinguish between *ex post* and *ex ante* schemes. In *ex post* housing allowances, the amount of payment to which the claimant is entitled is related to the amount of rent that they are being charged for their accommodation by the landlord. In this type of scheme, households whose rent is higher (or lower) than households whose circumstances are otherwise identical receive a larger (or smaller, as the case may be) housing allowance. In contrast, in *ex ante* schemes, the size of the payment is not a function of the recipient's actual rent. Instead, it is either a more or less arbitrary amount or is related to rent levels in the local area or region. Because *ex ante* housing allowances are based on an average or standard rent, rather than on recipient's actual rent, the amount of payment is by definition less tailored to the individual circumstances of the recipient. Hence, other things being equal, *ex ante* schemes are arguably less likely than *ex post* allowances to satisfy the affordability goal of housing allowance schemes.

Why Have Housing Allowances Become So Important?

Income-related housing allowances have become an increasingly important policy instrument compared with supply-side interventions such as rent controls and bricks and mortar subsidies. In the first few decades after the Second World War, in order to tackle housing shortages, many industrial nations introduced or expanded the provision of subsidies or tax reliefs to enable landlords to build dwellings and let them at below market rents. Meanwhile, rent controls were used to prevent landlords from raising rents to market levels at a time of severe housing shortage.

While these supply-side interventions were seen by many governments in the aftermath of the Second World War as the right way to tackle the housing shortage, they seemed less appropriate by the 1970s when dwellings had become less scarce relative to the number of households. During the last third of the twentieth century, therefore, many of the advanced welfare states began to phase out rent controls and to reduce or even eliminate bricks and mortar subsidies. This, in turn, led to higher rents in both the private rental and the social housing sectors, respectively. Income-related housing allowances made it possible to protect, at least to some extent, lower-income households from these rent increases. Hence the shift from supply-side to demand-side interventions was related, as the growth in the latter instrument helped make it possible to achieve the decrease in the former.

The shift from supply- to demand-side subsidies in the housing market did not only reflect the end of large-scale accommodation shortages. It also reflected the resurgence of neo-liberal ideas especially after the end of the postwar 'golden age' of economic growth and welfare state development in the 1970s. Since then, there has been a renewed belief in the market as an allocative device and a corresponding decline in the perceived ability of public and other nonmarket action to tackle public policy concerns. This shift in attitudes has had implications for perceptions of the relative merits of supply- and demand-side subsidies in housing. Supply-side subsidies enable social landlords to provide accommodation at below market rents. Meanwhile, rent controls prevent landlords from setting market rents and are thought to discourage housing provision by private landlords. In contrast, housing allowances help to underpin the market: in theory at least, they provide recipients with sufficient resources to be able to afford to pay a market rent.

Hence, housing allowances are more in tune with neo-liberal policy orientations. From the 1980s in particular, public perceptions of social housing in the liberal market economies (such as Australia, Britain, and the United States) had become less favourable. Particularly in the United States, 'public housing' had become highly stigmatised and associated with high levels of poverty, unemployment, crime, and other social problems. Instead of being seen as a solution, social housing had come to be seen as the problem. In this context, housing allowances were seen as a policy instrument that could help avoid the problems of poverty neighbourhoods and the stigma associated with living in them. Indeed, in the United States, housing vouchers were used as a way of helping low-income households to escape from such areas.

A related driver of the shift from supply- to demand-side assistance with housing costs has been the desire to achieve more efficient use of public funds. Economists have argued that housing allowances are more efficient than bricks and mortar subsidies in that they can provide help to a greater number of households for a given amount of money. Moreover, it has been claimed that bricks and mortar subsidies are often 'indiscriminate'.

They assist all tenants living in social housing irrespective of whether they need subsidised rents or not, though the force of this argument depends on the extent to which social housing is not targeted on the poor. In contrast, because housing allowances are income-related, only households that truly need help receive it.

Further, housing allowances are thought to encourage residential and labour mobility while rent controls and bricks and mortar subsidies are thought to inhibit housing moves (see article Housing and Labour Markets). Housing allowances are also believed to enable households to exercise choice – an important leitmotif in the neo-liberal era – in the housing market. This is because they enable recipients to move to the accommodation that is best suited to their preferences and circumstances. By contrast, social housing is typically allocated on administrative criteria that offer relatively limited scope for the household to choose their accommodation.

As well as housing and policy-related developments that have reduced the perceived need for interventions on the supply-side, the growing importance of housing allowances has also reflected an increase in the number of 'needy' households. The drivers here are common to those facing social security benefits in the modern era. These rising needs reflect socio-economic and demographic trends that have occurred over recent decades. These include the growth of unemployment since the 1970s, which led to an increase in the number of households needing help with their rent or mortgage payments. The associated rise in long-term unemployment meant that some claimants had exhausted their entitlement to social insurance and had to rely on less generous social assistance safety net benefits, which again increased the demands on housing allowance schemes. The increase in part-time jobs and the growth of more precarious forms of employment since the 1970s have also helped to increase the demand for housing allowances from people on the margins of the labour market. In addition, the growing numbers of economically inactive people of working age – including lone parents, early retirees, and people receiving long-term sickness and disability benefits – have also helped to increase housing allowance costs and caseloads. Finally, population ageing has resulted in an increasing number of low-income pensioners who are entitled to housing allowances.

What Are the Disadvantages of Housing Allowances?

Income-related housing allowances are arguably more efficient policy instruments than universal housing allowances because they are paid only to needy households. Depending upon the design of the scheme, they are confined to low- and moderate-income households; the means test upon which entitlement is calculated excludes better-off households, who are by implication not in need of such support.

However, income-related housing allowances also have disadvantages, one of which is low take-up. Although housing allowances are targeted on those living on a low income, many entitled households do not apply for them. Research has suggested that the reasons for low take-up are complex, but include lack of awareness of (entitlement to) the allowances; the time and inconvenience of claiming them; not wishing to rely on government subsidies; and the perceived stigma associated with being a benefit claimant. Some of these reasons for low take-up might also apply to universal housing allowances, but others (such as stigma) are specific to, or more salient for, income-related housing allowances.

In addition, the fact that the allowance is income-related can create undesirable disincentives, particularly in relation to work (see article Housing Subsidies and Work Incentives). One of these is known as the 'unemployment trap'. This occurs where people in receipt of out-of-work welfare benefits would be little or no better-off if they were to move into paid employment, taking into account the extra expenses involved in working such as commuting costs. The size of the unemployment trap is often measured using the 'replacement rate', that is, the amount of income that a welfare benefit recipient receives while out of work as a percentage of the amount they are likely to earn if they were to move into employment. High replacement rates are believed by many policy-makers to act as a disincentive for unemployed claimants to get a job.

The unemployment trap effect of housing allowances may be minimised or eliminated if low-income working households are eligible to claim them and not just those in receipt of unemployment benefits. Housing allowances that are payable to low-paid households can ensure that, when the claimants move off welfare and into work, their net income increases (or at least does not decrease), thereby guaranteeing that 'work pays'. This potential role of housing allowances in helping to avoid an unemployment trap from occurring is very important given the high cost of housing relative to earnings from low-paid employment.

However, the low take-up of housing allowances by people in work can undermine the 'work pays' benefits of such schemes. In Britain, for example, take up of Housing Benefit among people in work is estimated to be only about half that among people on welfare. One reason for this differential take-up is that, as qualitative research has shown, many low-paid worker incorrectly believe that only people on welfare are entitled to receive housing benefit.

A further reason for low take-up in Britain relates to the fact that entitlement is calculated on current (weekly or monthly) income, a fact that creates considerable difficulty for people in precarious jobs or whose hours of work vary from week to week. The relatively slow administration of Housing Benefit and delays that result from it, add further difficulties for such households. As a result, income and allowance receipt may be perpetually out of sync, creating shortfalls and overpayments that are difficult to cope with for people in low-paid and precarious work. For such households, Housing Benefit in Britain provides an insecure income pillar, thereby reducing its effectiveness in tackling the unemployment trap. Meanwhile, when housing allowances are 'rationed', as in the United States, there are also potential 'lock-in' effects. Eligible households join the queue to receive a housing allowance and may not search for work as they might otherwise because they fear loss of eligibility on accepting job offers that may prove temporary, in which case they must rejoin the queue.

Another work disincentive resulting from the income-related feature of housing allowances is the 'poverty trap'. It is inherent in the design of such schemes that the amount of payment varies according to the income of the recipients; it follows that, if their income increases, the amount of housing allowance to which they are entitled decreases. In effect, this withdrawal of the allowance as income rises is functionally equivalent to an income tax; it is often referred to as a 'tax back rate' or an income 'taper'.

Working households in receipt of housing allowances typically pay income tax and social security contributions on their income. Hence, if their gross income increases as a result of a pay rise or working extra hours, housing allowance recipients will have to pay increased tax and social security contributions on that extra income and lose some of their housing allowance. If they receive other 'in-work', income-related social security benefits or tax credits, they will also lose some of their entitlement to those too. The effect may be to create a very high 'marginal deduction rate' (or effective marginal tax rate) on their additional gross income. As a result, the increase in the household's net income after these deductions may be quite small relative to the increase in the gross income.

In Britain, the marginal deduction rate can be as high as 94% at present. Although this represents an extreme example of the poverty trap, it nonetheless graphically illustrates an inherent feature of income-related housing allowances. The problem is attenuated in countries where the allowance is calculated on annual income for a previous tax year, rather than on current income, in that the adjustment is undertaken annually in arrears. But, although this may delay the effect, and iron out within-year income fluctuations, it ultimately does not eliminate the problem altogether.

A further potential disadvantage of housing allowances – which particularly affects *ex post* schemes (see above) – is that they may reduce the incentive of households to shop around for accommodation. *Ex post* housing allowance entitlement is calculated (at least to some degree) on claimants' actual rent. It follows that, to the extent that it is based on their rent, the higher the rent, the larger is the allowance to which they are entitled. The cost of the higher rent is, in effect, shared between the claimant and the housing allowance scheme budget. Hence, the marginal cost of housing for allowance recipients is less (and often much less) than 100% of the rent. Perhaps the most extreme example of this is the British Housing Benefit scheme for social housing tenants, which can cover up to 100% of the rent, and in which the marginal cost of housing is nil (the payment increases by £1 for every £1 increase in rent, and decreases by £1 for every £1 decrease in rent).

Housing allowance schemes that subsidise a high proportion of the marginal cost of housing blunt, to some extent, recipients' incentive to shop around for accommodation in the rental housing market and to bargain with the prospective landlord over the rent level. Moreover, they can potentially incentivise claimants to move to unreasonably large or expensive accommodation, something referred to as 'upmarketing'. In order to counter this potential problem, most *ex post* housing allowance schemes incorporate devices to prevent over-consumption or upmarketing. These techniques fall into three main categories: rent ceilings, housing allowance maxima (caps), and administrative rules about what counts as 'unreasonably' large accommodation or an 'excessively' high rent.

With few exceptions – the United States is one – housing allowances are not cash-limited but demand-led schemes. That is to say, they do not usually have a fixed budget to be spent each year; instead, the amount spent on the scheme depends upon the number of households that claim the allowance and their particular circumstances (income, rent, etc.) that define how much they are entitled to receive. Consequently, when the level of unemployment increases, for example, the number of people claiming housing allowances increases and hence so too does the cost of the scheme; and vice versa when unemployment falls.

This demand-led feature of most housing allowance schemes means that they act as a counter-cyclical regulator or automatic stabiliser within the economy, helping to maintain effective demand during recessions (see article Housing Markets and Macroeconomic Policy). However, the corollary of this open-ended arrangement is that expenditure on housing allowances is difficult to control. This 'uncontrollability' can be especially problematic for finance ministries during periods of fiscal austerity.

A final potential disadvantage of housing allowances is that they may cause rents to rise within the housing market and thereby reduce the impact of the scheme on housing affordability. This is because housing allowances increase the purchasing power of recipient households; and if the number of recipients within a local housing market is substantial, the increase in demand could push up rents. In a perfectly competitive housing market, an increase in rent levels will induce an increase in the supply of dwellings, which in due course will bring rents back down to their original level. However, if new rental housing supply is not very elastic, at least in the short run, rents will stay at a higher level than before the housing allowance programme was introduced. Consequently, the financial benefit of the allowances will be captured by landlords rather than by recipients; and nonrecipient tenants will end up paying a higher rent.

Thus, the extent to which the benefit of the allowance programme lies with the recipients or with landlords depends upon the price elasticity of supply, that is, the degree to which supply increases in response to an increase in rents (see article Supply Elasticity of Housing). The research evidence of the impact of housing allowances on rents is mixed, however, with some studies finding no impact and others that rents have increased to some extent, at least in the short run.

Conclusions

Housing allowances have become a widely used policy instrument in the advanced welfare states and, in some countries, the most important one in the housing market. Improved housing conditions, increased income inequality, demographic trends, and the rise in nonemployment and precarious work, have all been important factors behind the growing emphasis on income-related housing allowances; a shift that has also reflected the neo-liberal zeitgeist. Such schemes are believed to have important advantages over supply-side approaches to providing help with housing costs, such as rent controls and bricks and mortar subsidies. Yet, they also have potentially negative impacts in relation to both the housing market and the labour market, which are not easily resolved. Nevertheless, for the foreseeable future, income-related housing allowances are likely to remain a key feature of housing policy in the advanced welfare states.

See also: Access and Affordability: Housing Vouchers; Access and Affordability: Rent Regulation; Housing and Labour Markets; Housing Markets and Macroeconomic Policy; Housing Subsidies and Work Incentives; Policies to Support Access and Affordability of Housing; Policy Instruments that Support Housing Supply: Supply-Side Subsidies; Supply Elasticity of Housing.

Reference

Kemp PA (1997) *A Comparative Study of Housing Allowances*. London: The Stationary Office. http://research.dwp.gov.uk/asd/asd5/rrep060.pdf (accessed 27 June 2011).

Further Reading

Bradbury KL and Downs A (eds.) (1981) *Do Housing Allowances Work?* Washington, DC: Brookings Institution.

Briggs X, de S, Popkin SJ, and Goering J (2010) *Moving to Opportunity*. New York: Oxford University Press.

Gibb K (1995) A housing allowance for the UK? Preconditions for an income-related housing subsidy. *Housing Studies* 10: 517–532.

Hulse K (2003) Housing allowances and private renting in liberal welfare regimes. *Housing, Theory and Society* 20: 28–42.

Kemp PA (1992) *Housing Benefit: An Appraisal*. London: Social Security Advisory Committee.

Kemp PA (2000) *'Shopping Incentives' and Housing Benefit Reform*. Coventry, UK: Chartered Institute of Housing and Joseph Rowntree Foundation.

Kemp PA (ed.) (2007) *Housing Allowances in Comparative Perspective*. Bristol, UK: The Policy Press.

Laferrere A and Le Blanc D (2004) How do housing allowances affect rents? An empirical analysis of the French case. *Journal of Housing Economics* 13: 36–67.

Oxley M (1987) The aims and effects of housing allowances in Western Europe. In: van Vliet W (ed.) *Housing Markets and Policies Under Fiscal Austerity*. London: Greenwood Press.

Shroder M (2002) Does housing assistance perversely affect self-sufficiency? A review essay. *Journal of Housing Economics* 27: 381–417.

Steele M (1998) Canadian housing allowances inside and outside the welfare system. *Canadian Public Policy – Analyse de Politues* XXIV: 209–232.

Stephens M (2005) An assessment of the British Housing Benefit scheme. *European Journal of Housing Policy* 5: 111–129.

Varady D and Walker CC (2007) *Neighborhood Choices*. New Brunswick, NJ: Center for Urban Policy Research.

Access and Affordability: Housing Vouchers

M Steele, University of Guelph, Guelph, ON, Canada; University of Toronto, Toronto, ON, Canada

© 2012 Elsevier Ltd. All rights reserved.

Glossary

Experimental housing allowance programme (EHAP) A large-scale, expensive US experiment carried out in the 1970s to test alternative housing allowance designs.

Fair market rent (FMR) In the United States, the 40th percentile rent for rental units occupied by recent movers. The FMR is calculated and set annually by HUD for units with different numbers of bedrooms by urban area; the set rent – payment standard – in the US voucher is usually equal to the FMR.

HUD The US Federal Department of Housing and Urban Development.

Low Income Housing Tax Credit A housing program run through the tax system. It subsidises most new non-profit housing construction in the US. Tax credits are competitively awarded – about a third to non-profits – to projects for low- and moderate-income tenants. Developers then sell the credits to investors to fund development.

Moving to Work (MTW) Demonstration programme authorised in the United States in 1996 to increase work incentives in housing programmes and allowing some local housing authorities wide latitude to change programme parameters and designs.

Section 8 certificate The initial form of US tenant-based subsidy in which the rent of a beneficiary's unit was not permitted to exceed the payment standard.

Introduction

Housing vouchers have been used in some Eastern European countries, and to a limited extent in the United States, to assist home purchase, but in this article we focus on their employment in rental housing subsidy programmes (see article Access and Affordability: House Purchase Certificates). A housing voucher in rental housing is defined as an *ex ante* housing allowance (see article Access and Affordability: Housing Allowances). In effect, it is a certificate entitling a household to a monthly subsidy that depends on the household's income and on a set rent – usually close to the median rent – for the urban area where the household lives. It also sometimes depends on the actual rent of the recipient's unit. The household receives the certificate before deciding where to live. The US Housing Choice Voucher, the major example of a voucher, differs from the typical housing allowance in several major respects. First, the subsidy cheque goes to the landlord, albeit on behalf of the tenant. Second, a voucher is not a right of all eligible households but instead vouchers are allocated to a waiting list and their number is determined by a vote of Congress. Further, unless the recipient finds a landlord with qualified units willing to take the voucher, she or he must return it. Third, the tenant is not required to pay rent before benefiting from the subsidy, while a housing allowance recipient usually must pay market rent up front, receiving the subsidy only *ex post*. Finally, the marginal cost to a tenant of a dollar increase in rent up to the set rent is zero, at which point it becomes a dollar, while the marginal cost is always more than zero in most housing allowance schemes.

The Role of the Voucher in US Housing Policy

The US Section 8 voucher, along with predecessor programmes, has been in place for over three decades, providing affordable housing to hundreds of thousands of low-income households. In 2008, two million families were assisted with vouchers worth over $14 billion; administrative costs added over 9%; in total, this is more than a third of federal government explicit housing subsidies. The subsidy per household is high, averaging almost $600 per month in 2008 and is about 80% of median (2007) US rent (plus utilities). The size of this subsidy is in part related to the miserly level of income assistance provided for those on welfare in many parts of the United States. On average, welfare income is much less than in Canada, Australia, and Western European countries. This means that the income on which some voucher holders' contribution to rent is based so low that the voucher pays almost all the rent. According to Kemp (2007c, table 12.6), while the average subsidy relative to rent in the United States is similar in order of magnitude to that of the UK housing allowance, it is far greater than that of housing allowances in most countries.

The History of Tenant-Based Subsidies in the United States

By the late 1960s, there was disenchantment in the United States with public housing. Many projects, far from providing good shelter for their inhabitants, were places of urban blight. Vandalism and crime were rife and the physical quality of the housing was poor. The source of the problems was judged to be the government ownership and management of projects, the large size and high-rise character of many buildings as well as their placement and design, and the concentration of welfare households – many of them multiproblem families – in projects without the moderating effect of a sufficient number of low- and moderate-income working families.

Section 8 of the 1974 Housing and Community Development Act was a response to this assessment. It introduced tenant-based subsidies in the form of certificates to assist eligible households to rent units of their choice. Selected households were required to pay their landlords 25% (later, 30%) of their incomes. The government paid landlords the residual rent. Under this programme, a recipient could not occupy a unit renting for more than a set rent and units were required to pass a housing quality inspection.

The Section 8 certificate had been introduced while the Experimental Housing Allowance Programme (EHAP) was underway. One EHAP finding was that the housing chosen by recipient renters was much less responsive to increases in income and reductions in rental prices than economists had expected. There was little improvement in quality in response to strong incentives. In experiments with a minimum quality requirement, improvements were typically minor. At the same time, this requirement reduced participation especially among the poorest households, and analysts concluded that it was, at best, of dubious merit. Recent assessments have not changed this conclusion.

After EHAP ended, the Section 8 certificate was retained, but a voucher was added. It provided that the landlord received a set subsidy amount and the recipient paid the residual rent, which could be less – or more – than 30% of its income. Every dollar of additional rent a recipient paid cost the recipient a dollar. Thus, the scheme reflected the economists' perspective that incentives are of paramount importance and, assuming market imperfections can be safely ignored, unconstrained consumer choice leads to the optimum outcome. Despite doubts cast by EHAP on the housing quality requirement, this feature was retained. Furthermore, Congress added an element untested in EHAP, payment of the subsidy directly to the landlord rather than to the tenant. Together with annual housing inspections, this linked the landlords of voucher and certificate recipients tightly to the local housing authority.

In later legislation, a limit of 40% of income was set on the amount voucher tenants are permitted to pay when they first move into a unit; while this may have been intended to protect recipients, it means that the poorest are restricted to a narrower part of the market than the better-off. For example, if the payment standard is $700 per month, at an annual income of $12 000, a recipient needs to find a unit with gross rent (contract rent + utilities) of less than $800 ($700 + 10% of $12 000/12) while a unit renting for up to $900 would be eligible to a recipient earning $24 000. This may make some units in Low-Income Housing Tax Credit (LIHTC) projects beyond the reach of extremely low-income recipients (see article Low-Income Housing Tax Credits).

The US Housing Choice Voucher: Critical Elements

The US voucher provides for payment to the landlord of the gap between a set rent (including utilities) and affordable rent, defined as 30% of the household's adjusted income. The set rent or 'payment standard' is at or close to fair market rent as determined by the US Department of Housing and Urban Development (HUD) for a unit of suitable size in the area where the household lives. If rent for the unit is $800 and the subsidy is $500, there will be a contract between the landlord and the government stipulating a payment of $500 to the landlord. The subsidised household pays the landlord the remainder, $300.

There is an asymmetry in the current US voucher which distinguishes it from a generic voucher. Prior to 1998, a voucher recipient pocketed the difference between the payment standard and a bargain rent. But there is a requirement in the Quality Housing and Work Responsibility Act of 1998 that the recipient must pay rent of at least 30% of income. If the recipient secures a bargain unit, the reward goes entirely to the housing authority. If the recipient secures a unit renting for more than the payment standard, the voucher recipient pays the extra in full. Thus, below the payment standard the marginal cost to the recipient of a dollar extra rent is zero, but above it the marginal cost is a dollar, until the cutoff at 40% of the recipient's income.

HUD allocates vouchers directly to thousands of local housing authorities and to a few state government agencies. These in turn award the vouchers to households on their waiting list and have some leeway in setting parameters and rules – for example, a local authority might decide to extend the 60-day period recipients are given to find a unit, or increase the payment standard to 110% of fair market rent. HUD allows further flexibility to housing authorities that are participants in its Moving to Work (MTW) programme. Under MTW the voucher can be changed to increase work incentives; for example, recipients may be required to pay a flat amount rather than 30% of their income (see article Mobility Programmes for Disadvantaged Populations: The Moving to Opportunity Programme).

Policy Motivations: Housing Quality, Mobility, and Affordability

Unlike the case in most countries with housing allowances, a major motivation for implementing the Section 8 certificate and voucher programmes was to improve the quality of housing. In most developed countries after the Second World War, initially there were major initiatives to deal with the shortage of housing. But, by the 1960s, overcrowding was no longer a major problem, the quality of housing had much improved, and attention switched to affordability. In the United States in the 1960s, while affordability was also a critical issue, extensive swaths of dilapidated housing persisted, much of it in distressed, inner city areas with a predominantly Black population. Perhaps, this was the reason why a central feature of Section 8 was a list of minimum physical specifications. Partly as a consequence, about three-quarters of those awarded a voucher move. They may move because they want to live in better housing or they may be forced to move because their existing landlord is unwilling to upgrade to meet the quality requirement, to submit to an inspection – or for other reasons wants no involvement in the programme. The proportion moving has been regarded as an indicator of success by many who view it as a sign of improved housing quality.

In recent years, the policy emphasis has shifted to good-quality neighbourhoods. The conventional view is that the voucher gives a family the chance to move to a better neighbourhood, one with good schools and a high level of social capital, which together will reduce unemployment and improve child outcomes, notably education levels. The Moving to Opportunity programme, where some eligible movers are given vouchers and special counselling, is based on this idea. Recent research indicates, however, that the voucher does not have the expected positive effects on work effort, at least in the initial years of receipt, or on child outcomes (see article Mobility Programmes for Disadvantaged Populations: The Moving to Opportunity Programme).

The emphasis on moving – and the general view that moving is desirable – is a uniquely American feature of housing policy. This emphasis may seem odd in view of the evidence that moving is detrimental to child outcomes, but there is deep concern about the concentration of Blacks in high-poverty neighbourhoods far from employment centres, and the impact of racial discrimination on their mobility. Furthermore, the US population is more mobile than most other countries' populations, and economists emphasise that a mobile labour force contributes to economic growth by facilitating speedy adjustment to shifting economic fundamentals.

The US Voucher and the Low-Income Housing Tax Credit

The voucher has played a critically important role in the success of the LIHTC that, despite its name, subsidises moderate-income households rather than low-income ones unless augmented by other assistance. For very low-income households, the maximum rents permitted under the tax credit programme are unaffordable. Developments built using the credit, however, must accept voucher households. Thus, although about two-thirds of credit units are owned by for-profit developers and investors, almost half of credit buildings, in a recent investigation, were found to have at least one voucher tenant. Indeed, the two programmes have a symbiotic relationship: the voucher helps ensure housing tax credit developments are filled and the latter helps ensure that voucher recipients will be able to use their voucher.

The Use of Set Rent but Not Actual Rent in the Formula

Effect of the Subsidy on Rents Paid: Theory

In the generic voucher – although as indicated earlier, not in the US voucher – there is no relationship between the subsidy and the actual rent for a recipient's unit. Economists generally like this design because of a belief that it minimises effects on market rents. In contrast, when an allowance depends partly on actual rent, recipients pay a discounted marginal price for better housing because the subsidy increases as rent does. This tends to increase the demand for housing and to exert upward pressure on market rents. Also, landlords have an incentive to increase rents at lease renewal time because they know their tenants bear only part of the increase and would face transaction costs if they moved.

Evidence of the US Voucher's Effects on Rents

Scott Susin, in a 2002 paper, finds large price effects – although it may be that these are upward biased because of inevitable technical problems – resulting from the US certificate–voucher programmes. Not only would such effects increase the cost of the programme, but they would also hurt low-income families who are not recipients. This would exacerbate the horizontal inequity implicit in the granting of vouchers to some but not all low-income households – poor nonrecipients may be left even worse off than they would have been had the programme not existed. This is also true for the large share – over one-third in some cities in years when markets are tight – of those awarded vouchers who end up returning them because they cannot secure qualifying units.

One possible reason for the effects Susin found is that publication of fair market rents each year acts as a signalling device prompting landlords to target their rents at published values. A more specific prompt can occur on the acceptance of a voucher recipient, or renewal of a recipient's lease: landlords know that the rules allow the recipient to pay 40% of income and know the income of the recipient because the rent split between housing authority and voucher recipient depends on it. This is markedly different from the typical housing allowance where the landlord may not know who receives the allowance, let alone what the income of a recipient is. Concern about turnover, the application of the programme's 'rent reasonableness' requirement, and the negotiation of rents between government housing authorities and landlords temper rent effects, but the very existence of negotiation indicates the importance of incentives to increase rents. Also, while negotiation protects recipients, it also belies the image of the voucher as a subsidy which unleashes recipients from the paternalism of the housing authority.

Actual Rents in the Formula, Programme Costs, and Affordability

An advantage of actual rent in housing allowance formulae is that it reduces programme costs below those of a voucher, at least in the short run, because of the wide dispersion of actual rents in any given market. Some low-income tenants pay above the median rent but many pay less. For example, there is abundant empirical evidence that continuing tenants tend to pay less than new ones. Other reasons for dispersion derive from imperfections in the housing market and variation in the cost of providing housing services that are due to actions of the tenant. Some tenants use more water and electricity than others. Some may perform maintenance for their landlords while others damage the property; some are easy to deal with because they speak the same language as the manager, while others do not understand unwritten, let alone written rules.

Rent dispersion sometimes takes the form of different rents in otherwise similar buildings in the same market that are traceable to different criteria in tenant selection. For example, some landlords accept only tenants with a good credit record, which means immigrants too recent to have a credit record are excluded. Some landlords in the United States do not accept vouchers. Some exclude tenants with children although this is almost always prohibited by law. Landlords employing loose selection criteria to fill their buildings have been found to have higher rents. This implies that households perceived as costly tenants will tend to pay a relatively high rent. Their predicament may result in a severe affordability problem.

Rent dispersion and the fact that some households may have to pay more than the median rent is the cause of a conundrum related to the leeway US housing authorities have in varying the payment standard. They are permitted to vary it within a range of plus – and sometimes more – or minus 10%. Setting the standard high is typically needed in cities where rental markets are tight and landlords are able to fill their buildings without accepting vouchers. Set the payment standard too low and many recipients with low and precarious incomes will have to pay 40% of income on rent, or be unable to secure any unit, forcing them to return the vouchers. Set the payment standard too high and the cost per recipient is unnecessarily high, reducing the number who can be served within a given budget.

Equity Issues

In the generic voucher programme, there are prima facie no equity issues unless higher rents in some cities reflect relatively high levels of amenities or other benefits – in which case recipients there would benefit more than recipients elsewhere. This is a potential horizontal equity issue. But there is a vertical equity advantage of the voucher over housing allowances that use actual rent in their formulas. Suppose the subsidy equals part of the affordability gap – for example, 75% of rent minus 30% of income where rent is actual rent up to some maximum – then it is possible for a higher-income recipient to receive a bigger subsidy than a lower-income recipient. This is not possible in the generic voucher.

A more subtle point is put by posing the following question: if racial minorities (because of discrimination) or immigrants (because of an absent credit record) or young people (because of a short time in a unit) pay a relatively high rent for a given level of housing service, is it equitable that their subsidy should be based on the same set rent as families without these characteristics? If the answer is no, there is an equity case for making a housing allowance dependent on actual rent.

In the case of the US voucher, the major inequity is the limitation of vouchers to only about 10% of eligible families not living in subsidised projects.

The *ex ante* Nature of the Voucher and the Nature of Assisted Households

The *ex ante* character of vouchers means that recipients need not be paying an unaffordable rent or indeed any rent to become eligible for the subsidy. For example, some young mothers paying nothing and living in cramped conditions with relatives may be recipients (enabling them to move to a place of their own). This is in contrast to most housing allowances where some evidence of rent already paid is needed. A voucher-like programme may be essential to alleviate overcrowding and to house the homeless – at the same time, *ex post* allowances would serve more resourceful households, those able to secure and retain housing and willing to devote a large part of their budgets to it. The latter almost all live in adequate housing but many have so little left after paying their rent that they are forced to restrict their diet or use food banks.

Difficulties in the US Voucher Associated with the Quality Requirement and Direct Payment to the Landlord

The housing quality requirement of the US voucher means that recipients benefit only if they are able to secure qualifying housing. In contrast to a subsidy that gradually declines as actual rent declines, the voucher is worthless – that is, must be returned – unless the family finds housing meeting minimum standards.

The relationship between the landlord and the recipient of the voucher is affected by the contract between the former and the housing authority. This guarantees the landlord receipt of a large part of rent but also reduces the tenant's bargaining power and reveals to the landlord changes in the tenant's income. After the UK reform of its Housing Benefit programme, payments directly to the landlord were prohibited for reasons like these. This leaves the US voucher almost alone among housing allowances in its payment method.

Payment of the voucher to the landlord along with the inspection requirement means that beneficiaries are necessarily identified and stigmatised, unlike the situation with housing allowances. It also means that administering the programme is complex – the *Guidebook* for local housing authorities is over 500 pages – and administrative costs – $1.3 billion in 2008 – are high. Administering the typical housing allowance is far cheaper and the administrative burden for private agents is minimal; for example, in the Canadian province of Quebec, there is usually a zero burden for landlords, and applicant families need only make a phone call, complete a simple application form, and enclose evidence of rent such as a rent increase notice. The income tax agency administers the programme and this lowers the cost of compliance and administration because details of income are already known to the government.

High Costs but Some Advantages Over *ex post* Housing Allowances

The very high cost per household of the US voucher is in part due to the use of a set rent close to median rent and to the zero marginal cost to recipients of an increase in rent to this level. But it may also be attributed to the very low income of a large fraction of recipients and to the housing quality requirements as well as the need for landlords to be legally linked to a government agency. The pre-2008 UK Housing Benefit shared some features with the voucher and was also high cost.

Direct payment to landlords is not without policy advantages. It means landlords have a direct, well-understood, and clear interest in ensuring that the set rent – the payment standard – keeps pace with rent inflation. In some housing allowance schemes where payment is made to the tenant, maximum rents have been left to languish, steadily eroding the real value of the allowance. Furthermore, some families, such as the homeless, require direct payments, and generous ones at that, to ensure success in accessing housing. It may be that a generous scheme for those in extreme housing distress should exist alongside a cheaper, administratively simple programme, for those already housed in accommodation which might not meet the US voucher's minimum housing quality standards. Difficult issues would be where to draw the line between the two and how to design co-existing programmes with minimal perverse incentives.

See also: Access and Affordability: House Purchase Certificates; Access and Affordability: Housing Allowances; Low-Income Housing Tax Credits; Mobility Programmes for Disadvantaged Populations: The Moving to Opportunity Programme.

References

Kemp PA (2007c) (ed.) Housing allowances in the advanced welfare states. In: *Housing Allowances in Comparative Perspective*, pp. 265–287. Bristol, UK: The Policy Press.

Susin S (2002) Rent vouchers and the price of low-income housing. *Journal of Public Economics* 83(1): 109–152.

Further Reading

Benjamin JD, Peter Chinloy G, and Sirmans S (2000) Housing vouchers, tenant quality, and apartment values. *The Journal of Real Estate Finance and Economics* 20(1): 37–48.

Bradbury KL and Downs A (1981) *Do Housing Allowances Work?* p. 412. Washington, DC: The Brookings Institution.

Carlson D, Haveman R, Kaplan T, and Wolfe B (2008) Long-term effects of public low-income housing vouchers on work, earnings, and neighborhood quality. University of Wisconsin Institute for Research on Poverty. *Discussion Paper No. 1338-08.* p. 51. Available at URL: http://www.ssc.wisc.edu/irpweb/publications/dps/pdfs/dp133808.pdf (accessed 30 October 2011).

Center on Budget and Policy Priorities (2009) Introduction to the housing voucher program. p. 9. Washington, DC. Available at URL: http://www.cbpp.org/files/5-15-09hous.pdf (accessed 30 October 2011).

Jacob BA (2004) Public housing, housing vouchers, and student achievement: Evidence from public housing demolitions in Chicago. *American Economic Review* 94(1): 233–258.

Kemp PA (ed.) (2007a) *Housing Allowances in Comparative Perspective*, p. 295. Bristol, UK: The Policy Press.

Kemp PA (ed.) (2007b) *Housing benefit in Britain: A troubled history and uncertain future*. In: Housing Allowances in Comparative Perspective, pp. 105–133. Bristol, UK: The Policy Press.

Khaduri J (2003) Should the housing voucher program become a state-administered block grant. *Housing Policy Debate* 14(3): 235–269.

Newman S (2007) Housing allowances American style: The housing choice voucher programme. In: Kemp PA (ed.) *Housing Allowances in Comparative Perspective*, pp. 87–104. Bristol, UK: The Policy Press.

Quadel Consulting Corporation (2001) *Voucher Program Guidebook: Housing Choice*. Produced for the US Department of Housing and Urban Development, Office of Public and Indian Housing. Washington, DC. Available at URL: http://www.hud.gov/offices/adm/hudclips/guidebooks/7420.10G/index.cfm (accessed 30 October 2011).

Steele M (2007) Canadian housing allowances. In: Kemp PA (ed.) *Housing Allowances in Comparative Perspective*, pp. 61–85. Bristol, UK: The Policy Press.

US Office of Management and Budget (2009) *The Fiscal Year 2010*. Appendix, Detailed Budget Estimates by Agency. Department of Housing and Urban Development. Available at URL: http://www.gpoaccess.gov/usbudget/fy10/pdf/appendix/hud.pdf (accessed 30 October 2011).

Wood M, Turnham J, and Mills G (2008) Housing affordability and family wellbeing: Results from the housing voucher evaluation. *Housing Policy Debate* 19(2): 367–412.

Access and Affordability: Mortgage Guarantees

R Van Order, George Washington University, Washington, DC, USA

© 2012 Elsevier Ltd. All rights reserved.

Introduction

Almost all American mortgages for decades have benefited from some sort of government guarantee, for example, directly via FHA insurance, or indirectly from deposit insurance for banks or guarantees for government-sponsored enterprises (GSEs) like Fannie Mae and Freddie Mac (see article Housing Finance: Deposit Guarantees). Guarantees promote housing by working through the financial system to make housing finance easier and cheaper – by limiting risk premia in interest rates and relaxing quantitative standards such as those on down payments. From an economic perspective, the role of housing guarantees should be to promote a housing finance system that allows housing to be financed in a way that equates the risk-adjusted social return on housing with the risk-adjusted returns on other assets. This requires adjusting to market inefficiencies and external benefits and costs.

That is not easy, and as we have found out with the failure of the savings and loan industry in the United States in the 1980s and Fannie Mae and Freddie Mac more recently, guarantees can have perverse and costly incentives, which make the housing policy case for guarantees a weak one. This article focuses on the basic principles supporting the use of guarantees to increase housing affordability. It does not analyse particular institutional setups. For a survey that deals with the wider institutional background, see Quigley's 2006 article in the *Federal Reserve Bank of St. Louis Review*.

If financial markets were perfect, or close to it, and transfer payments were easy to make, there would be no economic justification for the government to have much of a role in financing housing, and certainly no need to provide guarantees to get people into good housing. Anything that needed to be done could be done with housing vouchers or direct provision of housing services, letting the financing take care of itself by appropriate risk-based pricing. Guarantees can make sense outside of housing policy – deposit insurance, for example, as a way of stabilising financial markets – and they can be justified in a 'second best' sense as a way of promoting housing and homeownership when transfer payments are hard to make or there are inefficiencies in financing housing.

Individual guarantees are generally granted by government-backed agencies, while government extends guarantees to these agencies. That is the case with FHA insured loans. In other cases, such as with Fannie Mae and Freddie Mac and banks, guarantees are made directly to institutions. Because they are more common, the focus here is on institutional rather than individual guarantees.

Guarantees have two principal effects:

1. If not fully priced, they lower the cost of housing and alter resource allocation, redirecting investment into housing and away from other uses. When targeted, they promote housing for particular classes of households. This is 'good' to the extent that housing is under produced, which is a hard case to make, or when targeting is important, for instance, to encourage homeownership.
2. They help prevent financial panics by removing the motivation for 'bank runs'. However, if they are not well regulated, they lower the cost of risk-taking and promote excessive risk-taking.

The first effect is most closely associated with access to housing; the second is indirectly associated with it but also has broad macro effects. Both have potential costs in terms of misallocated resources and 'bailout' costs when institutions getting the guarantees fail. These two costs are related; the bailout costs typically go along with misallocated resources, but even without misallocation bailout costs are disruptive and unpopular. In the United States, a bailout of the savings and loans insurance fund ultimately costs taxpayers around $150 billion, and more recently the bailouts of Fannie Mae and Freddie Mac will cost a comparable amount (probably bigger in dollars and smaller relative to gross domestic product). In both cases, these represented costly transfer payments.

A key question in evaluating the role of guarantees is whether they can be expected to matter much. The point of departure on this is the Modigliani–Miller (MM) irrelevance theorem whose derivation is explained in their seminal 1958 article published in the *American Economic Review*. Briefly, the theorem is that under a set of assumptions, which mainly involve perfectly competitive markets, no transaction costs, and widely agreed on information, the liability structure of the firm is irrelevant in the sense that changing the way the firm finances its assets will not affect its total cost of funds, where that total includes the costs of hedging different risks for different strategies. This is because different liability strategies are simply different ways of rearranging the same cash flows from the firm's assets, and in a well-informed, competitive market competition and arbitrage will assure that all structures are priced so that none has an overall advantage; the sum of the parts will equal the whole.

Taken literally, the theorem, applied to mortgage markets, implies that, while there are lots of possible institutional structures for funding mortgages and lots of liability structures within the institutional structures, which institutions and structures are chosen does not affect mortgage rates. A softer version is that the advantages of different structures are likely to be small; if there are elastic supply curves, then small advantages of one source of funding (e.g., some sort of subsidy or slightly lower transaction costs) can have big effects on how the financing is done (who has the biggest market share), but small effects on interest rates on the loans and subsequent resource allocation.

The 'MM' theorem is one of those ideas that seem obvious, but, of course, it is wrong (markets are not perfect; e.g., some supply curves, in the short run at least, are not flat, although they are often rather elastic; asymmetric information is often the rule rather than the exception; and transaction costs matter). But the theorem is not a bad place to start. Regarding guarantees, it should remind us that there is more than one way to lower housing costs, but it also opens the door to guarantees to the extent that they help solve problems like asymmetric information by providing standardised information. For present purposes, the central point is that the size of the subsidy and incentive structure conveyed with a guarantee are more important than the particular institutional structure that employs it.

Rationales for Guarantees

The three central rationales for public intervention in housing finance are incomplete markets, externalities, and distributional concerns.

Incomplete Housing Finance Markets

There are a number of potentially incomplete markets in the provision of housing finance. For instance, because of concern with credit risk and information problems, lenders often ration mortgage credit. They do this mainly in two ways: first, they limit access to credit to those able to afford to make significant down payments, and second, they limit eligibility for loans to those able to pay less than a specific share of their income for repayments. The first type of constraint rations those households without savings for homeownership. The second rations out those households who have enough savings for the down payment but cannot satisfy the payment-to-income constraints lenders use to screen quality borrowers. An extensive literature indicates that in the United States and United Kingdom the first constraint is more binding.

The problem with rationing to determine loan eligibility arises because of lenders' reluctance to lend against borrowers' future income, or, alternatively, borrowers' inability to pledge their human capital. However, the down payment constraint has been relatively unimportant in the United States over the past decade as private lenders and insurers have been willing to accept the risk of low down payment loans. As policy the rationale has to be that particular groups, like low-income borrowers, need government support in this area.

Externalities

Housing has positive externalities in that good housing can have positive effects on neighbouring houses and access to loans to finance improvements can be important in promoting these externalities. An inability to finance basic improvements has often meant that investments in many slum neighbourhoods are not undertaken. A result is that in some cases private returns to housing are less than social returns, so that some subsidy can be justified.

Homeownership in particular

The existence and size of external social benefits from homeownership have been studied more intensively of late, and there is an emerging consensus that homeownership causes changes in people's behaviour that have positive externalities (see article Home Ownership: Economic Benefits). The more controversial question is whether or not guarantees are particularly good at providing the subsidy. Currently, the main vehicle for subsidising homeownership in the United States is the tax system. While the tax system can deliver large subsidies, it is inefficient if the goal is to promote homeownership among lower-income groups because the subsidy goes disproportionately to high-income, high-tax-bracket owners (see article Access and Affordability: Homeowner Taxation). Guarantee subsidies work by lowering mortgage rates so the impact on repayments is independent of marginal tax rates and therefore have a bigger effect on lower-tax-bracket homeowners.

Distributional Concerns

Housing has been used to correct income distribution concerns. Indeed, in a recently published book Rajan (2010) suggests that using housing policy as a way of solving income distribution policies was an important factor in the recent financial crunch. One does not have to go that far to see the importance of distributional concerns in US mortgage market policy. For instance, the Community Reinvestment Act has tried to influence bank lending towards 'underserved' areas and groups. Similar goals for lending to low-income and related groups have been a part of Fannie Mae and Freddie Mac's regulatory structure for some time. The appeal is that housing finance can be targeted on low-income groups but at the expense of a regulatory cost burden for financial institutions. Clearly, this is a sloppy way of doing the job, but it is likely to at least initially be off budget, and relatively easy to implement. It is clearly a second best relative to, say, housing vouchers (see article Access and Affordability: Housing Vouchers).

Behaviour: Options and Profits

As Merton demonstrated in his 1977 *Journal of Banking and Finance* article, guarantees have many of the characteristics of financial options in that the owners of guarantees get the upside from risk-taking but have limited liability on the downside. If a guarantee is not priced properly, then recipients get downside protection at below cost, essentially an underpriced insurance policy. This provides incentives to take on risk to maximise upside returns without having to worry about downside losses. Indeed, absent those other factors, like reputation or franchise value, maximising wealth will tend to involve maximising the value of the guarantee, which in turn means maximising risk. As a result, the subsidy that comes with guarantees changes incentives. Because risk-taking is hard to observe and control, the subsidy is hard to control.

A clear example of this was the savings and loans in the 1980s that took on lots of risks and ended up costing taxpayers a lot and redirected resources in clearly inefficient ways. More recently, Fannie Mae and Freddie Mac have ended up with a lot of risky assets, which will probably cost taxpayers well over a hundred billion dollars.

On the other hand, neither banks nor Fannie Mae and Freddie Mac were a source of systemic risk because the guarantees kept the values of their deposits or debt from falling, and diminished incentives to sell off or withdraw funding. That is the paradox of guarantees. They make it easier to take on risk, but they also limit systemic risk and bank runs. It is hard to have one without the other. In the Great Recession, systemic risk happened mainly in the private 'shadow banking' system, which was not guaranteed, but which still took on excessive risk and saw something akin to bank runs as investors lost confidence in that system's liabilities.

Policy

It is hard to justify guarantees on housing policy grounds alone. All of the above can be accomplished by taxes and subsidies, and without the perverse behavioural outcomes that guarantees can provide.

Guarantees may have important roles in financial systems that are prone to bank runs. The role of guarantees extends beyond housing; although one can argue that because of housing's importance, keeping housing finance markets open is especially important, not just for its macroeconomic effect but also because of its role in promoting housing (see article Housing and the Macroeconomy).

So there is a justification for guarantees, but it is a tricky one: splicing together the role of guarantees with externalities on the grounds that the two are complements. Given that guarantees are likely to persist, a remaining issue is control over the effective subsidy they deliver and the consequences for risk-taking. If guarantees are to be used, they need to be set up in a way that puts the government as far down the risk queue as possible.

Capital provides a cushion that protects debt holders and guarantors, and it provides incentives to control risk because more investor money is at stake. Clearly, minimum capital standards have been too low for all sorts of financial institutions, particularly those with guarantees. However, simply raising them allows institutions to increase risk subject to minimum levels as a constraint.

Regulators need more flexibility to raise and lower capital levels and to require higher levels of capital as the economy changes and as new business lines are introduced. Stress tests have been used with mixed success, as in the case of Fannie Mae and Freddie Mac. But something like them is necessary if rules are to be risk based.

Less costly, debt-like, forms of capital should be considered. A promising form is subordinated debt that can be converted into stock if stock price falls below some preset level. This creates a class of bond holders that cannot be bailed out and who will have an ongoing interest in controlling risk. This debt can be ahead of guaranteed debt in the risk queue. A good long-run structure is to have a first-tier equity capital requirement similar to what we have now, though better attuned to risk, for instance, at 5–10% of assets, then require that convertible bonds be the next 5 or 10% of banks' liabilities. Between the two, banks would have 10–20% in capital reserves in times of stress. Behind this can indeed be guaranteed debt or deposits that will attract investors or depositors at low rates while maintaining incentives to control risk.

See also: Access and Affordability: Homeowner Taxation; Access and Affordability: Housing Vouchers; Government Mortgage Guarantee Institutions; Home Ownership: Economic Benefits; Housing and the Macroeconomy; Housing Finance: Deposit Guarantees.

References

Merton R (1977) An analytic derivation of the cost of deposit insurance and loan guarantees. *Journal of Banking and Finance* 1: 3–11.

Modigliani F and Miller MH (1958) The cost of capital, corporation finance and the theory of investment. *American Economic Review* 48(3): 261–297.

Quigley JM (2006) Federal credit and insurance programs: Housing. *Federal Reserve Bank of St. Louis* 88(4): 281–309.

Rajan R (2010) *Fault Lines*. Princeton, NJ: Princeton University Press.

Further Reading

Black F and Scholes M (1973) The pricing of options and corporate liabilities. *Journal of Political Economy* 81(3): 637–654.

Green RK and White MJ (1997) Measuring the benefits of homeowning: Effects on children. *Journal of Urban Economics* 41(3): 441–461.

Haurin DR, Pacel TL, and Haurin RJ (2002) Does homeownership affect child outcomes? *Real Estate Economics* 30(4): 635–666.

Access and Affordability: Rent Regulation

M Haffner, M Elsinga, and J Hoekstra, Delft University of Technology, Delft, The Netherlands

© 2012 Elsevier Ltd. All rights reserved.

Glossary

First-generation rent regulation Strict rent regulation that often freezes all private rental sector rents. At best, it allows limited yearly rent increases that are lower than the inflation rate.

Imperfectly competitive markets Markets that are not perfectly competitive; for example, there may be asymmetric information between suppliers and consumers. Another example is negative externalities (undesired incidental effects) of decisions that are not reflected in prices.

Private renting Dwellings that are owned by private individuals or firms with a profit objective and that presently are not subsidised with bricks and mortar subsidies (possible subsidisation via the tax system is disregarded in this definition).

Rent control Policy to restrict rent setting and rent increases of private sector dwellings.

Rent regulation See rent control; used interchangeably with rent control.

Second-generation rent regulation Rent control that is typically more tailor-made than first-generation rent regulation: it allows for controlled rent increases; it usually differs between new and existing contracts; and it is often embedded in an additional set of regulations with regard to tenant security, housing quality, conversion, home improvement and maintenance, and landlord–tenant relations.

Tenancy rent control Rent regulation for existing rental contracts.

Welfare economics The field of economics that studies the functioning of the welfare state and the appraisal of alternative resource allocations.

Introduction

When rental dwellings are scarce in the housing market, a popular measure to prevent rents from increasing and dwellings from becoming too expensive used to be and sometimes still is rent control, also called rent regulation. Rent control restricts the rent of a (private) rental dwelling. It allows sitting tenants to stay where they are for as long as the contract lasts without a large increase in housing costs, and it may make private renting more affordable for new tenants. Rent regulation typically provokes a lot of discussion among social scientists and policy-makers. Critics of rent control – including many economists – see controls as a source of inefficiency that impose costs on landlords and society that outweigh the benefits for tenants. On the other hand, proponents of rent control argue that market failures in the rental housing market require corrective forms of government intervention that include some form of rent regulation and security of tenure provisions in the sense of some security of contract (see article Security of Tenure Legislation in Private Rental Housing).

In the first part of this article, the disadvantages and advantages of rent regulation are outlined in more detail. This is followed by a brief discussion of the history of rent regulation. We observe that in most countries, the rigid first-generation rent control systems of the postwar years have been gradually replaced by more moderate and sophisticated forms of rent regulation: second-generation rent control. In the second part of the article, the possible reasons for second-generation rent control are described and evaluated from the perspective of welfare economics. Various design options for second-generation rent control are then discussed.

Disadvantages and Advantages of Rent Regulation

Most economists would argue that rent regulation has many negative and market-distorting side effects. Standard economic analysis shows that rent regulation inevitably leads to lower returns for landlords because they cannot charge the market price for their property. This dissuades investors from supplying rental property and may result in undermaintenance of existing property, eventually leading to falling property values and degradation of neighbourhoods. Rent regulation may also cause rental housing shortages, because landlords cut back their supply and below-market rents raise the demand for rental housing. Thus, while rent regulation may improve the affordability of private rental dwellings for existing tenants, rental housing could become less accessible for new tenants who must search for longer periods before finding suitable housing opportunities. There may also be costs to society if existing tenants are unwilling to give up their affordable rent-controlled housing. This reduces residential and labour market mobility, with negative effects on efficiency and economic development. In short, critics argue that rent controls benefit existing tenants ('insiders') at the expense of landlords, society as a whole, and possibly also new tenants ('outsiders'). They also believe that the costs of rent regulation are far larger than the benefits, thus making the 'cure worse than the disease'. According to critics, society is served best by a private rental market in which rents are freely determined by the forces of supply and demand.

On the other hand, advocates of rent regulation argue that deregulated rental housing markets are vulnerable to market failures (imperfect competition, information asymmetry; see below) that give landlords a comparative advantage over tenants. They claim that some form of rent regulation will establish a better balance between the interests of landlords and tenants. Some proponents of rent regulation also stress the perceived social benefits of rent control; it may reduce spatial segregation and promote the social integration of disadvantaged tenants.

Empirical research has not yet been able to resolve the controversy between critics and advocates of rent regulation. Although most empirical studies invariably investigate the disadvantages of these kinds of interventions, they typically find that the impacts of rent regulation vary greatly between countries and regions, and are therefore specific to housing market situations. Moreover, it should be noted that the potential effects of rent regulation on social integration and spatial segregation are frequently ignored in the empirical models used to estimate the impacts of rent regulation.

Despite sustained criticism from academics and especially economists, many policy-makers remain favourably disposed towards rent controls. This is illustrated by the fact that many jurisdictions still apply rent controls, especially so in Europe. However, rent regulation has generally become more lenient over time.

First- and Second-Generation Rent Regulation

In the literature on rent regulation, a distinction is often made between first- and second-generation rent regulation. First-generation rent regulation generally applies a rent freeze to all private rental dwellings. At best, it allows limited yearly rent increases that are lower than the inflation rate. In the United States, first-generation rent regulations were prominent during the Second World War and for some years thereafter. The war led to massive migration of industrial workers and, after the war had ended, returning soldiers. Rent freezes were imposed to ensure access to affordable rental housing and prevent profiteering. However, a housing construction boom eased shortages, and so these rent freezes were abandoned in most jurisdictions by the late 1940s or early 1950s.

In many European countries, first-generation rent regulation started in the interwar period and continued long after the Second World War ended; indeed, in some countries, they persisted into the 1980s. In a few European countries, France and Portugal for instance, a part of the older private rental stock is still subject to first-generation rent regulation. Against a background of housing shortages, rent regulation was considered necessary to reduce the housing cost burden of the working and middle classes, and also to help curb wage and price inflation. First-generation rent regulation has had huge effects on the quality and quantity of housing in the European private rental sector. Investment in new private rental dwellings dried up, renovation and maintenance were neglected, and many landlords sold their dwelling as soon as they had the opportunity. The private rental sector declined while the social rental sector and the owner-occupied sector gained market share.

Since the 1970s, 'hard' first-generation rent controls have been gradually replaced by the 'softer' so-called second-generation rent regulation. Second-generation rent control is typically more sophisticated and tailor-made than first-generation rent regulation: it allows for controlled rent increases, it usually differs between new and existing contracts, and it is often embedded in an additional set of regulations with regard to tenant security (especially length of contract), housing quality, conversion, home improvement, maintenance, and landlord–tenant relations.

Welfare Economics Rationales for Government Intervention

The apparent popularity of second-generation rent controls suggests that some policy-makers are convinced that the benefits of regulation outweigh the costs. Welfare economics is one way of approaching the question of what these benefits and costs might be, and why intervention in the form of rent regulation could be justified. From the perspective of welfare economics, there are four main reasons for government intervention in welfare states, as presented by the liberal economist Barr in his influential (2004) book *The Economics of the Welfare State*. The first is about achieving economic efficiency in the sense that no-one's utility can be improved without a reduction in the utility of someone else. According to welfare economics, this is the most important reason for intervening in a market; intervention is justified if economic efficiency is improved. Efficiency has different dimensions, but all of them are about minimising distortions to the allocation of resources in markets, and avoiding cost explosions due to poorly organised and managed welfare-state institutions. It may also be about the efficient design of the public funding and benefits of institutions in order to minimise the adverse effects on employment. In all these cases, however, it must be recognised that government intervention is never without cost; indeed, government failure may be the cause of inefficiency. A careful balance of market- and government-caused inefficiencies will be a useful exercise.

If a market operates efficiently, society's total welfare will be maximised. The resulting distribution of welfare, however, may not be one that society or politicians are comfortable with. The distribution of income may be considered 'unfair'. If that is the case, government intervention could improve social equality between citizens by redistributing welfare, which represents a second rationale for intervention. Vertical redistribution is about the redistribution of income or consumption from higher- to lower-income households. Horizontal redistribution seeks to ensure equal access to certain goods and services and equality of opportunity. Equality of opportunity is not easy to put into practice. It could be about equality across households with respect to total cash and in kind income; or it could be about equality across households with respect to access to certain goods or services (education, for example); or it could be the price that households are charged or the public expenditure that is needed for the provision of that good or service. For each of these different concepts of equality of opportunity, the outcomes will vary; a more equal distribution of income may not deliver the same opportunities for households as public expenditure that guarantees equal provision of a good or service.

As a third goal, the welfare state could aim not only for redistributing income, but more broadly for improving the living standards of citizens. This can be achieved by fighting poverty in the sense that a minimum standard of living is available to all. It could also be about providing economic security by not allowing anyone to be faced with a large and sudden drop in living standards (insurance), or by allowing the smoothing of income of households to take place across time (e.g., with the help of a state pension).

Next to these more standard economic goals, welfare states can also help to realise broader social objectives, for example, benefit programmes that facilitate social integration. Preserving the social dignity of households (no stigmatisation) and fostering social solidarity regardless of the socioeconomic status of the recipient are important aims here.

Each of these goals of government intervention – efficiency, income redistribution, and broader social objectives – may be considered a rationale for rent regulation. It goes without saying that for any of these rationales, the argument could also be that disadvantages for tenants are not 'big enough' to warrant intervention or that tenants will be able to help themselves, by negotiating insurance contracts against rent increases, for instance (see below). Decisions on whether rent control is desirable always have a strong subjective component, since the costs and benefits of such interventions are hard to measure and may be weighted differently by different people. What the rationales for intervention could be – if it is decided that government intervention delivers more benefits than costs – will be discussed next.

Rationales for Rent Controls Based on Reasons of Efficiency

Perfect information, perfect competition, complete markets, and no market failures (such as negative externalities) ensure economic efficiency. If these criteria are not met, the idea is that government can improve economic efficiency by 'corrective' interventions that include regulation. Breaches of these criteria are likely in the private rental market.

Landlord information about tenants and tenant information about rental housing opportunities are inevitably imperfect. In both cases, rent regulation can play a role by preventing landlords from setting rents too high.

Information asymmetry will exist, when the dwelling stock is heterogeneous, and if the landlord has a greater knowledge of dwelling quality than tenants. Information advantages can then be opportunistically exploited by landlords who can make exaggerated statements about quality to justify higher rents, and they have the added advantage of market power, given that the transaction costs of moving are high, particularly if there is a lack of affordable alternatives. The information asymmetry can work in the other direction. A landlord does not know whether a tenant will take care of their house, or whether the tenant will meet future rent payments. These risks may encourage landlords to charge higher rents, particularly in neighbourhoods where such risks are perceived to be high.

The criterion of perfect competition is also unlikely to be met in the rental market. If a tenant becomes attached to his or her home, the landlord acquires monopolistic power that can be exploited by raising the rent. Tenants must incur high financial and emotional costs because they have to move if they are to avoid rent increases, and these costs give landlords market power. In his seminal article,

Arnott (1995) describes rental markets as imperfectly competitive. Last but not least, the criterion of complete markets needs to be considered in the rental market. Rental markets are arguably incomplete in the sense that there is no insurance available for cover against unanticipated and sharp rises in rent. Government may then consider introducing rent regulation to provide this insurance.

In summary, welfare economics suggests a rationale for rent regulation if markets are inefficient. It will be introduced by governments who believe that controls will protect tenants disadvantaged by the market power given to landlords as a result of market failures such as asymmetric information and imperfect competition.

Rationales for Rent Controls Based on Reasons of Income Redistribution

An unregulated private rental housing market can impose unreasonable housing cost burdens on the poor. As housing affordability is a key issue in housing policy debates in most parts of the world, rent controls might be used to redistribute (vertically) from landlords who in this scenario have high incomes to tenants who generally have low incomes. However, much of the literature shows that rent control is an ineffective instrument to improve affordability because it is invariably poorly targeted in comparison to other instruments. Olson (1972: 1096) states, "There is nothing approaching equal treatment of equals among the beneficiaries of rent control. In this sense, rent control is a very poorly focused redistribution device."

Given the poor targeting of rent regulation, housing allowances or vouchers (see articles Access and Affordability: Housing Allowances, and Access and Affordability: Housing Vouchers) have become more important in many countries as a policy instrument geared to improving housing affordability. Eligibility for these personal subsidies is typically restricted to lower-income groups, and they are therefore considered a more efficient and effective policy instrument than rent control. On the other hand, critics point out that personal subsidies of this kind can push up house prices and rents, and add to government expenditures. Rent controls can appeal to governments because subsidies are 'hidden', and they are perceived to have no inflationary impact.

The horizontal equity argument for rent controls is that an inefficient private rental market (see above) pushes up the housing costs of tenants relative to those of owner-occupiers. Rent controls help to equalise housing costs across tenures. If rent control is introduced because of market inefficiencies, this could be a side effect. Whether rent control can equalise costs across tenures is open to question because economic theory suggests that market forces will ensure that the present value of future rent income equals house price.

Rationales for Rent Controls Based on Other Social Reasons

The housing literature also emphasises how rent control can be motivated by concerns about social inclusion and social segregation. These reasons for rent regulation have been discussed in the social sciences literature, but are often neglected by economists, possibly because there is little evidence of their significance.

An aim of social policy can be that everybody should be able to afford to rent a dwelling in the more popular neighbourhoods. If all areas are accessible for the lowest-income groups, there is less chance that these groups will concentrate in segregated areas and become socially excluded with all the social and economic problems associated with exclusion.

Rent control prompted by social aims was more popular in the past; these days, other policy instruments are considered more effective because they are better targeted than rent control and can be used to encourage upward residential mobility. Housing allowances or vouchers are an alternative that can be used to encourage lower-income households to move into more popular neighbourhoods (see article Mobility Programmes for Disadvantaged Populations: The Moving to Opportunity Programme). Another policy option may be regulation of new construction that requires housebuilders to build both cheap and expensive dwellings in the same neighbourhood or housing project (see article Inclusionary Zoning to Support Affordable Housing).

A Typology of Second-Generation Rent Regulation

Second-generation rent regulation can take many forms. However, following Lind (2001), two criteria are crucial for characterising this type of rent regulation:

1. The type of contracts that are subject to regulation: existing or new rental contracts?
2. The basis for rent regulation: cost price based or market based?

Rent regulation that is only applied to existing rental contracts is also termed tenancy rent control. This form of rent regulation can be cost price based or market based. In cost price-based rent regulation, landlords may raise the rents in line with a rise in their costs (maintenance costs, management costs, etc.), and a

Table 1 Typology of rent regulation

	Cost price or quality based	Market based
Existing contracts	1	2
New contracts	3	4

return (capped) for the landlords may also be taken into account when calculating these costs. In practice, this usually means that the regulated annual rent increase may be no higher than the increase in a price index, such as, for example, the consumer price index. Cost price-based rent regulation for existing contracts (type 1 in **Table 1**) is now the most commonly used form of rent regulation.

The yearly permitted rent increases can also be based on market developments (type 2). In that case, one needs an indicator that measures these market developments. So-called reference dwellings are often used to calculate such an indicator. Reference dwellings can be defined as private rental dwellings of similar quality and characteristics as the dwelling whose rent increase needs to be determined. Germany is the best-known example of a country with this type of rent regulation system. In Ireland, market rent is also legally defined in relation to dwellings with similar characteristics.

Rent control (either cost price based or market based) is only effective if it is accompanied by strong tenant protection: indefinite or longer-term rental contracts, with the legitimate eviction of tenants allowed for only a limited number of reasons. The security of tenure offered by such protection prevents landlords from replacing sitting tenants by households that are willing to pay higher rents. Rent regulation for new contracts is now less common than rent regulation for existing contracts. Many countries have deregulated new rental contracts, but continue to apply rent controls with respect to the rents of existing contracts. Nevertheless, there are still some jurisdictions in which the rents of new contracts in the private rental sector are regulated as well. This regulation can be based on historic costs, or alternatively, on the quality of the dwelling (type 3). In the Netherlands, for example, the maximum permitted rent in the regulated private rental sector (about 85% of the private rental sector) is dependent on quality as assessed by a points rating of dwelling quality.

Finally, the rent of new contracts may be regulated on a market basis (type 4). This means that the rents of new rental contracts may not exceed current market rents. Reference dwellings are commonly used to apply this type of rent regulation, but it may also be enforced by prohibiting above-market (exploitative) rents, for example, through the penal code (e.g., England, Germany).

Conclusion

First-generation rent control was introduced in many countries as a way to protect the working-class and middle-class households in periods of housing scarcity. These first-generation rent controls have been heavily criticised on the grounds that they cause inefficiency. However, this type of rent control is often introduced to promote social equality and prevent segregation. These arguments are key ones for advocates of first-generation rent control systems.

More recently, discussion has focused on second-generation rent controls, often referred to as tenancy rent control that aims to curb adverse impacts on housing market efficiency. From a welfare economics perspective, rent controls can be interpreted as a corrective form of government intervention to overcome problems of asymmetric information and monopolistic power. However, even the more moderate second-generation rent controls are criticised, reflecting empirical evidence that often shows the costs of rent control for landlords to be higher than the benefits to tenants.

There is also a growing reliance on housing vouchers and housing allowances to address issues of housing affordability, accessibility, and segregation. Critics of rent control typically regard these instruments as more efficient and more effective in achieving housing policy goals.

Despite the widespread doubts about both first-generation and second-generation rent controls, rent regulation continues in many places and many forms. In practice, debate does not focus on reasons for introducing rent control but on whether or not to abolish rent control. The discussion is often heated and complicated because many (political) interests are involved. But the longevity of rent regulation might in the end be due to its use as an instrument that improves housing affordability without being a financial burden on the national budget.

See also: Access and Affordability: Housing Allowances; Access and Affordability: Housing Vouchers; Inclusionary Zoning to Support Affordable Housing; Mobility Programmes for Disadvantaged Populations: The Moving to Opportunity Programme; Security of Tenure Legislation in Private Rental Housing.

References

Arnott R (1995) Time for revisionism on rent control? *Journal of Economic Perspectives* 9: 99–120.

Barr N (2004) *The Economics of the Welfare State*, 4th edn. New York: Oxford University Press.

Lind H (2001) Rent regulation: A conceptual and comparative analysis. *European Journal of Housing Policy* 1: 41–57.

Olson EO (1972) An econometric analysis of rent control. *Journal of Political Economy* 80: 1081–1100.

Further Reading

Arnott R (2003) Tenancy rent control. *Swedish Economic Policy Review* 10: 89–121.

Basu K and Emerson PM (2000) The economics of tenancy rent control. *The Economic Journal* 110: 939–962.

Fallis G (1988) Rent control: The citizen, the market, and the state. *Journal of Real Estate Finance and Economics* 1: 309–320.

Frankena M (1975) Alternative models of rent control. *Urban Studies* 12: 303–308.

Glaeser EL (2003) Does rent control reduce segregation? *Swedish Economic Policy Review* 10: 179–202.

Haffner M, Elsinga M, and Hoekstra J (2008) Rent regulation. The balance between private landlords and tenants in six European countries. *European Journal of Housing Policy* 8: 217–233.

Haffner M, Hoekstra J, Oxley M, and van der Heijden H (2009) *Bridging the Gap between Market and Social Rented Housing in Six European Countries*. Amsterdam: IOS Press BV.

Hubert F (2003) Rent control: Academic analysis and public sentiment. *Swedish Economic Policy Review* 10: 61–81.

Jenkins B (2009) Rent control: Do economists agree? *A Journal of the American Institute for Economic Research* 6: 73–112.

Turner B and Malpezzi S (2003) A review of empirical evidence on the costs and benefits of rent control. *Swedish Economic Policy Review* 10: 11–56.

Actor–Network Theory

R Dankert, Delft University of Technology, Delft, The Netherlands

© 2012 Elsevier Ltd. All rights reserved.

Glossary

Actant–network Two or more actants that are connected and together form a new actant.
Actants Everything that accomplishes or undergoes an act. An actant can be a human, animal, object, or concept.
Agency The power of an actant to change other actants.
Translation The work through which actants are changed and displaced in order to make or break a connection with other actants.

Introduction

Actor–network theory (ANT) is used in science and technology studies. It was developed in the 1980s by Bruno Latour, Michel Callon, and John Law. Since the 1980s, ANT has been used in multiple variations. Although ANT carries 'theory' in its name, it is better looked at as a method for doing research. Still ANT does carry some substantive elements in it that cannot be neglected when doing ANT-driven research.

In short, ANT can be defined as a research method with a focus on the connections between both human and non-human entities. It describes how these connections lead to the creation of new entities that do not necessarily practice the sum of characteristics of the constituent entities. This can be compared to what happens if a chemist puts together two chemicals. Another example of such fusion of entities into another entity is the gunman example that was introduced by Latour in *Pandora's Hope*. Here, it is stated that a man and a gun can form a new entity when they are connected in a third entity: the gunman. In spite of what has been argued by the American pro-gun lobby, a man cannot shoot someone all by himself. However, it cannot be said either that the gun is the cause of all problems. Guns that shoot someone all by themselves are quit rare. The connection that ANT wants researcher to focus on is the connection that brings the man and the gun together, and thus creates a gunman. A gunman is different from both a man and a gun in the sense that a gunman is able to shoot someone whereas both the man and the gun cannot do this alone. This example also shows that ANT-driven research can come up with unexpected conclusions. From this example we could conclude that war is caused by neither man nor guns. It is the connection between the two entities that we have to blame for all the cruel incidents that happen with it every day. If we were able to break down the connections between men and guns the existence of both man and guns would not be a problem anymore.

The focus on connections shows ANT is a constructivist theory. Although the word actor suggests that the method is about networks of people, this is not the case. As we have seen from the example of the gunman, an actor can also be non-human. In this case, the actor gun is part of the actor-network gunman. As we shall see in the next section of this article, the word actant would therefore be more appropriate.

During fieldwork, connections between humans and non-humans can be traced. Only traceable connections from the empirical data will be part of the description that is made by the ANT researcher. This description reveals the connections that lead to the creation of a certain entity. For instance, a gunman. ANT also wants to focus on how connections were established. This can only be revealed through fieldwork, because it can be done differently every single time.

For ANT, existence is first, essence is second. The gunman from our example only is a gunman after the constituent elements were connected. Therefore, ANT does not search for essences, but rather for the connecting and reconnecting of entities that shape and reshape the essences of a certain entity. Understanding what this really means requires us to first go into the way ANT understands the concept of truth. In philosophy, there is a divide between modernist and postmodernist thinking about the definition of truth. ANT rejects both modernist and postmodernist thinking. Modernist philosophers believe that truth is something that is out there independent from humans. It only has to be discovered by scientists. Postmodernist philosophers do not believe in the concept of truth at all, or they think that every individual can create his own truth. For ANT, truth should be understood as a state of affairs that cannot be denied in a practical sense. In modern Western societies, for example, the statement that people do not need houses would thus be regarded as not true. For ANT, truth does exist, but it can change over time. That is, essences can change. When we keep in mind this conception of truth, it is logical that ANT does not want to focus on truth or essences themselves. Rather focus should be on the forces that shape and reshape the true essences the researcher faces when doing fieldwork.

In the following section we will first go into some basic terms of ANT. After that the article will show how ANT can be done in practice. Also some examples will be given. The article will conclude with some consideration on when ANT should be used, and when not.

Basics of ANT

In this section, I will introduce the most important terms the ANT works with. First, I will go into the formation of sociotechnical groups of entities. Then, this paragraph will go into actants with agency. The difference between objects and things, that is central to ANT, will be discussed. After that, I will go into the notion of actor–networks and the translations by which these actor–networks are made and remade.

Group Formation

Research in housing often starts with groups: the department, the homeowners, the housing association, and so on. Even a thing like a home could be regarded as a group of other entities. As we have seen already, the same is true for the gunman. These are all groups of human and non-human entities such as employees, building materials, and computers. These groups are mostly taken for granted. Following constructivism, in ANT these groups are to be deconstructed in order to see what is going on inside of them. Then it becomes clear that every single entity is in fact a group of other entities. For example, when we would unravel the group 'home', we would see a lot of building materials, paperworks, and efforts of builders, architects, and others.

For ANT, the point is that groups are not stable. They are, or at least can be, remade over and over again. However, if you stop making and remaking groups, you stop having groups. All kinds of groups, whether a department or a home, need to be remade every single day in order to keep alive. When the employees do not go to work anymore, the department does not exist anymore. When the walls of a house fall down, the house does not exist anymore. ANT-driven research wants to show the dynamics of the making and remaking of groups. Therefore, every now and then we have to wonder how groups have been formed by the actors involved.

Actants with Agency

Above, we have used the word actor. Actors form groups that ANT calls actor–networks. However, although it is in its name, ANT does not use the word actor in its regular meaning. The word actant would be more appropriate. An actant is that which accomplishes or undergoes an act. They differ from actors because an actant can not only be a human, but also an animal, object or concept that accomplishes or undergoes an act. Through the use of the word actant, humans, animals, objects, and concepts are treated equally in an analytical sense. ANT does not deny that there can be huge differences between different actants. However, if this is the case, the researcher should find evidence for this during the fieldwork.

ANT agrees on mainstream sociology when it states that actors have the power to change other actors. This power is called agency. When we act we always interact with others. As John Law has stated: 'interaction is all that there is'. During these interactions we change other actants. At the same time, however, we are being changed by other actants. ANT points out that not only humans but also non-human entities are influencing us constantly. Some people 'have to' watch when a television screen in their surrounding is turned on, and a computer that crashes from time to time can make you really desperate. On the other hand, people influence televisions by turning them off. And the system administrator can help to fix a computer. For buildings this also counts. Humans first shape buildings and then are being shaped by the same buildings. For example, through the sick building syndrome, buildings practice agency to influence humans.

The Difference between Objects and Things

The fact that ANT does not make an analytical distinction between humans and non-humans is sometimes regarded as weird or even as faulty. Sometimes these critics are bases on an incorrect view of how ANT deals with humans and non-humans. The differences between humans and non-humans are not neglected, but have no a priori relevance for ANT-driven studies. If we look into the argument in more detail, we will see that it is possible to make this statement. Therefore, we have to distinguish between objects and things. To most people an object is something that is stable. It does not change. Examples are a chair or a computer. However, 'things' is a more abstract term. It can also point at something that is not as stable as an object in the traditional definition. ANT does see objects as things that are the temporary result of a set of connections. As long as these connections hold, the object has the same essence. It is not changed by others, and it does not change others either.

Networks

By using the word actant, we have shifted the focus a little towards the actions rather that the entity that is the source of this action. The word network then focuses on the outcomes of these actions. When two or more actants are connected, they form an actant–network. For ANT, a network is always an actant–network. In a sense actant–network is similar to actant. If we zoom out till we cannot see the connections of an actant–network anymore, the actant–network will appear as one actant. The other way around: if we zoom in on any actant, we will be able to trace connections and thus see the actant–network. For example, if we watch a movie on the television, it appears to us as one actant. However, if the television breaks down and we have to open it, only then we see that it is also an actant–network that consists of a lot of materials and work of assembling. Actant–networks are thus constructed and reconstructed through interaction between actants. As long as the actants keep interacting the actant–network will look stable from the outside. The connections between their constituting actants will hold. However, if the interaction ends, the actant–network will break down. For ANT, no network is stable without the ongoing interactions between actants.

Translation

In the previous section, we have seen that interaction between actants is necessary to establish and hold the connections between them. In order to establish connections, actants have to be displaced and transformed in order to make them fit into an actant–network. The work that is necessary to displace and transform is called translation. For ANT, translation is understood as all the negotiations, intrigues, calculations, acts of persuasion, and violence through which an actant is changed. When actants have not been translated (or translate themselves), they are not part of the actant–network.

In the example of implementing housing management plans, thorough translation connections have to be made between visions of the alderman and the director of the housing association. And also connections between the rule of law and the floor plan. When translation is successful, the actants work together in order to change the actor–network from a plan on paper into a building of stone. However, if actants are not translated (i.e., displaced and transformed) there cannot be established an actant–network. In other words, if all actants stick to their original characteristics they will not be able to connect to each other in such a way that a new actant–network with other characteristics is created. Change can be present in many forms. When an architect changes his drawings, he has also become a different architect. And if the housing association agrees to a suggestion of the architect, the housing association has become a different constituent.

Immutable Mobiles

Interaction is like a flow: something flows from one actor–network to another. ANT-driven research wants to track these flows. To let something flow from one actant–network to another, it has to be put into a form. An example of this can be information. When we want to flow information from the desk of a researcher to the meeting of the management team at a company where important decisions are made, we have to put the information into a form that can be understood by the managers. Usually, scientists do so by writing a popular version of their reports. In that case, the report would function as an 'immutable mobile' as it is able to let the information flow from one actant–network to another.

Doing ANT

In the previous section, we have looked into the most important terms of the ANT method. When we actually want to do ANT-driven research, this knowledge is vital, but not enough. In this section, we go into the steps that have to be taken when doing ANT-driven research.

After the research question has been set, and ANT has been picked to be the research method, the first step is to choose a starting point. That is, to choose the actant from where the research departs. There is not much to guide this choice. For ANT, there is no best or worst choice. Theories and other presumptions are to be avoided at this stage in order to make sure that the full range of involved entities can be explored without the researcher being biased. So these cannot help either to choose the starting point. The only guide to choose the starting point is the theme, central question, and goal of the research. For example, in a research on the implementation of a policy, the policy document could be such a starting point.

Starting from the chosen actant, the research then begins by exploring and unravelling this actant and the human and non-human actants that relate to it. In this exploration, it is important to 'hear' the actants involved. This is usually done through interviews and the analysis of documents. When it is possible direct observations or diary keeping by the human actants involved could be added to these methods. In order to get the full picture, there are three requirements ANT-driven research should meet. In the first place, it should be acknowledged that ANT is a boundaryless and holistic approach. This means that context as such does not exist. The division between the direct surroundings of an actant and its context has to be overcome. Instead ANT creates a new divide between actants that leave traces and actants that do not leave traces. For ANT, only actants that leave traces really exist and are therefore part of the data. The second requirement of ANT is that the actants that leave traces should be regarded in the same way. For example, new regulations from the central government that affect a building project can be analysed in the same way as a group of tenants that have influence on a building project. Although their substance differs, they can be described through the same kind of vocabulary. The last requirement that has to be met during fieldwork is an emphasis on connections. It should be made clear how the regulation from the central government connects to a specific building project, and what the effect of this connection is. An example of such connection is an inspector from the government should give permission based on the regulations for a project.

After the fieldwork, a new phase starts. From the rich data that have been produced, it is hard to choose what is useful to the research and what is not. To do this the researcher must make clear what the goal of the research is. Is it to tell the story? Then almost all data could be used and there will be no concluding article. However, if the goal is to develop a model, to learn something from the research or to make recommendations, not all data will be useful. There has to be a selection based on the issues that the research wants to focus on. This focus should of course be introduced and substantiated. In these cases it also becomes important to go into the existing literature on the subject. Only then can the researcher show how ANT-driven results connect with the existing knowledge.

Examples of ANT-Driven Research

The use of ANT in housing research has been rather scarce. However, if we broaden the scope and also look into related fields, some interesting examples of ANT-driven research can be found.

An example that is close to organisation and institutional studies is the work of Barbara Czarniawska. Her research could also be of interest for researches on the institutions in housing and home. As Czarniawska points out, standard analysis on organisations begin with actors or organisations. However, following ANT, actors or organisations are not the sources, but the output of ongoing organising. For research on organisations this means that the employees have to be followed. That is, they have to be followed in a very literal sense over a period of some day or less literal through interviews or diary keeping over a longer period. In such research, the subject is approached through the eyes of the employees taken into the study.

In my own research on the implementation of housing management strategy, I take a measure from such strategy as the starting point to follow a project over a period of 10 years. Through multiple case studies at housing associations, it appears that a measure from their strategies changes over time. When everything goes according to the plan, a measure eventually will turn into a new or renovated building. Along the way measures change into floor plans, building permissions, and building materials. Because the measures that are followed in this research cannot talk, I use document analysis and interviews with human actants involved in the project to gather the data.

A third example of ANT-driven research has been carried out by Bruno Latour. In his book on Aramis – a metro system that was meant to be implemented in Paris but never succeeded – Latour gives Aramis himself a voice. Although not much research would cite things in this way, *Aramis* is a powerful example of how ANT-driven research can be practiced. Through document analysis and interviews with all human actants involved in the project, Latour tries to trace back the causes of the breakdown of the Aramis project. However, *Aramis* also shows a weakness of ANT-driven research. That is, it is difficult to set unambiguous conclusions from the rich palette of data. *Aramis* therefore also confirms the need to bring in some theory when it comes to writing down the findings from the fieldwork.

When to Use ANT, and When Not to Use it?

As we have seen during the course of this article, doing ANT-driven research is time consuming. Although it can result in surprising conclusions, there is no guarantee that this will be the case. Therefore one has to think twice before using ANT as a research method. It is well suited for exploratory research in areas that have not been investigated much already. The method can also be of use to go into complex issues that cannot be understood through the use of traditional theories and methods. Because of its boundarylessness, research that is ANT-driven is able to come up with new and sometimes unexpected conclusions.

However, there are – as with any scientific method – drawbacks that make ANT not a solution to everything. In the first place, ANT-driven research can never be quick and cheap. The method consumes lots of time (and thus money). Even if there is sufficient time, the number of cases to investigate will be rather small. The people and things that will be followed in the research need to have great commitment to the research as it also consumes some of their time. Doing multiple interviews and observations is more time consuming than a one simple questionnaire. Another drawback is that it cannot lead to statistical data that can be used to generalise conclusions.

See also: Case Studies; Ethnography; Qualitative Interviewing; Qualitative Methods in Housing Research.

References

Latour B (1996) *Aramis, or the Love of Technology*. Cambridge, MA; London: Harvard University Press.
Latour B (1999) *Pandora's Hope. An Essay on the Reality of Science Studies*. Cambridge, MA; London: Harvard University Press.

Further Reading

Bijker WE and Law J (eds.) (1992) *Shaping Technology, Building Society: Studies in Sociotechnical Change*. Cambridge, MA: MIT Press.
Callon M (1986) Some elements of a sociology of translation: Domestication of the scallops and the fishermen of St Brieuc Bay. In: Law J (ed.) *Power, Action and Belief: A New Sociology of Knowledge*. London: Routledge & Kegan Paul.
Callon M and Latour B (1981) Unscrewing the Big Leviathan: How actors macrostructure reality and sociologists help them to do so. In: Knorr-Cetina K and Cicourel AV (eds.) *Advances in Social Theory and Methodology: Towards an Integration of Micro- and Macro-Sociologies*, pp. 227–303. London: Routledge & Kegan Paul.
Czarniawska B (2004) On time, space and action nets. *Organization* 11(6): 773–791.
Gabriel M and Jacobs K (2008) The post-social turn: Challenges for housing research. *Housing Studies* 23(4): 527–540.
Latour B (2005) *Reassembling the Social. An Introduction to Actor-Network Theory*. Oxford, UK: Oxford University Press.
Law J (1992) *Notes on the Theory of the Actor Network: Ordering, Strategy and Heterogeneity*. Lancaster, UK: Centre for Science Studies, Lancaster University.
Law J (1999) *Traduction/Trahision: Notes on ANT*. Lancaster, UK: Centre for Science Studies, Lancaster University.
Law J and Hassard J (1999) *Actor-Network Theory and After*. Oxford, UK: Blackwell Publishing.
Mol AM (2002) *The Body Multiple: Ontology in Medical Practice*. Durham, NC: Duke University Press.

Adaptable Housing

E Støa, Norwegian University of Science and Technology, Trondheim, Norway

© 2012 Elsevier Ltd. All rights reserved.

Glossary

CIAM 'Congrès International d'Architecture' or 'International Congress of Modern Architecture' (1928–59) was a series of international conferences which became important platforms for the discussion of modern architecture and urbanism.

Dynamic dwellings The term is used to describe the possibility of both increasing and decreasing the size of a unit.

Elasticity The usable space can be extended and/or reduced through or without rebuilding.

Flexibility The layout of a dwelling, a building or an area is adaptable through changes or rebuilding.

Generality The layout of a dwelling, a building or an area permits multifunctional use and accessibility without requiring changes or rebuilding.

Open form A concept introduced by the Polish architect Oscar Hansen in 1957. It implied that buildings should consist of open grids or slabs where the specific solutions and detailing are not defined but can be designed on the basis of individual user needs and interpretations.

Polyvalancy A term introduced by the Dutch architect Herman Hertzberger in 1962, meaning that architectural space can be used in different ways over time or in different situations without having to undergo physical changes.

Situationalism Utopian, revolutionary architectural ideas that emerged in the 1960s, in which changeability, temporariness, and ambiguousness of urban structures are the main issues.

Structuralism Architecture based on a highly structured framework or grid system in which the buildings are regarded as a stage in a process and all parts in principle can continuously grow and develop further.

Introduction

The question of how housing and homes may adapt to societal changes has occupied architects, planners, and researchers since the early twentieth century. The adaptation of shelter to suit varying needs has, however, always been a part of human habitation, and vernacular dwellings worldwide are often characterised by the ability to change over time.

It seems, however, that the idea of adaptable or flexible housing is no matter of course in spite of the fact that our society is witnessing rapid changes and the unpredictability inherent in these changes has probably never been greater. There is a marked tendency, as stated by the British architects and researchers Tatjana Schneider and Jeremy Till in their book *Flexible Housing* from 2007, towards short-term profitability in new housing developments, with housing being regarded as a disposable commodity. These are obstacles towards a long-term perspective which is embedded in the idea of adaptable housing as well as in the overall objective of a more sustainable housing sector.

The aim of this article is to identify the main discussions and controversies regarding adaptable housing within professional debate since the early 1920s. It will furthermore argue for the need to still see adaptability as an important approach towards meeting contemporary challenges in the housing sector, and will finally present a number of possible models of adaptable housing on different levels, from the dwelling unit on one hand to the whole neighbourhood on the other.

The literature on adaptable housing is extensive, much of it in fact published during the last decades of the twentieth century, implying that there has been a revival of interest in the topic. It has been on and off the agenda of architects and planners since the 1920s. Common to much of the literature from 1990 to 2010 is the need to clarify concepts and decide which terms best cover the issue. 'Flexibility' seems to be the most widely used term, but 'adaptability' and 'time-based architecture' are used more or less as synonyms.

No matter which concept is used, there is a common understanding among most authors that one should distinguish between two ways of dealing with the issue of adaptable housing. One is by altering the physical structure of the building; the other is by altering the way we use the building. 'Adaptable', as in the heading for this article, is meant to cover both spatial and functional alterations. Another distinction is also commonly made between what may be called 'designed flexibility' and a more sensible way of designing buildings that may cope with changes. The last approach is embedded in the concept of 'polyvalency', which the Dutch architect Herman Hertzberger introduced in 1962 and which is defined by Gerard Maccreanor in the British-Dutch architectural practice MaccreanorLavington in 2005 as an approach that aims at creating buildings that are both 'transfunctional' and 'multifunctional'. This implies that they allow for the possibility of changing use over time as well as for different uses simultaneously. Accordingly, the concept of adaptability covers both what may be called 'designed flexibility' and 'flexible design' and may in fact include several different strategies. This will be elaborated more thoroughly later on in this article.

Short Historical Background

Although the idea of adaptable housing is far from new, the reasons and solutions have varied throughout history. In the following, a short review of the changing rationalities, concepts, and debates regarding adaptability within housing design and planning from the modern movement until today will be presented.

Modern Movement: An Open and Dynamic Dwelling

The Dutch architectural historians Jos van Eldonk and Helga Fassbinder trace the beginning of the modern history of adaptable housing to the American architect Frank Lloyd Wright. His open floor plans were inspired by traditional Japanese dwellings with rooms that were neither clearly limited nor had uniquely defined functional purposes. There were nonspecific zones, smooth transition from one zone to another, and large, open plans. The spatial continuum was made possible by a wooden frame structure, and the plan may be laid out in various ways by use of sliding walls. Wright searched for an alternative to interiors divided into 'boxes' with separate functions. Interior spaciousness and the open plan became one of the main symbols of early modernism, and flexibility was introduced as part of the design idea. This was made possible with new technologies and construction methods distinguishing between load-bearing structure and space divisions as manifested clearly by Le Corbusier's Domino-system from 1914. Le Corbusier stressed the distinction between the static building structure and the functional layout of the apartment. The system offered a possibility to develop floor plans independently of the structural framework: the open plan with ribbon windows and endless flexibility.

The avant-garde architects in the 1920s and 1930s questioned existing patterns of living, and part of the modernist approach was to regard the building as something that could change over time. Open and flexible plans were believed to bring liberation to their users and thus contribute to a rapidly changing and future-oriented society.

The Minimal Dwelling

Many architects in this period were socially committed and put a lot of effort into the development of housing for the underprivileged, which meant a focus on minimal cost and reduced space standards. Flexibility became one of the measures to reach the goal of creating adequate housing for the masses within restricted space. Among the principles that were explored was the idea of rooms with unspecified functions.

An important forum for the debate over the best solutions for space-efficient housing was the CIAM congress on 'Die Wohnung für das Existenzminimum' in Frankfurt, 1929. Several ideas from the most well-known architects of the time were presented. Ernst May experimented with how one unit could expand by connecting two or more temporary units. Victor Bourgeois had a proposal for how the same rooms could be used differently during the day and at night. Gerrit Rietveld transferred his concept from the Schröder house (1925) to a minimal dwelling, for example, by the use of foldable furniture. And Le Corbusier developed further the principle from the Domino-system for minimal dwellings.

The congress at Frankfurt resulted in different trends in different countries. In Germany the focus was on standardisation of the minimal dwelling with regard to dimensions of space and furniture, whereas in the Netherlands the architects dealt more with the processes of use, including the changeability in use on a daily basis as well as in longer time perspectives.

Industrialisation and Standardisation

The Second World War created a severe shortage of housing in most European countries. This fact, together with the development of industrialised production of housing, led to a shift from the focus on possibilities for individual adaptation and variation to standardised options. Emphasis was placed on principles and standardised floor plans that could make prefabrication possible, on the basis of the aims and needs of the building industry. A premise for rational construction was standardisation of pipelines and building elements and prefabrication of load-bearing elements. Module systems that might contribute to standardised floor plans based on functionalistic thinking were introduced. The process of manufacturing and building houses came to overshadow the idea of dwelling as a process.

Modularity and standardisation of housing units with a series of hierarchically organised components provided a framework to achieve formal as well as technical clarity and order. Among the arguments for mass production of housing were the potential efficiencies of repetition in manufacture. The use of standardised elements would allow adaptation over time and the possibility of elements being replaced or added to. The flexibility inherent in prefabricated systems was based on the principle of components that can potentially be arranged in an infinite number of ways, and it was believed that prefabrication would lead to wider choices being provided to the future user.

The result of the industrialised production of housing was, however, buildings and neighbourhoods marked by conformity and lack of identity. A new generation of architects opposed what they believed was a quantitative and technocratic approach towards housing. The CIAM congress in Otterloo in 1959 gathered several of them, and became a starting point for a critique against the functionalistic thinking that had been dominating planning and housing developments during the first postwar period.

Structuralism

'Open form' was introduced by the Polish architect Oscar Hansen in 1957. It implied that buildings should consist of open grids or slabs where the specific solutions and detailing were not defined but could be designed on the basis of individual user need and interpretations. In the early 1960s NJ Habraken published the book *Support – An Alternative to Mass Housing* in which he presented the idea that architecture is not a static product but rather an antiauthoritarian framework for continuous change. He became, together with the SAR Architectural Research Institute (established in the Netherlands in 1964), an important spokesperson for a dynamic approach to the built environment, in which the users' right to take part in the decision-making process, both during planning and after completion, was central. Habraken introduced a distinction between what had to be decided by professionals and the solutions that could be freely chosen and changed by the users, between 'support' and 'infill': the permanent structure and the changeable elements. The ideal was changeability, variation, and the unfinished – in contrast to the mass-produced suburban housing that was regarded as overdetermined, static, and authoritarian.

Habraken's principles are seen as part of the idea of structuralism, which was characterised by area plans and housing layout based on grid systems; the buildings were regarded as a stage in a process, and all parts could in principle continuously grow and develop further. This approach was criticised for leading to formal dictates, mechanised variations instead of new situations, and lack of architectural qualities as well as opportunities for residents to experience, use, and interpret housing environments as a magnitude of situations.

The Situationalists

Several other voices rose against the functionalistic planning ideas, among them were the situationalists. They sought more freedom of choice and indeterminacy, but according to the British architectural historian Adrian Forty, they regarded flexibility as a political strategy rather than a technical solution.

Situationalism is used to describe utopian, revolutionary architectural ideas in which changeability, temporariness, and ambiguousness are the main issues. The Dutch architectural historians Koos Bosma et al. describe these ideas as 'light' versions of urban design, often illustrated as megastructures, for example, by architects such as Archigram, Constant Nieuwenhuys, and Yona Friedman. They spoke up for open urban spaces that could offer situations for various actions and events, and mobility and a nomadic life were seen as alternatives to conventional ways of thinking about the development of cities. The architectural elements, and thus their flexibility, were regarded as preconditions for different and continuously changing events to take place.

Polyvalence as an Alternative to Flexibility

Among the critics who took part in the Otterloo congress in 1959 were the Dutch architects Herman Hertzberger and Aldo Van Eyck. They both questioned the way the ideas of flexibility and user appropriation found expression through structuralism, and disapproved of the view that architecture should be unfinished and indeterminate, left to the future to decide. Van Eyck wrote about 'false neutrality', and Hertzberger followed up with stating that flexibility had become a way for architects and planners to avoid taking clear standpoints and not committing themselves. He introduced the term polyvalency, understood as a permanent, given quality: that architectural space can be used in different ways over time or in different situations without having to undergo physical changes. According to Adrian Forty, Hertzberger's main concern was that architecture designed to be adaptable to all future possibilities becomes boring and difficult for people to identify with. Schneider and Till thus define polyvalency in architecture as leaving space for personalised interpretation by users, appropriation, and aiming at a higher degree of social empowerment and identification.

Democratisation of the Planning Process

From a belief in the future and universal solutions and a trust in new technology's ability to solve problems in society as well as a focus on large-scale housing developments, in the early 1970s there was a growing concern among architects and planners with historic and cultural values as well as with considerations for the local context. According to the Norwegian architect and researcher Jon

Guttu, 'small is beautiful' became a slogan in this period and the social life at a neighbourhood level became just as important as a criterion for housing quality as apartment layout. User participation became in this period an aim in itself, and adaptability implied that new housing could be developed in a direct dialogue with future residents, as a means to achieve the highest possible degree of democratisation in the planning process.

In the 1980s the trend was a greater focus on the individuality of each household and resident, often at the expense of the community. A part of this was a critique of the predominance of housing production aiming at standard, 'average' households (nuclear families). The needs of elderly and disabled people were put on the agenda, resulting in the concept of 'lifetime homes'. These were apartments and houses that could be used by everyone, in all stages of life and regardless of disabilities, without physical alterations. Some decades later, the term 'universal design' was incorporated in most public strategies as well as building requirements, meaning 'usability for all', which included not only people with physical disabilities, but also with orientation and environmental handicaps. This approach has common features with the idea of spatial adaptability to changing needs during lifetime.

Back to the City

The concern in adaptable housing has, in the 1980s, to a large degree been related to an increased interest in urban living. The quality and cultural diversity of urban life proved attractive and created a renewed status for urban dwelling. Adaptable housing was, and still is, seen as a way to achieve diversity and stability in urban settings. Urban dwellings should be suitable for all kinds of people and should be planned in interaction with other functions: public services as well as business activities and institutions. As stated by Gerard Maccreanor, adaptability is in fact an essential aspect of a vibrant urban structure because it is, and must be, continuously changing both when it comes to functions and character as well as social life.

Rationalities of Adaptable Housing at the Beginning of the Twenty-First Century

Schneider and Till elaborate in their book on some of the main reasons for still being occupied with this issue: changing demographics (e.g., decrease in traditional nuclear families, increased number of ageing users, more single-person households, more home-working, increased cultural heterogeneity); internal dynamics of households (e.g., changing family size and structure, changing lifestyles, ageing and disability during life course); long-term financial issues; and user opportunities (e.g., ability to customise as well as giving a sense of involvement and emotional identification). And, finally, they emphasise the significance of adaptability as a strategy towards a more sustainable housing sector. These aspects will be dealt with more thoroughly in the final section.

Models of Adaptable Housing

Schneider and Till use the terms 'soft' and 'hard' techniques of flexibility, which are somewhat parallel to the two strategies mentioned in the introduction, but not entirely, since both may be relevant for physical and spatial adaptability. With 'soft' they mean tactics that allow for a certain indeterminacy. The users may apply a solution according to their needs, with the designer effectively working in the background. It is even possible to talk about 'soft' technology, which implies systems and physical structures allowing freedom of choice and diverse uses and interpretations. 'Hard' techniques refer to elements that more specifically determine the way the design may be utilised. Here the designer works in the foreground, determining how spaces can or should be used over time. 'Hard' technologies are, according to Schneider and Till, those that are designed specifically to achieve flexibility and that also to a high degree determine the total layout of the scheme. As mentioned earlier, we may distinguish between 'designed flexibility' and 'flexible design'. Maccreanor comments that the first in most cases has failed to live up to the promise, a view that is supported by other writers.

However, when discussing adaptable housing as architects and planners, the focus is on how we may deal with time and uncertainty through architectural as well as technical means. We are not looking for social strategies. Bearing in mind the discussion above, we will return to the two main strategies: spatial and functional adaptability.

Risvollan Housing Cooperative – a Norwegian Example of Adaptable Housing

The Risvollan area (see **Figure 1**) was built in the city of Trondheim in 1974 and was designed by the Norwegian architects Brantenberg, Cold, and Hiorthøy. It consists of nearly 1200 apartments, mostly terraced houses (2–4 floors) grouped in eight neighbourhoods surrounding a common playground.

The building system of Risvollan consists of load-bearing partition walls with a distance of 540 cm. This gives room for diverse types and sizes of apartments as shown in **Figure 2**. The layout of apartments was meant to be as adaptable as possible, with the only fixed elements being the bathroom and the staircases. The inner walls were standardised and easily movable, so the residents could decide for themselves the sizes of rooms, where to have bedrooms and living rooms, and so on. The other, and perhaps just as important, aspect of adaptability at Risvollan is the great variation of apartment sizes. This means that people either growing out of their apartment or needing more space have been able to find another, more suitable place to live – within the same neighbourhood.

Figure 1 Terraced housing at Risvollan, fall 2006. Photo by Eli Støa.

In the Norwegian professional debate over adaptable architecture, the following three concepts are used to distinguish between the three main aspects of adaptability that cover the vast number of suggested categories and terms used in the literature:

1. **Generality** – the layout of a building or area permits multifunctional use and accessibility without requiring changes or rebuilding.

   Generality includes a number of approaches from polyvalency, the adaptability embedded in lifetime homes and universal design as well as the term 'redundancy' defined by Adrian Forty as a wasteful surplus of space. He refers to the Dutch architect Rem Koolhaas when he states that flexibility is about creating margins which enable different and even opposite interpretations and uses over time.

2. **Flexibility** – the layout of the building or area is adaptable through changes or rebuilding.

   The second category covers the possibility of making both internal and external physical alterations, varying from changing the position of a door or window, or moving or removing a wall to revising the entire internal layout. Flexibility can be consciously designed-in by the architect, for example, through support or carcass concepts, or it can be achieved by generic design principles, such as simple and robust construction techniques and the considered placing of staircases, service cores, and entrances. The Dutch architect Bernard Leupen suggests that 'semipermanent' buildings may also belong to this category, a term that includes industrially produced demountable buildings

3. **Elasticity** – the usable space can be extended and/or reduced through or without rebuilding.

The third category contains methods that meet the changing needs for living space through the different life phases of a family or household. This may imply enlarging the living space by adding new space as extensions or including attics or basements in the dwelling or it may include the possibility of reducing living space by separating parts of the original apartment. The term 'dynamic dwellings' is used to describe this possibility of both increasing and decreasing the size of a unit.

Each aspect has solutions that can imply either functional or spatial adaptability within both a housing area as a whole and a single house or dwelling unit. They are all related to the physical context, but do not necessarily imply physical changes. Below is presented a list of some of the solutions/models which are particularly relevant for the housing sector. See also **Table 1** for an overview.

Within the housing area/neighbourhood level:

- Universal design: accessibility for all user groups, and throughout the lifecycle of each individual.
- Varied composition of apartments: makes it possible to move to another apartment within the area when requirements and needs change.
- Premises that may be used and transformed for different functions.
- Common premises/rooms: may function as a 'buffer zone' that can reduce pressure on small apartments.
- Flexible area plan and structures: permit extensions of the units and densification through new units, functionally as well as aesthetically.

Within the house/dwelling unit:

- Universal design: accessibility for all user groups, and throughout the lifecycle of each individual.

of activities between different rooms on both a short-term and long-term basis (temporarily and permanently).
- Adaptability with or without rebuilding: solutions allowing for physical changes through rebuilding or the use of sliding walls and doors, movable and foldable elements, etc.
- Dynamic housing units: two units that can be joined together or be used separately with little rebuilding or even without.
- Extension of dwelling units through making use of secondary space: possibilities to include attics, storerooms, and so on, for dwelling purposes.
- Extensions by adding new space.

Adaptability: A Viable Approach Towards More Sustainable Housing

...flexible housing embeds itself into the heart of any sustainable approach to housing design. (...) flexible housing works across and integrates social, environmental and economic fields. (Schneider and Till, 2007: 44)

Sustainable development is a major issue of our time and has gained even more importance due to the recent focus on severe climate changes. First and foremost the concept of sustainability involves a long-term perspective in accordance with the Report of the World Commission on Environment and Development from 1987: a development that meets the needs of the present without compromising the ability of future generations to meet their own needs. That is what adaptability is all about: to create buildings that last through altering times and situations. Correspondingly, we may state that the tendency to reduce housing to a disposable product or commodity that will be abandoned once it has lost its attraction is a threat against both the long-term perspective of sustainability as well as the aim of viable and stable human communities.

Adaptable housing may be regarded as an approach towards meeting the challenges of contemporary society. It should, however, not be limited to a physical and technical issue that may support an optimal fit for individual households and their dwellings. To make the most of the potential of adaptability as an approach towards more sustainable housing, in the broadest sense of the term, we should focus on the models that are relevant on a larger scale, on the neighbourhood or even on the city level. Only then may adaptability contribute to reach the vision of a society that may change its direction and leave the planet in a better shape for future generations.

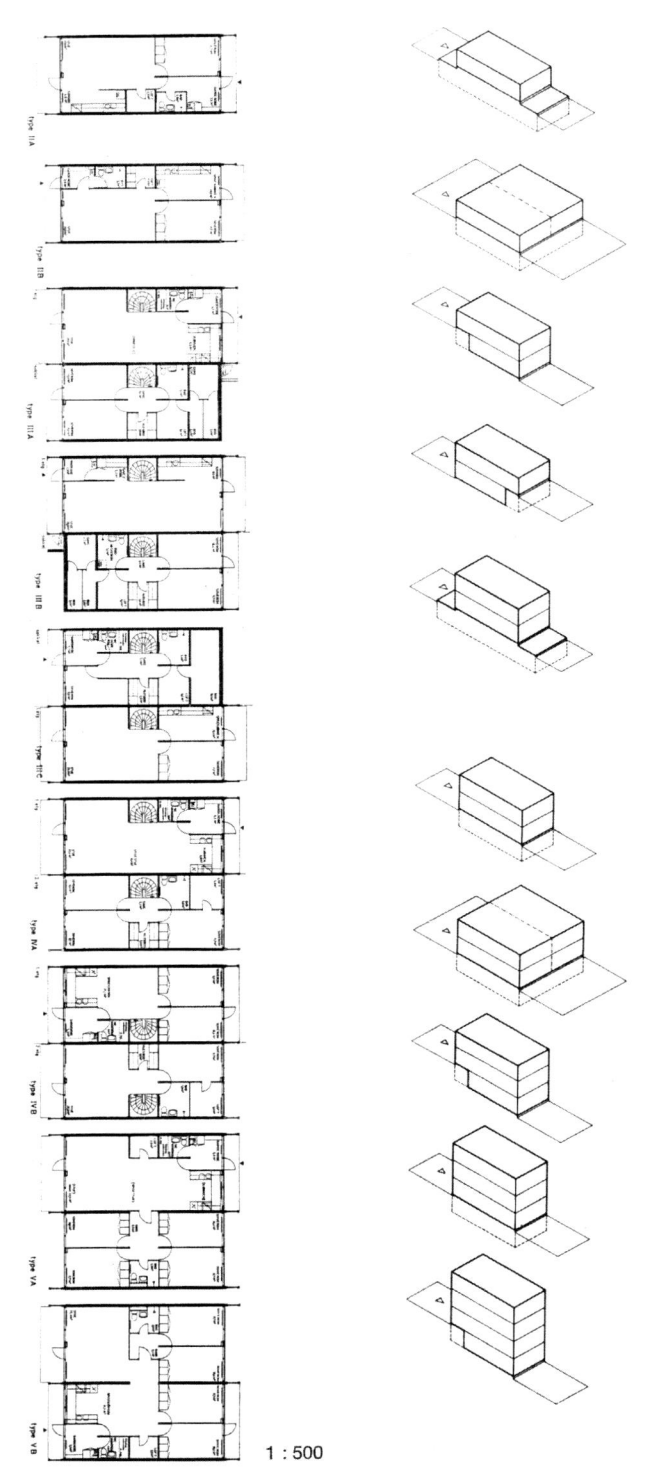

Figure 2 Principal drawings showing variations of apartments at Risvollan.
Reproduced with permission from a figure in Brantenberg and Hiorthøy (1972) *Risvollan Borettslag*, pp. 158–159. Byggekunst 5/1972. Oslo: Norske Arkitekters Landsforbund.

- Multifunctional rooms/areas: spatial composition and rooms that allow altering use and interchangeability

Table 1 Overview of the three different aspects of adaptability in housing, on the level of housing areas and dwelling units

		Generality	*Flexibility*	*Elasticity*
Housing area	Functional adaptability	• Universal design • Varied composition of apartments		• Common premises/rooms
	Spatial adaptability	• Premises that may be transformed for different functions	• Flexible area plan and structures that permit individual variation and changes	• Area plan and structures that allow for densification or division of units
Dwelling unit	Functional adaptability	• Universal design • Multifunctional rooms/areas		• Dynamic housing units
	Spatial adaptability	• Adaptability by use of moving elements	• Rebuilding within existing buildings • Changing architectonic expression	• Extension of dwelling units through making use of secondary space • Extensions by adding new space

Reproduced with permission from Støa E (2003) Adaptable housing areas: Improved quality with less space. *Open House International* 28(1): 43–51.

See also: Housing Developers and Sustainability; Sustainable Communities; Sustainable Housing Cultures.

References

Brantenberg and Hiorthøy (1972) *Risvollan Borettslag,* Oslo: Norske Arkitekters Landsforbund pp. 158–159. Byggekunst 5/1972.Oslo: Norske Arkitekters Landsforbund.
Schneider T and Till J (2007) *Flexible Housing*. Oxford: Architecural Press; Elsevier.

Further Reading

Bosma K, van Hoogstraten D, and Vos M (2000) *Housing for the Millions: John Habraken and the SAR (1960–2000)*. Rotterdam: NAI Publishers.
Forty A (2000) *Words and Buildings: A Vocabulary of Modern Architecture*. London: Thames & Hudson.
Friedman A (2002) *The Adaptable House. Designing Homes for Change*. New York: McGraw-Hill.
Guttu J (2003) *'Den gode boligen': fagfolks oppfatning av boligkvalitet gjennom 50 år*. PhD Dissertation, AHO, Oslo, Norway.
Hertzberger H (1962) Flexibility and Polyvalentie. *Forum* (3).
Hertzberger H (1991) *Lessons for Students in Architecture*. Rotterdam: 010 Publishers
Leupen B (2005) Towards time-based architecture. In: Leupen B, Heijne R, and van Zwol J (eds.) *Time-Based Architecture*, pp. 12–20. Rotterdam: 010 Publishers.
Leupen B (2006) *Frame and Generic Space*. Rotterdam: 010 Publishers.
Maccreanor G (2005) The sustainable city is the adaptable city. In: Leupen B, Heijne R, and van Zwol J (eds.) *Time-Based Architecture*, pp. 98–109. Rotterdam: 010 Publishers.
Støa E (2003) Adaptable housing areas: Improved quality with less space. *Open House International* 28(1): 43–51.
Støa E and Høyland K (2002) *Tilpasningsdyktige boligområder. Begrepsbruk og modeller for tilpasningsdyktighet* ['Adaptable housing areas. Concepts and models for adaptability', only available in Norwegian]. *SINTEF Report STF22 A02501*. Trondheim, Norway.
Van Eldonk J and Fassbinder H (1990) *Flexible Fixation. The Paradox of Dutch Housing Architecture*. Assen/Maastricht: Van Gorcum.

Affordable Housing Strategies

V Milligan and T Gilmour, University of New South Wales, Sydney, NSW, Australia

© 2012 Elsevier Ltd. All rights reserved.

Glossary

Affordable housing Affordable housing is housing that is provided at a rent or purchase price that does not exceed a designated standard of affordability. Affordability is usually defined by measuring whether housing costs exceed a fixed proportion of household income and/or whether household income is sufficient to meet other basic living costs after allowing for housing costs.

Not-for-profit organisations Not-for-profit organisations are independently governed, formally constituted entities that do not distribute their profits to shareholders or members.

Introduction

The need for affordable housing has grown as house prices have risen faster than the incomes of many housing consumers whose incomes fall in the lower bands of national income distributions (see article Policies to Support Access and Affordability of Housing). Now in many countries, there is evidence of a sizeable gap existing between the typical price of housing that is produced or traded in the housing market and an indicative price that is deemed affordable to lower-income households.

In response to this issue, contemporary affordable housing strategies employ multiple instruments and seek to engage actors and institutions across the public, private, and not-for-profit sectors. This article provides an overview of the changing approach to financing and delivering affordable housing that has emerged in recent decades and examines the respective contributions of public, private, and not-for-profit sector players. The focus is on housing systems where each of these sectors plays a significant part in providing affordable housing.

Much of the policy debate on strategies to provide affordable housing is framed by whether these support or regulate either the production (supply side) or the consumption (demand side) of housing. Often, strategies are also further classified and differentiated by tenure, that is, whether they support renters and renting or homeowners and homeownership. In this article, the range and mix of strategies used in contemporary societies to achieve more affordable housing is examined through a different lens, that of an institutional framework. This approach brings into focus the role and respective contributions of government, private sector, and not-for-profit agencies. It also helps to highlight how relationships between these sectors (such as public–private partnerships, intermediary organisations, and regulatory controls) are shaping the provision of affordable housing.

The underlying rationale for affordable housing strategies is to promote, produce, and protect appropriate housing that is affordable to households who face problems obtaining or sustaining housing in the market. How this is achieved can take many forms depending on the diagnosis of factors that are contributing to a shortage of affordable housing and the opportunities that are present in a particular institutional and geographical context for improving the prevailing situation. For example, in relation to supply shortages, strategies may focus on increasing the long-term supply of affordable housing for certain target groups or in particular locations where supply is inadequate, or they might be concerned with preserving (and/or replacing) an existing supply of low-priced housing in an area undergoing redevelopment and renewal. Also important are the ideologies and priorities of governments, which become manifest in the particular forms of subsidies and incentives that may be offered, the institutions chosen for service delivery and regulatory requirements. Strategies may also be designed to achieve additional supplementary objectives, for example, to promote more affordable housing in locations where there are labour market shortages or to increase social mix in desirable neighbourhoods that can offer more economic and social opportunities (especially jobs and services) to households, who may be disadvantaged by living in other more affordable but less well-endowed locations.

In relation to government priorities, there has been a widespread trend in recent decades to adopt policies that achieve goals for affordable housing through enabling 'affordable' forms of market-based homeownership, although policies in favour of rental housing and innovative tenures have reemerged in the first decade of the twenty-first century. This latest development has been given further impetus by the 'subprime' mortgage lending crisis in the United States, which impacted adversely on recent home buyers, as well as having much wider negative ramifications in housing markets and national economies around the globe.

The Changing Role of Public Institutions in Affordable Housing Provision

Over much of the twentieth century, many national, regional, and/or municipal governments played a direct role in owning and managing a share of housing to be allocated to a mix of working and nonworking households, often at low rents (compared to market levels). The historic share of government-owned housing in national housing systems varies considerably. High levels of social housing (50–90%) were reached in the state-controlled and -planned economies of China and Eastern Europe and in the special cases of Hong Kong and Singapore. Many Northern and Western European countries had moderate shares (10–50%). Low shares (less than 10%) were typical in most English-speaking countries, southern Europe and countries that have not developed modern housing systems. A variety of factors have been cited to help explain the historic role of governments in providing housing directly, including addressing wartime housing destruction and production shortages and replacing undeveloped or nonexistent housing markets. Provision of public housing was also used to support state-driven welfare goals – particularly to overcome public health problems that had been linked to poor housing quality, and the desire of governments to keep wages low in support of economic productivity and competitiveness.

Beginning in the 1970s, many governments with larger and smaller public housing systems began rethinking their direct role in housing in favour of market-based alternatives. Strategies aimed at both transforming existing public housing systems and adopting new ways of enabling the private and not-for-profit sectors to provide more affordable housing have been adopted widely, although at a variable pace and to different extents across countries, and with mixed results. Diverse and sometimes conflicting reasons are cited in the literature for this move including improving standards of service, avoiding debt in government accounts, leveraging additional resources from partners, and generating market-like cost efficiencies. The impacts of this policy transformation are reflected in new institutions and models of affordable housing, as discussed in the following sections. In time, these new institutional arrangements themselves have become influential in shaping housing strategies, sometimes constraining change and sometimes generating new ideas and dynamic responses.

The main kinds of adjustments to the role and strategies of governments that can be identified across many diverse countries over the last three decades include the following interconnected trends.

First, governments have shown a preference to provide income subsidies, incentives, or vouchers to individuals assessed as having a housing affordability problem, to boost their capacity to pay for their housing in the private market rather than to subsidise the production or purchase of housing directly. Key evidence of this trend is found in the large increases in expenditure on housing allowances in national accounts (see article Access and Affordability: Housing Allowances).

Second, governments have reduced their investment in the direct supply of social housing and linked this to policy settings that aim to increase targeting of the housing retained to those considered most needy, typically those on very low income or with special needs (such as a need for home-based support or modified housing) that are not catered to elsewhere in the housing system. Thus social housing sectors have shrunk as a proportion of all housing in a wide array of countries since peak levels of the second half of the twentieth century. As one consequence, many social housing sectors are now described as 'residualised', implying that they house a very limited range and mix of households and operate under highly prescribed rules of access and security of tenure.

Third, many governments have privatised significant amounts of their former public housing. Often this has been linked to a strategy to increase homeownership among lower-income households, by handing sitting tenants ownership or offering them 'a right to buy' and financial inducements (such as concessional loans or price discounts). This process has occurred most extensively in the former Soviet Bloc countries in the 1990s, whereby between 50 and 90% of state-owned housing in these countries was privatised, and also in urban China. However, it was also significant in Britain from the 1980s, where a third of the former stock of public housing had been sold to tenants, and in Australia at an even earlier time, where the majority of public housing that was built was tenanted and subsequently sold to sitting tenants, from the 1950s to the 1970s.

Fourth, commensurate with the deregulation of many national financial systems from the 1980s, the expansion of capital markets, and a diversifying mortgage industry, there has been a shift away from public lending for affordable housing (both renting and ownership forms) in favour of private financing. In a related move, many national governments have shifted responsibility for procuring and managing government-enabled affordable housing schemes to nongovernment vehicles and many former state-controlled financial institutions have been corporatised or privatised. The most prominent example is the giant American mortgage fund raiser, the Federal National Mortgage Association, known as Fannie Mae, which was founded in 1938 as a public institution with a charter to improve access to mortgage finance for low- and moderate-income households in the United States. Fannie Mae was corporatised in the 1960s but, along with another government founded and regulated private shareholder corporation, the Federal Home Loan Mortgage Corporation (Freddie Mac), has continued to address the public policy goal of increasing access to homeownership, especially for minority groups and in areas traditionally underserved by mortgage lenders. However, following the 2007 subprime mortgage lending crisis, the US government was forced to take control of both these corporations to prevent their collapse.

Finally, there have been trends in locating responsibility for housing policy across spheres and agencies of government. One discernible trend from the 1990s was devolution of responsibility for housing programmes to lower levels of government to encourage locally driven responses. However, where this was accompanied by a reduction in national funding, such as in Canada, Germany, Austria, and Australia (until recently), this has contributed to affordability problems. Somewhat paradoxically, there has been a growing recognition at the heart of central government that shortages of affordable housing are contributing to wider economic problems, including labour market shortages and reduced economic competiveness. Even before the Global Financial Crisis from 2008, this development had prompted the reengagement of government agencies, especially Treasuries, in affordable housing strategies in countries such as Britain, Ireland, and Australia.

While housing policy remains a sovereign issue, international and regional agencies are showing increasing interest. For example, the United Nations has several agencies, such as UN Habitat, that promote housing goals and provide information and advice to governments and other national institutions. The World Bank also assists national governments by providing housing information, expertise, and policy advice, which is particularly oriented to developing countries. There is also interest from regional agencies in the way that neighbouring governments organise their housing systems. For example, the European Union has been concerned recently to promote a level playing field between not-for-profit and private sector housing developers across member countries. Other networks, such as the European Liaison Committee on Housing (CECODHAS), promote policy development through strategic research and advisory activities. In the finance area, the Bank of International Settlements and the International Monetary Fund are active in assessing national financing systems for housing and advising on finance-related policies and institutional arrangements that will help to promote an adequate supply of finance for housing.

While many of the trends listed above may be read as suggesting a contraction of the role of governments in affordable housing in favour of private provision, a full assessment also has to take into account myriad other ways that governments continue to influence the financing, provision, allocation, and management of affordable housing through nongovernment models. The main contemporary roles that characterise the state's contribution can be grouped into three types. The first set involves provision of a variety of subsidies and financial incentives that are linked to the independent supply of additional affordable housing and/or the provision of other government resources, especially housing allowances and the allocation of public land for affordable housing. The second set is regulatory controls to help ensure that public policy goals for affordable housing are met by arm's length providers that receive government assistance. Thirdly, planning policies that are designed to meet affordability goals are applied. These can encompass developer levies for affordable housing, bonuses and concessions (e.g., less onerous parking provisions) for affordable housing providers, and requirements for inclusion of a component of affordable housing in designated new development and redevelopment areas. The potential of these mechanisms can be assessed in terms of the quantity of housing that can be produced; capacity to influence the quality of housing outcomes and to promote innovation (towards the achievement of affordability as well as a variety of social, economic, and environmental goals); value-for-money considerations; and, importantly, the longevity of affordability and other benefits that result from government investment.

The effectiveness of contemporary affordable housing strategies can also be related directly to how these diverse levers are brought together strategically to achieve affordability goals. Typically, each mechanism that is applied operates as one part of a structured package of financial and nonfinancial levers. For example, British planning policies have operated in conjunction with the provision of partial grants for construction to ensure that government-regulated affordable housing providers have access to well-located sites, while the provision of generous housing allowances to tenants means that low-income tenants can pay rents that cover the costs of a significant component of private financing in the projects.

Private Sector Institutions

The majority of residential accommodation in modern housing systems is built by the private sector. Traditionally, small firms and individual contractors have dominated provision but larger development companies, mortgage finance institutions, and specialised real estate professionals tend to become dominant as markets mature and institutional arrangements evolve.

In this context, questioning during the 1970s in many developed countries of public housing as the main source of low-income rental accommodation led to new strategies to use private sector institutions (and not-for-profit agencies, as described next). Many governments switched their emphasis to improving effective 'demand' by subsidising tenant income to help them to afford to rent in the private market. A prominent example was the introduction in 1974 in the United States of 'Section 8' housing vouchers where federal funds meet the gap between 30% of a household's income and market rents (see article Access and Affordability: Housing Vouchers). Though some vouchers are tied to particular properties, vouchers can allow tenants to move to different locations. The scheme's supporters claim that it passes the responsibility for property ownership to the private sector, increases labour mobility, and deconcentrates poverty. Critics point to the failure of these growing schemes to dampen rents and to help overcome shortages of affordable housing. In a more comprehensive scheme to that of the United States, in 1982 Britain introduced 'housing benefit' – an income subsidy available to all landlords whether public, private, or not-for-profit. Many other countries have followed a similar approach.

Private sector institutions have also been used to increase affordable housing supply. Contracting of private developers and builders by public and not-for-profit agencies to construct affordable properties on their behalf is longstanding and widespread and firms that work mainly in this part of the market have flourished in some countries, such as the United States. In many countries that have not established or retained a significant publicly owned social housing sector, private individuals and corporations have also been encouraged through government incentives and regulations to own properties for low-cost rental. The United States and Germany are two leading examples of countries taking mainly a market-based approach to the provision of low-cost rental housing. Much of the former West Germany's sizeable rental sector (around half of all dwellings) was developed from the 1980s under generous tax incentives offered to private investors who were required by law to set rents that were affordable for middle-income households. However, since unification, Germany has followed other countries in switching away from supply-linked incentives to housing allowances for low-income individuals. In the United States, the Low-Income Housing Tax Credit (LIHTC) scheme, introduced in 1986, uses tax breaks as incentives for private investors to build new affordable units with rents set at 30% of local salary levels. These properties are retained as affordable for a minimum 30 years, sometimes longer. During the last two decades some 1.7 million properties have been built through this method in the United States, with three-quarters of tax credits allocated to private institutions and one-quarter to not-for-profit agencies. Either private or not-for-profit institutions allocate and manage this housing on behalf of the investors in accord with policy requirements.

Contrasting with equity investment in the United States and Germany, the more common approach internationally has been to use private debt finance to support construction of affordable housing. Britain introduced private finance in 1988, and the mix of mainly medium-term bank loans coupled with a smaller volume of bond issues finances around half the cost of new affordable housing projects (the remainder is funded from government grants and provider surpluses). In continental Europe, private finance tends to come not directly through banks, but is channelled through state-sponsored intermediaries that are generally regulated, though run at arm's length from the government. France, for example, has a dedicated agency that directs tax-privileged deposits from individuals and a fixed share of payroll tax revenue to public and not-for-profit social housing agencies. Some countries, such as Switzerland, guarantee the housing bond-raising vehicle to enhance its credit rating and thereby reduce the cost of funds raised. Others, such as a jointly public and not-for-profit-sector-funded intermediary in the Netherlands, guarantee many of the loans made by banks to not-for-profit agencies.

The Global Financial Crisis from 2008 has challenged the viability of a number of schemes used over the last two decades to encourage private sector involvement in affordable housing. In particular, private finance has become harder to obtain and more expensive, and funds from developer levies and cross subsidies have declined as market activity fell. During 2008, many banks faced a liquidity crisis and were not able to make new loans. In Britain, the margin charged on loans to affordable housing providers increased from around 0.25 to 2%. In the United States, corporate losses led to a lack of investors in tax credit schemes and many affordable housing schemes have been kept on hold. Considerable investment has been required by governments to underpin private investment in affordable housing, including liquidity support for banks, direct grants or provision of public land for housing providers, and economic stimulus packages to protect construction industry jobs and to compensate for ailing private sector supply. One outcome has been that many governments that had wound back their housing role have been forced to increase their funding of housing.

Not-for-Profit Institutions

The involvement of not-for-profit institutions in the provision of affordable housing has been longstanding, though their role and scale has changed over time. Philanthropy has a long tradition in many countries, often linked with faith groups or secular interests such as trade unions, and became more important during industrialisation as social conditions worsened while governments made little provision for social welfare. In Western Europe and the United States towards the end of the nineteenth century, housing trusts and charitable societies funded by donations started to produce affordable rental housing at scale. These were supplemented by not-for-profit 'model housing companies', mixing business and philanthropy by paying below-market dividends or loan interest to socially minded investors. Unlike traditional philanthropic approaches that targeted provision at high-needs individuals, the model housing companies in Britain and the United States provided accommodation for people in regular employment. Governments supported these initiatives by exempting the organisations from paying income tax, and in Britain by providing public loans at below-market rates.

During the middle decades of the twentieth century, government funding for affordable housing provision in most countries was channelled more through public rather than not-for-profit agencies. Consequently, the sector remained small. The funding balance for new construction shifted during the 1970s due to increasing rejection of public housing, as described above. Britain switched funding towards not-for-profit 'housing associations' from 1974, leading to a wave of new organisation formation. In the United States, funds provided under the 1974 Community Development Block Grant Program led to an expansion of not-for-profit 'community development corporations' (CDCs) that increasingly focused on affordable housing rather than general neighbourhood issues. They became mandated after 1986 to receive a portion of funding from LIHTC tax credits, leading to further expansion of the not-for-profit housing sector. In the Netherlands, housing associations became the dominant providers of social housing after the 1970s as central government funds were directed exclusively to them along with extensive transfers of municipal housing. In other European countries, such as Switzerland, Denmark, France, and Austria, preexisting organisations such as housing cooperatives and other socially oriented organisations became the preferred vehicles for providing affordable housing.

With greater funding of not-for-profit providers came greater independence from government, and arguably the need for more complex systems of regulation, inspection, and intervention to achieve public policy goals and to manage risk. Many developed countries adopted systems of regulating providers by setting rules for their governance, business, and reporting. However, dismantling of public systems has not always been supported by capacity building in alternative institutions and enhanced regulation. For instance, in many former state-controlled housing systems in Eastern Europe, new institutional arrangements (such as for mortgage finance) have been slow to develop and adequate regulatory powers have not been put in place, resulting in a severe diminution in institutional control over housing functions and standards.

Consideration of the degree of control by government of not-for-profit agencies receiving public funds continues to be contested. Balance is needed between the prevention of organisational failure, which jeopardises investment and tenant occupation, and the ability of organisations to be entrepreneurial and innovative. Growing regulatory controls have led to greater professionalism and capacity building in the sector, allowing not-for-profit organisations to expand their range of activities. Many providers have taken advantage of access to private finance, as described above, with some undertaking for-profit activities (such as market-rate property development) to cross-subsidise provision of affordable rental housing. There has also been innovation with shared ownership and shared equity schemes, which offer pathways into homeownership for lower-income households. Innovative organisational forms, such as common equity cooperatives and tenant cooperatives in Europe and Canada, and community land trusts in Britain and the United States, offer new approaches to creating and preserving affordability by mixing community ownership and resident buy in. Other not for profit organisations have expanded their social remit, aiming to bring cohesion to troubled neighbourhoods by providing or supporting community facilities and offering training support and employment to their tenants.

In addition to not-for-profit organisations increasingly building new affordable housing stock, in some countries such as Britain, the United States, and the Netherlands, they have grown through the transfer of public housing assets. Britain has transferred ownership of over 1.3 million units to housing associations in the last two decades, with the programme accelerating from 1997 when extra funding was provided to allow the transfer of larger urban estates in poorer condition. Since 2000, British municipal governments have also transferred management (but not ownership) of a further one million public housing units to 'arm's length management companies'. These are constituted as not-for-profit organisations, although under the terms of their contract with municipalities can revert to public management if performance standards are not maintained. Similar arm's length companies have replaced municipal providers in many parts of Europe. Stock transfer in Britain has made not-for-profit providers the dominant force in affordable housing, eclipsing the role of the public sector. In both Britain and the Netherlands, some providers that have grown very large through merger have been criticised for losing neighbourhood connectivity, opaque accountability and growing wealth evidenced by high executive salaries and large balance sheets. This position can be contrasted with countries such as Ireland, Australia, New Zealand, Hong Kong, and Singapore, where most social housing remains in the public sector and not-for-profit providers are often small, neighbourhood organisations. In Canada, while not-for-profits own two-thirds of the social housing stock they too are mostly small local organisations that are unable to invest in their own growth. In the United States, the system of tax credit allocation has militated against the growth of more than a handful of national housing providers, and there is greater reliance on volunteering and philanthropic donation to support core activities. These examples highlight the diversity of approaches to the structuring of not-for-profit housing sectors across countries and the varying influence on affordable housing provision that may result.

Cross Sector Partnerships

Despite the distinction drawn so far in this article between public, private, and not-for-profit institutions, the provision and management of affordable housing is becoming increasingly complex and often involves cross-sector activities. This is not new, particularly the outsourcing of tasks such as property design, construction, and routine maintenance by the public (and increasingly the not-for-profit sector) to private entities. The rationale for this arrangement is normally the belief in private sector efficiencies, specialisation, and potential for scale economies. Outsourcing also allows competitive bidding for contracts, which should reduce costs. Critics of this type of arrangement cite potential problems with the quality of service provided by the private contractor, the complexity and costs of involving multiple agents and the public policy issues of private companies earning shareholder profits from public subsidy.

A more recent development has been the growth of risk/reward sharing arrangements such as public–private partnerships (PPPs) that, in the affordable housing sector, often also involve not-for-profit organisations (see article Public-Private Housing Partnerships). Though originally used for delivering physical infrastructure such as roads and bridges, PPPs have been used from the 1990s for social housing renewal in a number of countries. These schemes typically regenerate monotenure public housing estates, improving housing quality, mixing public, affordable, and market rate housing, and stabilising troubled communities, through better service and employment provision. The structure of consortia varies considerably, though generally involves a complex balancing of risk and reward depending on the capabilities of each partner. In Britain, the main model used for housing renewal during the last decade has been the 'private finance initiative' launched in 1992. In the United States, HOPE VI (1993) provided the framework for the restructuring of 224 public housing estates.

Conclusions

Meeting the growing need for affordable housing is one of the biggest challenges in both developed and developing countries. Contemporary national strategies involve many different institutional approaches, and are characterised by dynamic relations between the public, private, and not-for-profit sectors. Although these approaches are influenced by the country (or regional) context, especially historic tenure mix, the place of housing in the welfare system and local structures of housing provision, common themes, and converging trends are also evident. For example, there has been a general move away from direct provision of affordable housing by public agencies in favour of approaches involving the private and not-for-profit sectors, either separately or in partnership. This has resulted, in most countries, in a more complex landscape of affordable housing financing, ownership, and management. Nevertheless, public support remains significant using a mix of levers such as income support for housing, incentives offered through capital grants for providers and/or tax privileges for investors, and regulation of affordable housing providers. As evident during the recent global financial crisis, many governments have had to recommit to direct intervention to prevent systemic failure.

The growth of cross-sectoral relations and new institutions, coupled with the more general introduction of market forces into affordable housing provision, has led to what some commentators see as a move towards 'hybrid' organisations. Hybridity is the balancing within an institution of responsibilities to the state (public goals), the market (through using entrepreneurial approaches), and society (achieving good community outcomes). For example, not-for-profit organisations need to become financially astute in their use of commercial bank lending, public agencies need to understand market forces, and private firms need to address social responsibilities. The concept of hybridity is helpful as it suggests the traditional distinctions between institutions in the public, private, and not-for-profit sector are becoming more blurred, with particular benefits traditionally associated with one type of institution now potentially achievable in another. It also highlights the complexity and dynamic character of approaches to the institutional provision of affordable housing.

See also: Access and Affordability: Housing Allowances; Access and Affordability: Housing Vouchers; Policies to Support Access and Affordability of Housing; Public-Private Housing Partnerships.

Further Reading

CECODHAS (2007) *Housing Europe 2007: Review of Social, Co-Operative and Public Housing in the 27 EU Member States*. Brussels: CECODHAS.

Cummings JL and DiPasquale D (1999) The low-income housing tax credit: An analysis of the first ten years. *Housing Policy Debate* 10(2): 251–307.

Evers A and Laville J-L (2004) Social services by social enterprises: On the possible contributions of hybrid organizations and a civil society. In: Evers A and Laville J-L (eds.) *The Third Sector in Europe*, pp. 237–255. Cheltenham, UK: Edward Elgar.

Gruis V, Tsenkova S, and Nieboer N (eds.) (2009) *Management of Privatised Housing: International Policies and Practice*. London: Wiley-Blackwell.

Harloe M (1995) *The People's Home: Social Rented Housing in Europe and America*. Oxford, UK: Blackwell.

Kemeny J (1995) *From Public Housing to Social Renting: Rental Policy Strategies in Comparative Perspective*. London: Routledge.

Lawson J and Milligan V (2007) International trends in housing and policy responses. *Melbourne: Final Report No 110*. Melbourne, VIC: Australian Housing and Urban Research Institute.

Mullins D and Rhodes ML (2007) Special issue on network theory and social housing. *Housing, Theory and Society* 24(1): 1–13.

Pawson H, Mullins D, and Gilmour T (2010) *After Council Housing: Britain's New Social Landlords*. Basingstoke, UK: Palgrave Macmillan.

Pollitt C and Bouckaert G (2004) *Public Management Reform. A Comparative Analysis*. Oxford, UK: Oxford University Press.

Schwartz A (2006) *Housing Policy in the United States: An Introduction*. New York: Routledge.

Sørensen E and Torfing J (eds.) (2007) *Theories of Democratic Network Governance*. London: Palgrave Macmillan.

Tsenkova S (2009) *Housing Policy Reforms in Post-Socialist Europe: Lost in Transition*. Heidelberg, Germany: Physica-Verlag.

Whitehead C and Scanlon K (eds.) (2007) *Social Housing in Europe*. London: London School of Economics.

Anthropological Perspectives on Home

I Cieraad, Delft University of Technology, Delft, The Netherlands

© 2012 Elsevier Ltd. All rights reserved.

Glossary

Binary oppositions The basic premise in the anthropological theory of structuralism is that human thinking is structured in opposing (binary) language categories, the so-called binary oppositions of which some are universal, such as the opposition nature versus culture, life versus death, or male versus female, while others are specific for one culture only. The layout of houses and villages is structured according to the dominant binary oppositions (the language categories) and maps the culture, so to speak. A characteristic combination of universal and specific binary oppositions typifies each culture.

Ethnology In the European academic tradition ethnology stands for the study of folk customs and traditions of indigenous populations within the borders of a particular nation-state.

House The house in the anthropological interpretation is a model or map of the meaningful categories, which are mirrored in the layout and architectural structure of the dwelling.

Paradigm shift When basic premises within an academic discipline have been changed, one is likely to call it a paradigm shift, which refers to the seminal work of Thomas Kuhn on scientific revolutions. The change is often initiated by a new generation of scholars.

Anthropology and the Home: A New Combination

Only in the late twentieth century did the contemporary home (loosely defined as domestic space in an urban or suburban context) become an anthropological research setting in its own right, and as a consequence the word 'home' popped up more frequently in the titles of publications by anthropologists. On superficial reading it might seem a modern translation of the more traditional anthropological concept of the house, but actually it reflects a major shift within the anthropological discipline, not only in its focus, but also in research areas and research methods. The situation from which it emerged warrants description as a paradigm shift.

In the early twentieth century, anthropology developed from a Western armchair philosophy focused on grand schemes of cultural evolution into a semi-colonial academic discipline based on fieldwork studies in foreign cultures and societies. Although the discipline was coined 'social anthropology' in the United Kingdom, and 'cultural anthropology' in the United States and continental Europe, both slightly different academic traditions produced ethnographies which resulted from fieldwork studies applying the discipline's unique and most known research method of participant observation over a considerable period of time. The participatory element of doing-the-things-they-do proved to be very helpful for ethnographers in studying exotic communities in isolated regions, especially when the ethnographer had little or no command of the language of the people under scrutiny.

However, most ethnographers could not have participated and done their fieldwork without the help of native key-informants who also served as interpreters. In due course, the method of participant observation contributed to the discipline's hierarchy of trustworthiness in which actual behaviour has more credits than discourse. In other words, from an anthropological perspective the things people do are more important than the things they say.

Throughout the twentieth century the academic endeavour of anthropologists has been to find structure in, or reason behind, seemingly illogical practices, beliefs, and behaviours of more or less exotic people. The implicit difference and comparison between us and them has propelled the discipline since its inception. One of the assumed and implicit differences between us and them has been the idea that, unlike our behaviour, the behaviour of exotic others is symbolically motivated. Western people lost the symbolic drive in the course of the civilising process, and nineteenth-century urbanism and industrialisation have progressively wiped out the rural residues of popular symbolism in the West.

Parallel to the exotic-oriented anthropological traditions, national ethnological traditions developed, which focused not only on traditional crafts and material culture of the national peasantry, but also on folk traditions, customs, and the residues of symbolism. Especially in Scandinavia, Eastern Europe, and France the inward-oriented ethnology flourished even more than the outward-oriented anthropology. In some instances, ethnology also adopted the method of ethnographic fieldwork. Although at present ethnologists mainly operate under the guise of anthropology, their research has always reflected, and still does reflect, its national orientation. In 1984 the well-known Swedish ethnologist Orvar Löfgren was probably the first to address the topic of the contemporary home in his cultural analysis of the interior decoration of the Swedish working class. Ethnological data have become a source of information in anthropological research on the history of the contemporary home and domestic practices.

In the anthropological discipline, however, the house as a reflection of a culture became a topic in the 1960s. Both the French school of structuralism and the British school of structural functionalism saw spatial layouts and demarcations as a key to the understanding of a culture, because spatial layouts mirror the way people classify their living environment. In the perspective of the founding father of structuralism Claude Lévi-Strauss and his initial follower Pierre Bourdieu, not only the layout of compounds or villages, but also the spatial demarcations within houses mirrored major cultural distinctions and represented as such a variation of a number of so-called binary oppositions common to most cultures, like the oppositions of nature–culture, man–woman, life–death, dark–light, left–right, east–west, and raw–cooked. Especially, the spatial demarcations within the microcosm of the house were perceived as a reflection of the culture's cosmology and functioned as an analytical tool in the anthropologist's understanding of the culture.

The perspective of structural functionalists, such as Mary Douglas and Clark Cunningham, however, was less bi-polar, and more focused on behaviour that expressed ritual zoning and symbolic boundaries in and around the house. For instance, the behaviour regarding thresholds is a major focus of attention. Still in both perspectives the concept of the house is perceived as the conflation of a spatial and a symbolic structure, and acts as a shorthand for a cultural analysis of the symbolic kind.

The house – symbolic as it may be – lacks, however, the emotional connotation of home, which Westerners including anthropologists find so special about their own dwelling. Therefore the switch to the concept of the home in late twentieth-century anthropological writings is first and foremost explained by a change of research areas. Anthropology was literally brought home to the countries where the academic tradition of the discipline was founded. Fieldwork studies closer to home resulted not only from shrinking research funds in the 1970s, but also from fewer and fewer exotic research paradises left unspoilt by Western civilisation.

When the research focus of British and American anthropology shifted to their backyards (the Mediterranean and Latin America) the rigid disciplinary boundaries between anthropology, sociology, political science, and history blurred. This resulted in blends such as historic anthropology, political anthropology, and civilisation studies. In addition, the implicit cultural comparison between 'us' and 'them' changed more and more into an explicit historic comparison between now and then to explain an existing situation, or mind frame. The blending introduced sociological issues into the anthropological discipline, such as power, stratification, class, and the civilising process.

Although the symbolic perspective soon lost ground in anthropological studies of urban communities closer to home, it flourished in anthropological studies of traditional rural communities which were perceived as primitive isolates in modern societies. For a short while the research interests of anthropologists and ethnologists intertwined in their collective focus on traditionalism and its revival. The segregation of the sexes which pervaded every aspect of traditional rural society – as also represented in the respective domains within farmhouses – triggered the feminist aspirations of young female anthropologists to fight patriarchal dominance in their pursuit of a more activist agenda.

In women's studies, an offspring of the emerging feminist perspective in the social sciences of the late 1970s, not only the traditional house but also the modern home were perceived as patriarchal constructions. In bringing to the fore the relation between gender, power, and space Shirley Ardener's volume *Women and Space: Ground Rules and Social Maps* (1981) was ground-breaking. The twining of traditional symbolic and feminist perspectives in anthropology characterises the renewed interest in the home since the 1980s: for example, ethnology's interest in rural material culture blended into the material culture studies of anthropologists in their research of consumption practices and objects in the home.

By bringing anthropology 'home', anthropologists have put themselves in competition not only with a range of other social scientists interested in the contemporary home and its inhabitants, such as sociologists, ethnologists, environmental psychologists, and human geographers, but also with art, literary, design, cultural, and architectural historians interested in the historic development of the representations and material manifestations of the home, its domestic interior, furnishings, and domestic technology. Within this wide scholarly arena of research on the contemporary urban home and its historic development there are evidently interdisciplinary crossovers in methodology and sources. Anthropologists, however, seek for distinction in clinging to the discipline's ethnographic roots.

Anthropological Methods and the Home

One may wonder what makes research on the home distinctly anthropological when most of the research is practised in the anthropologist's home country, or in more or less familiar situations. It is not only a situation in which the traditional fieldwork method of doing-the-things-they-do has lost its urgency, but also a home situation in which prolonged participant observation of even an invited ethnographer will produce tensions. The ethnographer's stay in the narrow confines of the home will in the long run conflict with the inhabitants' feelings of hospitality and privacy. Other than making the research less invasive by shortening the stays and by reducing the participation, there is no real alternative to the ethnographic method of participant observation most anthropologists so strongly identify with. This also clarifies why participant observation in the home is seldom practised. Nevertheless, anthropologists tend to claim a distinctive approach.

In the mundane interpretation, however, anthropological methods describe the ways in which trained anthropologists 'do' research, and while this may result in distinctly anthropological perspectives, it will not necessarily do so. The prevailing research methods in the anthropological study of the contemporary home are for the most part qualitative in nature, and include a combination of home visits, in-depth interviews, photographic documentation, and to a lesser extent also video documentation. Although the claimed hierarchy of trustworthiness of behaviour over discourse is crumbling (due to the change of research methods) practices are still the anthropologist's main focus of attention.

Though modern technology enables observation of a non-participatory kind in the guise of video cameras installed in the home, this is generally disapproved of by anthropologists. The one-way video observation, introduced into the home by psychologists to monitor and research the interaction between parents and children, conflicts with the professional ethics of modern anthropology. Not only is communicative equality in research situations deemed to be of quintessential importance, but so also is sincere respectfulness towards the privacy of the research subject. There is, however, a trend towards a more interactive use of video documentation, as in the so-called 'show-us-your-home' approach, when the inhabitants handle the camera and document their home for anthropological research purposes. Afterwards the videos are discussed with the anthropologist.

One of the most frequently used research methods in present-day anthropological research in general, and in the study of the contemporary home in particular, continues to be the in-depth interview. However, the qualitative research method of the in-depth interview presupposes the near-native speaker qualities of the anthropologist, which were uncommon in the early days of the discipline. Although the in-depth interview is methodologically linked to the former role of key informants, it has balanced the communication between the researcher and the researched and reduced the anthropologist's dependence on key informants. Although the method of the in-depth interview can not in any way claim to be distinctly anthropological, the anthropologist's approach probably can. In contrast to the biographical approach of oral historians, for instance, anthropologists tend to search for meaning that transcends the individual interviewee. The anthropologist's interpretation is directed at a wider (sub)cultural meaning characteristic of a certain group of people, often addressed as identity. Although the identity concept is in origin a psychological concept it has been incorporated into the vocabulary of the social sciences and, in particular, to studies of migrant communities within national borders.

The historic anthropological study of the home is directed at understanding the present situation by taking into account the historic development. As such it might seem historical in method and approach, but again there is a definite anthropological twist. Anthropology, as a discipline rooted in the implicit cultural comparison between 'us' and 'them', thrives on the estranging effect of difference. In the historic anthropological approach it is the comparison of the seemingly self-evident present with the situation in the past that estranges the present and renders the self-evident intriguing. Western facilities like archives, museums, and libraries offer anthropologists an abundance of historic sources to draw on, from written sources to pictorial material, as diverse as paintings, photographs, drawings, movies, and advertisements. In contrast to historians, however, sources are only a means to an end, and not an end in itself. The anthropologist's rather indiscriminative attitude towards historical sources might conflict with the historian's more discriminative attitude. Being an insider in the culture under scrutiny the historic anthropologist takes the position of the key informant and co-constructor of meaning in the research.

Linked to the historic anthropological approach is the reverse anthropological approach in which Western cultural phenomenon are explained in reference to non-Western cultural phenomena, as described in ethnographies of societies once called primitive. The explicit reversal of the implicit comparison between us and them is the legacy of the 1970s generation of radical American anthropologists, who criticised not only the claimed superiority of Western civilisation in general and anthropology in particular, but also the colonial roots of the discipline. Although the penances of the white men's burden were mainly rhetoric, they did stimulate future generations of anthropologists to problematise their own societies and as such contribute to the homecoming of the discipline. In combination with a more critical stance towards anthropology's underlying assumptions it fostered a modern culture critique.

Anthropological Theories and the Home

The method of reverse anthropology also introduced the symbolic analysis of the house into the study of the contemporary Western home. As such it subverted the notion of an all-pervasive rationality in Western societies. In the reverse perspective, seemingly mundane household practices, such as laundering, cleaning, and clearing, are interpreted as domestic rituals restoring symbolic boundaries and meaningful categories. Meaning and meaning construction – either inside or outside the home – are not necessarily conscious affairs, but essentially related to and sustained in practice. Rituals are recurrent practices in which meanings are imbued and coined. Meaning dissolves when it is not enacted time and again. The importance of practices in the sustentation of meaning underlines anthropology's traditional focus on the things people do. The reverse perspective introduces more traditional anthropological issues and theoretical notions into the study of the contemporary home and its domestic practices, such as reciprocity and gift giving, kinship relations, and rites.

The homecoming of anthropology and the study of the contemporary home in Western consumer societies also resulted in a revival of material culture studies, which until then had been mainly researched in ethnographic museums or on archaeological sites. Notably, Daniel Miller's prolific research on consumption and the home has inspired a generation of European anthropologists in studying the meaning of mass-produced objects within the context of the home. Miller captures the power of individual consumers in the concept of appropriation in opposition to the powerless, mass-related concept of alienation in traditional Marxist rhetoric. Individual consumers appropriate mass-produced objects by incorporating them into a domestic universe of personal meaning: the material home.

In consumer studies like these, however, the concept of identity is often presented to designate the individual character of the creation or appropriation, while the essence of concepts like identity and also style refer to their social character, be it in opposition or in coalition, and as such it transcends individual homes. The complexity of identity creation is best exemplified in the formation of an ethnic identity, which is a complicated emotional process in which migrants not only define the difference between the host society and themselves, but also redefine the relation with their home country and its traditions vis-à-vis the host society. Anthropological studies of migrant homes mainly focus on material expressions of the migrant's native identity as displayed in decor and furniture, and to a far lesser extent on the use of domestic spaces or domestic practices which demand prolonged participant observation in the home.

Home: A Cultural Construct

The concept of home when used in ordinary speech has multifarious meanings. In general it refers to a strong emotional bonding with a place and a material environment, ranging in scale from a room, a dwelling, or a residential institution to a street, a neighbourhood, a village, a town, a region, or even a country. However, more often than not it will also include an emotional attachment to one or more living beings on that location, ranging from pets, significant others, family members and friends, to neighbours, fellow-citizens, and compatriots. Although there is a hierarchy in home attachments of ties to people over places, both commitments are not necessarily twinned, and both will change in the course of a lifetime. Cohabitation, marriage, birth, divorce, the moving out of adult children, and death will change not only the human home environment, or the so-called household composition, but most likely lead to a change in the material home environment too, such as moving house to another location, a renovation, or refurbishment.

In sum, the concept of home defies easy definitions, not only because it is layered and multifarious, but more so because it is deeply engrained in Western culture and societal organisation. Western culture and society thrive on the emotional, social, and spatial opposition between the domains of home and work. From an anthropological perspective home is no less than a cultural construct. It is the outcome of a cultural, societal, and historic development towards the progressive separation of two domains, represented in the separate urban domains of consumption and production as the respective spaces of living and working. These two domains were once united under one roof. The historic development in the layouts of European farmhouses is in turn a perfect illustration of the progressive separation of the two domains in one building. Town and country – once the dominant opposition in Western culture – is overshadowed by the modern opposition between home and work.

The importance of the home in Western culture finds its expression, among others, in the concept of privacy. Privacy in the home, however, is not a property of domestic space as such, but effectuated by demarcation practices of its inhabitants. The primary demarcation practices pertain to the shutting of doors and the closing of curtains, but they are in essence wilful, temporary, and reversible – otherwise the home will become a prison, and privacy a punishment. The modern family home in particular is an arena of demarcation practices by parents and children alike, for example, because demarcation practices in the home are used to underline the cherished male or female gender identities of children, as represented in the separate colour coding in the decoration of boys' and girls' bedrooms. While sex discrimination in the workplace is prohibited by law, it is justified in the decorational differences between boys' and girls' rooms at home. From an anthropological perspective, this illustrates the special character of the home domain in Western culture.

See also: Cultural Analysis of Housing and Space; Discourse Analysis; Ethnography; Feminist Perspectives on Home.

Further Reading

Ardener S (ed.) (1981) *Women and Space: Ground Rules and Social Maps*. London: Croom Helm.

Berreman GD (1974) Bringing it all back home: The malaise in anthropology. In: Hymes D (ed.) *Reinventing Anthropology*, 4th edn., pp. 83–98. New York: Vintage Books.

Birdwell-Pheasant D and Lawrence-Zúñiga D (eds.) (1999) *House Life: Space, Place and Family in Europe*. Oxford: Berg.

Blunt A and Dowling R (eds.) (2006) *Home*. London: Routledge.

Bourdieu P (1990) The Kabyle house or the world reversed. (1970) In *The logic of Practice*. pp. 271–283. Cambridge: Polity Press.

Carsten J and Hugh-Jones S (1995) *About the House: Lévi-Strauss and Beyond*. Cambridge: Cambridge University Press.

Cieraad I (ed.) (1999) *At Home: An Anthropology of Domestic Space*. Syracuse NY: Syracuse University Press.

Collignon B and Staszak J-F (eds.) (2003) *Espaces Domestiques: Construire, Habiter, Représenter*. Paris: Bréal.

Cunningham CE (1973) Order in the Atoni house (1964) In: Needham R (ed.) *Right and Left: Essays on Dual Symbolic Classification*, pp. 204–238. Chicago: Chicago University Press.

Daniels IM (2009) *The Japanese House: An Ethnography*. Oxford: Berg.

Löfgren O (1984) The sweetness of home: Class, culture and family life in Sweden. *Ethnologia Europeae* 14(1): 44–64.

Mallett S (2004) Understanding home: A critical review of the literature. *The Sociological Review* 52(1): 62–89.

Miller D (ed.) (2001) *Home Possessions: Material Culture Behind Closed Doors*. Oxford: Berg.

Nippert-Eng CE (1996) *Home and Work: Negotiating Boundaries Through Everyday Life*. Chicago: Chicago University Press.

Peirano MGS (1998) When anthropology is at home: The different contexts of a single discipline. *Annual Review of Anthropology* 27: 105–128.

Relevant Website

www.bergpublishers.com – *Home Cultures: The Journal of Architecture, Design and Domestic Space.*

Appraisal and Cost–Benefit Analysis

K Addae-Dapaah, National University of Singapore, Singapore

© 2012 Elsevier Ltd. All rights reserved.

Glossary

Appraisal The process of developing an opinion of value of an asset. It also refers to the assessed value – the estimated monetary worth – of the asset in question.

Evaluative complexity A system (such as society) consisting of multiple stakeholders (such as individuals) with different views of what is desirable and undesirable. Utility or value of a thing is thus in the eye of the beholder.

Externalities Uncompensated direct impacts of a project on nonusers of the project.

Pareto improvement A situation in which either all parties to a transaction gain or some gain and no one loses from the transaction.

Potential Pareto improvement A situation in which those who gain from a project compensate losers from the project to result in an overall net gain to all parties.

Shadow price A surrogate price where no market exists.

Foundations of Cost–Benefit Analysis (CBA)

The coexistence of the sustainability movement and the reality of limited resources for which there are many alternative competing uses makes accountability for the use of public funds a very important and sometimes an emotive issue. Governments can reasonably account for the use of public funds for public projects such as those on housing, neighbourhoods, and so on, if they can have an acceptable and reliable tool for appraising projects. Thus, the need for a sound appraisal technique for the appraisal of projects involving huge public funds cannot be overemphasised. CBA is one such method that is widely accepted and used for appraising large-scale public sector investments. CBA considers life-cycle costs and benefits of a project with the noble objective of revealing the economically efficient investment alternative or course of action. In other words, the objective of CBA is the identification of investment alternative or course of action that maximises net benefit to society. It is a tool for judging the efficiency of public sector's allocation of resources to public projects such as housing. Maximisation of net social benefits is tantamount to maximisation of social utility or social welfare. The emphasis on society introduces evaluative complexity to the analysis which incorporates:

1. Defining the objective function
2. Defining the life-cycle of the project(s)
3. Identifying options offered by each project
4. Identifying the costs and benefits of the project
5. Measuring costs and benefits
6. Appraising costs and benefits
7. Calculating the appropriate discount rate to be used in converting future costs and benefits to present values.

Notwithstanding the emphasis on society, the concept of efficiency by which the utilisation of public funds is judged is firmly rooted in the market economy.

Efficiency Concept

A hallmark of the market economy is the spontaneous transaction of goods and services in which no party loses out. Let us assume that John wants to buy a house which Mark wants to sell for a minimum (WTA) of 400 000 pounds sterling. John wants to pay a maximum (WTP) of 500 000 pounds sterling. As long as the house changes hands between the two at a price between 400 000 and 500 000 pounds sterling inclusive, either both John and Mark win in the transaction or John wins and Mark does not lose and vice versa. If the house sells for 450 000 pounds sterling, each party gains 50 000 pounds sterling – Mark gains 50 000 pounds more than his WTA, while John gains 50 000 pounds by paying that amount less than his WTP. Alternatively, if the house changes hands at 500 000 pounds sterling, Mark gains 100 000 pounds more than his WTA, while John does not lose anything. The reverse could also be true when John gains all the 100 000 pounds and Mark loses nothing.

The change that results from the above example is defined as 'Pareto improvement' to imply that an efficient market transaction has occurred. CBA applies the concept of efficiency to publicly supplied goods by equating any utility that people derive from such goods to the people's WTP. Thus WTP and WTA are, respectively, the benefits that people derive from, and the cost of supplying a public good. The supply of a public good is considered to be efficient if the aggregate social benefits exceed costs. Given the differences between private and public goods, the application of the concept of efficiency to public goods appears to be putting a square peg in a round hole. Individuals have a choice in the consumption of private goods but may not have a choice in the consumption of a local public good such as neighbourhood renewal. This is imposed on the people living in the neighbourhood who have no choice except to consume it. Such a renewal providing better environmental quality could be both beneficial and disadvantageous to the neighbourhood dwellers while conferring advantages to people outside the neighbourhood who frequent the area. People who pass through such neighbourhood would enjoy the improved amenities free of charge while the neighbourhood dwellers may pay higher rentals/prices for houses. In effect, some people suffer net losses in such a situation to negate the 'Pareto improvement' attendant to efficiency.

Thus, on the basis of strict 'Pareto improvement', it is unlikely that any public sector project will pass the efficiency test. This problem can be overcome through the compensation principle which introduces relativity to the efficiency concept. According to the compensation principle, a 'Pareto improvement' will be achieved if everyone can receive a net profit by compensating losers from the gains of winners. This does not mean that there is actual redistribution of gains to ensure that losers from a public project are compensated for their losses. Thus, the existence of a net social benefit does not necessarily mean that everybody in society is better off. All it means is that the total benefits to society are higher than losses. There are winners and losers which could widen the gap between the rich and the poor if losses occur among the poor and benefits occur among the rich. In such instances, efficiency could negate equality of distribution to cause injustice and unfairness in society. One way to address the problem is taxation. However, taxation is a political issue and whether fair distribution of net gains from public projects can be achieved through taxation is a debatable issue. The main point is that as long as CBA results in a net social benefit, the public project is deemed efficient in the allocation of resources. Implementing the project is a political decision.

What Is Society in CBA?

Another important issue in CBA is the definition of 'Society'. The individuals that constitute society in CBA may differ across nations. While most CBA restrict the definition of society to individuals of one nation, some studies include benefits and costs of other countries. Furthermore, individuals comprising the present society only are considered in CBA. This may militate against the interest of the future generation to undermine sustainability especially if present society is preoccupied with short-term gains. Moreover, by a strict definition of society, everyone's preference(s) must count in CBA. However, actions are frequently taken which only take account of informed opinion and thus disenfranchise most people in society from registering their preferences. This may be justified on the basis of practicality as it is not pragmatic to get everybody in a nation to register his/her preference in a CBA exercise. This may be cost-prohibitive. Notwithstanding, this means that the preferences reflected in a CBA do not necessarily reflect those of the society at large.

Furthermore, the concept of individual preference that is of relevance to CBA is the preference registered in the market place and/or via a survey. This implies that only the preferences of those with effective WTP and respondents to a survey are taken into account. This may not be compatible with democratic decision-making. Similarly, the term benefit to society appears to be a misnomer as society is subject to definition. There is also the danger of equating prices to social values or preferences.

Decision Rule

Two models of discounted cash flow (DCF) technique are used as decision criteria in CBA. These are the net present value (NPV) and the internal rate of return (IRR).

Mathematically, the NPV model is expressed as follows:

$$\text{NPV} = \sum_{i=1}^{n} \left(\frac{B_t}{(1+k)^t} \right) - \sum_{i=1}^{n} \left(\frac{C_t}{(1+k)^t} \right) > 0 \quad [1]$$

where B_t is benefit in period t, C_t is the cost of the project, k is the discount factor, and n is the economic life of the project. A project is accepted if NPV is greater than zero, that is, if the total value (benefits) of the project exceeds the total cost in today's money. When there are several mutually exclusive options or projects, the one with the highest NPV should be chosen.

The IRR model is expressed mathematically as follows:

$$\sum_{i=1}^{n} \frac{B_t}{(1+r)^t} = \sum_{i=1}^{n} \frac{C_t}{(1+r)^t} \quad [2]$$

or

$$\sum_{i=1}^{n} \frac{B_t}{(1+r)^t} - \sum_{i=1}^{n} \frac{C_t}{(1+r)^t} = 0 \quad [3]$$

where r is the internal rate of return to be solved for in eqns [2] and [3]. A project is accepted if r is greater than k. The IRR can lead to a wrong decision when faced with mutually exclusive projects because of problems inherent in the IRR (notably the possibility of multiple rates of return and the assumed reinvestment at the IRR). These problems can be resolved through mathematical manipulations via the modified/adjusted/terminal value internal rate of return (MIRR/AIRR/TVIRR) or the financial management rate of return (FMRR). MIRR and FMRR have been described as examples of mathematical overkill. It is far easier, however, to use the NPV model which leads to the correct decision without further mathematical manipulation as it provides only one NPV: positive, negative, or zero at any time.

Another criterion used in CBA is the benefit–cost ratio (BCR). This is the ratio of the present value of total benefits to the total cost of a project (i.e., present value of total benefits divided by present value of total costs). Where two options can achieve the same objective, the one with a higher benefit–cost ratio is to be chosen. However, one must be very careful in using ratios as a higher ratio could be a function of scale problem. Furthermore, unless there is consistency in the variables that enter the numerators and denominators of the options, benefit–cost ratios could mislead one to make a wrong decision.

Choice of Discount Rate

The DCF models require the use of a discount rate, called the social discount rate (SDR) in CBA as it is supposed to reflect the perception of society. It may be defined as the rate at which benefits from a project fall over time. In the case of NPV, the SDR is required to convert all future values (benefits) to the present, while in the case of IRR, the SDR is the hurdle rate. A low SDR (relative to the 'true' SDR) will result in accepting projects which are not beneficial to society. Alternatively, an unreasonably high SDR will result in the rejection of projects which are otherwise beneficial to society. Thus, the need for choosing an appropriate SDR cannot be overemphasized. Unfortunately, there is no consensus on how to derive the SDR. There are three main schools of thought: the social time-preference rate (STPR), the social opportunity cost rate (SOCR), and the synthetic or weighted-average cost rate.

STPR

This school argues that SDR should reflect society's preference for present consumption over future consumption. Thus, STPR is the rate that depicts the relative value that society as a whole assigns to present as opposed to future consumption at the margin. Time-preference smacks of 'pure myopia' which arises from fear of death and the belief that future generations will be wealthier than present society. According to the risk of death theory, people prefer to enjoy benefits today than tomorrow for fear that they may not live tomorrow. This implies that people of different ages will have different time preferences which are all subject to probabilities. Logically, the older you are, the higher will be your time-preference rate.

The risk-of-death position fails to consider the strong bequest motive of the aged which will considerably reduce their time-preference rate. Old people usually think more about the future of their children and grandchildren than themselves. Thus, they sacrifice present consumption for the future consumption of their children. Moreover, society is a great continuum. Thus, present society has a responsibility for future societies. This means that present society should not be selfish to dissipate resources to satisfy its needs at the expense of future societies.

Similarly, the contention that future generations will be wealthier is debatable especially in view of the fear that the earth will not be able to sustain human life in the future due to global warming and the rapid depletion of the earth's resources. This implies that any STPR must consider both the present and future societies. Moreover, since the analysis involves evaluation complexity, averaging individuals' time-preference rate will not represent the collective rate of society. It has been suggested within this school of thought that STPR should incorporate diminishing marginal utility over time by estimating a marginal utility of income function. Thus,

$$s' = \left(\frac{1+c}{1+n}\right)^e - 1 \qquad [4]$$

where s' is the STPR derived from the marginal utility argument, c is the consumption growth rate, n is population growth rate, and e is the elasticity of marginal utility function. The problem is whether the variables in eqn [4] are truly reflective of the society.

SOCR

It is argued that the SDR should be equal to the opportunity cost of government projects. Since public investment involves withdrawing resources from alternative investment opportunities in the private sector, the SDR must be equal to the rate of return obtainable from the alternative investment. However, the return on private investment is not based on social values and cost. Thus, the SOCR school may not be comparing an apple with an apple.

Synthetic or weighted-average rate
It is presumed that the STPR, s, will be less than the opportunity cost rate. Since both the STPR and the opportunity cost rates are relevant in CBA, both rates

must be reflected in the STPR through the use of a weighted-average r^* as SDR:

$$r^* = wr + (1-w)i \quad [5]$$

where w is the share of funds for the public project which is at the expense of investment, r is the opportunity cost rate, and i is the SDR. This approach attempts to merge SDR with shadow prices of capital to confuse the two issues.

Discount Rates in Practice

Given the different schools of thought and even disagreements within the same school, it is not surprising that SDRs used in practice varies from country to country and even within countries. For example, US government agencies use SDRs ranging from 0 to 12%. An SDR of 8% has been used by the Australian government, while in the United Kingdom, the HM Treasury Green Book recommends an SDR of 3.5% for projects with economic life of up to 30 years after which a declining schedule of discount rates is recommended. The use of one SDR for a public project that may have repercussions on future generations is problematic as the SDR, if it can be realistically estimated at all, is likely to change with time.

Appraisal of Costs and Benefits

The use of DCF as the decision criterion requires the specification of the quantity, variability, timing, and duration of benefits and costs in monetary units which are discounted at the chosen SDR to arrive at a net present value of social benefits. This requires the identification of all benefits and costs, tangible and intangible, local, regional, national, and all externalities. This is by no means an easy task as the social welfare benefits (if measurable at all) of public projects like housing are not certain. What is perceived as a benefit at the outset may turn out to be a cost in the long run. For example, low-income Glasgow families who were relocated to improved housing estates sacrificed food expenditure to pay doubled rents which resulted in increased mortality rate. Higher rents led to poorer nutrition and better housing led to a higher death rate! What would have been considered a benefit in CBA turned out to be a heavy cost in terms of human life. No amount of risk analysis could have predicted such an outcome in practice. Even where human life is predictably at risk, the valuation of human life is extremely problematic. Apart from moral connotations, it is questionable whether the metrics used in such valuation, for example, expected future earnings based on income, age, economic status, and so on, provide a fair valuation of human life. The worth of human life to his family, friends, and society in terms of help, happiness, comfort, and so on, offered is priceless.

Since the main objective of CBA is the maximisation of social welfare, the monetary values attached to the benefits and costs of a public project must reflect society's valuation of the final goods and resources involved in the project. Prices are often used in CBAs. In the United Kingdom, for example, the HM Treasury Green Book specifically states that real or estimated market values should be used in CBAs where markets exist for the public goods. The question is whether prices obtained from the market place fairly reflect social values. Second, if there are no markets for the public good, how do we derive surrogate prices that reflect social valuations? In evaluative complexity, collective view of society may not necessarily be the average of individual idiosyncratic views as people behave differently in a group from how they do when they are alone. This implies that even deriving and attaching weightages to individual preferences to calculate social preferences become somewhat questionable.

Since the commitment of public funds to a project entails an opportunity cost, the relevant price that must be used in CBA should be the price that reflects the opportunity cost of the project. The price which reflects the true social opportunity cost of using public funds for a project is called 'shadow' or 'accounting' price. A shadow price, S, may be defined as the increase in social welfare that results from any marginal change in the availability of a public good. Assuming public investment output good g is denoted by P_g, the shadow price is expressed as follows:

$$S_g = \frac{\Delta \, Social \; welfare}{\Delta \, Output \; of \; Good \; P_g} \quad [6]$$

A shadow price is not observable in actual markets. Thus, actual market prices may or may not approximate shadow prices. This implies that marginal social cost may not necessarily equate marginal private cost. The two are bound to vary as profit maximisation in the private sector does not account for externalities. Public projects such as housing low-income families have externalities. Ignoring external costs and benefits implies that the prices of private goods will not reflect true social cost. Moreover, using price as a measure of social welfare is somewhat problematic as price is not equal to value although economic analyses are based on price.

Another problem with the use of marginal costs as shadow prices for final goods is that optimality conditions can only be met if all final goods are priced at marginal costs. Since not all final goods are priced at the marginal cost because of market imperfection, the substitution of private marginal cost for social marginal cost (shadow price) in the public sector militates against Pareto optimum which is the foundation of CBA.

Valuation of Intangibles

Intangibles such as improved security, dignity, improved sanitation, and so on, associated with better housing environment need to be included in CBA. Surrogate market technique, the hedonic model, is often used to value a quality of the environment (e.g., improved sanitation) that has no explicit market.

Hedonic price function establishes a functional relationship between the market-clearing housing price and the attributes of the housing unit:

$$P(H) = f(h_1, h_2, \ldots, h_k)$$

where $P(H)$ is the price of the house and $h_1 \ldots h_k$ are the utility bearing attributes of the house. One can use the hedonic function to estimate people's WTP for a better housing environment. The problem is satisfying oneself that the better housing environment premium from the hedonic model is purely attributed to better housing environment. Furthermore, since the hedonic function uses market phenomena, only those who operate in the market have their preferences reflected in the model. Therefore, the premium may not reflect society's valuation of the attribute. Moreover, hedonic model holds all other attributes, except the one in question, constant. This is problematic as in evaluative complexity as pertains to society, unlike economics, all other things are not equal. Society epitomises complexity of the highest order. Thus, drawing a sample from better housing and relatively poor housing areas to determine the premium for better housing as a proxy for society's WTP for better housing is problematic as the sample differs markedly in social and economic status.

Another method for assessing people's WTP is contingent valuation (CV). CV is a method for establishing a monetary value for a good or service by asking people what they are willing to pay for it or accept as a compensation for losing it. CV takes several forms: bidding games, convergent direct questioning, trade-off games, moneyless-choice method, and priority evaluation method – all are based on surveys.

Note that expressing WTP is not the same as paying. In paying, a person parts with money (suffers a loss) to obtain something, while in expressing WTP, a person has no skin in the game. WTP may be overstated if benefits are to be received and understated if costs are to be incurred. Alternatively, respondents to a survey may give answers considered to be in accord with the interviewer's preferences just to please the interviewer. Thus, it is not surprising that CV methods have been subjected to severe criticism. Notwithstanding the caveats, CV has been used for projects in the United Kingdom, Australia, the United States, Madagascar, Morocco, Croatia, and so on, by several government bodies and international institutions including the World Bank.

Furthermore, the Delphi Technique which relies on the informed opinion of a group of experts is used to value intangibles. The Delphi technique suffers from being undemocratic. The values of experts could be divorced from society at large. Thus, some of the critical inputs in CBA are, at best, intelligent guesstimates to support or oppose a proposed public project.

Conclusions

CBA has received worldwide acceptance as a tool for judging the efficiency of public projects. Given that the efficiency concept on which CBA is founded is difficult to apply to public projects, the results of CBA are subject to interpretation. The use of WTP, the difficulty in ascertaining benefits and costs (which evolve over time) at the outset, the valuation methodologies which use questionable proxies to measure society's WTP and social welfare, introduces a lot of uncertainties in CBA which are difficult to handle through risk analysis. The uncertainties and valuation problems reduce the reliability of CBA as a strict quantitative technique. The phrase 'net social benefit' which CBA is aimed at maximising, is misleading as winners do not compensate losers to effect potential Pareto improvement that is pivotal to CBA. Thus, maximisation of net social benefits could lead to unfairness and injustice. However, the need to justify decisions on public projects on a transparent and objective basis calls for appraisals, and thus the wide use and acceptance of CBA. Although the philosophical and economic bases of CBA have been the subject of controversy over the years, CBA has been and can be effectively used to appraise public projects provided analysts pay heed to its effectiveness and limitations, and policy-makers use the results of CBA with care.

See also: Behavioural Economics; Critical Realism; Economics of Social Housing; Health, Well-Being and Housing; Neighbourhood Effects: Approaches; Politics of Housing; Residential Segregation and Ethnic Diversity in the United States; Social Justice.

Further Reading

Ackerman F and Heinzerling L (2004) *Priceless: On Knowing the Price of Everything and the Value of Nothing.* New York: The New Press.

Boardman AE, Greenberg DH, Vining AR, and Weimer DL (2006) *Cost-benefit analysis: Concepts and practice*, 3rd edn. Upper Saddle River, NJ: Pearson Education, Inc.

Brent RJ (2006) *Applied Cost-Benefit Analysis*, 2nd edn. Cheltenham, UK: Edward Elgar.

Layard R and Glaister S (ed) (1994) *Cost-Benefit Analysis*, 2nd edn. Cambridge, UK: Cambridge University Press.

Megbolugbe IF (1996) Understanding neighbourhood dynamics: A review of the contributions of William G. Grigsby. *Urban Studies* 33(10): 1779–1795.

Meyer PB (1994) Institutional myopia and policy distortions: The promotion of homeownership for the poor. *Journal of Economic Issues* 28(2): 567–576.

Michaels RG and Smith VK (1990) Market segmentation and valuing amenities with hedonic models: The case of hazardous waste sites. *Journal of Urban Economics* 28: 223–242.

Mishan EJ (1969) *Welfare Economics: London, An Assessment*. Amsterdam: North-Holland Publishing Company.

Mishan EJ and Quah E (2007) *Cost-Benefit Analysis*, 5th edn. London: Routledge.

Oka T (2003) Effectiveness and limitations of cost-benefit analysis in policy appraisal. *Government Auditing Review* 10: 17–27.

Architects

TG Lee, University of Calgary, Calgary, AB, Canada

© 2012 Elsevier Ltd. All rights reserved.

Glossary

Architect A person or entity registered, licensed, or otherwise authorised exclusively to use the title 'architect' to plan and design buildings, and who participates in supervising the construction of a building. The architect's decisions affect public safety and therefore he/she must undergo specialised training and education, and a practicum for practical experience in order to qualify for and earn a licence to practise.

Architectural technologist A person with technical training and experience, who provides building design services such as the design and drafting of houses. They can coordinate or manage the house construction process from conception through to completion. Architectural technologists can have their own house design firms or be employed in architectural offices or municipalities.

Beauty A house that is designed and constructed in balance and harmony that provides a perceptual experience of pleasure, meaning, or satisfaction and leads to feelings of attraction and emotional well-being. While there is some subjectivity with the concept of beauty based on culture and taste, it is generally recognised as an object such as a house that is admired, or possesses features well conceived and executed to achieve perfection.

Building envelope The building enclosure including all walls, windows, and roofs, and their components, which wraps the entire building to separate the interior from the exterior environment. The building envelope provides a weather barrier such that the interior space can be conditioned for occupant's comfort and health. Building envelopes perform the function of structure integrity and moisture, temperature, and air pressure controls.

House designer Anyone who designs a house. In most countries, anyone can call themselves and offer services as a house designer as there is no requirement for training, licensing, and liability. Thus the quality, competence, or the house design can greatly vary.

Plagiarism Is the imitation or outright copy of someone else's design, representing it as one's own original work. While plagiarism is frowned upon in academia, it is acceptable for architecture students and even architects to emulate (but not copy) the style of another architect.

Profession A vocation or calling, especially one that involves some branch of advanced learning or science. In some countries, the use of the word profession is limited only to those in specific disciplines, such as law, medicine, architecture, and engineering, that are given government licences.

Real estate agent A person hired by a prospective home purchaser to facilitate the finding and purchasing of a house, or to sell their house. They must be able to estimate the current cost of a house, and know the rules governing the sale and purchase of houses. Real estate agents work for real estate brokers who manage real estate offices.

The Profession of Architecture

Historically, the scholarly endeavours and practices of medicine, law, and theology were considered as (the so-called learned) professions since they had certain principles and characteristics distinct from other vocations. Architecture is the sole profession whose members are qualified to design and to provide advice, including technical and aesthetic judgement of the built environment. This profession endeavours to identify the public need, and to serve the public interest, in matters relating to the built environment, which is commonly called environmental design.

The architect is a person or entity registered, licensed, or otherwise authorised by local authorities to practise architecture and may have exclusive use of the title 'architect' whereby others cannot call themselves an architect. Having this restricted title comes with the privilege but also the responsibility of belonging to this selected profession. An architect has the ability to undertake many related services because of extensive training generally requiring 6 years of university education, plus 2–3 years of apprenticeship and a rigorous set of examinations. Government licensing of architects requires strict adherence to qualification (education and experience), a code of practice, ethics, and responsibility.

Unfortunately, the expression 'profession' or 'professional' is often misused and overused, being applied to virtually all vocations. Thus, draftspersons, house designers, or architectural technologists, who do not have the requisite training or limitations of licensure and regulation, cannot be called a professional, at least in countries that recognise the distinction. In granting this privilege to architects, the public expects the profession to provide services and solutions with technical competence and aesthetic sensitivity suitable to the physical, social, cultural, and economic environment, thereby inspiring the community and its citizens.

Practice of Architecture

The practice of architecture consists of the provision of professional services in connection with town planning as well as the design, construction, expansion, conservation, restoration, or alteration of a building or group of buildings. These professional services include, but are not limited to, planning and land-use planning; urban design; provision of preliminary studies, designs, models, drawings, specifications, and technical documentation; coordination of technical documentation prepared by others (consulting engineers, urban planners, landscape architects, and other specialist consultants) as appropriate and without limitation; construction economics; contract administration; monitoring of construction (referred to as supervision in some countries); and project management.

It is generally recognised by the public that architects are needed to design public and institutional buildings of obvious complexities. Most countries do not require an architect to design a house, especially single family houses. For many architects, the design of a house, despite the small size, is the most challenging and fraught with problems because of the intimate and personal nature of the clients.

Ethical Standards for Architects

Ethics is defined as the rules or standards for moral behaviour based on common values and moral laws such as religious doctrines, secular beliefs, and traditional philosophies, which are adhered to by individuals, groups, corporations, industry, and professions. Professions such as architecture have a Code of Ethics and Professional Conduct by which their members must abide, or face disciplinary action or even expulsion from the profession. The seriousness of violating the code and possible disbarment requires a very exact procedure for disciplinary hearings and appeal options. This code not only addresses life safety and public welfare issues but also includes rules of conduct between members and the public.

Ethics of Architectural Design

Architecture is basically about creating space for people – to live, work, play, and socialise. The problem of simply stating that architecture is about creating space is that there are buildings in which there is very little space, such as the pyramid since it is of solid masonry. Thus architecture is more than just creating space.

xThe building enclosure (commonly called the building envelope) separates us from the outdoor environment, so that occupants can be comfortable and function effectively within. A variety of materials are strategically positioned in the walls and roofs to provide a continuous weather-tight barrier to the transmission of heat, sound, vapour and air as well as water leaks. Durability of building materials should be checked during selection, and its erection must also be safe to the inhabitants. Thus the role of the architect is not merely to build a large sculpture but to ensure the built environment serves its precise functions.

In the United States and European Union buildings consume about 40% of the total energy while the rest is consumed by transportation and industry. Since architects design many of these buildings, as well as plan cities that impact transportation, they can have a significant influence on future energy needs. The extraction and manufacturing of building materials and its erection consume energy (embodied energy), and in the process produce waste, leading to pollution (embodied pollution). Architects have the choice of selecting exotic materials from anywhere in the world. The embodied energy of selecting, for example, Italian marble for a countertop requires enormous amounts of effort and energy to extract that material from Italy and transport it half way around the world. It seems absurd to think of a bird going over to Italy to bring back some marble to build its nest but that is exactly what humans have done. Just because architects can access any material from anywhere in the world does not imply that they should.

It is not just the design and construction of buildings that consume so much energy but operation over the life of the buildings, perhaps lasting 100 years or more. The design decision when the building was conceived will have enormous impact on the amount of energy required to operate that building. Therefore, it is imperative for the architects to take the lead in addressing issues of resource depletion.

It is believed that Buckminster Fuller said, "If you build a building, you rape the earth" or that "we rape the Earth each time we build!" However, Frank Waters (1902–95), an American writer, in his 1940 book entitled *The Dust within the Rock*, states, "We are all fools! Blinded with greed, we rape the earth and declare ourselves its masters. We glut ourselves with the riches, cut the forests down like wheat, and jingling our dollars, cannot hear the voice of intolerable unrest within us. Beware America! The earth too has a voice which someday we must answer." Regardless of who first coined this phrase, it reveals the enormous environmental consequence of constructing a building. In addition to the resources required for building materials and energy to operate, the ecosystem of the land is destroyed by placing a building on top of it.

The Image of the Profession

The design of multiple family apartments and townhouses generally requires the services of an architect and their engineering consultants. The vast majority of single family houses in the developed world (probably more than 95%) are not designed by an architect. They are designed by architectural technologists, or designers with minimal training, because developers (who build the vast majority of the single family houses) do not perceive the need to use architects.

Thus very few members of the public would experience a house designed by an architect, because such houses are extremely rare. Most people would consider the average house as somewhat functional and acceptable. Only when they experience a house designed by an architect would they consider a house to be unique and truly exceptional.

Architectural magazines often feature houses designed by architects but the public perception is that these houses are only for the wealthy. Only they can afford to hire an architect to design a custom, one-of-a-kind house uniquely suited for the site. While the cost of a custom-designed house is slightly more than the cost of an average house with the same finish, it is the cost of the site that often sets the house apart from the typical suburban house. Most people have not considered that the fee paid to the architect is recovered and even more when the house is sold.

Architects are admired for their artistic creativity and problem-solving abilities. Architects and their buildings play a social role in the history of civilisation and culture. On the one hand, architecture inspires and impacts society and, on the other hand, it reflects a moment in time of a particular era.

There are varying opinions of the image projected by the architectural profession. The profession has been both blessed with a certain mystique and cursed by public misconceptions. Although the profession is respected, architects can sometimes be viewed as impractical dreamers or as strong-willed individuals.

Architects who push the boundaries of modern design are even criticised by modernist painters such as the French impressionist painter Pierre-Auguste Renoir. At the turn of the twenty-first century, there was a rejection of ornamental architecture of the Renaissance. With new building materials and better understanding of structural design calculation, buildings became simpler starting with Walter Gropius adopting the Bauhaus style in Germany from 1919 to 1933. This style was brought to North America, enabling the creation of the modern skyscraper by the American architect Louis Henri Sullivan.

Intimacy of House Design

Designing a house is a very intimate activity. The client lets the architect know their particular lifestyles, hobbies, relationships with their in-laws (provide a suite far off to the other side of the house), attitude towards their children, drinking habits (the wine cellar), entertainment (theatre), sexual preference (mirrors on the ceiling and bathtub), and so on.

The architect is often put in an awkward position of acting as a referee between married couples who have personal issues and who differ in taste and opinion. The architect tries to find solutions that will satisfy both but it is a never satisfactory compromise. Thus the architect loathes taking sides because satisfying one is insufficient when the other one is upset with the opinion.

Architects are very good at convincing the potential client that he/she is the best architect for the project. Upon successfully getting the commission, he/she goes away, excited and energised to create this edifice, a monument to his/her talents, and incidentally will also fulfil the needs of the client. Upon completing a conceptual design, the architect unveils the masterpiece, expecting that the client will be utterly delighted with the design, recognising the architect's greatness and creation along with great admiration and applause and thereby forever be in debt to the architect. There is not one iota of change that needs to be done. It is just perfect. Unfortunately, and over and over again, the architect's creation is bastardised by the client. It is but a delusion.

It is understandable that everyone wants to be appreciated for their work. It is disheartening that the unsophisticated client with no real understanding of architecture critiques the masterpiece created by the architect, who has extensive and rigorous education, experience, and talent, which are so easily rejected or dismissed by a client. Painters and musicians have patrons but there are no patrons who collect architectural masterpieces.

Even knowledgeable clients who had their house designed by famous architects may become critical of the design. The Edith Farnsworth house designed by Ludwig Mies van der Rohe is one of the most influential and aesthetically appealing houses of our century. It is characterised by large expanses of glass, by which the building opens up to the surrounding natural landscape, potentially causing biophilic responses in the inhabitants. The design of the house is considered aesthetically neutral because the outside is colourful, which is suited for contemplation, but it was a radical departure and contradiction between architecture and home. Despite spending several years in designing the house with the architect, Dr. Edith Farnsworth did not find the design satisfactory as a home and launched a lawsuit against the architect. Fortunately the judge ruled in favour of the architect.

Despite the criticism of architects and their houses, there are benefactors of radical designs. In the book *Women and the Making of the Modern House*, Alice T. Friedman has offered examples of many women clients who played an important role as patrons of innovative domestic architecture including the Hollyhock House by Frank Lloyd Wright, the Truus Schröder House by Gerrit Rietveld, the Constance Perkins House by Richard Neutra, and the Vanna Venturi House by Robert Venturi.

Why Must Architects Design Their Own House?

The custom-designed house represents an edifice whereby the homeowners can enjoy the fruits of their labour and talent and, more importantly, impress their friends, colleagues, and business partners. When the architect designs his/her own house, there is complete freedom to incorporate features that may not be accepted or bastardised by the unsophisticated clientele. Architects love to create their own private space, to show off their design skills such that the house represents a legacy of the architect's existence. The creation of the architect's own house is very personal.

What Inspires Architectural Design?

The public does not understand how architects design buildings. An artist has complete freedom of expression limited by whatever medium or palette he/she chooses. The public may believe that a beautiful design suddenly appears to the architect. It is certainly not that easy to design a building as the process of design can be a difficult undertaking for the architect.

While architectural design can be inspired, the added purpose of making buildings functional and safe does not come easily. It is obvious that buildings must be structurally sound to hold up a roof and to withstand environmental forces. Architecture is therefore not merely aesthetics but serves very practical functions. Thus the architect is both an artist and a builder who has social significance.

Plagiarism

Students of architecture study the various design styles through the ages and the architects that are associated with that style. Although there are historical, cultural, and technological reasons for evolution of certain architectural styles, there is also some subjectivity. There may be some consensus of good architectural styles that inspires young designers to emulate these styles in their design.

In academia, plagiarism is frowned upon on grounds of academic misconduct. When architecture students emulate the building style of a famous architect, it is acceptable as a means of learning from them but copying their entire design is not encouraged. One can incorporate elements of the style into his/her own studio design project. Thus the student and even graduate architect can design in the style of Mies van der Rohe, Frank Lloyd Wright, Le Corbusier, and so on.

Architects and the Real Estate Agent

As noted above, the architect typically requires 6 years of university education, plus 2–3 years of apprenticeship and a rigorous set of examinations. The real estate agent does not require a university degree but only 30–90 hours (1 week to 3 months part-time) of classroom instruction.

The design fee of an architect is typically based on a percentage (10–15%) based on the construction cost excluding land cost. The real estate agent fee in North America is typically 5–7% of the house including land cost. For European countries, the real estate fee is about 2–3%, which is more reasonable. Of interest is that while the architect can only charge for the design of the house, the real estate agent or their colleagues reap additional money every time it is sold. Typically, a house will be resold every 5–7 years, resulting in a potential fee of another 6–7% commission for the real estate agent.

Assuming a typical house is sold every 15 years, and the house lasts 80–100 years, it may be sold at least six times in its life. A $300 000 house with a 5–7% commission fetches $15 000 − 21 000 × 6 = $90 000 − 126 000. This does not account for the normally escalating price of the property. Thus the realtor fee includes the cost of land, which in some cases is as much or more than the cost of the house. The architect charges for the cost of construction when the house is built, early on in its life and thus the cheapest it will likely be worth.

There is little difference in the amount of time the real estate agent and the architect spend with the client to visit sites, advising the client on the merits of the site or property. The largest difference is the time spent

Table 1 Comparison of effort, compensation, and liability between architects and real estate agents in North America

Item	Architect	Real estate agent
Educational requirement	6 years university	30 and 90 hours of classroom instruction
Duration of work	3 months design + 6–8 months construction	Weeks to months
No. of times fee charged	1	6
Initial commission fee	10–15% of construction cost	5–7% of building + land
Fee based on $200 000 construction + $100 000 land	$20 000–30 000	$15 000–21 000
Resale commission fee	None	5–7%
Number of resales for the life of house	None	6–7 times
Total fee for life of house	$20 000–30 000	$90 000–147 000[a]
Annual liability insurance	$5000–30 000	$500–3000
Time to produce documents	500–1000 hour construction drawings +20–50 hour construction administration	3–5 hours to fill out standard sale agreement forms
Time to meet with client and the project	30–100 hours design meeting +50–150 hours site reviews	10–50 hours (show 10 houses)
Hourly rate (fee per hour/2) (fee split with consultants or seller)	$7.20–25 per hour	$163.64–807.70 per hour
Statue of Limitation	6–10 years[b]	As soon as it is sold

[a]Not included is the escalating cost of the house.
[b]6–10 years contractual limitation for the client, and for the life of the house for third party injuries.

afterwards to complete the work till the client moves into the house. For the architect, he/she must spend several months to design the house, and then must continue to provide site review and management services until the house is built, maybe for another 6–8 months. If anything goes wrong with the house after it is built, the architect will be notified perhaps within a statutory limit of 6–10 years. For the realtor, once the house is sold, he/she can close the file and work on the next sale.

Real estate agents must split their fees between seller and buyer (unless he is acting as both). The architect's fee is no different as it is also split with mechanical, electrical, and structural engineers, and there is no opportunity to undertake both the work and receive full commission.

An interesting comparison regarding the amount of effort, compensation, and liability between the architect and the real estate agent is made in **Table 1**.

For a typical life of a house, the realtor will receive five times more fees than the architect, spend five times less time on the project, and has no liability after the house is sold. Thus the architect has significant disadvantage of effort, compensation, and liability as compared to the real estate agent.

Why then do people want to be architects and design houses? It is certainly not for the monetary rewards. It is for the love of creating and legacy. Eero Saarinen (20 August 1910 to 1 September 1961), a Finnish American architect, said, "The purpose of architecture is to shelter and enhance man's life on earth and to fulfill his belief in the nobility of his existence." For that it is priceless.

See also: Housing Careers; Home Environments: Aesthetics, Fashion, Status; Institutions that Represent Housing Professionals; Meanings of Home; People and the Built Form; Price Determination in Housing Markets; Real Estate Agents.

Further Reading

Demkin JA (ed.) (2008) *The Architect's Handbook of Professional Practice*, 14th edn. The American Institute of Architects. Hoboken, NJ: John Wiley & Sons, Inc.

Friedman AT (2007) *Women and the Making of the Modern House*. New Haven, CT: Yale University Press.

International Union of Architects (UIA) (1998) *UIA Accord on Recommended International Standards of Professionalism in Architectural Practice*, 2nd edn. Paris: UIA.

Levitt D (2009) *The Housing Design Handbook: A Guide to Good Practice*. London: Taylor and Francis.

Pekzar MJ and Solomon LC (eds.) (1984) *Keeping Graduate Programs Responsive to National Needs. New Directions for Higher Education 46*. San Francisco, CA: Jossey-baas.

Piotrowski A and Robinson JW (eds.) (2001) *The Discipline of Architecture*. Minneapolis, MN: University of Minnesota Press.

RAIC (2009) *Canadian Handbook of Practice*, 2nd edn. Ottawa, Canada: The Royal Architectural Institute of Canada.

Royal Institute of British Architects (2009) *Architect's Essentials Bundle*. London: RIBA Publishing.

Yannick J (2007) Architectural lessons from environmental psychology: The case of biophilic architecture. *Review of General Psychology* 11(4): 305–328.

Asset-Based Welfare

L Murphy, University of Auckland, Auckland, New Zealand

© 2012 Elsevier Ltd. All rights reserved.

Glossary

Asset-based welfare Asset-based welfare involves the expansion of asset holdings among low-income households as a means of reducing wealth inequalities and promoting wealth-creating behaviours among citizens.

Equity withdrawal Housing equity is the value of a house minus any debt (e.g., mortgage) secured on the property. Equity withdrawal refers to the process of releasing the equity tied up in a house either through the sale of a property (housing equity release) or using existing equity to secure additional mortgage funding for consumption needs (mortgage equity release).

Social investment state The social investment state refers to a hybrid welfare system that involves investment in social and human capital. State expenditure extends beyond income support to include investment in skills, technology, and asset holding. The purpose of this investment is to endow citizens with the capacity to deal with economic change and the ability to provide for their own welfare needs. The goal is to create a more prosperous, inclusive, and cohesive society.

Introduction

The rise of neoliberalism with its emphasis on privatisation, financialisation, and market provision, in conjunction with the prospect of ageing societies and the so-called looming 'pension crisis', have created substantial pressures for change in welfare states. Traditionally, welfare states have been based on the notion of collective provision and have focussed on income support, with welfare programmes primarily funded through the taxation of current incomes. However, it is argued that the prospect of ageing societies, with higher dependency ratios, threatens the financial basis of traditional welfare states. In response to these problems, policy analysts and governments have sought to refashion welfare provision. One popular agenda argues that the long-held focus on income security needs to be shifted to a focus on asset building. At its simplest, the notion of asset-based welfare centres on the belief that providing individuals with (financial) assets facilitates a reduction in wealth inequalities within societies and promotes financial behaviours among individuals that support wealth creation.

The rising interest in asset-based welfare programmes aligns well with long-held political commitments that have supported the development of homeownership internationally. Homeownership has been promoted across the world (from North America, Europe, and Australasia to Asia) traditionally as a means of securing appropriate housing services but increasingly as a means of developing a financial asset. Liberalised mortgage markets and the growing fungibility of housing as an asset have meant that housing is increasingly viewed as a key component in the development of asset-based welfare and the 'social investment state'. This article examines the basic tenets of asset-based welfare policies and the possible role of homeownership within an asset-based welfare system. I argue that welfare policies that are based around supporting homeownership are inherently problematic. The nature (and possible benefits) of homeownership varies significantly across national housing systems and, even within individual countries, the tenure is characterised by a high degree of fragmentation and differentiation. Relying on homeownership to meet welfare goals does not address the problems of those in greatest need and could exacerbate wealth inequalities. In addition, promoting the financial practices required to make housing a cornerstone of asset-based welfare may undermine the role of housing as a source of long-term wealth, as households could increasingly enter the retirement phase with sizeable mortgage debts and smaller assets.

Asset-Based Welfare

While there are significant differences in welfare states and their evolution, at a broad level welfare states are underpinned by a commitment to minimum income support and collective provision. In general, welfare programmes are designed to assist individuals and households with their current consumption needs and are usually funded by taxing the incomes of those in employment (**Figure 1a**). As societies are progressively ageing, the burden of taxing those in work to meet the pension needs of a growing population is increasingly being seen as unsustainable. Governments around the world are

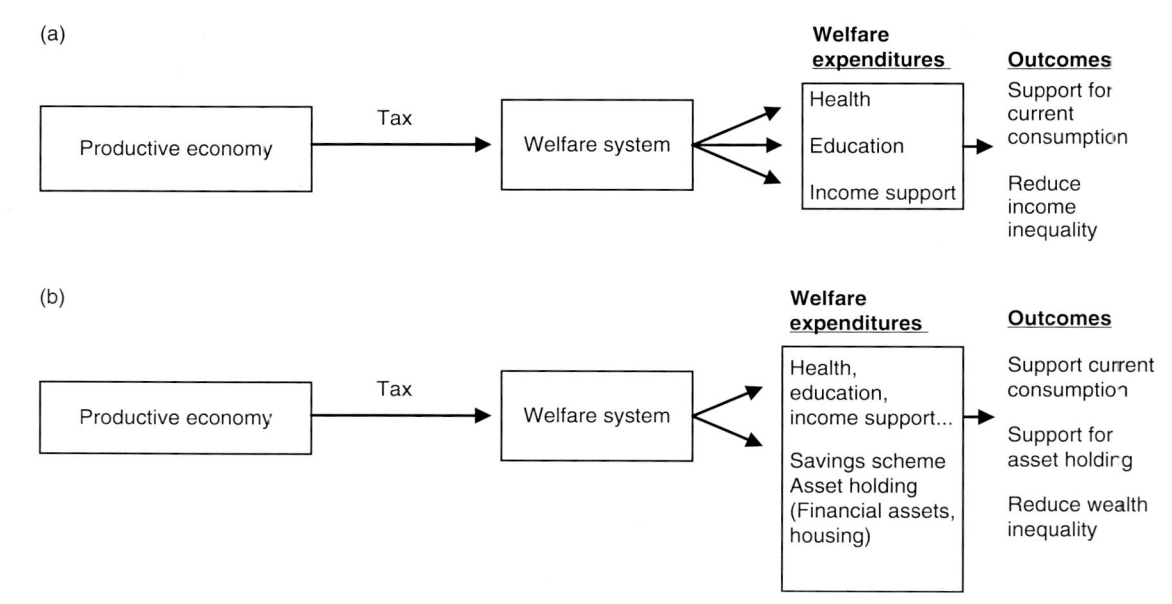

Figure 1 Simplified schema of traditional and asset-based welfare processes. (a) Traditional welfare state processes. (b) Asset-based welfare processes.

responding to the prospect of this 'apocalyptic demography' by introducing compulsory superannuation schemes as well as generally encouraging people to provide for their old age. In the context of a post-1980s consensus that markets are effective in meeting people's needs, governments are recasting welfare in terms of responsible citizens taking care of their own welfare.

Increasingly, asset-based welfare is being promoted as a possible policy response to the current problems of the welfare state. Sherraden (1991, 2003), a leading proponent of asset-based welfare, argues that policies that support the accumulation of assets (financial and physical) meet social protection goals (i.e., offer protection against hardship in times of need) and build capabilities (financial and entrepreneurial) within communities. In contrast to the traditional social welfare focus on income or consumption support, Sherraden suggests that asset-based welfare has the potential to increase people's capabilities and promote social and economic growth. Within this framework, governments are encouraged to promote and subsidise asset accumulation among the poor. In contrast to social welfare, that is viewed as a tax on growth, asset-based welfare is viewed as a form of welfare that contributes to long-term economic development (**Figure 1b**).

Sherraden acknowledges that asset-based tax benefits, designed to promote asset holding, are usually highly regressive in nature and often entrench existing wealth inequalities in society. In proposing the 'social investment state' he advocates progressive policies that are characterised by inclusiveness and a focus on developing the opportunities and capacities of low-income households.

Various asset-based welfare policies have emerged in recent years, including the Child Trust Fund in the United Kingdom and Individual Development Accounts (IDAs) in the United States. Under these schemes, eligible individuals are subsidised to save and can use their savings to purchase certain assets (e.g., housing, education, financial products). The schemes are designed to promote asset ownership in the long run and to encourage new attitudes to asset accumulation and self-management.

Asset-Based Welfare and Homeownership

Housing is the single largest asset class in the global economy. Internationally, homeownership rates have grown throughout the twentieth century, reflecting rising consumer demand and favourable housing policies. Governments have actively supported homeownership via financial incentives and tax policies because the tenure has traditionally been viewed as offering appropriate shelter outcomes and is believed to create positive individual and community effects. Political support for homeownership reflects a powerful ideology and discourse that surrounds the tenure. Within popular discourses, homeownership is often associated with economic development, wealth accumulation, self-reliance, good citizenship, and a variety of psychological and social benefits. Clearly, homeownership has long been promoted as a commodity that has substantial positive externalities but increasingly, and especially in the light of global financialisation processes, it is being viewed as a financial asset. For governments seeking to develop asset-based welfare policies, the connection between homeownership as an asset and individual/household welfare outcomes seems obvious.

In terms of asset-based welfare policies, support for homeownership represents support for asset accumulation, which in turn is believed to have positive welfare outcomes. At the very least, it is argued that elderly outright owners are likely to have low housing costs (apart from maintenance), which means that they can achieve higher consumption outcomes on fixed state pensions compared to elderly renters. In this context, outright homeownership has the potential to reduce poverty levels in old age and reduce pension demands within an economy.

Beyond this traditional view of homeownership as a form of economic security in old age, the post-1980s liberalisation of mortgage markets has altered the nature of housing as a financial asset. New and innovative mortgage products, aligned with liberal lending practices, have promoted increasing housing equity withdrawal (HEW) in certain housing markets (e.g., the United States, the United Kingdom) and helped to transform housing into the new ATMs (cash machines) of the post-2000 global consumer boom. In the United Kingdom, equity withdrawal amounted to £57 billion in 2003 and was estimated to account for 7% of consumer spending (Hamnett, 2010). The rise of HEW products points to an increasing sophistication in the operation of mortgage markets and in the practices of homeowners. From a policy point of view, these new practices raise the prospect of homeowners using HEW to support their incomes in old age or using equity from their housing asset to pay for welfare services, especially costly health services. In effect, homeownership has the potential to function as a type of pension. Underpinning this perspective is a belief that house prices are stable or rising over time. This has been called into question by the financial crisis of 2007–2009 and the subsequent sharp fall in house prices in some countries such as the United States, the United Kingdom, Ireland, and Spain, where generous mortgage lending had previously pushed up prices.

One of the most comprehensive asset-based welfare schemes in the world, which explicitly supports the expansion of homeownership as a welfare commodity, has been developed in Singapore (Groves et al., 2007; Ronald, 2008). The Central Provident Fund (CPF) is a mandatory savings scheme that was introduced by the government in 1955. As part of a welfare system that promotes individual and family responsibility, the CPF represents a key conduit for meeting social welfare needs. Originally a superannuation scheme, individuals are allowed to withdraw savings from the CPF for specific purposes (education, health insurance, housing, etc.). Withdrawals for housing have become a key component of the fund and this, in conjunction with state provision of housing units, has resulted in a homeownership rate of 92%. Although extremely successful in promoting households' savings and boosting homeownership, the emphasis on housing is problematic. Housing assets are illiquid and Singaporean homeowners are reticent to sell their properties to meet welfare needs. Moreover, since house price volatility has a significant effect on household wealth, the state is increasingly required to intervene in the market to manage house price performance.

While no country has adopted a comprehensive asset-based welfare system, many countries have adopted policies that align with the asset-based welfare approach. In the United Kingdom, the 'modernised welfare state' (Malpass, 2008: 9) emphasises self-reliance and self-management. Increasingly, the UK government's view of homeownership has emphasised its role as a financial asset that can be used to meet households' welfare needs. Significantly, a range of governments (e.g., the United Kingdom, Ireland, and New Zealand) have introduced asset tests on welfare programmes that require older households to use equity in their homes to fund various medical and residential care costs (Malpass, 2008; Robinson and O'Shea, 2010). Whereas once social rented housing was viewed as the key housing component of collectivised welfare provision, increasingly homeownership is being viewed as a tenure that can help people to pay for their own 'social welfare' needs (e.g., pensions) (Groves et al., 2007; Malpass, 2008). This aligning of private homeownership with welfare provision represents a significant, if problematic, policy transformation.

Homeownership: Asset versus Home

The notion of homeownership functioning as a pension has considerable political resonance but requires significant and ongoing financial innovation, especially in terms of equity release products, for it to become a reality. Despite considerable financial liberalisation in advance of the 2007 global financial crisis, reverse mortgages and other equity release products have not proved popular among elderly homeowners. In part, this reflects the limited benefits and the high cost of these schemes to date, but it also highlights the power of entrenched cultural and nationally differentiated understandings of homeownership.

Work in the United Kingdom, mainland Europe, and Asia highlight age-specific and nationally constituted differences in understandings of homeownership. Older homeowners adopt a somewhat risk-adverse stance when considering equity release products. Having achieved homeownership, these older homeowners perceive reduced housing costs as the main benefit of outright ownership and are keen to preserve equity in the property in order to pass on an inheritance to the next generation. The desire to pass on the family home as an inheritance is a significant challenge to the idea that homeowners will willingly spend their housing equity to meet welfare needs.

Depending on the national housing systems and the operation of mortgage markets, homeowners' understandings of the tenure vary. In a study of European housing markets (Toussaint and Elsinga, 2009), German homeowners were seen to view the welfare dimensions of homeownership primarily in terms of reduced housing expenditures in old age and were resistant to the notion of equity release, even in terms of selling and downsizing. In Sweden and the Netherlands, reduced housing cost in old age was considered a key benefit of homeownership and while owners were willing to access housing equity, this equity release was seen as a 'gift' from the housing market rather than as a basis for meeting welfare needs. In Portugal and Hungary, owners demonstrated a strong emotional attachment to their homes and were resistant to ever selling their properties. In reflecting on the findings of this eight-country study, the authors argued that it was only in the United Kingdom that homeowners expected to use equity release for welfare purposes.

While there is evidence of strong resistance to using housing equity as a pension, it must be remembered that the culture of homeownership is dynamic and changing. Work in Australia, the United Kingdom, the United States, and New Zealand has shown that younger owners, who entered the housing market under more liberalised mortgage market regimes, are open to extracting equity from their homes. The ways in which households spend this equity is unclear, but expenditures include servicing other debts and buying luxuries. This trend in equity withdrawal aligns with some of the basic arguments used by the proponents of asset-based welfare. It suggests that a new generation of homeowners are more attuned to the financial characteristics of homeownership and are more willing to use sophisticated financial products. It is argued that as homeowners become accustomed to using their housing equity to support their consumption, they will become more amenable to using their home as an income source in old age. However, the political vision of people "banking on housing" (Smith et al., 2008) for old age could be undermined by an increasing willingness to "spend the house" on current consumption.

The seemingly straightforward and logical linking of homeownership with asset-based welfare is premised on a temporally specific conceptualisation of the tenure. Within this conceptualisation, homeowners are assumed to amass a substantial financial asset that becomes available, via financial products, to support their incomes in old age. This view of homeownership is shaped within a traditional understanding of the tenure and historical patterns of ownership. However, as HEW increases, the realities of the tenure will change. If households use HEW (especially mortgage equity release products) for consumption purposes, they increase debt levels and delay the timing of becoming outright owners. This raises the prospect of homeowners entering retirement with high debt levels and lower equity. Moreover, HEW is facilitated by financial institutions on the premise that capital values rise over time. While financial institutions foster HEW, they are likely to exert pressures on owners to sell their homes to pay back debt in old age. Whether homeowners will have equity following a sale depends on the vagaries of the market, the timing of the sale, and their accumulated debts (Hamnett, 2010). Ironically, therefore, the current processes promoting an increasing financialisation of the home could result in older homeowners exiting homeownership with limited financial assets and an increased need for welfare support.

In another possible twist, the fostering of a more financially aware breed of homeowners could see the emergence of household strategies designed to avoid the use of equity to fund welfare expenditures. Asset-based welfare systems presuppose a more sophisticated and financially aware citizenry. In promoting asset holding, it is assumed that individuals will take responsibility for managing their resources and for providing for their own needs. Policies such as the UK, Irish, and New Zealand governments' requirement to sell one's home, or use housing equity, to fund residential care costs, are clearly aligned with the notion of asset-based welfare but are at odds with homeowners' desires to preserve their assets. In terms of housing, there is considerable evidence to show that people are emotionally attached to their homes and there are strong tendencies to hold onto their homes in order to pass it on to the next generation. A more financially sophisticated homeowner may be better equipped to protect their assets. For example, in New Zealand, over 160 000 households have transferred ownership of the family home to family trusts (Morrison, 2008). By doing so, they have legally alienated themselves from the home as an asset and avoided the prospect of having to sell the family home to cover residential care costs.

Home ownership: An Inappropriate Base for Social Welfare?

Superficially, the significant amount of household wealth locked up in housing assets represents a veritable untapped treasure trove for fiscally strapped governments faced with the prospect of rising welfare costs. Requiring wealthy homeowners to use their equity to meet their own welfare needs is not just politically expedient but is potentially politically acceptable. However, as clearly demonstrated by the fallout from the US subprime crisis, homeownership is not risk-free and the financial benefits of homeownership are temporally and spatially contingent. The disjuncture between the average benefits of homeownership and the individual experience of owning a home is crucial in determining the role of housing within an asset-based social welfare system (see Malpass, 2008).

Homeownership as a tenure is characterised by fragmentation and differentiation. As homeownership assumes a dominant role in a housing system, it necessarily incorporates a wider range of socioeconomic groups that are housed in properties characterised by variable quality. Although on average house prices may have a tendency to rise over time, this average masks substantial regional and local variation in prices (Malpass, 2008). Research on house prices clearly shows that the absolute returns to wealthy homeowners, who own expensive houses, exceed the returns from low-cost homeownership. In effect, the housing market works to entrench existing wealth inequalities (Hamnett, 1999).

The micro-geography of the housing market means that some households benefit from being located in 'boom areas', while other households struggle with the effects of persistent 'low demand'. Moreover, low-income households who have struggled to step onto the housing ladder may find that they remain on the bottom rung without any prospect of moving up, due to poor house price performance. This is particularly the case in periods of recession. Poor house price performance during a downturn can result in households experiencing periods of prolonged negative equity, such as those which occurred in the United Kingdom in the early 1990s and in Japan since the late 1980s. In a recession, households become increasingly vulnerable to problems associated with 'biographical disruption' (unemployment, sickness, divorce, death of an income earner, etc.) and the ability to stay in homeownership becomes more tenuous. In 2009, as a consequence of the subprime crisis and the ensuing recession, 3.9 million mortgage foreclosure filings were recorded in the United States. Widespread negative equity and rising mortgage defaults undermine the role that homeownership can play as part of any asset-based welfare system.

The differential lived-experiences of homeowners constitute a challenge to discourses that emphasise the universal benefits of homeownership. Significantly, and in contrast to traditional forms of welfare, which are designed to be progressive in nature, supporting homeownership is regressive. Wealthy homeowners benefit the most out of ownership and, due to their circumstances, usually have other financial assets to fall back on in times of need. In this context, supporting homeownership as a means of meeting welfare needs does not necessarily address the requirements of those in the greatest need. Moreover, relying on property market cycles to produce capital gains does not ensure that households will have sufficient incomes during times of need.

Conclusion

Proponents of asset-based welfare advocate for an extension of asset holding among low-income groups as a means of overcoming entrenched wealth inequalities in societies. Politicians, faced with rising welfare costs, have increasingly viewed homeownership as a key financial asset that could be mobilised to meet households' welfare needs. The increasingly dominant understanding of homeownership as a fungible asset aligns well with neoliberal ideas and the perception that markets are efficient and effective. It also aligns with third-way politics that advocate new models of citizenship based on self-regulation and personal responsibility. Housing is the largest asset class in the world and outright owners in many countries possess substantial, if highly illiquid, wealth. Facilitating the growth of homeownership and promoting economic practices that encourage homeowners to extract equity to pay for their welfare needs lie at the heart of an emerging asset-based welfare agenda.

However, relying on homeownership to meet welfare needs is problematic at a variety of levels. Homeownership cultures vary internationally and the tenure is highly fragmented in nature. The average financial gains accruing to homeowners mask substantial variations in experiences across countries and across localities. The operation of housing markets tends to exacerbate wealth inequalities. Housing markets do experience downturns that can result in widespread negative equity and repossessions, and housing market downturns are most likely to occur during periods when social welfare needs are at their greatest. Moreover, HEW for consumption, a practice encouraged by advocates of asset-based welfare, could erode the value of housing assets available in old age. In sum, the simple alignment of homeownership with asset-based welfare is riddled with potential problems and contradictions. Notwithstanding these issues, it is clear that households can, and do, use their housing wealth to meet welfare needs. The argument presented here is that while homeownership can convey welfare benefits, it is not the most appropriate foundation for developing a welfare system.

See also: Home Ownership: Economic Benefits; Housing and Wealth Portfolios; Housing Equity Withdrawal in the United Kingdom; Housing Subsidies and Welfare; Housing Wealth and Consumption; Housing Wealth and Inheritance in the United Kingdom; Housing Wealth as Precautionary Savings; Mortgage Equity Withdrawal.

References

Groves R, Murie A, and Watson C (eds.) (2007) *Housing and the New Welfare State: Perspectives from East Asia and Europe*. Aldershot, UK: Ashgate.

Hamnett C (1999) *Winners and Losers: Home Ownership in Modern Britain*. London: UCL.

Hamnett C (2010) Housing and the UK economy. In: Coe N and Jones A (eds.) *The Economic Geography of the UK*, pp. 110–122. London: SAGE.

Malpass P (2008) Housing and the new welfare state: Wobbly pillar or cornerstone? *Housing Studies* 23: 1–19.

Morrison P (2008) *On the falling rate of home ownership in New Zealand*. Report Prepared for the Centre for Housing Research, Aotearoa New Zealand (CHRANZ), Wellington, New Zealand.

Robinson DJ and O'Shea D (2010) Nursing home funding – deal or no deal? – an Irish perspective. *Age and Ageing* 39: 152–153.

Ronald R (2008) *The Ideology of Home Ownership: Homeowner Societies and the Role of Housing*. Basingstoke, UK: Palgrave Macmillan.

Sherraden M (1991) *Assets and the Poor: A New American Welfare Policy*. New York: M.E. Sharpe.

Sherraden M (2003) Assets and the social investment state. In: Paxton W (ed.) *Equal Shares: Building a Progressive and Coherent Asset-Based Welfare Policy*, pp. 28–41. London: IPPR.

Smith SJ, Searle BA, and Cook N (2008) Rethinking the risks of home ownership. *Journal of Social Policy* 38: 83–102.

Toussaint J and Elsinga M (2009) Exploring 'housing asset-based welfare'. Can the UK be held up as an example for Europe? *Housing Studies* 24: 669–692.

Further Reading

Doling J and Ronald R (2010) Property-based welfare and European homeowners: How would housing perform as a pension. *Journal of Housing and the Built Environment* 25: 227–241.

Smith SJ and Searle BA (2010) *The Blackwell Companion to the Economics of Housing: The Housing Wealth of Nations*. Chichester, UK: Wiley-Blackwell.

Relevant Websites

http://www.demhow.bham.ac.uk – DEMHOW (Demographic Change and Housing Wealth).

http://www.ippr.org – Institute for Public Policy Research (IPPR) (see Centre for Asset-Based Welfare).

http://www.oecd.org – OECD (see Directorate for Employment, Labour and Social Affairs pension data and reports).

Asset-Based Well-Being: Use Versus Exchange Value

BA Searle, St Andrews University, St Andrews, UK

© 2012 Elsevier Ltd. All rights reserved.

Glossary

Deregulation Reducing or eliminating government control of the operation of market forces; opening up markets to competition enabling more private operators to enter.

Equity withdrawal This is a generic description for transactions whereby a homeowner reduces the equity in their homes (i.e., the difference between what is owed (mortgage) and the value of the property). Equity may be withdrawn through four channels: selling up – selling a property and moving into rental accommodation, releasing funds from the previous house sale; trading down – selling a property and buying another property of a lower value and releasing the extra funds rather than investing them back into the new property; overmortgaging – selling a property and buying another property but increasing the mortgage by more than is needed to cover the difference in value of the traded properties; in situ equity borrowing – where no property transaction takes place, and homeowners increase their mortgage debt either through: remortgaging, taking out another loan higher than their current debt; or through using flexible features described above to borrow up against the existing mortgage.

House assets The value of residential property that is owned outright or is being bought through a loan.

Housing wealth/housing equity The value of a residential property minus all (mortgage) loans on the same property.

Mortgage A loan secured against a residential property. Traditionally mortgages are loans that are paid off on a monthly basis for the term of the mortgage, which is fixed at the time of taking out the loan. Recently, new products have been available that offer flexible features. These enable monthly payments to be increased (overpayments), decreased (underpayments), or for payments to be temporarily suspended (payment holidays), subject to agreements with the lending institution. They may also enable the mortgage debt to be increased (up to a fixed limit) without the need for re-mortgaging (and thus no additional costs) or changing the conditions of the original loan.

Subjective well-being A self-reported measure of individual state of mind. This is often measured by a single question that asks people overall how satisfied they are with their life, but may also consist of a score derived from several questions, for example, the General Health Questionnaire short-form 12 which asks about peoples' sense of self-worth, their ability to make decisions, their confidence, and overall happiness.

Wealth effects Where funds are withdrawn from assets (e.g., property) or investments (e.g. stocks and shares) and used to fund consumption.

Introduction

Home ownership has long been valued for its security. Whilst homeowners draw upon the emotional benefits and practical shelter the home provides throughout the life course, they also value the financial security that a home brings through providing a nest egg for retirement, and a final wealth contribution to the next generation through inheritance. During the latter years of the twentieth century, however, housing wealth was transformed into a potential resource, accessible throughout the lifecourse. New mortgage products with flexible payment options changed the way owners viewed and used the wealth (or equity) stored in their homes. This has given rise to a shift in emphasis away from use value towards exchange value as housing wealth is increasingly positioned as a supplement to household budgets and future welfare provision.

The ability of homeowners to access housing equity has, in many instances, provided a much-needed financial buffer as households manage increased demands on, or reductions to, household income. The new role of housing wealth has also entered the policy arena, with housing being placed as the asset base for welfare – providing the means to fund health care needs in older age. Whilst this newly available wealth may provide a boost to economies and government spending plans, it raises new questions about the availability of and access to home ownership, the sustainability of the housing stock and home values, and the extent to which housing wealth can provide welfare support to current as well as future generations.

House Assets

Homeownership expanded rapidly in many countries during the last half of the twentieth century. In many developed nations, over half of all households own their own home. For example, using the latest data available, 70% of households are owner-occupiers in the United Kingdom; 67% in the United States; 78% in Ireland, and 89% in Spain (**Figure 1**).

In these nations, on average, the value of housing increased substantially during the 2000s, and more than other measures of economic growth, such as GDP (**Figure 2**). Although the economic recession of 2007–08 saw house prices fall dramatically, for example, by 4% in the United Kingdom, 6% in the United States, and 11% in Ireland, prior to this downturn, house prices were generally rising at twice the rate of GDP.

For those households who own their home, their housing represents a major component of their overall wealth resources. The data from the OECD national figures for 2007 indicate that housing wealth accounted for 56% of total assets held by households in the United Kingdom; although data are patchy, generally in OECD countries housing wealth accounts for over half and up to three-quarters of all personal wealth. In nations like the United Kingdom, in which the majority of households are homeowners, housing thus represents the most widely distributed form of wealth. There are, however, regional variations. Homeowners in Scotland, Wales, and the North of England, for example, generally hold less wealth in their homes than those in London and the South East; even within London and the South East, most of this wealth is concentrated in the hands of half the population.

Notwithstanding these variations, many households are considered to be income poor but asset rich, that is, although the amount of money coming into the home (through wages or interest on savings/investments) is low, a lot of potential wealth is stored in their house. For many years, owner-occupiers envisaged that this wealth would be stored in

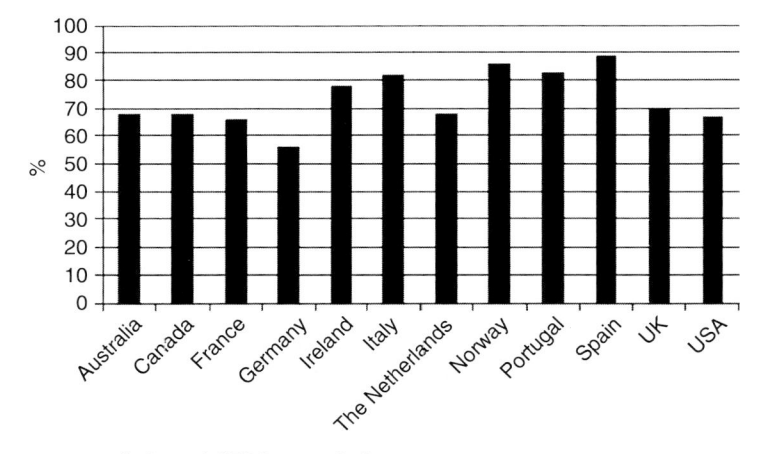

Figure 1 Proportion of homeowners (selected OECD countries).
Source: Australian Bureau of Statistics (series: 41300); Statistics Canada (series: 94-554-XWE2006001); Eurostat (SILC); Communities and Local Government, UK (Table 101); US Census Bureau.

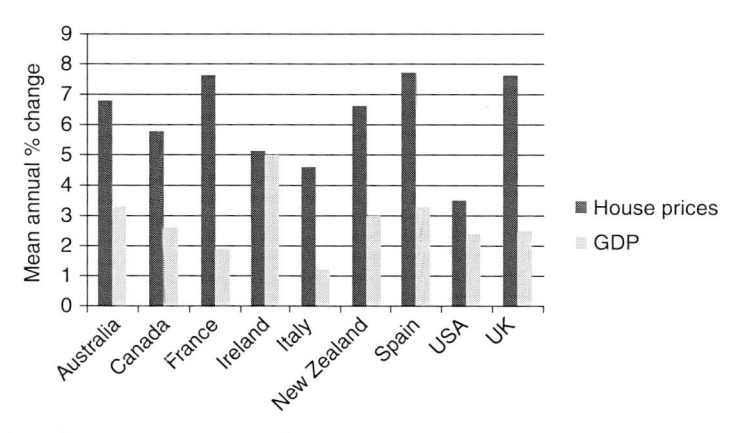

Figure 2 Average change in real house prices and real GDP 2000–08.
Source: OECD Economic Outlook No 87 Annex Tables 1 and 59, author's calculations.

their house until either they retired and sold the house for a cheaper one (downsized) and thus released some of their equity; or they would save the wealth until they died and it would be passed onto their children through inheritance.

This concentration of wealth into housing, particularly among an old, and, in many countries, ageing population, has fuelled policy debates about the potential release of equity to supplement incomes and fund support and care needs in older age. However, an asset-based welfare policy has encountered social and financial difficulties, associated with older homeowners' unwillingness to release their equity and the inappropriateness of some financial products that facilitate equity release. Qualitative evidence from the United Kingdom suggests that while some homeowners had successfully moved to smaller accommodation, others were sceptical of trading down and moving away from familiar neighbourhoods and friends, while selling up completely and moving out of the owner-occupied sector was generally viewed negatively (Rowlingson, 2006). Equity release was generally seen as good in theory – a means of avoiding poverty, however, issues of security and links to profit-making financial institutions, complexity, and poor value for money meant owners were generally adverse to such products. While these issues were still being debated at the turn of the twenty-first century, and generally reflected the views of people from a generation for whom homeownership was prized more for its security and emotional (use) rather than financial (exchange) value, housing finance was transformed, presenting the opportunity for housing wealth to become a resource that could potentially be accessed not only in old age, but also throughout the life course.

Changes in Mortgage Finance

Historically, housing finance has been provided by government-run entities and regulated local lenders; in the United Kingdom, for example, this was largely through building societies that operated under restrictive government policy and was generally shielded from market forces and wider economic fluctuations; in many European countries, housing finance systems were controlled by centralised banks who controlled saving and borrowing rates and restricted access to mortgage loans. In the 1980s, changes were made within the financial sector on a global scale that impacted not only on how mortgage loans were financed but also on who could sell mortgages; this introduced competitive markets such that mortgages, which had previously been rationed, became actively sold.

These changes also led to the development of a wide range of new mortgage products. Although homeowners had previously been able to re-mortgage to increase their debt (within tight criteria on how these additional funds may be spent), many of these new products included 'flexible' features that enabled homeowners to either pay more of their mortgage each month (overpayment) or increase the amount of their debt (drawdown) within agreed limits without the need for further approval from the lending company or without incurring additional costs. Increasing debt in this way (remortgaging or flexible drawdown) without moving home is referred to as 'in situ mortgage equity withdrawal' or 'equity borrowing'.

Housing Wealth Effects

Homeowners have for some time been able to extract equity from their homes, releasing funds through either last time sales or trading down. However, financial deregulation and changes within the mortgage markets (across many OECD nations) described above created new opportunities for in situ mortgage equity withdrawal and released the restrictions on secured lending, which meant housing equity could be channelled into other areas of consumption and not just reinvested back into the repair and maintenance of the housing stock.

The deregulation of housing finance markets, which coincided with both stock market and housing market bubbles and subsequent crashes, generated a renewed interest among economists over 'wealth effects' – the link between personal wealth and consumption (Case et al., 2001). Although these debates mainly focused on whether changes in stock market wealth or changes in housing wealth had the greatest impact on consumer behaviour, there was no denying that housing wealth increasingly featured in households' financial decisions around spending, saving, and debt management.

At the peak of the house price boom in the mid-2000s, around $318 billion was withdrawn in the United States, and, in the United Kingdom, the total was £57 billion. Further research shows that not only were the amounts of equity being withdrawn increasing but also that the proportion of homeowners using this resource was increasing. In the United Kingdom, for example, the proportion of households who withdrew equity increased from around a quarter (26%) in 1998 to a third (31%) in 2003. Data from Australia also show that between 2002 and 2005, 43% of homeowners released equity. Furthermore, this research shows that the amounts being released were substantial with average amounts of up to £7500 being released in the United Kingdom and $26 000 in Australia (Parkinson et al., 2009).

What this research shows is how attitudes towards housing wealth changed by the beginning of the twenty-first century. Homeowners were increasingly willing to use the value of their homes as a means of securing credit – facilitating levels of consumption that may not have otherwise occurred. While aggregate data are useful from an economic perspective in identifying the growing use of equity borrowing by households, what they do not show is why homeowners choose to increase their mortgage debt, and when they do, which areas of the economy they are redirecting the wealth from their homes into.

Housing Wealth: From Inheritance to Welfare

Initially much of the housing wealth withdrawn was channelled into home improvement rather than other consumption goods. In the United Kingdom, for example, among home buyers who reported taking out an additional mortgage or loan without moving property, 67% used some or all of their withdrawn equity on housing repairs in 1991, compared to 3% on cars, 3% on consumer goods, and 18% on 'other' expenditure. However, there is a notable trend that a considerable proportion of this equity is now being channelled away from the home and into other areas of consumption. By 2007, 42% of home buyers used their equity for housing repairs, the proportion spent on cars and consumer goods still accounted for less than 10% of spend, however, the proportion allocating funds to 'other' nonconsumer goods had more than doubled over the period, rising to 46% (Smith and Searle, 2008). What is difficult to recover from these data, however, is exactly what this 'other' category includes.

Further research is addressing this issue. Qualitative evidence from the United Kingdom (Smith et al., 2009), and later, Australia (Colic-Peisker et al., 2010), initially drew attention to the changing attitude of homeowners towards their housing wealth. This research highlighted how homes have become valued for the financial security they provide not just for later life, but as a resource that could be borrowed against at any time; an asset that may be called in 'if the worst came to the worst'. Many homeowners experienced such situations where housing wealth provided the kind of security and financial resource – which may previously have been sought or provided through welfare institutions – that tided them, or other family members, through periods of unexpected dips in income or increased expenditure. Quantitative studies in the United Kingdom (Benito, 2007), the United States (Hurst and Stafford, 2004), and the United Kingdom and Australia (Parkinson et al., 2009) are also showing that home equity may be performing the role of a financial buffer – when faced with financial shocks homeowners may have few other resources to call upon, other than unlocking some of the equity stored in their home.

This change in behaviour towards how and when equity is release from the home is reflected in changes in attitudes towards inheritance among homeowners. Evidence from qualitative studies in the United Kingdom (Rowlingson and McKay, 2005) suggest that while there is generally agreement that some wealth should be retained as a bequest, many homeowners are more relaxed about using some, or most, of their savings and housing wealth before retirement, or before they die. This research suggests that homeowners may give children their inheritance (lifetime gifts valued at £500 or more) early to assist with the costs of weddings or similar occasions, buying a car, education, or to help them with buying/maintaining property (although this may come from other savings or investments rather than housing wealth). Such decisions were, however, weighed up against their own needs in later life, where housing wealth may be needed to maintain a reasonable standard of living or pay for health care.

In Australia too, where homeownership has long been regarded as 'insurance for old age', attitudes are changing. Using quantitative analysis, Wood and Nygaard (2010) show that among older people (aged 65+) only 11% plan on releasing equity during retirement, while this rises to a quarter among middle-aged homeowners, who expect to trade down or sell up in order to finance retirement plans. Berry and Dalton (2010) also point towards a change in the bequest ethic: with many children having a better standard of living than their parents, older homeowners are more inclined to 'SKI' (spend the kids inheritance) or skip a generation and leave their wealth to their grandchildren.

Demographic and intergenerational aspects may become an increasingly important issue in respect of inheritance and the stage in the life course at which equity is accessed as populations age, younger people delay marriage and entry into the housing market, households have fewer children, and family formation becomes more complex. However, what the research to date is showing is that ideas about housing wealth are moving away from a traditional view of the home as an investment that is paid off over the life course with a view to being passed on through inheritance to the next generation. Instead homeowners, through the ability to increase mortgage debt, are more able and willing (or indeed may need) to use their housing wealth before retirement or before death. Housing wealth is being used as a resource not just for one-off events, but increasingly as part of day-to-day financial management and household budgeting. In this way, housing wealth is being viewed as a financial buffer or form of safety net against potential events that may impact on the household budget at any point during the life course.

This may have implications for the future redistribution of housing wealth. The effect of bequests on the transmission of wealth inequality has been a concern of economics for many decades (see Appleyard and

Rowlingson, 2010). The assumption that the current distribution of housing wealth will be reproduced in the next generation as the United Kingdom becomes 'a nation of inheritors' may not materialise for some time (Holmans, 2008). As home owners increasingly dip into their housing wealth before retirement, and governments pursue the use of housing equity to fund care in older age, this will not only reduce the level of finances being transferred but could also potentially lead to the inheritance of debt rather than wealth.

Home Maintenance and Equity Leakage

Interest in the 'wealth effects' of housing have focused on the generally perceived positive impact for national economies; however, relatively little attention has been given to the implications for housing policy and the housing stock. Where financial deregulation has opened up the opportunities to 'spend the home' on a variety of consumer goods and services, as demonstrated above, this has detracted from reinvesting back into the property itself.

While equity withdrawn from housing was initially closely monitored, and strictly regulated to ensure funds were reinvested back into housing, the deregulation of financial services removed these restrictions, opening up the opportunities for equity leakage into all areas of consumption. In the United Kingdom, for several years, national accounts have recorded the amount of equity that is 'reinvested' back into the housing stock. However, these data are based on broad definitions, whereby any expenditure within the housing sector constitutes 'reinvestment'. Given that this will include, among other items, transaction costs (such as legal fees, stamp duty, or removal expenses), these aggregate data potentially overestimate the extent to which equity withdrawals are being reinvested. Furthermore, the categories contained in household survey data that capture the direction of MEW spend – where they exist at all – broadly refer to 'housing maintenance and repair'. As discussed above, while these data show a notable trend away from spend on the home towards other nonspecified items; qualitative accounts also suggest that 'housing maintenance' may often include the finishing touches, which, while adding to the sale value of the property, may not constitute to its structural condition and repair (e.g., carpets, painting, furniture, and plasma TVs) (Smith et al., 2009).

As the occupation of housing increasingly moves towards homeownership, the responsibility for maintaining the quality and condition of the nation's housing stock transfers onto individual homeowners and their private finance. The availability of MEW may have added a boost to national economies and household budgets, however, as the evidence is showing, such funds are increasingly being directed towards welfare needs and diverted away from bricks and mortar. Where such trends continue and where governments actively encourage an asset-based welfare system, this draws attention to a potential crisis in maintaining the future quality and condition of the nation's housing stock.

Housing Wealth and Well-Being

The change in emphasis from use to exchange value, although potentially beneficial in providing a safety net through difficult financial periods and providing a consumption boost to flagging economies, has complex implications for the general welfare and well-being of homeowners.

Mortgage debt in itself is not necessarily a problem where owner-occupiers feel that their mortgage is manageable, something they feel that they are in control of, or that they have put the funds to good use. There are instances where housing wealth offers a protective effect; those who are altruistic in the way they spend the equity they have withdrawn (by, e.g., using the funds to support or help other family members) report high levels of well-being. This 'care-full' approach to spending housing wealth has positive benefits. However, the ease with which equity can be withdrawn, with the potential to borrow beyond a position where the debt continues to be serviceable, does give cause for concern. Adopting a more 'care-free' approach (e.g., increasing mortgage debt to maintain a credit lifestyle) can have detrimental outcomes in terms of people's reported subjective well-being.

The extent to which housing represents a household's financial resources can also impact on well-being. Those whose wealth and investment potential is constrained in housing, even during a period when house prices were continuing to rise, were more likely to report low well-being than those who are able to invest their wealth in a diverse portfolio (e.g., stocks and shares or other investment vehicles), or those who valued their home more for the emotional aspects than its investment or financial potential. This may be a reflection of the pressure or burden felt by those who (are only able to) invest in their home in that they have to keep their house in good repair in order to maintain its value (Searle et al., 2009).

Such findings point towards a tension in welfare policy between encouraging homeownership as a route to enhancing household financial well-being and increasing responsibility and risk on individuals in maintaining their home as an asset base for welfare. It raises questions for future welfare policy where younger homeowners are planning to (or may have to) spend their wealth before retirement; and where fluctuations in housing and financial markets determine how much equity is available and the ease and cost-effectiveness of its release.

See also: Asset-Based Welfare; Financial Deregulation; Home Ownership: Economic Benefits; Housing Equity Withdrawal in the United Kingdom; Housing Subsidies and Welfare; Housing Wealth and Consumption; Housing Wealth and Inheritance in the United Kingdom; Housing Wealth as Precautionary Savings; Housing Wealth Distribution in the United Kingdom; Housing Wealth Over the Life Course; Mortgage Default: Consequences; Mortgage Default: Well-Being in the United States; Mortgage Equity Withdrawal; Mortgage Innovation.

References

Appleyard L and Rowlingson K (2010) Home-ownership and the distribution of personal wealth. *JRF Programme Paper: Housing Market Taskforce*. York, UK: Joseph Rowntree Foundation.

Benito A (2007). *Housing equity as a buffer: evidence from UK households*. Bank of England Working Paper 324. London: Bank of England.

Berry M and Dalton T (2010) Trading on housing wealth: Political risk in an aging society. In: Smith SJ and Searle BA (eds.) *The Blackwell Companion to the Economics of Housing: The Housing Wealth of Nations*. Chichester, UK: Wiley-Blackwell.

Case K, Quigley J, and Shiller R (2001) Comparing wealth effects: The stock market versus the housing market. *Advances in Macroeconomics* 5(1): 1235.

Colic-Peisker V, Johnson G, and Smith SJ (2010) "Pots of Gold": Housing Wealth and Economic Wellbeing in Australia. In: Smith SJ and Searle BA (eds.) *The Blackwell Companion to the Economics of Housing: The Housing Wealth of Nations*. Chichester, UK: Wiley-Blackwell.

Holmans A (2008) *Prospects for UK Housing Wealth and Inheritance*. London: Council of Mortgage Lenders.

Hurst E and Stafford F (2004) Home is where the equity is: mortgage refinancing and household consumption. *Journal of Money, Credit and Banking* 36(6): 985–1014.

Parkinson S, Searle BA, Smith SJ, Stoakes A, and Wood G (2009) Mortgage equity withdrawal in Australia and Britain: Towards a wealth-fare state? *European Journal of Housing Policy* 9(4): 365–390.

Rowlingson K (2006) Living poor to die rich or spending the kids' inheritance? Attitudes to assets and inheritance in later life. *Journal of Social Policy* 35(2): 175–192.

Rowlingson K and McKay S (2005) *Attitudes to Inheritance in Britain*. York, UK: Joseph Rowntree Foundation.

Searle BA, Smith SJ, and Cook N (2009) From housing wealth to well-being? *Sociology of Health and Illness* 31(1): 112–127.

Smith SJ and Searle BA (2008) Dematerialising money? Observations on the flow of wealth from housing to other things. *Housing Studies* 23(1): 21–43.

Smith SJ, Searle BA, and Cook N (2009) Rethinking the risks of home ownership. *Journal of Social Policy* 38(1): 83–102.

Wood G and Nygaard CA (2010) Housing equity withdrawal and retirement: Evidence from the Household Income and Labour Dynamics in Australia Survey (HILDA). In: Smith SJ and Searle BA (eds.) *The Blackwell Companion to the Economics of Housing: The Housing Wealth of Nations*. Chichester, UK: Wiley-Blackwell.

Further Reading

Dvornak N and Kohler M (2007) Housing wealth, stock market wealth and consumption: A panel analysis for Australia. *Economic Record* 83(261): 117–130.

Smith SJ and Searle BA (eds.) (2010) *The Blackwell Companion to the Economics of Housing: The Housing Wealth of Nations*. Chichester, UK: Wiley-Blackwell.

Austrian Economics

D Maclennan, University of St Andrews, St Andrews, UK

© 2012 Elsevier Ltd. All rights reserved.

Glossary

Catallactics The essence of a catallaxy is the notion of a self-organising and self-regulating system. The Austrian economists, and Hayek in particular, argued that the study of market processes should be thought of as catallactics. Hayek took the view that the term 'economy' was better applied in its Aristotlean sense, that is, the organisation and management of resources within households or firms. In consequence, for Hayek, the catallaxy was the emergent order that arose from the complex interactions of each of these individual units.

Praxeology The study of human actions and conduct that lay at the core of the Austrian economics perspective. Their emphasis on praxeology led to their rejection of empirical methods of analysis, as they believed that behaviour observed in simple settings was unlikely to be replicated in more complex market processes.

Considering Housing and the Economy

In the aftermath of the Great Financial Crisis of 2008, housing research has shown an unprecedented interest in the role of housing in the economy. Economic historians, sociologists, geographers, political scientists, and, of course, mainstream economists have written much about the housing aspects of causes and consequences of the boom, bust, and slow recovery. In contrast, housing economics in Europe and the UK, as opposed to North America and Asia, has increasingly become a minority voice within housing debates. At the same time, some disciplines have become increasingly hostile to and dismissive of the relevance of 'economics' to understanding the economy. Much of modern human geography and planning, for instance, makes a casual and mistaken association of economics as an academic discipline with a technocratic, quantitative, disconnected approach that embeds and underpins essentially right wing views for policy.

That dismissal is unfortunate. In many ways with spatial economics, economic history and psychological economics, all attracting recent Nobel prizes, even the mainstream of economics has become more heterodox in this millennium. But older paradigms as well as newer perspectives in economics offer an intellectual diversity that casts light on economic processes and political economy debates (not that all, nor indeed any, need necessarily provide convincing and value free answers to the problems studied).

The 'Austrian' or neo-Austrian economics perspective is, in many ways, twice damned in this intellectual narrowing of vision. It is often used to underpin essentially libertarian views on economy and society. Yet, it has also been cast by mainstream economics into a corner marked historically interesting but methodologically and technically limited (see Samuelson, 1964). The same comment could also be applied to Marxian economics. A key intellectual question is whether, without subscribing to the consequent political economy positions, one can learn anything of import from understanding key aspects of Marxian or indeed Austrian economics.

This note explores the origins, core ideas, and strengths and weaknesses of Austrian economics in addressing housing system issues. (For the avoidance of doubt, I am not an Austrian economist. As an analyst I find some of its intellectual ideas useful, as a political economist I find most of its policy propositions negative and bleak.)

Origins, Key Proponents and Propositions

The core ideas of the Austrian School have clear roots in the classical economics tradition. Their focus on the functioning or markets and prices makes a clear connection back to Smith, and indeed forward to the current mainstream, and their philosophical emphasis on the individual and human behaviour has been traced back to the Salamanca School (Butler, 2010). (The positioning of Austrian economics outside of the economics mainstream means that much of the relevant literature emerges from sympathetic 'think tanks'. Butler is clearly sympathetic to the Austrian agenda but presents a clear, informed overview of the work of the School (see Keizer, 1997) for a more academic exposition.) They share their roots with mainstream neoclassical economic tradition but have branched down a different development path in a clearly identifiable way. And these divergences are not minor, but major, and define a distinct 'Austrian' approach. Milton Friedman once opined that there was no such thing as Austrian economics, just good and bad economics. This judgement is a good example of Chicago school intellectual imperialism and is unhelpful.

Carl Menger (1871) is regarded as a key founder of the intellectual tradition. Menger, with Jevons, Marshall, Walras, and others, was at the core of the marginal revolution in economic thinking and the application of mathematics and calculus to these ideas. However while the others underpinned modern neoclassical economics by arguing that objective, measurable factors explained cost curves in the economy, Menger adhered to the notion that supply curves, like demand schedules, were inherently subjective (the contrast to Marx's labour theory of value is stark).

This quickly gets to the nub of the Austrian approach. Menger and his Austrian contemporaries stressed the complex, subjective nature of human, economic, decision taking (Hayek, 1948; Von Mises, 1949). The key unit in economic understanding had to be the individual and, within firms, the entrepreneur (Kirzner, 1973). The core of human action was that individuals had plans that they used to guide market behaviour to achieve their subjective aims. Individuals were regarded as the only relevant economic plan makers and they had to deal with a constant state of change and imperfection in market knowledge while making these decisions. Indeed for the individual and the entrepreneur, the market, to use Hayek's phrase, was a discovery process.

Market processes rather than structures are at the core of the Austrian view. Prices became the key embodiment of relevant knowledge within the market process. And in that system constant attention to prices was essential as markets, even if they had self-correcting tendencies, never actually reached equilibrium and were always in a state of change. The Austrian interest in the market processes through which individuals pursued and adapted plans was labelled 'catallactics'.

The contrast of that view with the neoclassical mainstream, even as it exists now, is significant. What matters for Austrians about markets is the process, whereas for neoclassical economics the number of competitors (or degree of monopoly) was the key consideration in defining the market, its structures, and consequences. Whereas neoclassicists started from assumptions of perfectly informed market players, albeit the works of Stiglitz (1995) and Spence (1973) have significantly modified the received wisdom, and this contrasts sharply with the information seeking discoverer of Hayek's system of thought.

However, a more fundamental philosophical position underpinned the Austrian perspective that has shaped and cemented their separate existence. Their belief in the complexity of human behaviour (Von Mises, 1949) led them to reject the notion that much could be usefully measured. Indeed, there is something akin to a social version of Heisenberg's uncertainty principle in their view that any attempt to measure individual behaviour will change it. In consequence, their central philosophical method was deductive logic. This approach was labeled 'praxeology'. Hardin (2011) has recently argued that the emphasis on individualism and the role of knowledge in human action should have led to an Austrian 'sociology' as much as a different sense of economics.

The subjectiveness and complexity of human action dominates Austrian ideas. The only facts admitted are those that are subjective but widely believed. In consequence, the key aim of their inquiry is the understanding of human action rather than quantification and prediction. The Austrians reject the empirical testing/falsification approaches and econometrics that lie at the core of much modern applied economics. Ironically, this stance might place them somewhat closer to more left-leaning post-Keynesian economists or even the Foucauldian and other qualitative approaches that underpin much social research on housing.

The ideas underpinning individual choices quickly lead, in the Austrian view, to a rejection of the notion that collective choices are possible. Practically, there is no way of identifying and adding up the different views of those that make a collective choice, or indeed weight the views of a collective for which a choice is being made. In essence, there is no signaling device that will reveal what individuals will choose, nor indeed how they should revise their individual valuations of collective choices (leaving aside free-rider issues, etc.). In consequence, the Austrians usually end in a policy position that sees interventions in markets as distorting signals in ways that will lead to suboptimal outcomes. Von Mises (1949), arguably the most libertarian of the Austrians, argued that this approach was potentially value-free. That is, praxeology does not prescribe the best outcome but poses the question 'if this policy is pursued what will be the consequences'. In reality, the answer that practicing Austrian economists usually propose is minimal or no government intervention.

With that view on the 'collective' decision problem and the emphasis on market processes, the Austrian view is seen as supportive of private rather than public ownership of property and of avoiding policy actions that distort market price signals. Ironically, this is where the Austrian view has some use for others that take a different view. It reminds us of the need to spell out the nature of market failures and their extent (a task the Austrians would reject as philosophically invalid) and to identify these settings where price regulation or departure from market prices can have benefits.

These ideas lay at the core of the 1930s/1940s debates on the value or possibility of socialist planning, between Lerner and Hayek, for example (see Stiglitz, 1995). A knowledge of these debates would have sharpened the thinking of those who have set the social rents of millions of households in the last 50 years. The Austrians by questioning any intervention in markets espouse the notion of recognising the possibility of unintended consequences. That is, all decision takers will make mistakes between plan and outcome. Awareness of the actual as opposed to intended outcomes of policies, and some modesty about what is known *ex ante*, should encourage those who plan and provide housing to pursue prior analyses to the limit and be prepared to identify and amend mistakes. It is not essential to apply the Austrian approach to learn from it.

Austrian economics, despite the rejection of collective decision taking, is not limited to individuals and firms. It was articulated in, at least, three key areas of macroeconomic thinking. The Austrians were very influential in the development of the quantity theory of money. In that context, the concern that central banks would make decision mistakes led to an Austrian view that monetary regulation of fractional reserve banking systems could be problematic and that the gold standard was the preferred method for managing domestic and international aspects of monetary policy. The capacity for monetary policy to misprice money, and therefore fail to align individuals' time preferences with interest rates lay at the core of Bohm-Bawerk's (1890) theory of the business cycle. Schumpeter's (1942) notion of longer cycles and swarms of innovations typically set entrepreneurs and market processes at the core of major long-term changes in the economy.

Understanding Housing Systems

Ideas based on Austrian economics are most commonly articulated in housing debates that are concerned with political economy. Proponents of no or little intervention in housing markets and opponents of any form of rent controls and planning regulations are the most common expression of Austrianism. That is, in the absence of any belief in empirical observation and in the primacy of individual action and private property, Austrian contributions to housing debate are largely polemical. There is no well-established academic text assessing housing systems from the Austrian standpoint, though Webster et al. (2005) provide a well-argued set of pro and con views on neo-Austrian ideas in urban planning and related markets.

However, without abandoning the hope that government actions can provide societal benefits and the belief that quantitative, indeed mixed methods research, can be useful, it is still informative to ask whether and how Austrian ideas can contribute to an understanding of housing systems and policies.

There are a number of areas of research where an Austrian perspective has a weight of interest that the mainstream does not and is, in consequence, a useful reference point for developing questions, if not answers. These include the following:

1. Housing markets are often out of equilibrium and can take long periods of time to adjust to change. They also involve households in search processes for a complex commodity and some of that search behaviour has 'discovery' characteristics. Mainstream housing economics ignores most of these issues and needs to reflect on at least the questions the Austrians ask, for their view of markets is less reductionist.
2. Housing research, despite the complexity of markets and the sluggishness of supply processes, has paid little attention to the behaviour and role of market agents (the mainstream is weak on catallatics) and has no sense of entrepreneurial behaviour in the housing supply.
3. Much of social research on public and nonmarket housing has ignored the role of rents. They are viewed simply as a form of administrative charge, with no role to play in how households use or choose homes, and these schemes seldom have any coherence within and across such systems. The Hayek–Langer debates on the possibilities for pricing in any planned system should be essential for all those who are responsible for public rents so that they minimise the unintended consequences of what they offer poorer households. Nonmarket pricing schemes can be well designed, but they seldom are.
4. Planning for housing has important implications for affordability and accessibility. Yet housing planning, in reality, is not only weak on economic drivers but largely ignores the economic consequences of planning decisions. Local planners are frequently as polemical as Austrian high theorists. An understanding of how households behave in markets, the nature of market processes, and the consequences (negative as well as positive) should be essential in planning education.
5. Subsequent to the crash there has been some press comment on how the Austrian view on cycles has some pertinence. A long boom with cheap money certainly did lead to malinvestment, not least in US mortgage-backed securities, and booms in asset prices, not least housing. And this is consistent with an Austrian view, but also many other macroperspectives. The Austrian view of how to deal with the crash would have been to let market processes operate and 'malinvestments' fail (i.e., 'bad banks should not have been bailed out') and that price processes would have realigned interest rates, wages, and prices in the longer term. Most Keynesians reject this view of the 'hangover' theory of recessions. Arguably, it was an absence rather than excess of market regulation that permitted the crash of 2008. Once crashes occur it is imperative to deal with the labour and credit market failures that prevail so that unemployment and recession do not drop deeper. But with herd-like and

irrational behaviour cited by the mainstream as what shapes the form and timing of booms and busts, we still need to understand more about market processes. Austrian policy prescriptions may not be helpful once in recession but the questions they pose about consumers, markets, and ignorance are still unanswered by the mainstream in both housing market boom and bust.

Over long periods of time the economics mainstream has shown the capacity to absorb the insights of different theoretical strands and innovations. As economics again appears to have become more outward looking and more diverse in perspective, there may still be scope to show an interest in at least the market process questions that the Austrians set as their core. For, arguably, housing economics does not yet provide much insight about how consumers behave in housing markets and its whole theoretical and econometric modelling structures are built for a system in or close to equilibrium. That is, a convenient simplification for mainstream economics but it is an odd empirical judgement to make about the normal state of housing markets.

References

Bohm-Bawerk E (1890) *Capital and Interest: A Critical History of Economic Theory*. Smart WA (trans.). London: MacMillan.
Butler E (2010) *Austrian Economics: A Primer*. London: Adam Smith Trust.
Hardin R (2011) *How Do You Know? The Economics of Ordinary Knowledge*. Princeton University Press.
Hayek F (1948) *Individualism and the Economic Order*. University of Chicago Press.
Keizer W (1997) *Austrian Economics in Debate*. New York: Routledge.
Kirzner IM (1973) *Competition and Entrepreunership*. University of Chicago Press.
Menger C (1871) *Principles of Economics*. Vienna: Braumuller.
Samuelson P (1964) Theory and realism: A reply. *American Economic Review* 54: 736–739.
Schumpeter J (1942) *Capitalism, Socialism and Democracy*. New York: Harper.
Spence AM (1973) Job market signaling. *Quarterly Journal of Economics* 87(3): 355–374.
Stiglitz J (1995) *Whither Socialism*. Cambridge, MA: MIT Press.
Von Mises L (1949) *Human Action*. New Haven: Yale University Press.
Webster C, et al. (2005) The new institutional economics and the evolution of modern town planning. *Town Planning Review* 76(4): 455–502.

B

Behavioural Economics

K Gibb, University of Glasgow, Glasgow, UK

© 2012 Elsevier Ltd. All rights reserved.

Introduction

Behavioural economics (BE) is a diverse body of research that seeks to reposition economics through the deployment of more realistic or plausible assumptions about preferences, individual rationality, decision-making, and beliefs. It draws on a large and growing body of empirical, often experimental, research that is rooted in the study of human psychology. As such, it returns to earlier common interests between economics and psychology, but, to a greater or lesser extent, in its present guise it threatens to alter the underlying mainstream or neoclassical economics model. BE has considerable potential to contribute to housing economics and housing studies more generally.

BE has become fashionable within economics, policy-making, and popular discourses. Whether it will actually supplant or synthesise mainstream economic models, in particular, that of the probabilistic expected utility model of individual behaviour, remains to be seen. Several adherents, for example, Rabin (1998), expect that BE will augment and enlarge the neoclassical frame of reference rather than replace it. Other analysts, for example, Cassidy (2009), representing those most critical of the apparent recent failures of free markets such as the banking sector take a more radical perspective. They argue that the orthodoxy of positivist instrumentalism, wherein the reality of assumptions is argued not to matter in terms of model outcome accuracy, needs to be replaced with explicit realistic assumptions of behaviour premised on the corroborated findings of the BE literature.

Many economists are critical of the BE tradition and argue that it stems from an inductive bottom-up experimental methodology that veers too often towards the ad hoc. They also argue that it has to demonstrate that individual economic agents do not learn to become rational over time or indeed that competition in markets does not compel rational behaviour consistent with the grand unifying neoclassical theory. At the same time, there is probably only passing acknowledgement by noneconomists that BE is nonetheless situated in a positivist natural science methodological framework and is far removed from any social theory-based conception of knowledge. It remains much more mainstream to the core of economics than many heterodox or social scientists either realise or indeed would support.

BE is undoubtedly a significant development in economics. It has successfully applied experimental methods (and there is also an extensive and growing body of 'field' research), fits well with and extends game theory (and hence is at the centre in developments in microeconomics more generally), and applied behavioural research that has shone light in key public policy areas such as the financial markets and in social policy areas such as health, pensions, and, of course, housing. This entry does three things. First of all, we briefly trace the path of BE to its current eminent position. Second, the key ideas associated with BE are introduced. Third, we explore the ways in which BE can add to housing economics analysis, suggesting a forward research agenda.

The Rise of Behavioural Economics

The idea that economic agents are not calculating automatons but rather humans and prone to error (and that this may be systematically open to analysis) is not new in any way. Its growing relevance over the past 40 years parallels the colonisation of neoclassical optimising individualism as the working model underpinning mainstream economics. But, as an alternative, BE has only more recently grown to develop coherence and general principles that might either challenge the orthodoxy or in some way become synthesised into a broader economic research programme (see the recent textbook by Wilkinson, 2008). Certainly, in the 1950s, Herbert Simon raised fundamental questions about bounded rationality and others have argued that cognitive optimisation of information relevant to choices has an opportunity cost which will be rationed and managed. Others have of course developed ideas to do with incomplete and asymmetric information, though the latter tend to operate within an otherwise mainstream analysis.

In his review of the development of BE, Poundstone (2010) identifies important antecedents in the psychology research led by W. Edwards and colleagues at the Oregon Research Institute and S. S. Stevens at Harvard, the latter explicitly drawing on the nineteenth-century psychophysics ideas associated with, inter alia, Gustav Fechner and Ernst Weber (particularly the importance of reference level relative utility as opposed to absolute utility levels in decision-making). The advent of modern BE focuses on the work of two Israeli psychologists, Amos Tversky and Daniel Kahneman, who were seeking to reassess decision-making fundamentally. (A key anomaly identified by Lichtenstein and Slovic (1971) and then by others subsequently was that of preference reversal. Unlike economic choice orthodoxy, they found experimental evidence of inconsistent behaviour. This led both to increased interest in behavioural research and further anomalies and to doughty resistance from mainstream economists – further discussed in Poundstone (2010).) Subsequently, they have collaborated with several key behavioural economists and their work has been added to by many others, chiefly R. Thaler, M. Rabin, and C. Camerer among others. Adopting psychological experimental methods, Tversky and Kahneman produced ground-breaking work on biases in choice-making, developing a number of significant heuristics with which to systematise these biases. They then went on to develop an alternative to expected utility maximisation as a basis for decision-making, known as prospect theory that featured the ground-breaking concept of loss aversion in economic agents (the greater sensitivity to possible losses compared to possible gains). These innovations and other subsequent work ultimately led to Nobel recognition.

Although the growing body of work was asking fundamental questions about the mainstream modelling framework and its assumptions, BE found it hard to break through to the leading economics debates. However, and in parallel, one of the chief advantages of the BE paradigm became clear – it is particularly well suited to explaining puzzles in specific applied areas. One place where the behavioural approach blossomed was in finance, creating what became known as behavioural finance. This research sought to explain anomalies in the efficient market hypothesis (i.e., contested evidence about bubbles, volatility, and sustained excess returns), as well as other puzzles to do with equity premiums and apparently nonrational market behaviour by agents. Behavioural explanations of market performance by Shiller (2005) and others are now standard additions to the financial economics literature.

Why has BE been comparatively successful, so much so that it appears to be colonising some of the commanding heights of the economics landscape? One reason is the undoubted impact made in the field of financial markets (e.g., Shleifer, 2000) where the requirements of efficient markets have moved further away from reality or relevance, particularly in the past 4 or 5 years. Second, an ever-expanding literature speaks directly to theoretical and applied areas of economics in areas such as game theory and often fits directly into familiar economic problems. In this vein, third, the development of policy solutions based on incentive-compatible strategies involving behavioural revisions of standard assumptions appears to be paying policy dividends. Most notably, authors such as Thaler have tapped into something of the moment with the concept of 'nudging' policies in areas such as pensions and for preventative health care (in 2010 the new UK Government set up a high-level policy unit explicitly aimed at uncovering new areas that might benefit from such 'nudges'). Fourth, there has undoubtedly been a shift in the thinking in journals and amongst the profession in favour of (rigorously) exploring the consequences of behavioural assumptions (broadly speaking) in place of the standard model – particularly as evidence indicates that economic agents do not systematically overcome the sorts of biases and suboptimal decisions that standard theory would suggest will be eliminated by learning and by competition. Finally, BE can tap into new developments in social sciences and psychology that appeal to economists working at the frontiers of choice theory, for example, the opportunities presented by brain image scanning through neuroeconomics.

Key Ideas

In this section, several of the principal ideas associated with the BE tradition are outlined. We start with the Tversky and Kahneman (1974, 1981) heuristics that emerged as simpler methods of dealing with complexity and uncertainty. However, these heuristic devices also lead to bias and systematic error when attempting to assess the probability of an event occurring or when seeking to attribute value. The three original ideas (1974) are augmented with related concepts:

- *Representativeness*. This heuristic is concerned with the idea that when asked to judge whether some phenomenon (A) is representative of something else (B), the decision depends on the perception of how similar A is to B. This is often based on faulty comparisons or reasoning and an intuitive overconfidence in the representativeness of the comparison made. This approach can also lead to errors arising from the erroneous application of assumed statistical regularities, for instance, an insensitivity to the sample size judgements are drawn from (i.e., it may not be big enough to

generalise from); or misconceptions arising from the role of chance (e.g., the independence of successive coin tosses).
- *Availability.* Familiarity with an event can lead one to overestimate the probability of its occurrence. Biases in judgements can occur because specific outcomes are familiar or more salient than others. Tversky and Kahenman illustrate this by arguing that the subjective probability of a fire is likely to be greater if one has seen a fire rather than just read about it. Also relevant are the contexts within which we go about different tasks involving decisions since this shapes and filters the range of outcomes. Simple rules of thumb may be used to arrive at decisions where there is no prior memory to draw on and imagination can arrive at inaccurate probabilities of different contingencies but equally real risks may be underestimated if they are difficult to imagine.
- *Anchoring.* A theme running through BE is the importance of relative values as opposed to absolute levels. Ariely (2008) has called this 'arbitrary coherence'. We can judge how much difference there should be between two goods of different quality, but have difficulty assessing absolute value. Repeated evidence suggests that announcing arbitrary numbers can influence how agents value real entities – valuation is anchored to the initial arbitrary value. Valuations can be framed by the way questions are asked leading to quite contrary answers by so doing. This is thought to be important in a number of contexts, for instance, the damages awarded by juries and the valuation of properties without close substitutes.
- *Endowment effects.* The utility derived from a good or service is not independent of its ownership status (Wilkinson, 2008). Repeated experiments indicate that ownership seems to convey a higher value on an item compared to the valuation of an identical item by someone who does not possess it. This can lead to problems for sellers unwilling to accept, for instance, falling values of asset prices. There is a clear relevance here to housing market behaviour and property rights.
- *Herd, frenzy, or shoal effects.* Studies principally in the financial markets (but alluded to in the housing market too) suggest that market volatility can be exacerbated by herd-like behaviour in a clamour to follow fashion but also the fear of missing out before the market turns (or indeed a belief that it will not turn). To the extent that these transactions are based primarily on price expectations however formed – they can constitute bubbles in market prices.

A second theme of the work by Tversky and Kahneman arose out of prospect theory. In an acclaimed 1979 article in *Econometrica*, they critiqued expected utility theory and proposed prospect theory as an alternative model of decision-making under risk – later work extended this model to cases of genuine uncertainty. Wilkinson (2008: chapter 3) summarises the prospect theory as a two-stage process wherein agents first edit the prospects (i.e., a range of possible outcomes, gambles, or risky alternatives) into an ordered set which is then evaluated. In this second phase, in addition to the use of various heuristics, there are other important dimensions. First, the use of relative utility reference points, and gains and losses measured against that reference point. Second, the principle of 'loss aversion' (i.e., sensitivity is greater to losses than equivalent gains – Kahneman later argued that this was their single most significant idea). Third, agents exhibit diminishing marginal sensitivity to value differences as they get larger (either as gains or as losses) and this is associated with risk aversion.

Prospect theory seeks to be an alternative basis to expected utility decision-making under conditions of risk and uncertainty adopting more realistic assumptions about individual behaviour derived from the BE literature. It has been widely used by behavioural economists and specific elements of it, particularly loss aversion, has appeared as a motivating factor in many applied economics papers. Wilkinson (2008: 127–137) includes a useful account of the critical responses to prospect theory. These are really often fundamentally a methodological unwillingness to accept the premise of nonrational or optimising behaviour. Other economists simply oppose the very use of heuristics and principles such as bounded rationality which are argued to reduce the normative status of the theory, make it less parsimonious and even indeterminate given that an implication of the use of heuristics is that preferences may not be transitive (which is viewed by many economists as a step too far).

A third dimension of BE explores the extent to which and the circumstances when 'altruism' or fairness is a better basis of actor motivation than pure self-interest, the latter being the norm in mainstream economics. The behaviourists do continue to work in a self-interested motivational framework, but they have designed experiments and conducted research that test for anomalies in the selfish motivation theory, as well as examining more clear-cut versions of fairness as a guiding principle, exploring nonaltruistic ideas such as reciprocity and spite (Wilkinson, 2008: 359–363). While the evidence appears to find many flaws in the standard model in terms of anomalies that suggest simple self-interest breaks down as a guiding principle (e.g., repeated results from the so-called ultimatum and dictator games), it is quite hard to pin down evidence of the converse – of decisions based around fairness and altruism. This is a difficult area – empirically identifying motivations is inherently problematic and the research may serve simply to highlight the shortcomings of the experimental methods in designing incentives as opposed to making do with indirect inference from field research.

A fourth area of work is concerned with Thaler's concept of 'mental accounting'. This is a direct application of prospect theory. Thaler (1999) describes mental accounting as the set of cognitive operations put in place by agents to monitor, evaluate, and co-ordinate household finances – hence the direct relevance to decision-making choices. Thaler (1999) argues that mental accounting rules are not neutral in that they influence the relative attractiveness of different choices. In particular, he stresses the nonfungibility of money, that is, money held in one mental account is not a perfect substitute for money in another. Mental accounting is set in a BE prospect theory world where utility relative to a reference point rather than absolute utility is what matters, where there is diminishing sensitivity to the size of both gains and losses and loss aversion operates and has considerable influence on outcomes.

Thaler's work on mental accounting extends to look at a series of important topics. First, he distinguishes the consumer's valuation of a given purchase between 'acquisition utility' (i.e., the value of the good relative to the price paid) and 'transaction utility' (i.e., the perceived value of the 'deal' – the price paid relative to an expected reference price). A good deal can lead us to buy where the acquisition utility is low. Second, loss aversion can lead economic agents to resist selling assets when prices fall because of the pain associated with closing a mental account. Third, *ex post* evaluations of the purchase decision can lead to sunk costs playing a part in subsequent decisions (when mainstream economics says they should not) but that they appear to diminish over time. Fourth, paying by credit card or other noncash means decouples consumption from payment at least to a range of consumer preferences for flat-rate payment plans even where these are not the most efficient method. Fifth, separate accounts that are nonfungible help agents with self-control issues. Sixth, Thaler introduces the concept of 'myopic loss aversion', for instance, where investor worries over loss aversion lead them to reassess their portfolios too frequently and too conservatively. (Thaler also terms this 'narrow framing' after work by Kahneman and Lovallo (1993) where projects are evaluated one at a time rather than as one portfolio, leading to systematic reluctance to take risks.) Wilkinson (2008: 184–186) argues that several of these features of mental accounting alongside nonstandard discounting (see below) can help explain international evidence on mortgage equity withdrawal, consumption, and housing wealth impacts.

A final general idea in BE research concerns problems with intertemporal choice, and 'time-inconsistent preferences', exemplified by the concept of 'hyperbolic discounting'. The standard model of intertemporal choice is based on absolute utility (i.e., not relative comparisons with a reference level) and is governed by the discount rate by which economic agents discount (expected) future utility. There are many assumptions built into this model about psychology (Wilkinson, 2008: 194–198), but the two key points are that (1) it is assumed agents apply the same discount rate over their lifetimes (whereas evidence suggests that older people have lower discount rates) and (2) at any point in time the same discount rate is applied throughout the future in order to discount future expected utility (although again there is empirical evidence that these rates decline over time). These two assumptions ensure that rational time-consistent preferences hold. Wilkinson points out that several empirical anomalies with the standard model have been observed and evidenced. For instance, larger expected gains are in practice discounted at a lower discount rate than small prospects; and that agents have a preference for improving rather than declining sequences of utility per period (whereas the standard model posits a declining sequence as later periods are more heavily discounted).

As a result of these anomalies, BE research has looked at several alternative approaches to time-inconsistent discounting. One of the best-known alternative approaches is called hyperbolic discounting (Wilkinson points out that research on different types of discount function goes back as far as the 1960s). The standard discount rate is constant and this translates into a declining exponential function (with respect to time). A hyperbolic discount function, however, essentially has a higher initial discount rate before it flattens to a lower constant rate thereafter (depending on the specific parameters). This means that time preferences are not consistent and it raises important issues for decision-making over time for savings, assets, insurance, and so on.

Behavioural Economics and Housing

In the previous section, illustrations of how the emerging BE paradigm could be applied to housing research have been suggested and can be extended. Owner-occupiers may experience endowment effects, time-inconsistent preferences, relative reference point utility comparisons, anchoring, and other biases in their valuations and assumptions about the housing market. More generally, prospect theory may be a better basis to develop models of housing under risk or uncertainty. Equally in the mortgage market, policy nudges may be developed to promote more self-control and to encourage less speculative behaviour and generally more efficient outcomes for individuals and society. However, it is important to recognise that there is already housing research looking at these issues. In this final section, a brief selection of studies is highlighted for further exploration, alongside a possible research agenda.

Northcraft and Neale (1987) used both students and real estate professionals to generalise experiments with actual housing market data from Arizona to confirm anchoring adjustment biases in valuation (from both the amateurs and the experts). Genovese and Mayer (2001) and Engelhardt (2003) provide evidence of loss aversion where sellers in falling housing markets retain unrealistic values slowing down the normal functioning of the market because in Thaler's terms they cannot bear to close the mental account and accept the loss.

In a focus issue of *Housing, Theory and Society* (HTS), Marsh and Gibb (2011) develop a framework for analysing housing choices that embraces search theory, BE, bounded rationality, and aspects of institutionalism. They conclude with several ideas for a forward-looking empirical research agenda that would seek to parameterise several of the key ideas found in BE. Three examples might be:

- How are housing preferences developed and acted upon by economic agents?
- What role do market intermediaries have upon the decision-making of households active in housing markets?
- How are house price expectations formed and how do they influence decision-making?

This kind of inquiry might then lead on to a behavioural research agenda about reforming the housing market purchase process, mortgage choices, and even housing taxation. It may also contribute to debates about the role of housing within personal sector wealth portfolios and policies to ameliorate the formation of price bubbles. This is to say nothing of examining the decision-making behaviour of construction firms, landlords, and other governmental actors in the housing system. Thus far, the rich scope for housing market behavioural research, potentially both experimental and field-based, has barely been identified. The HTS focus issue also contains a contrasting paper on these questions from Smith (2011) and a series of comments and responses from the authors and others, drawing on issues such as the role of fundamentals in long-term house price determinations and the methodological difficulties associated with the combining of BE with other heterodox traditions, such as institutional economics.

Pryce et al. (2011) are concerned with how housing markets will respond to the greater frequency and severity of floods in the future and develop a conceptual framework derived from BE and the sociology of risk. In particular, they draw on ideas of myopia, amnesia, and path dependency. Although this is work in progress, it is a good example of the applicability of BE to different applied market contexts and questions, even one as challenging as future flood risk and housing markets.

There is a potentially rich agenda for housing researchers. First, there is tremendous scope to further analyse the heuristics and biases as they may or may not apply to different parts of the housing system. These lead on to questions about house price expectations, the formation of market bubbles, relative to economic fundamentals, valuation and home purchase behaviour and the asymmetries associated with equity withdrawal when house prices rise relative to when they fall. There are also fundamental questions regarding discounting behaviour in housing markets, and the scope for applying Thaler's mental accounting to housing consumption and choice decisions. Before one even considers the possible scope for marrying BE to other ideas such as evolutionary economics or institutional analysis such as property rights, there remains a major programme of work to fully explore prospect theory as the underlying choice under uncertainty basis for analysing housing markets and behaviour. Conceptually and empirically, this is a large prospective agenda but one well suited to the complexity of the housing commodity, its intertemporal nature and the widespread sense of market imperfections intrinsic to housing.

See also: Economic Approaches to Housing Research; Mortgage Choice: Behavioural Finance; Neoclassical Models of the Housing Market; Time and the Economic Analysis of Housing Systems.

References

Ariely D (2008) *Predictably Irrational: The Hidden Forces That Shape Our Decisions*. London: HarperCollins.
Cassidy J (2009) *How Markets Fail?* London: Penguin.
Engelhardt G (2003) Nominal loss aversion, housing equity constraints and household mobility: Evidence from the United States. *Journal of Urban Economics* 53: 171–195.
Genovese D and Mayer C (2001) Nominal loss aversion and seller behaviour: Evidence from the housing market. *Quarterly Journal of Economics* 116: 1233–1260.
Kahneman D and Lovallo D (1993) Timid choices and bold forecasts: A cognitive perspective on risk-taking. *Management Science* 39: 17–30.
Lichenstein S and Slovic P (1971) Reversals of preference between bids and choices in gambling decisions. *Journal of Experimental Psychology* 89: 46–55.
Marsh A and Gibb K (2011) Uncertainty, expectations and housing market choices. *Housing, Theory and Society* 28, forthcoming.
Northcraft G and Neale M (1987) Experts, amateurs, and real estate: An anchoring and adjustment perspective on property pricing decisions. *Organizational Behavior and Human Decision Processes* 39: 84–97.
Poundstone W (2010) *Priceless: The Hidden Psychology of Value*. Oxford, UK: Oneworld.
Pryce G, Chen Y, and Galster G (2011) The impact of floods on house prices: An imperfect information approach with myopia and amnesia. *Housing Studies* 26(2): 259–279.
Rabin M (1998) Psychology and economics. *Journal of Economic Literature* 36: 11–46.
Rabin M (2002) A perspective on psychology and economics. *European Economic Review* 46: 657–685.
Shiller R (2005) *Irrational Exuberance*, 2nd edn. Princeton, NJ: Princeton University Press.
Shleifer A (2000) *Inefficient Markets: An Introduction to Behavioural Finance*. Oxford, UK: Oxford University Press.

Smith S (2011) Home price dynamics: A behavioural economy? *Housing, Theory and Society* 28, forthcoming.

Thaler R (1999) Mental accounting matters. *Journal of Behavioural Decision Making* 12: 183–206.

Tversky A and Kahneman D (1974) Judgement under uncertainty: Heuristics and biases. *Science* 185: 1124–1131.

Tversky A and Kahneman D (1981) The framing of decisions and the psychology of choice. *Science* 211: 453–458.

Wilkinson N (2008) *An Introduction to Behavioural Economics*. Basingstoke, UK: Palgrave Macmillan.

Further Reading

Della Vigna S (2009) Psychology and economics: Evidence from the field. *Journal of Economic Literature* 47: 315–372.

Kahneman D and Tversky A (1979) Prospect theory: An analysis of decision under risk. *Econometrica* 47: 263–291.

Thaler R and Sunstein C (2008) *Nudge*. New Haven, CT: Yale University Press.

Brownfield Development and Housing Supply

TJ Dixon, Oxford Brookes University, Oxford, UK

© 2012 Elsevier Ltd. All rights reserved.

Glossary

Barker review UK government review of housing supply from 2003 to 2004, and named after Kate Barker, a senior economist.

Brownfields Previously developed land or buildings which may or may not be contaminated.

Contaminated sites Generally brownfield sites which suffer from contamination often as a result of previous use and which may pose a threat to human health.

Eco-town A new settlement designed to the highest standards, with particular emphasis on environmental issues such as conserving energy and water, reducing waste, and limiting carbon emissions.

Market failure A market failure exists when the production or consumption of goods and services by the market is not efficient.

Millennium community A joint programme between English Partnerships (now part of the Homes and Communities Agency) and UK government's Department for Communities and Local Government which was designed to create seven exemplar sustainable communities across the United Kingdom.

Sustainable communities Places where people want to live and work, now and in the future. They meet the diverse needs of existing and future residents, are sensitive to their environment, and contribute to a high quality of life. They are safe and inclusive, well planned, built and run, and offer equality of opportunity and good services for all.

Sustainable development A pattern of resource use that aims to meet human needs while preserving the environment so that the needs of both present and future generations can be met.

Brownfield Regeneration and Sustainable Development

In many countries, the regeneration of previously developed land and buildings has become a primary focus for underpinning the more effective reuse and redevelopment of major urban areas. Increasingly, this policy trend has also become entwined with national sustainable development and planning policies.

Despite this, there has been much debate over the terminology used to describe such sites. It is probably fair to say that the earliest use of the term 'brownfield' can be traced to the US steel industry in the 1970s. Later on, and certainly in the United States, the term brownfield became synonymous with urban sites (frequently industrial premises) which were derelict, underutilised, and suffering from contamination as a result of previous industrial processes. In Europe, brownfield sites were often (although not exclusively) redundant industrial sites, but they were not seen as being synonymous with contamination issues. Today, however, with policy evolution in the United States, under the Small Business and Liability Relief and Brownfields Revitalization Act of 2002, a brownfield site is seen as being:

real property, the expansion, redevelopment, or reuse of which may be complicated by the presence or potential presence of a hazardous substance, pollutant or contaminant.

This now coincides with the European understanding of brownfields, although it is fair to say that contamination is probably still seen as more of an issue with such sites in the United States than it is in parts of Europe. For example, in England, brownfield land was defined by the UK government in 2005 as (ODPM, 2005: 77):

land that is unused or may be available for development. It includes both vacant and derelict land and land currently in use with known potential for redevelopment. It excludes land that was previously developed where the remains have blended into the landscape over time.

Nonetheless, it is also true that in some European countries, particularly Scandinavia, there is no official definition for brownfield, perhaps reflecting the relatively small number of such sites in those countries. However, even here, in the areas bordering the Baltic, there are significant industrial legacies and accompanying contamination risks.

In the United Kingdom, the prominence of sustainable development is strongly linked to the emphasis on

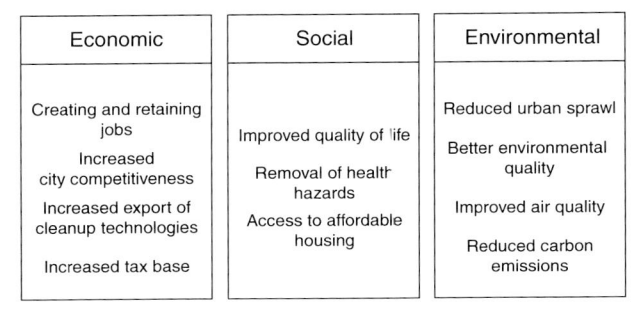

Economic	Social	Environmental
Creating and retaining jobs	Improved quality of life	Reduced urban sprawl
Increased city competitiveness	Removal of health hazards	Better environmental quality
Increased export of cleanup technologies	Access to affordable housing	Improved air quality
Increased tax base		Reduced carbon emissions

Figure 1 The benefits of brownfield regeneration.

brownfield regeneration and, in particular, the drive for new housing on such sites. In the UK government's 'Securing the Future' report of 2005, for example, brownfield redevelopment was viewed as vital in promoting environmental justice by removing environmental degradation in deprived communities. The same emphasis can also be seen in the context of a wider 'sustainable brownfield regeneration' agenda in Europe and elsewhere. For example, a study of western developed countries highlighted the key generic benefits of brownfield regeneration (**Figure 1**).

Brownfield redevelopment has therefore emerged as a key item on sustainable development agendas through its potentially beneficial impacts in preventing urban sprawl, keeping cities compact and reducing out-migration. It has also been promoted by key policy instruments, including planning and policy guidance in England, and that same country's 1998 60% annual target rate for the proportion of new housing to be built on brownfield land.

The extent of brownfield land varies from country to country. For example, current statistics from England suggest that there are 62 130 ha of brownfield land (or previously developed land (PDL)) in England, which represents about 5% of the total urban area. Additionally, there are some 300 000 ha of land (325 000 sites), or 2% of the land area, in England and Wales that are affected by industrial contamination (gasworks, chemical, or industrial plants), with two-thirds of this having undergone some kind of remediation or cleanup. In the United States, the extent of the contamination issue is greater, with some 500 000–1 000 000 sites affected. In Japan, research has shown that there are 900 000 potentially contaminated sites (i.e., brownfields), the equivalent of some 8.5% of urban areas, of which some 331 612 sites are contaminated.

It is also the case that the extent of national programmes dealing with brownfield land varies between countries, with the United States, the United Kingdom, and Germany most likely to be among those with more detailed and integrated policies currently in place.

Market Drivers and Barriers

For many actors in the development process, brownfield land and property markets have been characterised as 'dysfunctional' or suffering from 'market failure'. This may cause developers of brownfield sites to

- undervalue their commercial benefits – for example, developers may not take into account the positive impacts of redevelopment on the ability of other firms and assets in an area to produce wealth, or developers choosing between greenfields and brownfields may not recognise the cost savings from compact developments created by lower infrastructure costs because they do not necessarily accrue to the developer;
- overvalue their costs – for example, when buyers of land know more than sellers about the environmental risks of land, through the deployment of due diligence and environmental investigation processes, problems of adverse selection may be introduced and some exchanges of land might not occur; and
- exclude social and environmental benefits – for example, private markets may fail to capture collective benefits such as environmental gains, improved neighbourhoods, and better health (see article Economics of Housing Externalities).

Indeed, 'site abnormals' or additional costs of bringing brownfield sites back into use vary according to the precise nature of individual sites, so market failure is often symptomatic of cases where in economic terms the sites remain unviable in the long term.

A particular issue for the development industry is the risk of contamination on a site which usually becomes fully known only when site investigations are carried out. A number of developed countries or regions within countries have developed site contamination legislation either in response to dramatic and tragic contamination incidents such as Love Canal in the United States, Lekkerkerk in the Netherlands, or the Fischer site in Austria or more generally in response to a growing awareness of the extent of the problem. Examples of relevant legislation include:

- United States: The Comprehensive Environmental Response, Compensation, and Liability Act, 1980; Superfund Amendments and Reauthorization Act, 1986; and Brownfields Revitalization Act, 2002;
- England: Part 2A of the Environmental Protection Act, 1990; and
- Japan: The Soil Contamination Countermeasures Law, 2003.

Such legislation has frequently been based on detailed definitions of 'potentially responsible parties' which include the original polluters or the current owners of the contaminated sites, and a specific liability regime that operated retrospectively using strict liability and a command and control approach to serving orders on relevant parties to ensure cleanup of the site. In the case of the US contaminated site, legislation has also provided for the use of public funds (i.e., Superfund) to cover the cost of cleanup in certain cases. Often, however, cleanup has been undertaken outside the legislation. For example, on average, 87% of contaminated sites in England have been dealt with through the planning system (i.e., s106 agreements under the Town and Country Planning Act, 1990), 4% voluntarily, and 9% through Part 2A of the Environmental Protection Act, 1990. Moreover, in the United States, voluntary cleanup confers a degree of immunity from future liability under the current contaminated land legislation.

Besides legal incentives, financial incentives to redevelop brownfields also exist. In the European Union, for example, Structural Funds provide one possible source of financial assistance, and within countries, tax breaks and other types of incentives are also available for remediation or cleanup of sites. This is particularly important in areas where serious contamination exists, and where it is essential to allay the fears of the public because even after a site has been cleaned up, there are possible 'postremediation stigma' effects that can impact on land and property values.

The Big Picture: Is There Enough Brownfield Land for Housing?

Despite the uncertainties and risks associated with contamination, many sites have been cleaned up and many of these sites have subsequently been used for housing or for mixed use or commercial schemes. However, the cleanup standards and costs of remediation may, in some instances, still inhibit redevelopment for housing, although other types of use (e.g., retail, commercial, or light manufacturing) may be more viable. This is frequently a function of cost and required cleanup standards, though the latter would tend to be lower for nonresidential development.

In England, where the linkage between housing policy and brownfield regeneration is more highly evolved than in many other countries, there has been a particular focus on stocktaking nationally, regionally, and locally to determine how much brownfield land is available for housing. In 2007, some 77% of new housing development in England was built on such land compared with 76% in 2006, for example, although given the recent fall in house building activity, the number of brownfield completions has been relatively flat (**Figure 2**). In the face of falling house building activity, however, the 60% target (which is already exceeded) has met with justifiable criticism, as observers suggest the target should be tied to absolute figures on reuse rather than relative figures.

Nevertheless, the policy focus on targets and available brownfield stock was strengthened by Barker (2003, 2004), incorporating a wide-ranging review of housing supply, the reasons for underproduction, and a number of key recommendations. The review, which was heralded as the most important for housing policy in recent years, recommended substantial increases in new housing provision in the United Kingdom to reduce long-run increases in house prices and improve affordability.

However, a number of research reports subsequently questioned whether the supply of brownfield land could meet current market demand for housing in England. In

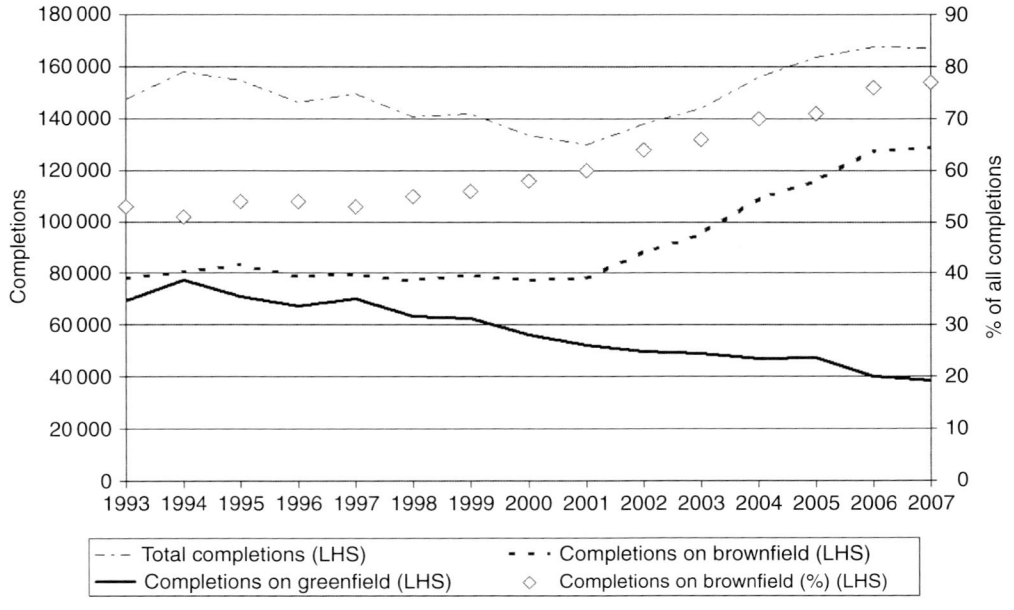

Figure 2 Completions of new dwellings: England (1993–2007).
Based on data from Department of Communities and Local Government (2008).

their 2008 study, Dixon and Adams used the National Land Use Database (NLUD) in conjunction with Barker projections to calculate a figure for 'notional years' supply' of brownfield stock that is suitable for housing. This formed the basis for calculations which are illustrated in **Figure 2**, and highlights the number of years' supply of brownfield remaining, treating the total 2007 'stock' figure of brownfield as a finite amount which contributes to the annual requirements for brownfield development for housing.

As **Figure 3** shows, under a Regional Spatial Strategy (RSS) (formerly Regional Planning Guidance (RPG)) scenario, there is just under 12 years' supply of brownfield land available if all brownfield land suitable for housing is included in the calculation. Under a 'low' Barker scenario, the figure is 10 years; under a 'medium' scenario, nearly 9 years; and under a 'high' scenario, 7 years. Regionally, there are variations with the North West at 21 years under the RPG-only scenario and 12 years under the high scenario. At the other extreme is the South West with a figure ranging from 7 years under RPGs to 4 years under the high scenario. It is important to stress that at the time of writing, the new UK coalition government has announced its intention to scrap the RSS system in favour of devolving strategic planning decisions to locally elected governments. Nonetheless, the example serves to highlight the limited extent of brownfield land available.

Although admittedly crude, such projections highlight the fact that pressures on brownfield stock are unavoidable if the house building projections in England are to be implemented. A key issue is the type of stock available, and the ease with which such land is likely to come on stream, in terms of, for example, available planning permission and complexity of cleanup. However, the stock of brownfield land has remained relatively stable, so as brownfield land is developed, more brownfield land flows replenish the overall stock figure. Nonetheless, it is clear that the focus on increased house building will have important ramifications for greenfield land: if Barker's requirements, and current house building projections, are to be satisfied in England, then greenfield sites will also need to be considered as potential opportunities.

Development Industry and Brownfield Regeneration for Residential Use

A strong driver for brownfield regeneration in the United Kingdom has been the Sustainable Communities Plan (see article Sustainable Communities). The term 'sustainable communities' came to the fore during the 1990s, based around Local Agenda 21. But this found a firmer policy focus with the announcement in February 2003 of

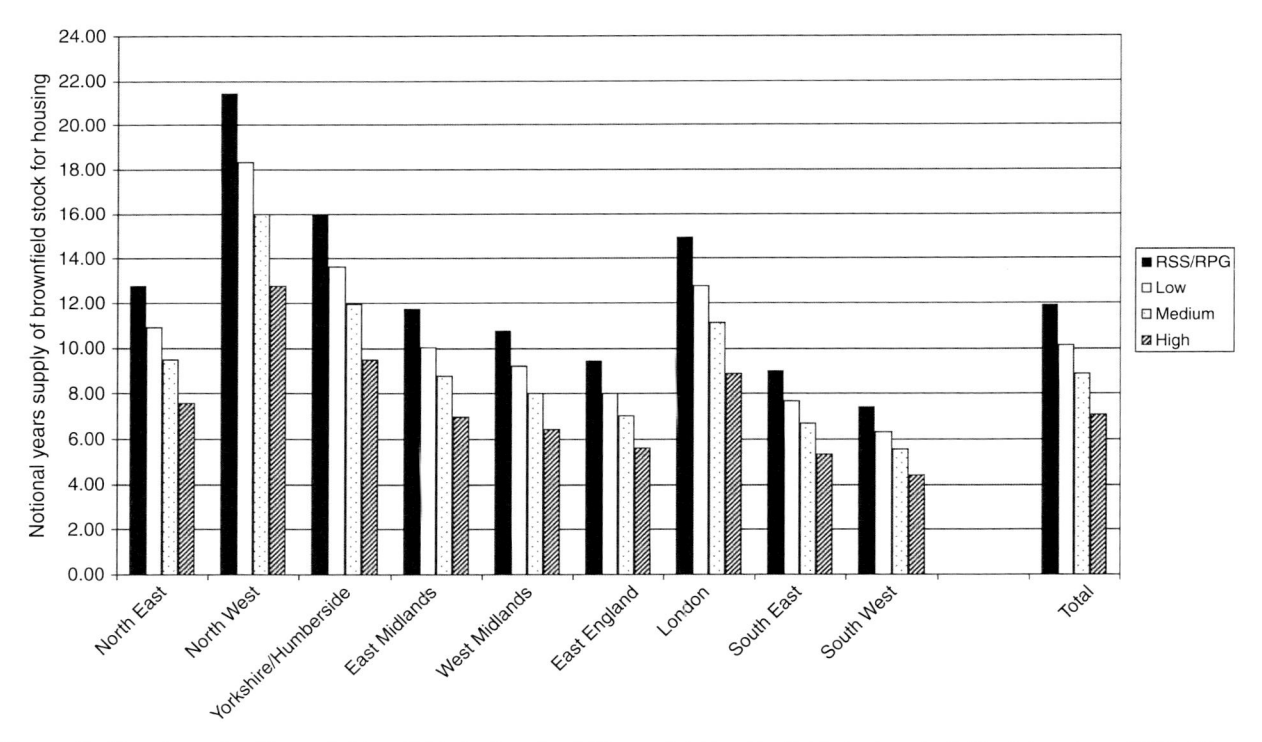

Figure 3 Years' supply of brownfield available for housing (all brownfield land 'suitable for housing') (English regions, 2006–16) (base = 2007 data).
Data from Dixon T and Adams D (2008) Housing supply and brownfield regeneration in a post-Barker world: Is there enough brownfield land in England and Scotland? *Urban Studies* 45(1): 115–139; and Communities and Local Government (CLG) (2008) *Previously-Developed Land That May Be Available for Development: England 2007*. London: CLG.

the UK government's 'Sustainable Communities Plan' (SCP). The government defined the term in its strategy document for sustainable communities for England (ODPM, 2003: 1):

> Sustainable communities are places where people want to live and work, now and in the future. They meet the diverse needs of existing and future residents, are sensitive to their environment, and contribute to a high quality of life. They are safe and inclusive, well planned, built and run, and offer equality of opportunity and good services for all.

The strategy was set out in the 2003 document 'Sustainable Communities: Building for the Future', which sought to tackle housing shortages in the greater South East, renew housing and land markets in low-demand areas of Northern England (i.e., the nine Pathfinder Renewal projects), and protect more rural areas from increasing development pressures. The key areas of growth in the plan are seen as Milton Keynes, Cambridge–Stansted, and Ashford, with substantial regeneration of the Thames Gateway also planned. The UK government has subsequently formulated the key constituents of sustainable communities as being:

- active, inclusive, and safe;
- well run;
- environmentally sensitive;
- well designed and built;
- well connected;
- thriving;
- well served; and
- fair to everyone.

Increasingly, therefore, the sustainable development and housing agendas have become interwoven in the United Kingdom. These ideas have underpinned the emergence of eco-towns, or what the government describes as new exemplar towns comprising 'green' developments of a minimum of 5000 homes. They will be designed to meet the highest standards of sustainability, including low and zero carbon technologies and good public transport. The original announcement of 15 eco-towns in 2008 was scaled back to 4 in 2009, to be completed by 2016: Whitehill Bordon in Hampshire, the China Clay Community at St Austell, Cornwall; Rackheath in Norfolk; and north-west Bicester in Oxfordshire, with the first two towns having a strong brownfield focus (Ministry of Defence land and former china clay workings, respectively).

Research in the United Kingdom has shown that residential developers, or house builders, have frequently struggled to come to terms with sustainability and that their response to the agenda is dependent not only on their individual culture but also on their engagement with the wider corporate social responsibility agenda (see article Housing Developers and Sustainability). Moreover, other barriers often hamper the successful regeneration of brownfield sites for residential development. For example, in the Thames Gateway in England, some commentators have observed that infrastructure issues are hampering efforts to regenerate the area in a holistic way, and governance structures provide a 'maze' which developers find difficult to navigate, despite the strong focus on sustainability in UK planning policy.

Given the market-driven nature of development, it is not surprising that compromises are often made in social and environmental sustainability. Nonetheless, some of the recent regeneration projects in Manchester in the United Kingdom (Higher Broughton, Hulme, and New Islington) offer good examples of an integrated approach to sustainability involving a range of development actors. For example, creating a new image and brand is seen as an important way of enhancing confidence in an area to overcome perceived 'stigma' relating to social deprivation and crime. But this can create problems for local communities, if too little affordable housing is provided or housing is built at too high a density, to the exclusion of 'family' housing. In some instances, schemes can become the victims of their own success, with high prices and unsuitable housing mix forcing out local people and creating 'transient' communities. There is an element of circularity here, however, because higher-density housing is encouraged centrally and locally to justify infrastructure provision.

Within the 'social' pillar of sustainable development, previous research has shown that joint venture schemes can be successful. The key examples of such schemes exist in the United Kingdom and elsewhere, but previous research suggests that there needs to be a balance between strong leadership and collaborative working to ensure success. As far as community engagement and development are concerned, active dialogue with key elements in the community is seen as a prerequisite for a successful project.

Best Practice Examples of Brownfield Redevelopment and Housing

Despite the problems associated with brownfield regeneration, there are a number of successful examples of projects from the United Kingdom, Europe, and elsewhere. Two such examples are New Islington and Hammarby Sjöstad.

New Islington, Manchester, United Kingdom

In 2002, the Ancoats area of East Manchester was identified as the site for the third Millennium Community. The £250 million New Islington Millennium Community development comprises a 12.5-ha site in East Manchester including the former Cardroom housing estate, which was characterised by high crime and social deprivation. Located between the Rochdale Canal and Ashton Canal, the 30-acre site is undergoing a substantial transformation which will feature over 1700 new homes, retail and leisure space, a new primary school, and health centre alongside an eco park. The development is due for completion by 2012. In the summer of 2003 work began, and the development work on the new canals that link to the Ashton Canal and the Rochdale Canal is now complete together with a new water park, 'Cotton Fields', which has been designed to promote a diverse wildlife, including a wetlands area, and a range of nesting boxes to attract a wide variety of birds. Both old mill workings and contamination proved challenging site conditions which have now been successfully resolved.

Hammarby Sjöstad, Stockholm, Sweden

The transformation of the former industrial and harbour area around the Hammarby Lake in Stockholm is one of the biggest urban development ventures in Europe. This is an urban extension to Stockholm's inner city and is often cited as an exemplar of integrated environmental urban design. The urban extension is based on a 200-ha brownfield site to the south of Hammarby Lake and will provide 11 000 homes and 200 000 square metres of commercial space when it is completed in 2018, with a total population of 30 000. The development is characterised by strong stakeholder engagement through what is known as the Hammarby Model, a systematic approach to integrating energy, water, and waste systems in a holistic way so that resources used in one part of the system are recycled for use in other parts of the system. The overall objective of the community is to reduce environmental impact by 50% compared with other suburban areas in Stockholm. The area was remediated using solidification and stabilisation techniques.

Conclusions

The key challenges for the development industry tackling brownfield sites to develop housing revolve primarily around cleanup costs, protecting public health, ensuring the compatibility of contiguous land uses, providing for an inclusive social mix, preserving local character, and addressing community concerns. Against the backdrop of a property market recession, more brownfield sites could become unviable as sites for housing, particularly at low densities. Despite these risks, many successful brownfield projects have led to residential development which has underpinned increased housing supply. In England, ensuring a sufficient supply of brownfield land to meet housing demand is a key policy issue. Successful case studies of brownfield site regeneration exist internationally, and it is also important to stress that although dealing with contamination is important, the most successful brownfield regeneration outcomes are also founded on sound community and transport infrastructure, leadership and vision, strong brand, and an effective private/public partnership with inclusive community engagement.

See also: Economics of Housing Externalities; Housing Developers and Sustainability; Housing Supply: Green Belts; Housing Supply; Housing Supply: Urban Growth Boundaries; Sustainable Communities.

References

Barker K (2003) *Review of Housing Supply: Securing Our Future Needs (Interim Report – Analysis)*. London: HM Treasury.
Barker K (2004) *Review of Housing Supply – Delivering Stability: Securing Our Future Housing Needs*. London: HM Treasury.
Communities and Local Government (CLG) (2008) *Previously-Developed Land That May Be Available for Development: England 2007*. London: CLG.
Dixon T and Adams D (2008) Housing supply and brownfield regeneration in a post-Barker world: Is there enough brownfield land in England and Scotland? *Urban Studies* 45(1): 115–139.
Office of the Deputy Prime Minister (ODPM) (2003) *Sustainable Communities: Building for the Future*. London: ODPM.
Office of the Deputy Prime Minister (ODPM) (2005) *Sustainable Communities: Homes for All, Cm 6424*. London: ODPM.

Further Reading

Adams D and Watkins C (2002) *Greenfields, Brownfields and Housing Development*. Oxford, UK: Blackwell Science.
De Sousa C (2008) *Brownfields Redevelopment and the Quest for Sustainability*. Oxford, UK: Elsevier.
Dixon T (2007) The property development industry and sustainable urban brownfield regeneration in England: An analysis of case studies in Thames Gateway and Greater Manchester. *Urban Studies* 44(12): 2379–2400.
Dixon T, Raco M, Catney P, and Lerner DN (eds.) (2007) *Sustainable Brownfield Regeneration: Liveable Places from Problem Spaces*. Oxford, UK: Blackwell Publishing.
Fowler RF (2007) Site contamination law and policy in Europe, North America and Australia: Trends and challenges. *Paper Presented at the 8th Meeting of the International Committee on Contaminated Land*. Stockholm, Sweden, 10–11 September.
National Round Table on the Environment and the Economy (2003) *Cleaning Up the Past, Building the Future: A National Brownfield Redevelopment Strategy for Canada*. Ottawa, ON: National Round Table on the Environment and the Economy.
Oliver L, Ferber U, Grimski D, Millar K, and Nathanail K (2007) *The Scale and Nature of European Brownfields*. www.cabernet.org.uk (accessed October 2009).
Syms P (2004) *Previously Developed Land*. Oxford, UK: Blackwell Publishing.
Thornton G, Franz M, Edwards D, Pahlen G, and Nathanail P (2006) The challenge of sustainability: Incentives for brownfield regeneration in Europe. *Environmental Science and Policy* 10: 116–134.
Vestbro DU (ed.) (2007) *Rebuilding the City: Managing the Built Environment and Remediation of Brownfields*. Stockholm, Sweden: Baltic University Press.

Relevant Websites

www.cabernet.org.uk – CABERNET (Concerted Action on Brownfield and Economic Regeneration Network).

www.communities.gov.uk – Communities and Local Government.

www.revit-nweurope.org – REVIT (Brownfield Revitalization).

www.subrim.org.uk – SUBR:IM (Sustainable Urban Brownfield Regeneration: Integrated Management).

Building Regulations for Energy Conservation

L Murphy, Delft University of Technology, Delft, The Netherlands

© 2012 Elsevier Ltd. All rights reserved.

Glossary

Building regulations A branch of legislation that details technical requirements and standards in the construction and renovation of buildings.

Energy plus house A house that is a net exporter of energy over a specified time.

Energy security The vulnerability of societies dependent on fossil fuels to price fluctuations, political instability, and the nonrenewable nature of fossil fuels.

Greenhouse gases Gases with properties that absorb and reemit thermal infrared radiation, for example, carbon dioxide (CO_2); the increasing concentration of these gases is linked to global warming and climate change.

Low energy house A house designed to consume approximately half the energy as one built to average building regulation standards.

Net zero energy house A house that generates as much energy as it consumes over a specified time, for example, annually, typically from on-site renewable sources.

Very low energy house A house designed to achieve significant reductions in energy use of between approximately 70–90% compared to average building regulation standards, for example, Passive House.

Energy and Buildings

Predictions related to peak oil; the environmental, economic, and social costs of fossil fuel dependence; and geopolitical security concerns have combined to make the de-carbonisation of society a key priority. Among these concerns, climate change is highly publicised. A share of current opinion states that greenhouse gas (GHG) emission reductions of 80% by 2050 (from 1990 levels) are required by industrialised countries if the CO_2 equivalent ceiling is to be maintained within levels presumed to be safe. Such reductions, and even more modest aims, require concerted action across the sectors. The building sector is identified as a key contributor of GHG emissions, being responsible for approximately 40% of global energy use (**Figure 1**). The majority of this energy consumption is in households. Alongside this, the building sector is promoted as offering the most cost-effective opportunities for reducing GHG emissions with associated environmental and social gains. In response, the role of building regulations is being reconceptualised as a tool to improve the quality of life of the current population and bequeath to future generations a less carbon-intensive housing stock.

The relationship between energy use and buildings reflects the same grave inequalities that characterise access to all resources. Regulating buildings to promote sustainable use of energy is a topic that directly impinges on the lives of less than a third of the world's population. Approximately the same share of the global population does not have access to electricity. Facts such as these bring into stark relief the urgency attached to tackling the challenges of sustainable energy provision and quality of life improvement on a global scale. At the same time, these statistics highlight the different priorities and conditions that characterise resource use and development across the world.

Energy Use in Buildings

Building regulations typically influence energy use associated with a building's operation. However, energy use characterises the entire building life cycle from the extraction of raw materials, to transport of materials after building demolition (**Figure 2**). Energy consumed during the various life-cycle stages can be subject to separate legislation or guidance. Nevertheless, the failure of regulations to reflect the entire energy consumption of a building forms a common criticism.

Energy use is typically pronounced during the operational phase of a building's life cycle. In residential buildings, operation refers to space heating and cooling, heating water, lighting, cooking, and appliance use. During a building's operational phase, energy use is dependent on a variety of factors including climate, economy, building type and size, fuel, and occupant behaviour. Within developed countries, energy is primarily used for space heating and/or cooling and is commonly based on fossil fuels. Poor energy performance of residential buildings in developed countries exposes households to fuel poverty and causes environmental harm that could often be reduced at low or negative cost. Within developing countries, the main

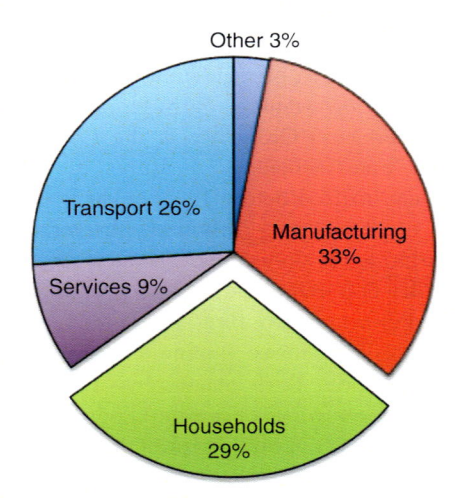

Figure 1 Total final energy consumption per sector. Households (excluding household transport) are responsible for approximately 30% of global final energy use.
Worldwide Trends in Energy Use and Efficiency. Key Insights from IEA Indicator Analysis. In support of the G8 Plan of Action. Copyright OECD/IEA, 2008, figure 2.1, page 17.

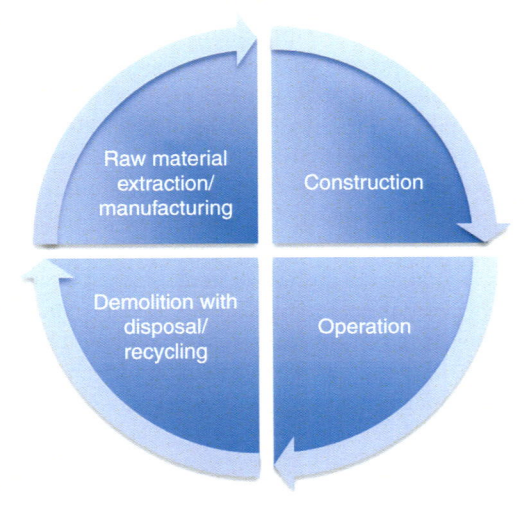

Figure 2 Energy use during a building's life cycle. Energy use features throughout a building's life cycle from extraction of raw materials to recycling at the end of a building's lifetime. As energy efficiency in buildings improves the significance of embodied energy, associated with raw material extraction and manufacture, will increase.

use of energy is cooking, with biomass as a common fuel type. The use of biomass can destruct habitats, remove valuable carbon sinks, lower the quality of life for women who are often responsible for collection, and severely compromise indoor air quality. In developing countries, informal building practices and lack of resources mean that regulations can be afforded low priority over meeting basic needs of shelter provision. In transition countries such as China, energy use in buildings is generally based on fossil fuels such as coal and a search of ways to decouple economic growth from environmental damage has secured a place for building regulations on the agenda.

The Evolution of Building Regulations and Energy

Building regulations can contain minimum standards to reduce unsustainable energy use in buildings. However, concern over the source and extent of energy use is a relative newcomer to regulations that govern the design and construction of buildings. Traditionally, the mainstay of regulations has been health and safety issues for building occupants and the public in terms of aspects such as fire, structural stability, and sanitation. Scandinavian countries were among the first to introduce energy aspects into regulation beginning in the late 1940s with insulation standards. However, the aim of this action was to improve indoor climate for occupants and not energy efficiency per se. The influence of energy concerns in regulations intensified as awareness of the environmental impact of buildings, both at the level of the building site and beyond its boundaries, developed. An external impetus came with the energy crisis of the 1970s when energy was launched into the building regulation agendas of many countries.

Over time, regulations became increasingly sophisticated moving steadily beyond a narrow concern with indoor climate quality towards strategic issues of energy security and climate change. In jurisdictions such as Wales and England modest specifications for elements such as insulation levels of the thermal envelope made way for complex computer simulation software predicting annual CO_2 emissions. More parties, such as nongovernment organisations and private companies, became involved in the design and enforcement of regulations in many countries in response to criticisms of insular and restrictive systems and as part of a wider shift towards governance. In some jurisdictions, for example European Union (EU) Member States, regulations moved from prescribing set standards for individual building elements to a performance-based approach. Building energy performance is based on an annual value of energy consumption. A performance-based approach promises more flexibility during the design process and is viewed as lending itself to innovation. On the other hand a purely prescriptive approach is regularly criticised for imposing rigidity on the design process and for stifling innovation.

More aggressive attempts to meet energy challenges have resulted in an increasing number of countries across the world adopting mandatory building standards combined with long-term ambitious objectives. The strengthening of building regulations has attracted both controversy and praise. A number of local and regional governments in Europe have championed the route towards more severe standards requiring the installation of microgeneration technologies during work to existing houses (Germany) or requiring energy-performance improvements to the whole house during extension developments (Uttlesford District Council, UK). Pioneering efforts such as these can meet opposition from both other levels of government and third parties with a common argument revolving around the violation of property rights. Recently, building regulations have attracted attention as a lever that can accelerate the drive to low energy or net carbon zero buildings. This manifests itself in numerous national and local government deadlines for achieving low energy or passive design standards in buildings within the next decades.

It remains that energy standards in building regulations are voluntary or absent within many countries. In the United States, voluntary standards operate in a number of states. Moreover, many countries lack the institutional framework and resources to formulate and adequately enforce building regulations. Several international organisations such as the United Nations work to assist countries with regard to developing such regulatory frameworks.

Energy Regulations and Existing Buildings

Regulations not only evolved in terms of style and content but also in terms of focus. Traditionally, new build construction reaped the attention of regulations, not surprising as at the design stage the most cost-effective elements can be factored in. Moreover, the established building/planning control processes of many countries mean that new construction is a viable target for regulations.

The effects of tougher standards for new buildings trickled to existing buildings due to, for example, the development of more energy-efficient building products incorporated during renovation. Nonetheless, existing houses have remained largely immune from systematic energy-performance improvement measures. The folly of this neglect has steadily attracted attention with the acceptance that buildings have long lives, 75–100 years in many countries, and without intervention, their poor energetic quality will characterise energy use in the sector for some time. This has resonance when the housing stock of 2050, when long-range GHG emission reductions are to be met, is considered. The reality is that much of the housing stock of 2050 is already standing today and largely consists of houses constructed before the 1970s when the mildest of energy standards entered building regulatory frameworks.

A number of cities in California are at the forefront of extending the reach of regulations to existing houses. San Francisco, for example, introduced a Residential Energy Conservation Ordinance in the 1980s requiring energy and water efficiency measures to be applied (to houses constructed before 1978) at the point of sale. Measures include fitting low-flow showerheads and weather-stripping of doors. The European Commission highlights the important role of the existing stock with the Energy Performance of Buildings Directive requiring Member States to enforce minimum standards during building renovation. With major renovation occurring every 25–40 years in European buildings, this requirement means that the opportunity presented by renovation can be exploited.

Challenges for Building Regulations and Energy

The integration of energy concerns into building regulations has sometimes been tumultuous. As just one aspect of a multithemed regulatory framework, energy-related objectives often vie for position. Achieving a balance between a range of competing objectives including flexibility, relevance, and political acceptability remains a challenge in the formulation of regulations. Regulations must include appropriate definitions for concepts such as a net zero energy house that are robust, limit unintended consequences, and maximise benefit while remaining flexible. In addition, building regulations are closely related to other established systems such as planning control where objectives can conflict. One commonly cited example in this regard is the installation of residential wind turbines which can clash with planning objectives to maintain visual uniformity of a street-scene.

Elements of Building Regulations

Building regulations contain scope to influence energy performance both in terms of energy demand and supply. At the design and construction stage, regulations can ensure that buildings follow passive design principles maximising natural lighting, heating, and shading. Regulations can stipulate that the building fabric, windows, and doors are high-performing and maximum air tightness is achieved. Regulations can set efficiency standards for technical installations like boilers, air-conditioning units, and ventilation systems. The integration of microgeneration technologies can be promoted as part of regulations. Additionally, building regulations can support the use of communication tools through the integration of smart meters or energy labels specifying real-time energy use and an energy rating for the building, respectively.

Following the prescriptive approach to regulation, requirements for each individual aspect such as a set insulation level in a certain climate can be set. Alternatively, following a performance approach, a performance level can be set which requires integrated design and operation across the different aspects. The European Commission promotes the performance approach through the Energy Performance of Buildings Directive. In a bid to establish a more holistic approach to building regulations and energy in EU Member States, a methodology to calculate energy performance in households must include the following aspects:

- Thermal characteristics
- Heating installation and hot water supply (including insulation)
- Air-conditioning installation
- Ventilation
- Position/orientation of buildings
- Passive solar systems and solar protection
- Natural ventilation
- Indoor climate conditions

It has to be stressed that specifications found in building regulations for energy performance are intended as minimum standards. Yet the standards found in regulations are often interpreted as the accepted target and have not stimulated a building sector, driven predominantly by construction costs instead of life-cycle costs, to strive beyond minimum standards. Even the most progressive building regulations for energy performance are dwarfed by voluntary schemes like the passive house standard developed in Germany.

Compliance and Enforcement

Testimony to the success of building regulations is how they are complied with, enforced, evaluated, and revised. Statistics regularly expound the virtues of tougher regulations stating that buildings of today are massively more energy efficient than their older counterparts. Such statements are often marred by findings that large proportions of buildings are noncompliant with regulations with discrepancies between plans and permit specifications and the final constructed product. Another issue is the frequent assertion that the energy aspect of regulations is a low priority for under-resourced building control departments.

There is much discussion on the style, content, and level of ambition of regulations; the degree to which they stimulate innovation; and the amount of resources they entail. Less attention is focused on the complete cycle of design, monitoring, evaluation, and revision which is required if regulations are to stay relevant and effective. The dearth of *ex post* analysis of building regulations and the surprising lack of monitoring programmes means that the actual effect of energy standards on energy consumption often remains unknown.

Cross-national studies, demonstration projects, and pioneering projects show that improving energy performance requires attention to detail at design and construction stage, commitment from stakeholders and adequate feedback mechanisms. These features must be obvious and transparent in building regulatory frameworks if confidence is to be attached to the more aggressive building regulations proposed to hasten the path to a low-carbon society.

While building regulations are plagued by the perennial problems attached to public law instruments there is consensus that they are required. It is widely accepted that without regulations market forces would allow unchecked business-as-usual development with resulting environmental damage and social and economic insecurity. What is more, given the scale of change required to meet ambitious GHG emission reduction targets there is strong opinion that regulations need to be stricter, noncompliance penalties stronger, and revision swifter if opportunities presented by regulations to represent the public good are to be achieved.

Policy Contexts and Tool Combinations

While building regulations can represent a significant measure defining requirements for energy performance in buildings it forms just one measure in a move towards a low-carbon society. Building regulations must sit within wider policy frameworks that promote and influence energy performance of buildings from different sectors and levels. In addition, the strength of building regulations will often depend on the presence and strength of measures that can offset inherent weaknesses.

Policy Context

The effect of building regulations is enhanced if the system sits within a co-ordinated strategic policy framework. Strategic planning policies can ensure that buildings are located in areas where energy can be received from sustainable sources and where public transport can be fully exploited. Strategic partnerships can be formed between governments, NGOs, and utility companies to generate safe, secure, and affordable energy supply to people living in substandard accommodation in developing countries. Financial models can be adapted using life-cycle costing for construction and renovation projects that can create logical support for sustainable energy measures. A combined strategic policy response can assist with the creation of buildings that protect occupier's health, confer adequate thermal comfort, provide household security against the vagaries of fossil fuel markets, and limit the environmental burden of buildings.

Complementary Tools

Building regulations can form one part of a combined response to achieving energy efficiency and sustainable energy supply in households. Alongside regulations, product standards can phase out energy-inefficient appliances; awareness campaigns can inform the public of why action is required; subsidies can promote the uptake of microgeneration technologies and assist low-income households with insulation costs; demonstration projects can push the boundaries of accepted norms to inform the building regulations of the future. In this way, tools can be combined to establish the minimum energy-performance standards in buildings and provide incentives for striving beyond the minimum. Working together these tools can affect market transformation, leading to more favourable conditions for sustainable energy technologies, products, and concepts.

Sustainability Issues

While building regulations are just one measure affecting the way in which energy is managed in buildings, operational energy use is just another measure of the environmental impact of a building. Looking at buildings from a holistic viewpoint of energy flows can ensure the energy implications of waste management, water resource use, and materials can be combined in designing, constructing, operating, demolishing, and recycling buildings. This means altering the way energy is conceptualised to reflect aspects such as embodied energy and the energy lifestyles of occupants. Furthermore, placing energy concerns within a wider sustainability assessment of buildings can manage balance and interaction between factors. In this regard, local biodiversity can be protected and enhanced by incorporating green roofs and materials can be sourced locally and sustainably.

The Future of Energy and Building Regulations

Building regulations are set to continue changing for years to come as countries explore different avenues for managing sustainable energy supply and demand and climate change adaptation and mitigation. Many countries are obliged to update regulations regularly or when technological change demands. Additionally, numerous forces exert an influence on energy use in buildings. Forces include demographic and social changes resulting in more households with lower occupancy rates in some developed countries and increased urbanism in developing countries. Other forces include the continuous growth in ownership of appliances and changes in climatic conditions. The influence of these forces means that regulations cannot remain static if effectiveness is to be maintained.

Major external forces come in the guise of looming GHG emission reduction targets and energy security concerns, placing pressure on building regulations to innovate. Innovation is captured with concepts such as low carbon, net zero carbon, energy plus, and passive houses, which push the boundaries of what is understood as conventional buildings. These building concepts demonstrate a range of creative solutions to reducing energy use such as turning building occupants from passive energy consumers to active energy producers and prioritising natural systems over conventional heating and cooling systems.

Forces also come from tools aiming to alter energy consumption by communication or economic means. Householders may be increasingly compelled to upgrade the energy performance of their homes as tools such as energy labels influence the marketability of houses. The use of tools following the polluter pays principle, such as personal carbon trading, may act as another force obliging owners to improve the energy performance of their homes to limit use of their allotted carbon credits.

So far, building regulations have been eclipsed in terms of an instigator of innovation in energy use by third-party voluntary certification schemes such as those developed by the various national Green Building Councils. These schemes have shown for a number of years that energy use in buildings can surpass minimum standards of regulations, provide improved thermal comfort and financial security in terms of energy billing for occupants, and respect boundaries of ecological systems. Building and planning policy systems in many jurisdictions have acknowledged the role and ambition of such schemes by, for example, aligning schemes with tax rebates or adopting standards into national or local policies.

Meanwhile, ways of attaching a high level of ambition to existing buildings and of capturing energy consumption associated with materials, water, and land throughout a building's life cycle must feature in regulations if the true extent of energy use in buildings is to be managed. A number of pioneering projects, such as the Zero Carbon Loft project described below, demonstrate that it is feasible to achieve the ambitious standards laid out for new buildings of the future in the existing houses of today. Furthermore, pioneering concepts such as Cradle to Cradle demonstrate the possibilities of constructing buildings that harmonise with natural processes.

Figure 3 Zero Carbon Loft. Retrofits of existing houses such as this loft development demonstrate the possibilities for achieving improved energy performance with benefits extending to local biodiversity, household recreational space, and water efficiency. (The award-winning Zero Carbon Loft project was designed by Thomas Lipinski and fully executed by Green Structures.)

Retrofits of the Future – Zero Carbon Loft

An award-winning project in London, UK, of a Zero Carbon Loft demonstrates improved energy and water efficiency, habitat creation, improved comfort and economic security for occupants, as well as the provision of additional recreational space (**Figure 3**). This project demonstrates how energy-performance ambitions can be directly aligned to wider environmental and social objectives and that achieving energy-performance improvement in existing houses is within reach.

Concepts of the Future – 'House Like a Tree'

In an emission reduction model of climate change policy, particularly one that espouses high ambitions, a justifiable expectation is that building regulations be stronger and enforced more rigidly. However, alternative models can also drive our understanding of how buildings are designed, constructed, and used. A deeper understanding of ecological systems based on the Cradle to Cradle concept, for example, could fundamentally alter the role and content of building regulations. Cradle to Cradle urges us to examine the physical constructs that we create in ecosystems in much greater detail. Designing products based on Cradle to Cradle principles means creating technical or biological nutrients, mirroring nature's cycle where nothing is a waste product and where energy is optimised.

The architectural firm of one of the founders of the Cradle to Cradle design paradigm, William McDonough, has designed a conceptual house of the future based on these principles, which gives instead of taking away from the environment (**Figure 4**). The Cradle to Cradle conceptual 'House Like a Tree' is designed to use renewable energy, nontoxic building materials that are safe for occupants, and the environment. The building components are biological nutrients, which break down naturally and benignly at the end of the building's operation, or technical nutrients, which can re-enter the product chain.

Figure 4 The Cradle to Cradle inspired 'House Like a Tree' concept. This concept was developed as part of a sustainable home of the future exercise run by *The Wall Street Journal*.
Copyright William McDonough + Partners, 2009.

Conclusion

Along with other government tools, building regulations are invested with a mandated power to influence mainstream thinking, to adopt and disseminate concepts that go beyond a brief of being simply fit for purpose. We are dependent on the strength and ambition of tools like building regulations acting in combination with tools within and across sectors from nongovernmental and private parties to steer, support, encourage, and enforce more sustainable energy use in buildings. We are also dependent on people, on homeowners, landlords, and renters, and their proactive engagement with tools that promote the sustainable use of energy.

See also: Climate Change; Climate Change: Adaptations; Ecological Footprint; Eco-Renovation; Energy Saving; Housing Developers and Sustainability; Housing Dynamics: Environmental Aspects; Sustainable Lifestyles; Sustainable Regeneration.

Further Reading

EC (2003) Council Directive 2002/91/EC of 16 December 2002 on the energy performance of building. *Official Journal of the European Communities* L1: 65–71.

Hitchin R (2008) Can building codes deliver energy efficiency: Defining a best practice approach. *A Report for the Royal Institute of Chartered Surveyors by the Building Research Establishment.* London: RICS.

Janda K (2009) Worldwide status of energy standards for buildings: A 2009 update. In: Broussous C and Jover C (eds.) *Proceedings of ECEEE 2009 Summer Study, Act! Innovate! Deliver! Reducing Energy Demand Sustainably*, pp. 485–491. Stockholm: ECEEE.

Lowe R and Oreszcyn T (2008) Regulatory standards and barriers to improved performance for housing. *Energy Policy* 36(12): 4475–4481.

McDonough W and Braungart M (2002) *Cradle to Cradle: Remaking the Way We Make Things*. New York: North Point Press.

OECD (2003) *Environmentally Sustainable Buildings: Challenges and Policies*. Paris: OECD Publications.

OECD/IEA (2008) *Energy Efficiency Requirements in Building Codes, Energy Efficiency Policies for New Buildings*. Paris: IEA Publications.

OECD/IEA (2008) *Worldwide Trends in Energy Use and Efficiency. Key Insights from IEA Indicator Analysis. In support of the G8 Plan of Action*. Paris: IEA Publications.

UNEP (2007) *Buildings and Climate Change, Status, Challenges and Opportunities*. Nairobi: UNEP.

Ürge-Vorsatz D, Koeppel S, and Mirasgedis S (2007) Appraisal of policy instruments for reducing building's CO_2 emissions. *Building Research and Information* 35(4): 458–477.

Visscher H and Meijer F (2008) *The growing importance of an accurate system of building control*. Paper Presented at the Construction and Building Research Conference of the Royal Institution of Chartered Surveyors COBRA 2008. Dublin, Ireland, 4–5 September.

World Business Council for Sustainable Development (2009) *Transforming the Market: Energy Efficiency in Buildings*. Geneva: WBCSD.

Relevant Websites

www.iisbe.org/ – International Initiative for a Sustainable Built Environment

www.aecb.net/ – The Sustainable Building Association

www.worldgbc.org/ – World Green Building Council

Case Studies

D Robertson, University of Stirling, Stirling, UK

© 2012 Elsevier Ltd. All rights reserved.

Glossary

Case A unit or example, which can be a sample, but not necessarily, that can be subjected to analysis by a range of different research techniques.

Comparative The comparing and contrasting of different real-life examples in order to elicit differences or similarities that help in the broader construction of knowledge.

Deductive theory The construction of theory based on the explicit testing of that theory through observation.

Grounded theory The construction of theory based on empirical, that is real-life, observation.

Research The systematic collection of data in order to subject it to considered analysis which is designed to facilitate understanding and knowledge.

Case Study Definitions

The recording of individual 'cases' in both a medical or welfare setting is a familiar one. Casework is considered an everyday work practice within health care, social work, and counselling. Within a social services or health context casework is employed as a means of assessing changing client needs, measuring the effectiveness of interventions, and providing a record of changes in an individual's circumstances. It is this meticulous recording of small everyday events, the minutiae of individual behaviour between client and service provider that generates the data. Subsequent careful analysis then helps improve understanding of activity patterns. Casework is also used within housing management, albeit to a lesser extent. Case notes are employed to provide a record of official interactions between the housing officer and the tenants in respect of rent arrears or tenancy condition matters. It is also common when managing special needs or vulnerable client groups, given the work practice demands set by health or social services in respect of these clients. In such instances, the case study approach is a core element of work practice, and the resulting records are then analysed to assist in refining care packages, management interventions, or predicting future patterns of behaviour, given previous analysis of similar data. This approach has long been considered the basis of 'grounded' theory – constructing inductive theory from empirical observation.

Packaging a series of individual cases together, in order to then test whether there are recurrent patterns, is one approach to case studies. The other, more common in housing research, is to try to select individual cases considered to be representative of a broader population. This approach, prevalent within all social science research, should not, however, be considered a distinct research method in itself. Rather, case study is an umbrella term for an approach to structuring the actual research exercise, within which the full range of research methods can be deployed (Robertson, 2008a). What case studies have in common is merely the researcher's decision to focus their inquiry around either a single instance or a set of individual cases. This is why the case study should always be considered an idiosyncratic combination of elements or events (Mitchell, 1983). It is the researcher who selects the actual element or event for case study examination. Cases can thus be defined spatially, organisationally, or by management practice to name but three approaches. It is this flexibility which is both the inherent strength and the obvious weakness of the case study approach.

Objectives

At its simplest, a case study merely provides the unit, or focus for further systematic analysis, as defined by the researcher. This can amount to a description of one or two cases or events, detailing what occurred within a specified timeframe. This snapshot, which occurred at one point in time, can then be reexamined at a later point in time, with any changes noted and appropriate explanations offered. By contrast, at their most complex, case studies are used to test experimental research within a natural setting, through controlling the influence of particular selected elements (Hakim, 1987). Case studies can, in this context, be used in deductive theory testing: that is where a theory is proposed and then tested through the examination of empirical examples, in contrast to grounded theory. So depending on how they are structured or utilised, case studies either can act as a microscope or alternatively provide a spotlight. They can be used to test deductive theory, or develop grounded theory. Thus their value depends entirely upon how well the researcher selects the case or cases, then utilises different methods to examine this case or cases, given the focus of the research task in hand.

Within housing research case studies are employed to allow for the exploration of complex interrelationships. They have proved particularly useful as a means of monitoring and evaluating a wide variety of policy and practice developments. Case studies are most commonly used in evaluative studies which seek to assess the impact of particular processes of change. Ensuring that there is relevant contextual material, which defines the case study within its specific setting, is also important as such information provides the means to assess the applicability of this particular case to other potentially similar contexts. It is thus crucial in such contexts that the cases are able to generate useful information about what exactly happened before and after the introduction of the specific intervention under examination.

Case studies also have the advantage of allowing the researchers the opportunity to appreciate what they are studying from the perspective of those being studied. There is never just one way of viewing the world. Through selecting appropriate methods, case studies can thus better help facilitate these wider perspectives. 'Official' interpretations of particular projects, policies, or events are often at variance with those who are actually working on them, or those whose life experience is touched by them. Research methods which draw out this material, and compare and contrast these varied interpretations, can act only to improve understanding of the various processes that are taking place, and in turn inform both practice and theory. The challenge here is to ensure the case study material is written up in a manner which is clear, accessible, and cuts away the mass of indigestible localised case-specific material to draw out the key conclusions. To work up from the mass of local case study data, which is required in order to explore the key questions and issues raised by the study, and then draw out select, robust, and central lessons is the real skill of research (Hakim, 1987). This is not a case of adding local colour to a study, which

undoubtedly has its own value and merit, but rather about improving and enhancing understanding. There is always a symbiotic relationship in the research process between description and explanation – getting that balance right is in the hands of the researcher.

Case studies can often involve detailed documentary studies, given that such material is often essential in setting the context for the case under consideration. If case studies are geographically based, then setting the context is enhanced by quantitative analysis, drawing from the various socioeconomic data sets held on a geographic basis. The more such data sets improve, the greater the capacity to generate both past and present socioeconomic information – a development that has clear advantages within any research context.

Case studies are also commonly applied as a means to engage in comparative analysis. When data from similar situations in different locations or countries are compared, common themes and patterns can be identified, leading to the generation of 'grounded' hypotheses. There are, however, limitations to the comparative capacity of case study work. Again this comes back to the problem of the specific case being used to predict what may be a general pattern. In cross-national comparisons the effects of national policy environments, which are culturally constructed, can severely limit the capacity to generalise (Robertson, 2008b). A useful discussion of the practical problems associated with international comparative housing research is provided by Harloe and Martens (1984). Comparisons within the one national context are generally more useful, but care has to be taken in how you express the links between the separate case studies and what you feel this reveals about the wider pattern.

Selection Methods

Case studies also have a logistical dimension, because they can provide a scale of research endeavour that an individual or team of researchers can easily handle. They also allow for one aspect of an issue, or a particular initiative, to be studied, in some depth, over a defined period. This is important, given the strict limits imposed on all research endeavours by the constraints of time and resources. That is not to say case studies cannot be employed over longer time periods. Many longitudinal studies undertake ongoing case study work, or revisit case studies at defined intervals, as previously noted. So it is the scale and, therefore, the ambition that distinguishes a case study approach from a larger, more comprehensive survey exercise. Given this, case studies are often viewed as a logistical compromise. But that ignores their adaptability and wide applicability, which helps to explain their ubiquity within social science research. This flexibility, however, needs to be properly understood if value is to be added to a specific research exercise.

In undertaking any case study work there are thus two clear objectives. Firstly, there is a need to provide a detailed description of each actual case study or studies employed. To achieve this goal, a variety of techniques should be deployed in order to delineate the focus of the research. The second objective is to expand knowledge and understanding of an issue, topic, or project, and in doing so help in the construction of concepts that have a wider applicability than just the specific cases being examined. A case study must, therefore, be distinguished from mere anecdote, or simple narrative, by the fact that it is not randomly selected and should have the potential for providing explanation of events or circumstances beyond just itself. This represents a challenge.

So if the study's purpose is to understand the impact brought about by altering the allocation arrangements of particular landlords, through a case study approach, it would first be necessary to detail the nature of the housing organisations under examination. Then in setting down the broader context it would also be necessary to detail what exactly these allocation changes were, and why it was felt necessary to amend previous arrangements. Only then could you set in place research instruments to explore what impact these changes had on the day-to-day experiences of the various participants engaged in the housing allocations task, in different organisations, as well as the experiences of those in receipt of such services. To do this properly it would be necessary to detail the roles and functions played by all participants, ideally prior to and after the allocations system was amended. Only then would it be possible to objectively detail the differential impacts of this particular change. Adopting a case study approach can thus enhance understanding of causality and the effects of particular actions and interventions. It is then up to those reading the cases to decide upon its relevance to their specific context. If similar patterns of change occur in different organisations then the research is enhanced by suggesting specific impacts, and these can then be generalised to a wider population.

The challenge presented here is that to be truly useful, a number of distinct research methods need to be deployed within any case study context. This may sound rather abstract, but an obvious example is provided when an estate management intervention is set up in a variety of different neighbourhoods in order to test which is the most appropriate in different contexts. Working out how many case studies are needed given the variety of neighbourhoods and interventions is the first challenge. Then devising ways of recording the various estate management interventions, writing this information up, and then evaluating the value of these different interventions illustrate a simple but useful example. As with all research, case study work is inherently incomplete.

Schuller (1988) in making this point sees much virtue in case study work for this very reason because, contrary to first impressions, it is forced to confront and make explicit that incompleteness (**Table 1**).

From the above examples it is clear that these categorisations are not mutually exclusive. Individual, group, and institution can, in certain circumstances, be interchangeable. While this illustrates the flexibility of case studies, it also aptly illustrates that any categorisation is, at best, arbitrary. What is critical is the justification used in applying a case study frame to a specific research project.

Case Study Contradiction

It is important to remember that each case study is 'unique', although it may contain some features that make it 'representative' of a group. Any case study, no matter the type, will display both common and unique features. So can any case study ever be seen to illustrate more than just itself? Does its uniqueness not act against it being seen as an exemplar for other cases that share its common features? In some instances a case study is selected precisely because it illustrates something that is quite different and unique. It may, for example, represent a specific point of view, or a particular approach. In other instances, case studies are selected to illustrate the experience of operating within a specific environment. But can they ever be anything but unique? Case studies are always unique, but the researcher can select them as being illustrative of wider patterns; the term 'illustrative' is used in preference to 'representative', as no case study should be described as being 'representative' of a specific type.

What case studies can often provide is a detailed snapshot of a piece of housing practice. In turn, this can be compared and contrasted by other managers and practitioners with their own experience. Whilst not producing 'blueprints' or 'templates', it can provide ideas and models that can be adapted and adopted to work in a variety of different settings. Any discussion should focus primarily upon what the case study itself has revealed. Extrapolating case study findings to the wider context demands great care. That is not to say it cannot or should not be attempted. Drawing out the broader patterns from the presented case study evidence is not only a goal, but also a challenge faced by the researcher analysing the mass of collected data.

Taking the example of a wide-ranging study of local authority housing management practice, it may be felt necessary to select a rural case study. If that rural local authority had a well-run housing department, operating exemplary management and maintenance systems, could this finding be taken to be indicative of the situation for all rural authorities? Clearly not: the case study could well

Table 1 Examples of case study types

Type	Description
Individuals or groups	Tracing the housing careers or histories of individual people. This approach has been used to illustrate the housing histories of young homeless people, the experiences of children in care, and those receiving other forms of intervention. A report by the Princes' Trust (2003) utilised a case study approach through interviews and focus groups to obtain the views of 19–25-year-olds in four categories: unemployed, educational underachievers, ex-offenders, and those in or leaving care. The research focused on how particular young people were doubly disadvantaged through their lack of qualifications, coupled with abuse of drugs and criminal records. The individual responses indicated that poor commitment to work or further education was exacerbated by their view that they were better off on benefits
Resource or institution	The use of case studies is common in project evaluations. Case studies can allow a detailed examination to be made of the role and impact of a particular facility or resource, such as a women's aid hostel. The practices adopted by similar statutory bodies when taking on new responsibilities, such as those arising from the 'Supporting People' initiative, provide further opportunities for institution-based case studies
	A good example of this type of case study work is provided by Cox (2006) who reviewed architectural practice in a number of supported housing developments across the United Kingdom designed specifically for people with dementia, in order to produce a good practice guide and dementia-friendly building evaluation tool
Intervention	The work of Pawson (2009) is an example of using different case studies to assess the impact of the housing stock transfer policy in the United Kingdom. This study selected a number of stock transfer case studies, and then evaluated them against their specific stated policy ambitions when transferring and then commented on how these findings tied to national policy ambitions for stock transfer
	Another example is the work of Anderson and Brown (2008) on antisocial behaviour, in producing a practitioners' action framework for dealing with the issue, detailing a number of case study examples of good practice. These include Edinburgh's use of floating support, various intensive family support and residential projects, diversionary activities for children and young people, youth shelters, employment of dedicated youth workers, the 'Manchester Youth Pod', Glasgow's Reidvale Housing Association's purchase of extra police time, and various neighbourhood warden schemes
Geographic	Often case studies are selected on the basis that they are used to represent a particular category of geographic area, such as rural or urban, or semiurban or semirural. These are sometimes referred to as exemplars
	Robertson et al. (2008) employed three geographic cases studies in Stirling to explore the issue of class and sustained association with specific locations. Each of the three neighbourhoods selected was a specifically planned community dating from the 1920s
	The issue of low-demand housing in the United Kingdom was examined by Holmans and Simpson (1999), first using national quantitative data sets supplemented by qualitative work in five geographic case studies, namely Blackburn, Bristol, Swansea, Inverclyde, and Belfast

have been selected precisely on the basis that it was illustrative of 'good practice'. So there are clear limits to how the material derived from case study contexts can then help develop explanations and approaches that are transferable. How the research work is constructed is core in this context.

The case study's purpose, given the focus of the research question being pursued, directly influences the selection criteria. Researchers, therefore, always need to make explicit the reasons that lie behind particular selection decisions. This allows the reader to consider and, where necessary, challenge the basis of selection and, in turn, this may lead them to reject the research conclusions.

It should also be borne in mind that, given the researcher selects the area for study, decides upon the data to be collected, and determines which material should be presented, it is very difficult to cross-check the data generated. Case studies can either consciously or unconsciously lead to distortion and bias. While bias is certainly not a problem unique to case-study-based research, it is more obvious. To avoid such criticism it is crucial that the researcher is explicit about the approach being adopted, and explain clearly why selection decisions were taken, and is clear about their potential broader applicability.

Strengths and Weaknesses

An emphasis does, as in all research contexts, need to be placed on the words 'best' and 'available' data. Time and resource constraints usually result in some sort of compromise which affects the final quality of the research work. The crucial point is that, at all times, ensuring quality should be the key objective in respect of data collection. In a research exercise, given limited funds, a large-scale survey may have to be reduced down to just eight cases. Such a selection is always a compromise, in that each of the cases must try to cover a range of contexts, which a larger, more comprehensive survey would have touched upon. In these cases, as with most case study selections, it is not a random selection.

Any selection also has an impact upon what is being researched. For example, in the aforementioned housing management study the imminent arrival of a researcher may result in the staff 'brushing-up' on their knowledge of administrative systems that are to be examined. Those involved in executing the day-to-day work may undergo individual, or organised, training to ensure that they all come up to speed. The researcher will always have an influence upon those being studied. While there is little that can be done about this, it is crucial that the researcher is fully aware of it. That said, solid interviewing technique can, on occasion, highlight inconsistencies and discrepancies in practices, thus breaking down such advance preparation. The best way to get round such a situation is again to ensure access to a range of data sources, so it is possible to cross-check information, thus highlighting any discrepancies.

There are other practical problems associated with organising research within a case study context, which Schuller (1988) detailed as follows. These examples were developed from his long experience of conducting such work. Firstly, the researcher goes in and gets nothing because access issues were not properly considered, or previous assumptions or guarantees failed to materialise. Secondly, the researcher goes in but only gets so far, because it proves to be a lot harder and more time-consuming to access the required data. Thirdly, data are easily accessed, but are sensitive and easily attributable to one specific case and, thus, hard to use. Finally, the researcher goes in and compiles so much data that it proves hard to retain a clear focus on the research topic at hand. The case study throws up a host of new ideas and this makes it necessary to rethink the basic assumptions of the study. Again, such issues are not unique to case-study-focused research but are applicable in all research contexts. What is important is to be aware of these potential problems, and try to plan out the research method in a way that avoids such pitfalls.

So the advantages of case studies are that they allow for an in-depth focus on particular relationships, and as such they can capture the complexities inherent in social situations. They allow a focus on the local understandings and a sense of participation in the case, and as such can produce a range of different data sets that bring research to life, articulating concerns and meanings which are germane to the situation under scrutiny. At their best they can generate data that assist in the development of a general hypothesis or theory. But to achieve this demands the careful collection of high-quality data, within a properly considered case study context – a task that requires time, focus, and much effort.

On the downside, case studies can be seen as an unwarranted intrusion into the affairs of others, given their potential for providing a detailed focus. At the same time, they are very much bound by their specific situation at a particular point in time. As a result, they may be so particular and unique that they fail to provide replicable practice, or useful management learning material, let alone advancing theory. Finally, there is a danger that the researcher becomes immersed in the case, compromising subsequent data analysis and focus.

As has been outlined above, the purpose of adopting a case study approach should be more than just providing the means to add colour and authenticity. A case study, if properly conducted, is much more than just a story about, or a description of, a particular event or state. It should be capable of providing more than generalisations. But to take a case study beyond such limited outcomes, as with all research, robust evidence has to be collected in a systematic manner and then subjected to considered analysis. Only through the methodical planning of data collection, via a case study frame, and its subsequent analysis, can the researcher hope, at a later stage, to prove whether there is a relationship between the variables which has a wider applicability. Case studies are often criticised as being 'soft subjectivity'. Yet, what should be clear from this article is that adopting a case study approach is no soft option.

See also: Appraisal and Cost-Benefit Analysis; Government Sponsored Enterprises in the United States; Housing Statistics; Qualitative Interviewing; Qualitative Methods in Housing Research; Small-Area Spatial Statistics; Visual Research Methods.

References

Anderson I and Brown A (2008) *Tackling Antisocial Behaviour in Scotland: An Action Framework for Social Housing Practitioners and Governing Bodies*. York, UK: Joseph Rowntree Foundation and Chartered Institute of Housing.

Cox S (2006) *Home Solutions 2: Housing, Care and Support for People with Dementia*. Stirling, UK: Dementia Services Development Centre, University of Stirling.

Hakim C (1987) *Research Design: Strategies and Choices in the Design of Social Research (Contemporary Social Research 13)*. London: Allen Unwin.

Harloe M and Martens M (1984) Comparative housing research. *Journal of Social Policy* 13(3): 255–277.

Holmans A and Simpson M (1999) *Low Demand: Separating Fact from Fiction*. York, UK: Joseph Rowntree Foundation and Chartered Institute of Housing.

Mitchell C (1983) Case and situation analysis. *Sociological Review* 31(2): 187–211.

Pawson H (2009) *The Impacts of Housing Stock Transfers in Urban Britain*. Coventry, UK: Chartered Institute of Housing.

Prince's Trust (2003) *Breaking the Barriers: Reaching the Hardest to Reach*. London: The Prince's Trust.

Robertson D (2008a) *Looking into Housing: A Practical Guide to Housing Research*. Coventry, UK: Chartered Institute of Housing.

Robertson D (2008b) Drawing out the issues. In: Scanlon K and Whitehead C (eds.) *Social Housing in Europe II: A Review of Policies and Outcomes*, pp. 287–300. London: LSE.

Robertson D, Smyth J, and McIntosh I (2008) *'Whaur are You Fae' Neighbourhood Identity in Stirling, Over Time and Place*. York, UK: JRF.

Schuller T (1988) Pot-holes, caves and lotusland: Some observations on case study research. In: Burgess R (ed.) *Studies in Qualitative Methodology*, Vol. 1, pp. 59–71. London: JAI Press.

Central Government Institutions

B Badcock, Housing New Zealand Corporation, Wellington, New Zealand

© 2012 Elsevier Ltd. All rights reserved.

Glossary

Housing legislation and statutes The codified written laws, such as a Housing Act, passed by the legislative branch of government, normally Parliament. For example, US Affordable Housing Laws and Regulations.

Housing regime Capitalist societies create distinctive housing regimes according to the decisions governments make in relation to housing subsidies, the allocation of housing, setting of rents, and the production and availability of new housing stock.

Mode of housing provision 'Mode' of housing provision is sometimes used interchangeably with 'structure' or 'form' in relation to the system of provision developed to house a nation's population. The construct was first used in 1983 by Michael Ball in his book, *Housing Policy and Economic Power: The Political Economy of Owner-Occupation*. At the time, he saw a need to switch the emphasis in housing studies away from the consumption of housing, specifically homeownership, and onto government policies and systems that form the framework of housing provision. This covers: forms of land tenure and property law; financial institutions and practices; the organisation of the home-building industry; and all the social agents involved in the production, marketing, and consumption of housing.

National housing plans and strategy Central governments develop national housing plans and strategies to set out a vision for the whole housing sector, and to provide guidance to regions and local authorities responsible for managing future growth.

Policy-making The process by which governments translate their political vision – often a housing manifesto – into programmes and activities to deliver outcomes (from the webpage of the Welsh Assembly Government).

Political ideology A reasonably coherent body of ideas, or 'world view', adopted by parties in power as a basis for political action. Adherence to a political ideology predisposes political parties to a particular view of how markets and civil society should be organised and function, and the role of the state in achieving the vision. Accordingly, governments tend to be characterised as left- or right-leaning, or centrist; although, inevitably, the formation of coalition governments leads to ideological compromise.

Power-sharing arrangements Strictly speaking, power-sharing arrangements refer to the formal constitutional provisions that enable significant minorities to participate in the political system. For example, the term 'consociationalism', as a form of power-sharing, is used to characterise democracies with multiparty cabinets and systems, political decentralisation, proportional representation, and proportionality in the distribution of legislative seats, civic service positions, and public funds. In the context of housing provision, power-sharing arrangements also apply to statutory provisions specifying the powers and responsibilities assigned to central government, regional government (states and provinces), and local authorities.

Public administration Government machinery and processes for managing the affairs of state. This includes framing legislation and regulations, developing and implementing public policy, and managing programmes whereby government facilitates the efficient functioning of markets and delivers services such as education, health, social security, and housing assistance.

State sector The state or public sector plays an important role in mixed economies by providing merit goods and services that the private sector is generally unable to supply profitably without government subsidies. The state sector is organised vertically, as well as horizontally, with the main functions of government split between national agencies, regions, and municipalities. The organisational and governance models found across the state sector can take many different forms, ranging from direct departmental control to publicly owned corporations, public–private partnerships, and the partial outsourcing of some public functions (e.g., IT and legal services).

Central Government and Housing Intervention

Central government comprises three branches: the executive branch, normally Cabinet, in which the authority to govern is vested; the legislative assembly, which is the law-making body; and the judiciary, which administers the body of laws and justice. These branches are supported by a state sector that is organised to develop and implement the government's policies and programmes.

The housing system is an important sector of the economy. Central government intervenes mostly to provide housing assistance to low-income households that are poorly served by the market. When markets are judged to have 'failed' in this way, the overriding purpose of housing policy is redistributive. Moreover, because housing costs form such a large part of everyday living expenses, government housing assistance is often regarded – along with health, education, and social security – as one of the pillars of the welfare state.

But governments have also used housing programmes as an instrument for economic development, or scaled up housing expenditure to stimulate growth during a recession. In the former case, Singapore remains a 'standout', having used the housing sector when it broke with Malaya in 1965 to successfully help stimulate economic development through the vehicle of the Housing and Development Board. In the latter case, the central governments in the United States, the United Kingdom, and Australia all boosted housing expenditure as part of economic recovery packages following the global financial crisis in 2007–09.

The nature and extent of intervention in the housing market ultimately mirrors the particular political system that has evolved over time to govern the nation state. Basically, there are three models that order relations between the central government and the lower tiers of government like states, regions, or municipalities: a unitary system, a confederation, and a federal system. In the case of unitary states – France, Great Britain, Italy, Japan, China, and Sweden – ultimate authority resides at the national level, such that central governments can direct and even override the decisions taken by lower-level jurisdictions. Unitary states typically centralise revenue raising and sharing, and develop national education, health, social welfare, and property systems. On the other hand, nation states with federal systems – the United States, Germany, Switzerland, India, Brazil, Mexico – have developed written constitutions specifying the division of law-making and fund-raising powers between central government and the constituent states. Even so, upholding 'states' rights' in the face of central government encroachment can be an underlying source of tension within a federal system. The European Union (EU) is an example of a confederated system.

Amongst the institutions of government, the state sector's central departments and agencies play a commanding role. In the case of housing, central government typically assumes responsibility for:

- legislation to stipulate the role and responsibilities of each tier of government or jurisdiction (namely, central or federal, regional or state, and local government);
- national housing plans and strategic frameworks;
- direct and indirect forms of housing subsidy;
- regulation and guidance; and,
- property and land management.

A few states like Northern Ireland and New Zealand have a central government agency that is directly engaged in supplying public housing and managing tenants; otherwise, it is more common for housing assistance to be delivered at arm's length through state/provincial or local/municipal organs of government. This is especially characteristic of federal systems such as the United States, Germany, Canada, and Australia where a mixture of arrangements are in place for power sharing, taxing, and funding. But even unitary states like the United Kingdom and France, where power is much more centralised, frequently devolve responsibility for housing delivery to local authorities.

There are limits, however, to what can be achieved in the name of housing intervention. Firstly, housing policy alone cannot always produce the housing outcomes sought by government. Policies affecting the money supply, fiscal capacity, labour markets, social assistance, transport, and planning, together with property law, all have the potential to exercise as much, and sometimes more, influence over housing outcomes.

Secondly, political ideology and the underlying principles governing the role of the state sector may exert an indirect, but often powerful, influence upon the way governments intervene in the housing sector. Outside of the former command economies of the Soviet Union and Eastern Europe, perhaps the most overt illustration of ideological sway over 'what is delivered by whom and how' in the housing sector can be taken from the Reagan era when the US Department of Housing and Urban Development marked the International Year of Shelter for the Homeless (1987) by exhorting markets to 'free the spirit of enterprise' (**Figure 1**).

Thirdly, nations are not always sovereign in all matters. This applies in the case of a confederation like the EU. Although the EU does not have a remit to frame housing policy for member states, other policies relating to competitive practices, construction, the energy performance of buildings, and air quality can impinge on housing provision. For example, in 2005, the arm of the European Commission that has responsibility for competition policy ruled that the Dutch social housing subsidy

Figure 1 Housing America: Freeing the spirit of enterprise.

system was at odds with European principles and needed adjustment in certain areas. In addition to this, EU member states have lost some of their autonomy in housing provision to the Committee for European Standardisation, the organisation responsible for standardising regulations across the 27 member states.

In this article, the primary focus lies on the policy-making, funding, and regulatory functions of central government together with the power-sharing arrangements struck with lower tiers of government. The account presented here is selective rather than exhaustive, focusing on largely English-speaking, and other similar industrially advanced societies. It provides, nonetheless, important observations and insights on how different states manage housing provision. There are, however, wide-ranging economic and cultural circumstances.

Housing Regimes

Some of the differences in the way central governments approach housing provision and management can be traced to the political consensus reached about overarching societal goals and limits to markets. In a seminal text on welfare provision in capitalist societies, Esping-Andersen (1990) distinguishes between:

- social democratic welfare regimes that offer comprehensive social protection (e.g., Sweden);
- liberal welfare regimes that favour market solutions, leaving a 'safety net' for the most vulnerable (e.g., the United Kingdom, Ireland, Canada, the United States, Australia, and New Zealand); and,
- a large middle group of countries with corporatist power structures where state and market mechanisms combine to produce hybrid welfare regimes (e.g., Germany and France).

These three models of welfare capitalism are ideal types based upon the exercise of political power and class relations in capitalist societies. Kemeny (2006) has pointed out that efforts to depict housing regimes in these terms have proven problematic. As a way forward, Hoekstra (2003) suggested that a housing regime is the sum of the systems devised by the state for subsidising and allocating housing, setting rents, and producing new housing stock. Also, an 'East Asian welfare model' has been proposed to account for the varying developmental paths taken by societies like Japan, Hong Kong, Singapore, South Korea, and Taiwan. In Japan, for example, both companies and families assume much greater importance as welfare providers – as does the privately owned family home – compared with other industrialised societies (Ronald, 2007).

There is a further reason for cautioning against over-simplifying the conceptualisation of housing regimes. Hoekstra (2003) and Malpass (2008) show just how much central government's housing role has changed in many European states since the 1970s crisis in welfare capitalism. In the Netherlands, since the beginning of the 1990s, a housing regime forged by social democratic institutions has been progressively 'corporatised'. More generally, there has been a widespread move in EU countries to transfer ownership to sitting tenants in the social housing sector as part of the transition to an 'asset-based' welfare state in which households are encouraged to build up their own welfare resources in the form of owner-occupied housing assets, rather than rely on public provision.

The most abrupt housing regime change has taken place in former Soviet bloc countries and in the People's Republic of China. In Eastern Europe, most governments have sold 75–95% of the housing that was formerly in state ownership to sitting tenants, usually on 'give-away' terms and even in the absence of property law covering multiunit housing. In China, homeownership has been centrally promoted via a series of reforms to both the housing and banking sectors – including the creation of a nationwide Housing Provident Fund.

Institutional Arrangements and Mechanisms

Before describing each of the functions performed by central government in pursuit of housing goals, some important differences can be noted in the institutional arrangements and mechanisms available to nation states for governance and public administration. When it comes to the central organs of the state, the institutional arrangements for administering and delivering housing programmes can vary widely. Constitutional arrangements between the differing tiers of government provide a framework for the sharing of powers and ultimately determine both the form and locus of housing intervention.

Housing allocation stands a better chance of achieving consistent outcomes if policy development and core funding are centralised. Regions and localities tend to be unevenly endowed, and their governing bodies often set differing priorities thereby denying some segments of a nation's population access to uniform levels and standards of housing assistance. The vastly differing capacity of nongovernmental organisations as housing providers – the community and voluntary sector – is another factor that contributes to uneven resource endowment at the community level. Nevertheless, tenants and citizens have a greater opportunity to shape housing outcomes when funding and decision-making powers are devolved to community housing providers that elect tenants to their governing bodies.

The Northern Ireland Housing Executive and Housing New Zealand Corporation are two nondepartmental statutory agencies responsible to central government through ministers and respectively through monitoring Departments for Social Development, and Building and Housing. While delivery may be regionalised, central agreement about common principles and criteria makes for more equitable treatment and consistency of outcome.

Of course, power-sharing arrangements can be fluid. Devolution in the United Kingdom has been accompanied by the transfer of greater autonomy in setting housing directions to the Welsh, Scottish, and Northern Ireland assemblies. In January 2007, Germany's Bund transferred some of its responsibility for housing provision to the 16 states, or Länders, along with an annual appropriation of 600 million euros. As a result, the Länders can now enact their own housing laws so long as they accord with federal housing legislation. But the municipalities remain bound by federal laws including those obliging them to fund housing for the 'particularly vulnerable'. Hence, under the federal Housing Act, while the Länders can now vary their housing assistance package, the responsibility for implementation lies with the municipalities.

Dutch housing reforms in the 1990s heralded a wholesale shift in the philosophy and role of central government and imposed sweeping changes on the social housing sector. Housing associations were effectively deregulated and their remaining public debt written off. This was the effect of the 1995 'Brutering', or 'balancing out', agreement negotiated between the state and the national federation of social housing organisations. Capital subsidies virtually ceased and housing associations were left to lever off their (mostly) very healthy balance sheets, whereas, prior to that, centrally mandated policy guidance determined housing outcomes by way of comprehensive regulation and control of the subsidy programmes that funded social housing.

Where they lack adequate revenue-raising powers, lower-tier jurisdictions can be hamstrung in implementing their housing programmes unless resources are also transferred from the centre. Following the retreat in the recent past of conservative administrations in the United States, Canada, and Australia from urban and housing aid, the states, provinces, and municipalities have struggled to make up the shortfall in funding. In the absence of federal leadership on rental housing policy in the United States, many local and state governments have stepped into the void as a matter of necessity because they recognise the connection between the availability of affordable housing and future economic prosperity.

The Obama and Rudd administrations in Washington and Canberra have begun to rebuild some of this lost capacity in housing assistance. The US Department of Housing and Urban Development is being resuscitated but time will tell whether future budgets can ever make up for deep funding cuts over the last two decades. In 2009, the Australian government replaced the Commonwealth State Housing Agreement with a National Affordable Housing Agreement that will have a significant bearing on the housing assistance programmes delivered by the states and territories. Funding has been voted to expand the community housing sector by 50 000 units and public housing by 20 000 units over the space of 5 years.

The institutions of central government reflect presumptions in public administration about the efficacy of 'agency'. Can bureaucratic agencies ever fully convert the intent of legislators into law on behalf of 'the people'? This variously manifests itself in the separation of funding agencies from organisations in government that are directly responsible for supplying and regulating social housing, or regulating the private housing sector (mortgage lenders, home builders, real estate agents, landlord-investors). Similarly, the establishment of independent monitoring and audit functions within central government is designed to uphold the principles of public accountability and transparency with respect to governance and operating procedures.

Such considerations have led to a major reorganisation of the housing portfolio in the United Kingdom. In May 2006, housing policy and strategy moved from the Office of the Deputy Prime Minister to a new Department of Communities and Local Government. This was followed by the formation of two new agencies in December 2008 – the Homes and Communities Agency and the Tenant Services Authority – in place of the Housing

Corporation. Apart from integrating housing management and area regeneration in a single agency and revamping tenant services, this was to prevent the conflict of interest that periodically arose within the Housing Corporation, given its dual roles as funder and regulator. The Housing Inspectorate in the Audit Commission retains responsibility for monitoring the performance of local authorities and registered social landlords.

Central government drafts and enacts legislation, some of which confers powers upon other jurisdictions so that they can create their own regulations and bylaws. As part of this process, proposed housing legislation and expenditure typically goes through several committee stages before being debated on the floor of a lower house, and then may be referred for further review to an upper house such as the Senate in the United States and Australia, or to the House of Lords in the UK parliamentary system. Where such checks and balances exist, radical shifts in public policy of the kind that occurred in New Zealand in the 1990s with the introduction of market mechanisms in health, education, and housing are less likely.

Housing Policy Instruments

The role and scope of central government housing policy mechanisms and programmes are influenced by market conditions, the degree of housing stress, and the sufficiency and quality of the housing stock. Only the central government is in the position to try, for example, to stabilise construction and business cycles or dampen violent swings in rents or asset prices. Monetary policy proved to be such a blunt instrument during the latest housing booms in the United Kingdom, Australia, and New Zealand, that all three governments commissioned major enquiries into affordable housing supply. None of the findings have led to direct measures that are capable of containing future house price inflation, partly because the solutions often lie in the realm of banking regulation or tax reform.

Housing policy instruments available to central governments run the gamut from housing plans and strategies, to direct and indirect subsidies (which may operate through the demand or supply sides), to regulation, and to land management and property law. Also, if crisis management requires, as was the case following the financial crisis in 2007–09, central government will step in and fund housing packages in an effort to help stimulate recovery, rescue the building industry, or prevent the repossession of 'at risk' mortgaged property.

All this policy development is subject to direction by ministers and to extensive interagency consultation. Treasuries or finance departments, along with other central agencies, have a significant input into this process prior to approving budget allocations (capital and operating) across portfolios.

Housing Plans and Strategic Frameworks

Central government may frame a national housing strategy or plan to support a visionary agenda such as 'nation building', a 'new deal', the 'ownership society', or a 'right to shelter'. Ultimately, much can be accomplished by directing most new housing investment to improving the bottom end of the stock, while arranging the financing and marketing so that a productive distribution of housing is balanced by a fair distribution of its costs (Stretton, 1974).

There are a number of recent examples. In December 2005, the Irish Government published a *Housing Policy Framework – Building Sustainable Communities* to provide a twenty-first-century vision for housing aimed at underpinning 'sustainable communities'. It followed up in February 2007 with a Statement on Housing Policy that coordinates increased housing investment under the National Development Plan 2007–13 and the National Action Plan for Social Inclusion 2007–16. Spain's Housing Plan for 2005–08 and France's 2004 Plan for Social Cohesion reflect the growing commitment of a number of EU member states to addressing worsening shortages of affordable housing and marginalised housing estates.

Direct and Indirect Forms of Housing Subsidy

Central governments generally operate two kinds of housing subsidy: direct expenditure and grants administered by government agencies and indirect expenditure that takes the form of tax relief for homeowners and tax credits for investors. In the United States, various tax expenditures for housing comprise the largest source of revenue foregone by the federal government. Indirect expenditure for homeowners and investors exceeds the total direct outlay for public housing projects, homeless shelters, and rent vouchers by about four to one. The major items comprise tax deductions on mortgage repayments and for property taxes on owner-occupied dwellings, and the tax exemption of capital gains on house sales.

Government support for homeownership in the form of untaxed benefits is not only a defining feature of liberal welfare regimes like the United Kingdom, Australia, and New Zealand. In the Netherlands too, the cost to government revenue derived from mortgage interest tax relief for homeowners is equivalent to around four times government expenditure on rental allowances for lower-income households.

The system in the United Kingdom is dominated by three main forms of central government funding: a means-tested Housing Benefit; provision of social housing at below-market rents; and generous tax concessions for owner-occupiers. Again, the net tax advantage granted to owner-occupiers together with the 'Right to Buy' discounts is roughly equivalent to the direct outlay on social housing and exceeds other forms of untied support for those with low incomes (**Figure 2**).

An important strategic issue for central governments to resolve is the most effective 'mix' of demand- and supply-side housing subsidies. Governments can give top priority to building a social housing portfolio (supply-side) or to providing income support to households (demand-side), or some combination of the two. Other demand-side subsidies can include home purchase discounts, subsidised mortgage rates, home buyer grants, and government housing loans. Following the Second World War, governments in Europe and Japan embarked on ambitious rebuilding programmes to replace housing destroyed by bombing, while governments in Allied countries concentrated on making good the housing backlog. But in the postwar years, many governments, notably the Netherlands, the United Kingdom, and West Germany, also controlled rents or established and deepened housing benefits to help with housing costs.

Later, in the 1970s, as welfare states began to downsize towards the end of the 'long boom', governments switched to demand-side subsidies in the belief that people housed by the state should be able to exercise greater tenure choice so long as a 'safety net' is provided for households who would otherwise be at risk, that is, homeless. **Table 1** illustrates the shift from supply-side to demand-side subsidies that gained momentum through the 1980s and 1990s, such that by 2003–04 in England one-third of the £16 billion total housing outlay was for supply-side subsidies (mainly capital grants to housing associations for new dwellings) and two-thirds for demand-side subsidies (mainly Housing Benefit).

Major changes in the United Kingdom's subsidy 'mix' over the period 1975–2000 have been evaluated by Gibb and Whitehead (2007: 197). They conclude that three in particular – the removal of mortgage tax relief, the Right to Buy, and modifications to the social housing funding model – helped to bring spending under long-term control, and that, while a revamped Housing Benefit may be prone to cyclical fluctuations, it acts as a "proper, if permeable, safety net". Even so, although the overall impact of the trade-offs was judged to be positive, completion targets have not been met in the social housing sector, and, as emphatically revealed by

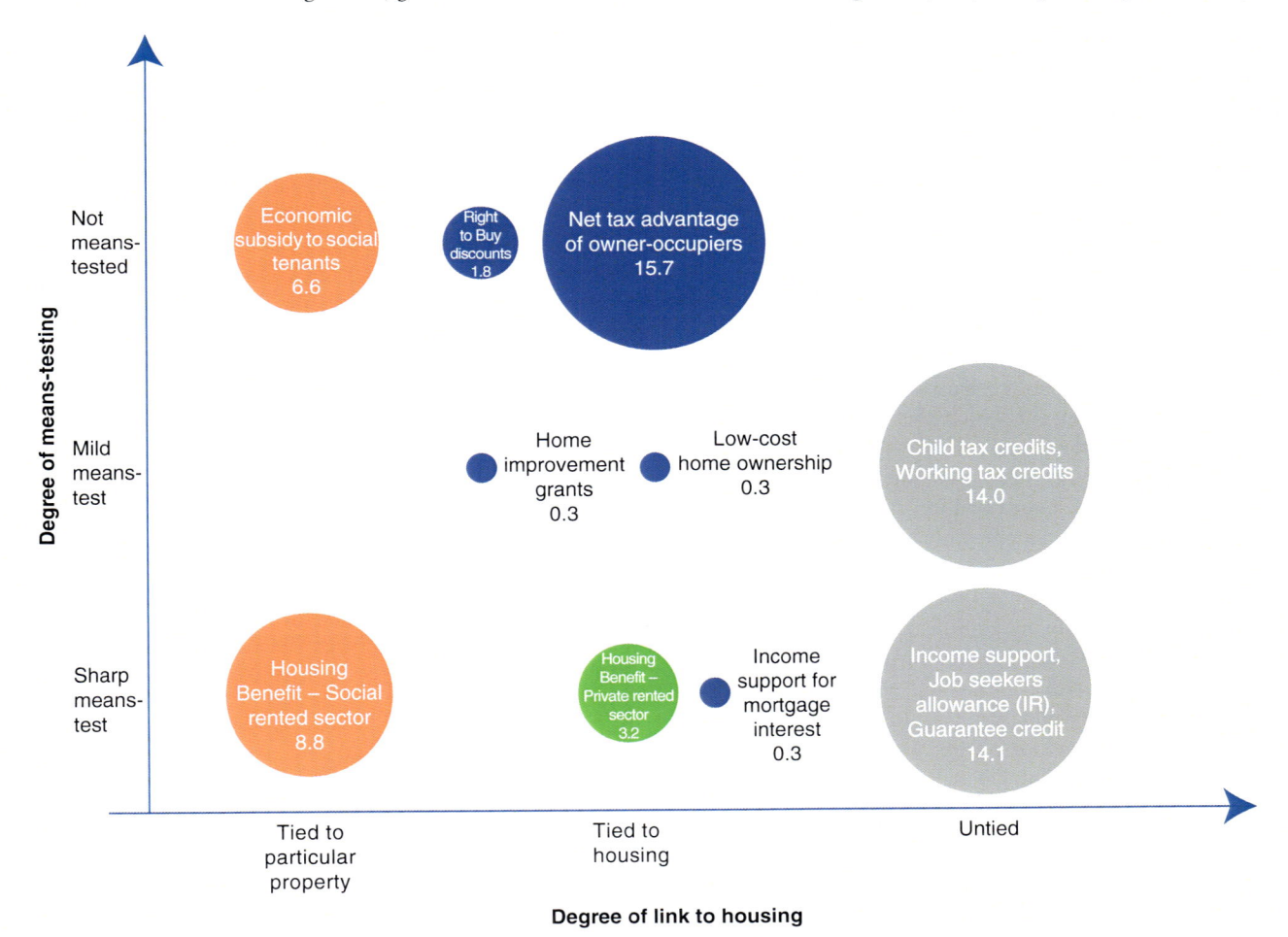

Figure 2 Scale and type of subsidies for housing in England (£ billion, 2004–05).
From Hills J (2007) *Ends and means: The future roles of social housing in England*. CASE Report 34. London: Centre for Analysis of Social Exclusion, Fig. 3.1, p. 25.

Table 1 Housing subsidy, 1975–76 to 2003–04 (£ billion, 2003–04 prices)

	1975–76	1980–81	1985–86	1992–93	1999–00	2000–01	2001–02	2002–03	2003–04
Capital[1]	10.7	6.3	5.2	5.8	3.0	3.9	4.2	5.0	5.2
LA revenue[2]	3.3	4.3	1.8	0.6	−1.0	−1.2	0.4	0.3	0.2
Total supply	**14.0**	**10.6**	**7.0**	**6.4**	**2.0**	**2.7**	**4.6**	**5.3**	**5.4**
Rent rebate[3]	0.6	0.7	4.4	5.0	4.7	4.5	4.4	4.4	4.1
Rent allowance[3]	0.1	0.1	1.7	4.0	5.5	5.6	5.8	6.4	6.3
Mortgage interest relief[4]	2.4	4.6	7.8	6.1	1.9	0	0	0	0
Income support for mortgage interest[5]	n/a	n/a	n/a	1.5	0.6	0.5	0.3	0.3	0.3
Total demand	**3.1**	**5.4**	**13.9**	**16.6**	**12.7**	**10.6**	**10.5**	**11.1**	**10.7**
Total	**17.1**	**15.9**	**20.9**	**23.0**	**14.7**	**13.3**	**15.1**	**16.4**	**16.1**

Notes:
[1] Figures taken from Wilcox S 2005, *Uk Housing Finance Review 2005/2006*, Chartered Institute of Housing.
[2] Communities and Local Government statistics: Logasnet Database (LA HRA).
[3] DWP Statistics.
[4] MIR was abolished in April 2000. Some financial costs were incurred in the 2000/01 financial year, but the precise figures are not available.
[5] Figures from 2000–01 onwards are based on those from *UK Housing Review 2005/2006*, deflated using the GDP deflator.
Source: Derived from Stephens M, Whitehead C, and Munro M (2003) *Lessons from the Past, Challenges for the Future for Housing Policy*. Loncon: ODPM, and updated by Hills J (2007, p. 56).

the credit crisis in 2007–09, "…the whole system is now far more dependent on the health of the private sector and the macro-economy".

Some rebalancing between demand- and supply-side subsidies is now underway again in the United Kingdom, Australia, and New Zealand as governments come to realise that subsidising households does nothing to generate sufficient affordable housing in those segments and areas of the housing market where it is most needed.

The low-income housing tax credit (LIHTC) programme, created by the Tax Reform Act of 1986, is the primary incentive for builders of affordable housing in the United States. Annual federal outlays are allocated by state and local agencies to companies willing to invest in low-income housing for which they receive 10 years of tax credits. Over the two decades 1987–2007, $8.3 billion in federal tax credits subsidised the construction of 1.6 million low-income housing units. But Katz (2008) argues that the federal government, which has the fiscal capacity, needs to do more to address the consequences for housing of stagnant wage growth and income inequality. He concludes that if the Obama administration were to address the demand-side of the housing affordability equation, the state and local jurisdictions could and should use both regulatory policies and supply-side subsidies to create incentives that repay 'for-profits' and 'nonprofits' to produce and maintain rental housing that is affordable for households with moderate incomes.

Regulation and Guidance

The state regulates the way finance and housing markets operate to achieve efficiencies in housing delivery and to protect consumers from unsafe or unhealthy housing, or from professional malpractice. Central governments use their statutory powers to mandate codes of practice and performance standards, or otherwise confer enabling powers on lower tiers of government. This provenance covers inter alia: minimum housing standards; the control of rents; the registration and regulation of nongovernmental social housing providers such as housing associations and housing trusts; tribunals and codes governing relations between landlords and tenants; terms and conditions relating to mortgage lending; professional practice in real estate and property management; building codes; and environmental performance of residential buildings. A few illustrations of the application of centrally administered housing regulations and guidance follow.

Perhaps the most comprehensive body of recent legislation to address housing standards is the Decent Homes programme. The programme was launched in 2000 to upgrade unfit social housing stock in the United Kingdom and was extended to cover noncompliant dwellings in the private sector as part of the 2002 Spending Review. Accompanying documentation specifies the criteria for a decent home and provides guidance for implementation. In 2005, a Fitness Standard was replaced with the Housing Health and Safety Rating System, which is designed to trigger action rather than prescribe a minimum decent home standard.

Also, in 2008 a review of social housing regulation in the United Kingdom led to the establishment of an independent social housing regulator, the Tenant Services Authority, with powers to oversee both standards and the overall level of rents in the social housing sector. Prior to that, the Department of Communities and Local Government, local authorities, the Housing

Corporation, and the Audit Commission all supervised the sector, using either regulatory or inspection powers or a combination of accreditation and contractual relationships. The statutory duties performed by the Tenant Services Authority include: ensuring continued provision of high-quality social housing; empowering and protecting tenants; expanding the availability of choice at all levels in the provision of social housing; collecting administrative data; and enforcing its decisions.

For the private housing sector, various Australian and New Zealand Acts regulate landlord–tenant relations and empower residential tenancies tribunals to resolve disputes. Most governments employ versions of coregulation or even self-administered codes to regulate real estate and property management practices. On the other hand, in many countries, removal of the controls that govern exchange rates and financial institutions, together with deregulation of mortgage markets, have worked in the opposite direction to inject greater competition at the expense of heightened risk into the home finance sector (Stephens, 2007).

Lastly, building regulations and codes are usually promulgated nationally to ensure that the health and safety of residents are safeguarded. Despite this, systemic 'weather tightness' problems in residential buildings that can endanger occupants and are traceable to performance failures have been reported in British Columbia, New Zealand, Ireland, and North Carolina. Increasingly, building legislation is being centrally reviewed in order for governments to meet environmental and energy performance targets.

Property and Land Management

There are two areas of law – contract law and planning law – where central government generally frames the Acts and statutes governing land and housing markets; otherwise, this may devolve to the state or provincial level. Contract law covers the many legal instruments that confer property rights and enable residential property to be transferred. These include title documents, contracts of sale, leases, operating agreements, mortgages, and deeds of trust. Planning law includes the Acts that stipulate how local jurisdictions zone for land use or subdivide land, and process and approve development applications.

Even though responsibility for planning and building activity mostly lies with local authorities, because land is frequently the leading source of cost escalation in housing production and because the affordability of housing has assumed such widespread political importance in recent decades, central governments can, and do, intervene in the market. In the 1990s, for example, the Dutch government earmarked specific housing expansion areas and indicated that subsidies would be available to support the desired development outcomes. German legislation imposes a legal duty upon municipalities to ensure a sufficient land supply for housing. The process of 'Umlegung' – literally the 'turning over of land', or land 'pooling' – although usually voluntary, is backed by statutory authority. Although the mechanism is mostly used to acquire land for 'greenfield' housing development, it also comes into its own in urban regeneration projects where landownership is fragmented.

In the United Kingdom, planning obligations are legal agreements between local planning authorities and developers as spelt out under section 106 of the Town and Country Planning Act (1990). Developers can be required to contribute in kind or in cash towards the provision of green space, play areas, access roads, and sites to support affordable housing. Since December 2006, a local authority can only obtain a Social Housing Grant if a certain number of the homes in a new development meet the Government's Planning Policy Statement 3 definition of affordable housing.

The Challenge Ahead

In the first decade of the twenty-first century, the liberalisation and deregulation of the banking and financial services sector presided over by central governments created the conditions that gave rise to structural imbalances in domestic economies around the globe. It was the mismanagement of monetary policy and the housing sector at a macrolevel by the US federal government that ultimately triggered the housing market collapse that, in turn, spilled over into the international financial system. At the same time, the reality of global warming and the contribution of domestic energy use were finally accepted by the international community.

Most governments developed rescue packages to address these twin 'crises' that included expanded spending on social housing, home insulation and modernisation, and to assist 'at risk' homebuyers. But beyond these short-term measures, to what extent will housing policy settings need to be revised and financial and housing markets reregulated? According to two British commentators, "National governments need to have a competence and understanding to design housing policies that create the right vehicles, governance structures and incentives to deliver big economic, environmental and social outcomes over the long term in a market-responsive way" (Cowans and Maclennan, 2008: 94).

See also: Civil Sector Institutions and Informal Settlements; Housing Policy: Agents and Regulators; Housing Policy Trends; Policies to Support Access and Affordability of Housing; Welfare States and Housing.

References

Cowans J and Maclennan D (eds.) (2008) *Visions for Social Housing: International Perspectives*. London: The Smith Institute.

Esping-Andersen G (1990) *The Three Worlds of Welfare Capitalism*. Cambridge, UK: Polity Press.

Gibb K and Whitehead C (2007) Towards the more effective use of housing finance and subsidy. *Housing Studies* 22: 183–200.

Hills J (2007) CASE Report 34. *Ends and Means: The Future Roles of Social Housing in England*. London: Centre for Analysis of Social Exclusion.

Hoekstra J (2003) Housing and the welfare state in the Netherlands: An application of Esping-Andersen's typology. *Housing, Theory and Society* 20: 58–71.

Katz B (2008) A perspective from the United States. In: Cowans J and Maclennan D (eds.) pp. 30–39.

Kemeny J (2006) Corporatism and housing regimes. *Housing, Theory and Society* 23: 1–18.

Malpass P (2008) Housing and the new welfare state: Wobbly pillar or cornerstone? *Housing Studies* 23: 1–19.

Ronald R (2007) Comparing homeowner societies: Can we construct an East–West model? *Housing Studies* 22: 473–493.

Stephens M (2007) Mortgage market deregulation and its consequences. *Housing Studies* 22: 201–220.

Stephens M, Whitehead C, and Munro M (2003) *Lessons from the Past, Challenges for the Future for Housing Policy*. London: ODPM, updated.

Stretton H (1974) *Housing and Government. 1974 Boyer Lectures by Hugh Stretton*. Sydney, NSW: The Australian Broadcasting Commission.

Wilcox S (2005) *UK Housing Finance Review 2005/2006*. Coventry, UK: Chartered Institute of Housing.

Further Reading

Allen Hayes R (1995) *The Federal Government and Urban Housing: Ideology and Change in Public Policy*, 2nd edn. Albany, NY: State University of New York Press.

Bratt RG, Stone ME, and Hartman C (2006) *A Right to Housing. Foundation for a New Social Agenda*. Philadelphia, PA: Temple University Press.

CECODHAS (2007) *Housing Europe 2007. Review of Social, Co-operative and Public Housing in the 27 EU Member States*. Brussels: European Social Housing Observatory.

Lai O-K (2001) The political economy of urban housing regime in transition: PR China, 1949–2000. *Journal of Policy Studies* 11: 205–218.

Scanlon K and Whitehead C (eds.) (2008) *Social Housing in Europe II: A Review of Policies and Outcomes*. London: London School of Economics.

Relevant Websites

www.cecodhas.org – Promoting Access to Decent Housing for All.

www.communities.gov.uk – Communities and Local Government.

www.hud.gov – US Department of Housing and Urban Development.

www.lse.ac.uk – The London School of Economics and Political Science.

www.usconstitution.net – This website outlines the nature of the US federal system.

www.whitehouse.gov – The White House, Washington.

Children and Parenting

C Holdsworth, University of Liverpool, Liverpool, UK

© 2012 Elsevier Ltd. All rights reserved.

Glossary

Boomerang kids Adult children who return to the parental home after leaving.

Denatured childhood Contemporary concerns in modern industrialised societies that children are becoming segregated from the outdoors and the damaging impacts this has on children's physical and mental health.

Positioning and personalising parenting Comparison of power relations in the family, derived from the sociological theories of Bernstein that contrast positional families associated with the authoritarian parenting style and strong boundaries with personalising families in which children have more of a say in rule making and boundaries are less strictly enforced.

Toxic childhood Concern that cultural and technological changes in modern industrialised societies, which while benefitting adults, are forcing children to develop in such a way that intensifies insecurity and development problems.

Home is the place where boys and girls first learn how to limit their wishes, abide by rules, and consider the rights and needs of others.

Sidonie Gruenberg

Introduction

Having children is often synonymous with creating a home; colloquially reference may be made to the ideal that a 'home is not a home without children'. This observation of the synergy between childhood and meanings of home is not only restricted to popular axioms but has also influenced philosophical writings on home and space. In particular, the French philosopher Gaston Bachelard in *The Poetics of Space* identifies the home as "our corner of the world" (1994: 4) and describes the magical 'cosmos' of the childhood home and its imaginary spaces. Bachelard explores the potential of both mundane domestic arrangements and particular spaces within the home, primarily attic, and cellar spaces, to provide refuge and stimulate imaginations. The power and emotional force of the childhood home and how its memory remains with us into adulthood are celebrated in Bachelard's writings. Yet this emphasis on the romantic idyll of the childhood home fails to recognise how the home can be a place of rules, authority, and power. The home, as Mary Douglas states (1991), rather than being an idyll, is a place of tyranny; it is a dystopic space and one that adult children cannot wait to leave. It would seem reasonable to suggest that neither perspective is sufficient to encompass fully the complexity of experiences of home during childhood. The significance of the childhood home and how it shapes subsequent transitions is an important motif in writings about home, particularly during young adulthood, yet the family home is always in construction, not only in individuals' imaginations but through the active emotional labour of all those involved. It is this sense of active participation in constructing meanings of home that can be usefully applied to understanding family practices within the home and the dynamic relationships between children and parents. In particular, this opens up the potential for the home to be simultaneously situated as both a nurturing and a disciplining space. During childhood, the home is not a neutral space but a space in which children learn to negotiate regulations of time and space.

This article develops this understanding of home as the social space of childhood through considering three aspects: children and parents at home, outside home, and on leaving home.

Children and Parents at Home

It is germane to begin an account of children and parents at home with the observation that the home is not a blank canvas on which parents and children impose their own rules and ideals. Rather, meanings of home are culturally contingent and the ways in which home spaces are conceived to shape and reframe childhood will reflect normative ideas about home and childhood. This is certainly not a new idea; for example, the fashion for nurseries in late Victorian England among middle-class families encapsulated the idea of the importance of children's spatial location within the home. Parents were encouraged to ensure that the design of nursery spaces would optimise children's health and mental development (Adcock, 2009). For the Victorians, the ideal location for the nursery was away from adult living spaces (preferably at the back of the house on an upper floor) and, as such, the spatial and temporal separation of children and parents ensured that the social spheres of adulthood and childhood were discrete. Parents were advised to furnish nurseries in a way that would promote health (with a particular emphasis on the importance of ventilation) as well as stimulate creative minds (with advice from colour schemes to the quantity and type of toys). The idea of creating a space exclusively for children (along with a nursemaid) and the spatial privatism of childhood that this practice entailed reflect wider processes of how spatial boundaries were reinforced both externally and internally in Victorian homes. As Gillis describes, the Victorian home came to be "put forward as a cure for the newly discovered malady of agoraphobia" (1997: 121), and the cosseting of children within the home exemplifies this practice. Yet the Victorian idyll of segregated childhood space was only accessible to the better-off, and the vast majority of children had to share cramped living conditions and continued to be victims of high infant and child mortality associated with exposure to environmental infection (particularly diarrhoea and respiratory disease). The nursery not only served to segregate children from parents but also reinforced the geographical segregation of middle-class from working-class children whose playground was the street and whose experience of home was very different from their upper-class peers.

Viewed from a contemporary perspective, the Victorian emphasis on segregated childhood seems quaint and amusing; in particular, the expression that children should not disturb their parents is one that might be seen as advantageous in some situations but would certainly not be advocated as 'best practice' in contemporary parenting. Since the Victorian era, modern industrialised societies have experienced rising living standards at the same time as the average household size has decreased, leading to a more equal distribution of resources and space, though inequalities in home life remain. Yet, although childhood might not be premised on either the inadequacy of home life or the segregation within the home, the importance of home, and how it shapes children's lives, has not diminished.

The conception of the contemporary home as a space for learning, challenging, and remembering rules is used in Wood and Beck's (1994) anthropological study of *Home Rules*. This book, written in conjunction with Denis Wood's family, is based on an ethnographic study of the living room in the Wood's family house. This study reveals how this room has three forms: values and meanings, rules, and material embodiment. These three forms are not experienced in isolation; for example, because children are not capable of appreciating the values and meanings embodied in the room and its artefacts, rules to protect these (e.g., 'don't touch' rules) introduce children to understanding the values that adults imbue in these material artefacts. As such, children's presence serves to highlight and reinforce the room's values and meanings for all occupants. The room should not be viewed as a static space but one that is continually unfolding. The rules incorporate adults' memories of their own childhood homes and, as such, the room is an "instantiation of a kind of collective memory" (Wood and Beck, 1994: xv). For children, home can only be undertaken as a 'field of rules'; yet as Wood and Beck argue, without these rules, a home would not be a home but a sculpture of woods and nails.

Rules are thus the result of negotiation between parents and children. Valentine's (1999) study of older children's negotiations with parents illustrates how rules can be broken and how children learn negotiating skills within the home. Children learn how to trade off one parent against another, often displaying a sophisticated understanding of gender dynamics, in order to manipulate the rules. Recognising the home as a dynamic product of both parents and children's negotiations is, therefore, important in unravelling how home unfolds over time as rules do not stay fixed and static. For example, temporal rules will shift, as children's bedtimes (and getting up times!) alter through late childhood into teenage years. Parents and children will often have conflicting needs within the home, which will vary temporally and might often lead to disagreements, particularly if lack of family resources means these needs cannot easily be accommodated. Sibley's (1995) analysis of home lives, using data from accounts of middle-class childhoods in the UK Mass Observation Archive, explores the tension between parents' desire for order and children's lack of concern for regulation and orderliness. Sibley associates the home, along with the boundary struggles that emerge from this tension, as a locus of power relations. Using a dichotomy of parenting styles derived from Basil Bernstein's distinction between positional and personalising families, he identifies different ways in which these power relations and associated modes of control are deployed within the home. The positional parents rely on their authoritative position to dictate what happens and where, thus maintaining strict boundaries, while personalising parents assume a more equal distribution of power, and, as a result, the use of space and time within the home becomes more flexible and negotiable. For example, a key feature of older children's negotiation at home is the need for privacy, yet achieving this has to be acknowledged by all family members; privacy is the 'gift' of parents, it cannot just be asserted by teenagers' needs (Gabb, 2008).

Our account of rules and negotiation needs to take into consideration that the processes of negotiations are not consistent in all households. Family structure is one important variable: for example, the home life of children living with a lone parent may differ from those living with more than one adult (not all of whom they may be related to). Within the same household, experiences may differ by sibling order, gender, and relational status. The increasing likelihood of partnership breakdown in industrialised societies has led to more children living between two homes, who may have to navigate and negotiate conflicting rules in different home spaces. The shift towards shared or co-parenting in postseparation families, rather than sole-custodial arrangements, has been encouraged in recent years as a way of promoting joint parental responsibility, although it has done little to assuage the notion that it is better for children to 'feel rooted' in one particular home as it is potentially damaging for children to have two homes. The assumption that this experience of moving between two homes is damaging for children is deep rooted; we describe children from such family arrangements as coming from a 'broken home', while research on the impact of separation on children's development underscores the expectation that this experience is damaging. Yet children's accounts of shared parenting arrangements demonstrate their resilience and ability to develop proficient negotiation skills. In particular, children may have to develop strategies to treat each parent equally and divide their time between two households (Wade and Smart, 2003). Some children may find that relationships with their parents (particularly fathers) may improve as they have more space and time to develop these relationships.

Parenting within the home is not just confined to internal negotiations, but rule-making practices, and adherence to them, are also shaped by community and social mores. The regulation of home spaces is not just restricted to children learning about negotiation but also facilitates the internalisation of public discourses about 'good' parenting. From providing a well-ventilated nursery in Victorian homes to the promotion of the 'naughty step' as an effective form of punishment and behavioural control in contemporary families, parenting practices are governed as much by common-sense notions of good parenting guided by parenting experts as they are by parents' own views and approaches.

Children and Parents Outside Home

To understand fully the spatial practices of negotiation between children and parents, it is not sufficient to focus on home spaces, but we also need to consider how these are shaped by the dynamics between home and outside spaces. Writers such as Sibley have argued that parental concerns in modern industrialised societies about the dangers facing children outside home are leading to more spatially restricted childhoods. Societal concern about stranger danger has resulted in children becoming cosseted in homes and being entertained with increasing reliance on technology. However, as Sibley remarks, parental observation about risk is highly subjective and does not necessarily reflect the quantitative distribution of risk. In England, at the beginning of the twenty-first century, about half of all deaths among children under the age of five occur in the home; however, for older children, car accidents are the most common cause of death, though compared with that for adults, these are most likely to occur closer to home. Each year in England, approximately 200 children die as pedestrians or cyclists and a similar number of children die as car passengers, though more children are injured as pedestrians than as car passengers (Department of Health, 1999). Yet it is not just anxiety about traffic that shapes parents' orientation to home-centred play, fears about abduction or molestation by strangers or members of the local community also feature heavily in parental accounts of childhood dangers. The result of such fears does not necessarily make children's lives any safer or healthier. Discourses about the risk to children from traffic position them as innocent victims, without recognising a vicious circle: as more children are driven between 'safe' spaces, that is, school to home, the volume of traffic on the road increases, which in turn increases children's risk of accident, as either pedestrians or passengers.

Moreover, the assumed impact on children's health is problematic. In the developed world recent increases in obesity throughout the population, though particularly among children, are associated with children leading more sedentary home-based lives. The need for safely regulated outdoor play and activity is promoted as a way of reducing the threat of the 'obesity epidemic'. Concerns about the health impact of home-centred childhoods are structured by prevailing social and environmental conditions. In Victorian England, for example, the main health risks to children were associated with environmental exposure and, as such, the nursery was designed to promote children's health through exposure to 'clean' air. In modern industrialised societies, the main identified health threat to children, particularly those from affluent neighbourhoods, is their own inactivity.

Yet unease about children becoming homebound is not just restricted to concern about their physical health but also relates to children's mental well-being and development. These concerns reflect a theoretical position that is clearly identified in Victorian commentaries on how space shapes children's development. This idea is endorsed in recent campaigns by education reformers against 'toxic' or 'denatured' childhood in both North America and Northern Europe. The argument is that contemporary parenting practices, in fashioning a childhood that is too home-centred and bereft of danger and risk, are damaging to children. From this perspective, outside play is associated with enabling children to take risks and with exposing them to dangers so that they can learn to negotiate risk and develop appropriate risk avoidance strategies. In the North American context, the importance of wilderness and access to wild natural spaces, in contrast to controlled urban space and suburban spaces, are identified as essential for 'healthy' childhood development. Eulogising about childhoods spent falling out of apple trees might fill up the comment spaces in newspapers but also reflect an assumed class bias. Children in less affluent neighbourhoods are more at risk in their immediate environment (e.g., from traffic and pollution) and may have less opportunities and resources to access natural spaces. The risks that children are exposed to outside their homes are not uniformly distributed.

The appeal of the natural environment is a common motif in children's imagined geographies, and the idea of children finding themselves and escaping adulthood in nature is an established literature genre. For example, Frances Hodgson Burnett's 1911 book, *The Secret Garden*, describes how Mary and Colin, two upper-class children abandoned by their guardian and father, are drawn out of their protected and uninspiring space within the nursery to experience the delights of the garden guided by Dickon, a local village boy. The garden, with its healing powers, is the central symbol of the book and provides a counterpoint to established focus on the nursery as the nurturing space for children. Escaping the home is a common theme in children's literature, which illustrates how home can be both comforting (e.g., Dorothy in *The Wizard of Oz* who learns through her travels in Oz that 'there is no place like home') and a restricted, adult-dominated space that does not afford children any freedom (e.g., Harry Potter's lonely childhood locked away in the cupboard under the stairs by his uncle and aunt). Children learn about themselves and the adults they encounter through their dialectical movement between home and spaces outside home. From this perspective, the boundary between the home and the outside is fluid, not fixed. As Massey (1992) rightly points out, this is a paradox of home; it is a space that is symbolised as bound but one that is, or has been, open in some way. Relations, communications, and movements that take place within the home are always stretched beyond the confines of its bound space.

The notion of home boundaries as fluid is certainly relevant for children's experiences, as Holloway and Valentine (2001) demonstrate. Although children might be homebound, their use of technology and communications allows them to go beyond the boundaries of home. Children are able to maintain complex networks with peers outside home, without necessarily leaving its space. Technology therefore has a diverse impact; it not only provides entertainment and an inducement to stay within the home but also opens up the home to the world outside.

Leaving Home

The final relational aspect to consider is what happens to child–parent relationships during the process of leaving home, and how relationships developed within the home continue to shape young adults' experiences of transitions to adulthood and independence.

Most of the literature on parenting and home focus on parenting in situ and the dynamic relationships between children and parents in shared space, yet the outcome of these interactions is not restricted to childhood experiences. The learning processes within the home that equip children with the skills of rule observance, negotiation, and breaking rules are recognised as essential preparation for adulthood. Yet, how and what children are expected to learn at home in preparation for adulthood is contingent on cultural contexts. In the North American and European contexts, children's learning within the home relates directly to supporting them to become independent adults. As children develop and move through the teenage years, a certain amount of mutual repelling is expected; teenagers withdraw into their rooms and demand privacy from the rest of the household. This stereotypical teenager is emblematic in much of North European and American popular culture, and phases of 'storm and stress' are essential for the formation of distinct adult identities. Young people have to develop their own identity independent of their parents, and this process starts at home. Yet this storm-and-stress model is culturally and social constructed. Holdsworth and Morgan's (2005) comparison of parents and young people in Britain, Spain, and Norway reveals how young people's experiences of home and relationships with parents before, during, and after leaving are distinctive in each country-specific context. Norwegian parents took a more active role in 'preparing' young people for eventual departure at relatively young ages. Colloquially parents explained that they 'should not sew pillows under their children's arms'; that is, children should not be spoilt but should be taught about responsibility and be encouraged to have some independence while at home, thus making their eventual departure less traumatic. The process of physical separation begins at home and continues through the process of leaving. Maintaining physical distance and reducing the frequency of contact are important for the leaving-home process, and both parents and children need to recognise each other's private space and maintain a physical barrier. One mother described how an adult child should live at such a distance that one 'needed to wear a coat to visit'. In contrast, Spanish young people and parents had a very different view of relationships between parents and adult children. Young people were not as prepared for leaving as their Norwegian counterparts; parents described relations based on friendship rather than separation and distance (and were critical of Northern European parents for their distance). Young people were not generally expected to help at home, although this was gendered, with men having fewer responsibilities than did women. In part, this lack of regulation and clear boundaries in the home was shaped by the importance of 'street life' for young people, as young people were able to develop their social lives outside their parental homes. After leaving home, which occurs at much older ages in Spain than in Norway, close relationship between parents and children was maintained through daily contact and with parents often shopping and cooking for their adult children as if they were living at home.

This comparison between Norwegian and Spanish families illustrates the cultural context of leaving home and how relationships between parents and children and their spatial manifestation are anticipated to shape young people's transition to adulthood. These processes start at home and continue throughout the process of leaving. The childhood home is not a fixed, defined space from which young people escape (or never want to leave); rather it is a space continually revisited and reframed through leaving home and transition to adulthood. Young people's ability to access resources to leave at the 'right time' can be regarded as a barometer of young people's economic and social welfare. For example, the recent increase in the proportion of young people in their twenties living at home in the United Kingdom, associated with either a delay in leaving or an increase in 'Boomerang kids' who return home after leaving, has received considerable attention in the media. This increase in coresidence is held up as an indicator of young people's lack of resources to become independent (in particular, access to affordable housing) or that young people lack the motivation to become independent of their parents and are procrastinating the process of leaving home.

Conclusions

The key theme throughout this article is negotiation in that the task of constructing and reconstructing childhood depends on recognising children's agency and understanding their social experience with adults (as well as with other children) and the particular spaces in which these relationships develop. The home is the locality associated globally as the social space of childhood. For some, the childhood home is distinctive from other spaces in providing an insulating and protective space that is forever present in their imaginations and memories. Yet, the home is also a space for learning: about boundaries and how to manipulate them, about the value of material objects and the need to protect them, and about negotiating between adults and the intricacies of power relations. How these processes are experienced is shaped by social and cultural contexts; the home life of a middle-class Victorian child was as different from a working-class counterpart as it is from contemporary middle-class youth. Yet, the home is not a bounded space, and while contemporary moral panics about childhood blame the intensified home-centredness of modern parenting, children develop their own competencies to navigate the boundaries of home. Negotiations between children and parents are part of the eventual process of leaving home, because the process of separation begins at home before leaving, to 'prepare' children for an independent adulthood. This process is mediated by cultural norms that shape relationships within the home as well as during the leaving process. Spatial separation and independence are valued in different ways that are shaped by prevailing economic, social, and cultural contexts, and how the home is experienced as the social space of childhood is not universal.

Acknowledgements

I am very grateful to Jamie Adcock for allowing me to use his analysis of Victorian child-care manuals in the writing of this article.

See also: Domesticity; Emotions at Home; Experiencing Home; Gender Divisions in the Home; Home as a Space of Care; Home as Leisure Space; Home: Unpaid Domestic Labour; Meanings of Home; Memory and Nostalgia at Home.

References

Adcock J (2009) *Cultivation and Nurture: The Nursery and Child Rearing Manuals*. Unpublished PhD Chapter, Department of Geography, Royal Holloway, University of London.
Bachelard G (1994) *The Poetics of Space*. Boston, MA: Beacon Press.
Department of Health (1999) *Saving Lives: Our Healthier Nation*. Command Paper 4386. London: The Stationery Office.
Douglas M (1991) The idea of home: A kind of space. *Social Research* 58: 287–307.
Gabb J (2008) *Researching Intimacy in Families*. Basingstoke: Palgrave Macmillan.
Gillis J (1997) *A World of Their Own Making*, ch. 6. Oxford: Oxford University Press.
Holdsworth C and Morgan D (2005) *Transitions in Context: Leaving Home, Independence and Adulthood*. Buckingham: Open University Press.
Holloway SL and Valentine G (2001) Children at home in the wired world: Reshaping and rethinking the home in urban geography. *Urban Geography* 22: 562–583.
Massey D (1992) A place called home. *New Formations* 17: 3–15.
Sibley D (1995) Families and domestic routines: Constructing the boundaries of childhood. In: Pile S and Thrift N (eds.) *Mapping the*

Subject: Cultural Geographies of Transformation, pp. 123–142. London: Routledge.

Valentine G (1999) 'Oh please mum. Oh please dad': Negotiating children's spatial boundaries. In: McKie L, Bowlby S, and Gregory S (eds.) Gender, Power and the Household, pp. 137–154. Basingstoke: Palgrave Macmillan.

Wade A and Smart C (2003) 'As fair as it can be?' Childhood after divorce. In: A-M Jensen and McKee L (eds.) Children and the Changing Family: Between Transformation and Negotiation, pp. 105–119. London: Routledge.

Wood D and Beck RJ (1994) Home Rules. Baltimore, MD: Johns Hopkins University Press.

Choice and Government Intervention in Housing Markets

M Cigdem and G Wood, RMIT University, Melbourne, VIC, Australia

© 2012 Elsevier Ltd. All rights reserved.

Glossary

Demand-side housing subsidy Government assistance to improve the ability of households to pay for housing or housing of a particular type and quality.

Deregulation The removal or relaxation of government controls that stipulate limits and/or requirements that market participants must observe.

Externalities Eventuate when the actions of consumers or producers incidentally affect other consumers or producers, but no compensation is paid or received for these incidental side effects.

Market failure Inefficient market outcomes that occur due to imperfections that prevent the optimal allocation of resources.

Merit goods Goods that are deemed to be intrinsically desirable and should be consumed at or above socially desirable minimum levels.

Neoliberalism A belief in market mechanisms as the best way of achieving an efficient and equitable allocation of resources.

Privatisation The transfer of the central government's ownership rights in enterprises, land, housing, and so on, to private investors.

Public housing Public housing is housing financed, owned, and managed by government agencies.

Social housing A form of housing that is supplied by not-for-profit providers, but typically fully or partly financed by government.

Supply-side housing subsidy Government assistance aimed at reducing the costs of producing or maintaining housing units.

Introduction

From as early as the late nineteenth century, governments have played an instrumental role in the housing sector, particularly in advanced Western countries. While the nature and degree of their involvement has varied over time and from country to country, governments of industrialised countries have deployed an array of housing policies in an effort to influence the production, consumption, financing, distribution, and location of dwellings. Policy-makers have experimented with alternative versions of the market–state relationship, some of which have emphasised the role of the free market relative to the state, and others that have enhanced the power of the state. In all of these relationships however, governments have exercised some degree of intervention in the housing sector. There are various justifications for the pervasiveness of government in housing. One of the more important is acknowledgement that shelter is a basic human need or merit good that is too pivotal for both individual well-being and social stability to be left solely to the free market. Housing is then often regarded as a merit good; if merit goods are under-provided in a market system, there is a case for government intervention (regulation, subsidies, taxation, or direct provision) to support their provision.

The concept of housing need has been a critical consideration for governments. Housing need can be defined as the quantity of housing required to provide accommodation of some minimum standard. Where a country's housing stock fails to meet all the nation's housing needs, homelessness, overcrowding, insecurity of tenure, and insanitary conditions can eventuate. Up until the 1970s, housing need and failure of markets to satisfy the housing needs of the poor tended to dominate housing policy debates and was an important influence shaping housing policy. It is only in the latter part of the twentieth century, as governments in industrial countries succeeded in meeting most housing needs, and housing shortages receded, that housing choice has attracted attention in housing policy debates.

The arrival of the Thatcher and Reagan governments brought with it the introduction of a neoliberal approach to housing, which holds as its most basic tenet the proposition that an efficient production and equitable distribution of goods and services is best achieved through the operation of markets. The advent of neoliberalism also witnessed a shift away from policies centred on meeting needs towards policies concerned chiefly with individual choice and housing affordability. This shift was also encouraged by a belief that direct government provision of housing (public housing) and the use of regulatory interventions (e.g., rent controls and security of tenure) stifled choice, and could even worsen housing conditions by deterring private investment in housing. Early examples of choice-based policies include the UK's 'Right to Buy' introduced in the 1980s (see article Privatisation of Social Housing), and the housing voucher programme implemented in the United States (see article Access and Affordability: Housing Vouchers). By 2000, housing choice was a key issue shaping housing policy debates in countries such as the United Kingdom, the Netherlands, the United States, Australia, and New Zealand. These countries were also among the first to promote demand-side subsidies as housing policy instruments that expand individuals' housing options (see article Policies to Support Access and Affordability of Housing).

The structure of the article is as follows. The first section asks why governments have intervened so pervasively in the housing sector. Next, we describe the various forms that government intervention typically takes. The next section presents a neoliberal critique of the role of governments in the housing sector, and examines the market-oriented policy approach to housing. Finally, we offer some observations on recent housing policy developments introduced by social democrat governments.

Housing Needs, Market Failure, and Government Intervention

Merit Goods and Housing Needs

This policy perspective is based on the belief that when low-income families and persons cannot afford to purchase or rent accommodation sufficient to meet housing need, government must intervene to ensure that housing needs are met. It is feared that if needs are not met, negative externalities such as ill-health, disease, homelessness, and inferior educational outcomes (for the children of those in housing need) will arise. The merit good argument is strengthened if low-income households are poorly informed with respect to the adverse effects of occupying housing at unsatisfactorily low levels. In such circumstances, a free market will underprovide housing. These arguments had a particular resonance in the late nineteenth and early twentieth centuries given the serious problems of poverty at this time. They tended to prompt government intervention on the supply side of the housing market that was more ambitious during eras and in countries with highly unequal distributions of income and wealth. The merit good rationale is commonly linked to issues of equity in housing markets. In the modern era, merit good arguments remain an important rationale for government intervention during economic recessions. This has been particularly apparent through the recent recession triggered by the global financial crisis.

Market Failure in Housing Markets

Housing has many of the characteristics likely to generate market failure and therefore negatively impact both productive and allocative efficiency. Housing is a durable, complex good that is spatially fixed. Its complexity and durability mean that problems of imperfect and asymmetric information are prominent features of housing markets. While housing is traded in private markets in much the same way as other durables, it is unusual in being responsible for the generation of important externalities. Externalities are incidental benefits and costs that can be nonexcludable and/or nonrival, for example, noise pollution or communicable diseases whose origin is poor housing conditions. Finally, while monopoly is not commonly associated with housing markets, it can be a source of market failure in rental tenures.

Externalities

Externalities are an important source of market failure in housing markets (see article Economics of Housing Externalities). Negative externalities are said to arise when one party's actions have adverse impacts on another party's utility or well-being. Because there is no market in the externality, the party adversely affected is not compensated. Externalities are not always negative. For example, gentrification can result in reduced crime, higher employment, better education outcomes, and typically have positive spillover effects on property values in the vicinity of the neighbourhood (see article Gentrification and Neighbourhood Change).

But it has been negative externalities that typically prompt housing policy interventions. In a housing context, externalities emanating from poor housing and overcrowding can impact on the wider neighbourhood, both monetarily and socially (see article Housing and Neighbourhood Quality: Urban Regeneration). Deteriorating housing can cause urban blight and decay that is capitalised into surrounding property values and deters financial institutions from lending to property buyers and investors (see article Policies to Address Redlining). Moreover, poor housing conditions can contribute to (1) health problems for adults and children (see article Health and Housing), (2) neighbourhood blight, (3) poor education outcomes for children (see article Residential Segregation and Education), and (4) inferior employment prospects for residents (see article Housing and Labour Markets).

Imperfect Information

Another problem that prevents markets from working optimally is imperfect information where consumers have inadequate knowledge of housing options, and are uncertain about future prices, incomes, and market conditions. Imperfect information has two characteristics: (1) incomplete information and (2) asymmetric information. Incomplete information occurs when consumers lack information on some aspects of a transaction that may affect their payoffs. Asymmetric information, on the other hand, occurs when one party to a transaction has valuable knowledge of some aspect of the transaction that is not disclosed to other parties involved in the transaction, and it would be costly for these other parties to verify this knowledge. Imperfect and asymmetric information are often associated with adverse selection and moral hazard market failures that are particularly prominent in mortgage markets and have prompted governments to intervene by regulating financial institutions that originate mortgages (see article Mortgage Markets: Regulation and Intervention).

Monopoly

A monopoly arises when one firm is responsible for all output in an industry and is protected from new competition by barriers to entry. Monopoly power prevents markets from operating efficiently because the monopolist can restrict output and thereby raise price to levels that are higher than would prevail if competition in and for the market were possible. This form of market failure is not prominent in the 'private housing sector' where there is typically more than one housing supplier, and entry by new firms is possible. But where a developer acquires substantial land banks and government regulations prevent release of more land for residential development in an area, there can be cause for concern. However, even in areas where there is a single developer, the exploitation of monopoly power will be constrained by the presence of developers in neighbouring areas and regions.

Private rental housing markets are generally considered to be competitive, but since housing is heterogeneous and moving costs are nontrivial, landlords can possess some monopoly power. But once again this power is held in check if there are ample alternative rental housing opportunities in terms of types of housing, in nearby locations and made available by numerous landlords. As long as housing consumers regard other types of housing, communities or neighbourhoods as close substitutes monopoly power will remain constrained.

What Form Does Government Intervention Take?

The above motives for government intervention have prompted a wide range of government policy measures in housing markets to promote equity and efficiency outcomes. The main instruments of government policy can be categorised as either demand-side or supply-side interventions. These are discussed in turn below.

Supply-Side Interventions

Interventions on the supply side take the form of 'bricks-and-mortar' subsidies that are granted to financiers, developers, or providers and designed to reduce the costs of housing supply, or government provision. These supply-side subsidies can take two forms, direct and indirect subsidies (see article Policy Instruments that Support Housing Supply: Supply-Side Subsidies). Direct supply-side subsidies involve a cash transfer from government to suppliers which lowers their costs of production. Indirect supply-side subsidies involve no cash transfer but instead use regulation or controls, for example, caps on interest rates that, in effect, lower costs of production. Government provision involves the financing and production of housing services by a state agency, as in public housing, for example.

Demand-Side Interventions

These types of intervention typically offer assistance to households (renters and homeowners) that facilitate affordability of and access to housing of a satisfactory standard (see article Demand Subsidies for Low-Income Households). These interventions aim to either lower the cost of housing, therefore making it more affordable, or lower the height of barriers, for example, discrimination, that impede access to housing opportunities (see article Discrimination in Housing Markets). Subsidies that lower the cost of housing include housing allowances, housing vouchers, rent controls, tax expenditures, and low-interest mortgages. Measures to improve access include legislation that aims to outlaw ethnic or racial discrimination, and regulation of housing standards.

The Neoliberal Critique

Since the 1970s, neoliberal ideas have become increasingly influential in shaping Western governments' approaches to housing policy. Government interventions in the housing sector have been criticised from a neoliberal perspective because:

- A government presence in housing markets tends to weaken competition and hence stifle innovation and choice. This is perhaps most evident in the large monolithic public housing estates built by Eastern European government agencies, but also apparent in Western developed countries with substantial public housing sectors
- The regulation of rents, interest rates, land use, and building standards distorts price signals and results in resource misallocation and the inefficient functioning of markets

- Clients of housing programmes can become welfare-dependent because of blunt incentives to work and save.

The critique is based on a philosophy that advocates the rights of the individual and, in particular, their right to exercise choice over what to purchase and consume, including residential location and housing services. Markets are viewed as the best vehicle guaranteeing these rights. In recent decades we have therefore witnessed a marked shift in housing policy, with a greater emphasis on market-based solutions. This change in approach towards housing policy is important for a number of reasons.

First, it seeks to empower households by facilitating the exercise of a greater degree of choice in housing markets. But what is meant by choice? Choice is an ability to exercise autonomy and responsibility in decision-making. Autonomy is the right to choose a preferred combination of consumption goods and services, given prices and incomes; responsibility in decision-making means that individuals are accountable for the consequences of their choices. The consequences of good or bad decisions are then borne by the individual responsible for making the decision.

Second, the neoliberal approach uses housing subsidies and other forms of government intervention in the housing market to fulfil different functions. Housing policy should facilitate the exercise of choice in housing markets rather than meeting needs that are defined by government.

Third, market-based solutions are the favoured approach. Policies should then assist low-income households' capacity to pay for housing, while relying on private markets to respond by supplying housing that meets the preferences of households. This implies that government should avoid intervention on the supply side of the market.

Market-Based or Neoliberal Approach to Housing Policy

With a market-based approach, government intervention is considered positive only insofar as it helps the market to operate freely, and assists the poor and disadvantaged who are unable to provide for themselves. There are three key elements to the market-based approach. First, the use of housing vouchers or housing allowance programmes (see article Access and Affordability: Housing Allowances) that assist poor households to move into housing of a satisfactory standard and in suitable locations (see article Mobility Programmes for Disadvantaged Populations: The Moving to Opportunity Programme). Second, there is an emphasis on privatisation measures that are designed to roll-back state involvement in the ownership and management of housing. Third, deregulation that relaxes or removes controls on housing rents, interest rates, building standards, land use, and any other aspect of housing and land markets. These three approaches are discussed below.

Housing Allowances and Housing Vouchers

Housing allowances are income-related subsidies that are designed to provide income support to low-income households and to assist them in obtaining housing accommodation of a quality that is beyond what would otherwise be affordable. They are paid either directly to eligible households or indirectly via landlords or mortgage lenders on the household's behalf. Eligibility is typically extended to low-income tenants and, less commonly, to low-income owner-occupied households. Because housing allowances improve a household's purchasing power, they are considered a demand-side subsidy. Payment of a housing allowance to eligible households can involve a cash payment, but another common method of payment is by housing voucher. A housing voucher takes the form of a promissory note issued by the administering agency to eligible tenants, who then use the voucher in place of cash to meet rent payments. In some developed countries including Australia, Canada, and Ireland, housing allowance programmes can provide housing assistance implicitly through income-related schemes. Also referred to as 'rents geared to income' or 'differential rent schemes', this form of housing allowance involves social housing landlords setting rents equal to some predefined percentage of the tenant's income.

While these housing policy programmes were commonly tied to housing of some minimum standard, the quality goal has become less of a concern, and they are increasingly geared to easing housing affordability and facilitating choice, including how much of income to devote to housing. From an income support point of view, policy-makers use housing allowance schemes to provide income assistance to low-income households by ensuring that low-income households do not spend a disproportionate share of their income on housing services. Thus, by reducing the rent-to-income ratio, housing allowances and vouchers allow households to allocate a larger portion of their income on nonhousing-related goods.

In recent years, the US policy focus has shifted further to a third dimension concerned with promoting greater spatial mobility among housing voucher recipients. Examples of such programmes include the 'Moving to Opportunity' programme and the 'Housing Choice Voucher' programme. One of the central features of these types of policy instruments is that the housing voucher is attached to the individual not the housing occupied by eligible tenants. As a result, recipients are not tied to a particular dwelling and can utilise their housing voucher entitlements wherever they go. This feature of the voucher-based programme is a particularly important one from a neoliberal perspective, as it allows households to exercise some choice over where they live, and the type of accommodation they wish to reside in. In a supply-side subsidy system, households often relinquish this right to public landlords who instead decide what type of housing the tenant will be offered, and where they will live. Since the recipient exercises choice, demand-side subsidies are regarded as more efficient than supply-side subsidies.

Privatisation and Consumer Sovereignty

Privatisation is another key component of the neoliberal approach and has been adopted by a growing number of countries, particularly over the last two decades (see article Privatisation of Housing: Implications for Well-Being). This trend is in stark contrast to the traditional postwar policy orientation based on expansion of the welfare state, planned development, and public-sector-led economic growth.

In a broad sense, privatisation occurs when the state transfers ownership or control over previously government-owned and -managed operations to the private sector. It has been extensively experimented with by different levels of government, and can take several forms. In the housing sector, privatisation has been associated with the sale of public and social rented housing and the contracting-out of management functions. This approach to privatisation was a particularly important theme in the UK housing agenda introduced by the Thatcher government elected in 1979. The 'Right to Buy' programme introduced a uniform national scheme whereby tenants of local authority housing and select housing associations were granted a 'right to buy' the property they occupied at a discounted rate. The size of the discount was positively related to the length of tenancy, and was as much as 70% of the market value in some instances. Applicants were given the right to buy their existing dwelling as well as the right to a 100% mortgage from the local authority at a rate of interest fixed by the Treasury (see article Privatisation of Social Housing).

Advocates of the privatisation of public housing maintain that private markets offer housing consumers a wider array of choices. Managers of public housing, on the other hand, are less responsive to consumer preferences. Furthermore, privatisation is believed to enhance consumer well-being through property ownership. Individuals who are owner-occupiers are able to exercise more control over the use of their dwelling, and through investing money in housing maintenance and improvements, they are also better placed to accumulate wealth. Governments of all persuasions tend to encourage the accumulation of wealth in housing by extending tax expenditures to owner-occupiers (see article Access and Affordability: Homeowner Taxation).

Privatisation programmes were subsequently introduced by a number of countries including the Netherlands, France, and Australia, among others, in an effort to promote increased homeownership. In the United States, however, privatisation efforts followed a somewhat different trend to that of other Western countries. While the Reagan government shared Thatcher's pro-market views, it sought to increase the role and influence of the market by deregulation and liberalisation rather than the sale of public housing. This reflects the traditionally smaller public housing tenure in the United States.

Deregulation

A third component of the neoliberal approach is housing market deregulation, which can be broadly defined as the removal or relaxation of government controls in housing markets with a view to increasing the role and influence of market processes. There are two key areas in the housing sector where deregulation has been prominent: (1) the housing finance sector and (2) rental housing.

Housing finance sector

Housing finance deregulation often features the removal of government restrictions on housing finance institutions' lending practices, the lifting of interest rate ceilings, and relaxation of reserve requirements. The removal of lending restrictions had important implications for banks in particular, allowing them to more vigorously compete with specialists in housing finance markets. Governments have also increasingly allowed the entry of international and nonbank lenders, leading to the opening up of the mortgage market to international competition and greater availability of funds. Deregulation is widely accredited with improving home buyers' access to credit, particularly low- and middle-income households. But it has also been blamed as a source of inflationary bias in housing markets.

Rental housing

Deregulation in rental housing typically features the relaxation or removal of rent controls and security of tenure regulations. Rent controls place caps on rents or rent increases, and are often accompanied by regulation of the terms of tenancies. In the early post-Second World War years, there was a popular measure adopted by governments struggling to meet housing shortages, and needing to curb the rising rents that inevitably accompany shortages. However, when landlords cannot charge the market rent because of rent controls, returns to investments in rental housing are lower than would eventuate in a free market. The attractiveness of private rental housing as an investment is further impacted if there are security of tenure provisions that prevent landlords from giving sitting tenants notice to quit during or even at the conclusion of lease contracts. These regulations have been blamed for shortages of good-quality rental housing on the grounds that they deter landlords from investing in new rental housing, and depress maintenance and improvement outlays on the established rental stock. Governments have moved to relax rent controls and security of tenure regulations as these adverse impacts became more apparent, and as the more severe post-Second World War housing shortages eased (see article Access and Affordability: Rent Regulation).

Conclusion

Until the early 1970s, governments in the Western world played a central role in the housing sector. That role was justified on two main grounds. First, that housing is a basic human need and therefore one that governments should ensure is sufficiently met for all individuals. The poor are particularly vulnerable so early forms of intervention tended to focus on supply-side interventions to meet the housing needs of the poorest. Second, housing is prone to market failures such as those associated with externalities and imperfect information. These failures have a strong spatial dimension that can be central to neighbourhood decline and the emergence of slum housing. Governments have introduced various subsidy programmes and regulatory controls to correct for these failures.

As housing shortages were eliminated and housing needs waned as a policy concern, housing choice began to emerge as an increasingly important influence in housing policy debates. This coincided with the growing importance of neoliberal ideas in both social and economic policy. The neoliberal critique posits that government intervention distorts price signals, which leads to resource misallocation, blunt incentives, and welfare dependency. Neoliberals also criticise government intervention on the grounds that it weakens competition and hence stifles innovation and choice. Their response was to develop policies advancing the rights of individuals to exercise choice in markets, including those such as housing where government involvement had been prominent. According to neoliberals, such outcomes are best achieved by market-based solutions, and in the housing sector this meant emphasis on housing allowances/vouchers, the sale of public housing, and removal or relaxation of regulatory controls such as those on rents and interest rates.

In more recent times social democrat governments have reacted by introducing reforms designed to make collective forms of housing provision more responsive to the needs and aspirations of clients. These developments encompass more decentralised models of public housing provision, the transfer of public housing to not-for-profit social housing providers, and increased tenant participation in the management of social housing. In some countries, particularly those in Western Europe, we witnessed a growing emphasis on neighbourhood renewal programmes that integrate housing and other public service programmes (such as employment services) to address urban decay. But even these initiatives have been shaped by neoliberal ideas. Public–private partnerships are a feature of many urban renewal interventions (see article Public-Private Housing Partnerships), while in social housing there is an increasing use of market principles in setting rents and guiding investment decisions. The exclusive reliance on large public sector programmes to address housing problems is now only resorted to in extreme conditions, such as the severe recession triggered by the meltdown in US financial markets in 2008.

See also: Access and Affordability: Homeowner Taxation; Access and Affordability: Housing Allowances; Access and Affordability: Housing Vouchers; Access and Affordability: Rent Regulation; Demand Subsidies for Low-Income Households; Discrimination in Housing Markets; Economics of Housing Externalities; Gentrification and Neighbourhood Change; Health and Housing; Housing and Labour Markets; Housing and Neighbourhood Quality: Urban Regeneration; Mobility Programmes for Disadvantaged Populations: The Moving to Opportunity Programme; Mortgage Markets: Regulation and Intervention; Policies to Address Redlining; Policies to Support Access and Affordability of Housing; Policy Instruments that Support Housing Supply: Supply-Side Subsidies; Privatisation of Housing: Implications for Well-Being; Privatisation of Social Housing; Public-Private Housing Partnerships; Residential Segregation and Education.

Further Reading

Aalbers MB (2004) Promoting home ownership in a social-rented city: Policies, practices and pitfalls. *Housing Studies* 19(3): 483–495.
Bradbury KL and Downs A (eds.) (1981) *Do Housing Allowances Work?* Washington, DC: Brookings Institution.
Clark WAV and Dieleman F (1996) *Households and Housing: Choices and Outcomes in the Housing Market*. New Brunswick, NJ: Rutgers University, Center for Urban and Policy Research.
Gibb K (1995) A housing allowance for the UK? Preconditions for an income-related housing subsidy. *Housing Studies* 10: 517–532.
Kemp PA (ed.) (2007a) *Housing Allowances in Comparative Perspective*, pp. 295. Bristol, UK: The Policy Press.
King P (2009) *Understanding Housing Finance: Meeting Needs and Making Choices*, 2nd edn. London: Routledge.
Leece D (2004) *The Economics of the Mortgage Market: Perspectives on Household Decision Making*. Oxford, UK: Blackwell Publishing.
Lindsay R (1970) The economics of interest rate ceilings. *Bulletin* 68–70.

Meijer FM and Visscher HJ (1998) The deregulation of building controls: A comparison of Dutch and other European systems. *Environment and Planning B: Planning and Design* 25: 617–629.

Steele M (1998) Canadian housing allowances inside and outside the welfare system. *Canadian Public Policy – Analyse de Politues* 24: 209–232.

Stephens M (2005) An assessment of the British housing benefit scheme. *European Journal of Housing Policy* 5: 111–129.

Turner B, Hedus J, and Tosics I (eds.) (1992) *The Reform of Housing in Eastern Europe and the Soviet Union*. New York: Routledge.

Varady D and Walker CC (2007) *Neighborhood Choices*. New Brunswick, NJ: Center for Urban Policy Research.

Wood G and Bushe-Jones S (1990) Financial deregulation and access to home ownership in Australia. *Urban Studies* 27(4): 583–590.

Yates J (1988) Housing finance and deregulation: Predictions and outcomes. *The Australian Economic Review* 21(1): 3–15.

Civil Sector Institutions and Informal Settlements

D Mitlin and D Satterthwaite, International Institute for Environment and Development (IIED), London, UK

© 2012 Elsevier Ltd. All rights reserved.

Introduction

In high-income nations, almost all new housing is designed by architects and built by private-sector building enterprises. The buildings they construct meet official norms – for instance, building codes and land-use regulations. And the buildings are served by roads, piped water supplies, and electricity connections and usually sewers. Civil society has little role here – although civil society organisations often have an important contribution in helping ensure accommodation for low-income groups and, historically, have had considerable importance in shaping current state structures and systems relating to housing.

In low-income and most middle-income nations, civil society institutions have more important roles in the construction of housing in urban areas, in the construction of infrastructure associated with housing, and in housing-related service provision (for instance, household solid waste collection). But this is mostly within the informal settlements where a high proportion of the urban population live. It is common for 30–60% of the population in cities in low- and middle-income nations to live in informal settlements. They live there because there is no suitable public or private housing that they can afford to rent, buy, or build within the formal legal system. In part, this is the result of their low incomes, but in large part, it is also because of the incapacity of government institutions. This can be seen in the lack of government action to ensure the availability of sufficient land for housing with infrastructure – and it is this lack of action which underpins the large proportion of housing built illegally. Poor-quality living conditions are also related to the refusal of some government agencies to work in informal settlements (which they often term 'slums'). Civil society organisations may be building houses or providing housing finance; they may be providing infrastructure (for instance, installing water systems) or services (including support for housing improvements, water and sanitation services, and solid waste collection). Civil society organisations are also generally active in making demands on governments in relation to the limited access to housing or to housing finance or land facing large sectors of the population (as in the work of the Urban Resource Centre in Karachi and other urban centres in Pakistan).

In relation to housing, the term civil society embraces a great range of organisations from small informal organisations (for instance, a savings group formed by some of the inhabitants of an informal settlement) through larger community organisations (for instance, resident associations) to a range of nongovernmental organisations (NGOs). NGOs working in housing range from small local NGOs to large national and international NGOs that include charities, some of which have hundreds of staff and annual budgets of millions or tens of millions of dollars.

The Development of Civil Society Organisations Related to Housing

The role of civil society organisations in urban housing in low- and middle-income nations gained more recognition from the 1970s onwards. Initially, this was in relation to the role of NGOs in housing, staffed by professionals, who worked direct with low-income groups. These organisations emerged as a result of the failure of government initiatives to address the housing needs of much of the low-income population. Early examples include two Mexican NGOs, CENVI and COPEVI, and the Orangi Pilot Project in Pakistan. In some cases, such as Planact in South Africa, NGOs emerged to defend groups under particular political threat. But from the 1970s, there was also a growing recognition of the roles of organisations formed by the urban poor to help address their own housing needs. These included groups formed to organise the occupation of land for housing – as in the land invasions that became common in many Latin American nations during the 1970s and 1980s. These and other civil society organisations also made housing-related demands – for instance, demands on the state to provide their informal settlements with infrastructure and services and land tenure or demands to prevent their eviction. A third grouping of civil society organisations was also important for housing although less directly – those engaged in making demands for political changes in nations with nondemocratic regimes, and challenging contraventions of civil and political rights. For instance, in Latin America, the shift or return to democratic governments and the internal reforms these brought have been an important factor in reducing the number of evictions from informal settlements and increasing the proportion of populations served by housing-related infrastructure (including piped water to the home and sewer connections).

Today, in many cities in low- and middle-income nations, there is a bewildering range of civil society organisations active in housing-related issues from grass-roots organisations through local NGOs to large international NGOs. In some cities, these work with government; in others, they work largely independent of government, especially where government institutions have little interest in or capacity to work with the urban poor on housing issues. The importance of local civil society organisations working within informal settlements and the many roles they have is probably underestimated as most of these operate below the radar of international agencies – and do not speak the language of these agencies. There are some international NGOs that work on housing although most international NGOs have little engagement in this, in part arising from what is an increasingly inaccurate assumption that there is little poverty in urban areas. There are some international NGOs that support local civil society organisations engaged in housing issues including preventing evictions – for instance, the Asian Coalition for Housing Rights (ACHR), the Habitat International Coalition (HIC), and the Centre on Housing Rights and Evictions (COHRE).

One obvious limitation of civil society organisations is that they lack the capacity to install needed city-wide infrastructure (for instance, trunk water mains, sewers, and drains) or to provide universal provision for services such as schools and health care. Ideally, civil society organisations should work within larger frameworks of government provision to make sure these serve those with the least income or groups facing discrimination; without this, the scale and scope of what civil society can do is always inadequate.

Rather than try to cover in detail the large and complex mix of civil society organisations active in housing-related issues, the sections below focus on one particular set of organisations – federations formed by slum and shack dwellers and homeless people that have affiliated with a transnational network, Slum/Shack Dwellers International. The growth in the number of these federations and the scale and ambition of their work programmes make them one of the most significant developments in housing policy and practice for low-income groups.

The National Federations of Slum/Shack Dwellers and Slum/Shack Dwellers International

One of the most important changes in civil society engagement with housing issues in urban areas is the emergence of grass-roots organisations formed by 'slum' or shack dwellers that form larger federations – at city and national levels. These have importance for what they undertake and in how they change state engagement with housing issues. Many of these federations and the local NGOs that work with them have formed their own international network known as Slum/Shack Dwellers International (SDI). SDI negotiates with international funding agencies on behalf of its member federations and helps manage external funding. It also supports exchanges and shared learning between the different national federations and with urban poor groups in other nations that want to learn about what these federations do. In 20 nations there are national federations allied to SDI, and in many other nations savings groups are active and in contact with these federations. Where governments and international agencies support these federations, the scale and scope of what they can achieve increases considerably.

The foundation for these federations is savings groups formed by slum or shack dwellers or homeless people, in which most savers and most savings group managers are women. These savings groups also allow members to draw small loans from the pool of savings to which they contributed. These savings groups join together to form local federations of savings groups, as they visit each other and learn from each other. These then develop to become citywide and then nationwide federations that pool some of their savings and develop their capacities to address housing issues and negotiate with government agencies. **Table 1** gives details of some of these federations. Many have set up their own national urban poor fund to help manage their savings and to help fund their initiatives. For instance, the Mchenga Fund in Malawi has supported land acquisition, house-building, and livelihoods with over 3000 households securing land in the last 5 years. In Zimbabwe, despite political and economic difficulties, the Gungano Fund has carried on lending for land development and infrastructure and has secured 4800 housing plots for its members. In the Philippines, the regionalisation of the fund has enabled thousands of members to negotiate for land in the 14 cities in which the Homeless People's Federation of the Philippines is active.

All the federations are actively engaged in addressing their members' needs for better-quality, more secure housing with good provision for water, sanitation, and drainage. In many nations, their savings groups have designed and built hundreds of new housing units; in some, they have built tens of thousands of new units. In Thailand, local slum dweller savings group-led initiatives have built or upgraded homes and neighbourhoods for 400 000 people since 2003 (see Upgrading Informal Settlements). The South African Federation of the Urban Poor has built over 20 000 homes and is developing new ways to upgrade existing informal settlements. Many other federations in Africa have large new house-building programmes including the federations in Kenya, Malawi,

Table 1 Examples of the savings and work programmes of some of the urban poor federations (2008)

	Year[a]	Number of settlements where there is a process[b]	Active savers[c]	Savings[d]	Houses built	Tenure secured (number of families)
India	1986	5 000	130 000	US$1.2 million	6 000[e]	80 000
South Africa	1991	750	30 000	US$1.2 million	15 800	23 000
Thailand	1992	42 700	5 000 000	US$206 million	40 000	45 000
Namibia	1992	60	15 000	US$0.6 million	1 500	3 700
Cambodia	1993	288	11 300	US$145 000	2 798	5 000
The Philippines	1994	148	42 727	US$631 830	547	26 166
Zimbabwe	1995	62	45 000	NA	1 100	4 035
Nepal	1998	396	3 147	US$173 402	50	85
Sri Lanka	1998	130	21 506	US$29 469	50	120
Colombia	1999	1	60	US$10 000	–	60
Kenya	2000	100	40 000	US$50 000	110	5 600
Zambia	2002	45	14 000	US$18 000	66	1 048
Ghana	2003	15	12 000	–	–	120
Uganda	2003	4	500	US$2 000	–	300
Malawi	2004	100	20 000	US$50 000	750	3 050
Brazil	2005	5	100	US$4 000	–	7 000
Tanzania	2004	16	1 000	US$2 000	–	500

[a]The year in which significant savings scheme activity began, and, in some instances, this precedes the year when the federation was established.
[b]This is the most meaningful measure of the scale of each federation – the number of settlements where grass-roots activities are taking place to build collective capacity and catalyse grass-roots-led development.
[c]The second indicator of scale, the number of people who save regularly.
[d]Local currency values converted to US dollars.
[e]A further 30 000 households in India have got new housing not constructed by the federations.

and Namibia. In India, the National Slum Dwellers Federation and Mahila Milan (the federation of women slum and pavement dwellers' savings groups) have built thousands of homes and have built and managed community toilets and washing facilities that serve hundreds of thousands of slum dwellers.

The federations have developed a set of tools and methods through which to engage with the government. One of the most powerful of these is the 'slum' enumerations that they undertake. Any initiative to improve housing or provide or improve (say) piped water supplies or provision for sanitation and drainage needs a detailed map and information about all households living there. But it is rare for informal settlements to have been mapped and enumerated. The federations have developed a capacity to undertake these enumerations and the enumerators are mostly the women who manage savings groups. The data collected and the detailed maps with plot boundaries also belong to the federation – so as they negotiate with governments, they also produce and own the information base the government needs. Some federations have developed the capacity to undertake citywide surveys to gather basic data about all the informal settlements. Through this profiling of all informal settlements, they expand their membership and can engage with the agencies responsible for managing informal settlements within the local and/or national governments and develop programmes that consider needs in all such settlements.

Almost all the federations have a local NGO that works with them; most such NGOs were also important for supporting the formation and expansion of each federation. These have professional staff and manage negotiations with international agencies and help the federation members manage the structures that are set up to support the expansion in their work – for instance, the funds and the external support. However, these NGOs have learnt that it is the federations that should lead and set the pace of work.

Women-Centred Movements That Want to Work with the Government

Two characteristics make these grass-roots federations unusual. The first is that they actively offer government partnerships. These are mass movements but they do not form simply to protest and to make demands (although they may do this); rather, they seek to offer governments the knowledge, skills, and capacities of their members with the belief that only solutions driven by local communities will work for the urban poor. They also demonstrate to governments what they can do – and how much the scale and effectiveness of their work increases if the government works with them. This is particularly important in changing how politicians and civil servants see the urban poor and their organisations and informal settlements – so they see them as creating solutions, not as 'the problem'. The second is that women are in the majority in all the federations and have key leadership roles. The strength and tenacity of the women-managed savings groups and their active role in finding land sites over which to negotiate and in building housing allows them to negotiate more equal roles with men.

In many nations, local governments now work in partnership with the federations and support substantial house-building or upgrading programmes – for instance, the federations in South Africa, Namibia, Malawi, Zambia, and Kenya (and also developing in Uganda and Tanzania) and in India, Thailand, the Philippines, and Cambodia (and many other Asian nations). In Brazil, a federation has developed in Sao Paulo and this is generating interest among the urban poor in other cities in Brazil and other nations in the region.

Grass-Roots Organisations within Illegal Settlements

In almost all informal settlements, groups of residents work together to address some of their needs – for instance, forming local savings groups or parent associations supporting local schools or groups that help manage garbage collection (because there is no government service). But there are obvious limits to what they can do without government support – for instance, setting up and managing their own piped water supplies, sewers, schools, and health-care centres (although there are good examples of resident organisations that have done so). Resident organisations are often active negotiating with government agencies – for instance, to extend a piped water supply to their settlement or to collect household waste or to stop a plan to evict them.

What makes the national slum/shack dweller federations unusual is that they provide citywide and national organisations that increase their members' capacity to negotiate with the government when this negotiation is around the joint development of the city. The methodology was pioneered by two federations in India during the 1980s – the National Slum Dwellers Federation and the federation of women's savings groups (Mahila Milan) that formed a partnership with a local NGO, Society for the Promotion of Area Resource Centres (SPARC). The National Slum Dwellers Federation had been set up to fight against the bulldozing of the homes of their members and to lobby for services and for more secure tenure. Their strength came from their numbers, their capacity to mobilise mass protests, and, in some instances, their capacity to get support from the courts. But under the leadership of their founder, Jockin Arputham, and with the partnership they developed with Mahila Milan, this strategy changed. There was a recognition that demands made to state organisations have limited value, if these organisations were incapable of fulfilling them. Negotiations by a grass-roots organisation with the water agency for providing piped supplies have limited value if the agency has no funds for this or is prevented by law from doing so. There was also a recognition by the slum leaders that even large coalitions of the urban poor have limited capacity to effect pro-poor change if both bureaucrats and politicians view them as the problem, as opponents, as trouble-makers, or as 'illegals'.

The National Slum Dwellers Federation and Mahila Milan began to offer government (especially local government agencies) the knowledge, strengths, and capacities of their members. These are mass organisations, with hundreds of thousands of members. But instead of protesting, they demonstrated to government that they could build or upgrade housing and community toilets better than government agencies or the contractors they used. They could also prepare the detailed household data and maps needed to plan upgrading – no easy task in very crowded settlements with no clear plot boundaries and a complex mix of 'structure owners', tenants, and subtenants. This change in strategy led to government-supported programmes being undertaken by these two federations, supported by SPARC. These illustrate a scale of action that is far beyond what civil society organisations usually engage in and far beyond what government agencies would usually support.

This did not mean that the National Slum Dwellers Federation and Mahila Milan lost their capacity for independent action, or that they were co-opted by the state – as can be seen in the current struggles over how Dharavi, the large informal township within Mumbai, will be developed. This struggle illustrates how the homes and livelihoods of the urban poor are threatened by both state power and market power. The state is prevented from bulldozing Dharavi and transferring the land to developers by democratic pressures and checks, even if there are developers, advisors, and politicians for whom this is the preferred 'solution'. But what is at issue is the proportion of Dharavi's residents and enterprises that will be rehoused when Dharavi is redeveloped and what influence they will have over the form and location of this rehousing. Without collective organisation and alliances with other slum dwellers and other civil society groups, the residents of Dharavi would have little possibility of influencing this.

From Making Claims to Coproduction

The federations chose collaboration with government agencies (what is often termed coproduction) because of how little conventional democratic processes deliver for them, even if they do provide more scope for urban poor organisations to organise, to make claims, and to protest.

Even politicians with progressive social agendas often distrust the federations because they will not align with the politician's political party or mobilise votes for them. Or once elected, the politicians assume they have the mandate to make decisions.

Even when the state responds positively to the needs of the urban poor, the responses are often inappropriate to their needs. Where the state allocates considerable resources to urban poverty reduction – for instance, in housing subsidies or in building public toilets and washing facilities in informal settlements – if these are built and managed by government bodies or by contractors, these are often inappropriate or of poor quality, unless urban poor organisations can shape what is provided and how it is designed and managed. The government of South Africa has supported one of the world's largest and most generous subsidy programmes to support low-income households in getting their own housing, but much of what has been built has been inappropriate, because low-income households had little influence on what was built and where it was located. In this instance, urban poor organisations, including the South African Federation of the Urban Poor, were able to change the way a proportion of the subsidies were allocated with the creation of a subprogramme, the People's Housing Process, so that federation members within savings groups, not contractors, designed and built the homes. The quality and management of public toilets in 'slum' areas in many Indian cities also improved greatly when Mahila Milan groups were able to influence their location and took over their design, construction, and management.

Coproduction allows the federations to show politicians and civil servants their potential as partners. It extends participatory democracy by extending to urban poor groups not only the right to influence decisions about priorities and the allocation of resources but also the right to design, implement, and manage responses. Coproduction also allows the development of solutions (house designs, building materials, plot layouts, infrastructure standards) that bridge the gap between what works for the poor and the formal rules and regulations governing land use and building and infrastructure.

Coproduction means the agreement by the state that local groups (in this case local savings groups formed by slum/shack dwellers and their federations) can be directly involved in the implementation of state policies for housing and service provision. It is now recognised that grassroots groups may be involved in the planning, design, management, implementation, and/or evaluation of services that are broadly considered to be the responsibility of the state – but which can be provided more effectively and to a higher standard if citizens are actively involved in aspects of delivery.

Funding and the Urban Poor Fund International

Most of what the federations do is generated by their own energy, capacities, and savings and by what support they can negotiate locally – for instance, for land on which they can build or guarantees that their homes will not be bulldozed. External funding has proved useful in many instances, as long as it supports these federations' priorities and its disbursement and use can be managed by them. The urban poor funds, mentioned already, are an important component of this. These independent financial institutions are set up by each federation and provide loan capital to local savings schemes, enabling them to undertake initiatives to show how informal settlements can be improved. These include the construction of toilet blocks, reblocking, land acquisition, and/or incremental housing construction. These urban poor funds also help negotiations with the city authorities. With an autonomous fund, it is possible to reach agreements for community-led initiatives with government agencies. The urban poor funds also provide external funders with the transparency and accountability they require, while ensuring that decisions over funding are retained by the federations.

One important support for the work of these federations has been the setting up of their own international fund, the Urban Poor Fund International. This provides support direct to the national federations. This is done through their membership of the SDI and the regular meetings organised by SDI where the federations present their plans and decisions are made about funding allocations. This presently has around US$5 million a year; it was initiated in 2001 with a grant from the Sigrid Rausing Trust (and this trust provided support each year between then and 2009). It received additional support from other sources, including in 2007 substantial support from the Bill and Melinda Gates Foundation. SDI is now institutionalising this international fund to demonstrate the potential for linking external assistance with community-led initiatives. The fund has a board of governors with representation from ministers from Brazil, Sri Lanka, Uganda, Norway, Sweden, and South Africa.

See also: Housing Policies in Developing Countries: Sites-and-Services and Aided Self-Help; Upgrading Informal Settlements.

Further Reading

Appadurai A (2001) Deep democracy: Urban governmentality and the horizon of politics. *Environment and Urbanization* 13(2): 23–43.

Bebbington AJ, Hickey S and Mitlin D (eds.) (2007) *Can NGOs Make a Difference? The Challenge of Development Alternatives*, 370 pp. London: Zed Books.

Burra S, Patel S, and Kerr T (2003) Community-designed, built and managed toilet blocks in Indian cities. *Environment and Urbanization* 15(2): 11–32.

Castells M (1983) *The City and the Grassroots,* 450 pp. London: Edward Arnold.

Environment and Urbanization (2008) Special issue on City Governance and Citizen Action 20: 2, see especially Mitlin D, With and beyond the state: Co-production as a route to political influence, power and transformation for grassroots organizations, pp. 339–360, and Arputham J, Developing new approaches for people-centred development, pp. 319–337.

Hasan A (2007) The urban resource centre, Karachi. *Environment and Urbanization* 19(1): 275–292.

Manda MAZ (2007) Mchenga – Urban poor housing fund in Malawi. *Environment and Urbanization* 19(2): 337–359.

Mayo M (2005) *Global Citizens: Social Movements and the Challenge of Globalization,* 224 pp. Toronto, ON: Canadian Scholars Press.

Mitlin D and Satterthwaite D (eds.) (2004) *Empowering Squatter Citizen; Local Government, Civil Society and Urban Poverty Reduction*. London: Earthscan Publications. This includes chapters on government housing programmes that work with civil society in Thailand, the Philippines, Mexico, and Nicaragua and chapters on civil society-led housing initiatives in Pakistan, Brazil, South Africa, and India.

Peattie L (1990) Participation: A case study of how invaders organize, negotiate and interact with government in Lima, Peru. *Environment and Urbanization* 2(1): 19–30.

Stevens L, Coupe S, and Mitlin D (2006) *Confronting the Crisis in Urban Poverty; Making Integrated Approaches Work*, Urban Management Series. 257 pp. Rugby, UK: ITDG Publishing.

Relevant Websites

www.achr.net – Asian Coalition for Housing Rights.
www.hic-net.org – Habitat International Coalition.
www.sdinet.org – Slum/Shack Dwellers International.
www.cohre.org – Centre on Housing Rights and Evictions.

Climate Change

T Fawcett, University of Oxford, Oxford, UK

© 2012 Elsevier Ltd. All rights reserved.

Glossary

Carbon dioxide equivalent (CO₂e) Total greenhouse gas emissions are measured in CO₂e (CO₂ equivalent). It is obtained by aggregating non-CO₂ greenhouse gas flows with those of CO₂ using weights which reflect the respective contribution of each gas to the change in net radiation in the upper troposphere. The figures include all sources of emissions, both energy and nonenergy, so emissions from deforestation are included.

Carbon intensity The amount of carbon dioxide emitted per unit of energy use.

Final (or delivered) energy The energy supplied to the consumer in each end-use sector, which is ultimately converted into heat, light, motion, and other energy services. It does not include transformation and distribution losses.

Intergovernmental Panel on Climate Change (IPCC) This is an international body of scientists and other experts which was formed to provide information and advice on climate change, and its reports have become the standard works of reference on the subject.

Introduction

This article concerns the relationship between the housing sector and climate change. Firstly the evidence for climate change, its effects to date, possible future effects, and limits to atmospheric concentrations of carbon dioxide are outlined (see section 'Climate Change'). Then the housing sector's contribution to climate change through its use of fossil fuel energy is explained, and the role of different activities within homes explored (see section 'Housing Sector Contributions to Climate Change'). This is followed by a longer discussion of mitigation – the options for reducing carbon emissions from the sector, from new housing, renovation of existing housing, energy use in lights, appliances, and hot water, and the personal and social side of energy use (see section 'Mitigation – Reducing Carbon Emissions'). Adaptation of homes to meet the challenges of inevitable climate change, particularly increasing temperatures, is the next topic (see section 'Adaptation – Reducing the Risks from Climate Change'). Finally, the opportunities and challenges facing the housing sector in reducing its emissions by 80% by 2050 are discussed (see section 'Discussion and Conclusions').

Climate Change

Introduction

Climate change is one of the most important issues facing the world today. The science supporting the existence of climate change is clear, as the Intergovernmental Panel on Climate Change (IPCC) in its Fourth Assessment Report in 2007 stated:

> Warming of the climate system is unequivocal, as is now evident from observations of increases in global average air and ocean temperatures, widespread melting of snow and ice, and rising global average sea level.

It is equally clear that wide-ranging changes in the climate have been caused by human actions, as the IPCC states:

> Most of the observed increase in globally averaged temperatures since the mid-20th century is *very likely* [i.e. with certainty greater than 90%] due to the observed increase in anthropogenic greenhouse gas concentrations.

This section explains briefly the science of climate change and why the climate is changing, presents data on how the climate is changing, looks at future scenarios, and describes future targets for greenhouse gas emissions reductions.

Why is the Climate Changing?

The climate is changing because the natural mechanism known as the 'greenhouse effect' which acts to warm the earth is being increased by human-induced emissions of greenhouse gases. The primary cause is use of fossil fuel energy (coal, oil, and gas), which releases carbon dioxide when burnt. Over the past several centuries, tropical deforestation and, to a lesser extent, other land use changes around the world have contributed to one-fifth of anthropogenic carbon dioxide emissions. In addition to carbon dioxide, there are five other important greenhouse gases: methane, nitrous oxide, hydrofluorocarbons, perfluorocarbons, and sulphur hexafluoride, of which the first two are most significant. Globally, carbon dioxide contributes to more than two-thirds of the warming and is generally a higher proportion of developed country emissions; for example, it accounts for five-sixths of US emissions of greenhouse gases. This article focuses on carbon dioxide emissions from fossil fuel burning as the largest single cause of climate change and that most closely linked to the housing sector.

Concentrations of carbon dioxide in the atmosphere are increasing, and have been doing so since the Industrial Revolution. They have increased from 280 parts per million (ppm) in 1750 to 387 ppm in 2009, a rise of more than a third. The increase since 1959 as measured at Mauna Loa in Hawaii (the meteorological station with the longest continuous recording of atmospheric carbon dioxide concentrations available in the world) is shown in **Figure 1**.

The carbon dioxide emissions leading to these concentrations can be seen in **Figure 2**. They show dramatic and accelerating growth, as the carbon deposits laid down over millions of years as fossil fuels are released into the atmosphere. Half the total emissions since 1850 have occurred since the mid-1970s. Annual emissions have doubled since the mid-1960s and trebled since the mid-1950s – a tripling in less than 50 years.

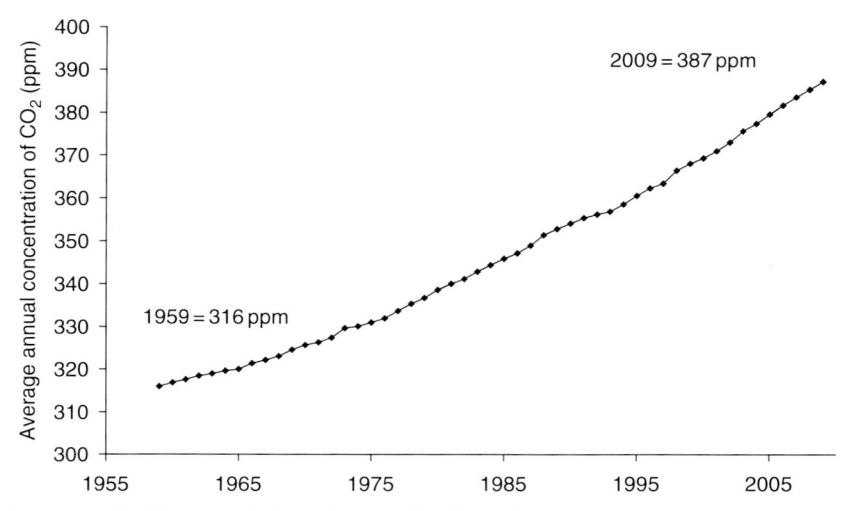

Figure 1 Atmospheric carbon dioxide concentrations since 1959, Mauna Loa.
Data from Tans P (2009) Atmospheric CO_2 samples. Mauna Loa, Hawaii: NOAA/ESRL. www.esrl.noaa.gov/gmd/ccgg/trends

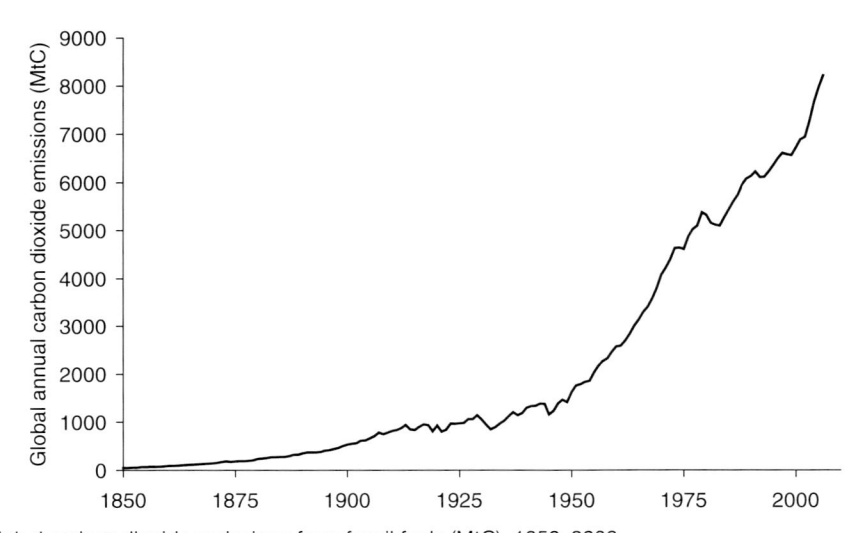

Figure 2 Annual global carbon dioxide emissions from fossil fuels (MtC), 1850–2006.
Data from Boden T, Marland G, and Andres RJ (2009) Global, regional and national fossil-fuel CO_2 emissions. In: *Trends: A Compendium of Data on Global Change. Carbon Dioxide Information Analysis Centre*. Oak Ridge, TN: Oak Ridge National Laboratory, US Department of Energy.

Table 1 Carbon dioxide from fossil fuel burning, emissions per capita, 2006

Country	Per capita emissions (tCO$_2$/person/year)
United States	5.18
Australia	4.90
Japan	2.80
Germany	2.67
United Kingdom	2.56
France	1.71
China	1.27
India	0.37
Bangladesh	0.08
Western Europe average	2.14
Global average	1.25

Data from Boden T, Marland G, and Andres RJ (2009) Global, regional and national fossil fuel CO$_2$ emissions. In: *Trends: A compendium of data on global change. Carbon Dioxide Information Analysis Centre.* Oak Ridge, TN: Oak Ridge National Laboratory, US Department of Energy.

Emissions per capita from fossil fuel burning vary widely across the world (**Table 1**). The United States is near the top of the league, with emissions 4 times the world average, and more than twice those of the average European. By contrast, Indians emit just over a quarter of the global average and Bangladeshis less than one-tenth.

At the start of the twenty-first century, emissions from North America (United States and Canada) made up over a quarter of the total, and those from Western Europe accounted for about one-tenth. In 2006, China, with its population of 1.3 billion, overtook the United States as the single biggest carbon emitter for the first time.

How is the Climate Changing?

Global temperature has risen by 0.7 °C in the 100 years 1906–2005, with land regions warming faster than oceans, and greater temperature increases at northern latitudes. **Figure 3** shows how global average surface temperature (over sea and land) has risen from 1850 to the present day. The data are set out in terms of the 'anomaly', that is the difference between each year and the average temperature in the period 1961–90. Before 1978, it was generally colder than the 1961–90 average, with all later years being warmer. Fourteen of the fifteen warmest years in the series have occurred in the past 15 years (1995–2009).

The climate system is driven by energy from the sun. Rising temperatures increase the amount of energy in the system and this has knock-on effects on many other aspects of climate. As a result of increasing temperatures, climate models predict changes in rainfall amounts and patterns, and increased occurrence of storms, heat waves, and other extreme events. Some of these expected changes can already be seen around the world. For example, in the United States, there is strong evidence of changing rainfall patterns over the last century. The well-known variability of the climate can make it difficult to be confident that individual extreme events, such as Hurricane Katrina which caused huge damage in New Orleans in 2005, are unusual and are specifically caused by climate change. However, as Mike Hulme, a leading British climate scientist, has said: "There is no longer such a thing as a purely natural weather event."

Climate change is now wide-ranging in its impacts. Higher temperatures have already had a measurable effect on land glaciers and sea ice. Mountain glaciers have been shrinking in almost all areas of the world. There has been a substantial thinning of Arctic sea ice in late summer: in August 2000, there was no ice at the North Pole – it was in a stretch of open water. The Greenland ice sheet has recently been found to be melting at a higher than expected rate. Other effects on the physical environment include rising sea levels, due to

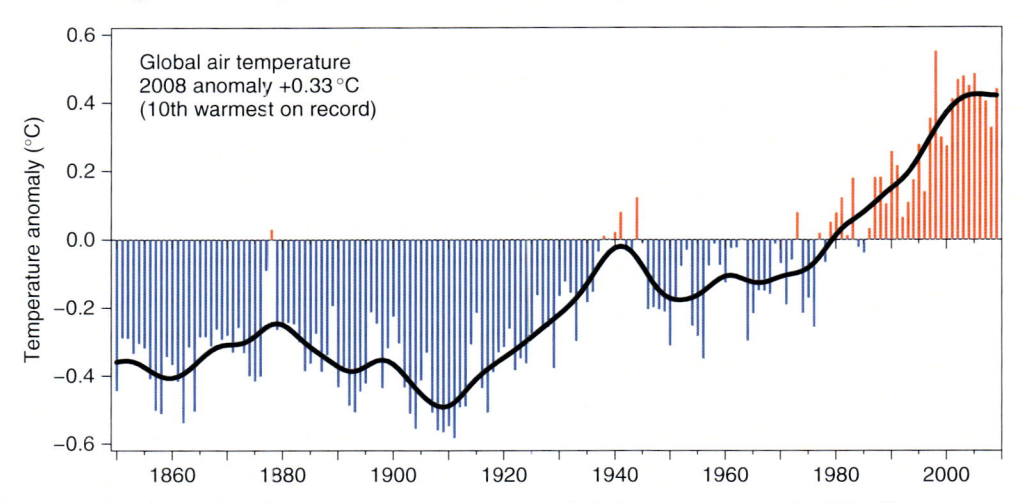

Figure 3 Changes in global average surface air temperature compared with the long-term average for 1961–90. Reproduced with permission from Jones P (2010) Global temperature record, Climatic Research Unit, University of East Anglia. www.cru.uea.ac.uk/cru/info/warming

both the expansion of warmer water in the oceans and the additional water produced by the melting land glaciers. Climate change is also leading to changes in the seasonal behaviour and geographical location of fauna and flora, with spring arriving early in many countries.

The Future Effects of Climate Change

What happens next with climate change depends on both the developing reaction of global ecosystems to the gases already emitted and the extent to which more carbon dioxide and other greenhouse gases are released into the atmosphere. Climate change does not have an instantaneous 'off-switch': its effects cannot quickly be reversed by reducing or even eliminating future emissions of greenhouse gases. This is for two reasons. Firstly, greenhouse gases stay in the atmosphere for long periods – hundreds of years in the case of carbon dioxide. Even if no additional carbon dioxide were emitted from now on, atmospheric concentrations would take centuries to decline to pre-Industrial Revolution levels. Secondly, the planet reacts to changes in temperature over a long timescale. Global increases in mean surface temperature, rising sea levels from thermal expansion of the ocean, and melting ice sheets are projected to continue for hundreds of years, in response to greenhouse gases already emitted. Even if all emissions of greenhouse gases ceased tomorrow, the climate would continue to change.

The IPCC's Fourth Assessment Report projection is that the world's temperature is likely to increase by 1.1–6.4 °C by the end of the century, relative to 1980–99, depending on which greenhouse gas emission scenario is realised. This average global temperature change will be unequally distributed and is expected to be greatest over land and at most high northern latitudes. A cautious projection of 'business as usual' trends suggests emissions concentrations of carbon dioxide and all other greenhouse gases could reach 750 ppm CO_2e by the end of the century. This would give around a 50% chance of temperature rise in the first half of the next century of more than 5 °C relative to 1850. Five degrees is the same temperature difference as there was between today and the previous Ice Age.

The likely effects on humans and the natural environment of the scenarios based on high emissions range from the death of coral reefs to the creation of millions of environmental refugees. Many countries will be under threat from rising sea levels, drought, storms, heat waves, and extreme economic and social disruption. Sea levels are predicted to rise by up to a metre over the next century, leading to heavily populated delta areas of the world such as those in Bangladesh and China becoming submerged.

Reduction Targets

The international community has agreed the world should achieve "stabilization of greenhouse gas concentrations in the atmosphere at a level that would prevent dangerous human-induced interference with the climate system" (via the 1992 UN Framework Convention on Climate Change). However, there is no legal definition of what might constitute 'dangerous'. A general scientific consensus is emerging around 2 °C as the maximum temperature rise required to avoid dangerous climate change. This is thought to be equivalent to atmospheric concentrations of 450 ppm CO_2 equivalent (a figure which includes all greenhouse gases, not just carbon dioxide). The problem is that atmospheric concentrations have already reached 430 ppm CO_2e and emissions are rising at a rate of 2.5 ppm CO_2e per year. The IPCC has calculated that in order to stabilise concentrations at 450 ppm CO_2e, developed country emissions would have to be reduced 25–40% from 1990 levels by 2020 (and by 80–95% by 2050). Developing country emissions would also need to be reduced. Given the difficulty of not breaching the 450 ppm CO_2e limit, it is suggested that emissions concentrations should be allowed to rise to 500 ppm CO_2e and then reduce to 400 ppm CO_2e. This would risk average global temperature rising by more than 2 °C.

While many developed countries (but not the United States) have agreed reduction targets under the Kyoto Protocol, these are generally modest, with the target over all signatory countries being a 5% reduction in greenhouse gas emission over 20 years. More significantly, countries have been adopting more ambitious mid- and long-term emissions reductions goals. For example, the United Kingdom has recently adopted a legally binding target of an 80% reduction in national greenhouse gas emissions by 2050, and a reduction of 26% of carbon dioxide by 2020, compared with a 1990 baseline. Germany has set a more challenging target of reducing emissions by 40% by 2020 compared with 1990. Many American states have their own reduction targets and nationally legislation is being proposed to reduce carbon emissions by 17% by 2020 compared with 2005 levels, but this has not yet been passed. These targets are hugely challenging, but, unlike the Kyoto targets, begin to respond appropriately to the scale of the problem. A global agreement incorporating developing as well as developed countries has yet to be achieved, despite high hopes for negotiations in Copenhagen during 2009.

Housing Sector Contributions to Climate Change

Introduction

By far the most significant contribution made by the residential sector to greenhouse gas emissions comes in the form of carbon dioxide emissions from fossil fuel energy use. Energy used within the sector for heating, cooling, lighting, cooking, and in appliances is 15–30% of national energy use in most developed countries. Within the EU-27 countries, an average of 27% of total delivered energy was used by the residential sector in 2006; in the United States the comparable figure in 2008 was 15% (resulting in 21% of national CO_2 emissions). Globally, household energy consumption accounted for 28% of final energy consumption in 2006 and 20% of carbon dioxide emissions.

Housing is also responsible for other environmental impacts. In addition to the energy used within homes, additional energy and carbon dioxide emissions are linked to the materials used for construction, repair, and renovation of homes. Figures are very uncertain, with studies differing by a factor of 10 on the energy embodied in a typical house. What is certain is that daily energy use is by far the most significant contributor to climate change over the lifetime of an average house. Clearly there are many environmental impacts of housing beyond its contribution to climate change, including loss of biodiversity and stored carbon due to land use change, increasing use of water, and exploitation of other natural resources. In developing countries, the use of unsustainable biomass for cooking and heating leads to problems including deforestation, increased soil erosion, and impacts on water resources. However, this article concentrates on the contribution to climate change of energy use in housing.

Energy Use and Carbon Emissions from Housing

Energy use within the home can be split into a number of major categories: space heating, space cooling (air conditioning and other methods), water heating, cooking, and lights and appliances. Figures from the United Kingdom, the United States, and Australia show average patterns of energy use in households (**Figure 4**). They demonstrate that in the United Kingdom and the United States energy use significantly influenced by the building shell – space heating and cooling – is responsible for more than half of household energy demand, and for just over 40% in Australia. The US national figures hide significant regional variations from the colder north where space heating is the dominant use, to the warmer south where cooling is more significant. Space heating is the largest component of household energy use in most developed countries, including all EU member states (except Malta). Other uses of energy, for water heating, cooking, and lights and appliances, are not generally related to the building structure, but rather depend on the technologies used to deliver these services, usage patterns, and ownership levels of energy-using equipment.

The amount of energy used per capita in the residential sector varies between countries. The Canadians, Americans, and Finns, at the top of the developed country league, use nearly 3 times as much per person as the Japanese, Spanish, and New Zealanders. Even when climate corrections are applied to the figures, differences remain, with average American energy use still being

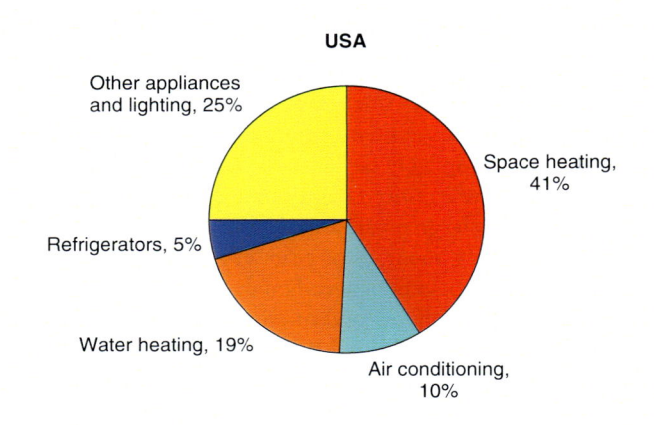

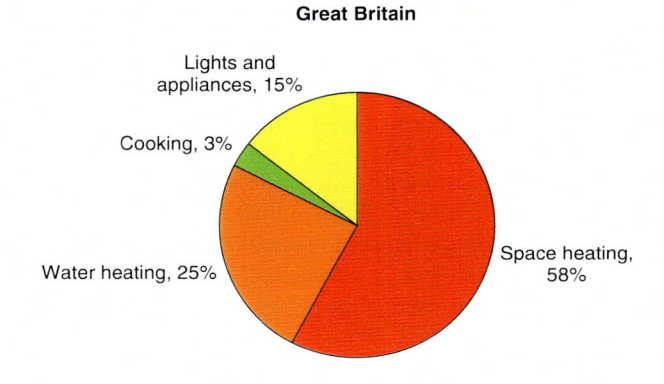

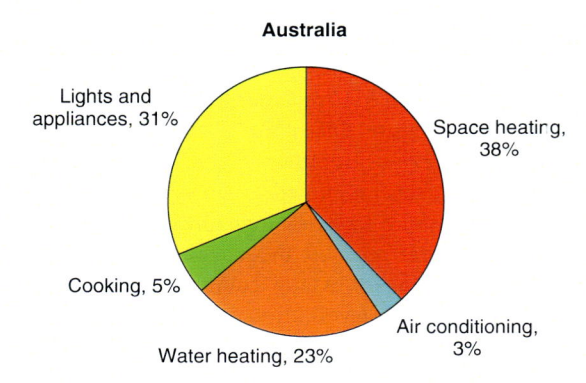

Figure 4 Percentage of delivered household energy use by end-use, USA (2005), Great Britain (2006), and Australia (2007). Data from EIA (2009) Residential energy survey 2005 Energy Information Administration, USA. www.eia.doe.gov/emeu/recs Utley JI and Shorrock L (2008) Domestic energy fact file 2008. Watford, UK: BRE, Energy Efficient Strategies (2008) Energy use in the Australian residential sector, 1986–2020. Canberra, ACT: Department of the Environment, Water, Heritage and the Arts.

two-and-a-half times those of a New Zealander, although countries such as Canada, Finland, and Sweden move from being near the top of the league to near average levels. Part of the explanation for this is that house size also varies considerably between countries. The average American home at 150–200 m^2 (depending on definitions used) is at least twice the size of the average dwelling in most European countries (80–100 m^2). Larger homes require more energy to provide heating, air conditioning, and lighting, and they tend to include more energy-using appliances, such as televisions and laundry equipment.

Energy use in housing is determined by a range of interrelated social, technological, geographical, demographic, and economic factors. These factors include: the thermal properties and air-tightness of the building, dwelling size, the types and quantities of energy-using equipment installed (e.g., how many TVs, what kind of heating system and fuels), the efficiency of the energy-using equipment, number of households, the number of residents per household, their patterns of occupying the house, the way in which they use their heating and cooling systems, lights and appliances, the climate, the cost of energy, and household income. In turn, these factors are linked to wider developments in society, such as the availability, social desirability, and cost of energy-using technologies, government energy and housing policy, and social norms around thermal comfort and personal cleanliness.

The relationship of carbon emissions to energy use depends on the fuels used to supply demand for energy. In most developed countries, fossil fuels provide the majority of energy used in the housing sector. Coal is the most carbon-intensive fossil fuel (i.e., its use results in more carbon dioxide per unit of energy), followed by oil and then natural gas. Nuclear, biomass, and renewable energy are low or zero carbon sources. Dominant fuels used for heating and electricity generation vary from country to country; for example, in the European Union access to a natural gas network (for heating energy) varies from around 10% of the population in Finland and Sweden, to almost 90% in the United Kingdom, the Netherlands, and Hungary. In most countries, electricity is more carbon intensive than the most common heating fuels (gas and oil) – although this is not true where nuclear or renewable energy dominates electricity generation, as is the case in France and Sweden for example.

Changing Patterns of Energy Use and Emissions

In general, energy use within the household sector has been rising since the 1970s. While there have been significant increases in energy efficiency of both the building shell and the energy-using equipment within it since that time, these have been offset by increasing household numbers due to both population increase and falling household size, strongly growing use of electricity for appliances, rising standards of thermal comfort (both heating and cooling), additional hot water use, and, in some countries, the increasing size of the average dwelling. While the rate of growth of energy use has not been as high as in some other sectors – most notably transport – it is nevertheless sobering that during a time of great improvements to energy efficiency, energy use has continued to rise. In countries whose fuel use mix has changed towards lower carbon sources, this increase in energy use may not have been matched by a rise in emissions. However, more generally, carbon dioxide emissions from the sector have also been rising.

In a 'business as usual' future, energy use in the sector would be expected to continue to grow. In several countries, energy use per household has now levelled out and has even begun to fall, driven primarily by energy efficiency improvements. However, the expectation of increasing household numbers means energy use in this sector is not guaranteed to fall even with increasing efficiency gains. As global temperatures rise, demand for space heating energy should fall at some point, but this may be replaced by increasing demand for space cooling. The possibility of a different, more positive, future for housing is discussed in the following section.

Mitigation – Reducing Carbon Emissions

Introduction

Energy use in housing is determined by a complex mix of factors, as described earlier. To outline the major opportunities for reducing energy use and carbon emissions from this sector, it is helpful to simplify the problem by splitting it into distinct parts: (1) new housing (see section 'New Build'), (2) existing housing (see section 'Upgrading the Existing Housing Stock'), (3) energy used in lights, appliances, and water heating (see section 'Lights, Appliances, and Water Heating'), and (4) people and social issues (see section 'Focusing on People'). While more attention is generally paid to innovative new housing, low-carbon refurbishment of existing housing is much more important in terms of the potential for reducing emissions. This is for two reasons: firstly most of the housing that will be used in 2050 has already been built (current housing will make up 80% of the United Kingdom's 2050 housing stock for instance) and secondly, new homes already use less energy than old homes. Finally, this section will conclude with examples of future visions for a low-energy housing sector (see section 'Visions for the Future').

New Build

Interest in low-energy housing began in the 1970s in response to the energy crises and consequent energy price rises. A number of different design philosophies were experimented with, including passive solar design, active solar design, super-insulation, thermally massive construction, use of renewable energy, and reducing energy demand from lights and appliances. Interest in developing low-energy homes fell away in the 1980s with that decade's lower energy prices. However, over recent years there has been much increased activity. Many of the design elements developed in the 1970s are being used in modern low-energy homes, in various combinations, with an additional focus on air-tightness (see Case Study 1). No new 'wonder' technology has developed since the 1970s, but prices of many technologies and building elements have fallen and performance has increased.

In developed countries, the importance of improving the efficiency of new homes is recognised and enforced through various legal mechanisms. In countries with widely varying climates, standards of construction may be set locally or regionally; in smaller countries, national standards apply. These standards are periodically reviewed and upgraded (see article Building Regulations for Energy Conservation). In the United Kingdom national minimum standards are set primarily through building regulations which define the minimum standard of heat loss in new buildings and major conversions (energy-using equipment is separately regulated). From 2016 onwards, the plan is that all new UK homes will have close to zero heating demand. This can be achieved, based on a combination of current technologies such as highly insulated walls, floors, and roofs; building air-tight dwellings with appropriate ventilation; maximum use of passive solar energy; highly efficient windows; passive cooling design; and installation of solar water heaters, solar PV, heat pumps, micro-CHP, and other micro-generation options.

With new homes, there is also the opportunity to consider whether larger scale issues – beyond the individual home – could significantly influence energy demand. Key approaches which might reduce carbon emissions for new housing schemes are optimum built form and community scale energy provision (see articles Sustainable Urban Development, Community Energy Systems). The built form of a property can have a significant effect on its heating energy use. A new detached home can use twice as much heating energy per square metre as a flat and 30% more than a mid-terrace (mid-row) house whose building

---

Case Study 1: Passive Houses (Passivhaus)

'Passive houses' are so named because the passive heat inputs – delivered externally by solar irradiation through the windows and provided internally by the heat emissions of appliances and occupants – essentially suffice to keep the building at comfortable indoor temperatures throughout the heating period. It is also part of the passive house philosophy that efficient technologies are used to minimise the other sources of energy consumption in the building, notably electricity for household appliances. The overall energy demand in a passive house is lower by at least a factor of 4 than the specific consumption levels of new buildings designed to the standards presently applicable across Europe (see the table below for passive house standards).

Passive house standard requirements

Area	Requirements
Space heating requirement	The building must not use more than 15 kWh m^{-2} per year
Air-tightness	With building depressurised to 50 Pa below atmospheric pressure by a blower door, the building must not leak more air than 0.6 times the house volume per hour
Total primary energy consumption	Primary energy for heating, hot water, and electricity must be less than 120 kWh m^{-2} per year

These high standards are achieved by improving the building envelope to a point where a central heating system becomes unnecessary, through a combination of eliminating all thermal bridging in construction, very high insulation standards, compact designs to minimise exterior surface area, and extremely air-tight construction with tiny heating systems integrated into the ventilation air distribution system.

By the end of 2007, there were more than 4000 residential units completed in Austria. Around 4% of all new residential buildings in Austria were constructed to the passive house standard in 2006. In the province of Vorarlberg, nearly 14% of new houses built in 2007 were to passive house standard. Since 2007 in Vorarlberg the passive house standard has been obligatory for social housing projects. Presently, Austria has the greatest number of passive houses on a per capita basis. In addition, it is estimated that more than 10 000 passive houses have been built in Germany, where the concept was originally developed, and 1500 in Sweden and Norway. Work is under way to extend the passive house concept and specifications to meet the need to reduce cooling demand in warmer countries.

Researchers have concluded that the development and diffusion of passive houses has not been simply a process of technological improvement and optimisation of construction processes but has been profoundly embedded in social and cultural contexts. Therefore, expanding the success of the passive house approach beyond a small number of European countries will take careful thought.

elements have the same heat loss standards. Community level combined heat and power (CHP)/district heating systems can result in lower emissions for electricity and heating than conventional single home systems, particularly if low-carbon biomass fuel is used. However, because of the social and functional differences between built forms, it is likely to be difficult to move towards more efficient forms for much of the housing market. In addition, the advantages of CHP may become less relevant as the heat demand in new housing progressively reduces. In conclusion, although optimum design of issues beyond the scale of the individual dwelling can contribute to energy and emissions reduction, the properties of individual dwellings remain key.

In addition to gradually increasing standards of new buildings, most countries have examples of pioneering demonstration low-energy/low-carbon homes, which may be funded by the government or built by private individuals (see article Eco-Communities). In some countries, including the United States and the United Kingdom, the number of such homes is very low in comparison with the total housing stock. In others, most notably Austria and Germany, these are becoming a significant sector of the market, as explained in Case Study 1. Exemplar homes have an importance much beyond their own energy and carbon savings. By demonstrating what is possible they can drive up standards nationally and internationally.

Upgrading the Existing Housing Stock

Achieving very low energy and carbon emissions standards is much more challenging for the existing housing stock than for new build. This is for technical, economic, and social reasons. The existing stock comes from a variety of eras, with different standards and methods of construction, which afford various degrees of upgrading. There are technical limitations on upgrading individual elements of many buildings, and in treating the building as a whole. Geographical orientation, which is important in maximising use of passive solar energy, is fixed. The costs of renovation to meet a given standard are higher, often prohibitively higher, than meeting the same standard in a new home. The policy and regulatory environment for low-energy renovation is very underdeveloped, for example, in contrast with new housing; there are no energy standards for refurbishment in the United Kingdom. In addition, the way in which renovation is undertaken is much more complex than raising construction standards for new homes. Low-carbon renovation relies on the individual decisions of millions of householders and thousands of landlords. It can involve considerable disruption (as well as expense), change to the aesthetics of a building, commitment to environmental improvement on behalf of the owner, and relies on a set of skills few builders or firms currently possess (see article Eco-Renovation).

Reducing heat loss (or gain) to a moderate degree in existing buildings is not necessarily technically challenging. Adding additional loft insulation and filling cavity walls is usually both straightforward and cost-effective, and in combination would be expected to reduce heating energy needs by a quarter or more. However, adapting an older building to become truly low energy, so that its carbon emissions reduce by 60–80% is much more difficult. Reaching this standard is likely to require a comprehensive and highly skilled approach which would include much improved air-tightness, greatly increased insulation standards for floors, walls, roofs, and windows, installation of low-carbon energy sources such as solar water heating, low-energy lights and appliances, and an efficient heating system with good controls. The standard which renovation needs to meet to qualify as an 'old home superhome' in the United Kingdom is a reduction in carbon emissions of 60%. Thus far fewer than 100 renovated homes have registered as meeting this requirement. While ambitious voluntary standards for refurbishment exist in Germany, Switzerland, and France, relatively few renovation projects are undertaken to these high standards each year. However, Case Study 2 suggests that exemplar eco-renovated homes can influence and inspire the wider public, despite their low number.

There are reasons to be cautious about how effective renovation is in practice. Research on efficiency measures installed in more than a thousand English homes showed actual space heating savings of 10–17%, compared with the theoretically predicted levels of 45–49% (where 'comfort taking' in the form of increased internal temperatures had already been accounted for). This discrepancy is thought to be due in part to the incomplete insulation of properties because, in practice, it is difficult to insulate 100% of the exterior wall and roof when insulation work is carried out as a retrofit measure. The great difference between modelled and monitored energy saving strongly suggests the need for further empirical research to assess the impact of energy-efficient improvements to dwellings. Levels of insulation may need to increase, and workmanship improve, if significant savings are to be achieved in real life.

Renovation of an existing home to a low-carbon standard is usually considerably more expensive than reaching a similar standard in new housing. Some types of insulation, including under-floor insulation and internal wall insulation, require considerable disruption to the existing house, which then has to be made good. Solid walls – which are present in pre-1930s UK housing – are expensive and time-consuming to insulate. Replacing windows with double- or triple-glazed options can be costly in older homes with period designs. Adding solar water heating requires scaffolding and usually a change of hot water tank and plumbing – neither of which would be required if installed in a new build. In addition, there are

> **Case Study 2: Leading by Example: Eco-Renovation Networks**
>
> In the United Kingdom there are relatively few examples of comprehensive low-carbon refurbishment projects. However, interest in this area is growing and new networks to promote existing examples are being developed. One such network operates in Oxfordshire, a central English county. The key activity is an annual 'open weekend' where eco-homes are opened to the public. This event is very successful, with thousands of people visiting the homes and learning from the owners and volunteer demonstrators what work has been undertaken and how effective it has been. The open homes events are backed up by website information, green homes trade fairs, eco-renovation clubs, information exchange events for builders, and other initiatives.
>
> Visitors enjoying an open day at an eco-renovation. Source: COIN & ClimateXchange
>
> There are a number of these networks throughout the United Kingdom. They all use the experience and enthusiasm of individual homeowners to inspire and inform the wider public about the opportunities for eco-renovation. While such activities can feel too small scale to influence the national scene, it may be that a bottom-up, community-led movement is exactly what is necessary to begin the transition to widespread low-carbon renovation.

few economies of scale. While social or private landlords may be able to access economies of scale if their stock is uniform, in privately owned housing each low-carbon renovation is a one-off job.

At present, low-carbon renovation, or 'eco-renovation' as it is often called, is a niche activity, undertaken by small operators. The industry carrying out eco-renovations is very much more decentralised and disaggregated than the house-building sector as a whole. Operators in this sector need a flexible portfolio of skills, as each house is different. One of the key findings of research in this area is that a massively improved skills base would be required before large-scale low-carbon upgrading work could be undertaken.

Lights, Appliances, and Water Heating

As highlighted in the section 'Housing Sector Contributions to Climate Change', in some countries over half the energy used in the housing sector is used in lights, appliances, and water-heating – end-uses which are not connected to the standard of construction or the age of the dwelling. Within the European Union, lighting and appliances – as traded goods – are subject to a range of policies including minimum efficiency standards and product labels, which apply equally in all 27 countries. In addition, at national level a range of subsidies, consumer information, innovation support, and R&D policies have been applied to many of these products. This is also true in the United States, Japan, Australia, and other developed countries, which have adopted a similar philosophy of 'market transformation', that is permanently transforming the product markets towards greater efficiency through the use of an integrated suite of policies. Despite the efforts made in this area over several decades, and significant improvements in the efficiency of many appliances, electricity use in lights and appliances is generally rising. This is largely explained by the expansion of uses for electricity, for example for entertainment and ICT equipment, increasingly high levels of product ownership, and expanding household numbers, none of which product-level market transformation policy seeks to address. Demand for hot water is also rising in many countries, driven by higher water use technologies, such as 'power showers', and changing standards of personal hygiene and cleanliness. Improving current strategies and developing new approaches to reducing energy use in these specific areas is of great importance for the housing sector; however, this is not the major focus of this article.

Focusing on People

The earlier focus on new and existing buildings may have seemed to imply that it is the buildings which use energy. In reality it is the interactions between people (seeking to live comfortable and socially normal lives within their homes), buildings, and energy-using technologies that result in energy use. The energy sources used combine with this to determine carbon emissions. The housing sector and elements within it such as the central heating system have been conceptualised as a 'sociotechnical' system. This concept stresses the interactions and interdependencies of social and technical features of a system of social provision. Accepting this description of the housing sector, reducing energy use and carbon emissions is not just a matter of altering the housing and energy-using technologies; it also requires changes in individuals, communities, and wider society, and in their relationships with their homes.

While most policy to reduce emissions from this sector is focused on changing buildings, there is some effort put into changing personal behaviour (see article Policies to Promote the Environmental Efficiency of Housing). In order to encourage behaviour change, people are appealed to in their role as:

- Economic actors – policies such as carbon and energy taxation, subsidies, loans, and other financial incentives are used to persuade people to cut down on energy use and invest in energy-saving measures in order to save money.
- Consumers/purchasers – the EU energy label and US Energy Star label are examples of using information (and other market transformation policies) to persuade/enable consumers to make more energy-efficient choices.
- Energy users – Feedback on energy use, smart meters, comparisons with peers are methods used to enable people to better understand and control their use of energy.
- Individuals lacking information – Energy advice services and public information campaigns run on the 'information deficit' model, assuming that if people understand what they can do to reduce their energy use and costs, they are more likely to go ahead and make those changes.

A new policy within the EU which gives people information on the efficiency of homes (Case Study 3) could appeal to people in several of these roles.

While governments and other agencies are using increasingly sophisticated communication techniques to engage with individuals, using findings from segmentation studies and social marketing tools, the understanding of an individual's relationship with his/her household energy use still seems rather limited. People are more than economic actors and consumers. They are also members of communities, citizens with responsibility for their own carbon emissions, have an emotional investment in their homes, and care about the long-term future of the planet. These perspectives, as well as a fuller appreciation of the sociotechnical nature of the housing system, could open up new opportunities for involving individuals more fully in reducing household carbon emissions.

Visions for the Future

Despite the many challenges posed in significantly reducing carbon emissions from the housing stock, there are a number of studies which demonstrate how savings of 80% or more from the sector could be achieved by 2050. The common element across various studies is the strong focus on energy efficiency improvements (using many of the techniques and technologies mentioned earlier). Some studies include elements of demand reduction (e.g., a decrease in winter heating temperatures), whereas others incorporate current or increasing energy service demands. What often differs across studies is the degree to which it is assumed the electricity grid has been 'decarbonised' and therefore which energy sources and technologies are used to provide heating, cooling, and hot water. The less optimistic authors are about the future carbon intensity of electricity, the more household-level renewable technology they assume is needed to achieve sufficient savings. Generally, it is not the technology needed to reach targets that is seen as most challenging, rather it is the social, political, and economic changes required.

Adaptation – Reducing the Risks from Climate Change

Introduction

Adaptation to climate change is sometimes seen as being in competition with mitigation efforts. However, the truth is that it is complementary to mitigation, and just as necessary. Regardless of future cuts in emissions, the world is already committed to at least 1.5 °C of additional warming due to carbon dioxide and other anthropogenic greenhouse gases already in the atmosphere. Along with increased temperatures, scientists are certain there will also be accompanying sea level rises and increases in heat waves and floods.

Case Study 3: Making Efficiency Visible: European Home Energy Labels

The implementation of the EU Energy Performance of Buildings Directive in the United Kingdom has resulted in the development of home energy labels, known as Energy Performance Certificates (EPCs). The British EPC mirrors the EU Energy Label for lights and appliances; it has categories A–G and has been a requirement on sale of all domestic property since December 2007.

This home's performance is rated in terms of the energy use per square metre of floor area, energy efficiency based on fuel costs and environmental impact based on carbon dioxide (CO_2) emissions.

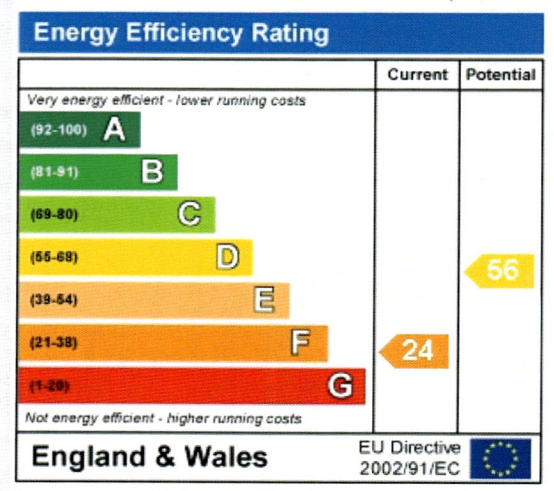

The energy efficiency rating is a measure of the overall efficiency of a home. The higher the rating the more energy efficient the home is and the lower the fuel bills will be.

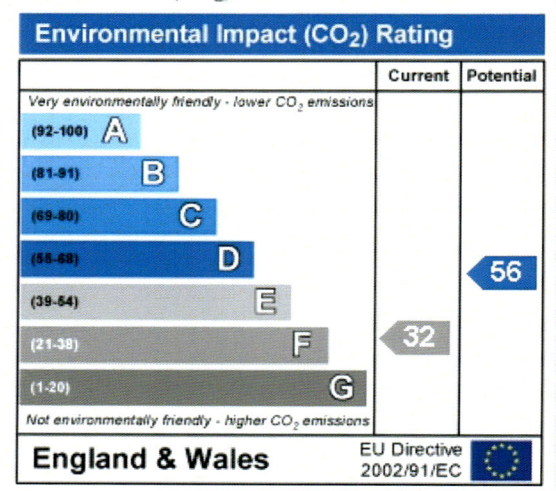

The environmental impact rating is a measure of a home's impact on the environment in terms of carbon dioxide (CO_2) emissions. The higher the rating the less impact it has on the environment.

Energy Performance Certificate as used in England and Wales.

The scale is from 1 to 100, with 100 being the best. This uses the United Kingdom's 'Standard Assessment Procedure' (SAP) and reflects the energy costs of providing space and water heating and fixed lighting. It does not include energy use in appliances and moveable lighting, which can change with ownership/tenancy. The carbon emissions that result from this use are shown besides the energy efficiency rating. For both energy efficiency and carbon emissions a 'potential' rating is also given, which is based on adoption of 'cost-effective' energy efficiency and low and zero carbon micro-generation measures. In addition to the label, the full EPC report contains further information on estimated energy costs, current building performance, and the potential for efficiency improvements. The certificates have to be provided by the building owner to the new occupant whenever a building is sold or rented. In all cases, the label is based on a theoretical calculation – for instance, what would be required to achieve a defined internal temperature – rather than reflecting the bills and unknown lifestyle of the occupants.

Across the EU, it is hoped that these energy labels can be an important step in the low-carbon transformation of the housing stock. By providing information on the energy performance of homes, this characteristic can be reflected in the cost (purchase or rental) for the first time. In addition, the whole suite of market transformation policies – regulation, subsidies, information, advice – can be implemented systematically based on the actual efficiency of individual properties. However, experience shows that the market transformation policy approach has worked best in the presence of minimum standards. Without these, the market may not be sufficiently transformed towards greater efficiency (as has been the case with lighting). The challenge for housing is the introduction of minimum standards – so that, for example, properties rated G/F/E could not be sold or rented by year X/Y/Z. Socially and politically, introducing such a policy would be hugely difficult.

As IPCC's Fourth Assessment Report noted, societies have a long record of managing the impacts of weather- and climate-related events. Nevertheless, additional adaptation measures will be required to reduce the adverse impacts of projected climate change and variability. Moreover, vulnerability to climate change can be exacerbated by other stresses. These arise from, for example, current climate hazards, poverty, and unequal access to resources, food insecurity, trends in economic globalisation, conflict, and incidence of diseases such as HIV/AIDS. There are sharp differences across regions and those in the weakest economic position are often the most vulnerable to climate change. New studies confirm that Africa is one of the most vulnerable continents because of the range of projected impacts, multiple stresses, and low adaptive capacity. Substantial risks due to sea level rise are projected particularly for Asian megadeltas and for small island communities. Some of these risks will have to be dealt with on a community or regional scale, for example via relocation of communities, provision of seawalls and storm surge barriers, dune reinforcement, and protection of wetlands and other existing natural barriers. However, adapting to increasing temperatures will largely need to be managed at the individual household level (see section 'Adapting Buildings'). In addition, societies will also need to adapt their patterns of economic activity and provision of support in order to reduce the impacts of climate change (see section 'Adapting Societies'; also see article Climate Change: Adaptations).

Adapting Buildings

While there are many potential threats from climate change, the universal one which will affect all housing will be increasing average temperatures and heat waves with the associated potential for increased thermal discomfort. Heat waves can have very serious consequences: it is estimated that 52 000 people died in Europe during the record heat wave in the summer of 2003. One way of adapting buildings to deal with increasing temperatures would be to install air conditioning or other active cooling systems. However, this would set in train a 'positive feedback' effect, whereby increasing carbon emissions leads to higher temperatures which encourage further use of fossil fuel energy, thereby further increasing carbon emissions, and so on. This needs to be avoided by better design of new buildings and passive adaptation strategies for existing buildings and neighbourhoods that will reduce heat transmission into dwellings in summer.

Fortunately, the housing sector is less vulnerable to overheating than many other building sectors; for example, offices and schools have more sources of 'waste heat' input – people, IT equipment, lighting – which make them more likely to overheat. New technological and design solutions to reducing overheating may well be developed for these sectors and diffuse into the housing sector.

A UK study which investigated passive cooling adaptation options found the most successful to be:

- Shading from the sun
- Making provision for controllable ventilation during the day and high levels of ventilation at night
- Using heavier-weight building materials combined with night ventilation to enable heat to be absorbed and released into the building fabric
- Improving insulation and air-tightness which enables undesirable heat flows to be controlled.

The study demonstrated that in temperate countries and regions it is possible to achieve acceptable levels of summertime thermal comfort under the projected warmer climates using passive cooling measures with modern building materials and design methods. In countries/regions which are already warmer, there is clearly a greater challenge and more innovation will be needed.

While most strategies to adapt to higher flooding risk are adopted at a city/regional/coastal area level, there is some initial thinking on how individual properties can reduce their vulnerability to damage by being 'flood proofed'. These strategies are designed to make it easier and cheaper to repair a property after flooding and include electrical and other services routed above floor level, solid flooring rather than carpets, waterproof plasterwork, plinths to raise kitchen appliances, and flood doors to delay the entrance of water into the property (see article Environmental Risks: Flooding).

Adapting Societies

Warm European countries have, thus far, managed high summer temperatures without recourse to widespread installation of air conditioning in homes. In part this has been achieved via traditional architecture, and its preoccupation with shade and shelter from the sun at both the building and city scale. Design features include window shutters, high thermal mass buildings, and narrow streets – providing shading. However, even traditional passive measures are not sufficient to completely avoid some level of thermal discomfort in the Mediterranean summer. Societal adaptations to the climate, such as siestas, early morning working/school times, and longer summer vacations, have also been an important part of dealing with the heat. Such societal patterns may have to be reinforced and more widely adopted as the climate gradually warms.

In addition to gradually warming temperatures, climate change brings with it greater risk of heat waves. Research from the 1995 heat wave in Chicago, and from France's 2003 experience (in which 15 000 people died) demonstrates that it is the elderly, the poor, and the isolated who are most at risk from these events. While improving the ability of housing to stay cool is part of reducing this risk, it also needs a wide social response including information and weather warning systems, targeting at-risk populations, and medical and social intervention when a heat wave is under way.

Discussion and Conclusions

Energy use in housing is a significant contributor to climate change and in many countries energy use is rising rather than falling. In order to contribute to avoiding dangerous climate change, carbon emissions from the sector are likely to have to fall by at least 80% by 2050, and by more than this per dwelling because of rising household numbers. This is a huge challenge. The sector faces the additional problem of needing to adapt housing to meet the changes in climate which are already inevitable regardless of future greenhouse gas emissions. Despite the scale of these challenges, there is hope. There are examples of new housing which can meet and even exceed the 80% reduction target, and some national and regional governments are putting policies in place to ensure low or zero carbon housing becomes the new standard. There are highly effective low-carbon refurbishment projects, and a great deal of bottom-up enthusiasm to spread knowledge about these. On mitigation, it is possible to achieve acceptable levels of summertime thermal comfort under the projected warmer climates using passive cooling measures with modern building materials and modern design methods. However, ensuring the housing sector plays its part in reducing emissions will require a great deal of commitment.

Making the transition to low-carbon new housing will be far easier technically, economically, and socially than transforming the existing stock. There is already a successful model in the 'passive house' design for countries with heating-dominated energy demand, and efforts are being made to develop an equally good solution for homes in warmer climates, where more energy is used for cooling. In order to speed the transition to low or zero carbon new housing, governments need to make this standard mandatory as quickly as possible, with the (government-aided) social housing sector being a good place to start. The standards set and reached for new housing will help drive development of technologies and approaches which can be used in renovation work, generate a more highly skilled workforce, and raise householders' expectations about the high environmental standards and low running costs which can be achieved in their homes.

Renovation of existing housing to a low-carbon standard, while possible, is challenging in many ways. Technical standards need to be improved: research demonstrates that expected savings are not always delivered in practice. Further research on postrenovation properties is needed to find out how well different improvements deliver energy savings, and how products and installation skills can be improved to deliver bigger savings. More challenging is the task of delivering a framework whereby all of the housing stock is renovated by 2050. In Europe, the home energy label provides a possible route for this, but only if national governments introduce tough minimum standards, requiring homeowners to upgrade their properties at the point of sale or rental. Knowledge gained through networks of existing eco-renovators provides reassurance that such renovation is possible and can result in a more attractive living environment. However, private individuals and landlords will have to invest money – perhaps a considerable amount of money – to reach the required standards, and careful policy will be needed to ensure this is socially and politically acceptable.

Householders, tenants, and landlords will have to play a full part in the transition to a low-carbon housing sector. At the very least, most householders are going to have to pay to upgrade their homes to a lower carbon standard. They may also need to use energy more carefully, accept different standards of thermal comfort, learn to make best use of new technologies (e.g., solar water heating, heat pumps), and take greater responsibility for their personal carbon emissions. Energy use in housing is not determined by technology alone, and carbon reduction approaches which do not include engagement of the population will not succeed. Taking action to reduce carbon at the household level brings the global problem of climate change directly into everyday lives.

While much adaptation to climate change will take place at a city or regional scale, adaptation measures will also be necessary at the building level. Fortunately, many of the changes needed to keep properties cool in a warming climate will also help reduce their heating energy needs (better insulation, air-tightness, ventilation controls). Designers of buildings and building standards will need to work with both climate mitigation and adaptation in mind.

It will be possible to reduce carbon emissions from the housing sectors in developed countries by 80% by 2050, but it will not be easy. Energy use and carbon emissions from the sector are still increasing in many countries, and there is continued upward pressure from population growth and increasing household numbers. In order to secure the necessary carbon savings, all the actors who influence housing will need to be engaged with the low-carbon agenda. This vital task cannot be left to energy experts, appliance designers, architects, builders, householders, and governments alone. City planners, social policy designers, financiers, local authorities, land owners, estate agents, mortgage companies, nongovernmental organisations, business, and all the other groups involved in housing must take on the task of responding to climate change. The need to reduce carbon emissions must become a core consideration in every decision made about housing. Only then will this sector be able to play a full part in preventing the emergence of dangerous climate change.

See also: Building Regulations for Energy Conservation; Climate Change: Adaptations; Community Energy Systems; Eco-Communities; Eco-Renovation; Energy Saving; Environmental Risks: Flooding; Policies to Promote the Environmental Efficiency of Housing; Sustainable Urban Development.

Further Reading

Boardman B (2007) Home truths: A low carbon strategy to reduce UK housing emissions by 80%.. *A Report for Friends of the Earth and the Cooperative Bank*. London: Friends of the Earth.

Boden T, Marland G, and Andres RJ (2009) Global, regional and national fossil-fuel CO_2 emissions Trends: *A Compendium of Data on Global Change, Carbon Dioxide Information Analysis Centre*. Oak Ridge, TN: Oak Ridge National Laboratory, US Department of Energy.

Energy Efficient Strategies (2008) Energy use in the Australian residential sector, 1986–2020. Canberra, ACT: Department of the Environment, Water, Heritage and the Arts.

EIA (2009) Residential Energy Survey 2005. Energy Information Administration, USA. www.eia.doe.gov/emeu/recs (accessed December 2009).

Hacker JN, Belcher SE, and Connell RK (2005) *Beating the Heat: Keeping UK Buildings Cool in a Warming Climate*. Oxford: UKCIP Briefing Report. UKCIP.

Hong SH, Oreszczyn T, and Ridley I (2006) The impact of energy efficiency refurbishment on the space heating fuel consumption in English dwellings. *Energy and Buildings* 38(10): 1171–1181.IEA (2007) *Energy Use in the New Millennium: Trends in IEA Countries*. Paris: International Energy Agency.

Jones P (2010) Global temperature record. Climatic Research Unit, University of East Anglia. www.cru.uea.ac.uk/cru/info/warming (accessed March 2010).

IPCC (2007) Climate Change 2007: Synthesis Report. Contribution of Working Groups I, II and III to the Fourth Assessment Report of the Intergovernmental Panel on Climate Change.Core Writing Team, Pachauri RK, and Reisinger A(eds.).Geneva, Switzerland: IPCC.

Killip G (2008) Transforming the UK's existing housing stock. *Environmental Change Institute, University of Oxford and Federation of Master Builders*. Oxford.

Ornetzeder M and Rohracher H (2009) Passive houses in Austria: The role of intermediary organisations for the successful transformation of a socio-technical system. *Proceedings of the European Council for an Energy Efficient Economy, Summer Study*. La Colle sur Loup, France: ECEEE.

Parker DS (2009) Very low energy homes in the United States: Perspectives on performance from measured data. *Energy and Buildings* 41(5): 512–520.

Shove E (2003) *Comfort, Cleanliness and Convenience: The Social Organisation of Normality*. Oxford, UK: Berg.

Stern N (2009) *A Blueprint for a Safer Planet: How to Manage Climate Change and Create a New Era of Progress and Prosperity*. London: The Bodley Head.

Tans P (2009) Atmospheric CO2 samples. NOAA/ESRL, Mauna Loa, Hawaii. www.esrl.noaa.gov/gmd/ccgg/trends (accessed December 2009).

UKERC (2009) *Energy 2050: Making the Transition to a Secure and Low-Carbon Energy System: Synthesis Report*. London: UK Energy Research Centre.

Utley JI and Shorrock L (2008) *Domestic Energy Fact File 2008*. Watford, UK: BRE.

Climate Change: Adaptations

R Gupta and M Gregg, Oxford Brookes University, Oxford, UK

© 2012 Elsevier Ltd. All rights reserved.

Glossary

Adaptation Adjustment of behaviour to limit harm or exploit beneficial opportunities, arising from climate change.

Adaptive capacity The ability of a system to adjust to climate change (including climate variability and extremes), to moderate potential damages, to take advantage of opportunities, or to cope with the consequences.

Climate Climate, put simply, is the average weather or, more rigorously, is the statistical description in terms of the mean and variability of relevant variables over a period of time ranging from months to thousands or millions of years. The classical period for averaging these variables is 30 years, as defined by the World Meteorological Organization. The relevant variables are most often surface variables such as temperature, precipitation, and wind.

Climate change Climate change refers to a change in the state of the climate that can be identified (e.g., by using statistical tests) by changes in the mean and/or the variability of its properties, and that persists for an extended period, typically decades or longer. Climate change may be due to natural internal processes or external forces or to persistent anthropogenic changes in the composition of the atmosphere or in land use.

Exposure Stimuli impacting upon a system and represents the background climate conditions within a system and any changes in those conditions.

Mitigation Action to reduce the sources (or enhance the sinks) of factors causing anthropogenic climate change, such as GHGs.

Resilience The ability of a social or ecological system to absorb disturbances while retaining the same basic structure and ways of functioning, the capacity for self-organisation, and the capacity to adapt to stress and change.

Risk Combines the likelihood an event will occur with the magnitude of its consequences. Consequences may be defined according to a variety of metrics including economic, social, and environmental. Risks can be either adverse costs or damages (true costs including nonmonetary costs) or beneficial opportunities.

Vulnerability Degree to which a system is susceptible to, and unable to cope with, adverse effects of climate change, including climate variability and extremes. Vulnerability is a function of a system's exposure, its sensitivity, and its adaptive capacity (see earlier definitions).

Introduction

The impacts of climate change are currently observable around the world and further change is projected to be increasingly unavoidable. According to the scenario of minimal greenhouse gas (GHG) emissions (B1), developed by the Intergovernmental Panel on Climate Change (IPCC), it would take the world 40 years to turn around emissions and to begin a downward trajectory resulting in a best estimate of 1.8 °C global average surface warming by the end of the century. The primary focus of both global and UK climate change response has reasonably been on mitigation, climate change intervention through reduction of GHG emissions, and/or reduction of atmospheric uptake of GHG emissions. Specifically, the United Kingdom has committed to mitigation efforts by planning to reduce GHG emissions to 80% below 1990 levels by 2050. Mitigation is an extremely important route to minimise the impacts of climate change globally; however, as some change is inevitable, it is clear that there needs to be a responsive adjustment to minimise or avoid the impacts and risks of climate change. This adjustment is referred to as adaptation. Mitigation and adaptation can be either synergistic or opposable, but in order to most effectively reduce the risk to future generations, it is essential that neither have negative consequences nor become contradictory.

Why Do We Need to Adapt Existing Housing for Climate Change?

Many buildings have shown through study and experience that they are unable to accommodate either gradual changes in average climatic conditions or extreme events, such as heat waves. Just as the housing sector is contributing to a significant proportion of CO_2 emissions as a result of energy consumed for heating, cooling, lighting, cooking, and use of electrical appliances, the housing sector is also inadequate in capacity to adapt to future climate change and in many ways is inadequate for even the variation in the current climate. These issues will clearly have an impact on the suburbs, which are the most common type of urban area in many developed nations. Nearly 80% of all homes in the United Kingdom, for example, are located in suburban areas, which are characterised by automobile-centred, low-medium-density housing that is generally energy and land intensive. The pace at which the built environment changes combined with the inclination for families to prefer the suburbs guarantees that the majority of dwellings in the suburbs will be around throughout the rest of this century. Herein, a majority (8/10 people) of the UK population's health, lifestyles, and property will be affected by gradual changes such as hotter drier summers and milder wetter winters and by extreme events such as more frequent high temperatures and precipitation.

Climate change adaptation has a clear role in climate change mitigation-oriented refurbishment approaches. One clear example is that a large majority of dwellings in the United Kingdom and northern Europe have no mechanical cooling. An increase in summer temperature has the potential to increase the vulnerability to overheating and the potential to increase energy use through the installation of air conditioning for occupant comfort. Flooding is also a problem for neighbourhoods around the world, through either the condition of neighbourhoods preexisting the full understanding of flood plains or lack of regulation. Increasingly every year countless homes are flooded around the world to varying degrees. This flood risk is only projected to become greater and more frequent where it already floods and to impact homes not yet exposed to the potential threat (**Box 1**).

Climate Change Risk

The necessity for adaptation of housing becomes clear when the risk that the changing climate presents is evaluated. There are varying degrees of scale for which risk, impacts, and adaptation strategies can be defined for the suburban typology. This scale can range from the global impact of climate change hazards down to the vulnerable

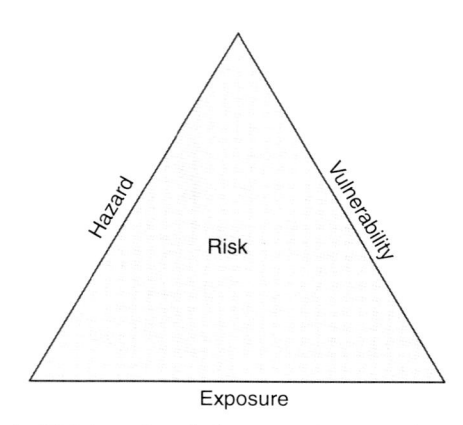

Figure 1 Risk-based analysis approach.

position of fuel poverty. At a fundamental level, the methodological approach to analysing the risk posed by climate change is based on the risk triangle developed in order to understand the implications of climate change for the insurance industry (**Figure 1**). With this approach, adaptation is successful when it is able to eliminate or reduce any one side of the triangle; risk is eliminated when the structure of the triangle collapses.

The hazard is the measurable effect of the changing climate on a suburban neighbourhood or an individual's home. Example hazards are a 5 °C increase in temperature combined with an increase in shortwave radiation (through reduced cloud cover) by the middle of the century. These hazards combined have the potential to create an overheating impact in homes. The exposure of a site or home is directly linked to the local environmental and microclimatic features of the site. These local environmental features (LEFs) localise the impacts of climate change for a site. Clear examples of exposure can be seen in a neighbourhood's historic tendency to flood or the neighbourhood's proximity to a dense urban area and the resultant UHI effect on the neighbourhood. The impacts of climate change hazards can be exacerbated by flood exposure and UHI. Vulnerability of the occupants to change in climate can be a factor of age, economic status, social status, and common local language proficiency, which can all interconnect and be related to health (mental or physical), access to resources, and inequality. Additionally, gender, cultural values, and belief systems

---

Box 1 Study: Climate change and future energy consumption in UK housing

Collins et al. modelled the impact of climate change on the UK housing stock (assuming a 50% uptake of air conditioning with no passive alterations and assuming heating methods would continue as they are currently) and found that there would be a 10% decrease in CO_2 emissions from the drop in heating demand. They, however, note later in the paper that another study suggests that one in four homes will be mechanically cooled by 2030 and that heat pumps (with cooling capacity) could become popular, placing pressure on electricity supply. Though a reduction in CO_2 emissions has been modelled, there are also other considerations (noted as not within the scope of the modelling research) such as noise pollution, power outages, and the effect of air conditioning on the local urban heat island (UHI) effect.

and the interrelationship between them can directly create vulnerability. Many of the vulnerabilities listed above can be determining factors for geographic location and access to resources; therefore, specific vulnerabilities, for example, can determine level of exposure, increasing or decreasing risk. Adaptive capacity is intimately linked with vulnerability. Adaptive capacity limits or eliminates vulnerability based on five possible capital influences: financial, built, natural, human, and social. Adaptive capacity for people is strengthened by social memory and the existence of social networks or bonds and shared knowledge.

Defining Hazards, Exposure, and Vulnerability for the Suburbs

Hazard Identification through Climate Change Scenarios and Downscaling

Climate change projections can be generalised for continents, countries, or regions, but in order to really understand risk, it is necessary to spatially downscale data so that real change projections can be relevant to a specific location. To be relevant to policy-makers, planners, and researchers, climate change hazards can be specified by state-of-the-art climate projection methods (explained in the case study example, **Box 2**) for an area as detailed as 5–25 km. This is referred to as spatial downscaling. Temporal downscaling, daily and hourly representation of data, is also necessary for quantifying thresholds within a climate change data set, for example, the frequency of a heat wave episode within a climate timescale. Temporal downscaling is also the method by which future climate data are manipulated to create 'future weather years' which are necessary for thermal building modelling (e.g., testing the impact of future external temperatures on the internal environment).

Exposure Identification through Site Analysis

As noted previously, the LEFs of a site point to the potential exposure of a specific neighbourhood or city. **Table 2** provides a list of city-scale LEFs that can be used to identify exposure, the results for the example of Oxford and the hazard that can have an effect or particularly be related to an LEF. When particular neighbourhoods are

Table 1 IPCC SRES designation of emissions scenarios for UKCIP02 and UKCP09 and corresponding atmospheric CO_2 concentrations at year 2100

E. Scenario	UKCIP02	UKCP09	CO_2 ppm^{-1}
Low	B1	B1	549
Medium-low	B2	–	621
Medium	–	A1B	717
Medium-high	A2	–	856
High	A1F1	A1F1	970

SRES, Special Report on Emissions Scenarios.
Source: Adapted from Hacker J, Capon R, and Mylona A (2009) Use of climate change scenarios for building simulation: The CIBSE future weather years. TM48: 2009. London: Chartered Institution of Building Services Engineers.

Box 2 UKCP09: A case study of climate projections in the United Kingdom

In order to evaluate the influence of climate change hazards, the hazards must first be defined through the use of climate science consensus-validated projection modelling. One such model, the most robust, extensive, and detailed publicly available climate change database in the world, has been developed for the United Kingdom. The UK Climate Projections (UKCP09) provides a wealth of information on climate change, detailed data for a number of climate variables, and capability for downscaling that data for detailed temporal or spatial analyses. The UKCP09 provides the best insight into how the climate system works and how it might change in the future with built-in logical uncertainties. The UKCP09 is the primary source in the United Kingdom for research groups, government, and the insurance industry to develop climate change scenarios for future preparedness and response. UKCP09 replaces the UK Climate Impacts Programme (UKCIP)02 and presents data as a result of three different possible future GHG emissions scenarios up to the end of the century: low, medium, and high. **Table 1** compares the emissions scenarios presented by both the UKCIP02 and the UKCP09 along with the IPCC Special Report on Emissions Scenarios (SRES) designations applicable to each scenario.

Based on historic climate evidence, the UKCP09 provides a range of possible outcomes defined regionally across the United Kingdom and the probabilities linked to each outcome for a number of climate variables. Key findings are presented for the 10, 50, and 90% probabilities; 50% is what is referred to as the 'central estimate' of probability, 10% is otherwise stated as 'very likely to be more than', and 90% is otherwise stated as, 'very likely to be less than'. To access climate data for a specific climate variable and location, a specific emissions scenario, climate time period, and temporal average must also be indicated. UKCP09 provides a user interface where climate data can be downloaded and/or downscaled through selection of a number of parameters. Data for change in climate over land (for individual 25 km grid squares) are available for the parameters presented in **Figure 2**; the order of selection towards an output can vary. Change in climate is used for hazard identification and climate absolutes (downscaling) are used for thresholds identification and temporal downscaling ('future weather years'). Spatially and temporally downscaling data within the UKCP09 can be done through the use of the weather generator (WG). The data from the WG can then be postprocessed to retrieve weather thresholds or extremes within a data set via the threshold detector.

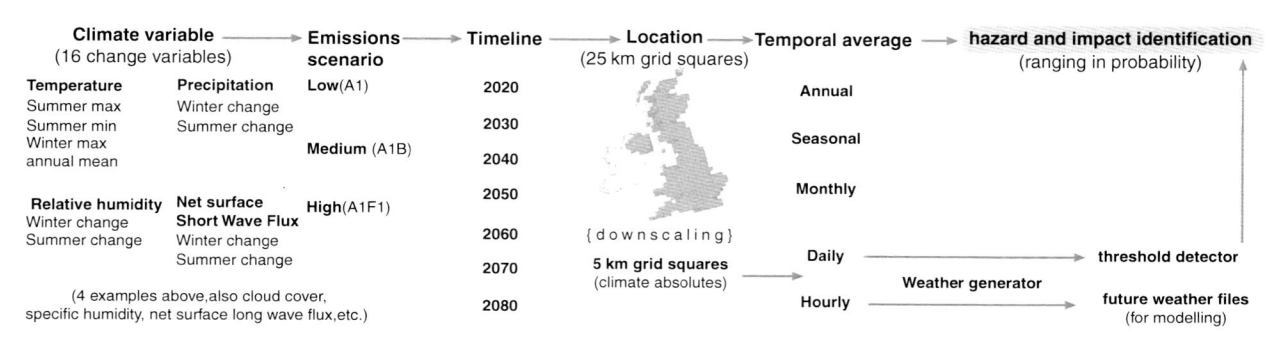

Figure 2 Parameters for which climate change data are available through the UKCP09. Adapted from Jenkins et al. (2009).

Table 2 Table of LEFs for example city: Oxford, United Kingdom

LEFs	Oxford	Hazard relevance
Latitude	51°	Temperature change and solar intensity change
Proximity to coast	>50 miles	Temperature increase and precipitation increase
Urban cover[a]	29% urban coverage[b]	Temperature increase, solar intensity increase, and precipitation increase
Urban cover pattern	Irregular	Temperature increase and precipitation increase
Elevation	Highest: 170 m, lowest: 60 m	Temperature change
Fluvial flood risk (EA, 2010)	Flood risk exists	Precipitation increase
Landslide potential (BGS, 2005)	Medium/low	Precipitation increase
Geology (clay soil – swell/shrink potential) (BGS, 2005)	High	Precipitation decrease/ground moisture content fluctuation
Water stress (EA, 2010)	High	Precipitation decrease and temperature increase
Wind driven rain potential (Graves and Phillipson, 2000)	Moderate: $33 > 56.5 \, \text{lm}^{-2}$ per spell	Precipitation increase/wind speed change

[a]Urban cover refers to built-up areas, for example, asphalt, concrete, and buildings, and has many implications for proximity to green space and urban heat island (UHI) potential. The urban coverage percentage is based on a 10 km grid square centred over the city centre of Oxford.
[b]The lower percentage of urban cover for Oxford increases the probability for a suburban area to be close to open green space, therefore reducing the potential impact of UHI.
LEF, local environmental features.

selected for in-depth analysis, additional LEFs can be identified including neighbourhood characteristics and location within the city. For example, depending on the city, older suburbs, generally closer to city centres with little to no outdoor space, could be exposed to greater UHI impacts. LEF analysis can be as specific as detailing the type of tree and shade it provides (during specific months) for a particular home and the resultant cooling (microclimate) it provides, decreasing the risk of overheating.

Vulnerability of the Occupants

Vulnerability is best understood when a neighbourhood is identified and the demographic is defined. With regard to age, affluence, and so on, housing type and home ownership is a large component of socioeconomic status; neighbourhoods generally represent a demographic standard for which vulnerabilities of occupants can be generalised based on affluence, social status, and access to resources. Additionally, suburban neighbourhoods present an interesting potential vulnerability for the whole. This is the vulnerability of divergence over how or willingness to adapt. In suburbia, defined by a large number of individually owned dwellings, it can be difficult to find agreement and implementation for collective action. Adaptive capacity of a neighbourhood can be a result of the success of a community and social connections and willingness to share knowledge and resources and work together. Exposure and vulnerability of a city, or even neighbourhood, can effectively be understood through the use of a methodology developed by the UKCIP for local authorities called the local climate impacts profile (LCLIP). LCLIPs help local authorities or communities recognise current and future exposure and vulnerability to weather events beginning with current exposure and vulnerability. The outputs of LCLIP are a schedule of location-specific consequences of weather events and analyses of important variables (location impact and weather type).

Key Climate Change Impacts

The large amount of published works on climate change in the built environment all commonly define four possible future impacts that can be identified for the cities, their suburbs, and homes:

- overheating
- unbalanced seasonal water surplus (e.g., flooding)
- water stress
- construction (material or structural) degradation.

Overheating will affect buildings and people above all other impacts. Flooding and water stress are more dependent on local exposure and in many cases current flood risk and water stress (although flood and water stress will impact in new places and not everyone will experience the impacts directly) (**Box 3**).

Overheating

Buildings can gain heat through a number of methods; these methods are internal gains, solar heat gain on exterior surfaces, solar gain transmitted through glazing on internal surfaces, and heat transmission through high external temperatures. The first three can be very advantageous for homes when maximised in the winter for many countries;

Box 3   Verifying climate change impacts in the United Kingdom through probabilistic projections

Key findings for selected regions in the United Kingdom are displayed in **Tables 3** and **4**. The regions, Scotland north (**Figure 3**) and southeast England (**Figure 4**), are selected for their location on the range of relative extremes for the United Kingdom with regard to summer temperature change, that is, the entire probabilistic range for change in summer mean temperature for the United Kingdom for the 2050s climate period is projected to be between 0.9 and 5.2 °C. Though not presented in tables below, change in net surface short wave flux (NSSWF) will also directly affect the significance of climate change impacts. Oxford, for example, will experience a summer average NSSWF increase of $9 W m^{-2}$ by the 2050s (central estimate, high emissions).

Given the evidence of the equal likelihood and unlikelihood of possible summer mean temperature increase (for example) by 2.4 °C averaged for the United Kingdom at medium emissions by the 2050s, overheating is a valid concern. Additionally, as can be seen in **Table 4**, summer water stress and winter flooding are also potential impacts.

Table 3   Change in temperature for Scotland north and southeast England

Climate change in	Summer mean temperature (°C)			Winter mean temperature (°C)		
Probability level (%)	10	50	90	10	50	90
Scotland north 2050s						
Low emissions	0.9	1.9	3.1	0.6	1.6	2.7
Medium emissions	0.9	2.0	3.4	0.6	1.6	2.8
High emissions	1.1	2.4	3.9	0.7	1.8	3.0
Southeast England 2050s						
Low emissions	1.4	2.6	4.3	0.9	2.0	3.1
Medium emissions	1.3	2.8	4.6	1.1	2.2	3.4
High emissions	1.4	3.1	5.2	1.4	2.5	3.8

Source: Adapted from Defra (2010).

Table 4   Change in precipitation for Scotland north and southeast England

Climate change in	Summer mean precipitation (%)			Winter mean precipitation (%)		
Probability level (%)	10	50	90	10	50	90
Scotland north 2050s						
Low emissions	−21	−8	6	−1	8	20
Medium emissions	−24	−11	2	3	13	24
High emissions	−24	−10	3	3	13	26
Southeast England 2050s						
Low emissions	−37	−14	9	1	13	30
Medium emissions	−41	−19	7	2	16	36
High emissions	−43	−19	9	3	19	40

Source: Adapted from Defra (2010).

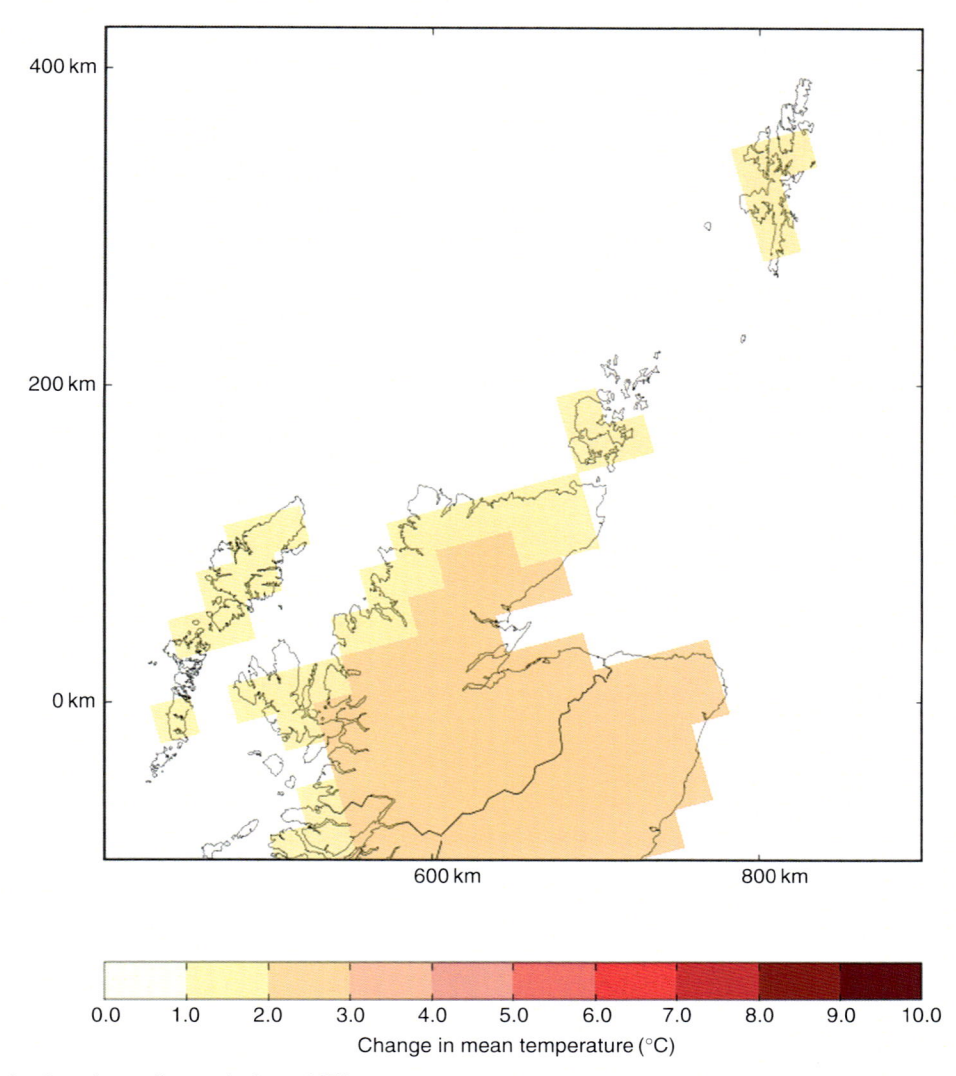

Figure 3 Scotland north, medium emissions, 2050.
Source: Defra (2010).

however, when external temperatures rise above a certain level (different for every building; dependent on many factors), the combination of all four of the methods mentioned above can lead to overheating. Exposure at the home level can range from lack of green space and trees, no shading elements, and construction type and age. Over long periods of high temperatures, health risks such as heat stress and heat stroke can impact vulnerable individuals. Many heat-related deaths are caused by heat (and pollution) exacerbating existing illness. In ages 65 and above, Hajat et al. found that risk to heat-related death had a greater impact on women than men and that risk to cold-related death (not showing as wide a gender gap as heat risk) provided much greater risk for all ages above 65 years. Risk usually involves heat exhaustion or heat stroke. Elderly (older women more so than men), bed bound, people with cardiovascular and mental illnesses, children particularly under the age of 4, and people required to take certain types of medication can be most vulnerable to overheating. Additionally, social isolation and the inability to adapt behaviour may exacerbate conditions of vulnerability. Furthermore, situational exposure such as home location (in urban or rural area), housing characteristics, and location or orientation in housing can exacerbate personal vulnerability (**Box 4**).

Most dwellings in cold and moderate climates utilise natural ventilation by opening windows to reduce interior temperatures, but as external temperatures rise, this will become more difficult. These homes will be unable to cope with these conditions and will either need to be adapted collectively with GHG reduction targets in mind (as a technically feasible addition to 'whole house' refurbishment programme packages) or the public will most likely adapt independently through more accessible means such as installing air-conditioning units in poorly insulated homes. Unless there is a significant

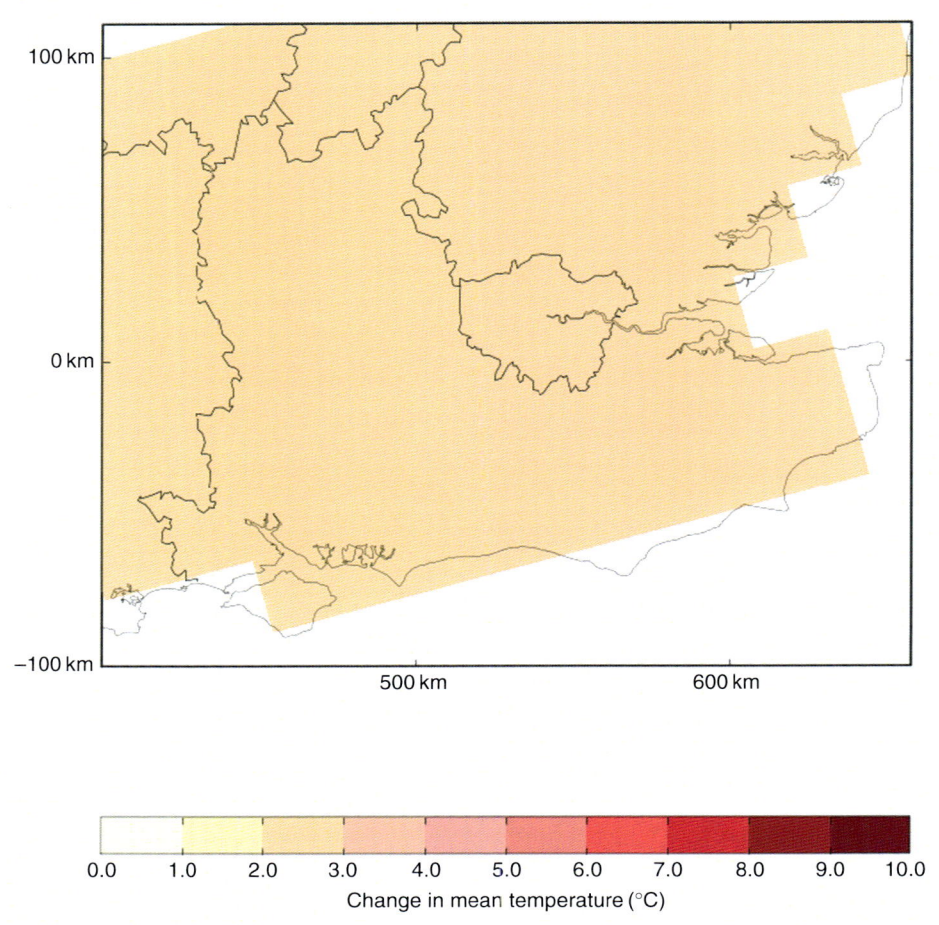

Figure 4 Southeast England, medium emissions, 2050.
Source: Defra (2010).

Box 4 Heat wave

When maximum daily temperature is greater than 30 °C and minimum daily temperature is greater than 15 °C for a minimum of three consecutive days. The heat wave threshold used by the UKCP09 is the heat wave threshold defined by the Met Office for Wales and much of the United Kingdom. Studies of climate change projections suggest that by the 2050s the United Kingdom will experience heat wave conditions every other year. To put this in perspective, CIBSE Guide A defines overheating in dwellings as 1% occupied hours over 28 °C for living areas and 1% occupied hours over 26 °C for bedrooms.

---

shift in GHG emissions and temperatures do not meet projections, it is suggested that effective passive cooling may not be enough and active cooling may be necessary by the end of the century. Even if active cooling may be unavoidable, many passive measures will be particularly effective in reducing the energy demand and CO_2 emissions.

Flooding

Every year flooding affects residential areas in both developed and developing countries alike. Flooding can occur as a result of water surplus in both waterways and urban drainage areas (where drainage cannot support the water flow level or is congested). In addition to personal vulnerabilities previously listed, situational vulnerability (exposure, social isolation, and location within a building) can contribute to flood risk as a result of lack of flood risk awareness or inability to receive or communicate information about risk and/or physical or mental inability to cope, recover, survive, or access aid for recovery. Not everyone will experience flooding; however, everyone in the United Kingdom, for example, will experience seasonal water surplus through increased winter precipitation. There are varying degrees to which the water surplus will affect a homeowner, but the term is used to shed light on the idea that in some cases the water surplus can be used to the advantage of some, for example, when dealing with water stress. Excesses in water can also lead to material degradation problems (explained later).

Water Stress

Water stress is the condition when water availability frequently falls below surplus. When water sources for a region cannot serve the population, limitations on water use are imposed causing difficulties for communities. Around homes and neighbourhoods, people could be dependent on vegetation for shading or sustenance that requires a specific amount of water to survive, which may change in a future climate. Individual vulnerability to water stress could result from the imposition of hosepipe bans where an individual or family may be dependent on food that they are growing in their garden or land plot. Increases in water costs could also result and be problematic for people that are economically vulnerable (**Box 5**).

Construction Degradation

Structural and material integrity could be impacted independently or in combination (over time) by all four hazards: temperature increase, precipitation increase, precipitation decrease, and NSSWF increase. Structural and material integrity can also be affected by change in wind and storm strength. It is important to note that wind and storm design standards have been improved in many areas based on observed weather events, and many existing homes may need to be updated to adapt to cope with even current climatic conditions. **Table 5** lists construction degradation impacts that may result from climate change hazards.

Case Study: Developing Packages for Adaptive Retrofitting of UK Homes

Effective adaptation strategies are available for existing homes to avoid overheating in the summer, to avoid or remain habitable after floods, to consume less water in times of water stress, and to ensure that the structure and materials of the dwelling are not compromised by the changing climate. The extensive variation in home type, condition, and age makes it difficult to communicate the idea of specific adaptation packages and costing. To avoid the dangerous impacts of climate change, a great number of individual assessments are necessary to contribute to effective adaptation. However, through statistical evaluation of construction materials and methods of housing categorised by age and type, a home's exposure and resultant impact to climate change can be modelled. Furthermore, given this information, mitigation and adaptation measures can be developed and modelled. As an example, U-values and construction methods, which can significantly impact

---

Box 5 Flooding and water stress in the United Kingdom

Only one in ten persons in the United Kingdom who is at risk is prepared in advance for a flood. Climate change is expected to make this situation even more problematic where, for example, flood risk in eastern England is expected to increase by 48%. Through the evaluation of historic weather accounts, similar to the process involved in developing an LCLIP, South Wales is shown to have experienced four disastrous flood events from 2006 to 2010. As a result of flooding (particularly extreme in 2008), many homes and offices throughout South Wales were damaged and evacuated, people were stranded in flood water, landslips occurred, train services were disconnected, and roads were closed. With winter precipitation projected to increase by 13% (central estimate, high emissions, 2050s) in Wales (for example), flood event impacts such as these can be expected to occur frequently and with more extreme results unless communities resolve the risk by either adapting to or abandoning the areas of exposure.

Projected future summer precipitation decrease combined with temperature and NSSWF increase (resulting in increased rapid evaporation) is expected to create drought conditions in some areas of the United Kingdom and exacerbate already existing water stress in areas such as the southeast of England. In areas of great water stress such as the southeast of England, the impact of reduced precipitation combined with increased population is placing great strain on the water supply to the region.

Table 5 Construction degradation impacts and relevant climate change hazards

Impact	Climate change hazards
Structural	
Foundation damage – change in soil moisture content (clay soils susceptible to shrinkage and expansion – location dependent)	Precipitation decrease or increase and temperature increase
Wind damage – older buildings are subject to the greatest risk (location dependent)	Wind change data currently not available
Material	
Rain ingress – rain or moisture can enter the dwelling and lead to mould and rot	Precipitation increase and wind
Material shrinkage, colour change, reduced integrity, etc.	Temperature increase and net surface short wave flux increase

Source: Adapted from Gething B (2010) Design for future climate: Opportunities for adaptation in the built environment. Swindon.

internal temperature and future flexibility for change to a building, can be derived from building regulations and standards attributed to dwelling age.

For the purpose of this article, three case study examples that were developed by ARUP for the Three Regions Climate Change Group will be used. The case studies represent a three-bedroom semi-detached house from the 1930s and a flat from the 1960s–70s; the third case is a low-rise block of flats of the same characteristics as the second case. Climate impacts and costs of the results of the case studies were specifically developed for the 'Three Regions,' east of England, London, and the southeast of England. According to the English Housing Survey, the most common housing type in the United Kingdom is the semi-detached house. Additionally, the largest number of low-rise flat blocks was produced during the period of the 1960s–70s. Assumptions for the house include owner occupied (family of two adults and three children), minimum standard insulation, suspended wooden floorboards (carpeted) with no basement, not renovated within the past 20 years, and no shading from trees. Assumptions for the flat include ground floor purpose-built flat rented by a young couple that do not have control over the fabric of the building and any adaptation measures would have to be negotiated with the landlord (the individual flat case study only considers what the occupiers can do apart from the landlord). The block of flats follows most of the same assumptions as the individual flat case; however, the block consists of 16 flats that are owned by a single individual who has the capacity to adapt the entire block. **Tables 6** and **7** list key characteristics of the three case study buildings. These characteristics along with specific occupancy patterns (not detailed here) were used to model the case study buildings to test effective adaptation measures. The final adaptation measures were selected for their appropriateness, given property type and tenure of the occupants.

Costing Adaptation Packages

The costs for adaptation packages developed for the case studies were produced by a quantity surveyor. Key references for costing were SPONS 2007 Builders and Mechanical and Electrical Price Guides. A majority of costs represent professional installation and it is suggested that 'do-it-yourself' installations should decrease some costs. Costing is supplied for overheating, flooding, and water stress; construction degradation, where price is grouped with the appropriate shared impact, for example, to protect doors from rot as a result of flooding, an adaptation measure, is presented as a flooding resilience measure.

The adaptation measures are presented in three bands (**Box 6**):

Though the costs are specific to the United Kingdom, the adaptation measures can logically be used in many other countries anticipating similar climate change impacts.

Table 6 Case study occupation classifications

Occupation					
House, semi-detached	Owner occupied	1930s	3 bed	5 person family	Southwest orientation
Purpose-built flat (ground and top floor)	Rented	1960s	2 bed	2 people (couple)	Southwest orientation
Block (16 flats)	Rented and all owned by single landlord, all other details same as flat				

Source: Adapted from ARUP (2007) LCCP: Retrofitting adaptation for climate change. Stage 3 report: Case studies. London: ARUP.

Table 7 Case study construction classifications

Construction	External walls	Party walls	Glazing	Ground floor	Roof
House, semi-detached	105 mm brick–50 mm cavity–105 mm brick	229 mm brick	Single	Suspended wooden floor – carpeted	Clay tiles–100 mm glass fibre–quilt loft insulation
Purpose-built flat (ground and top floor)	105 mm brick–50 mm cavity–100 mm concrete block	225 mm concrete block	Single	200 mm concrete–40 mm timber carpeted	19 mm asphalt–13 mm fibreboard–25 mm cavity–50 mm glass fibre quilt insulation
Block (16 flats)	Same construction as flat				

Source: Adapted from ARUP (2007) LCCP: Retrofitting adaptation for climate change. Stage 3 report: Case studies. London: ARUP.

> **Box 6 Cost bands**
>
> Low (**L**) – £1–100 | Medium (**M**) – £101–1000 | High (**H**) – £1001+

Adapting for Overheating

Table 8 lists adaptation measures to avoid overheating, possible limitation when implementing the measures and cost bands associated with each measure. The TRCCG report found that a house that has been retrofitted for maximising winter heat preservation (an important mitigation measure) can expect to pay half as much as an unretrofitted house in order to adapt to avoid overheating. Many of the mitigation measures that help conserve fuel and preserve heat in the winter can benefit a home at risk of overheating.

Table 9 lists the adaptation measures that were considered to be appropriate for each case. Measures were modelled using thermal building simulation software. ARUP modelled the case study dwellings using 'morphed' version of CIBSE's Design Summer Year for the 2050s. Morphing, or time series adjustment, is a downscaling method for constructing weather years for future climate scenarios. Morphing combines observed historical weather years and projected monthly changes in a process of stretching and shifting the present-day observed time series to produce a new time series. Overall, it was found that in all cases the initial cost of adaptation is significantly higher than air-conditioning installation. All adaptations only begin to look financially attractive after 10 years of running costs are calculated and compared.

Adapting for Flooding

When adapting for flooding, TRCCG is clear to differentiate between flood resistance measures and flood resilience measures. Flood resistance is a method of adaptation where the actual quantity of water that enters the home is either completely omitted or limited. Resistance measures are only successful when all entry points to a home are blocked; in order to be successfully resistant, these measures must be considered as a complete package (**Table 10**). Flood resistance is most appropriate for shallow and short duration flooding. In circumstances where there is potential for deep flood waters, the likely pressure on the structure of the home would suggest that water should be allowed to enter. The measures and packages presented are only for the case studies presented. Every site is different and will require professional analysis to ensure which measures are necessary to provide complete resistance. Flood resilience is when the time and cost of recovery from a flood event are reduced. Like with overheating, resilience measures are cumulative and can be implemented individually. Furthermore, there are external measures, which are listed as options. These external measures, such as the green roof, are not priced because the direct impact on flood mitigation and recovery savings is difficult to theoretically quantify at this level of study.

Table 8 Potential adaptation measures for overheating

Adaptation measures	Possible limitation	Cost
Reduce unused internal gains – turn off lights, appliances, equipment, etc.	–	Free–L
Naturally ventilate at night by opening windows	Security, noise, and air quality could be problematic	Free
Local cooling with fans (ceiling or floor fans)	–	L–M
Reduce solar gains through glazing with reflective blinds	–	L–M–H
Reduce solar gains with an awning	–	H
Reduce solar gains with shutters; also increases security	–	L–M
Replace carpets with (or expose) cool floors: concrete, tile, etc. (cover with rugs in winter)	–	H
Prevent heat absorption by increasing exterior wall and roof reflectivity and albedo	Changes the appearance of facades	L–M
Improve roof insulation	–	L–M
Install or improve cavity wall insulation	In flood risk area use closed cell insulation	M–H
Install double or triple glazing with low-e coatings to reduce heat gain	Must be balanced with adequate shading and ventilation or may increase overheating	M–H
Install secondary double glazing behind existing glazing	Only suitable where deep inset exists	H

Note: The last four shaded measures are typical fuel conservation measures made in low-carbon retrofits (mitigation).
Source: Adapted from Three Regions Climate Change Group (TRCCG) (2008) Your home in a changing climate: Retrofitting existing homes for climate change impacts. London.

Table 9 Case study selected adaptation measures and costs

Adaptation measures	House	Flat	Block[a]
Solar control			
Awning on southwest windows (external)	£1 700	–	–
Reflecting blinds or curtains with open window (internal)	–	Low[b]	Free–low
Shutters	–	–	£2 445
Air movement			
Natural ventilation through windows	Free	Free	Free
Ceiling fans (owner installed)	£545	–	£498
Desk fans	–	£60	–
Floor covering			
Replace carpet with wood or tile	£2 100	£2 800	–
Facade change			
Increase external wall reflectivity (painted)	£3 750	–	£1 500
Total adaptation for overheating only	*£8 095*	*£2 860*	*£4 442*
Full block total (16 flats)			£71 070
Winter fuel conservation measures			
Improve roof insulation	£2 200	–	£1 844
Improve wall insulation	£1 100	–	£401
Replace single glazing with low-e coated double glazing	£5 000	–	£2 575
Install secondary double glazing behind existing single glazing	–	£4 450[b]	–
Overall total	*£16 395*	*£7 310*	*£9 261*
Full block total (16 flats)			£148 180

[a]Pricing is per flat, block total is presented below flat total.
[b]Blinds and curtain costs are included in glazing price.
Source: Adapted from ARUP (2007) LCCP: Retrofitting adaptation for climate change. Stage 3 report: Case studies. London: ARUP.

Table 10 Potential adaptation measures for flooding

Resistance measures	Cost	Resilience measures	Cost
Know your flood risk: check the Environment Agency (EA) flood map/register with EA warning scheme	Free	Know your flood risk: check the Environment Agency (EA) flood map/register with EA warning scheme	Free
Drainage bungs for drains, sinks, and toilets	L	Store valuables and paperwork upstairs	Free
Install air brick covers	L	Turn off gas, water, and electricity supply	Free
Seal gaps around pipe and cable entries	L	Fit rising hinges so doors can be removed	L
Fit nonreturn valves on mains drains	M–H	Use dry-bags to protect furnishings	L
Install demountable door guards	M–H	Use water-resistant paint for internal walls	L–M
Move meters and electrical sockets above flood level	M–H	Rewire above flood level (with wiring drops from above)	M
Install a 'sump and pump' below ground level	H	Relocate meters and boiler above flood level (e.g., on a concrete plinth)	M
Install waterproof membrane on external walls (0.6 m below to 1 m aboveground)	H	Relocate domestic appliances above flood level (e.g., on a concrete plinth)	M
Repoint brick work on external walls	H	Replace carpets with vinyl or ceramic tiles	M–H
Apply waterproof render to external walls	H	Replace timber with solid concrete	H
Raise door thresholds	H	–	–
External adaptation measures			*Cost*
Use porous materials or open structures in place of driveway to allow water to drain in to ground			H
Ensure that surfaces around the house slope away from the home			H
Large-scale rainwater harvesting system			H
Green roof			H

Source: Adapted from Three Regions Climate Change Group (TRCCG) (2008) Your home in a changing climate: Retrofitting existing homes for climate change impacts. London.

Table 11 presents the total cost for resilience and resistance separately for each case. The total costs are compared to the cost saved through recovery, as number of flood events that a home should experience before payback of initial adaptation investment is realised. Though resilience can be individually considered for

Table 11 Case study selected adaptation measures and costs

Resilience adaptation measures	House	Flat	Block[a]
Moving appliances and other items within the home			
Locate boiler above flood level	£745	£640	£2 570
Raise electrical points and meter	£230	£275	£1 100
Place large appliances on a concrete plinth	£675	£675	–
Interior changes and furnishing/item protection			
Replace chipboard flooring with solid treated timber	£2 665	–	–
Fit rising hinges so doors can be removed (3 doors)	£30	–	–
Dry-bags (5)	£150	£150	–
Replace kitchen and bathroom units with plastic	–	£1 750	–
Total resilience	£4 495	£3 490	£3 670
Resistance adaptation measures			
Know your flood risk and register with EA warning scheme	Free	Free	Free
Fit nonreturn valves on mains drains	£5 490	–	£23 764
Install demountable door guards	£1 560	£655	£1 107
Raise door thresholds	£1 585	–	£4 300
Install waterproof membrane on external walls	£4 450	–	–
Install air brick covers	£635	£60	£336
Seal gaps around pipe, cable entries, doors, and windows	£30	£30	£120
Sandbags	–	£100	–
Drainage bungs for drains, sinks, and toilets	–	£95	–
Repoint brick work on external walls	–	£1 340	–
Apply waterproof render to external walls	–	–	£8 725
Total resistance	£13 750	£2 280	£38 352

[a]Pricing is the total for the four ground floor flats.
Source: Adapted from ARUP (2007) LCCP: Retrofitting adaptation for climate change. Stage 3 report: Case studies. London: ARUP.

Table 12 Payback for case study flood-related measure packages

	Total cost	Cost saved in recovery		Number of events until payback	
		Shallow flood <5 cm	Deep flood 5 cm > 90 cm	Shallow flood ≤5 cm	Deep flood 5 cm ≥ 90 cm
House					
Resilience	£4 495	£1 800	£4 270	2.5	1.1
Resistance	£13 750	£4 500	£23 100	3	1
Flat					
Resilience	£3 490	£3 900	£6 550	1	1
Resistance	£2 280	£4 500	£23 100	1	1
Block (4 flats)					
Resilience	£3 670	£2 800	£4 200	1.3	1
Resistance	£38 352	£18 000	£69 200	2	1

Source: Adapted from ARUP (2007) LCCP: Retrofitting adaptation for climate change. Stage 3 report: Case studies. London: ARUP.

payback, **Table 12** will simply present the measures as a package for payback calculation purposes.

Adapting for Water Stress

Adaptation for water stress will take place through water use reduction measures (**Table 13**). These reduction measures will be necessary to alleviate the water stress that already exists in some regions and is projected to become a problem in other regions as the climate changes. Cities in the southeast, for example, are familiar with occasional hosepipe bans where using collected rainwater for watering the garden would be an effective adaptation measure to combat drought. In most households, a majority of the water use is from shower (i.e., bathing) and toilet use; these two uses contribute to two-thirds of total household water use in the United Kingdom. Each case study situation dealt with toilet and shower use to some degree where either owners or renters can easily find ways to adapt whether through permanent toilet replacement or simply changing a shower head. Benefits for water efficiency like the adaptation measures for

Table 13 Potential adaptation measures for water stress

Adaptation measures	Potential water savings (l person yr^{-1})	Metered value of water saved (£ yr^{-1})	Cost
Ultralow flush toilet replacement	7 884	16	M
Cistern displacement device	Up to 5 256	10	Free[a]
Variable flush retrofit kit	Up to 7 834	15	L
Repair dripping taps	4 745	9	L
Low-flow bathroom taps	5 087	10	L
Low-flow shower or shower head	8 176	16	L–M
Low-flow kitchen tap adaptor	7 727	15	L
Water-efficient dishwasher	1 205	2	M
Water-efficient washing machine	4 592	9	M
Rainwater butts for garden watering	5 000	10	L
Rainwater butts for car washing	15 643	31	L

[a]Cistern displacement devices are offered free from some water service providers.
Note: The six shaded measures contribute to fuel conservation in addition to water conservation.
Source: Adapted from Three Regions Climate Change Group (TRCCG) (2008) Your home in a changing climate: Retrofitting existing homes for climate change impacts. London.

overheating (unlike resistance measures for flooding) are cumulative and can be considered as independent improvements or as an entire package.

In **Table 14**, adaptation measures for improving water efficiency are presented along with costs and payback period. The payback period only considers a decrease in main water costs and does not consider energy savings from decreased water heating as a result. The financial and carbon savings benefit of reducing water heating is much greater than the savings from reducing cold water use. In the case of the house (based on typical UK use for a family of five), for example, installing a low-flow shower would result in water savings of 40 880 l yr^{-1}. This reduction in heated water translates to energy savings of 1430 kWh yr^{-1}, a CO_2 savings of 600 kgCO$_2^{-1}$ yr^{-1} and a financial savings of £132 yr^{-1}.

Aside from the adaptations mentioned above, xeriscaping (low or no water-dependent landscaping) could be used in all garden spaces for the house or the block. No exterior water conservation measures can be recommended for the case study flat where the renter or owner has no control over the communal land.

Table 14 Case study selected adaptation measures, costs, and payback period

	House		Flat		Block[a]	
Adaptation measures	Cost	Years[b]	Cost	Years[b]	Cost	Years[b]
Bathroom						
New low-flow shower	£140	1.8	–	–	£140	3.7
Low-flow shower head adaptor	–	–	£15	0.5	–	–
Shower timer	–	–	£4	0.1	–	–
Ultralow flush toilet	£290	3.8	–	–	£290	7.9
Variable flush retrofit kit for toilet	–	–	£75	3.9	–	–
New bathroom taps (1.7 l flow)	£80	1.6	–	–	–	–
Low-flow bathroom tap adaptor	–	–	£20	2.7	£46	5.1
Replace washers for dripping taps	£2	0.2	£1	0.1	£2	0.2
Kitchen						
Low-flow kitchen tap adaptor	£20	0.3	£10	0.5		
Water-efficient dishwasher	£380	32.3				
Water-efficient washing machine	£380	8.5	£380	21.2		
Exterior use						
Rainwater butts (2) for garden and car	£80	8.2	–	–	–	–
Total adaptation	£1 392	–	£505	–	£478	–
Full block total (16 flats)					£7 648	–

[a]Pricing is per flat, block total is presented below flat total.
[b]Water reduction payback in years for each measure installed.
Source: Adapted from ARUP (2007) LCCP: Retrofitting adaptation for climate change. Stage 3 report: Case studies. London: ARUP.

A large-scale rainwater harvesting tank could also be recommended for the block of flats. Where there is sufficient space for one underground, the water could be used for flushing toilets and garden watering. The rainwater harvesting tank was not calculated in the report due to the complexities of the system and the need for water treatment but initial costing put the tank at £10 000–15 000 for a 6000 l tank.

Opportunities and Challenges of Combining Low-Carbon Retrofitting with Adaptive Retrofitting

As 27% of the UK's carbon dioxide (CO_2) emissions can be attributed to the nation's 26.1 million residential dwellings, it is clear that low-carbon retrofitting programmes are needed to meet GHG emissions reduction targets set by the government. Refurbishment programmes are underway, including the 'Great British Refurb', which takes a 'whole house' retrofitting approach to reducing CO_2 emissions by establishing comprehensive packages to address energy use, though it has been documented that the 'whole house approach' is missing the occupant adaptation to technological and energy use changes in the home. As adaptation becomes more pertinent to policy-makers, it could in theory be a smooth transition to consider both adaptation and mitigation together for retrofits. Additionally, as architectural adaptation is largely based on the occupant's health, safety, and comfort, the merging of both adaptation and low-carbon retrofitting would conceivably begin to be more considerate of the occupant's adaptation to technological use energy use changes, providing true 'whole house approaches'.

Mitigation and adaption can synergistically support each other and should attempt to never challenge the efforts of the other. It is possible that in some instances by the end of the century, active cooling will be unavoidable in many places where it is not currently necessary. With this in mind, every effort should be made to avoid the necessity for the use of active cooling and when it is unavoidable have prepared a building that is appropriately designed (or retrofitted) and ready to maximise the efficiency of any system that is deemed necessary to install. Adaptation in many respects can provide the necessary mitigation for the future climate along with improved comfort and safety. As can be seen, a number of adaptation options, particularly designed to deal with the impacts of overheating, share many commonalities with the typical measures that are recommended for all low-carbon retrofits. A large number of (if not all) adaptation measures that deal with water stress are also commonly a part of many sustainable building rating and certification systems, which are typically known for simply dealing with mitigation. Low-carbon retrofitting with passive measures is particularly advantageous where passive design can consider both adapting for overheating and maximising winter solar gain. Examples include, as mentioned, double glazing with low-e coating that both reduces heat gain in the summer and reduces heat loss in the winter.

Challenges of combining low-carbon and adaptation measures are clearly apparent in the costs involved in retrofitting. Some low-carbon retrofitting is not completed due to the costs; some payback period analyses show that certain buildings or homes are prohibitive to retrofit. In some cases, this issue can become even more complicated when combining low-carbon with the additional measures needed to adapt to climate change. Given the circumstance, some buildings or homes may need to be completely replaced to feasibly or practically meet the requirements of both mitigation and adaptation. Buildings that may need to be demolished are those with low thermal mass, low ceiling heights, or deep plans, particularly designed to be mechanically dependent. Others may include homes in flood zones that see considerable future increase in frequency and quantity of flooding where the area will be no longer habitable. As the Passivhaus standard is becoming increasing popular as a model for low-carbon design or retrofitting certification (e.g., Passivhaus UK, The Association of Environment Conscious Builders Gold standard and Energy Saving Trust Advanced Practice target – all of which use the Passivhaus standard as model), there is a concern that particularly the mechanical ventilation and heat recovery systems that are required will become unnecessary as the climate changes. Alternatively, testing and research by Passiv-On (EU-based) has studied the effectiveness of the Passivhaus standard in southern European locations such as Marseille, France. Results of their study showed that the high levels of insulation did assist in keeping the building cool during hot periods of the summer and that reverse cycle heat pumps used as active cooling could deliver a level of comfort (according to the Passivhaus Institut comfort criteria) without surpassing the Passivhaus energy demand limit.

Conclusions

Adaptation to climate change in the built environment is becoming increasingly important for researchers and policy-makers around the world. It has become apparent that though mitigation is still extremely significant for retrofitting, adaptation can be as important in many places where the risks of overheating, flooding, and water stress will in the future make daily life for some people more difficult or perhaps dangerous. The suburban typology, where a majority of the developed country's population tends to live, is an important area of the built environment in which to begin retrofitting for adaptation. Though there are many different types, ages, and conditions of homes, one study for the *Three Regions Climate Change Group* developed a methodology for modelling the costs of adaptation measures to meet three very import impacts: overheating, flooding, and water stress. The modelling assessed the impacts on three suburban typologies, the semi-detached house built in the 1930s and the low-rise block of flats built in the 1960s–70s. Typical living patterns, family sizes, and construction details characteristic of the building area and type defined how the homes were used and reacted to the impacts of climate change. Importantly, the tenure of the homes defined what adaptation measures would be most appropriate, acceptable, and feasible. Where the semi-detached house was owned by the occupier, it was assumed that most adaptation options would be acceptable, especially ones that provided a reasonable payback and were permanent. The block of flats was considered to be owned by a single owner that would also invest in permanent measures that were feasible. Conversely, a single ground floor flat was considered in a separate scenario where the owner only owned the single flat and had little or no interest in retrofitting. In this case, options were considered that allowed the occupants (renters) to make temporary inexpensive 'do-it-yourself' retrofits in order to adapt. These examples can prove to be useful when generalising adaptation options for meeting climate change impacts and challenges in many homes throughout the world; however, as adaptation to the changing climate is inseparably linked to a specific climatic region, the local environment, the specific hazards, exposure and vulnerabilities of the occupants, serious and thorough adaptation will need to be considered on a house-by-house basis or at least on a neighbourhood basis.

See also: Climate Change; Energy Saving; Environmental Consciousness; Environmental Risks: Flooding.

References

ARUP (2007) LCCP: Retrofitting adaptation for climate change. Stage 3 report: Case studies. London: ARUP.
British Geological Survey (BGS) (2005) *Hazards*. http://www.bgs.ac.uk/home.html (accessed 15 November 2010).
Defra (2010) *UK climate projections*. http://ukclimateprojections.defra.gov.uk/ (accessed 16 December 2010).
Environment Agency (EA) (2010) *Flood*. http://www.environment-agency.gov.uk/homeandleisure/floods/default.aspx (accessed 19 October 2010).
Gething B (2010) Design for future climate: Opportunities for adaptation in the built environment. Swindon.
Graves HM and Phillipson MC (2000) Potential implications of climate change in the built environment. *Report* 2nd edn. London, UK: Foundation for the Built Environment.
Hacker J, Capon R, and Mylona A (2009) Use of climate change scenarios for building simulation: The CIBSE future weather years.
TM48: 2009. London: Chartered Institution of Building Services Engineers.
Jenkins GJ, Murphy JM, Sexton DS, Lowe JA, Jones P, and Kilsby CG (2010) *UK Climate Projections: Briefing Report* 2nd edn. Exeter, UK: Met Office Hadley Centre.
Three Regions Climate Change Group (TRCCG) (2008) Your home in a changing climate: Retrofitting existing homes for climate change impacts. London: TRCCG.

Further Reading

Adaptation Sub-Committee (ASC) (2010) How well prepared is the UK for climate change? *First Report of the Adaptation Sub-Committee*. London, UK: Committee on Climate Change Adaptation.
Adger NW, Brooks N, Kelly M, Bentham G, Agnew M, and Eriksen S (2004) New indicators of vulnerability and adaptive capacity. *Tyndall Centre for Climate Change Research Technical Report 7*. Norwich, UK: Tyndall Centre for Climate Change Research.
BBC (2010) Snow thaw and rain bring floods in west and south Wales. *BBC News*. http://news.bbc.co.uk/1/hi/wales/8462984.stm (accessed 30 September 2010).
Brack CL (2002) Pollution mitigation and carbon sequestration by an urban forest. *Environmental Pollution*. http://www.sciencedirect.com/ (accessed 18 November 2010).
CIBSE (2006) *CIBSE Guide A: Environmental Design*. London, UK: CIBSE.
Collins L, Natarajan S, and Levermore G (2010) Climate change and future energy consumption in UK housing stock. *Building Services Engineering Research & Technology* 31(1): 75–90.
Crichton D (2001) *The Implications of Climate Change for the Insurance Industry: An Update and Outlook to 2020*. Watford, UK: Building Research Establishment.
Department for Communities and Local Government (DCLG) (2010) English housing survey: Housing stock report 2008. http://www.communities.gov.uk/documents/statistics/pdf/1750754.pdf (accessed 20 December 2010).
Department of Health (DH) (2010) Heatwave plan for England: Protecting health and reducing harm from extreme heat and heatwaves. http://www.dh.gov.uk/ (accessed 7 December 2010).
EPSRC (2010) LUCID. http://www.lucid-project.org.uk/ (accessed 26 November 2010).
EPSRC and UKCIP (2007) *Building Knowledge for a Changing Climate: Collaborative Research to Understand and Adapt to the Impacts of Climate Change on Infrastructure, the Built Environment and Utilities*. New Castle, DE: New Castle University.
French A (2006) Hosepipie ban in force from April. *The Oxford Times*. http://www.oxfordtimes.co.uk/news/705598.Hosepipe_ban_in_force_from_April/ (accessed 1 November 2010).
Gill SE, Handley JF, Ennos AR, and Pauleit S (2007) Adapting cities for climate change: The role of the green infrastructure. *Built Environment* 33(1): 115–133.
Greater London Authority (GLA) (2008) The London climate change adaptation strategy: Draft report. London, UK: Greater London Authority.
Gupta R (2005) Investigating the potential for local carbon emission reductions: Developing a GIS-based domestic energy, carbon-counting and carbon-reduction model. *Proceedings of Solar World Congress*. Orlando, FL, USA, 6–12 August 2005.
Gupta R and Chandiwala S (2009) A solutions-based simulation approach to test the technical and economic feasibility of achieving low and zero carbon homes in the UK. *ECEE 2009 Summer Study*, pp. 1607–1620.
Gupta R and Chandiwala S (2010) Understanding occupants: Feedback techniques for large-scale low-carbon domestic refurbishments. *Building Research and Information* 38(5): 530–548.
Gwilliam M, Bourne C, Swain C, and Prat A (1998) Sustainable Renewal of Suburban Areas. York: York Publishing Services Ltd.
Hajat S, Kovats RS, and Lachowycz K (2007) Heat-related and cold-related deaths in England and Wales: who is at risk? *Occupational and Environmental Medicine* 2007(64): 93–100.
House of Commons (HoC) (2008) Existing housing and climate change: Seventh report of session 2007-08. London, UK: The Stationary Office Ltd.

IPCC (2007) Climate change 2007: Synthesis report. In: Core Writing Team, Pachauri RK, and Reisinger A (eds.) *Contribution of Working Groups I, II and III to the Fourth Assessment Report of the Intergovernmental Panel on Climate Change.* Geneva, Switzerland: IPCC.

Jentsch MF, Bahaj AS, and James PAB (2008) Climate change future proofing of buildings – Generation and assessment of building simulation weather files. *Energy and Buildings* 40(12): 2048–2168.

Larson S (2010) Understanding the barriers to social adaptation: Are we targeting the right concerns? In: Hyde R (ed.) *Transforming Markets in the Built Environment: Adapting to Climate Change.* London, UK: Earthscan.

Mearns R and Norton A (2010) Equity and vulnerability in a warming world: Introduction and overview. In: Mearns R and Norton A (eds.) *Social Dimensions of Climate Change: Equity and Vulnerability in Warming World.* Washington, DC: The World Bank.

Smith I and Hopkins D (2010) *Adapting the English Suburbs for Climate Change: A Conceptual Model of Local Adaptive Capacity.* Helsinki, Finland: AESOP.

Three Regions Climate Change Group (TRCCG) (2008) *Your Home in a Changing Climate: Retrofitting Existing Homes for Climate Change Impacts.* London, UK: TRCCG.

University of Manchester (UoM): Centre for Urban Regional Ecology (n.d.). SCORCHIO. http://www.sed.manchester.ac.uk/research/cure/research/scorchio/ (accessed 4 October 2010).

Williams K (2007) New and sustainable communities in the UK. *A Report for the Cultural and Educational Section of the British Embassy.*

Williams K, Joynt J, and Hopkins D (2010) Adapting to climate change in the compact city: The suburban challenge. *Built Environment* 36(1): 105–115.

Wilson E and Piper J (2010) *Spatial Planning and Climate Change.* Abingdon, UK: Routledge.

Zero Carbon Hub (ZCH) (2010) Carbon compliance for tomorrow's new homes: A review of the modelling tool and assumptions. *Topic 3: Future Climate Change.* London, UK: Zero Carbon Hub.

Relevant Websites

http://ukcip-arcc.org.uk – The Adaptation and Resilience in a Changing Climate (ARCC) Coordination Network (ACN).

http://ukcip.org.uk – UK Climate Impacts Programme.

http://ukclimateprojections.defra.gov.uk – UK Climate Projections.

http://environment-agency.gov.uk – UK Environment Agency.

Collective Ownership

D Robertson, University of Stirling, Stirling, UK

© 2012 Elsevier Ltd. All rights reserved.

Glossary

Caveat emptor A legal principle derived from Latin that means 'let the buyer beware'. It is commonly used within a property purchase context and implies the basic premise that the purchaser buys at their own risk and, therefore, requires to fully examine and test the property themselves for obvious defects and imperfections. Consumer protection legislation often acts to challenge this presumption by setting down defined rights and expectations in respect of all consumer purchases.

Commonhold Legal definition for a property in which each owner has freehold entitlement of his or her 'unit' and is, through this arrangement, automatically a member of a company/association which owns the freehold of the development's common interest elements of the property, or alternatively has proportionate shares in these common interest elements.

Common interest property Property held jointly and in common by more than one owner who have undivided interest in the entire property.

Freehold Legal definition for the entitlement to hold a property with a perpetual right, that is, with no limit of time. Freehold property lies with the titleholder unless they transfer it of their own accord.

Governing documents These are typically legal covenants which constitute part of the title/ownership documentation for the property that specify both negative and affirmative obligations on the owner, and thus set in place the development's overall governance regime which determines both the management and maintenance of the common interest elements of the property.

Homeowners' association The homeowners' association is a legally constituted company or association which is charged through the governing documents to ensure that all the requirements set out within the development's governing documents are fully adhered to by all owners. These documents typically set down the constitution of the association and the governance rules for the management and maintenance of the common interest elements of the property.

Leasehold Legal definition for the entitlement to hold or use property for a fixed period of time at a given price, without transfer of ownership, on the basis of a lease contract. Leasehold is a fixed and marketable asset, but its value is affected by the length of the lease period.

Lien A charge made against the title of an individual's property which, in extreme circumstances, can result in the forced sale of the property to recoup the outstanding debts.

Property developer Individual or organisation that originally developed the housing project and set in place its governing documents which determine the governance system.

Property manager Commercial company that provides property management and maintenance services and, on occasion, specialist additional services to developers, individual owners, and/or homeowners' associations. They can be appointed by the original developer or, subsequently, by the owners' association.

Unit or lot Terms employed within a multi-owned private property to signify an individual asset holding within the development. A 'unit' or 'lot' can be both residential and commercial, depending on the nature of the specific development.

Introduction

In many countries, the pace and scale of multi-owned private housing development is quite breathtaking. This is particularly true in the United States. From a situation in 1970 when there were some 10 000 of these developments, encompassing some 700 000 'units', by 2000 this had grown to 223 000 developments encompassing nearly 18 million 'units'. In the following 8 years, the pace further quickened with respective figures rising to 301 000 developments with just over 24 million 'units', which represents almost 20% of the entire number of US housing 'units' (McKenzie, 2010: 54). In popular imagination new American housing was detached single-family suburban residences; now many new units are part of what are termed Community Interest Developments. While the United States perhaps represents the most striking example of this, rapid metamorphosis of private housing is evident throughout the developed world: in Australia, Canada, Israel, New Zealand, and South Africa, as well as the city-states of both Hong Kong and Singapore.

Ownership of an individual flat or 'unit' within such developments is markedly different from the ownership of an individual house (Van Der Merwe, 1994). The most obvious difference is that flat owners are typically 'physically' interdependent; those below provide support to those above, while those above shelter those below. It is this physical reality which demands that owners in multi-owned private property also be 'financially' interdependent. So while a houseowner may choose not to maintain their property, the inaction of flat owners would quickly prejudice the safety and financial security of adjoining owners. As a result of this reality, the rights of flat owners are tightly proscribed, and their responsibilities detailed: Property must be maintained to an agreed standard, and they are prevented from making internal structural alterations without securing the agreement of affected owners. Without such basic constraints in place, multi-owned private housing cannot function. A good illustration of such basic rules is provided by the recently revised common law provisions in the Scottish Law of the Tenement (Scottish Parliament, 2004). Homeownership within such developments demands that you adhere to a defined set of rules. Broadly speaking, this means that you are required to be part of an owners' association and through this contribute towards the cost of managing and maintaining the facilities held in common.

As Van Der Merwe (1994) observed, since "all systems of apartment ownership ultimately endeavour to solve the same practical problems, every legal system can only benefit from a comparative approach" (p. 15). The actual ownership rules and the resulting management arrangements that underpin this form of private housing only differ in detail depending on the legal jurisdiction. In France, for example, with some 20% of its housing stock in coownership units, a statutory system has been in place since the creation of the Napoleonic Code, as certain legal draftsmen came from Grenoble where flats were common in steep narrow valleys. More recently, specific 'co-propriété' legislation was first introduced in 1938, with the current statutory framework replacing it in 1965. Individual states in both Australia and the United States started introducing similar statutory systems from the 1960s onwards, with advisory Federal legislation following from the 1970s on. In both these cases, the emergent legal ownership arrangements took time to catch up with and, to a degree, regulate developer practice (Bailey and Robertson, 1996).

By contrast, in England, a statutory commonhold system was only just introduced in 2002, but is still not widely used in such multi-owned private housing developments (Blandy, 2010). Rather, the preference of both developers and their legal advisors is to stick with leasehold arrangements, whereby individual flats are sold leasehold and the block containing the flats, which constitutes the common building, is sold separately as a freehold. This effectively separates responsibility for common property management and maintenance from the leaseholders who are legally bound to pay for all works organised by the freeholder. This arrangement exists because until the introduction of commonhold, English property law was unable to oblige subsequent purchasers of the property to accept covenant obligations in respect of managing and maintaining the common property. Hence, the need to rely upon the leasehold–freehold relationship within multi-owned property, an arrangement that has been plagued by its fair share of problems, in large part because homeowners' cultural expectations of that tenure arrangement failed to accord with the reality of their actual ownership arrangement (Cole and Robinson, 2000; Robertson, 2006).

Despite English property law taking a long time to catch up with practice in other jurisdictions, it should be pointed out that there is a strong English common law element running through the majority of property law arrangements touched upon in this article. This reflects the legacy of the British Empire in some parts of the world. Each of these jurisdictions has what are broadly termed common interest developments which can embrace residential, commercial, or industrial usage. Mixed residential/commercial developments are not uncommon, with residential units being part of a development that can contain hotel, leisure complex, or retail components. In Australia, this model is also used to develop holiday home accommodation (Warnken et al., 2008). Within the residential context, there are four basic legally defined common interest housing arrangements:

'Condominium' ('strata titles' in Australia and Singapore, 'unit titles' in New Zealand, common condominium in Israel, coownership in Hong Kong). Here, the homeowner has a freehold interest in their residential unit coupled with a tenant-in-common interest in the common areas. Limited common area ownership can apply to parts of the common area (such as balconies, patios, and parking spaces) used by some, but not all owners. This arrangement is in contrast with the English leasehold system whereby the flats are sold on leasehold, and the common elements, on freehold, often to an owner who has no residential property interest in the block.

'Housing cooperative' ('company titles scheme' in Australia). Here, the cooperative, or corporation, owns the entire structure. Each individual owner has a lease for their unit within the building, coupled with an interest in the cooperative or corporation. This is similar to the situation in England and Wales where a group of leaseholders has used recent legal rights to collectively buy out the freehold. Although historically important in certain large American cities, co-ops are rarely created today because their legal structure can leave all co-op members liable if one defaults on their payment.

'Planned community' ('community titles' in New South Wales). The homeowner has a freehold interest in their 'unit' or 'lot' coupled with an interest in the community or owners' association that owns the common areas. As with condominiums, they can also own an interest in an area defined as a limited common area.

'Master planned communities'. Two or more of the above arrangements can coexist within a large development. In communities with more than one block, or with commercial element as well as residential units, this enables owners to vote on common matters which affect all of them, as well as on matters that only affect their particular block.

Most jurisdictions provide for a 'one unit–one vote' arrangement for all association election purposes, such as electing the office bearers charged with carrying out the functions of the association. Other arrangements can base voting rights on floor area, or on the value of the unit. The rights, rules, and responsibilities of the association, often legally constituted as a body corporate, are set down in the property's governing documents which, depending upon the specific legal jurisdiction, can be defined within statute, or set down in regulations that fall from statute, or through individual contracts (Robertson and Rosenberry, 2001).

Individual owners purchasing into such developments are therefore required to accept rights and responsibilities via negative and affirmative covenants. Examples of affirmative covenants include the obligation to become a member of the homeowners' association and pay the assessments which are levied in order to maintain the common interest property. Negative covenants normally set down use restrictions, such as not being allowed to keep pets or rent your property to a third party for longer than 6 months, or limiting putting washing out on balconies to certain specified days, to quote a few examples. These obligations and rules can also be enforced on any subsequent purchasers of the unit. As noted previously, a legal inability to do this in England helped ensure the emergence of the leasehold–freehold system within multi-owned property. In Scotland, property law allows title deed obligations to pass on to future owners. However, while there are common law provisions, these only apply if the properties' title deeds are silent in relation to that specific matter. It is the titles that set down the obligations that govern the common property, and these take precedence over the law of the tenement. Such title provisions vary markedly from block to block, and owners experience great difficulty in enforcing them (Robertson, 2010).

In other jurisdictions, unlike the situation in England and Scotland, specific statutes and regulations typically ensure a standardised and agreed procedure for organising the governance of these common interest elements. In theory, but as we shall see not always in practice, owners are more likely to know in advance of purchase what they are buying into and to understand the sanctions should they fail to play their part. They should also be made aware of the ongoing costs associated with living in this type of development, and not to budget solely on the basis of mortgage repayments. Most jurisdictions, therefore, require full disclosure when properties within such developments are sold rather than relying on 'caveat emptor' assumptions. Prospective purchasers thus receive a copy of the governing documents and should see the provision made for reserves, where such provisions exist. This report should detail all the major common building elements, estimates of their life expectancy, and the likely replacement costs. This can then be compared to the actual level of available reserves. Such jurisdictions generally have a stronger tradition of consumer protection. That said, despite having a statutory system in place, this is no guarantee that similar problems will not arise. Statutory systems also throw up a series of other challenges to notions of homeownership in such developments.

Common Problems with Multi-Owned Private Housing

As McKenzie (1994, 2010) has long argued, this quickening move towards multi-owned private housing has brought in its wake dramatic transformations in our understanding of the nature of 'home' and of homeownership; in the structure and conception of local government; and, consequently, the organisation and governance of urban space. He coined the term 'privatopia' to describe this process of change, by conceptualising such housing as a form of privatised residential governance. Although the governance regimes that operate are specific to a particular development, as will be clear by now, they do share many common characteristics and similar problems. Critical within this context are the power relations that operate through such arrangements. Power initially lies with the property developers, given that they set in place the governance regime. While these might not be explicitly designed to disadvantage homeowners, their modus operandi generally does, but to differing degrees. Owners serving on a homeowners' association will have a perspective different from that of those subject to their decisions. The inequality of these relationships is both illustrated and embedded within the governance documents and resulting regimes.

Property Developers

Given that it is the property developers, or more accurately, their lawyers who originally set in place the governance regime, they generally set down the rules to their advantage. When the rules are drawn up there are no home-owners, but upon purchase owners are contractually obliged to accept them. While some statutory systems set down guidelines regarding how the governance regime should function, lawyers generally have quite a degree of latitude in designing the governance framework. Where no statutory provisions exist, lawyers have free rein. When all the units are sold, the property developers' direct interest ceases, but their imposed governance regime outlasts them.

As lawyers cannot anticipate all the changes that might occur over the lifetime of a property, provision is made to amend the governing documents. That said, securing such amendments generally proves challenging. While some documents permit a simple majority to amend particular provisions, such as use restrictions, most operate variable majorities depending on the nature of the decision. What are termed 'supermajority' are typically required to amend provisions which are deemed to alter an individual's property interest. This mechanism, in effect, severely restricts the owners' collective capacity to bring about alterations because such a majority is very difficult to secure.

What appears peculiar is that while the local government is expected to regulate the physical construction of the building, through planning and development control mechanisms, it typically exercises no say in relation to the governance regime that applies to the building.

Property Managers

As a result of the above arrangements, within all jurisdictions there has long been a concern about the property developers' ability to embed lengthy contracts with property managers, some of whom have a direct business connection with the developer. This represents a major conflict of interest. During the initial period of occupation, owners may have a number of snagging issues, which the property developer is contractually bound to address. But if the property manager is dependent upon the developer for future work, or is part of their business, will owners get the service required? Further, when selling the units, it is in the developer's interest to deflate the property management and maintenance costs, but again this will not be in the owners' interests.

Property managers themselves have significant power, given that they deliver management and maintenance services to contractually agreed specifications set by the owners' associations. If they fail to meet these standards, the owners' association should be able to dismiss them and appoint someone new. However, the original contract signed with the developer may preclude this for many years.

Typically, it is these managers who also have control of sinking funds, monies paid by owners over time in advance of future major renewal works. Such funds, given their scale, attracted numerous fraud cases in France during the 1960s and 1970s, resulting in the introduction of strict regulations for both these funds and the property managers charged with managing them. Most jurisdictions, given such problems, have introduced some regulatory powers over property managers, although there is still more of an emphasis placed on self rather than statutory arrangements.

Homeowners' Associations

In most multi-owned developments, it is the associations' board of directors who are required to determine the level of service necessary to meet the defined governance requirements set within the governing documents in respect of common interest property. This in turn determines what owners are required to pay through monthly charges. These are, in some instances, subject to final approval by all owners at an AGM. Further, in some cases, the scale of increase is limited by statute.

These corporate bodies are also charged with enforcing the provisions set out in the governing documents. Such associations therefore have public, quasi-judicial, and charging functions which mirror local government. However, in this case, these powers are exercised within a relatively small private housing context: small, that is, when compared to the scale of the local government. By electing your neighbours, you empower them to determine the level of property services, enforce and revise the rules that govern behaviour within the development, set the monthly charge to cover the cost of these tasks, and, finally, deal with any disputes that arise.

In order to carry out these functions effectively, such bodies require to be both effective and fair. This can be difficult to achieve, given that most people are not at all clear about the governance arrangements they find themselves required to adhere to. It becomes very challenging when the association is required to notify owners of rule violations, and if necessary fine them for such breaches. In protracted disputes, where an owner refuses to pay their share of costs, a charge or lien can be placed upon their freehold interest. In extreme cases, a court can then instruct a foreclose sale of the property. So it is possible for your neighbours to force the sale of your property to recoup outstanding debts to the association. Given the challenges committee membership can throw up in dealing with such disputes and conflicts, as well as the associated personal liability and risks involved, not everyone will want to put themselves forward.

Conflicts that arise between unit owners can involve the association in internal and external dispute resolution mechanisms such as mediation, informal and formal arbitration, and when all else fails litigation. Arbitration is harder when it is the unit owners who are in conflict with the association. It is in such instances that the full implications as well as the limitations of the dual nature of their property ownership, being both individual and collective, become apparent. Again, these are not common occurrences for most owner-occupiers to engage with.

Homeowners

At the bottom rung of power relations are the owners who have no real say in determining the rights and responsibilities that apply to them, and a limited capacity to initiate revisions. This can limit their say in the quality of services provided for common interest property, and also the associated cost. More worryingly, the responsibilities which fall directly from ownership have not always been clearly articulated to them. When such properties are offered for sale, there is a detailed legal document setting out rights and responsibilities. However, it is also clear that the legal service offered by conveyancing lawyers is often inadequate, reflecting their reliance on 'caveat emptor' practice. Again, to address this failing, most jurisdictions have placed an emphasis upon improving advice and education on this housing form. Where such housing constitutes a significant segment of the market, and is regulated through statutory provision, such advice can be comprehensive, consistent, and uniform; but again this is not always the case.

Conclusions

As Clarke has observed, the "problem of finding an acceptable device to regulate relationships in communal-living situations is one that has had to be faced by all common law jurisdictions.... In most cases the devices are found to be wanting and inadequate, leading to reform and statutory solutions being introduced or proposed" (1998: 385).

A core issue here is that cultural expectations of ownership often fail to fully accord with this variant form. Homeownership within the United Kingdom, for example, is conceptualised on notions of freedom and not being beholden to anyone. Yet, within multi-owned private housing, while you own your home, you are also required to adhere to rules which proscribe your behaviour and how you use the space. In addition, you are required to make monthly payments to ensure the upkeep and maintenance of the common interest. Homeownership, in this form, can appear like a form of local 'state' housing. But this is private collective ownership, in that you, along with your neighbours, are required to govern the building to a defined set of rules which you had no say in drawing up, and have now little prospect of being able to change. You can try to influence matters, but that will demand time, effort, and knowledge. Trying to encourage others to play their part may prove a greater challenge given that most will opt out of taking an interest in such matters.

This is homeownership, but not as most people expect it. But that said, given future development pressures, and the need to properly embrace environmental considerations, this form of homeownership will constitute a greater part of the housing future.

So with individual property interests tied up within collective actions, there is a clear role for state intervention in setting in place the regulation of such developments. But given the evidence to date, we clearly need to get better at this task. Given the power interests involved, it is clear that we can never expect to get all matters right. Any system will always involve compromise. However, we should be able to mitigate the worst abuses of current arrangements; in doing so, we can learn much from the attempts of others to do just this. And yes, in time, we should be able to achieve greater residential satisfaction.

See also: Foreclosure Prevention Measures; Gated Communities; Gated Communities: Developed Countries; High-Rise Homes; Housing Developers and Sustainability; Housing Developers: Developed World; Master Plan Developers; Mortgage Market, Character and Trends: United States; Private Sector Housing Management: Asia Pacific; Private Sector Housing Management: Europe; Private Sector Housing Management: North America; Private Sector Housing Management: Post-Socialist; Self-Build: Global South; Tenant Cooperatives, Shareholders' Housing Companies.

References

Bailey N and Robertson D (1997) *Management of Flats in Multiple Ownership: Learning from Other Countries*. York, UK: Joseph Rowntree Foundation: Policy Press.

Blandy S (2010) Legal frameworks for multi-owned housing in England and Wales: Owners' experiences. In: Blandy S and Dupuis A Dixon J (eds.) *Multi-Owned Housing: Law, Power and Practice*, pp. 13–34. Farnham, UK: Ashgate.

Clarke D (1998) Occupying 'cheek by jowl': Property issues arising from communal living. In: Bright S and Dewar J (eds.) *Land Law: Themes and Perspectives*, pp. 377–405. Oxford, UK: Oxford University Press.

Cole I and Robinson P (2000) Owners yet tenants: The position of leaseholders in flats in England and Wales. *Housing Studies* 15(4): 595–612.

McKenzie E (1994) *Privatopia: Homeowner Associations and the Rise of Residential Private Government*. New Haven, CT: Yale University Press.

McKenzie E (2010) Emerging regulatory trends, power and competing interests in US Common Interest Housing Developments. In: Blandy S, Dupuis A, and Dixon J (eds.) *Multi-Owned Housing: Law, Power and Practice*, pp. 53–72. Farnham, UK: Ashgate.

Robertson D (2006) Cultural expectations of home ownership: Explaining changing legal definitions of flat 'ownership' within Britain. *Housing Studies* 21(1): 35–52.

Robertson D (2010) Disinterested developers, empowered managers and vulnerable owners: Power relations in multi-occupied private property in Scotland. In: Blandy S, Dupuis A, and Dixon J (eds.) *Multi-owned Housing: Law, Power and Practice*, pp. 35–52. Farnham, UK: Ashgate.

Robertson D and Rosenberry K (2001) *Home Ownership with Responsibility: Practical Governance Remedies for Britain's Flat Owners*. York, UK: Joseph Rowntree Foundation and YPS.

Scottish Parliament (2004) *Tenement (Scotland) Act, 2004*. Edinburgh: Scottish Parliament.

Van Der Merwe C (1994) Apartment ownership. In: Yiannopoulos A (ed.) *International Encyclopaedia of Comparative Law, Volume IV: Property and Trusts*, ch. 5. Tübingen: J.C.B. Mohr (Paul Siebeck).

Warnken J, Guilding C, and Cassidy K (2008) A review of the nature and growth of multi-titled tourism accommodation complexes. *International Journal of Hospitality Management* 27(4): 574–583.

Community- and Neighbourhood-Based Organisations in the United States

RM Silverman and KL Patterson, University at Buffalo, Buffalo, NY, USA

© 2012 Elsevier Ltd. All rights reserved.

Glossary

Common-interest community A housing development or planned neighbourhood where common areas and other amenities are mutually owned. Individual property owners are often required to be members of a homeowners' association and pay dues or assessments to maintain common areas and other shared amenities or improvements.

Intermediary organisation An organisation that facilitates linkages and transactions between other organisations. In relation to community-based organisations, intermediaries often connect local nonprofit developers with financial and other resources from larger institutions in the public, private, and nonprofit sectors.

Kibbutz A collective community in modern Israel based on cooperative enterprise. These communities represented the merging of socialism and Zionism. Initially, people lived and worked in communities that were engaged in agricultural production. Over time, other communities were organised around industry, technology, and other economic activities.

Low-income housing tax credit The LIHTC Program is an indirect federal subsidy used to finance the development of affordable rental housing for low-income households. The programme allows for proceeds from the sale of tax credits to private investors to be transferred to nonprofit organisations. These funds are used to develop affordable rental housing.

Neoliberal policies Policies that seek to transfer part of the control of the economy from the public to the private sector. These policies are based on the belief that private sector activity will produce a more efficient delivery of services. In terms of housing policy, neoliberalism focuses on eliminating public housing and other affordable housing programmes delivered directly through the government and replacing them with programmes that are delivered through private and nonprofit organisations.

Special assessment district A designated geographic area in a municipality where special purpose fees or taxes can be applied to property for public services or improvements not otherwise provided by the government.

Sweat equity A nonmonetary contribution made to a project or activity by people, usually in the form of work or time individuals commit directly to the completion of tasks.

Grassroots Advocacy and Community Development

Community- and neighbourhood-based organisations found in urban and rural settings may be considered central to the development of sustainable housing practices. They emanate from grassroots networks as well as formal organisations in the public, private, and nonprofit sectors. Community- and neighbourhood-based organisations can have a significant impact on social cohesion and housing development. The success of such organisations often depends on their ability to build capacity by leveraging human, financial, political, social, and cultural capital.

Although community- and neighbourhood-based organisations can be found across the globe, this article focuses on organisations found in the United States, although many similar organisations and models for community-based housing development discussed here are found in other countries. Thus, this article provides a framework for approaching the study of such organisations which can be applied to other settings.

Community- and neighbourhood-based organisations are subdivided into two broad categories in this article. The first focus is on grassroots organisations that derive from neighbourhood contexts. These types of organisations tend to emerge organically in response to local demands for improvements in housing and neighbourhood conditions. They are often led by residents and other indigenous groups. Grassroots organisations are also philosophically distinct. They tend to subscribe to decision-making models based on enhancing participation, local control, and neighbourhood governance.

In contrast to grassroots organisations, this article also identifies a group of community-based organisations that are designed to stimulate housing and economic development. These organisations are more formal in structure and are often sponsored by agencies in the public, private, and nonprofit sectors. Community development organisations link communities with resources and technical assistance from larger organisations in society, but this is sometimes at a cost. Because community development organisations are dependent on outside institutions for resources, local control of development can be diluted. Consequently, sustainable models for community-based housing development often rely on the presence of both types of organisations. Grassroots organisations fill a critical role in empowering residents and advocating for their interests, while community development organisations provide vital links to external resources and institutions.

Neighbourhood-Based Organisations

Grassroots and Neighbourhood-Level Organisations

There are a number of different types of grassroots and neighbourhood-level organisations found in communities across the United States. They include organisations such as block clubs, tenant associations, merchants associations, neighbourhood watch organisations, recreational and athletic clubs, community gardening clubs, parent–teacher associations, faith-based organisations, and a variety of informal groups organised by residents to improve housing and neighbourhood conditions. What unifies these groups is their geographic focus as well as their approach to decision-making and governance.

Grassroots and neighbourhood-level organisations are characteristically parochial in their focus. They emphasise tangible issues that impact the immediate surroundings of residents and basic concerns about housing maintenance, public amenities, and the general quality of life in communities. In many respects, the identity of a grassroots organisation is inseparable from the neighbourhood context. The definition of what constitutes a neighbourhood and its boundaries grows out of the manner in which residents use their physical surroundings to meet daily needs. Neighbourhood boundaries are defined in relation to housing, household consumption, recreation, education, social engagement, and spiritual and personal enrichment. From this perspective, the neighbourhood is both a distinct physical setting and a focal point for social interactions. At the same time, neighbourhood boundaries are porous. Unlike the boundaries of settlements that are demarcated by larger institutions in society for administrative purposes, organic neighbourhood boundaries are easily adjusted to meet the immediate needs of residents.

Closely related to local perceptions of, and identification with, 'neighbourhood' is the manner in which decision-making is approached in grassroots organisations. Governance is typically a deliberative process based on consensus building. Decision-making takes place in a fluid environment that encompasses both structured meetings and neighbourhood deliberations, as well as informal interactions in the community. Unlike more formal organisations, neighbourhood-based organisations practise democracy through a variety of mechanisms that include debating issues, voting on initiatives, and engaging in and crossing between public and private spheres. Grassroots and neighbourhood-based organisations also have a broad view of enfranchisement. Organisational membership encompasses most inhabitants of a community irrespective of age, gender, property ownership, income, or other distinctions. In contrast to more formalised institutions, the criterion for membership in grassroots organisations is tied to an individual's engagement in a community and his or her participation in the life of a neighbourhood. Like the definition of what constitutes a neighbourhood's boundaries, the decision-making and participatory processes in grassroots and neighbourhood-based organisations are relatively porous and fluid (**Figure 1**).

Grassroots and neighbourhood-based organisations essentially mobilise around parochial issues that are salient to community members. Many of these issues fall into the category of the mundane. For instance, block clubs engage in activities such as organising community dinners or social events. Merchants' associations advocate for the upkeep and beautification of community infrastructure. Recreational and athletic clubs sponsor sporting events and act as stewards for parks and open spaces. In a similar manner, other everyday activities are supported by faith-based organisations, parent–teacher associations, and other organisations.

In addition to mundane activities, grassroots and neighbourhood-based organisations can often serve as the first line of defence when neighbourhood threats emerge. These organisations typically identify and respond to parochial issues related to community threats such as crime, pollution, the deterioration of housing and infrastructure, inadequate public services, and other conditions that erode the quality of life. For instance, neighbourhood-based organisations in the Love Canal community of Upstate New York were the first to raise concerns about health risks due to hazardous waste. At a less extreme level, block clubs and other grassroots organisations often alert municipal officials when neighbourhood housing is in disrepair, parks require maintenance, crime is on the rise, and other immediate issues require attention at the neighbourhood level. Many of the issues that are salient to grassroots organisations are

Figure 1 Lawn sign and flower planter, the Andover Block Club in Buffalo, NY.

not often anticipated by larger institutions in society. In the absence of advocacy at the neighbourhood level, many of these issues would go unaddressed and contribute to the destabilisation of communities.

Neighbourhood Governance

A great deal of attention has been paid to the development of governance structures that are complementary to grassroots and neighbourhood-based organisations. In order to be truly grassroots in nature, these decision-making models must be based on expanding public participation and local control. During the 1960s, a body of scholarly writing emerged that examined the nature of grassroots governance and advocated for achieving it in urban neighbourhoods. In his seminal work *Neighborhood Government: The Local Foundations of Political Life*, Milton Kotler outlined a model for neighbourhood government. His model envisioned a neighbourhood government structure based on the creation of democratically controlled neighbourhood corporations with the power to make local policy, veto municipal decisions, regulate land use, raise revenue, deliver services, and implement programmes. In essence, Kotler and others envisioned a system of autonomous, self-governing neighbourhoods that would come to define American cities.

Over time, many of the elements articulated in the model for neighbourhood government have been applied to decision-making in local communities. In many cities across the United States, neighbourhood council systems have been created that formalise the role of neighbourhood-based organisations in the official decision-making processes of local government. The creation of neighbourhood council systems has promoted increased coordination between municipal governments and neighbourhood-based organisations, as well as greater grassroots influence over community and economic development policies. For example, the City of Los Angeles created a system of neighbourhood councils as a component of its 1999 charter reforms. This system incorporates 120 neighbourhoods into the City's policy-making process. Each neighbourhood receives funding and technical support from the City's Office of Neighborhood Empowerment (**Figure 2**). Another example is the Minneapolis Neighborhood Revitalization Program, which coordinates community development efforts and public participation across 67 neighbourhoods in the City of Minneapolis.

Similar efforts to augment neighbourhood control have been promoted through the creation of special assessment districts such as community benefit districts (CBDs) and business improvement districts (BIDs). In both cases, property owners agree to pay special assessments for enhanced services in their neighbourhoods. These services include things such as neighbourhood beautification, street and sidewalk cleaning, graffiti removal, special lighting, holiday decorations, special community fairs and

Figure 2 Logo of the Department of Neighborhood Empowerment in Los Angeles, CA.

events, tree maintenance, upkeep of public parks, and other improvements aimed at enhancing the quality of life. CBDs and BIDs are created through state enabling legislation and local ordinances. They are financed by property owners with additional taxes or fees, and are self-governing.

The first BID was created in 1970 to improve the condition of Chinatown in Los Angeles. Since then, over 1000 BIDs have emerged across the United States. They have also been influential in the development of similar organisations in other countries. Some examples of BIDs include the Times Square BID in New York City, the Metropolitan Improvement District in Seattle, and the Downtown Denver BID in Denver. CBDs function like BIDs, but focus on enhancing neighbourhood amenities as well as commercial districts. The City of Baltimore began incorporating CBDs in the early 1990s, and San Francisco followed suit in 2004. In both cases, numerous neighbourhoods voted to create CBDs and adopt special assessments that would be used to enhance the quality of life at the neighbourhood level.

Privatisation

In contrast to governance models based on the development of partnerships between local government and neighbourhoods, another trend that has emerged in the contemporary period has been the growing privatisation of neighbourhood-based organisations. This trend has been most visible with the emergence of gated communities across the United States. These communities are often referred to as common-interest communities and governed by homeowners' associations. Homeowners' associations manage common property in housing developments such as green space and recreational facilities. In addition to managing community amenities, they maintain storm drainage systems, streets, building facades, and other infrastructure. Homeowners' associations also provide private security and enforce neighbourhood covenants. Most controversially, they assess dues to property owners and establish rules and regulations pertaining to architectural standards and the use of private property.

Homeowners' associations have been a growing phenomenon in the United States since the 1970s. Today, more than 15% of housing units in the United States are located within common-interest communities. In a growing number of communities across the country, homeowners' associations fill a central role in the governance of neighbourhoods. The proliferation of common-interest communities represents an ongoing shift from public to private government. Among other things, this shift entails the privatisation of basic neighbourhood services. In 2000, over 126 000 homeowners' associations were registered with the United States Internal Revenue Service. For each of these communities, private government supplants a portion of the decision-making process related to how neighbourhood amenities are developed.

Although homeowners' associations represent a form of grassroots government, they have been criticised for their tendency to disenfranchise segments of local communities in decision-making and circumscribe local democratic processes. In most cases, participation in the governance of common-interest communities is limited to property owners. As a result, renters and other community members are blocked from participating in local decision-making. Because common-interest communities are private organisations, they do not have to represent broad public interests, pursue equity goals, or protect the rights of indigent groups, as many public sector agencies do. Private homeowners' associations are primarily focused on protecting property values and advancing parochial interests. As a result, they have been criticised for promoting the commoditisation of neighbourhoods and reducing their social function.

Nonprofit Community Development Organisations

Community Development Corporations

Another group of community-based organisations focuses on stimulating housing, workforce, and economic development in neighbourhoods. Although this group of organisations includes a variety of nonprofit developers and social service providers, individual organisations are often categorised as community development corporations (CDCs). These organisations are classified in this manner because their missions encompass a comprehensive focus on community development. CDCs often have formalised structures, bylaws, bureaucratic rules, professional staff, and implement a variety of programmes focused on neighbourhood revitalisation.

Many of the programmes that these organisations implement are funded by outside agencies in the public, private, and nonprofit sectors. Because of these funding arrangements, CDCs are sometimes argued to be coopted by their sponsors due to resource dependence. This is one reason that these organisations are not considered to be as grassroots oriented as other community-based organisations. Another reason CDCs are considered to be less grassroots in their orientation is because their work is heavily influenced by professional staff. While residents and grassroots organisations emphasise empowerment and neighbourhood advocacy, professional staff tend to focus more on administering community development programmes. Consequently, many CDCs have begun to make concerted efforts to connect with the communities they serve and expand opportunities for public participation (**Figure 3**).

Figure 3 The Cleveland Housing Network's Community Training Center in Cleveland, OH.

The tension between programme administration and advocacy can be traced to the history of CDCs in the United States. These organisations were initially rooted in urban communities and the Black Power movement during the 1960s. As an extension of this political movement, they were intended to play a pivotal role in levelling racial hierarchies, promoting black capitalism, and expanding grassroots control in black neighbourhoods. By 1966, the CDC model received national attention and federal funding was made available to support this approach to community development through the Special Impact Program sponsored by Senator Robert F. Kennedy. From that point onwards, these organisations shed much of their radical agenda and became more focused on the promotion of comprehensive community-building efforts in low-income neighbourhoods. CDCs became more narrowly focused on programme implementation during the 1970s, with many organisations specialising in affordable housing development and management. In the 1980s, CDCs began the process of restoring some of their comprehensive focus by adding economic development and social service programmes to their existing housing activities. Yet, through this transition, CDCs struggled to sustain their traditional advocacy functions. Many organisations had to scale back their community-organising activities in order to implement a broader range of programmes and services. As a result, CDCs became more institutionalised and less radical in their orientation.

Despite growing pressure to make trade-offs between grassroots advocacy and programme delivery, the CDC model flourished in the United States. In the late 1960s, there were fewer than 100 organisations in the United States. By the mid-1980s, the number of CDCs exceeded 1000 and by the early 1990s, there were over 2000 organisations. The number peaked at over 4600 in 2005. Much of the growth in the number of CDCs was driven by government retrenchment and the contracting out of public programmes. This shift in the relationship between government agencies and nonprofit organisations accelerated in the 1980s and continues to shape community development activities in the contemporary period. The growth in the number of CDCs was a reflection of this broader trend towards the privatisation and nonprofitisation of public programmes, which was driven by neoliberal policies.

The general expansion of CDCs has also masked some of the weaknesses in this approach to community development. Often larger and more productive organisations are cited by scholars and in the media as exemplifying the benefits that CDCs bring to neighbourhoods. For example, well-established organisations like the Bedford-Stuyvesant Restoration Corporation, the Dudley Street Initiative, and the Cleveland Housing Network are cited by boosters of the CDC movement. Despite the successes of a select group of high-capacity organisations, which some scholars have labelled the 'CDC Greats', the vast majority of CDCs are small with limited capacity. Moreover, the aggregate growth in the number of CDCs masks the fiscal instability of many smaller organisations, as well as a relatively high failure rate. In essence, a few high-capacity CDCs flourish, while smaller organisations remain relatively stagnant.

There have been incremental efforts to address weaknesses in the CDC model and build the capacity of these organisations. An early approach involved the creation of the Neighborhood Reinvestment Corporation (NRC) in 1978 by the US Congress. The NRC was renamed NeighborWorks® America in 2005. It serves as an intermediary organisation for a national network of CDCs. NeighborWorks America provides operating support and technical assistance to these local nonprofit developers in order to strengthen their affordable housing activities. Similar intermediary organisations have been created by sponsors in the nonprofit and private sectors. For example, the Local Initiatives Support Corporation (LISC) was organised by the Ford Foundation in 1979 to provide financial and technical support to CDCs. Among other activities, LISC has emerged as the largest syndicator of low-income housing tax credits (LIHTCs) for nonprofit developers in the United States. Similarly, the Enterprise Foundation was founded in 1982 by the private developer James Rouse and his wife Patty to function as an intermediary. Like LISC, the Enterprise Foundation provides financing and technical assistance to CDCs, and it is one of the largest syndicators of LIHTCs in the United States.

Other Models

There continues to be a great deal of experimentation with community-based organisations in the contemporary period. Beginning in the 1990s, faith-based organisations became more engaged in neighbourhood and affordable housing development. Churches, synagogues, and mosques began to form their own CDCs and pursue housing and economic development in order to revitalise declining neighbourhoods. Interest in faith-based development expanded in 2001 when President George W. Bush established the White House Office of Faith-Based and Community Initiatives. This initiative expanded access to federal funding for religiously sponsored community development organisations. The neighbourhood focus of this initiative was strengthened in 2009 by the Obama administration. This was symbolised with the renaming of the initiative as the White House Office of Faith-Based and Neighborhood Partnerships.

In addition to the growing presence of faith-based organisations in the areas of housing and community development, other approaches to neighbourhood revitalisation have emerged. One example is cooperative housing. Under this model, people purchase a group of homes, community buildings, and common spaces. A planned neighbourhood is created where individuals own their dwellings, but share common facilities. Cooperative housing is also governed democratically, with decision-making taking place through participatory processes. For example, residents contribute sweat equity in order to maintain common property. In some respects, the cooperative housing movement is a scaled-down version of the early Kibbutz movement in Israel, although it is exclusively focused on the shared management and governance of residential communities without agricultural or industrial components. In 1990, the first modern cooperative housing community was developed in the United States. This community was named Muir Commons in honour of the environmentalist John Muir. This cooperative community is located in Davis, CA (**Figure 4**).

Another approach to affordable housing development has been based on the community land trust (CLT) model. Under this approach, the ownership of land and housing is separated in order to reduce overall housing costs. While individuals own their homes, the land on

Muir Commons
Site Plan
1. Common House
2. Terrace
3. Tot Lot
4. Garden
5. Gathering Nodes
6. Wood and Auto Shop
7. Orchard

Figure 4 Site plan for the Muir Commons Cohousing Community in Davis, CA.

which the housing units are placed is held in trust by a tax-exempt, nonprofit organisation. Individuals lease the land their housing is placed on from the nonprofit trust for a nominal fee. The advantage of this arrangement is that land values are held relatively constant and are not included in the overall value of property when it is assessed for tax purposes by local jurisdictions. CLTs also operate under democratic governance structures, allowing residents to participate in decisions about how property held in trust is managed and developed over time. Some of the better-known CLTs are the Burlington Community Land Trust in Burlington, VT; the Sawmill Community Land Trust in Albuquerque, NM; and the Durham Community Land Trust in Durham, NC.

Future Directions

From a historic perspective, the development of community- and neighbourhood-based organisations is in its infancy. Nonetheless, many of the trends that have emerged in the evolution of these organisations have been shaped by neoliberal policies that have led to the retrenchment of public institutions and services in the contemporary period. In many instances, grassroots and neighbourhood-based organisations have rallied around issues tied to the quality and scope of public services. These organisations have advocated for improved public services. When the government had retreated from delivering such services, grassroots organisations developed partnerships between public, nonprofit, and private sectors to address their concerns. As the magnitude of neighbourhood revitalisation needs expanded, more formalised mechanisms to pursue community development have been adopted. In the area of housing, the CDC model has emerged as a mainstay in the United States.

Despite its inherent advantages in increasingly privatised and nonprofitised affordable housing markets, some scholars have begun to speculate about whether the CDC model has reached its limits. In response, efforts to build capacity among CDCs have been expanded. In addition, there is increased interest in new approaches to community-based affordable housing such as the development of cooperative housing and the use of the CLT model.

At a broader level, affordable housing is increasingly being linked to societal debates about neoliberal policies. In response to these policies, there are growing demands to link community development to progressive agendas for cities. This perspective is clearly articulated in the emerging 'right to the city' movement, which defines housing and popular access to public amenities as basic human rights. This perspective has a direct relationship to discussions of community- and neighbourhood-based organisations, since it highlights the underlying purpose of such organisations. Rights to public participation and input in neighbourhood governance are central to the development of sustainable communities. In short, this perspective argues that community- and neighbourhood-based organisations are at their best when they maximise the quality of life and expand opportunities for work, domestic pursuits, leisure, intellectual growth, and social development.

See also: Democracy and Accountability; Homeowners' Associations in Post-Socialist Countries; Neighbourhood Governance; Resident and Neighbourhood Movements; Social Movements and Housing.

Further Reading

Barton SE and Silverman CJ (1994) *Common Interest Communities: Private Governments and the Public Interest*. Berkeley, CA: Institute of Governmental Studies Press.
Brower S (2000) *Good Neighborhoods: A Study of In-Town and Suburban Residential Environments, by Sidney Brower*. Westport, CT: Praeger.
Frisch M and Servon L (2006) CDCs and the changing context for urban community development: A review of the field and the environment. *Community Development* 37(4): 88–108.
Glickman NJ and Servon LJ (1998) More than bricks and sticks: Five components of community development corporation capacity. *Housing Policy Debate* 9(3): 497–539.
Hyde C, Meyers M, and Cook D (2002) A new twist in nonprofit, for profit, and public sector relationships: The community benefits district. *International Journal of Sociology and Social Policy* 22(11/12): 55–76.
Kotler M (2005) *Neighborhood Government: The Local Foundations of Political Life*. New York: Lexington Books.
Marcuse P (2009) From critical urban theory to the right to the city. *City* 13(2/3): 185–197.
McKenzie E (1996) *Privatopia: Homeowner Associations and the Rise of Residential Private Government*. New Haven, CT: Yale University Press.
Medoff P and Sklar H (1999) *Streets of Hope: The Fall and Rise of an Urban Neighborhood*. Boston, MA: South End Press.
Patterson KL and Silverman RM (2007) Building a better neighborhood housing partnership. *Housing and Society* 34(2): 187–211.
Rohe WM and Bratt RG (2003) Failures, downsizing, and mergers among community development corporations. *Housing Policy Debate* 14(1/2): 1–46.
Silverman RM (ed.) (2004) *Community-Based Organizations: The Intersection of Social Capital and Local Context in Contemporary Urban Society*. Detroit, MI: Wayne State University Press.
Smith DH (2000) *Grassroots Associations*. Thousand Oaks, CA: Sage Publications.
Stoecker R (1997) The CDC model of urban redevelopment: A critique and an alternative. *Journal of Urban Affairs* 19(1): 1–22.
Vidal A (1992) *Rebuilding Communities: A National Study of Urban Community Development Corporations*. New York: Community Development Research Center.

Relevant Websites

www.restorationplaza.org – Bedford-Stuyvesant Restoration Corporation.
www.chnnet.com – Cleveland Housing Network.
www.caionline.org – Community Association Institute.

www.dsni.org – Dudley Street Neighborhood Initiative.
www.enterprisecommunity.org – Enterprise Community Partners, Inc.
www.livingcities.org – Living Cities.
www.lisc.org – Local Initiatives Support Corporation.
www.lacityneighborhoods.com – Los Angeles Department of Neighborhood Empowerment.
www.nrp.org – Minneapolis Neighborhood Revitalization Program.
www.muircommons.org – Muir Commons.
www.cltnetwork.org – National Community Land Trust Network.
www.ncced.org – National Congress for Community Economic Development.
www.nhtinc.org – National Housing Trust.
www.nw.org – NeighborWorks® America.
www.righttothecity.org – Right to the City.

Community Energy Systems

G Walker and N Simcock, Lancaster University, Lancaster, UK

© 2012 Elsevier Ltd. All rights reserved.

Glossary

Biomass A term used in the context of renewable energy to indicate that fuel is derived from living, or recently living, organisms, such as wood, waste, and alcohol fuels. For smaller-scale heating systems this usually takes the form of wood logs, wood chips or pellets, or agricultural wastes.

Combined heat and power A single system that generates both electricity and heating, as opposed to solely one or the other. These are often used in local district heating schemes, and are known to be far more efficient than single-generation systems.

Co-provision A term used to indicate where energy (or another resource service) is supplied by more than one route, such as through connections both to the national grid and from local microgeneration.

District heating Refers to a system for distributing heat from a centrally located device to the nearby stock of residential and commercial buildings.

Energy service company A business providing a range of comprehensive energy solutions including energy-saving projects, energy infrastructure outsourcing, power generation, and energy supply.

Heat pump A device that transfers heat from one location (the 'source') to another location (the 'sink' or 'heat sink') using mechanical work. Common examples beginning to be used to heat buildings include geothermal heat pumps that extract heat from underneath the earth's surface and air pumps that extract heat from outside air.

Microgeneration Defined in the United Kingdom as the generation of zero or low-carbon heat and/or power with a capacity of 50 kW or less.

Retrofitting A term used to describe the modification of existing buildings with additional or new components; in the context of this article, it refers to the installation of energy efficiency and/or renewable energy devices to current buildings.

Social capital The ability of an individual or group of individuals to mobilise group resources and to work together to achieve specified goals.

Introduction

The concept of community energy systems has been in place for some time in the form of local district heating networks supplying heat for homes and community buildings. Recent years have though seen a flourishing of other forms of community energy infrastructure, given an impetus by sustainable energy and carbon reduction programmes and by activists and entrepreneurs seeking to develop sustainable, low-carbon, community-based energy projects. Such initiatives can be readily identified in many different countries around the world and have been increasingly reported in both policy and academic literatures. They have been seen as a form of grassroots innovation that could provide alternative models for generating and supplying electricity and heat to homes, small businesses, and community buildings, which are radically different from centralised grid infrastructures that dominate advanced economies. It is clear though that some degree of political and policy support is needed to enable grassroots activities to flourish, with some countries such as Denmark, Germany, and Austria providing a more effective context for community energy than others.

Whilst this article concentrates on developed world contexts, it is important to note that local community-based energy generation and neighbourhood-scale electricity networks (formal and informal) also feature within urban and rural contexts in the developing world.

The Diversity and Meaning of Community Energy

Walker and Cass (2007) see community energy as one of a number of modes of deployment of renewable energy technologies – distinct from public or private utility supply, business microgeneration, and household microgeneration – but recognise that the boundaries between these modes are rather fuzzy. Indeed defining exactly what constitutes a community energy project is not entirely clear. This is for a number of reasons. First, the technologies involved now include many different methods of generating heat and electricity – various forms of wind turbines, wood and biomass burners, solar panels, hydroelectric turbines, geothermal heat, and combined heat and power (CHP) systems have all been deployed at a community scale. The amount of energy generation involved is typically small scale, but can range from under 100 kW to larger multi-megawatt projects.

Second, the energy generated from these projects can be used for a number of different purposes. Energy in the form of heat is always used locally for warming buildings through a local heat network. The same can also be true of electricity generation, but local electricity networks, except in remote island communities, are rarely entirely unconnected to a larger national electricity grid and normally some form of 'co-provision' arrangement is involved through which electricity can be sourced from both local generation and the wider grid. Furthermore, some larger-scale community energy projects, such as wind farms, seek only to supply electricity into the national grid, generating income for the local community through the sale of this energy but not directly supplying power for local uses.

Third, the models of social arrangement under which community energy projects are set up, developed, managed, and operated are very diverse. Cooperatives are often talked about in the context of community energy, with the Danish system of cooperative, locally owned wind farm development particularly significant. The cooperative model of local community ownership has now diffused into other places and contexts, including to wind farms in Japan, the Netherlands, Germany, the United States, and the United Kingdom, biomass heating systems in Austria, and small-scale hydroelectric power projects in the United Kingdom and elsewhere. However, the cooperative is only one particular model of a community project, with several other forms of social arrangement also being used. These include projects where local charities or social enterprises are set up to manage energy infrastructure, others where locally owned energy service companies (ESCOs) are established, and those where local authorities take a major role in developing and operating the energy infrastructure on behalf of the local community.

To illustrate some of this diversity, **Table 1** shows 10 community renewable energy projects from different parts of the United Kingdom.

This differentiation and diversity in the forms and scales of community energy project that have recently been developed is also mirrored in the range of objectives and drivers that can underpin their development and their labelling as 'community' in character. Walker and Devine-Wright (2008) analysed the range of different discourses promoting community energy in the United Kingdom and the characteristics that different actors saw as making energy projects distinctly in the community mode. They found little clear agreement and markedly different definitions at work. For example, some perspectives were legally driven such that community projects were simply defined as ones led by organisations with a charitable status and without commercial interests. Some had a physical rationale so that community projects had to

Table 1 Examples of community energy projects in the United Kingdom

Location	Technology and project purpose	Organisational arrangement
Llanwyddn, Wales	Biomass district heating network linking school and community centre plus 19 local houses	Public–private partnership
Bro Dyfi, Wales	One 75-kW wind turbine, grid-connected	Community cooperative
Kielder, north-east England	Biomass district heating network linking school, youth hostel, six houses, workshop, and castle	Public sector and local council
Gamblesby, north-west England	Ground source heat pump for renovation project on village hall	Village hall committee
Torrs Hydro, New Mills, Derbyshire	One 70-kW hydro system	Community cooperative
Sleat Renewables, Isle of Skye, Scotland	Biomass heater for community school and one planned wind turbine	Development trust
Knoydart, Western Isles, Scotland	One hydro system, not grid connected, selling energy to over 70 local buildings	Company limited by guarantee with charitable status
Bugle, Cornwall	Solar power system located at the village hall to provide a large percentage of its power	Public sector and local council
Galson Estate, Isle of Lewis	Three 900-kW wind turbines in development, selling the local community electricity and any excess to the grid	Development trust
Settle Hydro Ltd, North Yorkshire	One 50-kW hydro system, grid-connected, to generate community revenue by selling to the grid	Community cooperative

involve public buildings used by members of the community. Others stressed the importance of local people being involved, either in project development and/or in having a direct financial stake in a project through cooperative share issues.

Looking across these different perspectives they identified two key dimensions at issue: a process dimension concerned with who is involved and has influence in the development and running of a project, and an outcome dimension concerned with how the outcomes of a project are spatially and socially distributed (in other words who the project is for; who it is that benefits particularly in economic or social terms). These two dimensions are put together in **Figure 1** to form an indicative abstract space in which different combinations of 'process' and 'outcome', as exemplified in particular projects, can be represented. Three alternative views on the space that projects need to occupy in order to be classed as 'community' in character are shown. The first viewpoint (A) focuses on the process dimension and sees community projects as necessarily needing a high degree of involvement of local people in the planning, setting up, and, potentially, the running of the energy project. The second viewpoint (B) focuses on outcome and is less concerned with who is participating in the project than with whether the benefits are going to be concentrated locally rather than farther away.

The third viewpoint (C) is a more expansive perspective, open to many different forms of project being given a community label.

That these different viewpoints exist is not necessarily problematic (although conflicts can erupt in particular cases about what constitutes a 'true' community project and about misrepresentation of essentially commercial projects as community-driven). Diversity of projects – in both technical and social terms – is arguably necessary given the range of urban, rural, social, and political contexts in which community energy systems can be developed. Following only one model – such as insisting on a local community ownership or the local use of generated energy – would limit the extent of project development.

The Benefits of Community Energy Systems

It is clear therefore that there is a wide range of possibilities for community energy production and practices for implementing it. The potential benefits that can be derived vary with the context and form of each project, and go beyond just the direct impacts of the generated energy and avoided carbon emissions. The first of these additional benefits is that community energy production

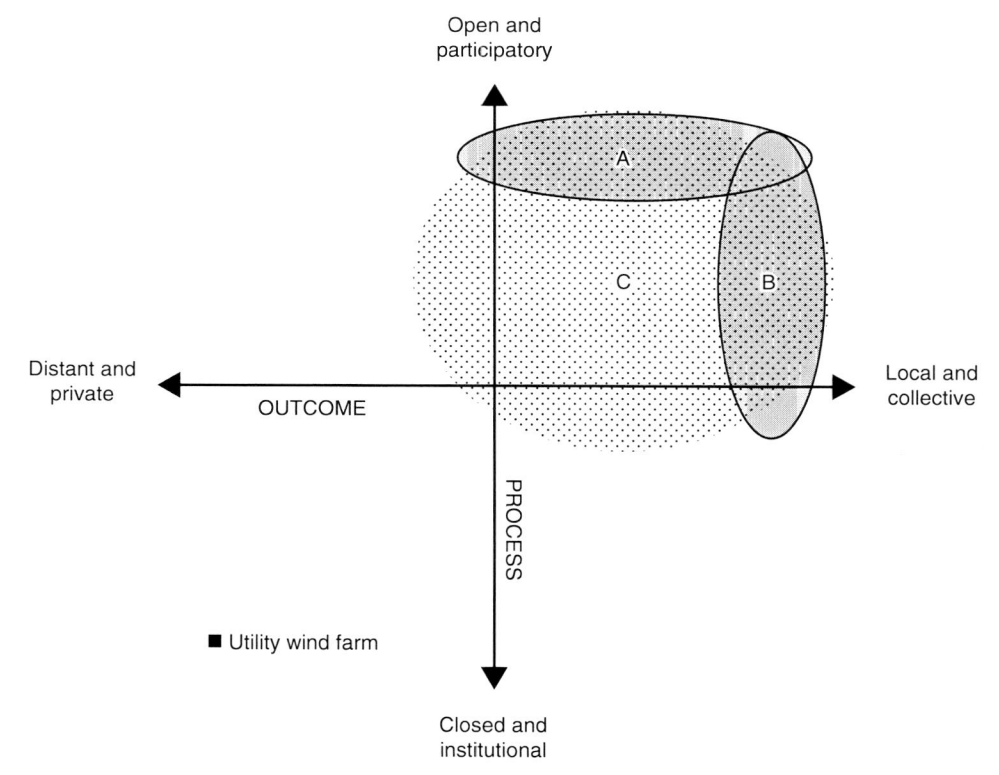

Figure 1 Understandings of community renewable energy in relation to project process and outcome dimensions. Source: Walker and Devine-Wright, 2008.

can generate income locally in a number of ways, through returns on investment and share ownership, the sale of generated energy in the form of electricity (either locally or to the national grid) or heat, or the creation of employment. Wind farms are by far the most profitable form of renewable energy and have generated proven returns through the sale of energy, as well as providing potential jobs in the management of the project and in the maintenance of the turbines, whilst biomass-fired energy projects have also been shown to generate local income, through sales of energy and by providing a market for local wood, agricultural wastes, and energy crops. If the project provides residents with more free money and greater spending power, as a result of higher employment or reduced fuel bills (see the next paragraph), economic benefits may also be derived if this extra income is spent on local goods and services, thus providing increased revenues for other neighbouring businesses. Community energy can therefore be part of more general local regeneration objectives.

A second possible benefit is that community projects based on renewable energy production may be able to provide energy more cheaply and reliably than the available alternatives, especially if grants can be obtained for upfront capital costs. This incentive operates particularly in rural areas where mains gas is unavailable and the electricity supply unreliable. The prospect of cheaper energy also means that some community energy projects have included fuel poverty objectives, targeting support and public investment on low-income communities that are vulnerable to fuel poverty and its associated health impacts. In the United Kingdom a number of projects led by local authorities or housing associations, involving solar panels, biomass heating systems, heat pumps, and other technologies along with highly energy-efficient new building designs or retrofitting of energy-saving devices to older ones, have been focused on addressing fuel poverty. An example of such a project is provided in **Box 1**.

Third, there is a widespread expectation and some evidence that projects fully or partly owned by the community will be more locally acceptable and will have fewer problems obtaining planning permission than other modes of project development. Some also point to the catalytic effect that community projects may have on the people who get involved, educating them about the benefits of sustainable energy and making them more aware of their own energy consumption practices in their own homes and daily lives.

Fourth, community cohesion and the deepening of local social capital are also often seen as outcomes of energy projects where the process dimension of significant local public participation is emphasised. Hoffman and High-Pippert (2005) particularly stress these beneficial outcomes in the context of community energy in the United States, whilst Walker et al. (2010) quote a community activist who argued that "we are raising a windmill, and symbolically the whole community comes and helps to raise the windmill . . . it's a bit like American barn raising, and I think that anything that brings a community closer together is a good thing". It can be the case that this is dependent upon the nature of the social organisation utilised in each scheme, with certain forms of ownership arrangement potentially supporting this benefit to a greater extent.

Challenges and Policy Issues

Whilst such benefits are readily promoted and emphasised in literature on community energy initiatives, there can be real and significant challenges in making community projects a success. Many practical difficulties exist and there are many examples of projects that have never got off the ground or have stumbled part way through. Such problems relate less to the innovative nature of the technology hardware involved (most being well proven) and more to

---

Box 1 The Glenshellach Community Heating Scheme

This project in Scotland involved a new housing estate built by the West Highland Housing Association with the aim of both making a significant contribution to affordable housing in the area and providing residents with a reliable and energy-efficient form of heating. An outside company, Vital Energi, was contracted in to provide the design, installation, and operation of a biomass community heating scheme which would meet the second of these aims. The heating system works through the use of a communal boiler located on the Glenshellach estate, utilising wood chips as a renewable fuel source, with the wood chips themselves being supplied from waste wood derived as a by-product of tree-felling and sawmilling in the Argyll region. Ninety homes are provided with heat and hot water through this scheme.

One of the most novel features of the scheme was the incorporation of a hydraulic interface unit (HIU) meter system, which monitors the amount of heat being used by each individual dwelling, and the use of a prepayment system in which residents purchase 'heat credits' from a local petrol station using a swipe card, which are then transferred into the heat meter within their home. The combination of these two features allows residents to more easily monitor their fuel consumption, purchasing 'heat' as and when they need it. Since it encourages energy efficiency and allows the cost of energy to be spread, it is argued this system provides a means to reducing fuel poverty in the area and that it is favoured by residents.

Alongside the objectives of tackling climate change and reducing fuel poverty, the scheme also aims to support local industry through the purchasing of fuel from a local business. It is then hoped that jobs will therefore be secured and the local economy will benefit.

complexity of the funding, installation, and operation arrangements that needed to be put in place in each particular project context. Some communities can largely 'do it for themselves', with local people taking the initiative in organising and managing projects, drawing on community skills and collective enthusiasm. Such cases are not though typical and most need more assistance, hand-holding, and guidance. This is particularly true where projects are more complex, larger scale, or risky (such as the biomass local heating networks) and where local skills and experience are limited. Projects which are only economically viable if they supply electricity to the grid can face significant problems as a small-scale generator entering the supply market, with a range of practical, financial, and regulatory barriers identified.

This all suggests that whilst community energy projects often have a grassroots, bottom-up character to them, a supportive policy environment is also needed to enable local initiatives to flourish. The different degrees of penetration of community energy projects across Europe have partly been attributed to the extent to which a supportive political and regulatory setting exists. In Denmark in 2001, an estimated 150 000 households owned or held shares in wind turbines, while in Germany an estimated 350 000 individuals owned shares in wind cooperatives (Lauber, 2004). In both countries various policy measures have been directly encouraging of cooperative ownership and small-scale generation. In contrast, in the United Kingdom only a relative handful of cooperative community-owned wind turbine projects are in place, and the regulatory environment has been seen as far more problematic.

The coming decades could see far more localised community energy infrastructures put in place with benefits that could then flow, but few observers are realistically envisaging a wholesale decentralisation of the energy system. There is a substantial potential for energy generation from community systems, and pressure for wider-scale engagement in carbon reduction and the likelihood for future instability in energy markets will provide drivers for sustainable and locally resilient energy supply. However, the incumbent regimes of major energy companies and centralised infrastructures present significant resistance to change, whilst the current economic recession does not provide a conducive environment either for large-scale financial support or for investment by individuals in local cooperative projects.

See also: Climate Change; Fuel Poverty; NIMBYism.

References

Hoffman S and High-Pippert A (2005) Community energy: A social architecture for an alternative energy future. *Bulletin of Science, Technology and Society* 25(5): 387–401.
Lauber V (2004) REFIT and RPS: Options for a harmonised community framework. *Energy Policy* 32: 1405–1414.
Walker G and Cass N (2007) Carbon reduction, 'the public' and renewable energy: Engaging with sociotechnical configurations. *Area* 39(4): 458–469.
Walker GP and Devine-Wright P (2008) Community renewable energy: What should it mean? *Energy Policy* 36: 497–500.
Walker GP, Hunter S, Devine-Wright P, Evans B, and High H (2010) Trust and community: Exploring the meanings, contexts and dynamics of community renewable energy. *Energy Policy* 38: 2655–2663.

Further Reading

Department for Trade and Industry (2004) *Co-Operative Energy: Lessons from Denmark and Sweden*. London: Department for Trade and Industry.
Hain JJ, Ault GW, Galloway SJ, Cruden A, and McDonald JR (2005) Additional renewable energy growth through small-scale community orientated policies. *Energy Policy* 33(9): 1199–1212.
Madlener R (2007) Innovation diffusion, public policy and local initiative: The case of wood-fuelled district heating systems in Austria. *Energy Policy* 35: 1992–2008.
Maruyama Y, Nishikido M, and Iida T (2007) The rise of community wind power in Japan: Enhanced acceptance through social innovation. *Energy Policy* 35: 2761–2769.
Rogers JC, Simmons EA, Convery I, and Weatherall A (2008) Public perceptions of opportunities for community-based renewable energy projects. *Energy Policy* 36: 4217–4226.
Sauter R and Watson J (2006) Microgeneration: A disruptive technology for the energy system? In: Murphy J (ed.) *Framing the Present, Shaping the Future*, pp. 110–128. London: Earthscan.
Seyfang G and Smith A (2007) Grassroots innovations for sustainable development: Towards a new research and policy agenda. *Environmental Politics* 16(4): 584–603.
Walker GP (2008) What are the barriers and incentives for community-owned means of energy production and use. *Energy Policy* 36(12): 4401–4405.

Relevant Websites

www.baywind.co.uk – Baywind.
www.geography.lancs.ac.uk – Community energy initiatives.
www.communityenergyscotland.org.uk – Community Energy Scotland.
www.dcw.org.au – Denmark Community Windfarm (Australia).
www.energy4all.co.uk – Energy4All Limited.
www.galsontrust.com – Galson estate renewables.
www.kennemerwind.nl – Kennermerwind cooperative (the Netherlands).
www.knoydart-foundation.com – Knoydart renewables.
www.ourwind.org – Our Wind Co-op (USA).
www.rccn.communitycarbon.net – Rural Community Carbon Network.
www.sleatcommunitytrust.co.uk – Sleat Community Trust.
www.torrshydro.org – Torrs Hydro.

Comparative Housing Research

M Oxley, De Montfort University, Leicester, UK; Delft University of Technology, Delft, The Netherlands
M Haffner, Delft University of Technology, Delft, The Netherlands

© 2012 Elsevier Ltd. All rights reserved.

Glossary

Comparative analysis An attempt to explain, rather than just describe, similarities and differences in two or more cases.
Housing markets The means by which dwellings are traded including the buying and selling, and the letting and renting of accommodation.
Housing policies The sets of objectives and instruments determined and applied by governments to achieve changes in housing conditions within a country.
Housing systems The combination of the housing markets, institutions, and policies within a country that together deliver housing.
Policy transfer The attempt to take a policy instrument initiated in one location (e.g., a country or region), and apply it in another location.

Introduction

Cross-national comparative housing research is defined, and the emphasis of such work on housing problems, markets, systems, and tenure is outlined. The reasons for comparative research including the generation of ideas for policy transference, the extension of knowledge of housing systems, and the propagation of new ideas are explained. The historic development of comparative housing research from the 1960s onwards is considered, the ideas of convergence and divergence are contrasted, and the search for typologies of housing systems is noted. The methods used in comparative work are examined, and the place of a scientific approach that includes hypotheses-testing is contrasted with descriptive approaches that simply present juxtaposing sets of information. The place of theory-building and the problems of quantification in comparative work are outlined. The role of comparative studies in an evidenced-based approach to policy analysis is considered.

What?

Types of Comparisons

Doling (1997) argued that all science is comparative. Here, we use comparative in the sense of cross-national. Comparative housing research is thus about more than one country, and it compares by applying research methods to questions or hypotheses. Most comparative housing research is about housing problems, policies, and markets. Much is about institutional arrangements and a good deal concerns housing tenure. The essence of comparisons between two or more cases is the similarities and the differences in the two situations.

Pickvance (2001) identifies four types of comparative analyses based on (1) whether they explain differences or similarities and (2) the assumptions they make about the causal patterns. Analysis is used to mean any attempt to identify causal relations. A causal relation exists when three conditions are met: (1) there is a theoretical reason for accepting a causal relation, (2) the causal variables are logically or temporally prior to the variables to be explained, and (3) the correlation between variables is as predicted by theory.

Pickvance, like Doling, argues that in a strict sense all analyses are comparative. Comparative analysis constitutes a situation in which two conditions are met: data are gathered for two or more cases and there is an attempt to explain, rather than just to describe. If there is the former without the latter, there is merely juxtaposition of cases and not analysis. Pickvance distinguishes universalising comparative analysis (that is used to make sense of similarities) from differentiating comparative analysis (that is used to explain differences). Both approaches assume that similarities must be explained by common processes and differences by variation. Alternative approaches arise by the introduction of the idea of plural causation where diverse chains of causation lead to the same event. This leads Pickvance to identify universalising comparative analysis with plural causation and differentiating comparative analysis with plural causation. To take a housing example to explain Pickvance's four categories: If we find similar levels of homeownership in several countries, a universalising comparative analysis would try to find similar causes in each country, whereas universalising comparative analysis with plural causation would acknowledge the possibility of different events leading to similar outcomes in different countries. Equally, if we observe different levels of homeownership in different countries, we might, through differentiating comparative analysis, seek to show that this is the result of variations in causal variables between the countries, whereas differentiating comparative analysis with plural causation would acknowledge the possibility of similar events leading to different outcomes in different countries. We will return to these methodology issues in the How? section of this article.

Policy Emphasis

What is it that is being compared in comparative housing research? Much of comparative housing research has been dominated by housing policy issues. In this sense, it is typical that within a society, housing problems are observed and governments attempt to take action to address these problems by the use of policy instruments that are seen to have policy outcomes. Housing problems include, for example, shortages in housing of a required standard; high levels of housing costs compared to incomes, that are typically said to be affordability problems; homelessness, meaning that certain households are without suitable accommodation or have no accommodation at all; a lack of housing options or choices for households; and low levels of housing production compared to household demands or needs. The policy instruments used include taxation, subsidies to producers and to households, regulations that influence rent levels, and standards and rules that influence the cost and availability of credit. Studies of policy outcomes seek to link changes in housing problems to changes in policy instruments. Similarities and differences between countries in housing problems, policies, and outcomes have been the subject of a large volume of housing research that has been driven by a variety of theoretical perspectives and has used a variety of methods. Again, we will return to this in the How? section.

Tenure

Studies of tenure have dominated much of the policy-oriented comparative housing analyses. The tenures considered have typically been owner-occupation, social renting, and private renting. This is despite the fact that the detailed definition of these tenures varies from country to country and several forms of tenure including condominium living, shared ownership, and social homeownership do not easily fit these divisions and some forms are specific to particular countries. Nevertheless, comparative research has attempted to investigate such questions as: why do homeownership levels vary between countries? what roles do homeownership play in welfare provision within countries? why is private renting more popular in some countries than others? and what differences are there in the way that social housing is allocated and subsidised in different countries? Understanding differences in the supply and allocation of social housing between countries means that comparative analysis has to consider the nonmarket as well as market forms of provision. The varying types of housing associations and public housing suppliers, as well as the ways in which they operate are, for example, the key aspects of several comparative studies.

Markets

Housing markets bring together the demand for and the supply of dwellings. Comparative investigations of housing markets consider the means by which dwellings are traded, including the buying and selling and the letting and renting of accommodation. Housing markets in different countries have been the subject of a good deal of comparative analysis. It is, however, usually not the market that is compared as a whole within a country, but an aspect of that market is compared with the aspect in another country. For example, there are several studies that look at variations in house prices between countries, taking a single average price indicator (with variations over time within a country, but, less often, geographical variations – north/south and urban/rural variations – at a comparative level are rare). Explanations are sought that link housing markets with other aspects of the economic and social systems within the relevant countries. Thus, links with finance markets, taxation policies, and demographic factors are common. Economists have attempted to compare price elasticity of demand (relationships between changes in prices and changes in amounts demanded) and price elasticity of supply (relationships between changes in prices and changes in amounts supplied – usually the amounts built) in order to discover why relationships vary between countries.

Institutions

Institutions have made an increasing contribution to comparative analysis. Here, institutions is used in a broad sense to encompass organisations such as firms, public bodies, and other agencies as well as the rules, norms, and regulations within societies. It could be the institutions themselves that are the topic of the research. Such a study might, for example, compare housing associations, mortgage lenders, homelessness agencies, or house-building firms among countries. Alternatively, institutions are seen to be part of the explanation for variations in some other set of outcomes between countries. This sort of institutional perspective on comparative housing analysis contrasts with data-driven approaches that seek explanations and/or predictions that are independent of variations in institutional arrangements.

Systems

It is possible to envisage the total housing system within a society comprising the markets, institutions, and policies that deliver housing. Understanding a housing system means that both the market and nonmarket organisations and forms of provisions will need to be considered. One approach to comparative housing analysis is to base comparisons on the explicit or implicit idea of a national housing system without any consideration for variations within the system or particular facets of the system within the country. Another is to acknowledge variations, especially of a geographic or thematic type, within countries. So far, we have referred to similarities and differences in housing phenomena between countries. Comparative housing research can consider comparisons between towns or regions or other localities in different countries, or can use such localities as the basis of case studies for comparing a given housing phenomenon between countries. Comparative housing research in short does compare between countries, but the comparisons need not be about whole countries. One can imagine, for example, a comparison of the nature and consequences of rent controls in Paris and Madrid that made no pretensions to be about a comparison between France and Spain.

Scope

English language comparative housing research has been dominated by studies focused on western, and more particularly north-western, Europe. Studies of central and eastern European countries are growing. Some countries in southern Europe, for example, Greece and Portugal, have been the subjects of relatively few studies. There have been several studies that have included North America and Australia, and comparative work in Asia is increasing. Studies that cover African and South American countries are scarce.

This article is concerned with research undertaken by social scientists. This includes economists, sociologists, and public administration specialists. Much of the work is interdisciplinary, bringing together several disciplines. More information on this aspect will be provided in the How? section.

Why?

General Aims

What are the aims of comparative research? It might be argued that policies are culturally, historically, and geographically distinct, and can rarely be exported. However, knowledge of policy instruments and outcomes in one country can inform analysis of similar issues in another country. Thus, with appropriate regard for the problems of transferability, comparative housing research can aim to improve policy application and outcomes. New policy ideas may arise from the stimulus of information about how things are done elsewhere, and exposure to different approaches can challenge insular beliefs about the causes of problems and the effects of policy instruments. Knowledge of the outcomes of the application of policy instruments in other countries thus may result in 'lesson learning' that will improve policy application. This can mean that lessons about how not to use the given housing policy instruments as well as how to use them successfully can arise ('best practices'). Understanding differences and similarities between societies can improve understanding of the processes at work within societies. The aims of comparative research in practice are frequently policy orientated, but they might be at a more general level related to a desire to understand how a housing market or system or part of that market or system operates. This could include understanding how different institutional arrangements contribute to different housing outcomes. The aims could also be technique- or theory-advancement orientated, with comparative method being used to build new theoretical concepts.

Specific Aims

At a more structured level, the following aims for comparative housing research have been suggested:

1. *Generally, extend knowledge by getting to know and letting others know.* This is about information gathering and extending knowledge that may lead to new ideas and analysis at a future date.
2. *Get ideas for new policies.* The explicit purpose in this case is to find instruments that might be transferred.
3. *Obtain material that can be used to reject arguments based on narrow perceptions.* Some policy ideas are the result of 'home-grown truths'. Beliefs about a policy instrument might be rebutted by an appeal to the facts in other countries.
4. *Examine theoretical techniques used by housing researchers in other countries and judge their applicability to one's own.* This is a narrower and more technical aim than the others. It may be an offshoot from pursuing one of the other aims.
5. *Investigate the operation of a professional activity in other countries in order to judge the potential for persons from one country competing as professionals in the other.*
6. *Examine the operation of some sort of system in a wide context to simply understand the system better or to find ways of making the system work better.* This system might be economic, political, or social in nature. The

interrelationships of the parts of such a system across countries might be investigated by pooling information to better understand how markets, governments, and societies function.
7. *Postulate a housing system and examine the interrelationships of housing system variables to other variables.* For example, what effect does the housing system have on the macro economy or the land-use system have on the housing system?
8. *Accumulate knowledge and ideas to formulate hypotheses.* The stimulation provided by new material in different countries may lead to new ideas. This is a necessary prelude to scientific hypothesis testing, but the hypothesis formulation process is not in itself scientific, it relies on judgement, hunch, and inspiration, all of which may be stimulated by international study.
9. *Test well-defined hypotheses.* The testing of hypotheses in a bigger framework than single countries may be a way of obtaining more data and using a cross-section approach or it might allow the pooling of cross-section and time series data (Oxley, 1991).

There are connections between this list and the 'curiosity, counselling, cumulativity' typology proposed by Lundqvist (1991). The point (1) given above is essentially curiosity and (2)–(5) have an element of 'comparing different ways of coping with similar problems' which, it is claimed, characterises counselling. The points (6)–(9) together constitute the search for systematic explanations which typifies cumulativity.

The objective (2) given above has become of interest to policy makers. Studies that look at the idea of housing policy transfer between countries have been undertaken to examine policies from other countries that might be applied in the hope of achieving a given objective more effectively. Policy transfer is also a key element of public policy texts (e.g., Hill, 2005; Hudson and Lowe, 2009). The need for contextualisation in transferability analysis is recognised in particular by Hantrais (2009). This point is expanded in the comments on methodology later in this entry.

When?

Historic Development

Many regard Donnison (1967) as one of the first to write systematically about comparative housing research (Oxley, 1991). He gave some first insights into policy in several countries. Selected events in European countries were used to illustrate a series of arguments about the nature of housing policies and the roles adopted by government. Others followed. For example, Fuerst (1974) edited a set of essays on public housing in Europe and America; and the OECD (1974) investigated certain housing finance issues.

Schmidt (1989a) characterised the decennium up to the late 1970s as one where comparative housing research lost its contact with the general theoretical and methodological developments in social sciences. It underwent a revival, for example, with Duclaud-Williams (1978) examining varying policy developments in France and Britain against a background of changing political circumstances, and Hallett (1977) comparing policy in West Germany and Britain. Many Western housing researchers 'discovered' the field of cross-national housing research from then on, widening the geographical coverage and deepening the analysis (e.g., Allen et al. 2004; Ball et al. 1988; Barlow and Duncan, 1994; Boelhouwer and van der Heijden, 1992; Donner, 2000, 2006; Haffner et al. 2009; Hallett, 1988; Kemeny, 1995; Lundqvist, 1991; Ronald, 2008; Stephens et al. 2002; van Vliet, 1987; Whitehead and Scanlon, 2007).

Convergence

Schmidt (1989b) set out to undertake a statistical analysis of the housing market developments in 18 countries to test the three modes of theoretical explanation, convergence theory, labour movement theory, and an institutional model based on theories of corporatism. The idea of convergence was propagated by Donnison (1967) and restated by Donnison and Ungerson (1982). The basic proposition is that the economic and demographic trends are leading to an increasing similarity of housing policies and markets in industrial societies. This is seen to occur irrespective of party-political, ideological, and institutional factors. Schmidt (1989b: 83) concludes that, "the results show that contrary to convergence theory and its associated thesis of a particular 'logic of industrialism', institutional and ideological factors loom large".

Before Schmidt (1989b), Burns and Grebler (1967) in effect also tested convergence in a quantitative way. They studied the stages or trends that countries follow in their relationship between housing investment and the state of economic development by using multivariate analysis. The basic idea is that economic advancement leads to a common route of development of the housing system. The rules that govern human behaviour everywhere will cause the links between welfare, economic development, and social and demographic factors.

Another research duo studying the movement of western European countries through more specific policy stages are Boelhouwer and Van der Heijden (1992). These policy stages run from reacting to scarcity on the housing market after the Second World War, to more emphasis on housing quality, and later greater emphasis on targeting support until possibly shortages reappear on the housing market. Even then, these authors explicitly indicate that housing systems are far too diverse for any convergence to take place.

The best-known, most coherent and clearly structured contribution to the convergence approach is Michael Harloe's 1985 book *The People's Home?* Using a political–economy approach, he emphasised the politically influenced national responses to the long-term dynamics of capitalism. According to this line of thinking, each expansion in capitalism will result in a particular set of social arrangements, including the one for the provision of social housing.

Divergence

Contrary to the structural determinism of the convergence approaches, the so-called divergence approaches assume that countries have a choice within the same stage of economic development. Such approaches with divergence perspectives are called theories of the middle range. Choice is based on the design of the market with social structures or constructs being either private or collectivist. Social and cultural heritage together with politics and ideology will determine the design. The divergence line of reasoning is most closely related to the work of Jim Kemeny (1995). According to him, much work was wrongly influenced by the Anglo-Saxon model of residualisation of the social rental sector. He called that making the 'Romeo error in comparative renting'. This involves using the taken-for-granted assumptions that underpin the operation of the researcher's 'home' society as the comparative epistemology through which the housing policy contexts of other societies are understood. Governments however have a choice; they can choose to have profit and nonprofit providers of rented housing that are in competition with one another (unitary rental market) or not (dual rental market). Only in the latter case will the social rented sector be marginalised. In the former case, the nonprofit sector may be dominating, leading, or influencing the rental market.

Kleinman (1996) arguing against policy convergence in the so-called Anglo-Saxon and Rhineland approaches introduced the concept of policy collapse followed by a bifurcation in housing policy. Housing policy, in its traditional sense of output targets and bricks and mortar subsidies, has collapsed to make way for poverty issues on the one hand and homeownership issues on the other, he argued, in line with broader welfare state developments. The policy collapse is taking place regardless of the starting point of different models. And even though common themes can be identified, Kleinman (1996) explicitly rejected policy convergence as an overarching explanatory concept. Instead, the common themes will be mediated by a context leading to path dependence of policy: history, policy, and institutions together determine 'new' policy which in turn influences the housing market and its actors, setting the scene for further policy changes.

Path Dependency

It has been shown that an understanding of differences in policies and institutional arrangements can be enhanced by considering the historical processes that have led to current outcomes. One way to do that is with the help of path dependence approaches which are rooted in political science, and are considered actor-based approaches. With an analysis from the viewpoint of elite actors reported by Bengtsson (2009), the surprising differences in the housing systems of five Nordic countries could be explained. He concludes that the inertia in public policy combines with the long lifetime and inflexibility of the housing stock and the regulation of the tenures to produce resistance to changes. The existence of limited profit housing enterprises in relation to their contexts (Lawson, 2010) has also been examined using such a path dependency approach. The explanation of the evolvement of housing allowance systems within their own context in different countries can also be classified as such an approach (Kemp, 2007).

Typologies

Theories of the middle range often propose typologies of housing systems. The study by Barlow and Duncan (1994) can be considered to be one of the best early examples of empirical analysis of divergence between housing systems. They follow the Esping-Andersen (1990) typology of welfare regimes: liberal, corporatist, and social democratic. One of the main criteria for making this typology is the degree to which social rights are decommodified, or independent of pure market forces. In a liberal welfare regime, decommodification is minimised; in a corporatist regime, the rights are based on class and status; and in a social-democratic regime, social rights are universal, and thus decommodified. Barlow and Duncan (1994) were one of the first to use this typology as a starting point for analysing the relative effectiveness of markets and governments in the provision of housing. Many others followed (e.g., Hoekstra, 2003; Kemp, 2007; Quilgars et al. 2009). In due course, other welfare regimes were introduced, like the 'radical' one, a southern European, Mediterranean or 'rudimentary' one, and an East-Asian one. Other researchers reshuffled or broke down regimes, such as Ronald (2008) who identified distinct homeownership ideologies in the United Kingdom, Australia, and the United States within the liberal regime and within the corporatist regime, and Hoekstra (2003) who distinguished labour-led conservative and modern corporatist welfare state regimes, the first with a dominant position for the state, the second with an important, if not dominant, position for the family, and the third with welfare services provided by both the market and the State.

Typologies have not only been used for welfare regimes, but also in approaches to explaining housing policy. Somerville (1994) compared four different approaches to explaining housing systems based on their characteristic ontology and epistemology. He argued that explanations in terms of systems of actors are inherently superficial. One needs to go beyond them in order to achieve an acceptable level of explanatory adequacy. Even though Somerville (1994) attempts to rescue hypothetico-deductive explanations from realist and culturalist criticisms, he concludes that they have serious limitations in terms of conceptual vagueness/ambiguity and contextual fragmentation. He uses regulation theory as an example of a realist explanation and concludes that it cannot meaningfully be applied to housing policy. His assessment of the culturalist explanations, using Kemeny's theory as an illustration, also yields ontological and epistemological problems.

An example of the systems approach can be found in the work of Ball and others. Ball et al.'s (1988) essay on the theory and research methods was very critical of comparative housing research, especially that dominated by a 'liberal interventionist' approach. A principal fault of such work is seen to be the 'lack of analysis of structures of housing provision'. This 'specifies the nature of the social agents involved in the provision of particular forms of housing and their interlinkages. Producers, consumers, and financiers in different guises all have their place within structures of provision'. Structures of provision can be viewed, like several other notions, as a device for 'tying things together' a sort of ordering framework or methodology. No theoretical basis is needed then. Donner's work (2000, 2006) constitutes examples of international housing information that is presented without a strong theoretical framework.

The study by Lawson (2003) applies realism to housing networks. It builds upon critical realist ontology of changing necessary and contingent relations, forming unique causal mechanisms in these networks. She argued that explanatory research requires the comparison and contrast of these clusters of relations over time and space. In order to identify differences between and changes within housing networks, such a study demands a concrete and historical approach to analysis.

How?

Methods

Despite the research typologies identified in the previous section, a good deal of comparative housing research is vulnerable to the criticism that is under-theorised with broad and often poorly structured descriptions rather than insightful analysis. The methodology is often unclear and this is linked to a lack of clarity in the purpose of the study. It has been argued that comparative research needs 'explorers, empiricists, theorists, and scientists' (Oxley, 1991). The explorers discover, describe, and report. There is less need for explorers as territory becomes known, but there are always changes in policies and structures to report on, and for some countries (as argued above) there is still a shortage of housing system information in the English language.

Empiricists

Empiricists who collate factual information according to consistent definitions have much to do. On many items, they face the problem of a lack of internationally consistent classification systems for crucial housing variables such as tenure, quality of the stock, and housing subsidies. There are many attempts to compare, in a tabular fashion, tenure in different countries. Typically, there are divisions between owner-occupation, social renting, and private renting. However, the meaning of these tenures and their definitions for the purpose of collecting data varies between states. Different sets of property rights are attached to the tenures in different countries. Social renting in particular takes a variety of institutional forms and is subject to varying allocation criteria between countries. In some nations, there are significant amounts of accommodation that might be classified as cooperative housing that is subject to some sort of collective ownership. In others, there are forms of social homeownership that is allocated according to needs-based criteria that are typical of social housing generally. Such housing may, however, have some property rights such as a claim to some or all of any capital appreciation in the property and an ability to trade the occupation rights that are more usually associated with owner occupation. These tenures that appear nonmainstream from the viewpoint of the internationally comparative empiricist tend to be either ignored, forced into a mainstream category (owner occupation, social renting, private renting), or lumped together as 'other' housing. As a matter of detail, some tenure tables compare all housing, whereas others compare permanent housing, and others set second homes to one side or include them in the main tables depending on the convention of the national data from which the comparative table is derived.

Data that attempt to represent differences on housing quality between countries are beset with similar problems that arise from national derivations of definitions and survey data. What counts as poor quality in one country may not, in short, count as poor quality in another country. This is not just about variations in the conceptualisation of physical standards; it is also about whether the experience of neighbourhoods as well as dwellings is considered and whether or not, in the case of rented housing, perceptions of the quality of management are included in the evaluation of quality. What counts as a housing subsidy within a country is often difficult to define and, thus, to measure. The problems are multiplied many times over when comparisons between countries are attempted. For example, tax relief on mortgage interest payments may be counted as a subsidy in some circumstances but not others. If all interest payments, and not just those for housing loans, are tax deductible, then the relative tax advantage for housing may be nonexistent. Comparisons without taking into account the structure of the tax system as a whole may be misleading. These examples of data problems illustrate the difficulty of measurement faced by empiricists. This does not mean that comparative measures are impossible. Rather, it suggests that they have to be undertaken with caution and regard for the peculiarities of varying national definitions and rules.

Theorists

Theorists provide ideas to make sense of facts and they build models and formulate hypotheses. When theory is explicit in comparative studies, it often comes from the discipline of the researcher. When comparisons are between countries, some sort of paradigm that conceptualises the totality that is to be examined, or part of which is to be examined, is needed. The dominant paradigms in comparative housing analysis have come from economics and sociology. There are claims for other disciplines, for example, political science, to be given more weightage (Bengtsson, 2009). Alongside the studies based on single disciplines, there are also attempts at multidisciplinary and interdisciplinary approaches to comparative housing studies. In debates about the relative merits of alternative methodological processes, comparative studies are bound by considerations within housing studies more generally as to the value of particular approaches. The application of a single discipline allows the methods of that discipline to be applied with some rigour. There have been arguments that housing has a claim to be a discipline in its own right and that the search for a theory of housing has some merit. Others have argued that housing is a field of activity, an area of policy and practice, and a complicated multifaceted phenomenon, but not a discipline, and therefore a theory of housing is inappropriate (Oxley, 2001). The application of a variety of disciplinary-based approaches to housing can provide many alternative and sometimes opposing theories about housing. If housing is viewed as an area of investigation rather than a discipline, international studies will continue to benefit from inputs from many disciplines. It has been argued that 'multidisciplinarity in housing studies is very difficult to justify' (Clapham, 2009: 2), because different disciplines are based on different assumptions about human behaviour and apply fundamentally different methods. A process whereby several disciplines work together simply glosses over these differences. The alternative way forward is to 'move as far as possible in the direction of interdisciplinarity' (Clapham, 2009: 3), which involves fresh approaches by which elements of different disciplines are integrated and applied to a common problem. This implies a unified and agreed theoretical approach. It may also require an approach that 'moves beyond the limits of positivism and is built around the relationship between humans and the material house' (Clapham, 2009: 9).

A Scientific Approach

Scientists do tend to accept at least a degree of positivism in that they test hypotheses that propose measureable relationships between variables. A lack of adequate data from empiricists and testable propositions from theorists helps to explain why scientists are a scarce phenomenon in comparative housing research. Where data are available or can be constructed in a reasonably consistent way for acceptably similar phenomena in different countries, there are theories that suggest relationships that hold good between societies, despite a whole host of historical, institutional, and cultural differences, there is scope for the cautious application of scientifically driven hypotheses-testing approaches. This does not mean ignoring the differences; it merely means exposing similarities and differences between relationships. If explanations for differences in observed quantitative relationships are required, these may well in turn be found in underlying conditions relating, for example, to institutional and cultural phenomena.

A scientific approach may well be compatible with what might be termed high-level comparative analysis. A distinction has been drawn between zero, low, middle, and high levels of comparative housing analysis (Oxley, 2001). In low-level comparisons, there may simply be descriptions of housing systems in different countries without any systematic attempt to compare and contrast. In middle-level comparisons, there is a significant level of systematic comparison with a given purpose. The purpose might be gaining policy or practice lessons from other countries for application in a given country or the key object of the study might be to examine the varying impact of a common external phenomenon in several countries. For example, the impact of European Union rules or a worldwide recession on housing outcomes in several countries might be the focus of such a study.

High-level comparative studies systematically examine intercountry similarities and differences. They apply an analytical approach that utilises explicit theory or theories and often relies on a high level of empiricism.

Conceptual Issues

Whatever the method that is adopted, comparative studies face several problems including those of conceptual equivalence, cultural explanation, and exceptionalism (Pickvance, 2001). It will be useful to consider each of these in turn.

Conceptual equivalence

To be compared, cases need not be identical but need to be commensurable. This means they can be placed at the same or different points on a dimension of interest. Thus, for example, the rights of a tenant may differ from one country to another. This does not mean that renting is so different that the cases cannot be compared. As long as there is, in both cases, some sort of legal basis for occupancy, there is arguably a common dimension within which comparison can occur. The issue of many different meanings and definitions of social housing was identified earlier. The issue of conceptual equivalence alerts one to these problems without saying that the problems are so big that no useful comparisons may be undertaken.

Cultural explanation

Pickvance argues that for those who consider culture a strong explanatory concept, cultural explanations of variations that reduce complexity to a few dominant features are acceptable. For others, such a cultural explanation may be insufficient. Thus, "What counts as comparative analysis depends on the perspective adopted. What for some is explanatory is for others a mere descriptive or classificatory step towards explanation that does not explain in itself" (Pickvance, 2001: 25–26). Cultural factors may be seen as part of an explanation for differences or they may be seen as reasons why explanations that ignore cultural factors can be unsatisfactory.

Exceptionalism

Exceptionalism is a label for cases that are not consistent with a dominant pattern. The recognition of exceptionalism like cultural explanation can be seen as a satisfactory conclusion in itself or be viewed as a spur to a further investigation. The latter is likely to be the more productive route. The additional investigation can usefully include a revision of the conceptualisation involved as well as additional empirical information.

Comparative Housing Methodology and Social Science Methodology

Work on comparative research methods in social sciences typically ignores comparative housing policy (e.g., Hantrais, 2009) and much of the theoretical and empirical work in comparative housing research ignores the theoretical developments in social sciences generally. For example, although policy transfer between countries is an increasingly significant feature of housing research, the vital relationship between comparative research methodology and policy transfer is marginalised despite the depth of policy transfer studies in the social sciences. The need for contextualisation in transferability analysis as recognised by Hantrais (2009) is frequently ignored by housing researchers.

This need for contextualisation suggests that neither (1) the universalistic and positivist approaches, relying heavily on quantification of dissimilar concepts nor (2) the culturalist approaches that identify each case as unique are useful in applied policy transfer analysis. Rather, taking the ladder of abstraction approach from 'universalism' to 'particularism' that puts the theory and practice of contextualisation at the centre of the methodology is more appropriate. The context-boundedness of specific policy instruments should, taking this approach, be a challenge to which comparative housing researchers are alert.

Method and Purpose: Qualitative and Quantitative Approaches in Comparative Housing Research

Any methodological decisions on how to compare will have to be accompanied by a methodological decision on the data to be used. In other words, what sources will be used and how will the data be collected? In principle, there are the decisions about using primary versus secondary data, using written sources (literature and internet) versus spoken sources (interviews), and using a qualitative versus a quantitative approach. Some comparative research will use a combination of these sources, starting with a literature search followed by ways to go beyond the information found in the literature and verify the hypotheses that were formulated.

The review of methodological problems does not suggest that there is a right or best methodology that can be applied in comparative work. The key issue is, rather, that the method is fit for purpose and that it helps answer whatever the research question happens to be. The method should be based in theory that is sound and coherent in relation to the research question. Useful theories do not provide good descriptions of the real world. That is not their purpose. By processes of abstraction and simplification they aid understanding of what has happened, what is happening and, what might happen in the future. The test of a good theory is whether it is useful in answering a question. For some questions, theoretical approaches that rely heavily on quantification may be helpful, for others, less quantification and more qualitative information may be useful, and for many, a combination of both is desirable. If the question is about how we got where we are, some historical perspective is of course necessary. If one is trying to understand the reasons for different levels of owner-occupation between countries, for example, a methodology that relies on current data on, say, financial incentives, property rights, and relative costs of owning and renting may fail to reveal the significance of historical facts in, for example, shaping the long-term structure of the housing stock (which may be more or less conducive, in varying circumstances, to individual ownership of dwellings) and determining cultural preferences for different tenures. The approach might still be quantitative but the data set used will include different factors than the one based on available secondary data sets. If, alternatively, the question is about current attitudes to owner-occupation, and if and why people in different countries feel that owner-occupation is more or less risky than other forms of investment, and indeed whether or not households think of owner-occupation as a form of investment, a different methodology and different sorts of information that might come, more appropriately, from qualitative attitude surveys than from the application of established data sets is required. Of course, the answer to the question about international variations in owner-occupation levels might also benefit from such information and might benefit even more from comparable survey data gathered in the past. The point is that, in the earlier question, attitudes were not the central question even though they might be part of a long-term historical explanation.

Some comparative studies are about the future. That is, they seek to forecast how the given housing phenomena will vary between countries at a given point of time in future. If this is the case, some sort of causal model of the phenomena might be used. Such models with good predictive value for items such as future homeownership levels, or future levels of house-building are usually complex when applied within countries. When applied between countries, they might give very poor predictions indeed. In such cases, one may have to contemplate the idea of differently specified models being used in different countries in an attempt to get reasonable predictive comparisons.

Many comparative studies are now conducted by teams that have expert knowledge of the several countries that are to be examined. Most studies are based on questions that are put before country experts either in spoken or written form (e.g., Donner, 2000). These interview type of methods could be loosely defined as qualitative methods, albeit methods that more or less miss transparency when the choices of the researcher are at stake. Examples of rigorous qualitative comparative housing research (Elsinga et al. 2007; Quilgars et al. 2009) may be as scarce as those of rigorous statistical testing (Horsewood and Neuteboom, 2006; Schmidt, 1989b).

Quantitative Sources

Quantitative sources, however, are manifold. But they often do not go very deep, usually because of differing definitions in different countries. The UNECE data on construction that go back some decades had many empty cells. Nowadays, they are presented under the title of Bulletin of Housing Statistics for Europe and North America. The bulletin relates population and households data to dwelling stock data, presents information on the dwelling stock (e.g., size of dwellings), as well as information on the construction of dwellings (number of dwellings, building material, value of construction). Some of the data are not later than the year 2002, however.

A more recent initiative is the one by the ministries responsible for housing within the European Union. Since about the early 1990s, every few years, irregularly, a new version of Housing Statistics in the European Union has been produced. Although the versions vary in the data they present, some data have been consequently reproduced, such as some economic and demographic data, data on the quality, availability, and affordability of the dwellings. The 2004 and 2005–06 versions also contain information on the role of the government, some of which had also been presented in the 1998 version. Other versions have included information on environmental aspects of housing and urban renewal (1998).

As housing is not considered a direct EU responsibility, Eurostat (the EU statistical body) does not produce very many housing statistics, but its involvement is in areas of social indicators or indicators for poverty. A new initiative along this line (2003–04) is SILC, the Eurostat Statistics on Income and Living Conditions. This is a longitudinal database based on a survey, sometimes completed with registered data. The aim is to provide information about the level and structure of social exclusion and poverty in the EU countries.

Next to the initiatives of pure production of statistics there are initiatives that intend to go further than presenting only numbers. They are mostly initiated by umbrella organisations such as the European Mortgage Federation which regularly publishes statistics on mortgage finance via country reports, fact sheets, and the annual Hypostat with data on the housing and mortgage markets that also describes some recent trends. The European Mortgage Federation also produces reports on an ad hoc basis on different aspects of housing finance, such as the cost of housing and the markets of covered bonds and mortgage-backed securities. Euroconstruct is another network. It consists of 19 European research institutes and provides construction market forecasts for all the main construction sectors: residential construction, nonresidential construction, and civil engineering.

CECODHAS, a network promoting the work of social housing organisations in the European Union, fosters the continuous exchange of ideas and experience among its members. Regularly publications appear on social housing; for example, in 2007, it was a review of social, cooperative, and public housing.

The RICS European Housing Review looks at the performance of European housing markets, analysing trends in areas such as inflation, building activity, mortgage markets, and turnover. The RICS publication has been appearing annually since 1999. Each version also gives a description of certain topics. The 2009 version, for example, contains a chapter on rent regulation (Ball, 2009).

Another initiative along these lines is the publication for which the ministries responsible for housing in the EU countries provided the information as addition to the Housing Statistics in the European Union (Norris and Shiels, 2004). It is entitled Regular National Report on Housing Developments in European Countries and contains information on recent housing policies and outcomes in a structured but brief fashion.

Another initiative is concerned with the Global Urban Indicators program. The United Nations Commission on Human Settlements (UN-Habitat) has developed an indicators system that contains a set of 30 quantitative key indicators and nine qualitative data which give an assessment of areas which cannot be easily measured quantitatively. These are the minimum data required for reporting on shelter and urban development. The indicators are supposed to measure performances and trends in the 20 selected key areas, and to measure progress in the implementation of the Habitat Agenda. The indicators provide a comprehensive picture of cities, which, with other indicators which may be chosen by countries, will provide a quantitative, comparative base for the condition of cities, and show progress towards achieving urban objectives. The UN-Habitat State of the World's Cities 2008–09 report contains international information on urban conditions, including housing, and shows, for example, that in 2005 half of the world's slum population resided in Asia, followed by sub-Saharan Africa and Latin America.

Concluding Comments

Comparative housing research analyses differences and similarities in housing problems, policies, markets, and systems in different countries. Some studies search for policy ideas that may be transferred between countries, some compare in order to deepen understanding of the housing systems and markets, and others search for new theoretical concepts or try to improve the abstract conceptualisation of housing phenomena. Although much comparative housing work has been done in western Europe, such research has extended worldwide. A variety of methods have been used including a range of quantitative and qualitative techniques with interdisciplinary teams occasionally constituted for major studies. The most sophisticated comparisons consider the contexts in which national housing phenomena such as policies and markets operate and take account of variations in contexts as well as differences in the prime housing phenomena. Detailed quantitative comparisons are sometimes hindered by the lack of comparable data, but the volume of usable data is growing. The interest in comparative research is evidenced by the increased significance of international housing organisations such as CECODHAS and by international housing research networks such as the European Network for Housing Research (ENHR) and the Asia Pacific Network for Housing Research (APNHR). It is also evident in the growth of journals such as the *European* (now *International*) *Journal of Housing Policy*, and the fact that journals such as *Housing Studies* and *Urban Studies* frequently publish articles based on comparative housing research. The significance of international comparisons for informing housing policy decisions has been increasingly realised by national governments that have commissioned work that depends on experiences in other countries. It is also apparent in the comparative work of national research organisations (such as AHURI in Australia) and the European Union. The European Union, for example, has commissioned the multicountry project Origins of Security and Insecurity (OSIS) that examined the interplay of housing systems with jobs, household structures, finance, and social security, and the DEMHOW study of the interactions between the ageing of European populations and the increasing significance of housing wealth. On a worldwide scale, UN-Habitat has also made use of international housing comparisons both to show the scale of problems in a comparative context and to seek solutions to those problems.

See also: Housing Policy Trends; Qualitative Methods in Housing Research; Research Networks and Professional Institutions in Housing; Tenure as an Institution.

References

Allen J, Barlow J, Leal J, Maloutas T, and Padavani L (2004) *Housing and Welfare in Southern Europe*. London: Blackwell.
Ball M (2009) *European Housing Review 2009*. London: Royal Institution of Chartered Surveyors (RICS).

Ball M, Harloe J, and Martens M (1988) *Housing and Social Change in Europe and the USA*. London; New York: Routledge.
Barlow J and Duncan S (1994) *Success and Failure in Housing Provision: European Systems Compared*. Oxford, UK: Elsevier Science Ltd.
Bengtsson B (2009) Political Science as the Missing Link in Housing Studies. *Housing, Theory and Society* 26(1): 10–25.
Boelhouwer PJ and van der Heijden HMH (1992) *Housing Systems in Europe: Part 1 A Comparative Study of Housing Policy*. Delft, The Netherlands: Delft University Press.
Burns LS and Grebler L (1967) *The Housing of Nations*. London: Macmillan.
Clapham D (2009) Introduction to the special issue – a theory of housing: Problems and potential. *Housing, Theory and Society* 26(1): 1–9.
Doling J (1997) *Comparative Housing Policy: Government and Housing in Advanced Industrial Countries*. Basingstoke, UK: Macmillan.
Donner C (2000) *Housing Policies in the European Union. Theory and Practice*. Vienna: Christian Donner.
Donner C (2006) *Housing Policies in Central Eastern Europe*. Vienna: Christian Donner.
Donnison D (1967) *The Government of Housing*. Harmondsworth, UK: Penguin.
Donnison D and Ungerson C (1982) *Housing Policy*. Harmondsworth, UK: Penguin.
Duclaud-Williams R (1978) *The Politics of Housing in Britain and France*. London: Heinemann.
Elsinga M, De Decker P, Teller N, and Toussaint J (eds.) (2007) *Home Ownership Beyond Asset and Security, Housing Related Security and Insecurity, Perceptions of Housing Related Security and Insecurity in Eight European Countries*. Amsterdam: IOS Press.
Esping-Andersen G (1990) *The Three Worlds of Welfare Capitalism*. Cambridge, UK: Polity Press.
Fuerst JS (ed.) (1974) *Public Housing in Europe and America*. London: Croom Helm.
Haffner M, Hoekstra J, Oxley M, and van der Heijden H (2009) *Bridging the Gap Between Social and Market Rented Housing in Six Countries?* Amsterdam: IOS Press.
Hallett G (1977) *Housing and Land Policies in West Germany and Britain*. London: Macmillan.
Hallett G (1988) *Land and Housing Policies in Europe and the U.S.A.: A Comparative Analysis*. London: Routledge.
Hantrais L (2009) *International Comparative Research; Theory, Methods and Practice*. Basingstoke, UK; New York: Palgrave Macmillan.
Harloe M (1985) *The People's Home: Social Rented Housing in Europe and America*. Oxford, UK: Blackwell.
Hill M (2005) *The Public Policy Process*, 4th edn. Harlow, UK: Pearson Longman.
Hoekstra J (2003) Housing and the welfare state in the Netherlands: An application of Esping-Andersen's typology. *Housing, Theory and Society* 20(2): 58–71.
Horsewood N and Neuteboom P (2006) *The Social Limits to Growth, Security and Insecurity Aspects of Home Ownership*. Amsterdam: IOS press.
Hudson J and Lowe S (2009) *Understanding the Policy Process*, 2nd edn. Basingstoke, UK: Palgrave Macmillan.
Kemeny J (1995) *From Public Housing to the Social Market, Rental Policy in Comparative Perspective*. London: Routledge.
Kemp P (ed.) (2007) *Housing Allowances in Comparative Perspective*. Bristol, UK: The Policy Press.
Kleinman M (1996) *Housing, Welfare and the State in Europe*. Cheltenham, UK: Edward Elgar.
Lawson J (2003) *Critical Realism and Housing Studies: An Explanation for Diverging Housing Solutions*. Amsterdam: AME, University of Amsterdam.
Lawson J (2010) Path dependency and emergent relations: Explaining the different role of limited profit housing in the dynamic urban regimes of Vienna and Zurich. *Housing, Theory and Society* 27(3): 204–220.
Lundqvist LJ (1991) Rolling stones for the resurrection of policy as the focus of comparative housing research. *Scandinavian Housing & Planning Research* 8(2): 79–90.
Norris M and Shiels P (2004) *Regular National Report on Housing Developments in European Countries*. Dublin: Stationery Office.
OECD (1974) *Housing Finance: Present Problems*. Paris: OECD.
Oxley M (1991) The aims and methods of comparative housing research. *Scandinavian Housing & Planning Research* 8(2): 66–77.
Oxley M (2001) Meaning, science, context and confusion in comparative housing research. *Journal of Housing and the Built Environment* 16(1): 89–106.
Pickvance C (2001) Four varieties of comparative analysis. *Journal of Housing and the Built Environment* 16(1): 7–28.
Quilgars D, Elsinga M, Jones A, Toussaint J, Ruonavaara H, and Naumanen P (2009) Inside qualitative, cross-national research: Making methods transparent in a EU housing study. *International Journal of Social Research Methodology* 12(1): 19–31.
Ronald R (2008) *The Ideology of Home Ownership: Homeowner Societies and the Role of Housing*. Basingstoke, UK; New York: Palgrave Macmillan.
Schmidt S (1989a) Book review of Housing and Social Change in Europe and the USA by Ball, Michael, Michael Harloe & Maartje Martens, London and New York, Routledge. *Scandinavian Journal of Housing and Planning Research* 6(2): 60–62.
Schmidt S (1989b) Convergence theory, labour movements, and corporatism: The case of housing. *Scandinavian Journal of Housing and Planning Research* 6(2): 83–101.
Somerville P (1994) On explanations of housing policy. *Scandinavian Housing & Planning Research* 11(4): 211–230.
Stephens M, Burns N, and MacKay L (2002) *Social Market or Safety Net, British Social Rented Housing in a European Context*. Bristol, UK: Policy Press; Joseph Rowntree Foundation.
van Vliet W (ed.) (1987) *Housing Markets and Policy under Fiscal Austerity*. Westport, CT: Greenwood.
Whitehead C and Scanlon K (eds.) (2007) *Social Housing in Europe*. London: London School of Economics and Political Science.

Further Reading

O'Sullivan A, Young G, Brittain A, et al. (2004) *Local Housing Systems Analysis: Good Practice Guide*. Edinburgh, UK: Communities Scotland.

Relevant Websites

http://web.hku.hk/~apnhr – Asia Pacific Network for Housing Research (APNHR).
www.ahuri.edu.au – Australian Housing and Urban Research Institute (AHURI).
www.cecodhas.org – European Liaison Committee for Social Housing (CECHODHAS).
www.enhr.ibf.uu.se – European Network for Housing Research (ENHR).
www.rics.org/ehr – Royal Institution of Chartered Surveys (RICS) European Housing Review.
www.unhabitat.org – United Nations Agency for Human Settlements (UN-Habitat).

Complexity

DS Byrne, Durham University, Durham, UK

© 2012 Elsevier Ltd. All rights reserved.

Complexity Science as a Frame of Reference

The first thing to appreciate in relation to the potential of 'complexity science' for assisting in our understanding of housing systems and the roles that housing and home play in people's lives is that such systems and their roles are dynamic. That is to say that they have the potential for change through time. What is important is the character of their trajectories. The term trajectory describes position through time. Systems change – or stay the same – but what matters is their path forward. In the social world what matters is change of kind rather than change of degree, and the trajectories of housing systems demonstrate that very clearly. All the entities of interest to us in relation to housing and home – households, neighbourhoods, and localities at the spatial level – are complex systems. We also have to think of housing markets as not so much complex systems in and of themselves but rather as manifestations of the complex interaction of the real systems which are households, neighbourhoods, localities, and local, regional, national, and global economies and cultures. Essentially the dynamic potential of systems of interest in relation to housing and home is a function of the status of those systems as complex systems, so a definition of a complex system is in order. Rosen (1987: 324) provides one:

> ... a simple system is one to which a notion of state can be assigned once and for all, or more generally, one in which Aristotelian causal categories can be independently segregated from one another. Any system for which such a description cannot be provided I will call *complex*. Thus, in a complex system, the causal categories become intertwined in such a way that no dualistic language of state plus dynamic laws can completely describe it. Complex systems must then process mathematical images different from, and irreducible to, the generalized dynamic systems which have been considered universal.

Important implications flow from this. Let us delineate them as listed below:

- Complex systems are inherently emergent. They cannot be understood by a process of analysis alone. Neither are they simply holistic. Understanding must address parts, the whole, interactions among parts, and interactions of parts with the whole.
- Complex systems are not chaotic. Therefore, they do not change radically and frequently in consequence of small changes in key determinant parameters.
- Complex systems are robust. Most of the time they continue to maintain the same general form with ongoing constant small changes within that form. In complexity terminology, most of the time their state space coordinates are located in a torus attractor. However, robustness is not the same as stasis, even with stasis understood as allowing change within an attractor. Robustness also resides in the capacity for radical change with continued existence.
- Significant change in complex systems is qualitative and radical, not incremental. In complexity terminology it takes the form of phase shifts. Change in complex systems can be thought of as a process of metamorphosis – the system changes radically whilst continuing to exist. In terms of state space it moves to a new attractor.
- Complex systems are nested and intersecting. All systems are contained within and intersect with other systems. Boundaries are fuzzy and plastic. Moreover, the nested character of a set of systems is not hierarchically deterministic. Nested systems have a recursive deterministic relationship with the systems within which they are nested. Potentially every level has implications for every other level.
- Complex systems display a high degree of autonomy. This does not mean that they can become anything, but it does mean that what they can and do become is in large part a function of the system, its own components, and systems nested within it.
- The range of potential future states for a system which undergoes phase shift transformation is greater than one, but nonetheless limited. There are alternative futures but not an infinity of possibilities. Future state is path dependent but not path 'determined' in the usual sense of determination as exact specification.

In relation to housing it has been asserted above that we are dealing with a large number of systems which intersect in important ways and that much of what we need to know about these systems and their potential behaviour can be understood only in relation to these intersections. This means that we need to pay attention to the nature of boundaries. Cilliers provides us with a crucial set of insights into the nature of boundaries in complex systems:

Boundaries [of complex systems] are simultaneously a function of the activity of the system itself, and a product of the strategy of description involved. In other words, we frame the system by describing it in a certain way (for a certain purpose) but we are constrained in where the frame can be drawn. The boundary of the system is therefore neither a function of our description, nor is it a purely natural thing. (Cilliers, 2001: 141)

So Cilliers understands boundaries as made for purposes but made in relation to reality rather than being a pure product of description alone. Reality has a voice. This is of course an essentially realist position.

Traditionally boundaries are understood as barriers, as points of separation. Cilliers uses Zeleny (1996: 133) to demonstrate that there is much more to them than this:

All social systems, and thus all living systems, create, maintain and degrade their own boundaries. These boundaries do not separate but intimately connect the system with its environment. They do not have to be just physical or topological, but are primarily functional, behavioural, and communicational. They are not 'perimeters' but functional constitutive components of a given system.

With boundaries understood not as separating so much as connecting, we must recognise that subsystems can be parts of multiple other systems, that there are multiple interconnections, that we might even have to think of systems as consisting of boundaries alone. In summary: "Everything is always interacting and interfacing with others and with the environment; the notions of 'inside' and 'outside' are never simple and uncontested" (Cilliers, 2001: 142). The back construction of the word 'liminal' from subliminal is an interesting illustration of how this kind of understanding of the nature of boundaries penetrates much of the contemporary episteme. Certainly in the spatial sciences we have become used to the idea of 'liminal spaces' at every level from the bioecological – think tidal zones – to the sociocultural – the liminal spaces of urban bohemia.

In continuation with the first part of this article, which consists essentially of a specification of terminology, let us consider the distinction between restricted and general complexity. These terms are due to Maurin (2006) but correspond to the terms 'simplistic complexity' and 'complex complexity' as these are deployed by Gerrits (Teisman et al. 2009: 20–21) after Byrne (2005):

Simplistic Complexity is essentially complexity within closed systems, with the emergence of structures and processes depending entirely on the (fixed) variables within the system. Such systems display complex behaviours but are deemed simplistic because the roots of this complexity always remain within the closed system. This means that the dynamics are confined by the variables that define the system. . . . .

In social reality, the number and nature of the variables defining an emerging structure or process is not fixed but rather changeable. Complex adaptive systems are considered to be open and constantly exchanging energy with other systems and with such systems, the constituent variables do not define its borders. . . . What constitutes and limits a system is relative to the agents' and observer's locality, which corresponds with the arguments on agency and boundary judgements . . . and as such is connected ad infinitum to other representations of systems.

Note the shift above from the term 'complex systems' to 'complex adaptive systems'. In the above discussion the term adaptive is used simply to refer to the potential for systems to change radically whilst maintaining their integrity as systems. We have to be careful here because the term 'complex adaptive system' is sometimes employed essentially to refer to systems where the complexity emerges entirely from interactions among the agents in the system with the behaviour of the agents delimited by rule sets. In such systems emergence is simply a product of the following of rule-defined behaviour by the agents. This is the version of complexity endorsed by Holland (1998) and has to be distinguished precisely from open systems operating in interaction with other systems which set of interactions constitute the environment of the systems themselves.

One conceptual tool of complexity theory which derives from our understanding of the character of open systems is the notion of coevolution. This has particular salience in relation to any process of governance in relation to complex systems and is defined by Gerrits et al. (2008: 134) thus: ". . . reciprocal selection between systems, a process during which future states of systems are selected reciprocally by other systems". Coevolution matters whenever we have systems which intersect with other systems, the general condition when we are dealing with anything which involves both the complex nesting of urban systems and the implications of differential processes of governance in application. Housing is an exact example here.

The Deployment of Complexity in the Study of Housing and Related Systems

It is of course possible to conceive of the housing system taken in isolation and this has most often been done in relation to housing markets. There is a body of research which has explored the dynamics of housing markets and related issues including land supply. Examples include Ma and Mu (2008) and Leung et al. (2007). This style of work is characterised by game theory and/or mathematical formalisms using nonlinear difference equations and related approaches. Baynes (2009) presents an overview of a range of methods with this kind of complexity colouring, which have been applied to issues of urban development and management with a particular focus on issues of prediction in relation to housing and population movement. The majority of work which has deployed complexity as a frame of reference has done so in a rather different way. Essentially we have two forms of discussion. One takes a broad issue and considers it in complexity terms. The other develops particular case studies and deploys the complexity perspective to interpret the dynamic development of those cases, often with a focus on the character of policy outcomes in relation to the emergent character of the consequences of complex social interventions. Both are characterised by an emphasis on narrative development. This is not to say that such work is wholly qualitative in the sense of taking the character of language-based textual presentation. It can and does deploy quantitative approaches both descriptively and sometimes even through the development of quantitative models. However, the models are embedded in and subordinate to the narratives rather than being taken as isomorphic scientific representations of the form of causation in reality itself. So we have on the one hand a 'scientistic' mode of complexity representation of housing and related systems, often carried out by mathematicians, physical scientists, and economists/econometricians and on the other a social mode of representation generally undertaken by social scientists with disciplinary backgrounds primarily in geography, sociology, and political sciences especially when they are practitioners of 'applied social science'. These are not so much dichotomous alternatives as ends of a continuum but there is heuristic value in the distinction.

Much of the work on complexity which has implications for understanding housing has been done in relation to urban systems taken as a whole. Portugali (2006) develops an argument for the relevance of the complexity frame by elaborating on the distinction between 'space' and 'place'. The first has been the focus of attention of a positivist tradition in geography, which has attempted to develop a nomothetic form of explanation modelled on the 'hard sciences'. In contrast humanistic geography has placed human understanding and meanings as central in articulating any understanding of spatial relations in the social world. Portugali argues that complexity in fact provides a bridge between these 'two cultures of science' since complexity's necessary emphasis on emergence admits agency and hence meaning into the causal nexus of the social world. It is worth remarking that whilst Portugali provides an elegant and coherent defence of this position, as he himself recognises, the language is perhaps new, the underlying understanding is not. Social theory since its first formal development in the nineteenth century, and certainly in the work of Marx himself, has always understood the social world as complex and subject to transformation in context by human agency – people make history even if not in circumstances of their own choosing. It is of course interesting that the structuralist turn in 'Marxism' lost sight of this entirely. Indeed there always has been a positivist current in 'Marxist' thought, clearly evident in, for example, the earlier Marxist writings of David Harvey, which lost sight of the agentic potential of human subjects. It is precisely through the reflexive capacity of human subjects – subjects in the sense of the actors in relation to the doing of things – that social complexity in all its forms is engendered.

An interesting and important study influenced by the thinking on complexity of Prigogine which addresses the development of city regions as systems is Allen's (1997) *Cities and Regions as Self-Organizing Systems*. Allen is by training a physicist but works in the much more philosophically open European complexity tradition following Prigogine in contrast to the generally more scientistic tradition associated with the Santa Fe school in the United States. His work in this text stands almost exactly at the midpoint of the continuum suggested above in which he develops complex mathematical models but always sets these in relation to the social context and even includes a wry recognition of the socially agentic potential of the models themselves. Allen's work provides a very useful and accessible introduction to the utility of the mathematically formulated ideas of complexity and at the same time is fully aware of the character of complex social systems.

An example of the thematic development of complexity in a housing-related domain is provided by Blackman in *Placing Health* (2005). This book is influenced in no small part by Blackman's advisory policy and practice role in relation to neighbourhood renewal and explores the relationships among neighbourhood character, policy interventions, and the emergence of states of health both for individuals and for social aggregates including households and communities. The argument is an important challenge to the tradition of linear modelling in social epidemiology, even when linear modelling takes on the sophisticated and much more appropriate form of multi-level modelling. Blackman takes a case-based view arguing after Byrne (2002) against the reification of variables outwith cases, and endorsing Ragin's (1987) approach in Qualitative Comparative Analysis (QCA), which provides a means for exploring complex and multiple causation through systematic cross-case comparison. Given the historic and contemporary salience of housing in relation to health inequalities, this is a particularly important policy arena. Housing is a vitally important territory for joined-up governance given the ways in which all of housing management, planning systems, and urban renewal strategies combine in overall urban management, and the reduction of health inequalities is a general target in most developed and functioning states.

Rhodes' (2008) study of urban regeneration in Ireland does not deploy a QCA method in any explicit sense but is in fact an excellent example of careful case-based comparison with a small but well-defined set of cases. Although Rhodes seems to start out with an understanding of complexity couched only in terms of agent interactions, in fact his narratives demonstrate not only the significance of the emergence of 'project-specific superagents' – in effect developed collaborative partnerships focusing on each project – for successful outcomes, but also the significance of the whole environment within which the projects operated. Rhodes uses, rather fruitfully, the biological complexity metaphorical apparatus of the 'fitness landscape' – that is a description of the possibility space for systems in terms of the energy required to achieve particular changes of state. He notes:

> ... the relationship between strategic choices and performance outcomes could vary over time and, in some cases, could be influenced by the efforts of one or more agents within the system, making the boundary between the environment and the system a rather more permeable one than conceived of in either Kauffman's (1993 – the original biological formulation) or Siggelkow and Levinthal's (2003 – where this was translated into a performance landscape formulation) formulations. (2008: 364)

His account resonates exactly with the notion of coevolution. The urban renewal schemes he examines are specifically housing related, dealing with scales varying from the very large – the Ballymun estate in North Dublin with thousands of units affected – to much smaller developments. He notes the contextual significance of religious sectarianism and segregation in his Northern Ireland cases, something unique in the United Kingdom and also unknown in the Republic of Ireland. He observed that the environment for the actors (a term perhaps to be preferred to 'agents' since it allows for much more autonomy than is the case with agents in agent-based modelling) comprised far more than the immediate policy decision space. Despite his citation of Holland's (1998) conception of agents' schema, Rhodes' cases sit far better with a complex or generalised complexity understanding of complex social interventions.

Rhodes' study, although not presented simply as an evaluation, indicates the significance of the complexity frame of reference for policy evaluation across the whole range of governance and related social processes. An important point here developed in a range of methodological discussions but summarised exactly in Haynes (2008) is the resonance of complexity with the general tenor of critical realism as a metatheoretical programme. This is particularly the case in relation to the close correspondence between critical realism's 'deep ontology' in which causes are to be understood in terms of the interaction between deep generative mechanisms and contingent contexts. The housing and health literature in relation to health inequalities (see, for example, Byrne, 2004, and Higgs et al., 2004) provides an excellent illustration of this issue.

At the level of whole system change Mullins and Pawson (2005) have deployed the complexity frame of reference to examine the major change in the allocation mechanisms for social housing, particularly but not exclusively in the United Kingdom, in the late twentieth century. They note how bureaucratic allocation on the basis of need rankings has been replaced by systems in which, whilst need criteria have not disappeared, market-style choices now have predominant saliency. Their account of Choice-Based Letting systems emphasises that these are not free markets but managed markets. What is particularly interesting is the way in which they show how the external factor, particularly important in the North of England's postindustrial conurbations, of low demand for social housing had an important interactive effect on allocation systems' forms but that change required alternative viable forms of management to become available – in complexity terms there was a need for an expansion of the potential attractor space for policy forms. The importation of the Delft-based model from the Netherlands provided such an expansion – as Mullins and Pawson (2005: 224) remark: " ... it is not so much overcoming resistance to change as stimulating viable alternatives to the status quo that can lead to sustaining system change".

Conclusion

Complexity has been described as the basis of twenty-first century science in what will increasingly be a postdisciplinary programme combining research and action. It is evident that not only academics but actually practitioners as well are finding the frame of reference of complexity useful. We can describe housing and related systems in complex terms, and we can use these descriptions to inform policy and practice which is directed towards the achievement of specific desired outcomes available to us in the potential future attractor state – a set greater than one but less than too many to comprehend. Of course a clear implication of this is that politics must be informed by a clear and coherent understanding not only of policy options but also of the differential consequences of such options not just for systems as a whole but for the people who live in and through such systems. This is not necessarily a recipe for consensus but it is a prescription for democratic determination in relation to conflicting social interests at every level.

See also: Critical Realism; Game Theory; Neighbourhood Effects; Simulation Models for Urban Economies; Systems Theory.

References

Allen PM (1997) *Cities and Regions as Self-Organizing Systems*. Amsterdam: Gordon and Breach.
Baynes TM (2009) Complexity in urban development and management. *Journal of Industrial Ecology* 13(2): 214–227.
Blackman T (2005) *Placing Health*. Bristol, UK: Policy Press.
Byrne DS (2002) *Interpreting Quantitative Data*. London: Sage.
Byrne DS (2004) Complex and contingent causation - the implications of complex realism for quantitative modelling: the case of housing and wealth. In: Carter R and New C (eds.) *Making Realism Work*, pp. 50–66. London: Sage.
Byrne DS (2005) Complexity, configuration and cases. *Theory, Culture and Society* 22(5): 95–111.
Cilliers P (2001) Boundaries, hierarchies and networks in complex systems. *International Journal of Innovation Management* 5(2): 135–147.
Haynes P (2008) Complexity and evaluation in public management, a qualitative systems approach. *Public Management Review* 10(3): 401–419.
Higgs P, Rees-Jones I, and Scambler G (2004) Class as a variable, class as a generative mechanism: the importance of critical realism for the sociology of health inequalities. In: Carter R and New C (eds.) *Making Realism Work*, pp. 91–110. London: Sage.
Holland JH (1998) *Emergence*. Reading, MA: Perseus Books.
Leung AYT, Tsui WS, and Xu JN (2007) Nonlinear delay difference for housing dynamics assuming backward-looking expectations. *Applied Mathematics and Mechanics* (English Edition) 28(6): 785–798.
Ma J and Mu L (2008) Dynamic analysis of the game between land supply and housing prices. *International Journal of Computer Mathematics* 85(6): 983–992.
Mullins D and Pawson H (2005) The land that time forgot?: Reforming access to social housing in England. *Policy and Politics* 33(2): 205–230.
Portugali J (2006) Complexity theory as a link between space and place. *Environment and Planning A* 38: 647–664.
Ragin C (1987) *The Comparative Method*. Berkley, CA: University of California Press.
Rhodes ML (2008) Complexity and emergence in public management – the case of urban regeneration in Ireland. *Public Management Review* 10(3): 361–379.
Rosen R (1987) Some epistemological issues in physics and biology. In: Hiley BJ and Peat FD (eds.) *Quantum Implications: Essays in Honour of David Bohm*, pp. 314–327. London: Routledge.
Siggelkow N and Griffen D (eds.) (2006) *Complexity and the Experience of Managing Public Sector Organizations*. London: Routledge.
Teisman G, van Buuren A, and Gerrits LM (2009) *Managing Complex Governance Systems*. London: Routledge.
Zeleny M (1996) On the social nature of autopoietic systems. In: Khalil EL and Boulding K (eds.) *Evolution, Order and Complexity*, pp. 122–143. London: Routledge.

Further Reading

Kauffman SA (1993) *The Origin of Order*. New York: Oxford University Press.

Construction and Demolition Waste

VWY Tam, University of Western Sydney, Sydney, NSW, Australia
CM Tam, City University of Hong Kong, Hong Kong, China

© 2012 Elsevier Ltd. All rights reserved.

Glossary

Building and housing waste Waste generated from building and/or housing activities, which can be on-site or off-site.

Recycling technology Methods for reusing or recycling the waste; these can also be ways to improve the reuseability or recyclability of the materials.

Introduction

As the promotion of environmental management and sustainable development has been overwhelming in recent years, there is a growing awareness of environmental issues and the potential problems from deterioration of the environment. Generally speaking, building and housing are not environmentally friendly activities. The effects of these activities include land use and land deterioration, resource depletion, waste generation, and various forms of pollution.

Building and housing debris resulting from building work constitutes a large proportion of the total solid waste, as shown in **Table 1**. In the United Kingdom, more than 50% of the waste deposited in a typical landfill comes from building; annually, about 70 million tonnes of waste arise from building and housing activities. In Australia, about 14 million tonnes of waste are being put into landfills each year, and about 44% of the waste is attributed to the building and housing industry. In the United States, around 29% of solid waste is from building and housing, and in Hong Kong, it is about 38%.

Building and Housing Waste Recycling Technology and Practice

Seven building and housing waste recycling technologies are investigated in this article. They include (1) brick, (2) concrete, (3) ferrous metal, (4) glass, (5) masonry, (6) nonferrous metal, and (7) plastic.

Brick

Bricks coming from demolition may be contaminated with mortar, rendering, and plaster, and are often mixed with other materials such as timber and concrete. Separation of the potentially valuable facing bricks is usually difficult and requires hand sorting. In Denmark, only 10–15% of the bricks from old buildings are facing bricks; hence, the sorting and cleaning of bricks tend to be more labour-intensive and costly. Any significant contamination of the bricks will render their use uneconomical, as cleanup costs far outweigh the cost of new bricks. The Japanese practice is to burn the bricks from demolition into slime burnt ash, whereas in Hong Kong, bricks are commonly crushed to form filling material and hardcore.

Concrete

The most usual way to recycle concrete rubble is to use it as recycled aggregate (RA). However, the deformation properties of concrete made with secondary aggregate are less favourable than those of concrete made with natural gravel. There are two potential solutions to this problem: (1) substitute 100% gravel by secondary aggregate and increase the dimensions of the structure by about 10% and (2) substitute only about 20% natural aggregate by mixed recycled aggregate, which, with a strength up to 65 MPa, does not reduce concrete quality.

Ferrous Metal

There is a highly developed market for ferrous metal recycling around the world. It is by far the most profitably recyclable material. The demand for ferrous metals has long been well established; therefore, the applications of this recycled material have been well accepted on-site.

Preferably, steel should directly be reused. If it is unsuitable for direct reuse, it is melted to produce new steel. More than 80% of the scrap is recycled, although almost 100% may be claimed to be recyclable. The Steel Organisation reports that roughly 100% of steel

Table 1 Comparison of the proportions of building and housing waste to total solid waste in various countries (1995–2010)

Country	Proportion of building and housing waste to total waste (%)	Waste recycled (%)
Australia	44	51
Brazil	15	8
Denmark	25–50	80
Finland	14	40
France	25	20–30
Germany	19	40–60
Hong Kong	38	nd
Japan	36	65
Italy	30	10
The Netherlands	26	75
Norway	30	7
Spain	70	17
United Kingdom	Over 50	40
United States of America	29	25

nd, not determined.

reinforcement and about 25% of steel sections are made from recycled scrap. Scrap steel is almost totally recycled and allows repeated recycling. In Japan, the steel used for building and housing, including steel form and rebar, is fabricated or cut to size off-site, with the cutting waste, 100% steel, being recycled to avoid waste generation at building sites.

Glass

In 1997, the glass industry recycled about 425 000 tonnes of glass in the United Kingdom (Coventry et al., 1999). However, the recycling rate is relatively low in Hong Kong (about 1%) in comparison to other countries (the rates in the United States, Japan, and Germany are about 20, 78, and 85%, respectively). Glass can be reused in the building industry for a number of applications:

(1) *Windows.* If care is taken during the demolition phase, glass window units can directly be reused, depending on how carefully they are handled, stored, and transported, and whether they are contaminated.
(2) *Glass fibre.* For enhancement of material properties, glass is recycled in the manufacture of glass fibre, which is used in thermal and acoustic insulations, or can be mixed in cement, gypsum, or resin products to strengthen them.
(3) *Filling material.* The UK practice is to use recycled glass as a fine material for cement replacement, called 'ConGlassCrete', which is used to improve concrete strength.
(4) *Tiles.* In the United States, the use of 100% recycled-glass tiles has been adopted. It gives an attractive reflective appearance to the surface after polishing.
(5) *Paving blocks.* In the United States, paving blocks are produced from recycled glass aggregate by crushing. Hong Kong is also developing this recycling technology, which can (1) provide an attractive reflective appearance to the surface after polishing, (2) reduce water absorption of concrete blocks, and (3) provide good compressive strength. However, the problems of instability, sharpness of aggregate, and expansion due to alkali–silica reaction need to be resolved. Adopting pulverised fly ash as a depressant for alkali–silica reaction and reducing impurities are necessary to improve paving block quality when adopting recycled glass aggregate.
(6) *Asphalt in road construction.* Old glass is crushed into a very fine material, which can replace asphalt in road construction. The Taiwanese practice is to replace about 15% of the asphalt used by recycled glass.
(7) *Aggregate in road construction.* Crushed glass has been developed for use as aggregate in bituminous concrete pavement; popularly known as 'glassphalt', it has been tested in the United States.
(8) *Aggregate in concrete.* In Sweden, a novel fine aggregate consisting mainly of glass has been developed for use in concrete. The presence of glass in secondary aggregate used for concrete or asphalt production may reduce the strength of the resulting material. 'Microfiller' is the result of an industrial process consisting of the steps for the purification of glass material by separation and washing. The glass is then dried, crushed, and ground to the required specification, and the particle size grading is defined to be between the size grading of cement and aggregate. The product is added to the concrete batch in the mixing process, along with the other constituents, and acts as a pozzolanic material. The addition of the microfiller will improve concrete properties in the fresh as well as in the hardened state.
(9) *Man-made soil.* The Japanese practice adopts waste glass as ultra-fine particles at high temperature.

Masonry

Masonry is normally crushed and recycled as masonry aggregate. A special application of recycled masonry aggregate is as thermal insulating concrete containing polystyrene beads, which is a light-weight type of concrete with high thermal insulation properties. Another potential application for recycled masonry aggregate is as aggregate in traditional clay brick as well as in sodium silicate brick. The following points may be noted regarding this application:

(1) A small portion of the recycled masonry aggregate is used as a replacement for clay in brick and as a sand replacement in sodium silicate brick.
(2) For use in traditional clay brick, this fraction should not contain any lime, to prevent the adverse effects on strength, shrinkage, durability, and colour.
(3) When used in sodium silicate brick, this fraction may contain lime; but the sodium silicate brick should be fabricated at a pressure of about 15 bar and at lower temperatures than that used for clay brick.

When the recycled masonry aggregate is used for sodium silicate brick, the adhering cement has to be removed by a mechanical or a thermal process. Interfacial stress is created when cement-covered brick is heated to about 900°C, and the cement can then be removed as fines. This material can be heated to produce clinker. The volume of carbon dioxide (CO_2) produced by this process is lower than that produced when natural material is used. Lime mortar can be reused after heating; but the adhesive has to be removed mechanically when processing the sodium silicate brick.

Nonferrous Metal

The main nonferrous metals collected from construction and demolition (C&D) sites are aluminium, copper, lead, and zinc. Once sorted, the products can be sold to scrap metal merchants for recycling or directly to end users after melting. In the United Kingdom, aluminium usage went up to 95 000 tonnes in 1997, about 70% of which being recycled metal. For copper, the quantity recycled is about 119 000 tonnes of copper and copper alloys out of a national market of about 262 000 tonnes used. A recycling rate of 100% can be achieved for copper. Lead also is highly recyclable and has a good scrap value; in 1997, about 228 700 tonnes of lead were recycled, representing over half of the total lead production. It is estimated that about 85% of lead used is recyclable. About 60 000 tonnes of zinc are used in the production of galvanised steel strips, and about 40 000 tonnes, for protecting steel galvanised after fabrication. A relatively small quantity of zinc sheet (about 2000 tonnes per year) is used for roofing, cladding, and, to some extent, flashing. Furthermore, a large quantity of zinc (representing about 30% of total composition) is used in the production of brass.

Plastic

High-level reuses of polyethylene, polypropylene, polystyrene, and polyvinylchloride (PVC) are possible for recycling if these materials are collected separately and cleaned. Recycling is difficult if plastic wastes are mixed with other plastics or contaminants. The scope for high-level recycling is limited owing to the deterioration of properties in old plastic. Virgin material has to be added for recycling. The recycled material is used for the production of new plastic profiles containing about 70% recycled material; about 30% virgin material is added to ensure sufficient UV-resistance. In future, it may be possible to improve this replacement ratio up to 80 or 90%.

There are several principal opportunities to address when considering recycling of plastic:

(1) Recycling of transparent PVC roofing panel started in 1992. Owing to contamination and the reinforcement used, the recycled material has poor quality, and therefore can only be used for the lower face. The old panel is converted to a powder by cryogenic milling. This powder is then mixed with plasticisers and other materials for the production of new panel.
(2) Plastic may be recycled and used in products specifically designed for the utilisation of recycled plastic, such as street furniture, roof and floor, piling, PVC window, noise barrier, cable ducting and pipe, panel, cladding, and insulation foam.
(3) Technology is being developed that will enable materials to be progressively infused with recycled plastic constituents to increase strength, durability, and impact resistance, and to enhance appearance. This has resulted in companies creating versatile products such as plastic lumber and plastic aggregate for asphalt and concrete.
(4) Plastic may be utilised for further building applications. However, owing to the volume, time, and economic constraints, recycled plastic applications are limited to landfill drainage and asphalt.
(5) The Japanese practice adopts burning waste plastic at high temperature and thus turning it into ultra-fine particles.

Summarising from the international experience in waste management and recycling, it is found that various types of construction materials are recycled, including aluminium, asphalt, concrete, steel, iron, wood, sand, brick, soil, paper, glass, and even car tyres. However, the adoption of these recycled materials only covers about 5% of the total materials consumed, and the recycled aggregate only accounts for <1%. Applications of these recycled materials are mainly confined to low-grade activities, for example, RA for sub-base in road construction.

To improve the existing recycling situation, the following measures are recommended:

(1) Legislations on the provision of mandatory waste management plans and on disposal tax are encouraged.
(2) Limited disposal areas and scarcity of primary materials can push the development of recycling industries. However, exorbitant waste treatment costs and long haulage of waste have restricted the recycling market in some countries. Hence, the use of innovative technologies by the industry needs to be encouraged.
(3) Installing recycling plants next to dumping sites is the most suitable measure for concrete recycling, which improves the recycling rates.

Acknowledgements

This article was published and reprinted from: Tam VWY and Tam CM (2006) A review on the viable technology for construction waste recycling. *Resources, Conservation and Recycling* 47(3), 209–221. Copyright Elsevier; Tam VWY and Tam CM (2008) *Reuse of Construction and Demolition Waste in Housing Development.* Nova Science Publishers, Inc.: United States. Copyright Nova Science Publishers, Inc.; and Tam VWY and Tam CM (2008) A review on the international requirements on waste management and recycling. *Progress in Waste Management: Research.* Copyright Nova Science Publisher, Inc.

See also: Housing Dynamics: Environmental Aspects; Sustainable Urban Development.

Reference

Coventry S, Wolveridge C, and Hillier S (1999) *The Reclaimed and Recycled Construction Materials Handbook.* London: Construction Industry Research and Information Association.

Further Reading

Cheung HK (2003) Use of recycled asphalt pavement: A practical approach to asphalt recycling. *Paper Presented at the Materials Science and Technology in Engineering Conference: Now, New and Next, Hong Kong, 15–17 January.*
Collins RJ (1993) Reuse of demolition materials in relation to specifications in the UK, demolition and reuse of concrete and masonry, guidelines for demolition and reuse of concrete and masonry. *Proceedings of the Third International RILEM Symposium on Demolition and Reuse of Concrete and Masonry.* Odense, Denmark: RILEM.
Forum for the Construction Industry (2001) Task Force B4: Recycling of Construction and Demolition Waste. *Final Report on the Development and Implementation of a Voluntary Construction Industry Programme to Meet the Government's Objectives for the Recovery of Construction and Demolition Waste.* Dublin, Ireland: Forum for the Construction Industry, Ireland Government.
German Standards (2002) *Aggregates for Mortar and Concrete: DIN 4226-100.* German Standards, German Government.
Hendrick CF (1994) Certification system for aggregate produced from building waste and demolished buildings. *Environmental Aspects of Construction with Waste Materials: Proceedings of the International Conference on Environmental Implications of Construction Materials and Technology Developments.* Maastricht, The Netherlands: Elsevier, 1–3 June.
Hendriks CF and Pietersen HS (2000) *Sustainable Raw Materials: Construction and Demolition Waste.* Cachan Cedex, France: RILEM Publication.
Kawano H (1995) The state of reuse of demolished concrete in Japan. *Integrated Design and Environmental Issues in Concrete Technology: Proceedings of the International Workshop 'Rational Design of Concrete Structures under Severe Conditions'.* Hakodate, Japan: RILEM, 7–9 August.
Lenssen N and Roodman DM (1995) *Making better buildings In: State of the World 1995.* New York: Worldwatch Institute.
Ofori G (1992) The environment: The fourth construction project objective? *Construction Management and Economics* 10(5): 369–395.
Rogoff MJ and Williams JF (1994) *Approaches to Implementing Solid Waste Recycling Facilities.* Park Ridge, NJ: Noyes.

Construction Methods

N Walliman, Oxford Brookes University, Oxford, UK

© 2012 Elsevier Ltd. All rights reserved.

Glossary

Foundations The underground construction that transfers the weight of the whole building to the ground in such a way that prevents movement and sinking.

In situ Constructed on site. Refers usually to concrete construction in which walls, floors, columns, and beams are made by pouring freshly mixed concrete into metal or timber forms (formwork) to create the correct shapes. The formwork is removed when the concrete has set.

Light timber framing Walls and floors constructed of closely spaced (600 mm) slender beams and posts nailed together to form load-bearing floors and walls. Plywood sheets are commonly used to provide stiffness against racking.

Load-bearing walls Walls that transmit the weight of floors and roofs down to the foundations.

Partitions Internal walls that divide up the space but do not normally carry any loads.

Prefabrication Construction of building parts, such as floors, walls, bathrooms, in a factory, which are then transported to the building site and assembled together, usually with the help of a crane. This form of construction is also called 'offsite construction' or 'modern methods of building'.

Reinforced concrete Concrete, used in elements such as foundations, floors, columns, and walls, that contains steel bars to provide strength in bending and tension.

Truss A triangulated frame for a pitched roof made of timber or steel members, the base of which spans between load-bearing walls or beams and the sloping sides providing support for the roofing materials (purlins, rafters, battens, tiles, etc.).

Introduction

Building construction is the way a building is assembled with different materials, how they fit together and form a stable construction, and how materials are utilised to perform particular functions within the construction.

Housing was traditionally constructed of building materials that could be obtained locally, such as timber, stone, earth, and reed, which created local vernacular building styles. Since industrialisation and transport improvements together with the decline of local sources of building materials, manufactured building materials have become available almost everywhere, resulting in a wide choice of construction options.

The types of construction used for housing depend on the size and shape of the buildings, the units of accommodation, their location and the ground conditions, available materials and relative costs, local traditions, developer and client preference, and sometimes planning regulations.

The variety of housing types can broadly be categorised by height as low rise (one to three storeys), medium rise (three to six storeys), and high rise (more that six storeys, requiring a lift for access to the upper floors).

Within these categories, there are several distinct types of housing configuration that relate to the way the accommodation is arranged within the buildings. The low-rise types of housing are detached (permanent or mobile homes, on land or water), semidetached (paired houses joined on one side), terrace (or town houses joined on both sides), apartments (or tenements, maisonettes, condominiums, etc., stacked above and next to each other). Medium-rise housing is usually in multioccupation (containing apartments or similar) and configured as freestanding villas, slabs, or city blocks, with staircase or balcony access. High-rise housing (containing apartments or similar) is in the form of slabs or towers.

Although these categories do not strictly define what type of construction can be used, some construction systems lend themselves particularly well to certain types of housing.

Two main factors distinguish the types of construction used – the structural system employed and the main construction materials used.

The structural system is the part of the construction which resists all the main loads and transfers them to the ground and thus stops the building from collapsing. A basic distinction can be made between a structural system that is based on a framework of columns and beams, or one that uses panels in the form of floor plates and load-bearing walls. Framed systems are generally used when large open interior spaces are required, which is not the case in housing, so are seldom used in this context, apart from for some very tall buildings or for special designs.

As with all types of buildings, the construction is designed to provide a durable system for protecting the interior from the weather and other outside influences, such as noise and pollution, to provide suitable, comfortable, and safe spaces for the activities within it, and to provide aesthetic aspects to the design. This can be accomplished using a wide range of materials.

There are normally two regulatory stages that need to be passed in order to construct housing (and most other buildings too). The first is at the planning stage, where the location, orientation, and overall design must be approved by the local authority, sometimes involving a democratic system of decision-making. The second is at the detail design stage, where the relevant building regulations must be complied with, covering such issues as structural integrity, weatherproofing, energy conservation, various health and safety precautions, fireproofing and escape, and access. These are enforced by trained building inspectors, to a greater or lesser extent depending on the bureaucratic and technical efficiency of the local authority.

Foundations

The foundations provide a stable base for the building and transfer all the loads from above to the ground. The type and depth of the foundations depend on the density and stability of the subsoil, and in clay soils the presence of tree roots, on the gradient of the ground, and on the structural system used in the building. Concrete, often reinforced with steel, is the commonest material used.

- Strip foundations are continuous linear foundations used under load-bearing walls. Two types are common – strip (about 150 mm thick and slightly wider than the wall placed at a depth) and trench fill (a concrete mass filling a trench dug along the line of the wall).
- Pad foundations are individual rectangular-shaped blocks used to support individual columns of framed structures.
- Raft foundations are strong and stiff reinforced concrete slabs extending the whole area of the building, used to support light buildings on unstable and variable subsoils.
- Piled foundations are circular-section reinforced concrete 'posts' that penetrate deep into the ground to find support for the building. They are used when the ground is weak and/or the building is heavy, particularly multistorey buildings. Friction piles act like nails, and rely on the resistance to movement provided by surface friction along the length of the pile. End-bearing piles act like columns, transmitting the loads to a firm stratum deep in the ground.
- Cassion foundations are large, usually reinforced concrete 'boxes' that are sunk into the ground by excavating beneath them usually from inside. These are used in soft ground often subject to saturation by water and are only economical for very large/tall buildings.

Construction Systems Based on Elements

The elements of construction are the main constituent parts of the building.

Basements

Usually constructed of reinforced concrete or concrete blockwork, the floor and walls being waterproofed to prevent ingress of ground water. They can act as the foundations for the building above.

Ground Floors

When supported by the ground, a concrete slab, usually reinforced, is laid on to a base of hardcore (small stones or broken bricks topped with sand) that replaces the topsoil. The slab is waterproofed with a plastic membrane and, in colder climates, thermally insulated with plastic foam insulation boards. A cement screed is normally added to provide a smooth top surface.

Suspended ground floors are supported by the surrounding walls and are similar in construction to upper floors, but with added thermal insulation.

Structural Frames

Structural frames in the form of columns and beams are constructed with hot rolled steel sections, reinforced concrete, or timber sections.

- Steel frames are occasionally used for one-off luxury villas, but more commonly for high-rise apartment buildings. The components are connected using bolts through predrilled holes using welded-on cleats (brackets).
- In situ concrete frames are widely used for single- and multistorey housing, particularly in warmer climates. Reinforced concrete slab floors are commonly combined with reinforced concrete columns.
- Oak or other hardwood is used to construct heavy timber-framed buildings of traditional style, combining beams with cross-braced columns to provide support for floors and roof. Mortice and tennon joints are used.

- Closely spaced small-section softwood columns and beams are commonly used, particularly in the United States, to form the framework for cladding and flooring for one- and two-storey houses (balloon frame). Nails are used to make connections.
- Light steel frames for walls and floors can also be made from thin cold-formed galvanised steel 'U'-shaped sections screwed together.

Load-Bearing Walls

Load-bearing walls carry the weight of the upper structure down to the foundations, and when used externally, to resist wind loads. A range of materials can be used to form these walls:

Masonry construction using brick, stone, or concrete blockwork, consisting of manually liftable units of these materials (i.e., bricks and blocks) 'glued' together with mortar. The external masonry walls are normally a cavity construction with the outer leaf providing the aesthetic appearance and weatherproofing. Thermal insulation is incorporated into the cavity between the outer and inner leaf. The inner leaf, normally of concrete blocks, is load-bearing, taking the weight of the upper floors and roof. Solid wall construction can also be used, together with added thermal insulation panels on the inside or outside.

Lightweight, aerated concrete block or cellular clay brick walls can dispense with insulation in mild climates.

Reinforced concrete panels are either poured in situ into temporary forms constructed from plywood or steel (formwork) or manufactured offsite and transported to the site when required. External reinforced concrete panel walls also need to be thermally insulated, either from the inside or from outside, usually with plastic foam boards glued or attached to the wall.

Storey-high timber panels consisting of studs (vertical rectangular 'sticks') faced with plywood on one side to provide stiffness are used. The external panels need to be supplemented with an exterior weatherproof finish, commonly of brick or timber weatherboarding. Thermal insulation, usually mineral fibre batts (stiffened quilt panels), is fitted between the studs, and water repellent/windproof sheeting is added to the outside face and a vapour-proof barrier to the inside, which is then covered with plasterboard to provide the internal surface. Recently, timber load-bearing walls in the form of thick, solid cross-laminated timber panels or structural insulated panels (SIPs) consisting of two plywood faces bonded to a core of plastic foamed insulation have been developed.

Earth walls are constructed using a variety of techniques, based either on forming the walls by compacting the earth in situ between wooded shuttering (pisé, rammed earth), or by building them up with unfired compressed earth blocks (adobe). Massive walls are required to provide stability and sufficient strength.

Non-Load-Bearing External Walls

These are supported by either the structural frame or the edge of the floor. A common construction for infilling concrete framing in warmer climates is to insert walls of hollow clay bricks which are then rendered on the outside and plastered inside. In cooler climates, masonry cavity walling is inserted, or insulated cladding panels of either steel or concrete construction are used. Heavy timber framing has insulated panels inserted into the frames, usually with a rendered external finish, though brickwork inserts are sometimes used. For timber balloon frames, the traditional external cladding is clapboard – horizontal overlapping weather boards, with the addition of fibre insulation batts between the studs and plasterboard internal finish. Coated weather-resistant plywood, mineral boards, or PVC planking are now commonly used in place of clapboard. Light steel framing has foil-faced foamed plastic insulation boards fitted on the outside of the framing and plasterboard to the inside. The walls are faced on the outside with a brick skin or a special reinforced rendered finish applied to the insulation boards.

In luxury developments, high-rise steel frames often have prefabricated storey-height insulated sandwich panel cladding mounted externally. The panels are made of a combination of sheets of steel, cement fibreboard or similar weatherproof materials on the outside, foamed thermal insulation, and plasterboard internal finish, and often incorporate windows.

Internal Walls and Partitions

Internal load-bearing walls can be of masonry, normally concrete blocks, reinforced concrete panels, or timber studs, laminated board or light gauge steel frame construction, depending principally on the main construction system of the house. The faces of the internal walls and partitions are either plastered or lined with plasterboard to provide a smooth finish. Non-load-bearing walls (partitions) can be of lightweight concrete block, cellular clay brick, timber, or light gauge steel stud construction, with plaster or plasterboard lining.

Upper (Suspended) Floors

Upper floors are supported by the load-bearing walls or a structural frame. They are either a slab construction, possibly with reinforced concrete (in situ or prefabricated planks) or laminated timber boards, or composed of a series of softwood timber beams with a boarded floor, commonly tongue and groove (T&G) timber boards, or chipboard sheets, with a plasterboard ceiling below. While all of these options are possible when supported by masonry or concrete supporting walls or frames, the timber-based flooring solutions must be used when supported by a timber-based structure. Additional layers and fibre matting infill may be required for acoustic reasons. Manufactured beams consisting of laminated timber flanges (top and bottom section) and plywood or steel lattice web (middle section) are used for larger spans.

For suspended ground floors, thermal insulation and resistance to damp are required. Concrete beams with lightweight concrete block or formed polystyrene infills are commonly used rather than timber or steel constructions.

Roofs

Roofs fall into two categories, flat and pitched. Flat roofs require a waterproof finish, while the slopes on pitched roofs allow overlapping tiles to fend off rainwater.

Flat Roofs

The construction of flat roofs (up to 3° inclination) is similar to that of suspended floors, using either a slab or beamed system. The additional requirements are those of waterproofing, condensation prevention, and thermal insulation. Waterproofing can be provided by:

- built-up roofing felt (three overlapping layers of bitumen felt bonded with bitumen emulsion) finished with a layer of stone chipping to protect against ultraviolet rays;
- a layer of asphalt poured in a molten state and spread over the roof to harden;
- a single ply plastic or rubber membrane glued at the joints;
- metal sheeting with standing seams (raised joints to prevent water ingress) – suitable metals are lead, copper, aluminium, and zinc.

Thermal insulation in the form of foamed plastic panels is usually placed just beneath the waterproofing, though an alternative system places waterproof closed cell foamed panels on top of a plastic waterproof membrane to protect it from extreme temperatures and ultraviolet rays from the sun. The panels need to be weighted down with gravel or concrete slabs to prevent them being blown away.

Pitched Roofs

These can vary in pitch from almost horizontal to near vertical. They are normally constructed from a triangulated framework of timber or steel sections, combined to form beams or trusses that span between the load-bearing walls or beams below. Modifications to the simple triangulations can be made to allow the roof space to be used for accommodation.

The trusses support purlins, beams that span horizontally between them to provide support for the rafters – the timber beams that form the roof slope which are spaced at about 600 mm centres. Prefabricated trussed rafters are slender, lightweight trusses spaced at rafter centres, obviating the need for purlins. The roof is thermally insulated either at the horizontal ceiling level with mineral wool or at the roof slope between the rafters, or with mineral wool or foamed plastic panels. The roof is finished with slates or tiles to provide waterproofing.

Prefabricated roofs can be made of trussed rafters or timber SIPs which are craned into place.

Components and Finishes

With the basic elements in place, numerous components are required to complete the housing.

Windows and external doors can be made of timber, metal, or plastics, alone or in combination, together with glass that can be single-, double-, or even triple-glazed, depending on climatic conditions. Local supply circumstances and economy will usually determine the materials and standards used, as well as the combination of opening and fixed panels, and whether the windows open inwards or outwards. Internal doors, skirtings, and architraves are usually timber-based, often using various forms of wood-derived boards.

Depending on location and use, stairs are constructed of timber, steel, or concrete, though glass has been used in luxury situations. Internal stairs in houses are usually of timber, while external and internal shared stairs are usually made of concrete due to its weather and fireproof qualities.

Floor finishes depend on local traditions and fashion. Tiled floors are usual in warm climates, while timber and carpets are common in more northerly climes. Stone has become a fashionable alternative in some more affluent sectors. Wall finishes are commonly plaster-based to form a smooth surface for painting or papering.

Services

All housing needs the basic provision of electric power and lighting, hot and cold water supply, and drainage. Heating is also necessary in cold climates, and cooling in hot climates. The trend is to increase the amount and sophistication of services provision to provide greater convenience and comfort. Mains electricity supply is generally available, and mains drainage is the norm in towns and cities, but in rural areas it is often necessary to provide onsite waste water treatment. Mains gas supply is also generally restricted to conurbations, with onsite storage required in other areas.

There is an increasing trend to harness renewable energy sources, particularly solar energy in hot climates. Solar hot water is most economically available in every climate, though ground source heat/coolth is feasible where there is enough space around the housing. Photovoltaic electricity generation is still only financially feasible with favourable government grants and generous buy-back tariffs, but technical advances promise a better return on the investment in this technology in the future.

Heating appliances for colder climates, especially gas-fired, have become increasingly efficient, which, when combined with high-grade thermal insulation and air tightness, result in minimal energy use and reductions in CO_2 emissions. Cooling, using electric-powered air-conditioning units, often as a retrofit solution, is now becoming universally adopted in hot climates, with the resultant huge increase in electric power consumption.

Modern Methods of Construction

Modern methods of construction aim to industrialise the construction process by moving most of the manufacturing of the building to factories. Obviously, the buildings cannot be transported whole to the site, so various levels of subdivision have been devised.

Panels. This is a 'flat-pack' approach that produces wall and floor panels that can be easily transported to site and erected to form the volumes of the buildings. Load-bearing panels are commonly made of light timber framing faced with plywood. For large multistorey apartments, precast reinforced concrete panels are used. The internal and external finishes are applied to the panels after erection, as they would be damaged during erection.

Volumetric. Whole rooms are constructed consisting of walls, floor, and ceiling, including windows and doors, and usually all internal finishes and services. Fully equipped bathroom and kitchen pods can be fabricated. The load-bearing units are then aligned and stacked to form the building. Units are commonly constructed from double-sided panels with timber or steel framework to provide strength. Concrete room units have also been fabricated, but are normally used where added durability is required, such as in secure units.

Kit of parts. This is a comprehensive system offered by some house manufacturers, principally in the United States, Western Europe, and Japan, that provide all the components of a house according to choice from a catalogue of designs, and deliver them to the prepared site in one process and erect the house as an integrated service.

Distinctive National Housing Construction Characteristics

Although westernisation has led to the general adoption of modern types of building construction for housing throughout almost all areas of the northern hemisphere, there still remain regional preferences and traditions which have influenced how these constructions are used. These preferences are commonly the legacy of historical precedent, and result in providing the distinctive characteristics of different places. In some areas, there are local regulations that determine the allowable construction types, normally restricting the scale and form of the buildings and types of materials used on the exterior. These are aimed at maintaining the built heritage, often in the context of increasing tourism. Elsewhere, it is the ready availability of certain building materials and particular skills on the part of the builders that lead to a predominance of a construction technique being the norm.

The United States and Canada

Two contrasting types of construction can be cited as indicative of North American housing developments, one based on the rural and suburban legacy and relating back to pioneering times, and the other based on urban high-density development.

Light timber construction based on frames of standard sawn sections is the norm for rural and suburban housing. 'Stick' construction, the classic building method of the 'wild west' is based on one- or two-storey walls consisting of timber verticals (6 × 2 inches being traditionally the most common) at 2 ft centres clad in timber weatherboarding (clapboarding). Timber floors of similar section beams at the same centres are finished with timber T&G boards. This lightweight timber-based approach to construction has been developed with increasing sophistication, now using advanced timber-based boards to stiffen the frames or to replace them altogether. This form of construction lends itself very well to offsite manufacturing techniques, thus industrialising the building process and providing copybook solutions to housing design.

High-rise housing is a feature of many North American cities, and commonly utilises the construction techniques developed for commercial buildings. Steel-framed structures clad in brick glass or concrete panels often replace the traditional townhouse developments of the past.

Mexico and Central America

The prevalence of informal settlements or slums in and around the large cities of Mexico and Central America is not untypical to that of other cities in developing countries experiencing the meteoric growth due to migration from rural areas and population increase. Construction in these developments relies on the availability of building and recycled materials, though simple reinforced concrete and brick constructions are generally aspired to.

However, a particular feature of traditional construction is the use of adobe, unfired earth blocks used as load-bearing walls, covered with an earth-based rendering. This remains a viable method of construction in more rural and suburban areas due to the ready availability and cheapness of the building material and the preservation of the skills needed for this type of construction. However, general adoption of this construction for new housing is unlikely.

Northern Europe

Three distinctive construction techniques based on the main structural material are evident in traditional housing construction in Northern Europe – heavy timber framing, stone, and brick. Where these occur tends to reflect the locally available raw materials, and leads to the distinctive character of housing and other buildings of the area. Timber frame construction is of the massive type using hardwood columns and beams to create a structural grid that is infilled with a choice of walling material. This can be found in the lowland areas of the continent where deciduous forests are common. Stone wall construction is utilised where good-quality limestone, sandstone, granite, and other building stone can be found. Today, the stone is used only as an external leaf of the external walls due to its expense, and cement-based substitutes using stone dust are often used where real stone is unaffordable. Brick is the choice in lowland areas where clay was traditionally extracted locally. Again, this is generally used only as an external facing material. Concrete blockwork and reinforced concrete components and softwood timber-based beams and roof structures are used to provide the main part of the construction.

Southern Europe

Rendered stonework and Roman pantile roofs are distinctive features of traditional houses in Southern Europe and around the Mediterranean. However, although the pantile roofs are retained in modern construction, the structure of the new houses tends now to consist of in situ reinforced concrete floor slabs and columns, infilled with cellular brick walls rendered on the outside and plastered on the inside. Floor tiles provide the floor finish.

North Africa and the Middle East

The distinctive flat-roofed houses with blank external walls and accommodation facing into enclosed courtyards are now no longer favoured for new housing. Earth construction using adobe and rammed earth is no longer considered acceptable despite being widely used in traditional housing. In situ reinforced concrete slabs and columns are used for almost all new residential buildings, whether luxury villas or low-cost apartment buildings. Concrete blockwork and cellular brick are used for infilling the concrete frames to provide external and internal walls. Little timber is used, even for roofs, which tend to be flat. Only doors, door frames, and windows are made of timber. Render and plaster are used for wall finishes and tiles for the floors.

North India and Bangladesh

In many areas of North India, there is a strong tradition of using brickwork for construction, including roof vaults. This is still a common modern constructional material, though often supplemented with in situ reinforced concrete to provide structural elements such as floors and roofs.

Urban informal and squatter settlements, with houses built mainly of reclaimed materials, are a feature of all the rapidly growing cities, though accelerating economic growth has led to numerous housing developments of apartment buildings built with in situ reinforced concrete floors and columns with brick infill walls, rendered on the outside, plastered inside.

Rural housing in the lowlands of Bangladesh is commonly constructed of a light bamboo framework with bamboo and reed walls and a thatched roof. The houses are often built on raised earthen platforms to avoid being flooded in the seasonal floods. The aspiration of many house owners is to clad their houses in galvanised corrugated iron sheets, seen as more durable though admittedly less comfortable in the hot climate.

Russia and Eastern Europe

The huge high-rise apartment developments of the Soviet era, 10–15 storeys high, were based on standard prefabricated concrete load-bearing panel systems that enabled a high degree of industrialisation of the construction and a fast erection process. Many of these are in need of repair and there is a shortage of new urban housing, now mostly built in in situ concrete. The more affluent city dwellers can afford to have a small country house (*dacha*), often little more than a cabin, constructed of a lightweight wooden framework clad in timber weatherboarding, and usually used only in the summer. The newly affluent class are building much more substantial country houses constructed with concrete and brickwork and high-class finishes inside and out.

Japan

The urban housing in many cities in Japan is distinguished by being low-rise individual houses densely packed together. The construction is based on lightweight timber framing. A sophisticated factory-based housing construction industry has developed to provide replacement houses for the short-lived units. When buying a property, it is commonplace to demolish the existing house and replace it with a new one. Pattern books provide a range of design options for the new houses, from which individual solutions can be devised. The houses are then prefabricated and transported to the site in finished panels or volumetric units and then quickly assembled. Based on timber construction, these houses increasingly contain modern timber-based boards and metal components to provide stiffness and weather resistance.

China and the Far East

Huge high-rise concrete apartment buildings are the feature of most rapidly developing cities in the Far East, particularly in those cities where space is at a premium, for example, Hong Kong and Seoul. Reinforced concrete is the standard construction material, and various techniques are used to speed up the building process. Factory precast façade panels which include windows are commonly used, as are prefabricated internal wall and floor panels and stairs. These are erected using tower cranes. The core of the apartments containing lifts, stairs, and service pipes and cables are normally of in situ concrete. A slip-formwork system can be used that is a semiautomated system of steel forms into which the concrete for the core walls were poured at storey-height stages. The formwork is moved up to create the next storey height as soon as the concrete is set. The walls and floors of the apartments are subsequently added around the core, commonly at a pace of one storey every 4–6 days.

Rural housing in Thailand, Malaysia, Indonesia, and other Far East countries was traditionally built with timber framing and bamboo and reed walls with thatched roofs. These materials are becoming increasingly more difficult and expensive to acquire, so modern manufactured materials such as concrete blockwork, concrete and clay tiles, and galvanised corrugated iron sheets are commonly substituted.

Natural Hazard Resistant Construction

In areas prone to occasional natural hazards such as earthquakes, floods, and hurricanes, special structural and design requirements are frequently enforced by the local governments. These include enhanced structural strength and integrity to withstand the extraordinary physical forces, and particular design features such as raised floors to overcome the effects of flooding. The specific regulations are formulated to respond to the particular nature of the anticipated hazard, and include not only the construction of the buildings, but also their siting, for example, away from known danger areas such as faultlines, landslip routes, and floodplains.

In the many areas of the northern hemisphere that are prone to earthquakes, precautions are taken to ensure that structural integrity is maintained despite severe shaking. Measures consist of providing a continuous structure throughout the building and strengthening the joints between materials. This is achieved using steel or reinforced concrete frames. Failure of any single component will not lead to progressive collapse.

See also: Building Regulations for Energy Conservation; Environmental Risks: Earthquakes; Environmental Risks: Flooding; High Rise; Modern Methods of Construction; Vernacular Housing.

Further Reading

Allen E and Ianno J (2008) *Fundamentals of Building Construction: Materials and Methods*. London: Wiley.
Allen E and Thallon R (2006) *Fundamentals of Residential Construction*. Hoboken, NJ: Wiley.
Aoyama H (ed.) (2002) *Series on Innovation in Structures and Construction, Vol. 3: Design of Modern Highrise Reinforced Concrete Structures*. London: Imperial College Press.
Ching F (2008) *Building Construction Illustrated*. Hoboken, NJ: Wiley.
Dietz A (1992) *Dwelling House Construction*, 5th edn. Chicago, IL: MIT Press.
Eisele J and Kloft E (eds.) (2002). *High Rise Manual: Typology and Design, Construction and Technology*. Basel, Switzerland: Birkhauser.
Eisele J and Kloft E (2003) *High-rise Manual: Typology and Design, Construction and Technology*. Basel, Switzerland: Birkhauser.
Marshall D and Worthing D (2006) *The Construction of Houses*, 4th edn. London: EG Books.
Mozas J, FernandezPer A, and Arpa J (2009) *HoCo: Density Housing Construction & Costs: a+t Density Series*. Madrid, Spain: a+t ediciones.
Riley M and Cotgrave A (2008) *Construction Technology 1: House Construction*, 2nd edn. Basingstoke, UK: Palgrave MacMillan.
Ross K (2005) *Modern Methods of House Construction: A Surveyor's Guide*. Garston, UK: BRE/CRC.
Taranath B (2005) *Wind and Earthquake Resistant Buildings: Structural Analysis and Design*. New York: Marcel Dekker.
VanderWerf P (2007) *The Concrete House: Building Solid, Safe & Efficient with Insulating Concrete Forms*. New York: Sterling.
Waite T (2010) *Steel-Frame House Construction*. Carlsbad, CA: NAHB Research Centre Craftsman Book Co.

Relevant Websites

www.homebuilding.co.uk/feature/construction-systems-masonry-vs-timber – Construction Systems: Masonry vs Timber.

www.cityu.edu.hk/CIVCAL/production/traditional – High-rise apartment construction options in Hong Kong.
www.homebuilding.co.uk/how-to/build – Build a house.
www.mcvicker.com/resguide/page000.htm – Single Family Residential Construction Guide (Canada).
www.youtube.com/watch?v=vfh6x6zUKMQ – Time lapse film of a prefabricated house construction (UK).
www.youtube.com/watch?v=690UMbr0y8 – Animation of brick/block wall construction (UK).

Construction of Housing Knowledge

C Allen, Manchester Metropolitan University, Manchester, UK

© 2012 Elsevier Ltd. All rights reserved.

Glossary

Epistemology The branch of philosophy concerned with the nature and scope of knowledge. Epistemology is concerned with questions such as 'What is knowledge?', 'How is knowledge acquired?', 'How do we know what we know?', and 'Why do we know what we know?'.

Feminism Theories of the social world that claim, amongst other things, that knowledge is gendered. Thus an understanding of gender relations is axiomatic to understanding why we know what we know, and why what we know reflects gender relations in society.

Knowledge What is known in a particular field or as a whole.

Marxism Theories of the social world that claim, amongst other things, that consciousness is false in capitalist societies. Revolution and liberation from capitalist oppression is axiomatic to the pursuit of truth.

Ontology The study of the nature of being, existence, or reality in general, as well as of the basic categories of being and their relations.

Social constructionism Sociological theories of knowledge that consider how social phenomena develop in social contexts. Within constructionist thought, a social construction (or a social construct) is a concept or practice that is the creation of a particular group.

Social science A form of knowledge gathering that uses formal theories and methods to guide the process of acquiring knowledge of the social world.

What is Knowledge?

Ontology

When we refer to our knowledge of housing, we are saying something about what we think we know about it. But to be able to make a statement that we think we know something about housing requires us to have ontological and epistemological commitments. Ontology is a theory of how the world is. Some social scientists subscribe to realist ontology. This is the belief that the social world is like the natural world. It is 'out there' to be discovered by us. Their task is rather like that of the natural scientist who studies things like the human body by observing it to find out how it works.

Realist ontology is contested by housing researchers who argue that there is no such thing as a world 'out there' that is simply waiting to be discovered by social scientists. They adhere to idealist, or what is sometimes called antifoundationalist, ontology. It is the belief that the world cannot be understood outside of the concepts that we use to make sense of it. The task of the social scientist is to understand what these concepts are and how they – rather than other concepts – are used to understand the world. Thus knowledge is conceptual rather than factual. Moreover, knowledge is contested and fallible (rather than factual and therefore verifiable) because we each employ different concepts to understand the social world. This means that we frequently argue with each other about what we know about the world by trying to convince others of the validity of our perspective. However, our tendency to understand the social world in different ways means that we are frequently unable to resolve our disputes. People tend, therefore, to take sides in disputes about what we think we know about social phenomena such as housing problems.

Epistemology

Having made our ontological commitments to realism or idealism, our next task is to decide how exactly we think we can find out about the social world that we think exists. This is our epistemology.

The key adherents to realist ontology are empiricists and positivists. In holding to the belief that the world is 'out there' to be discovered, empiricists treat our experience of the social world as our primary means of understanding it. In other words, they say that the social world is given to us in experience and that this is what enables us to know it. Crucially, they assume that social scientists can study the experiences that ordinary people have of the social world by asking them about their experiences. They may do this, for example, by interviewing people about their experiences of some phenomenon or other such as homelessness. They use what is called 'induction' to establish whether the experiences of homeless people are similar to each other and why. This enables them to make generalised statements about homelessness. Our knowledge resides in these generalised statements.

Positivists also hold the belief that the social world is out there to be discovered but they go about the task of finding out about it in a different way. Positivists believe that the only true knowledge of the world is the knowledge that is discovered by social scientists who study the world in order to find out about how it works. They believe that true knowledge resides in the coexistence and succession of observable phenomena. In other words, positivists believe that true knowledge resides in law-like statements (A + B = C) that can be verified with reference to the facts that have been collected by social scientists. Their approach to collecting these facts has been described as the 'hypothetico-deductive' approach – although they may also use inductive approaches. A hypothetico-deductive approach requires that the social scientist draw on their previous observations of social phenomena in order to formulate a hypothesis that they then test. They will test this by using a research method that is similar to an experiment in that 'data' are collected in a highly controlled manner that enables propositions to be verified or falsified. They may use 'structured questionnaires', where questions are always asked in the same way and in the same order, rather than interviews where the interviewee can exert more control over the data collection process by influencing the direction of the discussion. These questionnaires will provide 'respondents' with a list of possible answers so that they simply need to identify which answer applies to them.

Key adherents to idealist ontology in housing research have been Marxists and, more recently, social constructionists and to a lesser extent feminists and other existentialists. Proponents of these perspectives all agree with the ontological proposition that we can only understand the world by understanding the concepts that we use to make sense of it. However, they each have different epistemological commitments. Marxists believe that our knowledge of the world is 'false' because it is made available to us by a dominant ideology which teaches us to understand the world through the eyes of the capitalist. This leads us to hold beliefs, such as the idea that competition between people is natural and that success and failure are 'natural' outcomes of this natural competition. Marxists believe that there are alternative ways of knowing the social world which shows us that competition is anything but natural. It is a way of life that we adhere to because we are taught to accept it by the dominant ideology which makes competition seemingly natural. In other words, we have a false consciousness. Marxists believe that there are other ways of knowing the world and that the task of social science is threefold. First, the task of social science is to show how other ways of knowing the world are suppressed. Second, it is to make other ways of knowing the world available to people. Third, the social scientific task is to show that true knowledge (or consciousness) can be realised and that this knowledge will provide us with the path to working-class emancipation. Crucially, this means that they think working-class consciousness is 'false' when it is distorted by ideology, but that it can also speak a truth when it is allowed to understand what is in its own objective interests.

Adherents to 'feminist epistemologies' or 'standpoint epistemologies' argue a similar line. So whereas Marxists believe that the working class can access a truth that is produced from its own class position, unmediated by capitalist ideology, feminists believe that women can do likewise. In the same way that Marxists hold that truth is produced from class positions, then, feminists believe that truth is produced from gendered positions. Thus women are able to produce knowledge of the world that reflects their experience and understanding of it as women and that, moreover, challenges dominant understandings which are produced by men by drawing on men's experiences. For example, feminists might say that our knowledge of housing, and therefore housing policy, is based on masculine assumptions. Thus the design of houses reflects gendered assumptions that favour men. This emphasis on the social position of the knowledge producers has had influences across the social sciences. For instance, the disabled people's movement has taken it on board and has used it to argue that knowledge of housing, and therefore housing policy, is produced by able-bodied people. Thus, even though we might think that social science knowledge of housing is 'objective' or 'impartial', it is actually produced from the standpoint of able-bodied social scientists that make able-bodied assumptions when they study housing phenomena. Other truths exist, such as those produced by disabled people from their own experiences.

Social constructionists also believe that the social world is made up of competing discourses but, in contrast to Marxists and feminists, they make no commitment to any one of these discourses. This means that they do not believe that a true theoretical knowledge of the social world is attainable. They are concerned, rather, with how our understanding of the social world is produced in the way it is. That is to say, they are concerned to understand how knowledge of the social world is 'socially constructed'. There are different emphases in social construction. For instance, some social constructionists take seriously the ability of ordinary actors to produce their own understandings of housing. They suggest that knowledge is very fragmented because there is little evidence that a dominant perspective informs what people think and say. These social constructionists are influenced by perspectives, such as ethnomethodology, which emphasise the importance of taking ordinary actors' definitions of social phenomena seriously. Other social constructionists say that such an approach overlooks considering issues of power and authority. Thus they are interested in understanding how power works its effects, usually through political institutions, to produce understandings of social phenomena. They study how these institutions construct their own organisational perspective of social phenomena as objective and factual knowledge rather than what it is: one perspective amongst many possible alternatives. They also study how dominant understandings are forced upon, and taken on board by, ordinary people who make reference to them rather than their own direct experiences to understand the social world. Finally, they study how hegemonic understandings of social phenomena are challenged, and destabilised, by those with different perspectives.

The Search for 'Housing Facts'

If we go back to the origins of 'housing studies', we will see that it has always been shaped by realist ontology and that positivist and empiricist epistemologies have dominated. These influences can be detected in the earliest housing and poverty studies undertaken by Rowntree and Booth. These studies sought to counter myths about the working classes by providing facts about the conditions of poverty in which they lived.

The idea that social science could provide us with a factual knowledge of social phenomena, such as housing problems, gained currency after the Second World War when a Labour government was elected. This government was influenced by Fabian ideas, which highlighted the role of science in generating better understanding of social problems and in providing the means to solve them. The postwar Labour government established the Clapham Committee to examine the need to expand the social sciences and thereby enhance their capacity to undertake research into social and economic questions facing the government. The Clapham Committee provided the impetus for the growth of social science in the decades that followed. Universities grew in number, and as institutions. The expansion of the social sciences was a major part of this growth of universities. Moreover, the Social Science Research Council was created to provide social scientists with the resources to undertake research into the social issues and problems of the day. Housing research was a part of this growth in the social sciences.

Housing research was initially undertaken by social scientists who were located in a variety of university departments and disciplines, such as sociology, social policy, and geography. However, this changed in the 1980s and 1990s when a number of universities established housing research centres and appointed Professors of Housing Studies. This growth in the strength and position of housing research in the universities took place because it was attracting increasing amounts of government funding, which enabled it to branch out on its own.

This close relationship between government and housing research has shaped its development as a subject area. Thus housing researchers have mainly concerned themselves with the need to discover 'housing facts'. The purpose of this has been to provide government with knowledge of housing issues and problems as well as a means of solving housing problems in an informed way. This has meant that housing research has been overwhelmingly positivist and empiricist because it has sought to uncover the specific factors that can be observed to be regularly associated with housing problems – thereby establishing themselves as 'causes'. For instance, housing researchers have been concerned with discovering 'housing facts' that inform us about the causes of homelessness and housing need. They have been concerned with discovering the factors that produce unfair outcomes when council houses are allocated to people on the housing waiting list. There has also been a concern to discover why tenant participation in council housing tends to be better developed in some areas than others. More recently, housing researchers have concerned themselves with the need to discover housing facts about nature and causes of changing patterns of demand for housing and, in particular, the phenomenon of 'low demand' for certain types of housing in particular locations. Indeed the list of housing policy issues and problems that have been investigated by housing researchers, for the purposes of informing the policy-making process, is potentially endless!

So, housing researchers have been funded by government and other 'policy organisations' to uncover 'housing facts' about a range of housing issues and problems. They have been concerned with identifying the factors (such as the 'fact' that areas of low housing demand tend to be areas with a high proportion of terrace housing) that regularly appear to cause housing problems. This constitutes a factual knowledge of housing. In other words, the knowledge that has been produced by this type of housing research is based on 'facts' that have been subjected to hypothetical testing and therefore 'verified'. These housing facts are thought to 'speak for themselves'.

Struggles to Define Housing

The idea that 'housing facts' exist independently of housing researchers and are therefore 'out there' to be discovered has caused consternation amongst some housing researchers. These housing researchers argue that there is no such thing as a 'housing fact'. There are only perspectives on housing which inform the research exercises that provide us with 'knowledge' of housing issues.

They point out that different perspectives result in the production of different knowledges of housing and that the task of social science is therefore to study struggles to define housing issues rather than simply the housing issues themselves.

Some of the earlier advocates of this view in housing studies were influenced by the ideas of Marx and Marxist scholarship. They argued that positivists and empiricists were naive because they took what people told them about housing at face value and thereby treated them as 'housing facts' – especially when the same experiences or opinions were uttered by large numbers of people. For instance, they criticised housing researchers for assuming that people had a 'natural preference' for homeownership simply because a majority of survey respondents said that this was their preference. Marxists argued that this 'natural preference' for homeownership was ideologically constructed. They argued that the working classes had been encouraged to think that homeownership was superior to other ways of paying for housing, such as renting. According to them, the working classes were suffering from false consciousness because homeownership was in the interests of the capitalist class and not the working classes. Homeownership simply served to give the working classes a stake in the system which is what the capitalist class wanted in order to undermine the revolutionary potential of the working class. The key for Marxist scholars has been, therefore, to contest what passes as knowledge of housing in capitalist societies because they believe it is not knowledge at all but, rather, ideology. The other key task for Marxists has been to produce knowledge of housing that is true to the interests of the working class and that will enable the working class to see that things really can be different.

Marxist scholarship declined in housing studies, especially in the 1990s and afterwards. There are many reasons for this, such as the ever-increasingly close relationship between government and housing researchers. However, other factors are relevant such as the increasing popularity of post-Marxist perspectives such as social constructionism. The key proponent of social constructionism in housing studies has been Jim Kemeny. Kemeny used his influential book *Housing and Social Theory* to attack housing studies for its abstract empiricism and positivist orientation. He argued that too much housing research was dedicated to 'unearthing' housing facts that were assumed to exist 'out there', waiting to be collected by housing researchers. Kemeny argued that there was no such thing as housing facts – at least in the sense understood by empiricists and positivists. Insofar as housing facts existed, Kemeny argued that this was because powerful institutions had managed to transform their perspective of housing problems into accepted facts. Kemeny became concerned to understand how this happened and so set out, on his own and with his sometime collaborators Keith Jacobs and Tony Manzi, to understand the social construction of housing problems. His concern was to understand how state and other housing institutions managed to transform their definitions of housing problems, such as homelessness, into established facts upon which there was widespread agreement. Kemeny and colleagues used techniques such as historical analysis and discourse analysis to examine how discourses about housing problems are produced, circulated, and accepted and with what effects. Kemeny's work also sought to show how the social construction of housing problems resulted in the acceptance of some forms of knowledge of housing as legitimate and concomitant marginalisation of other forms of knowledge.

Some of the most significant work on the social construction of housing has been undertaken by David Clapham, Bridget Franklin, and Lise Saugeres. In a study of the social construction of housing management, they showed how housing managers engaged in 'boundary maintenance' practices. For instance, they showed that housing managers used technical language in order to keep 'outsiders' out of the realm of housing management and therefore unable to challenge their knowledge and practices of housing management. Saugeres has also shown how technical language is used by housing managers to represent their knowledge as 'objective' and therefore legitimise it in relation to other knowledges that do not meet these standards of objectivity. This is what enables housing managers to control what passes as knowledge of housing management. There are parallels with this and some of the work of Craig Gurney which has also analysed how language is used to construct knowledge of housing. Gurney pays particular attention to the use of analogy and metaphor in British housing discourse in order to show how some beliefs about housing ('an Englishman's castle is his home') sustain homeownership as the dominant tenure and thereby disadvantage other tenures, notably social renting.

So there is a key difference between social constructionist approaches to housing research and forms of housing research that are based on a search for housing facts. Housing researchers who devote their energies to the collection of housing facts focus on housing phenomena themselves. Housing researchers who devote their energies to examining how knowledge of housing is constructed focus on the processes that produce knowledge of housing phenomena rather than the housing phenomena themselves.

Finally, postscientific housing researchers are critical of housing research based on realist principles but also constructionist approaches as well. These housing researchers argue that the problem with each of these approaches is that they both are scientific. They are said to be 'scientific' because knowledge is either held to be verifiable (realism) or to provide a 'better' insight than 'common sense' because social theory is used to gain a more reflexive and in-depth understanding of how the social world works (theoreticism). The problem that postscientific housing researchers have with realist and constructionist housing research is that they believe scientific (empirical, theoretical) knowledge to be fundamentally flawed or, at least, limited. They argue that social science knowledge of all forms is produced at a distance from our experience of the world and, moreover, using principles that are radically different to those that apply in everyday life. It is also produced from positions (usually those of the white middle-class men who dominate university research) that, crucially, are not recognised as positions because housing researchers represent what they do as 'scientific research' rather than what it is, that is partial knowledge produced from class, gendered, and ethnocentric standpoints. This means that scientific knowledge misrepresents our experience of the world.

This becomes particularly problematic when scientific knowledge of housing is treated as the only legitimate knowledge of housing – which is what tends to happen in housing policy-making – yet it fails to adequately represent the experiences and opinions of the people who it is supposed to speak for. This is because ordinary people tend to be denied their voice in housing policy debate because they fail to use technical instruments to produce their knowledge and also fail to use technical language to articulate it. Advocates of postscientific perspectives argue that we need to take seriously what ordinary people say because it provides us with valuable insights into housing that social science does not provide. Critically, the voices of ordinary people that are flattened by the technical and objectifying techniques and language of housing research should be allowed to speak their own truth in their own language. A good example of this might be the technical language of housing research which is open to criticism because, as far as working-class people are concerned, it does not adequately describe how they feel about housing and therefore empties their worlds of their true meaning. They might argue that their knowledge can only be articulated through a form of language that is true to their feelings and experiences of housing. The same might apply to women. Social science knowledge of housing is produced in a rational way and, indeed, social scientists tend to insist on certain standards of rationality in order for claims to knowledge to succeed. Yet some women argue that the imposition of these standards is not done in the name of science at all because they actually represent a masculine hegemony. They argue that demands for knowledge to be produced in a rational way (e.g., by surveys that speak about housing in quantifiable ways or through a theoretical language that is highly technical) ignore other ways of knowing the world, for instance, emotional ways of knowing the world. The complaint here is that knowledge that is borne of an emotional engagement with the world is equally significant to our understanding, yet this form of knowledge is marginalised by social scientists who insist on certain standards of logic and rationality.

Conclusions

There are two main ways of understanding how we produce knowledge of housing. Realist approaches are based on the idea that housing phenomena exist independently of us and are 'out there' waiting to be discovered by housing researchers. This has been, and continues to be, the dominant approach to housing research. Idealist approaches emphasise the concepts that we use to make sense of housing phenomena. Marxists emphasise the issue of false consciousness and seek to provide the conditions in which a true knowledge of housing might emerge. They emphasise the role of class, and the working class and its sympathisers in generating this subversive knowledge. Many feminists have sympathies with this line of reasoning, pointing to the importance of learning from women's lives in their own terms rather than from the perspective of men. Social constructionists are not so much concerned to produce a knowledge that has more truth value when compared with dominant forms of knowledge, namely capitalist and masculine knowledge. Conversely, social constructionists are concerned with understanding how knowledge is produced and how it becomes established as accepted knowledge. They are also concerned with understanding how the process of establishing official knowledge results in the marginalisation of other alternative understandings of housing which are treated as nonknowledge. Finally, a third but marginal 'postscientific' perspective problematises 'all' forms of social science, including Marxist and feminist forms of it. They emphasise the idea that scientific knowledge in all of its forms is produced using different principles to those that are used to produce knowledge in everyday situations. This means that it does not adequately represent everyday knowledge of housing. This becomes problematic when science claims to speak on behalf of the people whom it collects its data from yet is unable to do so. It becomes particularly problematic when it is used to justify housing policies that damage these people. Advocates of a postscientific perspective therefore emphasise the importance of understanding these everyday knowledges of housing.

See also: Social Construction.

References

Allen C (2009) The fallacy of housing studies: Philosophical problems of knowledge and understanding in housing research. *Housing, Theory and Society* 26(1): 53–79.
Clapham D (1999) The social construction of housing management research. *Urban Studies* 34(5–6): 761–774.
Franklin B and Clapham D (1997) The social construction of housing management. *Housing Studies* 12(1): 7–26.
Greed C (1994) *Women and Planning: Creating Gendered Realities*. London: Routledge.
Gurney C (1999) Lowering the drawbridge: A case study of analogy and metaphor in the social construction of home ownership. *Urban Studies* 36(10): 1705–1722.
Harding S (1991) *Whose Science? Whose Knowledge? Learning from Women's Lives*. London: Routledge.
Jacobs K, Kemeny J, and Manzi T (2004) *Social Constructionism in Housing Research*. Aldershot, UK: Ashgate.
Kemeny J (1984) The social construction of housing facts. *Scandinavian Housing and Planning Research* 1(3): 149–164.
Kemeny J (1992) *Housing and Social Theory*. London: Routledge.
Lynch M (2008) *Scientific Practice and Ordinary Action: Ethnomethodology and Social Studies of Science*, 2nd edn. Cambridge, UK: Cambridge University Press.
Saugeres L (1999) The social construction of housing management discourse: Objectivity, rationality and everyday practice. *Housing, Theory and Society* 16(3): 93–105.
Smith M (2003) *Philosophy and Methodology of the Social Sciences II*. London: Sage.
Somerville P (1994) On explanations of housing policy. *Scandinavian Housing and Planning Research* 11(4): 211–230.

Contract Saving Schemes

R Ronald, University of Amsterdam, Amsterdam, The Netherlands

© 2012 Elsevier Ltd. All rights reserved.

Glossary

Central Provident Fund (CPF) A compulsory savings plan in which employees pay a fixed part of their salary along with an employer's contribution into a collective fund. Some funds are more explicitly designated for saving for housing, such as the Housing Provident Fund in China.

Good brothers Savers in a Contractual Savings Schemes for Housing (CSSH) who do not take out loans. A high number of good brothers reduces liquidity risks and allows CSSH banks to allocate loans more quickly.

Home Buyers' Plan (HBP) Allows first-time home-buyers (in Canada) to borrow from their retirement savings plan and repay the funds over an extended period.

Liquidity risk The risk that banks will have insufficient funds in their savings pools to meet future loan demands.

Loan multiplier A factor that determines the size of a loan in relation to the savings effort.

Saver–fund effort ratio (SFER) A formula which takes into consideration every individual's saving balance in relation to the amount of loans a CSSH bank grants to its customers.

Introduction

Governments have come under increasing pressure to support home purchase, especially where the availability of credit and purchasing power of low- and middle-income households has been limited. Housing policies can assist home-buyers through a diversity of schemes. This article considers 'contractual savings schemes for housing' (CSSH), which are known as one of the oldest and simplest collective funding mechanisms in housing finance. Rather than simply subsidising purchases, CSSH constitute a more stable mechanism that enhances the financial capacity of households by encouraging and supporting saving. They have largely been established where private finance and mortgage sectors have been undeveloped, or access to secure long-term loans has been limited for middle- and low-income working families.

CSSH schemes were pioneered in Western Europe, but have been adopted and adapted in developing and transition economies where governments have sought to promote savings behaviour at the household level, improve access to owner-occupied housing, as well as finance infrastructure at the institutional level. CSSH may represent a form of demand subsidy for housing as governments often provide beneficial interest rates and types of guarantees. They can also be considered policy mechanisms that promote stable housing consumption and consequently drive housing construction. This may also promote macroeconomic objectives. In developing societies, CSSH can also fulfil welfare functions. This is especially the case where welfare states are underdeveloped and owner-occupied housing assets provide resources that enhance informal family welfare exchanges, and supplement reduced incomes during unemployment or in retirement.

Features of CSSH are now examined. Particular attention is paid to key features as well as national variations among schemes. Consideration is also given to the risks associated with the regulation and management of CSSH. There is concern with social and systemic risks that have emerged in some contexts as a result of overemphasis on saving for housing and overinvestment in housing markets caused by contractual and compulsory saving schemes.

Types of CSSH Systems

CSSH in various guises have been established by governments in order to support home-buyers' accumulation of a deposit, as well as facilitating borrowing to meet the outstanding sum. Most schemes offer a dedicated loan-linked form of saving that combines a phase of contractual savings to the promise of a housing loan. Typically, after successful completion of the predetermined savings period, both the amount saved and the loan are disbursed to the saver who uses the funds for housing purposes. Some approaches utilise provident fund accounts in which finances are automatically deducted from wages along with an employer's contribution. In this case, accounts can be built up over time in order to pay for housing deposits, transaction costs, and housing renovation, while monthly contributions can also be transferred between different accounts to meet mortgage repayments.

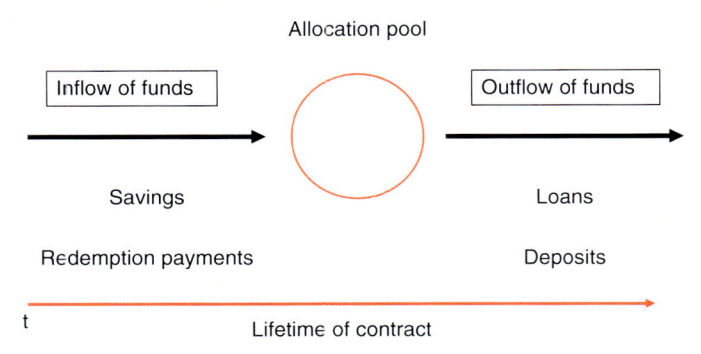

Figure 1 The CSSH mechanics.
Source: Roy F (2006) Contractual Savings Schemes for Housing (CSSH) – An assessment of past experiences and current developments. *Paper Prepared for World Bank/IFC Conference 'Housing Finance in Emerging Markets'*. Washington, DC, USA, 15–17 March.

The underlying design of CSSH products is more or less similar. The typical CSSH contract consists of three phases: (1) the savings period, (2) the waiting or allocation period, and (3) the loan period. **Figure 1** serves as an illustration. In the savings period, the saver agrees to save for a certain minimum episode and/or accumulate a certain amount (e.g., in a closed system, usually about 50% of the contract sum). The length of the waiting or allocation period may vary. It depends on available funds in the savings collective or other funding sources to which the collective has access to. During the loan period, the customer repays his CSSH loan in regular instalments.

Around this standard CSSH format there are numerous variations. **Table 1** shows examples of different CSSH types around the world. The most common CSSH types in Europe have their roots in the building society movement in the United Kingdom.

The two main forms of CSSH that dominate in Europe can be considered in terms of closed and open systems. In 'closed systems', the funding of CSSH loans exclusively relies on savings funds previously collected by the CSSH institution. The most prominent closed CSSH scheme in Europe is the German/Austrian Bauspar system, which has also been implemented in the Czech Republic, Slovakia, Hungary, Croatia, and Romania. Alternatively, in 'open systems', external funding is permitted when the inflow of savings does not meet CSSH contractual commitments to savers. Open systems have emerged in France (Épargne logement) and Slovenia.

The European CSSH schemes feature tight legislation as well as governmental support in the form of savings bonuses and/or other incentives. For example, interest is commonly exempt from tax (see article Access and Affordability: Homeowner Taxation). They are often managed by specialised institutions (except in France and Slovenia).

'Free savings schemes' are typically found in Asian, Latin American, or African countries. Sometimes they benefit from government support, such as tax advantages (e.g., Burkina Faso), but can be offered by private independent institutions. In such cases, there is no specific regulation and product designs may vary, although there are often similarities with classic CSSH schemes. A savings component is a popular feature among microfinance institutions that offer housing microfinance products. A savings period serves as a prerequisite for access to a housing loan. Typically, these schemes are linked to the financing of home improvements.

'Compulsory schemes' have appeared in Asian and African countries. In this case, CSSH are operationalised as monopolistic provident funds or are part of the product range of a housing bank (e.g., Iran). Typically, they are regulated by proprietary charter acts. In East Asia, Singapore has been a pioneer in developing contractual savings linked to the housing

Table 1 Types of CSSH systems

	Closed system	*Open system*	*Compulsory schemes*	*Free savings schemes*
Country examples	Germany Austria Czech Republic Slovakia Hungary Croatia Romania	France Slovenia Tunisia Morocco	China Nigeria Singapore Malaysia	Canada Chile Burkina Faso Democratic Republic of Congo India

> **Box 1 Country example: India**
>
> BHW Home Finance in India, a subsidiary of the German BHW Bausparkasse (now part of the German Postbank Group) implemented, in December 2002, a savings-linked credit product very similar to the German Bausparkassen Model (Easy Home Loan Deposit Scheme). The savings tenure varies between 3 and 5 years. The loan amount is limited by the savings amount accumulated and may not exceed the amount saved (a loan multiplier of 1). The loan period is 1 year longer than the savings period. The funds can be used for housing purposes only. Loan allocation depends on the saver's creditworthiness, a point system which measures the regularity of the payments during the savings period, and the size of the individual savings amounts. Irregular savings amounts lead to a lower loan amount (e.g., the loan amount will be reduced if the saving amounts in the later years are disproportionately higher than the saving amounts in the earlier years). There is no specific regulation of this scheme.

system. The Singapore Central Provident Fund (CPF) initially combined compulsory contributions from workers and employers in a pension fund that could be accessed at the end of the working career. The government subsequently approved transfers from individual CPF savings accounts to meet deposits and loan repayments for housing purchased from the state Housing and Development Board (HDB). Mortgages were also provided by the HDB for CPF account holders. Other East Asian countries that have adopted similar schemes include China and Malaysia.

Why Have CSSH Been Implemented?

CSSH have been normally introduced in countries at an early stage of economic development or transition. While their adaptation has been fuelled by the desire to develop housing finance more generally, CSSH have been advocated for the following reasons:

- Lack of long-term funding instruments since neither capital markets nor banks can provide long-term resources to refinance fixed rate mortgage loans.
- No loan supply in areas without standard mortgage finance, which are characterised by low loan volumes and high servicing costs (for banks).
- A further argument is that CSSH contribute to a broad mobilisation of savings This statement is, however, often contested since CSSH may also crowd out other savings products (especially when CSSH savings are subsidised).
- Low- and middle-income households have only limited access to home purchase because of high down payment requirements and high credit risk management costs.
- The promotion of owner-occupied housing consumption can boost housing construction which improves the housing stock and stimulates economic growth.
- A desire to stabilise family formation and life courses around a particular pattern of saving and consumption that encourages self-provision through more intensive saving in early life with an accumulation of substantial housing equity by old age.

Key Features of CSSH Systems

Open versus Closed Systems

The closed CSSH system can be described as a 'time–money' system. On conclusion of the CSSH saving contract, all conditions are fixed including the interest rate on both the savings and the loan, that is, the CSSH bank cannot use the interest rate to balance supply of and demand for funds. As **Figure 1** indicates, the allocation pool is the decisive management tool in a closed system because the CSSH institution can only distribute previously allocated funds in the form of CSSH loans, thus resulting in the already mentioned waiting period. The challenge for the CSSH institution in managing such an 'allocation pool' is to balance fluctuating inflows and outflows of funds in order to meet future loan demands within a reasonable time span. In order to attain short waiting periods, CSSH institutions normally stick to specific queuing rules, which determine the sequence of loan disbursements. Closed systems have often run into liquidity problems, especially when operating in high-inflation environments. As a result, semi-open schemes have evolved that combine aspects of open schemes (e.g., inflation indexation), with aspects of closed systems, such as fixed interest rates during the savings and lending periods.

In contrast to closed systems, managers of open CSSH schemes can access other funding sources (e.g., from the capital market) if a shortfall of deposits in the fund arises. As a result, waiting periods can be minimised. Since an open scheme may rely on different funding sources (e.g., personal savings and wholesale funds), the cost of funds may vary and, in the worst case, may lead to a deterioration of the scheme. Thus, open schemes do not often offer fixed rate contracts (for the savings and loan period) in order to avoid getting stuck in a high interest rate cost trap. Their main value is restricted to providing a savings product and an easier access to loans.

Although open and closed CSSH may resemble insurance contracts (in particular, life insurance) or any other form of contractual savings plans in their design and structure, funds are channelled towards housing purposes, that is, modernisation/renovation, construction, or purchase. However, since the savings and loan amount are in some way interrelated, the contract sum is often insufficient to finance larger housing investments (e.g., construction or purchase). Especially in closed systems, CSSH funds typically constitute only a part of the whole financing amount required. In the German Bauspar system, for example, the Bauspar loan is normally a second mortgage topping up a first mortgage loan from another lender. Due to the limited financing amount, CSSH loans have become popular in financing modernisation or renovation.

Savers who do not take out a loan are known as 'good brothers'. A high number of good brothers allow CSSH institutions to allocate loans more quickly, especially in a closed system. Since the number of good brothers is difficult to forecast, CSSH loans are only moderately higher than the savings amount. Open CSSH schemes are able to offer higher loan amounts, though only at variable interest rates to avoid liquidity shortfalls.

Although savers acquire entitlements to CSSH loans with the successful completion of a savings period, CSSH institutions still require assessment of the saver's creditworthiness. However, the savings prerequisite remains an important indicator of a saver's creditworthiness. It is particularly strong in housing microfinance schemes.

Compulsory Schemes

The compulsory schemes found in East Asian contexts are designed very differently from the open and closed systems of Europe. Provident funds are expected to accompany an account holder for their entire working life and funds can be inherited should the holder die. Contributions to savings accounts are often compulsory in East Asian countries as there are underdeveloped social security or public welfare mechanisms. CSSH often become the main means of social insurance and account holders are expected to eventually draw upon them as a pension in retirement. There is thus a strong link between employment, saving, and investment with an eye to fulfilling welfare functions.

Withdrawals before retirement age are normally restricted to housing purchase or property improvement. By splitting resources between a managed investment account and housing assets, risks are spread. Moreover, housing investment is also favoured by the state as it stimulates the construction and real estate sectors with the added bonus of multiplier effects in the rest of the economy. At the household level, the encouragement of home purchase is considered to have positive social and psychological impacts. It promotes saving and investment behaviour, individual and family self-reliance, and enhances feelings of community and belonging. Housing investments are also preferred as they have both consumption use (families can live in them and satisfy shelter needs) and investment use (an asset that accrues in value that can be realised by sale in the market).

The development of compulsory schemes along with intervention in the housing, planning, and development sector has also helped integrate circuits of funding between savings, mortgages, and construction. The capital accumulated in collective funds can be invested in housing development with profits increasing the value of the fund. At the same time, funds are used to finance individual lending which in turn stimulates housing and urban development. Singapore's compulsory savings and its public HDB is a monopolistic system where the government can draw from public savings at preferential (noncommercial) interest rates to fund lending and development activities. This has facilitated rapid urban growth and housing renewal, with more than 80% of the housing stock built by the state since 1961, and bought by citizens with publicly originated mortgages, with profits from both activities flowing back into provident funds. Commercial parties have largely been excluded, although the government has sought to reduce its exposure to market risks by expanding the role of the private sector in recent years, especially in providing mortgages.

In China, the Housing Provident Fund introduced in the early 1990s was initially used for short-term loans to work units, housing cooperatives, and developers to provide more affordable housing. Subsequently, housing funds have been used more in line with their original objective to assist individual employees with housing. In the late 1990s, the market for home loans was expanded through the promotion of new kinds of mortgage products. Housing provident fund loans, as well as a combination of commercial and housing provident fund loans, helped develop the emerging urban housing market.

An important feature in societies with compulsory CSSH is state intervention in the housing sector. Funds not only help individual home purchases but also the provision of affordable housing itself. There may also be a link to planning, slum clearance, and urban redevelopment with provident funds providing core finance for both development and purchase. Governments, through public agencies, are able to improve target areas or housing conditions for priority groups (considerable preference is normally given to working, family households), as well as mitigate risks (in Singapore the CPF intervenes in the case of mortgage default). Control over the housing system also extends the power of the state. In Singapore, housing improvement funds are sometimes withheld in districts where the electorate offers weaker support for the ruling party, and purchasers of new HDB housing have not received the keys to their properties until parking fines, and so on, have been cleared.

In view of housing market volatility, the deep link between savings and the housing system is now being reassessed. Overinvestment in the housing sector has become increasingly risky as it has undermined the spread of investments that, in principle, are meant to fund retirement. The CPF's role in funding retirement pensions has in recent years become a greater concern than housing development. The Singapore government has consequently restructured the system to ensure a minimum limit on savings retained in the account, capped withdrawals for housing, and introduced a greater diversity of investment and welfare products that CPF accounts can be used to purchase.

Risk Analysis of CSSH

CSSH systems are exposed to a host of risks. The following outlines different types of risk and the measures that can be introduced to mitigate them.

Credit Risk

Due to the pre-savings requirement, a high number of defaulting loans is unlikely. In 2004, default rates in Germany's bausparkassen amounted to around 0.04% of the total loan portfolio, whereas in Slovakia the rate was 0.56%.

Interest Rate Risk

In a closed system, interest rate risk is limited by the contract design. However, pricing of the contract must take into consideration capital market movements. If interest rates on the savings and the loans do not anticipate future market developments, attracting savings or selling loans may become difficult.

Box 2 Country example: Singapore

The Singapore approach to saving for housing has become a model for compulsory types of CSSH. Employees have, since 1955, been obliged to contribute a proportion of their wages, which is matched by employers, into a state-run Central Provident Fund (CPF). This fund was set up to provide, in principle, a lump sum payment on retirement. In 1968, the government approved the use of CPF savings for purchase of public owner-occupied properties, and later private ones. Since the 1960s the government Housing and Development Board (HDB, 1961) has been constructing apartments for sale to qualifying CPF account holders, and since the 1970s has regulated a second-hand market for HDB home purchase. The HDB has also provided mortgages for buyers. Around 61% of CPF withdrawals are for housing purchases (see **Figure 2**), the majority for HDB units.

Purchase of HDB homes facilitates the transfer of credit built-up in the compulsory saving scheme, the primary source of social insurance, into a housing account with transfers allowed for both down payments and mortgage repayments. CPF savings can also be used to cover survey and legal fees, renovation, or repair. HDB mortgage interest rates have been pegged close to CPF interest rates and reflect rates of government borrowing. Investment of CPFs in the HDB via transfers across government departments for the purpose of development, and the investment of CPFs from individual accounts into HDB housing properties, has funded expansion in the housing sector and stimulated increases in the asset values of owner-occupied properties.

When CPF transfers were introduced for home purchase in 1968, the gross national saving to GNP ratio was less than 10%. Increases in contribution ratios substantially accelerated the saving rate, which reached more than 50% of GDP by 2000. Nevertheless, there have been problems associated with overinvestment of CPFs in housing, and this became particularly evident after the 1997 Asian economic crisis. Property values dropped as much as a third. The government reacted by halting land sales and introducing new subsidies for purchases. In 2002, caps were placed on CPF withdrawals for housing to reduce risks of overexposure in the sector. Efforts have, in recent years, been made to spread CPF investments and risks including the liberalisation and diversification of investment options for retirement saving. A minimum is also now retained in CPF accounts on retirement to ensure a form of annuity income in old age.

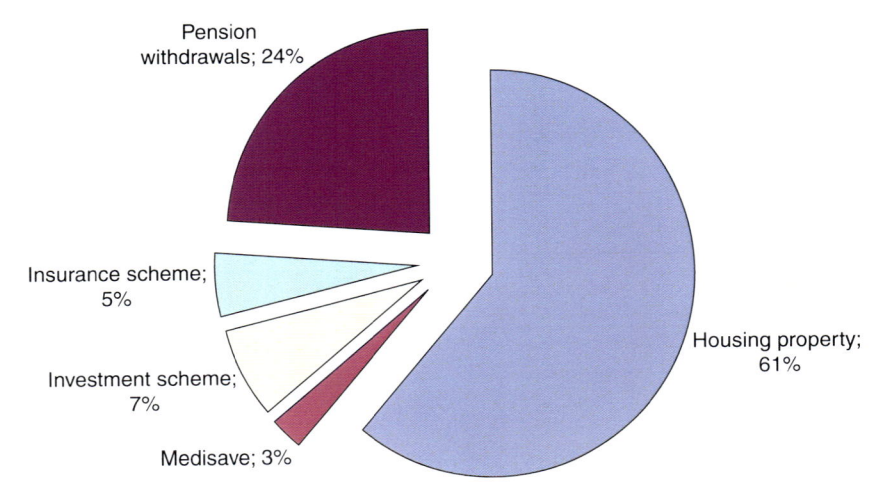

Figure 2 The CPF withdrawals, 2006.
Source: Singapore Central Provident Fund, 2006.

Liquidity Risk

The key risk that CSSH schemes are vulnerable to is liquidity risk, or the risk that banks will have insufficient funds to meet future demand for loans. Therefore, aggregate liquidity management depends on whether the products are individually viable and the credibility of the scheme as a generator of loans. The latter implies ensuring a sufficient ratio of loan allocations within the collective. Several factors are crucial to the liquidity management of a CSSH scheme. For example, the longer the lengths of savings and loan periods are, the more stable the scheme is (lower liquidity risk). Other important factors are as follows.

The nature of the loan commitment

The loan commitment (in time) is the only tool to balance the supply of savings with the demand for loans, especially in a closed system. Thus, the CSSH bank must determine when loans are ready for allocation.

Loan multiplier

This determines the size of loan relative to the savings effort. A higher multiplier requires a higher share of good brothers and/or access to external funding. The higher the numbers of good brothers, the more savings are available to meet the demand for loans. A high share of good brothers stabilises the CSSH pool of funds. The French Épargne logement system, for example, was built on a high share of good brothers. As the numbers of savers declined, the government was forced to adjust the scheme in order to maintain the stability of the system. **Figure 3** shows the change in liquidity status in a case where the CSSH banks decide to raise the multiplier from one to two. The model works with the following assumptions: both the savings and the loan period amount to 4 years; there is no waiting period; the number of newly concluded contracts per annum and loan takers are estimated at 1000 and 88%, respectively; the contract sum of the CSSH contract is 5000 currency units (CU). In the left figure, the borrower receives a loan worth 5000 CU, and in the right figure, they receive a loan amounting to 10 000 CU. According to the calculation, a multiplier increase results in a cash shortfall of about 4.5 billion CU for the CSSH banks, which would have to be covered through outside funding in order to meet the loan commitments. Since the multiplier is the crucial element of the system, it should not be higher than 1, especially in the set-up phase. Despite being fundamental to stability, this requirement is often violated in inflationary environments when no additional measures have been taken to preserve the real value of savings.

Prepayment Risk

For liquidity management reasons, CSSH loans are usually prepayable. These prepayments are reinvested in new CSSH loans, which stabilise the CSSH pool. If contract savings and loan rates are set too high, a drop in market rates may force the managing bank to reinvest large sums at low or negative spreads. The pricing of the CSSH product should therefore anticipate future interest rate movements to avoid massive prepayments. Restrictions (e.g., penalties) on prepayments may make the system less attractive.

Exchange Rate Risk

Normally, when both savings and loans are offered in one currency, exchange rate risk is absent. However, if there is

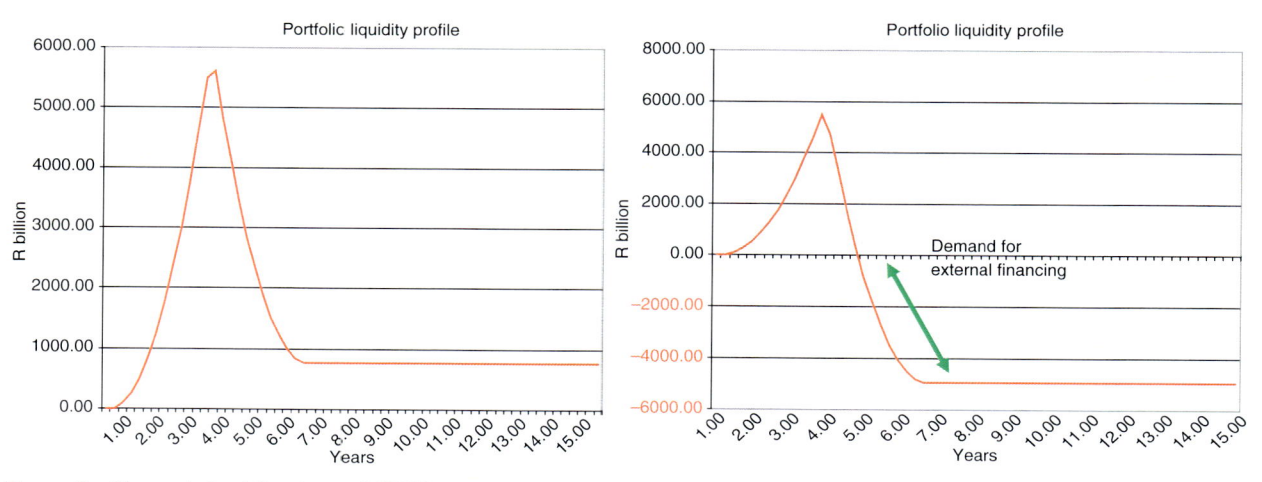

Figure 3 Change in liquidity status of CSSH pool when multipliers are raised from 1 to 2. The figure implies that 88% of the customers will take up a loan. Only 12% are so-called 'good brothers' who save in the system but do not take up the loan offer when the contract is ready for allocation.
Source: Dübel (2008).

external funding, wholesale funds in other currencies can leave the CSSH exposed. For example, if loans are denominated in US dollars in a given country, customers bear the exchange rate risk because salaries are likely to be denominated in their own national currency.

Overinvestment Risk

In compulsory systems in particular, where the purpose of CSSH is to stimulate housing construction and consumption as well as supplement pension provision, there has been overinvestment of provident funds in housing. Collective funds and housing equity in these contexts constitute a considerable amount of the national wealth. Housing market downturns have exposed funds and eroded aggregate asset wealth. Overinvestment by individuals in housing has also eroded the savings pool expected to provide an income in retirement.

Social and Political Risk

Many governments have relied on the success of their CSSH schemes to muster political support, invigorate urban redevelopment, and supplement rudimentary social insurance programmes. Failure in the housing market or the funds system can undermine the legitimacy of the state and has motivated efforts to stimulate the housing market and shore up the provident system at the expense of publicly provided social goods and social security benefits that ameliorate socioeconomic hardship.

Regulating CSSH Systems

The liquidity risk associated with CSSH systems clearly underlines the need for regulation and supervision. In Germany, for example, bausparkassen started their operations in the 1920s. The system became very popular throughout the whole country, resulting in the establishment of more than 400 bausparkassen. In the 1930s, many of them suffered severe liquidity gap traps due to high multipliers and short waiting periods, leading to unsustainable cash shortfalls. As a result, legislation to restore stability and credibility in the system was enacted. Consequently, separate laws or central bank directives have been established in order to improve the supervision and licensing of the CSSH. The precedent set in Germany constitutes a set of ideal regulatory practices requiring CSSH banks and schemes to embrace key guidelines, which have more or less guided the regulation of CSSH in other contexts. These guidelines include the following.

Definition of General Features and Principles

The objective of CSSH is the collection of savings and the granting of loans out of the savings pool (i.e., savings are a prerequisite to become eligible for a CSSH loan). CSSH funds are often restricted to housing finance purposes since other loan purposes may adversely affect the quality of loan portfolios. Management of CSSH funds (collective) is thus given over to a regulated financial institution that is specially licensed.

Definition of Balance Sheet and Cash Flow Principles

Typically, CSSH funds are separated from any other funds managed by the CSSH bank. CSSH banks are obliged to seek a balance between the inflow of savings and the outflow of loans. The saver–fund effort ratio (SFER) (a formula which takes into consideration every individual's saving balance in relation to the amount of loans a CSSH bank grants to its customers) and the assessment figure (allocations of CSSH loans are subject to a minimum savings period, minimum savings amounts, and a predetermined assessment figure) are adequate instruments to achieve this goal. A further prerequisite in this context is the equal treatment of all CSSH clients. Therefore, CSSH contracts usually refer to general contract conditions and are an integral part of the overall contract.

Fixing Conditions

A further measure, aimed at building trust in the system, is the commitment by CSSH banks to fix conditions during the lifetime of the contract. Changes in existing CSSH contracts can dilute confidence in the system as a whole. CSSH banks are generally able to introduce new CSSH products for new generations of savers in order to adapt to changing market conditions.

Relations between the CSSH Customer and the CSSH Bank

During the first years of its existence, a CSSH bank accumulates savings (before the first CSSH loans will be disbursed). Ideally, regulations define a minimum savings period (e.g., 2 years). Otherwise, asset–liability management (ALM) for the CSSH bank may become difficult. It would also contradict the underlying savings idea. Typically, CSSH banks have a slight surplus of free funds. Legislators often allow CSSH banks to invest these funds in clearly defined investments such as advances or bridging loans. There may also be some investment in secure assets, for example, highly rated bonds (from governments, for example). However, investment in shares and derivatives is regarded as too risky.

Risk Management (In Particular Liquidity Management)

Normally, managers of CSSH need to demonstrate their suitability as fund managers: they must prove certain risk management capabilities. In Germany, for example, CSSH board members need to undergo extra training before they can assume their positions. Underwriting standards are also set in place that ensure CSSH banks will decline loan requests where there is a significant probability of default. Control over timing (i.e., waiting period), especially in closed systems, is another important management tool that CSSH banks use to balance the inflow and outflow of funds (in contrast to normal banking practices). However, savers normally have the right to receive a loan, which is conditional on the availability of funds (from other savers). In the case of open schemes, a waiting period can be reduced or even eliminated if the interest rate on the CSSH loan is not fixed on conclusion of the initial savings contract, thus allowing the CSSH bank to seek finance through other funding tools (e.g., other deposits and bonds). Reserve funds are often used to balance fluctuating inflows of funds and keep the waiting periods equal in length and as short as possible.

Regulators

Ideally, there is transparency among those institutions that monitor and supervise CSSH banks and their related products. In addition, the rights of the supervising institution are clearly defined. Supervising institutions often have the right, in law, to enforce on- and offsite supervision, impose penalties, and remove managers from CSSH funds. Ideally, the central bank should assume this role. In order to facilitate the monitoring of the liquidity position of a CSSH bank, directives typically comprise some minimum reporting and auditing standards, for example, the CSSH fund should be disclosed separately in a balance sheet. This regulation is of particular importance in an open system in order to improve transparency. Like ordinary commercial banks, CSSH banks are subject to regular reporting of their liquidity position. An important issue in this regard is the mandatory approval of new contract terms (tariffs) by the supervisor before new CSSH products are launched. With detailed descriptions and liquidity projections under different scenarios, CSSH banks need to prove the viability of the new CSSH product. Tariffs that do not fulfil the minimum conditions set by the regulator can thus be refused.

State Support of CSSH

The choice of CSSH as housing policy instruments, or even 'subsidies', has sometimes been controversial. Advocates claim that the linkage between the savings process and access to subsidy is a necessary and efficient stimulus which both promotes the accumulation of household financial resources (required to buy a home) and makes mortgage financing more resilient with respect to unexpected irregularities (e.g., unemployment). However, subsidising owner-occupiers may also be criticised on the grounds that it sustains a tenure bias in policy towards those already well-off enough to accumulate substantial savings. From another perspective, CSSH also privileges finance designated for home purchase and distort market processes. Indeed, state support of housing finance institutions has featured in recent house-price bubbles and contributed to overinvestment in real estate.

CSSH are generally believed to be politically attractive, but government introduction of savings subsidy schemes has had mixed results in different countries. In some cases, the implementation of CSSH has in fact resulted in lower lending volumes. In the Czech Republic, the CSSH banks invested the major share of their deposits in other investments (e.g., bonds). After 10 years, the loan-to-deposit ratios of all CSSH banks reached 28% (as of 2002). In 2007, the loan-to-deposit ratio of the CSSH banks reached 45%. In Hungary, the government has increased subsidies to promote savings inflows, but the increases were from previously low and inadequate levels. CSSH have remained a niche market segment (a loan market share of 0.92% as of 2004) as CSSH products have been crowded out by other mortgage loan subsidies. In addition, CSSH loan interest rates were less favourable than those on other mortgage loans. After subsidisation, the interest rate on mortgage loans fluctuated between 3 and 6%, whereas for CSSH loans, interest rates were around 6%.

Subsidisation of CSSH has also had to take economic development directives into account. In Slovakia, for example, the subsidy amount has been repeatedly lowered to accommodate economic development and the increasing activities of Slovakian CSSH banks. In the early 1990s, CSSH banks were the first banks to offer long-term housing loans to private individuals, thus pioneering a new origination, servicing, and risk management infrastructure for the Slovakian housing finance market. As **Figure 4** shows, commercial banks have entered the mortgage loan market as economic development has progressed (e.g., rising incomes and improved legislation). As a result, the savings subsidy helped to support mortgage lending. Similarly, the burden on the budget has fallen due to repeated cuts to the individual subsidy amount. Nevertheless, total saving

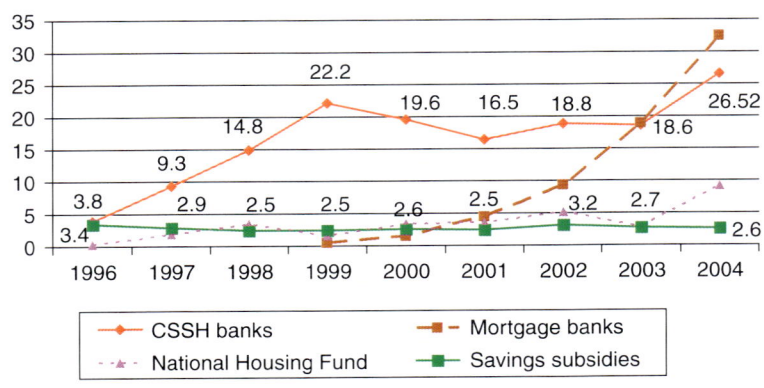

Figure 4 Mortgage lending versus savings subsidy payments in Slovakia (in billion SKK).
Source: National Bank of Slovakia (2010).

subsidy disbursements did not vary much because the reduced amount was offset by a higher number of beneficiaries. Had the entitlement not been reduced, the burden on the budget would have been higher.

In order to target the savings subsidy at lower- and middle-income groups in Germany, the government introduced income thresholds. To be eligible for the savings subsidy, the customer's yearly taxable income must not exceed certain limits (taxable yearly income up to €25 600 for a single person and €51 200 for a married couple in 2006). If the saver fulfils these criteria, they receive a bonus of 8.8% of their annual savings up to a maximum of €45.06 (for a single person) or €90.11 (for a married couple). The government does not grant any tax exemptions. In addition, there is a minimum saving period of 7 years.

The Canadian Government introduced the Home Buyers' Plan (HBP) in 1992 that allows first-time homebuyers to borrow from their registered retirement savings plan (RRSP) for home purchase, and repay the funds over an extended period of time. The drawdown represents an interest-free loan. The HBP is aimed at encouraging homeownership, savings in general, and savings for higher down payments. Although the HBP programme has been utilised by purchasers of more than 10% of all owner-occupied dwellings in Canada, it appears that high-income families have particularly benefited, while incentives for low-income groups have been considered weak.

Housing policy experts often recommend an efficiency analysis of saving subsidies that focuses on the investment multiplier which could be generated through CSSH funds. However, evaluation can only be conducted after the introduction of a savings subsidy scheme, but by then it is hard to repeal or radically reform. A recommendation has been to introduce CSSH products without a savings subsidy. The incentive to participate in the scheme can be embedded in the system itself by offering lower interest rates during the loan period, longer repayment terms, and higher loan amounts in relation to the savings amount (in an open system). Moreover, it has been suggested that banks can be supported in operating such schemes through a number of measures. First, lower capital requirements can be implemented for CSSH loans. Default rates on CSSH loans are lower than those of regular housing loans. Therefore, lower capital requirements can be justified and provide a significant incentive for banks. Since banks should separate CSSH funds from other activities, clear supervisory legislation is necessary in order to correctly track loans. Second, lower minimum reserve requirements may be acceptable. This measure could encourage more banks to launch CSSH products as long as regulation defines criteria for the administration of CSSH deposits, and prevents banks from benefiting from preferential reserve requirements for other types of deposits. It is further suggested that such measures should be temporary or at least regularly revised in order to maximise the effectiveness of subsidies or to identify an optimal point at which to abandon favourable treatment without harming the development of CSSH products.

CSSH Systems in Emerging Market Contexts

In many societies, CSSH have proved more effective during the early development of financial sectors because they stimulate home purchase practices and advance lending mechanisms. In these contexts, a significant question has been whether banks adopt CSSH as an opportunity to widen their customer base or to build up retail operations. In many cases, the state has remained a central player that some believe has inhibited development to maturity in the private finance sector. CSSH have also remained attractive within mature financial sector development contexts as a product which enhances access to credit, as well as nonstandard housing finance loans, for young and low-income households.

The case for CSSH is strongest when considering its use outside the standard mortgage market. CSSH generally offer small-volume loans, which are often not collateralised by mortgages and are therefore costly to securitise. In the Czech Republic and Slovakia, between 60 and 80% of loans are not collateralised and are given on a personal guarantee basis (renovation and modernisation loans make up about half of the portfolio). Even as financial systems develop, viable alternatives may never appear. CSSH banks are probably in a better position to overcome high origination and servicing cost through specialisation and a large number of loans.

From an economic perspective, low or, at least, stable inflation rates are essential. In volatile inflation contexts, it is more difficult to convince people to save because rising inflation erodes the value of their savings. In addition, an unstable and fragile banking sector is an impediment since people are reluctant to enter into long-term savings commitments in such circumstances. The introduction of CSSH may be less successful when interest rates are still high but are expected to decline as many people improve their access to a loan by simply waiting (or saving at market rates). A further obstacle to the introduction of CSSH can be rapidly increasing housing prices, especially when they rise faster than incomes. In this case, customers can be unwilling to wait (i.e., save) because they fear that housing will become even more expensive.

Conclusions

CSSH have been applied differently in varying national contexts. They remain popular and, in many cases, have been adapted in accordance with changing housing market conditions. From a financial institutional perspective, a strong argument for the implementation of CSSH has been their value as prescreening instruments in the selection of reliable borrowers. Germany and Slovakia have shown that CSSH borrower default rates are lower. The resulting decrease in credit risk thus requires lower reserves. Since the customer stays with the bank for a long time, CSSH products can also open the door for the sale of other financial products. Surveys in Germany have shown that customers with CSSH contracts typically buy at least two other products from their bank. From the saver's perspective, a CSSH contract may be a helpful hedge against rising interest rates. More importantly, they provide a secure means to accumulate savings, build creditworthiness, and acquire a loan. In some contexts, loans may only provide a supplement to another private loan in the purchase of a house, or may be used for the renovation or modernisation of a home. From the government's perspective, CSSH may be a useful instrument for developing finance opportunities outside the formal financial sector, thereby establishing a link to microfinance providers. As a housing microfinance product, it is well suited to funding steps in a progressive housing process. It thus helps extend the financial sector, increases individual homeownership rates, and stimulates economic growth more generally through the housing sector.

Acknowledgement

Thanks to Friedemann Roy, editor of Housing Finance International, for his contributions to this article.

See also: Access and Affordability: Homeowner Taxation; First Home Owner Grants; Policies to Support Access and Affordability of Housing.

References

Dübel A (2008) Contractual savings schemes for housing. In: Chiquiern L and Lea M (eds.) *Housing Finance in Emerging Markets*. Washington, DC: The World Bank.
National Bank of Slovakia (2010) http://www.nbs.sk/en/home (accessed 1 June 2011).
Roy F (2006) Contractual Savings Schemes for Housing (CSSH) – An assessment of past experiences and current developments. *Paper Prepared for World Bank/IFC Conference 'Housing Finance in Emerging Markets'*. Washington, DC, USA, 15–17 March.
Singapore Central Provident Bank (2010) http://mycpf.cpf.gov.sg/CPF/About-Us/CPF+Trends.htm (accessed 1 June 2011).

Further Reading

Burrell M (2006) China's Housing Provident Fund: Its success and limitations. *Housing Finance International* 20(3): 38–49.
Chua BH (2003) Maintaining housing values under the condition of universal homeownership. *Housing Studies* 18(3): 765–780.
Daphnis F (2004) Elements of product design for housing microfinance. In: Daphnis F and Ferguson B (eds.) *Housing Microfinance: A Guide to Practice*. Bloomfield, CT: Kumarian Press.
Diamond D (1999) Do bausparkassen make sense in transition countries? *European Mortgage Review, Issue No. 21*. London: Council of Mortgage Lenders.
Laux H (1992) *Die Bausparfinanzierung*, 6th edn, p. 61 et seqq. Heidelberg: Verlag Recht und Wirtschaft.
Lea M and Renaud B (1995) Contractual savings for housing: How suitable are they for transition economies? *Policy Research Working Paper No. 1516*, August. Washington, DC: The World Bank.
Merrill SR and Mesarina N (2006) Expanding microfinance for housing. *Housing Finance International* 21(2): 3–11.
Nilsson A (2008) Overview of financial systems for slum upgrading and housing. *Housing Finance International* 23(2): 19–26.
Steele M (2007) The Canadian home buyer's plan: Tax benefit, tax expenditure, and policy assessment. *Canadian Tax Journal* 55(1): 1–30.
Struyk R, Rabenhorst C, Roy F, and Butler S (2005) *Development of a Sustainable Market for Housing Finance in Armenia: Feasibility Study*. Commissioned by KfW. http://www.ceemortgagefinance.org/studies/Armenia_%20Feasibility_Study.pdf (accessed 1 June 2011).

Cooperative Housing/Ownership

D Clapham, Cardiff University, Cardiff, UK

© 2012 Elsevier Ltd. All rights reserved.

Glossary

Cooperative A form of housing, which offers collective responsibility for the ownership or management of dwellings.

Cooperative philosophy A political philosophy that extols the virtues of collective ownership or control over the production of goods or services such as housing.

Introduction

Cooperative housing is a long-established form of housing tenure found in many countries, including the United Kingdom and Scandinavian countries such as Sweden. It has taken many different definitions and forms, which vary in their legal forms, structures, and practical functioning. Cooperatives may be developed for pragmatic housing reasons or as part of the realisation of a political philosophy. Research on cooperatives has focused on their practical advantages and disadvantages when compared with other forms of tenure; on their practical functioning as the providers and managers of housing; and on their success – or otherwise – as instruments of collective resident involvement.

Forms of Cooperatives

The key feature that unites all cooperatives is collective responsibility for all or part of the duties involved in owning or managing one or more dwellings. There are many forms of housing cooperative that vary in the rights and duties of the residents and owners. One form is the par-value cooperative. Here residents jointly have an equal share in the ownership of the property (such as an apartment block). The payment required for ownership may be a symbolic sum or it may reflect the valuation of the dwelling. If a resident leaves, they will have their ownership share returned at its original value. In other words they do not benefit from any increase in property value. In some countries (such as the United Kingdom), many par-value cooperatives have been subsidised by governments.

In several other forms of common ownership, residents do share in increases in property values. These may be called co-ownership or equity-sharing cooperatives. Some forms of common ownership have evolved in particular countries to facilitate individuals to own an apartment and to share responsibility and ownership of the common parts and the external fabric. For example, in the United States condominium ownership fulfils this function, as do leasehold or commonhold ownership in the United Kingdom. These forms may not be called cooperatives but they share many essential features with cooperatives. Some cooperatives of this kind may have many jointly owned facilities, such as retirement villages or common-interest communities in the United States.

Cooperatives may be formed to manage dwellings; whereas ownership is vested in a landlord. This form is common in social housing in some countries, such as the United States, the United Kingdom, or Scandinavia and is usually called a tenant management cooperative. The rights and obligations of the residents and the landlord are usually laid down in a management agreement. Residents may have responsibility for full or part management of a particular housing block or scheme. For example, they may control repairs but not rent collection.

Cooperatives may be fully mutual, where all residents are members and all members are residents. In nonmutual cooperatives, there is not the exclusivity in membership and residence. In other words, some members may not be residents and vice versa.

Some cooperatives are established in existing housing, but others may be involved in the development of new housing. In self-build cooperatives, people usually undertake some or all of the building work themselves. They may also be involved in the design process.

All cooperatives involve some degree of collective responsibility and, sometimes, work. However in most, life is still focused on individual dwellings. Some cooperatives involve an element of shared living. This could involve the shared responsibility for aspects of everyday life, such as the provision of meals and other household tasks.

Some cooperatives exist for particular functions. For example, a common form in the United Kingdom has been the short-life cooperative that exists to lease property on a short-term basis for usually homeless people. This enables empty property to be brought into use, often while awaiting redevelopment or rehabilitation. Secondary cooperatives are organisations established to service mostly other cooperatives, by providing services such as housing maintenance or development or administrative support. Secondary cooperatives do not usually own dwellings themselves.

Reasons for Cooperative Formation

The motivation for the establishment of cooperatives varies from the pragmatic to the philosophical. The pragmatic reasons have often stemmed from the desire to find a legal structure that allows for individual ownership of dwellings, with joint responsibility for the common parts. In many countries, the pragmatic need to find a way to ensure the maintenance and repair of the external fabric of multidwelling buildings has coincided with the difficulty of defining the legal status of individual ownership of dwellings. A cooperative form provides a way of combining these elements. Some cooperatives have been a response to problems that have required a local solution involving residents. An example would be the management of a social housing estate, where various cooperative forms can provide resident involvement and local organisation. In some Eastern European countries under communist regimes, cooperatives allowed a form of individual ownership and investment, which fitted into the existing legal structure that had no place for private ownership. In less-developed countries, cooperatives can provide a form of collective sharing of resources and responsibilities, which can enable people on low incomes and little wealth to collectively build shelter. However, some cooperatives have been established by middle-class people to create a segregated environment.

Apart from the pragmatic reasons for the formation of cooperatives, there are philosophical ones. Housing tenures reflect general political philosophies. Individual owner-occupation reflects a liberal emphasis on the private ownership of property; whereas publicly owned housing reflects a socialist or communist idea of common ownership. Cooperative housing reflects the cooperative or communitarian political philosophy that has not been as influential as the other two. This relative lack of power may be responsible for the marginal status of cooperative housing in many countries.

Cooperative Philosophy

Communitarian or cooperative political philosophy is associated with a number of writers like Kropotkin, Proudhon, G. D. H. Cole, and Robert Owen. Owen is usually considered the first cooperative theorist. He was strongly influenced by the experience of the Industrial Revolution in Britain in the early nineteenth century. He considered the environment to be the determining factor in forming individuals' personalities. Therefore, in his writings and his practical work in New Lanark and New Harmony, he sought to promote the conditions under which human happiness could be experienced. He thought this could best be achieved in small, largely self-sufficient communities involved in agriculture and industrial production. This production could be bartered to procure goods that the communities could not produce themselves. In his later writings, Owen stressed the importance of self-government by the inhabitants as the best way of achieving his goals of harmony and equality. Owen's ideas were influential in the establishment of the cooperative retail movement in the United Kingdom by the Rochdale pioneers in 1844.

Other writers were stimulated by different circumstances. Proudhon was a contemporary of Karl Marx and his liberal form of cooperation was a response to his emerging socialist ideas. Proudhon argued strongly for individual responsibility and freedom and argued against any form of authority, whether from the state or elsewhere. However, he argued that free association of people was necessary to meet the needs of production, consumption, and security. Free association or mutualism should be reduced to the minimum to ensure the optimum of individual responsibility and freedom.

Kropotkin was born in Russia but was forced to flee when his ideas found favour neither with the Czar nor with the Bolsheviks. He was concerned to refute the interpretation of Darwinism, which held that individualism and the struggle for life were the primary motivating forces in animals and humans. He argued that humans had a basic need for sociability. This need brought with it a sense of mutuality and respect that was essential for their survival. Mutuality was not based on sympathy, but on a recognition of the dependency of everyone's happiness on the happiness of all and on a sense of justice or equity. Kropotkin was also critical of the economic specialisation or division of labour espoused by Adam Smith. He argued that this impoverished individuals. He thought that an ideal society would be based on an integration of labour, in which each person would have a mix of manual and intellectual work in both agriculture and industry.

G. D. H. Cole was a contemporary of Sidney and Beatrice Webb, who were influential in the construction of the Fabian version of social democracy. This version defined the policies of the twentieth-century Labour Party in the United Kingdom. Whereas the Webbs stressed the need for state intervention, ownership, and control, Cole followed Proudhon in arguing for the minimum of self-association to ensure maximum freedom. Nevertheless he argued that some level of association was necessary. Liberty could, however, be protected by dividing association along functional lines so that no individual would be totally reliant on one association. He espoused a system of worker cooperatives, consumer cooperatives, and housing cooperatives, which he thought would supersede traditional methods of representative democracy.

Despite their differences, the cooperative thinkers shared a common mistrust of the state, and a belief that representative democracy could lead to centralisation and authoritarianism. Instead, they put forward the idea of direct democracy based on self-governing groups. These groups should be small enough to involve all the members in decision-making processes and to be autonomous bodies outside the control of the state. Larger structures can be formed to pursue more general interests through the federation of smaller groups, which can render the state unnecessary. In this respect, cooperative ideas are in direct contrast to state socialism with its emphasis on a strong state.

Advocates of the cooperative system also share a common dislike of capitalism. They argue that individual freedom and equality are hindered by the exploitation inherent in the private ownership of property or capital. Marxism and communism were seen to merely replace capitalist exploitation by state exploitation in the accumulation of property. The writers who favoured cooperatives wanted the capitalist system with its large-scale and its highly developed specialisation of labour to be replaced by a system of smaller-scale cooperatives based on self-government and mutualism.

Cooperative ideas have never been in the mainstream of political dialogue in most countries; so the cooperative society has not emerged anywhere. However, cooperative movements have succeeded in establishing cooperatives in individual sectors, such as the British consumer cooperative sector or housing cooperatives. Some housing cooperatives have been sponsored by the state, often when there are sympathetic politicians or pragmatic reasons. However, many have been created by groups of grassroots activists committed to the cooperative ideal.

Cooperatives in Sweden

Sweden has one of the most established and largest cooperative sectors, which stretches back to urbanisation in the early part of the twentieth century. The first permanent housing cooperative, Stockholm Housing Cooperative Association (SKB) was established in 1916, in order to combat the shortage of small flats in Stockholm. In 1923, the National Tenants' Union created HSB (Tenants' Savings Bank and Housing Association), which remains one of the largest cooperatives today. The other major cooperative association, Svenska Riksbyggen, was founded in 1940 by building-trades unions at a time when unemployment in the construction industry was extremely high. The cooperative sector has been strongly supported by the state since the election of the first strong social democratic government in 1942.

There is a large and strong municipal rented sector in Sweden usually owned and managed by municipal housing companies. There can be strong links at a local level between the cooperative and the municipal sectors. In some areas, the municipal housing companies have transferred all or some of their stock to cooperatives. Some cooperatives such as HSB have diversified into the management of municipal housing. Riksbyggen has become much diversified, as it is active in the design of buildings – both domestic and commercial – as well as in property management. The cooperative sector has filled a space between the municipal rented sector and the owner-occupied sector of single-family houses. Cooperative ownership is the only way of being an owner-occupier of a single apartment in Sweden.

HSB and Riksbyggen are equity-sharing cooperatives. On being allocated a new cooperative house, residents are required to pay a deposit of 1%, which effectively buys them the right to dwell in a particular apartment. The cost of the deposit can be met by means of a loan from the cooperative organisation. On leaving the cooperative, members can sell their interests at market value, which can be high. Proposals have been made at various times to restrict the sale of cooperative apartments and to give the cooperatives the right to buy them back if they are sold within a short time of occupation.

HSB has a three-tier structure made up of the national organisation, local societies, and local cooperatives. The national organisation is controlled by representatives of the local societies. The local societies are the key structure, as they promote new cooperatives and support existing ones. Membership is made up of members of local cooperatives, as well as those on the waiting list for an apartment who have shown evidence of saving with the HSB savings bank. Local cooperatives vary in size, comprising 5–1000 dwellings, but the average size is around 90. Only 10% of the cooperatives have more than 200 dwellings. Local cooperatives are run by a board elected by members. These members can decide the level of management and maintenance services required – whether to buy services from the local society, employ their own staff, or buy in services from elsewhere. Local members can organise and undertake some of the work themselves. Rents are set on the basis of the need to repay the original loan, the costs of management, and maintenance services.

Housing Cooperatives in the United Kingdom

Britain has a long history of housing cooperatives. The earliest forms of these in the eighteenth and the early nineteenth centuries were the terminating building societies, where working people pooled their skills and capital to build a group of houses for themselves. Later they became more sophisticated, acting as savings organisations that issued shares to members enabling them to build a house. These building societies gradually became permanent savings-and-loan institutions, partly in response to growing government control and regulation.

There were many small housing cooperatives in the latter part of the nineteenth century – many with their roots in the mutual activities of friendly societies – which were institutions usually formed by small tradesmen and artisans in order to provide financial protection against sickness and unemployment. However, housing cooperatives were not linked to the growing consumer cooperative system and remained marginal in their impact. The increasingly important working-class political movements campaigned for and supported the provision of state rented housing through local authorities rather than cooperative provision.

During the nineteenth century, there were a number of middle-class experiments in cooperative housing. Cooperative villages were established by the followers of Robert Owen during the 1820s and the 1830s, but few lasted long. A number of cooperative housekeeping schemes were also established, some in conjunction with the Garden Cities movement pioneered by Ebenezer Howard. Also linked were copartnership societies, which were established, usually by wealthy enthusiasts. Through these, they would develop houses and let them on a co-ownership basis to working-class people. These were quite successful up to 1919. However, when public funding became available, they were outstripped by councils who were better able to make use of the new subsidies. Housing cooperatives became the forgotten tenure until the 1960s, when they started to receive attention and support from the state.

Government loans were made available to co-ownership societies from 1961. As described earlier, co-ownership is an arrangement whereby residents can each have an individual share in the equity of a small housing scheme. In addition, residents pay rent to cover the management and maintenance costs and the loan repayments incurred by a collective mortgage. On leaving, residents receive a sum based on their original down payment plus an allowance for the change in the capital values of their properties. The sector was modelled on the Swedish and Norwegian sector and was designed to help those who could not quite afford access to owner-occupation. The development of the sector was hindered by the lack of a stable institutional base (unlike in Sweden, the schemes were promoted by ad hoc groups of built-environment professionals who gained from the payment of professional fees). There were problems with the financing arrangements, which resulted in prices that were not much below owner-occupation. In addition, the collective aspects of the schemes were not fully developed. There emerged problems of inefficient and remote management with little resident control. In 1980, the government gave co-ownership members the right to buy out their societies and become owner-occupiers: very few co-ownership schemes still survive.

During the 1970s, there was political concern about the perceived problematical state of some council estates and the lack of a vital private rental sector. Therefore successive governments used the Housing Corporation (a quango established in 1964) to fund and regulate housing associations, in order to create an alternative to public renting. Some of the associations were cooperatives and, under an enthusiastic housing minister in 1974, the Housing Corporation was given a specific remit to foster cooperatives. Also during the 1970s, grassroots movements emerged to take over the management of problematic public-sector estates in tenant management cooperatives. The urgent housing problems in some inner-city areas also led to the creation of cooperatives to promote urban renewal and to use existing housing for homeless people. Although developed by local activists, the housing association framework gave them a source of funding while opening them to state regulation.

The development of cooperatives was focused on particular cities. Many were based in London where there were severe housing problems and strong community-action groups, such as the Holloway Tenant Cooperative and the Society for Cooperative Dwellings. In Liverpool a number of cooperatives were formed (such as the Eldonians and the Granby cooperatives) to counter the urban-renewal plans of the Militant-dominated city council. These were supported by the later Liberal-controlled council. In Glasgow, the city council supported the transfer of some areas of unpopular council houses to cooperatives and community-based housing associations under the Community Ownership programme.

Despite these local initiatives, the central government never provided consistent support for a cooperative sector and it has not grown into a major national tenure. The housing policy focus of successive governments has primarily been on promoting owner-occupation and supporting housing associations to develop new public rented property. Housing cooperatives have remained a minority form and, during the twenty-first century, have not received much political interest.

Researching Housing Cooperatives

Housing cooperatives are a minority tenure in most countries where they are found and have been adapted to fit the institutional context within which they operate. Therefore, the forms that cooperatives take have varied widely along a number of spectra. For example, Clapham and Kintrea (1992) drew the distinction between public rental and owner-occupation cooperatives, depending on which sector they most closely resembled. Public rental cooperatives are at the collective end of the spectrum: they are public; state-oriented; aimed at the working class; and oriented around consumption only. Owner-occupation cooperatives are at the individualist end of the spectrum: they are private; market-oriented; aimed at the upper and middle classes; and oriented around both consumption and investment. These are ideal types. Specific cooperatives would mostly be between the two extremes. For example, the Swedish HSB cooperatives are relatively collectivist; have both public and private elements, as they are independent; but are state-regulated and subsidised; are predominantly state-oriented although there is a market for secondhand apartments; are middle class; and are oriented towards consumption and investment. In contrast, a British tenant management cooperative is collectivist; public; state-oriented; geared to the working class; and only concerned with consumption.

Research on housing cooperatives has focused on a number of areas. Owing to their unique resident involvement, there has been much interest in how these are structured and in the reasons why residents want (or do not want) to be involved. Attention has focused on the motives of individuals – who are viewed either as rational agents in pursuit of practical rewards or as those motivated by gains from the participation process – such as self-realisation or the enjoyment of being part of a collective endeavour. A further focus has been on the institutional arrangements that can stimulate and support resident involvement. A distinction has been made between direct work (such as helping to clear up the area) or decision-making and policy-making roles for the cooperative, such as deciding on housing-management practices. The latter can be undertaken by the members as a whole or by an elected body accountable to the members at large. Research has shown great diversity in the extent and types of resident involvement in cooperatives. Some have extensive and widespread involvement. Others have problems in sustaining enough involvement to continue to operate. Opinions seem to differ on the types and extent of involvement, which is desirable or necessary.

Research has also focused on the relative efficiencies of cooperative forms of housing management. It has found that cooperatives outperform other forms of tenure in the quality of the service provided and in the tenant satisfaction gained. Many forms of cooperatives give tenants the choice over their managements and maintenance-service providers and enable effective mechanisms of control over service levels and standards. However, the less collective forms of cooperatives, such as the British co-ownership, may not in practice offer this advantage, as management may be vested in outside and unaccountable bodies. Also, the exertion of control may be dependent on a degree of collective involvement that may not always exist. Cooperatives are usually small in scale and this can lead to higher unit costs through an inability to enjoy economies of scale. This may be overcome through the establishment of larger secondary cooperatives or national organisations such as the Swedish cooperatives.

See also: Tenant Cooperatives, Shareholders' Housing Companies.

Reference

Clapham D and Kintrea K (1992) *Housing Co-operatives in Britain: Achievements and Prospects*. Harlow, UK: Longman.

Further Reading

Bengtsson B (2000) Solving the tenants' dilemma: Collective action and norms of co-operation in housing. *Housing, Theory and Society* 17: 175–187.
Birchall J (1988) *Building Communities the Co-operative Way*. London: Routledge and Kegan Paul.
Heskin A and Leavitt J (1995) *The Hidden History of Housing Co-operatives*. Los Angeles, CA: University of California.
Ospina J (1987) *Housing Ourselves*. London: Hilary Shipman.
Ward C (1974) *Tenants Take Over*. London: Architectural Press.

Cost Analyses of Homelessness: Limits and Opportunities

T Byrne and D Culhane, University of Pennsylvania, Philadelphia, PA, USA

© 2012 Elsevier Ltd. All rights reserved.

Glossary

Chronic homelessness Long-term or repeated homelessness. According to US federal law, a chronically homeless person is an individual with a disabling condition who has either been continuously homeless for a year or more or who has had at least four episodes of homelessness in the previous 3 years.

Cost–benefit analysis A form of analysis that compares the cost and effects of an intervention, with both costs and effects measured in monetary units. Cost–benefit analysis requires that some monetary value be assigned to all effects of an intervention, thereby allowing for a direct comparison of a programme's cost and consequences.

Cost-effectiveness analysis A form of analysis that compares the relative cost and effects of competing alternative courses of action, typically expressed in ratio form with cost as the numerator and some form of nonmonetary effect as the denominator. In cost analyses of homelessness, cost-effectiveness analysis is commonly assumed to include any analysis that compares the cost of service utilisation by homeless persons prior and subsequent to housing placement.

Homeless management information system (HMIS) Computer-based data collection application that uses unique identifiers to track individual-level public shelter utilisation.

Ten-year plans to end chronic homelessness Initiatives undertaken by communities to create and implement a comprehensive strategy for eliminating homelessness or chronic homelessness within their jurisdictions.

Introduction

Those advocating for increased attention and resources directed towards addressing homelessness face the challenge of highlighting the impact of the problem not just on the individuals and families experiencing homelessness but also on society at large. To achieve this end, there have been consistent claims that a failure to address homelessness comes at a far greater economic cost to society than implementing solutions. In the past decade, these claims have attracted substantial interest in the policy and planning arenas due in large part to the emergence and proliferation of a body of research that aims at analysing the costs of homelessness to society and the potential cost offsets of interventions targeted at homeless persons. These cost analyses have both academic as well as local, nonacademic origins and are having an impact on local and national policies. Nonetheless, while cost-related research provides important opportunities for expanded efforts to end homelessness in the United States, the approach comes with a number of drawbacks, which have not received adequate attention. The potential of cost research is undeniable, but communities must be aware of its limitations and cautious in how it is used for policy and planning purposes. In an effort to provide a full treatment of cost analyses of homelessness, this section first provides a background on cost analyses of homelessness and highlight relevant findings. After contextualising the issue, the article then explores the potential opportunities and benefits resulting from a cost-based approach to homelessness. Finally, it proceeds to a discussion of the limitations of such an approach and concludes with a brief discussion of the future trajectory of cost analyses.

Cost Analyses of Homelessness

Up to its reauthorisation in May 2009, the McKinney–Vento Homeless Assistance Act has been the major source of federal funds for homeless assistance programmes in the United States for over 20 years. Although largely perceived by Congress as merely a 'first step' in addressing homelessness upon its passage in 1987, the legislation is viewed as resulting in the institutionalisation of a parallel social welfare system comprised of programmes and services for which only already homeless persons are statutorily eligible. In response to the entrenchment of this system, advocates have consistently called for more permanent, housing-based approaches to homelessness. As part of their argument, they have made the claim that it is ultimately less expensive to end homelessness through housing-based interventions than to maintain the status quo of providing services to homeless individuals through shelters and other public facilities such as hospitals, mental health facilities, and correctional institutions. Despite these efforts, until recently, the cost of homelessness was not a primary factor influencing how policymakers formulated responses to the problem. In the past decade, however, cost analyses of homelessness have become important factors in the formulation of policy and programmes. The growth in academic research on the utilisation of acute care services of homeless persons and the cost effectiveness of housing interventions targeted at different subgroups of homeless persons has been important in this regard. However, less rigorously designed cost analyses conducted by local entities have perhaps been more important in terms of influencing local policy. These studies are most often part of communities' 'Ten-Year Plans to End Chronic Homelessness'. Over 250 plans have been created following the publication in 2000 of a national plan to end homelessness by the National Alliance to End Homelessness, a leading advocacy group. Despite their limitations, these local studies often carry more weight in terms of influencing policy as they are largely undertaken by community-based entities and provide tangible evidence of the impact of homelessness on local institutions and systems.

Both academic and locally generated cost studies can be divided into two broad categories. On the one hand are studies that aim to establish the extent and cost of service utilisation by certain subgroups of the homeless population. In effect, these studies test the assumption that not acting to end homelessness is likely to be quite expensive. On the other hand are studies that examine the cost effectiveness of interventions targeted at different subgroups of homeless persons.

Cost of Homelessness Studies

There is a modest body of academic research examining the service utilisation of homeless persons in the United States. A few studies have shown that in comparison to housed persons with similar characteristics, homeless persons use more emergency department services and experience greater numbers and longer durations of in-patient hospitalisations. Other research has provided evidence that there is a distinct subgroup of homeless persons who make a disproportionate use of emergency shelter resources relative to their share of the overall single-adult homeless population. These 'chronically' homeless persons constitute about one-tenth of shelter users overall, but account for half of all shelter days and costs. Similarly, studies using administrative data to track the multisystem service use of homeless persons who are chronically homeless and have a severe mental illness have found average annual per person service costs in the tens of thousands of dollars.

As a complement to academic research, since 2003, nearly 50 American communities have undertaken local studies to tabulate the costs of providing services across systems to chronically homeless persons. These efforts have produced estimates of the annual cost per person anywhere between $5360 from a study looking at the jail costs of incarcerated homeless persons in the city of Louisville, Kentucky, and $133 333 from a study of EMS, hospitalisation, and police charges of a group of chronic public inebriates in San Diego. Such a wide range of estimates is due more to the methodologies employed by the various studies than to actual variations in the cost of services used by homeless persons. Indeed, these studies largely rely on convenience samples of varying size and often select persons for inclusion on the basis of their perceived status as a heavy user of services. In addition, the studies monitor the service use of subjects for varying time periods and across different numbers of service types and systems. Consequently, the studies are not entirely rigorous from a scientific standpoint, and their results cannot be assumed to have a great degree of generalisability. Nonetheless, they are easily conducted by people without strong research training and provide clear evidence for local jurisdictions of the impact of homelessness on their communities.

Although existing studies suggest that the service utilisation of homeless persons can be quite costly, it is important to note that there is evidence that extremely heavy service use may be somewhat uncommon and confined to a small proportion of chronically homeless persons. Studies using large and inclusive samples of chronically homeless persons have found more modest service utilisation costs than studies using smaller, less inclusive samples. Understanding and comparing estimates of the cost of services utilisation by chronically homeless persons is further complicated by potential regional differences in the relative availability of public services for homeless persons. For example, varying levels of access to mental health services between regions as well as differences in the per capita spending by mental health systems certainly helps explain why some jurisdictions record higher service utilisation expenses than others.

Cost-Effectiveness Studies

In addition to studies that aim primarily to calculate the cost of services used by homeless persons, thereby effectively demonstrating the opportunity cost of not pursuing new interventions, a number of studies have sought to analyse the cost effectiveness of various interventions. Like research on the cost of homelessness, cost-effectiveness research has taken the form of both academic studies using rigorous methodologies and locally generated studies with less scientific approaches. Increasingly, research in this area is oriented towards showing that the cost of housing interventions targeted towards homeless persons may be entirely or partially offset by the reductions in service utilisation subsequent to housing placement. One way to characterise this frequently used approach is as a cost-accounting approach, which is one component of broader cost-effectiveness and cost–benefit analyses.

Academic research has examined the cost effectiveness of a number of interventions for homeless persons – although the focus has been largely on housing-based interventions for homeless persons – and on permanent supportive housing for chronically homeless persons in particular. Virtually all of these academic studies have experimental or quasiexperimental designs and have been conducted in urban settings, such as New York City, Chicago, and Seattle. Generally, they use administrative data or some combination of administrative data and self-report to analyse service utilisation by homeless persons in the time periods ranging anywhere from a few months to 2 years prior to and following placement in housing. Among these studies, the finding that homeless persons reduce their utilisation of acute care services such as inpatient hospitalisations and jail stays subsequent to housing placement is nearly universal. However, the degree to which the cost reductions associated with declines in service utilisation offset the cost of the housing interventions themselves varies. The results of some studies suggest that virtually the entire cost of an intervention can be offset through reduced service utilisation, while others have found more modest cost offsets. Undoubtedly, part of the variation in the extent of cost offsets is due to differences in the data available to researchers, as well as varying intervention costs. With greater access to records from multiple care systems, researchers are more likely to be able to demonstrate higher costs of homelessness and therefore are likely to find greater cost reductions in service utilisation and larger cost offsets resulting from housing placement. Likewise, lower intervention costs are easier to offset through cost reductions from reduced services utilisation.

In addition to the published academic research on the cost effectiveness of homeless programmes and housing interventions, local entities across the United States are increasingly interested in conducting cost analyses of interventions in their communities, as is evidenced by the rapid proliferation of such studies by local governments, planning authorities, and nonprofit organisations since 2003. These studies often use convenience samples that are likely to include heaviest users of services and present a wide variation in the cost reductions and cost offsets associated with housing placement. Recent local efforts undertaken in Colorado, Massachusetts, Maine, Illinois, and South Dakota, among others, have all shown that the cost of placing chronically homeless persons in permanent housing is more than offset through reduced service utilisation. Moreover, a recent study conducted in Maine also found annual net per person savings for a permanent supportive housing programme targeted at persons in rural areas experiencing homelessness. This is the first cost analysis study to be undertaken in a rural context and is indicative of the expansion of interest in cost-related research on chronic homelessness.

In sum, research on both the cost of homelessness and the cost effectiveness of interventions is growing rapidly and has had an influence on policy decisions. Locally generated studies are particularly useful in demonstrating the impact of readily identifiable persons on local systems and institutions and the potential for such systems and institutions to be positively affected through the targeting of housing solutions towards persons who make heavy use of their services. This has been important for garnering additional resources for new investments in housing programmes, especially in permanent housing for chronically homeless persons.

Opportunities and Benefits of Cost Analyses

The emergence and growth of cost analyses of homelessness presents a number of important opportunities for researchers, policymakers, and service providers alike. As has been noted, perhaps the primary benefit of these cost studies has been and continues to be the ability of local communities to leverage their findings to secure additional resources for new investments in housing, especially for chronically homeless persons. Indeed, there is evidence that these investments are paying off as the number of chronically homeless persons in the United States is estimated to have declined by 50 000 between 2005 and 2008. While increasing the political will and strengthening the fiscal commitment to homeless programmes are clearly important achievements, cost analyses of homelessness offer additional opportunities for deepening the understanding of effective and efficient ways to address both homelessness and other complex problems.

First, cost analyses of homelessness have helped underscore the value of establishing systems for collecting administrative data from shelters and other care systems. Indeed, the availability of administrative data has been of fundamental importance to the growth of cost analyses of homelessness in the United States. The existence of automated management information systems (MIS) that track public shelter utilisation and include unique identifiers (name, gender, ethnicity, social security number, and prior address) of shelter users allowed researchers to conduct some of the earliest cost research on homelessness. In turn, these early cost studies have highlighted the potential of using administrative data to strengthen the knowledge base about homelessness. In recognition of this potential, since 2000, the US Congress has required communities receiving federal funds for homeless programmes to implement homeless management information systems (HMIS). Few American cities have a long history of using such systems and a number of obstacles have led to the relatively slow adoption of HMIS in many localities. However, federal incentives have led to a recent growth in the number of communities with HMIS and more than half of US communities had a functioning HMIS as of 2008.

A clear benefit of HMIS is that it enables jurisdictions to calculate unduplicated counts of persons served by their homelessness services system, document their characteristics, identify their patterns of service use and lengths of shelter stay, and determine the outcomes of their services use. However, Congress also directed that HMIS be used to examine the connection between homelessness and mainstream social welfare systems. This points to the tremendous opportunity presented by the integration of administrative data from homeless assistance programmes and health, mental health, criminal justice, and other systems. The general idea is that personal identifiers contained in a community's HMIS can be used to merge shelter records with data from mainstream social welfare systems, thereby documenting the overlap between these systems. The potential utility of such data integration is large, and the most comprehensive cost analyses of homelessness have integrated administrative records from homeless assistance systems and multiple systems to demonstrate the impact of homelessness on mainstream systems and potential benefits to these systems associated with placing homeless persons in housing. Such research on the cost of homelessness has sparked interest within many communities in laying the groundwork for creating administrative databases that integrate records from multiple systems that may include public assistance, health and mental health services, criminal justice, public and assisted housing, child welfare, and public education. Ultimately, such data-integration efforts can be used both to better understand the relationship between homelessness and mainstream systems and to examine the extent to which mainstream systems are shifting their service obligations to the homeless assistance system. In this regard, data linkages may be useful in encouraging mainstream systems to allocate greater resources and services targeted towards other vulnerable groups.

A second benefit of cost analyses is that in demonstrating the potential economic efficiencies associated with permanent housing interventions, they have provided justification for the pursuit of interventions that, in placing 'housing first', invert the traditional linear model of homeless programmes. As such, cost research has helped drive what appears to be an emergent paradigm shift in policy and programmatic responses to homelessness in the United States. The federal government has increasingly displayed a preference for housing-based approaches for reducing homelessness. The reauthorization in May 2009 of the McKinney–Vento Act substantially expanded homelessness prevention and rapid rehousing programmes and strengthened an already-existing emphasis on creating permanent housing solutions for chronically homeless persons. Moreover, as part of the *American Recovery and Reinvestment Act of 2009*, Congress authorised $1.5 billion over 3 years for the 'Homelessness Prevention and Rapid Rehousing Program' (HPRP). In dedicating funds to prevention and rapid rehousing efforts, the HPRP marks a distinct break from the traditional approach of providing emergency and transitional housing before placing homeless persons in more permanent settings. By providing an economic rationale for implementing permanent housing solutions, cost analyses have helped create an opportunity for a fundamental change in the approach to homelessness in the United States.

Finally, both the general conceptual framework underlying cost analyses of homelessness – that a social problem can be quite expensive to society and solutions to the problem less expensive – and the methodology frequently employed in cost analyses – the integration of administrative records from multiple service systems – can be applied to the analysis of other complex social problems that also have an impact on multiple public systems and sectors. It is not difficult to imagine a community using a database linking administrative records to track any number of populations across multiple systems to better understand the true impact of a group or problem on multiple sectors. Examining the multisystem service utilisation of a cohort of youth exiting the child welfare system is one obvious example of the potential application of the approach. Developing the infrastructure and obtaining the necessary interagency cooperation for the creation of such integrated databases requires communities to commit to providing substantial time and resources to such a project, but having such a system could be quite useful in helping communities understand and formulate solutions to complex problems that they face.

Limitations and Drawbacks of Cost Analyses

As outlined earlier, the benefits and opportunities associated with cost-related research on homelessness are widely recognised and should continue to be emphasised.

Nonetheless, there has been less discussion of the potential shortcomings and limitations of such research. Failure to present a frank assessment of the drawbacks of both existing cost studies and the general underpinnings of the body of research can lead to a misunderstanding of the overall utility of cost research and comes with a number of additional risks. There are four primary reasons to cast a critical glance on cost analyses of homelessness and each merits discussion.

First, the extant body of cost-related research has a very limited scope. The service utilisation of homeless persons has not been tracked for longer than 2 years subsequent to placement in housing, suggesting that much remains to be learned about whether service reductions are sustained in the long term. Additionally, with a few exceptions, the focus of cost and cost-offset research has been on single adults with a serious mental illness. Evidence that persons with severe mental illness account for 20% of homeless single adults overall and 25% of the chronically homeless highlights significant gaps in knowledge about the costs of homelessness and the cost effectiveness of interventions. Put differently, researchers, policymakers, and service providers have a very limited understanding of the cost dynamics at play for the vast majority of homeless persons who do not have a serious mental illness and the potential economic benefits of programmes targeted towards these persons. The notable lack of research on homeless families, who comprise about 30% of the overall homeless population, is especially glaring and families are certainly one group that merits greater attention. Recent studies conducted in Seattle and Chicago indicate a promising trend as they evaluate the cost effectiveness of housing interventions for homeless persons who do not necessarily have a serious mental illness. Nonetheless, until research is significantly expanded beyond persons with a serious mental illness, it will remain challenging for communities to accurately and reliably use cost analyses for policy and programme planning purposes for a large share of the homeless population.

Second, research is not only limited in its scope but in the approach that it employs to evaluate cost effectiveness. Currently, studies that examine cost effectiveness simply compare the cost of providing housing to the reduction in services use and cost resulting from housing placement. In this regard, the relative cost effectiveness of an intervention is understood as the extent to which reductions in services utilisation offset the cost of the housing intervention itself. This does not entirely align with the framework for cost-effectiveness analysis used in health economics and other fields wherein the relative cost and effects of competing interventions are expressed in ratio form with cost as the numerator and some form of nonmonetary effect (e.g., years of residential stability gained, improved health status) as the denominator. Nor do cost analyses of homelessness fully fit the framework of a traditional cost–benefit analysis. Studies on the cost dynamics of homelessness typically measure effects in terms of the savings in acute services costs associated with housing placement. However, they do not attempt to monetise other impacts of housing placement, such as health improvements, as would be required in a traditional cost–benefit analysis. Likewise, findings are not frequently framed in terms of a ratio with monetised benefits as the numerator and costs as the denominator, wherein a positive ratio represents a beneficial programme and an indicator of the per-dollar value of an investment in an intervention is provided. Given that more comprehensive methods for conducting either cost-effectiveness or cost–benefit analyses exist, the current approach used in cost analyses of homelessness is incomplete. Evaluations of housing interventions could be strengthened by adopting methods used in cost–benefit and cost-effectiveness research conducted in other areas. In addition, cost analyses of homelessness should more closely examine benefits resulting from housing placement that go beyond reduced service utilisation, such as residential stability, increased employment opportunities, and improved health status or quality of life. The wide usage in health economics of the quality adjusted life year (QALY) as an outcome measure for assessing the per-dollar value resulting from a medical intervention is just one model for how cost analyses of homelessness might examine health-related impacts of housing.

Third, existing studies, especially those that employ less scientific designs and methods, may overstate the cost savings resulting from housing placement. In addition, advocates often overemphasise the potential cost savings associated with new investments in housing interventions and underemphasise their expense. These factors may create unrealistic expectations of cost savings among public agencies and residents in a community. Communities must not forget that it can be quite expensive to place homeless persons in permanent housing. In areas with tight housing markets, a full subsidy for an efficiency unit can cost as much as $8000 annually, and providing supportive services to persons with serious mental illness may require an additional $6000–12 000 annually. It may be unreasonable to expect that the entire cost of an intervention will be offset for every person placed in housing and indeed, there is evidence that this is likely the case. Nonetheless, there are certainly many heavy service users who are likely easily identified by local communities. Targeting these persons for housing interventions is a good starting place for most jurisdictions. Alternatively, net gains can be achieved even if cost offsets are not generated for each individual, and it therefore may be best to evaluate cost offsets based on the average case. Those whose service reductions more than fully offset the cost of housing placement may compensate for those whose reductions generate partial cost offsets. Appropriate targeting of housing interventions can help achieve an average cost offset per placement that is at the break-even point or better. Similarly, the degree of cost offsets depends on the package of housing and services in place. Chronically homeless persons do not constitute a homogenous population, and different subgroups of the chronically homeless population require service models with varying levels of services and expense. For example, persons with a severe mental illness who make extensive use of acute services may require a relatively expensive combination of housing and supportive services in comparison to persons with only a substance abuse disorder who need a simple shallow housing subsidy of a few hundred dollars a month in order to maintain residential stability. Such varying of service models in accordance with need increases the potential for cost offsets to be realised.

Certainly, advocating for the expansion of housing programmes on the basis of overstated estimates of potential cost savings runs the risk of undercutting continued support for such investments if the hypothesised cost savings do not materialise. Yet, the complex structure and siloing of public systems further complicates the issue. On the one hand, reductions in services use may not necessarily translate into cost savings, as systems and facilities such as jails may have operating costs that remain relatively unchanged even if individuals reduce their utilisation of the services provided by such systems. On the other hand, cost savings that do accrue through reductions in service utilisation may not easily be reinvested in housing solutions. Public funds are usually allocated separately to individual systems, and savings in one area cannot usually be easily transferred and reinvested in another. Further, these systems are all fluid, and offsetting service reductions for some may change accessibility of services and increase expenses for others.

Fourth, the growth in interest in cost analyses of homelessness carries with it the risk that policymakers and service providers may come to rely too heavily on cost offsets as a metric for evaluating the merit and value of solutions to homelessness. That a particular intervention may create net cost savings is undoubtedly one good reason for its implementation, but there are additional reasons for pursuing strategies to end homelessness that are equally as important and cannot be overlooked. Some argue that other moral and humanitarian concerns should compel society to take an interest in providing adequate housing for some of its most vulnerable members. Homelessness exacts a great toll on individuals through adverse health effects, marginalisation or exclusion from social processes, and increased risk of being victimised, especially through acts of violence. Providing for the housing and additional needs of homeless individuals and families must not be seen solely as a cost-saving endeavour, but more broadly speaking as a way to improve the residential stability, quality of life, employment opportunities, and social integration among persons at risk of experiencing homelessness. Given the importance of these other aims of housing programmes, fiscal considerations and cost offsets are clearly of interest in evaluating programmes and interventions, but should not weigh too heavily in assessing their overall value.

The Future Use of Cost Analyses

On the basis of the expanding interest in cost analyses of homelessness, it is clear that they will continue to play a role in policy and programme formulation for the foreseeable future. It is less clear, however, what exact role such studies will assume. Determining the appropriate role and level of importance attributed to cost analyses will be an important challenge for researchers and policymakers at the local and national levels. Decision makers must ultimately decide whether cost analyses will remain largely unscientific efforts, whose findings may not be entirely accurate. It is evident that these types of studies can be effective if the aim is to obtain the necessary fiscal support for expanded housing programmes in the short term. This approach may not be sustainable, however, especially if hypothesised cost savings do not result from new housing investments. A preferable alternative going forward would be for communities and governments to seize on the opportunity created by the interest in cost analyses to establish better data collection systems and to collaborate with service providers and researchers to engage in more rigorous efforts to analyse the costs of homelessness. More scientific studies would allow cost analyses to be used for better targeting in the planning and evaluation of housing interventions, which would result in the more efficient and effective allocation of resources. In the absence of a movement towards greater sophistication, cost studies are likely to encounter increasing scepticism and risk being charged with misleading taxpayers, especially if they make 'too good to be true' estimates for cost savings that subsequently do not pan out in practice.

See also: Economic Perspectives on Homelessness; Illicit Drug Use and Homelessness; Mental Health and Homelessness; Policies to Address Homelessness: Housing First Approaches.

Further Reading

Culhane DP (2008) The costs of homelessness: A perspective from the United States. *European Journal of Homelessness* 2: 97–114.

Culhane DP and Metraux S (2008) Rearranging the deckchairs or reallocating the lifeboats: Homelessness assistance and its alternatives. *Journal of the American Planning Association* 74(1): 111–121.

Culhane DP, Metraux S, and Hadley T (2002) Public service reductions associated with placement of homeless persons with severe mental illness in supportive housing. *Housing Policy Debate* 13: 107–163.

Culhane DP, Paker WD, Poppe B, Gross KS, and Sykes E (2008) *Accountability, Cost-Effectiveness, and Program Performance: Progress Since 1998*. Washington, DC: US Department of Housing and Urban Development.

Gulcur L, Stefancic A, Shinn M, Tsemberis S, and Fischer SN (2003) Housing, hospitalization, and cost outcomes for homeless individuals with psychiatric disabilities participating in continuum of care and housing first programs. *Journal of Community & Applied Social Pscychology* 13: 171–186.

Kuhn R and Culhane DP (1998) Applying cluster analysis to test a typology of homelessness by pattern of shelter utilization: Results from the analysis of administrative data. *American Journal of Community Psychology* 26: 207–232.

Kuno E, Rothbard AB, Averyt J, and Culhane DP (2000) Homelessness among persons serious mental illness in an enhanced community-based mental health system. *Psychiatric Services* 51: 1012–1016.

Kushel MB, Perry S, Bangsberg D, Clark R, and Moss AR (2002) Emergency department use among the homeless and marginally housed: Results from a community-based study. *American Journal of Public Health* 92: 778–784.

Martinez TE and Burt MR (2006) Impact of permanent supportive housing on the use of acute care health services by homeless adults. *Psychiatric Services* 57: 992–999.

National Alliance to End Homelessness (2000) *Ten Year Plan to End Homelessness*. Washington, DC: Author.

Rosenheck R (2000) Cost-effectiveness of services for mentally ill homeless people: The application of research to policy and practice. *The American Journal of Psychiatry* 157: 1563–1570.

Rosenheck R, Kasprow W, Frisman L, and Liu-Mares W (2003) Cost-effectiveness of supported housing for homeless persons with mental illness. *Archives of General Psychiatry* 60(9): 940–951.

Salit SA, Kuhn EM, Hartz AJ, Vu JM, and Mosso AL (1998) Hospitalization costs associated with homelessness in New York City. *The New England Journal of Medicine* 338: 1734–1740.

Schumacher JE, Mennemeyer ST, Milby JB, Wallace D, and Nolan K (2002) Costs and effectiveness of substance abuse treatments for homeless persons. *The Journal of Mental Health Policy and Economics* 5(1): 33–42.

United States Department of Housing and Urban Development (2009) *The 2008 Annual Homelessness Assessment Report: A Report to the US Congress*. Washington, DC: Author.

Covered Bonds

M Lea, Cardiff Economic Consulting, Cardiff, CA, USA

© 2012 Elsevier Ltd. All rights reserved.

Glossary

Cover pool Qualified assets on which investors have a priority claim.

Covered bond Instruments in which investors have a priority claim on a pool of assets along with a general claim against the issuing institution.

Dual recourse Investors have recourse to the cover pool and the issuing institution.

Prepayment Redemption of bond prior to contractual maturity due to early repayment of mortgage collateral.

Specialised issuer Nondepository financial institution that specialises in mortgage or public sector lending.

Substitute collateral Types of assets other than mortgages allowed in a cover pool.

Introduction: What Are Covered Bonds

Covered bonds are among the oldest forms of secured finance, having existed for more than 200 years in Europe. Mortgage covered bonds are an important source of long-term funding for mortgage lenders. They are the largest class of covered bonds that are also issued with public sector loans, ship loans, and agricultural loans as collateral.

Mortgage covered bonds are full-recourse debt obligations of the issuing financial institution, secured by a pool of performing eligible mortgage assets (the cover pool) that remain on the balance sheet of the issuer. Covered bonds are dual-recourse instruments. Investors have a priority claim on the cover pool assets in the event of an issuer default as well as a general claim on the institution. There are many types of covered bond with no universally agreed definition. The European Covered Bond Council, a trade group representing covered bond issuers, has listed four essential features of a covered bond:

- The bond is issued by a credit institution which is subject to public supervision and regulation.
- Bondholders have a claim against a cover pool of financial assets in priority to unsecured creditors.
- The credit institution has the ongoing obligation to maintain sufficient assets in the cover pool to satisfy the claims of bondholders at all times.
- The obligations of the credit institution in respect of the cover pool are supervised by public or other independent bodies.

The typical structure of a covered bond issuer is shown in **Figure 1**.

The cover pool and covered bonds are linked, not only in terms of priority claim but also through asset–liability matching requirements that ensure that the bonds are fully collateralised at all times and which limit the interest rate risk of the issuer. The cover monitor oversees the quality of the cover pool and the cover requirements. The covered bond securities are standardised, generally highly liquid and simple instruments (in most countries they are bullet bonds). As a result of dual recourse against a regulated financial institution and a cover pool of assets, the rating on covered bonds is usually higher than that of their issuer. Until the financial crisis of 2008, the vast majority of covered bonds were rated AAA or the equivalent.

Where Are Covered Bonds Issued?

Covered bonds represent a more than €2 trillion asset class in Europe with more than 55% backed by mortgages (**Figure 2**). Mortgage covered bonds have been the fastest growing segment of the market in recent years.

Covered bonds represent an important source of mortgage finance in many countries, as shown in **Figure** 3. They fund 16% of mortgage debt outstanding in the European Union (EU) and a significantly higher proportion in a number of countries.

The countries with the largest amounts of covered bonds outstanding are shown in **Figure 4**. Denmark has the largest amount of mortgage covered bonds outstanding followed by Germany, Spain, and Sweden. Covered bonds issued in these countries along with the United Kingdom accounted for more than 85% of total issuance in 2007, suggesting that the market is relatively concentrated.

Outside of Europe there are issuers in Canada (about €2 billion outstanding), the United States (about €12 billion outstanding), and Chile (about €5 billion outstanding). Several Central Eastern European countries

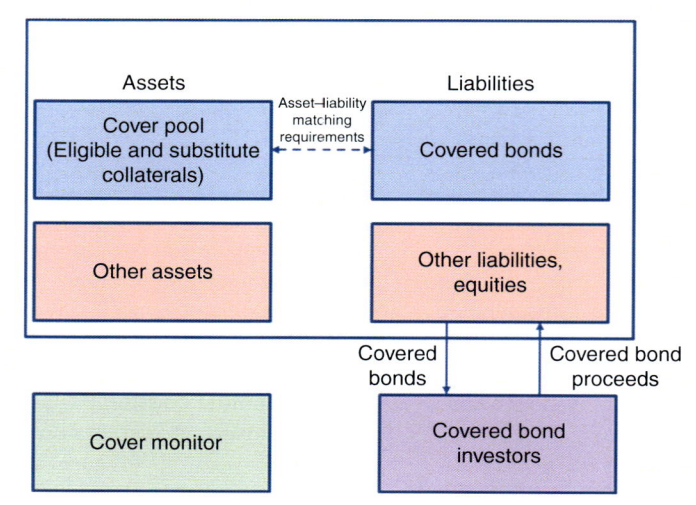

Figure 1 Covered bond issuer.

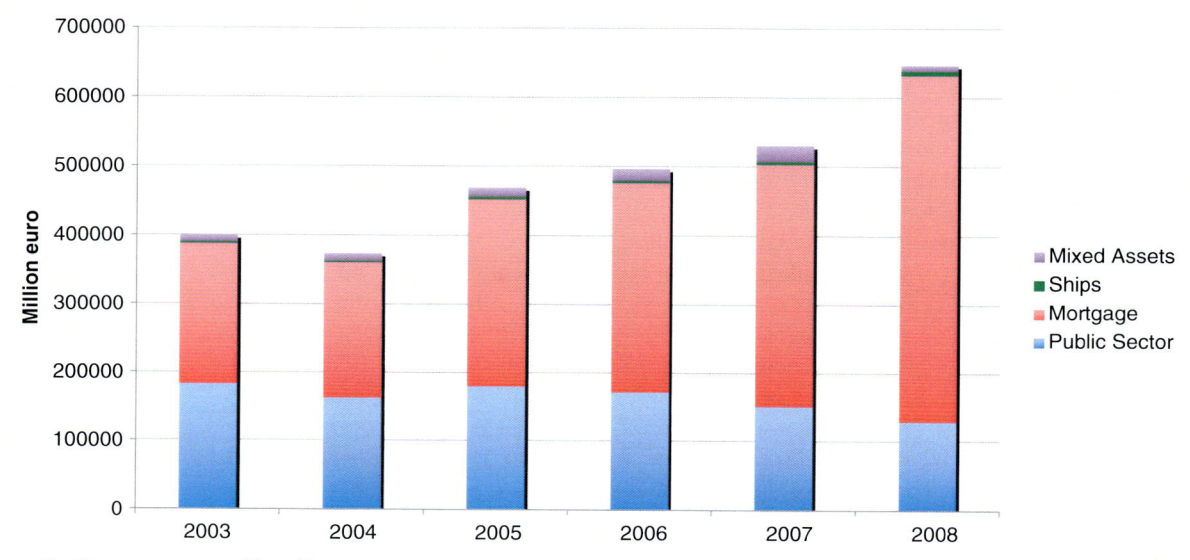

Figure 2 European covered bond issuance.
Data from ECBC and Sabine Winkler, Covered Bond Analyst; Alexander Batchvarov, CFA International Strategy Financial Strategist, Bank of America Merrill Lynch.

have been significant covered bond issuers led by the Czech Republic (€7.8 billion) and Hungary (€6 billion). Covered bonds have also been issued in Colombia, Mexico, and most recently Korea.

Key Design Features

A number of design features are important for the development of a covered bond market.

Legal Framework

Most countries which have covered bonds have special legislation that ensures the privileged position of covered bondholders in the event of issuer insolvency, defining the characteristics of the collateral and maintenance of sufficient collateral over the life of the bonds. At the end of 2008, there were 25 European countries with special legislation. In the EU, special legislation that is compliant with the UCITS directive (**Box 1**) facilitates a 10% capital risk weight for the bonds and a relaxation of investment limits for institutional investors.

Covered bonds can be issued without special legislation in five countries. The essential characteristics of a special law are replicated through contract and structuring in those countries. The rationale for issuing structured covered bonds is the absence of special legislation (Canada, United Kingdom before 2008, United States) and/or greater flexibility allowed outside regulatory framework (particularly asset

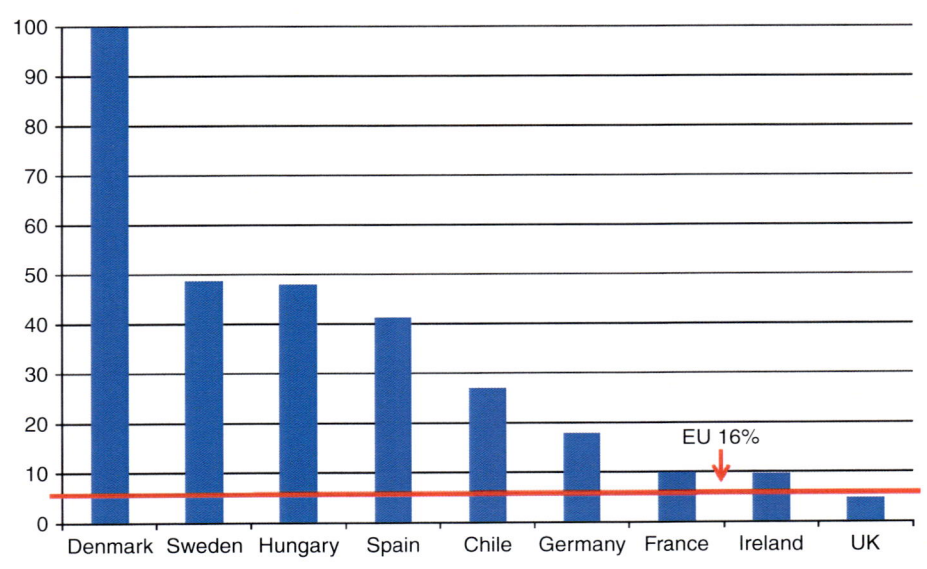

Figure 3 Percentage mortgages funded by covered bonds. Data from EMF, Banco Estado (Chile) 2007.

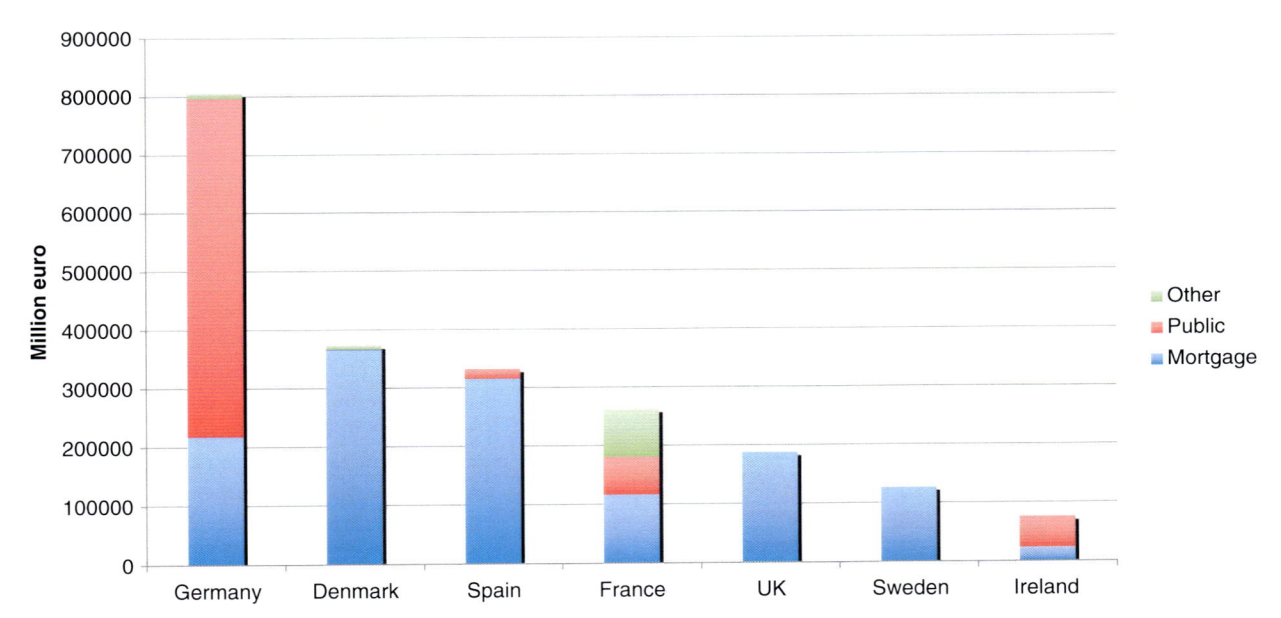

Figure 4 Largest covered bond markets. Data from ECBC and Sabine Winkler, Covered Bond Analyst; Alexander Batchvarov, CFA International Strategy Financial Strategist, Bank of America Merrill Lynch.

requirements and joint issuance arrangements (e.g., Spain)). However structured covered bonds do not qualify for special regulatory treatment in Europe and have not performed as well as bonds from special legislative countries during the recent global financial crisis.

Issuer

A defining characteristic of covered bond legislation is whether the issuer is a specialised or diversified (universal bank) institution. Historically and still in several countries issuance of covered bonds is allowed only by specialised credit institutions (mortgage banks). However, many countries now allow diversified banks to issue covered bonds. The advantages of specialised issuance include efficiency and transparency. The disadvantages are less economy of scope and diversification that can limit the competitiveness of specialised issuers. The trend in countries with specialised issuers is to incorporate them as subsidiaries in larger bank groups.

> **Box 1 UCTIS directive**
>
> Directive 85/611/EEC on undertakings for collective investments in transferable securities (UCTIS) provides limits on the concentration of investments in securities made by collective investment firms. According to article 22(4) of the directive, the general limit of 5% may be raised to a maximum of 25% in case of investments in covered bonds. In the directive, covered bonds are defined as bonds issued by a credit institution that is subject by law to special public supervision designed to protect bondholders. In particular, bondholders' claims must be secured during the whole maturity of the bonds by assets that, under the applicable law, would be used on a priority basis for the reimbursement of the principal and payment of the interest in the event of an issuer's failure.

Collateral

The characteristics of collateral eligible for the cover pool are defined in the legislation or contract and mandates that loans be secured by a first mortgage or public guarantee. In some cases, both commercial and residential mortgages can be included, whereas in others, it can only be residential. There are restrictions on the maximum loan-to-value (LTV) ratio. LTV ratios are generally set at 80% for mortgages secured by residential properties and at 60% for mortgage secured by commercial properties. Some countries set more stringent ratios (e.g., a maximum 60% LTV ratio on both types of properties). Legislation defines the way the valuation of properties is determined. In some cases, it is based on open market value and in others, sustainable mortgage lending value, which is a conservative approach to valuation emphasising the long-term nature of the mortgage contract. In some jurisdictions there are geographic restrictions and concentration limits.

Issuers can substitute other forms of collateral (e.g., cash, public debt, and in some cases derivatives and mortgage-backed securities). The purpose of such assets is as a temporary investment of excess liquidity within the cover pool or to replace noneligible assets (e.g., delinquent loans). The types and percentages of substitute collateral are defined in law or contract and are typically subject to limits (e.g., 10 or 20% of the cover pool).

Collateralisation and Matching

Issuers are required to maintain adequate collateralisation such that the value of the assets in the cover pool is always greater than or equal to the value of the bonds. The most common form of collateralisation is through dynamic pools in which the cover pool grows with new lending (and replacement collateral) and shrinks with repayment or default (in which case loans must be removed from the cover pool).

The simplest requirement is nominal value matching, but most covered bond laws and structures require more stringent matching to limit the interest rate (and/or currency) risk of the portfolio. Examples include yield matching requirements, duration gap limits, and requirements that the net present value of the assets be greater than or equal to that of the liabilities. Derivatives such as interest rate swaps may be allowed in the cover pool to facilitate meeting the matching requirements. In some jurisdictions, there are requirements to periodically stress test the portfolio. Bonds are issued periodically to fund new cover assets and to refinance loans in which the interest rate is being reset (e.g., loans with a 5-year fixed rate period would be financed through issuance of 5-year fixed rate covered bonds).

The most complete matching requirement is the pass-through-covered bond that is used in Chile and Denmark. In this form, there is a strict one-to-one match between a loan and a bond, with cash flows passed through from the borrower to the investor (the balance principle). There is no loan-to-bond correspondence in other covered bond models. In this model, there is no interest rate risk for the issuer – it is entirely absorbed by investors. The Danish model also allows for prepayment without penalty for borrowers, which is unique among covered bond countries (also recently introduced in Mexico). The prepayment option is symmetrical. If interest rates fall, the borrower can refinance the loan at par. If interest rates rise, the borrower can repurchase bonds at a discount and present them to the mortgage lender to repay the mortgage. The balance principle thus allows for de-leveraging when interest rates rise as borrowers. In Mexico, Hipotecario Total (HiTo) has introduced a modified version of the Danish model.

Recently, covered bond legislation has been modified to include a requirement for periodic revaluation of the underlying loan collateral. This can be done through indexes or automated valuation models. If current LTVs are found to be in excess of the legal limit, the issuer is required to add collateral to the cover pool.

Insolvency Protection

The cover pool must be excluded from the general bankruptcy mass upon bankruptcy or insolvency of the issuer. Covered bond holders must have an undisputed priority claim over the assets in the cover pool, including priority over governments and workers. Also, bankruptcy of the issuer should not trigger acceleration of the bond repayment.

The first goal is achieved by means of legal provisions or contractual agreements that stipulate the payment of principal and interest does not fall due, if the issuer enters into a bankruptcy procedure. This can be accomplished through asset segregation (ring fencing) in which cover assets are not included in the bankruptcy procedure or through appointment of a specific cover pool administrator who acts in the interests of bondholders. In structured covered bonds asset segregation is achieved by transferring assets to a special purpose vehicle (SPV) which is bankruptcy remote from the issuer.

The investor is also protected by a claim against the other assets of the issuer. This claim is usually ranked pari passu (equal rights to assets) with other unsecured investors.

There have been no instances of default on covered bonds, so these provisions are in fact untested. There have been issuer bankruptcies, but they have all been managed through transfer of the collateral and bonds. It is possible, in spite of statutory or contractually protections, that the issuer or administrator would not be able to maintain the quality of the assets or to manage cash flows and maturity mismatches effectively. The alternatives are to have the obligation to make payments and to manage the cover pool taken over by another credit institution (as has happened in Germany) or to accelerate the covered bonds and liquidate the cover assets to satisfy bondholders.

Supervision

Public supervision of the cover pool and bonds is mandatory to ensure compliance with solvency requirements, lending and valuation rules, and matching requirements. In many countries, both the bonds and cover assets are listed on a special register. The cover monitor can be a special auditor or trustee or a prudential supervisor. The prudential supervisor also authorises issuers and checks compliance with minimum capital requirements.

Rating agencies evaluate these design features to determine the rating of the covered bonds (specifically how many 'notches' the bond can be above the issuer's unsecured rating). The rating agency will evaluate the strength of the legal framework, the quality of the collateral, the performance of the cash flows of the cover pool and bonds in a stress scenario, and the issuer's access to liquidity in the event it cannot access the capital markets.

Issuer access to liquidity is a key issue in the current economic environment. Bond repayments must come from the cash flows of the cover pool, new issuance of covered bonds, or short-term borrowing. The disruption in the financial market in the fall of 2008 raised questions about whether issuers could obtain funds from the market or from third parties in the event the covered bond market closed. The rating agencies have been revising their rating standards to incorporate an assessment of issuer access to liquidity.

Another issue is the structural subordination of unsecured creditors (in particular deposit insurers). Some countries have placed limits on the proportion of issuer liabilities in the form of covered bonds, or they require issuers to discuss, in advance, their plans on the use of secured funding methods. At least one rating agency has stated that a reduced level of unencumbered assets available to cover senior unsecured obligations could have implications for a bank's senior unsecured debt rating. This issue does not exist with specialist, nondepository lenders.

Dealing with prepayment risk is a significant issue for issuers with fixed-rate mortgage cover pools. In most countries, this risk managed through penalties for or exclusion of prepayment or through issuance of callable bonds (Denmark). Penalties or exclusion reduce but do not limit prepayment risk leading to overcollateralisation requirements for issuers.

Advantages of Covered Bonds

Covered bonds are attractive to issuers, investors, and governments. For issuers they represent a long-term instrument facilitating funding and portfolio risk management needs. Issuers can access cheaper funding for longer maturities as they typically achieve a higher rating than the issuer's unsecured rating. The ability to obtain long-term fixed rate debt improves portfolio risk management, lowering both liquidity and interest rate risk. Covered bonds have low issuance costs as a result of their simple, standardised structure and, in most cases, direct issuance.

Covered bonds are attractive for investors because of their high credit quality (most are AAA rated at issuance), with protection against bankruptcy of the issuer. Their simplicity and liquidity are attractive features, but their private sector status allows investors to obtain a yield pickup over comparable maturity government bonds. The rapid growth of European covered bonds has been fostered by favourable European law. The 1988 UCITS directive noted earlier allows mortgage covered bonds to benefit from increased investment possibilities for institutional investors and relatively low (10%) regulatory risk weightings for banks (under the Capital Requirements directive).

Another institution factor supporting demand by banks is European Central Bank (ECB) repo eligibility (with low haircuts). The ECB recognises the high security of covered bonds and specifies that bonds that fulfil article 22(4) of the UCITS directive are eligible as collateral for monetary operations. In some countries, a large portion of covered bond issues are not sold but rather pledged as collateral at the ECB.

Liquidity has been enhanced through the jumbo market in Europe. Jumbos are typically issued for an initial amount of at least €1 billion, with a fixed coupon and bullet structure. In addition, jumbos are characterised by a market, making commitment of at least five traders, which requires continuous quoting of tight bid/ask prices depending on maturity. In 2007, the jumbo segment within the overall covered bond market accounted for 30% of the annual gross supply and 40% of the total volume outstanding. However in 2008 H2, the market making mechanism broke down significantly reducing jumbo covered bond liquidity.

Governments find covered bonds to be an attractive instrument for their capital markets. They augment the funding of housing and facilitate bond market development by providing a high-grade alternative to government bonds. Their relatively long duration make them attractive investments for institutional investors. Covered bonds can also be a tool for central bank operations. The ECB and many country central banks accept AAA-rated covered bonds as collateral for borrowing. In 2009, the ECB announced that it would purchase covered bonds in an attempt to stimulate the market.

Recent Developments

The financial crisis has impacted the covered bond market, albeit not as severely as the structured finance markets. Covered bond issuance dropped sharply in 2008, with no new issuance after the Lehman Brothers collapse in September (**Figure 5**). Issuance was sporadic in the early part of 2009, accelerating in June after the announcement that the ECB would purchase €60 billion during the year.

Covered bond spreads began widening in early 2008 with a dramatic widening after Lehman's bankruptcy (**Figure 6**). There were significant differences in the performance of bonds from different countries. Bonds issued under national legislation fared better than those that were not (United Kingdom and United States). Bonds with strong domestic demand (France and Germany) have performed better than those more dependent on international investors (Ireland and Spain). Bonds issued by lenders from countries with more stable housing markets have performed better than those with major boom-and-bust cycles. The maturity of covered bonds issued recently has been substantially shorter than before the crisis.

In addition to general market uncertainty with banks and bonds, several issues have affected covered bond issuance and spreads. The first is competition with government-guaranteed bank bonds. A number of issuers have substituted government-guaranteed debt for covered bonds. Investors that otherwise would purchase covered bonds have instead invested in government-guaranteed bank bonds in several countries. The second factor impacting covered bonds is ratings uncertainty. The three major rating agencies have adjusted their ratings methodology to place greater weight on issuer access to liquidity potentially leading to increased collateral requirements. Third, the market-making structure supporting covered bond liquidity has yet to be restored.

Conclusions

Covered bonds have been important source of funding for housing for over 200 years in Europe. More recently, a number of developed and emerging economies have introduced them. Although the funding through covered bonds has been under stress, it is likely to emerge strong, as the global financial crisis dissipates. As investors again become comfortable with banks as issuers and the supply of government guaranteed debt falls, it is likely that they will return to the covered bond market. This will lead to a resumption of issuance and a decline in covered bond spreads.

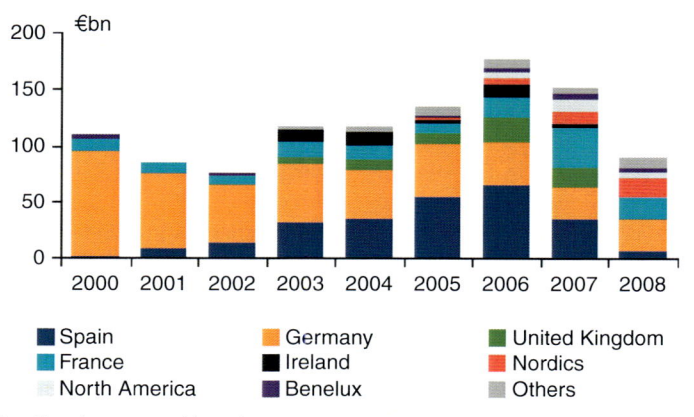

Figure 5 Annual gross supply of jumbo covered bonds. Reproduced from Bank of America Merrill Lynch 2009.

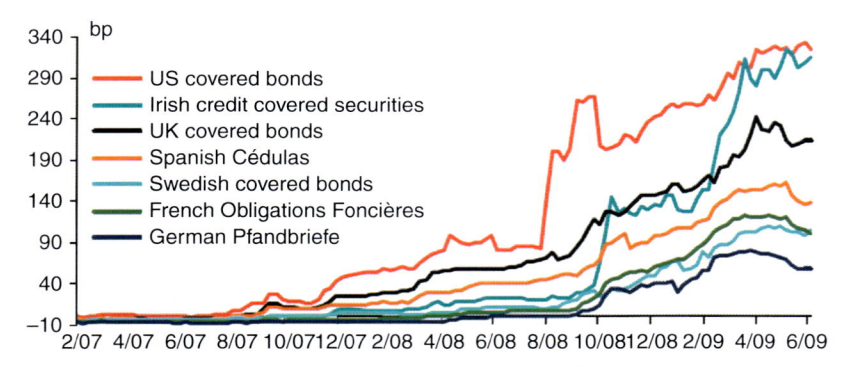

Figure 6 Secondary spreads of 5-year euro-denominated jumbo covered bonds (mid-swaps). Note that our spread calculations are based on Reuters' prices. The spreads are generic spreads of 5-year euro-denominated jumbos issued out of the respective jurisdictions. Consider that the calculations for France only consider obligations foncières, whereas those for Ireland and Germany take into account mortgage and public covered bonds.
Reproduced from Bank of America Merrill Lynch, 2009.

See also: Government/Public Lending Institutions: Asia-Pacific; Mortgage Choice: Classical Economics.

Further Reading

Avesani R, Pascual AG, and Ribacova E (2007) *The use of mortgage covered bonds. International Monetary Fund Working Paper 07/20, January*. Washington, DC: International Monetary Fund.
European Central Bank (2008) *Covered Bonds in the EU Financial System*. Frankfurt: ECB.
European Covered Bond Council (2009) *European Covered Bond Fact Book.*, 4th edn. Brussels: European Mortgage Federation.
European Mortgage Federation (2009) *Hypostat: A Review of Europe's Mortgage and Housing Markets*. Brussels: EMF.
Nykredit (2008) *Danish Mortgage Bonds*. Copenhagen: Nykredit.
Stöcker O (2008) *Covered Bonds in Europe Legal Structure and Transparency*. Barcelona: Presented at Curs du Crèdit Hipotecaria, Barcelona.
Winkler S and Batchvarov A (2008) *The Covered Bond Book*. London: Bank of America Merrill Lynch.

Relevant Website

www.ecbc.hypo.org – The Council publishes a comprehensive review of covered bonds including country summaries in *The Covered Bond Fact Book*, 2011, which is available on the website.

Credit Derivatives

A Rutledge, R&R Consulting, New York, NY, USA

© 2012 Elsevier Ltd. All rights reserved.

Glossary

Asset-Backed Securities (ABSs) Securities collateralised by the cash flows of a segregated (primarily) static pool of nonresidential mortgage receivables.

Collateralised Debt Obligations (CDOs) Securities collateralised by one or more varieties of debt, including loans (CLO), bonds (CBO), CDOs (CDO-Squareds), and ABS or RMBS (ABS or RMBS CDOs).

Credit Default Swap (CDS) Type of swap that facilitates the transfer of contingent default risk from the CDS buyer to the CDS seller at fair value (as of the transfer date). CDS are governed under ISDA.

Nationally Recognised Statistical Rating Organisations (NRSROs) Under US securities law, a licensed CRA (credit rating agency) whose ratings must be used in certain investment decisions and as credit risk measures by certain regulated financial institutions to calculate regulatory capital charges.

Securitisation A nonrecourse borrowing technique involving the simultaneous sale of securities and purchase of receivables to achieve funding cost savings, greater liquidity or other financial benefit.

Stochastic A property that describes phenomena with binary (yes–no) outcomes.

Introduction

Credit in finance, from the Latin 'credo' (I believe), refers to the *ex ante* likelihood that an obligor (be it an individual, corporation, or government) will repay a debt obligation on time and in full when it comes due.

For centuries, and through the 1970s, credit analysis was primarily a judgemental and static, balance-sheet-oriented risk assessment carried out by banks vis-à-vis their borrowers. By the end of the twentieth century, credit derivatives had emerged as products that replicate the value and risk characteristics of reference credit obligations in a continuous, mainly over-the-counter (OTC) trading environment.

This dramatic transformation in the character and concept of credit resulted from powerful, complex social and economic trends. Salient among these were the rise of information science paralleling the US investment in military intelligence during and after the Second World War; the movement of funding activity from banks to the capital markets and the parallel rise of securitisation in the early 1980s; implementation of the Basel capital regulatory framework by banks during the early 1990s; and the quest for yield when the financial markets were flooded with cheap capital in the early 2000s (**Table 1**).

The cumulative impact of such trends was to develop a continuous environment for credit analysis using data and concepts developed for market risk analysis. The medium that changed the most as a result of this shift in credit risk understanding was the liabilities side of the company balance sheet – the 'capital structure'. Hence the term 'structured finance' was given to credit restructuring and analysis.

From Securitisation to CDOs, to CDS, to Synthetic CDOs: A Short History of Credit Risk Transfer Ideas

In order to understand security structure credit derivatives, it is necessary to know something about how credit risk transfer ideas are evolved.

Securitisation

The original credit risk-redistribution transaction format was the Real Estate Mortgage Investment Conduit (REMIC) structure, which, under the US Tax Reform Act of 1986, made it possible to issue security structure (pay-through) transactions. The REMIC concept was for managing credit risk, not for interest rate risk. It legalised preferential transfers of default risk to certain classes of investors who knowingly and willingly accepted it, by creating multiple levels or 'tranches'.

REMICs were designed as off-balance sheet (OBS) vehicles that refinance, primarily, residential mortgage-backed securities (RMBSs) in a tiered capital structure with a bankruptcy-remote special purpose entity (SPE) issuer. However, the REMIC structure proved to be a starting point for refinancing all types of collateral, with the prototype of credit refinancing proceeding (financially) by the following three steps:

Table 1 OTC derivatives market value outstanding (USD TR).[a]

As of	Total	Interest rate	Equity	FX	CDS
Jun-01	$99.76	$67.47	$1.84	$16.91	–
Dec-01	$111.18	$77.57	$1.88	$16.76	–
Jun-02	$127.56	$90.00	$2.21	$18.08	–
Dec-02	$141.74	$101.70	$2.31	$18.47	–
Jun-03	$169.68	$121.80	$2.80	$22.09	–
Dec-03	$197.17	$141.99	$3.79	$24.48	–
Jun-04	$220.06	$164.63	$4.52	$27.00	–
Dec-04	$257.89	$190.50	$4.39	$28.29	**$6.40**
Jun-05	$281.49	$204.80	$4.55	$31.08	**$10.21**
Dec-05	$297.67	$215.24	$5.06	$31.61	**$13.70**
Jun-06	$370.18	$262.53	$6.78	$38.13	**$20.35**
Dec-06	$414.85	$291.58	$7.49	$40.27	**$28.65**
Jun-07	$516.41	$347.31	$8.59	$48.65	**$42.58**
Dec-07	$595.34	$393.14	$8.47	$56.24	**$57.89**
Jun-08	$683.73	$458.30	$10.18	$62.98	**$57.33**
Dec-08	$591.96	$418.68	$6.49	$49.75	**$48.87**

[a]© Bank for International Settlements, 'Acceleration of OTC derivatives market activity in the first half of 2002', 8 November 2002; 'OTC derivatives market activity in the second half of 2002', 8 May 2003; 'OTC derivatives market activity in the first half of 2003', 12 November 2003; 'OTC derivatives market activity in the second half of 2004', May 2005; 'OTC derivatives market activity in the second half of 2005', May 2006; 'OTC derivatives market activity in the second half of 2006', May 2007; 'OTC derivatives market activity in the second half of 2007', May 2008; 'OTC derivatives market activity in the second half of 2008', May 2009.

Step 1: Asset revaluation at the point of sale;
Step 2: Acquisition of the assets by issuing bonds in a capital structure crafted precisely to lower the overall cost of capital while maximising liquid interest using some combination of these mechanisms (with different costs and levels of protection).

- Excess spread (XS): the difference between the weighted average coupon on the assets and the weighted average funding cost of the security structure as of the time the transaction closes.
- Subordination: funds due to investors in the capital structure are available, first, to pay senior investors.
- Reserve funds: cash from proceeds at origination or accumulated XS, or some combination of the two, is held in the transaction for future drawdown. There are many permutations of reserving.
- Over-collateralisation (OC): the nominal principal value of the assets exceeds the amount of securities issued. This is similar to subordination (the 'equity' piece in **Figure 3**) but with lower proceeds and a lower weighted average interest cost because the seller is the investor.
- Triggers: covenants in the deal that redistribute risk and value when certain predefined scenarios materialise.

Step 3: Rating of the bonds by Nationally Recognised Statistical Rating Organisations (NRSROs) to validate the adequacy of capital for the risk-adjusted yield accepted by the investor.

Ultimately, of course, the collateral risk cannot be changed in these structures – only measured and redistributed. The risk measurement and redistribution methods deployed define both the transaction type and the riskiness of the securities.

For example, if the collateral blended and shaped into securities consists of private contracts, a 'securitisation' transaction issuing 'structured securities' will be the result. Securitisations of nonmortgage business receivables produce asset-backed securities (ABS) and securitisations of mortgage-related structured securities produce RMBS or commercial mortgage-backed security (CMBS). Here, Step 1 (asset revaluation) is carried out using historical performance data on the contracts supplied by the borrower as the basis of the credit risk measure.

Cash Collateralised Debt Obligations

By contrast, loans or securities on banks' balance sheets trade in the debt capital markets based on estimates of default probability associated with a public credit rating, risk grade, or credit spread. As these transactions do not transform private contracts into securities, they are a type of 'structured finance' but not securitisation. They, and their securities, are called 'collateralised debt obligations' (CDOs). Since the value discovery process of Step 1 is de-emphasised for CDOs, the focus shifts to Step 2, crafting the capital structure to redistribute risk efficiently. From the real estate investment trust (REIT) structure, where claims higher up in the capital structure investment are safeguarded by earlier principal return, the capital structure of OBS vehicles can be generalised abstractly as a continuum of the credit risk spectrum:

- a highly secure (AAA) range of payment risk at the very top, close to the source of repayment;
- a highly speculative risk ('equity') at the bottom, where defaults are first recognised; and
- an arbitrary number of gradations of payment risk in-between.

The utility of a CDO appears to be that it commoditises the analysis of capital structure, both for operating companies that have working capital needs and for banks that seek to leverage their capital as much as possible, using ratings. If this can be achieved, all types of structured securities can be traded or repackaged using a CDO structure. However, the validity of Step 3, the ratings on these securities, depends on the usefulness of credit ratings as risk measure inputs. For CDOs, this may be problematic due to deficiencies in the credit risk measure. A rating is derived from and not interchangeable with performance data. A backward-looking 'average' of the performance data, it is informationally an inferior substitute to the data itself.

Credit Default Swap

For banks, which have good access to liquidity and do not need to raise capital, structured finance is primarily useful as a tool to optimise their balance sheet by shedding 'risky' exposures synthetically, using credit derivatives. This allows them to leverage the liabilities as much as the Basel capital regulatory framework will allow. It is better for them to transfer the default risk of their assets, only, without the administrative burden and expense of transferring ownership.

The simplest credit derivative is a Credit Default Swap (CDS), a contractual arrangement made between two parties simultaneously to purchase and sell the default risk of a reference security or loan. In a CDS, the seller of the swap (said to be 'long' the CDS) is buying the risk of a contingent default, or selling credit protection, whereas the buyer of the swap (said to be 'short' the CDS) is selling the contingent risk of default, or purchasing credit protection. In case of default, the swap seller will pay the buyer the dirty price of the bond (the bond price at the end of the last payment period plus accrued interest) at the point of default, net of recoveries. Theoretically, the value of the swap is related to the price of the bond via the discount rate demanded by the market for bonds of a particular risk grade, which is higher than the rate on treasuries. A bond or swap premium that satisfies the buyer and seller of risk when the deal is struck is said to 'neutralise' the long swap counterparty's expected default risk over the time horizon of the credit.

CDS trades are 'unfunded' risk transfers, but a CDS can be transformed into a 'funded' synthetic risk transfer through the simultaneous issuance of bonds and reinvestment of the sale proceeds in highly rated government treasuries by a bankruptcy-remote SPE. What makes an SPE 'special' is that it is not an operating company – a blank slate. Bankruptcy-remote SPEs, created under specified legal and accounting rules, are required in order for OBS treatment to be granted and risk transfers to be recognised. For a funded synthetic risk transfer, the timing of principal and interest cash flows can be designed to match those of the purchased securities or customised via a swap. When the SPE is bankruptcy remote, its securities in aggregate will have the same risk as the reference pool of CDS. Credit default risk is thus transferred to buyers of the bonds, who receive scheduled interest and principal payments plus the agreed upon 'risk-neutralising' CDS premium. Investors in the naked default risk receive the CDS premium without the cash flows.

The latter scenario is illustrated in **Figure 1**: RMBS securities are issued in Vehicle I. The arranging bank keeps the Class B on its balance sheet but transfers its default risk

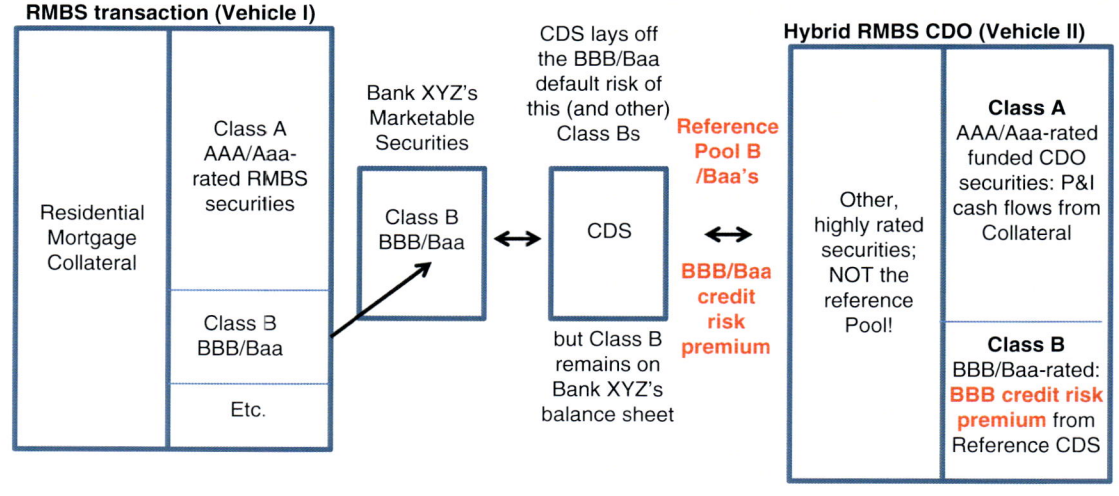

Figure 1 Partitioning cash flows into value/risk components.

Figure 2 Diagram of a CLN.

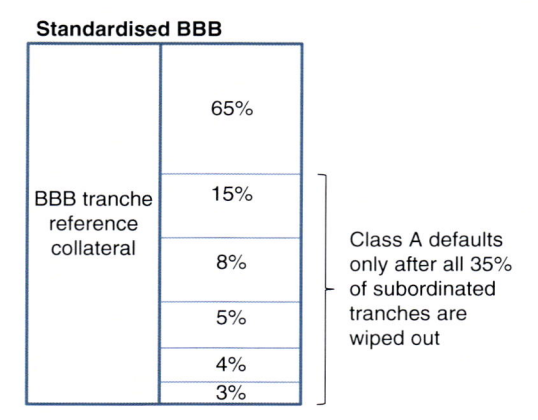

Figure 3 The hierarchy of payment claims.

by buying a CDS and pays the BBB credit risk premium. The CDS seller is the CDO, Vehicle II. In this case, the Class B investor in Vehicle II is not buying bonds, only default risk, and hence is receiving periodic CDS premium only. A funded Class B investor would receive principal and interest cash flows from the highly rated securities plus the BBB CDS premium. If each of the value/risk elements is properly rated and priced, the synthetic CDO is said to mirror the cash CDO, wherein the CDO buys the RMBS and pays investors with their proceeds. (But, this is a big 'if'.)

A one-tranche bond backed by CDS is known as a credit-linked note (CLN) (**Figure 2**). The investors rank pari passu in the bond structure, which means they are exposed to the default risk of the reference bond, in proportion to their invested amount. This is the simplest example of a credit derivative with a security structure.

CDS and CLNs transfer default risk but do not alter it. A payment default will adversely affect all investors in proportion to their investment since all rely solely on the same obligor for repayment. This observation brings the challenge of credit risk engineering into focus. For all the talk about *ex ante* default probability, there is nothing statistical about default when it happens. Credit risk is inherently stochastic – an all or nothing proposition. Herein lies the biggest impediment to building a science of credit risk reengineering on the foundation of price risk reengineering: but for the law of large numbers, the two risks are incommensurate. But, credit risk can be made more statistical, less stochastic, by creating synthetic portfolios: referencing multiple securities and transferring the risk using CDS. Even if one reference credit defaults, others in the portfolio are likely to go on paying. (How much diversification is achievable depending on the number of reference names and their correlation to future events, and to each other.) This is precisely the logic of a synthetic CDO.

Synthetic CDOs

A synthetic CDO has the same functional form as the cash CDO, but its purpose is to facilitate risk transfer not raise funds. The liabilities can be unfunded (CDS contracts only) or funded. The latter case follows the CLN concept, but the reference asset is a portfolio of CDS along with tranches at (usually) standardised intervals (**Figure 3**).

By the late 1990s, cash and synthetic CDOs were being produced, and, in the 2000s, the method was extrapolated to CDOs of ABS, RMBS, CMBS, and CDO-Squared (CDO^2). Meanwhile, coincident with the collapse of the hedge fund Long-Term Capital, a new type of repackaging called the 'market value CDO' came into existence.

Market value CDOs were constructed based on the amount of OC using traded security prices and collateral haircuts on the par value of the underlying securities, since the mechanism of repayment was resale of the collateral, not the cash collection. The advent of market value CDOs brought credit repackaging much closer to the goal of making it a continuous, tradable medium – the synthetic CDO.

Market value CDOs and synthetic CDOs are highly similar to each other in that both rely on the security price as the source of credit protection in the capital structure. But synthetic CDOs are incommensurate with cash flow CDOs: their principal and interest cash flows come from a source other than the reference portfolio. This discrepancy leads to challenges for the synthetic credit replication, in addition to the obvious opportunities.

On the opportunity side, synthetic CDOs are more uniform in their portfolio composition and security structure than cash CDOs, whose idiosyncratic motivations tend to result in one-off structures. The possibility of greater uniformity no doubt gave a boost to the development of traded credit indices, about which more will be said in the next section. Moreover, the decoupling of the capital structure with the portfolio of synthetic CDOs enabled them to issue liabilities in amounts unconstrained

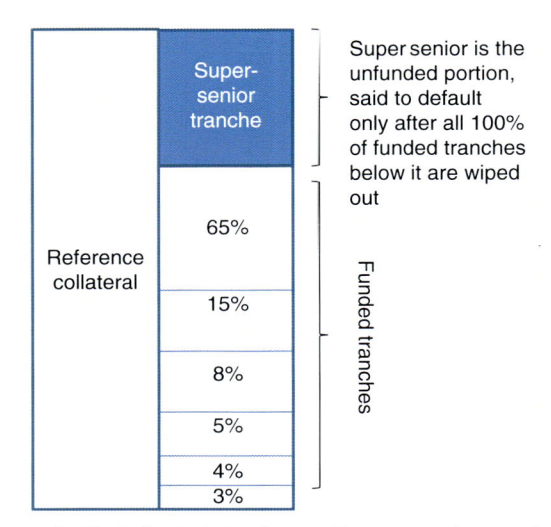

Figure 4 Underfunded structures with super-senior tranche.

by the size of the notional asset portfolio. Liabilities in excess of 100% of the asset balance could be issued (if sufficient demand existed) with the excess interest taking the form of an unfunded 'super-senior' tranche at the top of the capital structure (**Figure 4**). Prior to the collapse of the sub-prime market, the super-senior tranches of synthetic CDOs went to market with a *AAA/Aaa* rating by virtue of their position at the top of the capital structure and a financial guarantee from a highly rated counterparty. The market for such guarantees, issued by surety bond providers, has dried up since the collapse of the financial guarantee industry in the sub-prime crisis.

By the same logic as CDS, synthetic CDOs could also go to market unfunded, with the investors receiving no interest or principal cash flows, only the risk premium to match the rating on their particular tranche. Alternatively, they could go to market issuing only certain slices – bespoke tranches – but leaving the rest of the 'invisible capital structure' unsold (**Figure 5**). Cash transactions

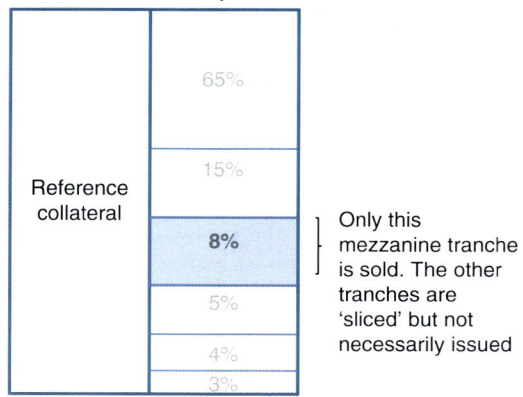

Figure 5 Partially funded structures with bespoke tranches.

lacked such flexibility because of the necessity of matching liabilities and assets.

On the other hand, the premise of the synthetic CDO posed a fundamental challenge: how to reflect the impact of portfolio defaults as they materialised. For cash flow CDOs, the impact of default is resolved organically through the distribution of diminished asset cash flows; investors are paid their amounts due until the cash collections and amounts held in reserve are used up. But with funded synthetic CDOs, the cash flows are not impaired. Carried to the limit, unfunded synthetic CDOs have no cash flow but only the abstraction of cash flow priority via subordination. The market-accepted solution to this challenge was to mirror the percentage of the defaulted notional principal balance in write-offs of commensurate percentages of the principal balance on the most junior tranche; with subsequent defaults, the write-downs would continue where they left off, going up the capital structure. This solution was broadly consistent with the intuition that junior securities carried proportionally greater risk. As a matter of fact, this is not necessarily true in cash market transactions; some did not rank order in risk redistribution. An example is turbo structures that, under good scenarios, eliminated the bottom tranches first so as to pare the weighted average interest cost. In such transactions, it is not enough to 'eyeball' the capital structure to determine relative risk because the interaction between cash flows and structure has a probabilistic nature. The cash flows must be modelled out to make an accurate relative risk determination. However, it introduced a permanent 'disconnect' or basis between synthetic and cash CDOs, whose periodic cash collections were distributed from the 'top' of the capital structure through the hierarchy of claims.

Duelling Paradigms

What is difficult to understand about CDO securities is how dramatically their intrinsic value can change after origination.

For cash market ABS and RMBS, credit risk decreases as a function of time when the underlying collateral is an amortising static pool, because uncertainty about performance goes away: the receivables that default, default; the receivables that prepay, prepay; and the receivables that remain follow the payment promise. Moreover, as the senior classes pay down, the structure de-levers, leaving more cash cushion for the riskier classes, whose endogenous risk decreases if the transaction is not infeasible (the cumulative collateral loss is contained by the equity tranche). In theory, the same should be true for RMBS CDOs, if they are structured to be feasible.

Synthetic CDOs are potentially more volatile. Designed to be traded, they are therefore potentially affected by exogenous shifts in CDS spreads, changes in the credit quality of reference securities, changes in the structure of correlation between the elements in portfolio, expiration of the time to maturity, and sensitivity given the extreme leverage in the capital structure (relative to the cash CDO) because the securities being referenced, themselves, have leverage.

All these factors can cause the intrinsic risk of the securities to change: hence the need for an analytic framework for security pricing that reflects endogenous credit risk transitions, which ratings do not provide.

To experienced derivatives traders, contingent price modelling provided such a framework. Fifty years before the advent of credit derivatives, academic finance began formalising theories of contingent pricing. By 1970, the thinking had coalesced around an approach today known as Black–Scholes–Merton modelling, whereby real prices of traded instruments are remapped to equivalent equilibrium prices linked to a risk-free rate (e.g., London Interbank Offered Rate (LIBOR) or other money market rates) so as to eliminate risk aversion as a demand factor, and allow prices to vary as a function of their objective risk factors, volatility, and time to expiration. The original formula has been modified and extended many times over the past three decades, evolving into a generalised approach to pricing contingent liabilities. It was adapted to explain capital structure as a combination of 'call option' (equity) and 'put option' (debt) on the assets of the corporation. The 'Merton default' or 'structural model' was adapted to the problem of dynamic valuation of CDS and CDS portfolios (baskets), where (consistent with CDO structuring conventions) the rating on the security formed the basis for establishing the CDS premium at origination.

Index-Traded CDO Security Structure

Standardisation and flexible risk transfer through synthetic CDOs made it possible to design CDS baskets representing a particular credit sector (geographic, risk grade, or collateral type) for trading or hedging. 'Credit baskets' could be placed in a capital structure of different credit tranches, with scheduled roll-over dates (rolls) as they came due. Tranches were standardised with fixed attachment points or given constant proportions. In this way, tradable synthetic indices of credit sectors in different credit grades – the ultimate form of credit standardisation – were born. The two largest commercial sponsors of synthetic CDO index products, Dow Jones and CDX, Inc. Co., a consortium of investment banks, developed a variety of corporate indices with proprietary levels and attachment points, for example:

- The iTraxx Europe products consisting of CDS on 125 European low-investment-grade corporate names are tranched into 0–3%, 3–6%, 6–9%, 9–12%, and 12–15% slices of risk.
- The CDX North American (NA) Investment Grade (IG) products with 125 reference names are tranched into 0–3%, 3–7%, 7–10%, 10–15%, 15–30%, and 30–100% slices.

When ABS, RMBS, CMBS, and CDOs securities began to be refinanced using the CDO method, a synthetic exotic CDO index industry soon followed. By 2003, the International Security Derivatives Association (ISDA) had finalised a comprehensive framework for derivatives of structured credits; and in 2005, ISDA published templates for documenting synthetic trading of ABS CDS. In early 2006, Markit, the derivative trade processing firm, launched synthetic indices on the sub-prime RMBS sector, on which it served as administration and calculation agent. Known as the ABX.HE indices, these were home equity (second lien) backed securities of vintages considered broadly representative of the sector, coming from 20 equally weighted transactions in five different credit grades: AAA, AA, A, BBB, and BBB-. Markit and CDX also collaborated in developing a traded ABX home equity (TABX.HE) index. The intervals on the security structures of lower-rated vintages were customised to be wider than those of corporate synthetic indices, allowing for more cushioning of risk

- TABX.HE BBB: 0–3%, 3–7%, 7–12%, 12–20%, and 20–35% levels.
- TABX.HE BBB-: 0–5%, 5–10%, 10–15%, 15–25%, and 25–40% levels.

In retrospect, it is clear that a synthetic market for credit suffers from some structural problems. A fundamental issue is that the market is one sided: banks have an innate advantage in making loans and disproportionate need to 'short' their credit exposures relative to other investors in the market. A related issue is that nonbank investors in the RMBS CDO and synthetic RMBS CDO or CDO^2 market did not use contingent price theory to assess the risks that they were taking on, and did not have access to underlying performance data on the mortgages that went into the RMBS.

The informational asymmetries in this market were therefore very large; the banks' motivation to misrepresent the credit quality of these CDO securities was very great; and their ability to control the disclosure of real risk by manipulating the prices of these securities at origination through ratings, and in the secondary market through traded indices, appears to have been quite comprehensive for a considerable time. A study of the information efficiency in prices on the ABX.HE 06-01 vintage published in 2009 in *The Journal of Structured Finance* concluded that discounted cash flow analysis of the indices based on real-time data produced the most information on security value, followed by raw collateral data on the indices, and that the traded prices had the most serious time lags.

The Past as a Guide to the Future of Security Structure Credit Synthetics

Corporate finance theory teaches that the debt of an operating company has a risk profile intrinsic to the company's franchise. Over the past 30 years, the static view of credit risk has been experimentally relaxed through financial engineering and the partially successful development of liquid, wholesale, near-continuous credit markets, to which synthetic replication techniques were added.

But, the onset of the sub-prime crisis, variously dated from the collapse of the Asset-Backed Commercial Paper (ABCP) market in August 2007 and the fall of Lehman Brothers in September 2008, brought trading and issuance to large sectors of the structured finance market to a halt. The ABX.HE market profiled in the last section failed to make its scheduled rolls beginning in January 2008. Congress, the Securities and Exchange Commission (SEC), and the Financial Industry Regulatory Authority (FINRA) investigated whether or not dealers that created synthetic CDOs did so in order to bet against the investors who bought them.

To date, the goal of credit standardisation and trading through financial engineering has fallen far short of what has been achieved in organised swap and option markets. Several reasons may be adduced to explain the difference. An OTC market does not have the same governance features of an organised derivatives exchange, which publishes trade data continuously so that the market participants all have access to the same information in the secondary market. (This feature would need to be adapted to traded credit markets by making timely and accurate performance data available, so that the credit risks can be reassessed or rerated to reflect endogenous shifts in quality.) A derivative exchange is also backed by a clearing house that is responsible for calibrating the level of margin (leverage) to price volatility; setting capital requirements for clearing members; ensuring that failed trades are resolved in an orderly fashion; and enforcing the responsibility for counterparty risk jointly and severally on clearing members, to avert market dislocation when a member fails. In contrast to the organised exchange model, the rules for banks trading in OTC derivatives resulted in undercapitalised CDS exposures after the passage of the Commodity Futures Modernization Act of 2000. The materiality of this change was evident in the revelation of American Insurance Group (AIG's) naked CDS exposures during its bailout by the New York Fed in September 2008.

Can these issues be properly addressed and resolved? Some answers may come from regulation. The Dodd–Frank Wall Street Reform and Consumer Protection Act has made several changes in how the market players are regulated, as well as imposing some conditions on leverage. A flash point is the requirement that securitising firms have 'skin in the game' in the form of a mandatory level of OC. The SEC's disclosure requirements for securitisation, known as Reg AB, in addition to adopting this and other Dodd–Frank requirements, has stiffened the rules on information disclosure to force the sellers and buyers to use the same information set. But, are buyers and sellers willing and able to play by the same set of rules, including the same set of risk measures? The liquidity and transparency of global structured credit markets may ultimately depend on the answer.

See also: Democracy and Accountability; Financial Deregulation; Financial Regulation; Hedging Housing Risk; Housing and the Macroeconomy; Housing Markets and Macroeconomic Policy; Industrial Organisation of the US Residential Mortgage Market; Mortgage Default: Consequences; Mortgage Default: Determinants; Mortgage Innovation; Mortgage Interest Rate Regulation; Mortgage Market Regulation: North America; Mortgage Markets: Regulation and Intervention; Price Dynamics in Housing Markets; Residential Property Derivatives; Subprime and Predatory Lending: Legal Regulation; Subprime Mortgages; Time and the Economic Analysis of Housing Systems.

Further Reading

Fons JS (2009) Shedding light on subprime RMBS. *The Journal of Structured Finance* Spring, 15(1): 81–91.

Morgenson G (2009) Banks Bundled Bad Debt, Bet Against It and Won. *New York Times*, 2 December.

Rutledge A and Raynes S (2010) *Elements of Structured Finance*. Section 5.2 The History of Structural Convergence of Chapter 5, Piecing the Credit Together. New York: Oxford University Press.

Teitelbaum R and Son H (2009) New York Fed's Secret Choice to Pay for Swaps Hits Taxpayers, Bloomberg, 27 October.

The Financial Crisis Inquiry Report (2011) Final Report of the National Commission on the Causes of the Financial and Economic Crisis in the United States, 'The CDO Machine', p. 149.

Credit Derivatives and the Housing Market

C King and A Pavlov, Simon Fraser University, Vancouver, BC, Canada

© 2012 Elsevier Ltd. All rights reserved.

Glossary

Alt-A mortgage borrowers This class of mortgage borrowers includes new immigrants without a credit rating or self-employed individuals who cannot verify either employment or income; specific mortgage products exist for this borrower class.

Collateral mortgage obligation This is a special purpose investment vehicle that as a legal entity owns mortgage assets within a pool. The mortgage assets represent the collateral and the mortgage pool provides cash flows for a bond issue sold to investors whereby specified tranches, for example senior, mezzanine, or equity, receive the distribution of cash flows subject to a contract which is referred to as the structure.

Credit default swap This swap contract is an unfunded credit derivative that results in a buyer of the credit default swap making a series of payments to the seller of the credit default swap to obtain insurance-like protection in the event of a credit default. However, credit default swaps are not insurance since the buyer of the credit default swap does not need to own the underlying asset and the seller may not be a regulated entity and is not mandated to set aside a reserve fund from the premium payments to pay claims in the event of a credit default.

Credit derivative This form of derivative is a bilateral contract and is negotiated over the counter, and not on an exchange, and is similar to other derivatives in that the seller of protection in a credit derivative contract receives premiums from the buyer of the protection until maturity, or until default, against the credit risk of the reference entity such as a mortgage pool. A credit derivative can be unfunded like a credit default swap or funded like collateralised debt obligations.

Credit enhancement The purpose is to enhance the credit rating of an investment often fundamental to the securitisation transaction in structured finance. Similarly, it can reduce credit risk and provide, for example, a lender or investor, with a guarantee of compensation if a borrower defaults by way of collateral, insurance, and/or some form of counterparty agreement.

Credit risk Credit risk in housing finance means the risk that the mortgage borrower will default on a mortgage loan and the mortgage lender is not able to cover its loss due to foreclosure.

Mortgage-backed security Referred to as MBS, this asset-backed security represents a claim on the principal and interest cash flows from a pool of mortgage loans originated from various financial institutions. MBS is typically sold as bonds and because mortgage borrowers can prepay mortgages there is the potential for prepayment risk. Credit risk also exists unless the mortgage assets are insured or guaranteed.

Mortgage loan insurance On high loan-to-value mortgages, typically where the mortgage borrower does not have a 20% downpayment, there is often a legislative mandate to require mortgage loan insurance to be obtained from a mortgage loan insurance supplier. Mortgage loan insurance is also integral to MBS. The premium is paid to the insurance company at the time of mortgage funding to insure or guarantee the mortgage lender against loss due to foreclosure.

Subprime mortgage lending The common misperception is that subprime mortgage borrowers can be defined by a type of mortgage product such as mortgages with zero downpayments, extended amortisations, or interest-only payments. Subprime mortgage borrowers are properly defined by their respective credit rating. A subprime mortgage borrower is someone that obtains a mortgage loan even though they have an impaired credit rating, usually due to a recent bankruptcy or when payments on personal debt obligations including taxes have been missed and are in arrears.

Housing Finance: Primary and Secondary Markets

Homeownership is acknowledged globally to be a key factor in political and economic stability, according to the International Monetary Fund (IMF). Due to high land and construction costs relative to wages, homeownership requires a stable housing finance and mortgage system to succeed. This reality seems to hold in any jurisdiction as reported by the IMF, and most new homebuyers seek out mortgages with terms of 15, 25, or more years and mortgages are often refinanced to pay for home maintenance, renovations, or other household consumption. The length of the mortgage amortisation period exposes borrowers to high interest costs and the potential for credit default is not insignificant as macroeconomic and personal fortunes can change.

Table 1 Mortgage funding sources

Retail	Wholesale
	Primary funding
Individual Bank Accounts	Raised from companies and capital markets
Current accounts	Short call deposits
	Certificates of deposit
	Commercial paper
	Bonds
	Secondary funding
	Residential mortgage-backed securities
	Mortgage-backed bonds and structured covered bonds

In most mortgage systems, government-regulated lenders are responsible for origination, servicing, funding, and portfolio management of mortgage loans. The sources of funds for the mortgage loans are debt obligations of the lender. These obligations are in most cases deposits but may also be in the form of mortgage (or nonmortgage) bonds, dedicated savings, and loans from other financial institutions or from special liquidity (warehouse) facilities, as outlined in **Table 1**.

Basel I and II set forth minimum regulatory capital requirements that financial institutions must adhere to as part of credit risk management. The mandated minimum capital requirement in most nations therefore

- limits mortgage lending that is carried on the balance sheet of a financial institution;
- influences whether financial institutions buy mortgage loan insurance as this reduces or eliminates the capital requirement for mortgages carried on the balance sheet; and
- results in a flow-through of mortgage loans into the secondary market, thus removing mortgage loans from the balance sheet.

Some mortgage lenders, which are referred to as monoline lenders, focus only on mortgage lending. They do not have funding available from retail sources and thus wholesale funding sources and securitisation are the only options to secure mortgage credit.

Consolidating loans or other debt instruments into single assets or securities is called securitisation. The secondary mortgage market has evolved mortgage finance to a more specialised activity and the originator of the loan often does not hold it until maturity. Residential mortgage-backed securities (MBS or RMBS), collateral debt obligations (CDOs), and asset-backed commercial paper (ABCP) are bought and sold in financial markets much like stocks. These assets are transferred from the balance sheet of the mortgage originator to a company that is legally separate, called a special purpose vehicle (SPV). With an MBS, the originating firm retains any excess interest over the all-in cost of the securitisation but removes the loans and any associated capital requirement from its balance sheet. It is the SPV that acquires legal title to the mortgages and issues the MBS where it is managed with payments then made to investors based on the performance of the specific pool of mortgages.

Figure 1 provides a graphic of a basic MBS. The cash flow from the mortgage pool is redistributed to the different tranches (known as 'tranche' from the French word for 'slice') based on a set of sequential payment rules, with

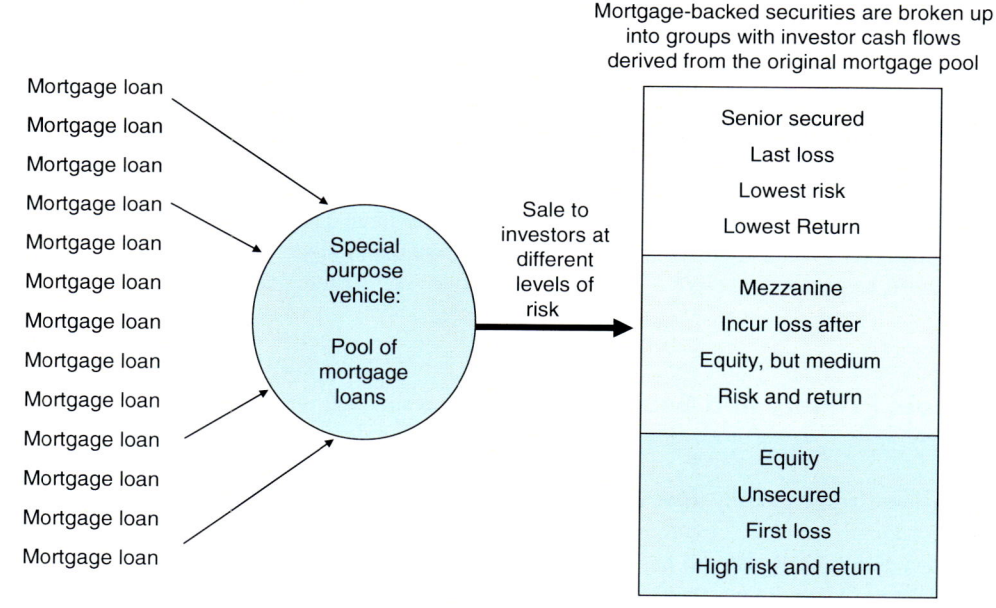

Figure 1 Mortgage-backed securities. Collaterised mortgage obligations divide mortgage pool into tranches.

interest and principal paid starting with the senior secured. Prepayment of mortgage loans can alter cash flow into each tranche. Some MBSs use an accrual tranche when one or more tranches do not purposefully receive a payment in a particular period. Different variations of accrual tranches relate to changes in lending rates. Floating rate tranches are created from fixed rate tranches, with London Interbank Offered Rate (LIBOR) often used as the reference rate. Inverse floaters or stripped MBSs segregate the cash flows from the underlying security and provide investors with cash flow from either interest-only or principal-only components. There are modifiable and combinable features that provide investors with synthetic coupon options, an effective hedging tool. Planned amortisation class (PAC) bonds allow for the payment of a stream of principal amounts.

Mortgage-backed bonds are secured debt securities issued by mortgage credit institutions supported by residential mortgages that remain on the balance sheet of the issuer. Individual mortgage-backed bonds can be substituted with other mortgage loans from the originator's portfolio. There are some substitution limitations, such as the requirement for a match in terms of duration and quality of the mortgage asset.

Managing Risk in the Housing Market

Credit risk in housing finance means the risk that the borrower will default and the lender is not able to cover its losses by means of foreclosure. Intermediary credit risk is the risk of default of the financial intermediary that attracts financing for mortgage loans from the market (capital or deposit markets). Interest rate risk is the risk that interest rates will change, leading to another risk, prepayment risk, which occurs when the mortgage holder pays off all or some of the mortgage ahead of the maturity date impacting the timing and amount of cash flows. Liquidity risk refers to the inability to sell an asset for an expected price in order to obtain cash when necessary or to minimise claims severity in the case of a mortgage default. Securitisation of mortgage lending does not make the fundamental credit risk disappear, but simply distributes this risk among various participants.

Credit insurance covers some or all of a loan obligation when certain things happen to the mortgage borrower such as unemployment, disability, or death. There is also mortgage loan insurance which a mortgage borrower may be required by legislation to obtain from a mortgage loan insurance supplier to insure the lender against default. Mortgage loan insurance is mandated typically on high loan-to-value mortgages, where the borrower has less than predetermined downpayment, typically 20%. Mortgage loan insurance is fundamental to housing finance throughout the world and there are public and private suppliers of mortgage loan insurance. While it is a form of credit insurance, credit insurance is more often used to refer to policies that cover other kinds of debt. Insured mortgages serve mortgage systems by reducing or eliminating capital requirements, and MBS-insured mortgages provide an extra security to investors.

The traditional view of lenders is that borrowers without a credit history or lacking ability to manage debt are not suitable candidates for mortgages at any loan rate. The recent performance of US private mortgage loan insurance providers suggests that mortgage underwriting can be challenging in a weak housing market when borrowers have little or negative home equity. Defaults for US insured mortgages among the largest mortgage insurers, with statistics tracked by the Mortgage Insurance Companies of America, ranged from between 210 000 and 350 000 per annum in the 1990s to more than 1 000 000 defaults in 2009. This is significant given that insured mortgages go through a dual underwriting process whereby the originating lender underwrites the mortgage loan and then forwards this to a mortgage loan insurer that again underwrites the application (except in the case of delegated underwriting common in the United States) so as to validate the application and charge an appropriate insurance premium.

International Housing Finance and Mortgage Securitisation

In an international context, credit derivatives influence housing markets to support mortgage lending by way of better integration of housing finance with capital markets. The reason is that the structure of mortgage lending among international economies has often been plagued by a lack of domestic bank deposits to ensure adequate mortgage credit. Even when bank deposits are available competing investments are sometimes considered more optimal to allocate capital. These include commercial loans which are often distributed as demand loans with full recourse, based on variable loan rates and shorter terms than mortgage loans. Consumers may avoid bank deposits due to rates on saving account deposits competition from mutual funds and retirement savings investments. This may constrain the amount of mortgage credit to consumers.

The international expansion of securitisation is complex. There is often no effective way to channel deposit savings into mortgages among many developed and developing economies. This reality has increased the global mortgage securitisation, linking the capital market with housing finance. The degree to which credit derivatives are used flows from the requirements of financial institutions and investors to manage risks of holding mortgage assets. Credit derivatives are one of many tools used globally to provide credit enhancement for mortgage assets. Government guarantees on mortgage loans, mortgage loan insurance, and other tools either used separately, or in combination with credit derivatives, are necessary to meet investor requirements for credit enhancement.

In the United States, there is a prominent role for government and government-sponsored enterprises (GSEs), such as Fannie Mae and Freddie Mac, to enhance credit and liquidity, facilitate mortgage securitisation, and expand homeownership as a national policy objective. (US GSEs Fannie Mae (Federal National Mortgage Association) and Freddie Mac (Federal Home Loan Mortgage Corporation) were 'nationalised' on 7 September 2008 through a conservatorship by the Federal Housing Finance Agency (FHFA) in response to the need for a liquidity injection to address the housing and mortgage market crisis in the United States.) The United States is the world's largest mortgage market and has a developed MBS market in which GSEs guarantee and purchase mortgage assets. Credit derivatives can be a fundamental instrument to elevate the credit rating of mortgage pools to meet investor requirements, particularly nontraditional mortgages that do not meet GSE guarantee requirements.

In Canada, there is a state-owned mortgage insurer and guarantor, Canada Mortgage and Housing Corporation (CMHC), which manages most of the securitisation of Canadian mortgages. CMHC operates in the secondary market through two programmes: MBS, which started in 1987, and the Canada Mortgage Bond (CMB) programme, which started in 2001. To be eligible for insured MBS or CMB, mortgages must be insured by way of federal statute, and this applies to all mortgages regardless of loan-to-value. In the case of CMB, the bonds are backed by pools of government-insured mortgages purchased by the Canada Housing Trust (CHT). The CHT was established in 2001 as a special purpose trust to purchase newly issued MBS pools and issue CMB, gaining the benefit of the government guarantee for mortgage loan insurance. This provides the basis for credit enhancement required by financial institutions and investors of Canadian mortgage assets.

Canada's approach is similar to that of both Japan, with the Government Home Loan Corporation, and Hong Kong, with the Hong Kong Mortgage Corporation. The government guarantee related to mortgage loan insurance is the dominant form of credit enhancement.

Australia and the United Kingdom restrict government participation to enabling legislation to achieve a market allocation of resources. The credit enhancement of mortgage assets is considered more flexible, but also more complex. While the pool size can be managed through bundling of assets and closed-end investment funds are common, there is little standardisation of the structure of securitisation contract. Australia allows for assignment programmes to pool mortgage loans on the balance sheet of a financial institution to an SPV. While some MBS is issued as a pass-through as in the United States, conduit programmes in Australia are the most common form of MBS, typically established by regional banks and financial intermediaries which lack the asset size to sponsor an assignment programme, without the credit support of a larger bank or facility provider. Among small financial institutions it is typical to warehouse mortgage pools until an adequate size is achieved to issue an MBS.

The securitisation of residential mortgages in the United Kingdom, which started in 1985, is similar to that in Australia, as it also facilitated strong mortgage credit growth. Even though UK mortgages are traditionally variable rate without prepayment penalties, a significant difference from North America, mortgage securitisation in the United Kingdom gained strong market presence. By 2000 residential mortgage securitisation was ready to advance into other European markets as banks went global to attract investors such as pension funds, insurance companies, and investment funds seeking high returns and diversification. The scale of residential mortgage securitisation in Europe has expanded. By 2008, there were a large number of market participants, including commercial banks of various sizes and monoline mortgage lenders.

Many European nations such as Denmark, Finland, Germany, Spain, Sweden, and France have mortgage bond legislation, supported by the central bank and a state-owned mortgage insurer and bank. European governments blend both direct and indirect actions to enhance mortgage lending, whereas the United States and Canada are more direct. For mortgage banks, covered mortgage bonds are an easy instrument to structure for residential mortgage lending, but require adequate pool size to achieve commercial attractiveness. Covered mortgage bonds are debt obligations issued by financial institutions for a pool of mortgages. They are subject to extensive statutory and supervisory regulation designed to protect covered bond investors from default risk. This legislative oversight has been generally lacking in the US mortgage system.

The main challenge for many emerging market economies is the relatively low credit rating of the financial institutions originating the mortgage pools. The first MBS in Russia was in 2006 for US $88.3 million with loans originated by JSC Vneshtorgbank (VTB), Russia's second largest bank. The credit enhancement for the 2006 VTB issue was provided by International Finance Corporation (IFC) in the form of a purchase of US $10.6 million Class B mezzanine notes. The active role of IFC as an investor, structurer, and credit enhancement provider assisted VTB in its goal to access long-term, cost-effective US dollar financing and to establish its name with European and US asset-backed investors. The increasing use of credit ratings, credit scoring, and market-standard securitisation structuring techniques by Russian originators is a necessary condition of financial intermediation in Russia.

It is still a reality that many regional housing markets often lack data on property valuation and the creditworthiness of the underlying assets and borrowers may be difficult to evaluate. This may be due to incomplete mortgage loans origination systems and limitations in underwriting that fail to fully account for the creditworthiness of borrowers. There are even institutional shortcomings in some nations that lack a system of land titles and mortgage registration. This highlights the importance of credit derivatives within international mortgage securitisation to market mortgage pools to investors. However, credit derivatives may not be enough and there are some limitations as to the breadth of international investment permitted as well as policies on asset quality among some investment groups.

Within the world banking community, securitisation is regarded as a way to not only enhance mortgage financing sources, as there is a limited retail deposit base, but also manage foreign exchange exposure and build global opportunities for growth. It is anticipated that a number of emerging economies will use residential mortgage securitisation to fill voids in retail lending directed towards housing finance to enhance homeownership. Government guarantees of mortgage pools; a combination of public and private mortgage loan insurance; and credit derivatives are considered essential for credit enhancement. In addition, the IFC will likely play a central role in the provision of credit enhancement for mortgage pools originating in emerging economies.

Structured Finance

The pricing of credit derivatives flows from the Black–Scholes option pricing model and the subsequent work of Robert Merton and others. The basis of this relation is the fact that a mortgage is a portfolio of a risk-free bond and an option to default. It is thus relatively straightforward to extend the traditional option pricing framework to mortgages and other fixed income instruments subject to default risk. Prior to Merton's 1974 work there was no systematic development of a theory for pricing bonds when there is a significant probability of default. Merton clarified and extended the Black–Scholes pricing model for options which at the time were just in their infancy in terms of importance as a financial instrument. Merton's work used comparative statics to develop graphs of the risk structure. The pricing of corporate liabilities is therefore derived from observable inputs, namely (1) the required rate of return on riskless debt, (2) the various provisions and restrictions contained in the indenture, and (3) the probability that the firm will be unable to satisfy some or all of the indenture requirements.

The market for credit derivatives has provided banks with new instruments for hedging and pricing loans. The link between credit default swaps and banks' pricing of syndicated loans illustrate that monthly changes in credit default swap spreads are very significant in explaining loan spread changes of the subsequent month.

Interest rate swaps and options along with cross-currency swaps have grown in importance and size since 1987, representing 75% of the derivatives market. Credit default swaps increased from $630 billion in 2000 peaking to $62 trillion in 2007, as **Figure 2** illustrates. The decline in the role of credit default swaps since 2007 highlights the market reality of the need to further restructure, refine, and regulate credit derivatives in general.

The vast amount of credit derivatives outstanding is not indicative of the exposure that any financial institution may have as there are typically offsetting hedge positions through the equity markets and through the use of options and debt-related instruments as well as collateral held against the potential failure of counterparties. However, credit default swaps are unique in that

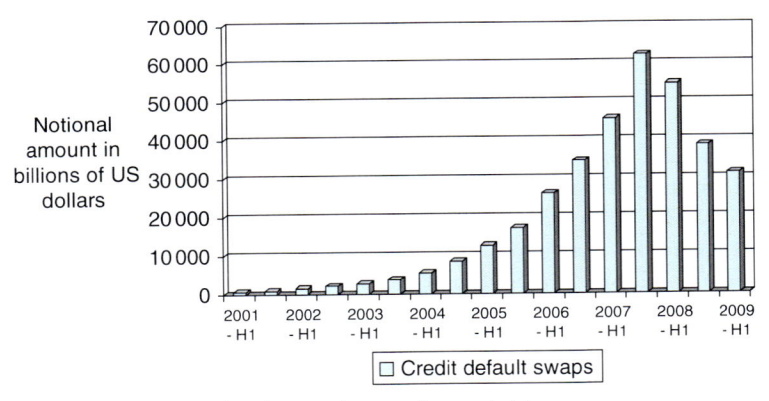

Figure 2 Credit default swaps outstanding: Notional amounts – semi-annual data.
Source: International Swaps and Derivatives Association. ISDA market survey, 2009.

collateral requirements require a strong credit rating to be maintained by the party taking on the credit risk. A downgrade in credit rating to a credit default or bond insurer triggers a collateral call and this can be sudden and significant, at amounts which could exceed capital reserves of financial institutions underwriting the credit default swap. (Lehman Brothers had an estimated $350 billion in credit derivatives settlement claims as of October 2008. AIG entered into credit default swaps to guarantee collateral debt obligations resulting in a $85 billion bailout from the federal government. The main basis for the financial threat at AIG came from several sources: (1) a decline in real estate prices and increasing mortgage defaults that reduced the market value of mortgage-backed securities; (2) the loss in investment value that impacted AIG's capital reserves, which would constrain AIG's ability to cover outstanding credit default swaps; (3) the downgrading of AIG's credit rating which triggered AIG's collateralisation requirements, which were conditions of the credit default swap contracts; and (4) collateral requirements that exceeded AIG's capital reserve and positioned AIG on the brink of collapse.)

The weakness in the system is that while the financial institution that issues the credit default swap can immediately recognise the premium to enhance the mortgage asset as income, it is not required to set aside an adequate capital reserve in the event of a settlement or collateral call. The financial incentive to write new credit default swaps can be suboptimal when there is no actuarial fund to secure the credit rating over time. The impact of this is heightened in the case of increasing mortgage defaults or other shocks that may impact the financial institution that issues credit default swaps.

Structured Housing Finance

The expansion of MBS issuances integrated the mortgage market with the capital market and enlarged the base for mortgage credit. This was important in nations where banks had seen a decline in bank deposits due to a rise in competing investments such as mutual funds. Multiple-class MBSs, known as collateralised mortgage obligations (CMOs), and real estate mortgage investment certificates/conduits (REMICs) offered investors different levels of prepayment risk, which made them a better match for investors with varying asset-liability preferences. These innovations in MBS, along with increased capital incentives for banks due to Basel minimum capital requirements, caused the composition of pass-through securities to increase since the 1970s. (An agency pass-through security is structured so that even under the worst circumstances regarding prepayments, the interest and principal payments from the collateral will be sufficient to meet the interest obligations of each tranche and pay off the par value of each tranche. Defaults are ignored because the agency that has issued the pass-through used as collateral is expected to make up any deficiency.) MBS/CMO can either be

- guaranteed by a government or government-sponsored (pass-through) agency (prior to September 2008, neither Freddie Mac nor Fannie Mae guarantees are backed by the full faith of the US government; however, each entity has a line of credit to the US Treasury); or
- private, nonguaranteed.

A common type of securitisation transaction is referred to as a lender swap transaction. Mortgage lenders that operate in the primary mortgage market will deliver pools of mortgage loans in exchange for, for example, GSE MBS backed by these loans. A GSE establishes a trust and takes a fee (retention of interest) to guarantee that principal and interest will flow to third-party investors. Private, nonguaranteed MBS/CMO increased in the 1990s. Investors typically made a trade-off between the guarantee of agency-sponsored MBS/CMO against the high return of private MBS/CMO. Counterparty risk involved in MBS/CMO comes from mortgage insurers; issuers, guarantors, and third-party providers of credit enhancements; mortgage investors; multifamily mortgage guarantors; and derivative counterparties. During the height of the subprime mortgage crisis in 2007, Freddie Mac reported ownership of almost $250 billion in nonagency MBSs; 27 different counterparties; and $1.3 trillion in derivatives largely to hedge benchmark interest rate risk. At the same time, Fannie Mae reported a $4.1 billion decline in the fair value of its derivatives (swap interest rates).

A credit derivative is unfunded in the case of a direct transaction where credit protection is bought and sold between bilateral counterparties. A funded credit derivative is a case of structured finance where a financial institution or an SPV uses securitisation techniques, such that a debt obligation is issued by the financial institution or SPV to support these obligations.

With GSE agency-sponsored MBS/CMO, investors do not bear credit risk and consumers benefit from low-cost mortgage loan rates. Nonagency MBS/CMO rely on subordinated tranches to provide credit loss protection, but still expose investors to institutional credit risk if the nature of the credit enhancement relies on a third-party credit default swap. Further protection comes by way of private bond insurance which had been rated AA or AAA, but in 2007 and 2008 bond insurers were downgraded by credit rating agencies (most notable was AIG's credit rating downgrade three levels on 16 September 2008 due to mortgage-linked derivatives). In the case of subprime mortgage the issuer could sell a quantity of bonds less than the value of the underlying pool of assets to account for a higher than expected default rate.

This protection is called overcollateralisation, but in the case of US subprime mortgages, as there was no history of default statistics, this was not deemed necessary as often no difference was distinguished among quality of residential mortgage classes when subprime mortgage originations were at their height in 2006 (see **Figure 6**). However, since 2007 investors began to recognise a substantial difference in quality among mortgage classes as defaults increased for Alt-A and subprime mortgage products (Alt-A or A-Minus are typically defined as self-employed borrowers (no documentation to verify income) or new immigrants to the United States (no US credit history) whereas subprime borrowers have little or no credit (below a Fair Isaac Corporation credit bureau score, FICO, of 580–620)) (see **Figure 6**). In some instances, a spread account is used as a measure to further protect investors. With a spread account the MBS issuer would pay a lower interest rate to investors than earned by the underlying pool of mortgages. The funds in the spread account are used to guarantee payments to the various tranches, thereby reducing credit risk, allowing some mortgage assets to become nonperforming without impacting cash flows.

Hedging instruments, such as options and futures, and institutions such as options and futures exchanges and clearinghouses allow financial institutions and investors to better manage cash flow risk from MBS/CMO. A decline in credit enhancements and credit downgrades used to support Alt-A and subprime mortgages restricts investment in the purchase of private MBS/CMO. **Figure 3** overviews CMOs which package mortgage pools in very complex structures to match investor returns and cash flow needs. Credit derivatives are an integral part of making these investments function.

CMOs are paid out subject to complex contracts. The senior tranche is represented by the highest credit rating, followed by the mezzanine tranche and finally the equity tranche. (It is apparent that credit rating agencies play a central role in the securitisation of mortgage assets as investors rely on accurate ratings as pension fund, endowments, and other investment policies strictly set forth the quality and grade of debt investments that fund managers can invest in. In the context of risk management, the bulk of the risks under the securitisation system are transferred to investors. Lenders keep only the liquidity risk and this may be a problem. The limitation of securitisation from a risk management perspective is that investors cannot measure borrower credit risk, but rely on third-party rating agencies. However, the quality and timeliness of the credit ratings have come into question. This raises the potential for misrepresentation of mortgage loan applications since investors and third parties do not have a direct role in underwriting. This can increase the liquidity risk and counterparty risk to very high levels.) Credit default swaps enhance the credit rating of underlying mortgage assets to achieve investor requirements. This further adds to the complexity of the payout of many mortgage pools. Valuing and hedging MBS is important, but typical models for pricing and hedging MBS focus principally on the effect of interest rates on mortgage prepayment. While MBS prices are primarily sensitive to interest rate fluctuations, house price movements also have a significant effect. Rising house prices stimulate mobility and may trigger prepayment. Conversely, falling house prices may trigger default. Prepayment and default must be regarded as substitutes when considering a model to price and hedge MBS. For example, a rise in the value of the default option must be accompanied by a fall in the value of the prepayment option. Support bonds absorb any principal prepayments that are made within a PAC tranche. However, when the support bonds are paid off due to prepayment, the PAC bonds schedule of planned

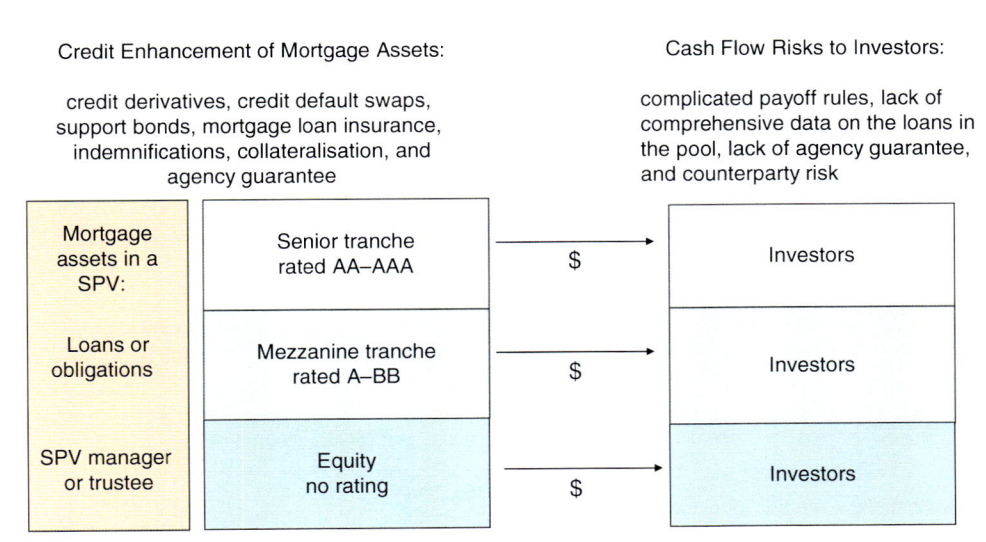

Figure 3 Collateral mortgage obligations packaging and payout on mortgage pools.

payments will not likely be maintained. PAC class bonds use different prepayment protection strategies and these are compared by investors.

Very accurately determined maturity bonds (VADMs) are supported by accrual or Z-bonds (Z because it is the last tranche to be paid out). In this instance, the interest that has accrued and not been paid out on a Z-bond protects the principal and interest on a VADM bond. In this regard the maximum final maturity can be determined in advance.

Mortgage Credit and Housing Markets

The synthetic securitisation process increased mortgage funding, particularly in the United States, the United Kingdom, and other European housing markets, with the most common being synthetic CDOs; credit-linked notes; single-tranche CDOs, and other similar products that increased private sector credit growth as noted in **Figure 4**.

Mortgage credit is regarded as an important determinant of the market demand for real estate. Deregulation, combined with phenomenal growth in the secondary mortgage sector, has resulted in a more liquid primary market that is now international in scope, as **Figure 5** illustrates. When the mortgage market mirrors the volatility of capital markets, lenders tend to offer significant front-end discounts on adjustable mortgages. (Financial market analysts often use the 10-year Treasury security rate as a surrogate for the long-term debt market. The size and liquidity of the Treasury market make it a good bellwether for other debt securities. Because Treasury bonds are free of default risk, the yield spread between mortgage rate and the 10-year Treasury rate is frequently used as a measure of the default risk premium on mortgages.) Overall, home price movements tend to track consumer credit levels.

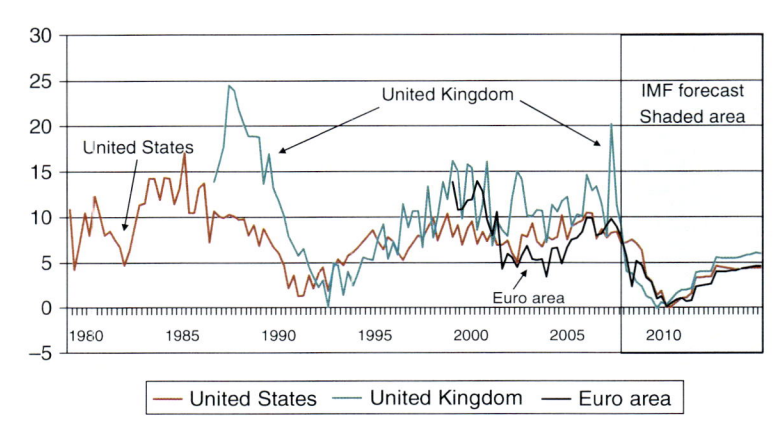

Figure 4 Private sector credit growth. Borrowing as a percent of debt outstanding, quarter on quarter annualised, seasonally adjusted.
Source: International Monetary Fund. Global Financial Stability Report, Financial Stress and Deleveraging, Macro-Financial Implications and Policy, 2008.

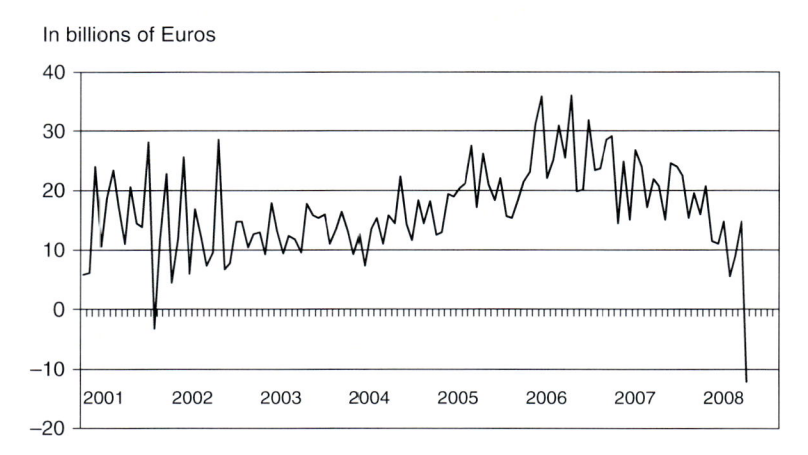

Figure 5 Euro area financial institution lending for house purchase.
Source: International Monetary Fund. Global Financial Stability Report, Financial Stress and Deleveraging, Macro-Financial Implications and Policy, 2008.

Credit derivatives have fundamentally changed housing finance globally, and the underlying housing markets served by the respective national mortgage system. Innovative mortgage products supported by credit derivatives have extended amortisations, kept downpayments to a minimum, and offered unique pricing features, to keep mortgage payments low.

The Complexities of Subprime Mortgage Lending

There is a hope that credit derivatives and loan pricing are subject to rigorous and complex pricing models. However, what has become apparent with subprime lending is that mortgage borrowers at the lowest range of the credit scale pose a substantial credit risk. These borrowers were traditionally excluded from obtaining mortgage credit. In fact, subprime mortgage products were introduced into housing finance without a history of credit default to ensure robust risk-based mortgage pricing. It may be that the secondary mortgage market and credit derivatives masked the problem, and combined with the US system of mortgage interest tax deductions, resulted in over-inflated US housing prices in markets exposed to subprime lending.

The ABX Index is useful to consider as it tracks a series of credit default swaps based on 20 bonds that consist of subprime mortgages. ABX contracts are commonly used by investors to speculate on or to hedge against the risk that the underlying mortgage securities are not repaid as expected. The ABX swaps offer protection if the securities are not repaid as expected, in return for regular insurance-like premiums. A decline in the ABX Index signifies investor sentiment that subprime mortgage holders will suffer increased financial losses from those investments. Likewise, an increase in the ABX Index signifies investor sentiment looking for subprime mortgage holdings to perform better as investments.

The ABX market illustrates that investors in mortgage pools can be exposed to potentially severe losses. The loss severity is large in a declining housing market where no- or low-credit-score mortgage borrowers with no downpayment, adjustable-rate mortgage (ARM) products, and extended amortisations found themselves in a negative equity position with little incentive or ability to keep current on mortgage payments. Subprime mortgage lending, which existed in only limited amounts until the late 1990s, exceeded 30% of mortgage loan originations in the United States by 2007 but only 5–10% in the markets of the United Kingdom, Australia, and Canada. The market reacted positively and more expeditiously than the regulators. As ABX market evidence indicates in **Figure 6**, investors became unwilling to hold subprime debt except at a deep discount during 2008. Financial institutions responded with a change to mortgage product offerings and more prudent underwriting practices and credit-granting rules.

Are Credit Derivatives Destabilising to Housing Finance?

The securitisation of mortgages is necessary for a well-functioning economy that supports homeownership. Credit derivatives are not destabilising, as these instruments do offer financial institutions various methods for hedging and transferring credit risks. What is problematic is the terms of some derivatives contracts which are often opaque, unregulated, and difficult to track on corporate financial statements by credit analysts. What appears to be destabilising is the magnitude of subprime lending which resulted in the pooling and

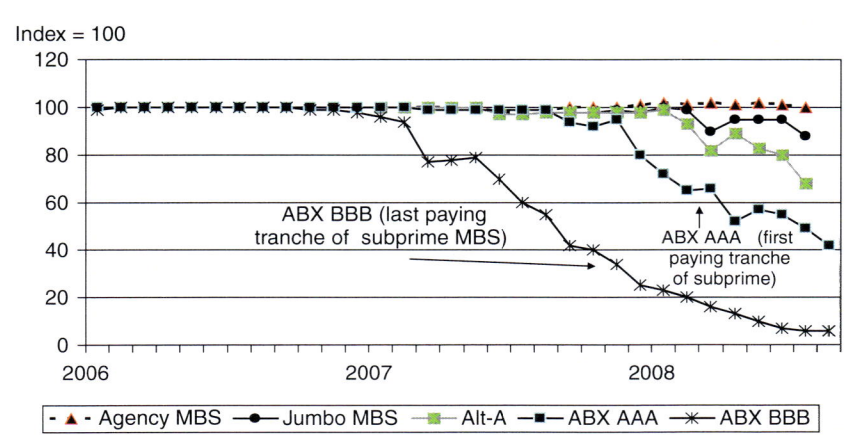

Figure 6 Prices of US mortgage-related securities (in US dollars). Note: Jumbo MBS in the United States include mortgage loans with values in excess of $417 000 (continental US) and as of February 2008 jumbo loans were substantially increased in some jurisdictions. Source: International Monetary Fund. Global Financial Stability Report, Financial Stress and Deleveraging, Macro-Financial Implications and Policy, 2008.

selling of mortgages to third parties within a system of complex payout schemes leading to government funding support.

Credit derivatives have come under scrutiny in recent years for a number of reasons:

1. The notional amount of financial instruments covered by over-the-counter derivatives exceeded $500 trillion by the end of 2008, according to the International Swaps and Derivatives Association (ISDA).
2. The settlement of credit derivative claims exposes potentially crippling losses to the impacted financial institutions, investors, and governments when there has not been a capital reserve set aside as part of the payment for the derivative (see **Figure 7**).
3. Public disclosure, comprehensive securitisation data, and regulatory oversight of credit derivatives have been lacking.
4. The decline in housing markets and rising default rate among mortgage markets coincided with a collapse in Alt-A and subprime MBS.

Figure 7 summarises both US bank mortgage assets and the 2008 US Treasury funding commitments to stabilise these assets. The federal takeover of two US GSEs which are at the forefront of the US mortgage system, Fannie Mae and Freddie Mac, took place on 7 September 2008 when losses at the two GSEs approached $15 billion and the disruption of the US mortgage credit system was at its height. The conservatorship of these GSEs is one of the most significant nonmarket actions of nationalisation in US history, and is directly related to the subprime mortgage market collapse. It was considered a necessary precondition by the US Treasury to commit up to $200 billion in preferred stock and extend credit through 2009 to keep the GSEs solvent to maintain mortgage credit for consumers. Between 2008 and 2010 the US Treasury extended $83.6 billion to Fannie Mae and $61.3 billion to Freddie Mac respectively, leading to an announcement in June 2010 by the FHFA that the shares of these GSEs be delisted from the New York Stock Exchange.

Legal Considerations

Although beyond the scope of this article, credit derivatives raise important legal considerations. For example, there are counterparty disputes where the seller of protection is trying to get out of its obligation to pay once a credit event occurs. There is also shareholder litigation where company shareholders that have entered into credit default swap contracts have had to make payments on the protection for which premiums were received, but claim that the company failed to disclose the risks posed by the credit default contracts. The US courts held in *Aon Financial Products v. Société Générale* (476 F.3d 90, issued in 2007 by the Second Circuit Court of Appeals; it relates to the financing of a condominium project in the Philippines) that credit default swaps are private contracts and this case among others illustrates that financial institutions and hedge funds can be exposed to substantial losses even following rigorous attempts to balance positions.

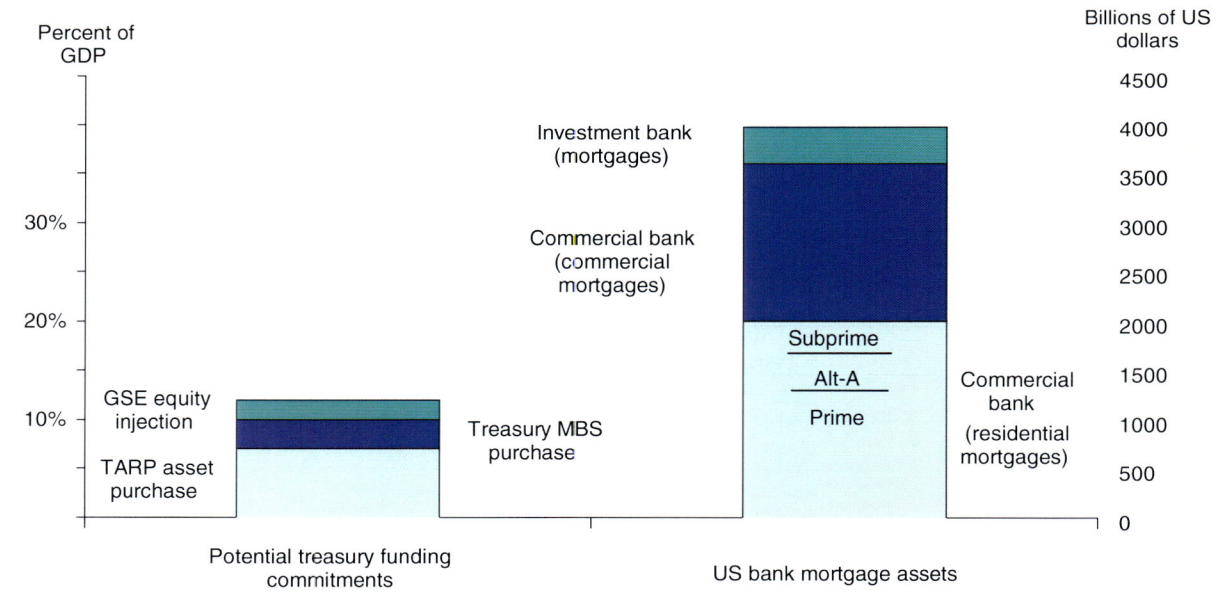

Figure 7 Potential US commitment in the mortgage market, 2008 and 2009.
Source: International Monetary Fund. Global Financial Stability Report, Financial Stress and Deleveraging, Macro-Financial Implications and Policy 2008. TARP: Troubled Asset Relief Program.

The legal specifics are even more complex as it becomes difficult to determine when a credit default swap contract legally triggers a credit default and payments are due to be made. The clearing of credit derivatives has become an important focus during the 2008 and 2009 financial crisis. Impacted financial institutions and investors commenced litigation to limit damages, claiming that there was misrepresentation and fraud during mortgage underwriting. Those who sold credit default swaps claim that these swaps are invalid if the mortgage origination was based on inaccurate property appraisals; false statements and omissions regarding borrower debt obligations; and unverified income for mortgage qualification.

Concluding Remarks

The credit derivatives market serves housing finance with important financial instruments that support new and innovative mortgage products and competitive mortgage loan rates. The consumer has benefited from the advances and changes to the mortgage system as homeownership rates in most nations have moved higher. Managing the fallout from failures in subprime mortgage lending is a challenging situation for financial institutions and regulators.

Credit derivatives, although complex and not without inherent shortcomings as the housing finance and mortgage system continues to evolve, have yet to be perfected. There is a need for financial institutions that issue credit default swaps to properly recognise potential liabilities at origination and set aside an adequate capital reserve to settle collateral requirements to support nonperforming mortgage assets. Mortgage securitisation may look to the corporate bond market for changes, resulting in more homogeneous and therefore less complex contracts, larger pool sizes, and more comprehensive data. This will allow credit analysts and investors a better opportunity to participate. Agency-sponsored CMO/MBS need to exercise prudence in terms of the mortgage products that qualify for these pools. Credit derivatives do not eliminate systematic risk in the economy and housing market downturns, and neither can they overcome risky mortgage products or flaws in mortgage loan origination and underwriting which can be the target of misrepresentation and fraud.

See also: Access and Affordability: Mortgage Guarantees; Government Mortgage Guarantee Institutions; Government Sponsored Enterprises in the United States; Mortgage Contracts: Flexible; Mortgage Contracts: Traditional; Mortgage Innovation; Mortgage Insurance; Mortgage Market Functioning; Mortgage Market, Character and Trends: United States; Mortgage Payment Protection Insurance; Post-Bubble Housing in Japan; Subprime Mortgages.

Further Reading

Black F and Scholes M (1973) The pricing of options and corporate liabilities. *Journal of Political Economy* 81: 637–654.

Childs PD, Ott SH, and Riddiough TJ (1997) Bias in an empirical approach to determining bond and mortgage risk premiums. *Journal of Real Estate Finance and Economics* 14(3): 263–282.

Downing C, Stanton R, and Wallace N (2005) An empirical test of a two-factor mortgage valuation model: How much do house prices matter? *Real Estate Economics* 33(4): 681–710.

Duffie D (2008) Derivatives and mass financial destruction. *Wall Street Journal* October 22: A 17.

Fabozzi F and Yuen D (1998) *Managing MBS Portfolios*. New Hope, PA: Frank J. Fabozzi Associates.

Green R, Sanders AB, and Wachter S (2008) Special issue on subprime mortgage lending. *Journal of Housing Economics* 17(4): 253.

Harrison DM, Noordewier TG, and Yavas A (2004) Do riskier borrowers borrow more? *Real Estate Economics* 32(3): 385–411.

Haworth H, Reisinger C, and Shaw W (2008) Modelling bonds and credit default swaps using a structural model with contagion. *Quantitative Finance* 8(7): 669–680.

International Monetary Fund (2008) World economic and financial surveys. *World Economic Outlook: Financial Stress, Downturns, and Recoveries*. October, Washington, DC: International Monetary Fund.

International Swaps and Derivatives Association (2009) *ISDA Market Survey*. New York: ISDA.

Merton R (1974) On the pricing of corporate debt: The risk structure of interest rates. *Journal of Finance* 29: 449–470.

Mints V (2007) Securitization of mortgage loans as a housing finance system: To be or not to be. *Housing Finance International* December: 23–28.

Mortgage Insurance Companies of America (2009) *2009–2010 Fact Book*. September, Washington, DC: Mortgage Insurance Companies of America.

Norden L and Wagner W (2008) Credit derivatives and loan pricing. *Journal of Banking and Commerce* 32: 2560–2569.

Pavlov A and Wachter S (2006) The inevitability of market-wide underpricing of mortgage default risk. *Real Estate Economics* 34(4): 479–496.

Shiller RJ (2008) *The Subprime Solution: How Today's Global Financial Crisis Happened, and What To Do about It*. Princeton, NJ: Princeton University Press.

Stiglitz JE and Weiss A (1981) Credit rationing in markets with imperfect information. *American Economic Review* 71: 393–410.

Relevant Websites

www.fanniemae.com – Fannie Mae annual reports.
www.freddiemac.com – Freddie Mac annual reports.
www.ifc.org – International Finance Corporation.
www.markit.com – Markit, the leading resource on the ABX market.
www.isda.org – International Swaps and Derivatives Association for market date on credit default swaps.

Crime Prevention through Environmental Design

G Steventon, Coventry University, Coventry, UK

© 2012 Elsevier Ltd. All rights reserved.

Glossary

Defensible space External spaces in residential areas that are linked to dwellings in a way that residents perceive a sense of proprietary concern over them, bringing them under residents' control such that they defend them against intrusion or threat.

Environmental determinism The doctrine that credits all social events, including those involving human choice, with causes that arise in the environment.

Informal social control The processes (active such as watching and taking action; passive such as social networks and the transmission of attitudes and values) by which conformity and self-policing is maintained in residential neighbourhoods, instigated by residents themselves without recourse to formal agencies of control such as the police.

Natural surveillance The watching over of a person or place by residents while going about their daily lives facilitated by good visibility of surrounding areas and properties.

Situational crime prevention Physical adaptations made to a context or environment to reduce the opportunity for crime.

Spatial theories Theories which seek to explain human behaviour as a product of the context or environment in which it takes place.

Zoning An aspect of town planning where specific land uses, such as housing, commercial, or industrial, are separated into discrete areas or zones.

Introduction

Crime prevention through environmental design (CPTED) is a globally adopted place-based approach to the design and effective use of the environment with the aim of reducing crime and the fear of crime and improving the quality of life for its users. Also known as designing out crime, the underlying assumption is that certain aspects of the built environment facilitate crime because they provide the opportunity for crime to take place, and/or inhibit the processes of informal social control, owing to the way that spaces are planned and subsequently used. By designing out the elements that facilitate crime and designing in those that encourage residents to adopt proprietary attitudes over spaces around their homes, it is argued that crime and its associated problems can be prevented or at least reduced in residential areas. As well as improving the physical security of individual properties, the objectives are also to make the offender visible, thereby increasing the risk of detection and apprehension, and provide a suitably well-maintained environment that signals residents' pride in their area such that a sense of ownership and belonging is conveyed. CPTED therefore aims to achieve both passive and active security of residential environments through a range of measures that focus on harnessing the territoriality of residents and building community solidarity and cohesion, including natural surveillance, access control, target hardening, image maintenance, and activity support.

Since its conception in the mid-twentieth century, CPTED has enjoyed growing popularity, becoming an integral part of government crime prevention policy in many countries, most notably the United States, United Kingdom, and Australia. However, it has also been subjected to criticism about the lack of rigour in its theoretical base, namely that its focus on the contribution of physical aspects of the environment to crime fails to take account of social factors, such as the demographics and resident dynamics of an area. As a result, later developments in CPTED have moved beyond what have come to be known as the first-generation CPTED strategies based purely on physical interventions to a more refined model known as the second-generation CPTED. This model of crime prevention incorporates measures to reinforce social cohesion through active citizenship and community participation and links informal social control with formal control measures such as community policing.

The Development of CPTED

Interest in CPTED as a crime prevention strategy developed in the United States from the early 1970s and became popularised through the work of spatial theorists, such as Oscar Newman, although its roots can be traced back a decade earlier to the work of Elizabeth Wood and Jane Jacobs.

Elizabeth Wood was a strong advocate of using the design of the physical environment to enrich the quality of life for its inhabitants. Through her work in deprived neighbourhoods for the Chicago Housing Authority, she observed the relationship between the physical characteristics of the environment, for example poor aesthetic quality, and the way people reacted to it. From these observations, she formulated some guidelines on security and crime prevention, including improving the visibility of and from residential apartments to increase surveillance and providing spaces for social interaction since areas that lacked use tended to be subjected to a breakdown in informal social control.

Jane Jacobs was an activist, writer, and commentator on urban life and city planning. From her observations of how cities work in some of the larger American conurbations, Jacobs argued that modern urban planning policies based on the zoning of land were destroying urban social life. By separating out what urban planners deemed to be incompatible uses (e.g., housing and commercial or industrial) into discrete areas necessitating increased car use, and the rebuilding of dilapidated areas with unsympathetically scaled developments, this process of sanitisation had removed much of the vitality of life that characterised older, mixed-use areas, thereby destroying the sense of neighbourhood community that often existed in them. Jacobs advocated a return to the design of cities based on the diversity of use and high density in order to bring back the dynamism of residential neighbourhoods that was lacking in zoned planning. She argued that the mixing of uses, such as inserting housing into retail and commercial areas (e.g., apartments over shops), in high-density configurations ensured vibrant patterns of activity for prolonged periods of day and night, thus ensuring safety and security through the presence of people and the natural surveillance that they provide. The emphasis on surveillance and social interaction in both Jacobs' and Wood's ideas on crime prevention influenced the subsequent development of spatial theories based on territoriality and defensible space. However, while their ideas have filtered through to contemporary thinking on CPTED, it was defensible space that had the greatest impact on the first-generation CPTED and led to it being framed in government crime prevention and planning policies, particularly in the United States in the 1970s and in the United Kingdom a decade later.

Although the term CPTED can be credited to American criminologist C. Ray Jeffery in 1971, his work had little influence on its development. Jeffery developed a multidisciplinary approach to crime prevention that linked external factors in the environment to the internal environment of the offender. Drawing on psychological learning theory, Jeffery emphasised the role of the physical environment in providing pleasurable or painful experiences that could impact on an individual's consequent behaviour. He suggested that control could be stimulated through a system of rewards and punishments administered in the environment through the interaction of the mind of the offender with these environmental stimuli. While these ideas gained little credence at that time, their influence is nevertheless apparent in the theoretical links with situational crime prevention – an approach that some argue forms part of the second-generation CPTED, while others suggest is a closely related but separate sphere of crime prevention because its focus has moved beyond the context of local environment into other areas, such as product design. The similarity in both approaches, however, is that prevention occurs from adjustments made to the physical environment to block the opportunity for crime by impacting on the rational decision making of the offender about the risk and reward of the crime.

While Jeffery's focus lay with the environment's influence on the motivation of the offender, his counterpart, Oscar Newman, was more interested in its influence on members of the community. Acknowledging Jeffery's contribution, Newman developed his defensible space theory in 1972, based on the notion that territoriality can be precipitated by the appropriate design of architectural features and building layouts, and it was this work that arguably established CPTED as a promising new approach to the study of crime and its prevention. As an architect, Newman's interest lay in the way in which certain features of building design facilitated crime. Through researching crime in medium-rise housing projects in New York, Newman noted how crimes were habitually located in certain areas of the housing blocks, such as stairways, elevators, and deck accesses, where little supervision by residents could occur because these areas were usually remotely situated from the routine observation and influence of individual units of accommodation. As a result, residents failed to adopt proprietary attitudes over these spaces. From these observations, Newman developed his theory of defensible space in which he claimed that the design of housing areas could be crucial in combating crime by facilitating natural surveillance and harnessing the territorial responses of residents to intrusion, providing an image of a close-knit community who cared about the spaces around their homes and were prepared to protect them. The defensible space approach not only became influential, but also enjoyed almost a cult status as a new way forward in dealing with crime, particularly in residential neighbourhoods. It also became embedded in social policy; for example, in UK planning policy from the early 1990s onwards, local authorities could require housing developers to consult with the police through a scheme known as Secured by Design, a police-inspired and administered scheme in which they provide advice according to a checklist of design principles based on defensible space. This approach to crime prevention was not without its critics, however, the main criticism being the overly deterministic assumptions about the causal powers of the environment to precipitate human behaviour that are inherent in defensible space theory – assumptions which take no account of social factors, such as communities divided by conflict or ethnic diversity, or neighbourhoods characterised by transience in which individuals or social groups have little vested interest and where a social sense of responsibility and belonging is absent. It was the lack of consideration of social factors in this form of CPTED that weakened its ability to deliver and led to a more robust approach that has shaped the contemporary crime prevention landscape.

Contemporary Principles of CPTED

In what is commonly referred to as the second-generation CPTED, contemporary approaches have acknowledged the problems inherent in the first-generation CPTED strategies based on spatial theories. However, that is not to say that the fundamental principles have been abandoned – territoriality and natural surveillance are still the cornerstone of CPTED-based initiatives, but included now are the need to carry out risk assessment, to assess socioeconomic and demographic issues, and to promote social cohesion and connectivity by establishing active community participation rather than assuming that these will simply arise from environmental adjustments alone. Six main areas of intervention can be identified as important in contributing to crime prevention efforts: territorial reinforcement, increased surveillance opportunity, access control, target hardening, image management, and activity support, all of which are interdependent.

Territorial reinforcement involves harnessing the natural defensive precepts that residents are considered to adopt when they are aware of outside intrusion into what they perceive as their space. The objective of design therefore is to organise spaces in a way that extends the sphere of influence of residents and increases their sense of control. In addition, spaces with clearly defined and designated purposes that are routinely cared for and monitored signal to intruders that they are at risk of identification or apprehension. Territorial definition can be achieved through clear demarcation of private and public spaces through the use of real and symbolic boundary markers, such as fences, walls, hedges, and landscaping. Surveillance is an integral part of territorial reinforcement and aims to heighten the visibility of spaces in order to ensure intruders are observable and therefore at greater risk. It may take the form of natural surveillance of public spaces and adjacent buildings by inhabitants through windows and doors of buildings, or by people moving through the environment, or it may take the form of systems such as closed-circuit television. Design can directly affect the monitoring capability within the environment by the layout of dwellings to optimise intervisibility, which has been found to be an important component in preventing crime. Good outdoor lighting coverage where glare and deep shadows are avoided increases surveillance after dark and has also been shown to improve street usage at night with benefits for informal social control.

Access control and target hardening are to all intents and purposes the same. They both aim to deny offenders access to targets and increase their risk in carrying out a crime in a specific place. Although target hardening as a generic term can be said to encompass all crime prevention activities that set out to achieve the aim of deterring the offender by making the target less attractive through increasing the risk or reducing the reward, in the context of CPTED it normally refers more specifically to security strengthening measures such as locks, bars, alarm installations, and other forms of physical barriers. Access control on the other hand sets out to restrict access through the use of informal and natural measures such as spatial definition, or formal and organised arrangements such as security patrols. First-generation CPTED strategies based on defensible space have tended to support access control through the elimination of through routes in residential developments to minimise access and escape for intruders, producing enclave housing formations, such as the cul-de-sac. However, in concurrence with Jane Jacobs' earlier observations, subsequent research has demonstrated the value of surveillance afforded by passing pedestrians on active streets that is rarely achieved in cul-de-sac configurations. Furthermore, housing environments with lack of pedestrian movement can increase the fear of crime of residents by heightening their awareness of strangers, and feelings of entrapment can arise in some cul-de-sacs with singular access/egress. In contemporary CPTED strategies, therefore, it is recognised that some access in itself is not a problem and may be beneficial provided adequate levels of surveillance are maintained; it is the unsupervised routes that facilitate crime and should be designed out.

Image management is based on the theory that cues of neighbourhood decline, such as graffiti, damage to property, and extensive littering, signal that an area is not cared for and lacks adequate informal social control. For residents this process increases fear of crime, whereas for offenders it indicates that they can operate with relative impunity, thus allowing the infiltration of petty crime, which can escalate into more serious crime and a spiral of decline if these processes are left unchecked. Image management is therefore important in ensuring that visible and social cues of decline are dealt with by routine maintenance to present a positive image.

Activity support sets out to ensure that spaces are used appropriately so that vulnerable activities can take place in the safest context. Research has suggested that places that appear safe will attract usage linking to the idea of busy streets being safe streets, and the increased usage adds to the safety. Of course, it is important to recognise that with the whole notion of designing out crime the types of crime likely to be prevented are mostly acquisitive crimes, such as burglary, theft and car crime, and criminal damage to property. Solutions to some problems may give rise to unintended consequences. For example, busy streets may help to reduce the incidence of burglary but may increase the risk of pickpocketing.

Theoretical Critique

The theoretical basis of CPTED states that for a criminal event to take place, three interrelated factors need to converge in time space: a motivated offender, a suitable target, and the absence of capable guardians. Known as routine activities theory, this proposition analyses the contribution each factor makes to the propensity for crime in a given place at a given time. Routine activities are important in the analysis of all three factors. First, offenders are known to commit crime in areas they inhabit on a regular basis, which allows them to form a cognitive awareness of what kind of elements of an environment provide opportunity and therefore identify suitable targets. Second, the routine activities of capable guardians, such as the residents of an area, dictate the level of guardianship available at any point in time. Opportunity for crime arises when the presence of an offender coincides with a vulnerable target that offers a sufficiently attractive reward at a time, or in a situation, when the likelihood of observation and apprehension are limited. The aim of designing out crime therefore is to address any or all of these issues to reduce or eliminate the opportunity.

From the point of view of the offender, the theoretical basis of CPTED has its foundations in Classical Theory, which emphasises the role of free will in human action and the fact that humans instinctively seek to maximise pleasurable or gratifying experiences and avoid painful or unpleasant ones. Motivation to commit an act such as a criminal offence is based on the rational decision-making process the offender undertakes when faced with an opportunity taking into consideration the extent of the risk involved in relation to the reward to be gained. Risk involves the likelihood of getting caught and punished and may be based on various constraining factors, such as the time available to the offender or his/her ability to carry out the crime. Reward is the pay-off for the crime that satisfies the needs or desires of the offender and may take the form of money, goods, status, sex, or excitement, or a combination of these factors. On the assumption that there will always be a supply of motivated offenders, the aim of CPTED is to remove the motivation in a given context by removing the opportunity for crime, by either increasing the risk or decreasing the reward for the offender or simultaneously achieving both. However, CPTED can never address the crime problem in its broader sense as it does not seek to resolve issues of poverty, deprivation, and social exclusion that arise from structural causes of inequality in society, with which most crime is associated. Nor can it address nonopportunist crimes that relate, for example, to alcohol and drug abuse where, perhaps through desperation, the offender is prepared to use whatever force is necessary to overcome the barriers that a CPTED strategy may erect.

The target and its guardianship are the aspects of routine activities theory on which designing out crime interventions focus. Target hardening is often a relatively simple and cost-effective measure but there is the possibility that excessive security can give rise to a fortress effect that may signal a crime problem where none exists. Problems of guardianship associated with zoned land use, whereby residential areas are devoid of occupation or activity for most of the working day, are gradually being tackled by planning objectives that utilise mixed-use developments, witnessing a return in favour of the empirical wisdom of Jane Jacobs. Acknowledgement of social factors that impact on local crime problems is a step forward in answering the critics of environmental determinist theories. However, successful strategies are those that allow not only for interrelationship between the social and the spatial, but also understand the social in terms of the way in which wider social forces and structural processes that derive from wider society impact on human behaviour at a local level. For example, designing out crime that is built around the notion of territoriality may serve to provide exclusive and excluding formations of housing layout that reflect separatist social desires, the realisation of which is most starkly represented in the gated community. Trends towards individualism can produce socially fragmented and atomised communities that challenge strategies which seek to engender citizenship, neighbourhood cohesion, and mutuality. Desires to lead privatised lives and the demand for screening of individual properties to avoid overlooking militate against strategies based on surveillance. Nevertheless, the move from the first-generation to the second-generation CPTED has brought improvements from a perspective that saw crime prevention largely as a defensive endeavour, in which the threat was external to the community and could therefore be designed out to one that acknowledges that crime may well flourish within and that brings different challenges.

The Future of CPTED

It is clear from its global ubiquity that CPTED in some form or other is here to stay. The fact that it has been able to develop from a limited theoretical base has given credence to its wide uptake and its contribution is generally seen to be worthwhile. However, some commentators are more guarded about where its future lies in crime prevention; its effectiveness has been demonstrated through research and yet it is not unequivocally supported. Part of the problem is the need for greater conceptual and definitional clarity, the lack of which has tended to result in varied application, and contradictions inherent in the conceptual framework as outlined earlier in this article have left the approach open to accusations of following fashion, which may then leave it open to shifts in political agenda.

A further concern is that strategies based on CPTED are self-limiting if they are interpreted and delivered by practitioners with little or no experience of the design process. Application in such a way invariably leads to design checklist solutions, whereas design should offer a more imaginative approach to overcoming specific problems, not only in the present but also in the future; in other words, adaptable to the changing trends in both context and crime in order to be responsive to need in a cost-effective way. It is also important to note that communities face issues other than crime, and enlightened policies set out to build capacity in communities with the ultimate aim of sustainability through a wide palette of social and spatial interventions, such as neighbourhood revitalisation and support for families, delivered through multiagency partnerships incorporating evidence-based practice. Within this framework, CPTED has a role and its contribution may be valuable, but it is far from all-encompassing; its effectiveness will always be a part of the wider strategy of crime prevention.

See also: Defensible Space; Gated Communities; Housing Dynamics: Environmental Aspects; Neighbourhood Incivilities; Neighbourhood Watch; Social Sustainability; Sustainable Communities; Sustainable Regeneration.

Further Reading

Brantingham PJ and Brantingham PL (1991) *Environmental Criminology*, Revised edn. Prospect Heights, IL: Waveland Press.

Clarke RV and Felson M (1993) *Routine Activity and Rational Choice*. New Brunswick, NJ: Transaction.

Cozens P, Saville G, and Hillier D (2005) Crime prevention through environmental design (CPTED): A review and modern bibliography. *Journal of Property Management* 23(5): 328–356.

Crowe T (2000) *Crime Prevention through Environmental Design: Applications of Architectural Design and Space Management Concepts*, 2nd edn. Oxford: Butterworth-Heinemann.

Ekblom P (1995) Less crime, by design. *The Annals of the American Academy of Political and Social Science* 539: 114–129.

Hillier B and Shu S (2000) Crime and urban layout: The need for evidence. In: Ballintyne S, Pease K, and McLaren V (eds.) *Secure Foundations: Key Issues in Crime Prevention, Crime Reduction and Community Safety*, pp. 224–248. London: Institute of Public Policy Research.

Jacobs J (1961) *The Death and Life of Great American Cities*. London: Penguin.

Jeffery CR (1971) *Crime Prevention through Environmental Design*. Beverly Hills, CA: Sage Publications.

Newman O (1972) *Defensible Space: Crime Prevention through Urban Design*. New York: Macmillan.

Plaster Carter S (2002) Community CPTED. *The Journal of the International Crime Prevention through Environmental Design Association* 1(1): 15–24.

Saville G and Cleveland G (2003a) An introduction to 2nd Generation CPTED: Part 1. *CPTED Perspectives* 6(1): 7–9.

Saville G and Cleveland G (2003b) An introduction to 2nd Generation CPTED: Part 2. *CPTED Perspectives* 6(2): 4–8.

Schneider R and Kitchen T (2002) *Planning for Crime Prevention: A Transatlantic Perspective*. London: Routledge.

Steventon GJ (1996) Defensible space: A critical review of the theory and practice of a crime prevention strategy. *Urban Design International* 1(3): 235–245.

Wilson JQ and Kelling GL (1982) Broken windows: The police and neighbourhood safety. *The Atlantic Monthly*, March: 29–38.

Criminological Perspectives on Homelessness

V Lyon-Callo, Western Michigan University, Kalamazoo, MI, USA

© 2012 Elsevier Ltd. All rights reserved.

Glossary

Broken windows legislation A theoretical approach to community development popular in the 1990s arguing that enforcing minor code violations and criminal ordinances could reduce violent crimes and spur economic development.

Criminalisation of homelessness The enactment of legislation resulting in criminal punishment for vagrancy or criminally prohibiting a variety of behaviours associated with homeless people.

English Poor Laws A series of policies enacted in England from the fourteenth to nineteenth centuries which specified punishments and, later, reforms for poor, homeless, or vagrant people.

Gentrification The process of policy interventions aimed at promoting more affluent people to move into a neighbourhood to displace poorer residents, thus promoting urban redevelopment.

Housing First A strategy for combating homelessness embraced by advocates for homeless people in the early twenty-first century which prioritised providing housing for homeless people prior to other criminal or social service interventions.

Quality of life policing Policing that built upon the broken windows framework to emphasise prosecution of minor offenses with the goal of decreasing overall crime and enhancing community development.

Introduction

To understand the experience of homelessness as well as responses to homeless people, it is important to consider the criminalisation of homelessness. Although criminalisation has taken different forms in different times and places, there is a several-century tradition in Europe and North America of criminalising public poverty. The punishing of homeless people has often been represented as a strategy for helping homeless people. At other points, it is clearly about assisting with social or economic development strategies. Exploring the historical and contemporary manifestations of criminalisation as well as alternative practices and policies helps to illuminate why criminalisation of homelessness occurs and how successful such strategies are at addressing the conditions producing homelessness.

History of Criminalisation of Poverty and Homelessness

Communities have responded to public poverty and homelessness in a range of ways throughout history. Sometimes homelessness has largely been accepted as a natural consequence of individual traits or social conditions. Alternatively, some religious orders, including Hinduism, Buddhism, mendicant orders of Catholicism, and some versions of Islam, have promoted poverty, begging, and giving alms to poor people as paths to spiritual enlightenment. A few political and governmental efforts have actively worked to ban or end homelessness by guaranteeing the right to housing. At other times, homelessness has been criminalised.

Responding to poverty and homelessness by criminalising behaviours of poor people can be traced back many centuries. One of the first such legislative efforts was the Ordinance of Labourers of 1349, which was the first of the English Poor Laws. Enacted in response to labour shortages due to high mortality resulting from the Black Death, this ordinance required that anyone under the age of 60 worked while setting restrictions on both begging and collective bargaining. The goals of increasing and maintaining the supply of potential labourers while keeping wages down were met by criminalising the efforts of poor people to either opt out of waged labour or to try to improve their economic well-being.

In 1495 a revised version of the Poor Laws added the punishment of 3 days in the stocks with a diet of bread and water for the crime of begging or being an idle person. After the 3 days, the person was made to leave town. A half century later, the 3 days in the stocks were replaced by a public whipping and then, in 1547, vagrancy became punishable with 2 years of servitude for a first offense and death for a second. Much like efforts to criminalise homelessness today, these legislative interventions did little to address structural conditions. Rather, they served to discourage one from not being employed and to remove homeless people from the community.

The Poor Laws were altered somewhat in the seventeenth and eighteenth centuries as workhouses were established to house, punish, and morally reform vagrants and other poor people. Similar efforts were made in the United States throughout the eighteenth and nineteenth centuries with poor houses and poor farms to care for and reform perceived shortcomings within poor people. The poor farms often focused on local members of a community. These were supplemented by antivagrancy laws which covered a range of behaviours such as loitering and drunkenness. Antivagrancy laws in the United States were also used to control the movement and labour of homeless former slaves following the end of slavery as well as itinerant workers and hobos in the early twentieth century.

The poor houses and poor farms in England and the United States were accompanied by an increasing pathologising of poverty during the nineteenth and twentieth centuries. Homeless people were increasingly represented as suffering from social, physical, or emotional pathologies, making them unwilling or unable to earn or retain enough money to house themselves. The criminalisation of some behaviours was accompanied by new professions such as social work aimed at governing and reforming the bodies and behaviours of poor people. This intervention strategy of medicalisation on the one hand being accompanied by criminalisation on the other hand came to dominate policy responses to homelessness by the end of the twentieth century.

Antivagrancy statutes in England went largely unenforced for most of the late twentieth century. But, as the number of homeless people began to increase in the 1980s and 1990s, enforcement increased. Legal challenges to antivagrancy laws occurred in the 1960s in the United States. These challenges resulted in the narrowing and clarifying of the specific crimes for which people could be prosecuted. As in England, as homelessness increased during the 1980s and 1990s in the United States despite the helping efforts aimed at reforming homeless people, communities across the United States increasingly adopted ordinances criminalising a wide range of behaviours associated with public homelessness. Communities in Canada, Australia, and elsewhere began to adopt similar strategies of criminalising homelessness during this period.

Criminalisation of Homelessness in the Twenty-First Century

The criminalisation of homelessness takes several different forms and occurs in nations throughout the globe. India, Australia, Canada, Brazil, England, Italy, Japan, Hungary, and Rwanda are some of the many nations actively enforcing legislation punishing behaviours associated with homelessness in the early twenty-first century. The forms differ slightly in each location, but what is fundamentally the same is that criminalisation takes the form of public policy designed to remove homeless people from being visibly poor in certain regions. The nation that has perhaps embraced criminalisation of homelessness the most is the United States.

Homelessness in the United States moved from an emerging public policy concern in the 1980s to a routine part of the social landscape across the nation by the late 1990s. Increased homelessness was met by a tendency for governments and business communities to advocate and enact legislation punishing the public behaviours of homeless people as a policy working in tandem with social service interventions increased. The early twenty-first century has seen both an increasing number of homeless people, with the number of homeless people often exceeding the space in homeless shelters, and escalating legislative interventions promoting criminal justice responses to homelessness. Furthermore, documented increased incidents of violent crimes against homeless people on the streets of cities across the United States have accompanied the increased criminalisation of homelessness.

As court rulings have held that the generalised antivagrancy statutes of early historical periods were too broad to be constitutional, municipalities have focused legislation on more specific behaviours. These often include:

- prohibitions against sleeping/camping in public spaces
- restrictions on where, when, and how begging or panhandling can take place; these are often focused on downtown shopping districts, tourist areas, or areas of cities undergoing gentrification
- limitations on how food can be distributed or shared
- prohibitions on sitting or lying on sidewalks
- enforcement of 'quality of life' laws such as jaywalking, squeegeeing, loitering, urinating in public, or open container laws; advocates for homeless people suggest that these laws are often selectively enforced against homeless people
- 'truth in begging' statutes which make it a fineable offence to misrepresent why you need money or what you intend to spend it on

These types of ordinances criminalising behaviours associated with homelessness are increasingly popular in communities throughout the United States. A 2009 report by the National Law Center on Homelessness & Poverty and the National Coalition for the Homeless – "Homes not Handcuffs: The Criminalization of Homelessness in U.S. Cities" – examined policies in 235 cities. The report found 49% with restrictions on begging or panhandling, 33% with prohibitions on camping in public places, and 30% with restrictions on sitting or lying in some public spaces. Santa Cruz, California, was one of the first few cities to pass a 'truth in begging' law. The 1994 ordinance outlawed lying about why they needed money or what they intended to do with it as well as forbidding panhandling at bus stops, public benches, or on public property.

In 2010, San Francisco's mayor Gavin Newsom proposed an ordinance which would ban sitting or lying on public sidewalks in 20 commercial districts throughout the city. The proposed ordinance was based upon similar laws in Santa Cruz, California; Seattle, Washington; and Portland, Oregon. Proponents explained that the aim was to increase safety and security for merchants and shoppers and not to punish homeless people. They explained that the city had many social service programmes to help homeless people who wanted the assistance including Mayor Newsom's 'care not cash' programme in which social service workers were teamed with police officers to offer social services followed by citations for people violating laws on littering, trespassing, urinating or defecating in public, public intoxication, or blocking sidewalks. Advocates for homeless people expressed concern about the teaming of social service workers with police officers as well as whether housed people would be treated the same as homeless under the effort.

Meanwhile, the city commission in Miami, Florida, debated a policy to enact a $300 fine for giving food to another person in the downtown area. Los Angeles made it illegal to sleep in public beaches after midnight in 2009. This was similar to a ban on public camping in Boulder, Colorado, which resulted in over 1500 nights in jail for those unable to pay the $100 fine between 2006 and 2010. Chicago banned all begging and Orlando, Florida, required a permit to ask for money in most areas of the community. Many communities have replaced park benches with new ones that contain bars dividing seats and thus discouraging lying down on benches. Others restrict the hours one can sleep in public parks, how close to ATM machines or banks people can beg, or what food can be salvaged from dumpsters.

Similar ordinances have been put in effect throughout Canada. Ontario, Canada, enacted the Safe Streets Act in 1999 which outlawed aggressive panhandling. Advocates for homeless people in Ontario suggest that the law primarily targeted homeless youth in Toronto who relied upon squeegeeing, or the cleaning of windshields in traffic to solicit money. The law was upheld despite several efforts to challenge the constitutionality of the ban. Windsor and Ottawa ban all panhandling. Vancouver, Hamilton, and Fredericton restrict panhandling in public parks while Kingston and Vancouver have regulations placing restrictions on loitering or gathering in public. Laws criminalising behaviours associated with homeless people became widespread and routine across North America during the early twenty-first century.

Criminalisation and the Olympics

An interesting, yet not widely discussed, example of the connection between gentrification and the criminalisation of homelessness relates to cities hosting the Olympics and similar large athletic events. At least since the 1992 Olympics in Barcelona, there has been a growing tendency for host cities to enact new legislative measures designed to clear the areas around the Olympic villages of poor and homeless people. Atlanta moved homeless shelters away from the Olympic area and instituted a series of ordinances, including one making it illegal to walk through a parking lot unless you had a car parked there, which were designed to drive homeless people from the area in preparation for the 1996 games. Sydney, Australia, followed this model and passed laws criminalising homelessness in areas where visitors to the Olympic Games were likely to visit. Beijing and Vancouver continued this precedent with the 2008 and 2010 games. In a similar move, India utilised the Bombay Prevention of Begging Act to clear Delhi of beggars for the 2010 Commonwealth Games. World Cup games have resulted in similar strategies such as Seoul's banning homeless people from particular parts of the city where attendees were likely to stay during the competitions.

Not only have recent Olympic events led to the criminalisation of homelessness in host cities, but there is also evidence that the buildup to the Olympics helps produce increased homelessness, which is then criminalised. Beijing's construction of Olympic facilities was used as a rationale for gentrification of the surrounding community through new construction which displaced many low-income people from their formerly affordable housing. Local advocates claimed that homelessness nearly tripled in Vancouver as a result of new construction and the removal of low-income housing leading up to the Winter Olympics in 2010. In response to Chicago's bid, advocates for the homeless expressed their lack of support for the 2016 games in the city due to the threat that the games posed to the rights of poor and homeless people.

A United Nations Human Rights Council report of March 2010 documented this tendency of city planners throughout the globe to use Olympic and World Cup events as opportunities for furthering particular strategies of urban economic development which are largely characterised by new construction, displacement of poor people, gentrification, and criminalisation of homeless people.

Why Criminalise Homelessness?

Although punishing and criminalising poor people has been a practice utilised in different times and places across the globe for centuries, the extent to which such policies are being implemented increased dramatically during the first few years of the twenty-first century. How do we understand that tendency?

Several different explanations are offered by policy-makers, advocates, and social scientists who study the trend of increased criminalisation. Interestingly, political and business leaders in communities which have embraced criminalisation as an intervention strategy often suggest that those policies are designed with benevolent intentions. There are three dominant ways in which an argument is made that criminalising behaviours of homeless people are helpful. These are often based upon an assumption that homeless people are in need of being policed or reformed for their own well-being and a perception that homelessness is caused by shortcomings within people who become homeless.

One popular argument suggests that homeless people are often in need of rehabilitative services that they are unable or unwilling to assess without prodding. Several cities have teamed police with social service outreach workers. People on the street are given a choice between getting their purported deficiencies repaired through social service interventions or being fined by the police. Policing is represented as an incentive to move homeless people to accept the services which are represented as helpful to them.

Not all proponents of criminalising homelessness advocate the need for social services. In this situation, homeless people are represented as lacking the work ethic or self-responsibility to get and maintain employment and housing. This is often accompanied by a sentiment that food programmes, people giving money to panhandlers, and allowing sleeping or sitting in public spaces make it too easy for homeless people to maintain that lifestyle choice. The suggestion is that the intervention of the criminal justice system would make it more difficult for those living on the streets to survive and, thus, more homeless people would choose to work themselves out of poverty.

A third rationale often stated for criminalising homelessness is that doing so will help foster economic development and gentrification. As can be seen with the Olympics or the 2010 effort to enact ordinances regarding sitting or lying on sidewalks in San Francisco, criminalisation efforts are often targeted at specific behaviours in what are represented as strategic locations of cities. Locations are most often downtown business districts, areas that cater to tourism, or regions targeted for gentrification or redevelopment efforts. The expressed logic is that people begging, sleeping on the streets, or urinating in public in those areas discourage business interests and curtail economic development. How does that help homeless people? The reasoning given is the purported belief that economic growth will lead to more job creation, which will then create more opportunities for people to become employed.

Of course, not all communities criminalising homelessness have expressed benevolent intent. Sometimes, the goal of supporting local businesses is stated without the accompanying rationale of helping local poor people. Aggressive panhandling is represented as a public nuisance that causes economic loss to businesses as it turns away potential customers. Likewise, there is often an explicit goal of simply removing the inconvenience of public homelessness from communities. This is sometimes expressed by local politicians arguing that less restrictive communities attract homeless people and allow poor people to be comfortable with their homelessness. The response is often one of simply removing homeless people from particular locations or, at least, controlling their public behaviour in those areas. A moral concern that able-bodied people should be working and self-supporting is often articulated as a rationale as well. Some cities in India, for example, make distinctions between those people who have to beg to support themselves and those who have other means of possible support but simply choose to beg instead.

Another reasoning stated for criminalising begging in some communities, especially in parts of Europe and Asia, is a belief that there are organised crime interests that prosper from organising and controlling people begging in cities. Purportedly, people are imported into cities explicitly to be exploited as beggars. In most cases, though, actual evidence supporting this as a widespread practice has been difficult for law enforcement personnel or policy-makers to obtain.

Finally, advocacy organisations and homeless activists offer a slightly different explanation for the laws becoming increasingly popular in the twenty-first century. The notion of compassion fatigue is expressed as an explanation. The thinking is that as homelessness has continued to remain pervasive after three decades, housed people have become increasingly tired of trying to help homeless people.

Social scientists who study the issue of criminalisation of homelessness often provide slightly different explanations than those offered by policy-makers, business leaders, or advocacy organisations. Some have suggested that it should not be surprising that citizens become tired of public homelessness considering the ways in which a social service solution to homelessness was often advanced during the 1980s and 1990s. Widespread homelessness began to occur in the early 1980s as affordable housing decreased and poverty increased, but a popular belief was that homelessness could be resolved through charitable and social service interventions aimed at fixing perceived deficiencies within homeless people rather than by addressing issues of increased systemic inequities. When social service solutions failed to be effective, communities turned to criminalising homelessness.

These scholars often suggest that in order to understand how compassion fatigue and the criminalisation of homelessness have come to make sense, it is necessary to consider the broader social and historical context within which policies are enacted. During that period in the United States, there was a marked increase in economic inequality, a globalisation of manufacturing jobs which once provided middle-class wages for many workers, declining real wages for much of the population, decreased tax rates, declining numbers of affordable housing units and support for publicly supported housing, and a dramatic increase in policing and the imprisonment of members of the population. It is suggested that shifting public policies and business behaviours have produced increased economic instability, declining community cohesion, and increased emotional insecurity. Policing has been represented as a possible source of regaining security and stability such that, within that context, criminalisation becomes laudable.

The quest for a return to economic and social stability through policing has been the focus of much policy discussion surrounding related efforts, most often connected with quality of life policing, the zero tolerance policing enacted in New York City in the 1990s under former Mayor Rudolph Giuliani, or the broken windows theory of economic development advanced by James Wilson and George Kelling. Each of these approaches advocates that serious crime can be prevented or economic development can be fostered by proactively policing minor offences (such as jaywalking, graffiti, or panhandling) and antisocial behaviours. Where programmes to repair broken windows, increase policing of minor offenses, and plant flowers on urban streets have been represented as key to a return to security and prosperity, some scholars suggest that policies that criminalise homelessness logically follow.

Effectiveness of Criminalising Homelessness

Measuring the effectiveness of any public policy largely depends upon a subjective interpretation of the goals of the intervention. With criminalisation of homelessness, there are a range of goals which are sometimes stated and sometimes not. Further complicating the matter is that decreased crime rates and economic development have sometimes been represented as being the result of quality of life or zero tolerance policing, which may also be read as more of a correlation than a causation according to some recent scholarly work. Therefore, it becomes difficult to assess how well the policies have worked. What can be acknowledged, however, is that criminalising homelessness has done little to actually decrease homelessness.

Advocacy organisations such as the National Coalition for the Homeless suggest that criminalisation policies do not decrease homelessness because they do nothing to address the underlying causes of homelessness. Of course, there is no clear agreement on the causes of homelessness, but advocates suggest that arresting and charging people who are homeless may make them less likely to receive needed services and more difficult for them to obtain employment and housing. Furthermore, when jobs that pay wages sufficient to afford housing are difficult to obtain, simply making it more difficult and uncomfortable to survive while homeless does not provide an alternative way of living for those people.

Alternatives to Criminalisation

There are several alternatives to criminalising homelessness that have been attempted. Finland, for example, decriminalised begging in 2003. Even within the United States, where many cities have recently embraced policies of criminalisation, there remain many other communities that do not do so. Several communities chose not to prosecute formerly housed people who began camping illegally on public property or sleeping in their cars in the wake of the severe economic recession that began in 2008. However, most often this camping did not occur in downtown business districts.

A 2009 report by the National Coalition for the Homeless and the National Law Center on Homelessness and Poverty on criminalisation describes several examples of municipalities where service providers, city officials, and business groups came together to provide housing and employment opportunities or access to coordinated food sharing programmes as alternatives to criminalising poor people.

Advocates have also suggested a housing first policy. The housing first approach would prioritise the strategy of housing homeless people as an alternative to criminalising or reforming people.

Another alternative to criminalisation would involve building the social movements necessary to move towards a just political and economic system that is less dependent upon exploitation thereby producing a society with less systemic inequities. That possible intervention, however, has thus far received little popular support.

Conclusions

Public policies that criminalise behaviours associated with homeless people, although common throughout recent history, became increasingly popular throughout the world in the early twenty-first century. The policies are often represented as resulting from desires to help homeless people overcome perceived deficiencies or dysfunctions on an individual level, spurring economic development in key areas of municipalities by improving quality of life, or resulting from housed citizens becoming tired of seeing other helping efforts prove unsuccessful. Social scientists studying these interventions suggest that, while quite popular, they have proven to be a failure at actually decreasing homelessness.

See also: Ethnographies of Home and Homelessness; Homelessness: Causation; Policies to Address Homelessness: Housing First Approaches; Rights, Citzenship, and Shelter; Social Justice; Social Movements and Housing.

Further Reading

Amster R (2008) *Lost in Space: The Criminalization, Globalization, and Urban Ecology of Homelessness*. El Paso, TX: LFB Scholarly Publishing.

Beckett K and Herbert S (2008) Dealing with disorder: Social control in the post industrial city. *Theoretical Criminology* 12(1): 5–30.

Duneier M (1999) *Sidewalk*. New York: Farrar, Strauss, and Giroux.

Gans H (1996) *The War against the Poor: The Underclass and Antipoverty Policy*. New York: Basic Books.

Hopper K (2003) *Reckoning with Homelessness*. Ithaca, NY: Cornell University Press.

Katz M (1900) *The Undeserving Poor: From the War on Poverty to the War on Welfare*. New York: Vintage Books.

Lensky HJ (2008) *Olympic Industry Resistance: Challenging Olympic Power and Propaganda*. Albany, NY: State University of New York Press.

Lyon-Callo V (2004) *Inequality, Poverty, and Neoliberal Governance: Activist Ethnography in the Homeless Sheltering Industry*. Guelph, ON: Broadview Press.

Mitchell D (2001) The annihilation of space by law: The roots and implications of anti-homeless laws in the United States. In: Blomley N, DeLaney D, and Ford RT (eds.) *The Legal Geographies Reader*. Malden, MA: Blackwell Publishers.

National Coalition for the Homeless (2006) *Hate Crimes and Violence against People Experiencing Homelessness*. Washington, DC: National Coalition for the Homeless.

National Law Center on Homelessness & Poverty and the National Coalition for the Homeless (2009) *Homes Not Handcuffs: The Criminalization of Homelessness in U.S. Cities*. Washington, DC: National Coalition for the Homeless and National Law Center on Homelessness & Poverty.

Wacquant L (2009) *Punishing the Poor: The Neoliberal Government of Social Insecurity*. Durham, NC: Duke University Press.

Wilson JQ and Kelling G (1992) Broken windows: Police and neighborhood safety. *The Atlantic Monthly*. March.

Critical Realism

P Somerville, University of Lincoln, Lincoln, UK

© 2012 Elsevier Ltd. All rights reserved.

Glossary

Critical realism The belief that reality exists independently of the human mind but cannot be completely or certainly known.
Epistemology A theory of knowledge, of how the world is known or can be known.
Fallibilism The belief that our knowledge of reality can always be shown to be false.
Foundationalism The belief that our knowledge of reality has sure foundations – that is, it can be proved to be true.
Idealism The belief that reality is to be identified with our ideas of it – that is, our conceptualisations, social constructions, discourse, and so on.
Neo-institutionalism The study of institutions as shapers of people's actions and perceptions, within broader social environments.
Ontology A theory of being or existence, of how the world is or can be.
System A set of entities that are necessarily related to one another.
Transcendental argument An argument that a proposition must be true in order for another proposition to be true, and the truth of the latter proposition is already known.

Critical Realism – A Critique

The nature of critical realism is disputed but is commonly associated with the work of Roy Bhaskar. Following Sayer, it can be characterised as a combination of a realist ontology (or theory of being, of how the world is) with a fallibilist epistemology (or theory of knowledge, of how the world is known). Realism here means the belief that reality exists independently of the human mind, with the latter being typically understood as perception (the observer), cognition (the knower), or thought (the thinker). Fallibilism is the belief that our knowledge of reality always has a chance of being proved wrong, that is, our knowledge has no sure foundations. Sayer argues that the two beliefs are logically connected in that it is precisely because reality exists beyond human thought that we cannot be sure of our knowledge of it.

Critical realism is usually assumed to be antifoundationalist, that is, as denying the possibility that knowledge has sure foundations. The belief that our knowledge has no sure foundations, however, itself lacks foundation, that is, it is fallible. In other words, we can never be sure whether or not our knowledge has sure foundations. Arguably also, fallibilism should hold for the belief in realism itself; that is, the belief that reality exists independently of the human mind has no sure foundations. Consequently, not only can we not be sure whether our beliefs about reality and our possible knowledge of it are true but we also cannot even be sure about how unsure we should be about the truth of these beliefs (I call this a nonfoundationalist position). Yet, as Hume recognised, life goes on as before – observing, naming, categorising, analysing, theorising, evaluating, acting, and so forth.

Realists assume that realism must be true in order to explain why our knowledge of reality is fallible – an example of what Kant called a transcendental argument. There are other possible reasons, however, why our knowledge is fallible: our capacity for knowing could be defective, for example, or reality could be constantly changing, or both. There does not seem to be any way of deciding which of these possibilities is more likely. The argument for the transcendental argument therefore appears unconvincing.

As well as offering beliefs about the world and our possible knowledge of it, critical realists make substantive claims about the world, for example, that it has different 'layers': empirical, actual, and real. On closer inspection, however, these terms appear to refer to things we already know in the world, namely, experiences, events, and objects. It is not clear that translation of these constituents of the world into 'layers of reality' adds anything to our knowledge. Similarly, with regard to social reality, critical realists appear to subscribe to a form of 'analytical dualism', according to which 'structure' and 'action' are interdependent and mutually constitutive but not reducible to each other. The precise nature of these structures and actions, however, is left to be specified by research.

It seems reasonable to assume that our knowledge is part of the world – because, if it were not part of the world, where would it be? So, if critical realism tells us nothing new about the world, then it follows that it tells us nothing new about our knowledge of the world. So what is it for? A common argument here is that critical realists function as 'under-labourers' for the sciences; that is, although they create no new knowledge themselves, they facilitate the creation of knowledge by others. It is by no means clear, however, that critical realists do perform such a facilitative role, or even that scientists are in need of their philosophical assistance. One might ask why it is not possible, or indeed preferable, for scientists to develop their own theories and research designs for themselves.

Perhaps, however, the value of critical realism lies in its function as critique, for example, of forms of positivism (crudely understood as seeking regularities, as in the search for statistical associations between variables) and interpretivism (crudely understood as seeking meaning rather than causes). Certainly, Sayer (2000) contains a good deal of criticism of variants of postmodernism, strong social constructionism, and anti-essentialism, to name but a few. The thrust of his criticism is that all of these currents of thought appear to deny that there is a reality outside of thought itself, with 'thought' being expressed in discourse or language or whatever. I take him to be saying that these currents of thought all involve varieties of idealism, that is, a belief that reality is to be identified with our conceptualisations (or social constructions) of it. Clearly, this belief contradicts realism.

The realist critique of idealism is problematic, however. Sayer seems to think that strong social constructionists, for example, although claiming to be antifoundationalist, must be foundationalists. In fact, however, critical realists, no less than strong social constructionists, seem to have foundational beliefs (namely, in favour of, rather than opposed to, the independent existence of reality). If we take fallibilism seriously, then neither realism nor idealism has sure foundations. One can be just as fallible about one's own social constructions as about the world that lies beyond those constructions. A more logical position, therefore, would be that of nonfoundationalism, as outlined above.

Critical realism also involves a distinctive approach to research. The argument is that if we conceive the world as consisting of dispositions, series of events, and systems of relations, then we are able to make more and better sense of it. Critical realists criticise traditional approaches in research, for example, those that attempt to identify regularities among sequences of events. This is expressed most forcefully by Sayer (2000: 14):

> . . . for realists, causation is *not* understood on the model of regular successions of events, and hence explanation need not depend on finding them, or searching for putative social laws. The conventional impulse to prove causation by gathering data on regularities, repeated occurrences, is therefore misguided; at best these might suggest where to look for candidates for causal mechanisms. What causes something to happen has nothing to do with the number of times we have observed it happening. Explanation depends instead on identifying causal mechanisms and how they work, and discovering if they have been activated and under what conditions.

There are some problems with this line of argument, however. First, the identification of such 'causal mechanisms' cannot prove that realism itself is true (or false) — the causal mechanisms may or may not exist independently of thought. The commitment to identify causal mechanisms is therefore not exclusive to a realist position (consider Kant's position of transcendental idealism). Second, if the causation has nothing to do with observational regularity, how does it come to be known in such a way that there is a chance of proving otherwise? If, say, we have observed something to happen only once or a small number of times, how can we be sure that this has not happened by chance? If we take fallibilism seriously, then arguably the postulating of causal mechanisms must be subject to observational testing of some kind.

In social research, the issue is often one of wanting to know the effects of a particular intervention without necessarily having much knowledge of the causal mechanisms involved. Interventions are made without clear understanding of their potential effects, with the result that it becomes difficult, if not impossible, to establish whether the observations that follow the intervention are actually effects of that intervention or not. So-called realistic evaluation does not help here because it appears to fall short of identifying particular causal mechanisms, let alone explaining what effects those mechanisms could have.

In the absence of a theory of the field (in Bourdieu's sense) in which the intervention takes place (such a theory needs to generate hypotheses that can be tested in the field), the most valid research method would appear to be that of randomised control trials (RCTs). This is because such trials rely on the random selection of a requisite variety of contexts in which the intervention is or is not to take place; statistical comparison of the differences between the contexts of intervention and nonintervention then enables the identification of real effects of the intervention. It is important to note, however, that the causal mechanisms whereby those effects are produced remain unknown. For this reason, RCTs cannot substitute for theory development, whether realist or otherwise.

Critical Realism and Housing (Homelessness and Housing Systems)

Critical realism has not figured greatly in housing research. Homelessness, however, has been a topic that has received some attention from critical realists, particularly in relation to the search for its causes. So, let us consider homelessness from a critical realist standpoint and see where the argument leads.

First of all, what is homelessness? Is it empirical, actual, or real; that is, is it an experience, an event, or an object? For critical realists, it is all of these things: it is experienced by those who become homeless, it is an event in their lives that can be observed by others, and it is a socially structured object that can be investigated and analysed by researchers. The nature of homelessness, however, is contestable: definitions and interpretations can vary. If we cannot agree on what homelessness is, then how can we agree on what its causes might be? Fitzpatrick (2005) argues that, although experiences and events vary, it is possible to identify 'real' homelessness as a condition that emerges from a range of separate and complex 'pathways' into and through homelessness. 'Real' homelessness exists whether or not it is experienced as such and whether or not people agree on what actually counts as homelessness. 'Real' homelessness is a state of being that results from specific sequences of interconnected events in people's lives.

Considered over time, therefore, homelessness is a 'realistic' category. If we assume this to be correct, what then could be the causes of homelessness? At this point, Fitzpatrick's account becomes problematic in a number of respects. First, criticising Williams (2003) for his rejection of homelessness as a realistic category, she writes "Homelessness [unlike Greekness, as used by Williams] is not a cultural phenomenon, but rather a signifier of objective material and social conditions." Unfortunately, this resurrects the old chestnut of the distinction between 'structure' and 'culture', with the former being equated with 'objectivity' and the latter with 'subjectivity'. In reality, however, 'culture' can have structure and 'structure' can include culture. In the case of homelessness, for example, it could be argued that it is possible only in a sedentary culture, where it is assumed that people should have fixed spaces in which they reside or dwell. In any case, Fitzpatrick's assertion is probably tautological, because she has already constructed homelessness as having to do with complex pathways, which are not be understood as 'cultural' products. Homelessness can, however, be defined in other ways, for example, as rootlessness, which looks more like a cultural phenomenon. Perhaps the lesson to be (re)learnt from this is that homelessness is not *just* a realistic category but also has cultural significance – or, to put it more correctly, the reality of homelessness is cultural as well as material.

A second problem for Fitzpatrick is that the category of homelessness lacks conceptual coherence. What is required here are "overlapping, shared (but not necessarily identical) experiences which give rise to similar impacts on individuals (that is, similar emergent attributes and causal tendencies)". It is interesting to note that this sounds remarkably similar to the observed regularities sought by nonrealists. Currently, however, it is not clear if what is generally regarded as the homeless population meets this regularity requirement. As Fitzpatrick puts it, there is a "question mark over the appropriate scope of the 'real' conceptualisation of homelessness".

Given this uncertainty about whether homelessness is a realistic category at all, or whether instead only realistic subcategories can be identified, such as single rough sleepers or occasional hostel dwellers or family bed-and-breakfast residents, it seems that further research may be required before it becomes possible to identify the mechanisms that cause homelessness. (The very concept of a realistic category, at least as outlined by Fitzpatrick, is suspect. What emerges from her analysis is a construction of homelessness, not as a state of being but as a sequential repeated pattern of specific experiences associated with specific emergent attributes. This is surely a variant of Hume's constant conjunctions, which she earlier criticised as positivist.) Fitzpatrick hypothesises a number of factors that could act as such mechanisms (economic structures, housing structures, patriarchy, and individual attributes). These mechanisms, however, with the possible exception of patriarchy, seem little more than an elaboration of the structural and individual factors that form the 'new orthodoxy' of homelessness explanation that she criticised earlier in her article.

The question here is how are the hypotheses to be operationalised and tested? In a process of what might be called retroductive testing, Fitzpatrick notes that poverty seems to be universally implicated in the causation of homelessness, not just directly through inability to afford housing but also indirectly "through an array of necessary ('internal') and contingent ('external') relationships" involving other causal mechanisms. The feedback loops involved "can be interpreted as increasing the 'weight of the weighted possibility' of homelessness amongst certain poor people".

Given the lack of specification of these feedback loops or of the weights of the different causal mechanisms apart from poverty, this analysis does not seem to say much more than that poverty is the primary risk factor for homelessness, while other factors are secondary. The relationship between primary and secondary factors and the relative importance of the different secondary factors (in different circumstances) are only briefly discussed. Consequently, it is not clear from this that whether introducing a critical realist interpretation adds anything to what is already known about homelessness. Indeed, an analysis of risk factors (criticised earlier in the article as positivistic) seems preferable in that it has, for example, clearer potential predictive value.

Arguing from the position of a critical realist model of contextual rational action theory, Nicholls (2009) provides evidence to show that homeless people themselves can be (partly) responsible for increasing the "weight of the weighted possibility" of their homelessness, in a variety of ways such as substance misuse, prostitution, noncooperation with the authorities, and transgression generally. This is important for showing how critical realism can take agency seriously, and this in turn reveals that homelessness as a realistic category may be even less coherent than envisaged. The sheer variety of individual experiences of, and responses to, homelessness suggests that the scope for overlapping, shared experiences giving rise to similar impacts may be very small indeed.

Nicholls ends her article with a challenge: "The next step is to theorise the causation of homelessness with social structures explicitly written back in." It is not clear how this is to be done, however, when social theory in relation to homelessness remains so undeveloped and when both the effects and capacity of agency continue to be so little understood. Moreover, if Fitzpatrick is right about poverty being the main cause of homelessness, there is an argument for giving more priority to identifying and tackling the causes of poverty than the causes of homelessness.

As noted above, Lawson (2006) is an exceptional piece of work in many ways. It acknowledges a considerable debt to critical realism in steering a course between positivism on the one hand and interpretivism on the other. It attempts to analyse the social relations of housing provision in Australia and the Netherlands, providing extremely rich and detailed case studies of the two countries. It distinguishes between necessary and contingent relations, and identifies causes in terms of the former. Its focus seems clearer than that of homelessness in that it studies each national housing system as a whole. In so doing, it provides an example of what a wider analysis of housing using a critical realist framework can look like.

The distinction between necessary and contingent relations, however, is insufficiently clear. Although Lawson talks of housing systems in terms of clusters of relations of both kinds, the concept of a (national) housing system remains unanalysed. Is it a realistic category or not? Once again, it seems that critical realism in itself does not help to identify real causes, and problems always remain about knowing whether causes have been correctly identified. (For example, Lawson identifies an underlying cause as associated with fundamental change, but the association only works "under the right contingent conditions". Critical realism does not help to identify what can count as fundamental change, what causes such change, or what can count as the right (or wrong) contingent conditions.) In any case, as already noted above, the identification of causes can be undertaken without necessarily subscribing to a realist position (for more details see article on Path Dependency).

Actually, Lawson inclines towards something more akin to a neo-institutionalist or systems approach because of the way, for example, she identifies 'roots' of causality in different forms of housing provision (based on historically and geographically specific relations of property, finance, and labour) and because of her use of neo-institutionalist concepts such as those of embeddedness, path dependency, and institutional fix. No doubt she found critical realism very helpful in her work but, with hindsight, it does not seem to have been necessary for her undoubtedly considerable achievement.

Conclusions

Critical realism is a philosophy that aims to assist the growth of scientific knowledge by clearing up conceptual confusions, removing obstacles to clear thinking, pointing to how science needs to be developed, and so on. Where it succeeds in its aim to act as underlabourer to the sciences, however, it does not appear to add anything of value to our knowledge. This is because, as argued here, critical realists have not reflected sufficiently on the foundations of their own knowledge. They consider themselves to be fallibilist, but they hold to the truth of realism, which appears to be unfalsifiable. They consider themselves to be antifoundationalist, but they believe that realism is the foundation of all (fallible) knowledge. They are critical of idealism, but they fail to see that it is a mirror image of their own position. They have a distinctive approach to research, which is laudable in many ways (e.g., the search for causes, the advocacy of fallibilism), but which does not need the realist belief that accompanies it and may not be entirely compatible with fallibilism itself.

On homelessness, for example, despite some sterling efforts, it appears that critical realists have not as yet significantly improved our understanding or even assisted others to do so. They have not pointed to new ways of doing research into homelessness that could be fruitful, nor have they suggested how new kinds of theory might be developed that would provide more satisfactory explanations of what causes homelessness. The causal mechanisms identified by Fitzpatrick lack precise specification, thus failing to supersede an analysis in terms of risk factors. Arguably, as Somerville and Bengtsson (2002), and Nicholls have advocated, more medium-range theorising such as contextual action theory could help to remedy our current lack of understanding of the complex causation of homelessness. Alternatively, research into the reasons why people become homeless could be broadened and deepened to include research into the reasons why they are (and by and large remain) poor.

Lawson is the exception here, in that, from a critical realist perspective, she has substantially increased our understanding of how housing systems work. In this case, however, it seems that critical realist thinking, except insofar as this involves an awareness of the limitations of positivism and interpretivism, was not crucial in producing this theoretical progress.

See also: Homelessness: Causation; Path Dependency; Philosophical Perspectives on Home.

References

Fitzpatrick S (2005) Explaining homelessness: a critical realist perspective. *Housing, Theory and Society* 22(1): 1–17.

Lawson J (2006) *Critical Realism and Housing Research*. London: Routledge.

Nicholls CM (2009) Agency, transgression and the causation of homelessness: a contextualised rational action analysis. *European Journal of Housing Policy* 9(1): 69–84.

Sayer A (2000) *Realism and Social Science*. London: Sage.

Somerville P and Bengtsson B (2002) Constructionism, realism and housing theory. *Housing, Theory and Society* 19(3–4): 121–136.

Stones R (2001) Refusing the realism-structuration divide. *European Journal of Social Theory* 4(2): 177–197.

Williams M (2003) The problem of representation: realism and operationalism in survey research. *Sociological Research Online* 8: 1. www.socresonline.org.uk/8/1/williams.html

Cultural Analysis of Housing and Space

D Lu, University of Sydney, Sydney, NSW, Australia

© 2012 Elsevier Ltd. All rights reserved.

Glossary

Material culture Refers both to the psychological role and the meaning of all physical objects in a particular culture and to the range of manufactured objects that are typical within a culture and form an essential part of cultural identity. Human beings perceive and understand the material things around them as they have learned to from their culture. It also refers to the approach that archaeologists adopt to understand the general articulation of past human societies by inferring what the less permanent aspects of cultures may have been like from the material record they have left behind.

Vernacular architecture Is a term used to categorise the dwellings and other buildings of the people constructed by using locally available resources and traditions to address local needs. Based on knowledge achieved by trial and error and handed down through local traditions, vernacular architecture reflects the climatic, geographical, economic, cultural, and social context in which it exists.

Housing, Culture, and Cross-Cultural Analysis

Amos Rapoport's book *House, Form and Culture* (1969) has been a pivot document in advancing the understanding of cultural variables in housing. Based on a wide range of examples across cultures, Rapoport demonstrates that there is a rich variety of housing even given similar functional, economic, technical, geographical, or climatic factors. While the form of housing is influenced by the interplay of all factors, cultural factors should be considered as primary. This is because a house is not just a physical structure but a cultural entity which supports a way of life. Through collective assent, certain ways of building and dwelling are accepted and obeyed in a traditional community, which express distinctive values and norms of the community. Although any one traditional society tends to be highly homogeneous, great diversity occurs cross-culturally.

In his subsequent research, Rapoport continued to explore the role of culture in the variability of housing from the perspective of Environment-Behaviour Studies (EBS). His approach was influenced by sociologist Talcott Parsons, whose theory of 'structural functionalism' explained human action as the result of four systems: the 'behavioural system' of biological needs; the 'personality system' of an individual's characteristics affecting their functioning in the social world; the 'social system' of patterns of units of social interaction; and the 'cultural system' of norms and values that regulate social action symbolically. Following the 'behavioural turn' in social sciences, Rapoport and other EBS scholars concentrated on the observable social manifestations of culture rather than its more vague traits. Rapoport conceptualised housing as a system of settings which accommodate certain systems of activities with four components: activities themselves, how they are carried out, how they are related to other activities, and their meanings. The different ways and meanings of food preparation, for instance, have a great impact upon the settings of the activity. As there are always many ways to meet certain needs, choice is an essential factor in understanding the cultural aspects of housing. In traditional society, choices in housing design are often made within severe constraints, but they nonetheless convey worldviews, values, behaviour patterns, identity, and social status of the owners. A social community living in a region often follows systematic choices, which result in a characteristic housing form. In modern society, choices made among a wide range of alternatives lead to specific lifestyles of special-user groups, such as the urban rich, the gay community, and the elderly. With cultural variables changing at a faster pace, and the increasing need to communicate individual identity, it is considered that open-endedness should be an important function of housing.

Cross-cultural analysis of housing has been an important approach among EBS scholars. Its basic premise is that there exist some comparable, universal patterns of traits despite variability, and it is possible to compare cultural traits taken out of their immediate context. A comparative method is adopted to test the hypotheses and theories that are proposed to explain the variation. Compared with holocultural studies, cross-cultural analysis allows researchers to measure cultural variables and draw correlations based on a range of variation in housing. There have been attempts to compare room arrangement, space use, rules of sex division, expressions of values, and social status in housing across cultures. These studies help to evaluate the range and distribution of cultural variables in housing. Roderick Lawrence's comparative study of a range of architectural, cultural, social, and psychological variables in housing design of several countries, for example, has convincingly illustrated the importance of the cultural dimension in housing policies.

Vernacular Architecture

In the field of architecture, the interpretations of housing and culture have been shaped by the circumstances of different times. The question of housing was central to interwar modernism. Architects claimed that new architecture was the best tool to alleviate housing scarcity and rehumanise the modern city. While they espoused new technologies to create the ideal 'minimal dwelling', many of them also studied local housing cultures and applied selected aspects in their designs. By the 1960s, however, most architects in Western societies had abandoned social agendas that characterised modern architecture of the previous era; housing gradually developed into a separate discipline. With the rise of consumption-orientated society amid post-Second World War prosperity in the West, earlier modernist doctrines were questioned, and new aesthetics and design principles were advanced to interrogate capitalist modernity in its new state. It was against this context that early studies of vernacular architecture were associated with the criticism of architectural modernism. The 1964 exhibition *Architecture without Architects* put on by the architect Bernard Rudofsky at the Museum of Modern Art, New York, was immensely influential. Accompanied by a book of the same title, the exhibition consisted of black and white photography of vernacular buildings in Africa, Asia, Saudi Arabia, and South America. These photographs presented dwellings and settlements around the world as instances of 'true functionalism', with uncorrupted essence that was considered long obscured by the complexities of modern architectural production. Adopting a similar critical attitude towards modernist architecture, Paul Oliver's edited volume *Shelter and Society* (1969) called for a broader geographical and historical horizon for architectural research and insisted that both domestic and monumental buildings should be seen as part of an integral totality.

While conventional historiography in architecture is marked by its codification of aesthetically exemplary buildings into stylistic categories, a new generation of scholars of vernacular architecture pay attention to a wide range of ordinary dwellings such as apartments, farmhouses, and modernist villas. Influenced by developments in humanities and social sciences, new methodologies have been developed to achieve a more sophisticated cultural understanding of housing and space since the 1960s. Structuralist anthropology, for example, considered that information was dichotomised for organisation and interpretation in the human brain, and this structure was embedded in the construction of culture. The folklorist Henry Glassie's book *Folk Housing in Middle Virginia* (1975) was among the first to employ this theory to study vernacular architecture, which looks into how the patterns of folk housing design were structured by the community mindset. Also influenced by this tradition was the theory of space syntax developed by Bill Hillier and his colleagues since the early 1980s. Space syntax analyses posit that spaces are ordered according to a set of relations and restrictions. It is possible to decode the rules of social organisation by investigating spatial connectivity and integration through diagrams and maps. Space syntax as an approach to housing and culture is most efficient when combined with other social analytical tools: researchers will examine not only the configuration of floor plans, but also issues such as household hierarchical structure, gender relations, and the division of public/private spheres.

Material culture has been another important approach to housing and culture among researchers of vernacular architecture since the 1980s. The approach posits that objects made purposefully reveal as much about people's ideas and practices as does a text document. Housing is considered one important type of artefact that marks the past ways of life. Studies adopting a material culture approach have contributed to the writing of a less elite-focused history through an investigation into tangible objects produced by those who left few if any written records. They have increasingly built up our knowledge on the housing of slaves, the working class, and other marginal populations. These studies in turn generate new theoretical insights for the further development of the approach. Dell Upton (1991), for instance, proposes a 'landscape' approach which takes the entire material world as its object of inquiry and stresses the multiplicity and fragmentation of meaning. He calls for attention to be paid to the users of buildings: "Once introduced into the landscape, the identity of a building and the intentions of its makers are dissolved within confusing patterns of human perception, imagination, and use...This process of creation goes on long after the crew leaves the site" (Upton, 1991: 197).

The rise of postcolonial scholarship has opened up new perspectives on housing and culture in recent years. While much of previous literature treats vernacular architecture as if it were purely a product of the internal dynamics of local society, recent studies examine geographically dispersed realities involved in housing production. With a flourishing vocabulary of mobility and hybridity, global links, flows, entanglements, and networks are treated as important factors that have influenced the evolution of dwelling forms. The art historian Anthony King's influential book *The Bungalow: The Production of a Global Culture* (1984), for example, reveals how the bungalow evolved from its initial forms in India to the popular dwelling style in America during the twentieth century. Seminal work by Nezar AlSayyad, Gwendolyn Wright, and Zeynep Çelik has also greatly contributed to the development of this approach. In recent years, the Berkeley-based journal *Traditional Dwellings and Settlements Review* has published many case studies on housing and culture in non-Western societies from this perspective. By traversing existing sociopolitical boundaries and establishing new connections between previously disjunctive historical narratives, postcolonial scholarship presents a new framework which views connection, dispersion, and mobility as important dimensions in analysing housing and culture.

Everyday and Domestic Spaces

Growing attention has been paid to the everyday as an approach to housing and culture in recent years. Everydayness, as Henri Lefèbvre proclaims, is a philosophical category that most intimately corresponds to experiences of modernity. Often defined as what it is not – not the extraordinary or the heroic, not the formal or the spectacular, not the transcendent or the philosophical – the everyday is the unarticulated habitat of the modern subject. It is through this amorphous and seemingly insignificant arena where average people do ordinary things that most social processes occur. Recent calls to adopt the everyday as an approach have taken diverse forms in response to different epistemological, methodological, and political concerns. The move has been related to a now-familiar turning in historiography and social analysis from privileging the actions of the state and public organisations to attending to the microcontexts of society, with the French Annales school of historiography and the German *Alltagsgeschichte* ('everyday life') school of social history as its two prominent variants. From the feminist contention that 'the personal is political' to the postcolonial recovery of the voices of the subaltern, the shift in focus has underscored the deinstitutionalisation of 'the political' in modern society.

Notably, French sociologist Pierre Bourdieu (1977, 1990) has developed a systematic framework to analyse everyday practice in direct reaction to structuralism. According to Bourdieu, the richness of everyday life does not stem from objective social laws, nor arise from the subjective decision-making of free subjects. Instead, it is a result of the operation of *habitus*, a set of bodily dispositions acquired through a gradual process of inculcation, which incline individuals to act and react in certain ways. As Bourdieu (1990: 68) puts it: "It is because agents never know completely what they are doing that what they do has more sense than what they know." As such, any adequate analysis of space and culture must include into it the nonrepresentational dimension of knowing, of which Bourdieu's theory of practice provides a constitutive account. Also influential among spatial disciplines is Lefèbvre's (1984) critique of everyday life, which points to an alternative approach to the everyday as an open-ended and provisional arena created by the political economy of modernity. At the core of his arguments, Lefèbvre holds that a sizable transition, from an industrial to urban base of capitalist production, has taken place in our time. Such a transition, which Lefèbvre terms 'the urban revolution', has enabled capitalism to expand into every aspect of daily life. The everyday as such is a product of controlled consumption but nonetheless holds desires necessary to generate transformation. Lefèbvre's emphasis on the materiality of the quotidian environment helps to rebuke the dominion of language over lived experience: "Everyday life is sustenance, clothing, furnishing, homes, neighbourhoods.... Call it material culture if you like" (Lefèbvre, 1984: 21). Others have addressed the issue of agency in everyday practice.

Recent attempts to understand housing and modernity through investigations into everyday space have proved to be productive. An acute sense of 'homelessness' has long been taken as an important attribute of modernity in Western thought (Berger et al., 1974). Yet such a metaphor of homelessness, according to Hilde Heynen (2005: 2), only "reinforces the identification of modernity with masculinity". While 'ordinary' dwellings were studied under the category of 'vernacular architecture' in the previous era, feminist writers, along with scholars of other fields, have worked to bring the research of domestic architecture back to the core of modernity studies in the last three decades. They show that the rise of modern society has been associated with the redefinitions of private and public spheres, the articulation of new gender relations in domestic settings, the development of new urban dwelling types in response to the experiences of uprooting, and the impact of consumption patterns upon housing and interior design. Compared with approaches of the previous era, current researchers put more emphasis on how people make meaning in their life worlds and assert their subjective agency in often heavily gendered domestic spaces. They also highlight the domestic sphere as the site where modernity is materialised and particularised. Jordan Sand's book *House and Home in Modern Japan* (2003), for example, uses domestic space for staging everyday experiences with the modern and the new bourgeois culture during the formation period of Japanese modernity.

Significantly, a flourishing literature of everyday and domestic spaces in socialist societies has offered more nuanced renderings of various dimensions of 'real existing socialism'. Focusing on the mechanisms of state power and planned economies, Western Cold War scholarship often depicts state socialism as a culture of dictatorship and surveillance, and a type of 'unmodernity' when measured with normative standards of capitalist modernity. Recent research into everyday experiences in socialist societies has debunked this totalitarian model and provided new insights into what modernity meant for socialist society. Scholars have revealed the dynamic interplay of individual subjectivity and the project of building modern socialism in the Soviet Union and other socialist bloc states. Duanfang Lu's book *Remaking Chinese Urban Form* (2006) brings into light a broad range of everyday textures and tensions under Maoist socialism by examining how the work unit (*danwei*) developed as a primary urban form which integrated work, housing, and social services, and how its characteristic spatiality in turn staged a modernity alternative to that of both the West and the Soviet Union. Linking socialism to global reconceptualisations of the modern, Katherine Pence and Paul Betts (2008) take issue with the longstanding Cold War modern/unmodern dichotomy between West and East Germany and prompt reconsideration of East German socialism as modern. They show that despite being "a severely circumscribed field of interaction", the GDR society was characterised by diverse lived spaces, occupied and transformed by ordinary people.

An important premise of the everyday approach concerns the liminal realm of human experience in which people are aware of certain occurrences but have not quite articulated them at the level of explicit consciousness. While other accounts of modernity focus on well-articulated social/structural mechanisms of one sort or another, the everyday approach seeks to discern how nuanced recognitions, social relations, and symbolic struggles are forged in the liminal space between the unseen and the seen, the submerged and the apprehended, and the unspoken and spoken. By looking into the actual doings of people rather than stereotypes, studies of everyday and domestic spaces have shown that experiences of the modern are differentiated by class, gender, ethnicity, and local settings, even within the same national or cultural space.

See also: Difference; Ethnography; Material Cultures of Home; People and the Built Form.

References

Berger PL, Berger B, and Kellner H (1974) *The Homeless Mind. Modernization and Consciousness*. New York: Vintage Books.
Bourdieu P (1977) *Outline of a Theory of Practice*. Cambridge, UK: Cambridge University Press.
Bourdieu P (1990) *The Logic of Practice*. Cambridge, UK: Polity.
Glassie H (1975) *Folk Housing in Middle Virginia: A Structural Analysis of Historic Artifacts*. Knoxville, TN: University of Tennessee Press.
King A (1984) *The Bungalow: The Production of a Global Culture*. London: Routledge.
Lefèbvre H (1984) *Everyday Life in the Modern World,* Rabinovitch S (trans.). New Brunswick, NJ: Transaction Books.
Lu D (2006) *Remaking Chinese Urban Form: Modernity, Scarcity and Space, 1949–2005*. London: Routledge.
Oliver P (1969) *Shelter and Society*. London: Barrie & Rockliff.
Pence K and Betts P (eds.) (2008) *Socialist Modern: East German Everyday Culture and Politics*. Ann Arbor, MI: University of Michigan Press.
Rapoport A (1969) *House, Form and Culture*. Englewood Cliffs, NJ: Prentice-Hall.
Sand J (2003) *House and Home in Modern Japan: Architecture, Domestic Space, and Bourgeois Culture, 1880–1930*. Cambridge, MA: Harvard University Press.
Upton D (1991) Architectural history or landscape history? *Journal of Architectural Education* 44(4): 195–199.

Further Reading

Heynen H (2005) Modernity and domesticity: Tensions and contradictions. In: Heynen H and Baydar G (eds.) *Negotiating Domesticity: Spatial Productions of Gender in Modern Architecture*. London: Routledge.
Hillier B and Hanson J (1984) *The Social Logic of Space*. Cambridge, UK: Cambridge University Press.
Lawrence R (1987) *Housing, Dwellings and Homes: Design Theory, Research and Practice*. Chichester: Wiley, UK.

Defensible Space

P Cozens, Curtin University of Technology, Bentley, WA, Australia
D Hillier, University of Glamorgan, Wales, UK

© 2012 Elsevier Ltd. All rights reserved.

Glossary

Capable guardians Can be anything, either a person or thing, that discourages crime from taking place. These can be formal or informal and include police patrols, security guards, neighbourhood watch schemes, doorstaff, vigilant staff and co-workers, friends, and neighbours.

Intervisibility The state or fact of being visible, the ability to give a relatively large range of unobstructed vision. For buildings which face each other across the street, windows and doors provide opportunities for intervisibility.

Zeitgeist The spirit of the time; general trend of thought which is characteristic of a particular period of time.

History and Background of Defensible Space

In 1960s America, the problem of ever-rising levels of crime pervaded and responses appeared to be both limited and ineffective and the future for American cities seemed bleak. There were fears of a crime-ridden society and a drift towards a 'lock-up' police state. There was also some evidence of migration by the middle classes away from the 'criminal' inner cities to the 'law-abiding' suburbs. In America, the President and the Congress passed the Safe Streets Act in 1968, which provided funding for research into new crime prevention techniques. This funding underpinned the research that is documented in Newman's book *Defensible Space* (1973). Developed largely from an architectural perspective, *Defensible Space* was based on critical observations of the built form (public housing) and the association between specific design features and how recorded crime rates varied.

Within the discipline of planning, there were growing concerns about some of the practices of the day and the potential links between crime and planning/urban design. Jane Jacobs' *The Death and Life of Great American Cities* (1961) criticised contemporary urban planning practices, such as land-use zoning and slum clearances, and she also observed how urban design could potentially promote surveillance by residents. Jacobs coined the now well-known phrase "eyes on the street" and claimed this principle could help to make places safer. Jacobs proposed that a sense of community cohesion, notions of territoriality, and a sense of responsibility/ownership for one's immediate area are essential for crime prevention. In opposition to a contemporary trend for 'zoning', she advocated mixed land uses. This would encourage more street-level activity, which, it is argued, would stimulate social control and increase opportunities for surveillance ('eyes on the street'), thereby reducing crime. Although largely anecdotal in content, Jacobs' work has had a significant influence upon subsequent researchers, in particular Newman. Some have suggested that Newman's work operationalised Jacobs' themes. However, despite the impact of Jacobs' observations in planning circles, her ideas did not resonate within the field of criminology or crime prevention until Newman published *Defensible Space*.

As an instructor at Washington University in the 1960s, Newman observed and analysed the decline of Pruitt-Igoe, a high-rise (11 storeys) public housing development of 2740 units in St Louis (see **Figure 1**). Crime problems and low levels of occupancy contributed towards its subsequent demolition within 10 years of its construction. Indeed, the abundance of undesignated communal interior and exterior grounds unintentionally became the focus of litter, graffiti, vandalism, antisocial behaviour, and crime. Occupancy levels did not exceed 60% and the residents were predominantly single-parent families relying on welfare payments. Adjacent to Pruitt-

Figure 1 The Pruitt-Igoe development in St Louis.
Reproduced with permission from Newman O (1973) *Defensible Space: People and Design in the Violent City*. London: Architectural Press; http://www.defensiblespace.com/book.htm.

Igoe, Newman observed the better-functioning Carr Square development, which was inhabited by residents of similar social characteristics but was older, smaller, and designed as rows of houses. It was fully occupied and relatively trouble-free and had significantly lower levels of recorded crime.

To test Newman's ideas on defensible space, the social housing projects of Brownsville and Van Dyke in New York (considered broadly similar, in social terms) were compared and analysed using their recorded crime rates. Van Dyke was a high-rise block (14 storeys), while Brownsville buildings were relatively low level (six storeys). According to the New York City Housing Authority (NYCHA) police statistics, the high-rise Van Dyke project experienced a crime rate of 51.4 per 1000, while the rate for Brownsville was 28.2 per 1000. Since the NYCHA's demographic and socioeconomic data for both tenant populations were broadly similar, Newman posited that the physical design of buildings was a causal factor, which could be used to explain the differing crime rates in the two housing projects. Important variables included the height of the building and the number of families sharing a common entry point.

Definitions and Concepts of Defensible Space

For Newman, defensible space is about restructuring residential environments to become liveable and controlled by the community rather than the police, and it argues that design can hinder or assist the criminal in the selection of both a crime site and a criminal act.

There are four elements of defensible space that act individually and in combination to assist in the creation of a safer urban environment:

- the capacity of the physical environment to create perceived zones of territorial influence;
- the capacity of physical design to provide surveillance opportunities for residents and their agents;
- the capacity of design to influence the perception of a project's uniqueness, isolation, and stigma; and
- the influence of geographical juxtaposition with 'safe zones' on the security of adjacent areas.

Territoriality is a key design concept directed at reinforcing notions of proprietary concern and a 'sense of ownership' in legitimate users of urban space, thereby reducing opportunities for offending by discouraging illegitimate users. Different forms of territoriality include symbolic barriers (e.g., signage and surface treatments) and real barriers (e.g., hedges, fencing, or design that clearly defines and delineates between private, semiprivate, and public spaces). A hierarchy of defensible space is illustrated in **Figure 2**.

Physical design has the capacity to promote informal or natural surveillance opportunities for residents and their agents, and surveillance is an integral part of capable guardianship. If offenders perceive that they can be observed (even if they are not), they may be less likely to offend, given the increased potential for intervention, apprehension, and prosecution. Different types include natural (e.g., residents' self-surveillance opportunities as facilitated by windows), formal or organised (e.g., security/police patrols), and mechanical surveillance strategies (e.g., street lighting and CCTV).

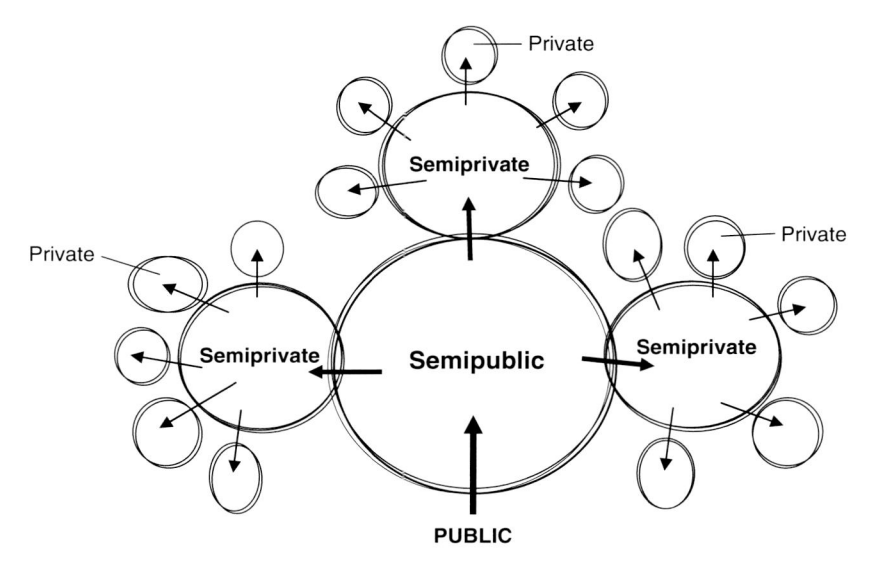

Figure 2 Hierarchy of defensible space. Arrows indicate entrance and exit points at different levels of the hierarchy. Reproduced with permission from Newman O (1973) *Defensible Space: People and Design in the Violent City*, p. 9. London: Architectural Press.

The perception of a project's uniqueness, isolation, and stigma relates to the promotion of well-maintained urban space that transmits positive signals to all users. The significance of the physical condition and 'image' of the built environment and the effect this may have on crime and the fear of crime have long been acknowledged, and an extensive body of research now exists. Furthermore, research suggests that vacant premises can represent crime 'magnets'.

Geographical juxtaposition refers to the location of a social housing project within the wider urban environment and the proximity to other land uses and activities, which might facilitate or discourage crime. Newman argues that it is possible to juxtapose schools and shops with housing so as to encourage walkability and to define territoriality of the residential area, and that scale is the key issue. For example, a long, narrow area of parkland can be juxtaposed with social housing such that houses on one side of the park have an uninterrupted view of the other side and vice versa.

The creation of defensible space therefore involves the use of design to enhance territoriality and promote a 'sense of ownership' by delineating between private and public space using real and symbolic barriers. It also promotes intervisibility between built structures and uses building and site design to increase both surveillance and 'eyes on the street'. The promotion of a positive image via the regular and routine management and maintenance of the built environment is also central to creating and sustaining defensible space and also serves to enhance territoriality. Finally, the influence of the wider environment on a specific component of urban space or its 'geographical juxtaposition' with surrounding land uses and activities is also important in the formation and maintenance of defensible space. As a design theory, defensible space is informed by human occupancy and use experience, a novel approach in architecture at the time.

Critics of Defensible Space

There are a range of criticisms of defensible space (for a review, see Cozens et al., 2001). Some have argued that Newman's methodology lacks an appropriate consideration for socioeconomic conditions. The selection of sites for investigation and his use and analysis of crime statistics have also been questioned on methodological grounds. On a theoretical level, some question the assumption that territoriality is a 'behavioural universal' and that Newman was too vague about the process by which residents define and defend territorial space.

Furthermore, the possibility of apprehension by residents may not deter all potential offenders. Properties affording surveillance may not be constantly occupied, and if they are, it does not necessarily mean that surveillance is routinely taking place, or that any direct action by citizens (e.g., challenging, reporting, or direct intervention) is guaranteed.

Some have argued that defensible space might merely displace or redistribute crime across the city. Crime can be displaced to an easier target (target displacement), to different places (spatial displacement), to another time (temporal displacement), and/or result in a change in the type of crime committed (crime type displacement) and in the tactics used to commit a crime (tactical displacement). More recent studies, however, identify a diffusion of benefits to surrounding areas rather than the displacement of crime, and the idea has emerged that displacement can be utilised as a positive tool rather than as a negative side effect. Moreover, it can also be argued that displacement occurs as a negative side effect of all existing crime prevention initiatives and is not a criticism that is exclusive to defensible space.

Criticisms also focused on the expensive, time-consuming nature of design modifications. Although modifications can be expensive, applying defensible space at the design stage is proactive and potentially reduces opportunities for crime. Indeed, a Home Office cost–benefit analysis of UK's Secured by design (SBD) scheme, which is based on defensible space, demonstrated that the additional expenditure on security features at the construction stage (estimated at £400) far outweighs the average cost of burglary to the victim (£2300 at 1999 prices) let alone the various costs to the wider community.

Finally, critics argued that Newman's concepts were too vague and ill-defined to be empirically tested. Many studies since the 1970s have attempted to probe elements of defensible space, often producing conflicting findings.

Since the 1970s, research has demonstrated how the varying levels of territoriality and the social dynamics of an area (particularly levels of fear of crime) can all affect the effectiveness of defensible space. Urban space, which is defensible and 'capable of being defended' by residents, can become 'undefended' as a consequence of fear of crime, for example (Merry, 1981). Furthermore, the same space can become defended and exploited by those who would seek to use it for their own illegal purposes (e.g., drug dens). This is referred to as 'offensible space' (Atlas, 1991). Finally, urban space can become 'indefensible' (Cozens et al., 2002), whereby it is 'incapable of being defended' by residents (e.g., urban riot). As the social dynamics of space changes, the effectiveness of defensible space both in theory and in application will also change.

Popularity and Development of Defensible Space

Initially, *Defensible Space* received considerable attention, but was predominantly ignored by criminologists despite the existence of numerous studies linking crime and urban design. Furthermore, *Defensible Space* was written by an architect and the ideas did not concur with most contemporary criminology, which as an offshoot of sociology (particularly in America) favoured social explanations for crime. Newman was not a social scientist and for some his ideas ignored the findings of traditional criminology. Indeed, before the 1960s planning and architecture did not routinely interact with criminology, and defensible space thinking challenged long-established assumptions across disciplinary boundaries, with a scientific rigour that was uncommon for the time (although both the methodology and the data analysis have subsequently been criticised).

Despite the criticisms of *Defensible Space*, Newman's ideas have had continuing appeal and several factors have been suggested to explain this popularity. First, the ideas resonated with current thought and the zeitgeist of the time. For academics, these ideas were reflective of a contemporary emphasis in psychology and criminology of the importance of the physical environment in determining behaviour. Second, *Defensible Space* was innovative in that it challenged the traditional criminological indifference to the role of the physical environment as a factor in understanding and tackling criminal behaviour. Third, *Defensible Space* was attractive, since it provided a well-illustrated and seemingly scientific demonstration of the influence of design on crime and offered practical strategies and applications to reduce crime, which other texts had not provided. Fourth, Newman's ideas were (and remain) attractive to politicians across the political spectrum. It appeals to those on the 'right' since environmental engineering provides immediate, visible, and clear evidence of a positive commitment to tackle crime in society. Also, it does not make any demands to reorganise the social structures. For politicians on the 'left', it represents an alternative to blaming the stereotypical vandal, the unemployed working-class youth. For all political parties, *Defensible Space* represented a highly visible, innovative, practical, and clearly positive approach to tackling crime.

Operationalising procedures to create defensible space was an attractive feature of Newman's thinking and may have influenced the continuing federal governments' financial sponsorship of his work in the United States. The Westinghouse Corporation extended research on the application of defensible space concepts to educational and commercial sites, but results proved disappointing. This may be explained by lower levels of territorial behaviour outside the residential setting. In America, government and academic research interest in defensible space dwindled in the 1980s and early 1990s but was used as a practical training tool for police.

In the United Kingdom, a Home Office study conducted by Sturman and Wilson (1976) analysed 52 housing estates in London and the findings largely supported Newman's work. However, this study reported that the density of children in the urban environment was more important than design characteristics – and this became the focus of British housing authorities and councils rather than design modifications.

The riot-prone inner cities in the United Kingdom of the 1980s, such as the Broadwater Farm Estate, seemed to vindicate defensible space ideas. This estate was a series of 12 high-rise and deck-access flats interconnected via overhead pedestrian walkways and with many 'alienating mechanisms' such as escape routes and isolated areas. Furthermore, residents were socially deprived; the estate was poorly maintained; and it exhibited various hotspots for crime, antisocial behaviour, and robbery. Following rioting in 1985, a £33m funding programme has transformed the estate, which has since reported significantly lower levels of crime than the surrounding areas. This funding supported the redesigning the estate's layout, various community initiatives and increased community participation. Supported by the then prime minister Margaret Thatcher, a series of defensible space modifications were conducted by Alice Coleman and colleagues at the Land Use Research Unit, King's College, London (Coleman, 1990). These included providing each block with a unique identity, demolishing the intimidating walkways, and installing concierge lobbies, landscaped gardens, a health centre, and an enterprise centre.

Interestingly, Taylor et al. (1980) identified a second-generation defensible space, which, in addition to a regard for the physical dimension, also considered the impact of other social and cultural features on fear of crime and victimisation rates. It argues that defensible space (physical) and local social dynamics interact and can therefore facilitate or discourage both the use of outdoor locations and affect levels of informal social control. Newman's publications around this time (e.g., Newman, 1980; Newman and Franck, 1980, 1982) also began to acknowledge the importance of social factors in determining the effectiveness of defensible space.

Globally, interest in defensible space diminished from the beginning of the 1980s and into the mid-1990s. Some assert that in important policy circles, strategies stressing physical change simply became unfashionable. Various developments have significantly altered this situation, and by the mid-1990s defensible space was once again popular, primarily under the banner of CPTED and SBD.

First, there was a growing body of evidence of the significance of the role of opportunity in crime and an increasing number of case studies indicating significant and continuing reductions in crime following environmental modifications (Newman, 1996). In 1996, the US Department of Housing and Urban Development commissioned Newman to produce *Creating Defensible Space* (1996), which was largely an upgraded monograph of his previous work. It discussed three case studies where defensible space ideas were put into practice. The first involved the reorganisation of an urban grid of residential streets into cul-de-sacs and minineighbourhoods in the Five Oaks community in Dayton, Ohio. The second case study related to Clason Point, a 400-unit public housing project located in the South Bronx, New York, and the final case study involved the dispersal of public housing in the Yonkers district of New York. It is reported that both crime and the fear of crime were reduced, property values increased, and there was no evidence of any displacement of criminal activity.

Second, this evidence was also underpinned by the emergence of new criminological theories such as routine activity theory (Cohen and Felson, 1979), crime pattern theory (Brantingham and Brantingham, 1981), and rational choice theory (Cornish and Clarke, 1986), which attached more importance to environmental determinants of crime.

Third, the displacement of crime associated with defensible space modifications was not demonstrated by research, as critics had previously suggested. Indeed, rather than influencing a change in the location, time, tactics, target, or type of offending, researchers have observed a diffusion of the benefits of defensible space to surrounding areas.

Current Status

Over the past 30 years, the application of defensible space has expanded beyond social housing projects to include other types of residential housing and to a variety of land uses such as retail, commercial, transportation nodes, schools, hospitals, town centres, and sporting locations (e.g., the Sydney Olympics). Defensible space theory has been further refined to include a clearly defined social dimension and many of its concepts are central to the modern approach to CPTED. Intriguingly, the term 'defensible space' is also central to the field of fire prevention in America and Australia. It refers to the well-maintained space around a home that has been cleared of trees, shrubs, and other flora and inflammable materials to reduce the potential impact of wildfires, which also provides safe space from which firefighters can seek to defend a property.

By the end of the twentieth century, defensible space, in the guise of CPTED in America, Canada, Europe, South Africa, and Australia, and SBD in Britain, has become contemporary and fashionable once again. There seems to be an increasing recognition of the role of design in crime reduction programmes. The International Crime Prevention through Environmental Design Association (ICA) has been established along with United Kingdom's Designing Out Crime Association (DOCA), E-DOCA in Europe, the Asia/Pacific CPTED Chapter, and a chapter based in Latin America. Defensible space and CPTED ideas now permeate and inform many planning processes in developed countries. Furthermore, the United Nations also recommends the use of these ideas in developing countries as the world becomes evermore urbanised.

CPTED ideas are based on Newman's defensible space, which has been referred to as the first-generation CPTED. Defensible space and CPTED both seek to manipulate the design of urban places in order to reduce opportunities for crime and there are many connections between these two approaches. The UK's SBD is firmly based upon defensible space ideas. The initiative was launched in 1989, whereby police provide defensible space advice to housing developers concerning specific new house-building projects. Three contemporary SBD evaluations have all reported positive results in terms of reduced crime levels. Crucially, SBD developments are generally more closely aligned with Newman's ideas of limiting access and reducing permeability through residential areas. A large body of evidence suggests that designing out crime using defensible space can lead to significant crime reductions (for detailed reviews of the evidence, see Cozens et al., 2001, 2005).

Newman's theory continues to be located within the complex interplay between the physical and social environment. Indeed, the development of the second-generation CPTED and the increasing focus on the social dynamics of urban space can arguably be traced to some of the original criticisms of defensible space.

The term 'defensible space' is well known in the United Kingdom and in the Netherlands, but appears to be less acknowledged within the CPTED movement, notwithstanding the recognition of its significant role in the history and development of CPTED ideas. The interpretation of defensible space as promoting enclavisation and limiting access as opposed to promoting permeability continues to undermine the development of both defensible space and CPTED. Indeed, several critical evaluations of defensible space have called for clarification of the theoretical framework. Moreover, CPTED is itself undergoing a reconceptualisation under the direction of Professor Paul Ekblom of the Design Against Crime Research Centre, Central Saint Martins College of Art and Design in London (Ekblom, 2006).

Future Research into Defensible Space

- First, local, contextualised research on the topic of 'undefended space', 'offensible space', and 'indefensible space' will contribute much to understanding how urban spaces change over time. Indeed, what factors convert an urban space which was once capable of being defended into one which is no longer defended by others or becomes incapable of being defended? These issues are also pertinent to understanding the development of CPTED and the idea of identifying the 'tipping point', where fear of crime, community withdrawal, urban decay, and out-migration can come to define a community and stigmatise an area of the city.
- Second, investigating and integrating the highly complex physical and social dimensions of crime continues to represent a common theme in both defensible space and CPTED and is an area of research that will continue to challenge academics, practitioners, politicians, and policymakers alike.
- Third, cross-disciplinary research between environmental criminology, planning and urban design, environmental psychology, and the social sciences could potentially develop a new model(s) for understanding crime and urban design that is more sustainable in both developed and developing cities.
- Fourth, in relation to accessibility and the issue of permeability, the routine activities in a place are the crucial mediating factor in the relationship between crime and spatial accessibility. Research that investigates defensible space in terms of understanding the dynamic use of urban spaces is therefore critical for the development and refinement of defensible space and CPTED both theoretically and operationally. Indeed, if defensible space is about the design, management, use of the built environment, then future research must reflect this complexity.
- Finally, research that probes the perceptions of defensible space (and undefended, offensible, and indefensible space) of different user groups in the city is also an area in need of further scrutiny. Crucially, research is particularly necessary in relation to perceptions of defensible space in different cultures in the developing world. The world is becoming increasingly urbanised and it is unlikely that the currently occidentally derived framework for CPTED and defensible space ideas will transfer unproblematically to developing countries, which possess very different cultures. Indeed, much of defensible space and CPTED in theory and in application is based upon Western ideas of individual property rights – which may (or may not) possess the same resonance or relevance for all urban locations.

In conclusion, much of the future research into defensible space concepts will potentially be conducted under the CPTED banner and the term 'defensible space' is likely to be used less frequently. However, defensible space remains a fundamental component of CPTED that can assist in the development and maintenance of safer, more sustainable, and more liveable urban communities, which are capable of being defended, valued, used, and self-policed by residents.

See also: Crime Prevention through Environmental Design.

References

Atlas R (1991) The other side of defensible space. *Security Management* March: 63–66.
Brantingham PL and Brangtingham PJ (1981) *Environmental Criminology*. Beverly Hills, CA: Sage Publications.
Cohen L and Felson M (1979) Social change and crime rates: A routine activities approach. *American Sociological Review* 44: 588–608.
Coleman A (1990) *Utopia on Trial*. London: Hilary Shipman Ltd.
Cornish DB and Clarke RVG (1986) *The Reasoning Criminal: Rational Choice Perspectives on Offending*. New York: Springer-Verlag.
Cozens PM, Hillier D, and Prescott G (2001) Crime and the design of residential property. Exploring the theoretical background. *Property Management* 19(2): 136–164 (paper 1 of 2).
Cozens PM, Hillier D, and Prescott G (2002) Criminogenic associations and characteristic British housing designs. *International Planning Studies* 7(2): 119–136.
Cozens PM, Saville G, and Hillier D (2005) Crime prevention through environmental design (CPTED): A review and modern bibliography. *Journal of Property Management* 23(5): 328–356.
Ekblom P (2006) Crime prevention through environmental design: Time for an upgrade? *Paper Presented at the International Environmental Criminology and Crime Analysis Symposium (ECCA)*, Chilliwack, BC, Canada, 26–29 July.
Jacobs J (1961) *The Death and Life of Great American Cities*. New York: Vintage Books.
Merry S (1981) Defensible space undefended: Social factors in crime prevention through environmental design. *Urban Affairs Quarterly* 16(3): 397–422.
Newman O (1973) *Defensible Space: People and Design in the Violent City*. London: Architectural Press.
Newman O (1980) *Community of Interest*. Garden City, NY: Anchor Press; Doubleday.
Newman O (1996) *Creating Defensible Space*. Washington, DC: US Department of Housing and Urban Development Office of Policy Development and Research.
Newman O and Franck K (1980) *Factors Influencing Crime and Instability in Urban Housing Developments*. Washington, DC: U.S. Department of Justice.
Newman O and Franck K (1982) The effects of building size on personal crime and fear of crime. *Population and Environment* 5(4): 203–220.
Sturman A and Wilson S (1976) Vandalism research aimed at specific remedies. *Municipal Engineering* 7: 705–713.
Taylor R, Gottfredson S, and Brower S (1980) The defensibility of defensible space: A critical review and a synthetic framework for future research. In: Hirschi T and Gottfredson M (eds.) *Understanding Crime*, pp. 53–71. Beverly Hills, CA: Sage.

Relevant Websites

www.defensiblespace.com – The Defensible Space Website
www.designagainstcrime.com – The Design against Crime Centre, London
www.designoutcrime.org – The Design Out Crime Research Centre, Western Australia
www.e-doca.eu – The European Designing Out Crime Network
www.cpted.net – The International CPTED Association
www.doca.org.uk – The United Kingdom's Designing Out Crime Association
www.securedbydesign.com – The United Kingdom's Secured by Design Scheme

Demand Subsidies for Low-Income Households

K Hulse, Swinburne University of Technology, Melbourne, VIC, Australia

© 2012 Elsevier Ltd. All rights reserved.

Glossary

Demand subsidies Government assistance to households (or on behalf of households) to assist in paying for their housing.

Direct demand subsidies Public expenditures to assist households with their housing costs through cash transfers, in-kind assistance (vouchers), or loans at below market rates.

Housing allowances Ongoing income-related subsidies to assist households with the cost of their housing.

Income security First tier of income support comprising payments to people who are unable to work due to older age, disability, or other approved reason.

Income support Government provided or guaranteed schemes to provide income to those who are unable to achieve a minimum standard of living through income from work or other private sources.

Indirect demand subsidies Tax concessions and expenditures designed to offset some of the costs of renting or buying dwellings.

Social assistance Second tier of income support comprising payments to people who are of workforce age but not currently in paid work or unable to support themselves through paid work.

Supply subsidies Government assistance to financiers, developers, or managers of housing to lower the cost of producing and providing housing.

Demand Subsidies

In economic terms, the rationale for government housing policies is that housing is a merit good whose consumption provides a range of benefits at societal level, such as a more productive workforce, a healthier population, or a more cohesive society. Governments aim to achieve greater levels of housing consumption, or particular types of consumption such as home ownership, than would otherwise be the case using various means including legislation, regulation, and financial subsidies.

There are two distinct types of financial subsidies targeted at housing: supply subsidies attached to dwellings (see article Supply-Side Subsidies for Affordable Rental Housing) and demand subsidies attached to households. Supply subsidies, also known as bricks and mortar or producer subsidies, are paid to the financiers, developers, or managers of housing to lower the cost of producing and providing housing. They aim to make dwellings available at a more affordable price than would otherwise be the case. Demand subsidies, also known as personal, consumer, or household subsidies, are paid to households. They assist households to pay for their housing. Both supply and demand subsidies may also have other objectives beyond housing affordability such as a minimum standard of housing quality, levels of amenity, or conditions of occupancy.

Most governments use a combination of supply and demand subsidies, with the relative importance of each type varying between countries and over time. Both supply and demand subsidies can be applied to either home ownership or various types of rental arrangements.

There are three distinguishing characteristics of demand subsidies. First, they provide additional purchasing power to households over and above usual sources of household income such as wages and government pensions and benefits. Second, they are paid to, or sometimes on behalf of, individual households. Third, they are portable between dwellings and housing providers, unlike supply subsidies, which are accessed through living in the dwellings that have attracted the subsidies.

Demand subsidies are not necessarily restricted to low-income households and may be targeted at specific groups such as first home buyers or people in particular age groups. This section, however, deals specifically with housing demand subsidies for low-income households.

A Hybrid Policy Instrument

Conceptually, demand subsidies are something of a hybrid policy instrument, addressing the problem of insufficient household income relative to the cost of housing, rather than insufficient income or insufficient affordable housing, as illustrated in **Table 1**. Governments are reluctant to see difficulty in affording housing as simply a matter of insufficient household income, in part because of the consequences for government-funded pension and benefit schemes and wages policies. Indeed, some demand subsidy schemes

Table 1 Comparison of features of income support, demand subsidies, and housing supply subsidies

Features	General income support	Housing demand subsidies	Housing supply subsidies
Perceived problem	Insufficient household income	Insufficient household income relative to the cost of housing	Insufficient affordable housing
Rationale	Basic income is required to live in a civilised society	Income should be sufficient to access housing meeting community standards	Decent housing is a basic requirement in a civilised society
Government policy focus	Income support	Income support and housing consumption	Housing supply and consumption
Objective	Untied income through income support to meet basic living expenses including housing	Provide income tied to housing consumption in some way, for example, affordability outcomes	Provide housing that meets agreed standards in terms of affordability, adequacy, and appropriateness
Treatment of expenditures on housing	Housing expenditures are the same as other expenditure categories	Housing expenditures differ from other types of expenditures (merit good)	Housing expenditures differ from other expenditures (merit good) but other aspects of housing important beyond price such as housing quality, secure occupancy, and location

Reproduced with permission from Hulse K (2002) Demand subsidies for private renters: A comparative analysis. Final Report No. 24, p. 5. Melbourne, VIC: Australian Housing and Urban Research Institute.

were originally introduced to provide a more targeted and less costly way of supplementing income support payments for particular types of households, such as old age pensioners. In contrast, supply subsidies typically embed a range of housing objectives beyond affordability, such as secure occupancy and quality standards. However, households may wish to trade off some of these items for other priorities. Demand subsidies provide an alternative in that although they provide additional income, this is tied in some way to housing consumption.

Types of Demand Subsidies

There are different types of housing demand subsidies. As illustrated in **Table 1**, a distinction can be made between direct and indirect demand subsidies. The former involve government expenditures, for example, the housing allowance schemes operating in many countries. The latter are typically provided through the tax system, such as mortgage interest tax relief and tax credits for low-income renters.

A further distinction can be made between once-only (capital) payments, such as assistance with payment of costs associated with moving into rental property such as rental bonds or assistance with a deposit to buy a home, and ongoing (recurrent) payments to enable households to meet the continuing costs of their housing such as rental support payments (**Table 2**).

Although four main types of demand subsidy are possible, using the typology in **Table 1**, only direct subsidies are regarded unambiguously as housing policy instruments. Indirect demand subsidies fall within the domain of taxation policy and are often used as an instrument in macroeconomic management. There is generally more scrutiny of, and information available about, direct subsidies to low-income households than those provided indirectly through the taxation system, which often benefit middle- and higher-income households.

Table 2 Examples of different types of housing demand subsidies

Demand subsidy type	Direct	Indirect
Once-only (capital)	Grants or loans to home purchasers (e.g., deposit assistance) Grants or loans to assist with up-front costs of accessing rental housing, for example, rental bond payments	Capital gains tax exemption
Ongoing (recurrent)	Subsidised loans to home buyers Mortgage relief payments (loans or grants) Rental assistance schemes (loans or grants)	Taxation relief on mortgage interest payments Taxation concessions via rental credits

Reproduced with permission from Hulse K (2002) Demand subsidies for private renters: A comparative analysis. Final Report No. 24, p. 4. Melbourne, VIC: Australian Housing and Urban Research Institute.

A Shift Towards Demand Subsidies

Housing policies in most developed countries in the period following the Second World War were directed at increasing the supply of affordable housing to meet accumulated shortages. Emphasis on supply, however, declined in some of these countries from the mid-1970s when immediate postwar shortages had been met. There was also a growing disenchantment with supply subsidies in the form of public housing in countries such as the United States and Canada. Governments increasingly saw the problem not as one of lack of supply but of the inability of lower-income households to afford housing.

In the countries of Northwest Europe, North America, and Australasia, progressive restructuring of the postwar welfare state from the 1970s was associated with a re-examination of the role of governments in providing housing directly to low-income households and in regulation of the housing sector. Demand subsidies were initially promoted in many countries as a safety net when rent controls were eased or phased out, although governments continued to invest in supply subsidies, particularly through not-for-profit or third sector organisations (e.g., Canada, Netherlands, UK).

Throughout the 1980s, the strategy of supply subsidies came under scrutiny as neoliberal ideas became dominant in public policy. These ideas promoted a withdrawal of governments from direct assistance and a more residual role in providing a social safety net. In the sphere of housing policy this translated into greater targeting of government assistance to those with the highest needs, using demand subsidies. By the 1990s, the rationale for demand subsidies became more explicitly pro-market, reflecting the view that consumer choice in private markets was the best driver of efficiency.

Demand subsidies were also introduced in other regions and for differing reasons. For example, they were adopted in some Central and Eastern Europe countries in the 1990s as rent regulation was withdrawn and house prices and rents have risen to market or near-market levels in the transition from socialist to market economies.

In some Latin American countries, housing demand subsidies have been seen as a policy instrument that can address low income and poverty more directly and efficiently than through supply subsidies. Chile moved to a system of up-front demand subsidies to assist home buyers in the mid-1970s, providing for one-off grants to assist low-income households to buy their own home. This replaced previous schemes in which the government had a direct role in financing the construction of specific new developments for home buyers and providing below market rate mortgage finance. These arrangements were criticised as being inefficient and benefiting middle-income households rather than those on low incomes. The so-called Chilean model was extended to other Latin American countries (e.g., Colombia, Costa Rica, Uruguay) and has subsequently been advocated by organisations such as the Inter-American Development Bank, which promotes economic development in Latin America.

Housing Allowance Schemes

The most common form of demand subsidies for low-income households is housing allowances, which are direct, ongoing subsidies to households to buy or rent their homes (see Access and Affordability: Housing Allowances). Although they are intended to boost the effective purchasing power of households in the housing market, specific objectives may vary. Housing allowances may be designed to reduce the portion of income devoted to housing costs, making housing more affordable, using conventional housing cost to household income ratios, a common objective of housing policies. Alternatively, housing allowances can increase the income households have available for other items after paying for housing, using residual income measures of housing affordability and addressing adequacy of income objectives. For this reason, some housing allowance schemes had their origins in antipoverty strategies. They may also have objectives beyond affordability, including the quality, amenity, and appropriateness of dwellings. In this case, the objective is to increase housing consumption to some agreed community standard.

Housing allowance schemes vary considerably between, and sometimes within, countries and are known by their local names such as Rent Assistance (Australia), Accommodation Supplement (New Zealand), Housing Choice Vouchers (USA), Housing Benefit (UK), and Wohngeld (Germany). A number of developed countries do not have a national housing allowance system (e.g., Austria, Belgium, Canada, Switzerland) while some countries have more than one housing allowance system (e.g., France). A small group of Anglo-Saxon countries have de facto housing allowances embedded within housing supply programmes through income-related rents for social housing (Australia, Canada, Ireland, New Zealand, USA).

Institutions

The institutional context for housing demand subsidies varies between countries, making cross-national comparison difficult, as the relatively small number of studies into the most common form, housing allowances, attests (see Further Reading). The hybrid nature of demand subsidies entails consideration of differences in the level and distribution of household incomes and the costs of buying and renting housing, both of which vary between and within countries. This complexity is exacerbated by differences in governance arrangements which reflect historical and political factors, such as the history of legislation and regulation, particularly in relation to the rental sector.

The design and implementation of demand subsidies for low-income households are shaped by the institutional context in which they are embedded. Demand subsidies are rarely stand-alone housing policy instruments: indirect subsidies are typically part of the taxation system while direct subsidies are often linked to income support systems. Not only are housing, taxation, and income support systems intertwined, but roles and responsibilities are shared between the national/federal, regional (e.g., state/provincial), and local government level, depending on the country, which adds further complexity. For example, demand subsidies may be financed centrally by a national/federal government, programme design may also reflect regional or local government preferences, and implementation may be a function of local government. Table 3 provides examples of the institutional arrangements for housing allowances in selected countries to illustrate this point.

Link with Income Support Systems

Housing costs are the single biggest items of household expenditure and vary not only because of household size, as with most other items of expenditure, but also by housing quality, tenure type, and location. A key issue in considering demand subsidies is how they relate to income support systems, which often are two-tiered, either explicitly or implicitly. The first tier (income security) provides cash transfers to people who are unable to work due to older age, disability, or some other reason, and may reflect contributions made while in the workforce. The second tier (social assistance) provides cash transfers, often with conditions attached, to people of working age who are not in the labour force. The former are typically national schemes while the latter may be a function of regional or even local government, particularly in large federal systems. Some income support systems are intended to cover reasonable housing costs incurred by households (e.g., Germany, Sweden) while others provide partial coverage within income support systems with supplementary demand subsidies, which recognise that additional assistance is required by some groups to meet their housing costs (e.g., Australia, Netherlands). In the United Kingdom, there is something of a mixed model with additional income provided for home owners as part of social assistance, but assistance to renters via Housing Benefit, a separate housing allowance programme.

Tenure Basis

Demand subsidies can be tenure neutral or encourage households to move into a particular tenure, reflecting the particular institutional configuration of housing tenure. In many developed countries, indirect assistance through the tax system provides greater financial incentives for households to purchase homes rather than rent. The design of direct demand subsidies varies according to the role and composition of different housing tenures in a country. Some schemes are tenure neutral, such as the housing allowance schemes that offer assistance to both low-income home owners and renters with their housing costs (e.g., France, Germany, New Zealand, Sweden). In other countries, demand subsidies predominantly assist renters rather than purchasers (e.g., Netherlands, UK) while some

Table 3 Institutional arrangements for housing allowance schemes in selected countries

Country	Wholly within income support	Additional payment for housing within income support (hybrid)	Housing programme
Australia	Yes (for home owners) Federal	Yes (private renters) Federal	Yes (IRR in public housing) State
New Zealand	No	Yes (home owners and private renters) National	Yes (IRR in public housing) National
Canada	Yes (shelter allowances) Province/local	Limited (shelter allowances) Province (Quebec)	Yes (IRR in social housing) Limited: shelter allowance programme (BC) Province/local
USA	Limited (shelter top-up) State/local	No	Yes (IRR in public housing) Yes: Housing vouchers for private renters Federal/state/local
UK	Yes (for home owners) National	No	Yes (all renters) National/local
Netherlands	Limited (all tenures) National	No	Yes (all renters) National

IRR is income-related rents, a form of de facto housing allowance.
Reproduced with permission from Hulse K (2002) Demand subsidies for private renters: A comparative analysis. Final Report No. 24, p. 20. Melbourne, VIC: Australian Housing and Urban Research Institute and Kemp P (ed.) (2007) Housing Allowances in Comparative Perspective, p. 271. Bristol: Policy Press.

have separate systems for home purchasers, private renters, and social housing tenants (e.g., Australia, USA).

Financial Risks

A key issue in designing demand subsidies is whether they are available as of right to eligible households or whether access is selective. This depends largely on whether they are budget limited or not. From this point of view, once-only demand subsidies are often considered preferable in that it is easier to contain costs. For example, substantial and temporary increases were made to once-only cash grants to first home buyers in Australia in 2008–09 to sustain demand for housing and provide support for the residential development and construction industries in the wake of the global financial crisis.

Many schemes are demand driven, that is, households are entitled to assistance if they meet defined eligibility criteria, unlike access to social housing, which is rationed even in countries with large social housing sectors such as the Netherlands. This provides some certainty to low-income households who experience difficulties in paying for their housing but presents risks to governments. Expenditure on direct demand subsidies increases at times of economic downturn when more households may be eligible for assistance. This is particularly the case where demand subsidies such as housing allowances are embedded within income support systems. The costs of demand subsidies can be difficult to control relative to supply subsidies. Some demand subsidies are rationed in order to mitigate this risk. An example of this is Housing Choice Vouchers in the United States, which are budget limited and therefore rationed. There is usually a waiting list for the vouchers and a system of setting priorities for assistance, which is more akin to the way in which social housing (a supply side programme) is administered internationally.

Moral Hazard

The design of demand subsidies for low-income households is often complicated in an attempt to provide an individualised assessment of household circumstances (household size and type, income, and housing costs) relative to housing costs. For example, most housing allowance schemes are variants of a 'housing gap' model. They are designed to address the gap between a minimum contribution that households could be expected to make to their housing costs and their actual housing costs (usually up to a maximum level). Typically housing allowance schemes do not cover the entire gap but some percentage, such as 75% of the gap in Australia and 70% in New Zealand. The rationale for the housing gap model is that, however constrained their circumstances, households have some choice in their housing and hence the level of housing payments. Thus households who choose more expensive housing have to pay at least part of the cost themselves.

Housing Benefit in the United Kingdom is unusual in that it is not based on the housing gap model. Households with incomes at or below social assistance levels can have all of their rent paid if they are social housing tenants, although this does not hold for private tenants. This is thought to be a problem of moral hazard because households have every incentive to get the best housing available and there is no incentive for 'shopping around' to find cheaper housing. For private tenants, rules about 'unreasonable rents' and more recently a Local Housing Allowance are intended to mitigate this risk. Likewise, in the United States, there are a number of design elements to try and address moral hazard including a 'rent reasonableness' test in which a dwelling's rent is assessed against comparable units available for rent in the area.

Unemployment/Poverty Traps

One of the challenges in designing ongoing (recurrent) demand subsidies that target low-income households is what happens as income from wages or salaries increases. This is a particularly important issue in the context of welfare reform in many countries, which aims to reduce dependency on welfare benefits and improve participation in paid work. A technical but important element of the design of such schemes is the rate at which these payments are withdrawn and how this relates to withdrawal of other income support payments and increase in taxation. If the rate of withdrawal is cumulative (stacking of taper rates), a large percentage of any increase in income is offset by withdrawal of income support payments and demand subsidies. This may act as a disincentive to entering work (unemployment trap) or earning more once in work (poverty trap). Ongoing demand subsidy schemes that are operated separately from income support schemes are more likely to have this effect.

Payment to Household or Landlord

By definition, demand subsidies are attached to households, but this does not mean that they are always paid directly to households. In some countries, rental allowances in particular are paid to the landlord on behalf of the household. For example, in the United States, Housing Choice Vouchers are paid to landlords and not to tenants and are only redeemable to assist with rent payments, which is aligned with a long tradition of in-kind rather than cash assistance, such as food vouchers. In other countries, such as Australia and New Zealand, housing allowances are paid as a cash transfer to the household, which means that they may well be spent on other nonhousing costs.

Effectiveness of Demand Subsidies

It is often difficult to gauge how effective demand subsidies are as a policy instrument to assist low-income households since often less information is available than for supply subsidies. There are a number of reasons why this is the case, including difficulty in obtaining reliable data on demand subsidies within income support systems and more particularly social assistance systems which may be implemented at a subnational level, and difficulty in obtaining specific data about the effects of indirect housing demand subsidies using tax data. Furthermore, governments may be reluctant to commit to specific and measurable objectives in schemes that are demand driven.

Housing Affordability

There is generally more information about housing allowances than for other types of demand subsidy, and assessment of effectiveness depends on the objectives of the scheme. All schemes address housing affordability but measure outcomes in different ways. In some cases, the effectiveness is measured as change in the percentage of household income spent on housing costs. However, treating the housing allowance as a housing payment (rent minus the housing allowance as a percentage of household income) produces a more favourable result than treating the housing allowance as an income supplement (rent as a percentage of income including housing allowance). A further way of measuring the effect of housing allowances on affordability is to use a residual income approach, which is to calculate to what extent housing allowances increase income available for other necessary expenditures after paying for housing. This is a measure of the extent to which housing allowances help address housing-related poverty. Using each of these means of measurement can make the same housing allowance schemes appear more or less effective in improving housing affordability.

Housing Choice Vouchers in the United States differ from many housing allowance schemes in that they include other objectives around changing housing consumption as well as addressing affordability problems. In the early years of the programme, the focus was on improving the standard of housing. More recently, a primary aim has been mobility, which has two related components: moving poor and minority households from areas with a high concentration of such households, and encouraging households to move to areas where there is job growth. There have also been a number of vouchers tied to specific objectives such as Welfare to Work and a transition to home ownership, although the scale of these initiatives has been small. Demand subsidies are more likely to be tied to housing quality standards in countries where the stock is in poor condition and does not meet minimum standards.

Housing Demand and Supply

There is surprisingly little information on the extent to which demand subsidies increase housing consumption or affect the supply of affordable housing. In terms of demand, a key piece of research was the Experimental Housing Allowance Program (EHAP) in the United States in the 1970s (Demand Experiment), which tested individual household responses to different types of housing allowances over 3 years in two metropolitan areas. It found that renter households made little change in their housing consumption patterns after receipt of a housing allowance and that only 20–25% of the allowance was spent on housing with the rest on other items. More recent research in the United States and elsewhere continues to support this view. In this respect, the effect of ongoing demand subsidies for rental seems to be releasing more income for nonhousing expenditures, at least in developed countries where housing quality is no longer a major problem.

EHAP also tested the market-wide effects of housing allowances for purchasers and renters on housing prices and rents through 'saturation' coverage in two specific housing markets (Supply Experiment). It found no measurable effect on house prices or rent levels beyond small increases in rent attributable to minor upgrading stimulated by the housing allowances and no increase in supply. More recent reviews in the United States have generally supported these findings, although noting that they did have a positive effect in reducing overcrowding. There is little evidence from elsewhere that demand subsidies elicit an increased supply of housing with rents affordable to households on lower incomes. Indeed, many countries with demand subsidies have reported a shortfall in affordable rental housing, which has escalated since the mid-1990s.

Housing Prices and Rents

In view of the increased reliance by government on demand subsidies, particularly over the last 20 years, an important issue is the extent to which demand subsidies are captured in increased housing prices or rents. The evidence particularly on rents is remarkably thin, and specific studies that have been undertaken are ambiguous in their findings. For example, a study in France where the scale of housing allowances was increased in the 1990s found that landlords and tenants in the private sector may tacitly agree to share the increase in payment by increasing rents, although the extent of the increase is unclear. In contrast, a study in New Zealand found it unlikely that increasing the scale of housing allowances led to increased rents or house prices.

It is likely that the market effects of demand subsidies depend on a number of factors including the market share of households with demand subsidies in either the purchase or rental market and the existence of specific submarkets in which landlords/managers know about and are able to set rents to capture some or all of the housing allowance payment, as is the case with social housing landlords. In a number of countries, demand subsidies for rental provide a significant income stream to social housing providers, particularly if they are paid directly to the landlord on behalf of the household. It has been estimated that about a third of the total rent bill in the United Kingdom is paid for through Housing Benefit, and almost 60% of the rent bill for public (council) housing. In this sense, demand and supply subsidies, while conceptually distinct, blur in practice. If governments seek to target demand subsidies further or reduce levels of payment, there is a flow-on effect in terms of the financial sustainability of social housing.

See also: Access and Affordability: Housing Allowances; Supply-Side Subsidies for Affordable Rental Housing.

Further Reading

Ditch J, Lewis A, and Wilcox S (2001) Social housing, tenure and housing allowances: An international review. In-house Report No. 83. London: Department for Work and Pensions.

Fallis G (1993) On choosing social policy instruments: The case of non-profit housing, housing allowances or income assistance. *Progress in Planning* 40(1): 1–88.

Ferguson B, Rubinstein J, and Vial V (1996) The design of direct demand subsidy programs for housing in Latin America. *Review of Urban and Regional Development* 8: 202–219.

Haffner M and Boelhouwer P (2006) Housing allowances and economic efficiency. *International Journal of Urban and Regional Research* 30(4): 944–959.

Haffner M and Oxley M (1999) Housing subsidies: Definitions and comparisons. *Housing Studies* 14(2): 145–162.

Howenstine E (1986) *Housing Vouchers: A Comparative International Analysis*. New Brunswick, NJ: Center for Urban Policy Research, Rutgers University.

Hulse K (2002) Demand subsidies for private renters: A comparative analysis. Final Report No. 24. Melbourne, VIC: Australian Housing and Urban Research Institute.

Hulse K (2003) Housing allowances and private renting in liberal welfare regimes. *Housing, Theory and Society* 20(1): 28–42.

Kemp P (1997) A comparative study of housing allowances. Department of Social Security, Research Report No. 60. London: The Stationery Office.

Kemp P (ed.) (2007) *Housing Allowances in Comparative Perspective*. Bristol: Policy Press.

Laferrère A and Le Blanc D (2004) How do housing allowances affect rents? An empirical analysis of the French case. *Journal of Housing Economics* 13: 36–67.

Lykova T, Petrova E, Sivaev S, and Struyk R (2004) Participation in a decentralised housing allowance programme in a transition economy. *Housing Studies* 19(4): 617–634.

Norris M, Healy J, and Coates D (2008) Drivers of rising housing allowance claimant numbers: Evidence from the Irish private rented sector. *Housing Studies* 23(1): 89–109.

Steele M (2001) Housing allowances in the US under Section 8 and in other countries: A Canadian perspective. *Urban Studies* 38(1): 81–103.

Relevant Websites

www.centrelink.gov.au – Centrelink (Australian Government), Rent Assistance

www.direct.gov.uk – Directgov (UK) Housing Benefit

www.hud.gov/offices/pih/programs/hcv – US Department of Housing and Urban Development, Office of Housing Choice Vouchers

www.workandincome.govt.nz – Work and Income New Zealand, Accommodation Supplement

www-wds.worldbank.org – World Bank, Demand Side Subsidies for Housing

Democracy and Accountability

M Taylor, University of the West of England, Bristol, UK

© 2012 Elsevier Ltd. All rights reserved.

Introduction

To analyse democracy, power, and accountability in any meaningful way requires far more space than an encyclopaedia of this kind allows. (At risk of considerable oversimplification, however, the article explores issues of legitimacy, accountability and representation raised by the inclusion of new actors in new governance arenas.) It ends by highlighting the continuing tensions in housing and other social policy fields between competing logics of accountability, and their implications for housing.

Models and Theories of Democracy

"Democracy", Stoker claims (2006: 20), "now has pole position as the world's preferred form of democratic governance", with democratic governance extended to some two-thirds of all countries. He defines democratic governance as "a political system that meets the following three criteria:

- Universal suffrage
- Governments chosen by regular, free, and competitive election
- The presence of a set of political rights to free speech and freedom to organise in groups."

Democracy, he argues, also demands a capacity for free exchange of views among citizens and an uncensored distribution of news and opinion.

Most accounts of the development of democracy begin in Athens with the ancient Greeks. The Athenian model of democracy was one in which all (male) citizens were said to be directly involved in decision-making in the city-state. But, despite being held up as an ideal, this involvement was only ever extended to free men and has in any case long been impractical as the polity has expanded, as the focus of power has moved beyond the city to the nation-state, and as societies have become more complex. Liberal democracy has instead emerged as a qualified form of democracy based on popular elections and representative government and founded, as Stoker reminds us above, in individual rights. Governmental powers are limited in various ways so that rights of individuals and minorities are balanced against majority rule.

However, many theorists have pointed out that this results in an elitist form of democracy where power is concentrated in the hands of a few rulers, and citizens only have the right to choose between elites every 4 or 5 years. It is also a blunt tool for representing the diversity of interests within society. Pluralist models of democracy, by contrast, see power as being dispersed throughout society. In these models, democratic decision-making is based upon bargaining between different interests, with the state acting as a neutral arbiter.

In corporatist models of democracy, the potential problems of mediating between fragmented and conflicting interests are addressed by institutionalising interests along religious or economic lines through peak organisations, which are then incorporated into the policy process. In return for direct channels of bargaining, leaders of key organised interests are expected to deliver support for agreed policies and keep their members firmly in line. However, this can still privilege certain interests over others and offers no guarantee against elitism within the peak organisations themselves.

The pluralist view of the state in liberal-democratic societies – as a neutral arbiter and agent of democratic social order, with no inherent bias towards any class or group – has attracted much criticism. As one dominant pluralist theorist argued in his later work (Dahl, 1989), pluralist politics is not played on a level playing field. The state is an active participant in the political process, primarily and inevitably the guardian and protector of dominant economic interests and elites. Public choice theory, meanwhile, has highlighted the power of the bureaucracy in a technically developed world, arguing that the bureaucracy has become self-serving rather than serving the public interest.

Regime theorists seek a middle way between models based on elite hegemony and those based on plural interests by emphasising the interdependence of governmental and nongovernmental forces. They argue that no government is likely to be able to exercise comprehensive control in today's complex world. Instead, they argue that power is mediated through informal yet relatively stable groups, which include those nongovernmental actors who can contribute the kind of institutional resources that enable them to have a sustained role in making governing decisions.

Another long-standing theoretical tradition, however, represented by writers such as Mill and Rousseau, has argued for models which would allow for more widespread political participation on the part of individuals and for direct and active involvement by citizens – the

Athenian model writ large. Drawing on this tradition, contemporary theorists have argued for associative forms of democracy, based on self-managed enterprises, "which allow their members control of the resources at their disposal without direct interference from the state, political agencies or other third parties" (Held, 1996: 323). They have also argued for new processes of decision-making, based on the Habermasian ideal of 'communicative action'. Habermas is critical of the instrumental rationality that pervades politics, arguing that it has crowded out other forms of reasoning and allowed abstract systems to invade the 'life-world'. Conscious of the inevitability of conflict between divergent world views, he argues instead for a democratic reasoning process based upon ongoing dialogue and the development of mutual understanding between different interests in what he calls an 'ideal-speech' situation, that is, between people who are equal in power and anchored in civil society.

While these are theoretical ideals, a number of factors have contributed to a growing interest in participatory models of governance in the world of policy and practice. Declining public confidence in the formal democratic system, combined with the complexity of contemporary society and the fragmentation of interests within it, mean that the state no longer has the resources, knowledge, or legitimacy to govern on its own. Governance theorists describe how new participatory spaces have emerged "at a distance from government", with policy communities and regimes opened up to a wider spread of actors – a phenomenon described by Rhodes (1997: 110) as "the ultimate in hands-off government".

More sceptical views of the potential of governance, however, argue that central control persists, despite the appearance of decentralised network forms of governing. Rather than being exercised overtly in an elite, however, new forms of control are more subtle. Thus Stephen Lukes (2005) identifies three levels of power, which can be simply characterised as follows:

- The first dimension, where A has power over B.
- The second dimension, where A sets the agenda and excludes B's issues from consideration – what has been called the 'mobilisation of bias'.
- The third dimension, where B internalises A's assumptions without question – where power-holders mould the way citizens think about what is possible or not possible.

Insofar as new governance spaces take on the assumptions and rules of engagement of the state and existing regimes, the mere presence of new actors is unlikely of itself to mean that power is shared more widely.

This analysis resonates both with Gramsci's earlier development of the idea of hegemony and Foucault's later analysis of power. Foucault explores how discursive practices and the development of 'regimes of truth' have moulded the perceptions and behaviour of 'subjects' and secured their willing compliance. Along with the governmentality school that he inspired, Foucault analysed the technologies through which individuals come to govern themselves. State power, he argued, had become decoupled from the state as government and was instead produced through a range of sites and alliances at a distance from the state. He did not present this as a conscious or totalising process nor did he equate power directly with the state. Indeed later, he and others have explored the potential for resistance and for participants to become 'active subjects', who are able to shape and influence the exercise of governing. However, Foucault did warn that forms of power outside the state can often sustain the state more effectively than its own institutions (Taylor, 2007).

These theories can be applied at any level of governance from the local to the global. But before leaving this brief survey of some of the major theories of democracy, it is important to consider how globalisation affects our thinking about democracy. Dahl (1989) has charted how 'first order' democracy, developed in the city-state, evolved into 'second order' democracy, developed in relation to the nation state. However, many of the policies that affect citizens at local and national level have their origins in wider global trends and are not amenable to the control of local – or even national – democratic processes. Globally, there is no state as such and no elected representative system. Indeed, it is difficult to imagine how a representative system would work at this level. The governance of global spaces, therefore, lacks democratic legitimacy. But globalisation frames the way in which decisions are taken at national and local levels. New approaches and models are therefore needed to make sense of the multiple levels of government that affect contemporary society.

Legitimating Participation

So far, this article has described how the theory and practice of democracy has evolved in parallel with the increasing complexity and diversity of interests within society. But what legitimates the decision-makers? In liberal models of democracy, the legitimacy of the governors is based on competitive elections and the right of citizens to vote. But if participatory models are now in the ascendant, who has legitimacy to govern and why?

Despite a largely positive rhetoric, the rationales for engaging 'the public' in governance are often overlapping and confused, leading to conflicting expectations and hence frustration. Goodlad et al. (2003) have described three main rationales: developmental, instrumental, and "due process". The developmental rationale promotes participation as fostering personal development, a democratic political culture, and social integration; the instrumental rationale promotes it as ensuring that decisions reflect the interests of the diversity of citizens but also that citizens 'buy into' and abide by decisions; the 'due process' rationale is based on the intrinsic right to participate, irrespective of outcome. But the public – or citizens – may be constituted in different ways by those who invite them into governance arenas (Barnes et al., 2007). Members of the public may be involved as service consumers, as citizens, or as co-producers of services, each of which implies a distinctive understanding of the rationale for their engagement and what is expected of them. Empowering people as individual consumers of particular services or drawing on their expertise as providers is a very different concept from empowering them as citizens who engage in the definition and pursuit of the common good. If we apply this analysis to housing, for example, members of the public may be involved in policy and the management of their housing as tenants (service recipients), as members of the local community, as service providers in the local community, or as tenant managers – each of which implies a different investment and different expectations. Members of the community, for example, may include people who are not tenants of public housing.

Related to this is the question of their legitimacy. Citizens may be invited to participate as individuals, as collective actors, or as an ill-defined 'public'. They may be expected to be 'representative' of particular interests or simply to 'reflect' the interests of particular population groups. Brown et al. (2001) distinguish between four types of legitimacy: political, moral, constitutional, and technical. Those involved in governance fora may have 'political' legitimacy – in that they are elected to represent a particular interest or population group. They may have 'constitutional' legitimacy (they have to be involved). They may have 'moral' legitimacy (they 'ought' to be involved). Or they may have 'technical' legitimacy – in that they bring particular kinds of knowledge to the table. Thus in the public housing field, legitimacy may be accorded to tenants' or community representatives because they are elected and mandated by other tenants or community members. It may be accorded them because legislation requires them to be involved. It may be accorded them because providers feel they should be involved as a matter of principle. Or it may be accorded them because of the knowledge they have as recipients of the housing service and members of the local community.

Particular tensions arise in relation to 'political' legitimacy. If members of the public are elected and mandated to be involved in governance, how does this relate to the legitimacy of the formally elected politician? It is not uncommon in community partnerships, for example, for community members to be challenged by others around the table in relation to their representativeness and their mandate. But as voting figures continue to fall and elected politicians become increasingly atypical of the population as a whole, claims to representative legitimacy are becoming increasing tenuous. Indeed, Saward (2005: 190) is highly critical of traditional representative models for their failure to reflect marginalised interests, emergent interests, or what he calls "intense interests", adding that "traditional geographic constituencies do not have the characteristics, faultiness or policy preferences that can be simply read-off by would-be elected representatives" (Saward, 2005: 181).

Rather than attempting to be representative, therefore, a more realistic aspiration for those engaged in decision-making arenas may be to be accountable – to those whose interests they are expected to reflect and to those who will be affected by their decisions. But the new governance poses a fundamental challenge also to the established principles and practice of public accountability and it is to this that we now turn.

Accountability

Accountability is a term that is being applied on an ever-widening scale, with an enormous growth of formal and informal accountability requirements. Unpacking accountability involves several elements. Leat (1996) has defined these as follows:

- To whom is accountability owed? Funders, consumers, the community, regulatory bodies, professional peers? (upwards, downwards, lateral)
- For what? Fiscal accountability (the proper use of money), process or procedural accountability, programme accountability (the quality of their work)?
- What type of accountability is required? Accountability with sanctions (being held to account), explanatory accountability (giving an account), responsive accountability (taking into account)?

However, in an increasingly complex environment even clarifying and applying these elements becomes increasingly challenging.

Accountability to Whom?

As well as recognising different legitimacy claims, as we have seen above, different players in new governance arenas will have multiple accountability claims – upwards, downwards, and lateral – which they will prioritise in different ways. In addition, as services are outsourced, accountability chains become attenuated and principal agent models become difficult to apply. There is no longer an automatic link to the electorate at large, which would give citizens the power to vote those running their services out of office. Potential users of outsourced services may also lose the rights that they had when these services were part of the state. When the Human Rights Act was introduced in the UK in 1998, for example, there were doubts as to whether housing associations and other non-state bodies would be covered as 'public authorities' under the Human Rights Act, 1998, despite significant levels of public resources into, and state oversight of, these organisations. The 1995/96 Nolan inquiries into *Standards in Public Life* in the UK, on the other hand, did treat housing associations as 'local public spending bodies' within the scope of its inquiry, suggesting that their activities should be more open to critical local scrutiny.

It is not only services that are outsourced. Increasingly, financial and regulatory functions are being outsourced to bodies at arm's length from the state. This again raises questions of accountability, as well as running the risk of regulator capture as relationships are established between providers and these new bodies. Richard Kaye (2006) also notes the growing phenomenon of 'meso-regulators' appointed by the state to oversee self-regulation in the professions. Again this raises questions of public accountability. Who, he asks, regulates the regulators?

While market principles threaten accountability to the public or to citizens, however, they do highlight the need for accountability to consumers, both through individual systems of redress and through representation on governance bodies. In the housing field in the UK, for example, housing associations and other social landlords are more likely to have their service users on their boards than most other public service providers. They may also involve other community members where their functions go beyond housing. However, questions remain about the control that part-time board members can exercise over professional staff. And as the logic of the market favours a shift away from locally based to regional and national bodies, links with the locality may themselves be attenuated, with implications for local accountability.

For What?

Day and Klein (1987) argue that effective accountability requires a common currency of expectations. But in an increasingly complex and fragmented policy environment, this common currency is becoming increasingly difficult to find. In public housing in the UK, for example, Mullins (2006) has identified two dominant institutional logics of accountability. Under the first, service providers are accountable to the market and to funders for providing value for money, which tends to be equated with scale and efficiency. Under the second — which he calls local accountability — service providers are expected to be responsive to their local communities and users and provide opportunities for local residents to be at the heart of decision-making. These, he argues, are contradictory.

While in the UK public funding has continued to be a central feature of housing provision despite the transfer of housing stock from the public to the third sector, local authorities have been represented in governance structures and local accountability has maintained a significant foothold. However, as the role of local authorities in housing is reduced, and private house-builders have entered the social housing market, Mullins argues that this representation is under threat.

What Type?

The increased dominance of the market in public services, along with a perceived need to restore public confidence in public services, has led to increased reliance on technical forms of accountability — performance management and audit. This has put increasing power into the hands of auditors and accountants. This might be seen to provide Day and Klein's common currency of expectations, accompanied as it is by targets and league tables. However, the judgements and assumptions on which this kind of accountability is based are largely unquestioned, seen instead to be objective and value-free — a demonstration perhaps of the operation of Lukes' third 'invisible' form of power. Critics maintain that technical forms of accounting are replacing responsibility and crowding out other virtues, such as democracy itself. Indeed an overreliance on technical accountability may also, instead of breeding greater transparency, simply breed new devices for circumventing audit requirements.

Martin (2006) suggests as an alternative that the overview and scrutiny functions introduced in the Local Government Act of 2000 may have the potential to develop a "dialogue of public accountability". In this she joins other voices who are sceptical of top-down technical systems of accountability, calling instead for bottom-up and lateral forms of accountability based on dialogue, learning, and development, which are compatible with the participatory and deliberative forms of democracy that are now in vogue. However, she notes that currently there is no duty for the executive to act on scrutiny or to recognise the authority of the citizenry. Dialogical models are also dependent on the quality of information flows through the system and on the building of informed publics who can analyse critically the information received. The various publics in decision-making forums will have differing information resources available to them and their capacity to hold decision-makers to account will also vary. Such dialogue also requires capacity on the part of decision-makers to communicate complex information effectively and to listen — by no means a foregone conclusion. Effective dialogue will require the skills, resources, time, and imagination both to engage participants and to mediate between different interests. These are skills too often overlooked in the training of housing professionals.

That said, however, there is a wealth of experience on which to draw both in the UK and beyond. More detailed discussion of developments in community and tenants' participation can be found elsewhere in this encyclopaedia.

Conclusions

The two competing logics that Mullins has described reflected a tension that is played out on in the governance of social policy worldwide – between the logics of the market and of business on the one hand and the logics of democracy and citizen participation on the other. Both feature strongly in the rhetoric of policy makers. On the one hand, we have witnessed the rise of the audit profession and of performance management based on what Habermas (1984) called instrumental rationality and predominantly technical forms of legitimacy; on the other, increasing interest in user engagement, community participation, and – in the housing field – tenants democracy, which has been accompanied by a greater emphasis on 'dialogues of accountability' and deliberative models of democracy. It is perhaps a reflection of the complexity of society today that what appear to be contrary trends – or competing logics – can co-exist both in the rhetoric and the practice of social policy. The way the dynamic between these logics plays out in the social housing field will vary from country to country according to the socio-political context and history. But they are global trends, and the tensions they create are likely to shape housing policy and practice – as well as providing fertile ground for research and debate – for some time to come.

See also: Politics of Housing; Power.

References

Barnes M, Newman J, and Sullivan H (2007) *Power, Participation and Political Renewal: Case Studies in Public Participation*. Bristol: The Policy Press.

Brown D and Associates (2001). Civil society legitimacy: A discussion guide. In Brown D (ed.) *Practice-Research Engagement and Civil Society in a Globalizing World*. Washington DC: Civicus; New York: The Hauser Center for Non-Profit Organizations.

Dahl R (1989) *Democracy and its Critics*. New Haven and London: Yale University Press.

Day P and Klein R (1987) *Accountabilities: Five Public Services*. London: Tavistock.

Goodlad R, Docherty I, and Paddison R (2003) Responsible participation and housing: Restoring democratic theory to the scene, Paper presented at the Housing Studies Association Autumn conference, Bristol, 9/10 September, http://www.york.ac.uk/inst/chp/hsa/papers/autumn03/Goodlad.pdf

Habermas J (1984) *The Theory of Communicative Action*, Boston, MA: Beacon Press.

Held D (1996) *Models of Democracy*. Cambridge: Polity Press.

Kaye R (2006) Regulated (self-)regulation: A new paradigm for controlling the professions. *Public Policy and Administration* 21: 105–119.

Leat D (1996) Are voluntary organizations accountable? In Billis D and Harris M (eds.) *Voluntary Agencies: Challenges of Organization and Management*. Basingstoke: Macmillan.

Lukes S (2005) *Power: A Radical View*. London: Palgrave Macmillan.

Martin J (2006) Overview and scrutiny as a dialogue of accountability for democratic local government. *Public Policy and Administration* 21: 56–69.

Mullins D (2006) Competing institutional logics? Local accountability and scale and efficiency in an expanding non-profit housing sector. *Public Policy and Administration* 21: 6–24.

Rhodes R (1997) *Understanding Governance Policy Networks: Governance, Reflexivity and Accountability*. Buckingham: Open University Press.

Saward M (2005) Governance and the transformation of political representation. In Newman J (ed.) *Modernising Governance: New Labour, Policy and Society*, pp. 179–196. Bristol: The Policy Press.

Stoker G (2006) *Why Politics Matters? Making Democracy Work*. London: Palgrave Macmillan.

Taylor M (2007) Participation in the real world: Opportunities and pitfalls in new governance spaces. *Urban Studies* 44: 297–317.

Further Reading

Hirst P (1994) *Associative Democracy: New Forms of Economic and Social Governance*. Cambridge: Polity Press.

Demographic Perspectives in Economic Housing Research

T Lindh and B Malmberg, Institute for Futures Studies, Stockholm, Sweden

© 2012 Elsevier Ltd. All rights reserved.

Glossary

Cohort effects Changes in behaviour or resources due to being born at different points in time, for example, younger birth cohorts have relatively higher income and therefore will have higher future housing demand.

Dynamic stock–flow model A model which predicts, in this case, how prices cause changes in the stock of housing by affecting the flow of housing, that is, the construction of new housing or the demolition of old housing.

Endogenously determined The variables have a mutual interaction, either directly or indirectly, that prevents a causal interpretation of a regression equation.

Indicator variable A variable taking the value of one if an observation has a certain property, or zero if the property is absent.

Rational expectations A technical term in economics asserting that individual agents on an average will correctly forecast future developments in, for example, prices.

Regression The computation of the statistical combination of explanatory variables with the least distance (based on the square of deviations from the average) to observations of a variable dependent on these variables.

Stationarity assumption The assumption necessary for regression analysis that the random variation in the relation between the dependent variable and the explanatory variables has a constant distribution around a constant level.

Introduction

Humans live in houses, and houses are structures where people live. Therefore, there will be a close link between the composition of the population and the residential stock of an area. The link goes both ways. Changes in the population will have an effect on the housing stock. But the housing stock will also influence demographic change. Both links are explored here.

First, the demographic effects from age structure change on house prices and residential investment are discussed. This discussion will start from a well-known research article that illustrates the problems involved in predicting house prices based on demographic data. Second, we discuss how the availability and affordability of housing as well as its quality may affect fertility, mortality, and migration.

There are other demographic connections to housing concerning gender, ethnicity, social stratification, and other issues which are discussed in other articles. The focus here is on the macro demographic development and its relation to overall housing development.

Demographic Effects on Housing Demand

Housing needs change over the life cycle and so does the income available for meeting housing costs. Having children affects the housing decisions of parents. Young adults form their own households, but their housing needs are relatively moderate and their purchasing power is limited. Access to credit is often restricted, at least until the young adult is firmly established in the labour market. Longer education implies a late entry into the labour market, thus pushing the housing career to start later. In family-forming ages, incomes start to grow and so does housing need. When children arrive, space becomes relatively more important than location, and leads to shifting to the suburbs. Around the age of 50, the need for space decreases as the children leave home. The dwelling as a capital asset also becomes more important and characteristics other than space become more desirable, for example, closeness to the workplace or leisure activities rather than closeness to schools and day care. For retirees, closeness to care centres and other social services takes over as desirable location attributes, and with decreasing income, the household budget restrictions tighten.

Age distribution, thus, becomes an important component summing up the total demand for housing. With a lot of people in economically active ages, housing demand is greater. An increase in fertility is associated with increased demand for space. Divorce rates also affect housing demand, but in the direction of increased demand for smaller units.

The demographic structure of the population has, therefore, always been an important consideration in social planning of housing construction. In Sweden, special multi-family housing for families with many children was, in the 1930s, a response to the miserable housing conditions that many saw as one of the most important reasons for decreasing fertility and reduction in reproduction rates for people with low income. In many countries, social housing with special conditions has been subsidised for similar reasons.

It would seem reasonable to expect that economic research on housing, long ago, should have incorporated demographic structure as a crucial factor that could explain developments in the housing market. But although there is some early work in the area, it is only in recent decades that demography has become prominent as a research issue.

The traditional way of transforming population data into housing demand forecast has been to use headship rates. The proportions of the age group that head different types of households are easily determined on the basis of survey data. If combined with population projections by age, the result is a projection of how the number of different types of households will change in the future. The method is simple but it has been criticised for being inadequate in many respects. Most importantly, headship rates do not stay constant over time, and it has proved difficult to project future changes in headship rates. On the other hand, it has been shown that a model that makes prediction of transitions in household status based on age and sex performs much better than the simple headship model. They also make it easier to incorporate assumptions about changing demographic parameters in the projection. The headship approach, however, is not strongly connected to economic theory. Instead, it is based on demographic–statistical modelling.

The focus here is on economic models of age distribution effects on the demand for housing. First, we review some of the more important international research and discuss some different complications that arise in the analysis of age distribution effects on price formation and new construction.

Mankiw and Weil (1989) published the article 'The Baby Boom, the Baby Bust, and the Housing Market'. This study brought a lot of attention to the connection between the American baby boom and own-home prices in the United States. A controversial debate raged and their results were questioned as they predicted a free fall in house prices during the 1990s (47%!). In *Regional Science and Urban Economics*, 1991, half a dozen critical articles were published contradicting this forecast.

Let us have a closer look at the analysis since its shortcomings are very instructive. Using census data and real estate registers, the value of an owned home was distributed to the household members by a regression approach. This was used to create an estimate of the average housing consumption in each age group. This housing consumption profile over age is more or less consistent with the loose intuition about life cycle change in housing needs sketched above. Housing demand is at its peak in the ages between 40 and 60 years. It has a sharp increase in connection to household formation between 20 and 30 years and is slowly decreasing among the elderly.

By summing up the number in each age group and multiplying with the average age-specific housing demand, a number can be given for the total housing demand contingent on age structure. Regressing house prices on this demand variable and a number of controls measuring user costs and incomes, the estimated demand coefficient is assumed to measure the age contingent change in house prices.

Formally it is assumed that the demand of household i, D_i, can be summed up from the age of the n household members' individual housing demand $D_{ij} = \sum_a \alpha_a D_{ij}^a$, where α_a measures average individual demand for each age group and include effects from rising income. If the age of the individual is a, the indicator variable D_{ij}^a is equal to 1, otherwise 0. Using information on household housing wealth and its age composition, the value of the age-specific housing demand can then be estimated. If the household owns its dwelling, tax values or market values are used otherwise, the rent for the dwelling is multiplied by a standard factor. For example, assume a household with a married couple 34 and 35 years old, with two children, 4 and 8 years old. The housing demand of the household is then computed as:

$$D_i = \alpha_{34} + \alpha_{35} + \alpha_4 + \alpha_8$$

The regression of the series D_i over households indexed by i on the age dummies for household composition D_{ij}^a provides the estimate for average demand in each age profile.

Using population data, we can then get an estimate of total demand D_t at time t, by simply multiplying the number of persons in each age group with the age-specific demand and sum over all ages.

In the next step, a price equation can be estimated where the price level of housing is explained by the demographic demand variable. When Mankiw and Weil then projected this equation forward using standard demographic projections and assumptions on income growth and user costs, they arrived at the sensational result that house prices would drop by 47% in the United States during the 1990s. This prediction was rather far from what actually happened and there were already plenty of critics when the article was published. In important aspects, it was also a well-founded critique. The empirical analysis was 'bold' not to say 'heroic', and the authors themselves had many qualifications already in the original article. There were several follow-up studies, however (on Canadian, Swedish, and Japanese data), that found quite a similar demand pattern with a peak in demand around the age of 40 years which then gradually decreased.

There are a number of different problems with the assumptions made in the study that provides a convenient focus to scrutinise the difficulties of predicting house prices by demography. In the ensuing debate after publication, three main points were made:

- Housing demand should depend on the cost of housing services, which is not necessarily the same as the house price. Housing costs depend on several factors apart from the asset price of the house, for example, operating costs, taxes, and subsidies, and such other factors that may vary quite a lot even in close neighbourhoods.
- Housing supply is often very elastic in the long run, and so demand changes should show up primarily as quantity adjustments, that is, new construction or demolition.
- Since the increase in household-forming individuals by the American baby boomers could be foreseen at least 20 years ahead, in expectation terms, the market should already have taken account of the demand shock and discounted it in prices.

The third argument was discussed already in Mankiw and Weil's original article, and their conclusion was that the market for owned homes is not characterised by rational expectations but rather adaptive expectations. This means that expectations on house prices on an average will not be correct but tend to be systematically wrong over long periods of time, creating both bubbles and busts in the housing markets. There are some good reasons why this may be the case, for example, information costs, uncertainty surrounding internal migration, asymmetric information on the housing market, and so on. This remains a controversial subject in the research literature though.

The first argument hinges on the extent of covariation between house prices and housing costs. The standard dynamic stock–flow model posits that the degree of covariation is rather strong, but does open for the possibility that, for example, large interest rate shocks may cause house prices to go in other directions than the housing costs and overshoot the equilibrium prices while the construction markets adapt to the new circumstances. Several of the other user cost factors like taxes should also be capitalised in the house prices. For example, a decreased real estate tax will at first lower both user costs and house prices, but prices will then turn up again without any further change in costs as residential construction can satisfy the increased demand for housing, only with a considerable delay.

This, like the second argument above, of course, depends on how fast the supply of owned homes reacts to demand changes. With immediate adaptation of the quantity, price would be entirely determined by production costs and no or small price effects would arise. But it takes time to build houses and there are location constraints on the quantity, and so it is reasonable to expect at least temporary price effects from demographic variation. Still some of the effects should also show up in residential investment variation. In fact, the forecasting properties of a residential investment equation based on demography seem to be a lot better than the corresponding performance of price equations.

But the price regression equation used by Mankiw and Weil also has a serious technical deficiency because the variables are trended and the stationarity assumption is violated. This is liable to substantially bias the estimated effects by covariation of trends that are unrelated to the relation between demography and housing prices. This is likely to be the decisive reason for the dramatic prediction of a major drop in the house prices. It has been shown that with a better method to handle the trends, the effects of age structure changes mainly show up in residential investment.

There are some other problems that have been less discussed in the debate. One is the shape of the age profile of housing demand. Most researchers agree that there should be an effect from household formation on housing demand, even if the exact age for household formation is endogenously determined. Falling demand in old age is, however, often claimed to be a cohort effect, that is, the observed lower demand from older people is a reflection of older birth cohorts having had a lower life cycle income than younger cohorts. Therefore, an ageing population would not have any effects on housing demand. It has also been demonstrated that elderly people do not move out of their own homes to the extent many would believe.

Some systematic studies on the issue of cohort effects find that a large part of the fall in demand is in fact a cohort effect due to older cohorts having less economic resources than young cohorts. Following a given cohort over time, housing demand does not start to fall around the age of 50 years as cross-section estimates would indicate, but considerably later between 60 and 70 years of age. At these ages, there is nevertheless a downward tendency that is probably due to the elderly starting to move into nursing homes and other facilities adapted to their health problems.

The conclusion would be that the actual age profile of housing demand over the life cycle has a rather sharp upturn between 20 and 30 years of age and then increases at a slower pace to reach a maximum somewhere between 40 and 70 years and then starts falling. The price effects are, however, related to the whole of the age distribution and depend on numerous other factors in the economy.

It seems that no study has solved the problem of macroeconomic feedback in a satisfactory way. Mankiw and Weil simply assume that the demand profile for a given year is constant in order to construct a demographic demand variable that is supposed to hold for every year. Yet, it is clear from the article that the demand profile for 1970 differs considerably from that of 1980. One plausible interpretation of these age profiles could be that middle-age groups are less price sensitive than the younger and the older age groups and therefore increase their housing demand more than these economically weaker groups when average incomes grow. There is micro-data evidence indicating that there really are considerable differences in price elasticity for housing between different age groups.

This difference in elasticities at different ages reflects that household formation and choice of housing tenure are intimately related to credit conditions and general macroeconomic conditions. These factors are of differential importance in different phases of the life cycle. An increase in the real interest rate means quite different things for a young adult starting a housing career with large loans at high interest and an older agent living in a house with low loan-to-value ratio and perhaps fixed interest on the loans. The young agent will tend to decrease housing demand while the latter has no such incentives. This is a simplification, of course, and in reality there are complications associated with tax rules and expectations for the future as well as the depressing effect that will follow the rise in user cost when capital costs increase. In general, we will, however, expect substantial differences in reaction between those who are established homeowners and those who have not yet become homeowners, as well as differences between those who have paid down their loans and those who have not, between those who still have children living at home and those who have not.

The influence of age distribution will, therefore, be modified quite considerably by indirect macroeconomic effects. Theoretically, we would therefore expect that the age profile of demographically based housing demand may vary quite a lot depending on upturns and downturns in prices. This kind of interaction cannot be controlled for in a regression just by compensating for the price trends, since the actual real quantity of housing services will vary more for the middle-aged households than for other groups.

Another way to express the same thing is to say that the age-specific demand is endogenously determined and consequently the residual in the price equation is correlated with the measure of demand, leading to bias in the estimated coefficient. Moreover, a large part of macroeconomic changes are dependent on the variation in the age distribution, and so further problems arise in identifying the quantitative effect on prices of age structure variation.

Finally, a rather obvious fact has been neglected in the debate. Mortality rate rises strongly around the age of 70 years in developed countries. First, when the number of old people in the population increases, the death rates rise and the flow of vacancies in the housing stock increases. This can either be seen in flow terms as an increase in the supply of housing available to those seeking new housing, or alternatively as a decrease in the demand for new residential investment.

Secondly, increased mortality rates in old age should in general lead to a decrease in consumption, since without perfect annuity markets rational individuals should discount future consumption heavier in the final stages of life. There is one obvious exception: health consumption, since that prolongs life and thus serves as an investment to decrease the mortality risk. Nonetheless, older people only exceptionally sell their houses. This fact is, however, perfectly consistent with a lower consumption of housing services by decreasing maintenance and operating costs. For example, elderly may be shutting off heating in some rooms in the winter or accepting flaws in comfort in order to save on repairs, and so forth.

The Effects of Housing on Demographic Change

Local population growth is determined by birth rates, death rates, and migration. Each of these factors, in turn, can be influenced by housing conditions. Historically, housing quality was an important factor in determining mortality. Overcrowding and unhygienic dwellings were the factors that kept mortality high in many cities during the early phases of industrialisation; so high, in fact, that the population would have dwindled were it not for a continuous supply of migrants from rural areas. Moreover, improved housing conditions have been singled out as a key factor behind the mortality decline that took place over the last two centuries.

Housing factors have also, recently, been given increased attention in migration research. Traditionally, employment opportunities and wages have been seen as the most important determinants of migration. Given the very large differences in house prices across regions that we can observe nowadays, changes in disposable real income (after housing costs) can be at least as dependent on differences in housing cost as on differences in labour income. Housing market effects are also a likely explanation why urban areas that serve as gateways for international migration often experience high rates of internal net out-migration. Moreover, if the supply of new housing is not elastic enough, large inward migration flows can lead to rapidly increasing house prices and housing shortages that will put a brake on further in-migration, and slow down employment growth. That may well be the case as crowding or housing regulations limit the scope for new construction.

The effects of the housing stock on mortality have long been acknowledged in academic research and especially in public health research. The importance of housing considerations for migration decisions is clear for anyone who has been considering migration. The effect of housing on fertility is more subtle. Malthus, for example, argued that the 'difficulty of procuring habitations' was one reason why England, in spite of its poor laws, had relatively low fertility by European standards in the beginning of the nineteenth century. But this has gone almost unnoticed in the shadow of his well-known dismal conclusion that population growth inevitably would lead to human living standards never exceeding the subsistence level in the long run. Research around the reasons for decreasing fertility has, instead, centred on the effects of education, female employment, urbanisation, and family planning.

During the last 10 years, there has, however, been an increasing interest in how housing market conditions can influence fertility. In many places, allocation of housing on the basis of family status has encouraged young people to have children relatively early. In a discussion of options for pronatalistic policies, prominent researchers now point to the fact that inadequate or expensive housing conditions is a major reason why young people choose to limit their fertility. In a recent US study, it is shown that housing cost, including the effects of housing subsidies, has a strong effect on the fertility decisions of economically vulnerable women. Another recent US study takes a broader perspective and analyses the effect of high rents on fertility behaviour in general. Their findings support the idea that housing costs act as a constraint on childbearing. In Europe, researchers have also looked at the effects of the type of housing on fertility and found a positive correlation between fertility and living in a single-family house and in the suburbs.

The recent appearance of studies that demonstrate the effects of housing market on fertility behaviour indicates that this is an area of research that could benefit from increased attention. In particular, since low birth rates in ageing countries are seen as an important future policy problem.

Conclusion

There are many different aspects of the linkage between demography and housing. Closely related to the migration issues are ethnic enclaves and housing, the functionality and mobility on the labour market, transportation and commuting. As already noted, there are many indirect links both at the individual and local levels and at the economy-wide and even global level that have been ignored in this article. One of the really central aspects is the fundamental role of real estate and mortgage markets in the determination of exactly how demography interacts with housing and construction. Financial crises may result from demographically induced decreases in demand in one country, with serious repercussions on the global markets. Moreover, since the construction sector often plays a key role in business cycle fluctuations, recessions may be triggered when the number of economically active adults decreases and the demand for new housing weakens, as will be the case in many major economies like Germany, Japan, and Italy. Residential investment is a major part of the investment activity in an economy and its connection to demography means that the domestic balance between saving and investment spills over into the external balances between economies.

Housing expenses are a major part of the household budget for nearly all people. Wealth in the form of owned homes is a dominant part of the wealth owned by most people, and so demographically induced fluctuations in house prices also affect the well-being and affluence of a great majority of individuals. Thus, the degree of inequality in welfare and life opportunities can be substantially affected by variations in housing demand. Moreover, the self-employed in many countries rely on their housing wealth as collateral for financing their business.

These examples serve only as a small sample in illustrating how important the structure of the population and the relation to the housing market is for the welfare of the population and ultimately to the global economy. Many of these links are insufficiently researched and still not well understood.

Although demography and housing are closely linked topics, this linkage is not strongly reflected in either housing research or demographic research. When the demography–housing link is ignored, there is a risk that both demographers and housing researchers will misjudge potentially important explanatory factors. In turn, this may lead economists and financial advisors to faulty policy conclusions. Politicians taking this advice ad notam then design policies that are unsustainable against the background of demographic change. On the other hand, and on a more positive note, one may argue that the intersection between demography and housing studies thus forms an important research field that is yet relatively unexplored and, therefore, one that offers rich opportunities for new and interesting studies.

See also: Forecasting in Housing Research; Housing Wealth Over the Life Course; Immigration and Housing: North-Western Europe; Immigration and Housing: United States; Life Course; Migration and Population Mobility; Older People: Well-Being, Housing and Neighbourhoods; Price Dynamics in Housing Markets.

Reference

Mankiw NG and Weil DN (1989) The baby boom, the baby bust, and the housing market. *Regional Science and Urban Economics* 19: 235–258.

Further Reading

Boyer GR (1989) Malthus was right after all: Poor relief and birth rates in Southeastern England. *The Journal of Political Economy* 97: 93–114.

DiPasquale D and Wheaton WC (1994) Housing market dynamics and the future of housing prices. *Journal of Urban Economics* 35: 1–27.

Engelhardt GV and Poterba JM (1991) House prices and demographic change: Canadian evidence. *Regional Science and Urban Economics* 21(4): 539–546.

Fair RC and Dominguez KM (1991) Effects of the changing U.S. age distribution on macroeconomic equations. *American Economic Review* 81(5): 1276–1294.

Frejka T and Ross J (2001) Paths to subreplacement fertility: The empirical evidence. *Population and Development Review* 27: 213–254.

Hendershott PH (1991) Are real house prices likely to decline by 47 percent? *Regional Science and Urban Economics* 21: 553–563.

Holland AS (1991) The baby boom and the housing market: Another look at the evidence. *Regional Science and Urban Economics* 21: 565–571.

Krieger J and Higgins DL (2002) Housing and health: Time again for public health action. *American Journal of Public Health* 92: 758–768.

Lindh T and Malmberg B (2008) Demography and housing demand – what can we learn from residential construction data? *Journal of Population Economics* 21(3): 521–539.

Mulder CH (2006) Population and housing: A two-sided relationship. *Demographic Research* 15: 401–412.

Muth RF and Goodman AC (1989) *The Economics of Housing Markets*. New York: Harwood Academic Publishers.

Pitkin JR and Myers D (1994) The specification of demographic effects on housing demand: Avoiding the age-cohort fallacy. *Journal of Housing Economics* 3: 240–250.

Poterba JM (1984) Tax subsidies to owner-occupied housing: An asset market approach. *Quarterly Journal of Economics* 99: 729–752.

Venti SF and Wise DA (1989) Aging, moving and housing wealth. In: Wise DA (ed.) *Economics of Aging*, pp. 9–54. Chicago, IL: University of Chicago Press.

Demolition

J Crump, University of Minnesota, St. Paul, MN, USA

© 2012 Elsevier Ltd. All rights reserved.

Glossary

Accumulation The profit earned through the circulation of money through the built environment of the city.
Demolition The purposeful destruction of buildings using mechanical or explosive means.
Displacement The involuntary movement of individuals, families, and/or communities in response to demolition.
Mega-event International events such as the Olympics or a World Cup that encourage host cities to demolish older structures.
Urban renewal A programme in the United States that targeted minority neighbourhoods for demolition and redevelopment.

Introduction

According to the Centre on Housing and Rights and Evictions (COHRE), in 2007 and 2008 over 1.5 million people were forcibly evicted from their homes when their houses and neighbourhoods were demolished. The large majority of these evictions and demolitions were carried out to clear land for urban regeneration schemes, for mega-events such as the Olympics or a World Cup, and to provide a superficial visual fix for deep-seated problems of urban poverty.

Evictions and demolitions frequently occur through government fiat and residents have little or no say in project planning. In addition, residents who lose their shelter via demolition often receive no assistance with relocation and frequently lose a substantial portion of the equity they have accumulated. The demolition of housing and the subsequent eviction and forced removal of residents constitute a major human rights violation.

In this article on demolition I focus on housing demolition in cities. I begin with an examination of the first instance of widespread demolition in the name of urban redevelopment: the Haussmannisation of Paris. Next, we will journey to Chicago and investigate the role of demolition in maintaining racial segregation in housing and promoting the urban development schemes of a powerful urban growth coalition. Next, I focus on the linkages between housing demolition and mega-events such as the Olympics. Here, the vast housing demolitions that preceded the Beijing games provide a recent example. Finally, I discuss the role of demolition in facilitating urban accumulation regimes under capitalism.

Demolition is part of a process of 'creative destruction' and the building and demolition of the built environment are, as David Harvey aptly notes, key moments in the urban process under capitalism. Demolition rids the city of places that stand in the way of accumulation. Old factories, for example, need to be cleared to make room for new entertainment districts intended to attract paying customers to the city spectacle. Used in this manner, demolition serves as a spatial fix to problems of capital accumulation.

Also often subject to demolition are slums, ghettos, and other neighbourhoods that are considered threatening (visually or otherwise) by the urban elite. Such demolitions are not intended as a way to address deep-seated problems of uneven development. Rather the goal is to push the poor out of sight and out of mind. In the United States, urban renewal, public housing 'transformation', and gentrification all lead to the demolition of housing.

Haussmann: The Demolition Artist

The first (and still the most famous) example of urban reconstruction and demolition on a massive scale is Haussmann's legendary remaking of Paris in the mid-nineteenth century. Known as the 'demolition artist' by his critics, Haussmann cut wide swathes through the medieval fabric of Paris to clear the way for the construction of wide boulevards that facilitated the accelerated movement of people and goods through the city. The sight lines created by Haussmann's boulevards allowed newly constructed monuments and buildings such as the Opera House to dominate the urban landscape. In a precursor to numerous urban redevelopment schemes to follow, thousands of affordable housing units were demolished to make way for the new development. However, critics note that housing conditions for neighbourhoods off the main boulevards remained abysmal for many residents.

The Haussmannisation of Paris not only stimulated capital accumulation via demolition and construction activities, but, the cutting of new streets, also provided the means whereby military units could be quickly moved throughout the city to contain any insurrections. The widespread destruction of working-class neighbourhoods also served to eliminate the territorial bases for protest, as the wide, defensible boulevards replaced the easily barricaded, narrow streets of many Paris neighbourhoods. Haussmann's demolitions facilitated capital accumulation in two ways: first, by using up excess capital via demolition and reconstruction; and second, by utilising urban design as a mode of social control. Needless to say, these two aspects of the demolition process are still with us today.

Haussmann used a set of biological metaphors to justify the widespread destruction of the Parisian built environment. Based on the fallacious reasoning that the city functions as a biological entity, Haussmann depicted Paris as a sick patient in need of surgery. According to Spiro Kostof, Haussmann used the term 'eventrement' to emphasise the need to perform surgery and excise the diseased portions of the landscape. Invariably this meant the demolition of many working-class neighbourhoods infected as they were with revolutionary fervour.

Following in the mode of Haussmann's Second Empire reconstruction of Paris, the fascist dictator Benito Mussolini was fond of wielding what he termed 'the healing pick'. In fascist Italy, massive demolitions were carried out. The purpose of demolition was to create a blank slate upon which the new history could be embroidered. Following Haussmann's Parisian model, Mussolini remade Italian cities with monumental architecture celebrating his regime's achievements. Urban design served the needs of fascism in recreating the city scene. As Marinetti (quoted in Kostof), "Get hold of picks, axes, hammers and demolish without pity, the venerated cities."

If Mussolini's approach to urban renewal was quite direct, in the United States more technocratic approaches to demolition have been utilised. To illustrate this point I will use Chicago as an example. Developed by a cadre of businessmen seeking to protect the interests of large retailers in the central business district, the implementation of urban renewal in Chicago set the pattern for most other US cities.

Urban Renewal, Public Housing, and Deconcentration by Demolition

During the Second World War, Chicago and other Midwestern industrial cities such as Detroit witnessed a massive influx of African Americans drawn by the availability of industrial jobs and the hope of a better life in the North. The housing choices of African Americans arriving in Chicago were very restricted because of racial discrimination in housing. Since African Americans could live only in a limited area, overcrowding was intense as over 300 000 people lived in a neighbourhood that only had enough housing units to safely house 100 000.

Although the post-Second World War housing shortage affected all racial and ethnic groups, the racial discrimination suffered by the African American population meant that they bore the brunt of the housing shortage. It should also be noted that racial discrimination in the sale and rental of housing is an extremely profitable enterprise. As David Harvey comments, segregated housing markets provide slumlords and other unsavoury actors in the housing market with a spatial monopoly, allowing the gathering of super profits because of the created (via discrimination) shortage of housing.

Because the discriminatory housing market limited their options, African Americans paid much higher rents than whites did for comparable accommodation. It is a sad but simple truism that racial discrimination is very profitable for landlords, real estate agents, and financial institutions.

In Chicago, some new public housing was constructed to ease the housing shortage for blacks. In addition, blacks attempted to break the bounds of the ghetto and seek housing in nearby white working-class districts. These attempts to shift boundaries were met with widespread violence on the part of white ethnics, who fought to prevent the integration of their neighbourhoods. There are numerous examples of white violence used to stop blacks from occupying houses and apartments in neighbourhoods considered white.

Although ethnic working-class whites used direct violence as a way to maintain segregated neighbourhoods, Chicago's urban elite used technocratic and legalistic means to achieve the same end. The implementation of urban renewal in Chicago provides an excellent example of the role of demolition in maintaining housing segregation and the linkages between housing demolitions and urban accumulation. Urban renewal practised Chicago style not only eliminated threats to the central business district but also provided an opportunity to construct densely populated public housing developments that served the important function of containing any potential threat to social order.

The legislative mechanism behind urban renewal was the model for federal legislation that set the tone for urban renewal throughout the United States. Urban renewal legislation allowed the city or designated entities (e.g., business development districts) to condemn 'blighted' neighbourhoods and use eminent domain to acquire the land. Demolition and land clearance were undertaken at public expense. Subsequently, the land was sold at a subsidised price to private developers. The urban renewal model was based on a significant expansion of government power with the public bearing the cost of land assembly and demolition while the private developers acquired potentially valuable urban space at a bargain price.

During the 1950s and 1960s cities throughout the United States utilised urban renewal to demolish the homes of African Americans in order to make way for business and industrial development as well as the construction of the interstate highway network. Urban renewal was clearly a tool designed to demolish minority neighbourhoods. So common was the demolition of minority neighbourhoods that critics of the programme dubbed it 'negro removal'.

In Chicago (as in other US cities) housing demolition could not proceed until replacement housing was found for those displaced. The solution to the need to provide replacement housing quickly led to the construction of large, high-rise public housing projects to provide shelter for the large numbers of blacks displaced by demolition of their neighbourhoods. Thus, the tragedy of urban renewal was compounded because rather than providing badly needed housing and neighbourhood improvement, public housing simply became the repository for the refugees of urban renewal.

A prominent example of how this worked was the construction of the Robert Taylor Homes on the south side of Chicago. After completing the building of the massive McCormick Place Convention Center, construction firms simply moved their concrete production equipment to the Robert Taylor site and began building a massive area of public housing.

The Robert Taylor Homes consisted of 28 high-rise structures that were 16 storeys tall. Many of the over 4000 units were three- or four-bedroom apartments and the project's peak population was 27 000. Over 20 000 of these residents were children, yet the project was constructed with only a single playground. In true modernist form, the buildings occupied only a fraction of the site and were surrounded by inhospitable zones of concrete.

Chicago's public housing was sited to maintain segregation and over 90% of the public housing was constructed in neighbourhoods that were already predominantly minority. Moreover, once Robert Taylor was built, Mayor Daley (the first) shamelessly constructed the Dan Ryan Expressway between Robert Taylor Homes and his native neighbourhood of Bridgeport. Suffice it to say, Chicago's public housing was constructed to maintain segregation, providing housing for the refugees of urban renewal and purposefully isolated from the rest of the city.

What is important to note here is that even though demolition is sold as a way to eliminate poor, minority neighbourhoods and thereby aid those who live in poverty, no real attempt is made to address the roots of urban poverty. Instead, new housing is constructed in the same neighbourhoods actually recreating the ghetto. Demolition does not actually ameliorate the problems caused by racial discrimination in housing. Rather, demolition is used as a spatial fix and simply moves individuals and families from one location to another while failing to deal with the underlying causes of urban problems.

It is also critical to recognise the decisive role of the state, in alliance with urban elites, in producing and reinforcing patterns of racial segregation in housing. The creation, demolition, and subsequent recreation of urban ghettos is a state-sanctioned activity. Demolition is an important tool used by the state to bolster accumulation and to maintain social order by relocating potentially unruly populations.

Those living in segregated public housing high-rises found themselves facing a very challenging environment. As Venkatesh notes, they had to learn how to cope with "project living" and raising families in 16-storey buildings was not easy. In particular, it was nearly impossible to adequately monitor children. In addition to the problems associated with living in poorly designed buildings, deindustrialisation cost many residents their jobs and by 1970 most found themselves without formal employment. However, as Venkatesh demonstrates so well in his ethnography of Robert Taylor, public housing residents found ways to cope with their situation.

Informal economic activity was key to economic survival for many tenants who employed a variety of means to make ends meet. In some ways, 'hustling' provided some earnings and a sense of personal efficacy. Yet, their very illegality meant that entrepreneurs were vulnerable to arrest and shakedowns by gangs demanding payment for protection. Widespread drug sales also meant that the community experienced an influx of addicts who added to the danger and stress of everyday life.

By the early 1990s a wide spectrum of policymakers, researchers, and federal and municipal officials agreed that high-rise public housing was a failed experiment. Researchers explained the alleged 'social pathology' of public housing residents as a result of the overconcentration of poverty. According to the staunchly neoliberal research policy community, to solve the problems allegedly associated with the spatial concentration of poverty, public housing, which concentrates low-income people in the inner city, must be demolished and the residents relocated to mixed-income communities.

The emphasis on social pathology and concentration effects ignores a bitter and ironic truth: as a matter of public policy African Americans were purposefully confined to isolated, densely populated, public housing projects. Thus, they were specifically deprived of the opportunity to live in areas with better schools and job opportunities. It is clear that most of the problems experienced by public housing residents have their root cause in government-sanctioned public policy.

To state the case baldly, the spatial concentration of African Americans decried by researchers in the 1990s was the result of public policy. Even a cursory perusal of the historical records reveals that during the 1950s, African Americans were confined to overcrowded ghettos by housing segregation. When urban renewal began in the late 1950s, blacks found their neighbourhoods targeted for demolition. Having few housing options, they were then steered into new public housing projects that were sited in segregated neighbourhoods and confined behind interstate walls.

Despite well-documented urban histories, in the 1990s the policy research community 'discovered' that African Americans were living in densely populated public housing projects in isolated locations. Deflecting the blame for this by utilising questionable theoretical formulations such as the 'concentration effects' and 'social pathology', housing policy researchers begin to advocate for the demolition of public housing as the solution to concentrated poverty!

Despite major methodological flaws in the available research, neoliberal policy research lends an aura of social scientific respectability, leading to radical changes in the US federal public housing policy. Reflecting the notion that the spatial concentration of poverty exacerbates the problem behaviours associated with low-income populations, the federal public housing policy is now focusing on a spatial fix: demolition of public housing projects and the dispersal of low-income residents. Federally sponsored deconcentration attempts to disperse poverty via two linked federal policy initiatives. First is the demolition of public housing and second is the use of housing vouchers intended to provide the displaced residents of public housing with greater economic opportunity through increased residential choice.

In Chicago, deconcentration via demolition is the explicit goal of the Chicago Housing Authority's (CHA) 'Plan for Transformation'. Utilising funding from the federal government's HOPE IV programme, Chicago has now demolished all nonsenior high-rise public housing units in the city. Approximately 20 000 units of family housing have been demolished. To replace these affordable units, mixed-income developments are being constructed. However, there will still be a net loss of 75% of the public housing units.

Advocates of demolition–deconcentration–dispersal use the results of the Gautreaux evaluation project to provide empirical support for their policy prescription. The basis for the Gautreaux experiment lies in a landmark lawsuit filed on behalf of public housing residents in 1966, wherein the plaintiffs charged that the Department of Housing and Urban Development (HUD) and CHA had practised discriminatory housing policies by purposefully limiting African Americans to public housing projects located in existing ghetto locations. In a 1976 Supreme Court ruling in favour of the plaintiffs, the Gautreaux settlement provided for the dispersal of public housing residents through the provision of Section 8 vouchers that would facilitate the plaintiff's residential mobility.

The emphasis on promoting geographic mobility was based on the idea that the personal habits of African American public housing residents would be remade if they were moved out of the environment of the urban ghetto and exposed to white suburban middle-class role models. To this end, the residential choices of African American relocatees were strictly regulated and the vouchers provided by the Gautreaux settlement could be used only in locations where the minority population was below 30%. According to the advocates of relocation, these restrictions were needed to prevent African Americans from 'reconcentrating' after their removal from public housing. Such a reconcentration, it was argued, would limit the desired social interaction between low-income African Americans and their white middle-class role models.

Mega-Events and Housing Demolition

Demolition of housing is frequently associated with the host cities of mega-events such as the Olympics or a World Cup. In the last 20 years it is estimated that over 2 million people have been forced from their homes to make way for the Olympic Games. Forced evictions and subsequent demolition have been reported in Seoul, Barcelona, Atlanta, Athens, Sydney, and Beijing. Also, in New Delhi, informal settlements have been demolished to clear ground for the Commonwealth Games; in South Africa, demolition is being used to make way for the 2010 FIFA World Cup. Here at least 20 000 people have lost their homes as Cape Town undertakes a 'beautification' project on the highway that links the city with the airport.

The displacement and demolitions that occurred in association with the 2008 Beijing Olympics are perhaps the most blatant example of human rights violations associated with a mega-event. It is estimated that 1.25 million residents have been evicted and had their housing demolished in preparation for the 2008 games. Beijing authorities are noteworthy for their use of propaganda, harassment, and violence used to force people out. A COHRE report also notes the threats used to discourage the efforts of housing rights activists to publicise the urban renewal efforts of the Beijing regime. This report indicates that in the years immediately preceding the Olympics an average of 60 000 homes per year were demolished. These demolitions are estimated to have forced 156 000 (on a yearly basis) people to move.

In addition, COHRE notes that demolitions are continuing even after the Olympics. These demolitions are being carried out in the name of 'cultural preservation' as buildings that are considered 'inappropriate' are eliminated. In reality, this amounts to a gentrification strategy as buildings are rehabilitated exclusively for higher-income occupants.

In Qianmen, a diverse neighbourhood of mixed use has been replaced by new structures that are intended by elite architects to depict what a traditional Chinese neighbourhood *should* have looked like. Ever in the thrall of moneyed interests, architects have designed 'traditional' buildings to house high-end retailers such as Nike and Starbucks. To accomplish the construction of an urban simulacrum, authentic neighbourhoods with historic value were demolished.

Housing Demolition and Human Rights

Adequate and affordable housing is essential for human well-being. The United Nations Declaration on Human Rights as well as the constitutions of over 30 countries declare that housing is a human right. Yet, housing rights are commonly trampled on. Demolition is a major method by which authorities promote accumulation by eliminating unprofitable or unsightly neighbourhoods. It is unfortunate, but accurate to say, that the poor and minority populations suffer the most from the violation of housing rights that occurs so frequently with housing demolition.

See also: Domicide; Eviction; Gentrification; Residential Segregation; Rights to Housing Tenure; Slum Clearance.

Further Reading

Byles J (2005) *Rubble, Unearthing the History of Demolition*. New York: Three Rivers Press.
Centre on Housing Rights and Evictions (2008) *One World, Whose Dream?* p. 35. Geneva, Switzerland: Centre on Housing Rights and Evictions.
Centre on Housing Rights and Evictions (2009) *Global Survey on Forced Evictions*. Geneva, Switzerland: Centre on Housing Rights and Evictions.
Crump JR (2002) Deconcentration by demolition: Public housing, poverty and urban policy. *Environment and Planning D: Society and Space* 20: 581–596.
Harvey D (2006) *Spaces of Global Capitalism, Towards a Theory of Uneven Geographical Development*. New York: Verso.
Hirsch AR (1983) *Making the Second Ghetto, Race and Housing in Chicago, 1940–1960*. Cambridge, MA: Cambridge University Press.
Porteous JD and Smith SE (2001) *Domicide: The Global Destruction of Home*. Toronto, ON: McGill-Queen's University Press.
Sebald WG (2004) *On the Natural History of Destruction*. New York: The Modern Library.
Sugrue TJ (1996) *The Origins of the Urban Crisis: Race and Inequality in Postwar Detroit*. Princeton, NJ: Princeton University Press.
Venkatesh SA (2000) *American Project: The Rise and Fall of a Modern Ghetto*. Cambridge, MA: Harvard University Press.
Vergara CJ (1999) *American Ruins*. New York: The Monacelli Press Inc.
Wacquant L (2008) *Urban Outcasts: A Comparative Sociology of Advanced Marginality*. Malden, MA: Polity Press.

Deposit Assistance Schemes for Private Rental in the United Kingdom

J Rugg, University of York, York, UK

© 2012 Elsevier Ltd. All rights reserved.

Glossary

Deposit guarantee A guarantee offered by a local authority or voluntary sector to a landlord prior to the start of the tenancy that recompense will be made up to a certain level if a tenant breaches predetermined conditions such as owing rent or damaging a property beyond what might be deemed fair wear and tear.

Rental deposit A sum of money required by a landlord or agent prior to the start of the tenancy. The deposit is not returned in full or at all at the end of the tenancy if the tenant breaches predetermined conditions such as owing rent or damaging a property beyond what might be deemed fair wear and tear.

Paying a Deposit to Rent Privately

In many countries it is commonly the case that a household seeking to rent a property on the open market will pay a sum of money termed a 'deposit' or 'bond' to the landlord. This sum of money often equates to the payment of 1 or 2 months' worth of rent. The landlord takes this sum prior to the start of the tenancy and returns it in full to the tenant on termination of the tenancy if certain conditions have been fulfilled. For example, a landlord will withhold some or all the deposit if the tenant owes rent, steals from the property, or damages the property beyond what might be deemed fair wear and tear. A deposit is not the only kind of payment required by a landlord before the start of the tenancy: 1 or 2 months' worth of rent in advance is generally also required. There are local variations in practice: in some areas of the United Kingdom the term 'bond' is preferred to deposit; a deposit may not always be asked for; and tenants may not always be clear about the exact purpose of a sum of cash required in advance by the landlord.

The confusion in terminology and in practice is reflected in confusion in policy responses to this aspect of private renting. It has been acknowledged that some households need assistance with paying a deposit – that can amount to sums that are difficult to pay for those on low or even moderate income. Ostensibly, therefore, help with deposits would simply require some kind of cash payment or loan. However, some welfare lobby groups have claimed that no assistance would be required if landlords did not fraudulently retain some or all the deposit when the tenancy terminated, meaning that tenants are then unable to use this money as deposit on their next property. This issue, in turn, brings forward more general concerns that the practice of unfairly retaining deposits is endemic in the sector. The conflation of two policy threads – supporting deposit payment and managing its fair return – means that policy responses have been framed in the context of ambiguity: it is not always certain which problem is being 'solved' by which initiative. It could be argued that this lack of clarity means the history of help with deposits presents a narrative of missed opportunity. A further and more complex theme is also evident in the history of policy development for deposit assistance: the subversion of an ideal. Both these themes are discussed below.

The Practice of Paying a Deposit

Little is known in quantitative terms about the prevalent practices in asking for and paying deposit on a rental property. Evaluation of a pilot tenancy deposit scheme in 2002 in the United Kingdom provided the context for qualitative research with landlords and tenants on deposit practice. Landlords themselves viewed asking tenants for a deposit as an element of good management. Although the sums being asked for as deposits can be large, it is not necessarily the case that the fee would adequately recompense a landlord for serious damage to a property: for example, where a tenant might leave the property very dirty, needing replacement of carpets, curtains, and redecoration. Rather, the ability to pay a deposit was seen by many landlords as an indication that the tenant is financially stable and so will be at lower risk of defaulting on their rent; it is then a signal that the tenant views the tenancy seriously and intends to act in a responsible manner, and ensures that the tenant's behaviour will be moderated by the desire to see the full return of their deposit.

In the United Kingdom, understanding the nature of the private rental market and its constituent sub- or niche markets is only just beginning to develop. Anecdotal evidence indicates that the practice of charging a deposit will vary substantially within those niche markets. The fact that there were, in 2008 and according to the Survey of English Housing (SEH), 2 982 000 privately renting households does not mean that this number of deposits has been paid. For example, tenants renting from their employer may not necessarily pay a deposit at the start of their tenancy. Many landlords are themselves sometimes inconsistent in their deposit-taking practice. Where a landlord might feel that a particular tenant is 'risky', a slightly larger deposit might be charged or the fee might be waived altogether by a landlord if they know the tenant, or if the landlord knew that an individual might be unable to pay the deposit, but would otherwise make a good long-term tenant.

Statistics on whether deposits are paid are not always collected by the SEH. The SEH report for 1999/2000, where this information was last reported, indicated that 71% of renters whose tenancy had begun since 1993 had paid a deposit; the mean value of the deposits paid was £450. It is uncertain whether the practice of taking a deposit has become more commonplace. An increasing number of tenancies are being managed by letting and managing agents, and as a consequence, it is quite probable that more tenants are being asked for deposits. Large franchised letting agencies – where a number of local offices are controlled centrally – will probably tend to have less flexible and more formal working practices, which mean that the payment of a deposit will always be a requirement.

Under the UK Housing Act of 2004, it became mandatory for all deposits paid on assured shorthold tenancies to be lodged by the landlord or agent into one of three national deposit schemes. Two of these schemes are industry-led and require landlords to take out insurance with respect to the event of a claim against the deposit they hold; the landlord or agent retains control of the deposit themselves. The third scheme is 'custodial' and holds the deposit on behalf of tenant and landlord. In all three cases, where there is a disagreement about the return of the deposit, the scheme offers mediation. It is uncertain how much of the deposit-paying segment of the private rental sector (PRS) is covered by the three schemes, although in total the schemes cover well over a million properties. The schemes reported in press releases early in 2009 that average deposit payments were over £1000.

Help with Paying a Deposit: A Missed Opportunity

As has been seen, the requirement to pay a deposit is commonplace in the private rented sector, but there is no universal assistance available through the UK welfare system. This help has been available in the past, but was removed in 1988. Until that time, it was possible for households to apply to the then Department of Health and Social Security for a one-off payment – termed a Single Payment – that could be used to cover the deposit cost. However, it appears that little effort was made to monitor either the payments or the ability of tenants to recover this cost at the end of the tenancy. It was argued that tenants and landlords colluded in claiming payments for large deposits, and the budget for this element of the Single Payment system had increased rapidly. When the Social Fund replaced the Single Payment system in 1988, it was no longer possible for households to apply for funds to help with deposits.

It was perhaps at this point that two related but not necessarily interconnected issues became married together in the search for a policy intervention that would offer assistance that was less vulnerable to fraudulent activity. In 1990, the National Consumer Council began to lobby for the introduction in the United Kingdom of a national bond board, similar to that operating in New South Wales. The bond board was the repository of all rental deposits, which were lodged by the landlord at the start of the tenancy. When the tenancy came to a close, the deposit was repaid to the tenant unless the landlord appealed and provided evidence of damage or owed rent. It was thought that this scheme would help those people on low incomes, since they would theoretically only need to provide a deposit once – the deposit could be moved from tenancy to tenancy within the scheme providing the landlord made no appeal.

Lobbying for a national deposit scheme took place through much of the 1990s, and by the end of the decade had attracted sufficient policy attention for the government to institute a pilot deposit scheme. Of particular importance was the production in 1998 of the National Association of Citizens Advice Bureau report *Unsafe Deposits: CAB Clients' Experience of Rental Deposits*. This report concluded that "half of all private tenants who paid a rental deposit may have experienced their deposit being unreasonably withheld." As a consequence, the case for reform was deemed to be 'overwhelming.' A great deal of rhetoric that garnered support for the notion of a national scheme was predicated on the presumption that the scheme would also act as an umbrella for assistance with deposits. It was assumed that the collation of all deposits nationally would bring together capital of such value that its interest would under-write a programme to provide deposit guarantees for tenants in need.

However, the scheme that was finally agreed carried no guarantee element. The pilot scheme tested the possibility of two options: a custodial scheme, where the deposits would be held centrally; and an insurance scheme, whereby landlords retain the deposit but purchase insurance that would cover them in the eventuality of a claim being brought against them with a decision found in favour of the tenant. The insurer would repay the tenant, and themselves recover the costs from the landlord. Following the

Housing Act of 2004, three separate schemes have been established, with the requirement that a landlord lodge the deposit or sign on to one of the schemes. How far has the Housing Act of 2004 helped households unable to meet deposit payments?

Ostensibly, the fair return of one deposit means a tenant is able to pay another. However, there is limited evidence that tenants manage their finances in this way. Deposits are often repaid well after the end of the tenancy. Indeed, some landlords may wait for a month before returning the deposit to ensure that the tenant has been up-to-date with their utility bills. A tenant's new landlord will normally require a deposit before the tenancy starts, which means that the tenant generally has to find money from their existing resources, or borrow on the strength of a deposit being returned. Evidence on the beneficial impact of deposit protection schemes for lower-income households has yet to be established, but it is certain that none offer any assistance with deposit payment.

It is therefore possible to argue that the development of mandatory deposit protection is a missed opportunity to establish universal assistance with deposit payments. Mandatory assistance with deposits could be resumed through the Social Fund and using the custodial scheme since fraudulent claims by landlords or tenants would be impossible to make. However, the willingness to pursue this policy development has been undermined somewhat by the availability of another kind of help with deposits: deposit guarantees.

Deposit Guarantees: A Subverted Ideal?

At the beginning of the 1990s, the notion of deposit guarantee schemes attracted government attention and a pilot scheme was launched in London in 1992. Under a deposit guarantee scheme, a landlord is offered a guarantee of payment in lieu of actual cash and up to a specified level, in the event of actions such as nonpayment of rent, damage, theft, and rent in lieu of notice. The guarantee would cover the first 6 months of the tenancy, after which time it was assumed that the tenant would have been able to save for their own deposit, or their good behaviour persuaded the landlord that a cash deposit would not be required. The virtue of the scheme, from the government's perspective, was that many more tenancies could be covered by a limited sum of money, and since cash was given to the landlord only in the event of their proving that conditions had been breached, the opportunity for fraud was minimised. The 1992 pilot was administered by the Notting Hill Housing Trust, using £110 000 from the Rough Sleeper Initiative. An evaluation of the scheme found it to be 'extremely effective'.

By 1994, 12 similar schemes – operated by local authorities and the voluntary sector – had been established throughout the country. A deposit guarantee scheme handbook published in 1993 was influential in spreading best practice, and was reprinted in 1994. In 1995, the National Rent Deposit Forum was established with a remit to spread best practice on assistance with deposits, and in 1997 the homelessness charity Crisis set up a franchise model named 'Smartmove'. By 1996, the value of the schemes was acknowledged by a broad spectrum of opinion. For example, Ann Winterton, MP, in a Commons debate on homelessness commented:

> One approach that is achieving impressive results is the introduction of rent and deposit guarantee schemes. They give landlords the reassurances that they may require to house low-income tenants and can dramatically increase the chances of such households gaining access to rented accommodation.

Since that time, government policy on deposit schemes has been to encourage the proliferation of local initiatives rather than institute any kind of national scheme. The number of schemes in operation in England is uncertain, but in 2006, Wales had 18 schemes in operation across their 22 local authorities. In 2002, the Homelessness Task Force in Scotland recommended that all Scottish local authorities should have a deposit guarantee scheme in place by 2004, and by 2008, there were 28 schemes in 32 local authorities. Ostensibly, it appears as if this history underlines the successful development and proliferation of an effective policy intervention. However, a wider context offers further options for analysis.

The growing interest in help with deposits reflects the increasing awareness of the potential of the private rented sector to accommodate households who might otherwise seek a long-term home in social housing. Indeed, deposit guarantee schemes are generally regarded as an important tool in local authority homelessness strategies, so reflecting growing certainty that – in the absence of a large-scale social house-building programme – private renting will comprise a long-term tenure for an increasing proportion of low-income families. This is not to say that the private rented sector does not already accommodate a large proportion of households on low income. Indeed, according to the SEH in 2006/07, 21% of tenants on assured shorthold tenancies were in receipt of housing benefit.

Nevertheless, a number of studies have underlined the difficulties encountered by benefit recipients seeking to secure good-quality, affordable private rented accommodation. The requirement to pay a deposit and rent in advance is one substantial obstacle. In addition, many landlords simply do not like the idea of letting to a benefit (income support) recipient, since landlords often conclude that a person on benefit reflects some kind of personal deficiency. Where an alternative supply of tenants is readily available, landlords will find it a straightforward task to operationalise their preference for a working tenant.

The difficulties faced by lower-income households have been met by a plethora of policy interventions: indeed, through much of the 1990s central government grants were available to local voluntary and social sector agencies that introduced a range of initiatives easing the pathways into private renting. For example, in the early 1990s, s73 funding was aimed at voluntary agencies that developed accommodation registers, which were – essentially – lists of landlords who were willing to let to housing benefit recipients and so accept rent payments at housing benefit levels.

However, it is important to recognise that, initially, the development of assistance with deposits was a measure intended to help households who had no priority for social housing. This group generally included single people, people who could not demonstrate a local connection to a given area, and people who were regarded as 'intentionally homeless'. From the mid-1990s, voluntary sector homelessness agencies in particular had begun to view private renting as an effective solution for this group. At that time, statutory agencies were perhaps less enthusiastic, largely because private renting was deemed to be a problematic tenure with rents that were higher than in social housing, with a lower standard of housing and limited security of tenure.

Nevertheless, partnership working between voluntary sector agencies and private landlords developed effectively through a multiplicity of local schemes. It should perhaps be remembered that deposit guarantee schemes offered a package of assistance to households, and often went far beyond what appears to be a simple financial requirement. In 1996, a study of 161 schemes that helped low-income families to access the private rented sector found that many schemes offered ongoing support to both tenant and landlord once a tenancy had started. Services to tenants included help with housing benefit forms, general befriending, guidance through the tricky process of setting up a tenancy, development of budgeting skills, and independent living. The schemes were often working with clients who had experience of hostel living and/or street homelessness, and this kind of help was an organic development from other kinds of outreach and support work. Landlords also saw substantial benefits to working with schemes, in getting access to fully referenced clients, to help with the often complex task of negotiation with the housing benefit system, and assistance with managing the beginning and end of tenancies.

The Subversion of an Ideal?

The notion that this ideal policy solution has become subverted follows from the changing context in which deposit guarantee schemes operate. Originally, schemes tended to focus help on marginalised non-statutory homeless households who were excluded from the statutory framework. Increasingly, it is now the case that schemes are being used by statutory authorities to deal with households who might otherwise have some priority for social housing. The 1996 survey of access schemes found that nearly half of the schemes that were operated by local authorities accepted only statutory homeless households. More up-to-date information is not currently available on the types of clients assisted by local authority or voluntary sector schemes. However, in 2009, Crisis produced a report that assessed the cost-effectiveness of deposit guarantee schemes in Scotland. This report noted the Scottish Government's consultation on local authorities' discharge of homelessness duties, which aims to enable wider use of the private rented sector. The success of deposit guarantee schemes was cited specifically as an indicator that the PRS was a 'viable option for homeless households'.

It could be argued that it is irrelevant to make any distinction between the types of client being assisted by deposit guarantee schemes. In actual fact, the distinction is extremely important. The supply of good-quality, affordable privately rented property is not infinitely elastic. Landlords who are willing to let in this market often seek long-term tenants: indeed, tenants at the 'bottom end' of the sector tend to stay in their tenancies longer than households in higher-income quartiles. It has been noted that many landlords prefer not to let to the recipients of housing benefit, and so many local authorities offer financial incentives. It could be argued that this kind of intervention distorts the operation of the bottom end of the market. There is anecdotal evidence that voluntary sector schemes that seek to house their nonpriority homeless clients are being edged out of the market. The ability to use deposit guarantee schemes to help marginal, nonstatutory homeless households has been undermined. At the same time, however, the proliferation of deposit guarantee schemes across local authorities persuades national policy-makers that a universal scheme is unnecessary.

Low-income households seeking to make a home in the private rented sector will invariably face the need to pay a deposit, particularly if they are seeking better quality property. This universal need is not well served by the existing policy framework although there have been opportunities to develop appropriate initiatives. Confusion around 'the problem' with deposits has diverted attention from what is a fairly pragmatic need; it is unlikely that more recent policy developments will resolve the issue.

See also: Housing Finance: Deposit Guarantees.

Further Reading

Crisis (2009) *Accessing the Private Rented Sector: The Cost Effectiveness of Deposit Guarantee Schemes in Scotland*. London: Crisis.

Phelps L (1998) *Unsafe Deposit: CAB Clients' Experience of Rental Deposits*. London: NACAB.

Rugg J (1996) *Opening Doors: Helping People on Low Income Secure Private Rented Accommodation*. York, UK: Centre for Housing Policy.

Rugg J and Bevan M (2002) *An Evaluation of the Pilot Tenancy Deposit Scheme*. London: Office of the Deputy Prime Minister.

Rugg J and Rhodes D (2008) *The Private Rented Sector: Its Contribution and Potential*. York, UK: Centre for Housing Policy.

Development Land Tax

M Oxley, De Montfort University, Leicester, UK; Delft University of Technology, Delft, The Netherlands

© 2012 Elsevier Ltd. All rights reserved.

Glossary

Development A change in land use. This may mean a new building being constructed on a plot or adaptations to an existing building. Such changes typically require official approval which in many countries is termed planning permission.
Development gains Increases in land values that result from development.
Development land taxation Taxes imposed on increases in land values that result from development.
Economic rent An increase in value of a factor of production, such as land, that is a surplus over and above the minimum amount required, in a market system, to ensure the supply of the factor to a given use.
Transfer earnings The minimum financial reward required, in a market system, to ensure the supply of the factor to a given use.

Introduction

Residential development can result in large increases in land values. These increases have for many years and in many countries been the subject of much debate by economists and politicians. In particular, the idea of a special tax on land value increases has been discussed and in several cases applied. This contribution considers both the theory and the application of such land value taxation. It shows the link to the concept of economic rent and it shows that taxes on land value enhancement can be levied in explicit or implicit forms.

Definition

Development Land Tax (DLT) can be viewed as a generic term for any sort of tax that is levied on land value enhancements when land is developed; it is also, specifically, the name of a tax that was applied in Britain from 1976 to 1985. Here it will be discussed mainly in its generic form.

Why Have Special Taxes on Land Development?

In any planning and development system, there are essentially two sets of reasons for imposing special taxes on the development process. One relates to externalities and the other to redistribution. The externalities argument is that the development imposes external costs on a local community and a tax can help to pay for these costs, or possibly encourage developers to mitigate the size or type of development in order to ameliorate the impact. The external costs might be environmental and/or social. The costs, for example, thus relate to the loss of green fields and to the need for a new school or road. Taxation might discourage environmentally harmful green field development or it might help to pay for a school or a road. When the tax is designed to pay for infrastructure and other public facilities that are required to service a new development, it may take the form of an 'impact fee' as used in the United States and several other countries (see article Impact Fees). Such fees, paid in advance of the completion of the development, are used to finance improvements off site but to the benefit of the development. In practice, such fees may be passed on to the land owner. Impact fees may therefore be capitalised into land values, and thus represent an extraction of the incremental value of land attributable to the higher value use made possible by new publicly provided facilities.

The redistribution argument for taxation is that there are gains that accrue to developers or landowners that are 'unearned' or 'unnecessary' and can, on grounds of equity, be appropriated. The gains can thus be taxed for the benefit of the community. The case for taxation in such cases can be additionally supported on efficiency grounds if the gain that is subject to taxation is 'economic rent' and thus a surplus which, when removed, will not affect output. Landowners who sell their land for residential use are typically the recipients of 'large windfall development gains', because the granting of planning permission tends to increase land values, and taxation can have a powerful role in capturing these economic rents for the wider community. Such taxation will not impact on housing supply or prices because it is passed on to land owners according to the standard neoclassical theory of economic rents. The burden of the tax is then expected to fall largely on landowners.

Theory and Thinkers

Economists from Adam Smith (1723–90) onwards have argued that land values are determined differently from other factors of production and are a suitable object for special taxation. Taxes on land rents were seen to be efficient in that they would be neutral in their resource allocation effects and equitable in that they provided a fair way to tax away surpluses that were not due to individual effort. Land values were seen to be partly due to good government and people should pay for advantageous government actions. David Ricardo (1772–1823) introduced the concept of derived demand for land, claiming that the rent of corn land was high because the price of corn was high and arguing that it was not true that corn prices were high because land prices were high. It follows that residential land values are high because house prices are high, rather than house prices are high because land values are high. Any surplus above the supply price (or transfer earnings) of land was viewed as an economic rent. JS Mill (1806–73) argued that landlords grew rich in their sleep without working, risking, or economising. Henry George (1839–97) in his *Progress and Poverty* (1879) provided some of the most influential arguments on land value taxation. Like some other nineteenth-century economists, he believed that land values were the result of natural and social values and that landlords had no moral rights to the benefits of rising values. However, he went further than others in arguing for land value taxation to be the sole source of government revenues. As a tax on economic rent it would, following Ricardo's arguments, be shifted to others and have no effect on resource allocation. George's arguments were important in supporting attempts by twentieth-century politicians to find a way of capturing land value enhancements and using them for the benefit of the public.

The Essence of Development Land Tax Arguments

DLT is essentially a tax on increases in land values that are associated with changes in the use of land. Where these changes in use require the permission of the state through planning controls, the tax may be associated with the granting of planning permission. The arguments in favour of such a tax flow from (1) propositions about the cause of the land value increase, and the associated ideological views about who has the rights to capture value enhancement, and (2) propositions about the consequences for resource allocation of imposing the tax. Proponents of DLT argue that the increases in land values are a result of the actions of society rather than land owners. The claims about the causes of land value changes are variously that social forces have brought about the changes in demand that raise land values, that public expenditure has funded infrastructure such as roads and drainage that has helped make land ready for development, and that society has sanctioned the change in use that has allowed value to be realised. The associated claim is that individual land owners have done little or nothing to bring about the higher values. They therefore have an inferior moral claim to the value enhancement than society as a whole. DLT is thus seen to be an equitable tax that can be part of a wealth redistribution process.

The propositions about resource allocation effects are based on the theory of economic rent. This assumes that payments to all factors of production, including land, can be divided into two elements: transfer earnings and economic rent. The former are payments that are essential to ensure that supply is forthcoming and the latter are payments over and above transfer earnings. The more inelastic is land supply with respect to price, the greater will be the economic rent and the smaller with be the transfer earnings. If the DLT falls only on economic rent, taxation of this surplus will have no consequences for how the land is used since transfer earnings continue to accrue in full. DLT is thus seen to be an efficient tax. These equity and efficiency arguments in support of DLT can be challenged by questioning both the theory behind these propositions and the practicality of implementing a form of DLT that is in accord with the propositions.

Arguments for and against DLT need to be seen in the context of the tax systems of particular countries. For example, under tax regimes with comprehensive capital gains taxation (no exemptions), DLT will double tax the increases in land value associated with the changes in land use, and weaken the case for DLT. Some countries have recurrent land taxes levied on site values and, in principle, if the land values on which taxes are based are regularly updated, such taxes will capture some of the value increases.

Propositions about the Cause of the Land Value Increase

On the causes of land value increases, it may be difficult to argue that none of any increase is due to the efforts of individual owners. The owner may have made some improvements and exercised judgment that has helped to make the land ready for a new use. When the argument is that society is responsible for value enhancement, it may be useful to distinguish three ways in which society has an impact; the arguments differ for each of these impacts. Society may (1) play a role by generally increasing demand for the goods or services generated by the new use for the land, (2) provide infrastructure that makes the land ready for the new use, or (3) grant the planning consent that allows development to occur. Sometimes, a combination of two or all three of these impacts will be apparent.

Impact (1) might through increased population and incomes, for example, raise housing demand and residential development land values. However, such increases in population and incomes will also raise the demand for many items and for other factors of production such as labour. So one has to ask: what is special in this case about land values? If the argument about taxing such value enhancements is to be applied consistently, should it be applied to all factors of production? To some extent, it can be argued that income taxes will capture the rise in wages, profits, dividends, and rents that flow to other factors of production. The issue of consistency also raises questions about what should happen when the demand for a current land use falls as a result of a general fall in demand. Should land owners then be compensated for a loss of value that is due to factors outside of their control, such as a general increase in unemployment in their locality? Critics can argue that this sort of taxation and compensation ultimately destroys a market system, because such a system relies on risk-taking entrepreneurs gaining and losing as a result of the way they have anticipated social changes. For impact (2) it can be argued that a specific charge levied on the land owner to cover infrastructure costs may be more appropriate than a tax on enhanced values. It is useful also to consider the proposition that the removal of infrastructure (say the closure of a road) results in lower land values. Consistency with the pro-DLT case again arguably means that land owners should be compensated in such cases. Impact (3) which means that the state allows development to occur on a specific plot that would not otherwise have been eligible for a newer higher value use can be seen as the state being the cause of the value increase. This may in some cases be deemed to be a windfall gain that was unexpected. However, the granting of planning permission may alternatively be seen simply as lifting a restraint on a new use that is needed because of changes in demand. If there are several options about where new development will occur and the state is seen as discriminating in favour of one owner rather than another, then the idea that a tax is appropriate in such a situation is supported by the notion of redressing the balance of advantage, or the redistribution of wealth, in favour of one party rather than another. A tax lessens the unequal impacts on wealth distribution that arise because some are granted permission, while others are not.

Propositions about the Consequences for Resource Allocation of Imposing the Tax

The arguments in favour of DLT, based on the idea that it will have no resource allocation effects, because it is a tax on economic rent, are sound as long as the tax is only a tax on economic rent. The counter arguments are largely practical. They are about the difficulties in practice of (1) identifying economic rent and separating it from transfer earnings and (2) imposing a tax that is levied only on economic rent and not on transfer earnings. Whether or not a payment is essential to ensure that land is provided for one use rather than another (the transfer earnings) is linked directly to how uses are defined, and how precisely one use is distinguished from another. The more broadly the uses are defined, the more inelastic is supply, the smaller are the transfer earnings, and the greater is the economic rent. The minimum amount required to prise land from agricultural to residential use will be quite different from the minimum amount required from one residential developer to ensure that this developer gets the land rather than another residential developer.

If DLT is to tax the change in land values on the granting of planning permission, then the values of the land in the pre-permission and post-permission uses must be established. The proportion of the change that is economic rent then has to be determined and a tax rate applied to this amount. If this is done on a plot-by-plot basis, there are complex and costly processes involved in establishing these values. If, alternatively, generic values are established in a locality for different uses and these values are used as the basis of the tax, the tax on individual plots may capture economic rent only in an approximate fashion; in some cases, it may be too low and in others too high.

Only if a practical way can be found of measuring and taxing economic rent, and only economic rent, in each and every case, can one be sure that the resource allocation effects of DLT are neutral. Many legislative attempts at imposing a form of DLT have foundered because in practice a solution to the measurement problems has proved elusive.

Explicit or Implicit DLT?

The problems of an exact specification and taxation of development gains have been avoided by governments who have chosen to tax in an implicit, rather than explicit, fashion. Implicit taxation occurs through arrangements whereby developers agree to provide a set of public benefits, such as new infrastructure or affordable housing, in return for permission to develop. In some cases, money is provided by the developer instead of such benefits in kind. In England, these sorts of arrangements have been put in place through Section 106 (S106) agreements (named after the relevant section of 1990 legislation).

S106 agreements are signed after negotiations between developers and local planning authorities. The amount that developers can afford to provide in these agreements is limited by the economic viability of the development. If the concept of residual valuation is applied, the maximum amount that the developer can afford to pay for the land is a function of the value of the completed development minus all nonland development costs, including S106 costs. If S106 costs are passed on to the landowner in the form of lower bids for land, the landowner is effectively paying the S106 costs. This cost to the landowner can be viewed as an implicit tax on the gains made through the granting of planning permission. In negotiating with a planning authority, the maximum value of S106 contributions that a developer is prepared to offer should be no greater than the economic rent that is apparent through the land value enhancement. What is delivered by the developer as a result of a S106 agreement is sometimes termed a planning obligation. S106 results in an implicit negotiated tax on economic rent or the enhancement in land value.

Implicit taxation through S106 agreements thus involves case-by-case bargaining. In favour of such arrangements it can be argued that negotiation will ensure that the sum that is taken in taxation, that is the cost to the developer or landowner, is no greater than the economic rent in that a developer would presumably not offer to bear costs that make the development unprofitable. The case against taxing economic rent in an implicit fashion is that it is ad hoc, uncertain, and from the point of view of both developers and local authorities the process is highly risky. Negotiations are often long and costly. The concept of a negotiated tax is peculiar. The outcome of negotiations and thus the amount paid is not strictly related to ability to pay or the benefits received; it is rather related to the skills and the relative bargaining position of the negotiators.

Who Pays? Questions of Incidence

There is a long and extensive literature on who pays taxes that fall in formal terms on development gains. There is no simple answer. The result depends on what exactly is taxed, when the tax is imposed, the conditions in the land market, and the conditions more generally in the property market or, in the case of housing, specifically in the housing market. The developer is the party who is required to pay the tax or, for example, deliver the affordable housing contribution. In principle, this reduces the net revenue that the developer receives from a site. If the developer knows this reduction in advance of the land purchase, we may expect the developer to try to pass this on to the seller of the land by offering a lower price for the land. If the developer is successful in passing the tax back to the land seller, the tax is borne by that seller. If the land seller is set to make a large gain because the site has previously been in a much lower value use, the seller may well accept an offer much below what the developer would have offered in the absence of a tax, or an affordable housing obligation, and still achieve a large after-tax gain. If the developer/house builder is able to raise the prices of the houses that are sold privately on a mixed tenure site, then some of the tax cost may be passed on to the purchasers of new houses. The extent to which this backward or forward shifting of the tax actually occurs depends on the relative market power of house purchasers, house builders, and land sellers in the housing and land markets. If, as is often assumed in the UK case, house builders are in the main price takers, because they face stiff competition from offers to sell from owners of established housing, the option of passing the tax on to house buyers will be very limited. Where supply from the existing housing stock is price inelastic, the likelihood of some of the tax being reflected in house prices is increased (see article Supply Elasticity of Housing).

With residential development values typically many times alternative use values the uplift in value when planning permission is granted is substantial. Average residential land values in England in 2004 were over 250 times agricultural values and nearly 4 times average industrial and warehousing land values. This uplift or economic rent is constrained in its upper limit by the maximum the developer is willing to offer, which we assume is the developer's valuation of the site in its new use, and in its lower limit by the minimum the landowner is willing to accept. This lower value we assume will not go below the current use value. The actual price at which the land changes hands will, as argued above, be determined by the relative bargaining position of the two parties. If taxation, in whatever form, tries to take more than the economic rent, then there will be no incentive for the land to move from its current use and development will not occur. As long as taxation does not exceed economic rent, the tax should have no disincentive effect, and the decision to develop will be unaffected by the tax. If the implicit tax imposed by planning obligations plus any explicit tax are more than economic rent, there will be a disincentive effect. It is important if planning obligations operate alongside explicit taxes that the sum of the two costs does not impede the economic viability of the development. The combined tax in these circumstances will be paid partly by the landowner and partly by the developer.

Application

There have been many attempts worldwide at capturing land value enhancements through some form of tax. For example, there have been several attempts in the United

Kingdom to impose taxation on development gains. These have been short-lived. Attempts in 1909 and 1932 at taxing increases in land values due to planning proved virtually inoperative because of the difficulty of proving that the value increases were due to planning. Land value taxation has, moreover, been short-lived because of a lack of political consensus. Measures introduced by one political party have usually been repealed by another. For example, a 100% charge on all land value changes due to planning, introduced by a Labour government in 1947, was abolished by a Conservative government in 1953. Similarly, a 40% levy introduced by Labour in 1967 was abandoned by a Conservative government in 1971. The last major attempt to explicitly tax development gains, DLT, introduced by Labour in 1976, was severely modified by a Conservative administration that came to power in 1979 and eventually scrapped in 1985.

In 2004, the *Barker Review* of housing supply in England said that Government should use tax measures to extract some of the windfall gain that accrues to landowners from the sale of their land for residential development. Government should impose a tax on the granting of planning permission. The *Barker Review* proposed a planning gain supplement (PGS) to tax the windfall gains that result from residential planning permission. It was suggested that this new tax should function alongside scaled back planning obligations that require developers to provide benefits in kind in return for planning permission. A major benefit in kind is the provision of affordable housing that is intended for households who cannot compete effectively in the housing market. This 'affordable housing through planning' now makes a substantial contribution to social housing provision in England. Having initially accepted these proposals and consulted on the implementation of a PGS, the government eventually reversed its commitment to the proposed PGS, but local planning authorities will be able to introduce a new community infrastructure levy (CIL) for all development (not just residential) alongside a reformed system of planning obligations. This idea was proposed by a Labour government and in 2010 accepted by a new Conservative/Liberal Democrat Coalition government. The reformed system will restrict the volume of items that a local authority could seek through planning obligations, but the list of acceptable items will still include affordable housing. The proposed CIL would be a standard charge on new development to support infrastructure delivery. The exact basis of the charge is yet to be determined, but it is proposed that it will be a certain amount per dwelling or per square metre of development. Local planning authorities will be able to use CIL if they wish, but they will not be compelled to do so. It will operate in England, and also potentially in Wales. For authorities who choose not to implement CIL, planning obligations will continue to provide a means of securing developer contributions. While CIL is proposed specifically as a way of financing infrastructure, developers will effectively pay the levy out of the profits made from development and will be able to pass the costs on to landowners in the form of lower bids for land. The CIL concept can thus be viewed as an indirect form of taxing increases in land values that are due to development. England is not peculiar in this context.

The planning system is used as a method of securing such public benefits in many countries and there are several similar uses of planning throughout Europe. In Ireland, for example, cross-subsidies from the private sector for social housing are provided through Part V of the Housing and Development Act (2000), whereby developers support provision as a condition of planning permission. Up to 20% of dwellings or sites are transferred to local authorities or equivalent financial compensation paid. Given that the costs of this provision are met from land value enhancements, this is again a form of implicit taxation of development gains. In the Netherlands, municipalities have traditionally acquired land, serviced it, and sold it to developers with the necessary infrastructure to commence building. Since the 1990s, private developers have started to acquire land and develop it themselves. But a significant volume of development still follows the traditional model where municipalities sell serviced land to developers. Under this system, the costs of construction are subtracted from the potential sales revenues to give a residual land value that is used to finance the acquisition and conversion of land, and the provision of local public goods. This system thus levies an implicit development tax on residential land for private construction. In the United States, developers can be encouraged or required to contribute to the affordable housing stock in return for enhanced development rights, including the opportunity to develop at higher than normal densities through inclusionary zoning (see article Inclusionary Zoning to Support Affordable Housing). Local inclusionary zoning ordinances in the United States set out what developers will be expected to provide and what they will get in return. More generally, there are worldwide struggles to find ways to tax, explicitly or implicitly, land value increases to fund local services. Searches for ways to implement this 'value capture' are ongoing at national and local levels in many countries.

Conclusions

Taxes on development gains or the increases in land values that occur when changes in land use occur have a long history in terms of theory and application. If increases in land values are due to the efforts of society, rather than individual owners, there is a case on redistribution grounds for levying a special tax. If the gain is deemed to be economic rent, there is an additional case on efficiency grounds as the tax will have no adverse resource allocation implications. However, it has been shown that imposing DLTs, whether they are explicit or implicit, poses several problems. As a matter of principle, it raises the question of whether consistency demands parallel compensation when values fall. As a matter of practical implementation, it raises major questions about how to measure and tax only gains that are economic rent.

See also: Impact Fees; Inclusionary Zoning to Support Affordable Housing; Supply Elasticity of Housing; Taxation Policy and Housing.

Further Reading

Barker K (2004) *Review of Housing Supply, Delivering Stability: Securing Our Future Housing Needs, Final Report – Recommendations*. London: HMSO.

Bowers JB (1992) The economics of planning gain: A re-appraisal. *Urban Studies* 29: 1329–1339.

Brown HJ (ed.) (1997) *Land Use and Taxation*. Cambridge, MA: Lincoln Institute of Land Policy.

Claydon J and Smith B (1997) Negotiating planning gains through the British development control system. *Urban Studies* 34: 2003–2022.

Crow S (1998) Planning gain: There must be a better way. *Planning Perspectives* 13: 357–372.

DCLG (2006) *Valuing planning obligations in England: Final report*. University of Sheffield and The Halcrow Group. London: Department for Communities and Local Government.

DCLG (2008) *The Community Infrastructure Levy*. London: Department for Communities and Local Government.

HMSO (2005) *Planning-Gain Supplement: A Consultation, HM Treasury, HM Revenue and Customs, ODPM, December*. London: HMSO.

ODPM (2005) *Circular 05/2005 Planning Obligations*. London: Office of the Deputy Prime Minister.

Oxley M (2004) *Economics, Planning and Housing*. London: Palgrave Macmillan.

Oxley M (2006) The gain from the planning-gain supplement: A consideration of the proposal for a new tax to boost housing supply in the UK. *European Journal of Housing Policy* 6: 101–113.

Oxley M (2008) Implicit land taxation and affordable housing provision in England. *Housing Studies* 23(4): 661–671.

Prest AR (1981) *The Taxation of Urban Land*. Manchester, UK: Manchester University Press.

Relevant Websites

www.henrygeorgefoundation.org – Henry George Foundation.
www.lincolninst.edu – Lincoln Institute of Land Policy.

Difference

M Harrison and L Hemingway, University of Leeds, Leeds, UK

© 2012 Elsevier Ltd. All rights reserved.

Glossary

Difference Differentiations and distinctions between groups or categories, generally other than those of class and socioeconomic status.

Ethnic clustering A process and situation whereby households with specific ethnic origins or affiliations live near to other households with similar backgrounds and connections.

Feminisation of social renting High levels of occupancy of social rented housing amongst female-headed households.

Particularism A perspective that stresses the particular needs, preferences, or outlooks of specific groups of people (and contrasts with more universalistic perspectives that emphasise shared values and standards).

Redlining The practice of financial institutions (especially mortgage lenders or insurance companies) of delineating geographical areas within which they are reluctant to invest (or will invest only on terms that are onerous for households).

Social model of disability An account that locates disablement primarily as a product of disadvantaging and systematic social and economic processes.

The Significance of Difference

Issues of difference have moved up the housing research and theory agenda in many countries in recent decades. Housing literature increasingly takes account of variations linked to disability, ethnicity, or gender, while an acknowledgement of these elements now parallels more longstanding interests in class or socioeconomic differentiation within theories. Adding to the growing portfolio of scholarly and policy concerns on difference have been further significant foci on age, sexual orientation, or religion. Of course, specific categories of households were often targeted by policy makers in earlier decades. Some elderly and disabled people, for example, have long been supported via specialised forms of provision (including sheltered housing). The shift we are referring to, however, is not simply about heightened priority or an increasing reach or range within policy responses, although these are important. For alongside these have often come greater sophistication and responsiveness, both in debate and performance. Thus, today's best practice in policy development, research, and service delivery is marked by greater cultural sensitivity, improved communication with many categories of users, and recognition of a diversity agenda. At the same time, awareness of difference has had an impact on the theoretical front within housing studies.

One reason for the increased attention given by scholars to difference has been a recognition that class-orientated analyses on their own might overlook or undervalue important elements of social relations. In effect, neither relative disadvantage nor patterns of experience are likely to be adequately described and accounted for by a simple model of class-based societal divisions or conflicts. Recognising the impact of other areas of differentiation – such as gender and ethnicity – is essential for stronger understanding of the complexities in daily life, and of variations in households' opportunities, strategies, and access to resources. Even so, we should not lose sight of institutional forces and patterns of socioeconomic differentiation that are linked firmly to wealth distribution or class. Thus, writers need to appreciate the limitations of those explanations of causation and context that rely narrowly on reference to specific areas of categorisation or group demarcation. At a general level, therefore, work emphasising difference can be seen ideally as complementing other approaches that also tackle social divisions. Meanwhile, at the detailed level it brings unique and essential insights into the impact of organisations and policies, the activities of particular groups of people, and the systematic differentiations that can arise in the patterning of outcomes for households.

Inevitably, our review must be highly selective, concentrating primarily on disability, ethnicity, and gender, rather than other dimensions of differentiation. Furthermore, it is difficult to capture realistically the diversity of situations and national information bases between countries or regions, and in-depth materials and exemplars are currently more readily available from

Western countries than elsewhere. In addition, there is often a disappointing lack of comparative work between Western countries, as far as links between housing and difference are concerned, and even more so with countries in other regions and with other cultural contexts. Any general claims below are therefore offered subject to reservations, particularly insofar as the information base remains underdeveloped.

Key Issues Related to Disability, Ethnicity, and Gender

To consider relationships between housing and our three highlighted dimensions of difference, we begin by identifying some key issues under four subheadings.

Conditions and Economic Positions

There are often strong associations between variations in housing situations on the one hand and ethnicity, disability, or gender on the other. Practices or patterns of differentiation relating to housing opportunities and circumstances have been reported from many countries, with accounts often indicating disadvantaged situations and histories for women or minorities (see Further Reading for examples from a range of societies). So far, however, disability seems to have received less attention as an issue of housing disadvantage. There are technical writings looking into relationships between specific impairments and features of housing provision, but these are underpinned more by a medical and individual model of disability than by one seeing disablement as a disadvantaging social and economic process. The rise of social model perspectives within disability studies (deploying a 'social model of disability') has encouraged increasing recognition of systematic processes of disadvantage and exclusion, but this has not yet had international impact on housing studies comparable with what seems to have been happening for gender and ethnicity.

When looking at housing and difference, it is difficult to compare in detail across countries, but easy to find specific locations where a relatively data-rich environment generates useful insights. In the United Kingdom, for example, a long quantitative and qualitative historical record shows relatively poor housing conditions for minority ethnic groups, when compared in overall terms with white households. Female-headed single-parent households, furthermore, have often faced housing difficulties, and many turn to social renting as the best hope for obtaining decent and affordable accommodation. This may happen too for some disabled people, as households containing disabled adults or children may struggle to meet their housing needs or find adapted dwellings in the private sectors. The central drivers for all these housing situations are in part financial.

In market-orientated societies, a household's relationship with labour markets and access to capital frequently shapes its housing prospects. Inequalities between categories of households – in terms of dwelling or neighbourhood quality, choice of tenure, and overcrowding – in many instances reflect an unequal patterning of labour market status and wealth. In effect, the price mechanism sifts and distributes households differentially according to their ability to pay. This is inevitable in most urban housing market systems, unless offset by financial resources or other interventions from governmental, family, community, or third sector sources. Since minority and migrant ethnic groups, female-headed households, and disabled people are often disproportionately found in the less advantageous and lower-income parts of labour markets, the members of such groups are also likely to be strongly represented in poor quality housing areas. This is to be expected in countries like the United Kingdom or United States. Many households lack the economic power to secure and hold better housing (although there is considerable variation within our three broad categories). In any event, the overlap between difference and socioeconomic positioning is crucial, and may be reinforced where a household is disadvantaged on more than one dimension of difference.

Culture, Discrimination, and Stereotyping

In many countries, cultural or religious histories and practices have material effects on housing opportunity, and these seem especially strong around gender. Socially constructed gendered practices are reported from many parts of the world, sometimes systematically disadvantaging women when compared with men. Even in Western countries, where law has increasingly protected equality of status, women may remain affected by stereotypical assumptions (although the impact of these on housing requires empirical exploration). Of course, culture or religion can have a positive as well as negative impact on the climate of thinking on housing policies and practices. Islamic values, for example, might lead to emphasising a fair approach to provision, linked with ideas about rights to decent accommodation. More generally, the entrenchment of specific social rights in housing can provide some degree of defence against inequalities.

For ethnicity, significant differentiations in housing opportunities and conditions have often been linked with racist views and practices manifested both within public policies and private sector activities. Perceptions by mainstream housing consumer groups of their material and cultural interests may reinforce a desire for ethnic separation on their part, and the idea that minorities represent something dangerous or deviant. The United States offers particularly strong evidence about such racism and its effects, including the reluctance of white people to live alongside those perceived as black. In the United Kingdom, one of the most difficult problems affecting daily life and housing opportunities is racist harassment, ranging from verbal abuse to physical assault on adults or children. We should be cautious, however, about overemphasising a simple identification of racist ill-treatment with reactions to in-migrants, or to those seen as nonwhite. Within the European Union, some indigenous minority groups – particularly the Roma – have experienced adverse housing conditions and negative treatment far out of line with what is seen as acceptable for the majority populations. For disabled people, stigmatisation and labelling can lead to housing disadvantage, and to exclusion and intimidation that parallel experiences of racism. In the United Kingdom, it has sometimes been felt that specific disabled people should not be considered appropriate to own or play a part in managing their accommodation, while care and support can be cast effectively as a form of custodial provision.

Institutional Behaviours

Marketised housing systems in principle have a capacity to reduce discrimination to a single dimension – the ability to input finance – and thereby to downgrade variables of ascribed colour, gender, origin, and so forth. In practice, however, institutional power in markets involves the application of forms of differentiation around concepts of risk, reliability, and status, linked to labels and stereotypes. Thus, particular categories of households may be characterised as presenting higher risks than others, or even as representing some kind of danger to other consumers, housing suppliers, or finance providers. Evaluations linked with risk or fear are not random, but patterned in ways that have historically worked against women, disabled people, and some minority ethnic groups. In the United States, the patterning of housing outcomes has led scholars such as Darden to refer to a black tax, implying increased housing costs and problems linked with being treated as people of colour (see discussion in Harrison et al. 2005: 18–20).

The problems facing specific groups of consumers are all the more severe because discrimination by organisations often aligns closely with economic disadvantage, derived from a lack of inherited wealth and poor labour market opportunities. One of the classic territories for analyses of institutional effects in housing has been the impact of lending for owner-occupation. Studies of redlining in the United States have related to areas demarcated as constituting high risks for loans, and within which loans were therefore harder to obtain. This problem could disproportionately affect minority ethnic groups. Similar studies elsewhere may face difficulties of accessing privately held data, although some work was carried out in this field in the United Kingdom in the past. Disabled people may also suffer disadvantage with finance organisations because of estimates about the risks associated with specific impairments. Apart from the finance sector, there are other institutions acting as intermediaries, service providers, or gatekeepers that have been found to have an impact in the private rented and ownership sectors (real estate agents, landlords, etc.). As well as problems of racism, there have been reported instances in private renting of harassment of women and lack of interest in accommodating disabled people.

Public and third sector organisations also have impacts on outcomes for categories of consumers. This was exemplified strongly in UK experiences amongst minority ethnic groups in the post-Second World War years, up to the 1990s. Direct and indirect discrimination practices were chronicled in several classic studies of social rented housing performance, some of which produced striking illustrations of negative perceptions and practices applied to nonwhite groups. The development of stronger equality and diversity laws and policies has diminished this overt discrimination in the United Kingdom. Established black and minority ethnic households are far better statistically represented today in many areas of social housing than in earlier years of settlement, although some newer migrants still encounter many problems. One conclusion from the United Kingdom is that the public and third sectors can be changed substantially through accumulating strengthened laws and regulatory practices, although private sector institutions and actors are more difficult to monitor and influence. Nonetheless, policies may also shift in ways that disadvantage particular categories of households (and claims could well be made against some economic liberal housing policies in this regard on behalf of women).

The United Kingdom also offers examples of the way that the climate of thinking has shifted in relation to gender and disability. Building regulations, for example, have been strengthened so that new dwellings are more physically accessible than before (albeit within limits). As far as obtaining affordable housing is concerned, an increasing emphasis on needs has facilitated entry into UK social renting for some chronically sick and disabled people, and for many female-headed households. The strong representation of female tenants with children has contributed to the view that there has been a feminisation of social renting in the United Kingdom. This reflects on the one hand the relative dependency that such households face because of economic disadvantage, and on the other the vital role that affordable and secure social renting plays in a context of difference.

Choices, Housing Pathways, and Segregation

Ideas about housing careers, pathways, stages, cycles, and the life course all point to the dynamic nature of housing experiences. Not only are there differences within as well as between broad categories of households (with socio-economic positions and resources being important), but positions may alter significantly over time for specific cohorts or groups. For example, as many settled minority groups in the United Kingdom have adapted and improved their positions in recent years, there has been a tendency to associate severe disadvantage more strongly with particular new arrivals, including asylum seekers and low-waged labour market migrants. By contrast, specific established groups are doing relatively well, moving ahead of many people in disadvantaged white neighbourhoods along with low-income minority ethnic households. Class is a key variable to consider alongside ethnicity and gender, and (bearing this in mind) it is important not to view the white category as a monolithic one. In any event, what we are seeing in the United Kingdom is a degree of fragmentation – and difference within difference – as far as housing achievements within broad ethnic categories are concerned. Fragmentation occurs especially along lines of citizenship status, socio-economic position, settlement history, and adaptation pathways. In addition, studies show not only diverse needs, preferences, and strategies amongst households, but also difference playing a part within households too (perhaps along gendered lines). What the home means can vary between and within communities and households, while a wide range of factors affect satisfaction.

For present purposes four points can be emphasised:

- First, the constraints and opportunities for most households will be affected by the scale and types of resources (economic, social, and interpersonal) that they can mobilise and bring to the home. Resources are distributed unevenly amongst households, and this reflects difference to some extent.
- Second, households vary in responsibilities and interdependencies, and there may be obligations to members that affect choices (for households with children, or to elders in an extended family, etc.).
- Third, households will try to be strategists and planners even in difficult circumstances. A fine account of harassment written by Chahal and Julienne illustrates this clearly (1999). More generally, the search for autonomy by housing users reflects the desire to influence surroundings, security, and control of the home and its meanings. This can be a challenge to practitioners, especially if they seek to determine needs in a top-down way for disabled people.
- Fourth, most households face some bounding or restricting of preferred choices at particular moments or more long term. Factors beyond the individual household are crucial in this, and there is an ongoing (albeit shifting) environment of opportunities and constraints that tends to affect categories of households differentially.

Bringing together these four points, we can see that housing pathways are likely to reflect interactions developing over time between household strategies, obligations and resources, and external influences creating opportunities and constraints. Factors can overlap and mutually affect each other in complex ways, and there is great individual diversity of prospects amongst households. Yet there is also some patterning of relative strength and disadvantage between broad household categories. Thus the pathways available to households over time are likely to be influenced by disability, ethnicity and gender, as well as by class.

One specific type of pattern in housing pathways is strongly associated with minority ethnic status and low incomes. This is the situation of spatial separation or segregation of disadvantaged groups that has been notoriously persistent in North America along lines of ethnic origin and ascribed colour. The inferior conditions occupied by some minority groups in the United States have contributed to widespread images of enclaves or ghettos, within which bad housing conditions are associated with the clustering of specific minority ethnic households. Care is needed before transferring any American model to other cultural and political settings, but the image of the ghetto is nonetheless a potent one that attracts some politicians or analysts in Europe too.

It is important neither to confuse the clustering together of similar households with a notion of problematic neighbourhoods, nor to assume any simple causative link between the two. Ethnic clustering can be a positive asset for households (as is frequently understood in the case of Jewish communities in parts of the United Kingdom or United States). As this suggests, the real problem is less about the separation of groups than about the economic disadvantages faced by disproportionate numbers of the residents of deprived areas. As already indicated above, people tend to live in bad housing mainly because of relative poverty, and because they face limited choices. Similar people (and close kin) living nearby may make life more manageable and reduce the likelihood of racist harassment. This will not adequately compensate for inferior job prospects, low-quality dwellings, or poor services, but may help a little. Historically, some disabled people also had very little choice about where they lived, being segregated out of ordinary housing and into separate schemes targeted around specific types of impairment. The key point here (as for ethnicity) is that the separation of a group can be voluntary or involuntary, but also often a mix of the two. The smaller the voluntary element becomes in the choice of residence, the more unfair and restricting the outcome may seem.

Some Options for Analysis and Theory

We have touched above on several key variables (including features of marketised relationships, cultural factors, access to property rights and wealth, individual strategies, and relationships with labour markets). It can be useful to develop a general picture by adopting a dual approach, catering for structure alongside human agency (and keeping in mind the ongoing interactions and overlaps between the two). On the one side, we can study the tendencies for housing outcomes to be patterned heavily by structural factors. These are forces that persist over time (albeit with potential for change) and are manifested especially through institutional practices, distribution and availability of resources, and external constraints and opportunities when households make their strategies. As we have indicated, patterns of opportunities may often work against specific minority groups, female-headed households, and some disabled people. Market relationships and wealth distribution play inevitable roles here, so that outcomes are rarely a result of irrational prejudices and hostilities alone.

As a concept, structure is primarily about the environments that people encounter, and this can include a wide range of features with a degree of persistence, including not just factors affecting access to material resources but also those in the realm of established ideas, official discourses, or entrenched cultural practice. Labour market circumstances, access to resources, and socioeconomic positions are often crucial in helping determine housing outcomes for households, but labelling and cultural expectations may also play roles. One way of interpreting the processes and outcomes is to think in terms of differential incorporation, whereby differing groups are drawn into the housing world with varying degrees of satisfaction and support. At the same time an important feature is that institutional effects can operate across the broad categories of households. Thus policies and organisations may negatively affect pathways of women as well as some minority ethnic groups, and the application of an evaluative principle (such as risk appraisal) may affect disabled people as well as people living in poor parts of a city.

On the other side of our picture, research can investigate how people continue to act on their own and families' behalf, and this tends to be characterised by the phrase human agency. The idea in essence refers to the capacity to have an effect. Households define what residence and the home mean to them, albeit within constraints. Thus their consciousness plays roles in determining what the dwelling means. Even where not taking particular actions, they are receiving and interpreting the physical and social environment of the home in a way that may not always coincide with how it has been seen by providers, developers, or other practitioners. In any event, attempts to explain the ongoing significance of issues of housing and difference need to take account of individual and collective strategies, perceptions, and household resources amongst consumers.

Conclusions

Understanding difference is essential for an adequate and balanced account of conditions and trends, and when addressing policy concerns. Housing scholars and researchers can help improve debates on areas such as social housing, housing needs, or housing subsidies by more fully stressing the significance of diverse needs and situations alongside the frequent commonality of disadvantaging experiences. It would be valuable to have fuller development not only of national and local studies, but of comparative work on several fronts. Key potential foci for cross-countries comparisons might include: differentiation of housing pathways; links with positions relating to labour markets; the impact of institutional behaviours; and the development of regulatory systems and forms of positive action strategies. At the same time, scholars need to keep in view the interrelations between other aspects of difference on the one hand and class and intraclass divisions on the other.

As far as policy development is concerned, one key to changes is to tackle institutional practices that work against groups, and that help negatively pattern their housing options. At the same time, analysts need to be wary about assumptions that social changes (such as increased integration and social mixing) can or should be generated through housing interventions, given the nature of clustering processes and bounded choices. It is also important to keep in mind the diversity of views and potential claims from different groups. Material conflicts over access to resources may heighten tensions, and an absence (or decline) of strong state welfare systems may make it more difficult to handle resentments (as when social housing is in short supply). An additional and abiding issue in management of intergroup relations and individual rights concerns the balances struck between particularism and universalism. On the one hand, the particular needs and preferences of specific groups point to policies that are culturally sensitive and that do not undermine positive benefit groups gain from their social solidarities and religious affiliations. On the other hand, there are always limits to relativism, and policies need to ensure fairness and some basic similarities of expectations, despite the benefits of multiculturalism and diversity.

See also: Discrimination in Housing Markets; Ethnic Minorities and Housing; Gender and Urban Housing in the Global South; Impairment and Experience of Home; Meanings of Home: Gender Dimensions; Older People: Well-Being, Housing and Neighbourhoods; Policies to Address Redlining; Residential Segregation and Ethnic Diversity in the United States; Social Class and Housing.

References

Chahal K and Julienne L (1999) *We can't all be White: Racist Victimisation in the UK*. York: Joseph Rowntree Foundation.

Harrison M, Phillips D, Chahal K, Hunt L, and Perry J (eds.) (2005) *Housing, 'Race' and Community Cohesion*. Coventry: Chartered Institute of Housing.

Further Reading

Clapham D (2005) *The Meaning of Housing: A Pathways Approach*. Bristol: Policy Press.

Connerly CE (2005) *'The most segregated city in America': City Planning and Civil Rights in Birmingham, 1920–1980*. Charlottesville: University of Virginia Press.

Harrison M and with Davis C (2001) *Housing, Socil Policy aDifference: Disability, Ethnicity, Gender and Housing*. Bristol: The Policy Press.

Hemingway L (2010) Taking a Risk? The Mortgage Industry and Perceptions of Disabled People. *Disability and Society* 25(1): 75–87.

Hirayama Y and Izuhara M (2008) Women and housing assets in the context of Japan's home-owning democracy. *Journal of Social Policy*. 37: 641–660.

Housing Studies (2004). *Special Issue on housing quality, disability and domesticity*. 19(5): 691–708.

Imrie R (2006) *Accessible Housing: Quality, Disability and Design*. London and New York: Routledge.

Klak TH and Hey JK (1992) Gender and State Bias in Jamaican Housing Programs. *World Development* 20(2), 213–227.

Olotuah AO and Ajayi MA (2008) Repositioning women in housing development in Nigeria. *Indian Journal of Gender Studies* 15(1): 101–113.

Phua L and Yeoh B (1998) Everyday negotiations: women's spaces and the public housing landscape in Singapore. *Australian Geographer* 29(3): 309–326.

Spicker P (1993/4) Understanding particularism. *Critical Social Policy* 13(39, Pt. 3): 5–20.

Tester G (2008) An intersectional analysis of sexual harassment in housing. *Gender and Society* 22(3): 349–366.

Yinger J (1995) *Closed Doors, Opportunities Lost: The Continuing Costs of Housing Discrimination*. New York: Russell Sage Foundation.

Relevant Websites

www.leeds.ac.uk/ – Disability Archive UK

www.equalityhumanrights.com/ – Equality and Human Rights Commission (EHRC)

http://fra.europa.eu/ – European Union Agency for Fundamental Rights (FRA)

http://fra.europa.eu/ – Harrison M, Law I, Phillips D (2006) *Comparative analysis on discrimination and racism in housing. Report on 15 countries to the European Union Monitoring Centre on Racism and Xenophobia*. EUMC (FRA).

www.sociology.leeds.ac.uk/ – International Research Network on Housing, Ethnicity and Policy (IRNHEP)

http://www.jrf.org.uk/ – Robinson D, Reeve K and Casey R (2007) The housing pathways of new immigrants. *Joseph Rowntree Foundation Findings*.

Disability and Enablement

R Jacinto, King's College London, London, UK

© 2012 Elsevier Ltd. All rights reserved.

Glossary

Independent-living movement This movement campaigns for the rights of disabled people so that they are given the means to live independently and/or to choose the conditions of their care and support system. The ILM also campaigns for disabled people to be considered primarily as citizens and not only as consumers of health care, special housing, and rehabilitation. The ILM was significantly influenced by the US civil rights movement in the 1960s and their activism also brought attention to the need of adopting universal design principles in the construction of the built environment. The first Centre for Independent Living was founded by disability activists in California, United States, in 1972.

Lifetime homes standard Lifetime homes standard are a series of 16 criteria aimed to make homes accessible and adaptable. The concept of a lifetime home was initially developed in 1991 by the Joseph Rowntree Foundation (United Kingdom). In 2008, the UK government announced its intention to make the criteria mandatory to all new-built homes at the national level by 2013.

Poverty line Poverty line is the minimum level of income, per day, considered to be necessary to achieve an adequate standard of living, in a given country. This level changes per country, but the common international poverty line is around US$1 a day (currently US$1.25), as set by the World Bank.

Public procurement Public procurement is the act of contracting or acquiring goods and/or services at the best possible price and quality, by using a public tender, also called a government procurement process. To prevent fraud and corruption, several countries possess laws to regulate the acquisition of goods and/or services by both the public and private sectors.

Social model of disability This model understands disability as the disadvantage or restriction of activity caused by a social organisation which takes no or little account of people with impairments, and therefore excludes them from mainstream social activities (UPIAS, 1976). Disability, according to this model, is caused by social restrictions and not by physical, sensory, or cognitive impairments. The phrase 'social model of disability' was coined by Mike Oliver in 1983.

Introduction

Home plays a crucial function in people's lives as it provides a sense of belonging and shelter, shaping our existence. The way we dwell influences how we access and explore the world. The domestic environment can enable us to succeed or fail, to win or lose, and to come back to a safe refuge. It can enable us to experience our capacities to the full and it can influence greatly the quality of our lives.

However, all too often, the absence of housing, and the absence of a home to dwell, severs people's chances and opportunities to conduct their lives, participate in their social, professional, and political interactions, and, in the broadest possible sense, to be capable of living the lives they wish for themselves. Housing is not only an individual act, it is also determined by the way governments intervene in the housing market, assist or penalise different households, regulate housing policies, building codes, land allocations and planning permissions, among many other aspects. Housing is dependent on the social rights governments define for their citizens, and also on what governments believe individuals are entitled to have as a home, particularly in terms of affordability, size, and location.

Postwar welfare framed housing responsibilities as a model where the male was the breadwinner and the female stayed at home. Today, this model is obsolete in the way it excludes a large proportion of the population living under different arrangements (Andersen, 2005; Lewis, 2001). Social, gender, religious as well as professional values and attitudes are changing, along with shifting understandings of social rights. Moreover, demographic changes are having an impact on housing needs. For instance, demographic changes in Europe are leading to an ageing population with increased need for social care, an increased proportion of single or single parents' households, and higher levels of immigration. All these factors have an impact on how states define the frameworks that enable citizens to have access to adequate housing and quality of life.

Housing for enablement cannot be limited to one narrow definition, as housing social contexts differ immensely; and these affect how housing and enablement are understood. Enablement depends on political, moral, and ethical values. Housing for enablement encompasses housing as a basic right, as a physical form, and as a process whereby individuals are provided the means to determine the conditions of their lives. The choices made by different governments to secure adequate accommodation for the most vulnerable social groups are issues facing governments across the globe. The way in which these issues have been approached varies between and within societies at different points in time.

This article will first address changes in the domestic environment, housing deprivation, and housing enablement strategies such as affordable housing. The second part will present the idea of disablement and choice in the housing sphere, as well as the contribution of the independent-living movement (ILM) to the understanding of housing enablement and independence. Finally, the third section will cover the work of authors that have contributed to housing design and community participation in housing projects, as well as discussing design standards and accessibility regulation, which are key to the enablement of residents inside and outside their homes.

Housing, Affordability, and Enabling Strategies

Housing has evolved over time. Wars, environmental risks, political structures, financial crises, and demographic changes have all shaped housing construction and design. At the beginning of the twentieth century, housing had a different form from what it is today. Together with other societal sectors such as transport, housing became central to the making of modern twentieth-century lifestyles. For instance, urban sprawl after 1945 was the consequence of modernist visions of the city, characterised by divisions between work and living space aided by changes in transportation and, in some cases, government policy.

However, this lifestyle did not necessarily reflect residents' aspirations for quality of life. As discussed in Rob Imrie's work, housing manifests what governments and the building industry understand as citizen's aspirations. For example, housing differences in Eastern and Western Europe until the 1990s were accentuated by different political regimes. Also, in the middle of the twentieth century, housing in Latin American, African, and Asian countries presented itself as a mechanism of social stratification, particularly for European colonies where the colony and the coloniser were allowed to dwell in very different housing arrangements.

As noted by Rowe (1993), the domestic environment has been shaped in the interests of social welfare. Welfare and economic policies have an extensive impact on what happens in the housing sphere. The concept of an enabling strategy towards housing or housing enablement was particularly evident at the City Summit (Habitat II) in 1996. In this context, an enabling strategy for housing is a concept that favours governments assuming the role of supporter rather than direct provider in the housing sector (Ogu, 1999), giving a foremost role to the private sector.

The emergence of the strategy covered in the City Summit of 1996 (Habitat II) was influenced by the rapid expansion of urban areas in developing countries, ineffective housing, and financial policies, together with an acute lack of affordable housing for a large proportion of the urban population. In addition, agencies such as the World Bank changed their funding policies, which affected the ways governments managed to provide housing in the 1990s. Some of the features of housing enablement strategies in developing countries (UNCHS, 1994) involved the granting of security of tenure to low earners and removal of inhibitive bureaucratic controls on housing development, and formulation of building standards and planning regulations and financial policies from small loans to flexible payment schedules. These were mainly aimed at poor communities so that these could access affordable plots and housing. Hamdi (1991) and Ogu (1999) have argued that these strategies are not a solution per se to housing deprivation in developing countries. Rather, the way these different aspects are addressed will influence the success of this programme.

However, it is not only developing countries that are affected by housing deprivation. This issue also affects developed countries. Housing deprivation is more acute when social inequality is accentuated (Winn and Morris, 1990); and social inequality is increasing in the world (de Miguel, 1998). The gap between the richest and the poorest groups of the population, within a country, has increased since the 1980s (de Miguel, 1998) and the proportion of people below the poverty line has also grown higher (**Figure 1**).

Gender and race divisions also affect housing deprivation. For instance, Winn and Morris (1990) conclude that in the United Kingdom single women are more likely to be subject to housing deprivation than men, frequently due to differences in participation in the labour force, employment discrimination, childcare responsibilities, and unpaid housekeeping work. This combination puts women at risk, particularly when a couple's relationship breaks down.

Affordable housing policies have also been associated with enablement strategies, in order to help those who cannot afford a suitable home. Harriott and Matthews (1998) have pointed out two key aspects for housing to be considered affordable or socially owned: (1) landlords are not profit-driven and (2) its administration and eligibility for residents is done on the basis of 'housing need'. Some countries have a large share of housing stock managed by social landlords, such as The Netherlands and Denmark.

Figure 1 Three siblings at the door of their home. Amazon, Brazil, 2007.
Photo by Thomas Merckx.

Nonetheless, rents in these countries are not necessarily much lower than the private market when compared to countries with a smaller share of social landlords, for instance, Portugal and Italy. Such price similarities between social and private rents in countries with a great share of social housing are often accompanied with rent prices set in relation to taxation, housing benefits, and other subsidies directly provided to households, which may help compensate higher social rents (Tsenkova and Turner, 2004). In addition, in countries where the share of social landlords is small compared to the share of the private sector, the government mainly targets low-income groups for the social rented sector. Because rent level is often dependent on the income of tenants, the average level of social rents is low in such countries.

Affordable or social market homes can be purposely built or be part of 'mainstream' housing projects. Some homes are sold or rented to the wider public, while others are allocated, by local or central government, to families in need. Denton (2006) has called attention to affordable housing strategies that do not resolve housing inequality; rather they can perpetuate it, particularly in relation to ethnic groups and racial discrimination. Denton's analysis of housing and race segregation in the United States concluded that if governments only focus on mortgage interests and tax deductions, while neglecting structural contexts responsible for social disadvantage, these strategies will be short-term solutions, and may subsidise housing for the wealthy.

Choice, Disablement, and Independence

Imrie (2001, 2006) and Gleeson (2001) suggest that much of the urban fabric, particularly housing stock, is inaccessible and perpetuates disabling values in the way it constructs physical and social discriminatory barriers to disabled people. Those who fall outside the 'Hellenic body ideals' are excluded from living or visiting most homes, either flats or houses, due to poor design and lack of consideration for the wide range of human needs.

Today's housing stock can prevent citizens from fulfilling their potential, when, for example, the single reason why individuals are hindered from being able to perform daily tasks is the lack of accessible design features. In addition, the World Health Organisation (WHO) suggests that inadequate housing is one of the mechanisms through which poverty can affect health and wellbeing. Living in overcrowded homes, or with damp and mouldy walls, has a negative impact on the health of its residents. For instance, it can cause chronic respiratory problems and mental health problems (WHO, 2009). The needs of disabled people are often forgotten, as are the growing needs of an ageing population and a multicultural society with different aspirations and ways of dwelling. For instance, children, adults, and older people may have different housing needs but homes are designed in the same way, with little sensitivity to the specific ways they may wish to use the dwelling space.

As Imrie (2006) notes, housing construction is primarily determined by the interests and constraints of the speculative building industry aligned to a generalised conceptualisation of the 'average human body', and of 'average housing needs' where impairment, illness, age, ethnicity, among other aspects, are not part of how housing design practices are understood. Among urban planners, architects, and housing design managers, the concept of housing need is often rooted in the same way as other products are conceived – as a financial product, to be marketed, sold, acquired, and distributed (**Figure 2**).

Ulrich Beck (1998) has argued that there is an architecture of apartheid not focused on race, but instead on the social exclusion created by the built environment, which only assures the needs of 'productive elites', discriminating against disabled people, older people, and all those not understood as part of the 'mainstream' functional body. Disabled people can be prevented from entering a home due to the lack of accessible ramps or lifts. However, while some homes may have a step-free entrance and fulfil minimum design standards, these

Figure 2 Apartment building, view from a nearby shopping centre. Lisbon, Portugal, 2007.
Photo by the author.

homes can still be inaccessible to live in once a person has access to the inside of the home.

Although architects and builders may consider corridor widths and step-free entrances when addressing accessibility aspects, in order to dwell most people need more. Disabled people need to be able to socialise with family and friends and carry on daily tasks such as doing their laundry, preparing meals, using the bathroom, and getting ready themselves to go out of the home every day. Furthermore, flexible environments and accessible features are not only relevant for physically disabled people. People may require a home where the different levels of light can be adjusted, where noise can be suppressed, or where a guide dog can be accommodated. Also, the way pipes and electrical installations are incorporated into a home should allow for a flexible use of rooms in case residents need to rearrange their living space.

In the United Kingdom, the ILM, allied to the social model of disability, has fought for a change in the way homes are designed and equipped as well as for alterations in the process by which individuals have access to care and support for their daily tasks. This movement has been driven by the work of activists and scholars, such as Mike Oliver, Jenny Morris, and Tom Shakespeare. As suggested by Morris (2001), many disabled people experience significant barriers to citizenship in relation to housing, such as imposed dependence.

This movement argues that to be segregated in residential homes, with imposed schedules and imposed care providers, represents a denial of the human right to a family life, to see friends, and to establish the relationships individuals choose to have. The key point is that for independence, people should have control over their lives, not that they perform every task independently. Independence is not necessarily associated with physical, sensory, or intellectual capacities to care for oneself without assistance; conversely, independence can be created by enabling people to have choice in the assistance provided.

Also, in the choice of support and care, individuals can be viewed as consumers who make rational decisions regarding their consumption of public goods or services, as pointed out by Marsh (1998). If people are seen as consumers, and they do not like what they obtain from a particular supplier, they can exercise what Hirschman (1970) termed the 'exit' option and require a particular service from another provider, in case they are available. However, as local authorities or municipalities shift from being direct providers to enablers (Harriott and Matthews, 1998), choice also plays a role in the provision of services. A number of concerns have been raised by scholars and policy-analysts about this strategy, such as governments replicating the inequality of market mechanisms by delivering good-quality services to some but denying access to adequate services to others (Marsh, 1998). It may be that only those with adequate resources are in a position to choose, and such people are not necessarily those in most need.

Moreover, the location of the home affects the access people have to hospitals, leisure centres, public transport, and schools in the way that many of these facilities provide a service only to those living nearby, falling under their catchment areas. In these circumstances, housing affects the other areas of life, acting as an enablement or disablement factor to quality of life. As noted by Gleeson (1999), an enabling environment aspires to create social independence and empower people to determine the conditions of their own existence, without imposed hierarchical social relationships.

Enabling People Inside Their Homes

There are several conventions and laws addressing the housing needs of people, particularly disabled people, as they are often deprived from living independently. Legislation against the discrimination of disabled people, including discrimination through the built environment, has been adopted in many countries across the globe. This has been adopted by the European Union countries and most American countries, such as the United States in 1990, Argentina in 1991, and Peru in 1998. In addition, Australia saw its Disability Discrimination Act approved in 1992, followed by India in 1993 and Pakistan in 2002. African countries are also working towards antidiscrimination legislation. Uganda passed an antidiscrimination bill in 2003 and Ghana in 2006.

Housing needs are particularly overlooked in environments where natural disasters, war, and civil conflicts have affected both the population and the condition of the built environment. The United Nations estimates that among 42 million forcibly displaced people worldwide an estimated 3.5 million are disabled people (UNHCR, 2009; WRC, 2009). The United Nations believe that the real number of disabled people uprooted is significantly higher, but these are not being properly accounted for during registration processes in refugees' camps. In 2006, the United Nations Convention on the Rights of Persons with Disabilities was adopted and all the European Union countries ratified this convention.

Furthermore, European countries can be subjected to public procurements with directives which require, for example, that contracting authorities should specify the accessibility criteria for people with disabilities or design for all users. In addition to this, many countries already had accessibility-specific legislation or accessibility standards incorporated into their building regulations. In Europe, Sweden was one of the first countries to require builders to comply with housing accessibility regulations, since the introduction of the adaptable home standards in 1977. However, the extent to which governments ensure that these laws are complied with, and assess whether these are being appropriately put into practice, varies greatly within and across countries.

These practices are highly dependent on institutional frameworks, accountability, compliance mechanisms, and reliance on juridical systems and get-out clauses. For instance, in the United States, the Americans with Disabilities Act applies to housing, but only if it is constructed with government funding. Of these, only 5% of housing units are expected to be accessible. Although the Fair Housing Act Amendments of 1988 (USA) requires all newly constructed multifamily housing to be accessible, this only applies to multifamily housing with four or more units in elevator-equipped buildings. Since a large proportion of town homes are single-family homes, these regulations exclude a large part of the housing supply (Pynoos and Nishita, 2006).

Moreover, many antidiscrimination bills require that reasonable adjustments must be made so that housing design accommodates for the needs of disabled people, or anyone with particular physical, sensory, or cognitive requirements. However, as argued by Imrie and Hall (2001), the understanding of what is a reasonable adjustment is dependent on complex processes and varies with different political views, financial constraints, social attitudes, and the interests of the building industry.

Culture plays a significant role in this process as well. In intimate spaces of the home, such as the bathroom, different cultures may require different designs and equipment. For instance, a Portuguese accessibility directive from 2006, created as part of a governmental policy for social inclusion of disabled people, preceded the national building regulations. It requires all new homes (houses and flats) to have at least one facility with a bath (or a shower), a toilet, a sink, and a bidet. All the equipments in this facility must meet the 2006 accessibility directive guidance. However, bathroom equipment is dependent on the country's culture and while relevant for some societies, it can be seen as redundant by others.

King (1996) has argued that part of the housing quality should be related to a vernacular housing process, where individuals can construct and self-make adjustments to their own homes, ways of dwelling, and experience their home in a different manner than that prescribed by developers and building regulations. John Turner (1977) has also made significant contributions to the value of self-construction in the domestic space, particularly influenced by his work in Peru (1957–65) with squatter settlements. His work contributed to the development of community participation in housing developments, as well as to the idea that people, as residents with different forms of interactions in a particular place, are the most significant part of a housing project.

Hamdi (1991) also notes that housing, as an enablement strategy, ought to leave some gaps in parts of development plans so that communities can have space for 'design improvisation'. As Hamdi suggests, because life inside and outside the home is intertwined, communities should be allocated space with margins of tolerance for the unknown, either in the private or in the public domain, as this will enable people to create their own specific demarcations and use of space as they feel the community needs. This margin should represent a negotiable space between potentially conflicting functional and social demands rather than lines of confrontation. This idea may, however, be more or less difficult to implement in a practical sense as it depends on local contexts (**Figure 3**).

With regard to key publications focused on arrangements for different rooms inside the home, Ernest Neufert, one of the first students of the German Bauhaus school, published Architects Data in 1936. This book included anthropometric data and ergonomics criteria to define principles of housing and spatial organisation that could enable homes to be designed for individuals of different sizes, and with different needs. Another key publication was by Selwyn Goldsmith in the United Kingdom in 1963, 'Designing for the

Figure 3 Roça Água Izé, São Tomé e Príncipe, 2009. Housing for cocoa plantation workers during the colonial period. Today, families still dwell in these houses.
Photo by the author.

Disabled', which, at its time, pioneered with the inclusion of anthropometric measurements for disabled people.

These publications, together with antidiscrimination laws, set the ground for the creation of the concept of universal design. The concept of universal design was first used in the United States by Ron Mace in 1985, and the term has become part of the literature, particularly by academics and policy-makers. The concept of 'universal design' is used mainly in the United States and in Nordic countries. In the United Kingdom, the term 'inclusive design' is more common, while in most European Union documents the term 'design for all' is adopted. Their meanings are similar, if not the same in many cases. The key idea is that products, spaces, housing, and equipment should be designed for the wide range of human beings without excluding disabled people, older people, children, and all those who usually fall into categories of 'special needs'. Inclusively designed homes are vital to assure that people can use and enjoy their domestic environment, and feel enabled to live their lives according to their aspirations.

In the United Kingdom, the government incorporated accessibility standards into the national Building Regulations, so that housing could better accommodate disabled people's needs, but this relates mainly to physically disabled people. In addition, the United Kingdom announced its intention to adopt the Lifetime Homes Standard (LHS) for all new-built homes by 2013. Although the LHS presents different and more flexible design features than the national Building Regulations, some authors have considered its design to be rigid and others find it too costly. There is no design plan that would satisfy the needs of all people. For instance, with regard to the flexibility of the rooms in a home built to the LHS, Imrie (2006) questions the lack of demountable walls or multifunctional rooms with integrated elements such as bathing and sleeping facilities so that the residents can adapt their home to their needs, even if temporary. Also, the building industry has argued that this significantly increases housing construction costs and that some of its criteria are obsolete.

Jon Christophersen's (2002) work has also addressed the many ways in which homes can be adapted, including for people with mental health problems. His work in Norway has demonstrated that adapting homes for people with mobility and cognitive disabilities does not need extraordinary measures and adapted dwellings do not differ greatly from ordinary dwellings. He has discussed the impact that even small changes in housing design can have on residents' lives, enabling them to live more independently and to exercise their capacities. Christophersen argues that the usual preconditions for good architectural planning are crucial, and in many occasions already present in accessibility standards. However, these are often overlooked by architects and planning authorities.

Conclusion

People's life stories are intrinsically related to their domestic space in the way housing can enable or prevent citizens to take control over their lives. Individuals choose different social paths within the wider constraints they face, and housing must be a part of individuals' existence that allows them to be self-determined in establishing the conditions that will ensure well-being and quality to their lives. The opportunities for individuals to control their circumstances ought not to be disunited due to one's home being designed without consideration for human needs, for instance, with inaccessible design features, with little consideration to ageing needs, or with no possibility for flexibility in the use of rooms.

Housing enablement strategies, such as providing affordable housing to the most vulnerable social groups, are essential to allow those in housing need to exercise their human rights. Public policies related to the way homes are designed, constructed, and managed are dependent on governments' establishment of design and building regulations, as also on a country's establishment of social rights, societal attitudes, and culture. The level of reliance that populations have on juridical frameworks and governmental regulating bodies is significant to the way housing policies are put into practice and how these policies effectively work as means to enable individuals to a decent home.

The understanding of the wide range of housing needs, by policy-makers, architects, builders, and society in general, is fundamental to ensure that homes are designed in a manner that enables citizens to live their lives, inside and outside the home, according to their values and aspirations. Only by doing so, can housing be for enablement.

See also: Impairment and Experience of Home; Older People: Well-Being; Social Justice; Urbanisation and Housing the Poor: Overview.

References

Andersen JG (2005) *The Changing Face of Welfare: Consequences and Outcomes from a Citizenship Perspective*. UK: Policy Press.

Beck U (1998) *Democracy Without Enemies*. Cambridge, UK: Polity Press.

Christophersen J (ed.) (2002). *Universal Design: 17 Ways of Thinking and Teaching*. Norway: Husbanken.

de Miguel JM (1998) *Estructura y cambio social en Espana*. Madrid: Alianza Editorial.

Denton NA (2006) Segregation and Discrimination in Housing. In: Bratt R, Stone M, and Hartman C (eds.) (2006) *A Right to Housing: Foundation for a New Social Agenda*. Philadelphia, PA: Temple University Press.

Gleeson BJ (1998) A place on earth: technology, space and disability. *Journal of Urban Technology*.

Gleeson B (2001) Disability and the open city. *Urban Studies* 38: 251–265.

Hamdi N (1991) *Housing without Houses*. London, UK: Intermediate Technology Publications.

Harriott S, Matthews L, and Grainger P (1998) *Social Housing: An Introduction*. UK: Longman.

Hirschman AO (1970) *Exit, Voice, and Loyalty: Responses to Decline in Firms, Organizations, and States*. Harvard, MA: Harvard University Press.

Imrie R and Hall P (2001) *Inclusive Design – Designing and Developing Accessible Environments*. London: Spon Press.

Imrie R (2001) Barriered and bounded places and the spatialities of disability. *Urban Studies* 38(2).

Imrie R (2006) *Accessible Housing: Quality, Disability and Design*. London: Routledge.

King P (1996) *The Limits of Housing Policy: A Philosophical Investigation*. UK: Middlesex University Press.

Lewis J (2001) The decline of the male breadwinner model: implications for work and care. *Social Politics: International Studies in Gender, State & Society* 8(2).

Marsh A (1998) Processes of change in housing and public policy. In: Marsh A and Mullins D (eds.) *Housing and Public Policy: Citizenship, Choice, and Control*. UK: Open University Press.

Morris J and Winn M (1990) *Housing and Social Inequality*. London: Shipman Ltd.

Morris J (2001) *That kind of life? Social exclusion and young disabled people with high levels of support needs*. UK: Scope.

Ogu VI (1999) Housing enablement in a developing world city: the case study of Benin City, Nigeria. *Habitat International* 23(2).

Pynoos J and Nishita CM (2006) The Elderly and a Right to Housing. In: Bratt R, Stone M, and Hartman C (eds.) (2006) *A Right to Housing: Foundation for a New Social Agenda*. Philadelphia, PA: Temple University Press.

Rowe PG (1993) *Modernity and Housing*. Cambridge, MA: MIT Press.

Tsenkova S and Turner B (2004) The future of social housing in Eastern Europe: reforms in Latvia and Ukraine. *International Journal of Housing Policy* 4(2).

Turner J (1977) *Housing by People: Towards Autonomy in Building Environments*. New York: Pantheon Books.

Union of the Physically Impaired Against Segregation (UPIAS) (1976) *Fundamental Principles of Disability*. UK: UPIAS.

United Nations High Commission for Refuges (UNCHS) (1994) *Shelter Forum Bulletin No 6*. Nairobi. United Nations Publications.

United Nations High Commission for Refuges (UNHRC) (2009) *Global Trends 2008: Refugees, Asylum-seekers, Returnees, Internally Displaced and Stateless Persons*. United Nations Publications.

Women Refugee Commission (WRC) (2009) *Refugees with disabilities: Key Facts*. USA: WRC Publications.

World Health Organization Regional Office for Europe (2009) *WHO Guidelines for indoor air quality: Dampness and Mould*. Denmark: WHO Publications.

Further Reading

Bratt R, Stone M, and Hartman C (eds.) (2006) *A Right to Housing: Foundation for a New Social Agenda*. Philadelphia, PA: Temple University Press.

Bretherton J and Pleace N (2008) *Residents' Views of New Forms of High Density Affordable Living*. York/Coventry, UK: Joseph Rowntree Foundation/Chartered Institute of Housing Publications.

Gleeson B (2001) Disability and the open city. *Urban Studies* 38: 251–265.

Hamdi N (1991) *Housing without Houses*. London: Intermediate Technology Publications.

Imrie R and Hall P (2001) *Inclusive Design – Designing and Developing Accessible Environments*. London: Spoon Press.

Imrie R (2006) *Accessible Housing: Quality, Disability and Design*. London, UK: Routledge.

Morris J and Winn M (1990) *Housing and Social Inequality*. UK: Biddles Ltd.

Peace S and Holland C (eds.) (2001) *Inclusive Housing in an Ageing Society*. Bristol, UK: Policy Press.

Swain J, French S, Barnes C, and Thomas C (2004) *Disabling Barriers, Enabling Environments*, 2nd edn. London: Sage.

Turner J (1977) *Housing by People: Towards Autonomy in Building Environments*. New York: Pantheon Books.

Yahya S, Agevi E, Lowe L, Mugova A, Musandu-Nyamayaro O, and Schilderman T (2001) *Double Standards, Single Purpose – Making Housing Regulations to Reduce Poverty*. London: ITDG.

Discourse Analysis

T Manzi, University of Westminster, London, UK

© 2012 Elsevier Ltd. All rights reserved.

Introduction

Discourse analysis has become an increasingly influential approach in housing studies. Mainly formulated as a response to positivism, discourse analysis formed part of what has been categorised as an interpretative or 'linguistic turn' (Fischer and Forrester, 1993) in urban studies in the 1980s. Since the 1990s, housing studies have attempted to draw upon a wider multidisciplinary theoretical tradition, providing detailed analysis, using interpretative frameworks, and qualitative methodologies. This article considers a number of questions: what do we mean by discourse analysis? What are its main philosophical and sociological foundations? Why has it become such an influential paradigm? What are its main limitations and how can these criticisms be countered?

Definitions of Discourse and Discourse Analysis

At the most basic level, discourse refers to language and patterns of speech; it is primarily connected with the analysis of meaningful social interaction. Discourse analysis that considers the significance of language, conversation, and text as well as wider social practices. However, the difficulty is that discourse can be defined so widely as to be almost meaningless. Take the definition offered by Howarth (1995): "The concept of discourse includes all types of social and political practice, as well as institutions and organisations, within its frame of reference" (p. 115). More helpful is the notion that discourse analysis examines the ways in which structures of meaning make possible certain forms of conduct. Hence, "it attempts to understand how the discourses which structure the activities of social agents are *produced*, how they *function*, and how they are *changed*" (Howarth, 1995: 115, emphasis in original).

Similarly, for writers such as van Dijk (1997), discourse moves beyond common-sense definitions of language use to encompass its functional aspects, using the concept of 'communicative events' to explain how language ideas, beliefs, or emotions are articulated through verbal interaction. The role of discourse analysis in social science is therefore to consider how social interactions are mediated through language use, communication, and cognition. Moreover, the ambiguity of discourse can refer to particular, specific conversations or texts or to a more general system or "order of discourse" (pp. 3–4), allowing a focus on both agency and structural features to consider issues of meaning, style, rhetoric, and schemata (or structure).

The main insight from discourse analysis (influenced by social constructionist theories) is that "our ways of talking do not neutrally reflect our world, identities and social relations but rather play an active role in creating and changing them" (Phillips and Jorgensen, 2002: 1). Language is therefore both generative and constitutive – changes in discourse are the means by which the social world itself is transformed.

Discourse Analysis in Philosophy and Social Theory

Theoretical interest in discourse can generally be traced to the influence of postwar 'ordinary language' philosophy which emphasised cultural practices; speaking languages involves engagement in social practices, rather than merely articulating particular combinations of words according to fixed rules of grammar. Moreover, access to reality is always through language, which has a productive function; it is not simply a representation of preexisting facts but is responsible for determining sense and understanding. Hence, the ascription of meaning through discourse works to constitute and change the world.

This recursive view of language considers our understanding of reality as fundamentally affected by the terminology used to describe, explain, evaluate, contest, and agree common understandings and definitions. Characterised as an 'antifoundationalist' philosophy, it maintained there are no entirely objective standpoints which guarantee truth or knowledge about the world. This contingent approach to epistemology implied that an essential truth for one generation may later come to be seen as accidental or empirical for another.

Sociological theories of discourse were strongly influenced by the development of 'symbolic interactionism' (Goffman, 1959), which provided an account of reality wherein identity was primarily explained through social interaction, that is, expressed through language. Accompanied by ethnomethodological research studies (Garfinkel, 1967), 'social constructionist' theories examined relationships between social agents and institutional structures and how these may determine our understanding of social reality. Social constructionism was highly influential in the development of discourse analysis by emphasising historical and cultural specificity, questioning 'taken for granted' knowledge, and demonstrating linkages between knowledge and social action.

Discourse analysis has been strongly influenced by the work of Foucault, in particular his view that discourses largely determine manifestations of power, revealed through 'discursive formations' and within 'discursive regularities', dispersed throughout social activities (Foucault, 1977). In providing 'the conditions of possibility for the social' (Phillips and Jorgensen, 2002: 13), power functions as both a productive and constraining force. These approaches in philosophy and social theory provided important theoretical innovations, allowing for the application of discourse analysis to public policy studies.

The Argumentative Turn in Public Policy

Whilst acknowledgement of the symbolic features of politics and the use of rhetoric in political ideology had been long established, discourse analysis placed particular emphasis on social change and political contestation. Laclau and Mouffe's (1985) notion of 'discursive struggle' illustrated how discourses could be transformed through social contact; in attempting to assert hegemony meaning is regularly manipulated to meet ideological ends. Interest in discourse as 'communicative action' (Habermas, 1981) or as part of symbolic capital (Bourdieu, 1991) encouraged a focus upon argumentation and negotiation strategies in both theory and practice.

The development of critical discourse analysis (CDA) has proved highly significant in the analysis of contemporary public policy. CDA, most closely associated with the work of Fairclough (1992), has studied the construction of 'narratives' in public policy and considered agenda-setting techniques, through the establishment of ways of thinking, speaking, and writing. Meaning is therefore related to social convention rather than being innate; individual texts draw on other texts and change occurs through combinations of discourses and their interaction with the wider social and cultural world. In methodological terms, discourse analysis has been extensively used to consider the significance of speeches, writings, interviews, and conversations.

At the same time, within political science, criticism of an orientation to empirically based, largely quantitative approaches to public policy led to the formulation of 'deliberative policy analysis' wherein public policy is viewed as a 'discursive construct'; these postempiricist approaches paid close attention to argumentation and the value-laden nature of political processes, examining concepts such as the 'mobilisation of bias', the creation of 'discourse coalitions' (Hajer, 2003), the significance of 'nondecisions', and the use of technocratic discourse and policy narratives within participatory democratic mechanisms. Interest in 'cognitive' discourse analysis or 'discursive institutionalism' (Schmidt, 2008) has examined power relationships, explaining how institutions are created and how they change and persist over time. Such approaches served to explain the creation of hegemonic relationships, providing an understanding of how political forces structure dominant forms of conduct and meaning within given social contexts.

Discourse analysis in urban policy was used to explain how rhetoric is used as a means of social action rather than as a vehicle for transparent communication. The use of detailed case studies in geography and planning illustrates ways in which deliberative analysis highlighted policy initiatives and identified the limitations of empirical analysis. Discursive struggles were seen as central to the articulation of urban problems, the range of solutions available, and the types of opposition and dissent expressed; discursive practices can often serve to reinforce existing power relations.

The Linguistic Turn in Housing Studies

The linguistic turn in housing studies emerged as an important research approach in the late 1990s. Influenced by social constructionism, discourse analysis was based on dissatisfaction with what was viewed as traditional empirically based and at times atheoretical approaches to housing studies. An interest in how narratives and myths serve to construct ideology (such as the preference for home ownership) helps to explain the development of cross-cultural differences in institutional arrangements for the delivery of housing. The work of Kemeny (1992) has been highly influential in arguing for a greater attention to be paid to issues of culture, knowledge, power, and ideology in discussion of housing processes. Discourse analysis therefore emerged in housing studies in an attempt to develop a nonpositivist epistemological approach, to enable wider cross-disciplinary models, and to engage with new empirical terrain (Hastings, 2000: 132).

One of the main reasons for the growth in interest in discourse analysis and housing from the late 1990s onwards was the emergence of new processes of governance. A more complex multilevel policy environment heralded an interest in processes of argumentation, determining the place of discourse in social interaction and the operation of power relationships in the design and implementation of policy. The focus on political communication included understanding the process of problem definition, the mobilisation of opinion, the formulation of strategy, and the selection of institutional delivery vehicles. Rhetorical strategies deployed by elite decision makers and the role of the media formed an important part of the housing research agenda. Additionally, an increased interest in resident participation in decision making necessitated wider attention to bargaining and interaction processes in determining policy outcomes among nonelite groups. Advocates of discourse analysis argued that its application helped to counter systematic, thematic biases in writing and discussion about housing issues, laying open the 'ideological work' undertaken in everyday housing practice (Hastings, 2000: 137).

Housing studies therefore began to pay close attention to understanding the linkages between cognition, ideas, normative strategies, and rhetorical persuasion. Textual analysis of key policy documents formed an important research tool alongside the use of conversation analysis to understand key concepts such as the 'labelling' of council tenants, revealing the differential application of normative standards in housing practice. Such studies have uncovered implicit and systematic class biases amongst elite decision makers, denying legitimacy to dissenting attitudes and demonstrating considerable tenure prejudice.

The process of negotiated order through the construction of boundaries and social antagonisms has played an important role in the development of a contemporary housing research agenda. Acknowledgement of the way in which political struggle is inherently linked to the creation of the 'other', including the delineation of clear distinctions between deserving and undeserving groups, has a long history in housing policy. The benefit of detailed discourse analysis is to identify the social processes though which such boundaries are routinely drawn to determine eligibility and restrict access to service provision. Discourses surrounding gypsies and travellers (Richardson, 2006) provide one illustration of the way in which conceptions of in and out groups are used to control and inhibit settlement, through a Foucauldian 'gaze' – utilised through media discourse, through statements made by policy makers, and shaping policy decisions. Within homelessness research, the use of 'manipulative silences' (Huckin, 2002) and 'hidden and emerging spaces' in rural localities (Cloke et al. 1999) provide discursive accounts of the marginalisation of specific groups and the neglect of certain categories of need. Such aspects have been traditionally neglected in positivist influenced, quantitative housing studies where the voices of service users (and front-line staff) were either ignored or misinterpreted. Similarly, the application of policy and legislation designed to tackle antisocial behaviour by United Kingdom social landlords, based on discourses of 'conditionality' and determining acceptable and unacceptable forms of conduct, demonstrates contemporary attitudes towards welfare provision, through the differential application of incentives and sanctions (Flint, 2006).

The role of discourse analysis in the construction of meaning therefore is valuable in understanding the experiential basis of housing policy. Acknowledging the importance of the individual, subjective domain, analysis of discourses used by different stakeholders has illustrated how attitudes, values, identities, and normative expectations have been shaped to determine organisational practices, communication strategies, and the wider housing policy process.

The Limitations of Discourse Analysis

The rise in interest in social constructionism and interpretative policy analysis has generated a variety of criticisms. First, discourse analysis is criticised on the basis that it offers a highly abstracted and vague set of statements. The theory can be seen as simply too broad: "the appeal of discourse analysis is also its greatest fault, namely its inclusiveness: everything is discourse, but as a result nothing is differentiated from anything else" (King, 2004: 37). However, this criticism rests on a misunderstanding: "the starting point is an explicit recognition that discourse is not everything" (Marston, 2002: 90). The main focus of discourse analysis is to understand language within its wider context at the levels of texts, social practices, and structures. Its theoretical utility is as a tool to understand the construction of meaning, identity, and the determination of problems in housing. Examples might include analysing the problem of 'social exclusion', questioning the use of 'evidence-based' policy, and interpreting the application of 'sustainability' as a catch-all solution; such examples can demonstrate how meaning is generated, how the definition of a housing problem influences decision making, and ways in which political power is exercised.

A second line of criticism is that the focus on historical contingency and political construction becomes essentially meaningless as notions of identity, truth, and meaning are subject to continual negotiation. However, this extreme relativism represents a caricature of both discourse analysis and social constructionism. As Laclau and Mouffe state: "the discursive character of an object does not by any means, imply putting its existence into question" (1987: 82). The material world is not rejected; discourse analysis merely contends that our *access* to the material world is mediated by language and social interaction. Moreover, whilst concepts of truth and meaning are subject to interaction, the boundaries of negotiation are nevertheless constrained. Most discourse analysts hold to a view that social life tends towards the rule-bound and regulative wherein knowledge and identities, although contingent, are relatively inflexible: "Specific situations place restrictions on the identities which an individual can assume and on the statements which can be accepted as meaningful" (Phillips and Jorgensen, 2002: 6).

A failure to engage with issues of power and justice represents a third criticism. However, this argument also rests on a misinterpretation of discourse analysis. Questions of power, control, and the maintenance of inequalities are central to critical discourse analysis; the adoption of a sociopolitical rather than a purely linguistic and narrowly technical mode of analysis is specifically designed to counter such criticism. Power relationships and social justice are explicitly highlighted in demonstrating how professional orthodoxies are developed, how received opinions are distorted, how certain interests are privileged over others, and how biases are manipulated. Discourse analysis thus provides a method for examining ideology, hegemony, and legitimation within the complexity and fluidity of power relations.

Finally, there is the argument that discourse has rarely been applied systematically in housing analysis – few articles on housing have been published in the main social science journals, *Discourse and Society* or *Critical Discourse Studies*. One reason for this may be that there have been relatively few clear attempts to rigorously apply specific techniques such as conversation analysis or to consider other methods such as nonvocal techniques of communication. Some have criticised a failure to study how texts may be interpreted differently by lay readers rather than academics (Hastings, 2000: 133). Moreover, discourse analysis has been accused of selective quotation; there is a risk of choosing a small number of examples of discourses as representative, thereby risking offering a range of confusing narratives (Jacobs, 2006). Such a criticism is only valid if underpinned by an inadequate methodological basis; these accusations can apply to qualitative methodologies on a wider scale. The important point is that discourses are clearly contextualised and carefully considered in relation to existing and changing social practices. The criticisms demand a more robust application of the techniques of discourse analysis, within a clear and reflexive set of methodologies accompanied by a need to be clear about data, method, and interpretation.

In relation to further research, one area that discourse analysis might fruitfully explore is that of international comparative policy analysis. Despite work on the discourse of globalisation and theorising comparative housing systems, there has been little substantive analysis of the way in which differences in language and translation have affected the form and content of housing policies in different countries; the relationships between different discourses, institutional structures, and a broader cultural milieu represent opportunities for more wide-ranging discourse studies. In addition, there may be considerable opportunity to reflect upon how new technologies and visual representations impact on deliberative processes in housing policy.

Conclusions

This article has shown that discourse analysis has proved to be both influential and subject to extensive application within a range of settings. It is particularly helpful in developing new techniques for housing research and providing an interdisciplinary locale for the study of policy and practice. In empirical terms it brings a reflective, critical, and detailed analysis to a variety of issues including ideology, preference formation, and social change at the level of both structure and agency, within a field that has long been dominated by positivist, empirically based and mainly practical analysis.

As the tools of government have changed from hierarchical and bureaucratic institutions to civil society and third-sector agencies, a focus on wider processes of governance demand a more nuanced approach to housing studies – one that considers ideas, interests, and processes of political argumentation and accounting for the dynamic nature of change. This explains the interest in the discursive practices of elite and nonelite groups in the framing of policy problems and solutions, emphasising the high level of interdependence in their social construction. Analysis requires an emphasis on techniques used to manipulate opinion as well as to build trust through rhetoric, persuasion, and the construction of formal and informal coalitions of interests, taking into account cognitive and normative dispositions. In this way the construction of 'taken for granted' knowledge and construction of orthodoxies in housing policy can be more clearly understood.

At the same time, it is clear that despite its increasing interest, discourse analysis in housing research is still in somewhat embryonic form. This is evident in the lack of systematic work in certain areas, such as conversation analysis. As noted above, these criticisms demand a more robust application of the techniques, within a clear and reflexive set of methodologies, using cross-cultural case studies as well as more traditional historically based approaches.

See also: Cultural Analysis of Housing and Space; Ethnography; Foucauldian Analysis; Power; Qualitative Methods in Housing Research; Social Construction; Social Theory and Housing; Structure and Agency; Textual and Linguistic Analysis.

References

Bourdieu P (1991) *Language and Symbolic Power*. Oxford: Blackwell.
Cloke P, Widdowfield R and Millbourne P (1999) The hidden and emerging spaces of rural homelessness. *Environment and Planning A* 32(1): 77–90.
Fairclough N (1992) *Discourse and Social Change*. Oxford: Blackwell.
Fischer F and Forrester J (eds.) (1993) *The Argumentative Turn in Policy Analysis and Planning*. London: Duke University Press.

Flint J (2006) Housing and the new governance of conduct. In: Flint J (ed.) *Housing, Urban Governance and Anti-Social Behaviour*, 19–37. Bristol: The Policy Press.

Foucault M (1977) *Discipline and Punish: The Birth of the Prison*. London: Allen Lane.

Garfinkel H (ed.) (1967) *Studies in Ethnomethodology*. New Jersey: Prentice Hall.

Goffman E (1959) *The Presentation of Self in Everyday Life*. Harmondsworth: Penguin.

Habermas J (1981) *The Theory of Communicative Action: Reason and the Rationalisation of Society*. Cambridge: Polity Press.

Hajer M (2003) Discourse coalitions and the institutionalisation of practice: the case of acid rain in Great Britain. In: Fischer F and Forrester J (eds.) *The Argumentative Turn in Policy Analysis and Planning*. London: Duke University Press.

Hastings A (2000) Discourse analysis: What does it offer housing studies? *Housing, Theory and Society* 17: 131–139.

Howarth D (1995) Discourse theory. In: Marsh D and Stoker G (eds.) *Theory and Methods in Political Science*, 115–133. Hampshire: Macmillan.

Huckin T (2002) Textual silence and the discourse of homelessness. *Discourse and Society* 13(3): 347–372.

Jacobs K (2006) Discourse analysis and its utility for urban policy research. *Urban Policy and Research* 24(1): 39–52.

Kemeny J (1992) *Housing and Social Theory*. London: Routledge.

King P (2004) Relativism, subjectivity and the self: A critique of social constructionism. In: Jacobs K, Kemeny J, and Manzi T (eds.) *Social Constructionism in Housing Research*, pp. 32–48. Aldershot: Ashgate.

Laclau E and Mouffe C (1985) *Hegemony and Socialist Strategy: Towards a Radical Democratic Politics*. London: Verso.

Laclau E and Mouffe C (1987) Post Marxism without apologies. *New Left Review I*, 166: 79–106.

Marston G (2002) Critical discourse analysis and policy-oriented housing research. *Housing, Theory and Society* 19(2): 82–91.

Phillips L and Jorgensen M (2002) *Discourse Analysis as Theory and Method*. London: Sage.

Richardson J (2006) Talking about gypsies: the notion of discourse as control. *Housing Studies* 21(1): 77–96.

Schmidt V (2008) Discursive institutionalism: the explanatory power of ideas and discourse. *Annual Review of Political Science* 11, 303–326.

Van Dijk T (1997) The study of discourse. In: van Dijk T (ed.) *Discourse as Structure and Process*. London: Sage.

Discrimination in Housing Markets

DE Sommervoll, Research Department of Statistics Norway, Oslo, Norway

© 2012 Elsevier Ltd. All rights reserved.

Glossary

Redlining The practice of denying or increasing the cost of services such as mortgage finance and insurance to residents in certain, often ethnically determined, areas.

Rental guaranty A third party, usually the government, guaranties payment of rent. The rental guaranty provides landlords with security against tenants defaulting on payments.

Rental risk The risk faced by the landlord when leasing a property. The two main components of rental risk are contract default (unpaid rents) and damaged property.

Statistical discrimination Individuals face prices that reflect the characteristics of their group, not their individual characteristics.

Taste for discrimination An agent acts as if he were willing to pay something either directly or in the form of reduced income to be associated with certain persons.

Rents and Price Discrimination

Shelter is a basic human need. It can be rented or owned. Obtaining a roof over our heads can therefore involve three different markets (owner-occupation, private, and social rental tenures), which in most countries are markets subject to regulations. The owner-occupied and rental tenure shares vary considerably across countries (see article Housing Policy Trends). However, in all countries, renters tend to have lower income and less wealth than homeowners. The cheaper rental segments are associated with poverty, and households living in these segments tend to be challenged in many other respects as well. Limited human and financial capital diminishes their bargaining power, for instance. In developed economies, recent migration from the Third World has created minority communities that can be conspicuous because generally unemployment is higher and low-pay jobs more prevalent among minority populations. Like other low-income households, the lower end of the rental market is their only housing option. If landlords refuse to lease property to ethnic minorities, or charge higher rents, their search costs and housing outlays are increased, and standards of living suffer among the already challenged households. Homeownership prospects can also be adversely affected because first home-buyers generally rely on mortgage finance, but the credit ratings of minorities are often too low.

The cheaper segments of the homeownership market resemble the rental market because low-income households naturally buy in these segments. Mortgage providers tend to adopt a more conservative policy towards low-income households, given their higher mortgage default rates. If credit institutions are also less accommodating towards certain ethnic groups, it will be even more difficult for the lower-income members to become homeowners. As minority households will also have fewer options in the rental market, housing markets are often segmented along ethnic lines, and accompanied by urban decay (see article Policies to Address Social Mix in Communities).

Discrimination by lenders in mortgage finance markets is not the only source of disadvantage for ethnic minorities aspiring to become homeowners. There are research studies showing that some ethnic groups pay more for dwellings, even after controlling for differences in the characteristics of housing (size, amenities, and so on) purchased by ethnic minorities. The price differential could arise because of sellers' (and their real estate agents') ethnic preferences. But there is conflicting evidence from studies documenting how minority ethnic groups pay less because white majority groups are willing to pay a premium to live distant from minorities. A comparison of house prices in neighbourhoods where ethnic minority and white majority groups dominate is far from straightforward, as prices reflect both property and neighbourhood attributes.

Definitions and Theories of Discrimination

Ethnic discrimination can manifest itself in different ways. There is overt discrimination when a market agent (lender, landlord, etc.) refuses to deal with members of certain groups. But discrimination can be covert and played out more subtly. An example would be an agent who is reluctant to negotiate prices with members of certain minority groups, but not consciously or at least not officially admitting that the action – or inaction – depends on group characteristics. Finally, discrimination may be the result of the disparate impact of policy if, for example, commercial practices or laws disproportionately harm certain groups.

If success and achievement depend on physical differences or sexual orientation, then equal opportunity is compromised.

The economics of discrimination originated in the study of labour markets (see article Discrimination in Mortgage Markets). Discrimination, however, is likely in any market where agent type influences the profitability or utility derived from a transaction. Apart from the housing market, insurance and health are pertinent examples. Competing theories suggest two main causes of differences in outcomes for otherwise comparable members of distinct groups. The first emphasises how some market participants are willing to pay either directly or through reduced income to be associated with some persons rather than others, and is often referred to as a 'taste for discrimination'. The second is driven by objective intergroup differences that are observable at the group level, but not at the level of the individual. Mortgagors from particular minority groups might have higher default rates, for example, but little is known about individual borrowers. Decision-makers may then proceed to make decisions based solely on information about the ethnic or minority group the individuals belong to. Borrowers from minority groups might be charged a higher interest rate because they belong to a group with a relatively high default rate. This is known as statistical discrimination. It is not confined to mortgage finance markets. For example, in the rental market, a tenant may be charged a rent that reflects the expected return of their group rather than their individual expected return.

Legislation and practices may also disproportionately and unreasonably hurt one group more than another. Owner-occupied housing is, for example, given favourable tax treatment under most countries' tax regimes and these tax arrangements normally benefit higher-income households more than lower-income households (see article Taxation Policy and Housing). Individuals belonging to ethnic groups and minorities overrepresented among the poor will receive little or no benefit. This is arguably unreasonable and unjust, but is not discrimination if one takes the view that this outcome is an incidental by-product of a tax design motivated by reasons unrelated to which groups in the population will benefit most. This article focuses on those forms of discrimination that are the basis for taste-based and statistical theories of discrimination.

A taste for discrimination and statistical discrimination are not mutually exclusive and so observed differences in rents and prices that correlate with membership of minority or ethnic groups could be due to both forms of discrimination. But only one form of discrimination is consistent with profit-maximising behaviour. Consider imperfectly informed landlords who rely on group characteristics with respect to contract default. Expected returns are maximised by setting a higher group rent to compensate for higher group risk. In the case of a taste for discrimination, rent differentials may simply reflect landlords' preference for tenants who belong to a preferred group. Rent-setting behaviour will not maximise expected return if rents are discounted to attract tenants from a preferred group.

Legal Issues

Most countries have antidiscrimination laws in place that comply with the UN Human Rights Charter. However, laws and courts set up to enforce antidiscrimination laws do not prevent discrimination per se. Discrimination in housing and rental markets is hard to prove because one never observes the counterfactual, that is, the same house cannot be sold (or rented) to two buyers (tenants) at the same time so that the price (rent) differential is observed. Proof of discrimination has to rely on a more or less well-founded comparison, which is likely to be challenged by the party accused of discrimination.

Risk and Discrimination in Rental Markets

Rental markets are prone to discrimination. Landlords want to avoid undesirable risky outcomes such as unpaid rent, damaged property, and potentially lengthy procedures to evict 'nonperforming' tenants. Landlords can therefore seek to offset the risk by setting rents that ensure a contract's anticipated profitability or utility. However, it is hard to distinguish performing from nonperforming tenants prior to the signing of rental contracts. But ethnicity, gender, presence of children, and sole parent status are all commonly perceived to be correlated with contract default and can be readily detected. The landlords' perceptions of contract default by group status could be erroneous; rents will nevertheless tend to reflect these landlords' expectations of default rates.

Rental markets tend to have a mix of large- and small-scale landlords. The size of the rental business can affect the potential for discrimination since small-scale landlords are likely to screen applicants carefully. Selection of just one nonperforming tenant could make deep inroads into the business's cash flow. Large-scale landlords, on the other hand, may be more willing to accept risky tenants and higher vacancy rates because cash flow is less affected, and overall profits could be higher than would result from a more intensive and costly screening strategy that ensures lower vacancy rates and less risky tenants.

Some small-scale landlords let accommodation in their own home. As living under the same roof tends to require some form of mutual understanding, discrimination is likely to eventuate as such landlords seek tenants with a similar and familiar cultural, social, and ethnic background to their own. This preference to mix with people from a familiar background may seem unimportant; it is after all something we are all prone to. Also, what some call discrimination is to others a legitimate attempt to preserve one's cultural heritage. In practice, this urge to live alongside neighbours who share the same values will cause market segregation, and the selection of tenants in such communities could transgress antidiscrimination laws. Economic models show that a slight preference for living in a neighbourhood where your ethnic or minority group is the majority can generate market processes that preclude ethnically diverse neighbourhoods (see article Policies to Address Social Mix in Communities).

Search Costs and Discrimination in the Market of Owner-Occupied Housing

The market for owner-occupied housing is intimately linked to the mortgage market. The latter resembles the rental market inasmuch as a mortgage implies a contract with future payments. Mortgage defaults may seriously hurt the profitability of a mortgage provider. The mortgage provider may be tempted to use ethnicity as a predictor of mortgage default if default rates differ across ethnic groups. Discrimination can take a spatial form when lenders avoid granting mortgages in neighbourhoods with a certain ethnic composition. The latter is called 'redlining' (for more details on these topics within the encyclopaedia, see article Policies to Address Redlining). This sort of conduct obviously generates ethnically biased mortgage outcomes and falls within the scope of antidiscrimination law.

Potential redlining and other ethnically biased conduct by mortgagees make the achievement of homeownership more difficult for minorities. Search costs may already be higher for certain groups if real estate agents treat ethnic groups differently. Intriguingly, there may be a discrimination feedback effect. A real estate agent may view a potential buyer as less likely to buy, because his/her ethnic background lowers his/her chances of obtaining a mortgage. In other words, disparate treatment by the real estate agent is conditional on discrimination in the mortgage market. The net effect of discrimination in these two markets may be considerable, although the mortgage providers and real estate agents base their actions on objective statistical information.

Testing for Discrimination in Housing Markets

Scholars rely on two main techniques to study discrimination in housing markets: regression analysis and audits. The regression methodology can be used on housing market transactions by regressing prices on a set of explanatory variables (see article Econometric Modeling). These variables include hedonic and neighbourhood characteristics. Tests for discrimination are performed by including ethnicity as an explanatory variable and seeing whether its contribution is economically and statistically significant. One of the methodological problems with this approach is the possibility of missing variables. If missing variables vary across ethnic groups, their influence on the market price will be wrongly attributed to ethnic price discrimination.

The same kind of regression analysis can be applied to rents in the rental market. One seeks here to explain rents by hedonic and neighbourhood characteristics. This approach is more easily challenged in the rental market, as landlords' assessment of rental risk will involve tenant type. Landlords may demand a risk premium for risky tenants. To allow for risk premiums in the regression analysis, we need to add features of the tenant as explanatory variables. It must be emphasised that setting rents to mirror risk based on 'individual' characteristics is legal, but rent setting based on 'ethnic group' characteristics is not. If ethnicity continues to be significant, statistically and economically, after controlling for relevant tenant characteristics, the analysis can be taken as an indication of ethnic discrimination.

The regression methodology can unravel discrimination in the market as a whole, and also whether discrimination lies behind exorbitant rents. But it does not tell us much about how discrimination works in these markets. The audit approach may fill this knowledge gap. Imagine an audit in which tenants whose only distinguishing feature is their ethnicity seek the same housing opportunities. We can compare outcomes and detect overt discrimination as well as differences in rents for the same dwelling.

Audits are costly, so sample sizes are usually small. Tenant enquiries and rent quotes may not result in true market transactions. The absence of a signed contract, sceptics argue, corrupts the bargaining and may not necessarily mirror real contracts. Audit results, moreover, can be affected by the attitudes conveyed by 'fake' tenants in the negotiation process. Internet audits, it can be argued, are free of such constraints. The responses of imaginary tenants to ads are identical, apart from the name of the sender. This gives unbiased estimates of the probability of call back, given the ethnic background.

Despite obvious challenges, regression and audits provide useful information. They can also, theoretically at least, distinguish between statistical and taste-based discrimination. Discrimination is taste based if price differences do not mirror differences between groups. In practice, as noted above, quantifying justified rent differences by observed differences between groups is far from straightforward even under the premise of efficient market outcomes.

Discrimination in Housing and Rental Markets in the United States

Despite the ethnic tapestry of the country, the United States has a long history of racial discrimination – African Americans in particular have suffered and continue to suffer unequal treatment. Agitation by the Civil Rights Movement of the 1960s resulted in a momentous trio of antidiscrimination laws. The first, the 1964 Civil Rights Act, was followed by the 1968 Fair Housing Act, which prohibited discrimination (whether based on race, colour, national origin, religion, sex, or familial status) in the sale, rental, and financing of dwellings, and other housing-related transactions. Finally, in 1976, the Equal Credit Opportunity Act was passed. These laws also criminalise indirect disparate treatment such as redlining. They forbid prices reflecting differences between groups, even when they generate efficient market outcomes. In other words, these laws reflect society's belief that enabling and facilitating social justice outweigh the potential cost of market inefficiency.

Unlike many developed economies, racial issues have been high on the political agenda in the United States. In response, there are a plethora of research studies purporting to show the actual extent of ethnic discrimination. Conducted mostly as audits, the work provides compelling evidence of discrimination. According to a 1989 audit, African Americans were 10.7% more likely to be excluded altogether from available rentals, and 23.5% more likely to be shown fewer potential rental dwellings. They were also much more likely not to be called back by the real estate brokers.

Similar disparate treatment is found in the market for owner-occupied housing, where there are estimates suggesting a price increase of 4000 USD for African Americans, all else being equal. The main challenge for any low-income household is the mortgage. Many households find the application process itself challenging enough as it requires a degree of both persistence and economic literacy. The likelihood of being turned down (repeatedly) is not only discouraging, but also humiliating. So fear of discrimination may well perpetuate it. Chicago's ShoreBank tried breaking this vicious circle by providing mortgages to residents of redlined neighbourhoods. As a business, the bank thrived until the financial crisis of 2008. In 2010, the ShoreBank was declared insolvent, and parts of the banks' operations are now managed by the Urban Partnership Bank. Although the global economic downturn affected many banks, the bankruptcy may be viewed as a sign of the high financial risk associated with providing mortgages to low-income households.

Recent analysis of data from the housing market suggests less disparate treatment than what was 20–30 years ago, one of the fruits of half a century of policy and legislative overhauls.

Ownership rates for African American households have risen from 45.6% in 1983 to 48.6% in 2007, but to a lesser extent than for white households which rose from 69.1 to 75.3% in the same period. Recent empirical analysis seems to indicate that most of the gap in ownership rates may disappear if family income, education, net wealth, and savings behaviour could be improved to the levels enjoyed by white households. If true, the gap in ownership rates can be significantly reduced in the long run by narrowing the gap in income and education.

Discrimination in Housing and Rental Markets in Europe

Europe has a long history of internal and external migration. Minority communities have lived in many of the major European cities for centuries. The postwar surge in migration from former colonies and other Third World countries has created new, and highly visible, minority communities, more culturally diverse than former European minorities. Migrants enter countries legally and illegally. Illegal migration is usually facilitated by criminal organisations, not only because European laws outlaw illegal migration, but also because illegal immigrants do not exist officially, and may have to rely on the black economy to make ends meet.

This is likely to perpetuate discrimination, since illegal immigrants are to the eye indistinguishable from the larger group of legal, hard-working immigrants. And if some ethnic communities find it hard to get rented accommodation or own their own housing, segregated communities are likely to spring up at the lower end of the housing market.

These challenges are a fairly recent occurrence for policy makers, and discrimination in housing markets is an underresearched area. A Swedish audit used three fictitious persons whose names were readily associated with certain ethnic groups. Call-back frequency differed significantly with ethnicity. An analysis of the Norwegian Rental Survey indicates that non-Norwegian tenants pay 7% more than Norwegians ceteris paribus.

Policy Measures

Discrimination is socially undesirable and violates basic rights and freedom, including the right to equal opportunity. It can fuel social unrest, harm the economic prospects and welfare of victims of discrimination, and also harm society as a whole. Legislation alone cannot prevent ethnic discrimination. Having said that, policies that actually prevent and reduce discrimination in rental and owner-occupied housing and mortgage markets are neither abundant nor foolproof, and some may require substantial government investment to police and enforce.

Statistical discrimination is possibly easier to address than taste-based discrimination, since it relies on true differences between groups. There are essentially two, although not mutually exclusive, ways to reverse statistical discrimination. The first and most important is to encourage agents to base commercial decisions on individual rather than group characteristics. A tenant register is an option for the rental market. A register could be routinely accessed by landlords for information on performing/nonperforming tenants. In some countries, such tenant databases are already in place and designed by private intermediaries. The downside of a tenant register is that past misdemeanours can be the source of impediments to affordable housing that locks nonperforming tenants out of rental markets, an outcome that could well prompt policy actions. This could be avoided by time-limiting tenant information and helping households with a 'record' find affordable housing. In the case of privately owned registers, legislation and government control may be needed to ensure tenant protection.

Statistical discrimination can also be addressed by what is known as a rental guaranty. Under this scheme, a third party, usually the government, guaranties payment of rent. A rental guaranty can extend to more than just paying rent. It may be in the form of head leasing wherein the guarantor, usually the government, also takes on maintenance responsibilities. The guaranty lowers rental and property maintenance risk for landlords, who adjust their reservation price accordingly. In some cases, the rental market may fail to provide housing for some groups altogether, in which case social housing may be the only solution in the short term.

Since mortgage markets tend to be dominated by large credit institutions, monitoring compliance with antidiscrimination legislation and bringing charges for violations should be feasible. In the United States, major credit institutions self-audit their lending practices, and a mortgage applicant is entitled to know on what grounds his/her application was turned down. Furthermore, government websites provide information on how to legally pursue cases of disparate treatment. Lessons learned in the United States in this respect are mixed, however, and at times legislation may not be sufficient to ensure equal treatment of all ethnic minorities by mortgage lenders. Policy-makers could initiate a credit scheme whose sole objective is to provide mortgage financing to groups that tend to be excluded from the ordinary mortgage market. These mechanisms, however well intended, risk inadvertently protecting discriminatory behaviour in the rest of the market. If minority mortgage schemes have a higher default threshold and milder sanctions, issues to do with moral hazard and adverse selection are likely to arise.

Statistical discrimination in housing markets is most likely driven by disparate treatment in the search process, inflating search costs and overall transaction prices. This being the case, mechanisms that lower search costs could be highly effective. The Internet has probably cut searching costs for all home seekers and narrowed the search cost gap between population subgroups. To reduce search costs in general, the government could initiate mechanisms to help minority households in their pursuit of owner-occupied housing.

Taste-based discrimination is not easily addressed by short-term policies. While overt discrimination takes place, in practice, it is difficult to prove in court. Rental guaranties and suchlike will not be effective and may be morally offensive to some, if they ultimately reward bigots. Long-term policies, such as encouraging minorities to gain qualifications and creating arenas enabling cross-ethnic interaction and understanding, could possibly reduce taste-based discrimination. Urban planning policy might also have a role in encouraging ethnically mixed neighbourhoods that in time will facilitate tolerance and help reduce discrimination.

See also: Discrimination in Mortgage Markets; Econometric Modeling; Housing Policy Trends; Policies to Address Redlining; Policies to Address Social Mix in Communities; Taxation Policy and Housing.

Further Reading

Ahmed AM and Hammarstedt M (2008) Discrimination in the rental housing market: A field experiment on the Internet. *Journal of Urban Economics* 64(2): 362–372.

Arrow KJ (1973) The theory of discrimination. In: Ashenfelter O and Rees A (eds.) *Discrimination in Labor Markets*, pp. 3–33. Princeton, NJ: Princeton University Press.

Beatty T and Sommervoll DE (2008) Discrimination in Europe: Evidence from the rental market. *Discussion Paper 547*. Research Department of Statistics: Norway.

Becker GS (1957) *The Economics of Discrimination*. Chicago, IL: University of Chicago Press.

Boem TP and Schlottsmann AM (2009) The dynamics of homeownership: Eliminating the gap between African American and white households. *Real Estate Economics* 37(4): 599–634.

Choi SJ, Ondrich J, and Yinger J (2005) Do rental agents discriminate against minority customers? Evidence from the 2000 housing discrimination study. *Journal of Housing Economics* 14(1): 1–26.

Dymski GA (2001) Is discrimination disappearing? Racial differentials in access to credit, 1992–1998. *International Journal of Social Economics* 28(10/11/12): 1025–1045.

Ondrich J, Stricker A, and Yinger J (1999) Do landlords discriminate? The incidence and causes of racial discrimination in rental housing markets. *Journal of Housing Economics* 42(3): 185–200.

Phelps E (1972) The statistical theory of racism and sexism. *American Economic Review* 62(4): 659–661.

Roed Larsen E and Sommervoll DE (2009) The impact on rent from tenant and landlord characteristics and interaction. *Regional Science and Urban Economics* 39: 316–322.

Schwab S (1986) Is statistical discrimination efficient? *The American Economic Review* 76(1): 228–234.

Yinger J (1986) Measuring racial discrimination with fair housing audits: Caught in the act. *The American Economic Review* 76(5): 881–893.

Yinger J (1998) Evidence on discrimination in consumer markets. *Journal of Economic Perspectives* 12(2): 23–40.

Discrimination in Mortgage Markets

GA Dymski, University of California Riverside, Riverside, CA, USA

© 2012 Elsevier Ltd. All rights reserved.

Glossary

Loan-flipping A predatory loan practice in which a lender continually refinances an existing home loan, earning upfront fees that are not offset by any benefit to the borrower.

Mortgage discrimination The failure of a lender to make decisions about which prospective borrowers should receive mortgage loans, and at what terms, on an equitable basis.

Predatory lending Loans, including mortgage loans, that impose interest rates, fees, and/or penalties for nonpayment on borrowers at levels higher than are justified by those borrowers' risk levels.

Redlining A situation in which a lender makes no (or disproportionately few) loans in an area that has been deemed excessively risky due to the racial/ethnic composition of its population.

Subprime loan A mortgage that requires borrowers to pay higher-than-average interest rates and fees, and that may impose higher-than-average penalties for nonpayment.

Introduction

Discrimination arises in mortgage markets when potential participants are denied equal access to housing finance because of those participants' racial/ethnic identity, gender, or some other shared characteristic prohibited by law. This unequal access can take different forms, such as high rates of mortgage-application denial, overly costly credit, unduly strict terms, or excessive fees. Discriminatory behaviour by lenders can be intentional or unintentional. It can have strong impacts on those affected, ranging from the denial of access to desirable communities to a higher likelihood of facing loan default and foreclosure.

No universally accepted guidelines have emerged about what causes such discrimination, how to measure it, and what to do about it when it is detected. Years of protests by activists, of studies by researchers, and of regulations by policy-makers have yielded much insight but no clear consensus.

Note that this article touches almost exclusively on racial discrimination against African Americans and Latinos in the United States. Discrimination in other countries, against other racial/ethnic minorities, and/or on the basis of gender or other factors, is mentioned only in passing.

The Legal Context

Discrimination occurs whenever agents who individually share some common characteristic can complete a market transaction only at a higher cost or more stringent terms than other agents. It also occurs when agents sharing this characteristic are less likely to succeed in an uncertain market transaction, such as a loan application, or have less access to resources. Instances of discrimination raise concerns about social injustice and legal propriety because they may conflict with the Constitutional guarantee that no person can be deprived of "life, liberty, or property without due process of law".

This guarantee notwithstanding, federal policies designed in the 1930s to expand access to home mortgages openly discriminated against racial/ethnic minority areas and individuals. This changed with the passage of civil-rights legislation in the 1960s. The Fair Housing Act of 1968 makes it "unlawful for any person or other entity whose business includes engaging in residential real estate-related transactions to discriminate against any person in making available such a transaction, or in the terms or conditions of such a transaction". This Act identifies seven classes protected by the law: race, colour, national origin, religion, sex, familial status, and disability. The Equal Credit Opportunity Act of 1974, in turn, makes discrimination against loan applicants unlawful.

Court cases and Congressional fine-tuning have clarified the legal meaning of these laws. Three legal types of discrimination have been identified:

- overt discrimination – refusing to initiate a transaction with a member of the protected class;
- disparate treatment – screening members of the protected class more harshly than others in application processes, or subjecting their applications to different application processes;
- disparate impact – conducting commercial practices that disproportionately harm one or more members of a protected class without being justified by a legitimate business need.

Overt discrimination rules out intentional behaviour aimed specifically at blocking members of the protected classes from access to housing or mortgage credit. Disparate treatment is also behavioural, and focuses on application processes that have nonneutral effects, even if there is no harmful intent. Disparate impact refers to situations in which procedures that are racially neutral on their face lead to *ex post* racial disparities. Unless a legitimate business-related reason for making racial distinctions can be identified, racial divisions in market outcomes are suspect under the law.

In the early 1970s, a broad-based movement of community-based groups protested against the 'redlining' of inner-city neighbourhoods – that is, the unwillingness of lenders to make mortgage credit in areas that have many minority residents and/or that are experiencing racial/ethnic transitions. Studies by academic researchers and community groups found evidence of redlining in several cities. This raised the question of whether redlining was widespread.

To answer this question, in 1975, Congress passed the Home Mortgage Disclosure Act (HMDA). Two years later, initial results from data collected under HMDA, together with continued grassroots pressure, convinced Congress to pass the Community Reinvestment Act (CRA), which requires banks to meet credit needs in their entire market area. The Act states that lenders "have a continuing and affirmative obligation to help meet the credit needs of the local communities in which they are chartered".

Reporting requirements under HMDA have been tightened twice. As of 1990, banks and other mortgage lenders have been required to report data on every mortgage loan application, including the applicant's race and income and the disposition of the application. And as of January 2004, reporting lenders have provided information about the loan rates they charge.

In the 1990s and 2000s, half the states and the federal government approved legislation in response to the growing problem of predatory lending. Congress passed the Home Ownership and Equity Protection Act (HOEPA) in 1994. This act covers high-rate mortgage loans, especially refinancing and home equity instalment loans. It empowers the Federal Trade Commission to establish guidelines and standards for home loans whose interest rates or fees were well in excess of those prevailing in the marketplace. Balloon payments, negative amortisation, and other arrangements that are not in the owners' best interest are prohibited under the regulations promulgated under this act. The Federal Reserve is empowered under HOEPA to adjust this act's regulations as it deems necessary; it made such adjustments as of October 2009.

HOEPA encompasses only a small percentage of mortgage loans, even predatory loans, because of its high trigger rates; for example, only first-lien loans whose annual rate is 8% above the prevailing market rate are covered. Consequently, about half the states have passed legislation aimed at banning a higher share of predatory lending practices. North Carolina passed the first such law in 1999; it banned both loan-flipping and prepayment penalties for home loans in excess of $150 000.

Theoretical Models

Economists, focusing primarily on racial inequality, have identified three reasons why discrimination can emerge in market processes:

1. Personal discrimination (bigotry): racially differential outcomes that are due to racial preferences unrelated to economic factors.
2. Rational discrimination: racially differential outcomes which arise when agents use race or characteristics correlated with race to make valid statistical inferences about the distinct market prospects of different racial groups.
3. Structural discrimination: racially differential outcomes that arise because of identifiable economic factors associated with the agents or property involved.

The second reason differs from the third in that it refers to *anticipated* disparities, and the third reason to *existing* disparities. These three factors (personal, rational, and structural discrimination) correspond approximately to the three types of legal discrimination identified above (respectively, overt discrimination, disparate treatment, and disparate impact).

Personal Discrimination (Bigotry)

The landmark treatment of the impact of bigotry on market outcomes is Gary Becker's 1957 book (later expanded in a 1971 second edition). Becker traces race effects in markets to individual agents' racial bigotry. The idea is that some whites so dislike minorities that they will pay a premium or accept lower wages or profits to avoid dealing with minorities in workplace, home, or business settings. Becker goes on to argue that with free entry, discriminators themselves bear the costs of discrimination. So discriminators will be driven out of business or tire of reduced profits; no policy intervention is needed to overcome it.

The results that Becker anticipates do emerge under one set of conditions in the mortgage market: the case in which some lenders are bigoted, but no current or potential residents are. Then bigoted lenders will make fewer profits and be driven out of the market. But under other conditions, this self-policing result is unlikely to arise. One special problem is that because most homes have fixed spatial locations, the mortgage market is intertwined with the housing market. Thus, whether or not lenders are bigoted, the viability of any loan depends on the value of the homes their loans support; and this in turn depends on residents' preferences regarding where and with whom they are willing to live.

If there is bigotry among the residents of a neighbourhood, a lender may deny credit to borrowers whose entry would cause property-value losses, or home sales and nonpayment by current residents. So Becker's perpetrator-pays scenario does not apply – and lenders may discriminate 'rationally' when they fear retaliation by bigoted existing borrower/residents.

Rational Discrimination

'Rational' discrimination, which minimises lenders' costs and thus enhances their profits, can arise for reasons other than residential mixing. Informational problems can lead to discrimination even when no agents are Becker-type bigots. Suppose first that minorities and whites (to focus on these two groups) reside in segregated communities: a disproportionate share of minorities live in some spaces, and of whites in others. Suppose further that mortgages are riskier in minority than in white communities. Then to minimise their exposure to default risk on mortgage loans, lenders might rationally decide not to make loans in the minority community. This decision is 'rational' in that lenders can avoid the costs associated with determining borrowers' creditworthiness. This outcome is termed 'redlining', as it connotes the idea that banks draw a 'red line' around areas their loan officers are to avoid. Indeed, if both minority and white applicants apply for loans in the redlined area, then there is no discrimination per se. If minorities are more likely to apply for mortgages in minority areas, then this practice also involves discrimination against minority borrowers.

Why would mortgages in the heavily minority community be riskier? Some possible explanations involve externalities: residents there might be more likely to lose their jobs, to remain unemployed, to spend time in the prison system, and so on. Another possibility is that housing values there are more variable, or homes there are harder to sell. These possibilities can be linked to banks' own behaviour: if lenders overall are reluctant to make loans in such areas, this could make it more difficult to market and sell new or existing homes there. That is, lenders' collective aversion to this community can itself create this excessive risk.

Rational discrimination can also arise when it is costly to acquire information about individual borrowers. Suppose again that significant racial segregation exists. Then if loan applicants' race and economic fundamentals are correlated, lenders can 'rationally' use neighbourhood racial composition as a low-cost substitute for costly information-gathering. This last idea is an application of the 'statistical' theory of discrimination.

Structural Discrimination

Racial imbalances in the volume or variability of wealth and income may explain why racial minorities receive systematically fewer loans than other applicants. In effect, racial wealth/income differences create groups of potential borrowers, some more capable of consistently making mortgage payments than others. Lenders who are members of racial majority groups may also privilege other group members so as to maintain their group members' advantage in access to wealth.

Empirical Studies of Redlining and Mortgage Discrimination

The loan-approval process can be divided into four stages: advertising and outreach; preapplication inquiries; loan approval/denial and/or terms and conditions; and loan administration. Discriminatory behaviour can arise in any of these stages. And discrimination in one stage can generate discriminatory behaviour in another stage. For example, bank branch closures in minority neighbourhoods can have a discriminatory effect.

The passage of laws against credit-market discrimination and the legal requirement that banks provide mortgages data have led to a robust empirical literature. Different empirical tests have been developed in attempts to measure the different types of discrimination. Most of these tests focus on lenders' mortgage volumes and on lenders' decisions about mortgage applications.

The Redlining Model

The HMDA, passed in 1975, initially required banks and thrifts to report the number and dollar volume of their mortgage loans in every calendar year by census tract. This made it possible to estimate equations testing whether mortgage flows in a given area are influenced by that area's racial/ethnic population, after taking into account the influence of that area's economic characteristics on these flows.

Such equations provide an indirect measure of redlining. That is, area economic variables should legitimately affect housing value, and hence mortgage flows. If mortgage decisions are based solely on economic fundamentals, then area social variables, including neighbourhood racial composition, should be insignificant. Thus there is evidence of redlining when area race affects loan flows, even after controlling for economic fundamentals.

A key problem in designing redlining tests is what constitutes an area. Researchers attempt to separate data into geographic subsets corresponding to community boundaries. This has to be done without falling into the trap of preselection bias. This bias arises when what an observer separates and analyses the data using spatial divisions than she expected in advance to find significant. In this case, the suspicion that a certain geographic area is subject to redlining is not independent of the statistical test for whether it is.

This preselection bias can be avoided by using a neutral method for sorting census tracts. A well-known study of Atlanta divided tracts into five tiers based on median income, and three distinct tiers based on minority population. This study found that loan flows were dramatically lower in high-minority tracts, holding area median income equal.

Redlining studies such as this have attracted numerous criticisms. They do not control for whether lower loan flows in minority areas are due to lower loan demand, nor is there any measure of whether apparently redlined areas pose greater lending risks. That is, sceptics have argued that redlining studies cannot show definitively that any type of mortgage discrimination is at work: efficient market forces may simply generate outcomes that resemble redlining.

Controversies about redlining studies in the 1980s shaped the subsequent course of empirical studies of mortgage discrimination. The burden of proof was shifted from the presumption that fair market outcomes 'should be' racially neutral to the presumption that efficient market outcomes, 'may be' racially nonneutral. Given their limitations, evidence of racial redlining constitutes at least a warning beacon, an indicator that credit flows are contributing to – not subtracting from – the balance sheet of American racial inequality.

Mortgage Discrimination Models

As of 1990, HMDA reporting requirements have required lenders to collect data on individual mortgage applicants. This permitted researchers to surpass the limitations inherent in redlining studies. It became possible to construct equations that probed the existence of discrimination against mortgage applicants. The most common such equation examined whether the approval or denial of loan applications was related to the economic and social characteristics of the area in which a home loan was being sought, applicants' economic characteristics, and applicants' social characteristics – especially their race/ethnicity.

Many studies of this type, using post-1989 HMDA data, have found that African American and Latino applicants are at a considerable, statistically significant disadvantage in applying for mortgages, even after controlling for other area- and applicant-specific factors. The consensus among most experts is that such evidence is consistent with either bigotry-based or rational discrimination, but cannot definitively prove that either exists in a specific case.

Very early on, a 1992 study by the Federal Reserve Bank of Boston attempted to break through this limitation. Researchers in that study had access to the actual loan files used by banks making mortgage loans in Boston in 1990. On the basis of this comprehensive grasp of what variables banks consider, these authors found that African American applicants had a 60% greater chance of loan denial than equally creditworthy whites.

For many analysts, this result was the statistical 'smoking gun' showing that banks do discriminate by race. However, critics have subsequently challenged this study's result, focusing on methodological flaws, including its use of a single equation. For some, because this test cannot definitively identify the presence or absence of bigoted behaviour by lenders, it cannot be labelled a test of discrimination. Other challengers have asserted that this approach does not estimate what lenders actually do, which is to set benchmark criteria that applicants may pass or fail. Still other critics observed that the lender's approve-or-deny decision is just one of several interlinked decisions by both lenders and mortgage applicants. These objections have been answered by defenders of the Boston study. However, disagreements over the significance of the Boston study – and hence over the significance of single-equation estimations of mortgage discrimination more broadly – continue. At root, these disagreements stem from the fact that different analysts have different understandings of what constitutes unlawful discrimination.

Researchers continue to do empirical studies of redlining and mortgage discrimination. Aside from their value in detecting discrimination per se, they are useful in exploring patterns of neighbourhood disinvestment, understanding patterns of inequality in credit flows, and establishing benchmarks for community-development efforts.

Audit Studies

'Audit' studies present an alternative empirical approach: white and minority subjects pose as home-mortgage applicants under carefully controlled conditions; their experiences are then recorded and compared. The testers' contacts must be randomised and their experiences standardised to allow data collection. Audit tests often expose disparate treatment and even bigotry in some of the submarkets that are involved in the home-search and mortgage acquisition process. While not without their limitations, these studies are useful tools for the detection of inadvertent or purposeful discriminatory behaviour.

Predatory Lending and the Rise of Subprime Mortgages

US mortgage markets were transformed in the 1980s. Increasingly, mortgages were made by nonbank or non-savings-and-loan lenders, who then sold them off to be securitised. Initially, FNMA and FHLCC were the primary purchasers of mortgages; these agencies established criteria that restricted the risk of default. This created a new divide in mortgage markets: between those who could and those who could not qualify for 'plain vanilla' mortgages by virtue of meeting down payment and loan-payment-to-income thresholds.

The 1990s then saw the creation of a new set of financial products targeting customers who lacked access to standardised – 'mainstream' – loan markets and banking services. While these products were aimed at high-risk customers, the interest rates, penalties for nonpayment or prepayment, and fees they entailed were often far higher than risk considerations alone warranted – that is, they were 'predatory'. These markets grew rapidly because earnings for participating lenders and for participants in the securitisation process were substantial, prior to the crash of the subprime market in 2007–08.

One common form of predatory lending consisted of payday loans – small, short-term loans to cash-short, credit-constrained (often unbanked) households. Payday lending grew explosively in the 1990s and 2000s. These loans' high rates and strict repayment terms turned many customers into chronic borrowers, enhancing profits for companies supplying this credit.

The dominant predatory-loan product, and the one that drew the most regulatory attention, was the subprime mortgage loan. This term refers generally to mortgages made to customers who are deemed more risky than usual, and who thus are ineligible for 'plain vanilla' loans.

Subprime mortgages were initially targeted to homeowners interested in second mortgages; they soon were adapted for use in home purchases. From 1993 to 1999, subprime mortgages increased by 900% in inner-city areas, while 'plain vanilla' lending there shrank. A nationwide study of 2000 HMDA data found that African Americans were more than twice as likely as whites to receive subprime loans, and Latinos at least 40% more likely.

These new instruments often led to excessive rates of nonpayment and personal financial distress. The higher rates imposed because of these loans' perceived riskiness contributed to the higher default rate. Subprime loans often led to foreclosures and home seizures, even on second mortgages. As such, they became a centre of controversy. Community-based advocates protested these as different forms of predatory lending, designed to extract excessive interest income and fees from those excluded from mainstream markets. Lenders responded that they were, to the contrary, offering products tailored to the circumstances of inherently riskier customers.

Two periods of subprime loan-making can be identified. The first period, ending in 1999, involved rapid growth in the most risky segments of the mortgage market. Many borrowers in this market lacked access to alternative mainstream sources of credit. In the second period, beginning in 2000, the subprime market grew due to the increasing number of subprime borrowers who had higher credit scores (lower levels of risk). As lenders shifted to less-risky borrowers, they were willing to lend larger amounts and to accept lower down payments. The increasing use of prepayment penalties and the emergence of credit-default swaps that reduced apparent risks for lenders led to ever-more-risky loans on an ever-thinner basis of objective information about borrower income.

A series of empirical studies have been done to determine whether the efforts of the federal government and of many states to curb predatory loan practices by regulating lending had any effect on the growth or geographic locus of predatory mortgage lending. Comparisons among these studies' findings are difficult because of the wide range of data sources, time-periods, and areas that have been examined. Some studies find little evidence that regulatory efforts had any effect. Others have shown that predatory lending was measurably reduced in states that passed predatory lending laws. Overall, these studies show that more restrictive anti-predatory-lending laws and more active enforcement of such laws, all else being equal, have reduced the volume of predatory subprime loans. Obviously, these legal restrictions did not curtail the explosive growth of the overall subprime market – which was accomplished by the collapse of housing prices and of the borrowing markets for securitised subprime loans.

Predatory Mortgage Lending and Discrimination

A disproportionate number of the borrowers were minorities; and subprime loans were often predatory – that is, they imposed rates and fees higher than considerations of borrower risk could account for. Thus, the question arises as to whether subprime lending, and especially predatory lending, involves racial/ethnic discrimination.

The question of discrimination is complicated by three factors. First, most subprime loans were made by nonbank lenders not subject to the Community Reinvestment Act. Second, the subprime market was linked to the rapid growth of securitisation in US credit markets. In the 1980s, only 'plain vanilla' mortgages could be securitised. The 1990s saw the evolution of far more extensive securitisation, which included subprime mortgages. Over the next decade, markets for securitised credit accepted an increasingly adventurous mix of loans, ranging from credit-card debt to educational and auto loans. Banks, especially very large banks, were involved in these markets primarily as bundlers, sellers, and in some cases buyers of securitised debt. It was often these banks' subsidiaries that made subprime mortgages.

The third complicating factor was that subprime mortgage loans were increasingly used to finance home purchases in the 2000s – in the subprime market's second phase – because of the rise of a US housing-price bubble. Housing prices rose precipitously in a number of US regions, notably Florida and the western states, exceeding borrowers' income-earning capacity. An ever-expanding assortment of subprime loans was invented to permit borrowers to buy homes that would have been unaffordable had 'plain vanilla' mortgages been required. These loans often featured reduced payment levels for several years – unpaid interest would then be rolled into the principal owed, and a longer-term loan locked in. Borrowers unable to afford plain-vanilla mortgages typically paid high fees for these contractual features, whose viability depended primarily on continually rising home prices.

During the run-up of the US housing market to its peak and crash in 2006–07, minorities were disproportionately represented among subprime borrowers. Studies showed that subprime lending was especially prominent not just in areas with rapid home-price appreciation, but also in areas with disproportionate numbers of minority home-buyers. Examples of the latter are industrial midwestern cities and the 'black belt' in the southern states. Studies also found that minority borrowers were more likely than whites, all things being equal, to receive subprime mortgages, and to have disadvantageous terms on these loans.

Two categories of potential racial/ethnic discrimination involving subprime lending can be identified: first, were minorities more likely than whites to be provided with subprime finance when they could have qualified for 'plain vanilla' mortgages?; second, among applicants for subprime loans, were minorities more likely than whites to be subject to predatory loan terms? Some preliminary studies have suggested that both forms of discrimination existed in the subprime mortgage market. However, studies responding to these questions have not unfolded in the systematic – if contentious – way of the earlier waves of redlining and of mortgage-denial discrimination studies. This is undoubtedly because this market imploded in 2007–08, and because that implosion coincided with the meltdown of the US housing market and the widespread insolvency of large portions of the US banking system. In the aftermath, minority borrowers and minority communities, after having been more likely to take on subprime mortgages, have been disproportionately victimised by the wave of foreclosures and housing-price collapses that has unfolded in the postbubble period. While lender bigotry or rational discrimination in the subprime market may thus never be established to analysts' satisfaction, there is no doubt that the consequence of the subprime era will be to worsen structural discrimination in the mortgage market.

Conclusion: A Moving Target

Mortgage discrimination has since the 1960s been an important focal point for civil rights law and a source of social and theoretical controversy. While this has been a constant, the form and remediation required in response to discriminatory behaviour has changed dramatically during this time frame. The empirical methods used to assess the extent of discrimination have changed remarkably as well. Researchers seeking evidence of mortgage discrimination and policy-makers interested in reducing its impacts on mortgage markets initially focused on redlining, then on loan denial in credit markets, and most recently on racial/ethnic biases in predatory lending. Undoubtedly the focus will shift again as mortgage markets continue to evolve.

And while huge literatures and bodies of case law on mortgage discrimination now exist, they remain incomplete, covering only a portion of the legal ground protected under the Constitution and the Civil Rights Act. There has been some limited study of mortgage discrimination on the basis of gender. This research indicates that women sometimes face discrimination, and problems are especially profound for minority female applicants. But much more work remains to be done on gender-based and other possible forms of discrimination.

Mortgage discrimination is also a moving target because the complementary but not identical legal principles of fairness for individuals (Civil Rights legislation) and fair access for communities (the Community Reinvestment Act) do not clearly identify which behaviours infringe the rights of well-identified sets of protected classes. Some regard an empirical study as successful when it depicts a clear pattern of racial difference in housing and credit flows; others define a study as successful only when it isolates predatory racial behaviour attributable to racial animus. These differing views are nested in some of the deepest questions about the sources of, and responses to, inequality that confront the American republic. These questions are far from settled; consequently, controversy about mortgage discrimination, and studies exploring this phenomenon, is likely to continue for years to come.

See also: Ethnic Minorities and Housing; Mortgage Market, Character and Trends: United States; Residential Segregation and Ethnic Diversity in the United States; Residential Segregation: Experiences of African Americans; Social Justice; Subprime Mortgages.

Further Reading

Arrow KJ (1998) What has economics to say about racial discrimination? *Journal of Economic Perspectives* 12(2): 91–100.

Becker GS (1971) *The Economics of Discrimination*, 2nd edn. Chicago, IL: University of Chicago Press.

Bostic RW (1997) *The Role of Race in Mortgage Lending: Revisiting the Boston Fed Study, Finance and Economics Discussion Series 1997-2*, January. Washington, DC: Division of Research & Statistics and Monetary Affairs, Federal Reserve Board.

Bostic RW (2003) A test of cultural affinity in home mortgage lending. *Journal of Financial Services Research* 23(2): 89–112.

Bostic RW, Engel KC, McCoy PA, Pennington-Cross A, and Wachter SM (2008) State and local anti-predatory lending laws: The effect of legal enforcement mechanisms. *Journal of Economics and Business* 60: 47–66.

Bradford C (2002) *Risk or race? Racial disparities and the subprime refinance market. A Report of the Center for Community Change*, May. Washington, DC: Center for Community Change.

Browne LE and Tootell GMB (1995) Mortgage lending in Boston – A response to the critics. *New England Economic Review* (September/October): 5–78.

Calem PS, Gillen K, and Wachter S (2004) The neighborhood distribution of subprime lending. *Journal of Real Estate Finance and Economics* 29(4): 393–410.

California Reinvestment Committee (2001) *Stolen Wealth: Disparities in California's Subprime Lending Market*. San Francisco, CA: California Reinvestment Committee.

Carr JH and Megbolugbe IF (1993) The federal reserve bank of Boston study on mortgage lending revisited. *Journal of Housing Research* 4(2): 277–314.

Chomsisengphet S and Pennington-Cross A (2006) The evolution of the subprime mortgage market, *Federal Reserve Bank of St. Louis. Review* January/February 88(1): 31–56.

Cloud C and Galster G (1993) What do we know about racial discrimination in mortgage markets? *Review of Black Political Economy* 22(1) Summer: 101–120.

Dedham B (1988) The color of money. *The Atlanta Journal-Constitution*, 1–4 May: A6.

Engel KC and McCoy PA (2002) A tale of three markets: The law and economics of predatory lending. *Texas Law Review* 80(6): 1255–1382.

Galster GC (1992) Research on discrimination in housing and mortgage markets: Assessment and future directions. *Housing Policy Debate* 3(2): 637–683.

Guttentag JM and Wachter SL (1980) *Redlining and Public Policy, Monograph Series on Finance and Economics. No. 1*. New York: Solomon Brothers Center for the Study of Financial Institutions.

Han S (2004) Discrimination in lending: Theory and evidence. *Journal of Real Estate Finance and Economics* 29(1): 5–46.

Ho G and Pennington-Cross A (2006) The impact of local predatory lending laws on the flow of subprime credit. *Journal of Urban Economics* 60: 210–228.

Hunter WC and Walker MB (1995) *The Cultural Affinity Hypothesis and Mortgage Lending Decisions, Working Papers Series: Issues in Financial Regulation*, Research Department, July. Chicago, IL: Federal Reserve Bank of Chicago.

Ladd HF (1998) Evidence on discrimination in mortgage lending. *Journal of Economic Perspectives* 12(2): 41–62.

Lang WW and Nakamura LI (1993) A model of redlining. *Journal of Urban Economics* 33: 223–234.

Munnell AH, Browne LE, McEneaney J, and Tootell G (1992) *Mortgage Lending in Boston: Interpreting HMDA Data.* Working Paper No. 92-7. Boston, MA: Federal Reserve Bank of Boston.

Schwemmer RG (1995) Introduction to mortgage lending discrimination law. *The John Marshall Law Review* 28(Winter): 317–332.

Staten ME and Yezer AM (2004) Introduction to the special issue. Special issue: 'Subprime lending: empirical studies'. *Journal of Real Estate Finance and Economics* 29(4): 359–363.

Stegman MA and Robert F (2003) Payday lending: A business model that encourages chronic borrowing. *Economic Development Quarterly* 17(8): 8–32.

Stiglitz J and Weiss A (1981) Credit rationing in markets with imperfect information. *American Economic Review* 71(3): 393–410.

Tootell G (1996) Redlining in Boston: Do mortgage lenders discriminate against neighborhoods? *Quarterly Journal of Economics* 111(4): 1049–1079.

Turner MA and Skidmore F (eds.) (1999) *Mortgage Lending Discrimination: A Review of Existing Evidence*. Washington, DC: Urban Institute.

Turner MA, Struyk RJ, and Yinger J (1991) *Housing Discrimination Study: Synthesis*. Washington, DC: U.S. Department of Housing and Urban Development.

Turner MA, Freiberg F, Godfrey E, Herbig C, Levy DK, and Smith RR (2002) *All Other Things Being Equal: A Paired Testing Study of Mortgage Lending Institutions – Final Report*. April. Washington, DC: Urban Institute.

Zenou Y and Boccard N (2000) Racial discrimination and redlining in cities. *Journal of Urban Economics* 48: 260–285.

Do-it-Yourself

M Watson, University of Sheffield, Sheffield, UK

© 2012 Elsevier Ltd. All rights reserved.

Glossary

Appropriation Processes through which someone takes possession or ownership, in the broadest sense, of a thing, including processes through which a house becomes home.
Arts and Crafts movement Movement that originated in England in the 1880s with widening international cultural influence to the 1930s, promoting craftsmanship as resistance to the social and cultural effects of industrialisation.

DIY Do-it-yourself – people providing for themselves services which they could be expected to pay a professional to do.
DIYer A person undertaking DIY.
Tradesperson Gender-neutral version of more conventional 'tradesman': a person practicing a skilled trade or craft professionally, for example plumber, electrician, joiner.

Introduction

Across diverse fields of activity, the term do-it-yourself (DIY) is used to refer to people providing for themselves services which they could be expected to pay a professional to do. However, the core field of reference for the term has always been and remains in relation to householders undertaking home maintenance and improvement themselves. As such, DIY fits uneasily in core categorisations of social scientific inquiry. It clearly involves household consumption, of tools, materials, fixings, and so on. Yet, in effecting material transformations generally resulting in some sort of added value, it is also clearly an activity of production. As an activity, it can fit into people's lives like a form of recreational leisure. Yet it can also be hard work, undertaken to serve inescapable obligations, whether to the house and its maintenance as a home, or to a spouse or other family members. It is by definition an amateur pursuit, but one which can sometimes be undertaken with craft skills and care beyond what would be expected of professional tradespersons. In relation to housing and home, DIY finds diverse expressions, from creative responses to the basic need for shelter through to the discretionary use of time and money to make superficial decorative changes to a comfortable home, to innovative approaches to integrating different architectural techniques and technologies in the pursuit of more affordable or more environmentally sustainable homes.

The Historical Emergence of DIY

People have of course maintained and altered their own homes across cultures and throughout history. However, the term 'do-it-yourself', and the possibility of identifying a more or less bounded range of activities and meanings as a reference for that term, is both historically recent and culturally specific. The phrase has been found to crop up in US advertising as early as 1912, but only really reached any level of common currency in Anglophone countries in the 1950s. The shortening of do-it-yourself to DIY and its stabilisation as a reference to a fairly definite set of activities appear to have been particular to the United Kingdom in the late twentieth century. This emergence of DIY home maintenance and improvement as a distinct cultural phenomenon can be seen as an effect of converging dynamics: from large-scale economic divisions of labour to how household tasks relate to gender relations and identities; shifting housing tenure patterns and the purposes of homeownership; and the development of DIY markets, technologies, and products.

To begin with, the concept of DIY only makes sense within an economic system where particular tasks are specialised and professionalised. It is the expectation that a task done by oneself would be done by someone else that sets it apart as DIY. Its emergence can therefore be seen to reflect the ongoing processes of professionalisation and the specialisation of paid work. The separation of home and work in space, through the development of suburbs, and in time, through the coalescence of the working day, operated substantially to reduce the amount of work householders did on their own homes. Through the nineteenth and early twentieth centuries, relatively affluent householders increasingly hired professionals to do even minor repairs and improvements about the home. It is against this historic backdrop that it makes sense to talk of doing it yourself as something distinctive, an active decision taken to some extent against the expected norm. In part, the historical rise of DIY can be seen as a form of resistance to, or recreation from, the ongoing evacuation of craft skills and substantive production from paid employment. This was particularly true for the types of paid work typical for the urban and suburban middle classes, which did not provide for particular ideas of fulfilment that are served by practical, hands-on, creative work. In their more skilled manifestations at least, the sorts of activities we now recognise as DIY were valorised by the artisanal ideals of the Arts and Crafts movement as it was popularised in the first decades of the twentieth century. DIY provided a form of productive skilled work in the home that was a recreational relief from the limited experience of paid work typical for the property-owning middle classes.

Discourses of labour, skill, and craft immediately resonate with discourses of gender. Indeed, DIY is inherently gendered. There have always been women participating in DIY, and female participation in DIY has rapidly increased in recent years, but it has always been and substantially remains understood as a man's pursuit. Indeed, some histories of what we now recognise as DIY place its emergence firmly within the dynamics of gendered divisions of labour in the home during the twentieth century. In postwar America, doing household maintenance and improvement provided a way for suburban husbands to answer growing cultural expectations that they should be actively involved in the home without compromising masculine identity. By being concerned with processes of material destruction and production, executed through manual labour with heavy tools, the activities we now identify with DIY provided a means to actively contribute more than a wage packet to the home without threatening a man's masculinity. In displacing paid professional help with maintenance, or undertaking improvements that otherwise could not be afforded, this work had evident economic value so fitted in to the legitimation of men's skilled labour. By the 1950s, undertaking home maintenance and improvement was a core element of typical American suburban masculinity. As such DIY emerged as part of the ongoing negotiation of domestic gender identities in the mid-twentieth century.

DIY also figured more subtly within domestic relations. For example, it can provide justification to carve out space for a bench or workshop, in a spare room, garage or shed, to spend time undertaking these legitimate tasks, or using the legitimated private space and time for other purposes. This enabled men to be an active part of the home while retaining separation, both in time and space, from the routines of daily domestic reproduction. At the more detailed level of the emotional economy within the family, the execution of DIY tasks can often take the form of a gift or the expression of care and love for another. DIY is sometimes more a matter of do-it-for-you than do-it-yourself.

The historical evolution of DIY over the twentieth century, and particularly its progressive normalisation, is also inextricable from the development of a distinct DIY industry and market. Before the 1970s, securing the tools, materials, and fixings for DIY tasks generally meant visiting the same retail outlets as professional tradespersons, such as builders' yards. For many people, these specialist retail spaces were frequently intimidating, with an approach to service developed for customers who know how to ask for what they need for the job in hand. From the 1960s, major dedicated DIY retailers – like B&Q in the United Kingdom (1969), Castorama in France (1969), and Home Depot in the United States (1978) – became established. From the start these shops provided a more accessible retail environment, aiming at providing a 'one-stop shop' for the DIYer. Progressively, they developed supermarket-style self-service product display and the provision of knowledge and expertise to amateur DIYers, whether in printed guides or the (not always dependable) availability of expert staff. In addition to the emergence of specialist retailers, the 1970s saw the real emergence of dedicated DIY magazines and manuals, both marking and enabling the normalisation of DIY as a social activity, and making the competence and confidence to undertake tasks more widely accessible. Along with retail changes came also changes in products themselves. Rather than having to use only tools and materials produced for professionals, and so attempt to take on tradespersons' competencies, the DIY market has diversified and specialised as it has grown.

Why DIY?

Much analysis of DIY assumes it represents a rational economic response on the part of those unable to afford to pay for professional labour and skills, or those seeking to maximise profit through increasing property value without having paid for external labour. This is supported by evidence, but only to a certain extent. To begin with, the assumption that DIY substantially results from desires to maximise property market value appears to be supported by the extent to which the varied distribution, frequency, and character of DIY substantially reflects differences in housing tenure. Inevitably, homeowners are typically more inclined to invest time, money, and sweat into their house than are tenants, as they stand to benefit most from their work, including through ownership of any capital value added. Consequently, rates of participation in DIY roughly correlate with rates of homeownership in a given country. For example, within Western Europe, Germany has both one of the lowest rates of participation in DIY and one of the lowest rates of homeownership. The correlation of DIY with homeownership is also reflected historically within countries, with the emergence of DIY as a recognisable social activity generally accompanying rising rates of homeownership over the twentieth century. The relation between DIY and the housing market continues, with corporate profits in the DIY sector generally mirroring the rise and fall of house-buying activity and prices. However, undertaking DIY is not so simply aligned with property as this broad correlation might suggest. While DIY projects entailing large-scale capital investment tend to be carried out exclusively by homeowners, DIY intended to adapt a property in detailed ways – such as improving storage or changing decoration – is frequently also carried out by tenants of rented property, where they are not prevented from doing so by the terms of their lease. This reflects the diverse ways in which DIY activity can serve purposes framed by different understandings, valuations, and practical demands of home. Clearly, DIY can be carried out entirely independently from concerns about maximising the market value of the home.

Income and ability to pay has a more complex relation with DIY. Some correlates with participation in DIY appear to be partly to do with disposable income. In particular, the relation of DIY with age reflects financial pressures to some extent. The highest rates of DIY occur in the years of life typically dominated by commitments like mortgages and family. Multi-adult households with children are particularly likely to be undertaking DIY, caught between continually changing demands for accommodation within the home, and typically limited financial resources. With retirement, whilst enthusiasts have more time particularly for the more craft-oriented forms of DIY such as cabinet making, typically householders are more ready to pay professionals to undertake general household maintenance and repair, reflecting typically higher disposable income as well as declining physical capabilities. However, a number of studies have shown that relative ability to pay under-determines the decision to DIY. DIY is clearly a cost to the individual, suffered to achieve pragmatic ends which could be more easily, but expensively, achieved through professional labour. DIY both in its material results and in the process of its execution clearly can bring additional benefits to the practitioner.

From a cultural approach, motivations for DIY home improvement can be related to identity in a number of ways, in addition to the points on gender outlined above. Physical transformation of a dwelling can be a means to shaping the home as an expression of personal identity. For example, the replacement of a plastic front door by a classic timber design with brass door furniture might be read as a statement of social position and aspiration to passers-by, to visitors, and to householders themselves. The remodelling of a sitting room with features such as storage, lighting, and decor could similarly be understood in identity terms, whether as a means of presenting respectability, hospitality, or demonstrating caring family relations. DIY can be a means to making a home cohere with the shared norms for the appearance of homes within a given social group. However, DIY can also be the means to distinctiveness and innovation, producing features of the home which could not be secured through mass-market products or mainstream professional services, at least within the householder's budget. Whether pursuing identity-related interests through achieving normality or pursuing uniqueness, DIY enables householders to use skill and time to bridge the gap between aspiration and what they can secure in the market.

However, a focus upon DIY as the means to symbolic expression reflects only a very partial framing of what a home is. Home is more centrally the physical and social space which must accommodate its residents' lives. A household's history of DIY within a home can sometimes be presented as the linear pursuit of a guiding logic, a vision for what the house should become. Such histories cohere with the implicit narratives of the home improvement television shows which proliferated from the 1990s, presenting DIY as grand design. However, DIY often results from a mismatch between the shifting needs and purposes of householders and the fabric of the building. Therefore, the reality of DIY activity within the house, especially over decades, is often the result of an ongoing conversation between a changing household – its composition, routines, tastes, and so on – and the fabric of the property. This is evident in the clustering of DIY activity over periods of residency. Typically, it is most prevalent when people take on a new home and reshape it to their needs, both structurally and aesthetically. Subsequent periods of DIY activity focus around life changes with direct effects on how the house is to be used as a home. For example, the decoration of a room repurposed as a nursery is an embedded ritual within preparation for parenthood, shortly followed by innumerable opportunities for small-scale DIY such as the erection of stair gates, to make the home 'childproof' against inquisitive toddlers. At the other end of childhood, children leaving home can be the prompt for material changes to the home, as can caring for elderly parents. Over time, new projects can continue to arise to make the home fit, not simply for the self-image of the householder, but also for the practical exigencies of the households' everyday life. The fabric of the house is itself a participant in the generation of DIY projects, providing limitations, affordances, inspirations, and attachments as part of its ongoing relationship with the household.

DIY as Practice

The accounts of DIY bring out a range of purposes which can be served by DIY. However, on interrogation, it becomes clear that they all focus on DIY as a means to an end. Whether increasing the value of property, redecorating to better express identity, or reshaping to better accommodate a changing family, the emphasis is on the physical change finally effected. The difference between a physical change being provided by the householder's own labour or through professional help is largely incidental to these accounts. To an extent, such explanations are more useful in understanding why home improvement is undertaken, than in understanding why householders might do it themselves. To better understand DIY as a social phenomenon, we need a clearer understanding of what is involved in the actual doing of DIY, one which takes account of the satisfactions, the frustration, the dust, and the sweat. While, for some, DIY is hard work suffered to realise particular ends, for a substantial minority, DIY is a source of challenge and satisfaction to the extent that it is recognised as a hobby. DIY is clearly about process, as well as result.

A focus on the practice of DIY first of all emphasises labour. DIY involves the active bringing together of human body and its capacities of physical and mental engagement with the physical fabric of the building. Mediated by tools, competencies, and materials, through labour the material world is changed. As such, DIY can act as a process of appropriation of a property, gaining a different sense of ownership and belonging through mixing one's labour with the house. For example, in his renowned ethnography of North London council flats, anthropologist Danny Miller identifies the transformation of kitchens as a means through which residents created a sense of belonging within their homes through their own labour, in the process countering a sense of alienation from flats built and decorated by the local authority.

The crucial roles of tools and technologies are similarly highlighted by attention to the doing of DIY. The dynamics of development and innovation in tools and materials designed for the DIY market has been a motor of the growth of DIY. A fundamental effect of such innovations has been to make it easier for the consumer to achieve a particular task. Over the history of DIY, the most emblematic innovation has been the power drill. Whilst electric hand drills emerged by the end of the nineteenth century, their appearance in the toolbox of handy householders had to wait for the mid-twentieth century. Like so much technology, electric drills underwent rapid development and proliferation in war time, when they were used to expedite production of armaments. Post-war, drills were available at high price to professionals and to enthusiastic amateurs with the means. As the DIY market took shape in the late twentieth century, drills were increasingly engineered to the cheaper tolerances needed by amateurs making occasional use, and sold through outlets targeting the DIYer. By the end of the twentieth century, globalised production meant power drills became available at unprecedentedly low prices, making them a viable purchase for even a very occasional user. A DIYer with a power drill clearly has far more capability to tackle jobs, particularly those involving making holes in things, than one without. The steadily increasing accessibility of power drills makes a wide range of tasks accessible to DIY leaving them less dependent on professional help. On a more recent timescale innovations in materials have similarly shifted the boundaries around what can be achieved by a DIYer. For example, push fit plastic plumbing has made a wider range of plumbing jobs accessible to people without the skills necessary to solder copper plumbing joints. Similarly, innovations in paints and varnishes have made it possible for the relatively unskilled to achieve good results on surfaces such as timber doors, where previously suitable paints demanded considerable skill and knowledge on the part of the person painting.

Despite such innovations shifting the requirements for capability on behalf of the person executing a particular task, DIY nevertheless continues to demand skill, as well as labour. In some expressions at least, DIY clearly has the character of craft activity. This of course lies in the roots of DIY identified above through the legitimation of activities we now recognise as DIY by the meanings and motivations of the Arts and Crafts movement. Craft involves the exercise of judgement, skill, and knowledge to produce something which is at least in part designed by the person making it. So far as DIY can be seen as craft production, it resonates with activities valued by thinkers such as Marx, Veblen, and Morris, for each of whom craft production represents an authentic expression of humanity, standing in contrast with the alienating production processes of industrial capitalism. While such ideals may seem a long way from the aisles of DIY superstores, something of them can nevertheless reside in people's experiences of undertaking skilled activities of home maintenance and improvement, particularly where they involve a responsive relationship to the affordances of materials mediated through the competent use of tools.

DIY Culture and Innovation in Housing

It is in these more idealistic understandings that the mainstream sense of DIY, framed within home maintenance and improvement, resonates with the broader uses and meanings of DIY as a cultural phenomenon. DIY has been a trope of counter-culture, alternative and resistance movements since the 1960s. Through free festivals, elements of hippy culture and later the centrality of DIY in punk, the principles of self-reliance, creativity and resistance to industrial capitalism that can be traced back to the Arts and Crafts movement found new forms of expression in response to the conditions of advanced capitalism. Indeed, the politics of a DIY approach found perhaps their most explicit expression in the punk movement from the late 1970s, where the music, the zines, and the clothes all represented a spirit of self-reliance, DIY production, and resistance to the corporate machine. DIY continues as a principle of alternative and resistance movements today, not least in the ethics and practices of the diverse movements falling under the labels of anticapitalist and antiglobalisation movements, as well as those of grassroots development and sustainability initiatives.

The connection of this wider understanding of DIY as ethic and principle may not seem immediately to resonate with concerns of housing and home. However, it is often in the expression of these ethics in relation to housing that alternatives to mainstream solutions and ideas persist, and in which innovations emerge and are nurtured. Alternatives to conventional models of housing based around homeownership or renting by conventional household units, such as through communal living and squatting, are kept alive in part through exercise of the DIY ethic in relation to housing. More visibly, innovations in house design and household-level technologies, particularly in relation to issues of sustainability, have been substantially driven over several decades by determined individuals ready to collaboratively design and develop technologies that the market signally failed to provide. DIY innovation in technologies which are becoming increasingly mainstream along with concerns of climate change and peak oil, like wind turbines, passive solar design, advanced insulation or solar energy, emerged and were nurtured in the innovation niches comprised by people ready to do it themselves.

Conclusions

For DIY to have meaning, it has to exist in opposition, as an alternative to another, often more dominant, mode of provision. People have always maintained and improved homes through their own labour, and continue to do so. However, without an economic system where it is both possible and normal to rely on a professional to provide the service, it does not make sense to talk of providing that service oneself as DIY. Analysed in terms of ideological roots and basic principles, DIY is in some senses a means of resistance, a means of claiming a measure of autonomy and capability, even creativity, in the face of an economic system that drives towards ever more specialised paid work as the means to pay someone else to provide the services we might provide for ourselves. Yet this is a form of 'resistance' that provides the market for multi-billion dollar national industrial and retail sectors, and one which is largely practiced without the anti-industrialisation of Morris or the anticapitalism of punk in mind. DIY thus occupies a strange middle ground, both production and consumption, both labour and leisure. It provides the means for householders to fill the gap between their needs for material changes to the home and what the market can afford with their own labour. It figures in the negotiation of relationships within the home and in the expression of identities. It provides satisfactions as well as frustrations, creativity as well as drudgery. It enables the pursuit of normality but also the means for the reproduction of radical alternatives and the emergence of new innovations. It will undoubtedly remain a source of dynamism and innovation in housing.

See also: Experiencing Home; Gender Divisions in the Home; Home as a Space of Care; Home as Investment; Maintenance and Repair; Rights to Housing Tenure; Self-Provided Housing in Developed Societies; Suburban Homes.

Further Reading

Clarke A (2001) The aesthetics of social aspiration. In: Miller D (ed.) *Home Possessions*, pp. 23–46. Oxford, UK: Berg.
Edwards C (2006) 'Home is Where the Art is': Women, handicrafts and home improvements 1750–1900. *Journal of Design History* 19: 11–21.
Gelber S (1997) Do-It-Yourself: Constructing, repairing and maintaining domestic masculinity. *American Quarterly* 49(1): 66–112.
Goldstein C (1998) *Do It Yourself: Home Improvement in Twentieth-Century America*. New York: Princeton Architectural Press.
Miller D (1997) Consumption and its consequences. In: Mackay H (ed.) *Consumption and Everyday Life*, pp. 13–64. London: Sage and the Open University.
Watson M and Shove E (2008) Product, competence, project and practice: DIY and the dynamics of craft consumption. *Journal of Consumer Culture* 8(1): 69–89.
Williams CC (2004) A lifestyle choice? Evaluating the motives of do-it-yourself (DIY) consumers. *International Journal of Retail & Distribution Management* 32(5): 270–278.

Relevant Website

http://www.doityourself.com – do-it-yourself.

Domestic Pets

P Carlisle-Frank, The Foundation for Interdisciplinary Research and Education Promoting Animal Welfare (FIREPAW, Inc.), Houston, TX, USA

© 2012 Elsevier Ltd. All rights reserved.

Overview of Scientific Research Findings: Pets and Housing

Prior to the economic crisis, estimates of companion animals euthanised at US shelters indicated that 4.2 million dogs and cats or 14.8 animals per 1000 Americans were euthanised each year (Clifton, 2003). Although some of these animals have untreatable health or behavioural issues, the majority of these animals could have been adopted if there had been homes available. The research indicates that a primary reason for companion animals to be relinquished to shelters is housing issues; researchers Salman et al. (1998) have estimated that nearly one-third of relinquishments are for 'housing issues'. And according to the National Council on Pet Population Study and Policy's Regional Shelter Survey, the top reason for dog relinquishment to shelters in the United States is moving house. It is the third most frequently cited reason for cat relinquishment to shelters. Landlord refusal to allow pets was the most common additional reason given for relinquishment (New et al., 1999). Another US study found that the primary reason for relinquishing cats and the third most common reason for relinquishing dogs is moving (Miller et al., 1996). A further recent study found that one of the most frequently given reasons for relinquishing companion animals to shelters was 'moving'. The authors found that 'landlord restrictions' was a critical factor in the decision to relinquish a companion animal (Shore et al., 2003).

The lack of available pet-friendly rental housing is puzzling when one considers the high numbers of US households with companion animals. According to the American Veterinary Association nearly one out of every two renters in the United States, for instance, has pets (Anonymous, 1996) and 35% of people without pets have stated they would own a pet if their rental units permitted them (Hart and Kidd, 1994).

Problems with 'No Pets' Policies

Recent national surveys have indicated that over one-half of the homes in the United States have pets. Yet, the majority of rental housing forbids pets (Anonymous, 2001). There is perhaps no other factor that makes finding housing more difficult than having pets. Due to a variety of misperceptions about animals many landlords are reluctant to rent out to tenants with pets. And if tenants have a large dog or multiple animals, landlords are even more likely to refuse to grant a tenancy – even if a person is the perfect rental applicant in every other respect. If renters with pets lack the time and ability to be persistent and resourceful they often give up on trying to find housing that welcomes their animals. Feeling devastated, they often see their only option is to turn their beloved animal family members in to a shelter. In fact, when it comes to housing and pets, renters are almost 3 times more likely to relinquish both dogs and cats as nonrenters are (Patronek et al., 1996).

The Companion Animal Renters Study: Examining the Realities of 'Pet-Friendly' versus 'No Pets' Rental Policies

In an effort to determine the factors influencing the availability of pet-friendly rental units, the Foundation for Interdisciplinary Research and Education Promoting Animal Welfare (FIREPAW), a 501(c)(3) nonprofit organisation, conducted a nationwide empirical research study. The results of the study indicate that the current shortage of pet-friendly rentals is frequently based on a misperception by many rental property owners that renting to tenants with animals is too costly and problem-ridden to justify (Carlisle-Frank et al., 2006). The results further demonstrated that rental property owners with pet-friendly rentals experience tenants who stay longer and are more loyal, have less turnover (meaning less time spent renting their units), spend less on advertising their rentals, and have their rental units filled more quickly. In short, this study found that for the majority of landlords it just makes good economic sense to make their rentals pet-friendly (**Table 1**).

Availability of Pet-Friendly Housing

According to the information reported by landlords in the FIREPAW study, approximately one-half of the rental housing is pet-friendly. However, most of the pet-friendly housing had some limitations regarding animal size or type. Only 9% of rental housing had no significant restrictions on size or type of animal permitted. Approximately one-half of rental housing allowed cats; cats were the easiest type of animal to get housing for. Having a large dog was the most difficult condition for renters to find rental housing, with only

Table 1 Annual costs and benefits per unit from allowing pets

Total costs	
Insurance	$150
Damage/unit[a]	$39
Time spent on pet issues (@ $30 h^{-1})	$29
Total costs	$218
Total benefits	
Increased rent	$2294
Decrease in lost rent from vacant units	$398
Decrease in time spent on marketing (@ $30 h^{-1})	$235
Decrease in advertising spending	$24
Total benefits	$2949
Net benefit per unit annually from allowing pets	**$2731**

[a]When all factors are taken into account, there may actually be a benefit rather than a cost in terms of average damage due to reduced turnover and increased deposit. However, the figures used here are intended to be conservative. All calculations are estimated averages that will vary by the specific situation.

11% of property owners allowing these animals (**Figure 1**). Most tenants with animals (82%) reported having trouble finding a rental unit that would take their pet(s). This number was even higher for tenants with dogs, with 100% of tenants with multiple dogs reporting having trouble.

Pet Deposits and Rent Differentials

The majority of pet-friendly rental property owners in the FIREPAW study charged a separate pet deposit. Using landlord survey data, 73% of pet-friendly housing required a pet deposit. The average pet deposit was between 40 and 85% of the rent. In addition to a separate pet deposit, the average total deposit was larger for pet-friendly housing relative to no-pets rentals.

The data indicate there was a clear rent differential between housing that allowed pets and housing that did not, with pet-friendly housing charging more in rent. This difference was found consistently using three different sets of data (national listings, landlord data, and tenant data), with the rent premium being statistically significant in all cases (**Figure 2**). Housing with limitations on the type and/or size of pets permitted (such as allowing cats only and limiting the animal size) was also found to be slightly cheaper (by an average of $100 per month) than other pet-friendly housing.

Length of Tenancy

From tenant surveys, it can be seen that tenants staying in pet-friendly housing units stayed an average of 46 months compared to 18 months for tenants residing in rentals

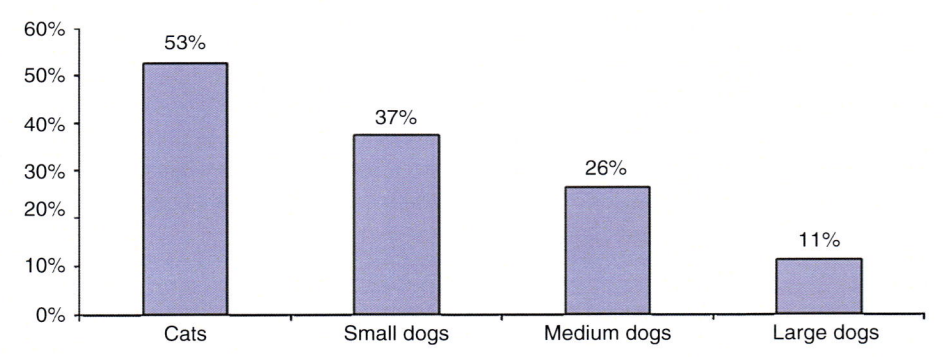

Figure 1 Percentage of rental units taking pets by type and size of animal.

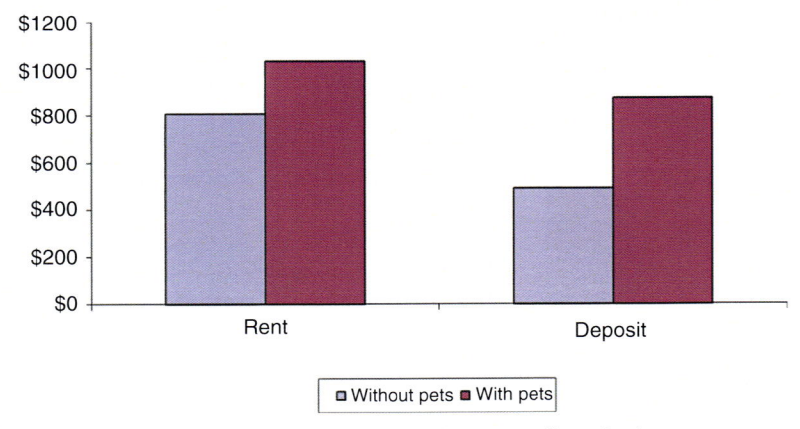

Figure 2 Average rent and deposit costs (in USD) for pet-friendly and no-pets-allowed units.

prohibiting pets. It should be noted that the increased length of tenancy did not occur for tenants who illegally kept pets. Tenants who illegally kept pets were closer in their length of tenancy to people who do not keep pets at all. Thus, the increased tenancy for people who keep legal pets appears to be out of loyalty or a desire not to have to search again for pet-friendly housing rather than because of any physical hardship of moving with animals.

Vacancy Rates

The vacancy rate for pet-friendly housing was significantly lower than that for 'no pets' rentals: 10% for pet-friendly housing compared to 14% for other housing. The amount landlords had to spend on advertising their units was lower for pet-friendly housing at $15 per unit compared to $32 per unit for no-pets housing. Landlords also needed to spend less than half the amount of time marketing pet-friendly housing. Pet-friendly housing also received about twice as many applicants for a vacant unit as no-pets housing. The average time it took to rent out a pet-friendly unit was 19 days compared to 29 days for non-pet-friendly units. Approximately 25% of applicants inquiring about rentals of non-pet-friendly housing were specifically seeking pet-friendly rentals (**Figure 3**).

Common Concerns: Permitting Pets

Among the landlords who did not allow pets, damage was the greatest concern by far, with approximately two-thirds of landlords citing damage as a major concern.

Noise was the second largest concern, followed by tenant complaints and insurance issues. Concerns about people leaving their pet behind or not cleaning common areas were rarely cited as reasons for not allowing pets.

Pet-friendly housing did have some costs for landlords. For example, landlords reported an average annual insurance premium of $150 more for pet-friendly housing. However, this annual cost is less than the premium received from the rent charged for pet-friendly housing in just 1 month. Of the potential problems pets could cause to housing, damage was the most commonly reported. However, even this was not that common, with approximately one-half of landlords who allowed pets stating that they had never experienced damage from companion animals allowed in their units. Slightly less than half of landlords had ever experienced complaints from tenants or neighbours regarding animals, about one-third of landlords ever had noise problems, and only approximately 15% had ever experienced any other problem associated with allowing pets. Although 85% of landlords reported having some amount of damage at some time, the worst damage reported by each landlord averaged just $430 – much less than the average rent or the average pet deposit. For half of the landlords who allowed pets, the worst case of pet-related damage they ever experienced was still fully covered by the deposit. In addition, FIREPAW's results suggest that a proper use of screening tools can significantly minimise the chance of suffering a loss that would ever exceed the deposit. A more important issue is whether overall damage is different for tenants with pets than for tenants without pets. The data suggest there is no difference in damage.

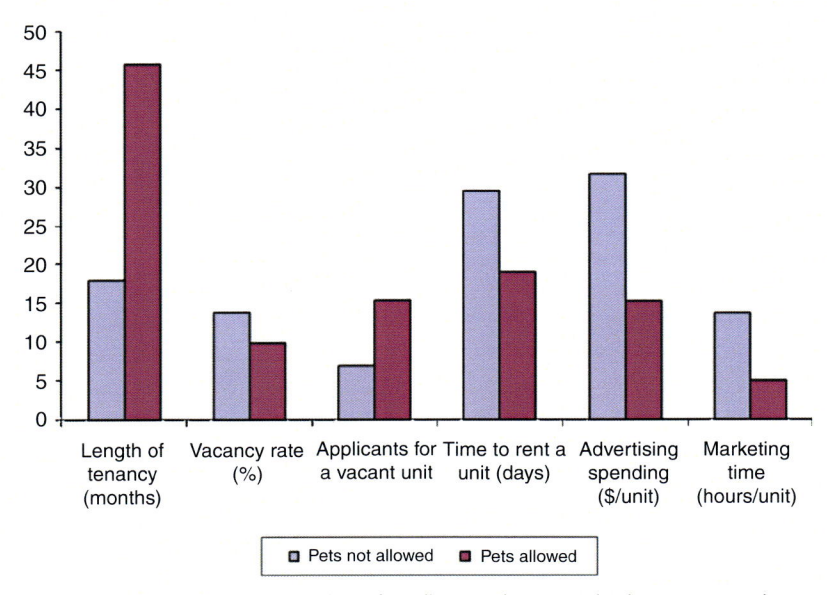

Figure 3 Average length of tenancy, vacancy rate, number of applicants, times required to rent out unit, cost of advertising (in USD), and hours required to market rental unit for pet-friendly and no-pets-allowed rental units.

Lack of Screening Procedures

Potentially useful tools for screening tenants with animals or limiting landlords' exposure to problems were rarely used. Only 3.7% of landlords required pet references, and only 7.4% required a 'pet résumé'. None of the landlords surveyed required training certificates, only 11% required health certificates (such as proof of rabies vaccinations or proof the animal had been spayed/neutered – a procedure which has been shown to dramatically reduce aggression, biting, spraying, and other unwanted, potentially problematic behaviours for landlords to deal with), and only 18.5% required a pet agreement/policy. Tenants gave some of these items more frequently than they were required – 18% of tenants offered a pet résumé, 22% offered pet references, and 4% gave certification of training.

Keeping Pets Illegally

When landlords who prohibit pets were surveyed, they estimated that 7% of their tenants keep pets in their rental units despite the no-pets policy. However, the tenant data show that over 20% of tenants are keeping pets illegally. This is quite a significant finding since landlords with tenants holding illegal pets receive none of the benefits, yet suffer all of the potential costs of having animals (**Figure 4**).

Making a Case for Going 'Pet-Friendly'

There is no denying the fact that there may be hassles involved in renting to tenants with pets. In addition, tenants without pets cause problems every day. So if the potential for hassles already exists, why should landlords add in yet another variable by accepting pets? The answer is simple: Because going pet-friendly can increase their bottom line and, just as important, it can also reduce landlords' hassles overall. Rental property owners who make their rental housing pet-friendly can make a significant difference in the amount of time, money, and aggravation they spend writing and placing ads, showing rentals, and interviewing prospective tenants. Pet-friendly properties will be rented far quicker and will offer a significantly larger pool of applicants to choose from once the transition to accepting pets is made.

The Economics of Pet-Friendly Housing

According to behavioural economists we are all consistently irrational in predictable ways. One of the key foundational insights from behavioural economics theory is that people do not actually make decisions by maximising the benefits. Instead, they do something called satisficing. The truth is that rental property owners and managers are busy people. And they are only human. For all the choices they face daily, they simply do not have the time or cognitive capacity to take full consideration of every possible course of action or look into all possible outcomes in every situation. Instead, they typically deal with problems as they arise. Only the most obvious options are considered. And once a satisfactory course of action presents itself, the manager will take it and move on to all the other issues they need to address.

Renters with animals may be a common victim of this satisficing. There may be a number of things landlords might be able to do to make more money, and they may even be aware of many of those possibilities. But pursuing those potential opportunities is another story. Allowing pets may be one of the last policies a landlord will spontaneously change in an effort to increase the bottom line because without the appropriate level of information it appears to involve a lot of uncertainty and risk. If they are satisfied with their current profitability, a landlord may think about squeezing a little more profit by raising rents, but it is unlikely they will consider going into the uncertain realm of changing pet policies. This is because typically landlords and property managers will be risk-averse. But the evidence suggests there may be a compelling reason for making the effort to switch: rental property owners will make more profit and save time.

Examining the Landlord–Tenant Relationship as It Relates to Pet-Friendly Housing

The landlord–tenant relationship for pet-friendly housing is no different than rental housing that prohibits pets. For the landlord it is a business intended to make a profit and for the tenant it is their private dwelling. As such, rules and boundaries – especially those concerning pets in both the residence and the common areas – should be clearly established and explicitly outlined in writing and agreed to by all parties. Beyond the establishing of rules, however, there are a number of other things landlords can

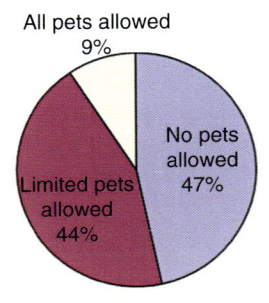

Figure 4 Rental housing distribution/percentage of rentals permitting pets.

do to help ensure happy, long-term tenants and reduce potential problems. Among these are educating tenants about how to make sure their pets are 'rental-ready', as well as their role in maintaining a positive pet-friendly rental experience for themselves, their pets, and their neighbours. Additionally, there are strategies that landlords can use to meet their tenants halfway. These include learning to be clear, fair, and consistent in setting and enforcing pet-related rules, being diplomatic and respectful of tenants' positions, becoming good managers adept at problem-solving and conflict resolution, and facilitating a happy, respectful, and pleasant business relationship with their tenants with pets.

Educating Tenants about Their Role in Maintaining a Great Pet-Friendly Rental Experience

It is the responsibility of landlords to educate their tenants about the rules and expectations for pet care within the rental environment and their role in maintaining a positive pet-friendly rental experience for themselves, their pets, and their neighbours.

There are a number of practical, tried-and-true techniques, tips, and strategies landlords can use to educate their tenants with pets to show how to maximise their rental housing experience and to assist them in the process of maintaining conflict-free, happy, and fulfilling housing arrangements for themselves, their neighbours, their landlords, and their animals. First and foremost is the utilisation of appropriate screening tools for ensuring the tenant selected has the best fit with the landlord's rental property. This includes landlords requiring prospective tenants to complete a 'tenants-with-pets application' and submit a 'pet résumé' that requires prospective tenants to give all of the key information so that rental property managers can call references and fact-check the information with veterinarians, previous landlords, and other relevant references to make an informed decision about the best applicant (see Relevant Websites).

Rental property owners will also need to clearly outline for their new tenants the key factors affecting the rental scenario, including the pet deposit and required extra rent, restrictions on the type, size, and weight of animals permitted, as well as the specific rules surrounding pets in the common areas and pets left unattended in the rental unit for extended periods of time. If landlords expect compliance with the rules there can be no ambiguity. New tenants should clearly understand the parameters such as what the pet deposit and extra rent does and does not cover, the specifics about use of common areas, and so on. Landlords must also learn how to set boundaries and hold tenants accountable for the behaviour of their animals. It is imperative that rental property owners not only clearly specify the rules and expectations for how tenants will behave with their animals but also clearly spell out the consequences of not following the rules. Only doing so will ensure that tenants with pets are active players in a pet-friendly experience.

Making Sure Tenants' Pets Are 'Rental-Ready'

Landlords should give all new tenants a copy of FIREPAW's rules for the road (see Relevant Websites). This booklet offers specific tips for teaching tenants to be responsible pet guardians and to ensure that they and their pets are mannerly, respectful residents.

The Landlord's Role: Meeting Tenants Halfway

Like any other business, there must be reciprocity between the parties involved in a landlord–tenant relationship. If rental property owners are to have a peaceful, problem-free, and profitable experience permitting pets, they need to meet their tenants halfway. This requires developing and maintaining the right rapport, which encourages compliance and creates a happy, trusting relationship where everyone, including the animals, wins. This entails landlords taking the lead in creating and maintaining open communication with tenants and developing effective problem-solving and conflict negotiation skills. Finally, landlords must also be responsible for setting firm limits, enforcing rules, and ensuring their assets are protected while facilitating a happy, respectful, and pleasant business relationship with their tenants with pets.

An Important Aside: Considering the Laws about Companion Animal Renters

Landlords considering switching to pet-friendly rentals are encouraged to check out their local, county, and state laws and regulations on the subject. This segment is not intended to be a legal text or reference, especially given the variation in regional law, but instead offers some very general, but important information about trends and tendencies in the law regarding deposits and rents in pet-friendly rental housing. When it comes to pet deposits and charging higher rents for pet-friendly rentals, landlords need to know their local laws. In some states or municipalities, requiring a separate pet deposit can be illegal. However, in some cases, landlords may be able to avoid this restriction by charging all tenants a higher deposit. This makes more sense anyway; allowing pets raises total demand, so the property managers can afford to tighten up their pricing, both on rents and on deposits. The justification for raising deposit requirements for all tenants is that bad tenants can cause damage regardless of whether they have pets. It is recommended landlords not charge a different rent for people with and without pets.

Such rent differentials may even be illegal in some cases. Instead, it is recommended landlords adjust their total rent to reflect the total demand. In general, it is recommended landlords keep the same rules and prices for people with pets as those charged for tenants without pets.

In any event, remember that a damage deposit is just that – money that is held to reimburse the owner in case there are damages. Keeping this money without cause is illegal. Routine maintenance between tenants is also not a cause for keeping the money. Only damages beyond normal wear and tear or unpaid expenses such as rent (including the next 30 days if 30-day notice is required in the contract) are causes for holding the deposit. Anything beyond that should be returned to the departing tenant. If a separate amount of money is explicitly defined as a pet deposit, then it can be kept only for that specific reason.

Strategies for Making Pet-Friendly Housing Work for Everyone

This section provides landlords with a starter kit: the tools, techniques, and strategies they need to begin the process of converting their rental properties to pet-friendly.

The Companion Animal Renters Program: The Logistics of Going 'Pet-Friendly'

Once landlords understand why going pet-friendly can be beneficial they must learn the logistics of how to do it. Drawn from FIREPAW's Companion Animal Renter Program, this subsection offers an at-a-glance version of the key features to developing and maintaining a successful pet-friendly rental business in the following pet-friendly landlord checklist:

1. *Economic feasibility.* Landlords should always conduct an economic assessment of their rental property so they recognise and understand the economic realities of their rental situation. Is converting to 'pet-friendly' rentals financially feasible? What conditions would make it work? Should there be pet deposit requirements? Monthly pet rental charges? (A rental property owner questionnaire has been provided by FIREPAW to assist landlords in beginning this economic feasibility process; see Relevant Websites).
2. *Needs assessment and determination of specifics.* Landlords should broadly assess their regional situation, market availability, competition, amount of potential tenants, and so on, to custom-tailor the specifics of pet-friendly rentals to their situation.
3. *Understand and use screening and assessment tools.* In order for rental property owners to find the best tenant-with-animals match and to screen out potentially problematic tenants with animals they should make regular use of screening tools such as pet résumés and a tenant-with-animals application (see Relevant Websites).
4. *Training in conflict resolution and problem-solving.* Obtain conflict resolution training (offered free of charge by many communities; check with your local chamber of commerce, police department, and community colleges) and learn how to resolve conflicts, mediate disputes, and head off problems before they arise.
5. *Requiring pet agreements and pet policies.* Customise the pet policy and pet agreement to fit your own local laws and unique circumstances and incorporate FIREPAW's 'How to be a good tenant-with-animals' booklet – requiring tenants to read, understand, and follow guidelines and attest to this in the pet agreement so that they are held accountable for their and their animal's behaviour (see Relevant Websites).
6. *Offering pet-related activities in complexes.* Establish a 'pet perks package'. Contact pet trainers, pet groomers, animal communicators, and so on, in your area and schedule them to make presentations (free of charge) at your rental community for tenants. This can be as basic or as sophisticated as the circumstances call for.
7. *Registering of rental properties.* Register your rental properties on the referral listing for pet-friendly rentals. Landlords can get free advertising in high-traffic pet-friendly rental listing sources simply by contacting their local humane society and animal welfare organisations and requesting to be added to their listings.
8. *Gaining support and assistance from the animal care community.* Once a landlord reaches out to the animal welfare organisations in their community to get on their listing of pet-friendly rental housing, they will find an abundance of support and assistance (including how to deal with potential problems that may arise) from the animal care community – all at no cost.
9. *Setting and maintaining strict rules for common areas.* Make the rules clear and easily visible. All tenants should be aware of the rules and the consequences for repeated offenses of breaking those rules.
10. *Requiring strict adherence that all pets have proof of spaying or neutering.* In addition to helping stop unwanted litters, this will greatly reduce unwanted behaviours from pets such as aggression, fighting, biting, spraying, and howling.

Resources for Landlords and Tenants Searching for Pet-Friendly Solutions

In addition to animal welfare organisations in your own local area, national organisations such as the Humane Society of the United States (HSUS), the Delta Society, and the American Society for the Prevention of Cruelty to Animals (ASPCA) promote excellent programmes designed to provide tips and strategies for landlords considering converting their properties to pet-friendly rentals. They can be found on the Internet and offer literature for free to rental property owners.

See also: Nature in the Home; Private Rental Landlords: North America; Rights to Housing Tenure.

References

Anonymous (1996) *The Veterinary Service Market for Companion Animals*. Schaumburg, IL: American Veterinary Medical Association.

Anonymous (2001) *Renting with Pets: How a Pets-Allowed Policy Can Work for You*. Washington, DC: The Humane Society of the United States.

Carlisle-Frank P, Frank J, and Nielsen L (2006) Companion animal renters and pet-friendly housing in the US. *Anthrozoos* 18(1): 59–77.

Clifton M (2003) Latest US data show shelter killing down to 4.2 million/year. *Animal People* 12(6): 17.

Hart L and Kidd A (1994) Potential pet ownership in US rental housing. *Canine Practice* 19(3): 24–28.

Miller D, Staats S, Partlo C, and Rada K (1996) Factors associated with the decision to surrender a pet to an animal shelter. *Journal of the American Veterinary Medical Association* 209: 738–742.

New J, Salman M, Scarlett J, Kass PH, Vaughn JA, Scherr S, and Kelch WJ (1999) Moving: Characteristics of those relinquishing companion animals to US animal shelters. *Journal of Applied Animal Welfare Science* 2(2): 83–96.

Patronek G, Glickman L, Beck A, McCabe G, and Ecker C (1996) Risk factors for relinquishment of cats to an animal shelter. *Journal of the American Veterinary Medical Association* 209: 582–588.

Salman M, New J, Scarlett J, Kass P, Ruch-Gallie R, and Hetts S (1998) Human and animal factors related to the relinquishment of dogs and cats in 12 selected animal shelters in the US. *Journal of Applied Animal Welfare Science* 1(3): 207–226.

Shore E, Petersen C, and Douglas D (2003) Moving as a reason for pet relinquishment: A closer look. *Journal of Applied Animal Welfare Science* 6(1): 39–52.

Further Reading

Anonymous (2000) No pets allowed: Fighting for pets in rental housing. *Animal Sense* Summer issue: 1–3.

Relevant Websites

www.firepaw.org/CARP_Brochure.pdf – FIREPAW rental property owner questionnaire.

www.firepaw.org/CARPTenants.PDF – FIREPAW sample for how to find, keep, and enjoy a pet-friendly rental.

Domestic Technologies and the Modern Home

L Spigel, Northwestern University, Evanston, IL, USA

© 2012 Elsevier Ltd. All rights reserved.

Glossary

The Bauhaus (translated as 'House of Building' or 'Building School') A school founded in post-First World War Germany that combined crafts and fine arts and became famous for its innovations in the field of design. Founded by architect Walter Gropius, the school was located in three German cities (Weimar from 1919 to 1925, Dessau from 1925 to 1932, and Berlin from 1932 to 1933), under three different architect-directors: Gropius from 1919 to 1928, Hannes Meyer from 1928 to 1930, and Ludwig MiesVan der Rohe from 1930 until 1933, when the school closed due to pressure from the Nazi government.

Cyberculture A term used to refer to the culture or cultures that have developed in relation to the rise of computer networks, digital devices, and digital forms of information, communication, and entertainment. It is often connected to the literary and film science fiction genre known specifically as cyber fiction.

Digital divide A term that came into usage in the mid-1990s and has been used to refer to unequal access to information technologies (especially computers and the Internet) among different social groups and world populations. The term not only refers to unequal access to hardware, but also refers to the educational and cultural opportunities that go hand in hand with technological literacy and access. The term has often been used in policy discussions of digital communication infrastructures.

Dystopia A place of doom or a vision of such a place, often associated with the end of the world and/or a nightmarish existence. Often imagined in science fiction stories.

Modernity A term used to explain the historical turn towards industrialisation, capitalism, secularism, nationalism, and rationalisation. While it relates to the forces of modernisation and to aesthetic modernisms, it is a distinct concept that is itself divided into a number of sub-eras. Following the early modern period (after the Middle Ages and through the 1700s), it is generally related to the Industrial Revolution in the eighteenth and nineteenth centuries. The late period of modernity refers to the social and cultural developments in late nineteenth- and early twentieth-century life, especially as that was experienced in the urban centres of Europe and the United States. Cultural theorists often use the term modernity to refer to the new sense of speed, mobility, and consumerism in modern cities, and to the new sensorial experiences of everyday life, including experiences offered by new transportation and communication technologies like the train, cinema, and telephone.

Modernism A term used to refer to movements in the arts and architecture that turn away from traditional ways of organising images, spaces, temporality, narrative, and sound. There are different kinds of modernism (or modernist movements) that have emerged in different historical, geographical, and sociopolitical contexts. While modernism is often associated with the term 'avant garde' and with a reaction against tradition, modernism is a distinct concept from avant gardism, and despite its associations with innovation in the arts, some forms of modernism have been used to uphold national or corporate agendas.

Introduction

The idea of home in the modern world is unthinkable apart from the array of technologies of which they are comprised. Even if technology seems anathema to sentimental notions of family life, for numerous populations around the globe, an increasing array of technological artefacts designed for use at home are central to the experiences of everyday life. Domestic technologies are not just useful tools; they have helped to define the very meaning of what it means to be at home – or conversely not at home – in the modern world.

From the telephone to the washing machine to the microwave oven to the flat screen TV, domestic technologies help to orchestrate daily activities and relationships among residents. For example, people sometimes turn on the television to punctuate their daily routines, and they also use media technologies to spark conversations or else to avoid them (Lull, 1990; Morley, 1985; Silverstone, 1994). So too, domestic technologies are central to the ways in which people experience relations between the private and public world. AT&T's famous marketing slogan 'Reach Out and Touch Someone' promised consumers a world of instant accessibility to distant loved ones through the wires.

As this already suggests, home technologies have an affective dimension. Like other objects in the home, they become embedded with family memories and they may even take on the status of family heirloom or antique. For example, people often integrate technologies into their homes by adorning them with family mementoes. People paste family snapshots or children's art on fridges, turning a highly standardised industrial appliance into a family scrapbook of sorts. Following this trend, the new 'smart' fridge industry offers models with LCD screens that allow consumers to upload personal photos and project them on the refrigerator door. Conversely, new technologies can also be a source of anxiety, and people often resist the changes they perceive will accompany new machines. Since the nineteenth century, fears about technology's effects on the home circulated in both intellectual and popular culture. Would the sewing machine threaten the sanctity of Victorian femininity by replacing domestic handicrafts with the dirt and grime of industrial machines? Would people contract diseases by talking to distant strangers on the phone? Would television (in the tradition of George Orwell's 'Big Brother') somehow peer into our private lives at home? Will computers turn kids into sedentary loners, robbing them of outdoor play? Accordingly, corporations often design and advertise technologies in relation to public perceptions, uses, expectations, and anxieties about machines.

In this sense, rather than determining social relationships in the home, domestic technologies become enmeshed in the fabric of the everyday. Although they open up a range of possible applications, not everyone uses them in the same way. For example, in some households, a computer can be a divisive force as family members argue over who gets to use it and where (Frohlich et al., 2003). But, other families report that they use media technologies to experience a sense of togetherness by, for example, sitting together doing e-mails and working on laptops (Morley, 2007). Yet, even if people use technologies in different ways, their choices are not entirely freewheeling. Given their historical relation to capitalist production and consumer culture, domestic technologies are part of wider sociopolitical struggles and power hierarchies, and not everyone has equal access to them. So, for example, today the digital divide means that Internet penetration is unevenly distributed among populations. For example, in 2009, Internet penetration (either at home or in public places) varied widely among national populations: roughly 90.9% in Norway; over 75% in the United States, Japan, and the United Kingdom; 32.3% in Russia; and 12% in Algeria.

More generally, domestic technologies are embroiled in national and global agendas, not only through political-economic dimensions (such as federal funding or corporate research and design), but also through symbolic dimensions. Just as with the space race or the military race for arms, home technologies have historically served as a symbol of progress and national supremacy. Promoted at world's fairs and international exhibitions since the nineteenth century, they represent modernisation and scientific advancement. Home technologies are therefore not just a matter of personal use or convenience; they exist at the intersection of private and public life.

In the remainder of this brief survey, I focus on how a range of domestic technologies have been designed and promoted in the context of larger social ideals about home, family, and modernisation since the nineteenth century. (As exemplified by some of the work cited herein, there are numerous qualitative studies and ethnographies of the use of specific technologies, but the results are typically case-specific and vary methodologically.) My sources are often advertisements and promotional practices, so that my goal is less to present empirical data on penetration rates and use, than it is to consider how technologies have been designed and inscribed with cultural meanings about what it means to be modern and to live in a modern home. This symbolic dimension is not just a trivial flourish applied to the hardware of machines; rather technologies mean something to their users and these meanings have social consequences. For example, the car has, for many years, been associated with freedom and escape, so when people buy a car it is possible (at least in fantasy) to seek not only mobility but also liberation. Similarly, the television set has long been associated with laziness and lowbrow tastes, and even if people like to watch TV, they often do not admit it (which makes it difficult for researchers to access exactly how people use it). Finally, as will become obvious, I focus on the United States, not simply because of my own national and linguistic expertise, but also because the United States was where domestic technologies were first integrated into and wed to the notion of the modern home.

Electrifying the Home: Progress and Nostalgia

Home technologies are a product of the wider context of modernity and the changes to daily life wrought by industrialisation, and in particular by electrification. In 1884, American inventor Thomas Alva Edison predicted that electricity would be harnessed to a range of appliances that would fundamentally change domestic labour. "With electricity", he enthused, "you will be able to drive sewing machines, shoe-cleaning machines and washing machines. You will be able to light your house and cook your food" (Edison cited in Sparke, 1987: 23). Like other industrialists, Edison's intended audience (the 'you' in his statement) was a burgeoning group of middle-class American consumers who would find such devices especially useful at a time when the labour pool for domestic servants was shrinking (a phenomenon especially on the rise in the early decades of the twentieth century) and when social reformers (many of whom were women) saw the family home as a microcosm of the American democracy, and American progress, at large.

In part because of the labour shortage, and also because of the availability of cheap manual labour in American factories, it was in the United States where the manufacture and dissemination of electrically powered domestic technologies first took place. By the end of the nineteenth century, the United States had developed an electrical industry with companies like Westinghouse (formed in 1886) and General Electric (formed in 1892) eager to sell electrical machines for domestic use. In 1917, only about one-quarter of the dwellings in the United States had been electrified, but by 1920 this figure had doubled (for nonfarm and urban dwellings) and by 1930 it had risen to roughly 80% (Historical Statistics of the United States, 1960: p. 510; Schwartz Cowan, 1976). By the 1920s, many of the electrical goods in use today were finding their way into American homes. While Britain, Germany, and a host of other nations did invent and/or promote electrical appliances in the first decades of the twentieth century, it was largely after the Second World War that the British, as well as other European nations, adapted home appliances on a grander scale. And while home appliances were in use in Japan in the early part of the twentieth century, they became widely popular after the Second World War when they were linked to ideals of Japanese nationalism and middle-class family life, but also to Americanisation (Shunya, 1999). By the 1980s, Japan became a leading centre for the manufacture of consumer electronics, so much so that it has now displaced the West as a symbolic centre for technological lifestyles and cyberculture. As this suggests, the history of domestic technologies is one of uneven development, and highly dependent on national as well as regional and even local contexts of innovation, promotion, and use.

In the United States, the promotion and dissemination of domestic technologies occurred alongside the rise of the private suburban home, the family car, and modern communications institutions (the telephone, radio, and movies), all of which became key indicators of modern life by the early decades of the twentieth century. In this regard, to understand home technologies, we should look less at the historical lineage of single machines than at the collection of ensemble technologies that together help to orchestrate patterns of everyday life. For early adaptors of electrical machines, the private home (constructed with the latest advances in building technologies), the automobile, labour-saving appliances, and an assortment of communications and media devices served as the key ensemble technologies for living a modern life.

That said, technologies in themselves are not domestic by some inherent property or essential nature. In fact, many domestic technologies (including radio, television, microwave ovens, and computers) were initially designed for business or military applications, and later only adapted for domestic use. As Fischer (1992) shows in his history of the telephone, AT&T initially marketed the phone as a business machine to be used mostly by men to convey information in highly rationalised efficient ways. But people (especially women) began to use the telephone to form social networks and maintain personal relations; that is, they used the device in ways that AT&T did not initially intend. In turn, these unintended uses transformed AT&T's marketing approach, and eventually AT&T designed phones in models and colours meant to appeal to female callers, so that a business machine intended for men in the public sphere became a device associated with female friendships in the domestic realm.

More broadly, the proliferation of domestic technologies in the twentieth century was based on larger social-political and economic conditions of power that favoured the private home over public housing and communal residences. Nevertheless, not everyone embraced this techno-domestic ideal. During the Progressive Era, a feminist reform movement argued that the single-family dwelling had led to women's exclusion from public life and the hardships of women of all classes. In response, the 'material feminists' proposed public laundries, communal kitchens, and cooperative housekeeping, all of which used new labour-saving machines by harnessing them to public spaces and collective housing (Hayden, 1982). But this collectivist solution gave way to government-sponsored privatised solutions envisioned most emphatically by then Secretary of Commerce Herbert Hoover's 'Own Your Own Home' campaign of the 1920s, which focused on improvements to the home as a means of augmenting the health and productivity of American workers.

While social reformers and politicians saw modern housing and building technologies as a boon to the American family and workforce, corporations were more interested in creating a mass market for machines, and they stirred public enthusiasm with promotional campaigns that tied enlightenment ideologies of progress to technological advances. This idea was epitomised in the 'homes of tomorrow' that appeared at fairs, international exhibitions, and in popular media, and which corporations like General Electric and Westinghouse used to sell to the public an array of wondrous machines. At the 1933–34 Century of Progress Exhibition in Chicago, visitors could explore a special 'Homes of Tomorrow' section of the fairgrounds, and by the end of the decade, in 1939, the New York World's Fair (dubbed the 'World of Tomorrow') presented an 'America at Home' exhibit with attractions like the Kelvin Home that invited fairgoers to "Step inside and the world of tomorrow awaits you! Daily living brought to the effortless, automatic perfection made possible by the complete electrical home equipment of the Nash-Kelvinator Corporation" (see **Figure 1**). (For the home and citation, see Relevant Websites.)

Despite its consumer ethos, the home of tomorrow was in part inspired by the utopian goals of modernist architects, and in particular the Swiss Architect Le Corbusier who famously pronounced, "The house is a machine for living in" (Le Corbusier, 1923). Applying industrial principles to residential architecture and towns, Le Corbusier saw the house as a central motor of progressive social change. In the United States, visionary architect Buckminster Fuller imagined affordable housing for all through his Dymaxion Dwelling Machine, an octagonal glass structure that he designed on the model of a navy ship with factory-like efficiency, complete with an appliance-filled 'service core'. Fuller's Dymaxion Dwelling Machines was first displayed in 1929 at Marshall Field's Department Store in Chicago. When marketed as a kit in the 1940s, it did not catch on. In the same period, Walter Gropius and Konrad Wachsmann's Packaged House (also a prefabricated mass produced home) was not popular and survived only for a short while. While these visionary architects were interested in the utopian potential of machine aesthetics and presented this with avant-garde designs, corporations were more concerned with selling commodities to consumers, so that despite its utopian gestures, the home of tomorrow functioned mostly as a sales gimmick.

Homes of tomorrow flourished after the Second World War in the context of the new consumer economy and the international competition for technological supremacy and scientific exploration. At the 1964–65 New York World's Fair, General Electric celebrated the history of home technologies with its Carousel of Progress pavilion (built by the Walt Disney Studios). Whisking fairgoers across a series of theatrical scenes of domestic life, the time travel ride featured 32 Audio-Animatronics figures who sang 'There's a Great Big Beautiful Tomorrow' while demonstrating how the American family benefited from electrical appliances over the course of the twentieth century. (The Carrousel of Progress became a central fixture in Disneyland in 1967, replacing MIT's Monsanto home of tomorrow.) The ride begins in a turn-of-the-nineteenth-century home, where dad sits in an easy chair marvelling at the advancements wrought by his new cast iron stove and icebox. Out in the kitchen, mom extols of the joys of her hand powered 'wash day marvel' that allows her to do the wash in 'Just 5 hours, Imagine!' But as the decades pass, the family trades in their old-fashioned iceboxes and coal-powered stoves for an assortment of ever more dazzling gadgets. An automatic washer-dryer, dishwasher, push button conveniences, and a TV set compose an electrifying spectacle of the modern family home by the ride's last stop. The future, GE reminded fairgoers, could be purchased today.

Despite such extraordinary corporate spectacles of social progress through domestic machines, the vision of modern life inscribed in domestic technologies tends to conserve – rather than disrupt – traditional modes of family life, and especially the kinds of families that corporations target as their consumer base. The Carousel of Progress is again a perfect example. While the ride portrays the future as a march of increasingly sophisticated machines, the family itself remains the same throughout the decades. It is consistently a suburban, white, heterosexual nuclear family – the exact kind of family that served as the reigning social ideal for everyday life in cold war America. In fact, in the latter decades of the twentieth century when the Disney theme park updated the Carousel of Progress for contemporary times, the final stop on the ride exhibited only surface adjustments. Although the contemporary home includes video games and has dad cooking in the kitchen, its central cast of characters is still the suburban, white, nuclear family that it had originally showcased in 1964. So, even while marketers promote home technologies as instruments of progress, they also assure consumers that traditional ways of life will remain virtually the same.

Consumer tastes in housing design also reflect this view. Average consumers have historically rejected the avant-garde styling associated with modern architects like Le Corbusier and Fuller, even while they embrace the new technologies on which modern housing is based. At the 'Town of Tomorrow' exhibit at the 1939 New York World's Fair, the architects for a home of tomorrow (built with new advances in insulation) claimed, "In the belief that the majority of people will in the future be still influenced in the selection of their homes by tradition and sentiment, we chose a modification of a Williamsburg Colonial and adapted the design to the modern problem of living... It is our belief that the modern home of tomorrow will be the development of the home of yesterday, adapting new materials, equipment, etc., to the design." (To see images of the house and the 1939 New York World's Fair, see Relevant Websites.)

Paradoxically in this respect, home technologies are based on a curious combination of progress and nostalgia. Certainly, from a marketer's point of view, there are good reasons for this. Aware that consumers may resist new technologies, marketers often associate machines with sentimental visions of family life that hark back to idealised images of bourgeois domesticity in some imagined past. For example, to mitigate fears that television would divide the family and cause conflicts over programme choices or other family squabbles, advertisers often depicted scenes of family togetherness, with mom, dad, and the kids gathered in a circle around the new appliance as if it were a Victorian hearth (Spigel, 1992; Tichi, 1992) (see **Figure 2**). Family circle iconography accompanied early marketing campaigns for television in a wide range

Figure 1 Kelvin home.

Figure 2 Family Circle iconography in an ad for RCA © Television, 1949.

of nations including the United States, Britain, Japan, India, Australia, China, and France, even while family life varied in these places. And despite the decline in nuclear family households (and the rise of single-parent families), it also accompanies the 1980s adverts for the computer, for twenty-first century home theatre devices, and even labour-saving devices. For example, the gourmet kitchen with microwaves, restaurant-style espresso machines, sub-zero wine coolers, flat screen TVs, and Internet access is promoted as a new form of family 'cocooning' that provides a family hub for work and play (Mills, 2008).

So too, in a wide variety of national contexts, advertisements for domestic machines often conjure up nostalgia for a preindustrial, pretechnological past. Writing about America's response to industrialisation more generally, Marx (1964) spoke of the American iconography that placed the 'machine in the garden', depicting technology within natural landscapes. Similarly, ever since the nineteenth century, manufacturers have designed and promoted household machines by adorning them with images of nature. This includes everything from an 1858 manually powered sewing machine designed to look like a squirrel to Samsung's recent ad campaign for 3D TV that shows exotic peacocks, Alaskan huskies, and breathtaking views of the sea on its flat screen plasma TVs. (For the plasma TV ad, see Relevant Websites.) Ironically, even the newest designs for 'smart homes' are often based on a nature motif. Speaking of his digitally enhanced mansion in his book *The Road Ahead*, Microsoft guru Bill Gates (1995) bragged of his use of simulated wood to capture the rustic feel of nature. As in this case, the modern and the premodern coexist.

Labour, Leisure, and Gender

Over the course of the twentieth and twenty-first centuries, domestic technologies have been enmeshed in the gendered practices of labour and leisure that define the modern home. In the early decades of the twentieth century, labour-saving devices were part of a broader philosophy of household efficiency professed by the domestic science movement and meant, in part, to address the shortage of domestic servants in the middle-class home. Orchestrated by Christine Frederick and Lillian Gilbreth (wife of Frank Gilbreth, a leader in the scientific management movement for industry), domestic science entailed the application of industrial factory procedures to the home, emphasising efficiency through a new organisation of domestic space and time. For example, dishwashing was standardised and simplified by breaking the job into three separate operations: scraping and stacking, washing, and drying and putting away. The legacy of the new domestic science was strongly felt both in the United States and in Europe, and it resonated not only with women reformers like Frederick and Gilman, but also with the male-dominated movement of modernist architecture. Time motion studies were of particular interest, for example, at Germany's Bauhaus School in the 1920s where they were applied to architectural designs that eliminated decoration (associated with the Victorian home and women's spaces) and now (in the eyes of the modernist architects) redefined as irrational 'feminine' clutter. In place of Victorian decoration, minimalism and streamlined factory-like kitchens became key to the imagination of a well-organised home. Despite the industrial and often anti-feminine associations of this streamlined factory aesthetic, industry counted on female consumers to buy the new labour-saving devices that went hand in hand with domestic science and streamlined design. Frederick popularised her new domestic science in a series of articles for *Ladies' Home Journal*. Her role as popular adviser expanded in the 1920s when she became an advertising consultant and published *Selling Mrs. Consumer* (1929), a kind of how to guide for admen that promised to teach them how to sell goods to the woman of the house.

In the 1920s and 1930s, marketers developed advertising and promotional campaigns aimed at Mrs. Consumer. Some ads flattered the housewife by elevating her status in the home from that of domestic drudge to household manager and engineer. For example, an ad for the appliance company N.W. Ayer & Son dubbed the 'the modern housewife' a 'General Purchasing Agent' congratulating her for running her home "quite as efficiently as her husband does the business—perhaps more so." (Marchand, 1986: 168–169). Other ads provoked anxiety by warning women that they would lose their girlish looks (and implicitly, therefore, their husbands) if they continued do the housework in the old-fashioned way. More upbeat ads assured the housewife that new electrical servants would liberate her from a life of tedium and isolation, allowing her to partake in exciting leisure-time activities associated with social mobility. Advertisements for stoves, percolators, dishwashers, and the like depicted women freed from labour, playing tennis or going shopping while their kitchens did the work (Marchand, 1986; Schwartz Cowan, 1976) (**Figure 3**).

By the 1940s, and especially in the postwar era, the idea of women's liberation through technical means came to a dramatic pitch in the 'kitchen of tomorrow'. After the consumer shortages of the Second World War, and as women wartime workers were being rechannelled back to their homes, advertisers were eager to convince women that being back at home with wondrous machines was the ultimate freedom in the free world. In England, the 1954 Ideal Home Exhibition promoted modern appliances as part of a postwar domestic ideal tied to national uplift. One publicity photo showed the newly married Queen Elizabeth gazing longingly at a dishwasher at the exhibit, implicitly tying the purchase of domestic machines to national agendas (Sparke, 1995: 170). Industrial ads and television commercials delivered a similar message. In 1952, the Whirlpool Corporation promoted its new washer-dryers in 'Mother Takes a Holiday', a short sponsored film featuring a group of high-school girls who sit around a kitchen table searching for topics to write about for their homework assignment. Inspired by the purchase of her family's new Whirlpool washer-dryer units, Marilyn (the cleverest girl in the group) suggests that they write about how household appliances have emancipated American women. (For the film, see www.archive.org.)

The advent of automation, push buttons, and remote controls served only to multiply such claims. Although such devices were already on the horizon by the late nineteenth century, it was in the mid-century period, in the context of the space race, that push buttons and remotes became associated with a new kind of space-age domesticity – the utmost in modern living. Advertisers showed women in command, navigating their automated kitchens as if they were astronauts flying to the moon. In 1956, General Motors presented one such space-age housewife in *Design for Dreaming*, an elaborate sponsored film that shows a woman in a dream kitchen who, by the press of button, cooks a meal, bakes a cake, and then flies off on a 'highway of tomorrow' where she drives in a rocket-powered car with her dreamboat date (who operates the futuristic steering wheel). (The film is available online at www.archive.org.) In scenarios like these (see **Figure 5**), the dazzling new technologies of space-age culture maintained familiar gender roles, even as they promised a spectacular escape. In fact, the idea of liberation through home technologies was so much part of the postwar world that in 1959, when then American Vice President Richard Nixon opened the American National Exhibition in Moscow, his attempted diplomatic gesture resulted in the shamefully famous 'kitchen debate' in which he touted the conveniences of American kitchen appliances while Soviet Premier Nikita Khrushchev boasted of his nation's substantial achievements in hard science and rocketry.

Meanwhile, for housewives, dreams of technologically enhanced liberation have never amounted to that in practice. In her historical study of women's work in the twentieth century, Schwartz Cowan (1983) found that the time women spent on unpaid household labour did not significantly decrease but was instead redefined so that even as labour-saving devices helped with chores, women were expected to spend more time on childrearing and other nurturing activities, including their new twentieth-century role as Mrs. Consumer. Today, a similar paradox holds true as the time saved from the use of labour-saving devices is channelled back into new forms of work, particularly at a time when the hours spent on paid labour have expanded (Schor, 1993) and when more people are doing work via digital technologies at home. Nevertheless, ideals of liberation and progress continue to ignite powerful sentiments about what it means to live in a modern home with modern machines, sentiments that are just as prevalent in twenty-first century digital culture as they were in the twentieth century, particularly (as we shall see) in relation to the new technologies of the smart home.

Figure 3 Westinghouse ©, 1923.

Media Technologies and Private/Public Spaces

Domestic technologies are not just confined to the four walls of the home; they are also intimately related to larger patterns of community and commerce in public life. Increasingly in the twentieth century, domestic appliances and other luxury goods replaced community facilities; refrigerators, for example, minimised the extent to which residents had to leave the home to purchase fresh goods, while washer-dryers made it unnecessary to visit public laundries. This dynamic is especially evident with communications and media technologies that connect the home to far off places and bring information and entertainment into the private world.

Considering the history of telecommunications, cultural theorist Raymond Williams (1975: 26–28) coined the term 'mobile privitisation', a phenomenon he tied to the simultaneous rise of privatised suburban housing and mobile urban industrial centres in the latter decades of the nineteenth century. The advent of telecommunications, Williams argues, offered people the ability to maintain ideals of privacy while providing the mobility required by industrialisation, and broadcasting in particular held out the promise of bringing the public world indoors. In this respect, media technologies like radio and television offer the ability to travel 'imaginatively' to distant locales (and to commune with virtual strangers) while ensconced in the safe space of the home.

In the most literal sense, television is often considered a replacement for theatrical experiences in the public sphere. In the United States, for example, television's rise in the 1950s correlated with decreased box office sales at the movies. But even before this, in the early 1900s, popular critics speculated on the ability of home technologies to approximate theatrical experiences for the resident (Boddy, 2004; Spigel, 1992). By the 1950s, when TV was heavily promoted in the United States and Britain, advertisers often referred to television as a 'home theatre', 'armchair theatre', 'family theatre' and like, while women's magazines and books on interior décor instructed homemakers on ways to arrange their rooms to approximate a theatrical viewing situation. Following the more general technological claims for women's liberation, advertisers often suggested that the new home theatres would provide women an imaginary escape from the isolating role of housewife. Ads in women's magazines showed couples dressed in ballroom gowns and tuxedoes while watching TV in their living rooms, as if they were out for a night on the town. Ironically, sociological studies revealed that women feared television's isolating effects on their lives, and numerous articles in women's magazines discussed television as a potential threat to romance that would compete for their husband's attention (Spigel, 1992).

Nevertheless, the home theatre concept continues through to the present, and its promise of simulated social life has morphed into elaborate forms of display with the contemporary 50+ inch flat screens and surround-sound components that promise to envelop the resident in a complete audiovisual environment. Magazines like *Electronic Home* and *Home Theater* show rooms designed to look like Hollywood movie palaces of the 1920s, sports bars, and the like. Home theatres are internationally marketed so that, for example, a 2001 ad for Samsung Digital TV shows an Indian family watching TV while sitting on the floor in front of a stack of pillows and an Indian-woven rug, summoning up nostalgia for traditional Indian life while embracing a global technology (Kumar, 2006: 89).

Although the 'home theatre' emphasises family cannoning, television has also often been promoted as a 'window on the world' that provides a kind of virtual tourism. Even before media guru McLuhan (1964) predicted that television and satellite technologies would create a new 'global village', in the late 1940s and 1950s marketers and industry spokespeople used the window analogy to promote TV. So too, advertisers placed TV sets against scenic backdrops suggestive of the exotic locales that television promised to make domestic. In 1953, Arvin's advertising campaign used the Eiffel Tower and Big Ben as backdrops for its TV sets while Emerson TV showed a television floating in outer space, offering consumers an imaginary trip to the moon (Spigel, 1992: 105). The DuMont Corporation even promoted its TV set as an 'Armchair Columbus' (see **Figure 4**). In Germany, a 1956 ad for Philips TV showed a housewife sitting in a modern-styled chair watching a TV set placed against a background that displays a futuristic car driving down a bridge on what appears to be a city of tomorrow. This fantasy of armchair mobility and virtual tourism continues with the global marketing for wide-screen TV. In 1996, the Indian company Videocon marketed its 'double wide window' TV that was, according to the ad, "bringing the world to India" (Kumar, 1996: p. 80).

In a related strategy, in the 1960s, advertisers for portable television sets promised consumers that TV was not only a window on the world, but also a way to extend one's private life into public places. Unlike the 1950s console model that was placed in the central area of the family home, ads for portable receivers often showed people on the move, carrying their tote-able TV sets to beaches, picnics, and even, in one humorous 1967 Sony ad, nudist colonies (Spigel, 2001: 77). Rather than homebodies gathered round the family tube, now spectators were presented as adventurous heroes toting portables on motorcycles or to the gym, or else as liberated women wearing mini-skirts accessorised by mini-TV's that looked like purses. Product design enhanced this experience as sets were made to look like luggage and adorned

YOU'LL BE AN ARMCHAIR COLUMBUS!

You'll sail with television through vanishing horizons into exciting new worlds. You'll be an intimate of the great and near-great. You'll sit at speakers' tables at historic functions, down front at every sporting event, at all top-flight entertainment. News flashes will bring you eye-coverage of parades, fires and floods; of everything odd, unusual and wonderful, just as though you were on the spot. And far-sighted industry will show you previews of new products, new delights ahead.

All this—the world actually served to you on a silver screen—will be most enjoyably yours when you possess a DuMont Television-Radio Receiver. It was DuMont who gave really *clear* picture reception to television. It will be DuMont to whom you will turn in peacetime for the finest television receiving sets and the truest television reception...the touchstone that will make you an armchair Columbus on ten-thousand-and-one thrilling voyages of discovery!

DuMONT *Precision Electronics and Television*

ALLEN B. DuMONT LABORATORIES, INC., GENERAL OFFICES AND PLANT, 2 MAIN AVENUE, PASSAIC, N. J.
TELEVISION STUDIOS AND STATION W2XWV, 515 MADISON AVENUE, NEW YORK 22, NEW YORK

Figure 4 DuMont ©, 1944.

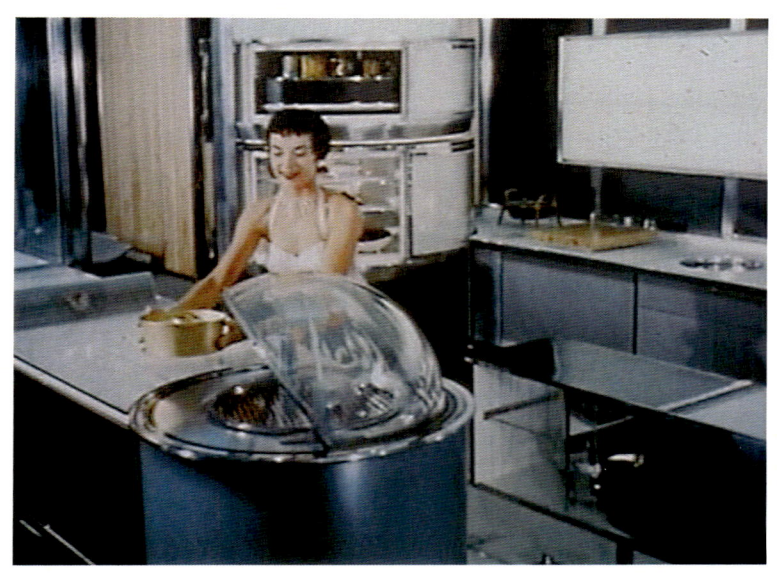

Figure 5 *Design for Dreaming*, 1956.

with product names like the RCA 'Globe Trotter' or GE 'Adventurer'. In this regard, the advent of portable TV inverted the experience of 'mobile privatisation' that Williams first associated with telecommunications. Instead, portable television offered people a fantasy of 'privatised mobility' in which residents could imagine being outdoors while actually still watching TV inside the home. Indeed, despite the new designs and advertising rhetoric, market research showed that people almost never moved the portable set inside the home, no less outdoors (Spigel, 2001).

Today, digital mobile technologies (like PDAs, lap tops, and iphones) continue to be promoted as means by which to transcend relations between domestic interiors and the outside world, and to experience forms of mobile privatisation and privatised mobility. Ads for the iphone and other mobile devices show people on the move, recalling much of the advertising rhetoric for portable TV (Dawson, 2007). Studies of mobile devices (from the car stereo system to the walkman to the cell phone to the ipod) suggest that people use them both to create private and even protective bubbles around themselves and to experience a sense of home while away (Bull, 2004; du Gay, Hall, Janes, and Mackay, 1997; Flichy, 1995). In her interview-based study of mobile phone use in Morocco, Kriem (2009) found that people who feel alienated in urban environments use the mobile phone to connect back to home and family. More broadly, Tomilson (2001: 17) argues that mobile phones should be seen as "technologies of the hearth ... by which people try to maintain something of the security of cultural location." Expanding this, Morley (2007: 224) observes that mobiles allow us to "take our homes with us, just as a tortoise stays in his shell, wherever it travels." In this respect, mobile communication devices promote a kind of homeless domesticity in which people are both away while at home and at home while in public. This double fantasy of spatial derealisation defines the contemporary moment, and is found most emphatically in the newest of household technologies – the fully digitised smart home.

Smart Homes: From Homes with Media to Homes as Media

Since the 1980s, dreams of progress and liberation through domestic technology have resurfaced, although in a mutated form, with the rise of the smart home and related smart technologies. A smart house is a networked house whose appliances interact with each other, adapt to dwellers, and allow residents, via the Internet, to communicate with the outside world and to speak to the home while away at work or travel. In their most elaborated form, smart homes work through post-desk-top ubiquitous computing in which information processing no longer is tied to a specific machine located in a central place, but is instead all around us, thoroughly integrated into everyday objects and activities. Cupboards, washing machines, doors, media screens, and windows can now interact with each other and with residents to perform chores, share information, and create an assortment of daily experiences.

The smart home also responds to the changing nature of community, and like communications and media technologies before it, the smart home is based on the paradox of mobile privatisation and privatised mobility. But rather than just a window on the world that brings vistas of reality into the home, the smart home interfaces with information and services in the outside world. In its 'House 2000' exhibit home in Tokyo, for example, Panasonic displayed a smart toilet that can analyse urine and call your doctor with the results. In more fantastic architectural projects, smart homes are imagined as extensions of human bodies and community formations. In a speculative (unbuilt) project called the 'Digital House' (which was commissioned by the magazine *House Beautiful*) architects Gisue Hariri and Mogin Hariri imagined a home whose smart skin (a high-tech edifice) welcomes in virtual guests and even a virtual chef (see **Figure 6**). Michael Trudgeon and Anthony Kitchener's 'Hyper House Pavilion 5' (unbuilt, 1998) transmits messages to its neighbours on its electrochromic glass walls, so that the house actually does the job of neighbourliness for its residents (Riley, 1999; Spigel, 2005). In this sense, whereas the twentieth-century home of tomorrow was a house filled with wondrous machines, today's smart home is itself a communication device through which artefacts and humans relate to each other and to the world at large.

Given the complexity of its aims, the smart house is the product of global alliances among architects, engineers, computer scientists, university research labs, the residential housing industry, telecommunication companies, computer and home entertainment manufacturers, and interior designers, all of whom are in the business of promoting new forms of social interaction among people and their things. Like previous homes of tomorrow, the smart house has been ushered in with a wave of utopian predictions. Key among these is the promise that smart homes will provide greener environments, more mobility (via telerobotics) for physically challenged and ageing populations, and increased safety for residents. Smart house engineers and product designers stress values of interactivity and human productivity over the leisure and sedentary lifestyles that twentieth-century electrical servants and automation promised. Yet, as with the older homes of tomorrow, the corporations sponsoring the research and design know that consumers are wary of unfamiliar futures. In response, they primarily envision the future in relation to middle-class residential housing and the people who can afford smart lifestyles.

Given their corporate control and prospective consumers, it is not surprising that the most advertised features of residential smart homes are the twin middle-class goals of homeownership – lifestyle enhancement and convenience on the one hand, and privacy and surveillance on the other hand. Elaborate home theatres, dream kitchens, and electronic eyes adorn the home with comfort and safety, thereby ensuring that while technology advances, once again domestic ideals remain the same. In this respect, the consumer promotion of smart homes and appliances is very much in line with the logic of nostalgia; like the Carousel of Progress, the smart house is a future where people can acquire new technologies without experiencing radical social change.

Still, even while smart homes conserve middle-class ideals of property and privacy, they are also a product of contemporary changes in everyday life. One of the key changes revolves around gendered patterns of housekeeping. Whereas the old electrical servants were promoted pragmatically as time-saving devices that could liberate housewives, the new intelligent appliances do not just do the chores. They virtually become the housewife as they perform the managerial and care-taking roles previously ascribed to women. For example, like ideal mothers, smart appliances anticipate your needs. Smart fridges do not just store food, they know when you have run out of milk or tuna and order more for you by sending a signal to the market. Corporations like IBM's subsidiary Home Director, Microsoft's Universal Plug and Play, Macintosh's Xtension home, and Intel's Digital Home Fund have hooked up with appliance companies like GE and Maytag to produce 'integrated systems' that orchestrate not only internal household tasks (like cooking or cleaning), but also dialogues (increasingly via Wi-Fi) between and among household devices and even between appliances and things. So, for example, the bar code on the frozen dinner you buy at the market will be able to prompt your microwave oven to follow manufacturer's cooking instructions.

Smart homes also respond to changing configurations of wage labour, and in particular, the increased entry of women into the labour force and the extension of the work clock (from the 9–5 schedule of Fordist factory time to post-Fordist extended work schedules in which work and leisure are increasingly coterminous). As opposed to the labour/leisure binary that accompanied the twentieth-century home of the future, architectural renderings and product advertisements for smart homes

Figure 6 Virtual chef. © Hariri and Hariri, Digital House, 1998.

show people engaged simultaneously in leisure and labour pursuits. A prototypical image here is the June 1996 cover of *Wired*. The cover shows Microsoft CEO Bill Gates floating in his pool, wearing smiley face swim trunks with his signature nerd glasses while talking on his mobile (Caruso, 1996). Lest the imagery fool you, the article reassures readers that Gates is not just sunning himself; he is actually quite busy turning his empire into a full-blown media company. This work-play imagery has since become an advertising convention in ads promoting smart homes and mobile technologies. For example, the August 2003 issue of *Digital Home* (**Figure 7**) shows a classically beautiful couple in swimwear at poolside while talking on mobiles and working on laptops while a 2001 issue of *Broadband House* shows dad swimming in a pool while doing business on his mobile (Digital Home, 2003: cover; Cleaver, 2001–2002: 59). Meanwhile, architectural designs show computer screens in bedrooms that display stock market reports or work schedules so that even sleep is colonised by the daily grind of labour (Spigel, 2010). Here as elsewhere, the truly successful business tycoon simultaneously works and plays. The ultimate paradox, then, is that the postmodern luxury home has become the ultimate work terminal – a place where the resident is in a perpetually interactive state of preparedness – never allowed to simply waste time. Whereas Thorstein Veblen (1899) famously coined the phrase 'conspicuous consumption' to characterise the bourgeois lifestyles at the turn of the nineteenth century, today media industries promote a lifestyle of 'conspicuous production' where leisure and labour activities are wholly intertwined.

The lifestyle aesthetic of conspicuous production circulates in a social context in which households are increasingly composed of two-parent or single-parent workers who juggle child rearing with careers. The installation of the home computer (which proliferated in the 1980s) and the subsequent marketing of mobile technologies allow people to place-shift and time-shift between work and family on a daily basis. (In the United States, for example, according to a September 2008 Pew Research Center study, "Nearly half of all working Americans do at least some work from home, and 'Overall, 56% of networked workers report some at-home work and 20% say they do so 'everyday or almost every day'." In addition, "networked workers ... are more likely than average Americans to have access to a wide array of technological assets outside the workplace" that enable work not just at home, but on the go (Madden and Jones, 2008).) To be sure, these technologies can offer people real advantages; nevertheless, smart homes are embedded in familiar gender divisions. In magazine articles and ads promoting smart technologies the labour of housekeeping is still imagined as women's work even as her work expands to include wage labour (in form of office work, telecommuting, etc). Marketing campaigns for smart home technologies typically show women in home offices multitasking as they mix housewife chores and mothering with paid labour at home. Rather than the 1920s ads that offered women liberation and leisure, today women are portrayed as superwomen who are able to maintain a successful career and family life through the skilful orchestration of labour-saving and home office technologies. Ads and articles in home electronics magazines show women working on their PCs while changing diapers or cooking meals while e-mailing into work. Studies suggest that even while some women may welcome the ability to work at home, women's multitasking roles, nevertheless, are creating personal tensions for them and their families (Burke, 2003; Lally, 2002).

More generally, despite their pro-social possibilities and the positive social advances they may perform, corporately engineered smart homes and devices raise important questions about the future of family life. Smart technologies are not just conveniences for the resident; they are also based on Internet feedback loops between residents and market researchers who track behaviours. For example, the digital video recorder (DVR) extracts personal data from the choices you make on your TV set and stores that data for future use (which sometimes also includes selling your data to other corporations). The same is true for numerous Internet shopping sites. An entire home based on this kind of feedback loop creates the potential for the increasing stronghold of observational science and market research in private life. So, at its most chilling extreme, the smart house opens up new questions about surveillance, control, and personal freedom in the domestic realm (Allon, 2004; Andrejevic, 2009; Heckman, 2008).

In addition, the smart house and smart technologies raise fundamental questions about social life and community relations. In neoliberal societies where individuals are asked to take responsibility for themselves and to accept (and even embrace) the waning of public services, smart homes suggest that more and more of these services will be privatised through technological band-aid solutions to deep social wounds. Insofar as the smart home future is expensive, the digital divide compounds the historical inequalities in housing and in this respect, despite the utopian claims of the engineers and product designers, the digital home may well aggravate social disparities (at least without any social polices to provide equitable access).

Conclusion: Fabulous Futures and Domestic Dystopias

As these concerns suggest, the utopian ideals of progress, liberation, and control that have accompanied the innovation

Figure 7 Cover of *Digital Home*, August 2003.

of domestic technologies are not without their detractors. Running parallel to the marketing and public enthusiasm for domestic technologies is a counternarrative that gives voice to fundamental fears and anxieties about the industrialisation of the home. Stories about domestic technologies out of control have multiplied over the course of the twentieth and twenty-first centuries. Take, for example, Buster Keaton's *The Electric House* (1922) where Keaton is outdone by a set of domestic contrivances including an escalator-like staircase on which he hilariously tumbles and an automated pool in which he nearly drowns. Similarly, Warner Brother's 'Merrie Melody' *Dog Gone Modern* (1939) features two cartoon dogs who visit a home of tomorrow only to be assaulted by an assembly of robot sweepers, overambitious dishwashers, and sentient napkin folders that inflict all kinds of harms and humiliations on the unsuspecting canines. Science fiction stories present comparable tales, but rather than laughter they provoke uncanny terror. Ray Bradbury's short story 'There Will Come Soft Rains' (1950) features a sentient home where a lonesome toaster and sorrowful stove mourn their missing residents who die in a nuclear blast. *Forbidden Planet*'s (1956) space-age dream house turns out, in the tradition of false utopias, to be a mad scientist's trap. *The Stepford Wives* (1975) depicts a seemingly ideal suburban community that turns out to be a corporate plot in which sinister husbands turn their women's lib'-inspired wives into docile housewife robots. Not surprisingly, in this regard, while today's consumer magazines, corporations, and smart home designers project utopian futures, films like Disney's *Smart Home* (1999) tell unnerving stories about digital homes with plans to destroy their owners, while others like Steven Spielberg's *AI* (2001) and Jon Favreau's *Iron Man* (2008), present uncanny visions of smart homes in corporately engineered futures.

While these spectacles of mechanised mayhem and uncanny dread are certainly hyperbolic, they exist alongside more sober apprehensions about mechanised society that have surfaced in both intellectual and popular circles over the course of modern times. Will automation put an end to human control and deskill the workforce? Will home office technologies disintegrate the separation between home and work and turn the home into a high-tech sweatshop? Will the telephone, television, computer, the Internet, and smart devices invade our private lives or corrupt our children? Or, in more positive terms, can new technologies help to sustain a greener environment, enhance independent living for physically challenged or elderly populations, or provide spaces better equipped to help single parents juggle home and work? Domestic technologies have historically opened up a whole series of debates about the future that go way beyond their technical possibilities, and into larger questions about the nature of home, family, and community in the modernised world.

Today, as new smart technologies are being ushered in with a wave of both utopian fanfare and dystopian dread, they provide an opportunity not only to think about technology qua technology, but also to think about housing, community, and the way people (ideally) want to live. Indeed, just as the material feminists of the early 1920s argued against the private home and its consumer technologies as a model for everyday life, today we can continue to question how the conjuncture between technological innovation and private residence will affect social welfare for all populations, and not just the propertied classes who have historically been the target consumers for domestic technologies and tomorrow's homes. To be sure, despite over a century worth of marketing and promotion, technologies on their own do not liberate people or create social progress, and they certainly do not ensure democratic housing for all. But they are also not the monstrous machines imagined in dystopian science fiction. Domestic technologies are not static things with closed and predictable effects; they are historically and geographically contingent tools that help to express, construct, maintain, and transform social ideals and practices of everyday life. As such, they are also tools through which to imagine alternatives to contemporary social disparities in housing and community across the globe.

References

Allon F (2004) An ontology of everyday control: space, media flows and "Smart" living in the absolute present. In: Couldry N and McCarthy A (eds.) *Mediaspace: Place, Scale and Culture in a Media Age*, pp. 253–275. London: Routledge.

Andrejevic M (2009) *I Spy: Surveillance and Power in the Interactive Age*: University of Kentucky Press, 2007.

Boddy W (2004) *New Media and the Popular Imagination: Launching Television, Radio, and Digital Media in the United States*. London: Oxford.

Bull M (2004) To each their own bubble: Mobile spaces of sound in the city. In: Couldry N and McCarthy A (eds.) *Mediaspace*, pp. 275–293. New York, NY: Routledge.

Burke C (2003) Women, Guilt and Home Computers. In Turow J and Kavanaugh Al (eds.) *The Wired Homestead: An MIT Sourcebook on the Internet and the Family*, pp. 325–336. Cambridge, MA: MIT Press.

Caruso D (1996) Microsoft morphs into a media company. *Wired*, cover and 126–130.

Cleaver J (2001–2002) Say hello to the house of tomorrow. *Broadband House*: 56–63.

Colomina B (2007) *Domesticity at War*. Cambridge, MA: MIT Press.

Dawson M (2007) Little players, big shows: Format, narration and style on television's smaller screens. *Convergence* 13(3): 231–250.

Digital Home (August 2003), cover.

Du Gay P, Hall S, Janes L, and Mackay H (1997) *Doing Cultural Studies: The Story of the Sony Walkman*. London: Sage.

Fischer CS (1992) *America Calling: A Social History of the Telephone to 1940*. Berkeley, CA: University of California Press.

Flichy P (1995) *Dynamics of Modern Communication*. London: Sage.

Forty A (1986) *Objects of Desire: Design and Society from Wedgewood to IBM*. New York: Pantheon.

Frederick CM (1929) *Selling Mrs. Consumer*. New York: Business Bourse.

Frohlich D, Dray S, and Silverman A (2003) Breaking up is hard to do: Family perspectives on the future of the home PC. In: Turow J and Kavanaugh AL (eds.) *The Wired Homestead*, pp. 291–324.

Gates B (1995) *The Road Ahead*. New York: Viking.

Giedion S (1955; Reprinted 1969) *Mechanization Takes Command*. New York: W.W. Norton & Co.

Hayden D (1982) *The Grand Domestic Revolution: A History of Feminist Designs for American Homes, Neighborhoods, and Cities*. Cambridge, MA: MIT Press.

Heckman D (2008) *A Small World: Smart Houses and the Dream of the Perfect Day*. Durham, NC: Duke University Press.

Historical Statistics of the United States (1960) Washington, DC: Government Printing Office.

Holiday LS (2001) Kitchen technologies: Promises and alibis, 1944–1966. *Camera Obscura* 47(2): 79–130.

Horrigan B (1986) The home of tomorrow, 1927–1945. In: Corn JJ (ed.) *Imagining Tomorrow, History, Technology, and the American Future*, pp. 137–163. Cambridge: MIT Press.

Kriem MS (2009) Mobile telephony in morocco: A changing sociality. *Media, Culture & Society* 31(3): 617–632.

Kumar S (2005) *Ghandi Meets Primetime: Globalization and Nationalism in Indian Television*. Champaign-Urbana: University of Illinois Press.

Lally E (2002) *At Home with Computers*. Oxford, UK: Berg.

Le Corbusier (1923; Reprinted 2007) *Toward an Architecture*. Los Angeles: Getty Publications.

Lull J (1990) *Inside Family Viewing*. London: Comedia.

Lupton E (1996) *Mechanical Brides: Women and Machines from Home to Office Princeton*. New York: Princeton Architectural Press.

Lupton E and Miller AJ (1996) *The Bathroom, The Kitchen, and the Aesthetics of Waste*. Princeton, NJ: Princeton Architectural Press.

Madden M and Jones S (2008). 'Networked Workers', Pew Internet and Life Project. http://www.perinternet.org/Reports/2008/Networked-Workers.aspx (accessed).

Marchand R (1986) *Advertising the American Dream: Making Way for Modernity, 1920–40*. Berkeley, CA: University of California Press.

Marvin C (1990) *When Old Technologies Were New: Thinking about Electric Communication in the Late Nineteenth Century*. New York: Oxford University Press.

Marx L (1964) *The Machine In the Garden: Technology and the Pastoral Ideal in America*. New York: Oxford.

McLuhan M (1964: Reprinted 1994) *Understanding Media: The Extensions of Man*. Cambridge, MA: MIT Press.

Mills K (2008) 'Tech Kitchens', *Home Entertainment*, November 27, 2008, http://www.hemagazine.com (accessed 1 February 2009).

Morley D (1985) *Family Television: Cultural Power and Domestic Leisure*. London: Routledge.

Morley D (2007) *Media, Modernity and Technology: The Geography of the New*, pp. 199–234. London: Routledge.

Oldenziel R and Zachman K (eds.) (2009) *Cold War Kitchen: Americanization, Technology, and European Users*. Cambridge, MA: MIT Press.

Riley T (1999) *The Un-Private House (exhibition catalog)*. New York: Museum of Modern Art.

Rutherford JW (2003) *Selling Mrs. Consumer: Christine Frederick and the Rise of Household Efficiency*. Georgia: University of Georgia Press.

Schor J (1993) *The Overworked American: The Unexpected Decline of Leisure*. New York: Basic Books.

Schwartz Cowan R (1976) The industrial revolution in the home: Household technology and social change in the twentieth century. *Technology and Culture* 17(1): 1–23.

Schwartz Cowan R (1983) *More Work for Mother: The Ironies of Household Technology from the Open Hearth to the Microwave*. New York: Basic Books.

Shunya Y (1999) Made in Japan": The cultural politics of "Home Electrification" in Postwar Japan. *Media, Culture & Society* 21(2): 149–171.

Silverstone R (1994) *Television and Everyday Life*. London: Taylor and Francis.

Silverstone R and Hirsch E (1992) *Media and Information Technologies in Domestic Spaces*. London: Routledge.

Sparke P (1987) *An Introduction to Design and Culture: 1900 to the Present*. London: Icon.

Sparke P (1995) *As Long as It's Pink: The Sexual Politics of Taste*. London: Pandora Press.

Spigel (1992) *Make Room for TV: Television and the Family Ideal in Postwar America*. Chicago, IL: University of Chicago Press.

Spigel (2001) *Welcome to the Dreamhouse: Popular Media and Postwar Suburbs*. Durham, NC: Duke University Press.

Spigel (2005) Designing the smart house: Posthuman domesticity and conspicuous production. *European Journal of Cultural Studies* 8(4): 403–426.

Spigel (2010) Digital lifestyles: Practiced and imagined. In: Grisprud J (ed.) *Relocating Television*, pp. 238–255. London: Routledge.

Tichi C (1992) *Electronic Hearth: Creating an American Television Culture*. New York: Oxford University Press.

Tomilson J (2001) *Instant Access: Some Cultural Implications of "Globalizing" Technologies*, University of Copenhagen: Global Media Cultures Working Paper No. 13.

Veblen T (1899; reprinted 2008) *The Theory of the Leisure Class*. London: Oxford.

Williams R (1975) *Television, Technology and Cultural Form*. New York: Schocken Books.

Further Reading

Baudrillard J (2006) *The System of Objects*. Trans. James Benedict. London: Verso.

Turow J and Kavanaugh Al (eds.) (2003) *The Wired Homestead: An MIT Sourcebook on the Internet and the Family*. Cambridge, MA: MIT Press.

Relevant Websites

http://library.duke.edu – Ad*Access, John W. Hartman Center for Sales, Advertising, and Marketing History, Duke University Libraries.

http://library.duke.edu – AdViews: A Digital Archive of Vintage Television Commercials, Duke University Libraries.

www.dsrny.com – Diller, Sofidio, and Renfro Slow House and Phantom House (speculative architecture for homes and digital media).

www.tvhistory.tv – Early German TV Ad.

www.haririandhariri.com – Hariri and Hariri Digital Home.

www.greatachievements.org – History of Household Machines.

http://architecture.mit.edu – MIT architecture.

www.internetworldstats.com – Internet World Statistics.

www.archive.org – Mother Takes a Holiday.

www.mztv.com – MZTV Museum of Television.

www.pmphoto.to – 1939 New York World's Fair – The Town of Tomorrow House # 15.

www.pmphoto.to – 1939 New York World's Fair – The Town of Tomorrow House # 16.

www.pewinternet.org – Pew Internet and American Life Project.

www.perinternet.org – Pew Internet and Life Project.

www.plasma.com – Plasma TV Ad.

Domestic Violence

P Meth, University of Sheffield, Sheffield, UK

© 2012 Elsevier Ltd. All rights reserved.

Glossary

Domestic violence Violence that occurs between former or current intimate partners or family members.

Introduction

The concept 'domestic violence' is contested and defined differently by individuals, institutions, and nations, but usually refers to violence between intimate partners. Domestic violence occurs within widely varying cultural, sociopolitical, and legal contexts across the world. In highly patriarchal societies, such as in the Middle East or Africa, the problematisation of domestic violence is often limited, legal sanctions may be weak, or ignored by the state, the community, perpetrators, and even victims. Conversely, where sociopolitical transition has occurred, an appreciation of domestic violence as a criminal problem may have risen, leading to its incorporation into criminal–legal frameworks (see, e.g., changes to legislation in South Africa following its progressive constitution post 1994).

Definitions of domestic violence change over time, for example, there is a current preference within global policy circles for the term 'intimate partner violence' (IPV) in place of domestic violence in an effort to emphasise the relational nature of the crime (WHO, 2005). Recognition of what constitutes domestic violence is culturally informed, and thus incorporating emotional abuse, and rape within marriage, has proved more difficult, in comparison with recognition of physical abuse.

The Home Office in the United Kingdom defines domestic violence as follows:

> 'any violence between current and former partners in an intimate relationship, wherever the violence occurs. The violence may include physical, sexual, emotional and financial abuse.' Domestic violence occurs across society regardless of age, gender, race, sexuality, wealth and geography. And the Crown Prosecution Service includes family members in addition to partners. (UK Home Office, 2009)

Domestic violence is distinguishable from other forms of violence, in particular stranger, civil, and state-sponsored violence. The social relationship between perpetrator and victim, that of current or previous partnership (or family), is a key feature. The UK Home Office definition acknowledges that violence can occur 'across society' and is symbolic of a more progressive awareness of differential relations of sexuality. This awareness counters the historic tendency to equate domestic violence with 'wife-bashing by men', as, although this gendered stereotype is statistically dominant, it has the negative effect of overlooking violence committed by women, violence between homosexual partners, and violence committed by other family members. This article, however, will focus largely on the relationship between men (as 'perpetrator') and women (as 'victim').

A focus on the home, housing, and homelessness is central to understanding the materiality and politics of domestic violence, although not necessarily in obvious ways. Domestic violence is not confined to the home space. Attacks take place in public and work places. However, the majority of incidences occur within the home (or the place where someone lives) and thus for scholars interested in problematising the home, and geographies of homelessness, the concept of domestic violence provides much scope for reflection. This article argues that the interconnections between home, homelessness, and domestic violence are complicated by the prevalence of multiple housing types and varied living arrangements, which sit within wider cultural, political, and economic contexts that intimately shape experiences of domestic violence. Home also has great symbolic meaning, and is imbued with emotion, and values about tranquility, privacy, and belonging. Experiences of domestic violence fundamentally challenge these meanings and in contrast can construct a home as a 'prison' or a space of fear. These emotional meanings of home intersect with the aforementioned wider institutional and material processes, and these are explored in relation to the consumption of home explained later. The article turns to an examination of these arguments, but first reminds the reader that domestic violence is a complex social and power relationship, which is shaped by, and in turn shapes spatial elements (particularly the home).

Power Relations and Domestic Violence

The power relations of domestic violence are not simply those of the (physical) inequality between perpetrator and victim; but rather the inequality borne of financial, social, and cultural dependency of women on men, and the wider politics of the social and political system within which domestic violence takes place. These power relations work to (often) disempower women and to undermine their ability to leave violent partners.

Domestic violence is inherently gendered, whereby gender is understood to be a social relationship between men and women. Violence between same sex partners is also gendered in complex ways as they are structured by relations of masculinity and femininity that embody power inequalities. Feminist academics and activists have contributed to rethinking domestic violence as something beyond a criminal offence and an act of violence, and have argued that its practice is tied to wider patriarchal dominance (the power of men over women). Domestic violence by men towards women forms one explicit component of this, across many societies in the world and is a way in which patriarchal structures, norms, and practices are entrenched and reinforced. In this respect, domestic violence is fundamentally a power practice, where the perpetrator uses violence to hold power over someone(s) else. Men use violence to maintain their control over household decision-making (expenditure, employment, consumption, etc.); choices over sexuality and reproduction; decisions about children, family, health, and education; and crucially to curb the freedoms or independence of women where this is perceived to undermine their (men's) power. In addition to the social relationship between men and women, the physical and biological differences between men and women, whereby women are generally weaker than men in contexts of self-defence, underpin the relative prevalence of domestic violence and the devastating outcomes for many female victims. The home is intimately implicated in the power relations of domestic violence because of its multiple social, material, cultural, and economic functions. The home is a gendered space, and the politics of homemaking, homeownership, family, affordability, and housing support, all intersect with the power relations identified earlier. The home is not simply the stage on which domestic violence unfolds, but rather it is part of the relation.

The power relations of domestic violence are not, however, unidirectional: perpetrator over victim. In addition to the power dynamics of wider community and social norms (which can work to uphold and/or challenge domestic violence), women themselves also practice power in their efforts to resist domestic violence. Women's agency is central to understanding domestic violence, and various support organisations prefer the term 'survivors' to victims in recognition of their efforts to resist; women are not simply passive victims. Women adopt a myriad of strategies to divert, avoid, ignore, limit, and halt practices of violence, and the home is often bound up within these resistances. Women use physical elements of the home to protect themselves (locks, doors, etc.), and the threat of perpetrator eviction from the home is a key leverage for some women. The home, however, can also work to undermine women's resistance.

A final key power element of domestic violence is that of the differentiation between women who experience domestic violence and the significant role played by the politics of marginalisation in shaping women's capacities to manage domestic violence. The power of communities and the state to condone or resist domestic violence was highlighted earlier. Politics of marginalisation is often tied to particular social relations that serve to entrench inequality and uneven power relations. Here, race, sexuality, age, religion, poverty, migration, and health (both mental and physical) all structure and complicate experiences of domestic violence.

Prevalence of Domestic Violence Globally and Institutional Responses

Multicountry and local area studies of domestic violence corroborate the finding that domestic violence is phenomenally widespread globally. Figures of women who have experienced domestic violence range between countries, between urban and rural areas and between the educated and less educated, but stand at around 29–62% of all adult women. These figures are higher when measuring emotional abuse (up to 75%); and the large proportion of all forms of domestic violence is severe and occurs frequently (WHO, 2005). In global criminal and health terms, this is an epidemic, and has significant human rights and health costs.

Measuring domestic violence at the global or local scale has always been difficult because of the so-called 'private' nature of the crime. Across the world, women are discouraged or prevented from reporting experiences of violence, and criminal justice systems globally have a pathetic success rate of prosecuting perpetrators. Women globally tend to either keep their experiences to themselves or inform their wider family, neighbours, or friends when desperate. It is estimated that 55–95% of women have never reported their experiences of domestic violence to a formal or professional representative (police, health worker, etc.) (WHO, 2005). This global trend of significant underreporting profoundly complicates understandings of domestic violence. Women too are implicated in this, as in particular societies, such as Jordan and elsewhere in the Middle East, a significant proportion of women (e.g., 30%) argue that the beating of wives by husbands is justified in many circumstances (Al-Nsour et al., 2009).

National institutional responses to domestic violence vary widely, although most countries adopt a legal framework wherein domestic violence is recognised as a crime, even within countries where there is significant inequality between men and women. This advancement is in part a function of the globalisation of ideas of 'human rights' and rising awareness of gender inequalities. In practice, however, legal frameworks can prove meaningless, and there is limited evidence globally of women benefitting from legal resolutions to experiences of domestic violence, even in the global North. For legal frameworks to be meaningful, they must be upheld by state institutions, such as the police, the judiciary, and the health care system. In many countries this support is absent, and the police in particular are often implicated in exacerbating women's vulnerability through insensitive requests, disbelief, and a failure to protect and support 'victims'.

Spaces of Domestic Violence

Domestic violence is, as are other social practices, spatially inscribed. Its spatial relations are, however, not simply a function of the common location of domestic violence within the home, that is, the home as a stage for domestic violence. As indicated earlier, the home is bound up with domestic violence through its materiality as well as its politics (of ownership, possession, use, and meaning). This article goes on to examine some of the complexities of this relationship through a focus on four key themes: domestic violence and homelessness; materiality and housing type; social and spatial living arrangements; and the politics and consumption of home.

Domestic Violence and Homelessness: Consequence and Context

Bearing in mind that homelessness is a contested concept (see Watson and Austerberry, 1986), it is shown to be a common consequence of domestic violence: evidence from Shelter in 2002 suggests that 40% of all homeless women stated that domestic violence contributed to their homelessness (Blunt and Dowling, 2006: 126). Victims of domestic violence may be forced to leave their homes (by violent partners or family members), or they may 'choose' to leave in an effort to safeguard themselves and/or their children. Women are also forced to move house by landlords, or the state, because of the damage caused to property by violent partners. Violent men (or women) can also be made homeless when forced to leave their homes, either through local sanction or enforceable legal practices such as Protection Orders.

One of the limitations, however, of exploring the interconnections between domestic violence and homelessness (as a consequence) is that this conjures up a linear process: that is, living with a violent perpetrator, leaving the house because of this violence, being homeless. In reality, this relation is multidimensional in varying ways. Just because a woman leaves a violent home does not mean the violence ends, and many, if not most, women return to their violent partners for different reasons (usually financial dependency). Because domestic violence is a social relation, it can follow a woman wherever she lives, through abusive phone calls, text messaging, as well as physical encounters. Domestic violence thus spills over, and out of, the domestic space of the home. Women often move in with relatives or friends and their spaces become part of the power relations of domestic violence.

Aside from the causality between domestic violence and homelessness, homelessness also works as a key context within which domestic violence takes place, shaping social relations through the characteristics of homelessness. Women who are already homeless (or insecurely housed) also experience domestic violence, but their violence is often experienced in public or semipublic spaces. This contextual relation can be used to describe the living situations of women who have been forced out of their homes and continue to experience domestic violence (across the world), but more importantly it should be used to understand the lived experiences of millions of women across the global South who live in relatively homeless conditions (shack dwellers, street sleepers, hostel residents, etc.). Being homeless as an a priori condition shapes how domestic violence can be managed and usually points to extensive poverty and political marginalisation, both of which severely limit the extent to which homeless victims of domestic violence can seek protection or alternative safe accommodation. The role of domestic violence shelters, discussed later, pursues some of these concerns.

Materiality and Multiple Housing Types

Key dimensions in the relationships between home, housing, and domestic violence are the material and spatial properties of housing and the roles these play in practices of domestic violence. In general, analyses of domestic violence fail to problematise the qualities of the house and overlook the impact of housing type on practices and experiences of domestic violence. This limitation may be a function of the adoption of narrow western ideas of housing type within global literature on domestic violence, whereby a house is assumed to be a formal structure (with a door, walls, separate rooms and subsequent capacities for privacy, protection, and imprisonment). Domestic violence takes place in a range of spatial contexts within and beyond the formal home, including hostels, homeless shelters, and informal housing, many of which exist across the global North and South. I turn to the significance of different living arrangements below, but key here are the complex ways in which materiality shapes power relations.

The absence of solid structures (walls, doors, roof) and divisions between living spaces (bedrooms, bathroom, kitchen, garden, etc.), all potentially fitted with lockable barriers, affects how women experience and manage domestic violence, though not always in obvious ways. Informal shacks are inherently vulnerable and victims of domestic violence suffer because of this. Violent partners can easily break in, either through the door, the walls, or the roof, and once inside, there are often no spaces for escape or barricade, fabric or furniture divide rooms (if any), and there are usually no lockable internal doors. However, informal housing also affords little privacy. They are usually densely located in close proximity to other informal housing and even normal conversation can be heard between structures as a result (Meth, 2003). Shrieks for help in situations of domestic violence have a far higher chance of being heard and (depending on cultural relations) hence a higher chance of being assisted. This is by no means insignificant, as homicide rates following domestic violence are high, and the propensity for neighbours or friends to intervene is a key determinant of the outcome of violent incidences of domestic violence.

A formal brick or stone built structure that offers elements of protection (e.g., locking oneself in a bathroom) also significantly increases risks of imprisonment and the inaudibility associated with isolation. The case of Austria's Elisabeth, who was imprisoned for 24 years and was a victim of domestic violence and rape by her father, Josef F, that came to light in 2008 is a gruesome illustration of the power of materiality to shape domestic violence. The layout of Josef's home served to facilitate the structuring of his practices of domestic violence through his use of a sealed reinforced concrete electronic trap door, walls thickened with rubber, and the inaudibility associated with underground cellars. In addition, the detached nature of the house meant that its contextual location benefitted the perpetrator. Formal housing, both materially, but also through its complex relationship with privacy (as a social and physical relation) can prove highly detrimental to the safety of domestic violence victims. Furthermore, the materiality of housing can work to entrench or counter the interconnections between private space and domestic violence. More flimsy structures, or indeed sleeping on the street, effectively forces domestic violence into the public arena. Housing type thus shapes the power circumstances within which violence, or the threat of violence, occurs.

The interconnections between the materiality of different housing types and cultural and social relations are also fundamental to experiences of domestic violence and illustrate how different cultural practices shape the meaning and use of housing types. Detached formal housing can perform very different roles in different societies. For example, where women frequently work or engage in social activities with nonfamily members either inside or outside the home their capacity for support is potentially higher than women who are prevented from working or engaging socially with others. In societies where women suffer limited freedoms in public space (e.g., Afghanistan), and where the majority of their time is spent within extended formal courtyard-style compounds, their strategies for managing domestic violence differ and are usually curtailed. In these contexts, women are controlled both within private space and also in public space, and the courtyard home is a symbolic container of family values: privacy, solidarity, and reputation (Douki et al., 2003: 166).

Finally, as indicated above, the materiality of housing is also structured by the context of housing, its relative positioning in relation to other housing, other people, and other built form. The aforementioned examples of densely settled informal settlements and detached formal homes illustrate the significance of locational context. Distinctions between rural and urban locations are also important, as rural contexts specifically entrench social relations of privacy and isolation but also potentially construct strong and supportive communal relations between residents. Research in America points to debates over the significance of architecture, density, location, and environmental disorder in shaping domestic violence and argues that a chaotic and dense environment, such as that found in dense public housing, can exacerbate domestic violence (Menard, 2001).

Social and Spatial Living Arrangements

Closely related to the significance of housing type and the materiality of home are the relations between living arrangements and domestic violence. Although not explicitly stated, much of the Western literature, and indeed literature written about the global South, draws and rests on the living arrangements of the nuclear family in narratives of domestic violence. This assumption of heterosexual parents with 'two' children, for example, limits an understanding of the complex sociopolitical realities of domestic violence.

Living arrangements vary extensively across the world but are key to the ways (materially and socially) in which domestic violence is experienced and a purposefully long selection is listed here to illustrate this point: nuclear family, communal, single, foster, homosexual, migrant (both original home and migrant residence), illegal, holiday, and extended-family households; hostels (single sex and/or family hostels); institutionalised residences (social care housing, housing for mentally or physically disabled, the elderly, the homeless, refugees, victims of domestic violence); live-in or onsite domestic workers or au pairs; households with children; ad hoc living arrangements with friends and family; bed-and-breakfast arrangements; backyard shack tenancies; university accommodation; traveller sites; emergency camps; and such. In addition, forms of tenancy (formal and informal renting, outright ownership, mortgage ownership, joint or individual ownership, illegal squatting, etc.) overlay this wide variety, shaping further the power relations structuring domestic violence.

Different sociopolitical relations operate within all of these examples. Different types of people are present in these different contexts, and different social norms and daily practices are evident. Of particular significance is the way in which these varying sociospatial arrangements structure power relations, in particular the capacity of victims of domestic violence to resist and manage violence. Different living arrangements afford differential access to legal protection. This access is restricted or absent for residents who are illegal or for homosexual victims in societies where same-sex relations are not protected constitutionally. Where women access social housing, the unreported (or illegal) presence of a male partner may place her at risk of losing her housing, thereby undermining her willingness to report abuse.

Different living arrangements have a temporality, and, in turn, the timing of these shapes the temporal qualities of domestic violence. Household members change over time, not only at the temporal scale of the day but also the week, month, and year. For example, migrant workers move between different 'homes' at different times and thus practice differential domestic living arrangements. Gold mine workers in South Africa, for example, often come to the city of Johannesburg for employment and choose to reside with a girlfriend or make use of sex workers in their place of employment. They make tri- or biannual trips to their 'home' (often rural) wherein a different set of relations are adopted with their wives and children.

The Politics and Consumption of Home

Finally, the relations between domestic violence and the home are acutely shaped not only by how the state treats housing as an item of consumption and production and a symbol of a 'human right' but also by how users produce and consume housing. State treatment relates to the affordability of housing subsidy schemes; decisions about location, design, and planning; housing finance; tenure and ownership legislation, particularly that which is gendered; and policies about informality and the control of illegal structures. There is a great variability in the extent to which affordable housing alternatives are available for women, and the decisions made by a state about investment in public housing directly shape the capacity and abilities of women to manage their experiences of violence. Domestic violence shelters, although key for some, globally address <1% of the housing needs of women (WHO, 2005) and are largely a short-term solution. Rather, it is the provision of public housing, or services to protect women within existing housing (through responsive policing) that are key. In some countries of the global North, there has been a sustained effort to provide for victims of domestic violence, but in countries where homelessness and informal housing is dominant (i.e., much of the global South), the state cannot be relied upon to provide (as they already have decades of housing backlog to deal with). The politics of this housing reality means rethinking the notion of 'shelter', which assumes that a home will be found on departure. This can seldom occur if one is homeless (or informally housed) prior to shelter.

The home is also a key site of production and consumption for its users: it serves as a social, economic, and emotional resource for many. This multiple function exacerbates women's difficulties with leaving their homes in situations of violence and is not necessarily tied to the risk of homelessness. Affluent women, for example, who live in luxurious homes find leaving their home space very difficult. Their homes symbolise extensive personal, creative, and emotional investment, and women fear 'giving up' the significant advantages of such domestic environments. This burden of the consumption of home is often tied to the economic dependency of women on men, where women are not financially able to sustain a home environment independent of their male partner, who may be the sole breadwinner. This is compounded by many women's (re)productive role as mother and homemaker, both of which are unpaid. The home as a site of production and consumption is structured thus by gendered power relations, which are often unequal and a source of vulnerability for women. These are exacerbated in contexts where families are so poor that the loss of the male partner's income throws a household into financial crisis. The symbolic weight and meaning of a home also shapes women's experiences of domestic violence. The loss of their 'haven' or 'sanctuary' affects women's emotional well-being as well the construction of their fears of place.

In conclusion, this article has pointed to the multiple intersections between domestic violence and home, beyond the outcome of homelessness because of domestic violence. The materiality and politics of home are key to experiences of domestic violence. Readers are urged to appreciate the vast differences globally in cultural and political approaches to both domestic violence and housing and to maintain awareness of the inequalities between experiences of domestic violence both locally and globally. At the global scale, violence within the home is prevalent in more than a quarter of all homes, thus as a social, health, criminal, emotional, and material fact, it must be examined in analyses of home and homelessness.

See also: Feminist Perspectives on Home; Feminist Perspectives on Homelessness; Women and Housing Organisations.

References

Al-Nsour M, Khawaja M, and Al-Kayyali G (2009) Domestic violence against women in Jordan: Evidence from health clinics. *Journal of Family Violence* 24: 569–575.

Blunt A and Dowling R (2006) *Home*. Oxford: Routledge.

Douki S, Nacef F, Belhadj A, Bouasker A, and Ghachem R (2003) Violence against women in Arab and Islamic countries. *Archives of Women's Mental Health* 6: 165–171.

Menard A (2001) Domestic violence and housing: Key policy and program challenges. *Violence Against Women* 7: 707–720.

Meth P (2003) Rethinking the 'domus' in domestic violence: Homelessness, space and domestic violence in South Africa. *Geoforum* 34: 317–327.

UK Home Office (2009) Crime Reduction, UK Home Office www.crimereduction/homeoffice.gov.uk (accessed 9 September 2009).

Watson H and Austerberry H (1986) *Housing and Homelessness: A Feminist Perspective*. London: Routledge; Kegan Paul.

WHO (2005) WHO multi-country study on women's health and domestic violence against women. *Summary Report.* World Health Organization.

Relevant Websites

www.un.org – UN Division for the Advancement of Women. Country-by-country data and policy initiatives on the prevalence and prevention of domestic violence are given in this site

www.who.int/ – World Health Organisation

Domesticity

J Hollows, Nottingham Trent University, Nottingham, UK

© 2012 Elsevier Ltd. All rights reserved.

Glossary

Domestic feminism Associated with some nineteenth-century feminists who believed that women's caring role in the home was the basis for moral authority over public life.
Heteronormativity The prescription of heterosexual familial living arrangements as the norm.
Mobile privatisation Coined by Raymond Williams to refer to the seemingly contradictory impulses towards increased mobility and increased privatisation in modern societies.
Second-wave feminism Associated with the Women's Movements of the late 1960s and the 1970s.
Sexual division of labour Presumption that social roles are differentiated along the lines of sex and/or gender.

Introduction

The meaning of home is frequently seen as timeless and natural. For many people, home signifies comfort, security, warmth, privacy, intimacy, and family; an escape from a harsh and calculating world of work, and from chaotic and impersonal urban life. Yet these ideas are far from timeless and natural but are the result of wide-ranging social, economic, and cultural processes associated with modernity that have fundamentally changed many people's experiences of the world. More specifically, these ideas of home are a product of discourses of domesticity that emerged alongside modernisation and offered specific ways of understanding the meanings, values, and functions associated with home. Discourses of domesticity also associated home with specific identities and relationships between people. Although domesticity is frequently associated with a conception of home as distinct and separate from the public sphere, the meanings of domesticity have frequently been constructed through public institutions, industries, policies, and representations. Likewise, although domesticity is frequently associated with a privatised and inward-looking conception of home, it also helps to create – and sometimes challenge – the experience of public life.

Struggles over the meaning of domesticity are struggles over the meaning of home and how we conduct everyday life. These are also struggles about who is responsible for producing and maintaining the values associated with domesticity and the experience of home. Yet discourses of domesticity frequently equate home with particular kinds of family life, an association which can exclude or pathologise both people and homes that do not fit these normative conceptions of domestic life.

This overview traces the changing meaning of domesticity from the late eighteenth century onwards. It begins by exploring how discourses of domesticity emerged alongside ideas about separate spheres and how they positioned women as homemakers, responsible for producing the aesthetic, moral, and cultural universe of a specific kind of home. The following section explores in greater detail how homemaking practices were understood to produce particular values associated with domesticity in the period. However, as the discussion progresses, I identify how domesticity becomes a site of struggle as different voices speak through different discourses about the meaning and value of domesticity. Therefore, while suburban domesticity operated as a model of the ideal home for much of the twentieth century, a range of voices condemned domesticity as a form of conservative mass culture. Among these voices were those of feminists who saw domesticity as an ideology that worked to sustain unequal power relations between men and women. However, I conclude by not only considering feminist critics who have asserted the value of domesticity and its potential as a source of critique of the values associated with the public sphere, but also a range of popular texts and practices that have reclaimed and reimagined the value of domesticity in contemporary life.

Separate Spheres and the Production of Domesticity

While there are multiple competing accounts of the history of home, many historians and theorists have identified a dramatic shift in the meaning of domestic space as a result of capitalist modernisation. The preindustrial home is frequently seen as a sociable rather than privatised space in which family members and other members of the household mingled. Most crucially, the preindustrial home is usually seen as a site of production (work) with all household members – men, women, and children – contributing to the production process. For many critics, under capitalist modernisation, the home acquired much more specialist functions: it was a private family retreat and was identified with child-rearing and the consumption, rather than the production, of goods. These changes occurred at different times in different national contexts and they were neither immediate nor uniform even within nations.

These new functions of home were given meaning through a wider opposition between the private sphere and the public sphere, realms that were imagined as separate and distinctive. The distinction between the public and private spheres offered a new way of imagining the social and cultural world and people's place within it. The public sphere was not only identified with the world of production, commerce, and city life, but was also associated with chaos and danger, fleeting and impersonal contacts, and immoral behaviour. In direct contrast, the private sphere of the home was associated with family and a wide range of moral values and attributes. By the mid-nineteenth century, in both the United States and the United Kingdom, home came to be seen as a special place: a place to be yourself and put down roots; a place of innocence, warmth, and intimacy; a site devoted to marriage and the family, to religion and morality, to leisure rather than labour; and as a stage to display your status and taste through appropriate consumption. These ideas were all central to the notion of domesticity that emerged in the United Kingdom and France in the late eighteenth century, and in the United States from the early nineteenth century. While the idea of separate spheres undoubtedly shaped the nineteenth-century imagination in a significant number of modernising Western nations, the extent to which the public and the private spheres were really distinct and separate has been challenged – an idea that is developed below.

Public and private spheres were not only associated with specific functions and meanings but also specific identities. If the public sphere of work was identified with the figure of the masculine breadwinner, the private domestic sphere was identified with the feminine homemaker. Many feminist critics argue that this marked a profound shift in gender relations. As production and business moved out of the household into the public sphere, they became increasingly identified as masculine activities. In the process, women were identified with the responsibility for maintaining domestic and family life and, because they did not work for an income, they became economically dependent on men. For some feminist critics, this was a decisive moment in women's history, producing deeply embedded inequalities between men and women. Furthermore, it is frequently claimed that women's identification with domestic life acted as a form of spatial segregation, effectively making them prisoners of domestic life.

Feminist historians have identified how discourses of domesticity which produced the meaning of home in modern life – and positioned women as homemakers – were produced through texts such as women's magazines and evangelical Christian literature and worked to legitimate the gendering of spheres. However, many critics have questioned whether these ideas about domesticity were directed at all women and argued that they not only identified women with the home but also played a key role in the formation of new and distinctively middle-class identities and cultures (and, in the United States, these identities were also distinctively white and likely to be urban). Whereas most theories of modernity assume that class identities and class cultures were primarily a product of a (masculine) public sphere, this ignores the extent to which domestic cultures have also played a central role in producing both classed and gendered identities.

For example, in Leonore Davidoff and Catherine Hall's *Family Fortunes*, they explore how the meaning of domesticity was shaped by evangelical religion that promoted new modes of domestic femininity and new meanings of home to the emerging middle-class population in provincial England between 1780 and 1850. These religions promoted the idea that the home was a necessity in promoting 'moral order' to combat the 'amoral world' of the public sphere (Davidoff and Hall, 2002: 74). Women were seen to be uniquely suited to sustain the morality of home because they were assumed to be inherently more nurturing and hence more Christian, gentle, and passive (qualities that made them unsuited to participate in the more competitive and amoral public sphere). These meanings of domesticity helped to legitimise a sexual division of labour based on men as breadwinners and women as economically dependent homemakers: masculinity was defined in terms of a 'man's ability to support and order his family' while 'a woman's femininity was best expressed in her dependence' (Davidoff and Hall, 2002: 144). This rested on the idea that women's natural place was in the home and that they should be economically dependent on men (ideas that would prove remarkably resilient to change); and through their responsibility for domestic life, women were seen to perform an equally important social and cultural role.

In the nineteenth-century discourses of domesticity, the home was also important because it was the site of marital and family life. Davidoff and Hall argue that middle-class women were positioned not only as wives who would save the souls of their husbands but as mothers who were entrusted with socialising their children into Christian, middle-class values. The importance of family life was also reinforced in the new status given to children who were now freed from any adult responsibilities that they may have undertaken in the preindustrial home and who were identified with 'innocence'. Yet if the home was primarily identified with women and children, men also had a key role to play in the middle-class domestic cultures. As breadwinners, men were most likely to experience the home as a 'haven' from the public sphere and as a site of leisure and freedom from work, and fathers were seen to have a vital role to play in family life. In this way, discourses of domesticity did not only produce specific feminine identities but also masculine ones.

Like many other historians of domestic life in the period, Davidoff and Hall draw many of their conclusions from an analysis of representations of domesticity in sources such as evangelical tracts and domestic advice literature. However, we cannot assume that these meanings of domesticity were accepted unquestioningly by middle-class women and there is significant evidence to suggest that the gendered separation of spheres was never as secure in practice as it was in such representations. Although most public spaces were represented as no place for 'respectable' women, significant numbers of middle-class women carried out philanthropic work in the city and, from the mid-nineteenth century, new feminine spaces such as the department store emerged within the city. Furthermore, some middle-class women participated in their husband's businesses, suggesting that "public was not really public and the private not really private" (Davidoff and Hall, 2002: 330). Just as public life shaped the meaning of domesticity, so also was domesticity used to shape and to challenge the meaning of public life. For example, some women used their domestic role as consumers as the basis for political action in the public sphere — for example, through consumer boycotts and protests. In this way, the public and the private are never distinct. Domesticity has often been seen to play a key role in building or maintaining the ideas of a nation. This is well-illustrated by Alison Blunt (1999) who demonstrates how domesticity "in British India was inextricably bound up with imperial rule" (p. 438).

The idea that domestic and work cultures were distinct and separate depended on classifying women's activities within the home as consumption rather than labour (and, in the process, ignoring the labour involved in consumption). Although many middle-class women were employers of labour, they were still involved in household management and child-rearing. Furthermore, the middle-class home was often a workplace for working-class women who were employed as servants. Indeed, working-class women's very position as workers problematises any straightforward idea that all women were confined to the home and economically dependent on men (although they were frequently paid significantly less than men). Joanna Bourke (1994) has suggested that becoming a full-time housewife may have offered working-class women a greater sense of power, autonomy, and control than their paid work afforded them. In the United States, black women living under slavery in the South were excluded from the ability to participate in domesticity and what was considered to be conventional family life because they were seen as part of slave-owners' families. After the abolition of slavery, African American women's investment in domesticity has been interpreted as a response to racism rather than an adoption of white middle-class definitions of domesticity. If African American women often had little option but to engage in paid work, Sharon Harley (1990) suggests that they also refused to identify themselves with their jobs and claimed domestic work as their source of identity and self-worth. Therefore, it should be evident that class and race impact on women's relationship to domesticity. This suggests that, far from being uniformly oppressive for all women, domesticity can operate as a resource to respond to other modes of inequality and resist class and racial positioning.

Discourses of domesticity offered ways of understanding a distinctively modern conception of home and its relationship to the public sphere and these discourses continue to shape many of the meanings we associate with home such as family, leisure, intimacy, and security. These discourses also produced new modes of feminine identity identified with the home. While the public and the private spheres were not strictly bounded spaces, domesticity offered ways of understanding the role of home in the modern world and, as the next section examines, offered guidance on the practices of making homes.

Domesticity and Homemaking in the Nineteenth Century

Accounts of the separation and gendering of the public and the private spheres frequently argue that the home shifted from being a site of production to a site of consumption and that women were transformed from active producers to passive consumers of goods. Domestic advice guided middle-class women on how to use consumer goods to create homes that embodied particular meanings, values, and identities. However, the meaning of domesticity was also negotiated in the practice of making homes. Consumption practices do not simply reproduce the meanings that have been ascribed to goods by producers or experts but are active homemaking practices through which people produce the meaning of home. Through domestic consumption practices, people use consumer goods to make homes and identities and to establish relationships within — and beyond — the home. In this way, consumption practices may be used to negotiate or resist dominant meanings of domesticity.

As industrialisation and increasing global trade created an ever-expanding range of consumer goods, middle-class women were the targets for advice from domestic experts about how to select between – and use – these goods to create homes that exhibited good taste and appropriate values. New forms of domestic experts emerged – in some ways similar to the experts who populate lifestyle media today – and offered women guidance on how to consume appropriately. In both the United States and the United Kingdom in the early- to mid-nineteenth century, domestic advice literature frequently focused on how women could use their consumption practices to create a home based on an aesthetic that embodied Christian values.

Ideas about appropriate forms of domesticity also underpinned the practices of planners and architects who shaped the meaning of domestic spaces. New suburban developments aimed at the expanding middle classes reinforced the idea of separate spheres by creating a spatial separation between home and work and a distance from urban life was reinforced symbolically through an association with nature, most clearly visible in suburban gardens and echoed in references to nature in domestic interiors. Ideas about separate sphere were also reproduced in domestic architecture through the identification of public and private spaces within the home: clear distinctions were made between work spaces such as the kitchen, private spaces such as bedrooms, and more public rooms appropriate for receiving guests, such as the parlour.

In the early- to mid-nineteenth century, the furnishing of the middle-class home also reinforced the distance of domestic life from the industrial city. Textures, colours, and shapes were frequently soft and gentle, reinforcing the associations between home and femininity, while heavy upholstery and voluminous curtains reinforced the values of comfort and privacy. Yet by the mid- to late nineteenth century, in both the United States and the United Kingdom, there was an increasing sense of struggle about what values the middle-class home should represent. New styles of heavily gilded and ornamental French furniture offered the middle-class people the opportunities to display their wealth and status. However, for their critics, these styles were seen as vain and ostentatious and a betrayal of the idea that the home should embody wholesome moral values and restrained good taste.

Struggles about appropriate domestic consumption also emerged as middle-class reformers set about improving the moral character of the working class by teaching them middle-class values of domesticity. In the United Kingdom, concerns about the appalling living conditions of the working class in overcrowded, unsanitary, and unhealthy slums were frequently articulated with concerns that such conditions bred immorality and insurrection. The solution was to improve working-class housing conditions as a way of improving their morals: for example, segregating adults from children and boys from girls in different bedrooms was seen as a way of combating sexual depravity and reinforcing the value of privacy. Likewise, reformers in the United States began to draw on scientific discourses to promote a more minimal aesthetic which, it was believed, would not only be morally uplifting in its simplicity and sobriety but also promote hygiene, cleanliness, and efficiency.

However, just because particular meanings of domesticity were advocated by domestic advisors and reformers – and built into housing and goods by designers, architects, and planners – does not mean that these were reproduced by homemakers. Instead, people frequently use domestic consumption practices to represent their own identities and relationships and their own values as they appropriate housing and goods to construct meaningful ways of life. Such practices may not always resist dominant meanings of domesticity, but they always involve an active engagement with them. Yet occupants sometimes do explicitly challenge the ideas about appropriate domestic life built into their housing. Lizabeth Cohen's (1980) study of a late-nineteenth-century US urban housing development demonstrates how Italian-American working-class residents resisted the use of architectural engineering to transform their domestic cultural practices. The residents resisted the meanings of domesticity built into their clean, sparse, hygienic, and efficient homes with strictly demarcated spatial divisions between different functional spaces by installing less hygienic and elaborate soft furnishings and by reclaiming the functional space of the kitchen as a social space. The domestic consumption practices of these residents represented a form of ownership of, and investment in, mass working-class housing and drew on their own cultural resources and practices to resist middle-class reformers' claims to cultural authority over domestic life.

Cohen's work demonstrates that far from being uniform and prescriptive, the meaning of domesticity is also a site of struggle and contestation about different ways in which to conduct domestic life. These homemakers' domestic culture also incorporated a rural and Italian heritage that was now geographically distant, using objects and practices as markers of people, places, and values that are absent but whose symbolic presence was necessary to maintain their conception of home. In this way, the meaning of home within their place of residence was stretched to include memories, values, and people from elsewhere.

Suburban Domesticity and its Critics

By the interwar period, the meaning of domesticity was increasingly inflected by new ideas from science, technology, and business, which had transformed the public sphere. Modes of domestic femininity were also reimagined: as middle-class women were increasingly without domestic servants, they were no longer distinguished by their distance from domestic labour. The figure of the middle-class homemaker was transformed into a skilled and professional housewife, now distinguished by her ability to harness the power of science and technology to manage the home in a rational manner. Although many of the core values associated with domesticity were central to everyday domestic practices, domesticity also came increasingly under attack. Furthermore, as suburban housing developments expanded and became available to more sections of the population, domesticity was increasingly interpreted as a celebration of the mundane and trivial and, at worse, as compliance with capitalist ideology and a retreat from political and social responsibilities in the public sphere.

Ideas about the need to rationalise domesticity had their roots in the nineteenth century and new disciplines such as 'domestic science' and 'home economics' advocated the importance of adopting principles from the industrial workplace to modernise the home. New domestic experts such as Christine Frederick wanted to use science to improve everyday life, arguing for more rational design to improve the efficiency of the household while Lillian Gilbreth applied ideas from industrial management to increase productivity in the home and professionalise the homemaker's role. Popular magazines such as *Good Housekeeping* offered technological and scientific solutions to household problems, encouraging their readers to use their knowledge of science, business, and medicine in their role as rational and professional housewives. A range of new and allegedly labour-saving household technologies such as fridges and vacuum cleaners were increasingly seen as central to the modern home (although many people did not have access to them), and the modern housewife was encouraged to see these as indispensable to her work. New media technologies such as radio and television also stretched the boundaries of home. While domestic media consumption was frequently seen to encourage families to become home-centred and privatised, the concept of mobile privatisation enables us to think about how people can be simultaneously home-centred and mobile. TV may be consumed within the home, but it also enables people to experience national public life within their homes and to travel to distant places without leaving their living rooms.

While middle-class women's magazines such as *Good Housekeeping* articulated a scientific approach to housewifery with the creativity that characterised nineteenth-century discourses of domesticity, in other quarters a war was being waged against the characteristics of the Victorian home. Privileging minimal and utilitarian aesthetics, architects such as Le Corbusier and Walter Gropius sought to banish the clutter and decoration that had been used by homemakers to signify domestic values such as family, privacy, comfort, and warmth. As the rest of this section goes on to document, this critique formed part of a wider attack on domesticity as a series of fears were projected on to developing forms of suburban domesticity.

In the United States, nineteenth-century suburban developments often reproduced ideas about separate spheres. While many suburbs in the period certainly represented a separation from urban and industrial public life and reinforced the value of privacy through a physical and symbolic separation from other people, some early suburbs were also based on principles of communitarian living, exploring new forms of domesticity. By the late nineteenth and early twentieth century, new transportation systems contributed to the expansion of suburban housing developments for the middle classes. However, there were also less planned developments based around prefabricated and self-built housing that enabled the white working class and African Americans to have some level of participation in suburbia, challenging the idea that suburban domestic cultures are inherently white and middle class. Yet, despite the heterogeneity of suburban developments prior to the Second World War, cultural critics such as Adorno and Horkheimer focused on the motif of standardisation to criticise suburban housing, suburban domesticity, and suburbia's residents.

These critiques gained force after the Second World War, a period associated with a massive building boom which offered the experience of suburban domesticity to a far larger number of people. This boom was led by large-scale developers who built huge suburban developments, the most famous of which were the Levittowns which acted as a synecdoche for everything critics thought was wrong with suburbia. For example, the architect and cultural critic Lewis Mumford railed against the physical uniformity of both suburban developments and their residents, arguing that suburban domesticity promoted a privatised existence that blinded people to their wider public and political responsibilities. Cultural critics such as Philip Wylie claimed that immersion in suburban domesticity emasculated men and led to a femininisation of society. Numerous other commentators highlighted the role television played in suburban domesticity, claiming that it not only colonised people's leisure time to accentuate people's level of privatisation but also that TV promoted a mode of domestic culture centred around consumption.

Indeed, for most of its critics, consumption was pathologised as a key feature of what was wrong with suburban domesticity. A domestic culture centred around consumption, it was claimed, produced a superficial form of cultural life centred around keeping up with the Joneses. For some feminist critics such as Betty Friedan (see the following section), this deskilled the housewife because her existence became identified with consumption and reinforced a mode of suburban domesticity that condemned women to a privatised existence, isolated in their own homes. Yet studies of the domestic culture of the period suggest a rather more complex picture, indicating how consumption practices were far from privatised and could be used to build support networks and community and promote sociality. Tupperware parties are frequently cited as an example here.

There is considerable evidence to dispute the idea that postwar suburban domesticity in the United States was simply conformist, standardised, and privatised. However, while the early-twentieth-century suburban developments were more socially mixed, it is less easy to dismiss claims about the social homogeneity of later suburban residents. Suburbia is clearly implicated in a wider history of racial segregation in the United States, accentuated by White Flight from urban areas and by racial discrimination in the allocation of home loans. Yet, while suburbs remain segregated by race and class, suburban domesticity cannot simply be dismissed as inherently conformist and conservative, nor can it simply be understood as a retreat from the public sphere. Such thinking not only rests on the idea that there is a rigid separation between the public and the private spheres but it also ignores the extent to which, for many people, suburban domesticity offered an escape from overcrowded, slum conditions. To criticise people for wanting a quality of housing that the middle-class people take for granted is rather elitist.

British intellectuals levelled similar criticisms against suburban domesticity, but they identified a particular culprit as responsible for its key characteristics – the lower middle class. The expansion of suburban housing in the United Kingdom in the interwar period coincided with the expansion of lower-middle-class occupations and owning a home in the suburbs enabled this class fraction to signify it had achieved middle-class status. They used external and internal decorative features of their homes to signify their individuality and their pride in achieving homeownership. Yet cultural critics such as George Orwell represented suburban domesticity as a fake and impoverished form of culture based around the insubstantial foundations of mass-produced consumer goods. These scathing attacks on lower-middle-class domesticity had a class basis because, as Judy Giles (2004) argues, they were "a form of modernity that was not of middle-class making" (p. 43).

Whereas ideologies of separate spheres identified femininity with domesticity, in the interwar period some cultural critics were concerned that women had been given too much authority over domestic life and, as British culture became more home-centred, the nation was becoming feminised. Orwell vividly portrayed how suburban domesticity, presided over by consumption-obsessed materialistic women, threatened to emasculate men. Yet the seemingly superficial mass-produced goods which cultural critics scorned were deeply meaningful to new suburbanites for whom acquiring a home of their own was the realisation of a dream. Suburban domesticity celebrated these hopes and dreams: as Judy Giles suggests, suburban semidetached modernity offered many people "the pride of being, at last, worthy of citizenship", to be seen as respectable and ordinary, and may have been "as significant as the vote in enabling people to see themselves as full members of modern society" (p. 44).

During the 1950s, large sections of the white working class in the United Kingdom moved to the suburbs as either owner-occupiers or tenants in new state-owned suburban developments. Many critics on the left argued that these new suburbanites underwent a process of embourgeoisement, adopting middle-class values as they built new lifestyles around consumer goods. Many of these critics identified the emphasis on privacy in suburban domesticity as a problem: the working class became cut off from the traditional forms of community and collective identity that gave them a sense of class consciousness in their older patterns of residence. Social realist films such as *The Loneliness of the Long Distance Runner* (1962) and *Saturday Night and Sunday Morning* (1960) reproduced this critique and identified how suburban domesticity emasculated the worker, trapping him in a feminine, privatised, and consumption-dominated world. However, left critics were primarily concerned with the impact of home-centredness on working-class men: spending time with their families, watching TV instead of going to the pub and doing DIY, it was claimed, meant they lost any sense of radical political identity and became more conservative.

These debates, like the earlier critiques of suburban domesticity, were frequently underpinned by the assumption that where you live – and what type of house you live in – determines your culture, identity, and politics. Furthermore, critics in the period were particularly concerned about the impact of home ownership on political values, concerns that would reemerge during the 1980s as analysts attempted to explain why significant numbers of the working class supported the Thatcherite government. However, just as some recent research suggests caution in making any straightforward connection between home-ownership and political allegiances, it is also necessary to be wary of reading the meaning of domestic cultures from the system under which they are produced. Most people's homes in the West are undoubtedly produced by large-scale capitalist building industries, but the meaning of domestic practices cannot simply be read off from this mode of production. While the ways in which housing is produced and distributed – and the form that housing takes – inform the meaning of domesticity, they do not determine it. People adapt, rework, negotiate, and transform the places they live in, to produce meaningful domestic cultures. Likewise, just because suburban domestic practices may appear to those at a distance to take place in pseudo-individualised but standardised housing does not mean that their occupants are uniform and conformist. Finally, when critics equate privatisation with a retreat from the sphere of politics, they ignore the extent to which the home is also a site of politics, a theme that is developed in the following section.

Feminism and the Politics of Domesticity

Domesticity has not only been seen as a problem in relation to class politics, but has also been seen to both produce and reproduce gendered power relations and inequalities. As discussed earlier, many feminist critics understand the ideology of separate spheres and the corresponding rise of discourses of domesticity as shaping the distinctive character of modern gender inequalities and power relations and, for some critics, it is the root cause of women's oppression. Feminist scholarship and activism have demonstrated how the home is a site of labour rather than leisure; can operate as a site of conflict and danger rather than a haven; and that the sexual division of labour is predicated on – and reproduces – gender inequalities (issues addressed in greater detail elsewhere in this encyclopaedia). While the works of feminist historians in understanding the significance of domesticity have already been discussed, this section focuses on a series of debates within feminism about the value of domesticity.

Judy Giles (2004) observes that in many second-wave feminist narratives of the 1960s and 1970s, "leaving home" is represented as "a necessary condition of liberation" (pp. 141–142). For many second-wave feminists, home is portrayed as a place of confinement, isolation, and powerlessness, associated with a life of drudgery and a loss of identity. Domesticity is characterised, Giles argues, "as something that must be left behind if women were to become 'modern', emancipated subjects" (p. 142). Therefore, second-wave feminism frequently reproduced the assumptions of other theories of modernity that privileged the public sphere as the site of politics, identity, and history and found little to value in the home or in housewives whose lives were assumed to be defined by domesticity.

One of the best-known examples of this position can be found in one of the foundational texts of second-wave feminism. Betty Friedan (1963) argued that a 'feminine mystique', promoted through women's magazines and advertising, persuaded women to invest in suburban domesticity and turn their backs on paid work. But this investment in domesticity, she argued, was far from rewarding and instead made women ill: it produced feelings of failure and nothingness and the drudgery involved in housework led to fatigue and breakdown. For Friedan, women could only find fulfilment by rejecting domesticity and seeking a sense of identity and achievement through paid work in the public sphere. While Friedan wrote as a housewife herself, she shows little regard for them and refuses to recognise any social or cultural value in domestic labour. She also ignores the extent to which full-time domesticity was only open to those women with access to the economic resources which enabled them to choose not to engage in paid work, a privileged position to which many working-class women could only aspire.

Although Friedan's work has been subject to many criticisms, her assumptions about the (lack of) value of domesticity and the housewife's role have been reproduced in some feminist studies of the sexual division of labour. For example, in her notable studies of housework, socialist feminist and sociologist Ann Oakley reproduces the idea that housework offers little more than drudgery, monotony, and exploitation, arguing that it has no social value and offers no opportunities for self-actualisation. Not only did domesticity offer none of the opportunities for creativity that it promised, she argued, but it also secured women's complicity with their own subordination. For Oakley, to embrace the housewife role and to express contentment with it was to be antifeminist because it was to be happy with one's own subordination.

The legacy of these arguments is important in understanding many feminist positions on home and domesticity. Because the identities of the feminist and the housewife are represented as mutually exclusive, it becomes difficult to conceive of a mode of domestic femininity informed by feminism. This assumes that the meanings of domesticity, housework, and the housewife's role are fixed and monolithic rather than open to contestation and change. Although Oakley argues that domesticity offers no opportunities for any meaningful form of creativity and self-identity, other studies have shown how it can offer ways of demonstrating skill or be a source of power and pleasure. As Joan Williams (2000) argues, "Feminists' imagery of the family as the locus of subordination seems most convincing to women otherwise privileged by class and race; to working-class women, it may seem instead (or as well) a haven against the injuries of class" (p. 157). Likewise, some black feminists have argued that African-American women's investment in producing a caring environment in the home is a means of countering their experience of racism and sexism in the public sphere. Finally, approaches that dismiss domestic labour as having little social or cultural value inevitably identify the interests of feminism with the public sphere: as Johnson and Lloyd (2004) argue, "the feminist resolves the tension between domesticity and public achievement by leaving the former at home for the latter" (p. 17).

An alternative feminist position on domesticity has its roots in the ideas of nineteenth-century domestic feminists who reproduced the idea of gendered and separate spheres to argue that women's sense of virtue and self-sacrifice cultivated in the home made them morally superior to men. It was claimed that it was precisely the moral qualities cultivated by domesticity that equipped women to arbitrate on matters in the public sphere. Some second-wave feminists drew on these ideas to celebrate women's domestic role, arguing that the home operated as a site for fostering feminine virtues that offered a critique of the patriarchal values of the public sphere. In a more theoretically developed version of this argument, Carol Gilligan argued that it was women's role as mothers that made them morally superior to men because they were inherently more selfless, caring, and self-sacrificing. While the public sphere was governed by masculine self-interest, she claimed, domesticity nurtured more humane values, values that had been lost in the pursuit of individual achievement in the public sphere. However, while these ideas offer the possibility of thinking more positively about the value of domesticity for feminism, they are also dependent on some deeply problematic assumptions. Crucially, these arguments rest on the assumption that there are essential – maybe even biological – differences between masculinity and femininity, and can be used to legitimate the idea that women are best suited to caring roles in the home and unsuited to the competitive world of the workplace.

The discussion so far has identified two opposing feminist positions on domesticity, one which argues that women should reject domesticity in favour of achievement in the public sphere and the other which defends the value of domesticity but argues that women are psychologically ill-equipped for participation in the public sphere. As should be clear, both of these positions are problematic: while it is important to recognise that domestic cultures are of value, the responsibility for the maintenance of these cultures should not simply lie with women. As Johnson and Lloyd argue, rather than abandoning all the values associated with domesticity, "feminism has a responsibility to reassert the importance of these values in the public world in a way that challenges the separation of home and work life, and the relegation of humane values" such as caring to the home (p. 160). Rather than rejecting the domestic, Joan Williams challenges us to think about what domesticity could be made to mean in different ways and "bending domesticity into new configurations" (pp. 198–199). Drawing on the work of Judith Butler, she argues that the values associated with domesticity need to be used in a self-conscious way to "destabilize" the ways in which relationships to the public and the private spheres continue to be gendered. Rather than attacking domesticity, she suggests that feminists need to offer "a new interpretation of it ... identifying the parts of domesticity that must be left behind if we are to move closer to our ever-elusive ideals of equality" (p. 160).

These ideas offer the opportunity to think about how some of the values associated with domesticity can be used as a resource for not only rethinking gendered relationships to – and between – the public and the private spheres, but also rethinking what domesticity can be made to mean in a diverse range of living arrangements beyond normative family structures. For example, research by Andrew Gorman-Murray (2006) has explored what domesticity may mean for both gay and straight men, exploring how the concept – and home, more generally – can be "*diversely* gendered and sexualized" (p. 66). While narratives of leaving home are frequently central to gay and lesbian identities, domestic cultures are not inherently heterosexual. Indeed, Gorman-Murray argues that domesticity can operate as a sanctuary "from heteronormativity" (p. 54).

Mobilising Domesticity

Although a series of twentieth-century commentators have criticised the values associated with domesticity, another challenge to the centrality of domesticity in everyday life has come from wide-ranging social, economic, and cultural changes associated with the late twentieth century. As a result, the meaning and value of domesticity is a site of tension in contemporary culture. This section explores how domesticity has become more mobile and dislocated from the private sphere while, at the same time, dispositions and practices associated with the workplace have increasingly shaped the home. Despite (or maybe because of) these shifts, there has also been a new interest in the meaning of domesticity and what it can offer as a resource in contemporary life.

New communication technologies have enabled larger numbers of people to do more of their work from home. As domestic and working spaces become increasingly merged for more people, this challenges the opposition between the meaning of work and home that was central to discourses of domesticity. Research indicates that many homeworkers attempt to negotiate the meaning of domesticity in relation to these changed conditions: they not only attempt to segregate working life from domestic life through the identification of paid work with particular zones within the home, but also negotiate fragile and complex temporal regimes to distinguish between work and home. Yet these forms of organisation are often difficult to sustain and many homeworkers recount experiences of permanently multitasking, combining the activities associated with home and work.

Yet the experience of home as a site where there are too many tasks to juggle in too little time does not simply apply to people who primarily work from home. In one of the classic studies of changing relations between home and work in the United States, Arlie Russell Hochschild

(2000) suggests that home is no longer experienced as a haven from work and a site of leisure because the temporal demands of the industrial workplace have become part of contemporary domestic experience. The middle-class workers she interviewed felt that their time at home was so hassled and squeezed that they outsourced elements of domesticity such as childcare and homemaking to other people in order to create pockets of quality time for the experience of family life. If the idea of scheduling time for family is antithetical to discourses of domesticity in which femininity is identified with caring for others, then it is unsurprising that women experienced these changing relationships between work and home most keenly. While neoliberalism promotes family values, the assumption that everyone has an active role to play in the workforce undermines the value of caring work that has been central to domesticity. Moreover, many workers in Hochschild's study turned to the workplace to experience the characteristics once associated with home: work not only appeared to offer the experience of belonging to a community or family, but it also made employees feel more valued and secure than they did at home. As Hochschild argues, "a tired parent flees a world of unresolved quarrels and unwashed laundry for the reliable orderliness, harmony and managed cheer of work" (p. 44). This suggests that the qualities associated with domesticity are increasingly becoming attached to public life and vice versa.

While these debates suggest that domesticity might be losing its purchase in the home, there are countertrends which celebrate a reinvestment in domesticity, maybe precisely because it seems to be under threat. While TV dramas such as *Mad Men* (2007) and movies such as *Revolutionary Road* (2008) have been used to explore the meanings of earlier forms of suburban domesticity from a historical distance, there has been a proliferation of lifestyle media formats devoted to domestic life and press reports that suggest increased participation in more traditional domestic activities such as knitting, cooking, and crafts. Some commentators have interpreted this preoccupation with domesticity as evidence of a backlash against women's professional success in the workplace and the relative success of feminism, and have claimed that these forms of domesticity herald a new traditionalism that seeks to reposition women within the home. However, the fascination with domesticity can also be interpreted as a response to the changing experience of home documented above and as a critique of the values associated with the public sphere.

Given that a shortage of time has been highlighted as a feature of many people's experience of home, the appearance of TV shows such as *Kirstie's Homemade Home* and books such as Nigella Lawson's *How to be a Domestic Goddess* may appear to be perverse. Yet activities such as home baking can also be seen as an attempt to produce a form of domesticity based on a slower and more focused temporal experience than that found in harried and multitasking households. For example, Lawson explicitly advocates using baking as a means of combating time scarcity by creating periods of temporal control in order to temporarily experience forms of domesticity unavailable in many contemporary homes. Rather than juggling tasks in a frenzied way, she demonstrates how baking can offer respite from feminine responsibilities for time management by enabling an, albeit fleeting, experience of temporal abundance. While such solutions are undoubtedly more open to the middle-class people who can buy other people's labour to relieve themselves from the less pleasurable aspects of domesticity, the appeal of Lawson's book lies in its ability to imagine taking pleasure in domesticity rather than simply enduring the hassle of home.

Rather than simply attempting to revive older forms of domesticity and domestic femininity, Lawson reclaims baking as a way of rethinking the significance of domesticity in contemporary life and for contemporary women. Some critics have indicated how the resurgence of interest in knitting can be understood as part of a wider pursuit of slowness, offering opportunities for more attentive use of time by investing identity in everyday activities. Furthermore, because knitting is a more mobile practice, it offers ways of making domestic values more public. This has been capitalised on by craftivists who have staged knit-ins on the London Underground and who have consciously mobilised the homely values of knitting as a critique of consumer culture and a form of eco-activism. These craftivists frequently reject the idea that domesticity and feminism have inherently antagonistic values and are part of a wider process through which the meanings of domesticity – and domestic femininities – are being destabilised.

As the meaning of domesticity is interrogated, it also offers opportunities to rethink the relationship between masculinity and domesticity. Some commentators have seen the rise of television chefs such as Jamie Oliver as evidence of new modes of domestic masculinity. *The Naked Chef* works to imagine a feminised domestic practice such as cooking as a cool masculine lifestyle activity. While this offers new ways of articulating masculinity and domesticity, it is also achieved through distancing Oliver from the more mundane and repetitive aspects of domestic labour and the obligation to care for others that frequently characterises domestic femininities. Nonetheless, shows such as *The Naked Chef* alongside other lifestyle programmes such as *Queer Eye for the Straight Guy* begin to think about the relationships between masculinity and domesticity in new ways.

Conclusion

The meaning, value, and significance of domesticity have been shaped by different discursive formations at different historical moments. Therefore, there is no fixed meaning of domesticity. While domesticity can be used as a resource to resist other forms of oppression, it has undoubtedly played a role in producing and reproducing unequal gender relations. However, because its meaning cannot be fixed, the meaning of domesticity – and the identities associated with it – can be reimagined to offer new ways of thinking about the meaning of home and everyday life in contemporary culture. This involves destabilising the association between domesticity and femininity – and also home and the nuclear family – so that both the responsibility for, and the pleasures of, home are more equally distributed.

See also: Feminist Perspectives on Home; Gender Divisions in the Home; Home: Unpaid Domestic Labour; Ideal Homes; Kitchens; Nature in the Home; Privacy, Sanctuary and Privatism; Suburban Homes.

References

Blunt A (1999) Imperial geographies of home: British domesticity in India, 1886–1925. *Transactions of the Institute of British Geographers* 24(2): 421–440.

Bourke J (1994) Housewifery in working-class England. *Past and Present* 143(1): 167–197.

Cohen L (1980) Embellishing a life of labour: An interpretation of the material culture of American working-class homes. *Journal of American Culture* 3(4): 752–775.

Davidoff L and Hall C (2002) *Family Fortunes: Men and Women of the English Middle Class, 1780–1850*, 2nd edn. London: Routledge.

Friedan B (1963) *The Feminine Mystique*. New York: Dell.

Giles J (2004) *The Parlour and the Suburb: Domestic Identities, Class, Femininity and Modernity*. Oxford, UK: Berg.

Gorman-Murray A (2006) Homeboys: Uses of home by gay Australian men. *Social and Cultural Geography* 7(1): 53–69.

Harley S (1990) The good of the family and race: Gender, work and domestic roles in the black community, 1880–1930. *Signs* 15(2): 336–349.

Hochschild AR (2000) *The Time Bind: When Work Becomes Home and Home Becomes Work*. New York: Owl Books.

Johnson L and Lloyd J (2004) *Sentenced to Everyday Life: Feminism and the Housewife*. Oxford, UK: Berg.

Williams J (2000) *Unbending Gender: Why Family and Work Conflict and What to Do about It*. New York: Oxford University Press.

Further Reading

Cott N (1977) *'Woman's Sphere' in New England, 1780–1835*. New Haven, CT: Yale University Press.

Gillis S and Hollows J (eds.) (2009) *Feminism, Domesticity and Popular Culture*. New York: Routledge.

Hollows J (2008) *Domestic Cultures*. Maidenhead, UK: Open University Press.

Leavitt SA (2002) *From Catherine Beecher to Martha Stewart: A Cultural History of Domestic Advice*. Chapel Hill, NC: University of North Carolina Press.

Domicide

R Atkinson, University of York, York, UK

© 2012 Elsevier Ltd. All rights reserved.

Glossary

Domicide The intentional destruction of dwellings and homes through human agency and resultant human suffering and victimisation.

What is Domicide?

The term domicide was coined by Douglas Porteous and Sandra Smith in 2001 to refer to the "deliberate destruction of home by human agency in pursuit of specified goals, which causes suffering to the victims" (p. 12). The term therefore refers to processes which have a long social history, yet which have arguably not been studied in significant detail. The suffix of the word itself, 'cide', comes from the Latin, meaning to cut, or to cut down. The power of the word thus stems from its resonance with other words suggestive of murder or death (such as suicide and homicide), but is also used in relation to the deep, affective connection between householders and the dwelling they call home.

The term domicide was coined to generate greater interrogation and empirical analyses of processes that not only affect significant numbers of people but which have also tended not to see systematic consideration. Acts such as dam construction or urban redevelopment have frequently involved large-scale and compulsory destruction of, often poorer, people's homes. In addition, many of the most extreme events in social history, such as war and ethnic cleansing, have led to the destruction of homes and the expulsion of large populations, both within and across national boundaries. So domicide, taken within these wide reference points, encompasses some of the most significant faultlines of human experience and misery, extending back across many centuries. The idea of domicide adds both emotional and sociolegal weight to acts which 'cut down' or deprive us of our private home or homeland and the deep emotional, physical, and physiological impacts that such deprivation implies.

While the home is often considered the core social space, protected by property relations, it is also overlain by significant variations in tenurial security, by the varying incomes and circumstances of the inhabiting household, and by broader social, political, and economic forces which may serve to undermine or finally destroy the links between dweller and dwelling. Since home expresses significant aspects of affective development, identity formation, and physical and income security, the idea of domicide presents us with a critical concept through which we can explore the destruction and loss of a foundation point of our broader social lives. Understanding the depth and nature of such a relationship is critical to a subsequent comprehension of the immiseration generated by such destruction, and the urgency of projects by which such aggression might be halted. Continued and extensive warfare, megaprojects (such as dam, airport, and road construction), and the restructuring of urban fabrics globally continue to make the concept of domicide a live and somewhat neglected issue.

Porteous and Smith distinguished two forms of domicide, the extreme and the everyday. Their intention here was to distinguish between irregular and extensive acts of domestic destruction (extreme), such as that generated through war, from those woven into the daily patterns of capitalist, urban political economy and property relations (the everyday), including compulsory purchase and neighbourhood renewal. Under the former they include the examples of South Africa's Bantustans where 15 million Blacks were concentrated within 13% of the nation's land, and Israel's forced displacement of around a million Palestinian households and the physical destruction of many of their homes and villages. The latter includes widespread dam building projects, which have been cited as generating the displacement of up to 80 million households globally.

Domicide brings into the housing researcher's lexicon the theatres of war, human aggression, and the destructive elements of everyday life in most regions of the globe. It sets conventional, often Western, notions of the tacitly understood perpetuity and stability of domestic life against such threats. The statistics (see below) relating to acts of domicide highlight an extensive, regular, and intrinsic part of our geoculture. Capitalist land relations, the power and expansion of corporate commodity extraction, as well as major income inequalities act as the fertile ground upon which domicide is permitted or carried out by political and industrial elites. The embedding of continued warfare and civic strife in many regions underscores that acts of domicide continue with depressing regularity, often used to take revenge in ethnic conflicts or deemed in the interests of the greater good in the contexts of many development projects.

The Scale of Domicide

In the early 2000s Porteous and Smith's estimate was that more than 30 million people globally were affected by domicide but that the issue remained neglected due to the complexity and lack of coherence of research in this area. However, global statistics on refugees and forced migrants by the United Nation's High Commissioner for Refugees (UNHCR) and United States Committee for Refugees and Immigrants (USCRI) have used a variety of different sources (government, other agencies, site visits, camp registration) to generate estimates that are relevant to this project of basic enumeration. Yet the scale of such estimates is so overwhelming that a consideration of the nature, or even possibility, of concerted policy responses remains a major challenge.

Recent figures on the scale of domicide can be determined to some extent via an examination of the reports of the UNHCR. Their latest, covering 2008, concluded that there were 42 million people forcibly displaced, and that this figure included 15.2 million refugees (though it is not clear how many of these people's homes were destroyed and therefore what proportion can be considered to be linked to acts of domicide in the strict sense of its meaning). The UNHCR itself was also offering protection or assistance to 25 million such people. The United Nations Office for the Coordination of Humanitarian Affairs (OCHA) has also estimated that there are an additional 25 million people who have been displaced due to natural disasters (see Relevant Websites). This brings in a related but conceptually distinct process, the unhousing of people through such catastrophes.

Porteous and Smith note that many of those affected by domicide remain internally displaced in the countries they come from. Figures for 2009 from the International Committee of the Red Cross estimate that there are 26 million internally displaced people globally – casualties of war feeling the terror of possible or actual attack on homelands and dwellings. The Red Cross cite the use of starvation, attacks on civilian sites, and the obstruction of relief as key tactics driving these human flows, often to informal or 'containment camps' run by agencies like the Red Cross itself. To take one key example they suggest that 40 000 internally displaced people were generated by the Israeli war in Lebanon in 2007. To these enormous tolls the same report adds a further 25 million people displaced by natural disaster and a further 11.4 million international refugees.

The UN has noted dramatic increases over time in these figures, with ongoing violence in countries like Iraq, which has generated the greatest number of refugees (2.2 million), and Afghanistan (1.9 million) (UN estimates for 2007). Estimates taken as early as 2000 show that there are still 7 million Palestinian refugees in the world, many seeking a right to return to settlements that were systematically destroyed in the war of 1948 to form the independent state of Israel.

Data issues clearly remain a challenge; many refugees have not suffered domicide in the strict sense of the word intended by Porteous and Smith. Refugees are easier to monitor and catalogue, while those internally displaced are harder to categorise and are not considered legal refugees by the UN, and so do not qualify for aid. Yet not all refugees will be led to seek shelter as a result of the actual destruction of their home, and yet the possibility of their continued existence and sustenance within the dwelling has been made impossible, often because their sociopolitical life has been compromised.

Estimates relating to the domicide of homes to enable, often Western-funded, megaprojects have been gathered by some researchers. In relation to dam construction, for example, it has been estimated that some 40–80 million people have been displaced. In early 2007 the BBC reported that the Chinese Three Gorges Dam project alone would displace around 1.4 million people, yet, shortly after, the UK Guardian newspaper detailed plans for a further 4 million people who were to be moved from their homes to ensure the 'environmental safety' of the dam, one of the biggest resettlements in modern history. Ironically at least one key rationale for the dam is to reduce China's reliance on coal-fired power stations, themselves part of a broader conflagration of forces generating the climate change that has made settlements on the steeply sided areas adjacent to the dam more vulnerable to mudslides.

A key example of the destruction of homeland linked to domicide was witnessed in the plight of the marsh Arabs of southern Iraq. It was here that Saddam Hussein drained the marshes, creating one of the first groups to be recognised as environmental refugees. Estimates of the number of Arabs displaced by these acts vary significantly, from around 40 000 to 1 000 000. Domicide also relates to the relationship between informal settlements, tenure, and questions of national sovereignty and migration. This complex amalgam was raised in the destruction of the 'jungle' camp close to the Channel Tunnel where those already displaced from countries like Afghanistan and Iraq saw the French state dismantle their temporary homes, leading to a second round of homelessness and dispossession from even the slenderest handhold on shelter that they had provided for themselves.

In countries like the United Kingdom the postwar period was marked by a move to rehabilitate and clear many sections of bomb-damaged and blighted urban areas, often of poor building standards, which were constructed by private developers in earlier decades. The slum clearance of this period moved many tens of thousands of households, particularly in the larger cities, such as London, Birmingham, and Glasgow. In the name of the common good many people were moved to areas of new public housing in order to improve their conditions and health. Yet such programmes, given the grieving for social systems of support documented in books like Willmott and Young's *Family and Kinship in East London*, highlighted an often misguided policy that generated many secondary problems. Yet whether we would seek to call such policies acts of domicide would no doubt generate significant debate given the genuine problems of these areas. Older examples of domicide abound and include the Scottish Highland clearances, the complex relationships between land, economy, and ethnicity that resulted in the potato famine in Ireland, and even the resiting of smaller English villages within country estates, often carried out to improve the views of the landed gentry.

Current policies in the United Kingdom for housing market renewal have raised these problems again. These have designated just under 50 000 demolitions in nine areas across the postindustrial landscape of northern England. The key question here revolves around the use of compulsory purchase, demolition, and the remaking of areas with more affluent characteristics seen to be more palatable by local political elites. In many cases evidence has arisen that people do not want to be forced to leave their homes.

Conceptual Issues

Domicide can be seen as a subset of complex forces that generate the loss of home. Such loss may be generated by a range of sources. For Porteous and Smith their concern is with the misery and victimisation caused by the intentional, human destruction of home. Many studies of such phenomena have been carried out, such as those on dam building, indigenous peoples, the impact of war, and so on. It is not clear whether the concept requires, or would benefit from, some refinement to encompass other processes through which the home is lost, or whether destruction of the home and human intentionality should be considered its hallmarks. Porteous and Smith certainly see domicide as analytically distinct from unintentional and nonhuman generated sources of homelessness and displacement. Yet this raises further questions.

Let us examine two key examples of possible confusion. First, while genocide is not considered to be an act of domicide, because victims of such acts are killed and dwellings may not be destroyed, it may be the case that genocidal acts considered under the UN definition (which includes the statement "deliberately inflicting on the group conditions of life calculated to bring about its physical destruction in whole or in part") might well force the abandonment of homes. Second, do we need to see the physical destruction of homes as the hallmark of domicide, or would the act of unhousing itself not be enough for us to deem that an act of domicide had occurred (i.e., that a sense of home has been cut down or lost)?

While Porteous and Smith did not include a discussion of gentrification per se there are a number of features of gentrification-related displacement that seem relevant to this debate. Could we not consider the eviction of tenants in order for a property to be sold to more affluent owners a process of domicide? While the house has not been destroyed it may well be that a home has been (precisely the affective dimension of the experience of dwellings that drove the creation of the neologism itself), and that grief, identity, and a place of refuge are swept away for those exiled through market dislocation, mediated by property relations. Certainly the talk of loss by victims of such displacement mirrors many of the accounts provided in direct efforts at describing the impact of domicide.

It would seem useful to distinguish between intentional and unintentional domicide and human/nonhuman forms, and that the actual act of destruction could be extended to include processes of unhousing that may or may not involve the physical disassemblage of a person's or household's dwelling. Yet even here things are blurred by the relationship between human agency itself and other forces. A clear example of this would be climate change, which has been responsible for the significant destruction of homelands and, more directly, property, such as that seen in Hurricane Katrina's impact on New Orleans, and the social geography of its impact on the city's black population. Similarly the broader impact of catastrophes, like the tsunami of 2007, highlights the interplay of social geography and national and social inequalities, which has mediated and amplified the effect of such disasters. Where such catastrophes have interacted with local variations in official responses the effect has been domicide by nature, compounded by the inadequacy or even overt racism of responses in cases like that of Katrina.

So the question arises as to how we can understand and explain the destruction of home, but perhaps also its more generalised and forced loss. If we require a sense of intentionality we should also recognise the broad range of rationalities driving such intentions. To include vicious acts against civilian populations by military personnel in

Darfur alongside households knocked down for a highway may suggest an overelasticity of the concept, even if we attach the tags of 'extreme' and 'everyday' to it.

Conclusion

Housing studies in the West have often focused on socioeconomic, problem-based questions, such as affordability, quality, and supply among many others. Yet, taken in a global context, such questions inevitably appear somewhat inconsequential when set alongside questions of internal displacement, household education and malnutrition, disease, homelessness, warfare, and political instability. The intersection of these factors with rapid urbanisation and social inequality of the global 'south' provides us with a salutary correction to the perhaps often insulated nature of housing studies in the global north. Refugees, informal settlements, domicide, and ecological catastrophe (variously mediated through human-political systems) highlight some of the largest housing problems globally. The figures associated with estimating the scale of such events have become a parade of epic and ungraspable statistics that belie individual human tragedy and persistent suffering amidst warfare, asymmetries of power, and property rights systems.

Stephen Graham has discussed in detail the purposive destruction of settlements and cities, using the term urbicide. This suggests the further possible scalar escalation of issues of human unhousing and the need to discuss and embrace such concepts in the face of overwhelming human need and policy and community responses to such problems. For all the raw, emotive power of the term domicide, and its connection with some of the most significant existential questions of human habitation, it is worrying that it has generated remarkably little direct literature.

In an age in which terrorism has been foregrounded and state crimes more clearly made visible by international media, the almost daily visualisation of the destruction of homes has become widespread and unsettling. One of the key contributions of this neologism has been to highlight the mundane quality of the kind of violence, destruction, and political power that unsettles Western notions of the stability of home and its ontological centrality. Like homelessness and displacement, domicide raises a concern with the antisocial forces that deny the most critical human symbiotic relationship – that between the physical shell and sheltering function of a dwelling, and the lives and nurturance of diverse household units within.

See also: Demolition; Gentrification; Home and Homelessness; Residential segregation; Social Justice.

Further Reading

Allen C (2007) *Housing Market Renewal*. London: Routledge.
Graham S (ed.) (2004) *Cities, War and Terrorism: Towards an Urban Geopolitics*. Oxford, UK: Blackwell.
Hewitt K (1983) Place annihilation: Area bombing and the fate of urban places. *Annals of the Association of American Geographers* 73(2): 257–284.
ICRC (2009) *Internal Displacement in Armed Conflict: Facing Up to the Challenges*. Geneva, Switzerland: International Committee of the Red Cross.
Porteous J and Smith J (2001) *Domicide: The Global Destruction of Home*. Montreal, QC: McGill-Queens.
Prebble J (1982) *The Highland Clearances*. Harmondsworth, UK: Penguin.
Robinson C (2005) Grieving home. *Social and Cultural Geography* 6(1): 47–60.
UNHCR (2009) *2008 Global Trends: Refugees, Asylum Seekers*. Geneva, Switzerland: UNHCR.
Willmott P and Young M (1957) *Family and Kinship in East London*. Harmondsworth, UK: Penguin.

Relevant Websites

www.fmreview.org – Forced Migration Review #20.
www.unhcr.org – United Nation's High Commissioner for Refugees.
www.refugees.org – United States Committee for Refugees and Immigrants.